ers'

CompTIA A+ Guide: Essentials
(Exam 220-601)

Mike Meyers

Mike Meyers'

CompTIA A+® Guide: Essentials

(Exam 220-601)

Mike Meyers

New York Chicago San Francisco
Lisbon London Madrid Mexico City Milan
New Delhi San Juan Seoul Singapore Sydney Toronto

The McGraw·Hill Companies

Cataloging-in-Publication Data is on file with the Library
of Congress

Sponsoring Editor
TIMOTHY GREEN

Editorial Supervisor
PATTY MON

Project Editor
LAURA STONE

Acquisitions Coordinator
JENNIFER HOUSH

Technical Editor
ED JENNINGS

Copy Editors
LAURA STONE, LISA THEOBALD,
LEEANN PICKRELL, ANDY CARROLL

Proofreaders
SUSIE ELKIND, PAUL TYLER

Indexer
JACK LEWIS

Production Supervisor
JAMES KUSSOW

Composition
INTERNATIONAL TYPESETTING AND
COMPOSITION

Illustration
INTERNATIONAL TYPESETTING AND
COMPOSITION

Art Director, Cover
JEFF WEEKS

Cover Designer
JEFF WEEKS

Cover Photograph
KEN DAVIES/MASTERFILE

McGraw-Hill books are available at special quantity discounts to use
as premiums and sales promotions, or for use in corporate training
programs. For more information, please write to the Director of
Special Sales, Professional Publishing, McGraw-Hill, Two Penn
Plaza, New York, NY 10121-2298. Or contact your local bookstore.

Mike Meyers' CompTIA A+® Guide: Essentials (Exam 220-601)

Copyright © 2007 by The McGraw-Hill Companies. All rights reserved.
Printed in the United States of America. Except as permitted under the
Copyright Act of 1976, no part of this publication may be reproduced or
distributed in any form or by any means, or stored in a database or
retrieval system, without the prior written permission of publisher, with
the exception that the program listings may be entered, stored, and
executed in a computer system, but they may not be reproduced for
publication.

1234567890 QPD QPD 01987

ISBN-13: Book P/N 978-0-9816217-0-8
        and CD P/N 978-0-07-226354-1
        of set 978-0-07-226352-7

ISBN-10: Book P/N 0-9816217-0-8
        and CD P/N 0-07-226354-7
        of set 0-07-226352-0

Information has been obtained by McGraw-Hill from sources believed to be reliable. However,
because of the possibility of human or mechanical error by our sources, McGraw-Hill, or others,
McGraw-Hill does not guarantee the accuracy, adequacy, or completeness of any information and is
not responsible for any errors or omissions or the results obtained from the use of such information.

McGraw-Hill is an independent entity from CompTIA. This publication and CD-ROM may be
used in assisting students to prepare for the CompTIA A+ Essentials (220-601) exam. Neither
CompTIA nor McGraw-Hill warrants that use of this publication and CD-ROM will ensure
passing any exam. CompTIA and CompTIA A+ are registered trademarks of CompTIA in the
United States and/or other countries.

■ About the Author

Mike Meyers, lovingly called the "AlphaGeek" by those who know him, is the industry's leading authority on CompTIA A+ certification. He is the president and co-founder of Total Seminars, LLC, a provider of PC and network repair seminars, books, videos, and courseware for thousands of organizations throughout the world. Mike has been involved in the computer and network repair industry since 1977 as a technician, instructor, author, consultant, and speaker. Author of numerous popular PC books and videos, including the best-selling *CompTIA A+ Certification All-in-One Exam Guide*, Mike is also the series editor for the highly successful Mike Meyers' Certification Passport series, the Mike Meyers' Computer Skills series, and the Mike Meyers' Guide to series, all published by McGraw-Hill/Osborne.

■ About the Contributors

A number of people contributed to the development of *Mike Meyers' A+ Guide to Managing and Troubleshooting PCs*.

Scott Jernigan wields a mighty red pen as Editor in Chief for Total Seminars. With a Master of Arts degree in Medieval History, Scott feels as much at home in the musty archives of London as he does in the warm CRT glow of Total Seminars' Houston headquarters. After fleeing a purely academic life, he dove headfirst into IT, working as an instructor, editor, and writer. Scott has edited and contributed to more than a dozen books on computer literacy, hardware, operating systems, networking, and certification. His latest book is *Computer Literacy – Your Ticket to IC³ Certification* (2006). Scott co-authored the best-selling *A+ Certification All-in-One Exam Guide*, 5th edition, and the *A+ Guide to Managing and Troubleshooting PCs* (both with Mike Meyers). He has taught computer classes all over the United States, including stints at the United Nations in New York and the FBI Academy in Quantico.

Alec Fehl (BM, Music Production and Engineering, and MCSE, A+, NT-CIP, ACE, ACI certified) has been a technical trainer, computer consultant, and Web application developer since 1999. After graduating from the prestigious Berklee College of Music in Boston, he set off for Los Angeles with the promise of becoming a rock star. After ten years gigging in Los Angeles, teaching middle-school math, and auditioning for the Red Hot Chili Peppers (he didn't get the gig), he moved to Asheville, North Carolina with his wife Jacqui, where he teaches computer classes at Asheville-Buncombe Technical Community College and WCI/SofTrain Technology Training Center. Alec is author or coauthor of several titles covering Microsoft Office 2007, Microsoft Vista, Web design and HTML, and Internet systems and applications.

Darril Gibson has been a technical trainer for over eight years, specializing in delivering leading-edge technical training. He has developed several video training courses for Keystone Learning on topics such as A+, MCSE 2003, and Exchange 2003. He has taught as an adjunct instructor at several colleges and universities. Darril is currently working on a key government contract providing extensive training on a wide array of technologies to Air Force personnel in support of a major Network Operations Support Center. He holds almost 20 current certifications including A+, Network+, MCT, MCSE, MCSD, and MCITP.

Technical Editor

Ed Jennings has 25+ years experience in information technology. His career has been spent with such leading firms as Digital Equipment Corporation and Microsoft Corporation. Ed is CompTIA A+, Network+, and Certified Technical Trainer+ certified. Ed is also a Microsoft Certified Systems Engineer (MCSE). He has published several planning and design services for a national services company and is a certified courseware designer. He has published and delivered several online courses. Ed is currently employed as a technical instructor in the computer information technology program at Branford Hall Career Institute (www.branfordhall.com), a division of Premier Education Group (www.premiereducationgroup.com).

Peer Reviewers

Thank you to the reviewers, past and present, who contributed insightful reviews, criticisms, and helpful suggestions that continue to shape this textbook.

Donat Forrest
Broward County Community
  College
Pembroke Pines, FL

Brian Ives
Finger Lakes Community College
Canadaigua, NY

Farbod Karimi
Heald College
San Francisco, CA

Tamie Knaebel
Jefferson Community College
Louisville, KY

Keith Lyons
Cuyahoga Community College
Parma, OH

Winston Maddox
Mercer County Community College
West Windsor, NJ

Rajiv Malkan
Montgomery College
Conroe, Texas

Scott Sweitzer
Indiana Business College
Indianapolis, IN

Randall Stratton
DeVry University
Irving, TX

Thomas Trevethan
CPI College of Technology
Virginia Beach, VA

■ Acknowledgments

Scott Jernigan, my Editor-in-Chief, Counter-Strike Foe, Master Bard, and *Bon Vivant*, was the glue that made this product happen. There's not a word or picture I put into this book that he hasn't molded and polished into perfection.

My acquisitions editor, Tim Green, did a fabulous job keeping me motivated and excited about this project. Tim, you're the poster child for "Californians who can actually get along with loud, obnoxious Texans." Let's do another one!

My in-house Graphics Guru and Brother Tech, Michael Smyer, took every bizarre illustration idea I could toss at him and came back with exactly what I needed. To top it off, his outstanding photographs appear on nearly every page in this book. Great job, Michael!

Cindy Clayton's title might be "Editor" but it should be "Go to Gal," as she was always there for any job we needed to get done.

Cary Dier and Brian Schwarz came in at the 11th hour to save our bacon with copy edits and technical editing. Thanks, guys!

On the McGraw-Hill side, their crew worked with the diligence of worker bees and the patience of saints to put this book together.

Laura Stone did it all this time, a true pleasure to work with as project editor, copy editor, and frequent long-distance companion during many late nights. Your words of encouragement and praise—and laughter at my bad jokes—helped me finish this book with sanity and a smile. I could not have asked for a better editor, Laura. Thanks!

Jenni Housh offered a quiet voice and helpful spirit as acquisitions coordinator. I enjoyed our Monday meetings and am looking forward to the next project.

My technical editor, Ed Jennings, kept a close eye on me throughout the book and made great suggestions and corrections. Thanks for the excellent work!

To the copy editors, page proofers, and layout folks—Lisa Theobald, LeeAnn Pickrell, Andy Carroll, Susie Elkind, Paul Tyler, and the folks at ITC—thank you! You did a marvelous job.

■ *To my wonderful daughter, Emily— even though you're far away, you're always in my thoughts. I love you. —Mike Meyers*

■ CompTIA Authorized Quality Curriculum

The logo of the CompTIA Authorized Quality Curriculum (CAQC) program and the status of this or other training material as "Authorized" under the CompTIA Authorized Quality Curriculum program signifies that, in CompTIA's opinion, such training material covers the content of CompTIA's related certification exam.

The contents of this training material were created for the CompTIA A+ exams covering CompTIA certification objectives that were current as of November 2006.

CompTIA has not reviewed or approved the accuracy of the contents of this training material and specifically disclaims any warranties of merchantability or fitness for a particular purpose. CompTIA makes no guarantee concerning the success of persons using any such "Authorized" or other training material in order to prepare for any CompTIA certification exam.

How to Become CompTIA Certified:

This training material can help you prepare for and pass a related CompTIA certification exam or exams. In order to achieve CompTIA certification, you must register for and pass a CompTIA certification exam or exams.

To become CompTIA certified, you must:

1. Select a certification exam provider. For more information, please visit http://www.comptia.org/certification/general_information/exam_locations.aspx

2. Register for and schedule a time to take the CompTIA certification exam(s) at a convenient location.

3. Read and sign the Candidate Agreement, which will be presented at the time of the exam(s). The text of the Candidate Agreement can be found at http://www.comptia.org/certification/general_information/candidate_agreement.aspx

4. Take and pass the CompTIA certification exam(s).

For more information about CompTIA's certifications, such as its industry acceptance, benefits or program news, please visit www.comptia.org/certification.

CompTIA is a not-for-profit information technology (IT) trade association. CompTIA's certifications are designed by subject matter experts from across the IT industry. Each CompTIA certification is vendor-neutral, covers multiple technologies, and requires demonstration of skills and knowledge widely sought after by the IT industry.

To contact CompTIA with any questions or comments, please call (1) (630) 678 8300 or e-mail questions@comptia.org.

About This Book

■ Important Technology Skills

Information technology (IT) offers many career paths, leading to occupations in such fields as PC repair, network administration, telecommunications, Web development, graphic design, and desktop support. To become competent in any IT field, however, you need certain basic computer skills. Mike Meyers' A+ Guide builds a foundation for success in the IT field by introducing you to fundamental technology concepts and giving you essential computer skills.

Cross Check questions develop reasoning skills: ask, compare, contrast, and explain.

Tech Tip sidebars provide inside information from experienced IT professionals.

Try This! exercises apply core skills in a new setting.

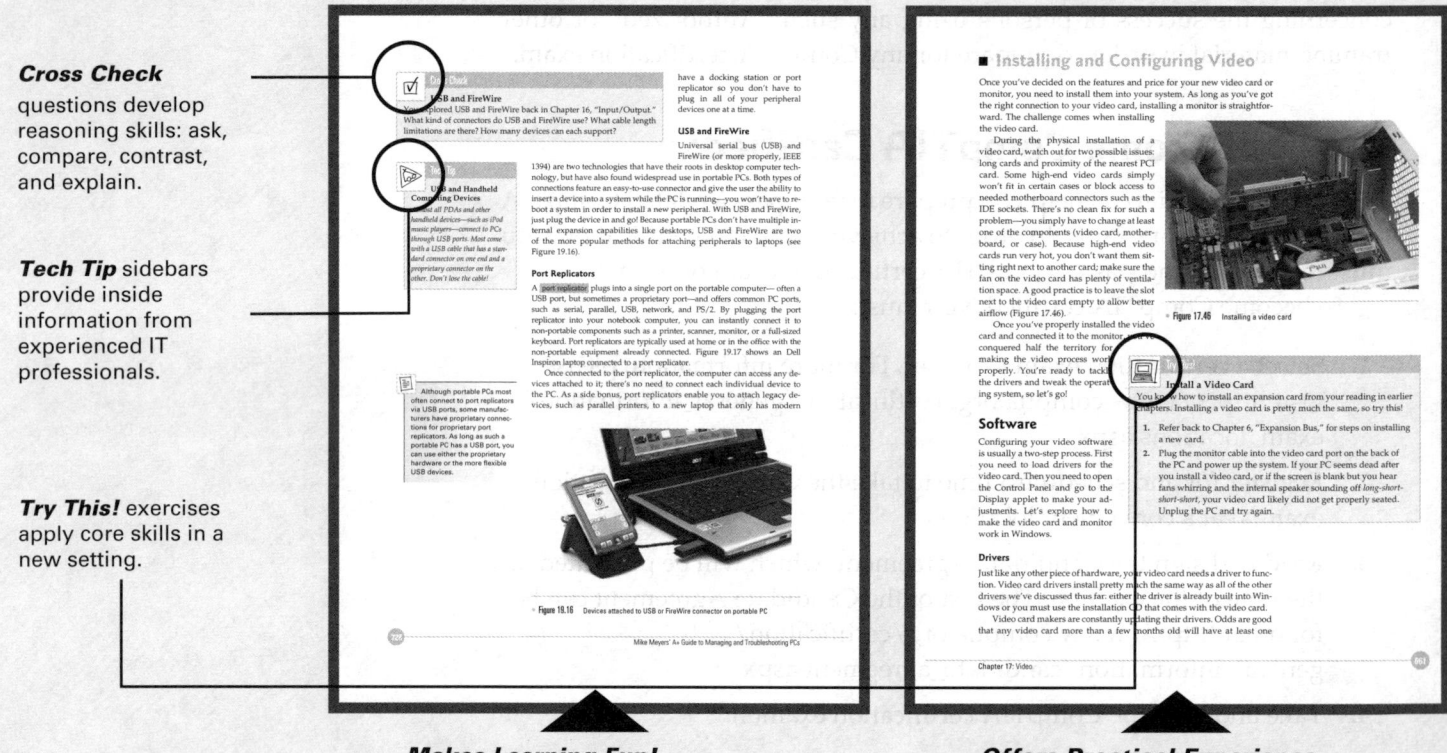

Makes Learning Fun! — Rich, colorful text and enhanced illustrations bring technical subjects to life.

Offers Practical Experience — Tutorials and lab assignments develop essential hands-on skills and put concepts in real-world contexts.

Proven Learning Method Keeps You on Track

Mike Meyers' A+ Guide is structured to give you comprehensive knowledge of computer skills and technologies. The textbook's active learning methodology guides you beyond mere recall and, through thought-provoking activities, labs, and sidebars, helps you develop critical-thinking, diagnostic, and communication skills.

Effective Learning Tools

This pedagogically rich book is designed to make learning easy and enjoyable and to help you develop the skills and critical-thinking abilities that will enable you to adapt to different job situations and troubleshoot problems.

Mike Meyers' proven ability to explain concepts in a clear, direct, even humorous way makes these books interesting, motivational, and fun.

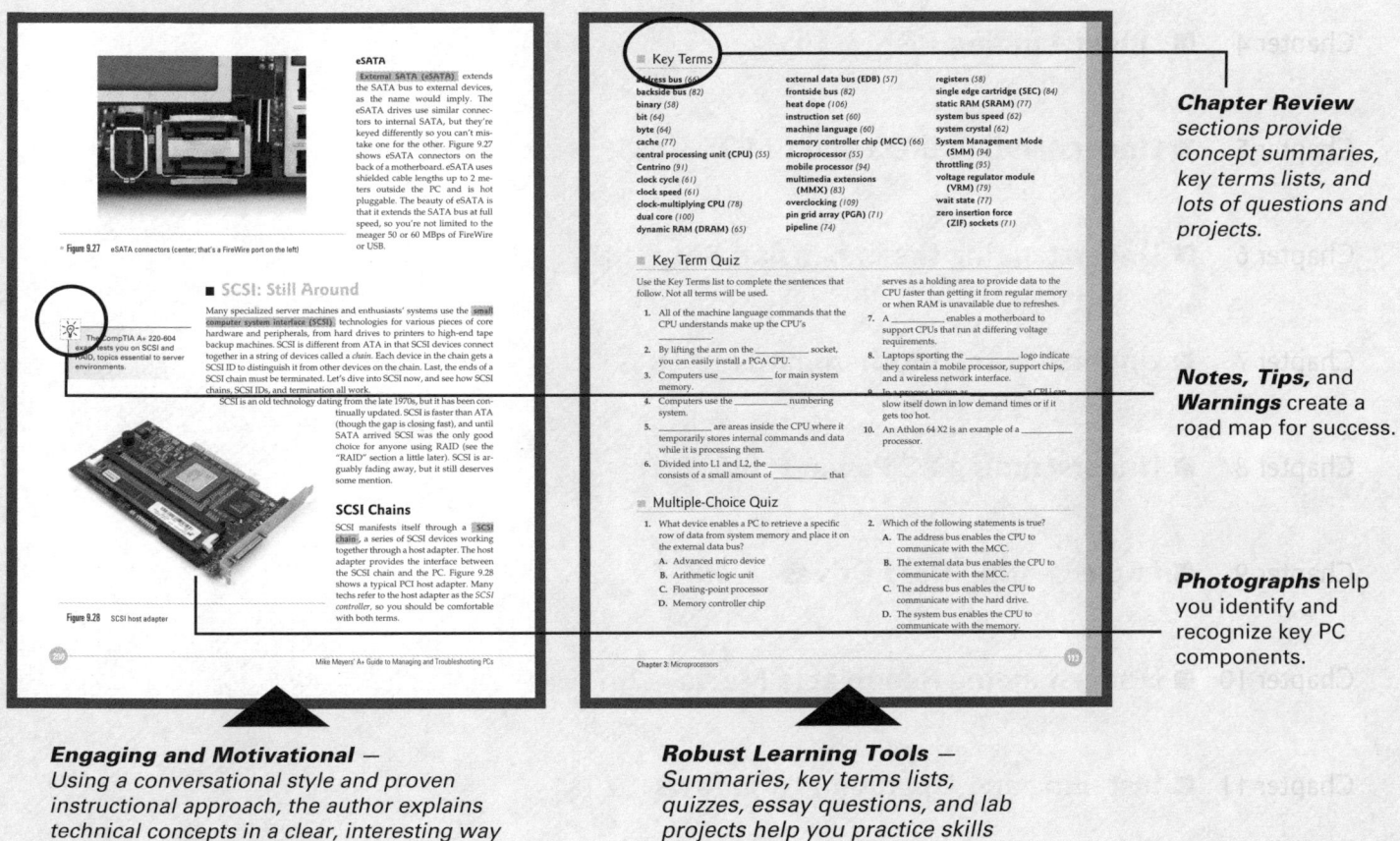

Chapter Review sections provide concept summaries, key terms lists, and lots of questions and projects.

Notes, Tips, and **Warnings** create a road map for success.

Photographs help you identify and recognize key PC components.

Engaging and Motivational —
Using a conversational style and proven instructional approach, the author explains technical concepts in a clear, interesting way using real-world examples.

Robust Learning Tools —
Summaries, key terms lists, quizzes, essay questions, and lab projects help you practice skills and measure progress.

Each chapter includes...

- **Learning objectives** that set measurable goals for chapter-by-chapter progress

- Plenty of **photographs** and **illustrations** that provide clear, up-close pictures of the technology, making difficult concepts easy to visualize and understand

- **Try This!**, **Cross Check**, and **Tech Tip** sidebars that encourage you to practice and apply concepts in real-world settings

- **Notes**, **Tips**, and **Warnings** that guide you through difficult areas

- **Highlighted Key Terms, Key Terms lists, and Chapter Summaries** that provide you with an easy way to review important concepts and vocabulary

- **Challenging end-of-chapter tests** that include vocabulary-building exercises, multiple-choice questions, essay questions, and on-the-job lab projects

CONTENTS AT A GLANCE

Chapter 1 ■ **Getting to Know the A+ Exams** 1

Chapter 2 ■ **The Visible PC** 17

Chapter 3 ■ **Understanding CPUs** 51

Chapter 4 ■ **Understanding RAM** 105

Chapter 5 ■ **Understanding BIOS and CMOS** 125

Chapter 6 ■ **Understanding the Expansion Bus** 147

Chapter 7 ■ **Understanding Motherboards** 168

Chapter 8 ■ **Understanding PC Power** 186

Chapter 9 ■ **Implementing Hard Drives** 208

Chapter 10 ■ **Understanding Removable Media** 267

Chapter 11 ■ **Installing and Upgrading Windows** 292

Chapter 12 ■ **Understanding Windows** 335

Chapter 13 ■ **Maintaining Windows** 394

Chapter 14 ■ **Input/Output** 433

Chapter 15 ■ **Understanding Video** 464

Chapter 16 ■ Portable Computing 494

Chapter 17 ■ Understanding Printing 532

Chapter 18 ■ Understanding Networking 552

Chapter 19 ■ Computer Security 600

Chapter 20 ■ The Complete PC Tech 643

Appendix A ■ Installing and Troubleshooting Printers 663

■ Glossary 682

■ Index 719

CONTENTS

Preface xix

Chapter 1
■ Getting to Know the A+ Exams 1

The Importance of Skill in Managing and
    Troubleshooting PCs 1
    The Concept of Certifications 1
The Importance of CompTIA
    A+ Certification 2
    What Is CompTIA A+ Certification? 2
    Who Is CompTIA? 3
    The Path to Other Certifications 3
How Do I Become CompTIA
    A+ Certified? 4
    The Basic Exam Structure 5
    Help! Which Exam Should I Take Next? . . . 7
    How Do I Take the Exams? 8
    How Much Does the Exam Cost? 8
    How to Pass the CompTIA A+ Exams . . . 8
Chapter 1 Review 14

Chapter 2
■ The Visible PC 17

Historical/Conceptual 18
How the PC Works 18
    Input 19
    Processing 20
    Output 20
    Storage 20
    The Art of the PC Technician 21
Tools of the Trade and
    ESD Avoidance 21
    Tools of the Trade 21
Essentials 22
    Avoiding Electrostatic Discharge 22
    Anti-static Tools 22
The Complete PC 25
    External Connections 25
    Devices and Their Connectors 30
Inside the System Unit 36
    Case 36
    CPU 38
    RAM 39
    Motherboard 40

    Power Supply 41
    Floppy Drive 42
    Hard Drive 42
    Optical Media 44
    Know Your Parts 45
Chapter 2 Review 46

Chapter 3
■ Understanding CPUs 51

Historical/Conceptual 52
CPU Core Components 52
    The Man in the Box 52
    Registers 54
    Clock 56
    Back to the External Data Bus 59
Memory 59
    Memory and RAM 60
    Address Bus 61
Essentials 65
Modern CPUs 65
    Manufacturers 65
    CPU Packages 66
    The Pentium CPU: The Early Years 68
    Original Pentium 76
    Pentium Pro 77
    Later Pentium-Class CPUs 79
    Pentium II 80
    Pentium III 82
    Early AMD Athlon CPUs 83
    Processing and Wattage 84
    CPU Codenames 84
    AMD Athlon Thunderbird 84
    AMD Duron 85
    Intel Pentium 4 Willamette 86
    *AMD Athlon XP (Palomino and
        Thoroughbred)* 87
    Intel Pentium 4 (Northwood and Prescott) . . 87
    AMD Athlon XP (Thorton and Barton) . . . 89
    Pentium 4 Extreme Edition 89
    Mobile Processors 90
    Intel Xeon Processors 91
    Early 64-Bit CPUs 92
    Dual-Core CPUs 96
    Intel Core—Goodbye, Pentium 98
    Know Your CPUs 99
Chapter 3 Review 100

Chapter 4
■ Understanding RAM 105

Historical/Conceptual 106
Understanding DRAM 106
   Organizing DRAM 107
   Practical DRAM 108
   DRAM Sticks 109
   Consumer RAM 111
Essentials 111
Types of RAM 111
   SDRAM 111
   RDRAM 112
   DDR SDRAM 114
   DDR2 116
   RAM Variations 116
Chapter 4 Review 120

Chapter 5
■ Understanding BIOS and CMOS 125

Historical/Conceptual 126
We Need to Talk 126
   Talking to the Keyboard 126
Essentials 130
CMOS 133
   Updating CMOS: The Setup Program 133
   A Quick Tour Through a Typical
    CMOS Setup Program 134
Option ROM and Device Drivers 140
   Option ROM 140
   Device Drivers 141
   BIOS, BIOS, Everywhere! 141
Chapter 5 Review 142

Chapter 6
■ Understanding the Expansion Bus 147

Historical/Conceptual 148
Structure and Function of the Expansion Bus . . 148
   PC Bus 150
   ISA 150
Essentials 151
Modern Expansion Buses 151
   False Starts 152
   PCI 152
System Resources 156
   I/O Addresses 156
   Interrupt Requests 158
   COM and LPT Ports 161
   Direct Memory Access 161
   Memory Addresses 163
Chapter 6 Review 164

Chapter 7
■ Understanding Motherboards 168

Historical/Conceptual 169
How Motherboards Work 169
   Form Factors 169
Essentials 172
   Chipset 176
   Motherboard Components 179
Chapter 7 Review 182

Chapter 8
■ Understanding PC Power 186

Historical/Conceptual 187
Understanding Electricity 187
Essentials 189
Powering the PC 189
   Supplying AC 189
   Supplying DC 195
Chapter 8 Review 203

Chapter 9
■ Implementing Hard Drives 208

Historical/Conceptual 209
Hard Drive Partitions 209
Essentials 209
   Basic Disks 210
   Dynamic Disks 214
   When to Partition 215
Hard Drive Formatting 217
   File Systems in Windows 217
   FAT 218
   FAT32 223
   NTFS 224
The Partitioning and
  Formatting Process 228
   Bootable Disks 228
   Partitioning and Formatting with the Windows
    Installation CD 229
   Partitions and Drive Letters 233
   Disk Management 235
   Dynamic Disks 240
   Mount Points 243
   Formatting a Partition 245
Maintaining and Troubleshooting Hard Drives . 246
   Maintenance 246
   Troubleshooting 249
Beyond A+ 255
   Third-Party Partition Tools 255
Chapter 9 Review 259

Chapter 10
■ Understanding Removable Media 267

Historical/Conceptual 268
Floppy Drives 268
  Floppy Drive Basics 269
Essentials 270
  Installing Floppy Drives 270
Flash Memory 273
  USB Thumb Drives 274
  Flash Cards 274
Optical Drives 277
  CD-Media 278
  DVD-Media 284
Chapter 10 Review 287

Chapter 11
■ Installing and Upgrading Windows 292

Historical/Conceptual 293
Functions of the Operating System 293
  Operating System Traits 293
  Communicating with Hardware 294
  Creating a User Interface 295
  Accessing and Supporting Programs 296
  Organizing and Manipulating
    Programs and Data 296
Essentials 297
  Today's Operating Systems 297
Installing and Upgrading Windows 304
  Preparing for Installation or Upgrade 304
  Performing the Installation or Upgrade 309
  Post-Installation Tasks 310
  Installing or Upgrading to Windows
    2000 Professional 311
  Installing or Upgrading to Windows
    XP Professional 312
  Upgrading Issues for Windows 2000
    and Windows XP 315
  The Windows 2000/XP Clean Install Process . 316
  Automating the Install 320
Troubleshooting Installation Problems 326
  Text Mode Errors 326
  Graphical Mode Errors 327
  Lockups During Install 327
  No Installation Is Perfect 328
Chapter 11 Review 329

Chapter 12
■ Understanding Windows 335

Essentials 336
The Windows Interface 336

User Interface 336
Tech Utilities 347
OS Folders 362
Features and Characteristics of
  Windows 2000/XP 370
  OS Organization 370
  NT File System (NTFS) 371
  The Boot Process 377
  System Partition Files 378
Windows Versions 381
  Windows XP Professional 383
  Windows XP Home 383
  Windows XP Media Center 384
  Windows 64-Bit Versions 385
Beyond A+ 386
  Windows Vista 386
  Windows Mobile 386
  Windows XP Tablet PC 387
  Windows Embedded 387
Chapter 12 Review 388

Chapter 13
■ Maintaining Windows 394

Essentials 395
Maintaining Windows 395
  Patches, Updates, and Service Packs 395
  Managing User Accounts and Groups 398
  Error-Checking and Disk Defragmentation . . 406
  Temporary File Management
    with Disk Cleanup 407
  Registry Maintenance 408
  Security: Spyware/Antivirus/Firewall 409
Optimizing Windows 409
  Installing and Removing Software 409
  Installing/Optimizing a Device 411
  Resource Tracking 416
  Preparing for Problems 419
Chapter 13 Review 427

Chapter 14
■ Input/Output 433

Essentials 434
Supporting Common I/O Ports 434
  Serial Ports 434
  USB Ports 436
  FireWire Ports 442
  General Port Issues 443
Common I/O Devices 445
  Keyboards 445
  Mice 447
  Scanners 449

Digital Cameras 452
Web Cameras 455
Specialty I/O Devices 456
Biometric Devices 456
Bar Code Readers 457
Touch Screens 458
Chapter 14 Review 459

Chapter 15
■ Understanding Video 464

Video Displays 465
Historical/Conceptual 465
CRT Monitors 465
Essentials 466
LCD Monitors 470
Projectors 476
Common Features 477
Power Conservation 481
Video Cards 481
Modes 484
Motherboard Connection 485
Chapter 15 Review 489

Chapter 16
■ Portable Computing 494

Essentials 495
Portable Computing Devices 495
LCD Screens 495
Desktop Replacements 496
Desktop Extenders 497
PDAs 498
Tablet PCs 500
Portable Computer Device Types 503
Enhance and Upgrade the
Portable PC 504
PC Cards 505
Limited-Function Ports 507
General-Purpose Ports 507
The Modular Laptop 509
Managing and Maintaining Portable Computers 514
Batteries 514
Power Management 516
Cleaning 518
Heat 519
Protect the Machine 520
Troubleshooting Portable Computers 522
Beyond A+ 523
Centrino Technology 523
Origami—Ultra-Mobile PCs 523
Chapter 16 Review 525

Chapter 17
■ Understanding Printing 532

Essentials 533
Printer Technologies 533
Impact Printers 533
Inkjet Printers 534
Dye-Sublimation Printers 536
Thermal Printers 537
Laser Printers 537
Solid Ink 541
Printer Languages 542
Printer Connectivity 543
Chapter 17 Review 546

Chapter 18
■ Understanding Networking 552

Historical/Conceptual 553
Networking Technologies 553
Topology 554
Essentials 555
Packets/Frames and NICs 555
Coaxial Ethernet 557
UTP Ethernet (10/100/1000BaseT) 560
Fiber Optic Ethernet 565
Token Ring 565
Parallel/Serial 567
FireWire 568
USB 568
Network Operating Systems 568
Network Organization 569
Protocols 573
Client Software 575
Server Software 575
Installing and Configuring
a Wired Network 575
Installing a NIC 576
Configuring a Network Client 576
Configuring Simple Protocols 577
Configuring TCP/IP 578
Sharing and Security 588
Chapter 18 Review 593

Chapter 19
■ Computer Security 600

Analyzing the Threat 601
Historical/Conceptual 601
Unauthorized Access 601
Data Destruction 601
Administrative Access 602
System Crash/Hardware Failure 602
Virus/Spyware 602

Essentials 602
Local Control 602
    What to Back Up 603
    Migrating and Retiring 605
    Social Engineering 607
    Access Control 608
Network Security 611
    User Account Control
        Through Groups 611
    Security Policies 613
    Malicious Software 615
    Firewalls 624
    Encryption 624
    Wireless Issues 629
    Reporting 629
Beyond A+ 633
    Security in Windows Vista 633
Chapter 19 Review 636

Chapter 20
■ The Complete PC Tech 643

Essentials 644
How Computers Work 644
    Computing Process 644
    Troubleshooting 650
Dealing with Customers 651
    Eliciting Answers 651
    Integrity 652
    Respect 653
    Assertive Communication 654
Troubleshooting Methodology 654
    Tech Toolkit 655
    Backup 655
    Steps 655
Chapter 20 Review 658

Appendix A
■ Installing and Troubleshooting Printers 663

The Laser Printing Process 663
    The Physical Side of the Process 663
    The Electronic Side of the Process . . . 666
Installing a Printer in Windows 667
    Setting Up Printers 668
    Optimizing Print Performance 669
Troubleshooting Printers 670
    General Troubleshooting Issues 670
    Troubleshooting Dot-Matrix Printers . . 673
    Troubleshooting Inkjet Printers 673
    Troubleshooting Laser Printers 674

■ Glossary 682

■ Index 719

I started writing computer books for the simple reason that no one wrote the kind of books I wanted to read. The books were either too simple (Chapter 1, "Using Your Mouse") or too complex (Chapter 1, "TTL Logic and Transistors"), and none of them provided a motivation for me to learn the information. I believed that there were geeky readers just like me who wanted to know *why* they needed to know the information in a computer book.

Good books motivate readers to learn what they are reading. For example, if a book discusses binary arithmetic but doesn't explain why I need to learn it, that's not a good book. Tell me that understanding binary makes it easier to understand how a CPU works or why a megabyte is different from a million bytes—then I get excited, no matter how geeky the topic. If I don't have a good motivation to do something, then I'm simply not going to do it (which explains why I haven't jumped out of an airplane!).

In this book, I teach you why you need to understand the technology that runs almost every modern business. You'll learn to build and fix computers, exploring every nook and cranny, and master the art of the PC tech. In the process, you'll gain the knowledge you need to pass the CompTIA A+ Essentials exam.

Enjoy, my fellow geek.

—Mike Meyers

Getting to Know the A+ Exams

chapter
1

"It does not matter how slowly you go, so long as you do not stop."
—Confucius

In this chapter, you will learn how to

- **Explain the importance of gaining skill in managing and troubleshooting PCs**
- **Explain the importance of CompTIA A+ certification**
- **Describe how to become a CompTIA A+ Certified Technician**

Computers have taken over the world, or at least many professions. Everywhere you turn, a quick dig beneath the surface sawdust of construction, the grease of auto mechanics, and the hum of medical technology reveals one or more personal computers (PCs) working away, doing essential jobs. Because the PC evolved from novelty item to essential science tool to everyday object in a short period of time, there's a huge demand for a workforce that can build, maintain, troubleshoot, and repair PCs.

The Importance of Skill in Managing and Troubleshooting PCs

The people who work with computers—the information technology (IT) workforce—do such varied jobs as design hardware, write computer programs that enable you to do specific jobs on the PC, and create small and large groupings of computers— networks —that enable people to share computer resources. IT people built the Internet, one of the most phenomenal inventions of the 20th century. IT people maintain the millions of computers that make up the Internet. Computer technicians, or PC techs as those of us in the field call each other, make up the core of the IT workforce. Without the techs, none of the other stuff works. Getting workers with skill in building, maintaining, troubleshooting, and fixing PCs is essential for success for every modern business.

In the early days of the personal computer, anyone who used a PC had to have skills as a PC tech. The PC was new, buggy, and prone to problems. You didn't want to rely on others to fix your PC when the inevitable problems arose. Today's PCs are much more robust and have fewer problems, but they're also much more complex machines. Today's IT industry, therefore, needs specialized workers who know how to make the machines run well.

The Concept of Certifications

Every profession requires specialized skills. For the most part, if you want to *get* or *keep* a job that requires those specialized skills, you need some type of certification or license. If you want a job fixing automobiles, for example, you get the *Automotive Service Excellence (ASE)* certification. If you want to perform companies' financial audits, you get your *Certified Public Accountant (CPA)* certification.

Nearly every profession has some criteria that you must meet to show your competence and ability to perform at a certain level. While the way this works varies widely from one profession to another, all of them will at some point make you take an exam or

 Try This!

Six Degrees of Personal Computers

As a fun exercise, divide up your class or your study partners and try this. One side comes up with a profession that seemingly doesn't use or depend on personal computers. The other side then, within six steps, tries to knock that argument down. Here's an example.

Side A: Poets don't need computers.

Side B: Sure, the poet could handwrite his or her poetry, but eventually would want the poems typewritten, thus a computer.

Side A counters: The poet could use an old-fashioned typewriter.

Side B: Okay, then to submit the poem for publication, the poet would have to use the mail—the mail is sorted electronically by computers.

Side A counters: The poet could hand-deliver the typed manuscript.

Side B: To get into print, the poem would have to be made electronically, whether by someone at the publisher's typing it in or even using a scanner to get it into electronic form.

Side A: Arghh!!!

You get the idea? Have fun and let your imagination run the game. By the end of a few minutes, you'll probably be convinced that computers are indeed everywhere and involved in just about every aspect of modern life.

series of exams. Passing these exams proves that you have the necessary skills to work at a certain level in your profession, whether you're an aspiring plumber, teacher, barber, or lawyer.

If you successfully pass these exams, the organization that administers those exams grants you certification. You receive some piece of paper or pin or membership card that you can show to potential clients or employers. This certification gives those clients or employers a level of confidence that you can do what you say you can do. Without this certification, either you will not find suitable work in that profession or no one will trust you to do the work.

■ The Importance of CompTIA A+ Certification

Although microcomputers were introduced in the late 1970s, for many years PC technicians did not have a universally recognized way to show clients or employers that they know what to do under the hood of a personal computer. Sure, there were vendor-specific certifications, but the only way to get them was to get a job at an authorized warranty or repair facility first, and then get the certification. Not that there's anything wrong with vendor-specific training; it's just that no one manufacturer has taken enough market share to make IBM training, for example, something that works for any job. (Then there is always that little detail of getting the job first before you can get certified!)

The software/networking side of our business has not suffered from the same lack of certifications. Due to the dominance of certain companies at one time or another (for example, Microsoft and Novell), the vendor-specific certifications have provided a great way to get and keep a job. For example, Microsoft's *Microsoft Certified Systems Engineer (MCSE)*, Novell's *Certified Novell Engineer (CNE)*, and Cisco's *Cisco Certified Internetwork Expert (CCIE)* have opened the doors for many.

But what about the person who runs around all day repairing printers, repartitioning hard drives, upgrading device drivers, and building systems? What about the PC hobbyists who want to get paid for their skills? What about the folks who, because they had the audacity to show that they knew the difference between CMOS and a command prompt, find themselves with a new title like "PC Support Technician" or "Electronic Services Specialist"? On the other hand, how about the worst title of them all: "The Person Who Doesn't Get a Nickel Extra but Who Fixes the Computers"? CompTIA A+ certification fills that need.

What Is CompTIA A+ Certification?

CompTIA A+ certification is an industry-wide, vendor-neutral certification program developed and sponsored by the Computing Technology Industry Association (CompTIA). The CompTIA A+ certification shows that you have a basic competence in supporting microcomputers. You achieve this certification by taking two computer-based, multiple-choice examinations. The tests cover what technicians should know after nine months of full-time PC support experience. CompTIA A+ certification enjoys wide recognition throughout the computer industry. To date, more than 600,000 technicians have become CompTIA A+ certified, making it the most popular of all IT certifications.

Who Is CompTIA?

CompTIA is a nonprofit, industry trade association based in Oakbrook Terrace, Illinois. It consists of over 20,000 members in 102 countries. You'll find CompTIA offices in such diverse locales as Amsterdam, Dubai, Johannesburg, Tokyo, and São Paulo.

CompTIA provides a forum for people in these industries to network (as in meeting people), represents the interests of its members to the government, and provides certifications for many different aspects of the computer industry. CompTIA sponsors A+, Network+, i-Net+, Security+, and other certifications. CompTIA works hard to watch the IT industry and constantly looks to provide new certifications to meet the ongoing demand from its membership. Check out the CompTIA Web site at www.comptia.org for details on the other certifications that you can obtain from CompTIA.

Virtually every company of consequence in the IT industry is a member of CompTIA. Here are a few of the biggies:

Adobe Systems	AMD	Best Buy	Brother International
Canon	Cisco Systems	CompUSA	Fujitsu
Gateway	Hewlett-Packard	IBM	Intel
Kyocera	McAfee	Microsoft	NCR
Novell	Panasonic	Sharp Electronics	Siemens
Symantec	Toshiba	Total Seminars, LLC (that's my company)	Plus many thousands more!

CompTIA began offering CompTIA A+ certification back in 1993. When it first debuted, the IT industry largely ignored CompTIA A+ certification. Since that initial stutter, however, the CompTIA A+ certification has grown to become the de facto requirement for entrance into the PC industry. Many companies require CompTIA A+ certification for all of their PC support technicians, and the CompTIA A+ certification is widely recognized both in the United States and internationally. Additionally, many other certifications recognize CompTIA A+ certification and use it as credit toward their certifications.

The Path to Other Certifications

Most IT companies—big and small—see CompTIA A+ certification as the entry point to IT. From CompTIA A+, you have a number of certification options, depending on whether you want to focus more on hardware and operating systems, or move into network administration (although these aren't mutually exclusive goals). The following three certifications are worth serious consideration:

- CompTIA Network+ certification
- Microsoft Certified Professional certifications
- Cisco certifications

CompTIA Network+ Certification

If you haven't already taken the CompTIA Network+ certification exam, make it your next certification. Just as CompTIA A+ certification shows you have solid competency as a PC technician, CompTIA Network+ certification demonstrates your skills as a network technician, including understanding of network hardware, installation, and troubleshooting. CompTIA's Network+ certification is a natural step for continuing toward your Microsoft, Novell, or Cisco certifications. Take the CompTIA Network+: it's your obvious next certification!

Microsoft Certified Professional Certifications

Microsoft operating systems control a huge portion of all installed networks, and those networks need qualified support people to make them run. Microsoft's series of certifications for networking professionals are a natural next step after the CompTIA certifications. They offer a whole slew of tracks and exams, but you should first pursue the Microsoft Certified Professional (MCP). The MCP is the easiest Microsoft certification to get, as it only requires you to pass one of many different exams—and all of these exams count towards more advanced Microsoft certifications.

When it comes to advanced certifications, Microsoft's ever-popular Microsoft Certified Systems Engineer (MCSE) certification holds a lot of clout in the job market. The MCSE consists of seven exams: six core exams covering three study areas—client operating system, networking system, and design—and one elective. You can find more details on Microsoft's training Web site at www.microsoft.com/learning/mcp/default.asp.

Cisco Certifications

Let's face it, Cisco routers pretty much run the Internet and most intranets in the world. A *router* is a networking device that controls and directs the flow of information over networks, such as e-mail messages, Web browsing, and so on. Cisco provides three levels of certification for folks who want to show their skills at handling Cisco products. Nearly everyone interested in Cisco certification starts with the Cisco Certified Network Associate (CCNA). The CCNA can be yours for the price of only one completed exam, after which you can happily slap the word Cisco on your resume! After your CCNA, you should consider the Cisco Certified Networking Professional (CCNP) certification. See the Cisco certification Web site here for more details: www.cisco.com/web/learning/le3/learning_career_certifications_and_learning_paths_home.html.

■ How Do I Become CompTIA A+ Certified?

You become CompTIA A+ certified, in the simplest sense, by taking and passing two computer-based, multiple-choice exams. No prerequisites are required for taking the CompTIA A+ certification exams. There is no required training course, and there are no training materials to buy. You *do* have to pay a testing fee for each of the two exams. You pay your testing fees, go to a local testing center, and take the tests. You immediately know whether you have passed or failed. By passing both exams, you become a `CompTIA A+ Certified Service Technician`. There are no requirements for professional experience. You do not have to go through an authorized training center. There are no annual dues. There are no continuing education requirements. You pass; you're in. That's it. Now for the details.

The Basic Exam Structure

CompTIA offers three tracks to CompTIA A+ certification: a primary (referred to as the IT Technician track) and two secondary (Help Desk and Depot Technician tracks). All three tracks require you to take two exams, the first of which is called the `CompTIA A+ Essentials`.

The Essentials exam concentrates on understanding terminology and technology, how to do fundamental tasks such as upgrading RAM, and basic Windows operating system support.

To follow the primary track, you would also take the `CompTIA A+ 220-602` exam, called the "602" or "IT Technician exam." The IT Technician exam builds on the Essentials exam, concentrating on advanced configuration and troubleshooting, including using the command line to accomplish tech tasks. This exam also includes network and Internet configuration questions.

To attain CompTIA A+ certification on one of the two secondary tracks, you would take Essentials and follow with either the `CompTIA A+ 220-603` exam (Help Desk Technician) or the `CompTIA A+ 220-604` exam (Depot Technician). Both exams test on a subset of the information covered in the IT Technician exam, but go more in depth on some subjects and have less coverage on other subjects. Nearly a third of all questions on the Help Desk Technician exam ask about managing, configuring, and troubleshooting operating systems, for example, whereas only one in five questions on the IT Technician exam hits that subject.

All of the exams are extremely practical, with little or no interest in theory. All questions are multiple choice or "click on the right part of the picture" questions. The following is an example of the type of question you will see on the exams:

A dot-matrix printer is printing blank pages. Which item should you check first?

A. Printer drivers

B. Platen

C. Print head

D. Ribbon

The correct answer is D, the ribbon. You can make an argument for any of the others, but common sense (and skill as a PC technician) tells you to check the simplest possibility first.

The 2006 tests use a regular test format, in which you answer a set number of questions and are scored based on how many correct answers you get, rather than the adaptive format used in recent years. These exams will have no more than 100 questions each.

Tech Tip

The Big Change in CompTIA A+ Certification

In June of 2006, CompTIA announced the most comprehensive changes to the CompTIA A+ certification exams. Up to this point, the CompTIA A+ certification consisted of two exams very different from what we now use. CompTIA gave these two exams a number of different official names over the years, but regardless of the name they boiled down to what we called the "hardware" exam and the "operating system" exam. That split always seemed forced because you can't have a functional computer without both hardware and operating systems working together to get things done.

In keeping with the idea of a PC as a single system instead of the PC as two separate entities—a pile of hardware and a pile of software—CompTIA reshaped the exams into a basic, conceptual exam followed by a more in-depth configuration/maintenance/repair exam, for which you have three choices.

Tech Tip

Numbers and Names

The CompTIA exams have a rather unique naming system. The first exam, the one you must take regardless of which track you choose, is called CompTIA A+ Essentials. There is no number associated with this exam in any CompTIA literature, although many people (including the author) refer to this exam incorrectly as the "601 Exam." The other three exams are called the 220-602, 220-603, and 220-604 exams. There is no name for these other three exams, although people (again, including the author) tend to call them the IT Technician, Help Desk, and Depot Technician exams, respectively. If you can get anyone at CompTIA to explain why they chose such a strange naming system, please email the author: michaelm@totalsem.com.

Be aware that CompTIA may add new questions to the exams at any time to keep the content fresh. The subject matter covered by the exams won't change, but new questions may be added periodically at random intervals. This policy puts stronger emphasis on understanding concepts and having solid PC-tech knowledge rather than trying to memorize specific questions and answers that may have been on the tests in the past. Going forward, no book or Web resource will have all the "right answers" because those answers will constantly change. Luckily for you, however, this book does not just teach you what steps to follow in a particular case, but how to be a knowledgeable tech who understands *why* you're doing those steps, so that when you encounter a new problem (or test question), you can work out the answer. Not only will this help you pass the exams, you'll be a better PC tech!

To keep up to date, we monitor the CompTIA A+ exams for new content and update the special Tech Files section of the Total Seminars Web site (www.totalsem.com) with new articles covering subjects we believe may appear on future versions of the exams.

The Essentials Exam

This book is designed to help you pass the Essentials exam. The questions on the CompTIA A+ Essentials exam fit into one of eight categories or *domains*. The number of questions for each domain is based on the following percentages shown in Table 1.1.

The Essentials exam tests your knowledge of computer components, expecting you to be able to identify just about every common device on PCs, including variations within device types. Here's a list.

- Floppy drives
- Hard drives
- CD- and DVD-media drives
- Solid state drives
- Motherboards
- Power supplies

- CPUs
- RAM
- Monitors
- Input devices, such as keyboards, mice, and touchscreens
- Video and multimedia cards

Table 1.1	Essentials Exam Domains and Percentages
Domain	**Percentage**
1.0 Personal Computer Components	21%
2.0 Laptop and Portable Devices	11%
3.0 Operating Systems	21%
4.0 Printers and Scanners	9%
5.0 Networks	12%
6.0 Security	11%
7.0 Safety and Environmental Issues	10%
8.0 Communication and Professionalism	5%

- Network and modem cards
- Cables and connectors
- Heat sinks, fans, and liquid cooling systems
- Laptops and portable devices

- Printers
- Scanners
- Network switches, cabling, and wireless adapters
- Biometric devices

The Essentials exam tests your ability to recognize, understand, and install all the standard technology involved in a personal computer. The emphasis is on installing devices on the outside of the computer—items such as printers, monitors, and mice. Sure, you need to know what a hard drive does and how it works, but the Essentials exam will not aggressively test you on how to actually install a hard drive. You do, however, need to know how to set up an already installed hard drive and configure devices in Windows 2000 or Windows XP. You also have to understand drivers. You have to know your way around Windows and understand the tasks involved in updating, upgrading, and installing the operating systems. You need to know the standard diagnostic tools available in Windows—not so you can fix everything, but so that you can work with higher-level techs to fix things.

You're tested on your knowledge of very basic computer security, including identifying, installing, and configuring security hardware and software. You need to know security tools and diagnostic techniques for troubleshooting. Again, you're not expected to know everything, just the very basics.

Finally, the Essentials exam puts a lot of emphasis on safety and environmental issues, and on communication and professionalism. You need to know how to recycle and dispose of computer gear properly. You have to understand and avoid hazardous situations. The exam tests your ability to communicate effectively with customers and coworkers. You need to understand professional behavior and demonstrate that you have tact, discretion, and respect for others and their property.

Help! Which Exam Should I Take Next?

With three different tracks to becoming a CompTIA A+ Certified Technician, the inevitable question revolves around choosing the proper track. *The bottom line is that unless you have an employer specifically telling you otherwise, do the primary track.* Take Essentials and follow that with the 220-602 IT Technician exam. This is by far the more common track and the one the vast majority of employers will want to see on your résumé! When you complete a track, your test results will show which track you chose.

If you choose the primary IT Technician track, potential employers will know they're getting a properly well-rounded tech who can be thrown into pretty much any IT situation and handle it well. The Help Desk and Depot Technician tracks target very specific jobs, so unless that job is yours, completing one of these tracks—and not doing the IT Technician track—limits your employment opportunities.

A glance at the competencies for the three Technician exams (602, 603, and 604) might suggest that it would be easier to take 603 or 604 because they have fewer domains than 602, but that assumption could prove very painful indeed. The Help Desk and Depot Technician exams test you on the

same material as the IT Technician exam, but emphasize different aspects or different ways to tackle personal computer issues.

How Do I Take the Exams?

Two companies, **Prometric** and **Pearson/VUE** , administer the actual CompTIA A+ testing. There are thousands of Prometric and Pearson/VUE testing centers across the United States and Canada, and the rest of the world. You may take the exams at any testing center. Both Prometric and Pearson/VUE offer complete listings online of all available testing centers. You can select the closest training center and schedule your exams right from the comfort of your favorite Web browser:

> www.prometric.com
> www.vue.com

Alternatively, in the United States and Canada, call Prometric at 800-776-4276 or Pearson/VUE at 877-551-PLUS (7587) to schedule the exams and to locate the nearest testing center. International customers can find a list of Prometric and Pearson/VUE international contact numbers for various regions of the world on CompTIA's Web site at www.comptia.org by selecting the Find Your Test Center link on the CompTIA A+ certification page.

You must pay for the exam when you call to schedule. Be prepared to sit on hold for a while. Have your Social Security number (or international equivalent) and a credit card ready when you call. Both Prometric and Pearson/VUE will be glad to invoice you, but you won't be able to take the exam until they receive full payment.

If you have special needs, both Prometric and Pearson/VUE will accommodate you, although this may limit your selection of testing locations.

How Much Does the Exam Cost?

The cost of the exam depends on whether you work for a CompTIA member or not. At this writing, the cost for non-CompTIA members is $158 (U.S.) for each exam. International prices vary, but you can check the CompTIA Web site for international pricing. Of course, the prices are subject to change without notice, so always check the CompTIA Web site for current pricing!

Very few people pay full price for the exam. Virtually every organization that provides CompTIA A+ training and testing also offers discount **vouchers** . You buy a discount voucher and then use the voucher number instead of a credit card when you schedule the exam. Vouchers are sold per exam, so you'll need two vouchers for the two CompTIA A+ exams. **Total Seminars** is one place to get discount vouchers. You can call Total Seminars at 800-446-6004 or 281-922-4166, or get vouchers via the Web site: www .totalsem.com. No one should ever pay full price for CompTIA A+ exams!

How to Pass the CompTIA A+ Exams

The single most important thing to remember about the CompTIA A+ certification exams is that CompTIA designed the exams to test the knowledge of a technician with only nine months' experience—so keep it simple! The exams aren't interested in your ability to overclock CAS timings

in CMOS or whether you can explain the exact difference between the Intel 975X Express and the NVIDIA nForce590 SLI chipsets. Don't bother with a lot of theory—think in terms of practical knowledge. Read the book, do whatever works for you to memorize the key concepts and procedures, take the Quizzes and the Essays at the end of the chapter, review any topics you miss, and you should pass with no problem.

Some of you may be in or just out of school, so studying for exams is nothing novel. But if it's been a while since you've had to study for and take an exam, or if you think maybe you could use some tips, you may find the next section valuable. It lays out a proven strategy for preparing to take and pass the CompTIA A+ exams. Try it. It works.

Those of you who just want more knowledge in managing and troubleshooting PCs can follow the same strategy as certification-seekers. Think in practical terms and work with the PC as you go through each chapter.

Obligate Yourself

The very first step you should take is to schedule yourself for the exams. Have you ever heard the old adage, "heat and pressure make diamonds"? Well, if you don't give yourself a little "heat," you'll end up procrastinating and delay taking the exams, possibly forever! Do yourself a favor. Using the information below, determine how much time you'll need to study for the exams, and then call Prometric or VUE and schedule them accordingly. Knowing the exams are coming up makes it much easier to turn off the television and crack open the book! You can schedule an exam as little as a few weeks in advance, but if you schedule an exam and can't take it at the scheduled time, you must reschedule at least a day in advance or you'll lose your money.

Set Aside the Right Amount of Study Time

After helping thousands of techs get their CompTIA A+ certification, we at Total Seminars have developed a pretty good feel for the amount of study time needed to pass the CompTIA A+ certification exams. Table 1.2 provides an estimate to help you plan how much study time you must commit to the CompTIA A+ certification exams. Keep in mind that these are averages. If you're not a great student or if you're a little on the nervous side, add 10 percent; if you're a fast learner or have a good bit of computer experience, you may want to reduce the figures.

To use the table, just circle the values that are most accurate for you and add them up to get your estimated total hours of study time.

To that value, add hours based on the number of months of direct, professional experience you have had supporting PCs, as shown in Table 1.3.

A total neophyte usually needs around 200 hours of study time. An experienced tech shouldn't need more than 40 hours.

Total hours for you to study: _____.

A Strategy for Study

Now that you have a feel for how long it's going to take, it's time to develop a study strategy. I'd like to suggest a strategy that has worked for others who've come before you, whether they were experienced techs or total newbies. This book is designed to accommodate the different study agendas of these two different groups of students. The first group is experienced techs who already have strong PC experience, but need to be sure they're ready to be tested on the specific subjects covered by the CompTIA A+ exams. The second group is

Table 1.2	Analyzing Skill Levels			
		Amount of Experience		
Tech Task	None	Once or Twice	Every Now and Then	Quite a Bit
Installing an adapter card	12	10	8	4
Installing hard drives	12	10	8	2
Installing modems and NICs	8	6	6	3
Connecting a computer to the Internet	8	6	4	2
Installing printers and scanners	4	3	2	1
Installing RAM	8	6	4	2
Installing CPUs	8	7	5	3
Fixing printers	6	5	4	3
Fixing boot problems	8	7	7	5
Fixing portable computers	8	6	4	2
Building complete systems	12	10	8	6
Using the command line	8	8	6	4
Installing/optimizing Windows	10	8	6	4
Using Windows 2000	6	6	4	2
Using Windows XP	6	6	4	2
Configuring NTFS permissions	6	4	3	2
Configuring a wireless network	6	5	3	2
Configuring a software firewall	6	4	2	1
Installing a sound card	2	2	1	0
Using OS diagnostic tools	8	8	6	4
Using a Volt-Ohm Meter	4	3	2	1

those with little or no background in the computer field. These techs can benefit from a more detailed understanding of the history and concepts that underlie modern PC technology, to help them remember the specific subject matter information they must know for the exams. I'll use the shorthand terms Old

Table 1.3	Adding Up Your Study Time
Months of Direct, Professional Experience...	To Your Study Time...
0	Add 50
Up to 6	Add 30
6 to 12	Add 10
Over 12	Add 0

Techs and New Techs for these two groups. If you're not sure which group you fall into, pick a few chapters and go through some end-of-chapter questions. If you score less than 70%, go the New Tech route.

I have broken most of the chapters into two distinct parts:

- **Historical/Conceptual** Topics that are not on the CompTIA A+ exams, but will help you understand what is on the CompTIA A+ exams more clearly.
- **Essentials** Topics that clearly fit under the CompTIA A+ Essentials exam domains.

The beginning of each of these areas is clearly marked with a large banner that looks like this:

Historical/Conceptual

Those of you who fall into the Old Tech group may want to skip everything but the Essentials area in each chapter. After reading that section, jump immediately to the questions at the end of the chapter. The end-of-chapter questions concentrate on information in the Essentials section. If you run into problems, review the Historical/Conceptual section in that chapter. Note that you may need to skip back to previous chapters to get the Historical/Conceptual information you need for later chapters.

If you're a New Tech or if you're an Old Tech who wants the full learning experience this book can offer, start by reading the book, *the whole book,* as though you were reading a novel, from page one to the end without skipping around. Because so many computer terms and concepts build on each other, skipping around greatly increases the odds you will become confused and end up closing the book and firing up your favorite PC game. Not that I have anything against PC games, but unfortunately that skill is *not* useful for the CompTIA A+ exams!

Your goal on this first read is to understand concepts, the *whys* behind the *hows.* It is very helpful to have a PC nearby as you read so you can stop and inspect the PC to see a piece of hardware or how a particular concept manifests in the real world. As you read about floppy drives, for example, inspect the cables. Do they look like the ones in the book? Is there a variation? Why? It is imperative that you understand why you are doing something, not just how to do it on one particular system under one specific set of conditions. Neither the exams nor real life as a PC tech works that way!

If you're reading this book as part of a managing and troubleshooting PCs class, rather than a certification-prep course, then I highly recommend going the New Tech route, even if you have a decent amount of experience. The book contains a lot of details that can trip you up if you focus only on the test-specific sections of the chapters. Plus, your program might stress historical and conceptual knowledge as well as practical, hands-on skills.

The CompTIA A+ certification exams assume that you have basic user skills. The exams really try to trick you with questions on processes that you may do every day and not really think about. Here's a classic: "In order to move a file from the C:\WINDOWS folder to the A:\ drive using Windows Explorer, what key must you hold down while dragging the file?" If you can answer that without going to your keyboard and trying a few likely keys, you're better than most techs! In the real world, you can try a few wrong answers before you hit on the right one, but for the exams, you have to *know* it! Whether Old Tech or New Tech, make sure you are proficient at user-level Windows skills, including the following:

- Recognizing all the components of the standard Windows desktop (Start Menu, System Tray, etc.)
- Manipulating windows—resizing, moving, and so on
- Creating, deleting, renaming, moving, and copying files and folders within Windows
- Understanding file extensions and their relationship with program associations
- Using common keyboard shortcuts/hotkeys

Any PC technician who has been around a while will tell you that one of the great secrets in the computer business is that there's almost never anything completely new in the world of computer technology. Faster, cleverer, smaller, wider—absolutely—but the underlying technology, the core of what makes your PC and its various peripheral devices operate, has changed remarkably little since PCs came into widespread use a few decades ago. When you do your initial read-through, you may be tempted to skip the Historical/Conceptual sections—don't! Understanding the history and technological developments behind today's PCs really helps you understand why they work—or don't work—the way they do. Basically, I'm passing on to you the kind of knowledge you might get by apprenticing yourself to an older experienced PC tech.

After you've completed the first read-through, go through the book again, this time in textbook mode. If you're an Old Tech, this is where you start your studying. Try to cover one chapter at a sitting. Concentrate on the Essentials sections. Get a highlighter and mark the phrases and sentences that bring out major points. Be sure you understand how the pictures and illustrations relate to the concepts being discussed.

Try This!

Windows Vista

Microsoft's Windows Vista operating system debuted in January 2007, and although CompTIA won't immediately put it on the CompTIA A+ certification exams, every tech will need to know it. Do yourself and your customers a favor and work with Windows Vista as soon as you can *after* you finish getting CompTIA A+ certified, even if it means using a school computer or making a lot of trips to computer stores.

I suggest waiting only because you'll want to keep the details of how to do things in Windows 2000 and Windows XP as fresh as possible before you take the exams. If you're studying simply to gain knowledge and are not worried about getting certified, then jump right in!

Once you have access to a Windows Vista computer, skim through this book and ask yourself these questions. What's different about setting up drives? What about installation? What diagnostic and troubleshooting tools does Vista offer that you can't find or that differ significantly from tools in Windows 2000 or Windows XP?

If you have any problems, any questions, or if you just want to argue about something, feel free to send an e-mail to the author—michaelm@totalsem.com, or to the editor—scottj@totalsem.com.

For any other information you might need, contact CompTIA directly at their Web site: www.comptia.org.

Tech Tip

Study Strategies

Perhaps it's been a while since you had to study for a test. Or perhaps it hasn't, but you've done your best since then to block the whole experience from your mind! Either way, savvy test-takers know there are certain techniques that make studying for tests more efficient and effective.

*Here's a trick used by students in law and medical schools who have to memorize reams of information: write it down. The act of writing something down (not typing, **writing**) in and of itself helps you to remember it, even if you never look at what you wrote again. Try taking separate notes on the material and recreating diagrams by hand to help solidify the information in your mind.*

Another oldie but goodie: make yourself flash cards with questions and answers on topics you find difficult. A third trick: take your notes to bed and read them just before you go to sleep. Many people find they really do learn while they sleep!

Chapter 1 Review

Chapter Summary

After reading this chapter and completing the exercises, you should understand the following about the CompTIA A+ exams.

The Importance of Skill in Managing and Troubleshooting PCs

- The IT workforce designs, builds, and maintains computers, computer programs, and networks, the basic information tools of the early 21st century. PC techs take care of personal computers, so they represent an essential component in that workforce. As PCs become more complex, the IT workforce needs specialized PC techs.

- Certifications prove to employers that you have the necessary skill to work in your chosen field. If you want a job fixing automobiles, for example, you get the *Automotive Service Excellence (ASE)* certification. To get certified, you take and successfully pass exams. Then the organization that administers those exams grants you certification. This is particularly important for IT workers.

The Importance of CompTIA A+ Certification

- In the early days of the personal computer, you could get vendor-specific certifications such as "IBM Technician," but nothing general for PC techs. Worse, you often had to have a job at that company to get the vendor-specific certification.

- CompTIA A+ certification is an industry-wide, vendor-neutral certification program that shows that you have a basic competence in supporting microcomputers. You achieve this certification by taking two computer-based, multiple-choice examinations. The tests cover what technicians should know after nine months of full-time PC support experience. CompTIA A+ certification enjoys wide recognition throughout the computer industry.

- CompTIA is a nonprofit, industry trade association based in Oakbrook Terrace, Illinois. It consists of over 20,000 members in 102 countries. CompTIA provides a forum for people in these industries to network, represents the interests of its members to the government, and provides certifications for many different aspects of the computer industry. CompTIA sponsors A+, Network+, i-Net+, Security+, and other certifications.

- The CompTIA A+ certification is the de facto entry point to IT. From CompTIA A+, you have a number of certification options, depending on whether you want to focus more on hardware and operating systems, or move into network administration. You can get CompTIA Network+ certification, for example, or go on to get Microsoft or Cisco certified. CompTIA Network+ certification is the most obvious certification to get after becoming CompTIA A+ certified.

How to Become CompTIA A+ Certified

- You become CompTIA A+ certified, in the simplest sense, by taking and passing two computer-based, multiple-choice exams. No prerequisites are required for taking the CompTIA A+ certification exams. There is no required training course, and there are no training materials to buy. You *do* have to pay a testing fee for each of the two exams.

- CompTIA offers three tracks to CompTIA A+ certification, a primary (referred to as the IT Technician track) and two secondary (Help Desk and Depot Technician tracks). All three tracks require you to take two exams, the first of which is called the CompTIA A+ Essentials. The Essentials exam concentrates on understanding terminology and technology, how to do fundamental tasks such as upgrading RAM, and basic Windows operating system support. The IT Technician exam builds on the Essentials exam, concentrating on advanced configuration and troubleshooting.

- To attain CompTIA A+ certification on one of the two secondary tracks, you would take Essentials and follow with either the CompTIA 220-603 exam (Help Desk Technician) or the CompTIA 220-604 exam (Depot Technician). Both exams test on a subset of the information covered in the IT Technician exam, but go more in depth on some subjects and have less coverage on other subjects.

- All of the exams are extremely practical, with little or no interest in theory. All questions are multiple choice or "click on the right part of the picture" questions. CompTIA may add new questions to the exams at any time to keep the content fresh, although the subject matter covered by the exams won't change.

- Of the three tracks to becoming a CompTIA A+ Certified Technician, most techs take the Essentials plus 220-602, IT Technician. Take one of the secondary tracks only if an employer specifically requires it.

- Two companies, Prometric and Pearson/VUE, administer the actual CompTIA A+ testing. You can schedule exam time and location via the Web site for either company, www.prometric.com or www.vue.com. Check CompTIA's Web site for international links.

- To achieve success with the CompTIA A+ certification exams, think in terms of practical knowledge. Read the book. Work through the problems. Work with computers. Take the practice exams. You should obligate yourself by scheduling your exams. This keeps you focused on study.

Key Terms

certification (1)
Cisco Certified Network Associate (CCNA) (4)
CompTIA A+ 220-602 (IT Technician) (5)
CompTIA A+ 220-603 (Help Desk Technician) (5)
CompTIA A+ 220-604 (Depot Technician) (5)

CompTIA A+ certification (2)
CompTIA A+ Certified Service Technician (5)
CompTIA A+ Essentials (5)
CompTIA Network+ certification (4)
Computing Technology Industry Association (CompTIA) (2)
information technology (IT) (1)

Microsoft Certified Professional (MCP) (4)
network (1)
PC tech (1)
Pearson/VUE (8)
Prometric (8)
Total Seminars (8)
vouchers (8)

Key Term Quiz

Use the Key Terms list to complete the sentences that follow. Not all terms will be used.

1. The folks who design, build, program, and fix computers are the _____ workforce.

2. You can become a CompTIA A+ Certified Service Technician by passing the _____ and CompTIA A+ 220-602 (IT Technician) exams.

3. A _____ gives clients and employers a level of confidence that you can do what you say you can do.

4. A casual term for a person who builds and maintains computers is _____.

5. Prometric and _____ administer the CompTIA A+ certification exams.

Multiple-Choice Quiz

1. Which of the following is a vendor-specific certification? (Select all that apply.)
   A. Certified Cisco Network Administrator
   B. CompTIA A+
   C. CompTIA Network+
   D. Microsoft Certified Systems Engineer

2. Which of the following certifications is the de facto requirement for entrance into the PC industry?
   A. Certified Cisco Network Administrator
   B. CompTIA A+
   C. CompTIA Network+
   D. Microsoft Certified Systems Engineer

3. John loves the Internet and wants a career working on the machines that make the Internet work. He's completed both CompTIA A+ and Network+ certifications, so which of the following certifications would make a good next step?

   A. Certified Cisco Network Associate

   B. Certified Cisco Network Professional

   C. CompTIA Security+

   D. Microsoft Certified Systems Engineer

4. At which of the following Web sites can you register to take the CompTIA A+ certification exam?

   A. www.comptia.org

   B. www.microsoft.com

   C. www.totalsem.com

   D. www.vue.com

5. Which of the following companies are members of CompTIA? (Choose all that apply.)

   A. IBM

   B. Intel

   C. Microsoft

   D. Hewlett-Packard

Essay Quiz

1. Write a short essay on the benefits of certification in the field of computers. Include discussion on how the CompTIA certifications function within the broader category of computer certification.

   Why do you suppose people get certifications rather than (or in addition to) two- and four-year college degrees in IT?

Lab Projects

If you have access to the Internet, do some searching on computer certifications. Make a personal certification tree or pathway that maps out a series of certifications to pursue that might interest you. What certifications would be useful if you wanted to be a graphics designer, for example? What if you want to create computer games?

The Visible PC

chapter 2

"The true mystery of the world is the visible, not the invisible."
—Oscar Wilde

Mastering the craft of a PC technician requires you to learn a lot of details about the many pieces of hardware in the typical PC. Even the most basic PC contains hundreds of discrete hardware components, each with its own set of characteristics, shapes, sizes, colors, connections, and so on. By the end of this book, you will be able to discuss all of these components in detail.

This chapter takes you inside a typical PC, starting with an overview of how computers work. Because it's always good to follow the physician's rule, "First, do no harm," the second section of the chapter gives you the scoop on how to avoid damaging anything when you open up the computer.

Remember the children's song that goes, "Oh, the leg bone connects to the thigh bone…"? Well, think of the rest of the chapter in that manner, showing you what the parts look like and giving you a rough idea as to how they work and connect. In later chapters, you'll dissect all these PC "leg bones" and "thigh bones" and get to the level of detail you need to install, configure, maintain, and fix computers. Even if you are an expert, do not skip this chapter! It introduces a large number of terms that will be used throughout the rest of the book. Many of these terms you will know, but some you will not, so take some time and read it.

In this chapter, you will learn how to

- **Describe how the PC works**
- **Identify the essential tools of the trade and avoid electrostatic discharge**
- **Identify the different connectors on a typical PC system unit**
- **Identify the major internal and external components of a PC**

It is handy, although certainly not required, to have a PC that you can take the lid off of and inspect as you progress. Almost any old PC will help—it doesn't even need to work. So get thee a screwdriver, grab your PC, and see if you can recognize the various components as you read about them.

Historical/Conceptual

■ How the PC Works

You've undoubtedly seen a PC in action—a nice, glossy monitor displaying a picture that changes according to the actions of the person sitting in front of it, typing away on a keyboard, clicking a mouse, or twisting a joystick. Sound pours out of tiny speakers that flank the screen, and a box whirs happily beneath the table. The PC is a computer: a machine that enables you to do work, produce documents, play games, balance your checkbook, and check up on the latest sports scores on the Internet.

Although the computer is certainly a machine, it's also `programming`: the commands that tell the computer what to do to get work done. These commands are just ones and zeroes that the computer's hardware understands, enabling it to do amazing actions, such as perform powerful mathematic functions, move data (also ones and zeroes), realize the mouse has moved, and put pretty icons on the screen. So a computer is a complex interaction between hardware and computer programming, created by your fellow humans.

Ever heard of Morse code? Morse code is nothing more than dots and dashes to those who do not understand it, but if you send dots and dashes (in the right order) to a guy who understands Morse code, you can tell him a joke. Think of programming as Morse code for the computer. You may not understand those ones and zeroes, but your computer certainly does! (See Figure 2.1.)

There's more to the ones and zeroes than just programming. All of the data on the computer—the Web pages, your documents, your e-mail—is also stored as ones and zeroes. Programs know how to translate these ones and zeroes into a form humans understand.

Programming comes in two forms. First are the applications—the programs that get work done. Word processing programs, Web browsers, and e-mail programs are all considered applications. But applications need a main program to support them. They need a program that enables you to start and stop applications, copy/move/delete data, talk to the hardware, and perform lots of other jobs. This program is called the operating

I *know* this. This is binary! It all makes sense now.

● **Figure 2.1** Computer musing that a string of ones and zeroes makes perfect sense to him

system (OS). Microsoft Windows is the most popular OS today, but there are other computer operating systems, such as Apple Macintosh OS X (Figure 2.2) and the popular (and free) Linux. Computer people lump operating systems and applications into the term **software** to differentiate them from the hardware of the computer.

Understanding the computer at this broad conceptual level—in terms of hardware, OS, and programs—can help you explain things to customers, but good techs have a much more fundamental appreciation and understanding of the complex interplay of all the software and the individual pieces of hardware. In short, techs need to know the processes going on behind the scenes.

From the CompTIA A+ tech's perspective, the computer functions through four stages: input, processing, output, and storage. Knowing which parts participate in a particular stage of the computing process enables you to troubleshoot on a fundamental and decisive level.

The CompTIA A+ certification exams focus on hardware and operating systems; other certifications cover many of the programs in common use today. Two examples are the Microsoft Office Specialist (MOS) and Macromedia Certified Professional certifications.

Input

To illustrate this four-step process, let's walk through the steps involved in a fairly common computer task: preparing your taxes. [Insert collective groan here.] February has rolled around and, at least in the United States,

• **Figure 2.2**   OS X interface

• **Figure 2.3** TurboTax is an example of software.

millions of people install their favorite tax software, TurboTax from Intuit, onto their computers to help them prepare their taxes (Figure 2.3). After starting TurboTax, your first job is to provide the computer with data—essential information, such as your name, where you live, how much you earned, and how many dollars you gave to federal and state governments.

Various pieces of hardware enable you to input data, the most common of which are the keyboard and mouse. Most computers won't react when you say, "Hey you!"—at least anywhere outside of a *Star Trek* set. Although that day will come, for now you must use something decidedly more mechanical: a keyboard to type in your data. The OS provides a fundamental service in this process as well. You can bang on a keyboard all day and accomplish nothing without the OS translating your keystrokes into code that the hardware can understand.

Processing

Next, the computer processes your data. It places information in various appropriate "boxes" in TurboTax, and then it does the math for you.

Processing takes place inside the system unit—the box under your desk—and happens almost completely at a hardware level, although that hardware functions according to rules laid out in the OS. Again you have a complex interaction between hardware and software.

The processing portion is the magical part—you can't see it happen. The first half of this book demystifies this stage because good techs understand all the pieces of the process. I won't go through the specific hardware involved in the processing stage here because the pieces change according to the type of process.

Output

Simply adding up your total tax for the year is useless unless the computer shows you the result. That's where the third step—output—comes into play. Once the computer finishes processing data, it must put the information somewhere for you to inspect it. Often it places data on the monitor so you can see what you've just typed. It might send the data over to the printer if you tell it so you can print out copies of your tax return to mail to the Internal Revenue Service (or whatever the Tax Man is called where you live). A hardware device does the actual printing, but the OS controls the printing process. Again, it's a fundamental interaction of hardware and software.

Storage

Once you've sent in your tax return, you most likely do not want all that work simply to disappear. What happens if the IRS comes back a couple of months later with a question about your return? Yikes! You need to keep permanent records; plus, you need to keep a copy of the tax program. The fourth stage in the computing process is storage. A lot of devices are used in the storage process, the most visible of which are the external storage parts, such as floppy diskettes and CD-R discs (Figure 2.4).

The Art of the PC Technician

Using the four stages of the computing process—input, processing, output, and storage—to master how the PC works and, in turn, become a great technician, requires that you understand all the pieces of hardware and software involved **and** the interactions between them that make up the various stages. You have to know what the parts do, in other words, and how they work together. The best place to start is with a real computer. Let's go through the process of inspecting a typical, complete PC, including opening up a few important pieces to see the components inside. Hopefully, you've got a real computer in front of you right now that you may dismantle a bit. No two computers are exactly the same, so you'll see differences between your PC and the one in this chapter—and that's okay. You'll gain an appreciation of the fact that all computers have the same main parts that do the same jobs even though they differ in size, shape, and color.

By the time you reach the end of this book, you'll have a deeper, more nuanced understanding of the interaction of hardware and software in the four-stage computing process. Just as great artists have mastered fundamental skills of their trade before creating a masterpiece, you'll have the fundamentals of the art of the computer technician and be on your road to mastery.

• **Figure 2.4**   Typical storage (CD-R discs)

■ Tools of the Trade and ESD Avoidance

Before we dive into the PC, you need two pieces of information: an overview of the most common tools you'll find in a tech's toolkit and how *not* to destroy hardware inadvertently through electrostatic discharge.

Tools of the Trade

The basic technician toolkit consists of a Phillips-head screwdriver and not much else—seriously—but a half dozen tools round out a fully functional toolkit. Most kits have a star-headed Torx wrench, a nut driver or two, a pair of tweezers, a little grabber tool, and a hemostat to go along with Phillips-head and flat-head screwdrivers (Figure 2.5).

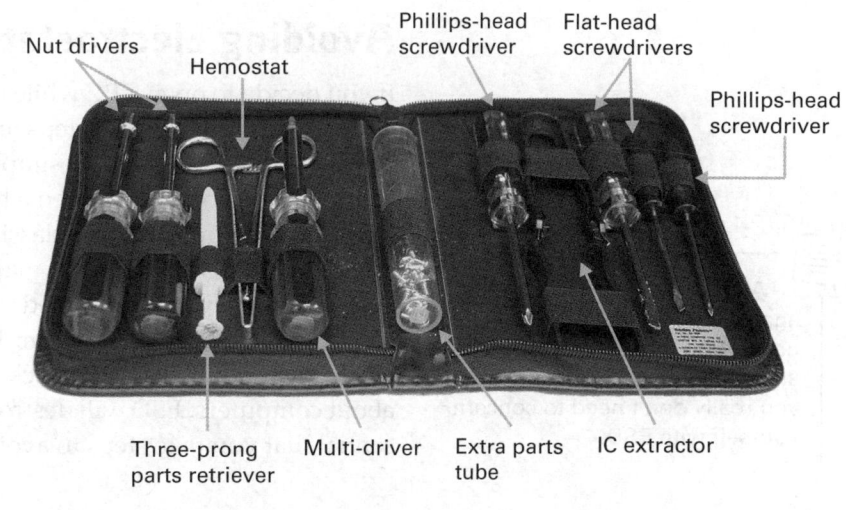

• **Figure 2.5**   Typical technician toolkit

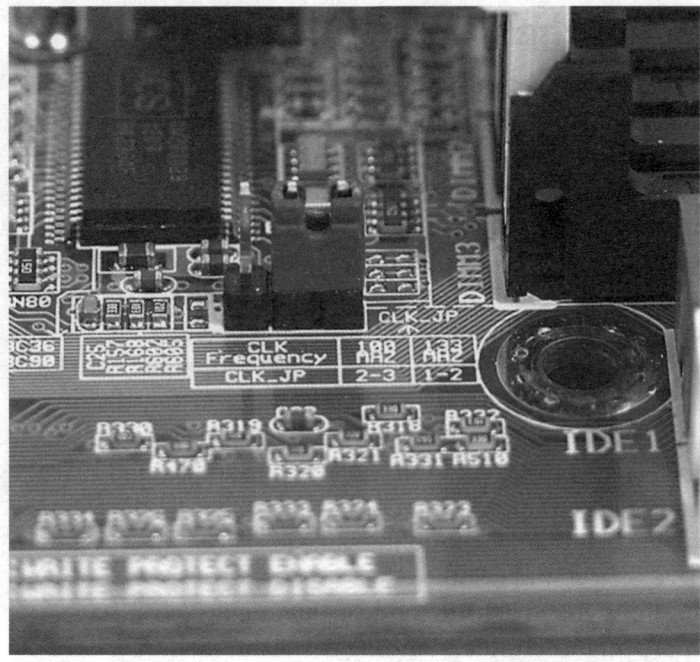

• **Figure 2.6**   Close-up of a printed circuit board (PCB)

A lot of techs will throw in a magnifying glass and a flashlight for those hard-to-read numbers and text on the printed circuit boards (PCBs) that make up a large percentage of devices inside the system unit (Figure 2.6). Contrary to what you might think, techs rarely need a hammer.

Essentials

Avoiding Electrostatic Discharge

If you decide to open a PC while reading this chapter, as I encourage you to do, you must take proper steps to avoid the greatest killer of PCs—**electrostatic discharge (ESD)**. ESD simply means the passage of a static electrical charge. Have you ever rubbed a balloon against your shirt, making the balloon stick to you? That's a classic example of static electricity. When that static charge discharges, you may not notice it happening—although on a cool, dry day, I've been shocked so hard by touching a doorknob that I could see a big, blue spark! I've never heard of a human being getting anything worse than a rather nasty shock from ESD, but I can't say the same thing about computers. ESD will destroy the sensitive parts of your PC, so it is essential that you take steps to avoid ESD when working on your PC.

All PCs are well protected against ESD on the outside—unless you take a screwdriver and actually open up your PC, you really don't need to concern yourself with ESD.

Anti-static Tools

ESD only takes place when two objects that store different amounts (the hip electrical term to use is **potential**) of static electricity come in contact.

The secret to avoiding ESD is to keep you and the parts of the PC you touch at the same electrical potential. You can accomplish this by connecting yourself to the PC via a handy little device called an anti-static wrist strap . This simple device consists of a wire that connects on one end to an alligator clip and on the other end to a small metal plate that secures to your wrist with an elastic strap. You snap the alligator clip onto any handy metal part of the PC and place the wrist strap on either wrist. Figure 2.7 shows a typical anti-static wrist strap in use.

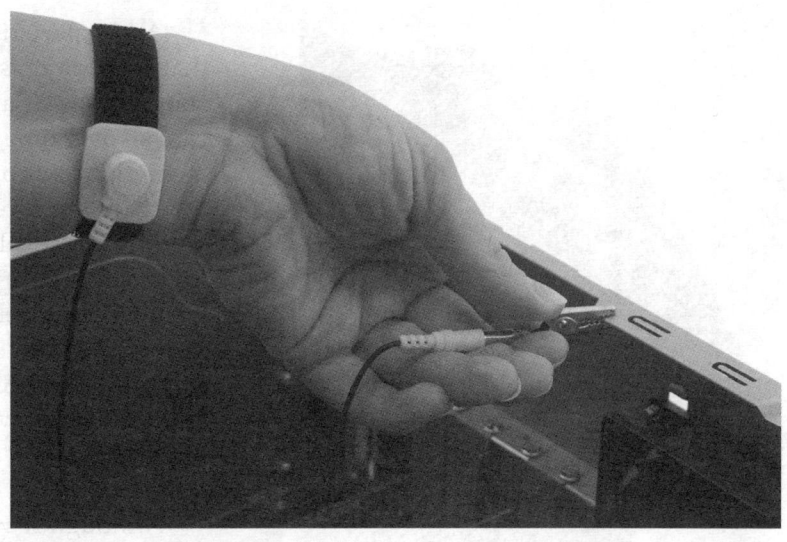

• **Figure 2.7**   Anti-static wrist strap in use

Anti-static wrist straps are standard equipment for anyone working on a PC, but other tools might come in handy. One of the big issues when working with a PC stems from the fact that in many situations you find yourself pulling out parts from the PC and setting them aside. The moment you take a piece out of the PC, it no longer has contact with the systems and may pick up static from other sources. Techs use anti-static mats to eliminate this risk. An anti-static mat acts as a point of common potential—you can usually purchase a combination anti-static wrist strap and mat that all connect together to keep you, the PC, and any loose components at the same electrical potential (Figure 2.8).

Static electricity, and therefore the risk of ESD, is much more prevalent in dry, cool environments.

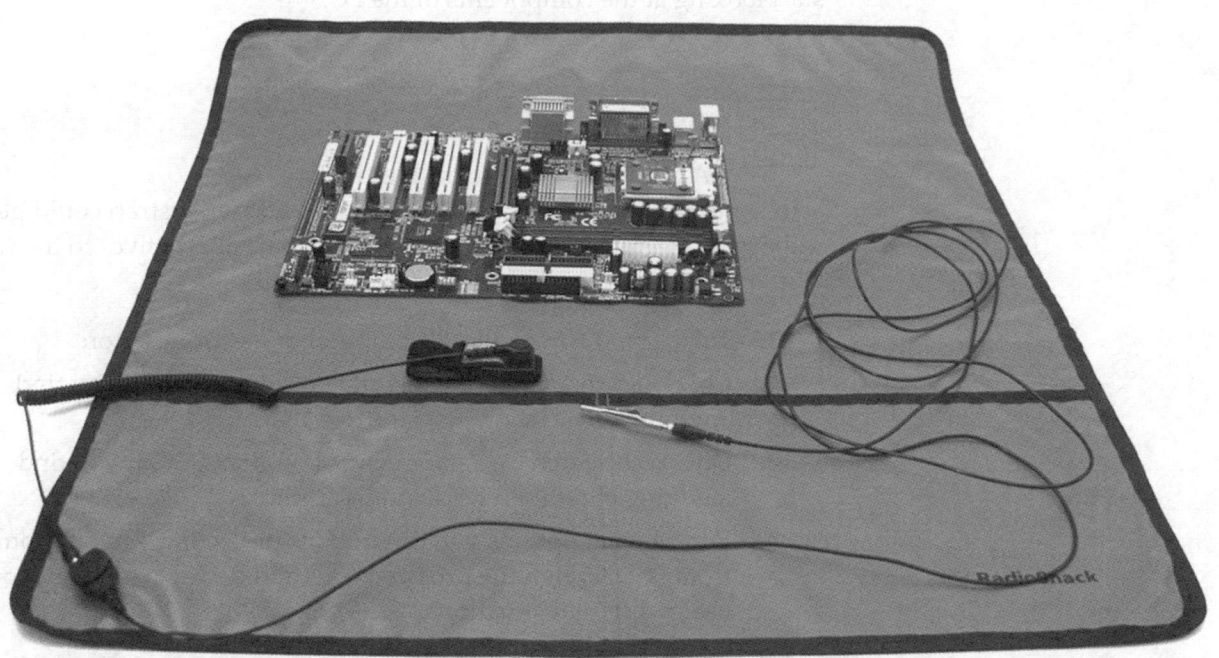

• **Figure 2.8**   Anti-static wrist strap and mat combination

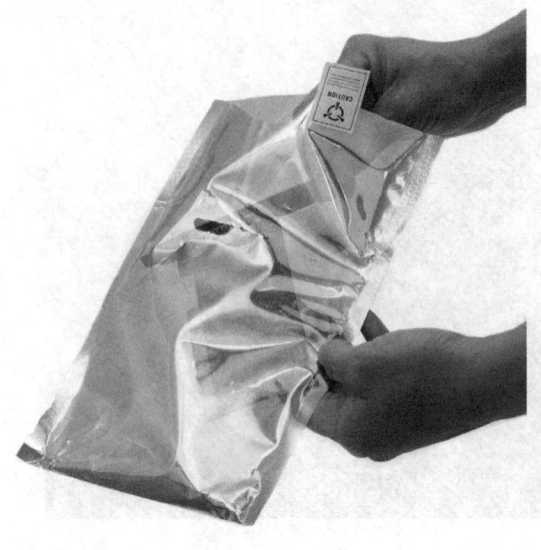

Anti-static wrist straps and mats use tiny resistors—devices that stop or *resist* the flow of electricity—to prevent anti-static charge from racing through the device. These resistors can fail over time, so it's always a good idea to read the documentation that comes with your anti-static tools to see how to test those small resistors properly.

Any electrical component not in a PC needs to be stored in an anti-static bag, a specially designed bag that sheds whatever static electricity you have when you touch it, thus preventing any damage to components stored within (Figure 2.9). Almost all PC components come in an anti-static bag when purchased. Experienced techs never throw these bags away, as you never know when you'll want to pull a part out and place it on a shelf for a while!

Although it would be ideal to have an anti-static wrist strap with you at all times, the reality is that from time to time you'll find yourself in situations where you lack the proper anti-static tools. This shouldn't keep you from working on the PC—if you're careful! Before working on a PC in such a situation, take a moment to touch the power supply—I'll show you where it is in this chapter—every once in a while as you work to keep yourself at the same electrical potential as the PC. Although this isn't as good as a wrist strap, it's better than nothing at all!

The last issue when it comes to preventing ESD is that never-ending question—should you work with the PC plugged in or unplugged? The answer is simple—do you really want to be physically connected to a PC that is plugged into an electrical outlet? Granted, the chances of electrocution are slim, but why take the risk?

Have I convinced you that ESD is a problem? Good! So now it's safe to start looking at the components of the PC.

• **Figure 2.9** Anti-static bag

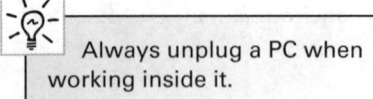

Always unplug a PC when working inside it.

Try This!

Anti-static Protection Devices

In some circumstances, wearing an anti-static wrist strap could get in the way. Manufacturers have developed some alternatives to the wrist strap, so try this:

1. Take a field trip to a local computer or electronics store.

2. Check out their selection of anti-static devices. Can you find anything other than wrist straps or mats?

3. Do a Web search for "static control products." Can you find anything other than wrist straps or mats?

4. Report what options you can find for protecting your equipment from ESD. Weigh the pros and cons and decide what you would use in different situations.

■ The Complete PC

Sometimes I hate the term "personal computer." That term implies a single device, like a toaster. A typical PC is more than one device, and you need all the parts (or at least most) to make the PC work. The most important part of the PC is the box that usually sits underneath your desk—the one that all the other parts connect to, called the system unit . All of the processing and storage takes place in the system unit. All of the other parts of the PC—the printer, the keyboard, the monitor—connect to the system unit and are known collectively as peripherals . Figure 2.10 shows a typical desktop PC, with the system unit and peripherals as separate pieces.

● **Figure 2.10**   Typical desktop computer with peripherals

Most computers have a standard set of peripherals to provide input and output. You'll see some variation in color, bells, and whistles, but here's the standard set:

- **Monitor**   The big television thing that provides a visual output for the computer.

- **Keyboard**   Keypad for providing keyed input. Based on a typewriter.

- **Mouse**   Pointing device used to control a graphical pointer on the monitor for input.

- **Speakers**/headphones   Speakers provide sound output.

- **Printer**   Provides printed paper output.

A typical PC has all of these peripherals, but there's no law that requires a PC to have them. Plenty of PCs may not have a printer. Some PCs won't have speakers. Some computers don't even have a keyboard, mouse, or monitor— but they tend to hide in unlikely places, such as the inside of a jet fighter or next to the engine in an automobile. Other PCs may have many more peripherals. It's easy to install four or five printers on a single PC if you so desire. There are also hundreds of other types of peripherals, such as Web cameras and microphones, that you'll find on many PCs. You add or remove peripherals depending on what you need from the system. The only limit is the number of connections for peripherals available on the system unit.

External Connections

Every peripheral connects to the system unit through one of the many types of ports. The back of a typical system unit (Figure 2.11) has lots of cables running from the system unit to the different peripherals. You may even have a few connectors in the front. All these connectors and ports have their own naming conventions, and a good tech knows all of them. It's not acceptable to

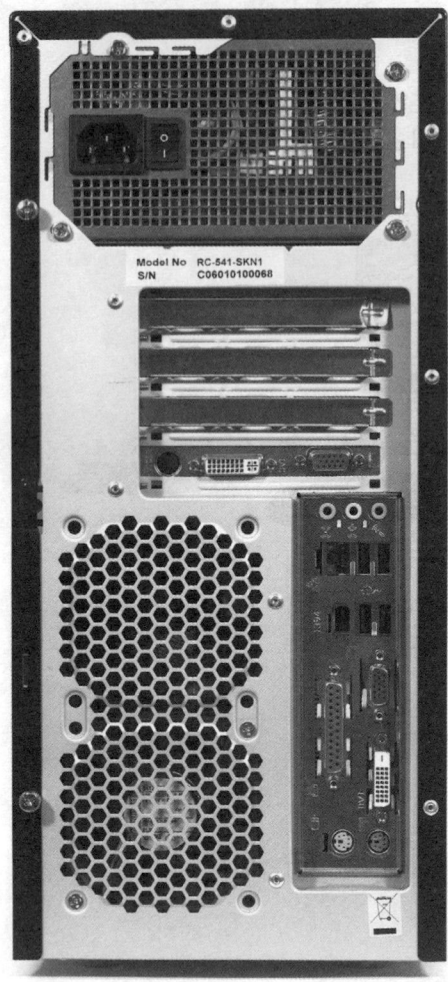

• **Figure 2.11** Connections in the back of a PC

go around saying things like "that's a printer port" or "that's a *little-type* keyboard connector." You need to be comfortable with common naming conventions so you can say "that's a female DB-25" or "that's a USB connector."

Plugs, Ports, Jacks, and Connectors

Although PCs use close to 50 different types of connections, almost all fit into one of six major types: DIN, USB, FireWire, DB, RJ, and audio. Read the next paragraph to get your terminology straight, and then you can jump into the various connectors with gusto.

No one seems to use the terms *plug, port, jack,* or *connector* correctly, so let's get this right from the start. To connect one device to another, you need a cable containing the wires that make the connection. On each device, as well as on each end of the connecting cable, you need standardized parts to make that connection. Because these are usually electrical connections, you need one part to fit inside another to make a snug, safe connection.

A `plug` is a part with some type of projection that goes into a `port`. A port is a part that has some type of matching hole or slot that accepts the plug. You never put a port into a plug; it's always the other way around. The term `jack` is used as an alternative to port, so you may also put a plug into a jack. The term `connector` describes either a port or a plug. (See Figure 2.12.) As you progress through this chapter and see the different plugs and ports, this will become clearer.

Mini-DIN Connectors

Most PCs sport the European-designed `mini-DIN connectors`. The original DIN connector was replaced by mini-DIN a long time ago, so you'll only see mini-DIN connectors on your PC (see Figure 2.13). Older-style keyboards and mice plug into mini-DIN ports.

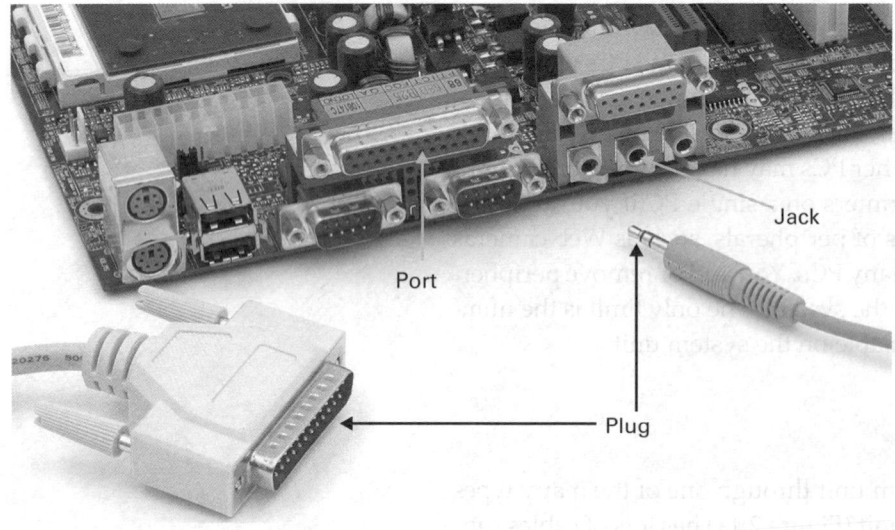

Port

Jack

Plug

• **Figure 2.12** Plug, port, and jack

• **Figure 2.13** Mini-DIN connector

• Figure 2.14   USB A connector and port

USB Connectors

Universal serial bus (USB) provides the most common general-purpose connection for PCs. You'll find USB versions of many different devices, such as mice, keyboards, scanners, cameras, and printers. USB connections come in three different sizes: "A" (very common), "B," and "mini-B" (less common). The USB A connector's distinctive rectangular shape makes it easily recognizable (Figure 2.14).

You never see a USB B connector on your computer. USB B connectors are for the other end of the USB cable where it attaches to the USB device (Figure 2.15).

The USB B connector's relatively large size makes it less than optimal for small devices such as cameras, so the USB folks also make the smaller mini-B–style connector, as shown in Figure 2.16.

USB has a number of features that make it particularly popular on PCs. First, USB devices are **hot-swappable**, which means you can insert or remove them without restarting your PC. Almost every other type of connector requires you to turn the system off, insert or remove the connector, and then turn the system back on. Hot-swapping completely eliminates this process.

Tech Tip

Downstream and Upstream

You'll sometimes hear USB ports and plugs described as upstream *or* downstream, *terms that create rather amusing conversation and confusion. It's all about whether you refer to the plug or the port, so here's the scoop. The USB A plugs go upstream to USB A ports on the host or hub. USB A ports provide downstream output from the host or hub. So, the plug is upstream and the port is downstream.*

Just to add more fun to the mix, USB B plugs go downstream to devices. USB B ports provide upstream output from the device to the host or hub. My advice? Stick with A or B and nobody will get confused.

• Figure 2.15   USB B connector

• Figure 2.16   USB mini-B connector

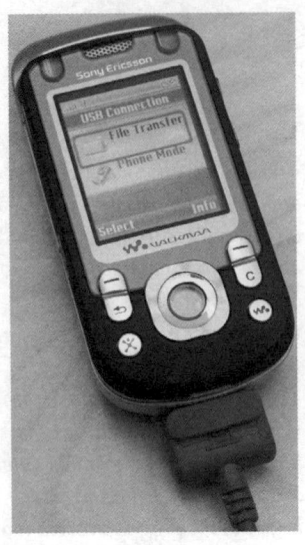

• **Figure 2.17**   Cell phone charging via
a USB connection

Tech Tip

**D-Subminiature
Naming Scheme**

*Each size D-sub connector—
called the* shell size*—has a specific name in the D-sub manufacturing world. A 2-row, 9-pin
connector, for example, is officially a DE-9 connector, rather
than a DB-9. The E refers to the
9-pin shell size. Why all the DA,
DB, DC, DD, and DE connectors
became DB-x in the world of personal computers is a mystery,
but most techs simply call them
DB connectors.*

Second, many USB devices get their electrical power through the USB
connection, so they don't need batteries or a plug for an electrical outlet. You
can even recharge some devices, such as cellular telephones, by plugging
them into a USB port (Figure 2.17).

FireWire Connectors

FireWire , also known as IEEE 1394 , moves data at incredibly high speeds,
making it the perfect connection for highly specialized applications, such as
streaming video from a digital video camera onto a hard drive. FireWire
consists of a special 6-wire connector, as shown in Figure 2.18. There's also a
smaller, 4-pin version, usually seen on peripherals. Like USB, FireWire devices are hot-swappable.

DB Connectors

Over the years, DB connectors have been used for almost any type of peripheral you can think of, with the exception of keyboards. They have a
slight *D* shape, which allows only one proper way to insert a plug into the
socket and makes it easier to remember what they're called. Technically,
they're known as *D-sub* or D-subminiature connectors, but most techs call
them DB.

Each male DB plug has a group of small pins that connect to DB ports.
Female DB plugs connect to male DB ports on the system unit. DB connectors in the PC world can have from 9 to 37 pins or sockets, although you
rarely see a DB connector with more than 25 pins or sockets. Figure 2.19
shows an example. DB-type connectors are some of the oldest and most
common connectors used in the back of PCs.

It wasn't that long ago that a typical PC used at least three or more different DB connectors. Over the past few years, the PC world has moved away
from DB connectors. A typical modern system might only have one or two,
usually for a printer or video.

• **Figure 2.18**   FireWire connector and port

• **Figure 2.19**   DB-25 connector and port

RJ Connectors

You have more than likely seen an RJ connector, whether or not you knew it by that name. The little plastic plug used to connect your telephone cord to the jack (techs don't use the word "port" to describe RJ connectors) is a classic example of an RJ plug. Modern PCs use only two types of RJ jacks: the RJ-11 and the RJ-45. The phone jack is an RJ-11. It is used almost exclusively for modems. The slightly wider RJ-45 jack is used for your network connection. Figure 2.20 shows an RJ-11 jack (top) and an RJ-45 jack (bottom).

Audio Connectors

Speakers and microphones connect to audio jacks on the system unit. The most common type of sound connector in popular use is the mini-audio connector. These small connectors have been around for years; they're just like the plug you use to insert headphones into an iPod or similar device (Figure 2.21). Traditionally, you'd find the audio jacks on the back of the PC, but many newer models sport front audio connections as well.

 Keep in mind that the variety of connectors is virtually endless. The preceding types of connectors cover the vast majority, but many others exist in the PC world. No law or standard requires device makers to use a particular connector, especially if they have no interest in making that device interchangeable with similar devices from other manufacturers.

• **Figure 2.20**   RJ-11 (top) and RJ-45 (bottom)

● **Figure 2.21** Mini-audio jacks and plug

Almost all connectors are now color coordinated to help users plug the right device into the right port. These color codes are not required, and not all PCs and devices use them.

Devices and Their Connectors

Now that you have a sense of the connectors, let's turn to the devices common to almost every PC to learn which connectors go with which device.

Cards Versus Onboard

All of the connectors on the back of the PC are just that—connectors. Behind those connectors are the actual devices that support whatever peripherals plug into those connectors. These devices might be built into the computer, such as a keyboard port. Others might be add-on expansion cards that a tech installed into the PC.

Most PCs have special expansion slots inside the system unit that enable you to add more devices on expansion cards. Figure 2.22 shows a typical card. If you want some new device and your system unit doesn't have that device built into the PC, you just go to the store, buy a card version of that

Try This!

Feeling Your Way Around Connectors

Given that most system units tend to sit on the floor under desks, a good PC tech learns to recognize most every PC connector by touch. This is a great exercise to do with a partner!

1. Look at all of the connectors on the back of any PC's system unit.

2. Turn the system unit around so that you can no longer see the connections.

3. Try to identify the connectors by feel.

● Figure 2.22   Typical expansion card

device, and snap it in! Later chapters of the book go into great detail on how to do this, but for now just appreciate that a device might be built in or it might come on a card.

Keyboard

Today's keyboards come in many shapes and sizes, but connect into either a dedicated mini-DIN keyboard port or a USB port. Many keyboards ship with an adapter so you can use either port. Most keyboard plugs and mini-DIN ports are colored purple (see Figure 2.23).

Monitor

A monitor connects to the video connector on the system unit. You'll usually see one of two types of video connectors: the older 15-pin female DB Video Electronics Standards Association (VESA) connector or the unique digital video interface (DVI) connector. VESA connectors are colored blue, whereas DVI connectors are white. Many video cards have both types of connectors (Figure 2.24), or two VESA or two DVI connectors. Video cards with two connectors support two monitors, a very cool thing to do!

● Figure 2.23   Keyboard plug and port

● Figure 2.24   Video card with both a DVI port (the white connector in the center) and VESA port (right); the port on the left is a proprietary video port

• Figure 2.25   HDMI connector

Occasionally you'll run into a video card with a mini-DIN connector, such as the S-Video connector you can see at the left in Figure 2.24. These mini-DIN connectors support all sorts of interesting video jobs, such as connecting to output to a television or input from a video camera.

The newest video connector is called High-Definition Multimedia Interface (HDMI), shown in Figure 2.25. HDMI is still very new to the video scene, but brings a number of enhancements, such as the ability to carry both video and sound on the same cable. Primarily designed for home theater, you'll see video cards with HDMI connectors growing more common over the next few years.

Sound

The sound device on your card performs two functions. First, it takes digital information and turns it into sound, outputting the sound through speakers. Second, it takes sound that is input through a microphone and turns it into digital data.

To play and record sounds, your sound device needs to connect to at least a set of speakers and a microphone. All PCs have at least two miniature audio jacks: one for a microphone and another for stereo speakers. Better cards provide extra miniature audio jacks for surround sound. A few sound cards provide a female 15-pin DB port that enables you to attach an electronic musical instrument interface or add a joystick to your PC (see Figure 2.26).

Adding more and more audio jacks to sound cards made the back of a typical sound card a busy place. In an effort to consolidate all of the different sound signals, the industry invented the Sony/Philips Digital Interface Format (S/PDIF) connection (Figure 2.27). One S/PDIF connection replaces all of the mini-audio connections, assuming your surround speaker system also comes with an S/PDIF connection.

• Figure 2.26   Legacy joystick/MIDI port

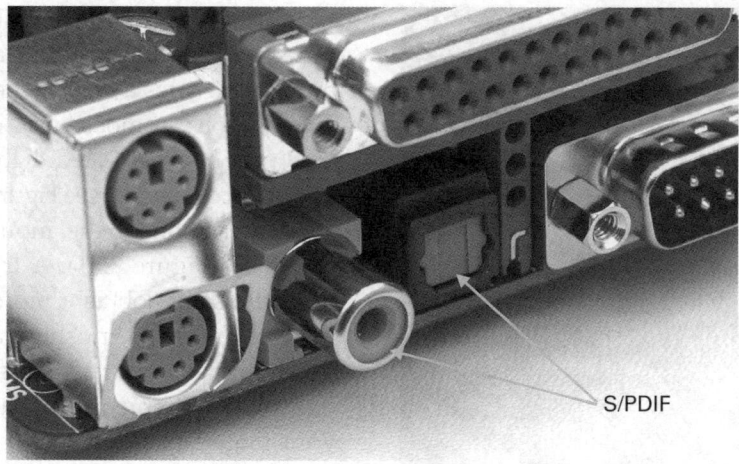

• Figure 2.27   S/PDIF connection

The color scheme for sound connections is complex, but for now remember one color—green. That's the one you need to connect a standard pair of stereo speakers.

Network

Networks are groups of connected PCs that share information. The PCs most commonly connect via some type of cabling that usually looks like an extra-thick phone cable. A modern PC uses an RJ-45 connection to connect to the network. Figure 2.28 shows a typical RJ-45 network connector. Network connectors do not have a standard color.

Mouse

Most folks are pretty comfortable with the function of a mouse (Figure 2.29)—it enables you to select graphical items on a graphical screen. A PC mouse has at least two buttons (as opposed to the famous one-button mouse that

Modern PCs have built-in network connections, but this is a fairly recent development. For many years, network devices only came on an expansion card, called a network interface card (NIC). The term is so common that even built-in network connections—which most certainly are not cards—are still called NICs.

• Figure 2.28   Typical network connection

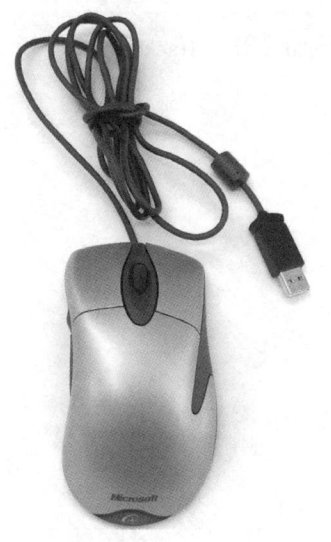

• Figure 2.29   Mouse

● **Figure 2.30**   Typical mouse mini-DIN connection

came with Apple Macintosh computers until recently), while a better mouse provides a scroll wheel and extra buttons. A mouse uses either a USB port or a dedicated, light-green mini-DIN connector (see Figure 2.30).

A variation of the mouse is a **trackball** (Figure 2.31). A trackball does the same job as a mouse, but instead of being pushed around like a mouse, the trackball stays in one place as you roll a ball with your fingers or thumb.

Modem

A **modem** enables you to connect your PC to a telephone. A modem is another easily identifiable device in PCs. Most modems have two RJ-11 sockets. One connects the modem to the telephone jack on the wall, and the other is for an optional telephone so that you can use the phone line when the modem is not in use (see Figure 2.32).

Serial Ports

External modems traditionally connected to a male 9-pin or 25-pin D-subminiature port on the system unit called a **serial port** (Figure 2.33).

Serials ports were the first general-purpose port used on PCs. Only in the last few years has the dominance of the far faster and easier-to-use USB finally made serial ports obsolete. Even though almost no new systems come with serial ports, you'll still find them occasionally.

● **Figure 2.31**   Trackball

● **Figure 2.32**   Internal modem

• **Figure 2.33**   Serial port

Printer

For many years, printers only used a special connector called a parallel port . Parallel ports use a 25-pin female DB connector that's usually colored fuchsia (see Figure 2.34).

After almost 20 years of domination by parallel ports, almost all printers now come with USB ports. Some better models even offer FireWire connections.

Joystick

Joysticks (Figure 2.35) weren't supposed to be used just for games. When the folks at IBM added the 15-pin female DB joystick connector to PCs, they envisioned joysticks as hard-working input devices, just as the mouse is today. Except in the most rare circumstances, however, the only thing a joystick does today is enable you to turn your PC into a rather expensive game machine! But is there a more gratifying feeling than easing that joystick over, pressing the Fire button, and watching an enemy fighter jet get blasted

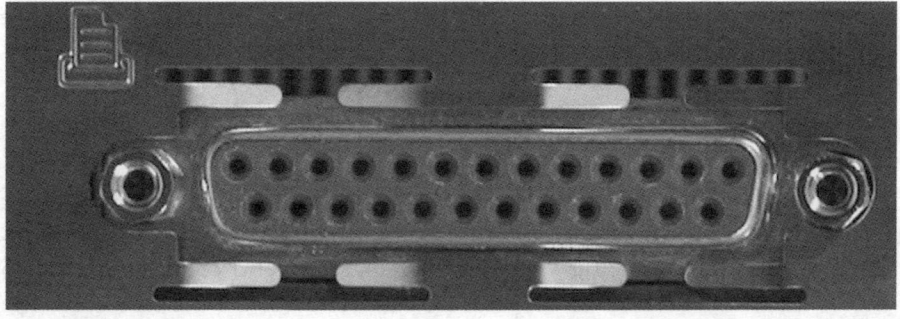

• **Figure 2.34**   Parallel port

● **Figure 2.35**   Joystick

by a well-placed Sidewinder missile? I think not. Traditional joystick connectors are colored orange, but most joysticks today connect to USB ports.

Plenty More!

Keep in mind that there are lots more devices and connectors out there! These are only the most common and the ones you're most likely to see. As we progress through this book, you'll see these less common connectors and where they are used.

■ Inside the System Unit

Now that you've seen the devices that connect to the PC, let's open up the system unit to inspect the major internal components of a typical PC. A single PC is composed of thousands of discrete components. Although no one can name every tiny bit of electronics in a PC, a good technician should be able to name the major internal components that make up the typical PC. Let's open and inspect a system unit to see these components and gain at least a concept of what they do. In later chapters, you'll see all of these components in much more detail.

Case

The system unit's case is both the internal framework of the PC and the external skin that protects the internal components from the environment. Cases come in an amazing variety of styles, sizes, and colors. Figure 2.36 shows the front and back of a typical PC case. The front of the case holds the buttons used to turn the system on and off, lights to tell you the status of the system, and access doors to removable media drives such as floppy, CD-ROM, and DVD drives. This system also provides USB, FireWire, and

Tech Tip

Front Connections

Front connections are most commonly used for temporary devices, such as headphones. If you have a device you don't intend to remove very often, you should install it in one of the back connections.

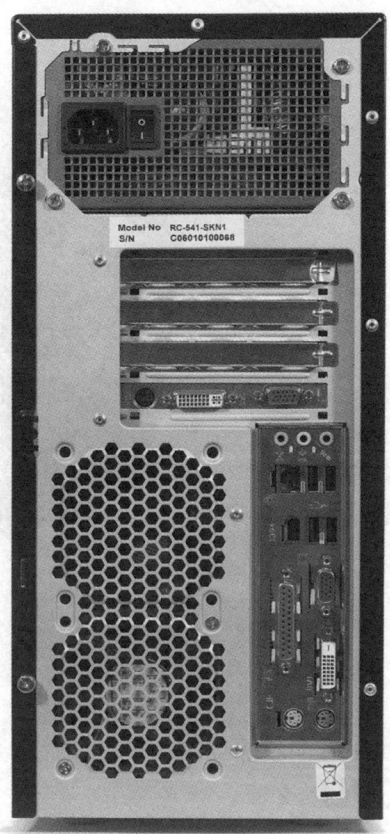

• **Figure 2.36**   Case—front and back

You'll hear the PC case be called the *enclosure,* especially at the more expensive end of the spectrum. Case, enclosure, and system unit are interchangeable terms.

audio connections in the front for easy access if you want to use a device that needs these connections.

The back of the case holds the vast majority of the system unit connections. You will also notice the power supply—almost always at the top of the case—distinguished by its cooling fan and power plug. Note that one area of the back of the case holds all the onboard connections, while another area contains slots for cards. The onboard devices need holes so you can plug in those devices (see Figure 2.37). Similarly, the case uses slots to enable access to the external connectors on cards installed in the system unit.

Opening a case is always…interesting. There's no standard way to open a case, and I'm convinced that the folks making system units enjoy some sick humor inventing new and complex ways to open them. In general, you detach the sides of a case by removing a few screws in the back of the system unit, as shown in Figure 2.38. Use common sense and you won't have too many problems. Just don't lose track of your screws or where each one was inserted!

Once you've opened the case, take a look inside. You see metal framework, all kinds of cables, and a number of devices. As you inspect the devices, you may gently push cables to the side to get a better view. Don't forget to wear an anti-static wrist strap or touch the metal case occasionally to prevent ESD.

• **Figure 2.37**   Onboard devices

• **Figure 2.38**   Opening a system unit

CPU

The **central processing unit (CPU)** , also called the **microprocessor** , performs all the calculations that take place inside a PC. CPUs come in a variety of shapes and sizes, as shown in Figure 2.39.

Modern CPUs generate a lot of heat and thus require a cooling fan and heat sink assembly to avoid overheating (see Figure 2.40). A heat sink is a

• **Figure 2.39**   Typical CPUs

• Figure 2.40   CPU with fan in PC

big slab of copper or aluminum that helps draw heat away from the processor. The fan then blows the heat out into the case. You can usually remove this cooling device if you need to replace it, although some CPU manufacturers have sold CPUs with a fan permanently attached.

CPUs have a make and model, just like automobiles do. When talking about a particular car, for example, most people speak in terms of a Ford Taurus SHO or a Toyota Camry LE. When they talk about CPUs, people say Intel Core 2 or AMD Athlon XP. Over the years, there have been only a few major CPU manufacturers, just as there are only a few major auto manufacturers. The two most common makes of CPUs used in PCs are AMD and Intel.

Although only a few manufacturers of CPUs have existed, those manufacturers have made hundreds of models of CPUs. Some of the more common models made over the last few years have names such as Celeron, Athlon XP, Pentium 4, and Core 2.

Finally, CPUs come in different packages. The package defines how the CPU looks physically and how it connects to the computer. The predominant package type is called *pin grid array (PGA)*. Every package type has lots of variations.

Chapter 3, "Understanding CPUs," goes into great detail on CPUs, but for now remember that every CPU has a make, a model, and a package type.

RAM

Random access memory (RAM) stores programs and data currently being used by the CPU. The maximum amount of programs and data that a piece of RAM can store is measured in units called *bytes*. Modern PCs have many millions, even billions, of bytes of RAM, so RAM is measured in units called *megabytes (MB)* or *gigabytes (GB)*. An average PC will have from 256 MB to 2 GB of RAM, although you may see PCs with far more or far less RAM. Each piece of RAM is called a *stick*. One common type of stick found in today's

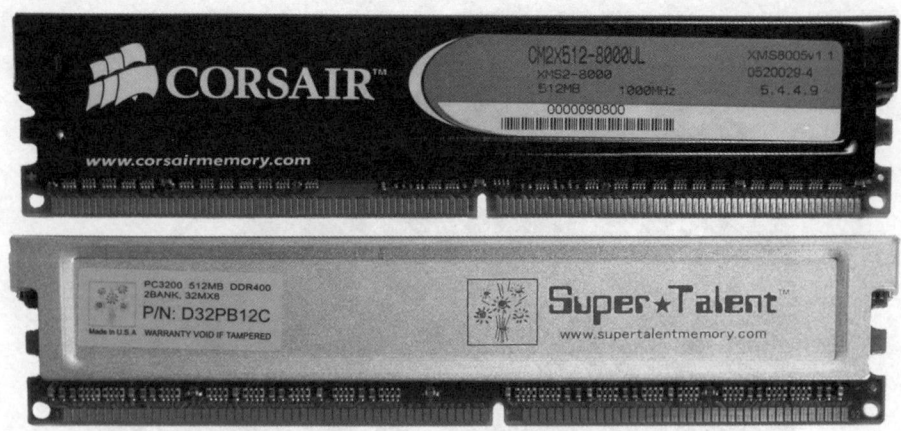

● **Figure 2.41** Two DIMMs

⚠ Some parts of your PC are much more sensitive to ESD than others. Your CPU and RAM are very sensitive to ESD. If you touch the metal parts of your CPU or RAM and you have even the tiniest amount of charge, it can destroy them.

PC is called a *dual inline memory module (DIMM)*. Figure 2.41 shows two examples of DIMMs used in PCs.

Your PC takes only one type of DIMM, and you must know the type so you can add or replace RAM when needed. Chapter 4, "Understanding RAM," covers everything you need to know to work comfortably with RAM.

Motherboard

You can compare a motherboard to the chassis of an automobile. In a car, everything connects to the chassis either directly or indirectly. In a PC, everything connects to the motherboard either directly or indirectly. A **motherboard** is a thin, flat piece of circuit board, usually green or gold, and often slightly larger than a typical piece of notebook paper (see Figure 2.42).

A motherboard contains a number of special sockets that accept various PC components. The CPU and RAM, for example, plug directly into

● **Figure 2.42** Typical motherboard

the motherboard. Other devices, such as floppy drives, hard drives, CD and DVD drives, connect to the motherboard sockets through short cables. Motherboards also provide onboard connectors for external devices such as mice, printers, joysticks, and keyboards.

All motherboards use multipurpose expansion slots that enable you to add adapter cards. Different types of expansion slots exist for different types of cards (see Figure 2.43).

Power Supply

The power supply, as its name implies, provides the necessary electrical power to make the PC operate. The power supply takes standard (in the United States) 110-volt AC power and converts it into 12-volt, 5-volt, and 3.3-volt DC power. Most power supplies are about the size of a shoebox cut in half and are usually a gray or metallic color (see Figure 2.44).

• **Figure 2.43**   Expansion slots

A number of connectors lead out of the power supply. Every power supply provides special connectors to power the motherboard and a number of other general-use connectors that provide power to any device that needs electricity. Figure 2.45 shows both the motherboard power and typical general-use connectors. Check out Chapter 8, "Understanding PC Power," for more information.

• **Figure 2.44**   Power supply

• **Figure 2.45**   Power connectors

Floppy Drive

The `floppy drive` enables you to access removable floppy disks (diskettes). The floppy drive used in PCs today is called a 3.5-inch floppy drive (Figure 2.46). Floppy drives only store a tiny amount of data and are disappearing from many PCs.

The floppy drive connects to the computer via a *ribbon cable,* which in turn connects to the motherboard. The connection to the motherboard is known as the *floppy drive controller* (Figure 2.47).

Hard Drive

`Hard drives` store programs and data that are not currently being used by the CPU (Figure 2.48). Even though both hard drives and RAM use the same

• **Figure 2.46**   Floppy drive

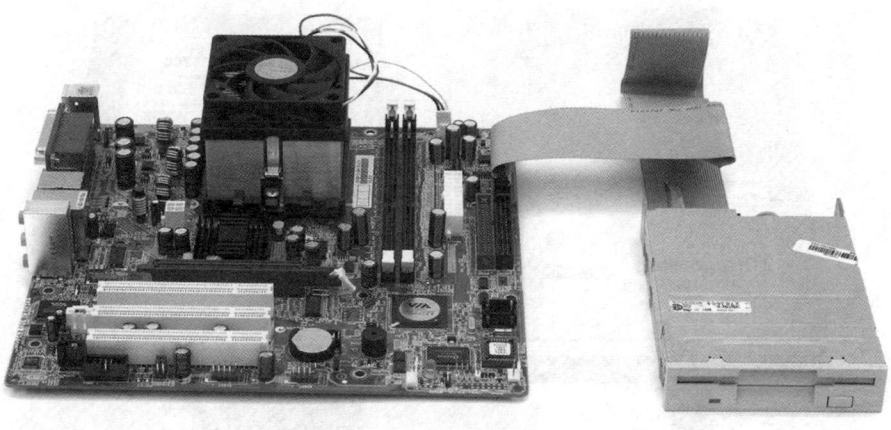

• **Figure 2.47**   Floppy drive connected to motherboard

storage units (megabytes and gigabytes), a PC's hard drive stores much more data than a typical PC's RAM—up to hundreds of gigabytes.

An average PC has one hard drive, although most PCs accept more. Special PCs that need to store large amounts of data, such as a large corporation's main file storage computer, can contain many hard drives—8 to 16 drives in some cases.

By far the most common types of hard drive seen in today's PCs fall under the *AT Attachment (ATA)* standard. These drives come in two types: the older *parallel ATA (PATA)* or the more modern *serial ATA (SATA)*. PATA drives use a ribbon cable very similar to the one used by floppy drives, whereas SATA drives use a very narrow cable. Figure 2.49 shows a SATA drive (left) next to a PATA drive (right). Most motherboards come with connections for both types of drives.

 Tech Tip

SCSI

A very few PCs use small computer system interface (SCSI) drives. SCSI drives are generally faster and more expensive, so they usually show up only in high-end PCs such as network servers or graphics workstations.

• **Figure 2.48**   Typical hard drive

• **Figure 2.49**   SATA and PATA drives

Almost all CD-ROM and DVD drives are actually PATA drives and connect via a ribbon cable just like a PATA hard drive. Figure 2.50 shows a DVD drive connected to a ribbon cable with a PATA hard drive—a very common sight inside a PC.

Optical Media

CDs, DVDs—there are so many types of those shiny discs to put in computers! The term optical media describes all of them (Figure 2.51). Generally, you may break optical media into two groups: CDs and DVDs. CDs store around 700 MB and come in three varieties: CD-ROM (*read only memory:* you can't change the data on them), CD-R (*recordable:* you can change the data once),

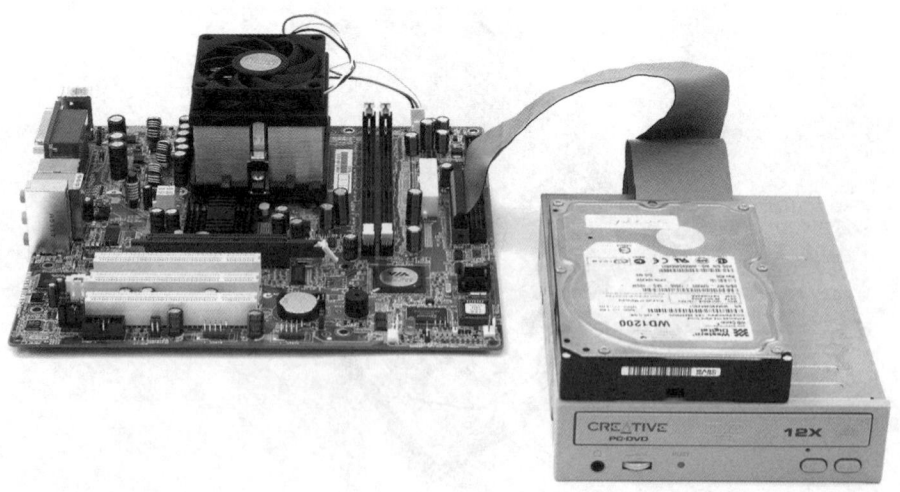

• **Figure 2.50**   Hard drive and DVD drive

● Figure 2.51   Assorted optical-media discs

and CD-RW (*rewritable:* you can change the data on them over and over). DVDs store much more data—around 4 GB, enough for a Hollywood movie—and come in even more varieties: DVD-ROM, DVD+R, DVD-R, DVD+RW, and DVD-RW, just to name the more famous ones.

All of these different optical-media discs require an optical drive that knows how to read them. If you want to do anything with a CD-RW disc, for example, you need a CD-RW drive. If you want to use a DVD+R disc, you need a DVD+R drive. Luckily, most optical drives support many different types of discs, and some support every common type of optical media available! Figure 2.52 shows typical optical drives. Note that some of them advertise the types of media they use. Others give no clue whatsoever.

 Chapter 10, "Understanding Removable Media," goes into great detail on the assorted discs and drive types.

Know Your Parts

The entire goal of this chapter was to get you to appreciate the names and functions of the different parts of the PC: peripherals, connectors, and components. You also learned about ESD and other issues that come into play when working with a PC. By starting with the Big Picture view, you may now begin breaking down the individual components on a chapter-by-chapter basis and truly understand at great depth how each component works and how they interconnect with the PC system as a whole.

● Figure 2.52   Optical drives

Chapter 2 Review

Chapter Summary

After reading this chapter and completing the exercises, you should understand the following about the visible PC.

How the PC Works

- The two parts of the PC—hardware and software—work intimately together to enable you to do work. The computer tech knows the four stages of computing: input, processing, output, and storage. Understanding how the various pieces of hardware and software interact in each stage enables you to master the art of the PC tech.

Tools of the Trade and ESD Avoidance

- The typical tech toolkit consists of Phillips-head and flat-head screwdrivers, a star-headed Torx wrench, a nut driver or two, a pair of tweezers, a little grabber tool, a hemostat, a magnifying glass, and a flashlight.

- Electrostatic discharge (ESD) can damage or destroy computer components. ESD only takes place when two objects that store different amounts (potential) of static electricity come in contact. You can avoid ESD by using proper tools, such as an anti-static wrist strap and anti-static bags.

Connectors on a Typical PC System Unit

- Most computers have a standard set of peripherals to provide input and output. Typical devices include the monitor, keyboard, mouse, speakers, and printer.

- PCs use many kinds of external connectors, but most fit into one of six major types: mini-DIN, USB, FireWire, DB, RJ, and mini-audio. A plug goes into a port or jack. Connectors are often identified by their shape (such as DB connectors that look like a capital D), gender (male or female), and by the number of pins. Most PCs have two round mini-DIN connectors, one for the keyboard and the other for the mouse.

- Universal Serial Bus (USB) connectors come in three sizes, A, B, and mini-B. Many devices plug into USB ports, including keyboards and cameras. USB is hot-swappable, so devices may be inserted or removed without restarting the computer.

- Also known as IEEE 1394, the FireWire interface is perfect for high-speed devices, such as digital video cameras. PCs rarely have built-in 4- or 6-wire FireWire connectors, so users typically purchase a FireWire adapter card.

- DB connectors come in a variety of sizes, but only one shape. You'll find only a few DB connectors on modern PCs, primarily for printers and video.

- The telephone jack is an RJ connector, called an RJ-11. Most network cards have a wider RJ-45 jack.

- Speakers and microphones connect to mini-audio jacks. You'll always find these on the back of the system unit; newer models have connectors on the front as well.

- Keyboards connect into either a dedicated mini-DIN keyboard port or a USB port. Monitors connect to VGA or DVI ports. Mice and trackballs use the mini-DIN or USB ports as well. Keeping with the same trend, printers come in one of two common varieties—those that plug into a DB-25 port and those that plug into a USB port. A joystick plugs into either a 15-pin female DB port or a USB port.

Major Internal and External Components of a PC

- Everything fits inside or connects to the case, more technically called a system unit. The system unit provides the framework for buttons, lights, drives, access doors, and so forth. Opening the case is usually a matter of unscrewing screws and pulling one side open.

- The central processing unit (CPU), also called the microprocessor or brain of the computer, has a make, a model, a speed, and a package. AMD and Intel are the two most common makers of CPUs. CPU speed is measured in megahertz (MHz) or gigahertz (GHz). The pin grid array (PGA) is the most common CPU package. A CPU cooling fan or heat sink is essential to dissipate the heat.

- Random access memory (RAM) contains the current programs and data that the CPU is using. Most PC memory is installed on sticks called dual inline memory modules (DIMMs). RAM capacity is measured in megabytes (MB).

- The motherboard contains soldered components, expansion slots, and sockets for the CPU, RAM, and other components. Expansion slots are connectors for expansion cards that enable optional devices to communicate with the PC.

- The power supply takes AC power from the wall outlet and converts it into 12-volt, 5-volt, and 3.3-volt DC power for the computer components. The power supply has a number of connectors for the motherboard and other devices.

- A floppy drive uses a ribbon cable to connect to the floppy drive controller on the motherboard. The most common type is the 3.5-inch floppy drive.

- Hard drives store programs and data that are not currently being used by the CPU. An average PC has one hard drive, although most PCs accept more. Most PCs use either PATA or SATA drives, both of which commonly connect to controllers built into the motherboard.

- Optical drives enable the computer to access optical-media discs. Some optical drives can record CDs, such as the Compact Disc-Recordable (CD-R) or the Compact Disc-Rewritable (CD-RW) drives. Many PCs now have digital video disc (DVD) drives that support capacities large enough for a full-length movie.

Key Terms

anti-static bag *(24)*
anti-static mat *(23)*
anti-static wrist strap *(23)*
central processing unit (CPU) *(38)*
connector *(26)*
DB connector *(28)*
digital video interface (DVI) *(31)*
D-subminiature *(28)*
electrostatic discharge (ESD) *(22)*
expansion slot *(30)*
FireWire *(28)*
floppy drive *(42)*
hard drive *(42)*
**High-Definition Multimedia
    Interface (HDMI)** *(32)*
hot-swappable *(27)*
IEEE 1394 *(28)*

jack *(26)*
joystick *(35)*
keyboard *(25)*
microprocessor *(38)*
mini-audio connector *(29)*
mini-DIN connector *(26)*
modem *(34)*
monitor *(25)*
motherboard *(40)*
mouse *(25, 33)*
network interface card (NIC) *(33)*
optical media *(44)*
parallel port *(35)*
peripherals *(25)*
plug *(26)*
port *(26)*

potential *(22)*
power supply *(41)*
printer *(25)*
programming *(18)*
random access memory (RAM) *(39)*
resistor *(24)*
RJ connector *(29)*
serial port *(34)*
software *(19)*
**Sony/Philips Digital Interface
    Format (S/PDIF)** *(32)*
speakers *(25)*
system unit *(25)*
trackball *(34)*
universal serial bus (USB) *(27)*
VESA connector *(31)*

Key Term Quiz

Use the Key Terms list to complete the sentences that follow. Not all terms will be used.

1. The monitor attaches to the _____ with a 15-pin female connector.

2. If you install a DIMM stick, your computer will have more _____.

3. The _____ has a make, a model, a speed, and a package.

4. Always place an expansion card or other computer part into a(n) _____ when it's not in use to protect against electrostatic discharge.

5. Two RJ-11 connectors identify the _____.

6. When attaching a peripheral, put the plug into the _____ or jack.

7. The _____ takes AC voltage from the wall outlet and converts it to DC voltage for the computer components.

8. If an expansion card contains an RJ-45 jack, it is a(n) _____.

9. A 25-pin female DB connector with a printer attached to it is a(n) _____.

10. An internal storage device that typically holds 20 GB or more is a(n) _____.

■ Multiple-Choice Quiz

1. Which of the following connections can replace all the mini-audio jacks on a system unit?
   A. FireWire
   B. HDMI
   C. S/PDIF
   D. VESA

2. A modern keyboard generally connects to which of the following ports? (Select all that apply.)
   A. FireWire
   B. Mini-DIN
   C. USB
   D. VESA

3. USB connectors come in which of the following sizes? (Select all that apply.)
   A. A
   B. B
   C. Mini-A
   D. Mini-B

4. Which of the following devices attaches with a ribbon cable?
   A. CPU
   B. CD-ROM drive
   C. RAM
   D. Sound card

5. Which of the following devices measure(s) storage capacity in megabytes or gigabytes?
   A. Floppy disk and hard disk
   B. NIC
   C. CPU
   D. Modem

6. Which of the following devices has enough storage capacity to hold a movie?
   A. CD-ROM
   B. CD-R
   C. CD-RW
   D. DVD

7. Which of the following connector types enable you to plug a device into them and have the device function without your restarting the computer? (Select all that apply.)
   A. FireWire
   B. Mini-DIN
   C. Serial
   D. USB

8. Which of the following ports would you most likely find built into a motherboard?
   A. A keyboard port
   B. A DVI port
   C. An HDMI port
   D. An RDA port

9. What's the best practice when working inside a system unit and installing and removing components?
   A. Wear an anti-static wrist strap
   B. Touch a door knob to ground yourself before going into the case
   C. Place components onto the motherboard to keep them grounded
   D. Use plastic tools

10. Which of the following tools would you find in a typical PC tech's toolkit? (Select all that apply.)
    A. Phillips-head screwdriver
    B. Torx wrench
    C. Hammer
    D. File

11. What's a resistor?

   A. A device that resists change, stopping AC electricity from becoming DC electricity.

   B. A device that resists the flow of electricity, helping anti-static devices protect against ESD.

   C. A tool used for extracting difficult-to-remove components.

   D. A person fighting against the invaders.

12. Which of the following ports can handle a connection from a monitor?

   A. DVI

   B. FireWire

   C. Mini-DIN

   D. USB

13. Which of the following ports enables a modern PC to connect to a network?

   A. Mini-audio

   B. Mini-DIN

   C. RJ-13

   D. RJ-45

14. What term describes the flow of a static electrical charge from a person to the inside of the PC?

   A. EMI

   B. ESD

   C. HDMI

   D. TTFN

15. Of the following, what do USB and FireWire connections have in common?

   A. Both are used for connecting keyboards

   B. Both support dual monitors

   C. Both support hot-swapping devices

   D. Both use D-subminiature connectors

Essay Quiz

1. Although serial and parallel ports have been around forever, newer and faster ports such as USB and FireWire are now available. At the same time, new computers have faster CPUs, more RAM, and larger-capacity hard drives. What factors do you think are driving the PC market for these improvements? Do you feel that you need to have the newest and the greatest PC? Why or why not?

2. Jason, one of your co-workers who knows nothing about computer hardware, needs to move his computer and will be responsible for reassembling it himself in his new office across town. What advice can you give him about disassembly steps that will help him reassemble the computer successfully? List at least five things that Jason should do as he disassembles the computer, transports it, and reassembles it. Do shapes and colors help him?

3. A floppy drive has been a standard component for personal computers from their beginning. Now some manufacturers, such as Dell, have decided to build PCs without a floppy drive.

Would you want to purchase a PC without a floppy drive? Why or why not? If so, what kinds of alternative devices would you want your computer to have?

4. Hearing that you are taking a computer hardware course, Aunt Sally approaches you about helping her select a new computer. She wants to use the computer primarily for office applications, to track her budget, to receive and send e-mail, and to surf the Internet. What are you going to tell her about the kind of PC to buy? What peripherals should she purchase? Why?

5. Your worksite currently has no ESD protection. In fact, your supervisor doesn't feel that such protection is necessary. Write a proposal to purchase ESD protection equipment for the computer assembly/repair facility that will convince your supervisor that ESD protection is necessary and cost-effective in the long run. What kinds of protection will you recommend?

Lab Projects

Lab Project 2.1

FireWire is a relatively new kind of port, so many personal computers do not normally include it. Check the following three Web sites: www.dell.com, www.hp.com, and www.lenovo.com. Is a FireWire port standard built-in equipment on their new computers? If so, how many FireWire ports are included? If not, do the sites offer FireWire as an optional add-on?

Lab Project 2.2

Find an advertisement for a new personal computer in a current newspaper or magazine and examine it to determine the following:

- What make, model, and speed of CPU does it have?

- How much RAM does it have?

- What is the storage capacity of the hard drive?

- Does it include a CD-ROM, CD-R, CD-RW, or DVD drive?

- Does it come with a network interface card?

- Is a monitor included? If so, what kind and size?

Understanding CPUs

*"I have a theory about the human mind. A **brain** is a lot like a **computer**. It will only take so many facts, and then it will go on overload and blow up."*

—ERMA BOMBECK

For all practical purposes, the terms `microprocessor` and `central processing unit (CPU)` mean the same thing: it's that big chip inside your computer that many people often describe as the brain of the system. From the previous chapter, you know that CPU makers name their microprocessors in a fashion similar to the automobile industry: CPU names get a make and a model, such as Intel Core 2 Duo or AMD Athlon 64. But what's happening inside the CPU to make it able to do the amazing things asked of it every time you step up to the keyboard?

In this chapter, you will learn how to

- ■ **Identify the core components of a CPU**
- ■ **Describe the relationship of CPUs and RAM**
- ■ **Explain the varieties of modern CPUs**

CPU Core Components

Although the computer might seem to act quite intelligently, comparing the CPU to a human brain hugely overstates its capabilities. A CPU functions more like a very powerful calculator than a brain—but, oh, what a calculator! Today's CPUs add, subtract, multiply, divide, and move billions of numbers per second. Processing that much information so quickly makes any CPU look quite intelligent. It's simply the speed of the CPU, rather than actual intelligence, that enables computers to perform feats such as accessing the Internet, playing visually stunning games, or creating graphics.

A good PC technician needs to understand some basic CPU functions in order to support PCs, so let's start with an analysis of how the CPU works. If you wanted to teach someone how an automobile engine works, you would use a relatively simple example engine, right? The same principle applies here. Let's begin our study of the CPU using the granddaddy of all CPUs: the famous Intel 8088, invented in the late 1970s. Although this CPU first appeared over 25 years ago, it defined the idea of the modern microprocessor and contains the same basic parts used in even the most advanced CPUs today. Stick with me, my friend. Prepare to enter that little bit of magic called the CPU.

The Man in the Box

Let's begin by visualizing the CPU as a man in a box (Figure 3.1). This is one clever guy in the box. He can perform virtually any mathematical function, manipulate data, and give answers *very quickly*.

This guy is potentially very useful to us, but there's a catch—he lives closed up in a tiny black box. Before he can work with us, we must come up with a way to exchange information with him (Figure 3.2).

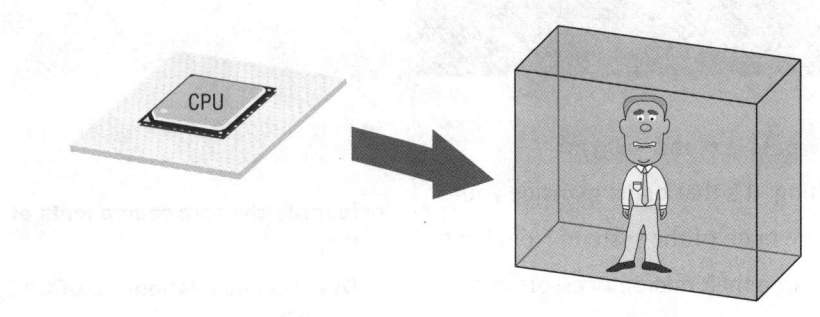

• **Figure 3.1**   Imagine the CPU as a man in a box.

• **Figure 3.2**   How do we talk to the Man in the Box?

Imagine that we install a set of 16 light bulbs, 8 inside his box and 8 outside his box. Each of the 8 light bulbs inside the box connects to one of the 8 bulbs outside the box to form a pair. Each pair of light bulbs is always either on or off. You can control the 8 pairs of bulbs using a set of 8 switches outside the box, and the Man in the Box can also control them using an identical set of 8 switches inside the box. This light bulb communication device is called the external data bus (EDB).

Figure 3.3 shows a cutaway view of the external data bus. When either you or the Man in the Box flips a switch on, *both* light bulbs go on, and the switch on the other side is also flipped to the on position. If you or the Man in the Box turns a switch off, the light bulbs on both sides are turned off, along with the other switch for that pair.

Can you see how this will work? By creating on/off patterns with the light bulbs that represent different pieces of data or commands, you can send that information to the Man in the Box, and he can send information back in the same way—*assuming that you agree ahead of time on what the different patterns of lights mean*. To accomplish this, you need some sort of codebook that assigns meanings to the many different patterns of lights that the external data bus might display. Keep this thought in mind while we push the analogy a bit more.

Before going any further, make sure you're clear on the fact that this is an analogy, not reality. There really is an external data bus, but you won't see any light bulbs or switches on the CPU. You can, however, see little wires sticking out of the CPU (Figure 3.4). If you apply voltage to one of these wires, you in essence flip the switch. Get the idea? So if that wire had voltage, and if a tiny light bulb were attached to the wire, that light bulb would glow, would it not? By the same token, if the wire had no power, then the light bulb would not glow. That is why the switch-and-light bulb analogy may help you picture these little wires constantly flashing on and off.

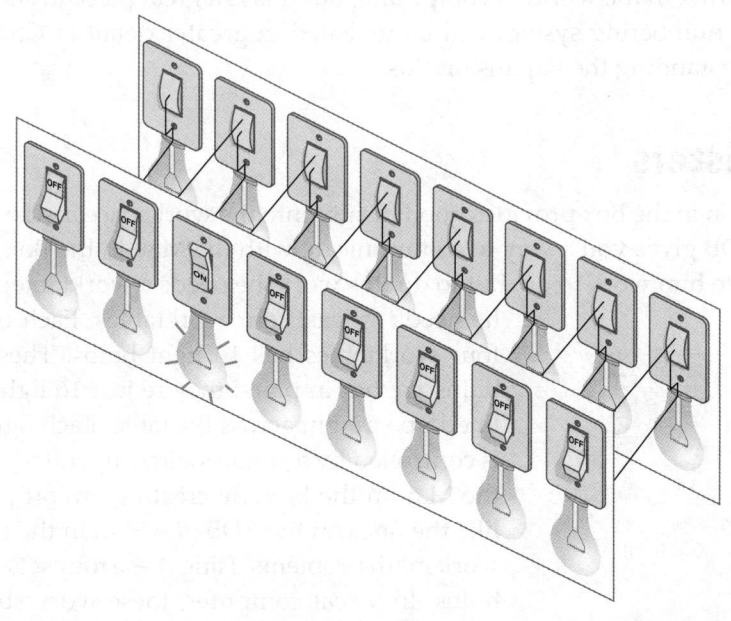

• **Figure 3.3** Cutaway of the external data bus—note that one light bulb is on

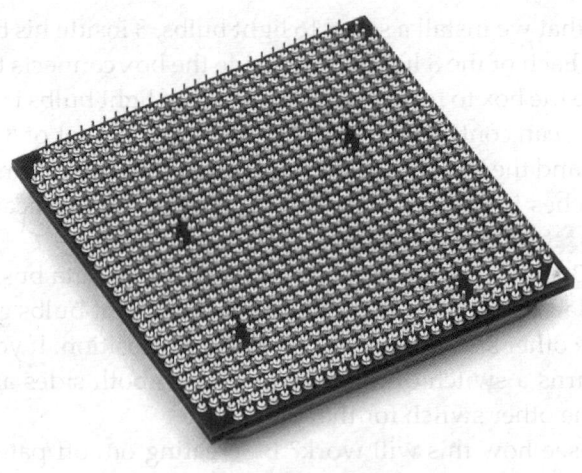

● **Figure 3.4** Close-up of the underside of a CPU

Now that the external data bus enables you to communicate with the Man in the Box, you need to see how it works by placing voltages on the wires. This brings up a naming problem. It's a hassle to say terms such as "on-off-off-off-on-on-off-off" when talking about which wires have voltage. Rather than saying that one of the external data bus wires is on or off, use the number 1 to represent on and the number 0 to represent off (Figure 3.5). That way, instead of describing the state of the lights as "on-off-off-off-on-on-off-off," I can instead describe them by writing "10001100."

In the world of computers, we constantly turn wires on and off. As a result, this "1 and 0" or **binary** system is used to describe the state of these wires at any given moment. (See, and you just thought computer geeks spoke in binary to confuse normal people! Ha!) There's much more to binary numbering in the world of computing, but this is a great place to start. This binary numbering system will be revisited in greater detail in Chapter 6, "Understanding the Expansion Bus."

Registers

The Man in the Box provides good insight into the workspace inside a CPU. The EDB gives you a way to communicate with the Man in the Box so you can give him work to do. But to do this work, he needs a worktable; in fact, he needs at least four worktables. Each of these four worktables has 16 light bulbs. These light bulbs are not in pairs; they're just 16 light bulbs lined up straight across the table. Each light bulb is controlled by a single switch, operated only by the Man in the Box. By creating on/off patterns like the ones on the EDB, the Man in the Box can work math problems using these four sets of light bulbs. In a real computer, these worktables are called **registers** (Figure 3.6).

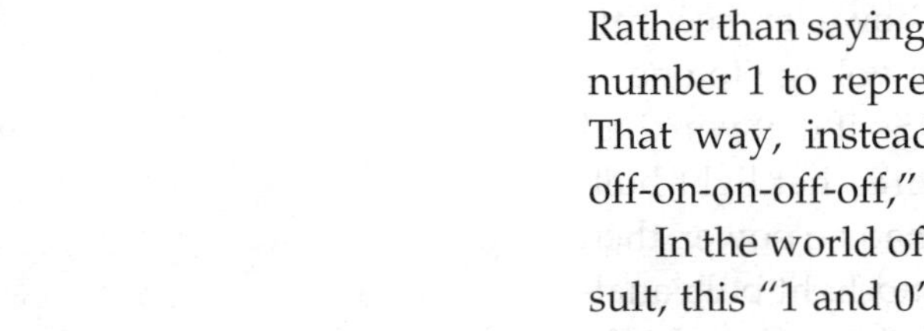

1   0   1   0   1   1   0   0

● **Figure 3.5**   Here "1" means on; "0" means off.

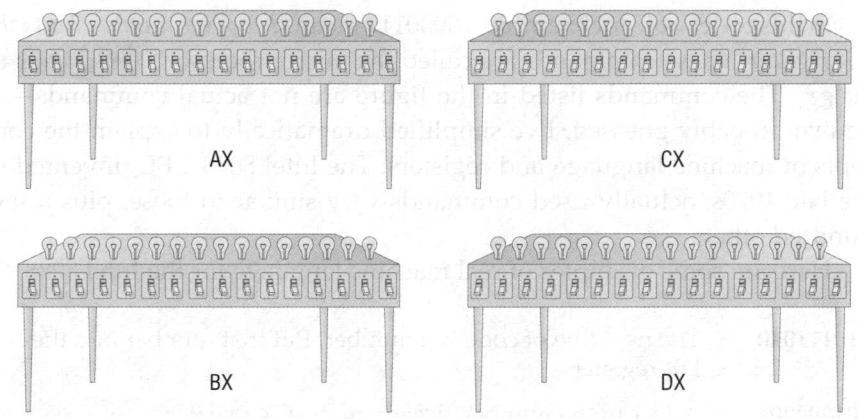

AX

CX

BX

DX

● **Figure 3.6**   The four general-purpose registers

Tech Tip

General-Purpose Registers

The 8088 was the first CPU to use the four now famous AX–DX general-purpose registers, but they still exist in even the latest CPUs. (But they've got a lot more light bulbs!)

Registers provide the Man in the Box with a workplace for the problems you give him. All CPUs contain a large number of registers, but for the moment let's concentrate on the four most commonly used ones: the *general-purpose registers*. Intel gave them the names AX, BX, CX, and DX.

Great! We're just about ready to put the Man in the Box to work, but before you close the lid on the box, you must give the Man one more tool. Remember the codebook we mentioned earlier? Let's make one to enable us to communicate with him. Figure 3.7 shows the codebook we'll use. We'll give one copy to him and make a second for us.

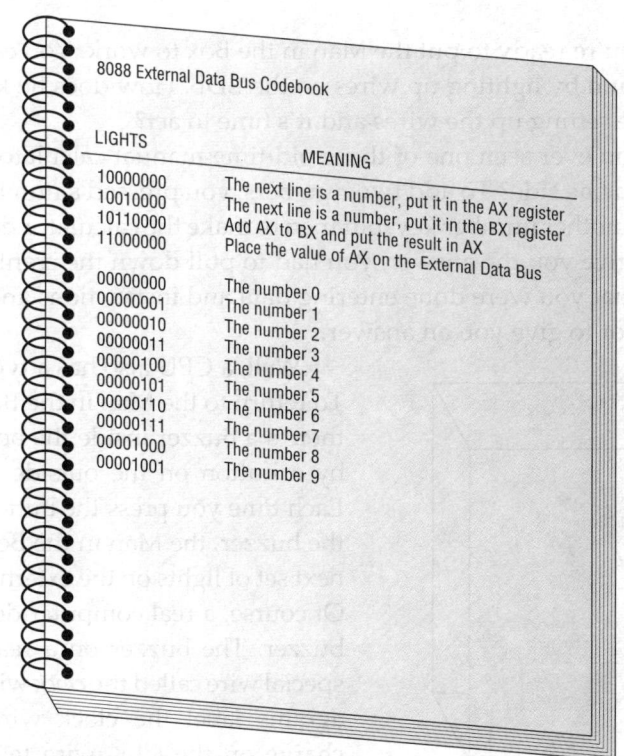

8088 External Data Bus Codebook

LIGHTS	MEANING
10000000	The next line is a number, put it in the AX register
10010000	The next line is a number, put it in the BX register
10110000	Add AX to BX and put the result in AX
11000000	Place the value of AX on the External Data Bus
00000000	The number 0
00000001	The number 1
00000010	The number 2
00000011	The number 3
00000100	The number 4
00000101	The number 5
00000110	The number 6
00000111	The number 7
00001000	The number 8
00001001	The number 9

● **Figure 3.7**   CPU codebook

In this codebook, for example, 10000111 means *Move the number 7 into the AX register*. These commands are called the microprocessor's machine language. The commands listed in the figure are not actual commands—as you've probably guessed, I've simplified dramatically to explain the concepts of machine language and registers. The Intel 8088 CPU, invented in the late 1970s, actually used commands very similar to these, plus a few hundred others.

Here are some examples of real machine language for the Intel 8088:

10111010	The next line of code is a number. Put that number into the DX register.
01000001	Add 1 to the number already in the CX register.
00111100	Compare the value in the AX register with the next line of code.

By placing machine language commands—called *lines of code*—onto the external data bus one at a time, you can instruct the Man in the Box to do specific tasks. All of the machine language commands that the CPU understands make up the CPU's instruction set.

So here is the CPU so far: the Man in the Box can communicate with the outside world via the external data bus; he has four registers he can use to work on the problems you give him; and he has a codebook—the instruction set—so he can understand the different patterns (machine language commands) on the external data bus (Figure 3.8).

Clock

Okay, so you're ready to put the Man in the Box to work. You can send the first command by lighting up wires on the EDB. How does he know when you're done setting up the wires and it's time to act?

Have you ever seen one of those old-time manual calculators with the big crank on one side? To add two numbers, you pressed a number key, the + key, and another number key, but then to make the calculator do the calculation and give you the answer, you had to pull down the crank. That was the signal that you were done entering data and instructions and ready for the calculator to give you an answer.

Well, a CPU also has a type of crank. To return to the Man in the Box, imagine there's a buzzer inside the box activated by a button on the outside of the box. Each time you press the button to sound the buzzer, the Man in the Box reads the next set of lights on the external data bus. Of course, a real computer doesn't use a buzzer. The buzzer on a real CPU is a special wire called the *clock* wire (most diagrams label the clock wire CLK). A charge on the CLK wire tells the CPU there's another piece of information waiting to be processed (Figure 3.9).

> Every CPU maker will gladly sell you a book that lists every machine language code for a particular CPU. Luckily, PC techs don't need to read these huge, boring books!

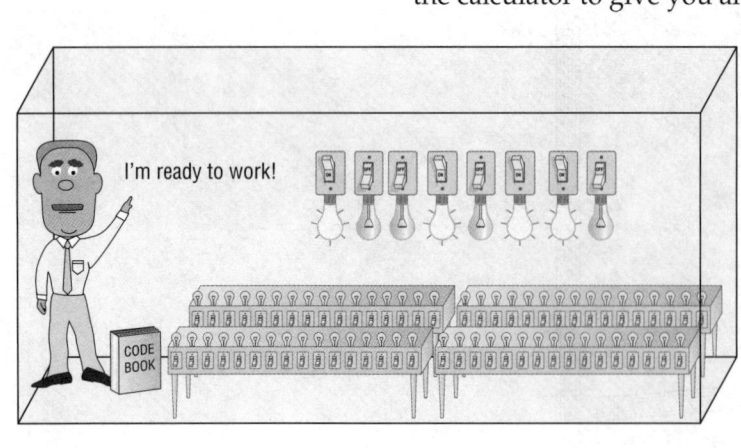

I'm ready to work!

CODE BOOK

● **Figure 3.8**   The CPU so far

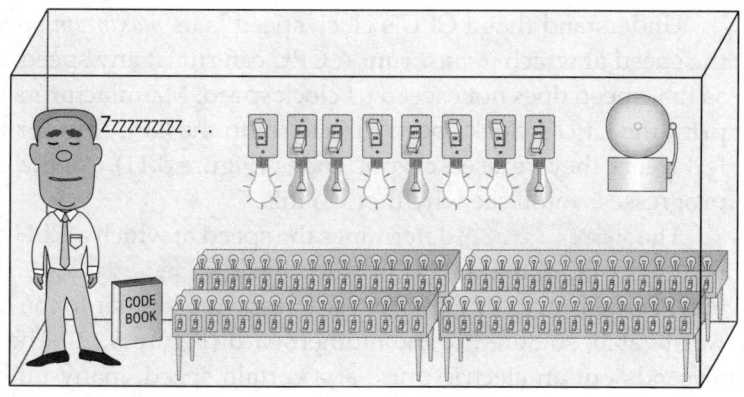

● **Figure 3.9**   The CPU does nothing until activated by the clock!

For the CPU to process a command placed on the external data bus, a certain minimum voltage must be applied to the CLK wire. A single charge to the CLK wire is called a clock cycle. Actually, the CPU requires at least two clock cycles to act on a command, and usually more. Using the manual calculator analogy, you need to pull the crank at least twice before anything happens. In fact, a CPU may require hundreds of clock cycles to process some commands (Figure 3.10).

The maximum number of clock cycles that a CPU can handle in a given period of time is referred to as its clock speed. The clock speed is the fastest speed at which a CPU can operate, determined by the CPU manufacturer. The Intel 8088 processor had a clock speed of 4.77 MHz (4.77 million cycles per second), extremely slow by modern standards, but still a pretty big number compared to using a pencil and paper! CPUs today run at speeds in excess of 3 GHz (3 billion cycles per second).

1 hertz (1 Hz) = 1 cycle per second
1 megahertz (1 MHz) = 1 million cycles per second
1 gigahertz (1 GHz) = 1 billion cycles per second

 Tech Tip

Processor Variations

CPU makers sell the exact make and model of CPU at a number of different speeds. All of these CPUs come off of the same assembly lines, so why different speeds? Every CPU comes with subtle differences—flaws, really—in the silicon that makes one CPU run faster than another. The speed difference comes from testing each CPU to see what speed it can handle.

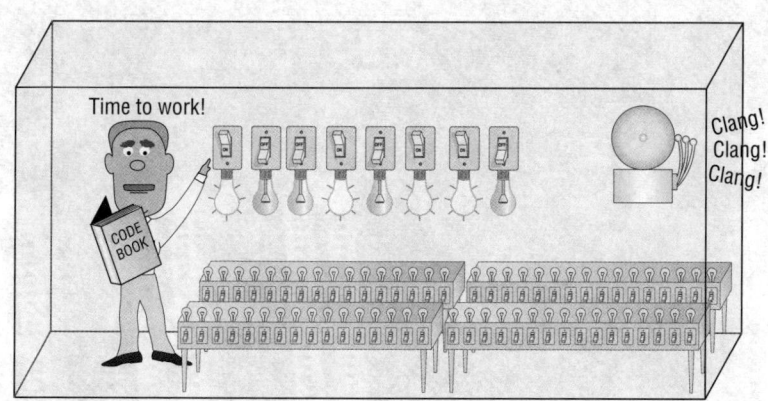

● **Figure 3.10**   The CPU often needs more than one clock cycle to get a result.

AMD Athlon™64
ADA3200AEP5AP
CAAKC 0334TPMW
9441535240617

• **Figure 3.11**   Where is the clock speed?

Aggressive users sometimes intentionally overclock CPUs by telling the clock chip to multiply the pulse faster than the CPU's designed speed. They do this to make slower (cheaper) CPUs run faster. This is a risky business that can destroy your CPU, but those willing to take that risk often do it.

Some motherboards enable you to override the default or automatic settings by changing a jumper or making a change in CMOS. A few enthusiasts' motherboards even enable you to make software changes to alter the speed of your CPU.

Understand that a CPU's clock speed is its *maximum* speed, not the speed at which it *must* run. A CPU can run at any speed, as long as that speed does not exceed its clock speed. Manufacturers used to print the CPU's clock speed directly onto the CPU, but for the last few years they've used cryptic codes (Figure 3.11). As the chapter progresses, you'll see why they do this.

The system crystal determines the speed at which a CPU and the rest of the PC operate. This is called the system bus speed . The system crystal is usually a quartz oscillator, very similar to the one in a wristwatch, soldered to the motherboard (Figure 3.12). The quartz oscillator sends out an electric pulse at a certain speed, many millions of times per second. This signal goes first to a clock chip that adjusts the pulse, usually increasing the pulse sent by the crystal by some large multiple. (The folks who make motherboards could directly connect the crystal to the CPU's clockG wire, but then if you wanted to replace your CPU with a CPU with a different clock speed, you'd need to replace the crystal too!) As long as the PC is turned on, the quartz oscillator, through the clock chip, fires a charge on the CLK wire, in essence pushing the system along.

Visualize the system crystal as a metronome for the CPU. The quartz oscillator repeatedly fires a charge on the CLK wire, setting the beat, if you will, for the CPU's activities. If the system crystal sets a beat slower than the CPU's clock speed, the CPU will work just fine, but it will operate at the slower speed of the system crystal. If the system crystal forces the CPU to run faster than its clock speed, it can overheat and stop working.

Before you install a CPU into a system, you must make sure that the crystal and clock chip send out the correct clock pulse for that particular CPU. In the not so old days, this required very careful adjustments. With today's systems, the motherboard talks to the CPU (at a very slow speed), the CPU tells the motherboard the clock speed it needs, and the clock chip automatically adjusts for the CPU, making this process invisible.

• **Figure 3.12**   One of many types of system crystals

Mike Meyers' CompTIA A+ Guide: Essentials (Exam 220-601)

Back to the External Data Bus

One more reality check. We've been talking about tables with racks of light bulbs, but of course real CPU registers don't use light bulbs to represent on/1 and off/0. Registers are tiny storage areas on the CPU, microscopic semiconductor circuits. When one of these circuits holds a charge, you can think of the light bulb as on; no charge, the light bulb is off.

Figure 3.13 is a diagram of a real 8088 CPU, showing the wires that comprise the external data bus and the single clock wire. Because the registers are inside the CPU, they can't be shown in this figure.

Now that you have learned what components are involved in the process, try the following simple exercise to see how the process works. In this example, you tell the CPU to add 2 + 3. To do this, you must send a series of commands to the CPU—the CPU will act on each command, eventually giving you an answer. Refer to the codebook in Figure 3.7 to translate the instructions you're giving the Man in the Box into binary commands.

Did you try it? Here's how it works:

1. Place 10000000 on the external data bus (EDB).
2. Place 00000010 on the EDB.
3. Place 10010000 on the EDB.
4. Place 00000011 on the EDB.
5. Place 10110000 on the EDB.
6. Place 11000000 on the EDB.

When you finish Step 6, the value on the EDB will be 00000101, the decimal number 5 written in binary.

Congrats! You just added 2 + 3 using individual commands from the codebook. This set of commands is known as a *program*, which is a series of commands sent to a CPU in a specific order for the CPU to perform work. Each discrete setting of the external data bus is a line of code. This program, therefore, has six lines of code.

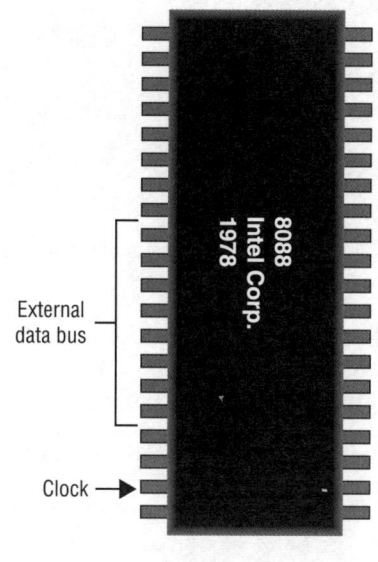

Figure 3.13 Diagram of an Intel 8088 showing the external data bus and clock wires

■ Memory

Now that you've seen how the CPU executes program code, let's work backward in the process for a moment and think about how the program code gets to the external data bus. The program itself is stored on the hard drive. In theory, you could build a computer that sends data from the hard drive directly to the CPU, but there's a problem—the hard drive is too slow. Even the ancient 8088, with its clock speed of 4.77 MHz, could conceivably process several million lines of code every second. Modern CPUs crank out billions of lines every second. Hard drives simply can't give the data to the CPU at a fast enough speed.

Computers need some other device that takes copies of programs from the hard drive and then sends them, one line at a time, to the CPU quickly enough to keep up with its demands. Because each line of code is nothing more than a pattern of eight ones and zeroes, any device that can store ones and zeroes eight across will do. Devices that in any way hold ones and zeroes that the CPU accesses are known generically as *memory*.

Many types of device store ones and zeroes perfectly well—technically even a piece of paper counts as memory—but computers need memory that does more than just store groups of eight ones and zeroes. Consider this pretend program:

1. Put 2 in the AX register.
2. Put 5 in the BX register.
3. If AX is greater than BX, run line 4; otherwise, go to line 6.
4. Add 1 to the value in AX.
5. Go back to line 1.
6. Put the value of AX on the EDB.

This program has an IF statement, also called a *branch* by CPU makers. The CPU needs a way to address each line of this memory—a way for the CPU to say "Give me the next line of code" or "Give me line 6" to the memory. Addressing memory takes care of another problem: the memory must store not only programs, but also the result of the programs. If the CPU adds 2 + 3 and gets 5, the memory needs to store that 5 in such a way that other programs may later read that 5, or possibly even store that 5 on a hard drive. By addressing each line of memory, other programs will know where to find the data.

Memory and RAM

Memory must store not only programs, but also data. The CPU needs to be able to read and write to this storage medium. Additionally, this system must enable the CPU to jump to *any* line of code as easily as to any other line of code that it stores. All of this must be done at or at least near the clock speed of the CPU. Fortunately, this magical device has existed for many years: *random access memory (RAM)*.

In Chapter 4 the concept of RAM is developed in detail, so for now let's look at RAM as an electronic spreadsheet, like one you can generate in Microsoft Excel (Figure 3.14). Each cell in this spreadsheet can store only a one or a zero. Each cell is called a **bit**. Each row in the spreadsheet is eight bits across to match the external data bus of the 8088. Each row of eight bits is called a **byte**. In the PC world, RAM transfers and stores data to and from the CPU in byte-sized chunks. RAM is therefore arranged in byte-sized rows. Here are the terms used when talking about quantities of bits:

1	0	0	0	0	0	1	1
0	1	0	0	0	0	0	0
0	0	0	0	1	1	0	1
0	1	0	1	0	0	0	0
0	0	0	0	0	0	0	1
0	1	0	1	1	0	1	0
0	0	1	1	1	1	0	0
0	0	0	0	1	0	0	1
1	1	1	0	0	0	0	0
0	0	1	0	1	1	1	0
1	0	0	0	0	0	0	0
1	0	1	0	1	0	1	0

- Any individual 1 or 0 = a *bit*
- 4 bits = a *nibble*
- 8 bits = a *byte*
- 16 bits = a *word*
- 32 bits = a *double word*
- 64 bits = a *paragraph* or *quad word*

• **Figure 3.14** RAM as a spreadsheet

The number of bytes of RAM varies from PC to PC. In the earlier PCs, from around 1980 to 1990, the typical system would have only a few hundred thousand bytes of RAM. Today's systems usually have billions of bytes of RAM.

● **Figure 3.15**   Typical RAM

Let's stop here for a quick reality check. Electronically, RAM looks like a spreadsheet, but real RAM is made of groups of semiconductor chips soldered onto small cards that snap into your computer (Figure 3.15). In the next chapter, you'll see how these groups of chips actually make themselves look like a spreadsheet. For now, don't worry about real RAM and just stick with the spreadsheet idea.

The CPU accesses any one row of RAM as easily and as fast as any other row, which explains the "random access" part of RAM. Not only is RAM randomly accessible, it's also fast. By storing programs on RAM, the CPU can access and run programs very quickly. RAM also stores any data that the CPU actively uses.

Computers use **dynamic RAM (DRAM)** for the main system memory. DRAM needs both a constant electrical charge and a periodic refresh of the circuits, otherwise it loses data—that's what makes it dynamic, rather than static in content. The refresh can cause some delays, as the CPU has to wait for the refresh to happen, but modern CPU manufacturers have clever ways to get by this issue, as you'll see when you read about the generations of processors later in this chapter.

Don't confuse RAM with mass storage devices like hard drives and floppy drives. You use hard drives and floppy drives to store programs and data permanently. Chapters 9 and 10 discuss permanent storage in intimate detail.

 Cross Check

RAM

You learned a few essentials about RAM in Chapter 2, "The Visible PC," so check back in that chapter and see if you can answer these questions. How is RAM packaged? Where do you install the PC's primary RAM, called the *system RAM*, in the system unit?

Address Bus

So far, the entire PC consists of only a CPU and RAM. But there needs to be some connection between the CPU and the RAM so they can talk to each other. To do so, extend the external data bus from the CPU so that it can talk to the RAM (Figure 3.16).

Wait a minute. How can you connect the RAM to the external data bus? This is not a matter of just plugging it into the external data bus wires! RAM is a spreadsheet with thousands and thousands of discrete rows, and you only need to look at the contents of one row of the spreadsheet at a time, right? So how do you connect RAM to the external data bus in such a way that the CPU can see any one given row, but still give the CPU the capability to look at *any* row in RAM? We need some type of chip between RAM and the CPU to make the connection. The CPU needs the ability to say which row of RAM it wants, and the chip should handle the mechanics of retrieving that row of data from RAM and putting it on the external data bus.

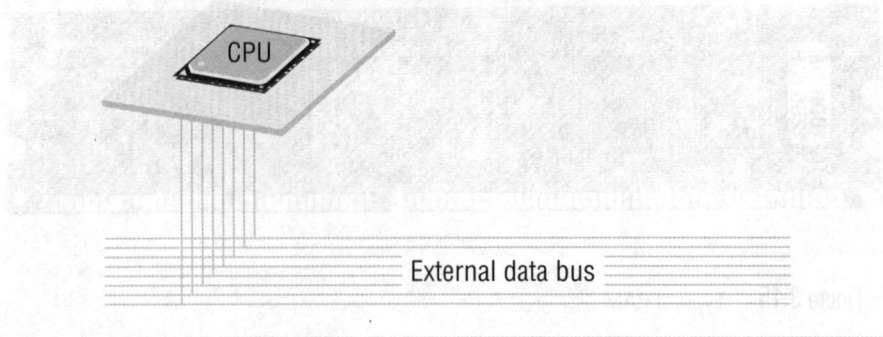

• **Figure 3.16** Extending the EDB

Wouldn't you know I just happen to have such a chip? This chip comes with many names, but for right now just call it the **memory controller chip (MCC)**.

The MCC contains special circuitry that enables it to grab the contents of any single line of RAM and place that data or command on the external data bus. This in turn enables the CPU to act on that code (Figure 3.17).

Once the MCC is in place to grab any discrete byte of RAM, the CPU needs the capability to tell the MCC which line of code it needs. The CPU therefore gains a second set of wires, called the **address bus**, that enables it to communicate with the MCC. Different CPUs have different numbers of wires (which, you will soon see, is very significant). The 8088 had 20 wires in its address bus (Figure 3.18).

By turning the address bus wires on and off in different patterns, the CPU tells the MCC which line of RAM it wants at any given moment. Every different pattern of ones and zeroes on these 20 wires points to one byte of RAM. There are two big questions here. First, how many different patterns of "on" and "off" wires can exist with 20 wires? And second, which pattern goes to which row of RAM?

How Many Patterns?

Mathematics can answer the first question. Each wire in the address bus exists in only one of two different states: on or off. If the address bus consisted of only one wire, that wire would be at any given moment either on or off.

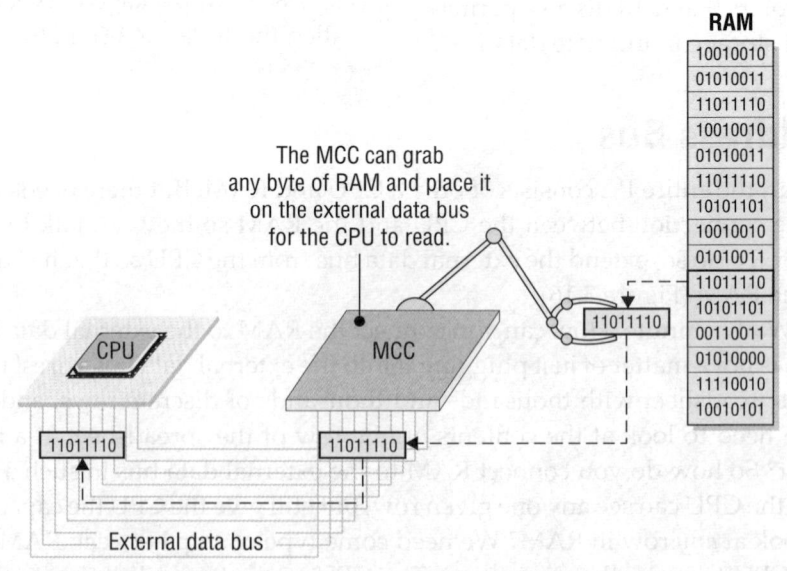

The MCC can grab any byte of RAM and place it on the external data bus for the CPU to read.

• **Figure 3.17** The MCC grabs a byte of RAM.

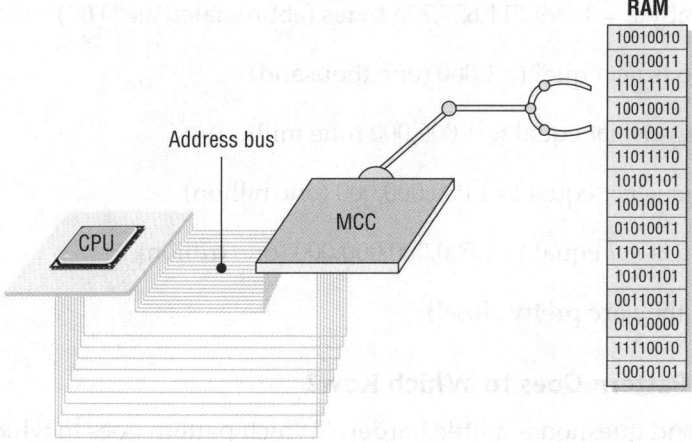

RAM

```
10010010
01010011
11011110
10010010
01010011
11011110
10101101
10010010
01010011
11011110
10101101
00110011
01010000
11110010
10010101
```

Address bus

CPU

MCC

Figure 3.18   Address bus

Mathematically, that gives you (pull out your old pre-algebra books) $2^1 = 2$ different combinations. If you have two address bus wires, the address bus wires create $2^2 = 4$ different combinations. If you have 20 wires, you would have 2^{20} (or 1,048,576) combinations. Because each pattern points to one line of code and each line of RAM is one byte, *if you know the number of wires in the CPU's address bus, you know the maximum amount of RAM that a particular CPU can handle.* Because the 8088 had a 20-wire address bus, the most RAM it could handle was 2^{20} or 1,048,576 bytes. The 8088, therefore, had an *address space* of 1,048,576 bytes. This is not to say that every computer with an 8088 CPU had 1,048,576 bytes of RAM. Far from it! The original IBM PC only had a measly 64 kilobytes—but that was considered plenty back in the Dark Ages of Computing in the early 1980s.

Okay, so you know that the 8088 had 20 address wires and a total address space of 1,048,576 bytes. Although this is accurate, no one uses such an exact term to discuss the address space of the 8088. Instead, you say that the 8088 had one *megabyte* (1 MB) of address space.

What's a "mega"? Well, let's get some terminology down. Dealing with computers means constantly dealing with the number of patterns a set of wires can handle. Certain powers of 2 have names used a lot in the computing world. The following list explains:

1 kilo = 2^{10} = 1,024 (abbreviated as "K")

1 kilobyte = 1,024 bytes (abbreviated as "KB")

1 mega = 2^{20} = 1,048,576 (abbreviated as "M")

1 megabyte = 1,048,576 bytes (abbreviated as "MB")

1 giga = 2^{30} = 1,073,741,824 (abbreviated as "G")

1 gigabyte = 1,073,741,824 bytes (abbreviated as "GB")

1 tera = 2^{40} = 1,099,511,627,776 (abbreviated as "T")

Tech Tip

Kilos

Of course 1 kilo is equal to 1,000 when you talk in terms of the metric system. It also means 1,000 when you talk about the clock speed of a chip, so 1 KHz is equal to 1,000 Hz. When you talk storage capacity, though, the binary numbers kick in, making 1 KB = 1,024 bytes. Got it? This same bizarre, dual meaning applies all the way up the food chain, so 1 MHz is 1,000,000 Hz, but 1 MB is 1,048,576 bytes; 1 GHz is 1 billion Hz, but 1 GB is 1,073,741,824 bytes; and so on.

Bits and bytes are abbreviated differently. Bytes get a capital B whereas bits get a lowercase b. So, for example, 4 KB is four kilobytes, but 4 Kb is four kilobits!

1 terabyte = 1,099,511,627,776 bytes (abbreviated as "TB")

1 kilo is *not* equal to 1,000 (one thousand)

1 mega is *not* equal to 1,000,000 (one million)

1 giga is *not* equal to 1,000,000,000 (one billion)

1 tera is *not* equal to 1,000,000,000,000 (one trillion)

(But they are pretty close!)

Which Pattern Goes to Which Row?

The second question is a little harder: "Which pattern goes to which row of RAM?" To understand this, let's take a moment to discuss binary counting. In binary, only two numbers exist, 0 and 1, which makes binary a handy way to work with wires that turn on and off. Let's try to count in binary: 0, 1 … what's next? It's not 2—you can only use 0s and 1s. The next number after 1 is 10! Now let's count in binary to 1000: 0, 1, 10, 11, 100, 101, 110, 111, 1000. Try counting to 10000. Don't worry; it hardly takes any time at all.

Super, you now count in binary as well as any math professor. Let's add to the concept. Stop thinking about binary for just a moment and think about good old base 10 (regular numbers). If you have the number 365, can you put zeroes in front of the 365, like this: 000365? Sure you can—it doesn't change the value at all. The same thing is true in binary. Putting zeroes in front of a value doesn't change a thing! Let's count again to 1000 in binary. In this case, add enough zeroes to make 20 places:

00000000000000000000

00000000000000000001

00000000000000000010

00000000000000000011

00000000000000000100

00000000000000000101

00000000000000000110

00000000000000000111

00000000000000001000

Hey! This would be a great way to represent each line of RAM on the address bus, wouldn't it? The CPU identifies the first byte of RAM on the address bus as 00000000000000000000. The CPU identifies the last RAM row with 11111111111111111111. When the CPU turns off all the address bus wires, it wants the first line of RAM; when it turns on all the wires, it wants the 1,048,576th line of RAM. Obviously, the address bus also addresses all the other rows of RAM in between. So, by lighting up different patterns of ones and zeroes on the address bus, the CPU can access any row of RAM it needs.

Essentials

■ Modern CPUs

Modern CPUs retain the core structures of the Intel 8088, such as registers, instruction sets, and, of course, the *arithmetic logic unit (ALU)*—our friend, the Man in the Box. But in the decades of the personal computer, many manufacturers have risen to challenge Intel's dominance—some have even survived—and all processor makers have experimented with different processor shapes, connectors, and more. The amazing variety of modern CPUs presents unique challenges to a new tech. Which processors go on which motherboards? Can a motherboard use processors from two or more manufacturers? Aren't processors all designed for PCs and thus interchangeable?

This section maps out the modern processor scene. I'll start with a brief look at the manufacturers, so you know who the players are. Once you know who's making the CPUs, we'll go through the generations of CPUs in wide use today, starting with the Intel Pentium. All modern processors share fundamental technology first introduced by Intel in the Pentium CPU. I use the Pentium, therefore, to discuss the details of the shared technology, and then add specific bonus features when discussing subsequent processors.

Manufacturers

When IBM awarded Intel the contract to provide the CPUs for its new IBM PC back in 1980, it established for Intel a virtual monopoly on all PC CPUs. The other CPU makers of the time faded away: Tandy, Commodore, Texas Instruments—no one could compete directly with Intel. Over time, other competitors have risen to challenge Intel's market segment share dominance. In particular, a company called Advanced Micro Devices (AMD) began to make clones of Intel CPUs, creating an interesting and rather cutthroat competition with Intel that lasts to this day.

Intel

Intel Corporation thoroughly dominated the personal computer market with its CPUs and motherboard support chips. At nearly every step in the evolution of the PC, Intel has led the way with technological advances and surprising flexibility for such a huge corporation. Intel CPUs—and more specifically, their instruction sets—define the personal computer. Intel currently produces a dozen or so models of CPU for both desktop and portable computers, most of which use the name Pentium, such as the Pentium 4 and the Pentium M. Their lower-end CPUs use the Celeron branding; their highest-end ones are called Xeon.

AMD

You can't really talk about CPUs without mentioning Advanced Micro Devices—the Cogswell Cogs to Intel's Spacely Sprockets. AMD makes superb CPUs for the PC market and has grabbed roughly half of the CPU market.

Like Intel, AMD doesn't just make CPUs, but their CPU business is certainly the part that the public notices. AMD has made CPUs that "clone" the function of Intel CPUs. If Intel invented the CPU used in the original IBM PC, how could AMD make clone CPUs without getting sued? Well, chipmakers have a habit of exchanging technologies through cross-license agreements. Way back in 1976, AMD and Intel signed just such an agreement, giving AMD the right to copy certain types of CPUs.

The trouble started with the Intel 8088. Intel needed AMD to produce CPUs. The PC business was young back then, and providing multiple suppliers gave IBM confidence in their choice of CPUs. Life was good. But after a few years, Intel had grown tremendously and no longer wanted AMD to make CPUs. AMD said, "Too bad. See this agreement you signed?" Throughout the 1980s and into the 1990s, AMD made pin-for-pin identical CPUs that matched the Intel lines of CPUs (Figure 3.19). You could yank an Intel CPU out of a system and snap in an AMD CPU—no problem!

In January 1995, after many years of legal wrangling, Intel and AMD settled and decided to end the licensing agreements. As a result of this settlement, AMD chips are no longer compatible—even though in some cases the chips look similar. Today, if you want to use an AMD CPU, you must purchase a motherboard designed for AMD CPUs. If you want to use an Intel CPU, you must purchase a motherboard designed for Intel CPUs. So you now have a choice: Intel or AMD.

• **Figure 3.19**   Identical Intel and AMD 486 CPUs from the early 1990s

CPU Packages

One of the many features that make PCs attractive is the ability for users (okay, maybe advanced users) to replace one CPU with another. If you want a removable CPU, you need your CPUs to use a standardized package with matching standardized socket on the motherboard. CPUs have gone through many packages, with manufacturers changing designs like snakes shedding skins. The fragile little DIP package of the 8088 (Figure 3.20) gave way to

• **Figure 3.20**   The dual inline pin package of the Intel 8088

● **Figure 3.21**   An AMD Athlon Slot A processor

rugged slotted processors in the late 1990s (Figure 3.21), which have in turn given way to CPUs using the now prevalent grid array packaging.

The grid array package has been popular since the mid-1980s. The most common form of grid array is the **pin grid array (PGA)**. PGA CPUs are distinguished by their square shape with many—usually hundreds—of tiny pins (Figure 3.22).

Collectively, Intel and AMD have used close to 100 variations of the PGA package over the years for hundreds of different CPU models with names like staggered-PGA, micro-PGA, BGA (ball grid array, which uses tiny balls instead of pins), and LGA (land grid array, which uses flat pads instead of pins). There are also many different varieties of PGA CPUs based on the number of pins sticking out of the CPU. These CPUs snap into special sockets on the motherboard, with each socket designed to match the pins (or balls or pads) on the CPU. To make CPU insertion and removal easier, these sockets—officially called **zero insertion force (ZIF) sockets**—use a small arm on the side of the socket (Figure 3.23) or a cage that fits over the socket (Figure 3.24) to hold the CPU in place. ZIF sockets are universal and easily identified by their squarish shape.

The first generations of sockets used a numbering system that started with Socket 1 and went through Socket 8. The hassle of trying to remember how many pins went with each type of socket made it clear after a while that the CPU makers might as well give all sockets a name based on the number

 Although there are many types of PGA packages, most techs just call them all "PGA."

 AMD CPUs and sockets have totally different numbering systems than Intel CPUs and sockets, so techs often use the name of the socket instead of AMD or Intel. For example: "Hey, did you see that Socket 775 motherboard?"

● **Figure 3.22**   Samples of PGA packages

• **Figure 3.23**   ZIF socket with arm on side

of pins. Most sockets today have names like Socket 940 and Socket 775 to reflect the number of pins.

It's very important to know the more common CPU/socket types. As you go through each type of CPU in this chapter, pay attention to the socket types used by those particular CPUs.

The Pentium CPU: The Early Years

Since the advent of the 8088 way back in the late 1970s, CPU makers have added a large number of improvements. As technology has progressed from the 8088 to the most current CPUs, the sizes of the external data bus, address bus, and registers have grown dramatically. In addition, the clock speeds at which CPUs run have kept pace, getting faster and faster with

• **Figure 3.24**   ZIF socket with cage over the top

● **Figure 3.25** Old CPUs

each successive generation of processor. The 1980s were an exciting time for CPU technology. The 8088 CPU was supplanted by a series of improved processors with names such as 80286, 80386, and 80486 (Figure 3.25). Each of these CPU families incorporated wider buses, increasingly higher clock speeds, and other improvements.

In the early 1990s, Intel unveiled the Pentium CPU. Although no longer manufactured, the Pentium CPU was the first Intel CPU to contain all of the core functions that define today's modern CPUs.

> Many of the CPU features attributed here to the Pentium actually appeared earlier, but the Pentium was the first CPU to have *all* of these features!

Man in Box Redux

Let's take a look at these improvements by evolving the friendly Man in the Box to the standards of an Intel Pentium processor. The Pentium retained the core features of the 8088 and subsequent processors, although the clock was much faster, the address bus and external data bus were wider, and the registers had more bits. You'll also see a number of other improvements that simply didn't exist on the original 8088.

The Rise of 32-bit Processing

The old 8088 had 16-bit registers, an 8-bit EDB, and a 20-bit address bus. Old operating systems (like DOS and early versions of Windows) were written to work on the 8088. Over the years, later CPUs gradually increased their address bus and general-purpose register sizes to 32 bits, allowing much more powerful operating systems (such as Linux, Windows XP, and Windows Vista) to work with the Pentium to process larger numbers at a single time and to address up to $2^{32} = 4,294,967,296 =$ four gigabytes of RAM. (See Figure 3.26.) Running 32-bit operating systems on 32-bit hardware is called *32-bit processing*.

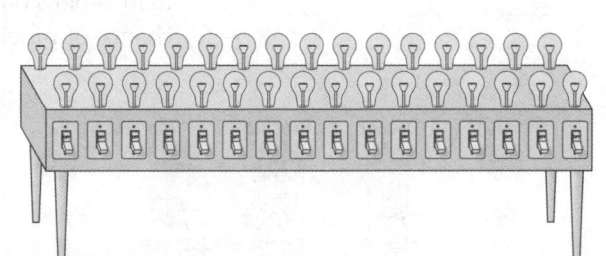

● **Figure 3.26** A 32-bit register

For the most part, modern PCs run 32-bit operating systems, like Windows, but that's about to change. Both AMD and Intel now make 64-bit processors that address up to 2^{64} = 18,446,744,073,709,551,616 bytes of RAM. You'll learn more about 64-bit processors later in this chapter.

Pipelining

Remember earlier when we talked about the idea that you needed to pull the crank multiple times to get an answer out of the CPU? The main reason for this stems from the fact that the CPU's process of getting a command from the EDB, doing the calculation, and then getting the answer back out on the EDB requires at least four steps (each of these steps is called a *stage*):

1. **Fetch**   Get the data from the EDB
2. **Decode**   Figure out what type of command needs to be done
3. **Execute**   Perform the calculation
4. **Write**   Send the data back onto the EDB

Smart, discrete circuits inside your CPU handle each of these stages. In early CPUs, when a command was placed on the EDB, each stage did its job and the CPU handed back the answer before starting the next command, requiring at least four clock cycles to process a command. In every clock cycle, three of the four circuits sat idle. Today, the circuits are organized in a conveyer belt fashion called a `pipeline`. With pipelining, each stage does its job with each clock cycle pulse, creating a much more efficient process. The CPU has multiple circuits doing multiple jobs, so let's add pipelining to the Man in the Box analogy. Now, it's *Men* in the Box (Figure 3.27)!

Pipelines keep every stage of the processor busy on every click of the clock, making a CPU run more efficiently without increasing the clock speed. Note that at this point, the CPU has four stages—fetch, decode, execute, and write—a four-stage pipeline. No CPU ever made has fewer than four stages, but advancement in caching have increased the number of stages over the years. Current CPU pipelines contain many more stages, up to 20 in some cases.

Pipelining isn't perfect. Sometimes a stage hits a complex command that requires more than one clock cycle for the stage to calculate the answer, forcing the pipeline to stop until that stage is done. These stops, *called pipeline stalls*, are something your CPU tries to avoid. The decode stage tends to cause the most pipeline stalls—certain commands are complex and therefore harder to decode than other commands. The Pentium used two decode stages to reduce the chance of pipeline stalls due to complex decoding (Figure 3.28).

Tech Tip

Lengthening Pipelines

After the Pentium, pipelines kept getting longer, reaching up to 20 stages in the Pentium 4. Since then, Intel and AMD have kept CPU pipelines around 12 stages (although this could change again).

• **Figure 3.27**   Simple pipeline

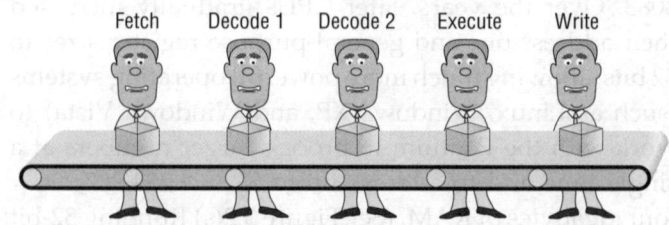

• **Figure 3.28**   Pentium pipeline

Pipelining certainly helped the Pentium run more efficiently, but there's another issue—the execute stage. The inside of the CPU is composed of multiple chunks of circuitry to handle the different types of calculations your PC needs to do. For example, one part, the *integer unit*, handles integer math—basic math for numbers with no decimal point. $2 + 3 = 5$ is a perfect example of integer math. The typical CPU spends more than 90 percent of its work doing integer math. But the Pentium also had special circuitry to handle complex numbers, called the *floating point unit (FPU)*. With a single pipeline, only the integer unit or the floating point unit worked at any execution stage. Worse yet, floating point calculation often took many, many clock cycles to execute, forcing the CPU to stall the pipeline until the floating point finished executing the complex command (Figure 3.29).

Execute

Integer

Floating point

Floating point

• **Figure 3.29**   Bored integer unit

To keep things moving, the folks at Intel gave the Pentium two pipelines— one main, "do everything" pipeline and one that only handled integer math. Although this didn't *stop* pipeline stalls, it at least had a second pipeline that kept running when the main one stalled! (See Figure 3.30.)

The two pipelines on the old Pentium were so successful that Intel and AMD added more and more pipelines to subsequent CPUs, to the point that most CPUs today have around eight pipelines, although there's tremendous variance from CPU to CPU.

You'll see the integer unit referred to as the arithmetic logic unit (ALU) in many sources. Either term works.

One of the biggest differences between equivalent AMD and Intel processors is the pipelines. AMD tends to go for lots of short pipelines whereas Intel tends to go with just a few long pipelines.

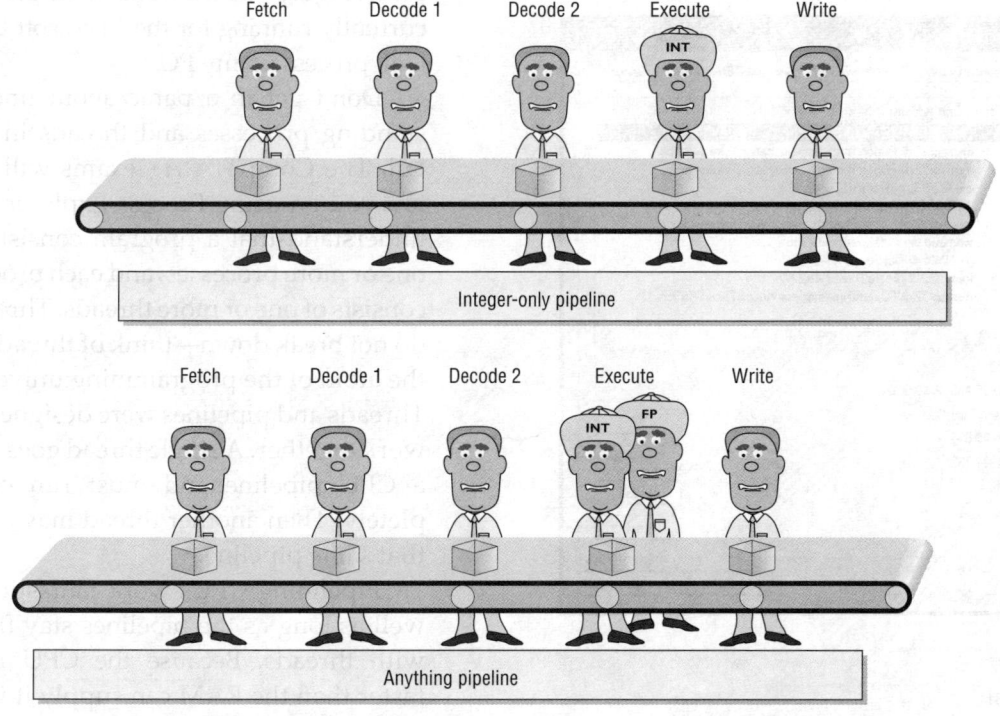

Fetch   Decode 1   Decode 2   Execute   Write

INT

Integer-only pipeline

Fetch   Decode 1   Decode 2   Execute   Write

INT   FP

Anything pipeline

• **Figure 3.30**   The Pentium dual pipeline

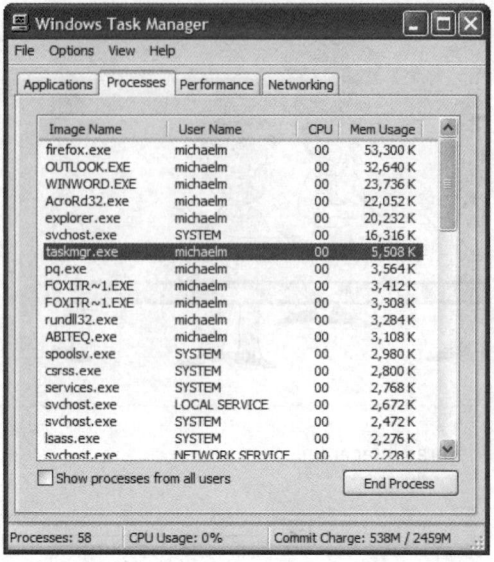

● **Figure 3.31**   Task Manager showing processes

CPU Cache

When you start your Web browser or some other program, Windows copies the program from the hard drive and stores it in RAM. The moment your program is stored in RAM and prepared to run through the CPU, it's no longer considered program—we now call that chunk of code a *process*. A single process doesn't need to know how to do everything—for example, Microsoft Word doesn't need code to know how to make scrollbars, respond to the mouse, and so on. Each process simply talks to other processes to know how to do the boring stuff. If the requested process is not running, Windows automatically loads it for the requesting process. Every process breaks down into one or more little pieces of code called *threads*. Each thread is a tiny part of the whole process, designed to do a particular job.

The Windows Task Manager (Figure 3.31) shows most of the processes running in RAM (Windows hides some of them). To access the Task Manager, press CTRL-ALT-DEL, click the Task Manager button, and then select the Processes tab. Note that different processes take up different amounts of RAM.

Threads are harder to see, as there's no program built into Windows to show threads, but you can download the free Process Explorer for Windows at www.microsoft.com/technet/sysinternals/utilities/ProcessExplorer.mspx. It's a fun, safe program that's a little hard to use, but will enable you to see the threads currently running on your computer. Figure 3.32 shows all of the threads currently running for the Microsoft Outlook process on my PC.

Don't get in a panic about understanding processes and threads in detail. The CompTIA A+ exams will not test you on using Process Explorer. Do understand that a program consists of one or more processes, and each process consists of one or more threads. Threads do not break down—think of threads as the atom of the programming universe. Threads and pipelines were designed to work together. A single thread goes into a CPU pipeline and must run completely. Then another thread may enter that same pipeline.

Pipelining CPUs work fantastically well as long as the pipelines stay filled with threads. Because the CPU runs faster than the RAM can supply it with threads, however, you'll always get a

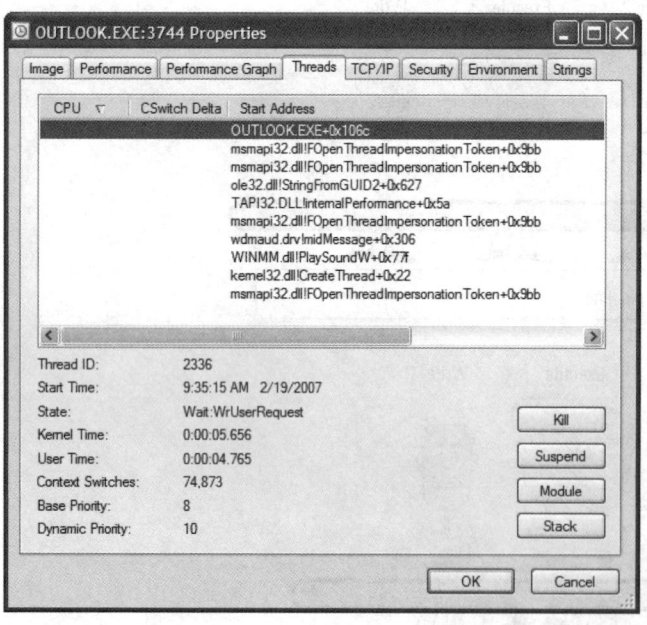

● **Figure 3.32**   Lots of threads!

special type of pipeline stall—called a `wait state`—due to the RAM not keeping up with the CPU. To reduce wait states, the Pentium came with built-in, very high speed RAM called `static RAM (SRAM)`. This SRAM would preload as many threads as possible and would also keep copies of already run threads in the hope that the CPU would need to run it again (it's very common for a process to run a thread over and over). See Figure 3.33. SRAM used in this fashion is called a `cache`.

The SRAM cache inside the CPU was tiny, only about 16 KB, but it helped tremendously with performance. In fact, it helped so much that many motherboard makers began adding cache directly to the Pentium motherboards. These caches were much larger, usually around 128 to 512 KB. When the CPU looked for a line of code, it first went to the built-in cache, but if the code wasn't there, the CPU would go to the cache on the motherboard. The cache on the CPU was called the *L1 cache* because it was the one the CPU first tried to use. The cache on the motherboard was called the *L2 cache*; not because it was on the motherboard, but because it was the

> You'll hear cache referred to as Level 1, Level 2, and Level 3 for L1, L2, and L3 cache, respectively. Any of the terms is acceptable.

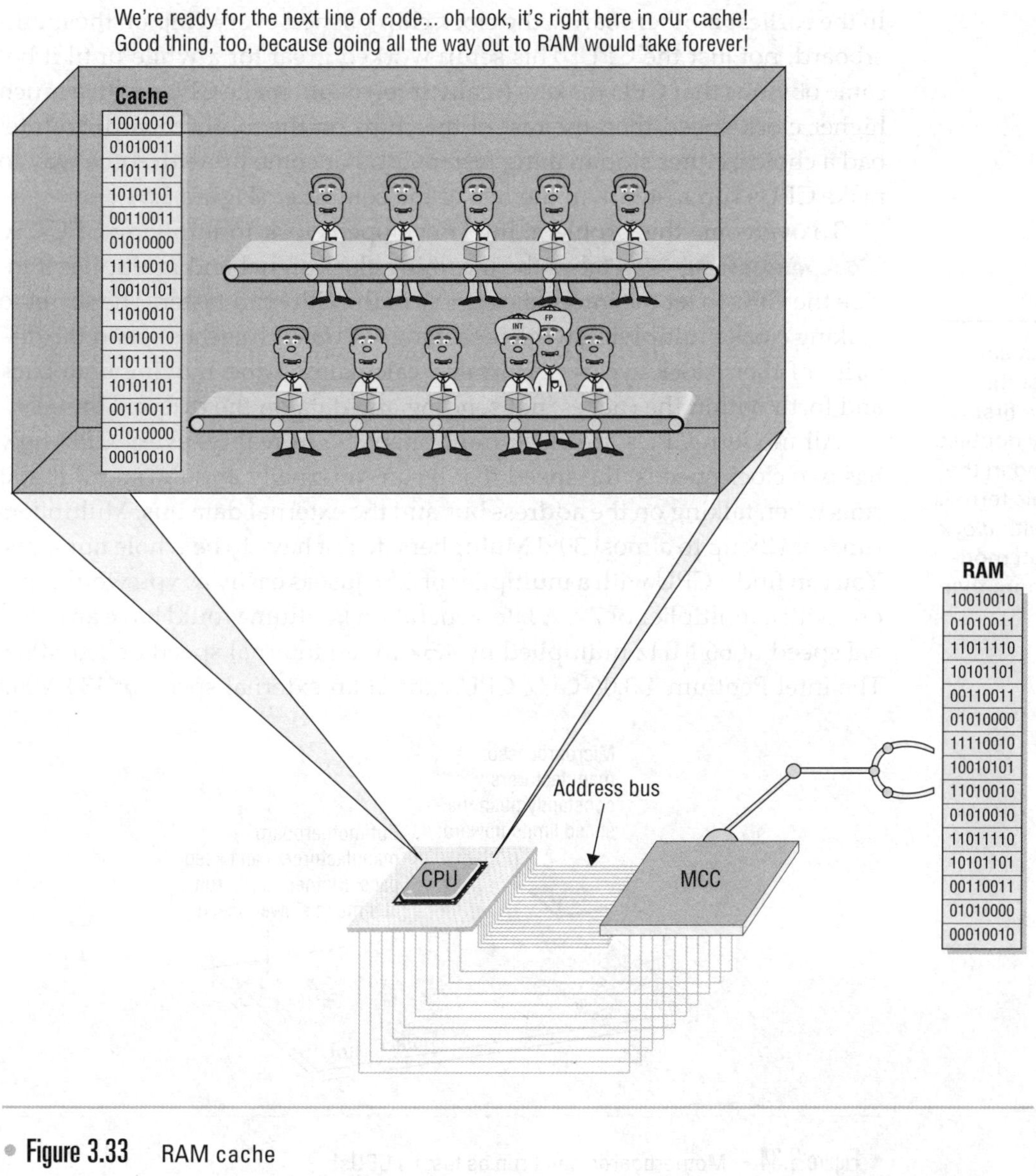

Figure 3.33 RAM cache

Tech Tip

It's Not Just Size That Matters

It's tempting to ask why processor manufacturers didn't just include bigger L1 caches instead of making onboard L1 and L2 caches. The answer is that a very small L1 and a larger L2 are much more efficient than a single fast L1!

Clock multiplying first surfaced during the reign of the Intel 80486 CPUs. All the first clock multipliers exactly doubled the clock speed, resulting in the term *clock doubling*. This term is used interchangeably with *clock multiplying*, even though modern CPUs multiply far more than just times two!

second cache the CPU checked. Later engineers took this cache concept even further and added the L2 cache onboard the CPU. A few CPU makers even went so far as to include three caches: an L1, an L2, and an L3 cache on the CPU. L3 caches are only seen on very powerful and specialized CPUs—never on more common CPUs.

The Pentium cache was capable of *branch prediction*, a process whereby the cache attempted to anticipate program branches before they got to the CPU itself. An IF statement provides a nice example of this: "If the value in the AX register = 5, stop running this code and jump to another memory location." Such a jump would make all of the data in the cache useless. The L1 cache in the Pentium could recognize a branch statement. Using a counter that kept a record about the direction of the previous branch, the L1 would guess which way the branch was going to go and make sure that side of the branch was in cache. The counter wasn't perfect, but it was right more often than it was wrong.

Clock Speed and Multipliers

In the earliest motherboards, the clock chip pushed every chip on the motherboard, not just the CPU. This setup worked great for a while until it became obvious that CPU makers (really Intel) could make CPUs with a much higher clock speed than the rest of the chips on the motherboard. So Intel had a choice: either stop making faster CPUs or come up with some way to make CPUs run faster than the rest of the computer (Figure 3.34).

To overcome this problem, Intel developed clock-multiplying CPUs. A **clock-multiplying CPU** takes the incoming clock signal and multiplies it inside the CPU to let the internal circuitry of the CPU run faster. The secret to making clock multiplying work is caching. CPUs with caches spend the majority of their clock cycles performing calculations and moving data back and forth within the caches, not sending any data on the external buses.

All modern CPUs are clock multipliers. So in reality, every CPU now has two clock speeds: the speed that it runs internally and the speed that it runs when talking on the address bus and the external data bus. Multipliers run from 2× up to almost 30×! Multipliers do not have to be whole numbers. You can find a CPU with a multiplier of 6.5× just as easily as you would find one with a multiplier of 7×. A late-generation Pentium would have an external speed of 66 MHz multiplied by 4.5× for an internal speed of 300 MHz. The Intel Pentium 4 3.06-GHz CPU runs at an external speed of 133 MHz

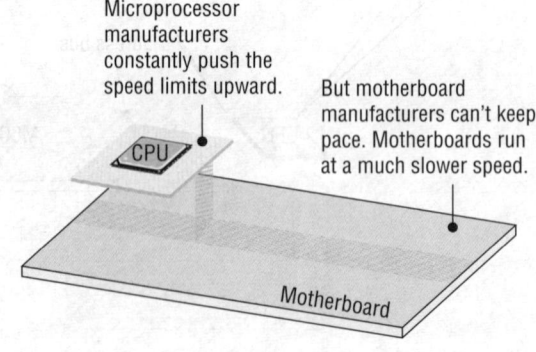

Microprocessor manufacturers constantly push the speed limits upward.

But motherboard manufacturers can't keep pace. Motherboards run at a much slower speed.

CPU

Motherboard

● **Figure 3.34**   Motherboards can't run as fast as CPUs!

with a 23× multiplier to make—yes, you've got it—3.06 GHz. Without the invention of multiplying, modern CPUs would be nowhere near their current blazing speeds.

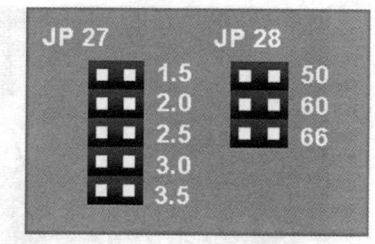

The system bus speed and the multiplier on Pentium CPU systems had to be manually configured via jumpers on the motherboard (Figure 3.35). Today's CPUs actually report to the motherboard through a function called *CPUID (CPU Identifier)*, and the system bus speed and multiplier are set automatically.

For years, users pushed for faster and faster CPU clock speeds, as clock speed was considered the most important way to differentiate one CPU from another. By 2003, advancements in caching, pipelining, and many other internal aspects of the CPU made using clock speed an inaccurate way to compare one CPU to another. CPU makers give their processors model numbers—nothing more than marketing names—to tell one processor from another. The Intel Core Duo T2300, for example, actually runs 1.66 GHz (166 MHz external speed with a 10× multiplier). If you want to know the speed of a particular processor, you must go to the CPU maker's Web site or other source.

• **Figure 3.35** Jumper settings on an old motherboard

CPU Voltages

In the simplest sense, a CPU is a collection of *transistors*, tiny electrical switches that enable the CPU to handle the binary code that makes up programs. Transistors, like every other electrical device, require a set voltage to run properly. Give a transistor too much and you fry it; too little and it doesn't work. For the first ten years of the personal computer, CPUs ran on 5 volts of electricity, just like every other circuit on the motherboard. To increase the complexity and capability with new generations of CPUs, microprocessor developers simply increased the number of transistors. But eventually they altered this strategy to increase the efficiency of the CPUs and keep the size down to something reasonable.

Intel and AMD discovered that by reducing the amount of voltage used, you could reduce the size of the transistors and cram more of them into the same space. Intel released the Pentium, for example, that required only 3.3 volts. AMD responded with its versions of the Pentium-class CPUs with even lower voltages.

Motherboard manufacturers had to scramble to adapt to the changing CPU landscape by creating motherboards that could handle multiple voltages of CPUs. All the logic circuits still ran at 5 volts, so manufacturers started installing a **voltage regulator module (VRM)** that damped down voltages specifically for the CPUs.

Because the new and improved motherboards handled many CPU voltages, initially techs had to install a VRM specific to the CPU. As manufacturers got better at the game and built VRMs into the motherboards, techs just had to change jumpers or flip switches rather than install a VRM (Figure 3.36).

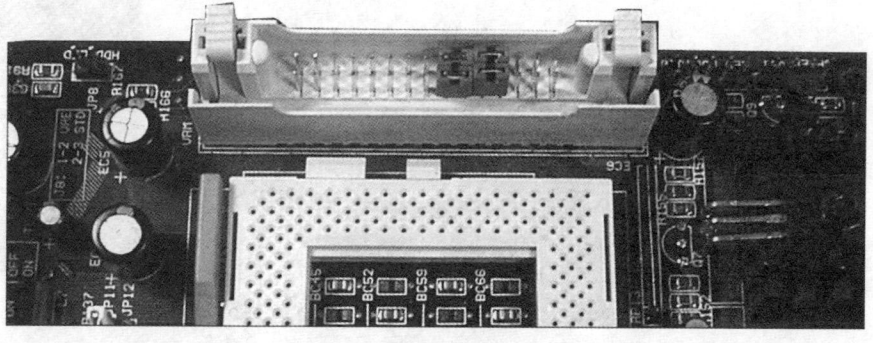

• **Figure 3.36** Voltage regulator module

• Figure 3.37 Typical motherboard voltage regulators

• Figure 3.38   An early Pentium

Getting the voltage right on today's CPUs is no longer a concern. Just as for clock speed and multiplier, today's CPUs tell the motherboard the voltage they need automatically. The integrated VRMs take care of the rest (Figure 3.37).

The feature set of the early Pentium CPUs continues to beat at the heart of every subsequent processor. Newer processors have a 64-bit data bus, 32-bit or larger address bus, 32-bit or larger registers, multiple pipelines, and L1 and L2 caches. All run at some multiple of the system clock. So, now that you've got the scoop on the Pentium, let's check out subsequent CPU models.

Original Pentium

The Pentium is not a new chip; it's been around since 1990, and the last versions of the Pentium chip were discontinued in 1995. The original Pentium was the springboard for the Pentium Pro, however, probably the most important CPU ever made, and thus it makes sense to start there. In the rest of this chapter, we look at all the popular CPUs developed since the Pentium and see how they've built on this legacy CPU (Figure 3.38).

Early Intel Pentiums

- External speed range: 50–66 MHz
- Internal speed range: 60–200 MHz
- Multiplier range: 1×–3×
- L1 cache: 16 KB
- Package: PGA
- Socket(s) used: Socket 4, Socket 5

AMD made a competitor to the Pentium called the AMD K5 (Figure 3.39). The AMD K5 was pin-compatible with the Pentium, but to keep Intel from suing them, AMD made the K5 very different on the inside, using a totally different method of processing. The AMD K5 had some success, but was rather quickly upstaged by better AMD CPUs.

• Figure 3.39   AMD K5

AMD Pentium Equivalents

- External speed range: 50–75 MHz
- Internal speed range: 60–150 MHz
- Multiplier range: 1.5×–2×
- L1 cache: 16 KB
- Package: PGA
- Socket(s) used: Socket 7

Pentium Pro

In 1995, Intel released the next generation of CPU, the Pentium Pro, often called the P6. The Pentium Pro was a huge CPU with a distinctive, rectangular PGA package (Figure 3.40). The P6 had the same bus and register sizes as the Pentium, but three new items made the P6 more powerful than its predecessor: quad pipelining, dynamic processing, and an on-chip L2 cache. These features carried on into every CPU version that followed, so many people consider the Pentium Pro to be the true "Father of the Modern CPU."

Intel Pentium Pro

- External speed range: 60–66 MHz
- Internal speed range: 166–200 MHz
- Multiplier range: 2.5×–3×
- L1 cache: 16 KB
- L2 cache: 256 KB, 512 KB, 1 MB
- Package: PGA
- Socket(s) used: Socket 8

Superscalar Execution

The P6 had four pipelines, twice as many as the Pentium. These pipelines were deeper and faster. With this many pipelines, the P6 was guaranteed to always, no matter what, run at least two processes at the same time. The ability to run more than one process in any one clock cycle is called *superscalar execution*.

Out-of-Order Processing/Speculative Execution

From time to time, a CPU must go to system memory to access code, no matter how good its cache. When a RAM access takes place, the CPU must wait a few clock cycles before processing. Sometimes the wait can be 10 or 20 clock cycles. Plus, because system memory is dynamic RAM and needs to be refreshed (charged up) periodically, this can cause further delays. When the P6 was forced into wait states, it took advantage of the wait to look at the code in the pipeline to see if any commands could be run while the wait states were active. If it found commands it could process that were not dependent on the data being fetched from DRAM, it would run these commands out of order, a feature called

■ **Figure 3.40**   Pentium Pro

out-of-order processing. After the DRAM returned with the code, it rearranged the commands and continued processing.

The P6 improved on the Pentium's branch prediction by adding a far more complex counter that would predict branches with a better than 90 percent success rate. With the combination of out-of-order processing and the chance of a branch prediction so high, the CPU could grab the predicted side of the branch out of the cache and run it out of order in one pipeline, even before the branch itself was run! This was called *speculative execution*.

On-Chip L2 Cache

The P6 had both an L1 and an L2 cache on the CPU. Because the L2 cache was on the chip, it ran almost as fast as the L1 cache (Figure 3.41). Be careful with the term "on-chip." Just because it was on the chip, that doesn't mean that the L2 cache was built into the CPU. The CPU and the L2 cache shared the same package, but physically they were separate.

The inclusion of the L2 cache on the chip gave rise to some new terms to describe the connections between the CPU, MCC, RAM, and L2 cache. The address bus and external data bus (connecting the CPU, MCC, and RAM) were lumped into a single term called the frontside bus , and the connection between the CPU and the L2 cache became known as the backside bus .

Figure 3.42 shows a more modern configuration, labeling the important buses. Note that the external data bus and address bus are there, but the chipset provides separate address buses and external data buses—one set just for the CPU and another set for the rest of the devices in the PC. No official name has been given to the interface between the RAM and the chipset. On the rare occasions when it is discussed, most techs simply call it the *RAM interface*.

The Pentium Pro had a unique PGA case that fit into a special socket, called Socket 8. No other CPU used this type of socket. The Pentium Pro made strong inroads in the high-end server market, but its high cost made it unacceptable for most people's desktop computer.

• **Figure 3.41**   A P6 opened to show separate CPU and L2 cache *(photo courtesy of Intel Corp.)*

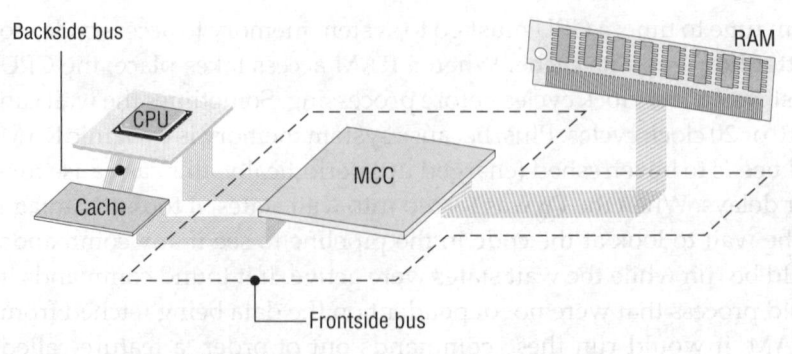

• **Figure 3.42**   Frontside and backside buses

Although the Pentium Pro never saw a large volume of sales compared with the Pentium, many people in the industry consider it to be the most important chip ever created by Intel. Its feature set was the prototype for all CPUs designed ever since.

Later Pentium-Class CPUs

Intel's usual game plan in the rough-and-tumble business of chip making is to introduce a new CPU and simultaneously declare all previous CPUs obsolete. That did not happen with the Pentium Pro, however, because Intel never really developed the P6 for most users. It was to be the CPU for powerful, higher-end systems. This kept the Pentium as the CPU of choice for all but the most power-hungry systems.

While the Pentium Pro languished on the high end for several years, Intel and AMD developed new Pentium-class CPUs that incorporated a series of powerful improvements, some of which were taken from the Pentium Pro. These improvements required that they be regarded as a new family of CPUs, which I call the "later Pentium-class CPUs" (Figure 3.43). Although certainly some profound differences exist between these CPUs, they all have three groups of similar improvements: multimedia extensions (MMX), increased multipliers/clocks, and improved processing.

Later Pentium-class CPUs

- External speed range: 66–75 MHz
- Internal speed range: 166–200 MHz
- Multiplier range: 2.5×–4.5×
- L1 cache: 32 KB
- Package: PGA
- Socket(s) used: Socket 7

Later-generation Pentiums were pin-compatible with earlier Pentiums, but included a large number of improvements. The most important improvement was increases in multipliers, and therefore clock speeds, but other improvements took place—some borrowed from the P6 and some developed just for this new breed of Pentium.

MMX

In 1996, Intel added a new enhancement to its Pentium CPU, called multimedia extensions (MMX), in response to the large number of programs with heavy graphic needs coming out at this time. MMX was designed to work with large graphics by calculating on large chunks of data and performing vector math (vector math is needed to handle graphical issues such as spinning a 3D object). MMX was not heavily supported by the folks who wrote graphics programs, but MMX did start the idea that CPUs should have special circuitry just for such programs. Over time, the graphics community began to work with Intel to improve MMX, eventually replacing it with better solutions.

• **Figure 3.43**   Later-generation Pentium

Increased Clocks and Multipliers

Later Pentiums all have vastly increased multipliers, resulting in higher speeds. Most early Pentiums used 2.5× multipliers at best, but later Pentium-class processors had up to 4.5× multipliers.

Pentium II

Intel's next major CPU was the Pentium II. Although highly touted as the next generation of CPU, the Pentium II was little more than a faster Pentium Pro with MMX and a refined instruction set. The Pentium II came in a distinctive **single edge cartridge (SEC)** that gave more space for the L2 cache and made CPU cooling easier while freeing up more room on the motherboard (Figure 3.44). Aggressive advertising and pricing made the Pentium II extremely popular.

Intel Pentium II CPUs

- External speed range: 66–100 MHz
- Internal speed range: 233–450 MHz
- Multiplier range: 3.5×–4.5×
- L1 cache: 32 KB
- L2 cache: 512 KB
- Package: SEC
- Socket(s) used: Slot 1

The Pentium II initially achieved the higher clock speeds by using high multiples of a 66-MHz external speed. During this time, however, AMD began to sell CPUs designed to run on 100-MHz motherboards. Although the final Pentium II models also ran on 100-MHz motherboards, Intel's slow adoption of 100-MHz external speed CPUs lost market share for Intel.

The SEC cartridge also created another problem: it was not free to copy. This prevented other CPU manufacturers from making CPUs that fit in the SEC's special Slot 1 connection. This move forced AMD to create its own SEC packages that were incompatible with Intel's. From the Pentium II to today, AMD and Intel CPUs are no longer interchangeable. We live in a world where AMD CPUs have motherboards designed for AMD, while Intel CPUs must have motherboards designed for Intel.

• **Figure 3.44**   Pentium II *(photo courtesy of Intel Corp.)*

AMD K6 Series

From 1997 to 2000, AMD produced a series of processors called the K6 that matched—and in many people's view, surpassed—the Pentium II, propelling AMD into serious competition with Intel (Figure 3.45). Four models were included in the K6 series: the K6, K6-2, K6-2+, and K6-III, each incorporating more advanced features than the previous model. The K6 processors incorporated a number of improvements, including 64-KB L1 cache, extremely advanced pipelining, and support for motherboard speeds of up to 100 MHz (on later models). The K6-2 added AMD's proprietary 3DNow! instruction set—a direct competitor to Intel's MMX and a significant advancement in graphics-handling capabilities—and increased clock speeds. The K6-III included even more advancements in pipelining and added a 256-KB L2 cache, all on a standard Socket 7 PGA package.

• **Figure 3.45** AMD K6 *(photo courtesy of AMD)*

AMD K6-Family CPUs

- External speed range: 66–100 MHz

- Internal speed range: 200–550 MHz

- Multiplier range: 3×–5.5×

- L1 cache: 32 KB or 64 KB

- L2 cache: 256 KB (some had none)

- Package: PGA

- Socket(s) used: Socket 7

Intel Celeron (Pentium II)

In an attempt to capture more market share of low-end PCs, Intel developed an offshoot of the Pentium II called the Celeron (Figure 3.46). The first Celerons were SEC, but lacked the protective covering of the Pentium II. Intel called this the *single edge processor (SEP)* package.

Although touted by Intel as a low-end solution and limited to only a 66-MHz bus speed, the Celeron CPU's cheap price made it a huge success in the marketplace.

> ⚠ Intel uses the name Celeron for its entire family of lower-end CPUs. There's a Celeron based on the Pentium II, a Celeron based on the Pentium III, and a Celeron based on the Pentium 4; and they are all called Celeron. When in doubt, ask.

• **Figure 3.46** Pentium II Celeron

Intel Pentium II–Based Celeron CPUs

- External speed range: 66 MHz
- Internal speed range: 266–700 MHz
- Multiplier range: 4×–10.5×
- L1 cache: 32 KB
- L2 cache: None in the first versions. Later versions had 128 KB
- Package: SEP, PGA
- Socket(s) used: Slot 1, Socket 370

Pentium III

The Pentium III improved on the Pentium II by incorporating *Streaming SIMD Extensions (SSE)*, Intel's direct competitor to AMD's 3DNow!; a number of internal processing/pipelining improvements; full support for 100-MHz and 133-MHz motherboard speeds; and high-speed L2 cache. The Pentium III was first produced using an SEC package, but improvements in die technology enabled Intel to produce (Figure 3.47) PGA versions later, ending the short reign of the SEC-package CPUs.

Intel Pentium III CPUs

- External speed range: 100–133 MHz
- Internal speed range: 450 MHz–1.26 GHz
- Multiplier range: 4×–10×
- L1 cache: 32 KB
- L2 cache: 256 KB or 512 KB
- Package: SEC-2, PGA
- Socket(s) used: Slot 1, Socket 370

Just as the Pentium II had a Celeron, so did the Pentium III. Unfortunately, Intel makes no differentiation between classes of Celerons, making buying a challenge unless you ask. The Pentium III–based Celerons were PGA and used Socket 370 (Figure 3.48).

• **Figure 3.47** Intel Pentium III

• **Figure 3.48** Intel Pentium III Celeron

Intel Pentium III–Based Celeron CPUs

- External speed range: 66–100 MHz
- Internal speed range: 533–700 MHz
- Multiplier range: 8×–11.5×
- L1 cache: 32 KB
- L2 cache: 128 KB
- Package: PGA
- Socket(s) used: Socket 370

Early AMD Athlon CPUs

The Athlon CPU has evolved from the name of a single class of CPUs into a term covering a number of very different CPUs that compete head to head against the latest Intel chips. The Athlon was AMD's first product to drop any attempt at pin compatibility with Intel chips. Instead, AMD decided to make its own AMD-only slots and sockets. The first Athlon used an SEC-style package called *Slot A* (Figure 3.49).

Early AMD Athlon CPUs

- External speed range: 100 MHz
- Internal speed range: 500 MHz–1 GHz
- Multiplier range: 5×–10×
- L1 cache: 128 KB
- L2 cache: 512 KB
- Package: SEC
- Socket(s) used: Slot A

• **Figure 3.49**   Early Athlon CPU

Processing and Wattage

To make smarter CPUs, Intel and AMD need to increase the number of microscopic transistor circuits in the CPU. The more circuits you add, the more power they need. CPUs measure their power use in units called watts, just like a common light bulb. Higher wattage also means higher heat, forcing modern CPUs to use very powerful cooling methods. Good techs know how many watts are needed by a CPU, as this tells them how hot the CPU will get inside a PC. Known hot CPUs are often avoided for general-purpose PCs, as these CPUs require more aggressive cooling.

CPU makers really hate heat, but they still want to add more circuits—so they constantly try to reduce the size of the circuits because smaller circuits use less power. CPUs are made from silicon wafers. The electrical circuitry is etched onto the wafers using a process called photo lithography. Photo lithography is an amazingly complex process, but basically requires placing a thin layer of chemicals on the wafer. These chemicals are sensitive to ultraviolet light—if a part of this mask gets exposed to UV light, it gets hard and resistant. If it doesn't get exposed, it's easy to remove. To make the circuitry, a mask of the circuits is placed over the wafer, and then the mask and wafer are exposed to UV light. The mask is removed and the wafer is washed in chemicals, leaving the circuits. If you want microscopic circuits, you need a mask with the pattern of the microscopic circuits. This is done through a photographic process. The old 8088 used a 3-micrometer (one millionth of a meter) process to make the mask. Some of today's CPUs were created with a 65-nanometer process, and 45-nanometer is just around the corner. The same CPU created with a smaller process is usually cooler.

As you read the wattages for the various CPUs, imagine a light bulb with that wattage inside your system unit!

A nanometer is one billionth of a meter.

CPU Codenames

The Pentium 4 and the Athlon started the most aggressive phase of the Intel/AMD CPU wars. From the year 2000 and continuing to today, Intel and AMD fight to bring out new CPUs with an almost alarming frequency, making the job of documenting all these CPUs challenging. Luckily for us, the CPU makers use special CPU codenames for new CPUs, such as "Willamette" and "Barton" to describe the first version of the Pentium 4 and the last version of the 32-bit Athlon, respectively. These codenames are in common use, and a good tech should recognize these names—plus they make a dandy way to learn about what's taking place in the CPU business!

You've already seen up to this point how Intel and AMD were trying to one-up each other with earlier processors. Now you'll see how the Intel/AMD wars really got going!

CPU codenames predate the Pentium 4 and Athlon, but the slower pace of new CPU models made them less important.

AMD Athlon Thunderbird

AMD's first major improvement to the Athlon CPU was codenamed Thunderbird (Figure 3.50). The Thunderbird Athlon marked AMD's return to a PGA package with the adoption of the proprietary 462-pin socket called *Socket A*.

The change between the Classic and the Thunderbird wasn't just cosmetic. Thunderbird had an interesting *double-pumped frontside bus* that doubled the data rate without increasing the clock speed. Athlon Thunderbird CPUs have a smaller but far more powerful L2 cache, as well as a number of other minor improvements.

AMD Thunderbird Athlon CPUs

- Process: 180 nm
- Watts: 38–75
- External speed range: 100–133 MHz (double-pumped)
- Internal speed range: 650 MHz–1.4 GHz
- Multiplier range: 6.5×–14×
- L1 cache: 128 KB
- L2 cache: 256 KB
- Package: PGA
- Socket(s) used: Socket A

● **Figure 3.50**   Athlon Thunderbird *(photo courtesy of AMD)*

AMD Duron

Duron is the generic name given to lower-end CPUs based on the Athlon processor. Basically an Athlon with a smaller cache, the Duron supported the same 200-MHz frontside bus as the Athlon, giving it a slight edge over the Celeron. The Duron connected to the same 462-pin Socket A as the later Athlon CPUs (Figure 3.51).

AMD Duron CPUs

- Process: 180 nm
- Watts: 21–57
- External speed range: 100 MHz (double-pumped)

● **Figure 3.51**   AMD Duron *(photo courtesy of AMD)*

- Internal speed range: 600 MHz–1.8 GHz
- Multiplier range: 6×–13.5×
- L1 cache: 128 KB
- L2 cache: 64 KB
- L3 cache: No
- Package: PGA
- Socket(s) used: Socket A

Intel Pentium 4 Willamette

While the Pentium II and III were little more than improvements on the Intel Pentium Pro, the Pentium 4 introduced a completely redesigned core, called *NetBurst*. NetBurst centered around a totally new 20-stage pipeline combined with other features to support this huge pipeline. Each stage of the pipeline performed fewer operations than typical pipeline stages in earlier processors, which enabled Intel to crank up the clock speed for the Pentium 4 CPUs. The first Pentium 4s included a new version of SSE called SSE2, and later versions introduced SSE3.

The Pentium 4 achieved a 400-MHz frontside bus speed—twice the Athlon's 200 MHz—by using four data transfers per clock cycle on a 100-MHz bus. Intel used this same *quad-pumped frontside bus* technology on a 133-MHz bus to achieve a 533-MHz frontside bus.

There were two packages of early Pentium 4 CPUs. The first Pentium 4 CPUs came in a 423-pin PGA package and had a 256-KB L2 cache. These were replaced by the 512-KB L2 cache Pentium 4 with a 478-pin PGA package (Figure 3.52). Even though the new package has more pins, it is considerably smaller than the earlier package.

Intel Pentium 4 Willamette CPUs

- Process: 180 nm
- Watts: 49–100
- External speed range: 100 MHz, 133 MHz (quad-pumped)
- Internal speed range: 1.3–2.0 GHz
- Multiplier range: 13×–20×
- L1 cache: 128 KB
- L2 cache: 256 KB
- Package: 423-pin PGA, 478-pin PGA
- Socket(s) used: Socket 423, Socket 478

• **Figure 3.52** Pentium 4 (423- and 478-pin)

AMD Athlon XP (Palomino and Thoroughbred)

Not to be left in the dust by Intel's Pentium 4, AMD released an upgraded version of the Athlon Thunderbird called the Athlon XP, codenamed Palomino, quickly followed by the Thoroughbred. Both processors used the 462-pin PGA package, but AMD incorporated a number of performance enhancements to the Athlon core, including support for Intel's SSE instructions. The Thoroughbred increased the external speed to a double-pumped 166 MHz and increased the clock speeds, while its 150-nm process reduced wattage.

One interesting aspect of the Athlon XP was AMD's attempt to ignore clock speeds and instead market the CPUs using a *performance rating (PR)* number that matched the equivalent power of an Intel Pentium 4 processor. For example, the Athlon XP 1800+ actually ran at 1.6 GHz, but AMD claimed it processed as fast or better than a Pentium 4 1.8 GHz—*ergo* "1800+."

AMD Athlon XP CPUs

- Process: 180 nm (Palomino), 150 nm (Thoroughbred)
- Watts: 60–72 (Palomino), 49–70 (Thoroughbred)
- External speed range: 133 MHz, 166 MHz (double-pumped)
- Internal speed range: 1.3 GHz (1500+)–2.2 GHz (2800+)
- Multiplier range: 13×–16.5×
- L1 cache: 128 KB
- L2 cache: 256 KB, 512 KB
- Package: 462-pin PGA
- Socket(s) used: Socket A

Intel Pentium 4 (Northwood and Prescott)

The Pentium 4 versus Athlon XP war really started to heat up with the next generation of Pentium 4 processors. These P4s increased the frontside bus speed to 800 MHz (200 MHz quad-pumped) and introduced hyperthreading.

With *hyperthreading*, each individual pipeline can run more than one thread at a time—a very tricky act to achieve. A single Intel P4 with hyperthreading looks like two CPUs to the operating system. Figure 3.53 shows the Task Manager in Windows XP on a system running a hyperthreaded Pentium 4. Note how the CPU box is broken into two groups—Windows thinks this one CPU is two CPUs.

Hyperthreading enhances a CPU's efficiency, but has a couple of limitations. First, the operating system and the application have to be hyperthreading-aware to take advantage of the feature. Second, although the CPU uses idle processing power to simulate the actions of a second processor, it doesn't double the processing power because the main execution resources are not duplicated. Even with the limitations, hyperthreading is an interesting advancement in superscalar architecture.

P4 Prescotts and Northwoods came in hyperthreaded and non-hyperthreaded versions.

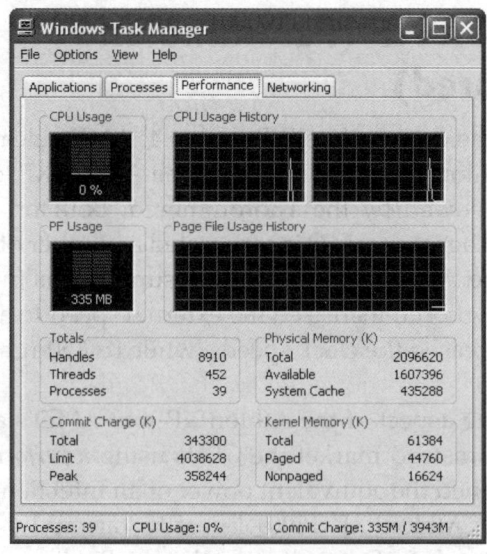

Figure 3.53 Windows Task Manager with the Performance tab displayed for a system running a hyperthreaded Pentium 4

Tech Tip

Deciphering the Numbers

Give it up. Intel must have some scheme for their CPU numbering, but it doesn't match the processor speed. They call a 2.66-GHz CPU a 506, for example, which might lead you to believe that the "6" reflects the "66" in the speed. But the 2.8-GHz CPU that followed was named the 511. Go figure!

Here's what Intel says on http://developer.intel.com: "The processor number is not a measurement of performance, nor is it the only factor to consider when selecting a processor. The digits themselves have no inherent meaning, particularly when looking across processor families. For instance, 840 is not 'better' than 640 simply because 8 is greater than 6."

The Northwood used a 130-nm process, and the Prescott used a 90-nm process. The Northwood had the same 478-pin PGA package (as did the very first Prescotts), but Intel switched to the *Land Grid Array (LGA) 775* package with the Prescott CPUs (Figure 3.54). Even though the LGA 775 package has more pins than a Socket 478 package, it is considerably smaller.

Starting with the LGA 775 Prescotts, Intel dumped the convention of naming CPUs by their clock speed and adopted a very cryptic three-digit model-numbering system. All Prescott Pentium 4s received a three-digit number starting with a 5 or a 6. One of the 2.8-GHz Pentium 4 CPUs is a 521, for example, and one of the 3-GHz processors is called the 630.

These Pentiums reached the apex of clock speeds, approaching 4 GHz. After this, Intel (and AMD) stopped the CPU clock speed race and instead began to concentrate on parallel and 64-bit processing (both to be discussed later in this chapter).

Figure 3.54 Pentium 4 LGA 775

Intel Pentium 4 CPUs

- Process: 130 nm (Northwood), 90 nm (Prescott), 65 nm (Cedar Mill)

- Watts: 45–68 (Northwood), ~84 (Prescott), 86 (Cedar Mill)

- External speed range: 100 MHz (quad-pumped), 133 MHz (quad-pumped), 200 MHz (quad-pumped)

- Internal speed range: 1.3–3.80 GHz

- Multiplier range: 13×–23×

- L1 cache: 128 KB

- L2 cache: 256 KB, 512 KB

- Package: 478-pin PGA, 775-pin LGA

- Socket(s) used: Socket 478, Socket LGA 775

AMD Athlon XP (Thorton and Barton)

The Athlon XP Thorton and Barton CPUs were the last generation of 32-bit Athlon XPs and the last to use the 462-pin PGA package. The only major difference between the two was the L2 cache. The Thorton had a 256-KB cache whereas the Barton had a 512-KB cache. Using a 130-nm process, AMD could produce faster CPUs without any real increase in wattage. Later versions of each processor increased the frontside bus to 200 MHz (double-pumped).

AMD Athlon XP CPUs

- Process: 130 nm

- Watts: 60–70

- External speed range: 133 MHz, 166 MHz, 200 MHz (double-pumped)

- Internal speed range: 1.6 GHz (2000+)–2.2 GHz (3100+)

- Multiplier range: 10×–16×

- L1 cache: 128 KB

- L2 cache: 256 KB (Thorton), 512 KB (Barton)

- Package: 462-pin PGA

- Socket(s) used: Socket A

After the Barton Athlon XPs, AMD stopped making 32-bit processors, concentrating exclusively on 64-bit. Intel, on the other hand, continued to make 32-bit processors.

Pentium 4 Extreme Edition

The Pentium 4 Extreme Edition was designed to place Intel at the top of the CPU performance curve. The Extreme Edition CPUs used a Socket 478 or LGA 775 package, making them identical to other Pentium 4s, but packed some powerful features. Most interesting was the 2-MB L3 cache—the only non-server CPU to carry an L3 cache. The Pentium 4 Extreme Edition also had some of the highest wattages ever recorded on any Intel desktop

CPU—over 110 watts! Extreme Edition CPUs ran incredibly fast, but their high price kept them from making any significant impact on the market.

Pentium 4 Extreme Edition

- Process: 130 and 90 nm
- Watts: 85–115
- External speed range: 200 MHz (quad-pumped), 266 MHz (quad-pumped)
- Internal speed range: 3.2 GHz–3.7 GHz
- Multiplier range: 14×–17×
- L1 cache: 128 KB
- L2 cache: 512 KB
- L3 cache 2 MB
- Package: 478-pin PGA, 775-pin LGA
- Socket(s) used: Socket 478, Socket LGA-775

Mobile Processors

The inside of a laptop PC is a cramped, hot environment, where no self-respecting CPU should ever need to operate. Since the mid-1980s, CPU manufacturers have endeavored to make specialized versions of their processors to function in the rugged world of laptops. These are called **mobile processors**. Over the years, a number of CPU laptop solutions have appeared. Virtually every CPU made by Intel or AMD has come in a mobile version. You can usually tell a mobile version by the word "mobile" or the letter "M" in its name. Here are a few examples:

- Mobile Intel Pentium III
- Intel Pentium M
- Mobile AMD Athlon 64
- AMD Turion 64 (All Turions are mobile processors, but don't say "mobile" or "M" in their name. AMD usually adds "mobile technology" as part of the Turion description.)
- Intel Core Duo (See the "Intel Core" section later in the chapter.)

A mobile processor uses less power than an equivalent desktop model. This provides two advantages. First, it enables the battery in the laptop to last longer. Second, it makes the CPU run cooler, and the cooler the CPU, the fewer cooling devices you need.

Almost every mobile processor today runs at a lower voltage than the desktop version of the same CPU. As a result, most mobile CPUs also run at lower speeds—it takes juice if you want the speed! Mobile CPUs usually top out at about 75 percent of the speed of the same CPU's desktop version.

Reducing voltage is a good first step, but making a smart CPU that can use less power in low-demand situations will reduce power usage even more. The first manifestation of this was the classic **System Management Mode (SMM)**. Introduced back in the times of the Intel 80386 processor, SMM provided the CPU with the capability to turn off devices that use a

Tech Tip

Centrino

Intel uses the marketing term **Centrino** *to define complete mobile solutions including a mobile processor, support chips, and wireless networking. There is no Centrino CPU, only Centrino solutions that include some type of Intel mobile CPU.*

lot of power, such as the monitor or the hard drives. Although originally designed just for laptops, SMM has been replaced with more advanced power management functions that are now built into all AMD and Intel CPUs.

CPU makers have taken power reduction one step further with throttling —the capability of modern CPUs to slow themselves down during low demand times or if the CPU detects that it is getting too hot. Intel's version of throttling is called *SpeedStep*, while AMD's version is known as *PowerNow!*

Intel Xeon Processors

Just as the term *Celeron* describes a series of lower-end processors built around the Pentium II, Pentium III, and Pentium 4, the term *Xeon* (pronounced "Zee-on") defines a series of high-end processors built around the Pentium II, Pentium III, and Pentium 4. Xeon CPUs built on the Pentium II and III core processors via the addition of massive L2 caches, but their strength comes from strong multiprocessor support. Both the Pentium II Xeon and the Pentium III Xeon used a unique SEC package that snapped into a Xeon-only slot called *Slot 2* (Figure 3.55). In general, people buy Xeons because they want to run a system with more than one processor. Most modern CPUs can run with one other identical CPU, but putting together two CPUs that were never designed to work together requires an incredibly complex MCC. Xeon processors, on the other hand, are carefully designed to work together in sets of two, four, or even eight CPUs. Although very expensive, their immense power lets them enjoy broad popularity in the high-horsepower world of server systems.

The Pentium 4 Xeon is quite a different beast from the previous Xeon types. First, the Pentium 4 Xeon's caches are smaller than other Xeons; advancements in pipelining make anything larger less valuable. Second, Intel sells two lines of Pentium 4 Xeons. One line, simply called the *Pentium 4 Xeon*, is for single or dual processor systems; and the second line, called the *Pentium 4 Xeon MP*, is for four or eight multiprocessor systems. Last, Intel went back to the PGA package with the Pentium 4 Xeons, a Xeon-only 603-pin package (Figure 3.56).

• **Figure 3.55**   Intel Pentium III Xeon *(photo courtesy of Intel Corp.)*

● **Figure 3.56**   Intel Pentium 4 Xeon *(photo courtesy of Intel Corp.)*

Early 64-Bit CPUs

Both AMD and Intel currently produce the newest thing in microprocessing: 64-bit CPUs. A 64-bit CPU has general-purpose, floating point, and address registers that are 64 bits wide, meaning they can handle 64-bit-wide code in one pass—twice as wide as a 32-bit processor. And, they can address much, much more memory.

With the 32-bit address bus of the Pentium and later CPUs, the maximum amount of memory the CPU can address is 2^{32}, or 4,294,967,296 bytes. With a 64-bit address bus, CPUs can address 2^{64} bytes of memory, or more precisely, 18,446,744,073,709,551,616 bytes of memory—that's a lot of RAM! This number is so big that gigabytes and terabytes are no longer convenient, so we now go to an exabyte (2^{60}). A 64-bit address bus can address 16 exabytes of RAM.

No 64-bit CPU uses an actual 64-bit address bus. Right now, the most RAM anybody uses is 4 GB, so there's not much motivation for creating a CPU or a motherboard that can handle and hold 16 EB. Every 64-bit processor gets its address bus "clipped" down to something reasonable. The Intel Itanium, for example, only has a 44-bit address bus for a maximum address space of 2^{44}, or 17,592,186,044,416 bytes.

Initially, both AMD and Intel raced ahead with competing 64-bit processors. Interestingly, they took very different paths. Let's look at the two CPUs that made the first wave of 64-bit processing: the Intel Itanium and the AMD Opteron.

Intel Itanium (Original and Itanium 2)

Intel made the first strike into the 64-bit world for PCs with the Itanium CPU. The Itanium was more of a proof of concept product than one that was going to make Intel any money, but it paved the way for subsequent 64-bit processors. The Itanium had a unique 418-pin *pin array cartridge (PAC)* to help house its 2- or 4-MB Level 3 cache (Figure 3.57).

• **Figure 3.57**   Intel Itanium *(image courtesy of Intel Corp.)*

The Intel Itanium 2 was Intel's first serious foray into the 64-bit world. To describe the Itanium 2 simply in terms of bus sizes and clock speeds is unfair. The power of this processor goes far deeper. Massive pipelines, high speed caching, and literally hundreds of other improvements make the Itanium 2 a powerful CPU for high-end PCs. The Itanium 2 uses a unique form of PGA that Intel calls *organic land grid array (OLGA)*. See Figure 3.58.

Intel Itanium 2

- Physical address: 50 bits
- Frontside bus width: 128 bit
- External speed range: 100 MHz (quad-pumped)

• **Figure 3.58**   Intel Itanium 2 *(image courtesy of Intel Corp.)*

- Internal speed range: 900 MHz, 1 GHz
- Watts: 90–100
- Multiplier range: 9×–10×
- L1 cache: 32 KB
- L2 cache: 256 KB
- L3 cache: 1.5 MB, 3 MB
- Package: OLGA
- Socket(s) used: Socket 611

Intel made a bold move with the Itanium and the Itanium 2 by not making them backward compatible to 32-bit programming. In other words, every OS, every application, and every driver of every device has to be rewritten to work on the Itanium and Itanium 2. In theory, developers would create excellent new applications and devices that dump all the old stuff (and problems) and thus would be more efficient and streamlined. If a company has a lot invested in 32-bit applications and can't make the jump to 64-bit, Intel continues to offer the Pentium 4 or Pentium Xeon. If you need 64-bit, get an Itanium 2. AMD didn't agree with Intel and made 64-bit processors that also ran 32-bit when needed. Intel would eventually follow AMD in this decision.

AMD Opteron

Coming in after the Itanium, AMD's Opteron doesn't try to take on the Itanium head to head. Instead, AMD presents the Opteron as the lower-end 64-bit CPU. But don't let the moniker "lower-end" fool you. Although the Opteron borrowed heavily from the Athlon, it included an I/O data path known as HyperTransport. Think of HyperTransport as a built-in memory controller chip, providing direct connection to other parts of the PC—and to other CPUs for multiprocessing—at a blistering speed of over 6 GB per second! The Opteron comes in a micro-PGA package, looking remarkably like a Pentium 4 (Figure 3.59).

AMD Opteron CPUs

- Physical address: 40 bits
- Frontside bus width: 128 bit
- External speed range: 6.4 GHz (HyperTransport)
- Internal speed range: 1.4–1.8 GHz
- Watts: 82–103
- Multiplier range: 14×–20×
- L1 cache: 128 KB
- L2 cache: 1 MB
- Package: micro-PGA
- Socket(s) used: Socket 940

• Figure 3.59   AMD Opteron *(image courtesy of AMD)*

Unlike the Itanium, the Opteron runs both 32-bit and 64-bit code. AMD gives customers the choice to move slowly into

64-bit without purchasing new equipment. This was the crucial difference between AMD and Intel in the early days of 64-bit processing.

Intel and AMD pitch the Itanium 2 and Opteron CPUs at the server market. This means that as a CompTIA A+ tech, you won't see them unless you go to work for a company that has massive computer needs. Newer CPUs from both companies fight for the desktop dollar.

Athlon 64

It's hardly fair to place the Athlon 64 with the early generation CPUs. The Athlon 64 was the first for-the-desktop 64-bit processor, so in that aspect it is an early 64-bit CPU. Through careful evolution it continues on as AMD's top-of-the-line desktop CPU offering (Figure 3.60). AMD makes two lines of Athlon CPUs: the "regular" Athlon 64 and the Athlon 64 FX series. The FX series runs faster than the regular Athlon 64 CPUs, uses more wattage, and is marketed to the power users who are willing to pay a premium. Underneath those two lines, AMD has almost 20 sublines of Athlon 64 CPUs in different codenames, making the act of listing all of them here unwieldy. To simplify, let's just break down all Athlon 64 CPUs into two groups based on the processes used in all Athlon 64 CPUs to date: 130 nm and 90 nm.

The Athlon 64 CPUs have a number of enhancements beyond simply moving into the 64-bit world. The most fascinating is the inclusion of a memory controller into the CPU, eliminating the need for an external MCC and for all intents also eliminating the idea of the frontside bus! The RAM directly connects to the Athlon 64. The Socket 754 and 939 Athlon 64 CPUs support DDR RAM; the Socket AM2 CPUs support DDR2. All Athlon 64 CPUs support Intel's SSE and SSE2 graphics extensions (later versions support SSE3).

The various mobile Athlon 64 processors offer AMD PowerNow! technology to reduce the wattage used and to extend the battery life in portable PCs. The two models to date are the Mobile AMD Athlon 64 processor and the AMD Athlon 64 for DTR. DTR stands for *desktop replacement*, the highest of the high end in portable PCs.

While regular Athlon 64 processors use the AMD PR numbers to describe CPUs, Athlon 64 FX processors uses a two-digit model number that's just as cryptic as Intel's current three-digit numbers.

AMD Athlon 64 130-nm CPUs

- Watts: 89
- Physical address: 40 bits
- External speed range: 200 MHz (System clock)
- Internal speed range (Regular): 1.8 (2800+)–2.4 (4000+) GHz
- Internal speed range (FX): 2.2 (FX-51)–2.6 (FX-55) GHz
- Multiplier range: 14×–20×
- L1 cache: 128 KB
- L2 cache: 512 KB, 1 MB
- Package: micro-PGA
- Socket(s) used (Regular): Socket 754, Socket 939
- Socket(s) used (FX): Socket 940, Socket 939

Tech Tip

Athlon 64 Clock Speed

Although the Athlon 64 may not have a true frontside bus, it does have a system clock that runs at 200 MHz to talk to RAM. This is still multiplied to get the internal speed of the CPU.

● **Figure 3.60**   Athlon 64

AMD Athlon 64 90-nm CPUs

- Watts: 67
- Physical address: 40 bits
- External speed range: 200 MHz (System clock)
- Internal speed range (Regular): 1.8 (3000+)–2.4 (4000+) GHz
- Internal speed range (FX): 2.6 (FX-51)–2.8 (FX-57) GHz
- Multiplier range: 9×–12×
- L1 cache: 128 KB
- L2 cache: 512 KB, 1 MB
- Package: micro-PGA
- Socket(s) used (Regular and FX): Socket 754, Socket 939, Socket AM2

AMD Sempron CPUs

AMD produces various Sempron CPUs for the low end of the market. Semprons come in two socket sizes and have less cache than the Athlon 64, but offer a reasonable trade-off between price and performance.

AMD Sempron CPUs

- Watts: 35–62
- Physical address: 40 bits
- External speed range: 200 MHz (double-pumped)
- Internal speed range: 1600–2000 MHz
- Multiplier range: 8×–10×
- L1 cache: 128 KB
- L2 cache: 128 KB, 256 KB
- Package: micro-PGA
- Socket(s) used: Socket 754, Socket AM2

Dual-Core CPUs

CPU clock speeds hit a practical limit of roughly 4 GHz around 2002–2003, motivating the CPU makers to find new ways to get more processing power for CPUs. Although Intel and AMD had different opinions about 64-bit CPUs, both decided at virtually the same time to combine two CPUs into a single chip, creating a dual-core architecture. Dual-core isn't just two CPUs on the same chip. A dual-core CPU has two execution units—two sets of pipelines—but the two sets of pipelines share caches (how they share caches differs between Intel and AMD) and RAM.

> Putting more than two execution cores onto a single chip is called *multicore*.

Pentium D

Intel won the race for first dual-core processor with the Pentium D line of processors (Figure 3.61). The Pentium D is simply two late-generation Pentium 4s molded onto the same chip with each CPU using its own cache—although they do share the same frontside bus. One very interesting aspect to the Pentium D is the licensing of AMD's *AMD64* extensions—the "smarts" inside AMD CPUs that enables AMD CPUs to run either 64- or 32-bit code. Intel named their version *EM64T*. Even though the Pentium D is technically a 32-bit processor, it has extra address wires and 64-bit registers to accommodate 64-bit code. There are two codenames for Pentium D processors: the "Smithfield" (model numbers 8*xx*), using a 90-nm process, and the "Presler" (model numbers 9*xx*), using a 65-nm process. Pentium Ds use the same LGA 775 package as seen on the later Pentium 4s.

Intel Pentium D

- Process: 90 nm and 65 nm
- Watts: 95–130
- External speed range: 166 MHz, 200 MHz (quad-pumped)
- Internal speed range: 2.6 GHz–3.6 GHz
- Multiplier range: 14×–20×
- L1 cache: Two 128-KB caches
- L2 cache: Two 1-MB caches or two 2-MB caches
- Package: 775-pin LGA
- Socket(s) used: Socket LGA-775

● **Figure 3.61**   Pentium D *(photo courtesy of Intel Corp.)*

Athlon Dual Cores

AMD's introduction to dual core came with the Athlon 64 X2 CPUs. The X2s are truly two separate cores that share L1 caches, unlike the Intel Pentium D. Athlon 64 X2s initially came in both "regular" and FX versions packaged in the well-known AMD Socket 939. To upgrade from a regular Athlon 64 to an Athlon 64 X2, assuming you have a Socket 939 motherboard, is often as easy as simply doing a minor motherboard update, called *flashing the BIOS*. Chapter 5, "Understanding BIOS and CMOS," goes through this process in detail, or you can simply check your motherboard manufacturer's Web site for the information on the process. In 2006, AMD announced the *Socket AM2*, designed to replace the Socket 939 across the Athlon line (Figure 3.62).

AMD Athlon 64 X2

- Watts: 89–110
- Physical address: 40 bits
- External speed range: 200 MHz (System clock)
- Internal speed range: 2.0 (3800+)–2.4 (4000+) GHz

● **Figure 3.62**   Socket AM2 *(photo courtesy of Nvidia)*

- Multiplier range: 10×–12×
- L1 cache: 128 KB
- L2 cache: Two 512-KB caches or two 1-MB caches
- Package: micro-PGA
- Socket(s) used: Socket 939, Socket AM2

Intel Core—Goodbye, Pentium

Intel signaled the end of the Pentium name in 2006 with the introduction of the *Intel Core* CPUs. They followed up with the Core 2 processors, the first generation of CPUs to use the Intel Core architecture. Are you confused yet? Let's look a little closer at the Core and Core 2 CPUs.

Intel Core

Intel based the first generation of core processors, simply called "Core," on the Pentium M platform. Like the Pentium M, Core processors don't use the NetBurst architecture, instead falling back to a more Pentium Pro–style architecture (codenamed "Yonah") with a 12-stage pipeline. Core CPUs come in single- (Solo) and dual-core (Duo) versions, but they all use the same 478-pin FCPGA package. Core also dispenses with the three-digit Pentium numbering system, using instead a letter followed by four numbers, such as T2300.

Intel Core

- Process: 65 nm
- Watts: 5.5–31
- External speed range: 133 MHz, 166 MHz (quad-pumped)
- Internal speed range: 1.06 GHz–2.33 GHz
- Multiplier range: 8×–14×
- L1 cache: One (Core Solo) or two (Core Duo) 32-KB caches
- L2 cache: One 2048-KB cache
- Package: 478-pin microFCPGA
- Socket(s) used: Socket microFCPGA

Intel Core 2

With the Core 2 line of processors, Intel released a radically revised processor architecture, called Core. Redesigned to maximize efficiency, the Core 2 processors spank their Pentium D predecessors by up to 40 percent in energy savings at the same performance level. To achieve the efficiency, Intel cranked up the cache size (to 2 or 4 MB) and went with a wide, short pipeline. The CPU can perform multiple actions in a single clock cycle and, in the process, run circles around the competition.

Intel has released two Core 2 versions for the desktop, the Core 2 Duo and Core 2 Extreme, as well as a mobile version (Figure 3.63). At the end of 2006, Intel released a

Tech Tip

Core versus Core 2

Intel's naming conventions can leave a lot to be desired. Note that the Core Solo and Core Duo processors were based on the Pentium M architecture. The Core 2 processors are based on the Core architecture.

Figure 3.63 Intel Core 2 CPU *(photo courtesy of Intel Corp.)*

quad-core version of the Core 2 Extreme. All versions incorporate AMD's 64-bit technology, rebranding it as EM64T, so they can run Windows Vista in 64-bit mode natively.

Core 2

- Process: 65 nm
- Watts: 45–95
- External speed range: 266 MHz (quad-pumped)
- Internal speed range: 1.8 GHz–3.2 GHz
- Multiplier range: 7×–12×
- L1 cache: Two 64-KB caches
- L2 cache: One 2048-KB or 4096-KB cache
- Package: 775-pin LGA
- Socket(s) used: Socket LGA-775

Try This!

Comparing CPUs

AMD and Intel are in a constant battle to have the fastest and cleverest CPU on the market. One result is that computer system vendors have a range of CPUs for you to choose from when customizing a system. So how do you know what you can and should choose? Try this:

1. Surf over to one of the major computer vendor's Web sites: dell.com, gateway.com, hp.com, and ibm.com all have customization features on their sites.

2. Select a low-end desktop from the available offerings and pretend you're considering purchasing it. Select the customization option and record the CPU choices you're given, as well as the price differentials involved: Note which CPU comes as the default choice. Is it the fastest one? The slowest?

3. Now start again, only this time select a high-end model. Again choose to customize it as if you're a potential purchaser. Record the CPU choices you get with this model, the price differentials, and which choice is the default.

4. Finally, do an Internet search for benchmarking results on the fastest, slowest, and at least one other of the CPU choices you found. What differences in performance do you find? How does that compare to the differences in price?

Know Your CPUs

In this chapter, you have seen the basic components and functions of a PC's CPU. A historical view has been provided to help you better understand the amazing evolution of CPUs in the more than 20-year life span of the personal computer.

The information in this chapter will be referred to again and again throughout the book. Take the time to memorize certain facts, such as the size of the L1 and L2 caches, CPU speeds, and clock-doubling features. These are facts that good technicians can spout off without having to refer to a book.

Chapter 3 Review

■ Chapter Summary

After reading this chapter and completing the exercises, you should understand the following about CPUs.

CPU Core Components

■ The central processing unit performs calculations on binary numbers to make the magic of computers work. The CPU interfaces with the motherboard and other components through the external data bus or frontside bus.

■ CPUs contain several areas of internal memory, known as registers, in which data and addresses are stored while processing. The commands a CPU knows how to perform are dictated by its instruction set.

■ A quartz crystal soldered to the motherboard and known as the system crystal provides a constant pulse known as the clock. The frequency of this pulse, or clock speed, dictates the maximum speed at which a processor can run, measured in megahertz or gigahertz. The processor typically runs at some multiple of this clock pulse, known as the internal clock speed. The internal clock speed is set by adjusting the multiplier (which multiplies the clock speed by some number) by configuring motherboard jumpers or making a change to a CMOS setting, or is set automatically via CPU circuitry. Setting the clock speed higher to force the CPU to run faster than its rating is known as overclocking.

Memory

■ A computer uses random access memory to take copies of programs from the hard drive and send them, one line at a time, to the CPU quickly enough to keep up with its demands. The CPU accesses any one row of RAM as easily and as fast as any other row, which explains the "random access" part of RAM. RAM is not only randomly accessible, but also fast. By storing programs on RAM, the CPU can access and run programs very quickly. RAM also stores any data that the CPU actively uses.

■ The CPU communicates with RAM on the motherboard via the address bus. The number

of wires comprising the address bus dictates the amount of memory the CPU can access.

Modern CPUs

■ Most CPUs in modern PCs are manufactured by Intel or AMD.

■ CPUs come in two main form factors: pin grid array (PGA) and single edge cartridge (SEC).

■ PGA CPUs connect to the motherboard by way of a zero insertion force (ZIF) socket, which allows the CPU to be inserted with no force. ZIF sockets work by way of a mechanical arm that locks the CPU in place.

■ The original Intel Pentium was introduced in 1990 and discontinued in 1995. AMD's competing CPU was the AMD K5.

■ Pipelining enables a CPU to perform calculations as an assembly line. No longer does one calculation need to be completed before the next can begin. Modern CPUs have multiple pipelines.

■ Modern CPUs contain small amounts of high-speed SRAM called cache. As CPUs advanced, the capacities of cache increased as did the number of cache areas itself. CPU cache is also known as L1, L2, or L3 cache. Data and instructions are stored in cache while they await processing. This increases performance, as the CPU can access data in cache more rapidly than data in motherboard RAM.

■ In 1995 Intel released the Pentium Pro. It improved upon the original Pentium by offering quad pipelining, dynamic processing, and on-chip L2 cache. With four pipelines, it was guaranteed to run at least two processes at the same time. The ability to run more than one process in a single clock cycle is called superscalar execution. The Pentium Pro's advanced branch prediction allowed it to run processes out of order to increase performance in a procedure called speculative execution.

■ In 1996 Intel released the Pentium II. It improved upon the Pentium Pro by offering multimedia extensions (MMX) and a refined instruction set. The AMD K6 (and its varieties) was the main competitor.

- The Intel Celeron is a low-end processor. The generic name of Celeron, with no identifying letters or numbers to indicate which version, made purchasing one difficult unless you asked the right questions.

- Intel's Pentium III improved upon the Pentium II by offering Streaming SIMD Extensions (SSE). AMD responded with the 3DNow! instruction set.

- The AMD Athlon was the first AMD CPU to use AMD-only slots and sockets. If you wanted an AMD Athlon, you had to purchase a motherboard with the special AMD slot/socket.

- The AMD Duron is similar to the Intel Celeron in that it was marketed toward the low-end PCs. The Duron is similar to the Athlon but contains a smaller cache.

- The Intel Pentium 4 came in several varieties identified by codenames Willamette, Northwood, and Prescott.

- The Athlon XP came in several varieties—Palomino, Thoroughbred, Thorton, and Barton.

- The Intel Pentium 4 Extreme Edition was the first non-server CPU to offer L3 cache.

- Mobile processors, or CPUs for laptops, are usually identified by the word "mobile" or the letter "M" in their names. A mobile processor uses less power than a desktop CPU, allowing for longer battery life and cooler running. They run on a lower voltage than a desktop CPU, which usually translates to lower speeds. The term Centrino defines a complete mobile solution consisting of a mobile processor, support chips, and wireless networking. There is no Centrino CPU.

- Intel's SpeedStep and AMD's PowerNow! technologies enable CPUs to slow themselves down during times of low demand or if the CPU senses it is getting too hot. Generically, this is called throttling.

- The Intel Xeon is a high-end processor aimed at the server or power-user market. Xeons are intended to be used in PCs with multiple processors. The Pentium 4 Xeon is for single or dual processor systems, while the Intel Pentium 4 Xeon MP is for four or eight multiprocessor systems.

- The original Intel Itanium was Intel's first 64-bit processor. The Itanium and the follow-up Itanium 2 were not backwardly compatible with 32-bit systems, so users had to use a 64-bit operating system, 64-bit software, and 64-bit drivers.

- The AMD Opteron, AMD's first 64-bit processor, was backwardly compatible with 32-bit systems.

- The AMD Athlon 64 comes in two varieties, Athlon 64 and Athlon 64 FX, with the FX being faster and more expensive. The AMD Sempron is AMD's low-end 64-bit processor.

- Dual-core CPUs combine two CPUs into a single chip. The two CPUs have different sets of pipelines, but share common caches. The Intel Pentium D (codenames Smithfield and Presler) is one such processor that can run both 32- and 64-bit code. AMD's Athlon 64 X2 CPUs are dual-core.

- The Pentium name was retired in 2006 with the release of the Intel Core and Core 2 CPUs, which are available in single- and dual-core versions.

Key Terms

address bus (62)	**dynamic RAM (DRAM)** (61)	**registers** (54)
backside bus (78)	**external data bus (EDB)** (53)	**single edge cartridge (SEC)** (80)
binary (54)	**frontside bus** (78)	**static RAM (SRAM)** (73)
bit (60)	**instruction set** (56)	**system bus speed** (58)
byte (60)	**machine language** (56)	**system crystal** (58)
cache (73)	**memory controller chip (MCC)** (62)	**System Management Mode (SMM)** (90)
central processing unit (CPU) (51)	**microprocessor** (51)	**throttling** (91)
Centrino (90)	**mobile processor** (90)	**voltage regulator module (VRM)** (75)
clock cycle (57)	**multimedia extensions (MMX)** (79)	**wait state** (73)
clock speed (57)	**pin grid array (PGA)** (67)	**zero insertion force (ZIF) socket** (67)
clock-multiplying CPU (74)	**pipeline** (70)	
dual core (96)		

Key Term Quiz

Use the Key Terms list to complete the sentences that follow. Not all terms will be used.

1. All of the machine language commands that the CPU understands make up the CPU's _____.

2. By lifting the arm on the _____ socket, you can easily install a PGA CPU.

3. Computers use _____ for main system memory.

4. Computers use the _____ numbering system.

5. _____ are areas inside the CPU where it temporarily stores internal commands and data while it is processing them.

6. Divided into L1 and L2, the _____ consists of a small amount of _____ that serves as a holding area to provide data to the CPU faster than getting it from regular memory or when RAM is unavailable due to refreshes.

7. A _____ enables a motherboard to support CPUs that run at differing voltage requirements.

8. Laptops sporting the _____ logo indicate they contain a mobile processor, support chips, and a wireless network interface.

9. In a process known as _____, a CPU can slow itself down in low demand times or if it gets too hot.

10. An Athlon 64 X2 is an example of a _____ processor.

Multiple-Choice Quiz

1. What device enables a PC to retrieve a specific row of data from system memory and place it on the external data bus?
   A. Advanced micro device
   B. Arithmetic logic unit
   C. Floating-point processor
   D. Memory controller chip

2. Which of the following statements is true?
   A. The address bus enables the CPU to communicate with the MCC.
   B. The external data bus enables the CPU to communicate with the MCC.
   C. The address bus enables the CPU to communicate with the hard drive.
   D. The system bus enables the CPU to communicate with the memory.

3. Which of the following CPUs was the first microprocessor to include both an L1 and an L2 cache?
   A. Pentium
   B. Pentium Pro

C. Pentium II
D. Pentium III

4. What do 64-bit processors expand that 32-bit processors, such as the Pentium 4, do not have?
   A. System bus
   B. Frontside bus
   C. Address bus
   D. Registers

5. What is the first stage in a typical four-stage CPU pipeline?
   A. Decode
   B. Execute
   C. Fetch
   D. Write

6. Which of the following terms measures CPU speed?
   A. Megahertz and gigahertz
   B. Megabytes and gigabytes
   C. Megahertz and gigahertz
   D. Frontside bus, backside bus

7. Which of the following CPUs was designed for systems with four to eight processors and also features a large Level 3 cache?

   A. Pentium 4

   B. Itanium

   C. Xeon MP

   D. Opteron

8. Which processor comes in an SEC package that fits into Slot A?

   A. Pentium II

   B. Pentium III

   C. Athlon

   D. Celeron

9. What's the main difference between the Itanium and the Opteron CPUs?

   A. The Itanium is a 32-bit processor whereas the Opteron is a 64-bit processor.

   B. The Itanium can run only 64-bit code whereas the Opteron can run both 32-bit and 64-bit code.

   C. The Itanium is made by AMD whereas the Opteron is made by Intel.

   D. The Itanium fits in Slot 1 whereas the Opteron fits in Slot A.

10. What connects on the backside bus?

    A. CPU, MCC, RAM

    B. CPU, MCC, L1 cache

    C. CPU, L1 cache

    D. CPU, L2 cache

11. What improvement(s) have CPU manufacturers put into processors to deal with pipeline stalls?

    A. Added multiple pipelines

    B. Increased the speed of the SRAM

    C. Created new die sizes with more pins

    D. Bundled better fans with their retail CPUs

12. Which of the following CPU manufacturing processes offers a final product that most likely uses the least amount of electricity for the same number of circuits?

    A. 3 micrometer

    B. 45 nanometer

    C. 65 nanometer

    D. 90 nanometer

13. What improvement does the Athlon 64 offer over the Athlon XP?

    A. Lower wattage

    B. Larger L1 cache

    C. Larger process size

    D. 64-bit processing

14. Which CPUs are made by Intel?

    A. Williamette and Barton

    B. Thunderbird and Duron

    C. Palamino and Thoroughbred

    D. Northwood and Prescott

15. Which processors combine two CPUs on the same chip? Choose all that apply.

    A. Intel Pentium 4 Extreme Edition

    B. Intel Pentium D

    C. AMD Opteron

    D. AMD Athlon 64 X2

Essay Quiz

1. Juan wants to buy a laptop computer, but he finds that laptops are more expensive than desktop computers. Moreover, he is complaining that he can't find a laptop that is as fast as the newest desktop PCs. Explain to Juan three special considerations that make a laptop more expensive and less powerful than desktop computers.

2. On the bulletin board outside your classroom, your friend Shelley notices two flyers advertising used computers. The first one is a 700-MHz Celeron that runs on a 100-MHz system bus, 32 KB of L1 cache, 128 KB of L2 cache, and 128 MB of RAM. The other one is an 800-MHz Athlon that runs on a 200-MHz system bus, 128 KB of L1 cache, 512 KB of L2 cache, and 256 MB of RAM. Shelley does not know much about computer hardware, so she asks you which one is the better computer and why. In simple terms that Shelley will understand, explain five differences that determine which computer is better.

3. You're forming a study group with a few of your friends to review microprocessors. Each one of you has decided to study a particular aspect of this chapter to explain to the group. Your responsibility is buses, including the address bus, backside bus, and frontside bus. Write a few sentences that will help you explain what each bus does and the differences among the buses.

Lab Projects

• Lab Project 3.1

Perhaps newer and faster CPUs have come out recently. Go to www.intel.com and to www.amd.com and investigate the newest CPUs for desktop computers from each manufacturer. Write a paragraph comparing the newest Intel CPU with the newest AMD CPU. Try to include the following information:

- What is the size of the address bus?
- What is the speed of the CPU?

- What is the speed of the frontside bus?
- What are the sizes of the L1 and L2 caches?
- Do either offer L3 cache?
- What kind of chip package houses each CPU?
- What kind of slot or socket does each use?
- What other new features does each site advertise for its newest CPU?

Understanding RAM

"Many complain of their memory, few of their judgment."
—BENJAMIN FRANKLIN

Anytime someone comes up to me and starts professing their computer savvy, I ask them a few questions to see how much they really know. Just in case you and I ever meet and you decide you want to "talk tech" with me, I'll tell you my first two questions just so you'll be ready. Both involve *random access memory (RAM)*, the working memory for the CPU.

1. "How much RAM is in your computer?"
2. "What is RAM and why is it so important that every PC has some?"

Can you answer either of these questions? Don't fret if you can't—you'll know how to answer both of them before you finish this chapter. Let's start by reviewing what you know about RAM thus far.

In this chapter, you will learn how to

■ **Identify the different types of RAM packaging**

■ **Explain the varieties of DRAM**

■ **Recognize RAM speed and capacity**

The CompTIA A+ certification domains use the term *memory* to describe the short-term storage used by the PC to load the operating system and running applications. The more common term in the industry is *RAM*, for random access memory, the kind of short-term memory you'll find in every computer. More specifically, the primary system RAM is *dynamic random access memory (DRAM)*. For the most part, this book uses the terms RAM and DRAM.

☑ **Cross Check**

Dynamic and Random Access

You encountered DRAM back in Chapter 3, so see if you can answer these questions. What makes DRAM "dynamic"? What does "random access" mean?

When not in use, programs and data are held in mass storage, which usually means a hard drive, but could also mean a USB thumb drive, a CD-ROM, or some other device that can hold data when the computer is turned off (Figure 4.1). When you load a program by clicking an icon in Windows, the program is copied from the mass storage device to RAM and then run (Figure 4.2).

You saw in the previous chapter that the CPU uses **dynamic random access memory (DRAM)** as RAM for all PCs. Just like CPUs, DRAM has gone through a number of evolutionary changes over the years, resulting in improved DRAM technologies with names such as SDRAM, RDRAM, and DDR RAM. This chapter starts by explaining how DRAM works, and then moves into the types of DRAM used over the last few years to see how they improve on the original DRAM.

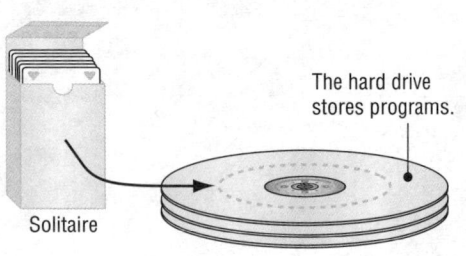

The hard drive stores programs.

Solitaire

● **Figure 4.1** Mass storage holds unused programs.

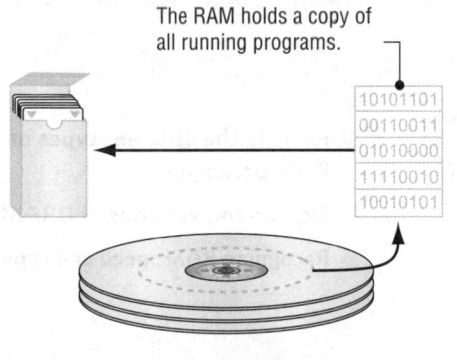

The RAM holds a copy of all running programs.

10101101
00110011
01010000
11110010
10010101

● **Figure 4.2** Programs run in RAM.

Historical/Conceptual

■ Understanding DRAM

As discussed in Chapter 3, DRAM functions like an electronic spreadsheet, with numbered rows containing cells and each cell holding a one or zero. Now let's look at what's physically happening. Each spreadsheet cell is a special type of semiconductor that can hold a single bit—one or zero—using microscopic capacitors and transistors. DRAM makers put these semiconductors into chips that can hold a certain number of bits. The bits inside the chips are organized in a rectangular fashion using rows and columns.

Each chip has a limit on the number of lines of code it can contain. Think of each line of code as one of the rows on the electronic spreadsheet; one chip might be able to store a million rows of code while another chip can store over a billion lines. Each chip also has a limit on the width of the lines of code it can handle, so one chip might handle 8-bit-wide data while another might handle 16-bit-wide data. Techs describe chips by bits rather than bytes, so ×8 and ×16, respectively. Just as you could describe a spreadsheet by the number of rows and columns, memory makers describe RAM chips the same way. An individual DRAM chip that holds 1,048,576 rows and 8 columns, for example, would be a *1 M × 8* chip, with

"M" as shorthand for "mega," just like in mega-bytes (2^{20} bytes). It is difficult if not impossible to tell the size of a DRAM chip just by looking at it—only the DRAM makers know the meaning of the tiny numbers on the chips (although sometimes you can make a good guess). See Figure 4.3.

Organizing DRAM

Due to its low cost, high speed, and capability to contain a lot of data in a relatively small package, DRAM has been the standard RAM used in all computers—not just PCs—since the mid-1970s. DRAM can be found in just about everything, from automobiles to automatic bread makers.

• **Figure 4.3**   What do these numbers mean?

The PC has very specific requirements for DRAM. The original 8088 processor had an 8-bit frontside bus. All the commands given to an 8088 processor were in discrete, 8-bit chunks. Therefore, you needed RAM that could store data in 8-bit (1-byte) chunks, so that each time the CPU asked for a line of code, the memory controller could put an 8-bit chunk on the data bus. This optimized the flow of data into (and out from) the CPU.

Although today's DRAM chips may have widths greater than 1 bit, back in the old days all DRAM chips were 1 bit wide. That means you only had sizes like 64 K × 1 or 256 K × 1—always 1 bit wide. So how was 1-bit-wide DRAM turned into 8-bit-wide memory? The answer was quite simple: just take eight 1-bit-wide chips and electronically organize them with the memory controller chip to be eight wide. First, put eight 1-bit-wide chips in a row on the motherboard (Figure 4.4), and then wire up this row of DRAM chips to the memory controller chip (which has to be designed to handle this) to make byte-wide memory (Figure 4.5). You just made eight 1-bit-wide DRAM chips look like a single 8-bit-wide DRAM chip to the CPU.

 Cross Check

Riding the 8088 Bus

You first saw the Intel 8088 CPU in Chapter 3, "Understanding CPUs," and now it pops up again. What components inside the 8088 handle the data once the CPU gets it from RAM? How does the CPU know when the data is complete and ready to take?

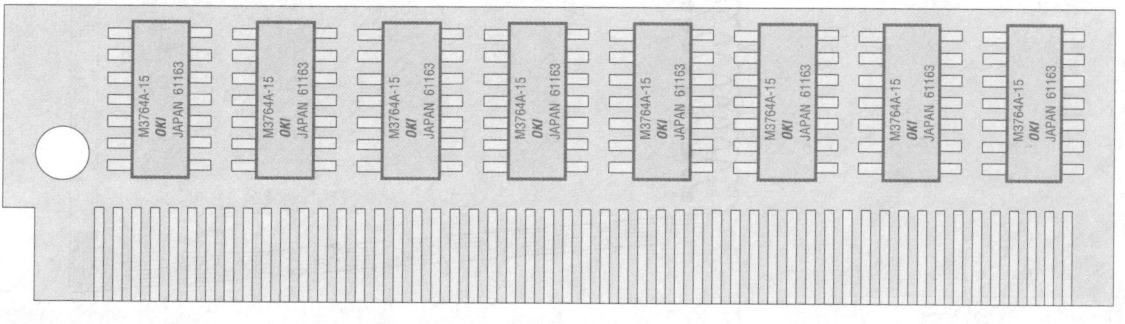

• **Figure 4.4**   One row of DRAM

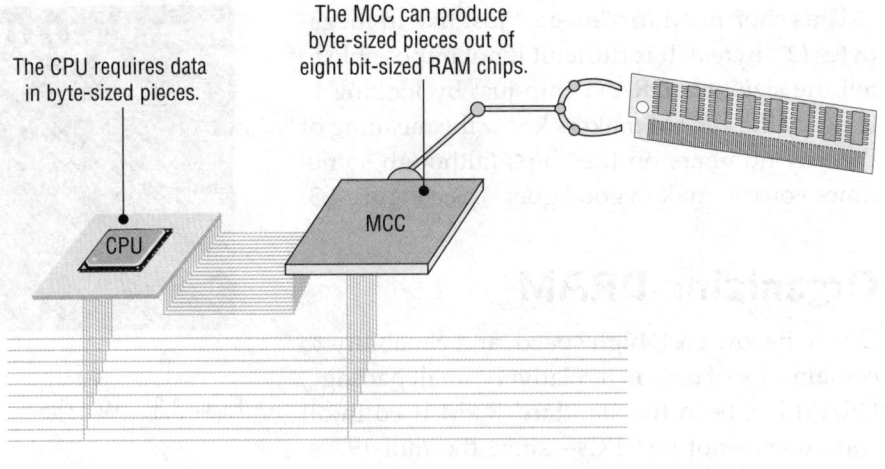

The CPU requires data in byte-sized pieces.

The MCC can produce byte-sized pieces out of eight bit-sized RAM chips.

CPU

MCC

• **Figure 4.5** The MCC in action

Practical DRAM

Okay, before you learn more about DRAM, I need to make a critical point extremely clear. When you first saw the 8088's machine language in the previous chapter, all the examples in the "codebook" were exactly 1-byte commands. Figure 4.6 shows the codebook again—see how all the commands are 1 byte?

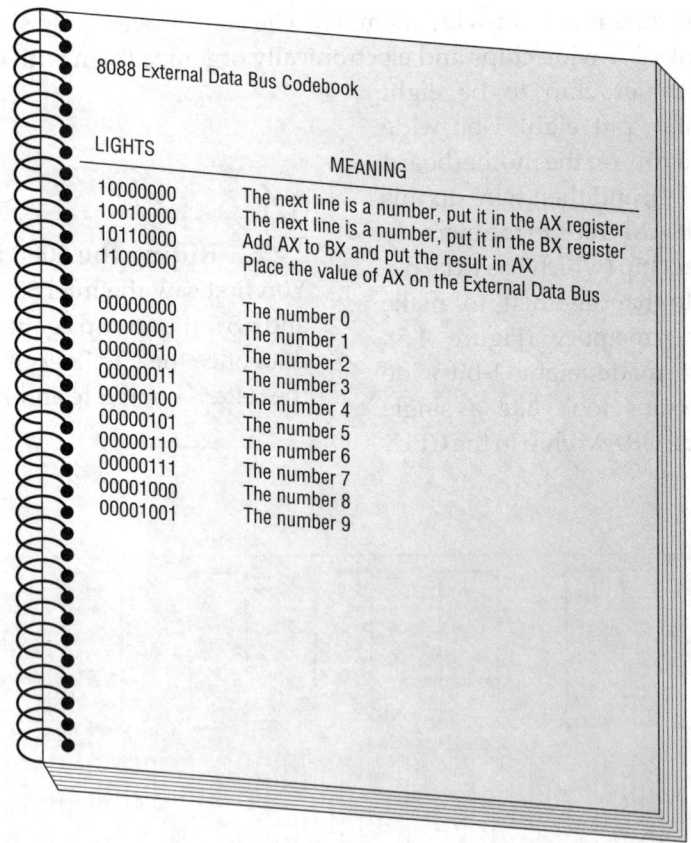

8088 External Data Bus Codebook

LIGHTS	MEANING
10000000	The next line is a number, put it in the AX register
10010000	The next line is a number, put it in the BX register
10110000	Add AX to BX and put the result in AX
11000000	Place the value of AX on the External Data Bus
00000000	The number 0
00000001	The number 1
00000010	The number 2
00000011	The number 3
00000100	The number 4
00000101	The number 5
00000110	The number 6
00000111	The number 7
00001000	The number 8
00001001	The number 9

• **Figure 4.6** Codebook again

Well, the reality is slightly different. Most of the 8088 machine language commands are 1 byte, but a few more complex commands need 2 bytes. For example, the command below tells the CPU to move 163 bytes "up the RAM spreadsheet" and run whatever command is there. Cool, eh?

1110100110100011

The problem here is that the command is 2 bytes wide, not 1 byte wide! So how did the 8088 handle this? Simple—it just took the command 1 byte at a time. It took twice as long to handle the command because the MCC had to go to RAM twice, but it worked.

Okay, so if some of the commands are more than 1 byte wide, why didn't Intel make the 8088 with a 16-bit frontside bus? Wouldn't that have been better? Well, Intel did! Intel invented a CPU called the 8086. The 8086 actually predates the 8088 and was absolutely identical to the 8088 except for one small detail—it had a 16-bit frontside bus. IBM could have used the 8086 instead of the 8088 and used 2-byte-wide RAM instead of 1-byte-wide RAM. Of course, they would have needed to invent a memory controller chip that handled that kind of RAM (Figure 4.7).

Why didn't Intel sell IBM the 8086 instead of the 8088? There were two reasons. First, nobody had invented an affordable MCC or RAM that handled two bytes at a time. Sure, chips were invented, but they were *expensive* and IBM didn't think that anyone would want to pay US$12,000 for a personal computer. So IBM bought the Intel 8088, not the Intel 8086, and all our RAM came in bytes. But as you might imagine, it didn't stay that way too long.

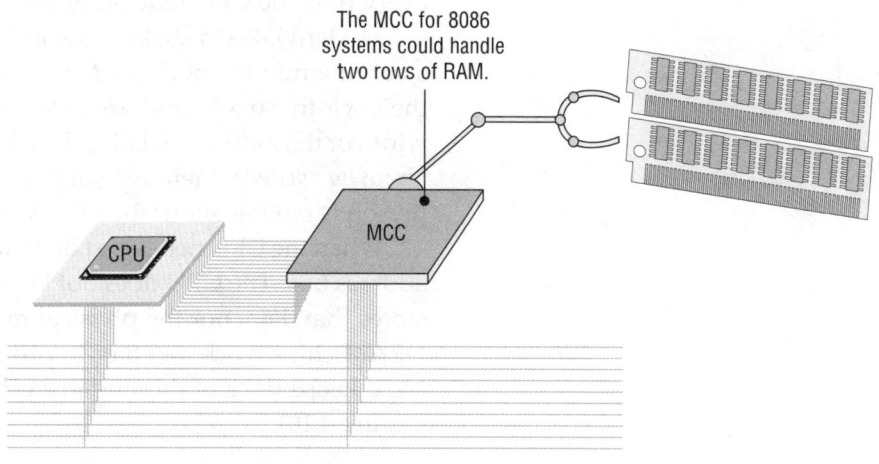

The MCC for 8086 systems could handle two rows of RAM.

• **Figure 4.7**   Pumped-up 8086 MCC at work

DRAM Sticks

As CPU data bus sizes increased, so too did the need for RAM wide enough to fill the bus. The Intel 80386 CPU, for example, had a 32-bit data bus and thus the need for 32-bit-wide DRAM. Imagine having to line up 32 1-bit-wide DRAM chips on a motherboard. Talk about a waste of space! Figure 4.8 shows motherboard RAM run amuck.

DRAM manufacturers responded by creating wider DRAM chips, such as ×4, ×8, and ×16, and putting multiples of them on a small circuit board called a **stick** or **module**. Figure 4.9 shows an early stick, called a *single inline memory module (SIMM)*, with eight DRAM chips.

• **Figure 4.8**   That's a lot of real estate used by RAM chips!

• **Figure 4.9** A 72-pin SIMM

Some MCCs are 128 bits wide.

To add RAM to a modern machine means you need to get the right stick or sticks for the particular motherboard. Your motherboard manual tells you precisely what sort of module you need and how much RAM you can install.

Modern CPUs are a lot smarter than the old Intel 8088. Their machine languages have some commands that are up to 64 bits (8 bytes) wide. They also have at least a 64-bit frontside bus that can handle more than just 8 bits. They don't want RAM to give them a puny 8 bits at a time! To optimize the flow of data into and out of the CPU, the modern MCC provides at least 64 bits of data every time the CPU requests information from RAM.

Modern DRAM sticks come in 32-bit- and 64-bit-wide form factors with a varying number of chips. Many techs describe these memory modules by their width, so ×32 and ×64. Note that this number does *not* describe the width of the individual DRAM chips on the module! When you read or hear about *by whatever* memory, simply note that you need to know whether that person is talking about the DRAM width or the module width.

When the CPU needs certain bytes of data, it requests those bytes via the address bus. The CPU does not know the physical location of the RAM that stores that data, nor the physical makeup of the RAM—such as how many DRAM chips work together to provide the 64-bit-wide memory rows. The MCC keeps track of this and just gives the CPU whichever bytes it requests (Figure 4.10).

 Try This!

Dealing with Old RAM

Often in the PC world, old technology and ways of doing things get reimplemented with some newer technology. Learning how things worked back in the ancient days can stand a tech in good stead. Perhaps more importantly, many thousands of companies—including hospitals, auto repair places, and more—use very old, proprietary applications that keep track of medical records, inventory, and so on. If you're called to work on one of these ancient systems, you need to know how to work with old parts, so try this.

Obtain an old computer, such as a 386 or 486. Ask your uncle or cousin or Great Aunt Edna if they have a PC collecting dust in a closet that you can use. Failing that, go to a secondhand store or market and buy one for a few dollars.

Open up the system and check out the RAM. Remove the RAM from the motherboard and then replace it to familiarize yourself with the internals. You never know when some critical system will go down and need repair immediately—and you're the one to do it!

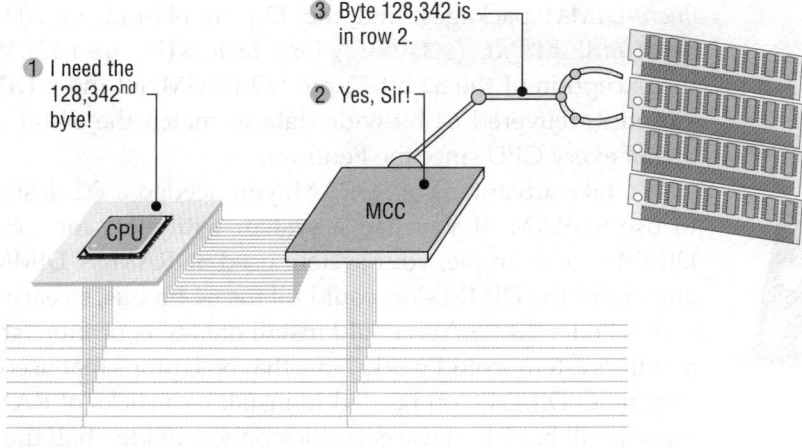

① I need the 128,342nd byte!

③ Byte 128,342 is in row 2.

② Yes, Sir!

CPU

MCC

• **Figure 4.10**   The MCC knows the real location of the DRAM.

Consumer RAM

So if modern DRAM modules come in sizes much wider than a byte, why do people still use the word "byte" to describe how much DRAM they have? Convention. Habit. Rather than using a label that describes the electronic structure of RAM, common usage describes the *total capacity of RAM on a stick in bytes.* John has a single 512-MB stick of RAM on his motherboard, for example, while Sally has two 256-MB sticks. Both systems have a total of 512 MB of system RAM. That's what your clients care about, after all, because having enough RAM makes their systems snappy and stable; not enough and the systems run poorly. As a tech, you need to know more, of course, to pick the right RAM for many different types of computers.

Essentials

■ Types of RAM

Development of newer, wider, and faster CPUs and MCCs motivate DRAM manufacturers to invent new DRAM technologies that deliver enough data at a single pop to optimize the flow of data into and out of the CPU.

SDRAM

Most modern systems use some form of synchronous DRAM (SDRAM) . SDRAM is still DRAM, but it is *synchronous*—tied to the system clock, just like the CPU and MCC, so the MCC knows when data is ready to be grabbed from SDRAM. This results in little wasted time.

SDRAM made its debut in 1996 on a stick called a dual inline memory module (DIMM) . The early SDRAM DIMMs came in a wide variety of pin sizes. The most common pin sizes found on desktops were the 168-pin variety. Laptop DIMMs came in 68-pin, 144-pin (Figure 4.11), or 172-pin

> Old RAM—really old RAM—was called *fast page mode (FPM)* RAM. This ancient RAM used a totally different technology that was not tied to the system clock. If you ever hear of FPM RAM, it's going to be in a system that's over a decade old. Be careful! CompTIA likes to use older terms like this to throw you off!

• **Figure 4.11**   144-pin micro-DIMM *(photo courtesy of Micron Technology, Inc.)*

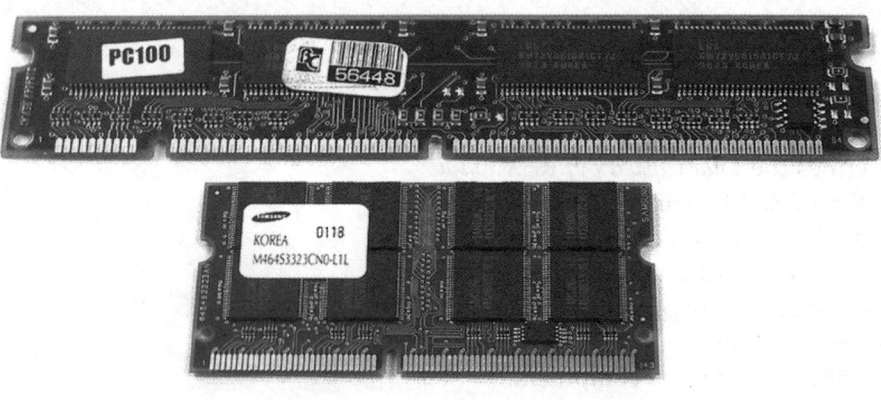

• **Figure 4.12**   A 168-pin DIMM above a 144-pin SO-DIMM

micro-DIMM packages; and the 72-pin, 144-pin, or 200-pin **small outline DIMM (SO DIMM)** form factors (Figure 4.12). With the exception of the 32-bit 72-pin SO DIMM, all these DIMM varieties delivered 64-bit-wide data to match the 64-bit data bus of every CPU since the Pentium.

To take advantage of SDRAM, you needed a PC designed to use SDRAM. If you had a system with slots for 168-pin DIMMs, for example, your system used SDRAM. A DIMM in any one of the DIMM slots could fill the 64-bit bus, so each slot was called a **bank** . You could install one, two, or more sticks and the system would work. Note that on laptops that used the 72-pin SO DIMM, you needed to install two sticks of RAM to make a full bank because each stick only provided half the bus width.

SDRAM tied to the system clock, so it had a clock speed that matched the frontside bus. Five clock speeds were commonly used on the early SDRAM systems: 66, 75, 83, 100, and 133 MHz. The RAM speed had to match or exceed the system speed or the computer would be unstable or wouldn't work at all. These speeds were prefixed with a "PC" in the front based on a standard forwarded by Intel, so SDRAM speeds were PC66 through PC133. For a Pentium III computer with a 100-MHz frontside bus, you needed to buy SDRAM DIMMs rated to handle it, such as PC100 or PC133.

RDRAM

When Intel was developing the Pentium 4, they knew that regular SDRAM just wasn't going to be fast enough to handle the quad-pumped 400-MHz frontside bus. Intel announced plans to replace SDRAM with a very fast, new type of RAM developed by Rambus, Inc. called **Rambus DRAM** , or simply **RDRAM** (Figure 4.13). Hailed by Intel as the next great leap in DRAM technology, RDRAM could handle speeds up to 800 MHz, which gave Intel plenty of room to improve the Pentium 4.

• **Figure 4.13**   RDRAM

Cross Check

Double-Pumped and Quad-Pumped

You've seen double-pumped and quad-pumped frontside buses in Chapter 3, "Understanding CPUs," so see if you can answer these questions. What CPU—by codename—started the double-pumped bus bandwagon? What socket did it use?

The 400-MHz frontside bus speed wasn't achieved by making the system clock faster—it was done by making CPUs and MCCs capable of sending 64 bits of data two or four times for every clock cycle, effectively doubling or quadrupling the system bus speed.

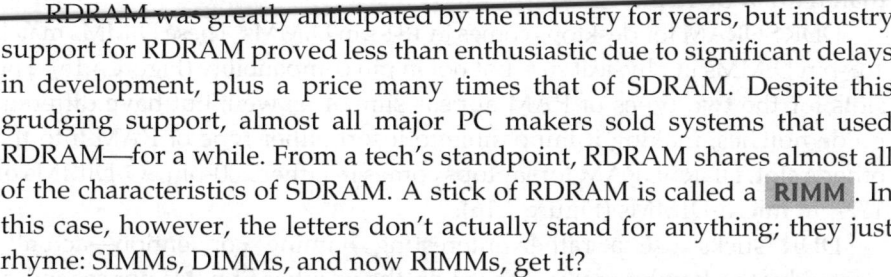

RDRAM was greatly anticipated by the industry for years, but industry support for RDRAM proved less than enthusiastic due to significant delays in development, plus a price many times that of SDRAM. Despite this grudging support, almost all major PC makers sold systems that used RDRAM—for a while. From a tech's standpoint, RDRAM shares almost all of the characteristics of SDRAM. A stick of RDRAM is called a RIMM . In this case, however, the letters don't actually stand for anything; they just rhyme: SIMMs, DIMMs, and now RIMMs, get it?

RDRAM RIMMs came in two sizes: a 184-pin for desktops and a 160-pin SO-RIMM for laptops. RIMMs were keyed differently from DIMMs to ensure that even though they are the same basic size, you couldn't accidentally install a RIMM in a DIMM slot or vice versa. RDRAM also had a speed rating: 600 MHz, 700 MHz, 800 MHz, or 1066 MHz. RDRAM employed an interesting dual-channel architecture. Each RIMM was 64 bits wide, but the Rambus MCC alternated between two sticks to increase the speed of data retrieval. You were required to install RIMMs in pairs to use this dual-channel architecture.

RDRAM motherboards also required that all RIMM slots be populated. Unused pairs of slots needed a passive device called a continuity RIMM (CRIMM) installed in each slot to enable the RDRAM system to terminate properly. Figure 4.14 shows a CRIMM.

RDRAM offered dramatic possibilities for high-speed PCs, but ran into three roadblocks that betamaxed it. First, the technology was owned wholly by Rambus—if you wanted to make it, you had to pay the licensing fees they charged. That led directly to the second problem, expense. RDRAM cost substantially more than SDRAM. Third, Rambus and Intel made a completely closed deal for the technology. RDRAM worked only on Pentium 4 systems using Intel-made MCCs. AMD was out of luck. Clearly, the rest of the industry had to look for another high-speed RAM solution.

Betamaxed is slang for "made it obsolete because no one bought it, even though it was a superior technology to the winner in the marketplace." The term refers to the VHS versus Betamax wars in the old days of video cassette recorders.

• **Figure 4.14**   CRIMM

Tech Tip

RAM Slang

Most techs drop some or all of the SDRAM part of DDR SDRAM when engaged in normal geekspeak. You'll hear the memory referred to as DDR, DDR RAM, and the weird hybrid, DDRAM.

DDR SDRAM

AMD and many major system and memory makers threw their support behind double data rate SDRAM (DDR SDRAM). DDR SDRAM basically copied Rambus, doubling the throughput of SDRAM by making two processes for every clock cycle. This synchronized (pardon the pun) nicely with the Athlon and later AMD processors' double-pumped frontside bus. DDR SDRAM could not run as fast as RDRAM—although relatively low frontside bus speeds made that a moot point—but cost only slightly more than regular SDRAM.

DDR SDRAM for desktops comes in 184-pin DIMMs. These DIMMs match 168-pin DIMMs in physical size, but not in pin compatibility (Figure 4.15). The slots for the two types of RAM appear similar as well, but have different guide notches, making it impossible to insert either type of RAM into the other's slot. DDR SDRAM for laptops comes in either 200-pin SO-DIMMs or 172-pin micro-DIMMs (Figure 4.16).

DDR sticks use a rather interesting naming convention—actually started by the Rambus folks—based on the number of bytes per second of data throughput the RAM can handle. To determine the bytes per second, take the MHz speed and multiply by 8 bytes (the width of all DDR SDRAM sticks). So 400 MHz multiplied by 8 is 3200 bytes per second. Put the abbreviation "PC" in the front to make the new term: PC3200. Many techs also use the naming convention used for the individual DDR chips; for example, *DDR400* refers to a 400-MHz DDR SDRAM chip running on a 200-MHz clock. Even though the term DDR*xxx* is really just for individual DDR chips

RAM makers use the term *single data rate SDRAM (SDR SDRAM)* for the original SDRAM to differentiate it from DDR SDRAM.

and the term PC*xxxx* is for DDR sticks, this tradition of two names for every speed of RAM is a bit of a challenge as both terms are commonly used interchangeably. Table 4.1 shows all the speeds for DDR—not all of these are commonly used.

Following the lead of AMD, VIA, and other manufacturers, the PC industry adopted DDR SDRAM as the standard system RAM. Intel relented and stopped

• **Figure 4.15**   DDR SDRAM

Try This!

DRAM Availability

The DRAM market changes fairly rapidly at the higher end, but products tend to linger at the low end, seemingly well past their usefulness. What do your class systems need? What's available in your area today? Try this.

Check out the RAM requirements for the PCs available in your class (or home or office). You can open them up for physical examination or read the motherboard books. Then go to your friendly neighborhood computer store and see what's available. Does the store offer memory that your system cannot use, such as EDO DRAM on 72-pin SIMMs or registered DDR SDRAM? What does this tell you about the PCs available to you?

• **Figure 4.16**   172-pin DDR SDRAM micro-DIMM *(photo courtesy of Kingston/ Joint Harvest)*

Mike Meyers' CompTIA A+ Guide: Essentials (Exam 220-601)

Table 4.1	DDR Speeds	
Clock Speed	DDR Speed Rating	PC Speed Rating
100 MHz	DDR200	PC1600
133 MHz	DDR266	PC2100
166 MHz	DDR333	PC2700
200 MHz	DDR400	PC3200
217 MHz	DDR433	PC3500
233 MHz	DDR466	PC3700
250 MHz	DDR500	PC4000
275 MHz	DDR550	PC4400
300 MHz	DDR600	PC4800

producing motherboards and memory controllers that required RDRAM in the summer of 2003.

There's one sure thing about PC technologies—any good idea that can be copied will be copied. One of Rambus' best concepts was the **dual-channel architecture**—using two sticks of RDRAM together to increase throughput. Manufacturers have released motherboards with MCCs that support dual-channel architecture using DDR SDRAM. Dual-channel DDR motherboards use regular DDR sticks, although manufacturers often sell RAM in matched pairs, branding them as dual-channel RAM.

Dual-channel DDR works like RDRAM in that you must have two identical sticks of DDR and they must snap into two paired slots. Unlike RDRAM, dual-channel DDR doesn't have anything like CRIMMs—you don't need to put anything into unused slot pairs. Dual-channel DDR technology is very flexible, but also has a few quirks that vary with each system. Some motherboards have three DDR SDRAM slots, but the dual-channel DDR works only if you install DDR SDRAM in two of the slots (Figure 4.17).

• Figure 4.17   An nForce motherboard showing the three RAM slots. The two slots bracketing the slim space can run as dual channel as long as you don't populate the third slot.

If you populate the third slot, the system will use the full capacity of RAM installed, but turns off the dual-channel feature—and no, it doesn't tell you! The dual slots are blue; the third slot is black, which you could clearly see if this weren't a black-and-white photo.

DDR2

The fastest versions of DDR SDRAM run at a blistering PC4800. That's 4.8 gigabytes per second (GBps) of data throughput! You'd think that kind of speed would satisfy most users, and to be honest, DRAM running at approximately 5 GBps really is plenty fast—for now. However, the ongoing speed increases ensure that even these speeds won't be good enough in the future. Knowing this, the RAM industry came out with DDR2, the successor to DDR. **DDR2 SDRAM** is DDR RAM with some improvements in its electrical characteristics, enabling it to run even faster than DDR while using less power. The big speed increase from DDR2 comes by clock doubling the input/output circuits on the chips. This does not speed up the core RAM—the part that holds the data—but speeding up the input/output and adding special buffers (sort of like a cache) makes DDR2 run much faster than regular DDR. DDR2 uses a 240-pin DIMM that's not compatible with DDR. You'll find motherboards running both single-channel and dual-channel DDR2 (Figure 4.18).

The following table shows some of the common DDR2 speeds.

Core RAM Clock	DDR I/O Speed	DDR2 Speed Rating	PC Speed Rating
100 MHz	200 MHz	DDR2-400	PC2-3200
133 MHz	266 MHz	DDR2-533	PC2-4200
166 MHz	333 MHz	DDR2-667	PC2-5300
200 MHz	400 MHz	DDR2-800	PC2-6400
250 MHz	500 MHz	DDR2-1000	PC2-8000

RAM Variations

Within each class of RAM, you'll find variations in packaging, speed, quality, and the capability to handle data with more or fewer errors. Higher-end systems often need higher-end RAM, so knowing these variations is of crucial importance to techs.

Double-Sided DIMMs

Every type of RAM stick, starting with the old FPM SIMMs and continuing through to 240-pin DDR2 SDRAM, comes in one of two types: single-sided and double-sided. As their name implies, **single-sided RAM** sticks only have chips on one side of the stick. **Double-sided RAM**

• **Figure 4.18**   240-pin DDR2 DIMM

sticks have chips on both sides (Figure 4.19). The vast majority of RAM sticks are single-sided, but there are plenty of double-sided sticks out there. Double-sided sticks are basically two sticks of RAM soldered onto one board. There's nothing wrong with double-sided RAM other than the fact that some motherboards either can't use them or can only use them in certain ways—for example, only if you use a single stick and it goes into a certain slot.

Latency

If you've shopped for RAM lately, you may have noticed terms such as "CL2" or "low latency" as you tried to determine which RAM to purchase. You might find two otherwise identical RAM sticks with a 20 percent price difference and a salesperson pressuring you to buy the more expensive one because it's "faster" even though both sticks say DDR400 (Figure 4.20).

● **Figure 4.19**   Double-sided DDR SDRAM

RAM responds to electrical signals at varying rates. When the memory controller starts to grab a line of memory, for example, there's a slight delay; think of it as the RAM getting off the couch. After the RAM sends out the requested line of memory, there's another slight delay before the memory controller can ask for another line—the RAM sat back down. The delay in RAM's response time is called its latency. RAM with a lower latency—such as CL2—is faster than RAM with a higher latency—such as CL3—because it responds more quickly.

From a tech's standpoint, you need to get the proper RAM for the system on which you're working. If you put a high latency stick in a motherboard set up for a low latency stick, you'll get an unstable or completely dead PC. Check the motherboard manual and get the quickest RAM the motherboard can handle and you should be fine.

CAS stands for *column array strobe*, one of the wires (along with the *row array strobe*) in the RAM that helps the memory controller find a particular bit of memory. Each of these wires requires electricity to charge up before it can do its job. This is one of the aspects of latency.

● **Figure 4.20**   Why is one more expensive than the other?

Parity and ECC

Given the high speeds and phenomenal amount of data moved by the typical DRAM chip, it's possible that a RAM chip might occasionally give bad data to the memory controller. This doesn't necessarily mean that the RAM has gone bad. This could be an occasional hiccup caused by some unknown event that makes a good DRAM chip say a bit is a zero when it's really a one. In most cases, you won't even notice when such a rare event happens. In some environments, however, even these rare events are intolerable. A bank server handling thousands of online transactions per second, for example, can't risk even the smallest error. These important computers need a more robust, fault-resistant RAM.

The first type of error-detecting RAM was known as parity RAM (Figure 4.21). **Parity RAM** stored an extra bit of data (called the parity bit) that the MCC used to verify if the data was correct. Parity wasn't perfect—it wouldn't always detect an error, and if the MCC did find an error, it couldn't correct the error. For years, parity was the only available way to tell if the RAM made a mistake.

Today's PCs that need to watch for RAM errors use a special type of RAM called **error correction code (ECC) RAM**. ECC is a major advance in error checking on DRAM. First, ECC detects any time a single bit is incorrect. Second, ECC fixes these errors on the fly. The checking and fixing come at a price, as ECC RAM is always slower than non-ECC RAM.

ECC RAM comes in every DIMM package type. You might be tempted to say "Gee, maybe I want to try this ECC RAM!" Well, don't! To take advantage of ECC RAM, you need a motherboard with an MCC designed to use ECC. Only expensive motherboards for high-end systems use ECC. The special-use-only nature of ECC makes it fairly rare. There are plenty of techs out there with years of experience who've never even seen ECC RAM.

Buffered/Registered DRAM

Your average PC motherboard accepts no more than four sticks of DRAM because more than four physical slots for sticks gives motherboard designers some serious electrical headaches. Yet some systems that use a lot of RAM need the capability to use more DRAM sticks on the motherboard, often six or eight. To get around the electrical hassles, special DRAM sticks add a buffering chip to the stick that acts as an intermediary between the DRAM and the MCC. These special DRAMs are called **buffered** or **registered DRAM** (Figure 4.22). The DDR2 version is called *fully buffered*.

Some memory manufacturers call the technology *Error Checking and Correction (ECC)*. Don't be thrown off if you see the phrase—it's the same thing, just a different marketing slant for error correction code.

Tech Tip

Counting Chips

To determine if a DRAM stick is parity or ECC, count the individual chips on the stick. If you can divide the number of chips on the stick by 3 or 5, you have either ECC or parity RAM.

• **Figure 4.21**   Ancient parity RAM stick

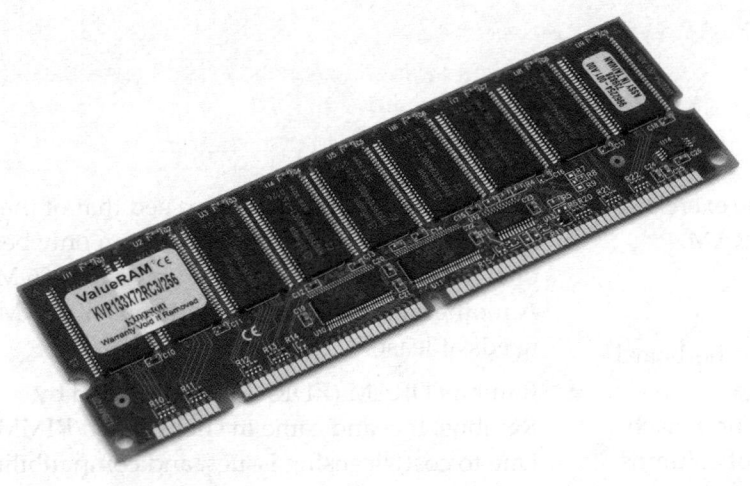

● **Figure 4.22** Buffered DRAM

Like ECC, you must have a motherboard with an MCC designed to use this type of DRAM. Rest assured that such a motherboard will have a large number of RAM slots. Buffered/registered RAM is rare (maybe not quite as rare as ECC RAM), and you'll never see it in the typical desktop system.

Chapter 4 Review

■ Chapter Summary

After reading this chapter and completing the exercises, you should understand the following about RAM.

Understanding DRAM

■ The sticks of RAM snapped into your motherboard are DRAM. DRAM can be thought of as a spreadsheet in which each cell holds a 1 or 0. Each cell represents a single bit. The number of columns and rows are finite.

■ If a chip contains 1,048,576 rows and eight columns it can be described as a 1 M × 8 chip. A chip containing 2,097,152 rows and 16 columns can be described as a 2 M × 16 chip.

■ DRAM needs to be able to fill the data bus. A 1 M × 8 DRAM chip is only 8 bits wide and would provide the CPU with only 8 bits of data. You would need eight of the 1 M × 8 chips to fill a 64-bit data bus.

■ DRAM chips are soldered to a circuit board called a stick or module, and when these chips are combined, a single stick can fill the data bus. Modern DRAM sticks come in 32-bit- and 64-bit-wide varieties.

Types of RAM

■ Synchronous dynamic random access memory, or SDRAM, is tied to the system clock. The CPU, memory controller, and RAM all work in tandem with the clock pulse. This results in little wasted time when the CPU requests data from RAM.

■ SDRAM comes in sticks called dual inline memory modules (DIMMs). SDRAM DIMMs come in a variety of pin sizes, with 168 pins being the most common for desktop systems. DIMMs are 64 bits wide so that they match the 64-bit data bus of modern CPUs. DIMMs snap into slots on the motherboard. Each DIMM is 64 bits, so snapping in a single DIMM will fill the data bus; therefore, each slot is called a bank.

■ SDRAM is advertised by capacity and speed. The speed is prefixed with "PC"; for example, PC66 runs at 66 MHz. A stick of SDRAM advertised as 256 MB PC133 has a capacity of 256 MB and runs at 133 MHz. Five clock speeds are commonly used: 66, 75, 83, 100, and 133 MHz.

■ RAM speed must match or exceed that of the system. For example, PC66 RAM can only be used on a motherboard running at (or below) 66 MHz. A motherboard with a frontside bus of 100 MHz needs at least PC100 RAM.

■ Rambus DRAM (RDRAM) was created by Rambus, Inc. and came in sticks called RIMMs. Due to cost, licensing issues, and compatibility, RDRAM is now obsolete.

■ RIMMs are 64 bits wide and come in speeds of 600 MHz, 700 MHz, 800 MHz, and 1066 MHz. Different notches prevent you from snapping a RIMM into a motherboard DIMM slot or vice versa.

■ The RIMM memory controller uses a dual-channel architecture: it alternates between two banks to increase the speed of data retrieval. You need to install RIMMs in pairs to accommodate this feature.

■ All RIMM slots on the motherboard must be filled with either a RIMM or a CRIMM. A CRIMM, or continuity RIMM, is simply a stick with no memory chips on it.

■ Double Data Rate SDRAM (DDR RAM) is faster than regular SDRAM because it doubles the throughput. Desktop PCs use 184-pin DDR DIMMs whereas laptops use either 200-pin or 172-pin small outline DIMMs (SO-DIMM). DDR RAM modules have notches that differ from both regular SDRAM and RDRAM, so DDR RAM will only snap into DDR slots on a motherboard.

■ DDR RAM is advertised one of two ways. One way is with "DDR" followed by the speed; for example, DDR400 for a stick of RAM runs at 400 MHz. Because DDR RAM runs at twice the clock speed, DDR400 is meant for a 200-MHz frontside bus. DDR RAM is also advertised by "PC" followed by the throughput; for example, PC3200. The number is determined by multiplying the speed by eight (as all DDR sticks are 64 bits, or 8 bytes, wide). Thus, DDR400 has a throughput of 3200 bytes per second (400 MHz × 8 bytes). DDR400 and PC3200 are equivalent.

- Dual-channel DDR improves upon DDR by using the DIMMs in pairs, much like RDRAM. For systems to use dual-channel DDR, the motherboard and memory controller must support dual-channel DDR RAM, and the DDR DIMMs must be identical. Dual-channel DDR does not require dummy modules like a CRIMM. Dual-channel slots are identified on a motherboard by their blue color. Some motherboards offer a third slot in black, but filling that third slot to increase your total system RAM will also turn off the dual-channel feature.

- DDR2 is an improvement of DDR. DDR2 runs faster than DDR and uses a 240-pin form factor that is not compatible with DDR. You need a motherboard with DDR2 slots to use DDR2 RAM. DDR2 is rated by speed or throughput. Thus DDR2-400 is the same as PC2-3200 and is meant for a 200-MHz frontside bus.

- RAM modules are either single-sided or double-sided. Single-sided sticks have chips on only one side, whereas double-sided sticks have chips on both sides. Most RAM is single-sided.

- Latency refers to the time lag between when the memory controller starts to fetch data from RAM

and when RAM actually sends out the requested data. Another lag occurs when the memory controller asks for the next line from RAM. The shorter this lag time, the faster the system. CL2 indicates a shorter lag time, or lower latency, than CL3, so CL2 is faster. Check your motherboard documentation and get the lowest latency RAM your system will support.

- When RAM gave bad data to the memory controller, parity RAM was able to detect this error most of the time, but could not fix it.

- Error correction code (ECC) RAM improved upon parity RAM by being able to fix single-bit errors on the fly. ECC RAM is always slower than non-ECC RAM due to the overhead of the correcting code. Only high-end motherboards and memory controllers can use ECC RAM.

- Buffered or registered RAM adds a buffering chip to compensate for the electrical interference that can result from using more than four DIMMs on a single motherboard. The motherboard and memory controller must be designed specifically to support buffered or registered RAM. You are not likely to see it in a typical desktop system.

Key Terms

bank *(112)*
buffered/registered DRAM *(118)*
continuity RIMM (CRIMM) *(113)*
double data rate 2 SDRAM
 (DDR2 SDRAM) *(116)*
double data rate SDRAM
 (DDR SDRAM) *(114)*
double-sided RAM *(116)*

dual inline memory module
 (DIMM) *(111)*
dual-channel architecture *(115)*
dynamic random access memory
 (DRAM) *(106)*
error correction code RAM
 (ECC RAM) *(118)*
latency *(117)*
module *(109)*

parity RAM *(118)*
Rambus DRAM (RDRAM) *(112)*
RIMM *(113)*
single-sided RAM *(116)*
small outline DIMM
 (SO DIMM) *(112)*
stick *(109)*
synchronous DRAM
 (SDRAM) *(111)*

Key Term Quiz

Use the Key Terms list to complete the sentences that follow. Not all terms will be used.

1. If your motherboard uses RDRAM, you must fill each slot with either a(n) _____ or a(n) _____.

2. _____ sticks contain chips on both sides.

3. A special kind of memory stick for laptops is called a(n) _____.

4. Memory that makes two data accesses during each clock tick is called _____.

5. Unlike regular DRAM, _____ is tied to the system clock.

6. Unlike regular DRAM, _____ enables error checking and correcting.

7. The time lag between when the memory controller starts to fetch a line of data from RAM and when the RAM actually starts to deliver the data is known as _____.

8. _____ detects errors, but cannot fix them.

9. Motherboards that support more than four sticks of RAM may require _____ to compensate for the additional electrical interference.

10. Memory chips are soldered to a small circuit board called a(n) _____ or a(n) _____.

Multiple-Choice Quiz

1. What is the correct throughput of DDR-SDRAM, and what is the resulting actual speed of PC1600 RAM?
   A. 4 bytes per second, 133 MHz
   B. 8 bytes per second, 200 MHz
   C. 4 bits per second, 400 MHz
   D. 8 bits per second, 200 MHz

2. How many sticks of RAM do you need to fill a bank in a computer that can use 168-pin DIMMs?
   A. One
   B. Two
   C. Four
   D. Eight

3. What does the CPU use to access the system's RAM?
   A. The system bus
   B. The frontside bus
   C. The address bus
   D. The expansion bus

4. Which of the following statements is true about RDRAM?
   A. It uses dual-channel architecture.
   B. It offers speeds ranging from 200 MHz to 600 MHz.
   C. It is less expensive than SDRAM.
   D. It is used by AMD but not Intel processors.

5. Which of the following SDRAM speeds would not work with a 100-MHz motherboard?
   A. 66 MHz
   B. 100 MHz
   C. 133 MHz
   D. 200 MHz

6. Which of the following is a valid package size for desktop RDRAM RIMMs?
   A. 160-pin
   B. 172-pin
   C. 184-pin
   D. 200-pin

7. What package does DDR-SDRAM use for desktop PCs?
   A. 30-pin
   B. 72-pin
   C. 168-pin
   D. 184-pin

8. Why is SDRAM faster than regular DRAM?
   A. It makes two processes per clock cycle.
   B. It runs synchronously with the system clock.
   C. It uses dual-channel architecture.
   D. It has fewer pins, resulting in fewer corrupt bits.

9. What is true about a double-sided DIMM?
   A. It has memory chips on the front and back.
   B. It can be installed forward or backwards.
   C. It is twice as fast as a single-sided DIMM.
   D. It has half the capacity of a quad-sided DIMM.

10. What is another name for DDR400?
    A. PC200
    B. PC400
    C. PC1600
    D. PC3200

11. Which statement best describes dual-channel architecture?
    A. Using two sticks of RAM together to increase throughput
    B. Using two memory controllers to speed RAM access
    C. Using the address bus in full-duplex mode
    D. Using double-sided RAM to increase capacity

12. What is the fastest version of DDR SDRAM?
    A. PC4200
    B. PC4800
    C. PC5200
    D. PC5200b

13. Joaquin wishes to upgrade the DDR RAM in his system with DDR2. Angela says he can't because sticks of DDR2 won't fit in the motherboard slots that currently hold Joaquin's DDR RAM. Ben says he can use DDR2 in his system, but won't see any speed benefit because the motherboard only supports DDR. Who is correct?
    A. Angela is correct.
    B. Ben is correct.
    C. Both Angela and Ben are correct.
    D. Neither Angela nor Ben is correct.

14. Which statements about CAS latency are correct? Choose two.
    A. You can use CL3 RAM in a system set up for CL2 without any problems.
    B. You can use CL2 RAM in a system set up for CL3 without any problems.
    C. CL3 RAM is faster than CL2 RAM.
    D. CL2 RAM is faster than CL3 RAM.

15. Clarice is building a high-end system for her company to run an important database application that can't risk any errors in data. What type of RAM should she use?
    A. Buffered
    B. ECC
    C. Parity
    D. Registered

Essay Quiz

1. Celia tells you she just received a new motherboard for the system she is building. She is confused about the RAM slots. The motherboard has three of them, but two are blue and one is black. What can you tell her about the RAM slots on her motherboard?

2. Now that Celia has built her system and installed the RAM, she notices a strange setting in CMOS Setup referring to CAS Latency with choices of CL1, CL2, CL3, and CL4. How would you explain this setting and the ramifications of changing the setting?

Lab Projects

• Lab Project 4.1

To learn more about memory, go to the Web site www.kingston.com, select Memory Tools from the buttons at the top of the screen, and examine the "Ultimate Memory Guide." This resource contains information about all aspects of computer memory. After using this guide, answer the following questions:

1 Why do memory prices vary so frequently?

2 What are the differences in tin- and gold-edged memory sticks, and how does one know which to choose when upgrading?

3 Describe the notches on a 30-pin SIMM, a 72-pin SIMM, a 168-pin DIMM, and a 184-pin DIMM. What function do the notches serve?

Understanding BIOS and CMOS

"When the apocalypse comes... beep me."

—BUFFY, *BUFFY THE VAMPIRE SLAYER* (1997)

In Chapter 3, you saw how the address bus and external data bus connect RAM to the CPU via the memory controller chip (MCC) in order to run programs and transfer data. Assuming you apply power in the right places, you don't need anything else to make a simple computer. The only problem with such a simple computer is that it would bore you to death—there's no way to do anything with it! A PC needs devices such as keyboards and mice to provide input, and output devices such as monitors and sound cards to communicate the current state of the running programs to you. A computer also needs permanent storage devices, such as hard drives and optical drives, to store programs and data when you turn off the computer.

In this chapter, you will learn how to

- **Explain the function of BIOS**
- **Distinguish among various CMOS setup utility options**
- **Describe option ROM and device drivers**

Historical/Conceptual

■ We Need to Talk

Simply placing a number of components into a computer is useless if the CPU can't communicate with them. Getting the CPU to communicate with a device starts with some kind of interconnection—a communication bus that enables the CPU to send commands to and from devices. To make this connection, let's promote the MCC, giving it extra firepower to act as not only the interconnection between the CPU and RAM, but also the interconnection between the CPU and the other devices on the PC. The MCC isn't just the memory controller anymore, so let's now call it the **Northbridge** because it acts as the primary bridge between the CPU and the rest of the computer (Figure 5.1).

Your PC is full of devices, so the PC industry decided to delegate some of the interconnectivity work to a second chip called the **Southbridge**. The Northbridge only deals with high-speed interfaces such as the connection to your video card and RAM. The Southbridge works mainly with lower-speed devices such as the USB controller and hard drive controllers. Chip makers design matched sets of particular models of Northbridge and Southbridge to work together. You don't buy a Northbridge from one company and a Southbridge from another—they're sold as a set. We call this set of Northbridge and Southbridge the **chipset**.

The chipset extends the data bus to every device on the PC. The CPU uses the data bus to move data to and from all the devices of the PC. Data constantly flows on the external data bus among the CPU, chipset, RAM, and other devices on the PC (Figure 5.2).

The first use for the address bus, as you know, is for the CPU to tell the chipset to send or store data in memory and to tell the chipset which section of memory to access or use. Just like with the external data bus, the chipset extends the address bus to all the devices, too (Figure 5.3). That way, the CPU can use the address bus to send commands to devices, just like it sends commands to the chipset. You'll see this in action a lot more in Chapter 6, "Understanding the Expansion Bus," but for now just go with the concept.

It's not too hard to swallow the concept that the CPU uses the address bus to talk to the devices, but how does it know what to *say* to them? How does it know all of the different patterns of ones and zeroes to place on the address bus to tell the hard drive it needs to send a file? Let's look at the interaction between the keyboard and CPU for insight into this process.

Talking to the Keyboard

The keyboard provides a great example of how the buses and support programming help the CPU get the job done. In early computers, the keyboard connected to the

> Chipset makers rarely use the terms "Northbridge" and "Southbridge" anymore, but because most modern chipsets consist of only two or three chips with basically the same functions, techs continue to use the terms.

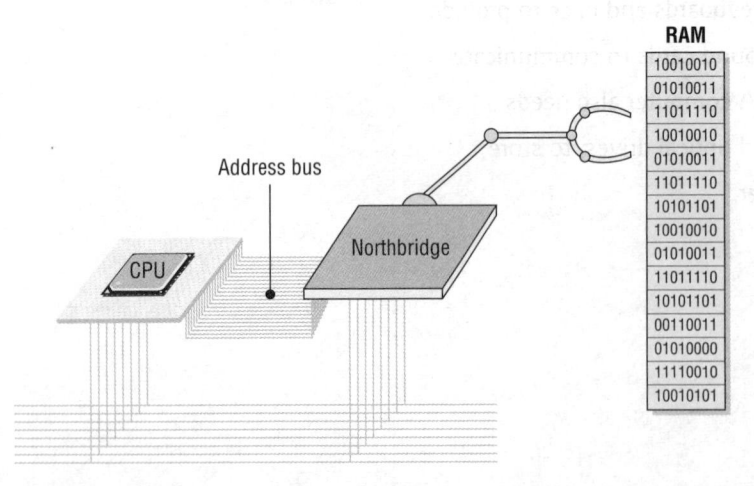

• **Figure 5.1**   Meet the Northbridge

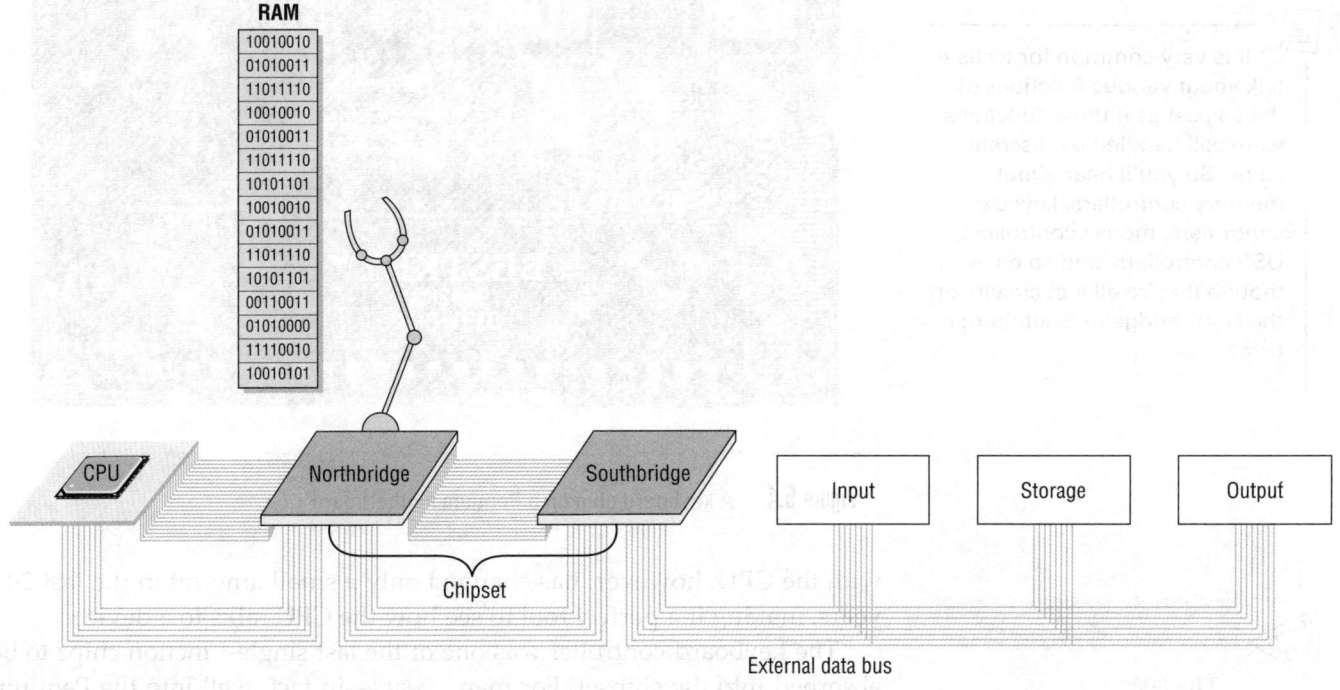

Figure 5.2   The chipset extending the data bus

external data bus via a special chip known as the *keyboard controller*. Don't bother looking for this chip on your motherboard—the keyboard controller functions are now handled by the Southbridge. The way the keyboard controller—or technically, the keyboard controller *circuitry*— works

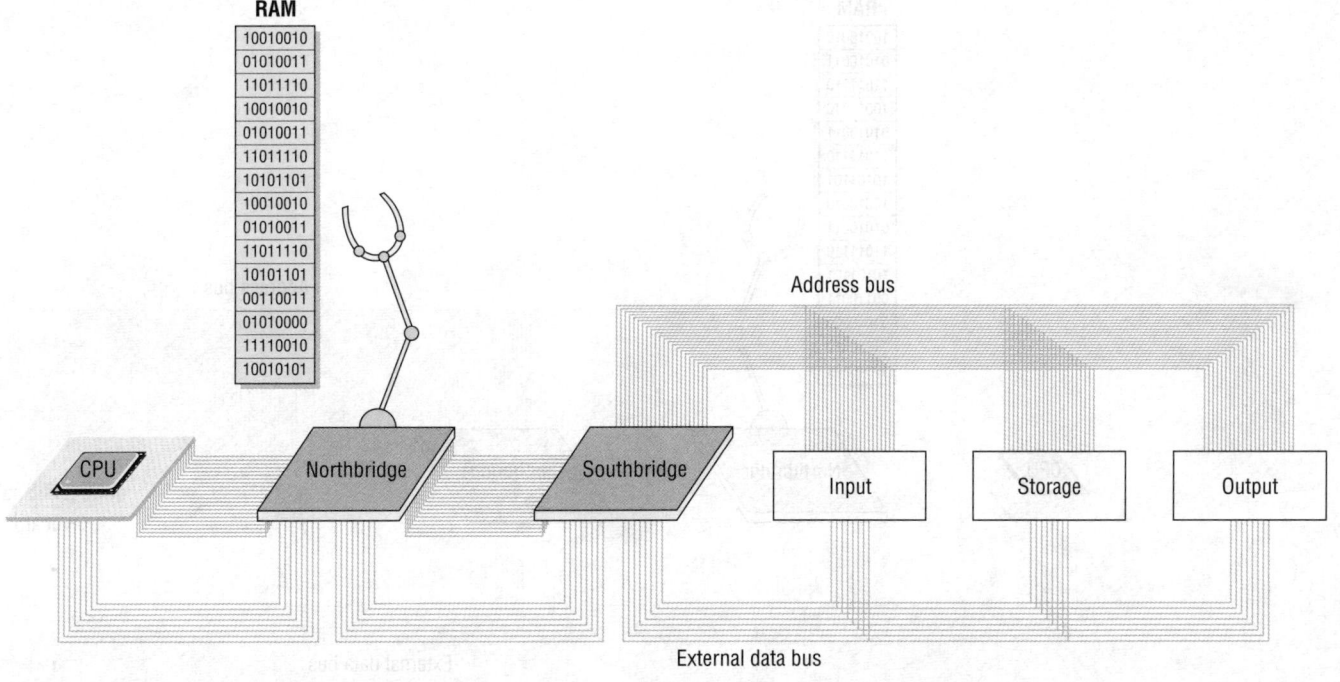

Figure 5.3   Every device in your computer connects to the address bus.

It is very common for techs to talk about various functions of the chipset as if those functions were still handled by discrete chips. So you'll hear about memory controllers, keyboard controllers, mouse controllers, USB controllers, and so on, even though they're all just circuits on the Northbridge or Southbridge chips.

• **Figure 5.4**   A keyboard chip on a Pentium motherboard

Tech Tip

The 8042

Even though the model numbers changed over the years, you'll still hear techs refer to the keyboard controller as the 8042, after the original keyboard controller chip.

with the CPU, however, has changed only a small amount in the last 20+ years, making it a perfect tool to see how the CPU talks to a device.

The keyboard controller was one of the last single-function chips to be absorbed into the chipset. For many years—in fact, well into the Pentium III/Early Athlon era—most motherboards still had separate keyboard controller chips. Figure 5.4 shows a typical keyboard controller from those days. Electronically, it looked like Figure 5.5.

Every time you press a key on your keyboard, a scanning chip in the keyboard notices which key has been pressed. Then the scanner sends a coded pattern of ones and zeroes—called the *scan code*—to the keyboard controller. Every key on your keyboard has a unique scan code. The keyboard controller stores the scan code in its own register. Does it surprise

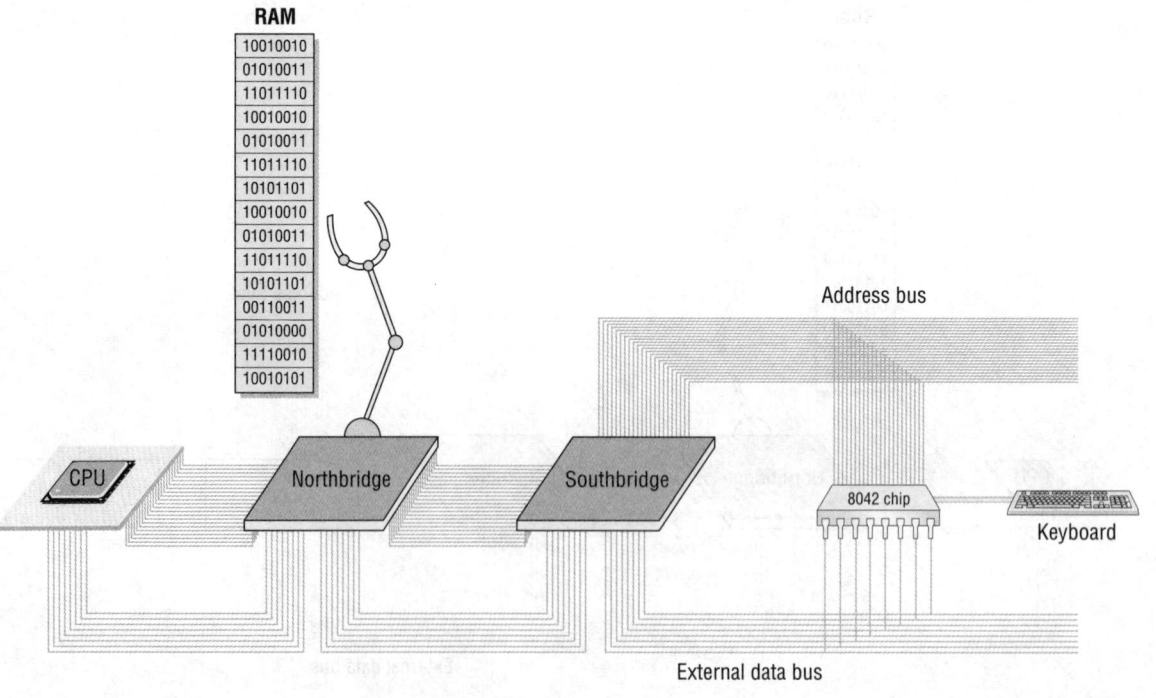

• **Figure 5.5**   Electronic view of the keyboard controller

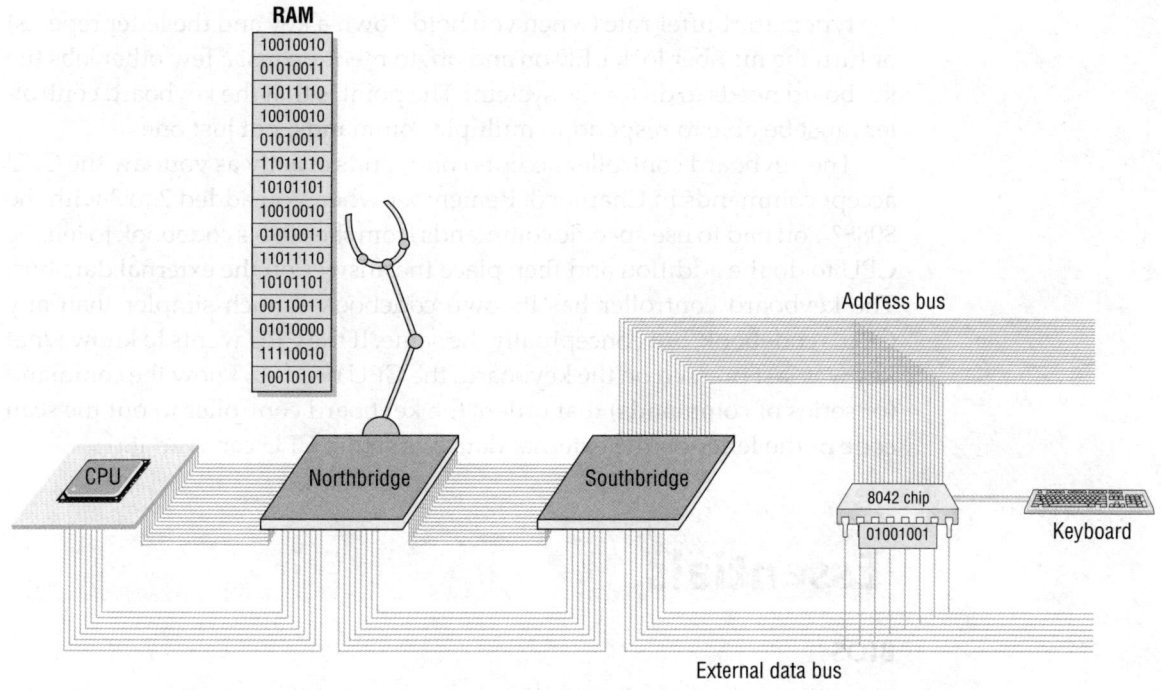

RAM

10010010
01010011
11011110
10010010
01010011
11011110
10101101
10010010
01010011
11011110
10101101
00110011
01010000
11110010
10010101

Address bus

CPU

Northbridge

Southbridge

8042 chip

01001001

Keyboard

External data bus

• **Figure 5.6**   Scan code stored in keyboard controller's register

you that the lowly keyboard controller has a register similar to a CPU? Lots of chips have registers—not just CPUs! (See Figure 5.6.)

How does the CPU get the scan code out of the keyboard controller? (See Figure 5.7.) While we're at it, how does the CPU tell the keyboard to change

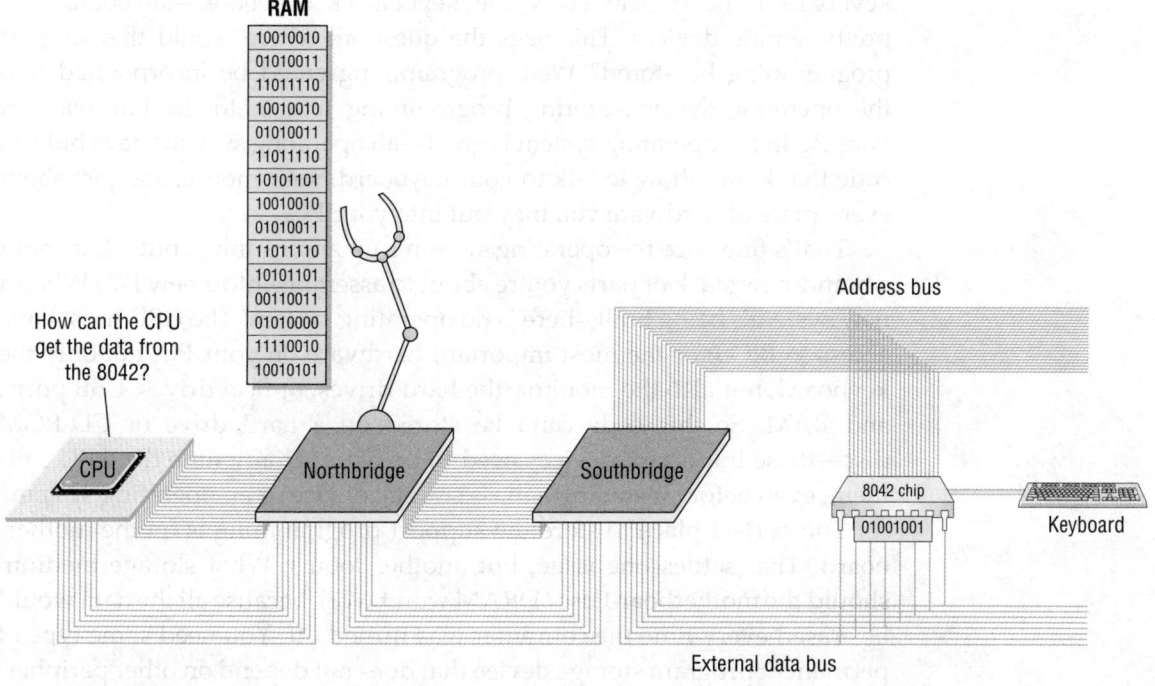

RAM

10010010
01010011
11011110
10010010
01010011
11011110
10101101
10010010
01010011
11011110
10101101
00110011
01010000
11110010
10010101

How can the CPU get the data from the 8042?

Address bus

CPU

Northbridge

Southbridge

8042 chip

01001001

Keyboard

External data bus

• **Figure 5.7**   The CPU ponders its dilemma....

the typematic buffer rate (when you hold down a key and the letter repeats) or turn the number lock LED on and off, to mention just a few other jobs the keyboard needs to do for the system? The point is that the keyboard controller must be able to respond to multiple commands, not just one.

The keyboard controller accepts commands exactly as you saw the CPU accept commands in Chapter 3. Remember when you added 2 to 3 with the 8088? You had to use specific commands from the 8088's codebook to tell the CPU to do the addition and then place the answer on the external data bus. The keyboard controller has its own codebook—much simpler than any CPU's codebook, but conceptually the same. If the CPU wants to know what key was last pressed on the keyboard, the CPU needs to know the command (or series of commands) that orders the keyboard controller to put the scan code of the letter on the external data bus so the CPU can read it.

Essentials

BIOS

The CPU can't magically or otherwise automatically know how to talk with any device, but rather needs some sort of support programming loaded into memory that teaches it about a particular device. This programming is called **basic input/output services (BIOS)**. The programs dedicated to enabling the CPU to communicate with devices are called *services* (or *device drivers*, as you'll see later in the chapter). This goes well beyond the keyboard, by the way. In fact, *every* device on the computer needs BIOS! But let's continue with the keyboard for now.

Bringing BIOS to the PC   A talented programmer could write BIOS for a keyboard if he or she knew the keyboard's codebook—keyboards are pretty simple devices. This begs the question: where would this support programming be stored? Well, programming could be incorporated into the operating system. Storing programming to talk to the hardware of your PC in the operating system is great—all operating systems have built-in code that knows how to talk to your keyboard, your mouse, and just about every piece of hardware you may put into your PC.

That's fine once the operating system's up and running, but what about a brand-new stack of parts you're about to assemble into a new PC? When a new system's being built, there is no operating system! The CPU must have access to BIOS for the most important hardware on your PC: not only the keyboard, but also the monitor, the hard drives, optical drives, USB ports, and RAM. So this code can't be stored on a hard drive or CD-ROM disc—these important devices need to be ready at any time the CPU calls them, even before installing a mass storage device or an operating system.

The perfect place to store the support programming is on the motherboard. That settles one issue, but another looms: What storage medium should the motherboard use? DRAM won't work because all the data would be erased every time the computer was turned off. You need some type of permanent program storage device that does not depend on other peripherals in order to work. And you need that storage device to sit on the motherboard.

ROM Motherboards store the keyboard controller support programming, among other programs, on a special type of device called a **read-only memory (ROM)** chip. A ROM chip stores programs exactly like RAM: that is, like an 8-bit-wide spreadsheet. But ROM differs from RAM in two important ways. First, ROM chips are **non-volatile**, meaning that the information stored on ROM isn't erased when the computer is turned off. Second, traditional ROM chips are read-only, meaning that once a program is stored on one, it can't be changed. Modern motherboards use a type of ROM called **flash ROM** that differs from traditional ROM in that you can update and change the contents through a very specific process called "flashing the ROM." Figure 5.8 shows a typical flash ROM chip on a motherboard. When the CPU wants to talk to the keyboard controller, it goes to the flash ROM chip to access the proper programming (Figure 5.9).

• **Figure 5.8** Typical flash ROM

Every motherboard has a flash ROM, called the **system ROM** chip because it contains code that enables your CPU to talk to the basic hardware of your PC. As alluded to earlier, the system ROM holds BIOS for more than just the keyboard controller. It also stores programs for communicating with the floppy drives, hard drives, optical drives, video, USB ports, and other basic devices on your motherboard.

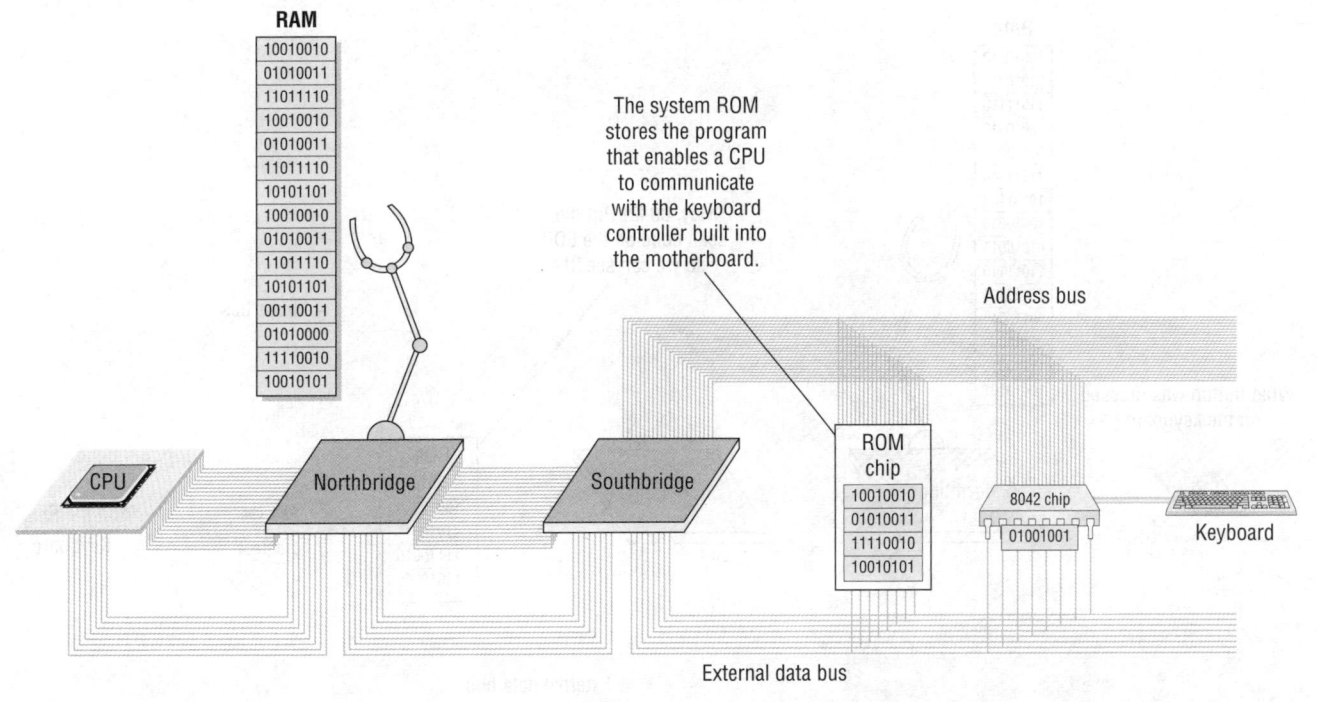

• **Figure 5.9** Function of the flash ROM chip

Programs stored on ROM chips—flash or any other kind of ROM chip—are known collectively as *firmware*, as opposed to programs stored on erasable media that are collectively called *software*.

To talk to all of that hardware requires hundreds of little services (2 to 30 lines of code each). These hundreds of little programs stored on the system ROM chip on the motherboard are called, collectively, the **system BIOS**. (See Figure 5.10.) Techs call programs stored on ROM chips of any sort **firmware**.

The system ROM chips used on modern PCs store as much as 2 MB of programs, although only 65,536 bytes are used to store the system BIOS. This allows for backward compatibility with earlier systems. The rest of the ROM space is put to good use doing other jobs.

System BIOS Support

Every system BIOS has two types of hardware to support. First, the system BIOS supports all the hardware that never changes, such as the keyboard. (You can change your keyboard, but you can't change the keyboard controller built into the Southbridge.) Another example of hardware that never changes is the PC speaker (the tiny one that beeps at you, not the ones that play music). The system ROM chip stores the BIOS for these and other devices that never change.

Second, the system BIOS supports all the hardware that might change from time to time. This includes RAM (you can add RAM), hard drives (you can replace your hard drive with a larger drive or add a second hard drive), and floppy drives (you can add another floppy drive). The system ROM chip stores the *BIOS* for these devices, but the system needs another place to store information about the specific *details* of a piece of hardware. This enables the system to differentiate between a Western Digital Caviar 500-GB hard drive and a Seagate Barracuda 60-GB drive, and yet still support both drives right out of the box.

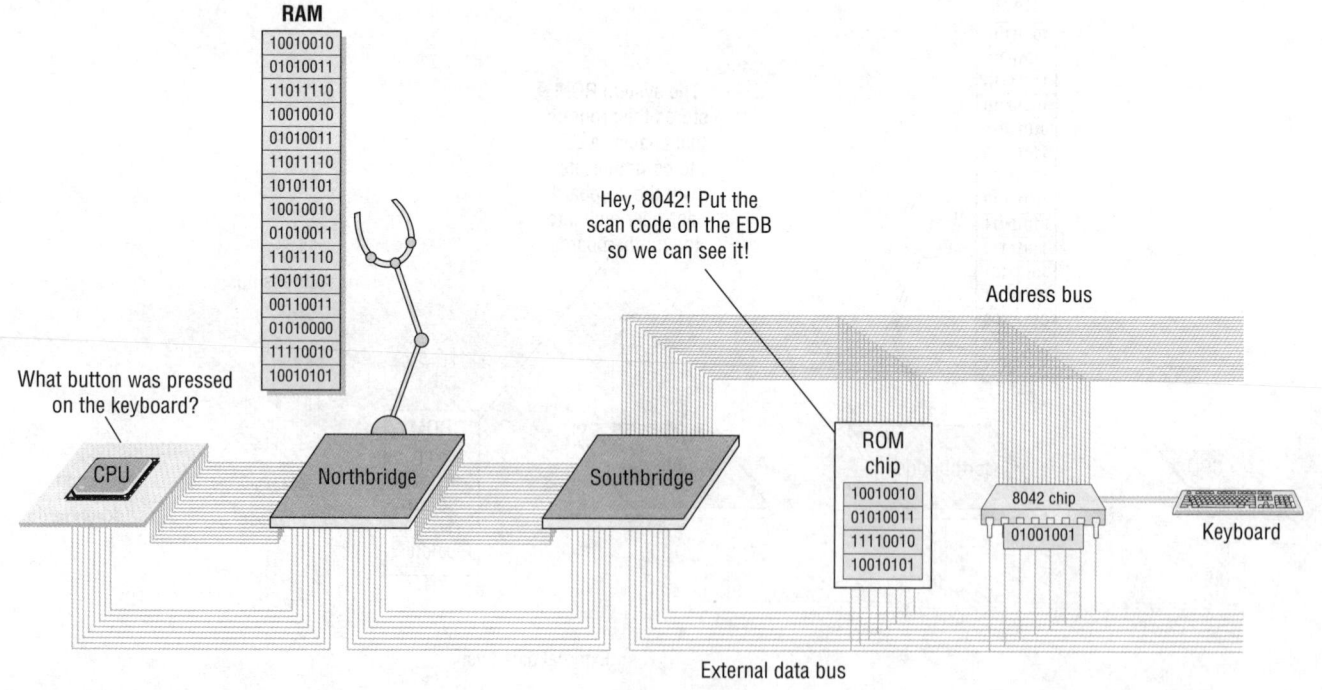

• **Figure 5.10**   CPU running BIOS service

■ CMOS

A separate memory chip, called the **complementary metal-oxide semiconductor (CMOS)** chip, stores the information that describes specific device parameters. CMOS does *not* store programs; it only stores data that is read by BIOS to complete the programs needed to talk to changeable hardware. CMOS also acts as a clock to keep the current date and time.

Years ago, CMOS was a separate chip on the motherboard, as shown in Figure 5.11. Today, the CMOS is almost always built into the Southbridge.

● **Figure 5.11**   Old-style CMOS

Most CMOS chips store around 64 KB of data, but the PC usually needs only a very small amount—about 128 bytes—to store all the necessary information on the changeable hardware. Don't let the tiny size fool you. The information stored in CMOS is absolutely necessary for the PC to function!

If the data stored on CMOS about a particular piece of hardware (or about its fancier features) is different from the specs of the actual hardware, the computer will not be able to access that piece of hardware (or use its fancier features). It is crucial that this information be correct. If you change any of the previously mentioned hardware, you must update CMOS to reflect those changes. You need to know, therefore, how to change the data on CMOS.

Updating CMOS: The Setup Program

Every PC ships with a program built into the system ROM, called the **CMOS setup program** or the *system setup utility,* which enables you to access and update CMOS data. When you fire up your computer in the morning, the first thing you will likely see is the BIOS information. It might look like the example in Figure 5.12 or perhaps something like Figure 5.13.

> The terms *CMOS setup program,* CMOS, and *system setup utility* are functionally interchangeable today. You'll even hear the program referred to as the *BIOS setup utility* or *CMOS setup utility.* Most techs just call it the CMOS.

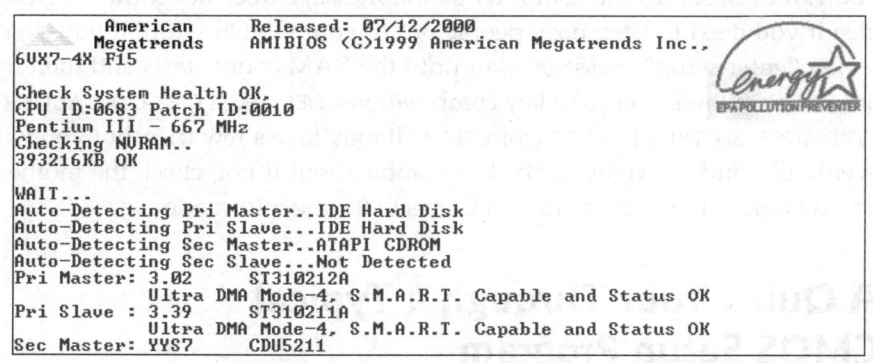

● **Figure 5.12**   AMI BIOS information

Tech Tip

Term Limits

Okay, I've thrown a whole bunch of terms at you describing various pieces of hardware and software and what does what to whom. Here's the scorecard so you can sort out the various pieces of data.

1. *The system ROM chip stores the system BIOS, programs needed by the CPU to communicate with devices.*

2. *The system ROM chip also holds the program that accesses the information stored on the CMOS chip to support changeable pieces of hardware. This program is called the CMOS setup program or the system setup utility.*

3. *The CMOS holds a small amount of data that describes the changeable pieces of hardware supported by the system BIOS. The CMOS today is in the Southbridge chip of the chipset.*

It's perfectly fine to access the CMOS setup utility for a system, but do not make changes unless you fully understand that system!

```
●Award Modular BIOS v6.00PG, An Energy Star Ally
↗ Copyright (C) 1984-2003 Phoenix Technologies, LTD


Main Processor : AMD Athlon(tm) 64 Processor 3200+
Memory Testing : 1048576K OK
CPU0 Memory Information: DDR 400 CL:3 ,1T Dual Channel, 128-bit

IDE Channel 1 Master : WDC WD1200JB-75CRA0 16.06V16
IDE Channel 1 Slave  : None
IDE Channel 2 Master : SONY     CD-RW  CRX175E2 S002
IDE Channel 2 Slave  : TOSHIBA CD=DVDW SDR5372V TU11

IDE Channel 3 Master : None
IDE Channel 4 Master : None

Detecting IDE drives ...




Press DEL to enter SETUP, ESC to Enter Boot Menu
07/01/2005-MF-CK804-6A61FA1DC-10
```

● **Figure 5.13**   Award/Phoenix BIOS information

Who or what is AMIBIOS, and who or what is Phoenix Technologies? These are brand names of BIOS companies. They write BIOS programs and sell them to computer manufacturers. In today's world, motherboard makers rarely write their own BIOS. Instead, they buy their BIOS from specialized third-party BIOS makers like Award Software and Phoenix Technologies. Although several companies write BIOS, two big companies control 99 percent of the BIOS business: American Megatrends (AMI) and Phoenix Technologies. Phoenix bought Award Software a few years ago and still sells the Award brand name as a separate product line. These three are the most common brand names in the field.

You always access a system's CMOS setup program at boot. The real question is, how do you access the CMOS setup at boot for your particular PC? AMI, Award, and Phoenix use different keys to access the CMOS setup program. Usually, BIOS manufacturers will tell you how to access the CMOS setup right on the screen as your computer boots up. For example, at the bottom of the screen in Figure 5.13, you are instructed to "Press DEL to enter SETUP." Keep in mind that this is only one possible example. Motherboard manufacturers can change the key combinations for entering CMOS setup. You can even set up the computer so the message does not show—a smart idea if you need to keep nosy people out of your CMOS setup! If you don't see an "enter setup" message, wait until the RAM count starts and then try one of the following keys or key combinations: DEL, ESC, F1, F2, CTRL-ALT-ESC, CTRL-ALT-INS, CTRL-ALT-ENTER, or CTRL-S. It may take a few tries, but you will eventually find the right key or key combination! If not, check the motherboard book or the manufacturer's Web site for the information.

A Quick Tour Through a Typical CMOS Setup Program

Every BIOS maker's CMOS setup program looks a little different, but don't let that confuse you. They all contain basically the same settings; you just

Try This!

Accessing CMOS Setup

The key or key combination required to access CMOS setup varies depending on your particular BIOS. It's important to know how to access CMOS setup, and how to find the BIOS information once you're in, so try this:

1. Boot your system and turn on your monitor. Watch the information that scrolls by on the screen as your computer boots. Most BIOS makers include a line indicating what key(s) to press to access the CMOS setup program. Make a note of this useful information! You can also check your motherboard book to determine the process for accessing the CMOS setup program.

2. Reboot the system, and this time watch for information on the BIOS manufacturer. If you don't see it, and if it's okay to do so, open the system case and check the name printed on the system ROM chip. Make a note of this useful information.

3. Reboot one more time, and this time use the key or key combination you found to run the CMOS setup program. Locate and make a note of the manufacturer, date, and version number of your PC's current BIOS.

4. If you can, make a note of the exact model information for your system and visit the Web site of the company that manufactured your PC. Search their support files for the specs on your specific system and see if you can locate your BIOS information. Now take the detailed BIOS information and search the BIOS manufacturer's Web site for the same information.

have to be comfortable poking around. To avoid doing something foolish, *do not save anything* unless you are sure you have it set correctly.

As an example, let's say your machine has Award BIOS. You boot the system and press DEL to enter CMOS setup. The screen in Figure 5.14 appears. You are now in the Main menu of the Award CMOS setup program. The setup program itself is stored on the ROM chip, but it edits only the data on the CMOS chip.

If you select the Standard CMOS Features option, the Standard CMOS Features screen appears (Figure 5.15). On this screen, you can change floppy drive and hard drive settings, as well as the system's date and time. You will learn how to set up the CMOS for these devices in later chapters. At this point, your only goal is to understand CMOS and know how to access the CMOS setup on your PC,

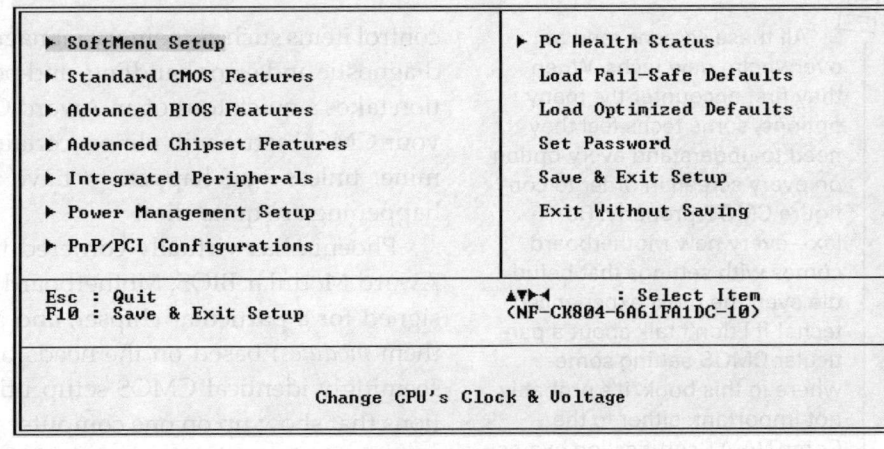

● **Figure 5.14** Typical CMOS Main screen by Award

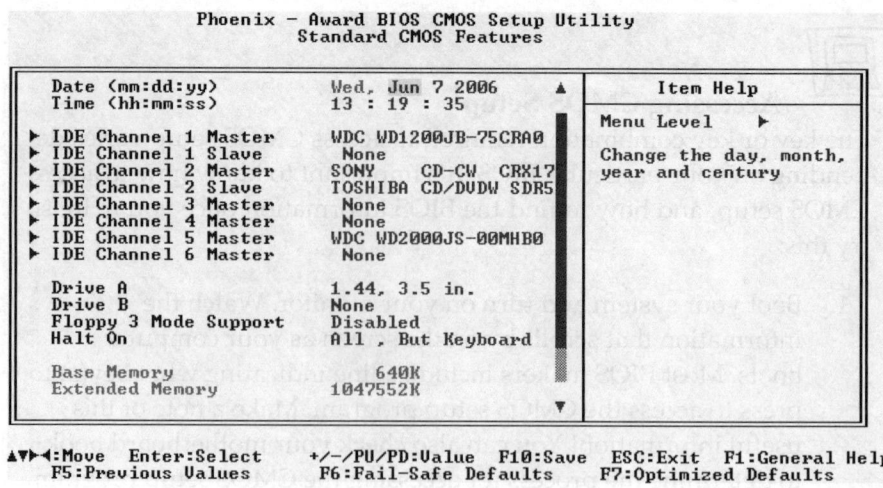

● **Figure 5.15** Standard CMOS Features screen

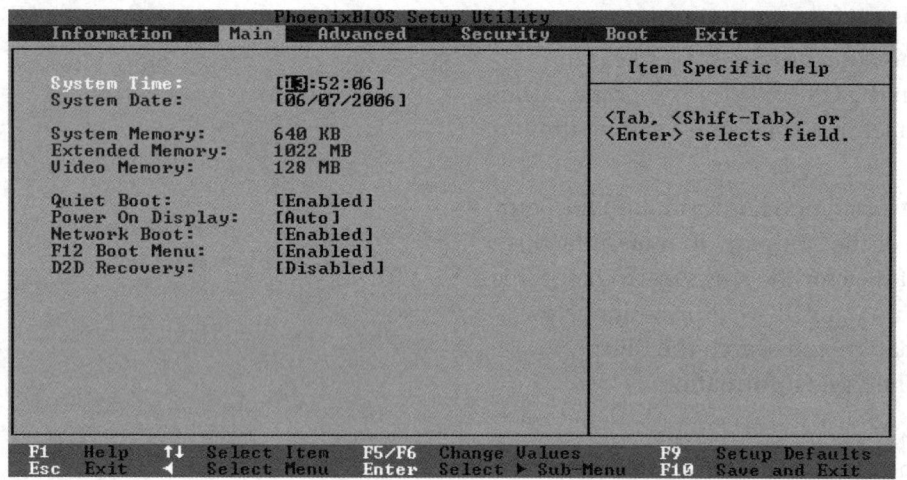

● **Figure 5.16** Phoenix BIOS CMOS setup utility Main screen

All these screens tend to overwhelm new techs. When they first encounter the many options, some techs feel they need to understand every option on every screen in order to configure CMOS properly. Relax—every new motherboard comes with settings that befuddle even the most experienced techs! If I don't talk about a particular CMOS setting somewhere in this book, it's probably not important, either to the CompTIA A+ certification exams or to a real tech.

so don't try to change anything yet. If you have a system that you are allowed to reboot, try accessing the CMOS setup now. Does it look anything like these examples? If not, can you find the screen that enables you to change the floppy and hard drives? Trust me, every CMOS setup has that screen somewhere! Figure 5.16 shows the same standard CMOS setup screen on a system with Phoenix BIOS. Note that this CMOS setup utility calls this screen "Main."

The first BIOS was nothing more than this standard CMOS setup. Today, all computers have many extra CMOS settings. They control items such as memory management, password and booting options, diagnostic and error handling, and power management. The following section takes a quick tour of an Award CMOS setup program. Remember that your CMOS setup will almost certainly look at least a little different from mine, unless you happen to have the *same* BIOS. The chances of that happening are quite slim!

Phoenix has virtually cornered the desktop PC BIOS market with its Award Modular BIOS. Motherboard makers buy a "boilerplate" BIOS, designed for a particular chipset, and add or remove options (Phoenix calls them *modules*) based on the needs of each motherboard. This means that seemingly identical CMOS setup utilities can be extremely different. Options that show up on one computer might be missing from another. Compare the older Award screen in Figure 5.17 with the more modern main Award CMOS screen in Figure 5.14. Figure 5.17 looks different—and it

Mike Meyers' CompTIA A+ Guide: Essentials (Exam 220-601)

```
                    ROM PCI/ISA BIOS (2A69HQ1A)
                       CMOS SETUP UTILITY
                     AWARD SOFTWARE, INC.

    STANDARD CMOS SETUP            INTEGRATED PERIPHERALS

    BIOS FEATURES SETUP            SUPERVISOR PASSWORD

    CHIPSET FEATURES SETUP         USER PASSWORD

    POWER MANAGEMENT SETUP         IDE HDD AUTO DETECTION

    PNP/PCI CONFIGURATION          HDD LOW LEVEL FORMAT

    LOAD BIOS DEFAULTS             SAVE & EXIT SETUP

    LOAD SETUP DEFAULTS            EXIT WITHOUT SAVING

  Esc : Quit                   ↑ ↓ → ←   : Select Item
  F10 : Save & Exit Setup      (Shift)F2 : Change Color
```

● **Figure 5.17**   Older Award setup screen

should—as this much older system simply doesn't need the extra options available on the newer system!

The next section starts the walkthrough of a CMOS setup utility with the SoftMenu, followed by some of the Advanced screens. Then you'll go through other common screens, such as Integrated Peripherals, Power, and more.

SoftMenu

The SoftMenu enables you to change the voltage and multiplier settings on the motherboard for the CPU from the defaults. Motherboards that cater to overclockers tend to have this option. Usually, you just set this to Auto or Default and stay away from this screen (Figure 5.18).

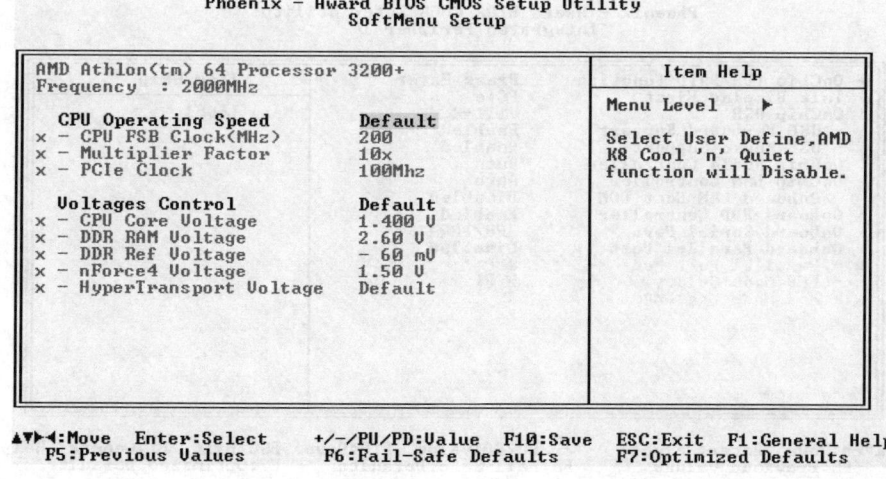

● **Figure 5.18**   SoftMenu

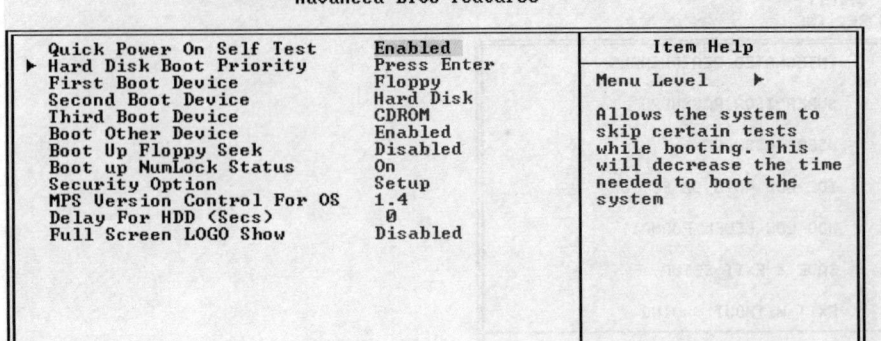

```
               Phoenix - Award BIOS CMOS Setup Utility
                        Advanced BIOS Features

    Quick Power On Self Test      Enabled            ┌───────────────────┐
  ▶ Hard Disk Boot Priority       Press Enter        │     Item Help     │
    First Boot Device             Floppy             ├───────────────────┤
    Second Boot Device            Hard Disk          │ Menu Level    ▶   │
    Third Boot Device             CDROM              │                   │
    Boot Other Device             Enabled            │ Allows the system to
    Boot Up Floppy Seek           Disabled           │ skip certain tests
    Boot up NumLock Status        On                 │ while booting. This
    Security Option               Setup              │ will decrease the time
    MPS Version Control For OS     1.4               │ needed to boot the
    Delay For HDD (Secs)          0                  │ system
    Full Screen LOGO Show         Disabled           │


▲▼▶◄:Move  Enter:Select    +/-/PU/PD:Value  F10:Save    ESC:Exit  F1:General Help
    F5:Previous Values         F6:Fail-Safe Defaults    F7:Optimized Defaults
```

● **Figure 5.19**   Advanced BIOS Features

```
               Phoenix - Award BIOS CMOS Setup Utility
                       Advanced Chipset Features

  ▶ HT Frequency                 Auto               ┌───────────────────┐
  ▶ DRAM Configuration           Press Enter        │     Item Help     │
    SSE/SSE2 Instructions        Enabled            ├───────────────────┤
    System BIOS Cacheable        Disabled           │ Menu Level    ▶   │


▲▼▶◄:Move  Enter:Select    +/-/PU/PD:Value  F10:Save    ESC:Exit  F1:General Help
    F5:Previous Values         F6:Fail-Safe Defaults    F7:Optimized Defaults
```

● **Figure 5.20**   Advanced Chipset Features

```
               Phoenix - Award BIOS CMOS Setup Utility
                        Integrated Peripherals

  ▶ OnChip IDE/RAID Function     Press Enter        ┌───────────────────┐
    Init Display First           PCIe               │     Item Help     │
    OnChip USB                   V1.1+2.0           ├───────────────────┤
    - USB Keyboard Support       Enabled            │ Menu Level    ▶   │
    - USB Mouse Support          Enabled            │
    OnChip Audio Controller      Auto
    OnChip LAN Controller        Auto
    - Onboard LAN Boot ROM       Disabled
    Onboard FDD Controller       Enabled
    Onboard Serial Port          3F8/IRQ4
    Onboard Parallel Port        Disabled
  x - Parallel Port Mode         SPP
  x - EPP Mode Select            EPP1.7
  x - Ecp Mode Use DMA           3


▲▼▶◄:Move  Enter:Select    +/-/PU/PD:Value  F10:Save    ESC:Exit  F1:General Help
    F5:Previous Values         F6:Fail-Safe Defaults    F7:Optimized Defaults
```

● **Figure 5.21**   Integrated Peripherals

Advanced BIOS Features

Advanced BIOS Features is the dumping ground for all the settings that aren't covered in the Standard menu, but don't fit nicely under any other screen. This screen varies wildly from one system to the next. You most often use this screen to select the boot options (Figure 5.19).

Advanced Chipset Features

The Advanced Chipset Features screen strikes fear into most everyone because it deals with extremely low-level chipset functions. Avoid this screen unless a high-level tech (like a motherboard maker's support tech) explicitly tells you to do something in here (Figure 5.20).

Integrated Peripherals

You will use the Integrated Peripherals screen quite often. It's here where you configure, enable, or disable the onboard ports, such as the serial and parallel ports. You can use this screen to get important work done (Figure 5.21).

Power Management

As the name implies, you can use the Power Management screen to set up the power management settings for the system. These settings work in concert (sometimes in conflict) with Windows' power management settings to control how and when devices turn off and back on to conserve power (Figure 5.22).

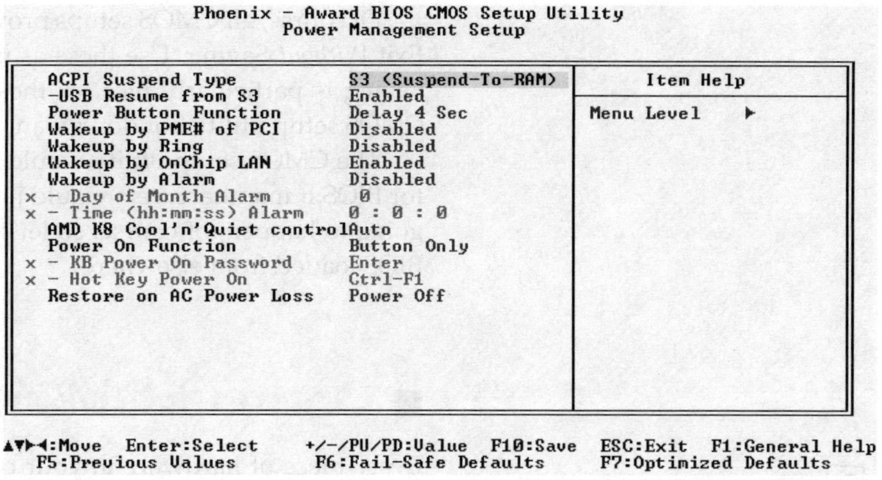

PnP/PCI Configurations

All CMOS setup utilities come with menu items that are for the most part no longer needed, but no one wants to remove. PnP/PCI is a perfect example. Plug and play (PnP) is how devices automatically work when you snap them into your PC. PCI is a type of slot used for cards. Odds are very good you'll never deal with this screen (Figure 5.23).

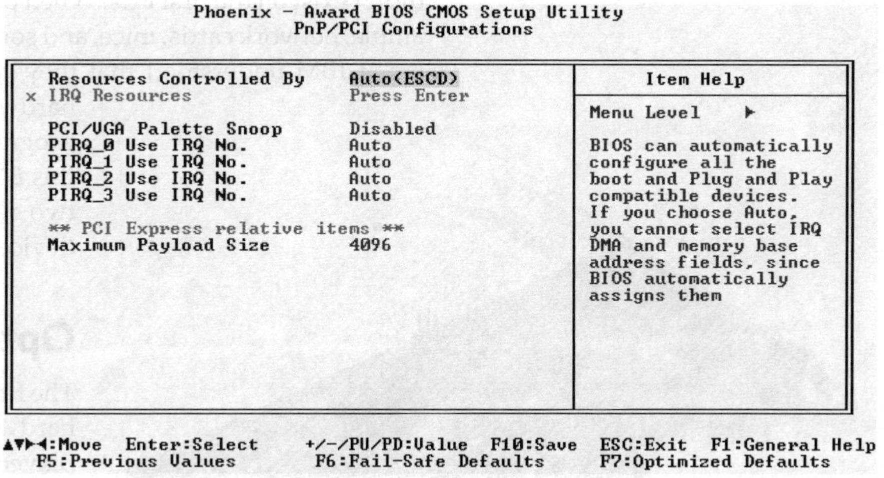

And the Rest of the CMOS Settings....

The other options on the main menu of an Award CMOS do not have their own screens. Rather, these simply have small dialog boxes that pop up, usually with "Are you sure?" messages. The Load Fail-Safe/Optimized defaults options keep you from having to memorize all of those weird settings you'll never touch. Fail-Safe sets everything to very simple settings—you might occasionally use this setting when very low-level problems like freeze-ups occur, and you've checked more obvious areas first. Optimized sets the CMOS to the best possible speed/stability for the system. You would use this option after tampering with the CMOS too much when you need to put it back like it was!

Many CMOS setup programs enable you to set a password in CMOS to force the user to enter a password every time the system boots. Don't confuse this with the Windows logon password. This CMOS password shows up at boot, long before Windows even starts to load. Figure 5.24 shows a typical CMOS password prompt.

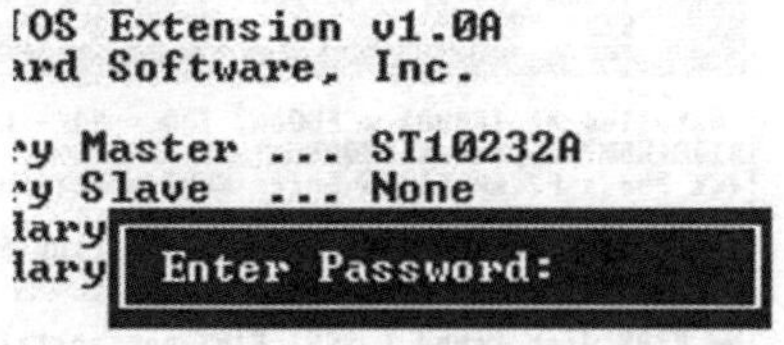

Some CMOS setup utilities enable you to create two passwords: one for boot and another for accessing the CMOS setup program. This extra password just for entering CMOS setup is a godsend for places such as schools where non-techs tend to wreak havoc in areas (like CMOS) that they should not access!

```
                Phoenix - Award BIOS CMOS Setup Utility
                          Power Management Setup

    ACPI Suspend Type           S3 <Suspend-To-RAM>    │      Item Help
     -USB Resume from S3        Enabled                 │
    Power Button Function       Delay 4 Sec             │  Menu Level    ►
    Wakeup by PME# of PCI       Disabled                │
    Wakeup by Ring              Disabled                │
    Wakeup by OnChip LAN        Enabled                 │
    Wakeup by Alarm             Disabled                │
  x  - Day of Month Alarm         0                     │
  x  - Time (hh:mm:ss) Alarm     0 : 0 : 0              │
    AMD K8 Cool'n'Quiet controlAuto                      │
    Power On Function           Button Only             │
  x  - KB Power On Password     Enter                   │
  x  - Hot Key Power On         Ctrl-F1                 │
    Restore on AC Power Loss    Power Off               │

  ▲▼►◄:Move  Enter:Select   +/-/PU/PD:Value  F10:Save  ESC:Exit  F1:General Help
    F5:Previous Values        F6:Fail-Safe Defaults     F7:Optimized Defaults
```

• **Figure 5.22**   Power Management

```
                Phoenix - Award BIOS CMOS Setup Utility
                          PnP/PCI Configurations

    Resources Controlled By     Auto(ESCD)             │      Item Help
  x IRQ Resources               Press Enter            │
                                                        │  Menu Level    ►
    PCI/VGA Palette Snoop       Disabled                │  BIOS can automatically
    PIRQ_0 Use IRQ No.          Auto                    │  configure all the
    PIRQ_1 Use IRQ No.          Auto                    │  boot and Plug and Play
    PIRQ_2 Use IRQ No.          Auto                    │  compatible devices.
    PIRQ_3 Use IRQ No.          Auto                    │  If you choose Auto,
                                                        │  you cannot select IRQ
    ** PCI Express relative items **                    │  DMA and memory base
    Maximum Payload Size        4096                    │  address fields, since
                                                        │  BIOS automatically
                                                        │  assigns them

  ▲▼►◄:Move  Enter:Select   +/-/PU/PD:Value  F10:Save  ESC:Exit  F1:General Help
    F5:Previous Values        F6:Fail-Safe Defaults     F7:Optimized Defaults
```

• **Figure 5.23**   PnP/PCI

```
  [OS Extension v1.0A
  ard Software, Inc.

  ·y Master ... ST10232A
  ·y Slave  ... None
  lary┌─────────────────────┐
  lary│ Enter Password:     │
      └─────────────────────┘
```

• **Figure 5.24**   CMOS password prompt

Of course, all CMOS setups provide some method to Save and Exit or to Exit *Without* Saving. Use these as needed for your situation. Exit Without Saving is particularly nice for those folks who want to poke around the CMOS setup utility but don't want to mess anything up. Use it!

The CMOS setup utility would meet all the needs of a modern system for BIOS if manufacturers would just stop creating new devices. That's not going to happen, of course, so let's turn now to devices that need to have BIOS loaded from elsewhere.

■ Option ROM and Device Drivers

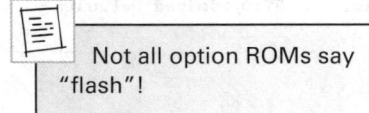

Not all option ROMs say "flash"!

Every piece of hardware in your computer needs some kind of programming that tells the CPU how to talk to that device. When IBM invented the PC more than a quarter century ago, they couldn't possibly have included all the necessary BIOS routines for every conceivable piece of hardware on the system ROM chip. How could they? Most of the devices in use today didn't exist on the first PCs! When programmers wrote the first BIOS, for example, network cards, mice, and sound cards did not exist. Early PC designers at IBM understood that they could not anticipate every new type of hardware, so they gave us a few ways to add programming other than on the BIOS. I call this *BYOB*—Bring Your Own BIOS. There are two ways you can BYOB: option ROM and device drivers. Let's look at both.

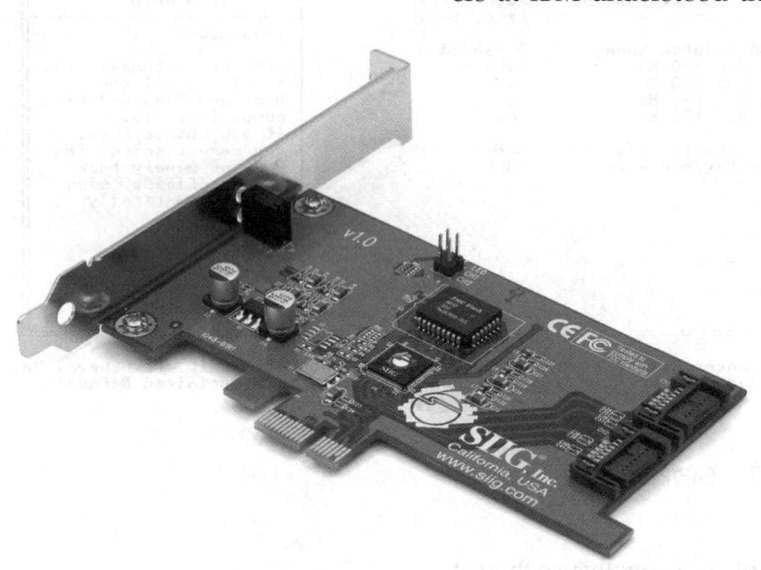

Option ROM

The first way to BYOB is to put the BIOS on the hardware device itself. Look at the card displayed in Figure 5.25. This is a serial ATA RAID hard drive controller—basically just a card that lets you add more hard drives to a PC. The chip in the center with the wires coming out the sides is a flash ROM storing BIOS for the card. The system BIOS does not have a clue about how to talk to this card, but that's okay because this card brings its own BIOS on what's called an **option ROM** chip.

• **Figure 5.25**   Option ROM

Most BIOS that come on option ROMs tell you that they exist by displaying information when you boot the system. Figure 5.26 shows a typical example of an option ROM advertising itself.

In the early days of the PC, you could find all sorts of devices with BIOS on option ROMs. Today, option ROMs have mostly been replaced by more flexible software methods (more on that in the next section), with one major exception: video cards. Every video card made today contains its own BIOS. Option ROMs work well, but are hard to upgrade. For this reason, most hardware in PCs relies on software for BYOB.

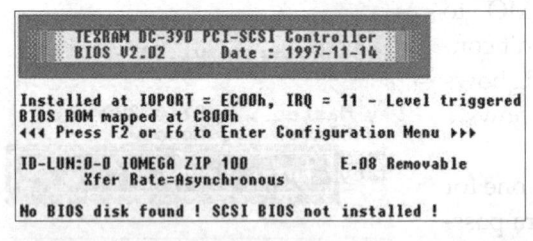

```
TEKRAM DC-390 PCI-SCSI Controller
BIOS V2.02        Date : 1997-11-14

Installed at IOPORT = ECOOh, IRQ = 11 - Level triggered
BIOS ROM mapped at C800h
◄◄◄ Press F2 or F6 to Enter Configuration Menu ►►►

ID-LUN:0-0 IOMEGA ZIP 100       E.08 Removable
      Xfer Rate=Asynchronous

No BIOS disk found ! SCSI BIOS not installed !
```

• **Figure 5.26**   Option ROM at boot

Device Drivers

A device driver is a file stored on the PC's hard drive that contains all the commands necessary to talk to whatever device it was written to support. All operating systems employ a method of loading these device drivers into RAM every time the system boots. They know which device drivers to install by reading a file (or files) that lists which device drivers the system needs to load at boot time. All operating systems are designed to look at this list early on in the boot process and copy the listed files into RAM, thereby giving the CPU the capability to communicate with the hardware supported by the device drivers.

Device drivers come with the device when you buy it. When you buy a sound card, for example, it comes with a CD-ROM that holds all the necessary device drivers (and usually a bunch of extra goodies). The generic name for this type of CD-ROM is installation disc. In most cases, you install a new device, start the computer, and wait for Windows to prompt you for the installation disc (Figure 5.27).

There are times when you might want to add or remove device drivers manually. Windows uses a special database called the registry that stores everything you want to know about your system, including the device drivers. You shouldn't access the registry directly to access these drivers, but instead use the venerable Device Manager utility (Figure 5.28).

Using the Device Manager, you can manually change or remove the drivers for any particular device. You access the Device Manager by opening the System applet in the Control Panel; then select the Hardware tab and click the Device Manager button. Make sure you know how to access the Device Manager. You'll see lots more of the Device Manager as you learn about different types of devices in the rest of the book.

BIOS, BIOS, Everywhere!

As you should now understand, every piece of hardware on a system must have an accompanying program that provides the CPU with the code necessary to communicate with that particular device. This code may reside on the system ROM on the motherboard, on ROM on a card, or in a device driver file on the hard drive loaded into RAM at boot. BIOS is everywhere on your system, and you will need to deal with it occasionally.

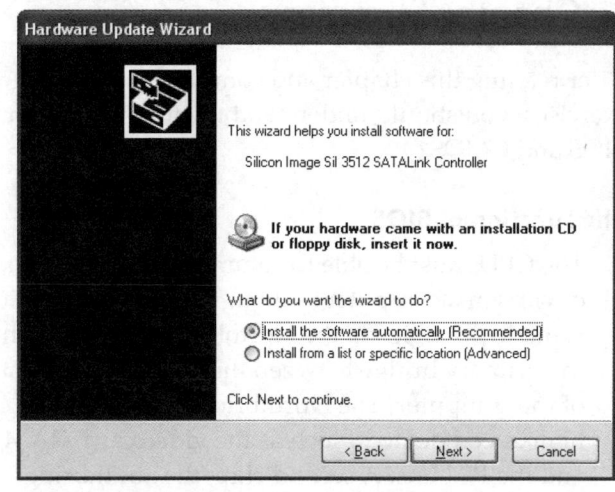

• **Figure 5.27**   Windows asking for the installation disc

You can also access the Device Manager by right-clicking My Computer and selecting Manage. When the Computer Management dialog box comes up, click on Device Manager.

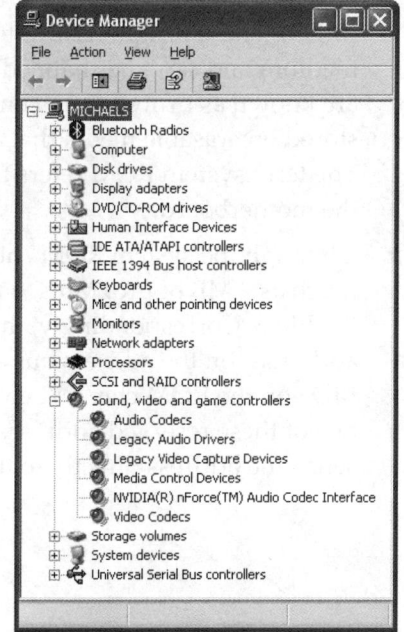

• **Figure 5.28**   Typical Device Manager

Chapter 5 Review

■ Chapter Summary

After reading this chapter and completing the exercises, you should understand the following about BIOS and CMOS.

The Function of BIOS

■ The CPU must be able to communicate with all devices in a computer system. This communication is made possible via the Northbridge chip, which is the primary bridge between the CPU and the rest of the computer. The Northbridge deals with high-speed devices, such as the video card, RAM, and the PCI bus. A second chip, the Southbridge, works with the other devices. The Northbridge and Southbridge chips are manufactured as a set called the chipset. The chipset extends the data and address buses to every device in the PC.

■ A ROM (read-only memory) chip is non-volatile, meaning it retains the information stored on it even when the power is turned off. Usually attached to the Southbridge, the ROM chip stores hundreds of little programs that enable the CPU to communicate with basic devices like the floppy drive, CD and DVD drives, hard drives, video card, and others. These programs, called *services*, are collectively referred to as the basic input/output services (BIOS). These programs are stored on a read-only medium and can't be changed by the user, so they are known as firmware, in contrast to programs stored on erasable media that are called software. The term system ROM refers to the ROM chip on the motherboard.

■ Although the system ROM chip has room for as much as 2 MB of programs, only 65,536 bytes store the BIOS. Correspondingly, the last 65,536 addresses on the address bus are reserved for the BIOS on the ROM chip. When the CPU indicates one of these reserved addresses, the Northbridge sends the address directly to the ROM BIOS.

■ The ROM BIOS includes programs that enable the CPU to talk to many basic hardware devices such as the keyboard, but other devices not supported by the ROM BIOS may have their own ROM chips.

■ Each piece of hardware in the computer needs programs for everything that piece of hardware performs. The CPU must access these programs to get the hardware to do its job. IBM also devised other methods to get BIOS to the hardware of the computer. If the hardware is common, necessary, and does not change, such as the keyboard, the system ROM chip stores the BIOS. If the hardware is common and necessary but may change from time to time, such as when you install a larger hard drive or add more RAM, the BIOS for the general type of device (e.g., a hard drive) can be on the system ROM chip. The information describing specific features unique to that particular device (e.g., a Seagate Barracuda 60-GB drive), however, must be stored on a changeable storage medium such as a complementary metal-oxide semiconductor (CMOS) chip.

CMOS

■ Your motherboard includes a changeable chip, capable of storing about 64 KB of data, called the complementary metal-oxide semiconductor (CMOS) chip. CMOS does not store programs. It stores the data that is read by BIOS, and that data is used by the programs residing in BIOS. Although CMOS used to be a separate chip on the motherboard, it is almost always built into the Southbridge on modern motherboards. The CMOS chip also keeps track of the date and time. CMOS requires a constant trickle of electricity to maintain its data. This is supplied by a small battery on the motherboard. If the data you have stored in CMOS continues to disappear or if the date/time resets itself, it may be time to change the motherboard battery.

- Within the system ROM is a CMOS setup program that lets you access and update the data on the CMOS chip. The terms CMOS setup program, CMOS, and system setup utility are functionally interchangeable today. Most techs just call it the CMOS. Two major manufacturers control 99 percent of the BIOS business: American Megatrends (AMI) and Phoenix Technology (which includes Award Software). The CMOS setup program can be started in many different ways, depending on the brand of BIOS you have on your computer. Pressing DEL when the computer boots is the most common way to access the CMOS setup program. The screen itself usually tells you how to access setup. If it doesn't, you can check the motherboard book or the Web site of your PC or BIOS manufacturer.

- All CMOS setup programs have basically the same main options. On the Standard CMOS Features screen, you can change floppy drive, hard drive, and date/time settings. Today's setup programs have extra CMOS settings that control items such as memory management, password and booting options, diagnostic and error handling, and power management. The Award Modular BIOS enables motherboard manufacturers to add or remove options from the setup program.

- Among the other things you can configure in CMOS setup are the voltage and multiplier settings for the CPU (the CPU Soft menu), boot options (check the Advanced BIOS Features menu), power management, password protection, and ports (the Integrated Peripherals menu). All setup programs include options to *Save and Exit* or *Exit Without Saving*. You should not change CMOS settings unless you know exactly what you're doing.

- On older systems, if the information on the CMOS chip was lost or erased, the computer would not boot. The most common cause was a dead onboard battery, but other factors such as electrical surges, chip creep, or a dirty motherboard could also erase CMOS data. Lost CMOS information produces errors such as *No boot device available* or *CMOS date/ time not set*. Making a backup copy of the CMOS data enabled you to restore the information and recover from this catastrophe.

- Unlike earlier ROM chips that you had to replace when you wanted to upgrade the BIOS programs,

today's computers use flash ROM chips that you can reprogram without removing. If you install a CPU or other new hardware that the flash ROM chip does not support, you can run a small command-line program combined with an update file to change your BIOS. The exact process varies from one motherboard maker to another. If the flash ROM utility allows you to make a backup of your BIOS, you should always do so. Don't update your BIOS unless you have a good reason. As the old saying goes, "If it ain't broke, don't fix it!"

- Many CMOS setup programs enable you to set a boot password, a password to enter the CMOS setup program itself, or both. These passwords are stored in CMOS. If you forget your password, you simply need to clear the CMOS data. Unplug the AC power from the PC and remove the motherboard battery. This will remove the trickle charge that enables CMOS to store information and clear all CMOS data, including the passwords. Reinstall the battery, plug in the power cord, boot up the computer, and re-enter your CMOS settings. Alternatively, many motherboards provide a "clear CMOS jumper" that enables you to clear the CMOS data without removing the battery. Small padlocks on the system chassis can prevent unauthorized users from accessing the motherboard and clearing CMOS data.

Option ROM and Device Drivers

- Newer hardware devices that are not supported by the system BIOS have other ways to BYOB—bring your own BIOS. A hardware device, such as a SCSI host adapter, may contain its own BIOS chip or ROM chip known as option ROM. Every video card contains its own BIOS for internal functions. A more flexible way to BYOB is to use files called device drivers that contain instructions to support the hardware device. Device drivers load when the system boots.

- Many devices come with device driver files on installation discs. These drivers must be loaded for the PC to recognize and use the devices. Windows keeps a list of what drivers should be loaded in a database called the registry. Editing the registry directly is dangerous (a mistake can prevent Windows from booting up), but you can safely install or remove drivers by using the Device Manager.

Key Terms

basic input/output services
(BIOS) *(130)*

chipset *(126)*

CMOS setup program *(133)*

complementary metal-oxide
semiconductor (CMOS) *(133)*

device driver *(141)*

Device Manager *(141)*

firmware *(132)*

flash ROM *(131)*

installation disc *(141)*

non-volatile *(131)*

Northbridge *(126)*

option ROM *(141)*

read-only memory (ROM) *(131)*

registry *(141)*

Southbridge *(126)*

system BIOS *(132)*

system ROM *(131)*

Key Term Quiz

Use the Key Terms list to complete the sentences that follow. Not all terms will be used.

1. Loaded when the system boots, a(n) _____ is a file that contains instructions to support a hardware device.

2. The combination of a specific Northbridge and a specific _____ is collectively referred to as the _____.

3. A(n) _____ chip can be reprogrammed without removing the chip.

4. Unlike RAM that loses all data when the computer is shut down, a ROM chip is _____, retaining the information even when the power is off.

5. The hundreds of programs in the system ROM chip are collectively called the _____.

6. The _____ is a database used by Windows to store information about what software is installed, what hardware is installed, and which device drivers should be loaded at startup.

7. The low-energy chip that holds configuration information and keeps track of date and time is called the _____ chip.

8. Some devices have their own built-in BIOS in the form of _____.

9. Programs stored on ROM are known as _____.

10. You can access and update the CMOS data through the _____ stored in the BIOS.

Multiple-Choice Quiz

1. Jack decided to go retro and added a second floppy disk drive to his computer. He thinks he got it physically installed correctly, but it doesn't show up in Windows. Which of the following options will most likely lead Jack where he needs to go to resolve the issue?

   A. Reboot the computer and press the F key on the keyboard twice. This signals that the computer has two floppy disk drives.

   B. Reboot the computer and watch for instructions to enter the CMOS setup utility (for example, a message may say to press the DELETE key). Do what it says to go into CMOS setup.

   C. In Windows, press the DELETE key twice to enter the CMOS setup utility.

   D. In Windows, go to Start | Run and type "floppy." Click OK to open the Floppy Disk Drive Setup Wizard.

2. What does BIOS provide for the computer? (Choose the best answer.)

   A. BIOS provides the physical interface for various devices such as USB and FireWire ports.

   B. BIOS provides the programming that enables the CPU to communicate with other hardware.

   C. BIOS provides memory space for applications to load into from the hard drive.

   D. BIOS provides memory space for applications to load into from the main system RAM.

3. Which of the following statements is true about CMOS?

   A. CMOS is a configuration program that runs from the hard drive during booting.

   B. CMOS is a low-energy chip that draws power from a battery while the computer is turned off.

   C. CMOS includes the power-on self test (POST) routines.

   D. CMOS is the Southbridge chip that controls input and output devices.

4. Which of the following most typically enables you to upgrade a flash ROM chip?

   A. Remove the chip and replace it with a different one.

   B. Reboot the computer.

   C. Install a different operating system.

   D. Run a small command-line program combined with a BIOS update file.

5. Henry bought a new card for capturing television on his computer. When he finished going through the packaging, though, he found no driver disc, only an application disc for setting up the TV capture software. After installing the card and software, it all works flawlessly. What's the most likely explanation?

   A. The device doesn't need BIOS, so there's no need for a driver disc.

   B. The device has an option ROM that loads BIOS, so there's no need for a driver disc.

   C. Windows supports TV capture cards out of the box, so there's no need for a driver disc.

   D. The manufacturer made a mistake and didn't include everything needed to set up the device.

6. Which chip does the CPU use to communicate with high-speed devices such as video cards or RAM?

   A. Complementary metal-oxide semiconductor

   B. Northbridge

   C. Southbridge

   D. Scan code

7. When your computer boots up and you press the appropriate key to enter the CMOS setup utility, a small program loads, allowing you to specify settings for various hardware devices. Where is this small program permanently stored?

   A. In the BIOS

   B. In CMOS

   C. On the hard drive

   D. In RAM

8. When you enter the CMOS setup utility (as in the previous question) and make changes, where are your settings stored?

   A. In the BIOS

   B. In CMOS

   C. On the hard drive

   D. In RAM

9. Which key combination will always allow you to access the CMOS setup program in any IBM-compatible computer?

   A. DEL-ESC

   B. CTRL-ALT-ESC

   C. F9

   D. There is no universal key combination that always works.

10. Which ROM chip enables the PC to communicate with basic hardware?

   A. Static ROM

   B. System ROM

   C. CMOS ROM

   D. Device ROM

11. How can you update the data stored in CMOS?

   A. Access the CMOS setup program.

   B. Access the BIOS setup program.

   C. Use third-party software.

   D. Data stored in CMOS is permanently burned into the chip and cannot be updated.

12. While system ROM chips can store as much as 2 MB of programs, how much space is allocated to storing the system BIOS?

   A. 65,536 bits

   B. 65,536 kilobits

   C. 65,536 bytes

   D. 65,536 kilobytes

13. Which CMOS setup option is used to configure onboard ports such as serial and parallel ports?

   A. Integrated Peripherals

   B. Legacy Ports

   C. External Connections

   D. System Resources

14. Where is information about installed device drivers stored?

    A. BIOS

    B. CMOS

    C. Device Manager

    D. Registry

15. What are the three most common brand names of BIOS?

    A. AMD, Intel, IBM

    B. Microsoft, Apple, Motorola

    C. Dell, Gateway, Compaq

    D. AMI, Phoenix, Award

■ Essay Quiz

1. From this chapter you learned that every piece of hardware in the computer needs BIOS to make it work. Explain three different ways in which these essential programs may be provided to the CPU.

2. Your instructor has asked you to give a report on the Northbridge and Southbridge chips, their functions, and how they use the address bus. Write a short essay on the subject that you can use in class.

Lab Projects

● Lab Project 5.1

Watch closely as your computer boots to see if it displays a message about how to reach the setup program. If it does not, consult your motherboard book to try to locate this information. Then, using the method appropriate for your system BIOS chip, access the setup program and examine the various screens. Do not change anything! Usually, your motherboard book includes default settings for the various setup screens and perhaps includes explanations of the various choices. Compare what you see on the screen with what the book says. Are there any differences? If so, how do you account for these differences? As you examine the setup program, answer the following questions:

1. How do you navigate from one screen to the next? Are there menus across the top or do you simply jump from one page of options to the next? Are there instructions on the screen for navigating the setup program?

2. What is the boot sequence for your computer?

3. What is the core voltage of the CPU?

4. What mode does the parallel port use?

5. What IRQ does COM 1 use?

When you have finished, choose "Exit Without Saving."

Understanding the Expansion Bus

Blackadder: "*Right, Baldrick, let's try again shall we? This is called adding. If I have two beans, and then I add two more beans, what do I have?*"

Baldrick: "*Some beans.*"

Blackadder: "*Yes … and no. Let's try again shall we? I have two beans, then I add two more beans. What does that make?*"

Baldrick: "*A very small casserole.*"

—EDMUND BLACKADDER AND BALDRICK, *BLACKADDER II* (1986)

Expansion slots have been part of the PC from the very beginning. Way back then, IBM created the PC with an eye to the future; the original IBM PC had slots built into the motherboard—called expansion slots —for adding expansion cards and thus new functions to the PC. The slots and accompanying wires and support chips are called the expansion bus , which can be found on all PCs, from the first to the latest and greatest.

The expandability enabled by an expansion bus might seem obvious today, but think about the three big hurdles a would-be expansion card developer needed to cross to make a card that would work successfully in an expansion slot. First, any expansion card needed to be built specifically for the expansion slots—that would require the creation of industry standards. Second, the card needed some way to communicate with the CPU, both to receive instructions and to relay information. And third, the operating system would need some means of enabling the user to control the new device and thus take advantage of its functions. Here's the short form of those three hurdles:

- Physical connection
- Communication
- Drivers

In this chapter, you will learn how to

- **Identify the structure and function of the expansion bus**
- **Describe the modern expansion bus**
- **Explain classic system resources**

This chapter covers the expansion bus in detail, starting almost at the very beginning of the PC—not because the history of the PC is inherently thrilling, but rather because the way the old PCs worked still affects the latest systems. Installation today remains very similar to installation in 1987 in that you must have a physical connection, communication, and drivers for the operating system. Taking the time to learn the old ways first most definitely helps make current technology, terminology, and practices easier to understand and implement.

Historical/Conceptual

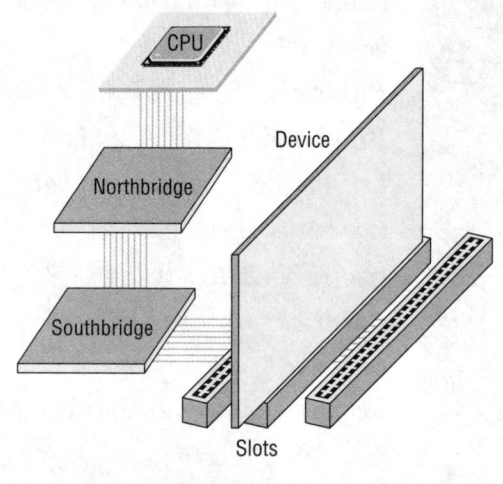

• **Figure 6.1** Expansion slots connecting to Southbridge

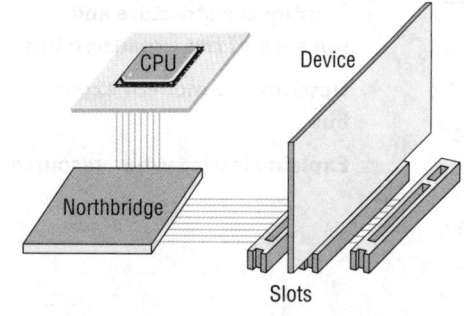

• **Figure 6.2** Expansion slots connecting to Northbridge

■ Structure and Function of the Expansion Bus

As you've learned, every device in the computer—whether soldered to the motherboard or snapped into a socket—connects to the external data bus and the address bus. The expansion slots are no exception. They connect to the rest of the PC through the chipset. Exactly *where* on the chipset varies depending on the system. On some systems, the expansion slots connect to the Southbridge (Figure 6.1). On other systems, the expansion slots connect to the Northbridge (Figure 6.2). Finally, many systems have more than one type of expansion bus, with slots of one type connecting to the Northbridge and slots of another type connecting to the Southbridge (Figure 6.3).

The chipset provides an extension of the address bus and data bus to the expansion slots, and thus to any expansion cards in those slots. If you plug a hard drive controller card into an expansion slot, it will function just as if it were built into the motherboard, albeit with one big difference: speed. As you'll recall from Chapter 3, the system crystal—the clock—pushes the CPU. The system crystal

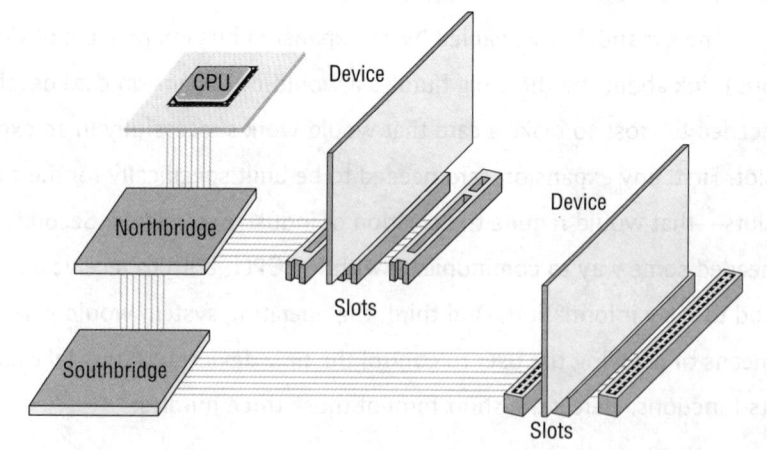

• **Figure 6.3** Expansion slots connecting to both Northbridge and Southbridge

provides a critical function for the entire PC, acting like a drill sergeant calling a cadence, setting the pace of activity in the computer. Every device soldered to the motherboard is designed to run at the speed of the system crystal. A 133-MHz motherboard, for example, has at least a 133-MHz Northbridge chip and a 133-MHz Southbridge, all timed by a 133-MHz crystal (Figure 6.4).

Clock crystals aren't just for CPUs and chipsets. Pretty much every chip in your computer has a CLK wire and needs to be pushed by a clock chip, including the chips

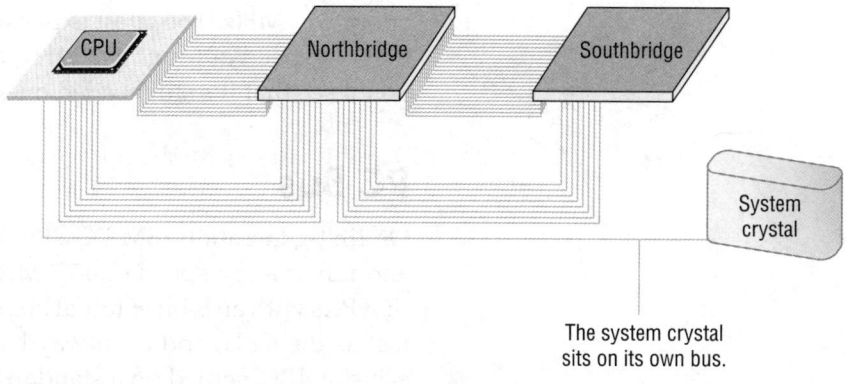

• **Figure 6.4**   The system crystal sets the speed.

on your expansion cards. Suppose you buy a device that did not come with your computer—say, a sound card. The chips on the sound card need to be pushed by a CLK signal from a crystal. If PCs were designed to use the system crystal to push that sound card, sound card manufacturers would need to make sound cards for every possible motherboard speed. You would have to buy a 100-MHz sound card for a 100-MHz system or a 133-MHz sound card for a 133-MHz system.

That would be ridiculous, and IBM knew it when they designed the PC. They had to make an extension to the external data bus that *ran at its own standardized speed*. You would use this part of the external data bus to snap new devices into the PC. IBM achieved this goal by adding a different crystal, called the **expansion bus crystal**, which controlled the part of the external data bus connected to the expansion slots (Figure 6.5).

The expansion slots run at a much slower speed than the frontside bus. The chipset acts as the divider between the two buses, compensating for the speed difference with wait states and special buffering (storage) areas. No matter how fast the motherboard runs, the expansion slots run at a standard speed. In the original IBM PC, that speed was about 14.318 MHz ÷ 2, or

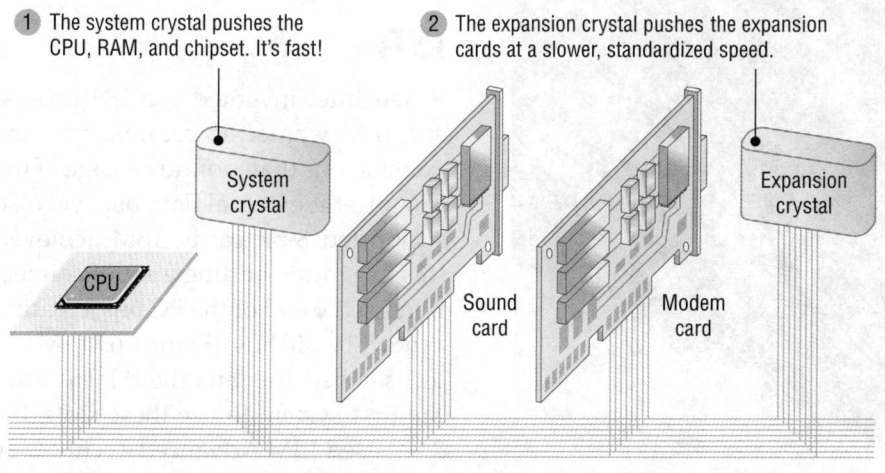

• **Figure 6.5**   Function of system and expansion bus crystals

about 7.16 MHz. The latest expansion buses run much faster, but remember that old speed of roughly 7 MHz; as you learn more about expansion slots, you'll see that it's still needed on even the most modern systems.

PC Bus

On first-generation IBM PCs, the 8088 CPU had an 8-bit external data bus and ran at a top speed of 4.77 MHz. IBM made the expansion slots on the first PCs with an 8-bit external bus connection. IBM wanted the bus to run as fast as the CPU, and even way back then 4.77 MHz was an easy speed to achieve. IBM settled on a standard expansion bus speed of about 7 MHz—faster than the CPU! (This was the only occurrence in the history of PCs that the expansion bus was faster than the CPU.) This expansion bus was called the **PC bus** or *XT bus*. Figure 6.6 shows these ancient, 8-bit expansion slots.

IBM certainly didn't invent the idea of the expansion bus—plenty of earlier computers, including many mainframes, had expansion slots—but IBM did something no one had ever done. They allowed competitors to copy the PC bus and make their own PCs without having to pay a licensing or royalty fee. They also allowed third parties to make cards that would snap into their PC bus. Remember that IBM invented the PC bus—it was (and still is) a patented product of IBM Corporation. By allowing everyone to copy the PC expansion bus technology, however, IBM established the industry standard and fostered the emergence of the clone market. If IBM had not allowed others to copy their patented technologies for free, companies such as Compaq, Dell, and Gateway never would have existed. Equally, component makers like Logitech, Creative, and 3Com would never be the companies they are today without the help of IBM. Who knows? If IBM had not opened the PC bus to the world, this book and the A+ Certification exams might have been based on Apple computers!

PC Bus

- 8 bits wide
- 7-MHz speed
- Manual configuration

ISA

When Intel invented the 286 processor, IBM wanted to create a new expansion bus that took advantage of the 286's 16-bit external data bus, yet also supported 8-bit cards. IBM achieved this by simply adding a set of connections to the end of the PC bus, creating a new 16-bit bus (Figure 6.7). Many techs called this bus the *AT bus* after the first system to use these slots, the 286-based IBM Advanced Technology (AT) computer. The AT bus ran at the

• **Figure 6.6**   Eight-bit PC/XT slots

same speed (approximately 7 MHz) as the earlier PC bus.

Even though IBM allowed third parties to copy the PC and AT expansion bus architecture, they never released the complete specifications for these two types of expansion buses. A number of clone makers got together in the early 1980s and pooled their combined knowledge of the PC/XT and AT buses to create the **Industry Standard Architecture (ISA)**.

The ISA bus enabled manufacturers to jump the first of the three hurdles for successful expansion cards, namely connectivity. If a company wanted to build a new kind of adapter card for the PC, they simply followed the specifications in the ISA standard.

ISA Bus

- 16 bits wide
- 7-MHz speed
- Manual configuration

● **Figure 6.7** Sixteen-bit ISA or AT slots

Essentials

■ Modern Expansion Buses

The ISA expansion bus was both excellent and cutting edge for its time, and was *the* expansion bus in every PC for the first ten years of the PC's existence. Yet ISA suffered from three tremendous limitations that began to cause serious bottlenecks by the late 1980s. First, ISA was slow, running at only about 7 MHz. Second, ISA was narrow—only 16 bits wide—and therefore unable to handle the 32-bit and 64-bit external data buses of more modern processors. Finally, techs had to configure ISA cards manually, making installation a time-consuming nightmare of running proprietary configuration programs and moving tiny jumpers just to get a single card to work.

Manufacturers clearly needed to come up with a better bus that addressed the many problems associated with ISA. They needed a bus that could take advantage of the 33-MHz motherboard speed and 32-bit-wide data bus found in 386 and 486 systems. They also wanted a bus that was self-configuring, freeing techs from the drudgery of manual configuration. Finally, they had to make the new bus backward compatible, so end users wouldn't have to throw out their oftentimes substantial investment in ISA expansion cards.

False Starts

In the late 1980s, several new expansion buses designed to address these shortcomings appeared on the market. Three in particular—IBM's Micro Channel Architecture (MCA), the open standard Extended ISA (EISA), and the Video Electronics Standards Association's VESA Local Bus (VL-Bus)—all had a few years of modest popularity from the late 1980s to the mid 1990s. Although all of these alternative buses worked well, they each had shortcomings that made them less than optimal replacements for ISA. IBM charged a heavy licensing fee for MCA, EISA was expensive to make, and VL-Bus only worked in tandem with the ISA bus. By 1993, the PC world was eager for a big name to come forward with a fast, wide, easy-to-configure, and cheap new expansion bus. Intel saw the need and stepped up to the plate with the now famous PCI bus.

PCI

Intel introduced the **peripheral component interconnect (PCI)** bus architecture (Figure 6.8) in the early 1990s, and the PC expansion bus was never again the same. Intel made many smart moves with PCI, not the least of which was releasing PCI to the public domain to make PCI very attractive to manufacturers. PCI provided a wider, faster, more flexible alternative than any previous expansion bus. The exceptional technology of the new bus, combined with the lack of a price tag, made manufacturers quickly drop ISA and the other alternatives and adopt PCI.

PCI really shook up the PC world with its capabilities. The original PCI bus was 32 bits wide and ran at 33 MHz, which was superb, but these features were expected and not earth-shattering. The coolness of PCI came from its capability to coexist with other expansion buses. When PCI first came out, you could buy a motherboard with both PCI and ISA slots. This was important because it enabled users to keep their old ISA cards and slowly migrate to PCI. Equally impressive was that PCI devices were (and still are) self-configuring, a feature that led to the industry standard that became known as plug and play. Finally, PCI had a powerful burst mode feature that enabled very efficient data transfers.

• **Figure 6.8** PCI expansion bus slots

Before PCI, it was rare to see more than one type of expansion slot on a motherboard. Today, this is not only common—it's expected!

There was a 64-bit version of the original PCI standard, but it was quite rare.

PCI Bus

- 32 bits wide
- 33-MHz speed
- Self-configuring

The original PCI expansion bus has soldiered on in PCs for over ten years. Recently PCI has begun to be replaced by more advanced forms of PCI. Although these new PCI expansion buses are faster than the original PCI, they're only improvements to PCI, not entirely new expansion buses. The original PCI might be fading away, but PCI in its many new forms is still "King of the Motherboard."

AGP

One of the big reasons for ISA's demise was video cards. When video started going graphical with the introduction of Windows, ISA buses were too slow and graphics looked terrible. PCI certainly improved graphics at the time it came out, but Intel was thinking ahead. Shortly after Intel invented PCI, they presented a specialized, video-only version of PCI called the accelerated graphics port (AGP). An AGP slot is a PCI slot, but one with a direct connection to the Northbridge. AGP slots are only for video cards—don't try to snap a sound card or modem into one. You'll learn much more about this fascinating technology in Chapter 15, "Understanding Video." Figure 6.9 shows a typical AGP slot.

> The AGP slot is almost universally brown in color, making it easy to spot.

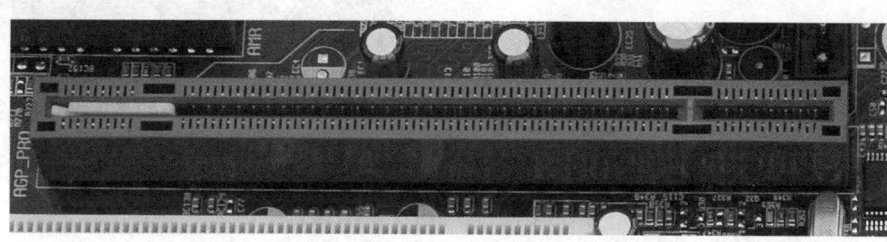

● **Figure 6.9**   AGP slot

PCI-X

PCI-X, already available in systems such as the Macintosh G5, is a huge enhancement to current PCI that is also fully backward compatible, in terms of both hardware and software. PCI-X is a 64-bit-wide bus (see Figure 6.10). Its slots will accept regular PCI cards. The real bonus of PCI-X is its much enhanced speed. The PCI-X 2.0 standard features four speed grades (measured in MHz): PCI-X 66, PCI-X 133, PCI-X 266, and PCI-X 533.

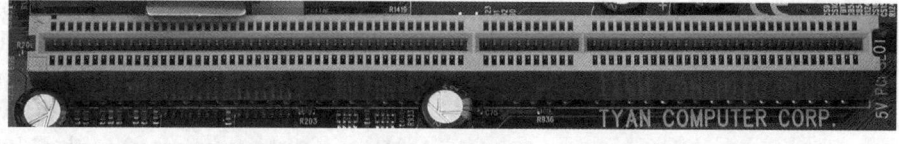

● **Figure 6.10**   PCI-X slot

The obvious candidates for PCI-X are businesses using workstations and servers, because they have the "need for speed" and also the need for backward compatibility. Large vendors, especially in the high-end market, are already on board. HP, Dell, and Intel server products, for example, support PCI-X. A quick online shopping trip reveals tons of PCI-X stuff for sale: gigabit NICs, Fibre Channel cards, video adapters, and more.

Mini-PCI

PCI has even made it into laptops in the specialty Mini-PCI format (Figure 6.11). You'll find Mini-PCI in just about every laptop these days. Mini-PCI is designed to use low power and to lie flat—both good features for a laptop expansion slot! Mini-PCI returns in Chapter 16, "Portable Computing."

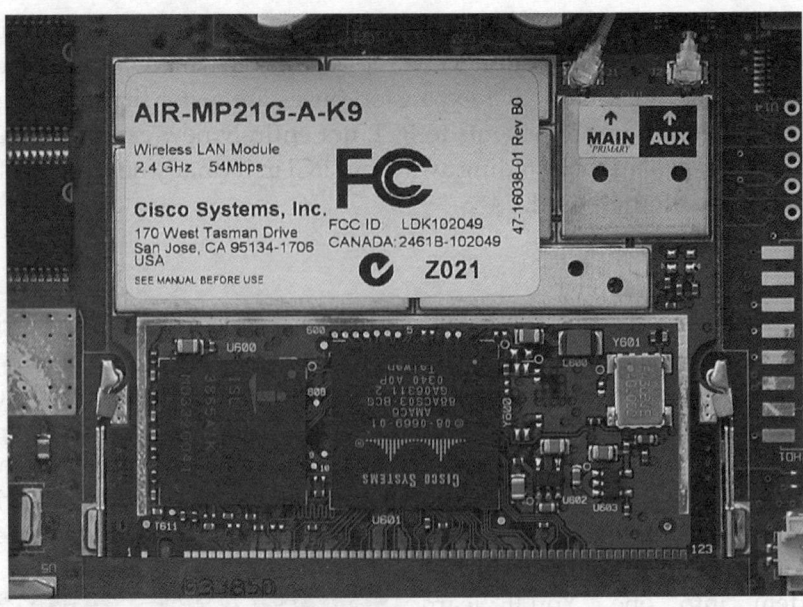

● **Figure 6.11**   Tiny card in a Mini-PCI slot. See the contacts at the bottom of the picture?

PCI Express

PCI Express (PCIe) is the latest, fastest, and most popular expansion bus in use today. As its name implies, PCI Express is still PCI, but it uses a point-to-point serial connection instead of PCI's shared parallel communication. Consider a single 32-bit chunk of data moving from a device to the CPU. In PCI parallel communication, 32 wires each carry one bit of that chunk of data. In serial communication, only one wire carries those 32 bits. You'd think that 32 are better than one, correct? Well, first of all, PCIe doesn't share the bus. A PCIe device has its own direct connection (a point-to-point connection) to the Northbridge, so it does not wait for other devices. Plus, when you start going really fast (think gigabits per second), it's difficult to get all 32 bits of data to go from one device to another at the same time because some bits get there slightly faster than others. That means you need some serious, high-speed checking of the data when it arrives to verify that it's all there and in good shape. Serial data doesn't have this problem, as all the bits arrive one after the other in a single stream. When data is really going fast, a single point-to-point serial connection is faster than a shared, 32-wire parallel connection.

And boy howdy, is PCIe ever fast! A PCIe connection uses one wire for sending and one for receiving. Each of these pairs of wires between a PCIe controller and a device is called a *lane*. Each lane runs at 2.5 Gbps. Better yet, each point-to-point connection can use 1, 2, 4, 8, 12, 16, or 32 lanes to achieve a maximum bandwidth of 160 Gbps. The effective data rate drops a little bit because of the *encoding scheme*—the way the data is broken down and reassembled—but full duplex data throughput can go up to a whopping 12.8 GBps on a ×32 connection.

The most common PCIe slot is the 16-lane (×16) version most commonly used for video cards, as shown in Figure 6.12. The first versions of PCIe

> When you talk about the lanes, such as ×1 or ×8, use "by" rather than "ex" for the multiplication mark. So "by 1" and "by 8" is the correct pronunciation. You'll of course hear it spoken as "ex 8" and "8 ex" for the next few years until the technology has become a household term.

● **Figure 6.12**   PCIe ×16 slot (black) with PCI slots (white)

motherboards used a combination of a single PCIe ×16 slot and a number of standard PCI slots. (Remember, PCI is designed to work with other expansion slots, even other types of PCI.)

The bandwidth generated by a ×16 slot is far more than anything other than a video card would need, so most PCIe motherboards also contain slots with fewer lanes. Currently, ×1 (Figure 6.13) and ×4 are the most common general-purpose PCIe slots, but PCIe is still pretty new—so expect things to change as PCIe matures.

 Try This!

Shopping Trip

So, what's the latest PCIe motherboard out there? Get online or go to your local computer store and research higher-end motherboards. What combinations of PCIe slots can you find on a single motherboard? Jot them down and compare with your classmates.

● **Figure 6.13**   PCIe ×1 slots

■ System Resources

All devices on your computer, including your expansion cards, need to communicate with the CPU. Unfortunately, just using the word *communication* is too simplistic, because communication between the CPU and devices isn't like a human conversation. In the PC, only the CPU "talks" in the form of BIOS or driver commands—devices only react to the CPU's commands. You can divide communication into four aspects called `system resources`. The system resources are I/O addresses, IRQs, DMA channels, and memory addresses.

Not all devices use all four system resources. All devices use I/O addressing and most use IRQs, but very few use DMA or memory. System resources are not new—they've been with PCs since the first IBM PC over 25 years ago.

New devices must have their system resources configured. Configuration happens more or less automatically now through the plug and play process, but in the old days configuration was handled through a painstaking manual process. (You kids don't know how good you got it! Oops! Sorry—Old Man Voice.) Even though system resources are now automated, there are a few places on a modern PC where you still might run into them. On those rare occasions, you'll need to understand I/O addresses, IRQs, DMAs, and memory to make changes as needed. Let's look at each system resource in detail to understand what they are and how they work.

I/O Addresses

The CPU gives a command to a device using a pattern of ones and zeroes called an `I/O address`. Every device responds to at least four I/O addresses, meaning the CPU can give at least four different commands to each device. The process of communicating through I/O addresses is called, quite logically, `I/O addressing`. Here's how it works.

The chipset extends the address bus to the expansion slots, which makes two interesting things happen. First, you can place RAM on a card, and the CPU can address it just like it can your regular RAM. Devices like video cards come with their own RAM. The CPU draws the screen by writing directly to the RAM on the video card. Second, the CPU can use the address bus to talk to all the devices on your computer through I/O addressing.

Normally the address bus on an expansion bus works exactly like the address bus on a frontside bus—different patterns of ones and zeroes point to different memory locations. If the CPU wants to send an I/O address, however, it puts the expansion bus into what can be called I/O mode. When the bus goes into I/O mode, all devices on the bus look for patterns of ones and zeroes to appear on the address bus.

Back in the old Intel 8088 days, the CPU used an extra wire, called the *input/output or memory (IO/MEM) wire*, to notify devices that it was using the address bus either to specify an address in memory or to communicate with a particular device (Figure 6.14). You won't find an IO/MEM wire on a modern CPU, as the process has changed and become more complex—but the concept hasn't changed one bit! The CPU sends commands to devices by placing patterns of ones and zeroes—I/O addresses—on the address bus.

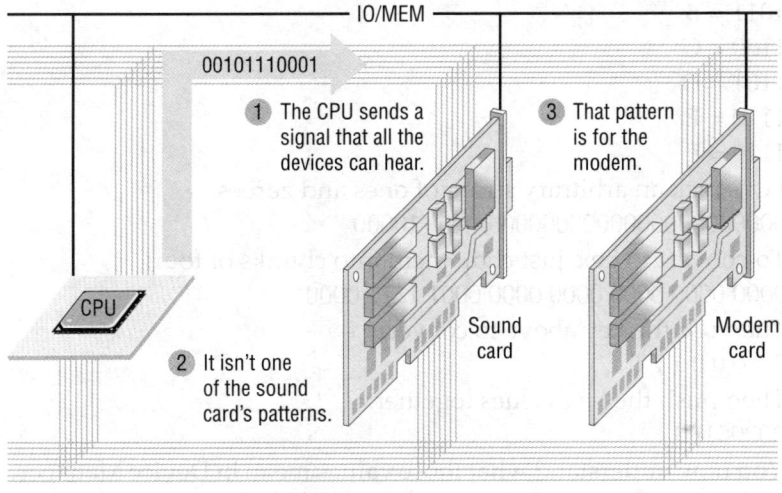

IO/MEM

00101110001

1 The CPU sends a signal that all the devices can hear.

3 That pattern is for the modem.

CPU

Sound card

Modem card

2 It isn't one of the sound card's patterns.

● **Figure 6.14** Sending out an I/O address on an old-fashioned IO/MEM wire

No two devices share the same I/O address because that would defeat the entire concept. To make sure no two devices share I/O addresses, all I/O addresses either are preset by standard (for example, all hard drive controllers use the same I/O addresses on every PC) or are set at boot by the operating system. You can see the I/O addresses for all the devices on your computer by going into Device Manager. Go to the View menu option and select *Resources by type.* Click on the plus sign directly to the left of the Input/output (IO) option to see a listing of I/O addresses, as shown in Figure 6.15.

Whoa! What's with all the letters and numbers? The address bus is always 32 bits (even if you have a 64-bit processor, the Northbridge only allows the first 32 bits to pass to the expansion slots), so instead of showing you the raw ones and zeroes, Device Manager shows you the I/O address ranges in hexadecimal. Don't know hex? No worries— **hexadecimal** is just quick shorthand for representing the strings of ones and zeroes—*binary*—that you *do* know. One hex character is used to represent four binary characters. Here's the key:

0000 = 0
0001 = 1
0010 = 2
0011 = 3
0100 = 4
0101 = 5
0110 = 6
0111 = 7
1000 = 8
1001 = 9
1010 = A

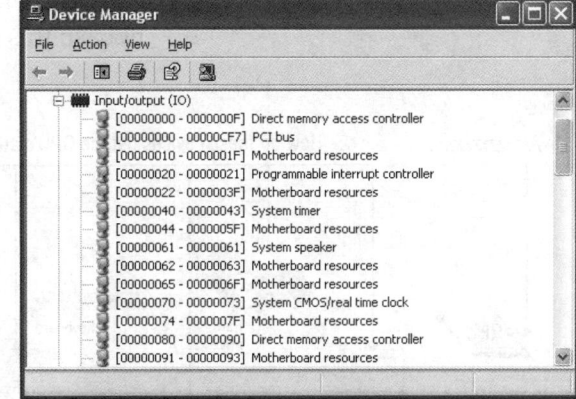

● **Figure 6.15** Viewing resources by type, with I/O addresses expanded

1011 = B
1100 = C
1101 = D
1110 = E
1111 = F

Let's pick an arbitrary string of ones and zeroes:

00000000000000000000000111110000

To convert to hex, just chop them into chunks of four:

0000 0000 0000 0000 0000 0001 1111 0000

Then use the key above to convert:

0 0 0 0 0 1 F 0

Then push the hex values together:

000001F0

You now understand what those values mean in Device Manager. Scroll down until you find the "[000001F0 - 000001F7] Primary IDE Channel" setting. Notice that there are two I/O addresses listed. These show the entire range of I/O addresses for this device; the more complex the device, the more I/O addresses it uses. Address ranges are generally referred to by the first value in the range, commonly known as the I/O base address.

Here are the most important items to remember about I/O addresses. First, every device on your PC has an I/O address. Without it, the CPU wouldn't have a way to send a device commands! Second, I/O addresses are configured automatically—you just plug in a device and it works. Third, no two devices should share I/O addresses. The system handles configuration, so this is done automatically.

All I/O addresses only use the last 16 bits (they all start with 0000). Sixteen bits makes 2^{16} = 65,536 I/O address ranges—plenty for even the most modern PCs. Should PCs begin to need more I/O addresses in the future, the current I/O addressing system is ready!

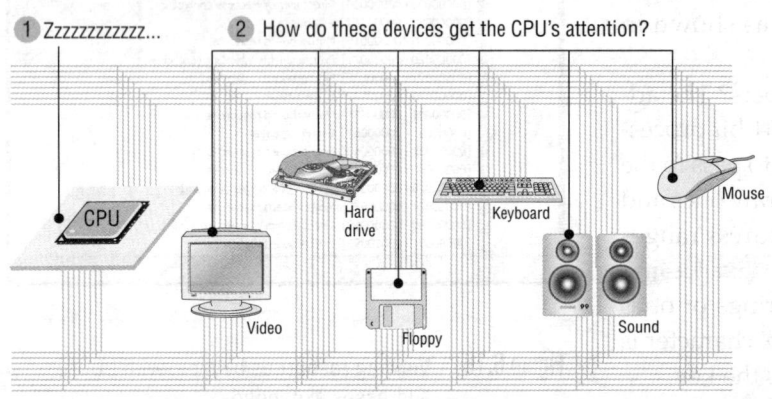

① Zzzzzzzzzzzz...   ② How do these devices get the CPU's attention?

CPU
Hard drive
Keyboard
Mouse
Video
Floppy
Sound

• **Figure 6.16**   How do devices tell the CPU they need attention?

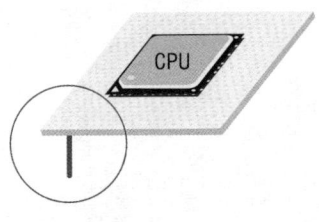

CPU

• **Figure 6.17**   The INT wire

Interrupt Requests

Between the standardized expansion bus connections and BIOS using I/O addressing, the CPU can now communicate with all of the devices inside the computer, but a third and final hurdle remains. I/O addressing enables the CPU to talk to devices, but how does a device tell the CPU it needs attention? How does the mouse tell the CPU that it has moved, for example, or how does the keyboard tell the CPU that somebody just pressed the J key? The PC needs some kind of mechanism to tell the CPU to stop doing whatever it is doing and talk to a particular device (Figure 6.16). This mechanism is called *interruption*.

Every CPU in the PC world has an INT (interrupt) wire, shown in Figure 6.17. If a device puts voltage on this wire, the CPU will stop what it is doing and deal with the interrupting device. Suppose you have a PC with only one peripheral, a keyboard that directly connects to the INT wire. If the user presses the J key, the keyboard charges the INT wire. The CPU temporarily stops running the browser (or whatever program is active) and runs the necessary BIOS routine to query the keyboard.

This would be fine if the computer had only one device. As you know, however, PCs have many devices, and almost all of them need to interrupt the CPU at some point. So the PC needs some kind of "traffic cop" to act as an intermediary between all the devices and the CPU's INT wire. This traffic cop chip, called the **I/O Advanced Programmable Interrupt Controller (IOAPIC)**, uses special interrupt wires that run to all devices on the expansion bus (Figure 6.18).

If a device wants to get the CPU's attention, it lights the interrupt wires with a special pattern of ones and zeroes just for that device. The IOAPIC then interrupts the CPU. The CPU queries the IOAPIC to see which device interrupted, and then it begins to communicate with the device over the address bus (Figure 6.19).

These unique patterns of ones and zeroes manifest themselves as something called **interrupt requests (IRQs)**. Before IOAPICs, IRQs were actual wires leading to the previous generation of traffic cops, called PICs. It's easy to see if your system has a PIC or an IOAPIC. Go into Device Manager and select Interrupt request (IRQ).

Figure 6.20 shows 24 IRQs, numbered 0 through 23, making this an IOAPIC system. IRQ 9 is special—this IRQ is assigned to the controller itself and is the IOAPIC's connection to the CPU. If you look closely, you'll also notice that some IRQs aren't listed. These are unused or "open" IRQs. If you add another device to the system,

IOAPIC functions are usually built into the Southbridge.

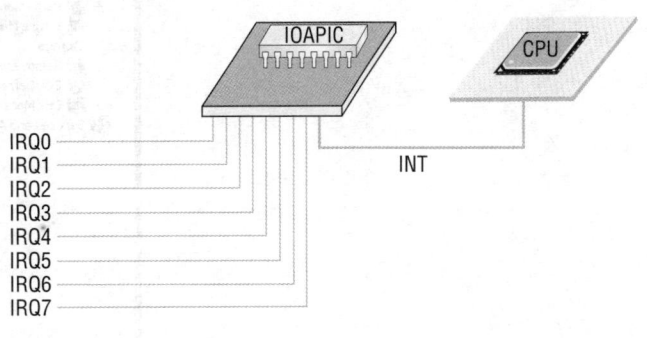

• **Figure 6.18**   Eight interrupt wires (IRQs) run from the expansion bus to the IOAPIC.

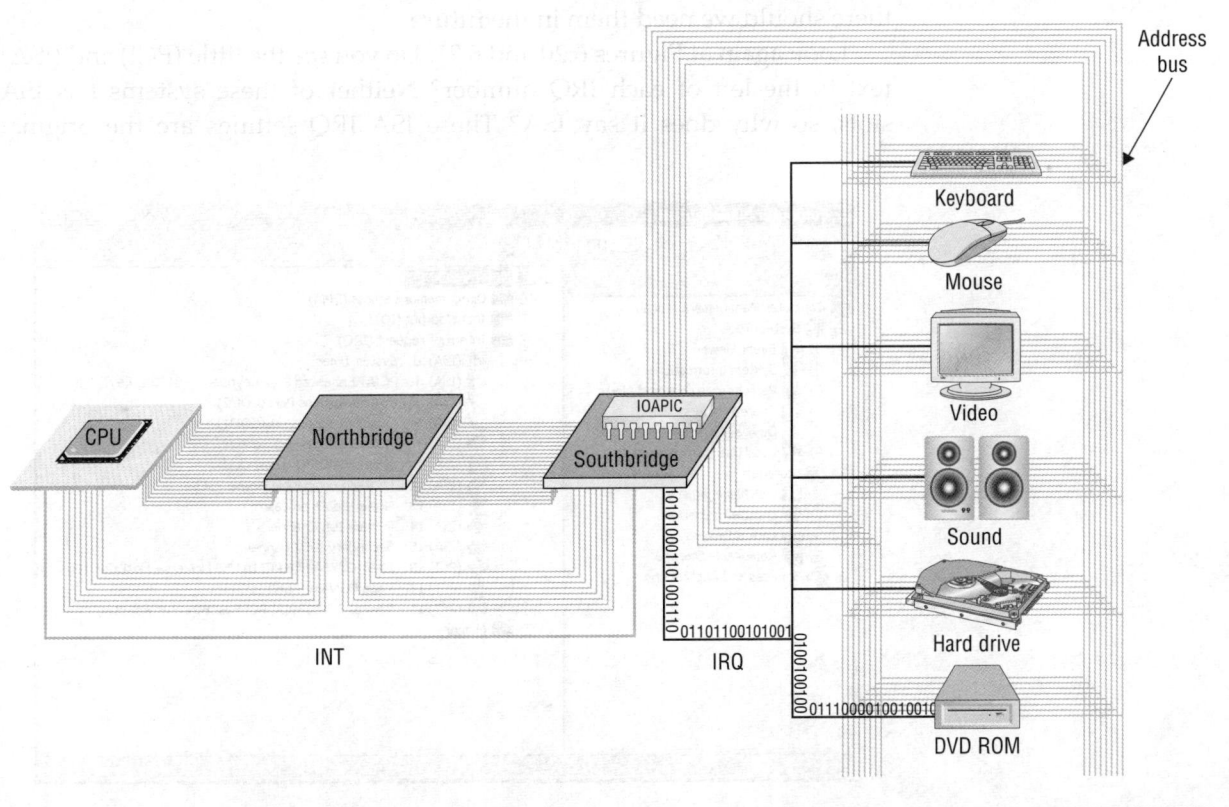

• **Figure 6.19**   IOAPIC at work

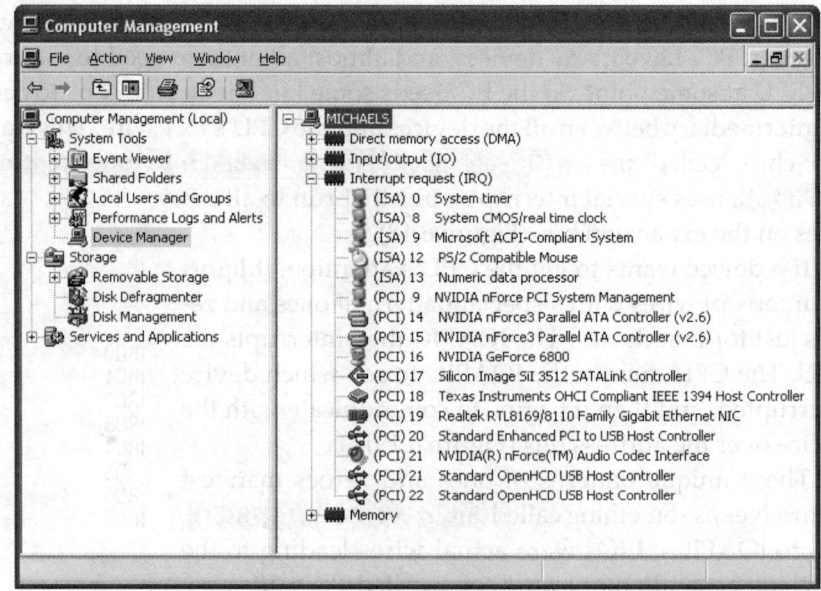

Figure 6.20   IRQs in an IOAPIC system

the new device will take up one of these unused IRQs. Now look at the older PIC system in Figure 6.21—note that it only shows 16 IRQs.

Don't freak out if you have a PIC system—they work just fine, but with fewer IRQs. As of now, very few systems take advantage of the extra IRQs provided by IOAPIC systems. But like the extra I/O addresses, they are there should we need them in the future.

Look again at Figures 6.20 and 6.21. Do you see the little (PCI) and (ISA) text to the left of each IRQ number? Neither of these systems has ISA slots, so why does it say ISA? These ISA IRQ settings are the original

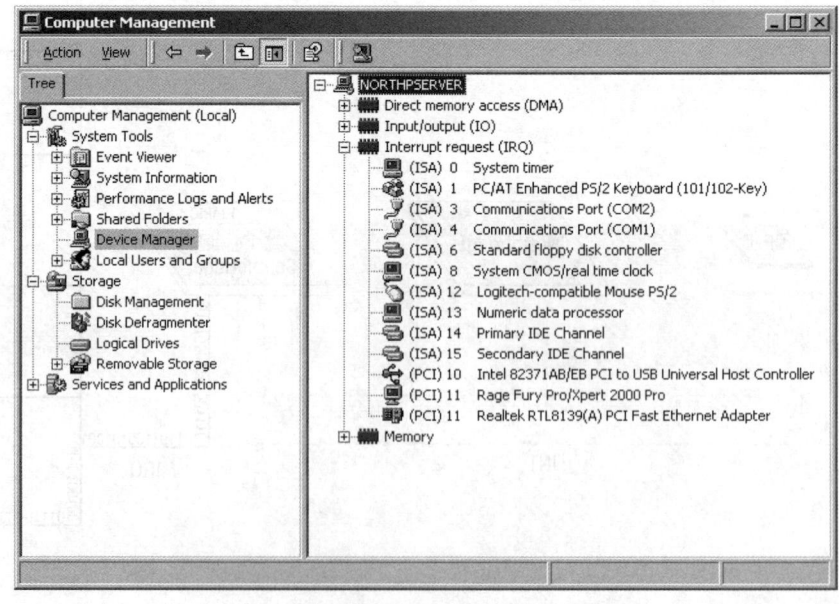

Figure 6.21   IRQs in a PIC system

IRQ numbers defined for these devices a long time ago. For backward compatibility with older equipment and older programs, your system makes these classically ISA devices look as though they use the old-style IRQs. As soon as the last few old devices go away, Microsoft will most likely remove these ISA values. What's interesting here is that you can still manually adjust the resources for a few of the old ISA devices, in particular the serial ports and the parallel ports. Let's look at the last serious vestige of the "bad old days" on your PC: COM and LPT ports.

COM and LPT Ports

When the PC first came out, every device had to have its I/O addresses and IRQ manually configured. How you did this varied from device to device: you moved jumpers, turned dials, or ran weird configuration programs. It was never easy. IBM tried to make configuration easier by creating preset I/O address and IRQ combinations for the serial and parallel ports, because they were the most commonly used ports on the original PC. These preset combinations were called **COM ports** for serial connections and **LPT ports** for parallel ports. Table 6.1 lists the early preset combinations of I/O addresses and IRQs.

 The term "COM" for serial ports came from "communication," and the term "LPT" for parallel ports came from "line printer."

Notice that the four COM ports share two IRQs. In the old days, if two devices shared an IRQ, the system instantly locked up. The lack of available IRQs in early systems led IBM to double up the IRQs for the serial devices, creating one of the few exceptions to the rule that no two devices could share IRQs. You could share an IRQ between two devices, but only if one of the devices would never actually access the IRQ. You'd see this with a dedicated fax/modem card, for example, which has a single phone line connected to a single card that has two different functions. The CPU needed distinct sets of I/O addresses for fax commands and modem commands, but as there was only the one modem doing both jobs, it needed only a single IRQ.

Direct Memory Access

CPUs do a lot of work. They run the BIOS, operating system, and applications. CPUs handle interrupts and I/O addresses. CPUs also deal with one other item: data. CPUs constantly move data between devices and RAM. CPUs move files from the hard drive to RAM. They move print jobs from RAM to laser printers, and they move images from scanners to RAM, just to name a very few examples of this RAM-to-device-and-back process.

Moving all this data is obviously necessary, but it is a simple task—the CPU has better things to do with its power and time. Moreover, with all of the caches and such on today's CPUs, the system spends most of its time waiting around doing nothing

Table 6.1	COM and LPT Assignments	
Port	**I/O Base Address**	**IRQ**
COM1	03F8	4
COM2	02F8	3
COM3	03E8	4
COM4	02E8	3
LPT1	0378	7
LPT2	0278	5

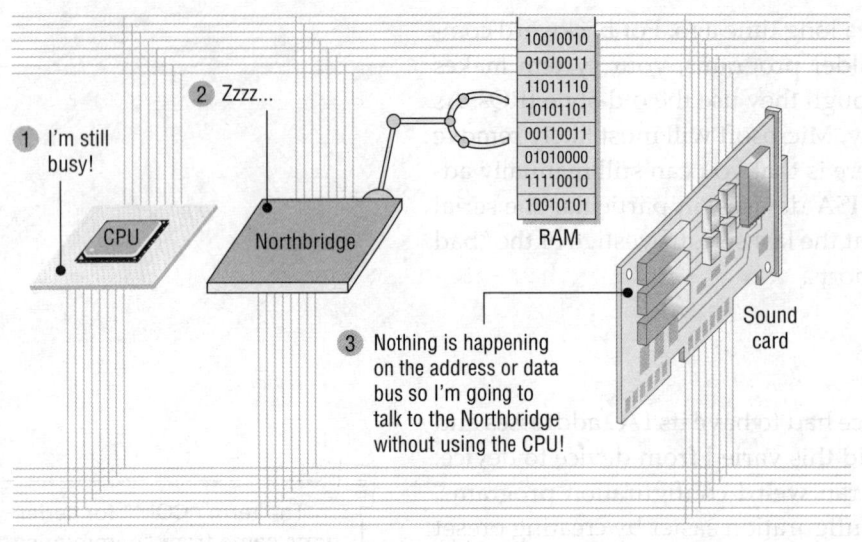

Figure 6.22   Why not talk to the chipset directly?

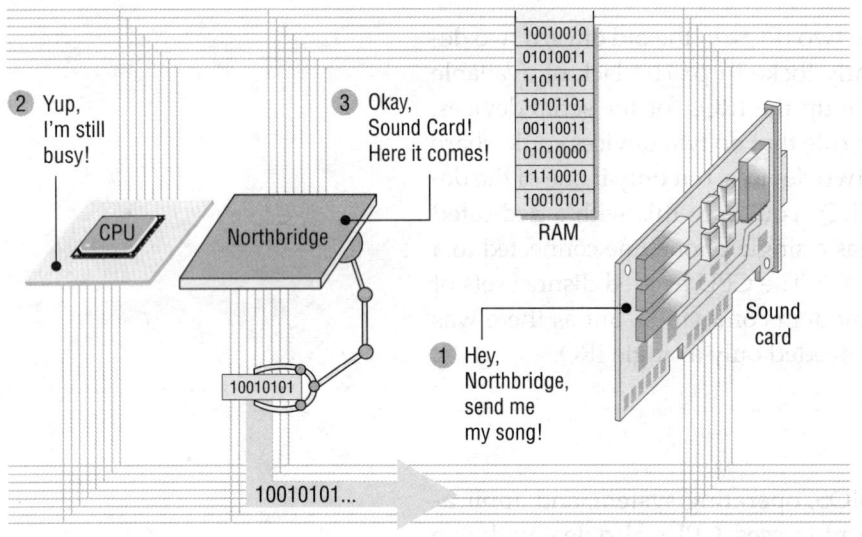

Figure 6.23   DMA in action

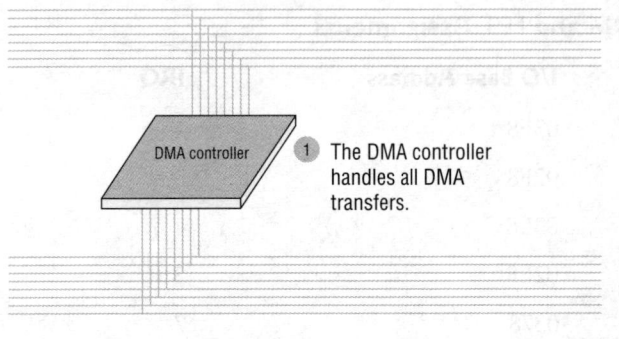

Figure 6.24   The DMA controller

while the CPU handles some internal calculation. Add these facts together and the question arises: Why not make devices that access memory directly, without involving the CPU (Figure 6.22)? The process of accessing memory without using the CPU is called **direct memory access (DMA)**.

DMA is very common, and is excellent for creating background sounds in games and for moving data from floppy and hard drives into RAM (Figure 6.23).

Nice as it may sound, the concept of DMA as described above has a problem—there's only one expansion bus. What if more than one device wants to use DMA? What keeps these devices from stomping on the external data bus all at the same time? Plus, what if the CPU suddenly needs the data bus? How can you stop the device using DMA so the CPU, which should have priority, can access the bus? To deal with this, IBM added another traffic cop.

The *DMA controller*, which seasoned techs often call the *8237* after its old chip name, controls all DMA functions (Figure 6.24). DMA is similar to IRQ handling in that the DMA controller assigns numbers, called DMA channels, to enable devices to request use of the DMA. The DMA also handles the data passing from peripherals to RAM and vice versa. This takes necessary but simple work away from the CPU, so the CPU can spend time doing more productive work.

The DMA chip sends data along the external data bus when the CPU is busy with internal calculations and not using the external data bus. This is perfectly acceptable because the CPU accesses the external data bus only about five percent of the time on a modern CPU.

The DMA just described is called "classic DMA"; it was the first and for a long time the only way to do DMA. Classic DMA is dying out because it's very slow and only supports 16-bit data transfers, a silly waste in a world of much wider buses. On most systems, only floppy drives still use classic DMA.

All systems still support classic DMA, but most devices today that use DMA do so without going through the DMA controller. These devices are known as bus masters. **Bus mastering** devices have circuitry that enables them to watch for other devices accessing the external data bus; they can detect a potential conflict and get out of the way on their own. Bus mastering has become extremely popular in hard drives. All modern hard drives take advantage of bus mastering. Hard drive bus mastering is hidden under terms such as *Ultra DMA*, and for the most part is totally automatic and invisible. See Chapter 9, "Implementing Hard Drives," for more details on bus mastering hard drives.

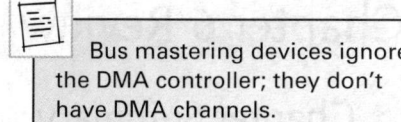

Bus mastering devices ignore the DMA controller; they don't have DMA channels.

If you want to see your DMA usage, head back to Device Manager and change the view to *Resources by type.* Click on Direct memory access (DMA) and you'll see something like Figure 6.25. This system has only two DMA channels: one for the floppy drive and one for the connection to the CPU.

One interesting note to DMA is that neither PCI nor PCIe supports DMA, so you'll never find a DMA device that snaps into these expansion buses. A hard drive, floppy drive, or any other device that still wants to use DMA must do so through onboard connections. Sure, you can find hard drive and floppy drive cards, but they're not using DMA.

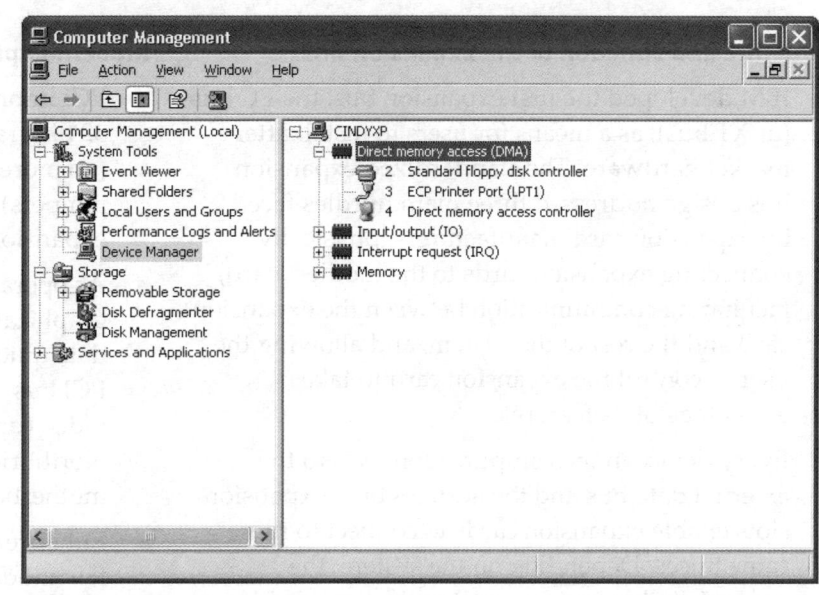

• **Figure 6.25**   DMA settings in Device Manager

Memory Addresses

Some expansion cards need memory addresses, just like the system RAM. There are two reasons a card may need memory addresses. First, a card may have onboard RAM that the CPU needs to address. Second, a few cards come with an onboard ROM, the so-called adapter or option ROM you read about in Chapter 5. In either of these situations, the RAM or ROM must steal memory addresses away from the main system RAM to enable the CPU to access the RAM or ROM. This process is called **memory addressing**. You can see memory addresses assigned to expansion card by clicking on Memory in Device Manager when viewing resources by type.

The key fact for techs is that, just like I/O addresses, IRQs, and DMA channels, memory addressing is fully automatic and no longer an issue.

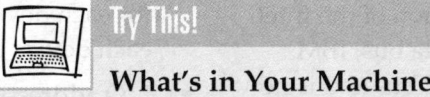

Try This!

What's in Your Machine?

If you haven't already, open up Device Manager and check out the resources assigned to your devices. Does anything use an IRQ? How many devices use the same IRQ? What about memory addresses? Where are all those devices located?

Chapter 6 Review

■ Chapter Summary

After reading this chapter and completing the exercises, you should understand the following about the expansion bus.

Structure and Function of the Expansion Bus

■ IBM developed the first expansion bus, the PC bus (or XT bus), as a means for users to install after-market hardware. The standardized expansion bus design addressed three main hurdles faced by expansion card manufacturers: physically connecting expansion cards to the motherboard, facilitating communication between the expansion card and the rest of the system, and allowing the user to control the expansion card to take advantage of its features.

■ Every device in the computer connects to the external data bus and the address bus. Expansion slots enable expansion cards to connect to these same buses. Depending on the system, the expansion slots may connect to the Southbridge or the Northbridge. Many systems have more than one type of expansion bus with slots connecting to both the Southbridge and the Northbridge. It is the chipset that extends the address bus and data bus to the expansion slots.

■ Expansion buses run at a standardized speed, depending on the type of expansion bus. This speed, which is much slower than the frontside bus, is dictated by the expansion bus crystal. The chipset uses wait states and buffers to compensate for the difference in speed between the expansion and frontside buses.

■ The original IBM PCs ran an 8088 CPU with an 8-bit external data bus at a speed of 4.77 MHz, which was actually slower than the 7-MHz expansion bus. With the introduction of the Intel 286 CPU and its 16-bit external data bus, IBM developed what was called the AT bus and is now known as the ISA bus. The ISA expansion bus was 16 bits and ran at about 7 MHz. ISA cards required tedious manual configuration.

■ The limitations of the ISA bus led to the development of other buses including MCA, EISA, VL-Bus, and the PCI bus.

Modern Expansion Buses

■ PCI improved upon ISA in several ways. It was 32 bits, ran at 33 MHz, and was self-configuring (no more manual configuration of expansion card jumpers). Additionally, it could coexist with other expansion buses.

■ As operating systems like Windows became more graphically intense, the demand for sending video data quickly was too much for the ISA or standard PCI bus. The AGP slot is a special PCI slot for video cards, with a direct connection to the Northbridge. You can easily find the AGP slot on a motherboard—a lone slot that's brown in color.

■ Enhancements to the PCI bus paved the way for a few modern variations. PCI-X is 64 bits wide, backward-compatible with PCI, and available in a variety of speeds up to 533 MHz. Mini-PCI is designed for laptops with an emphasis on low power consumption and a small, flat physical design. Finally, PCIe, with its point-to-point serial connection, touts speeds as high as 16 Gbps.

System Resources

■ Devices in a computer system communicate via the four system resources: I/O addresses, IRQs, DMAs, and memory addresses. Not all devices use all four system resources. Earlier systems required manual configuration of each device's system resources through jumpers, DIP switches, dials, or software. Modern systems feature plug and play, which automatically configures system resources for each device. The system resources assigned to each device can be seen in Device Manager.

■ I/O addresses enable the CPU to send commands to devices. These addresses are configured automatically, and no two devices may share an I/O address. A single device may be assigned a range of I/O addresses; the first address in the range is called the I/O base address.

- IRQs enable devices to signal the CPU that they need attention. Before reaching the CPU, all interrupts pass through the I/O advanced programmable interrupt controller, which manages all the incoming interrupts and forwards them to the CPU. In older systems, scarce IRQs and manual resource allocation meant that IRQ conflicts (and subsequent system lockups) were common. This is not a problem in modern systems, which have more IRQs and handle them automatically to avoid such conflicts.

- COM and LPT ports are simply presets of an IRQ–I/O address combination developed to make configuration of common devices easier. COM ports are for serial connections and LPT ports are for parallel connections.

- DMA enables devices to communicate with RAM without involving the CPU. The DMA controller sits between the devices and RAM and handles the DMA requests much like IRQ requests are handled. Newer systems use a type of DMA called bus mastering, which works without the need of a DMA controller.

- Memory addresses are used by devices that have either their own RAM (like video cards) or ROM (like the option ROM discussed in Chapter 5). When devices have their own RAM or ROM, they get memory addresses just like system RAM so the CPU can access their onboard memory.

Key Terms

accelerated graphics port (AGP) *(153)*
bus mastering *(163)*
COM port *(161)*
direct memory access (DMA) *(162)*
expansion bus *(147)*
expansion bus crystal *(149)*
expansion slots *(147)*
hexadecimal *(157)*

I/O address *(156)*
I/O addressing *(156)*
I/O Advanced Programmable Interrupt Controller (IOAPIC) *(159)*
I/O base address *(158)*
Industry Standard Architecture (ISA) *(151)*
interrupt request (IRQ) *(159)*

LPT ports *(161)*
memory addressing *(163)*
Mini-PCI *(153)*
PC bus *(150)*
PCI Express (PCIe) *(154)*
PCI-X *(153)*
peripheral component interconnect (PCI) *(152)*
system resources *(156)*

Key Term Quiz

Use the Key Terms list to complete the sentences that follow. Not all terms will be used.

1. The _____ bus was designed for laptop computers.

2. A shorthand system for binary numbers is called _____.

3. The _____ is an expansion slot, normally colored brown, that is used exclusively for a video card.

4. The CPU uses the _____, a unique pattern of ones and zeroes on the address bus, to communicate with a device.

5. The most common bus on today's computers, whether PC or Apple Macintosh, is the flexible _____.

6. Parallel ports that have been assigned a particular IRQ and I/O address, traditionally for a printer, are called _____.

7. A device uses its _____ to get the attention of the CPU.

8. _____ devices access RAM directly without passing through a DMA controller.

9. A(n) _____ is a preset combination of an IRQ and I/O address.

10. _____ is the newest and fastest expansion bus in use today with speeds up to 16 Gbps.

Multiple-Choice Quiz

1. Which of the following enables you to add more devices to a computer? (Select the best answer.)
   A. Device bus
   B. Expansion bus
   C. Peripheral bus
   D. Yellow bus

2. John argues that expansion slot wires always connect to the Southbridge. Is he correct?
   A. Yes, expansion slots always connect to the Southbridge.
   B. No, expansion slots always connect to the Northbridge.
   C. No, expansion slots connect to both the Northbridge and the Southbridge.
   D. No, expansion slots connect to the Northbridge in some systems and the Southbridge in others.

3. Which of the following devices sets the speed for expansion slots?
   A. Component crystal
   B. Expansion bus crystal
   C. Expansion slot crystal
   D. Peripheral crystal

4. You could find 16-bit ISA slots on which of these buses?
   A. AT bus
   B. BT bus
   C. PC bus
   D. XT bus

5. What advantages did PCI have over ISA? (Select two.)
   A. Faster (33-MHz versus 7-MHz)
   B. Longer (2 m versus 1 m)
   C. Shorter (1 m versus 2 m)
   D. Wider (32-bit versus 16-bit)

6. Which of the following slots offer 64-bit-wide data transfers? (Select the two most common.)
   A. AGP
   B. PCI
   C. PCIe
   D. PCI-X

7. What's the minimum number of I/O addresses a device will have?
   A. One
   B. Two
   C. Four
   D. Eight

8. Which of the following slots features serial data transfers?
   A. AGP
   B. PCI
   C. PCIe
   D. PCI-X

9. How many IRQs does the typical device use?
   A. One
   B. Two
   C. Four
   D. Eight

10. What are the standard system resource assignments for COM1?
   A. I/O address 03F8 and IRQ3
   B. I/O address 03F8 and IRQ4
   C. I/O address 02F8 and IRQ3
   D. I/O address 02F8 and IRQ4

11. Which of these devices is likely to still use DMA?
   A. USB flash drive
   B. Floppy drive
   C. Hard drive
   D. CD-ROM drive

12. Which type of expansion card requires manual configuration?
   A. ISA
   B. PCIe
   C. AGP
   D. DMA

13. How can you visually discern between PCI and AGP slots?
   A. A motherboard typically has more AGP slots than PCI slots.
   B. AGP slots are brown whereas PCI slots are white.

C. AGP slots are white whereas PCI slots are brown.

D. You can't tell the difference just by looking.

14. Which ports share a common IRQ?

   A. COM1 and COM2 share IRQ3.

   B. COM1 and COM3 share IRQ3.

   C. COM1 and COM2 share IRQ4.

   D. COM1 and COM3 share IRQ4.

15. Lloyd argues that Ultra DMA hard drives actually use bus mastering. Is he correct?

A. Yes, Ultra DMA is another term for bus mastering.

B. No, Ultra DMA simply uses DMA addresses above 4.

C. No, Ultra DMA hard drives use a point-to-point serial connection to communicate with the DMA controller.

D. No, there is no such thing as an Ultra DMS hard drive.

Essay Quiz

1. Although today's computers use plug and play to assign system resources automatically, CompTIA still expects you to know about system resources. Why is this knowledge important? Briefly explain two scenarios where your knowledge of system resources may help solve computer problems.

2. Write a short essay comparing PCI and PCIe. Describe the interfaces and speeds, and also explain the benefits offered by both. Why is PCI still important? What's so special about PCIe?

Lab Projects

• Lab Project 6.1

As technologies improve, manufacturers are continually upgrading their products. Use the Internet to find three prebuilt computer systems, each from a different manufacturer. (You may want to try www.dell.com, www.hp.com, www.gateway.com, www.alienware.com, or www.voodoopc.com

to name a few.) Do your three systems offer the same expansion buses? Do any support ISA? PCI? PCI-X? PCIe? If one supports PCIe, what version or speeds does it support? Do any systems support AGP?

Understanding Motherboards

"Man is most nearly himself
when he achieves the seriousness
of a child at play."

—HERACLITUS, CIRCA 500 B.C.

In this chapter, you will learn how to

- **Explain how motherboards work**
- **Identify the types of motherboards**
- **Explain chipset varieties**

The **motherboard** provides the foundation for the personal computer. Every piece of hardware, from the CPU to the lowliest expansion card, directly or indirectly plugs into the motherboard. The motherboard contains the wires—called **traces**—that make up the different buses of the system. It holds the vast majority of the ports used by the peripherals and it distributes the power from the power supply (Figure 7.1). Without the motherboard, you literally have no PC.

Historical/Conceptual

■ How Motherboards Work

Three variable and interrelated characteristics define modern motherboards: form factor, chipset, and components. The `form factor` determines the physical size of the motherboard as well as the general location of components and ports. The `chipset` defines the type of processor and RAM required for the motherboard, and determines to a degree the built-in devices supported by a motherboard, including the expansion slots. Finally, the built-in components determine the core functionality of the system.

Any good tech should be able to make a recommendation to a client about a particular motherboard simply by perusing the specs. Because the motherboard determines function, expansion, and stability for the whole PC, it's essential that you know your motherboards!

Form Factors

Form factors are industry standardized shapes and layouts that enable motherboards to work with cases and power supplies. A single form factor applies to all three components. All motherboards come in a basic rectangular or square shape, for example, but vary in overall size and the layout of built-in components (Figure 7.2). You need to install a motherboard in a case designed to fit it, so the ports and slot openings on the back fit correctly.

Tech Tip

Layers of the PCB

Modern motherboards—officially printed circuit boards (PCBs)—come in multiple layers and thus mask some of their complexity. You can see some of the traces on the board, but every motherboard is two or more layers thick. There's a veritable highway of wires in the layers, carrying data and commands back and forth between CPU, Northbridge, RAM, and peripherals. The layered structure enables multiple wires to send data without their signals interfering with each other. The layered approach allows the manufacturer to add complexity and additional components to the board without having to extend the overall length and width of the board. Shorter traces also allow signals to travel faster than they would if the wires were longer, as would be necessary if motherboards did not use layers. The multiple layers also add strength to the board itself, helping prevent it from bending when used.

● **Figure 7.1**   Traces visible beneath the CPU socket on a motherboard

● **Figure 7.2**   Typical motherboard

The power supply and the motherboard need matching connectors, and different form factors define different connections. Given that the term "form factor" applies to the case, motherboard, and power supply—the three parts of the PC most responsible for moving air around inside the PC—the form factor also defines how the air moves around in the case.

To perform motherboard upgrades and provide knowledgeable recommendations to clients, techs need to know their form factors. The PC industry has adopted—and dropped—a number of form factors over the years with names such as AT, ATX, BTX, and others. Let's start with the granddaddy of all PC form factors, AT.

AT Form Factor

The `AT` form factor (Figure 7.3), invented by IBM in the early 1980s, was the predominant form factor for motherboards through the mid-1990s. AT is now obsolete. The AT type of motherboard had a large keyboard plug in the same relative spot on the motherboard, and it had a unique, split power socket called `P8/P9`.

The AT motherboard had a few size variations, ranging from large to very large (Figure 7.4). The original AT motherboard was huge, around 12 inches wide by 13 inches deep. PC technology was new and needed a lot of space for the various chips necessary to run the components of the PC, such as the keyboard.

The single greatest problem with AT motherboards was the lack of external ports. When PCs were first invented, the only devices plugged into the average PC were a monitor and a keyboard. That's what the AT was designed to handle—the only dedicated connector on an AT motherboard was the keyboard plug (Figure 7.5).

Over the years, the number of devices plugged into the back of the PC has grown tremendously. Your average PC today has a keyboard,

● **Figure 7.3**   AT-style motherboard

● **Figure 7.4**   AT motherboard (bottom) and Baby AT motherboard (top)

a mouse, a printer, some speakers, a monitor, and if your system's like mine, four to six USB devices connected to it at any given time. These added components created a demand for a new type of form factor, one with more dedicated connectors for more devices. Many attempts were made to create a new standard form factor. Invariably, these new form factors integrated dedicated connectors for at least the mouse and printer, and many even added connectors for video, sound, and phone lines.

One variation from the AT form factor that enjoyed a degree of success was the `slimline` form factor. The first slimline form factor was known as `LPX` (defined in some sources as *low profile extended*, although there's some disagreement). It was replaced by the `NLX` form factor. (NLX apparently stands for nothing, by the way. It's just a cool grouping of letters.) The LPX and NLX form factors met the demands of the slimline market by providing a central riser slot to enable the insertion of a special `riser card` (Figure 7.6). Expansion cards then fit into the riser card horizontally. Combining built-in connections with a riser card enabled manufacturers to produce PCs shorter than 4 inches.

The main problem with form factors like LPX and NLX was their inflexibility. Certainly, no problem occurred with dedicated connections for devices such as mice or printers, but the new form factors also added connectors for devices like video and sound—devices that

● **Figure 7.5**   Keyboard connector on the back of an AT motherboard

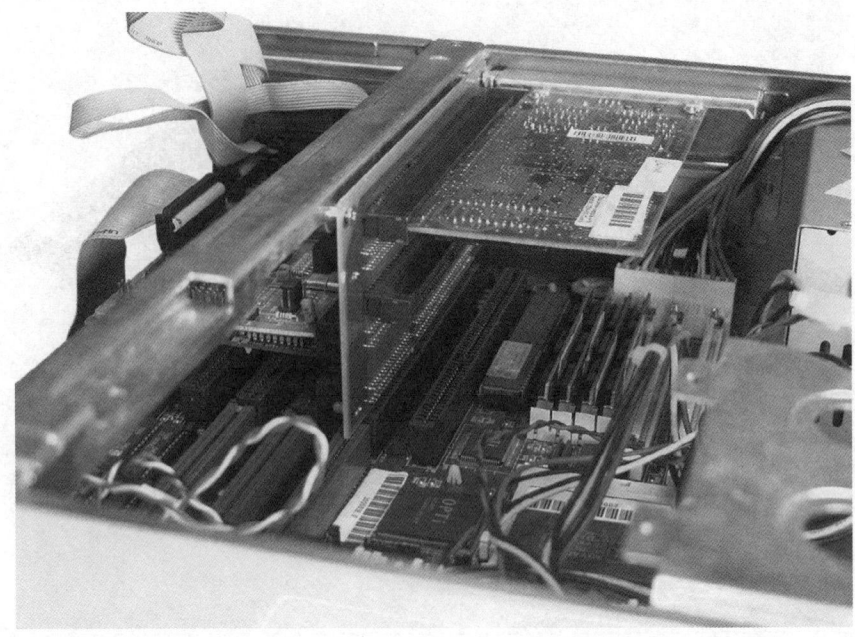

• **Figure 7.6**   Riser card on an older motherboard

were prone to obsolescence, making the motherboard out of date the moment a new type of video or sound card came into popularity.

Essentials

ATX Form Factor

There continued to be a tremendous demand for a new form factor—a form factor that had more standard connectors, but at the same time was flexible enough for possible changes in technology. This demand led to the creation of the ATX form factor in 1995 (Figure 7.7). ATX got off to a slow start, but by around 1998 ATX overtook AT to become the most common form factor used today.

Tech Tip

Soft Power

ATX motherboards use a feature called soft power. *This means that they can use software to turn the PC on and off. The physical manifestation of soft power is the power switch. Instead of the thick power cord used in AT systems, an ATX power switch is little more than a pair of small wires leading to the motherboard. We delve into this in more detail in Chapter 8, "Understanding PC Power."*

Cross Check

High-Speed CPUs and RAM

With the newly shortened wire lengths between CPU, Northbridge, and RAM, manufacturers could crank up at least that part of the motherboard speed. CPU and RAM manufacturers quickly took advantage of the new speed potential. Refer to Chapters 3 and 4, on "Understanding CPUs" and "Understanding RAM," respectively, and see if you can answer these questions.

1.   Which CPUs can take advantage of such speed increases?

2.   What type(s) of RAM can you put in those same systems to optimize the flow of data to the CPU?

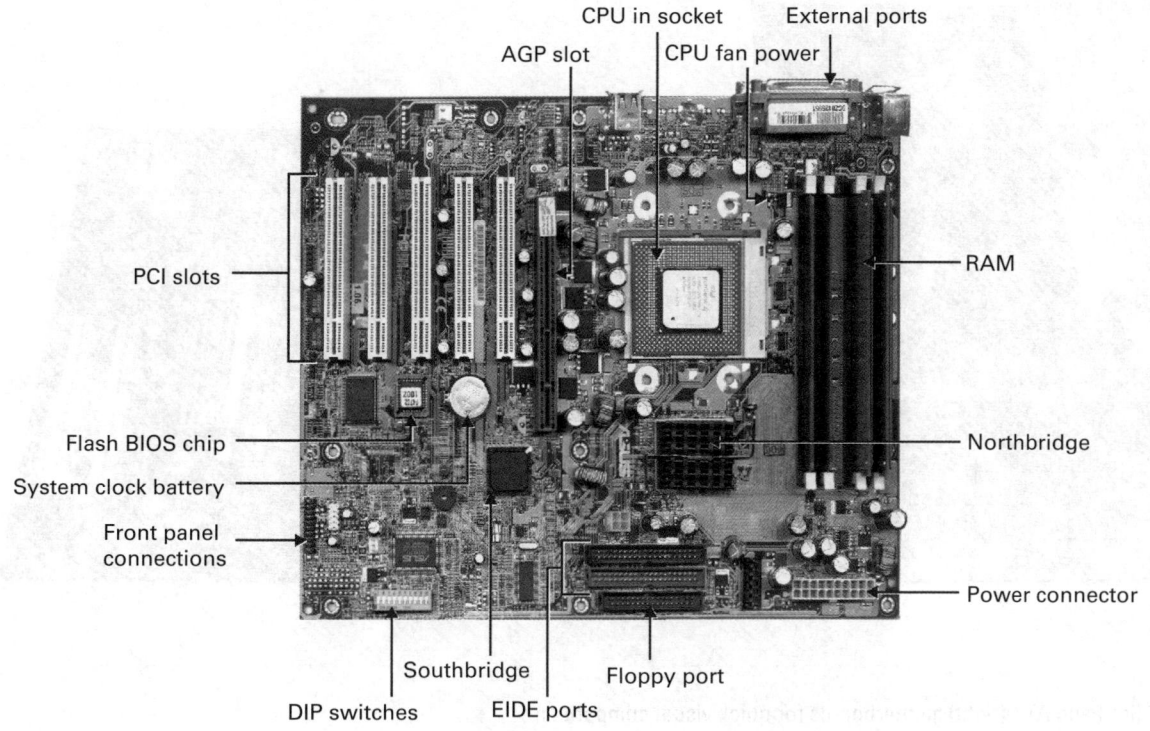

CPU in socket External ports
AGP slot CPU fan power
PCI slots
RAM
Flash BIOS chip
System clock battery
Northbridge
Front panel
connections
Power connector
Southbridge Floppy port
DIP switches EIDE ports

- **Figure 7.7** Early ATX motherboard

ATX is distinct from AT in the lack of an AT keyboard port, replaced with a rear panel that has all necessary ports built in. Note the mini-DIN (PS/2) keyboard and mouse ports in Figure 7.8, standard features on almost all ATX boards.

The ATX form factor includes many improvements over AT. The position of the power supply enables better air movement. The CPU and RAM are placed to enable easier access. Other improvements, such as placement of RAM closer to the Northbridge and CPU than on AT boards, offer users enhanced performance as well. The shorter the wires, the easier to shield them and make them capable of handling double or quadruple the clock speed of

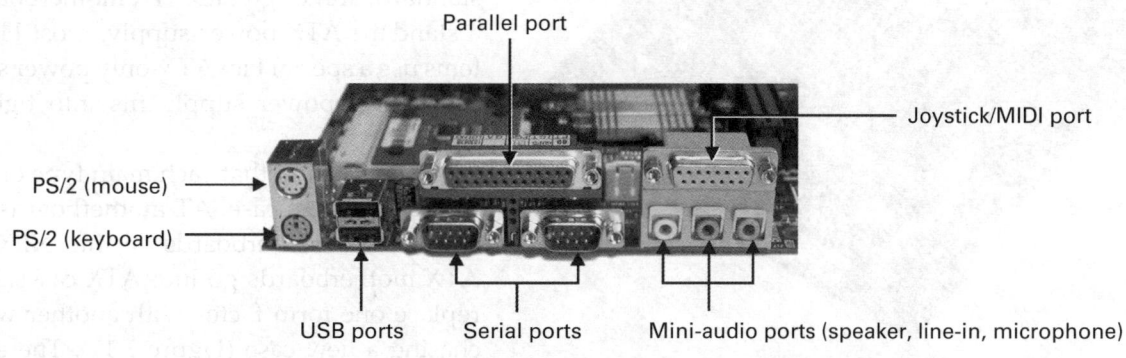

Parallel port
Joystick/MIDI port
PS/2 (mouse)
PS/2 (keyboard)
USB ports Serial ports Mini-audio ports (speaker, line-in, microphone)

- **Figure 7.8** ATX ports

Figure 7.9 AT (left) and ATX (right) motherboards for quick visual comparison

You'll find many techs and Web sites use the term *mini-ATX* to refer to motherboards smaller than a full ATX board. This is technically incorrect. The specifications for these small boards use only the terms *microATX* and *FlexATX*.

Figure 7.10 MicroATX

the motherboard. Figure 7.9 shows an AT and an ATX motherboard—note the radical differences in placement of internal connections.

The success of ATX has spawned two form factor subtypes for specialty uses. The **microATX** motherboard (Figure 7.10) floats in at a svelte 9.6 by 9.6 inches or about 30 percent smaller than standard ATX, yet still uses the standard ATX connections. A microATX motherboard fits into a standard ATX case or in the much smaller microATX cases. Note that not all microATX motherboards have the same physical size. You'll sometimes see microATX motherboards referred to with the Greek symbol for micro, as in µATX.

In 1999, Intel created a variant of the microATX called the FlexATX. **FlexATX** motherboards have maximum dimensions of just 9 by 7.5 inches, which makes them the smallest motherboards in the ATX standard. Although FlexATX motherboards can use a standard ATX power supply, most FlexATX systems use a special FlexATX-only power supply. This diminutive power supply fits into tight FlexATX cases.

Keep in mind that each main type of form factor requires its own case. AT motherboards go into AT cases, NLX motherboards go into NLX cases, and ATX motherboards go into ATX cases. You cannot replace one form factor with another without purchasing a new case (Figure 7.11). The exception to this rule is that larger form factor ATX cases can handle any smaller-sized form factor motherboards.

BTX Form Factor

Even though ATX addressed ventilation, faster CPUs and powerful graphics cards create phenomenal amounts of heat, motivating the PC industry to create the "coolest" new form factor used today—the Balanced Technology eXtended (BTX) form factor (Figure 7.12). BTX defines three subtypes: standard BTX, microBTX, and picoBTX, designed to replace ATX, microATX, and FlexATX, respectively.

At first glance, BTX looks like ATX, but notice that the I/O ports and the expansion slots have switched sides. You can't put a BTX motherboard in an ATX case! BTX does not change the power connection, so there's no such thing as a BTX power supply.

Everything in the BTX form factor is designed to improve cooling. BTX cases vent in cool air from the front and warm air out the back. CPUs are moved to the front of the motherboard so they get cool air coming in from the front of the case. BTX defines a special heat sink and fan assembly called the thermal unit. The thermal unit's fan blows the hot CPU air directly out the back of the case, as opposed to the ATX method of just blowing the air into the case.

• **Figure 7.11**   That's not going to fit!

Many manufacturers sell what they call "BTX power supplies." These are actually marketing gimmicks. See Chapter 8, "Understanding PC Power," for details.

• **Figure 7.12**   microBTX motherboard

Try This!

Motherboard Varieties

Motherboards come in a wide variety of form factors. Go to your local computer store and check out what is on display. Note the different features offered by ATX, microATX, and FlexATX (if any) motherboards.

1. Does the store still stock any AT motherboards?

2. What about NLX, BTX, or proprietary motherboards?

3. Did the clerk use tech slang and call the motherboards "mobos"? (It's what most of us call them outside of formal textbooks, after all!)

The BTX standard is clearly a much cooler option than ATX, but the PC industry tends to take its time when making big changes like moving to a new form factor. As a result, BTX has not yet made much of an impact in the industry, and BTX motherboards, cases, and thermal units are still fairly rare. BTX could take off to become the next big thing or disappear in a cloud of disinterest—only time will tell.

Proprietary Form Factors

Several major PC makers, including Dell and Sony, make motherboards that work only with their cases. These *proprietary* motherboards enable these companies to create systems that stand out from the generic ones and, not coincidently, push you to get service and upgrades from their authorized dealers. Some of the features you'll see in proprietary systems are riser boards like you see with the NLX form factor—part of a motherboard separate from the main one, but connected by a cable of some sort—and unique power connections. Proprietary motherboards drive techs crazy as replacement parts tend to cost more and are not readily available.

Chipset

Every motherboard has a chipset. The chipset determines the type of processor the motherboard accepts, the type and capacity of RAM, and what sort of internal and external devices the motherboard supports. As you learned in earlier chapters, the chips in a PC's chipset serve as electronic interfaces through which the CPU, RAM, and input/output devices interact. Chipsets vary in feature, performance, and stability, so they factor hugely in the purchase or recommendation of a particular motherboard. Good techs know their chipsets!

Because the chipset facilitates communication between the CPU and other devices in the system, its component chips are relatively centrally located on the motherboard (Figure 7.13). Most modern chipsets are composed of two primary chips—the Northbridge and the Southbridge.

• **Figure 7.13**   Northbridge (under the fan) and Southbridge (lower right, labeled VIA)

The Northbridge chip on Intel-based motherboards helps the CPU work with RAM, as mentioned in earlier chapters. On AMD-based motherboards, the Northbridge provides the communication with the video card, rather than memory, because the memory controller is built into the CPU. Current Northbridge chips do a lot and thus get pretty hot, so they get their own heat sink and fan assembly (Figure 7.14).

The Southbridge handles some expansion devices and mass storage drives, such as hard drives. Most Southbridge chips don't need extra cooling, leaving the chip exposed or passively cooled with only a heat sink. This makes the Southbridge a great place to see the manufacturer of the chipset, such as Intel (Figure 7.15).

Most motherboards support very old technologies such as floppy drives, infrared connections, parallel ports, and modems. Although supporting these old devices was once part of the Southbridge's job, hardly any modern chipsets still support these devices. Motherboard manufacturers add a third chip called the **Super I/O chip** to handle these chores. Figure 7.16 shows a typical Super I/O chip.

The system ROM chip provides part of the BIOS for the chipset, but only a barebones, generic level of support. The chipset still needs support for the rest of the things it can do. So, how do expansion devices get BIOS? Software drivers, of course, and the same holds true for modern chipsets. You have to load the proper drivers for the specific OS to support all the features of today's chipsets. Without software drivers, you'll never create a stable, fully functional PC. All motherboards ship with a CD-ROM disc with drivers,

● **Figure 7.14**   Heat sink and fan on a Northbridge

   Super I/O chips work with chipsets but are not part of the chipset. Motherboard makers purchase them separately from chipsets.

● **Figure 7.15**   An Intel NH82801 Southbridge chip on a motherboard

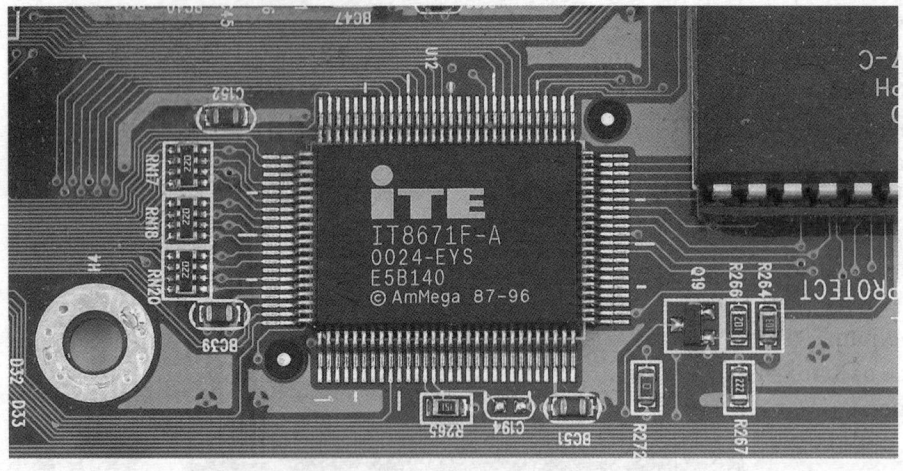

• **Figure 7.16**   Super I/O chip on ASUS motherboard

Tech Tip

AMD and ATI

Due to the purchase by AMD of chipset (and video card) maker ATI in 2006, the chipset field has the potential to change again. ATI makes a nice line of mobile and desktop chipsets. Backed by AMD's muscle, the combined companies might give VIA and NVIDIA a run for their money. Only time will tell, but it's something for informed CompTIA A+ certified techs to watch.

In an average year, chipset makers collectively produce around one hundred new chipset models for the PC market.

support programs, and extra special goodies such as anti-virus software (Figure 7.17).

There are a limited number of chipset makers. Both AMD and Intel make chipsets, but although they may control the CPU market, they have some serious competition in the chipset market. Two third-party chipset makers, VIA Technologies and NVIDIA Corporation, make some very popular chipsets. Motherboard manufacturers incorporate the chipsets into motherboards that match the feature set of the chipset. Some of the companies produce chipsets designed for both Intel and AMD CPUs, whereas others choose one or the other company to support. Chipset companies rise and fall every few years, with one company seeming to hold the hot position for a while until another company comes along to unseat them.

Chipset makers don't always use the terms Northbridge and Southbridge. Chipsets for AMD-based motherboards tend to use the terms, but Intel-based motherboards prefer to use the terms Memory Controller Hub (MCH) for the Northbridge and I/O Controller Hub (ICH) for the Southbridge. Regardless of the official name, Northbridge and Southbridge are the commonly used terms. Figure 7.18 shows a schematic with typical chipset chores for a VIA K8T900 chipset.

It would be impossible to provide an inclusive chipset chart here that wouldn't be obsolete by the time you pick this book up off the shelf at

• **Figure 7.17**   Driver disc for ASUS motherboard

your local tech pub (doesn't everybody have one of those?), but Table 7.1 gives you an idea of what to look for as you research motherboards for recommendations and purchases.

So why do good techs need to know the hot chipsets in detail? The chipset defines almost every motherboard feature short of the CPU itself. Techs love to discuss chipsets and expect a fellow tech to know the differences between one chipset and another. You also need to be able to recommend a motherboard that suits a client's needs.

Motherboard Components

The connections and capabilities of a motherboard sometimes differ from that of the chipset the motherboard uses. This disparity happens for a couple of reasons. First, a particular chipset may support eight USB ports, but to keep costs down the manufacturer might include only four ports. Second, a motherboard maker may choose to install extra features—ones not supported by the chipset—by adding additional chips. A common example is a motherboard that supports FireWire. Other technologies you might find are built-in sound, hard drive RAID controllers, and AMR or CNR slots for modems, network cards, and more.

USB/FireWire

Most chipsets support USB and most motherboards come with FireWire as well, but it seems no two motherboards offer the same port arrangement. My motherboard supports eight USB ports and two FireWire ports, for example, but if you look on the back of the

Try This!

VIA Makes What?
The giant Taiwan-based VIA Technologies produces many chips for many different markets and competes directly with Intel on several levels. Some of these might surprise you. Try this: go to VIA's Web site (www.via.com.tw) and see if you can answer the following questions.

1. VIA chipsets support which CPUs?
2. What technological innovations does VIA push? What about form factors?
3. Does VIA produce processing chips of the non-chipset variety, such as for video, sound, or general computing? What are they called?

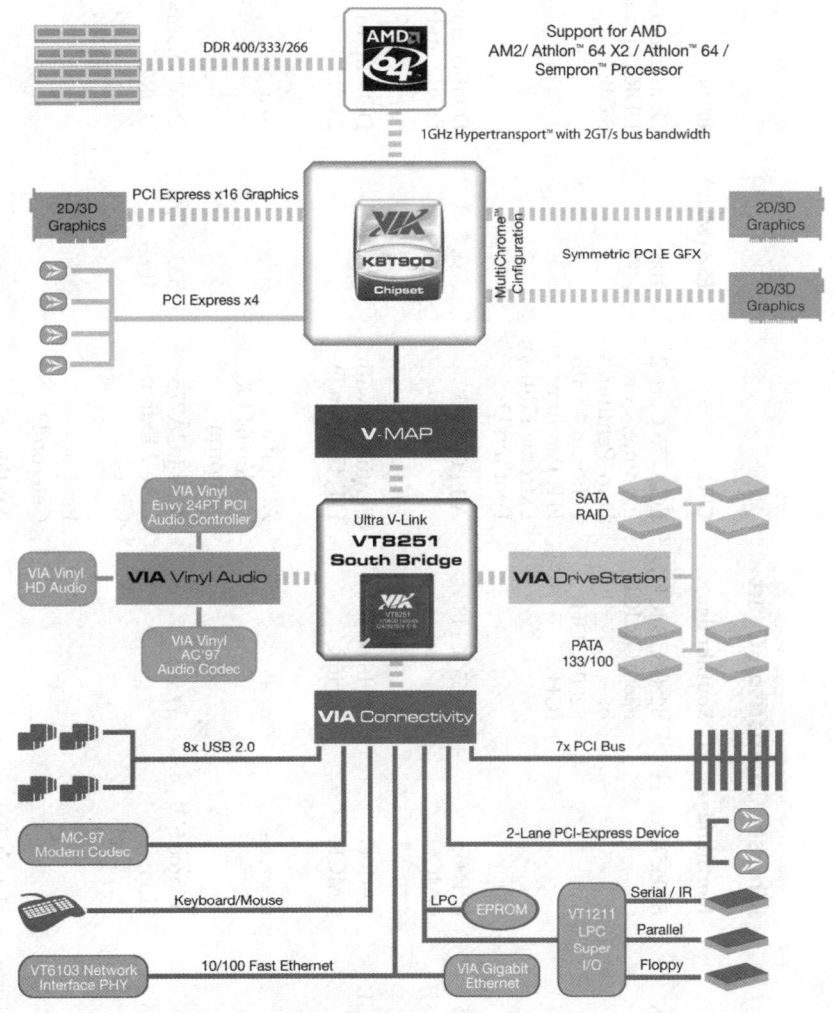

• **Figure 7.18**   Schematic of a modern chipset *(courtesy of VIA Technologies)*

Table 7.1   Chipset Comparison Chart

Chipset	Northbridge	Southbridge	CPU	FSB (MHz)	RAM	PCIe	AGP	HDD	USB	FireWire
Intel 975X Express	82955X MCH	82801GB ICH, 82801GR ICH, or 82801GDH ICH	LGA775 Core 2 Extreme, Core 2 Duo, Pentium 4, Pentium 4 with HT, Pentium Extreme Edition, Pentium D	1066 800	Dual-channel DDR2 up to 8 GB	SLI	No	4× SATA 3 Gbps	8× USB 2.0	No
Intel P965 Express	82P965 GMCH	P965 ICH8	All LGA775	533, 800, 1066	Dual-channel DDR2 up to 8 GB	Yes	No	6× SATA 3 Gbps	10× USB 2.0	No
Intel 910GL Express	82910G GMCH	ICH6 or ICH6R	Pentium 4 with HT, Celeron D	533	DDR up to 2 GB	Yes only 1×	No	4× SATA 1.5 Gbps	8× USB 2.0	No
NVIDIA nForce4	nForce4[1]	n/a[1]	Athlon 64, Athlon 64 FX, Sempron	n/a[2]	n/a[2]	Yes	No	4× SATA 1.5 Gbps	10× USB 2.0	No
NVIDIA nForce 570 SLI Intel	nForce 570 SLI[1]	n/a[1]	Intel LGA775: Core 2 Extreme, Core 2 Duo, Pentium D, Pentium 4, Celeron D	533, 800, 1066	Dual-channel DDR2	SLI	No	4× SATA 3 Gbps 4× PATA	8× USB 2.0	No
NVIDIA nForce 590 SLI AMD	nForce 590 SLI[1]	n/a[1]	Athlon 64, Athlon 64 FX, Athlon 64 X2	n/a[2]	n/a[2]	SLI	No	6× SATA 3 Gbps 2× PATA	10× USB 2.0	No
VIA K8 Series	K8T900	VT8251	Opteron, Athlon 64, Athlon FX, Sempron	n/a[2]	n/a[2]	SLI	No	4× SATA 3 Gbps 4× PATA 133 MBps	8× USB 2.0	No
VIA P4 Series	PT890	VT8237A	Pentium 4, Celeron	400, 533, 800, 1066	SDRAM with ECC, DDR, DDR2 up to 4 GB	Yes	No	2×/4× SATA 1.5 Mbps 4× PATA 133 MBps	8× USB 2.0	No

1. NVIDIA does not make a Northbridge/Southbridge distinction with the nForce chipset.
2. Because the Athlon 64 varieties and the Sempron CPUs have the memory controller built into the CPU, the frontside bus and memory clock speeds depend on the motherboard speed rather than the chipset. The speed between the CPU and the chipset runs up to 1066 MHz, hyperthreaded. The amount of RAM supported likewise depends on the CPU rather than the chipset.

motherboard, you'll only see four USB ports and one FireWire port. So, where are the other ports? Well, this motherboard has special connectors for the other four USB and one FireWire port, and the motherboard comes with the dongles you need to connect them (Figure 7.19). These dongles typically use an extra slot on the back of the case.

These dongle connectors are standardized, so many cases have built-in front USB/FireWire ports that have dongles attached. This is very handy for USB or FireWire devices you might want to plug and unplug frequently, such as a thumb drive or digital camera. You can also buy add-on front USB and FireWire devices that go into a 3.5-inch drive bay, like a floppy drive (Figure 7.20).

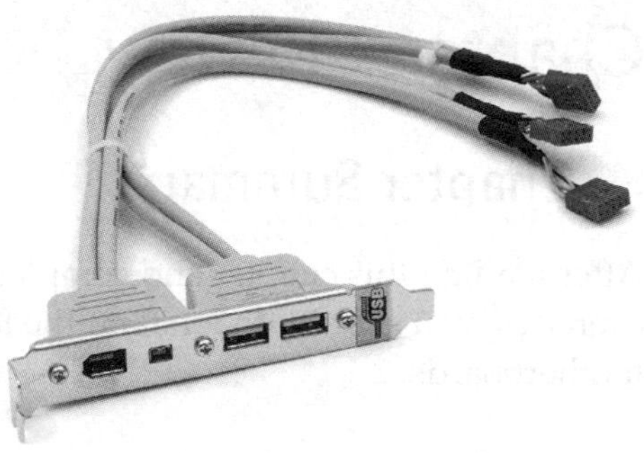

Sound

Quite a few motherboards come with onboard sound chips. These sound chips are usually pretty low quality compared to even a lower-end sound card, but onboard sound is cheap and doesn't take up a slot. These connectors are identical to the ones used on sound cards.

RAID

RAID stands for *redundant array of independent devices* and is very common on motherboards. There are many types of RAID, but the RAID on motherboards usually only supports *mirroring* (the process of using two drives to hold the same data, which is good for safety because if one drive dies, the other still has all the data) or *striping* (making two drives act as one drive by spreading data across them, which is good for speed). RAID is a very cool but complex topic that's discussed in detail in my other book, *Mike Meyers' CompTIA A+ Guide: PC Technician (Exams 220-602, 220-603, & 220-604)*.

● **Figure 7.19**   USB/FireWire dongle

● **Figure 7.20**   Front USB and FireWire drive bay device

AMR/CNR

The U.S. Federal Communications Commission (FCC) must certify any electronic device to ensure that it does not transmit unwanted electronic signals. This process is a bit expensive, so in the very late 1990s Intel came up with a special slot called the audio modem riser (AMR). See Figure 7.21. An AMR slot was designed to take specialized AMR devices (modems, sound cards, and network cards). An AMR device would get one FCC certification and then be used on as many motherboards as the manufacturer wanted without going through the FCC certification process again. AMR was quickly replaced with the more advanced communications and networking riser (CNR). Many motherboard manufacturers used these slots in the early 2000s, but they've lost popularity because most motherboard makers simply use onboard networking and sound.

● **Figure 7.21**   AMR slot

Chapter 7 Review

Chapter Summary

After reading this chapter and completing the exercises, you should understand the following about motherboards.

How Motherboards Work

■ Every piece of hardware connects either directly or indirectly to the motherboard. Wires called traces make up the different buses on the system, enabling hardware to communicate. Motherboards are several layers thick with traces running across each layer, creating a veritable highway of wires.

■ Motherboards are defined by their form factor, chipset, and components. The form factor defines the physical size and airflow; the chipset defines what type of CPU, what type and how much RAM, and what components a motherboard will support.

Types of Motherboards

■ The Advanced Technology (AT) form factor, though now obsolete, was the predominant form factor for motherboards through the mid-1990s. Its identifying features included a large keyboard plug and a split power socket called P8/P9.

■ LPX and NLX were slimline form factors, meaning they were ideal for low-profile cases. They offered a central riser slot to accept a special riser card into which expansion cards fit horizontally.

■ The Advanced Technology Extended (ATX) form factor replaced the AT as the form factor of choice by the late 1990s. It offered several improvements over the AT, including repositioning the power supply for better airflow, easier access to CPU and RAM slots, and better performance by moving RAM closer to the Northbridge and CPU. The microATX (µATX) and FlexATX are subtypes of the ATX and are considerably smaller than the ATX.

■ The Balanced Technology eXtended (BTX) form factor is newer than ATX and was designed to improve cooling. BTX cases take cool air in from the front and blow warm air out the back. As BTX motherboards place the CPU towards the front of the case, the CPU receives additional cooling from the improved airflow. Standard BTX, microBTX, and picoBTX are designed to replace ATX, microATX, and FlexATX respectively.

■ Several PC manufacturers make proprietary motherboards, meaning they do not adhere to a standard form factor like ATX or BTX. Servicing a system like this can be frustrating, as parts may be difficult to find and are often available only from authorized dealers.

■ Motherboards come with differing features or components such as USB/FireWire ports, audio, video, RAID, or AMR or CNR slots for modems and network cards. Sometimes a motherboard will support several USB/FireWire ports, but will not have rear ports for all of them. In this case, the motherboard likely has connections for the additional ports to be used in conjunction with a dongle to create front-mounted ports.

■ Popular motherboard manufacturers include Abit, Asus, Biostar, DFI, Gigabyte, Intel, MSI, and Shuttle.

Chipset Varieties

■ Every motherboard has a chipset that determines the type of CPU the motherboard supports, the type and capacity of RAM, and what devices the motherboard supports without an expansion card. Most modern chipsets are composed of two primary chips—the Northbridge and the Southbridge. As the Northbridge works with the CPU and RAM, it gets very hot, and therefore needs its own heat sink and fan. The Southbridge usually does not require any extra cooling and is thus exposed, making it a great place to find the stamp of the chipset manufacturer.

■ As almost no modern chipset supports old technologies like floppy disk drives, infrared connections, and parallel ports, motherboards contain a third chip called the Super I/O chip to support these technologies. The Super I/O chip is not part of the chipset.

■ The system ROM chip provides basic support for the chipset, but to benefit from all the features of a chipset, you need to install the operating system–specific driver for the chipset once you've installed the operating system.

- Chipset manufacturers for AMD-based motherboards tend to use the terms Northbridge and Southbridge, whereas Intel-based boards tend to use different terminology. You might see the Northbridge referred to as the Memory Controller Hub (MCH) and the Southbridge referred to as the I/O Controller Hub (ICH).

- Popular chipset manufacturers today include Intel, AMD, NVIDIA, and VIA.

Key Terms

AT *(170)*

ATX *(173)*

audio modem riser (AMR) *(181)*

Balanced Technology eXtended (BTX) *(175)*

chipset *(169)*

communications and networking riser (CNR) *(181)*

FlexATX *(174)*

form factor *(169)*

I/O Controller Hub (ICH) *(178)*

LPX *(171)*

Memory Controller Hub (MCH) *(178)*

microATX (μATX) *(174)*

microBTX *(175)*

motherboard *(168)*

NLX *(171)*

NVIDIA Corporation *(178)*

P8/P9 *(170)*

picoBTX *(175)*

riser card *(171)*

slimline *(171)*

Super I/O chip *(177)*

thermal unit *(175)*

traces *(168)*

VIA Technologies *(178)*

Key Term Quiz

Use the Key Terms list to complete the sentences that follow. Not all terms will be used.

1. The _____ defines the type of processor and RAM required for the motherboard and determines to a degree the built-in devices supported by a motherboard, including the expansion slots.

2. The AT type of motherboard had a unique, split power socket called _____.

3. The _____ form factor replaced the LPX slimline form factor.

4. Everything in the _____ form factor is designed to improve cooling.

5. The _____ determines the physical size of the motherboard as well as the general location of components and ports.

6. The smallest ATX motherboard form factor is the _____.

7. The smallest BTX motherboard form factor is the _____.

8. The fan of the BTX _____ blows the hot CPU air directly out the back of the case.

9. Small wires on the motherboard, called _____, make up the different buses on a system.

10. Older technologies, such as the floppy drive and parallel ports, are now handled by the _____.

Multiple-Choice Quiz

1. Which of the following are part of the ATX form factor? (Select two.)

   A. FlexATX

   B. macroATX

   C. microATX

   D. picoATX

2. Which of the following form factors dominates the PC market?

   A. AT

   B. ATX

   C. BTX

   D. NLX

3. The nonprofit where Sid works received a half-dozen new motherboards as a donation. When he went to install one into a case, however, it didn't fit. The ports and expansion slots seemed to be switched. What's most likely the issue?

   A. Sid's trying to install a proprietary motherboard into an ATX case.

   B. Sid's trying to install an LPX motherboard into an ATX case.

   C. Sid's trying to install a microATX motherboard into an ATX case.

   D. Sid's trying to install a microBTX motherboard into an ATX case.

4. Troubleshooting a system, Sarah finds that everything works except the floppy drive and parallel port. Even using a known good floppy drive and cable, and a working parallel Zip drive, she can't get either device to function. What is most likely at fault?

   A. Floppy/parallel bridge

   B. Northbridge

   C. Southbridge

   D. Super I/O

5. On Intel-based motherboards, which chip enables the CPU to interact with RAM?

   A. Memorybridge

   B. Northbridge

   C. Southbridge

   D. Super I/O

6. Brian bought a new motherboard that advertised support for eight USB ports. When he pulled the motherboard out of the box, however, he found that it only had four USB ports. What's likely the issue here?

   A. The extra four USB ports will connect to the front of the case or via a dongle to an expansion slot.

   B. The extra four USB ports require an add-on expansion card.

   C. The FireWire port will have a splitter that makes it four USB ports.

   D. The motherboard chipset might support eight USB ports, but the manufacturer only included four ports.

7. Which of the following chips enables an Athlon 64 to use dual-channel DDR RAM?

   A. ATI 200 Express

   B. NVIDIA nForce 570 SLI Intel

   C. NVIDIA nForce 590 SLI AMD

   D. None of the above

8. Steve has been tasked to upgrade ten systems at his office. The systems currently have microATX motherboards with 512 MB of DDR RAM and Athlon XP CPUs.
   Primary objective: Upgrade ten systems.
   Optional objectives: Use the current cases and use the current RAM.
   Proposed solution: Purchase ten microATX motherboards with NVIDIA nForce 570 SLI Intel chipsets and ten Pentium D CPUs.
   The proposed solution:

   A. Accomplishes only the primary objective.

   B. Accomplishes the primary objective and one of the optional objectives.

   C. Accomplishes the primary objective and both of the optional objectives.

   D. Accomplishes neither the primary nor the optional objectives.

9. Which of the following companies make chipsets?

   A. AMI

   B. Gigabyte

   C. MSI

   D. VIA

10. How are expansion cards installed on LPX and NLX motherboards?

   A. Via the onboard ISA and PCI slots

   B. Via a riser card

   C. Via MCA and XT slots

   D. Expansion cards cannot be installed in LPX and NLX motherboards.

■ Essay Quiz

1. This chapter talks about motherboards made in layers that contain the wires or traces. If necessary, find an Internet site that talks about the motherboard manufacturing process. Why do you think motherboards are made in layers? What advantages do the layers provide?

2. Some people believe that selecting a motherboard based on the motherboard chipset is an even more important decision than basing the decision on the kind of processor. Do you agree or disagree and why?

Lab Projects

• Lab Project 7.1

Examine all the ports and connectors on the back of your computer. With the computer turned off, you may disconnect the cables from the ports. (If necessary, document where and how the cables are connected so you can replace them correctly.) Determine the kinds of ports that are built in and those that are provided by expansion cards. From this information alone, ascertain whether your motherboard is an AT or an ATX form factor. Draw a diagram of the back of your system and label every port and all connectors. State if their sources are from the motherboard or from an expansion card. Lastly, state the form factor of the motherboard.

• Lab Project 7.2

One of the most important skills that a PC technician can possess is the ability to read and interpret documentation. No single piece of documentation is as important as the motherboard book. Let's see how well you can understand this documentation. Consult your motherboard book or use one that your instructor provides. (If you do not have the motherboard book, try to download it from the manufacturer's Web site.) Then write a paragraph about your motherboard that includes answers to the following questions:

- What make and model is the motherboard?

- What chipset does it use?

- What kinds of RAM slots does it contain?

- What kinds of expansion slots does your motherboard have and how many of each kind does it have?

- What kinds of onboard ports does it have?

- What kinds of CPUs does it support and what kind of processor slot does it have?

- Does your motherboard use jumpers or dip switches for configuration? If so, what do the jumpers or dip switches control?

- The motherboard book probably contains an illustration of the way that the motherboard components are laid out. By examining this illustration, determine what form factor your motherboard uses.

- Does your motherboard have any unusual or proprietary features?

Understanding PC Power

"I meant to kill a turkey, and instead, I nearly killed a goose."
—BENJAMIN FRANKLIN ON SHOCKING HIMSELF UNCONSCIOUS WHILE TRYING TO KILL A TURKEY WITH ELECTRICITY

In this chapter, you will learn how to

- **Explain the basics of electricity**
- **Describe the details about powering the PC**
- **Explain the different PC power supply standards**

Powering the PC requires a single box—the power supply or **power supply unit (PSU)**—that takes electricity from the wall socket and transforms it into electricity to run the motherboard and other internal components. Figure 8.1 shows a typical power supply inside a case. All the wires dangling out of it connect to the motherboard and peripherals.

● Figure 8.1 Typical power supply mounted inside the PC system unit

As simple as this appears on the surface, power supply issues are of critical importance for techs. Problems with power can create system instability, crashes, and data loss—all things most computer users would rather avoid! Good techs, therefore, know an awful lot about powering the PC, from understanding the basic principles of electricity to knowing the many variations of PC power supplies. Plus, you need to know how to recognize power problems and implement the proper solutions. Too many techs fall into the "just plug it in" camp and never learn how to deal with power, much to their clients' unhappiness.

Some questions on the CompTIA A+ certification exams could refer to a power supply as a *PSU*, for power supply unit. A power supply also falls into the category of *field replaceable unit (FRU)*, which refers to the typical parts a tech should carry, such as RAM and a floppy disk drive.

Historical/Conceptual

■ Understanding Electricity

Electricity is simply a flow of negatively charged particles, called electrons, through matter. All matter enables the flow of electrons to some extent. This flow of electrons is very similar to the flow of water through pipes; so similar that the best way to learn about electricity is by comparing it to how water flows through pipes! So let's talk about water for a moment.

Water comes from the ground, through wells, aquifers, rivers, and so forth. In a typical city, water comes to you through pipes from the water supply company that took it from the ground. What do you pay for when you pay your water bill each month? You pay for the water you use, certainly, but built into the price of the water you use is the surety that when you turn the spigot, water will flow at a more or less constant rate. The water sits in the pipes under pressure from the water company, waiting for you to turn on the spigot.

Electricity works essentially the same way as water. Electric companies gather or generate electricity and then push it to your house under pressure through wires. Just like water, the electricity sits in the wires, waiting for you to plug something into the wall socket, at which time it'll flow at a more or less constant rate. You plug a lamp into an electrical outlet and flip the switch, electricity flows, and you have light. You pay for reliability, electrical pressure, and electricity used.

The pressure of the electrons in the wire is called *voltage* and is measured in units called **volts (V)** . The amount of electrons moving past a certain point on a wire is called the *current* or *amperage,* which is measured in units called **amperes (amps or A)** . The amount of amps and volts needed by a particular device to function is expressed as how much **wattage (watts or W)** that device needs. The correlation between the three is very simple math: $V \times A = W$. You'll learn more about wattage a little later in this chapter.

Wires of all sorts—whether copper, tin, gold, or platinum—have a slight **resistance** to the flow of electrons, just like water pipes have a slight amount of friction that resists the flow of water. Resistance to the flow of electrons is measured in **ohms (Ω)** .

- Pressure = Voltage (V)
- Volume flowing = Amperes (A)
- Work = Wattage (W)
- Resistance = Ohms (Ω)

A particular thickness of wire only handles so much electricity at a time. If you push too much through, the wire will overheat and break, much like an overloaded water pipe will burst. To make sure you use the right wire for the right job, all electrical wires have an amperage rating, such as 20 amps. If you try to push 30 amps through a 20-amp wire, the wire will break and electrons will seek a way to return into the ground. Not a good thing, especially if the path back to ground is through you!

Circuit breakers and ground wires provide the basic protection from accidental overflow. A circuit breaker is a heat-sensitive electrical switch rated at a certain amperage. If you push too much amperage through the circuit breaker, the wiring inside will detect the increase in heat and automatically open, stopping the flow of electricity before the wiring overheats and breaks. You reset the circuit breaker to reestablish the circuit and electricity will flow once more through the wires. A ground wire provides a path of least resistance for electrons to flow back to ground in case of an accidental overflow.

Many years ago, your electrical supply used fuses instead of circuit breakers. Fuses are small devices with a tiny filament designed to break if subjected to too much current. Unfortunately, that breaking meant fuses had to be replaced every time they blew, making circuit breakers much more preferable. Even though you no longer see fuses in a building's electrical circuits, many electrical devices—such as a PC's power supply—often still use fuses for their own internal protection.

Electricity comes in two flavors: **direct current (DC)** , in which the electrons flow in one direction around a continuous circuit, and **alternating current (AC)** , in which the flow of electrons alternates direction back and forth in a circuit (see Figure 8.2). Most electronic devices use DC power, but all

An electrical outlet must have a ground wire to be suitable for PC use!

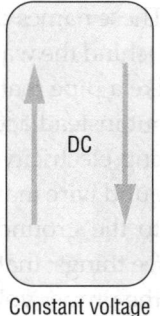

DC — Constant voltage in one direction

AC — Voltage in both directions, constantly switching back and forth

● **Figure 8.2**   Diagrams showing DC and AC flow of electrons

power companies supply AC power because AC travels long distances much more efficiently than DC.

Essentials

■ Powering the PC

Your PC uses DC voltage, so some conversion process must take place so that the PC can use AC power from the power company. The power supply in a computer converts high-voltage AC power from the wall socket to low-voltage DC. The first step in powering the PC, therefore, is to get and maintain a good supply of AC power. Second, you need a power supply to convert AC to the proper voltage and amperage of DC power for the motherboard and peripherals. Finally, you need to control the byproduct of electricity use, namely heat. Let's look at the specifics of powering the PC.

Supplying AC

Every PC power supply must have standard AC power from the power company, supplied steadily rather than in fits and spurts, and protection against accidental blurps in the supply. The power supply connects to the power cord (and thus to an electrical outlet) via a standard **IEC-320** connector. In the United States, standard AC comes in somewhere between 110 and 120 volts, often written as ~115 VAC (volts of alternating current). The rest of the world uses 220–240 VAC, so most power supplies have a little switch in the back so you can use them anywhere. Figure 8.3 shows the back of a power supply. Note the three switches, from top to bottom: the hard on/off switch, the 115/230 switch, and the IEC 320 connector.

Before plugging anything into an AC outlet, take a moment to test the outlet first using a multimeter or a device designed exclusively to test outlets. Failure to test AC outlets properly can result in inoperable or destroyed equipment, as well as possible electrocution. The IEC-320 plug has three holes,

  Flipping the AC switch on the back of a power supply can wreak all kinds of havoc on a PC. Moving the switch to ~230 V in the U.S. makes for a great practical joke (as long as the PC is off when you do it)—the PC might try to boot up, but probably won't get far. You don't risk damaging anything by running at half the AC that the power supply is expecting. In countries that run ~230 standard, on the other hand, firing up the PC with the AC switch set to ~115 can cause the power supply to die a horrid, smoking death. Watch that switch!

Figure 8.3 Back of power supply showing typical switches and power connection.

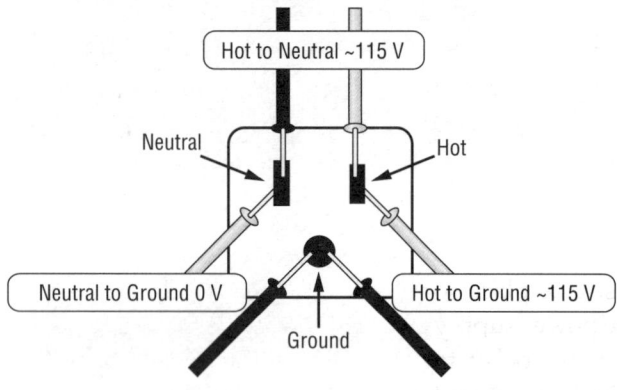

Hot to Neutral ~115 V

Neutral

Hot

Neutral to Ground 0 V

Hot to Ground ~115 V

Ground

Figure 8.4 Outlet voltages

called hot, neutral, and ground. These names describe the function of the wires that connect to them behind the wall plate. The hot wire carries electrical voltage, much like a pipe that delivers water. The neutral wire carries no voltage, but instead acts like a water drain, completing the circuit by returning electricity to the local source, normally a breaker panel. The ground wire makes it possible for excess electricity to return safely to the ground. When testing AC power, you want to check for three things: that the hot outputs approximately 115 V (or whatever the proper voltage is for your part of the world), that the neutral connects to ground (0 V output), and that the ground connects to ground (again, 0 V). Figure 8.4 shows the voltages at an outlet.

A **multimeter**—often also referred to as a *volt-ohm meter (VOM)* or *digital multimeter (DMM)*—enables you to measure a number of different aspects of electrical current. A multimeter consists of two probes: an analog or digital meter, and a dial to set the type of test you want to perform. Refer to Figure 8.5 to become familiar with the different components of the multimeter.

Note that some multimeters use symbols rather than letters to describe AC and DC settings. The *V* with the solid line above a dashed line, for example, in Figure 8.6, refers to direct current. The *V~* stands for alternating current.

Every multimeter offers at least four types of electrical tests: continuity, resistance, AC voltage (VAC), and DC voltage (VDC). Continuity tests whether electrons can flow from one end of a wire to the other end. If so, you have continuity; if not, you don't. You can use this setting to determine if a fuse is good or to check for breaks in wires. If your multimeter doesn't have a continuity tester (many cheaper multimeters do not), you may use

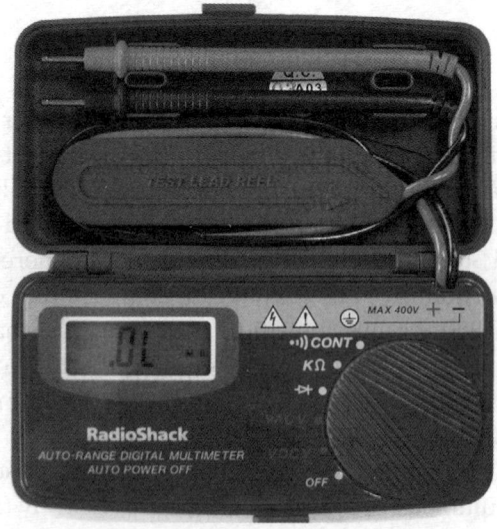

Figure 8.5 Digital multimeter

• **Figure 8.6**   Multimeter featuring DC and AC symbols

Tech Tip

Using a Multimeter to Test AC Outlets

Every competent technician knows how to use a multimeter, so if you haven't used one in the past, get hold of one and Try This!

First, you need to set up the meter for measuring AC. Follow these steps:

1. Place the black lead in the common (–) hole. If the black lead is permanently attached, ignore this step.
2. Place the red lead in the V-Ohm-A (+) hole. If the red lead is permanently attached, ignore this step.
3. Move the selector switch to the AC V (usually red). If multiple settings are available, put it into the first scale higher than 120 V (usually 200 V). *Auto-range* meters set their own range; they don't need any selection except AC V.

Once you have the meter set up for AC, go through the process of testing the various wires on an AC socket. Just don't put your fingers on the metal parts of the leads when you stick them into the socket! Follow these steps:

1. Put either lead in hot, the other in neutral. You should read 110 to 120 V AC.
2. Put either lead in hot, the other in ground. You should read 110 to 120 V AC.
3. Put either lead in neutral, the other in ground. You should read 0 V AC.

If any of these readings is different from what is described here, it's time to call an electrician.

Tech Tip

AC Adapters

Many devices in the computing world use an AC adapter rather than an internal power supply. Even though it sits outside a device, an AC adapter converts AC current to DC, just like a power supply. Unlike power supplies, AC adapters are rarely interchangeable. Although manufacturers of different devices often use the same kind of plug on the end of the AC adapter cable, these adapters are not necessarily compatible. In other words, just because you can *plug an AC adapter from your friend's laptop into your laptop does not mean it's going to work!*

You need to make sure that three things match before you plug an AC adapter into a device: voltage, amperage, and polarity. If the voltage or amperage output is too low, the device won't run. If the polarity is reversed, it won't work, just like putting a battery in a flashlight backwards. If the voltage or amperage—especially the latter—is too high, on the other hand, you can very quickly toast your device. Don't do it! Always check the voltage, amperage, and polarity of a replacement AC adapter before you plug it into a device.

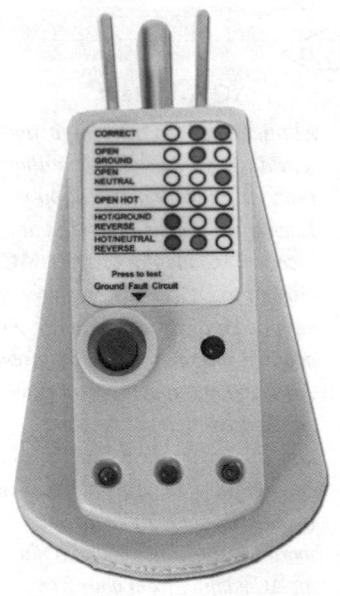

• **Figure 8.7** Circuit tester

the resistance tester. A broken wire or fuse will show infinite resistance, while a good wire or fuse will show no resistance. Testing AC and DC voltages is a matter of making sure the measured voltage is what it should be.

Using Special Equipment to Test AC Voltage

A number of good AC-only testing devices are available. With these devices, you can test all voltages for an AC outlet by simply inserting them into the outlet. Be sure to test all the outlets the computer system uses: power supply, external devices, and monitor. Although convenient, these devices aren't as accurate as a multimeter. My favorite tester is made by Radio Shack, catalog number 22-141 (see Figure 8.7). This handy device provides three light-emitting diodes (LEDs) that describe everything that can go wrong with a plug.

If all power companies could supply electricity in smooth, continuous flows with no dips or spikes in pressure, the next two sections of this chapter would be irrelevant. Unfortunately, no matter how clean the AC supply appears to be to a multimeter, the truth is that voltage from the power company tends to drop well below (sag) and shoot far above (surge or spike) the standard 115 V (in the U.S.). These sags and spikes usually don't affect lamps and refrigerators, but they can keep your PC from running or can even destroy a PC or peripheral device. Two essential devices handle spikes and sags in the supply of AC: surge suppressors and uninterruptible power supplies.

Surge Suppressors

Surges or spikes are far more dangerous than sags. Even a strong sag only shuts off or reboots your PC—any surge can harm your computer, and a strong surge destroys components. Given the seriousness of surges, every PC should use a surge suppressor device that absorbs the extra voltage from a surge to protect the PC. The power supply does a good job of surge suppression and can handle many of the smaller surges that take place fairly often. But the power supply takes a lot of damage from this and will eventually fail. To protect your power supply, a dedicated surge suppressor works between the power supply and the outlet to protect the system from power surges (see Figure 8.8).

Most people tend to spend a lot of money on their PC and for some reason suddenly get cheap on the surge suppressor. Don't do that! Make sure your surge suppressor has the Underwriters Laboratories UL 1449 for 330 V

• **Figure 8.8** Surge suppressor

rating to ensure substantial protection for your system. Underwriters Laboratories (www.ul.com) is a U.S.-based, not-for-profit, widely recognized industry testing laboratory whose testing standards are very important to the consumer electronics industry. Additionally, check the joules rating before buying a new surge suppressor. A **joule** is a unit of electrical energy. Joules are used to describe how much energy a surge suppressor can handle before it fails. Most authorities agree that your surge suppressor should rate at a minimum of 800 joules—the more joules, the better the protection! My surge suppressor rates out at 1,750 joules.

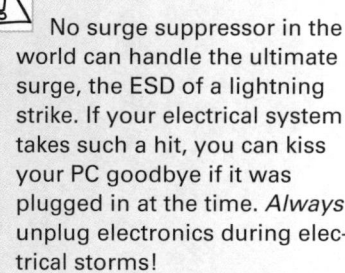

No surge suppressor in the world can handle the ultimate surge, the ESD of a lightning strike. If your electrical system takes such a hit, you can kiss your PC goodbye if it was plugged in at the time. *Always* unplug electronics during electrical storms!

While you're protecting your system, don't forget that surges also come from telephone and cable connections. If you use a modem, DSL, or cable modem, make sure to get a surge suppressor that includes support for these types of connections. Many manufacturers make surge suppressors with telephone line protection (see Figure 8.9).

No surge suppressor works forever. Make sure your surge suppressor has a test/reset button so you'll know when the device has—as we say in the business—turned into an extension cord. If your system takes a hit and you have a surge suppressor, call the company! Many companies provide cash guarantees against system failure due to surges, but only if you follow their guidelines.

If you want really great surge suppression, you need to move up to **power conditioning**. Your power lines take in all kinds of strange signals that have no business being in there, such as electromagnetic inter-

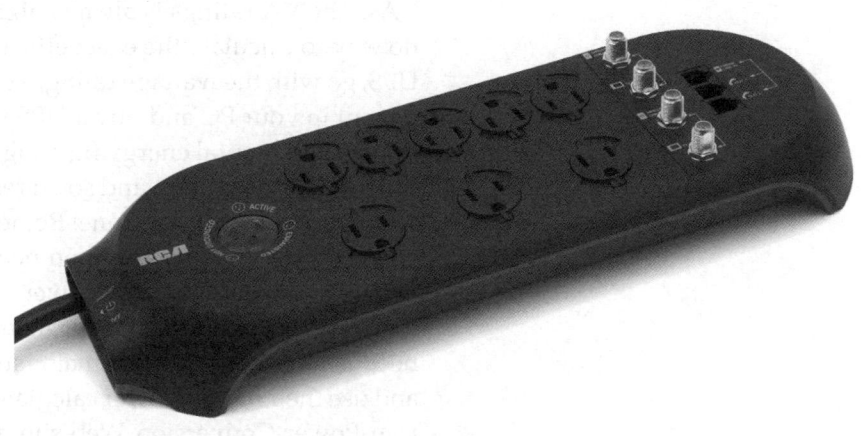

• **Figure 8.9**   Good surge suppressor

ference (EMI) and radio frequency interference (RFI). Most of the time, this line noise is so minimal that it's not worth addressing, but occasionally events (such as lightning) generate enough line noise to cause weird things to happen to your PC (keyboard lockups, messed up data). All better surge suppressors add power conditioning to filter out EMI and RFI.

UPS

An **uninterruptible power supply (UPS)** protects your computer (and, more importantly, your data) in the event of a power sag or power outage. Figure 8.10 shows a typical UPS. A UPS essentially contains a big battery that will provide AC power to your computer, regardless of the power coming from the AC outlet.

• **Figure 8.10**   Uninterruptible power supply

All uninterruptible power supplies are measured in both watts (the true amount of power they supply in the event of a power outage) and in *volt-amps (VA)*. Volt-amps is the amount of power the UPS could supply if the devices took power from the UPS in a perfect way. Your UPS provides perfect AC power, moving current smoothly back and forth 60 times a second. However, power supplies, monitors, and other devices may not take all the power the UPS has to offer at every point as the AC power moves back and forth, resulting in inefficiencies. If your devices took all the power the UPS offered at every point as the power moved back and forth, then VA would equal watts. If the UPS makers knew ahead of time exactly what devices you planned to plug into their UPSs, they could tell you the exact watts, but different devices have different efficiencies, forcing the UPS makers to go by what they can offer (VAs), not what your devices will take (watts). The watts value they give is a guess, and it's never as high as the VAs. The VA ratings is always higher than the watt rating. Since you have no way to calculate the exact efficiency of every device you'll plug into the UPS, go with the wattage rating. You add up the total wattage of every component in your PC and buy a UPS with a higher wattage. You'll spend a lot of time and mental energy figuring precisely how much wattage your computer, monitor, drives, and so on require to get the proper UPS for your system. But you're still not done! Remember, the UPS is a battery with a limited amount of power, so you then need to figure out how long you want the UPS to run when you lose power.

The quicker and far better method to use for determining the UPS you need is to go to any of the major surge suppressor/UPS makers' Web sites and use their handy power calculators. My personal favorite is on the American Power Conversion Web site: www.apc.com. APC makes great surge suppressors and UPSs, and the company's online calculator will show you the true wattage you need—and teach you about whatever new thing is happening in power at the same time.

Every UPS also has surge suppression and power conditioning, so look for the joule and UL 1449 ratings. Also look for replacement battery costs—some UPS replacement batteries are very expensive. Finally, look for a **smart UPS** with a USB or serial port connection. These handy UPSs come with monitoring and maintenance software (Figure 8.11) that tells you the status of your system and the amount of battery power available, logs power events, and provides other handy options.

Table 8.1 gives you a quick look at the low end and the very high end of UPS products (as of November 2006).

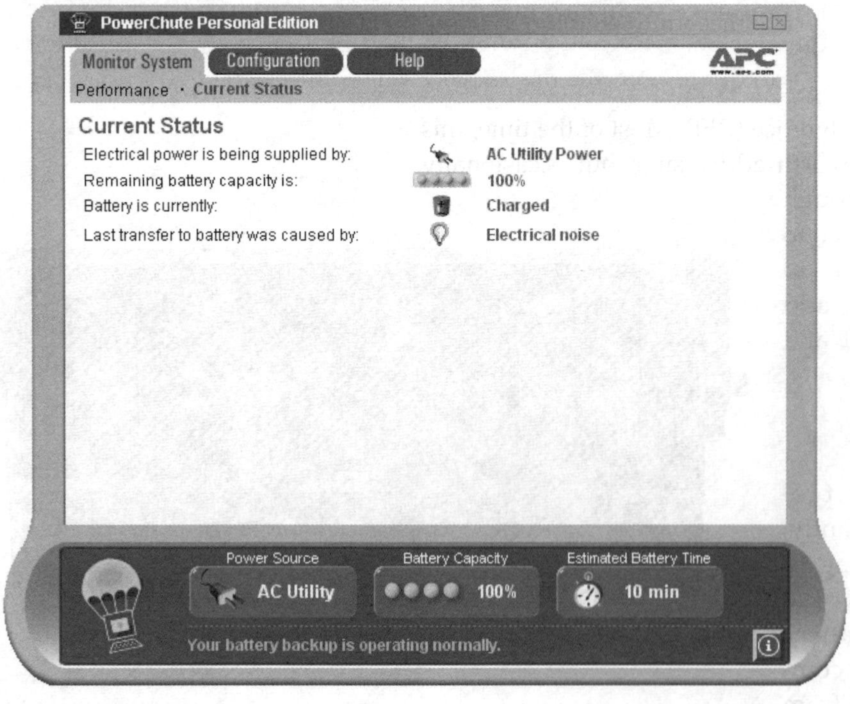

• **Figure 8.11**   APC PowerChute software

Table 8.1	Typical UPS Devices				
Brand	Model	Outlets Protected	Backup Time	Price	Type
APC	BE350U	3 @ 120 V	2 min @ 200 W, 21 min @ 50W	$39.99	Standby
APC	BE725BB	4 @ 120 V	4 min @ 400 W, <1 hour @ 50W	$99.99	Standby
CyberPower	CPS825AVR	3 @ 120 V	25 to 60 minutes	$136.12	Line Interactive?
APC	SYH2K6RMT-P1	12 @ 120 V 2 @ 240 V	11.9 min @ 1400 W	$2,835.00	Online

Supplying DC

After you've assured the supply of good AC electricity for the PC, the power supply unit (PSU) takes over, converting high-voltage AC into several DC voltages (notably, 5.0, 12.0, and 3.3 volts) usable by the delicate interior components. Power supplies come in a large number of shapes and sizes, but the most common size by far is the standard 150 mm × 140 mm × 86 mm desktop PSU, shown in Figure 8.12.

The PC uses the 12.0-volt current to power motors on devices such as hard drives and CD-ROM drives, and it uses the 5.0-volt and 3.3-volt current for support of onboard electronics. Manufacturers may use these voltages any way they wish, however, and may deviate from these assumptions. Power supplies also come with standard connectors for the motherboard and interior devices.

Power to the Motherboard

Modern motherboards use a 20- or 24-pin P1 power connector. Some motherboards may require special 4-, 6-, or 8-pin connectors to supply extra power (Figure 8.13). We'll talk about each of these connectors in the form factor standards discussion later in this chapter.

Power to Peripherals: Molex, Mini, and SATA

Many different devices inside the PC require power. These include hard drives, floppy drives, CD- and DVD-media drives, Zip drives, and fans. The typical PC power supply has up to three different types of connectors that plug into peripherals: Molex, mini, and SATA.

Try This!

Shopping for a UPS

When it comes to getting a UPS for yourself or a client, nothing quite cuts through the hype and marketing terms like a trip to the local computer store to see for yourself. You need excuses to go to the computer store, so Try This!

1. Go to your local computer store—or visit an online computer site if no stores are nearby—and find out what's available.

2. Answer this question: How can you tell the difference between an online and a standby UPS?

• Figure 8.12   Desktop PSU

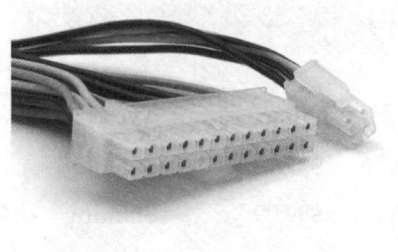

● **Figure 8.13** Motherboard power connectors

● **Figure 8.14** Molex connector

 As with any power connector, plugging a mini connector into a device the wrong way will almost certainly destroy the device. Check twice before you plug one in!

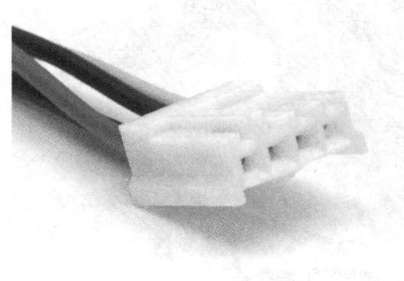

● **Figure 8.15** Mini connector

Molex Connectors   The most common type of power connection for devices that need 5 or 12 volts of power is the Molex connector (Figure 8.14). The Molex connector has notches, called *chamfers*, that guide its installation. The tricky part is that Molex connectors require a firm push to plug in properly, and a strong person can defeat the chamfers, plugging a Molex in upside down. Not a good thing. *Always* check for proper orientation before you push it in!

Mini Connectors   All power supplies have a second type of connector, called a mini connector (Figure 8.15), that supplies 5 and 12 volts to peripherals, although only floppy disk drives in modern systems use this connector. Drive manufacturers adopted the mini as the standard connector on 3.5-inch floppy disk drives. Often, these mini connectors are referred to as floppy power connectors.

Be extra careful when plugging in a mini connector! Whereas Molex connectors are difficult to plug in backward, you can insert a mini connector incorrectly with very little effort. As with a Molex connector, doing so will almost certainly destroy the floppy drive. Figure 8.16 depicts a correctly oriented mini connection.

SATA Power Connectors   Serial ATA (SATA) hard drives need a special 15-pin SATA power connector (Figure 8.17). The larger pin count supports the SATA hot-swappable feature, and 3.3 V, 5.0 V, and 12.0 V devices.

Try This!

Testing DC

It is common practice for techs troubleshooting a system to test the DC voltages coming out of the power supply. Even with good AC, a bad power supply can fail to transform AC to DC at voltages needed by the motherboard and peripherals. So grab your trusty multimeter and Try this! on a powered-up PC with the side cover removed. Note that you must have P1 connected to the motherboard and the system must be running (you don't have to be in Windows, of course).

1.   Switch your multimeter to DC, somewhere around 20 V DC, if you need to make that choice. Make sure your leads are plugged into the multimeter properly, red to hot, black to ground. The key to testing DC is that it matters which lead you touch to which wire. Red goes to hot wires of all colors; black *always* goes to ground.

2.   Plug the red lead into the red wire socket of a free Molex connector and plug the black lead into one of the two black wire sockets. You should get a reading of ~5 V. What do you have?

3.   Now move the red lead to the yellow socket. What voltage do you get?

4.   Testing the P1 connector is a little more complicated. You push the red and black leads into the top of P1, sliding in alongside the wires until you bottom out. Leave the black lead in one of the black wire ground sockets. Move the red lead through all the colored wire sockets. What voltages do you find?

● **Figure 8.17** SATA power connector

● **Figure 8.16** Correct orientation of a mini connector

SATA power connectors are *L*-shaped, making it almost impossible to insert one incorrectly into a SATA drive. No other device on your computer uses the SATA power connector.

> It's normal and common to have unused power connectors inside your PC case.

Splitters and Adapters You may occasionally find yourself without enough connectors to power all of the devices inside your PC. In this case, you can purchase splitters to create more connections (see Figure 8.18). You might also run into the phenomenon of needing a SATA connector but having only a spare Molex. Because the voltages on the wires are the same, a simple adapter will take care of the problem nicely.

ATX

The original **ATX** power supplies had two distinguishing physical features: the motherboard power connector and soft power. Motherboard power came from a single cable with a 20-pin P1 motherboard power connector. ATX power supplies also had at least two other cables, each populated with two or more Molex or mini connectors for peripheral power.

When plugged in, ATX systems have 5 volts running to the motherboard. They're always "on" even when powered down. The power switch you press to power up the PC isn't a true power switch like the light switch on the wall in your bedroom. The power switch on an ATX system simply tells the computer whether it has been pressed. The BIOS or operating system takes over from there and handles the chore of turning the PC on or off. This is called **soft power**.

Using soft power instead of a physical switch has a number of important benefits. Soft power prevents a user from turning off a system before the operating system's been shut down. It enables the PC to use power-saving modes that put the system to sleep and then wake it up when you press a key, move a mouse, or receive an e-mail. (See Chapter 16, "Portable Computing," for more details on sleep mode.)

● **Figure 8.18** Molex splitter

Cross Check

ATX Form Factor

The power supply form factor alone does not define a system as ATX or one of the later varieties. You've got to discuss the motherboard as well. Flip back to Chapter 7, "Understanding Motherboards," and see if you can put the full picture of the ATX standard together. What defines a system as ATX? What improvements did ATX incorporate over AT? What ATX form factors can you purchase?

All of the most important settings for ATX soft power reside in CMOS setup. Boot into CMOS and look for a Power Management section. Take a look at the Power On Function option in Figure 8.19. This determines the function of the on/off switch. You may set this switch to turn off the computer, or you may set it to the more common *4-second delay*.

ATX did a great job supplying power for more than a decade, but over time more powerful CPUs, multiple CPUS, video cards, and other components began to need more current than the original ATX provided. This motivated the industry to introduce a number of updates to the ATX power standards: ATX12V 1.3, EPS12V, multiple rails, ATX12V 2.0, other form factors, and active PFC.

ATX12V 1.3   The first widespread update to the ATX standard, ATX12V 1.3, came out in 2003. This introduced a 4-pin motherboard power connector, unofficially but commonly called the P4, that provided more 12-volt power to assist the 20-pin P1 motherboard power connector. Any power supply that provides a P4 connector is called an ATX12V power supply. The term "ATX" was dropped from the ATX power standard, so if you want to get really nerdy you can say—accurately—that there's no such thing as an ATX power supply. All power supplies—assuming they have a P4 connector—are ATX12V or one of the later standards.

```
                  Phoenix - Award BIOS CMOS Setup Utility
                          Power Management Setup
  ┌──────────────────────────────────────────┬───────────────────────┐
  │ ACPI Suspend Typr      S3 (Suspend-To-RAM)│      Item Help         │
  │  - USB Resume from S3  Enabled            │                        │
  │ Power Button Function  Delay 4 Sec        │ Menu Level      ▶      │
  │ Wake by PME# of PCI    Disabled           │                        │
  │ Wakeup by Ring         Disabled           │                        │
  │ Wakeup by OnChip LAN   Enabled            │                        │
  │ Wakeup by Alarm        Disabled           │                        │
  │ x - Day of Month Alarm     0              │                        │
  │ x - Time (hh:mm:ss) Alarm  0 : 0 : 0      │                        │
  │ AMD K8 Cool'n'Quite controlAuto           │                        │
  │ Power On Function      Button Only        │                        │
  │ x - KB Power On Password  Enter           │                        │
  │ x - Hot Key Power On    Ctrl-F1           │                        │
  │ Restore on AC Power Loss Power Off        │                        │
  │                                           │                        │
  │                                           │                        │
  │                                           │                        │
  └──────────────────────────────────────────┴───────────────────────┘
  ▲▼◄:Move   Enter:Select    +/-/PU/PD:Value  F10:Save   ESC:Exit  F1:General Help
     F5:Previous Values         F6:Fail-Safe Defaults    F7:Optimized Defaults
```

• **Figure 8.19**   Soft power setting in CMOS

The ATX12V 1.3 standard also introduced a 6-pin auxiliary connector—commonly called an *AUX* connector—to supply increased 3.3- and 5.0-volt current to the motherboard (see Figure 8.20). This connector was based on the motherboard power connector from the precursor of ATX, called *AT*.

The introduction of these two extra power connectors caused the industry some teething problems. In particular, motherboards using AMD CPUs tended to need the AUX connector, whereas motherboards using Intel CPUs needed only the P4. As a result, many power supplies came with only a P4 or only an AUX connector to save money. A few motherboard makers skipped adding either connector and used a standard Molex so people with older power supplies wouldn't have to upgrade just because they bought a new motherboard (Figure 8.21).

The biggest problem with ATX12V was its lack of teeth—it made a lot of recommendations but few requirements, giving PSU makers too much choice (such as choosing or not choosing to add AUX and P4 connectors) that weren't fixed until later versions.

EPS12V Server motherboards are thirsty for power and sometimes ATX12V 1.3 just didn't cut it. An industry group called the Server System Infrastructure (SSI) developed a non-ATX standard motherboard and power supply called EPS12V. An EPS12V power supply came with a 24-pin main motherboard power connector that resembled a 20-pin ATX connector, but it offered more current and thus more stability for motherboards. It also came with an AUX connector, an ATX12V P4 connector, and a unique 8-pin connector. That's a lot of connectors! EPS12V power supplies were not interchangeable with ATX12V power supplies.

EPS12V may not have seen much life beyond servers, but it introduced a number of power features, some of which eventually became part of the ATX12V standard. The most important issue was something called *rails*.

• Figure 8.20   Auxiliary power connector

• Figure 8.21   Molex power on motherboard

Rails Generally, all of the PC's power comes from a single transformer that takes the AC current from a wall socket and converts it into DC current that is split into three primary DC voltage rails : 12.0 volts, 5.0 volts, and 3.3 volts. Individual lines run from each of these voltage rails to the various connectors. That means the 12-volt connector on a P4 draws from the same rail as the main 12-volt connector feeding power to the motherboard. This works fine as long as the collective needs of the connectors sharing a rail don't exceed its capacity to feed them power. To avoid this, EPS12V divided the 12-volt supply into two or three separate 12-volt rails, each one providing a separate source of power.

ATX12V 2.0 The ATX12V 2.0 standard incorporated many of the good ideas of EPS12V into the ATX world, starting with the 24-pin connector. This 24-pin motherboard power connector is backward compatible with the older 20-pin connector so users don't have to buy a new motherboard if they use an ATX12V 2.0 power supply. ATX12V 2.0 requires two, 12-volt rails for any power supply rated higher than 230 watts. ATX12V 2.0 dropped the AUX connector and required SATA hard drive connectors.

In theory, a 20-pin motherboard power supply connector will work on a motherboard with a 24-pin socket, but doing this is risky in that the 20-pin connector may not provide enough power to your system. Try to use the right power supply for your motherboard to avoid problems. Many ATX12V 2.0 power supplies have a convertible 24-to-20-pin converter. These are handy if you want to make a nice "clean" connection as many 20-pin connectors have capacitors that prevent plugging in a 24-pin connector. You'll also see the occasional 24-pin connector constructed in such a way that you can slide off the extra four pins. Figure 8.22 shows 20-pin and 24-pin connectors; Figure 8.23 shows a convertible connector. Although they look similar, those extra four pins won't replace the P4 connector. They are incompatible!

The other notable additional connector is a 6-pin PCI Express (PCIe) connector (Figure 8.24). Some motherboards add a Molex socket for PCIe, and some cards come with a Molex socket as well. Higher-end cards have a dedicated 6-pin connector.

> A few updates have been made to the ATX12V 2.0 standard, but these are trivial from a PC tech's standpoint.

• **Figure 8.22**   20- and 24-pin connectors

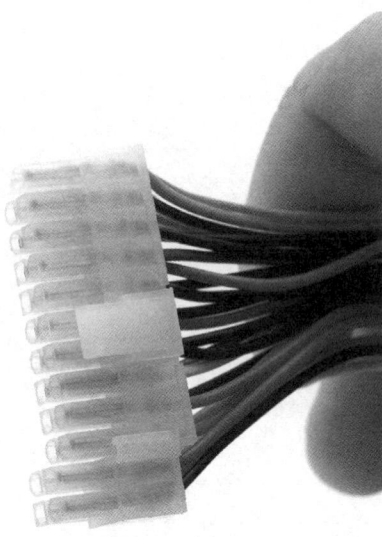

• **Figure 8.23**   Convertible motherboard power connector

• **Figure 8.24**   PCI Express 6-pin power connector

Niche Market Power Supply Form Factors   The demand for smaller and quieter PCs and, to a lesser extent, the emergence of the BTX form factor has led to the development of a number of niche market power supply form factors. All use standard ATX connectors, but differ in size and shape from standard ATX power supplies.

- **TFX12V**   A small power form factor optimized for low-profile ATX systems

- **SFX12V**   A small power form factor optimized for systems using FlexATX motherboards (Figure 8.25)

- **CFX12V**   An L-shaped power supply optimized for microBTX systems

- **LFX12V**   A small power form factor optimized for low-profile BTX systems

Active PFC   Visualize the AC current coming from the power company as water in a pipe, smoothly moving back and forth, 60 times a second. A PC's power supply, simply due to the process of changing this AC current into DC current, is like a person sucking on a straw on the end of this pipe, taking gulps only when the current is fully pushing or pulling at the top and bottom of each cycle, creating an electrical phenomena—sort of a back pressure—that's called *harmonics* in the power industry. These harmonics create the humming sound that you hear from electrical components. Over time, harmonics damage electrical equipment, causing serious problems with the power supply and other electrical devices on the circuit. Once you put a few thousand PCs with power supplies in the same local area, harmonics can even damage the electrical power supplier's equipment!

Good PC power supplies come with active power factor correction (active PFC), extra circuitry that smoothes out the way the power supply takes power from the power company and eliminates harmonics (Figure 8.26). Never buy a power supply that does not have active PFC—all power supplies with active PFC will proudly show you on the box.

You'll commonly find niche market power supplies bundled with computer cases (and often motherboards as well). These form factors are rarely sold alone.

The CompTIA A+ 220-602 and 220-604 exams test you pretty heavily on power supplies. You need to know what power supply will work with a particular system or with a particular computing goal in mind.

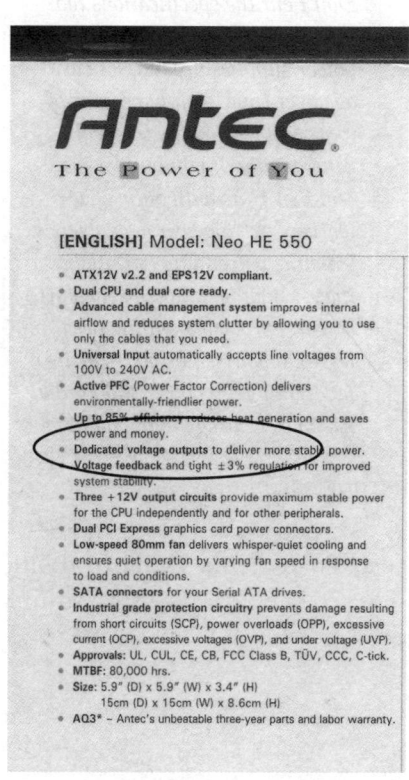

● **Figure 8.26**   Power supply showing active PFC

● **Figure 8.25**   SFX power supply

The CompTIA A+ Certification exams do not require you to figure precise wattage needs for a particular system. When building a PC for a client, however, you do need to know this stuff!

Tech Tip

Build in Aging

Don't cut the specifications too tightly for power supplies. All power supplies produce less wattage over time, simply because of wear and tear on the internal components. If you build a system that runs with only a few watts of extra power available from the power supply initially, that system will most likely start causing problems within a year or less! Do yourself or your clients a favor and get a power supply that has more wattage than you need.

Wattage Requirements

Every device in a PC requires a certain amount of wattage in order to function. A typical hard drive draws 15 watts of power when accessed, for example, whereas some Athlon 64 X2 CPUs draw a whopping 110 watts at peak usage—with average usage around 70 watts. The total wattage of all devices combined is the minimum you need the power supply to provide.

If the power supply cannot produce the wattage needed by a system, that PC won't work properly. Because most devices in the PC require maximum wattage when first starting, the most common result of insufficient wattage is a paperweight that looks like a PC. This can lead to some embarrassing moments. You might plug in a new hard drive for a client, for example, push the power button on the case, and nothing happens—a dead PC! Eek! You can quickly determine if insufficient wattage is the problem. Unplug the drive and power up the system. If the system boots up, the power supply is a likely suspect. The only fix for this problem is to replace the power supply with one that provides more wattage (or leave the new drive out—a less-than-ideal solution).

No power supply can turn 100 percent of the AC power coming from the power company into DC current. So all power supplies provide less power to the system than the wattage advertised on the box. ATX12V 2.0 standards require a power supply to be at least 70 percent efficient, but you can find power supplies with better than 80 percent efficiency. More efficiency can tell you how many watts the system puts out to the PC in actual use. Plus, the added efficiency means the power supply uses less power, saving you money.

One common argument these days is that people buy power supplies that provide far more wattage than a system needs and therefore waste power. This is untrue. A power supply provides only the amount of power your system needs. If you put a 1000-watt power supply (yes, they really exist) into a system that needs only 250 watts, that big power supply will put out only 250 watts to the system. So buying an efficient, higher wattage power supply gives you two benefits: First, running a power supply at less than 100 percent load lets it live longer. Second, you'll have plenty of extra power when adding new components.

As a general recommendation for a new system, use at least a 400-watt power supply. This is a common wattage and will give you plenty of extra power for booting as well as for whatever other components you might add to the system in the future.

Chapter 8 Review

Chapter Summary

After reading this chapter and completing the exercises, you should understand the following about PC power.

Understanding Electricity

- The power supply takes electricity from the wall outlet and transforms it into the kind of electricity that the motherboard and other internal components use. To remove the power supply, unscrew the four screws in the back of the case and lift it out. Installing it is just as simple. Be careful never to open the power supply itself as the capacitors inside can store a dangerous electrical charge.

- Techs need to know basic principles of electricity and how to recognize power problems. Electricity is a flow of negatively charged particles or electrons through matter. Metallic wire is a good conductor, allowing electrons to move freely. The pressure of the electrons in the wire is called voltage and is measured in volts (V). Measured in units called amperes (amps or A), current or amperage is the amount of electrons flowing past a certain point on a wire. Wattage (watts or W) refers to the amount of amps and volts a particular device needs. The formula $VA = W$ expresses the correlation among the three. Resistance to the flow of electrons is measured in ohms. Fuses and ground wires set limits for the flow of electrons. A ground wire provides a path of least resistance to allow the electrons to flow to the ground.

- Electricity may be either direct current (DC), with electrons flowing in one direction around a continuous circuit, or alternating current (AC), with electrons flowing back and forth in a circuit.

Powering the PC

- While the power companies supply high-voltage AC, the computer's power supply converts AC to low-voltage DC that is then portioned out to the internal devices. Heat is a byproduct of electricity and must be controlled in the computer.

- The power supply connects to the electrical outlet via a standard IEC-320 connector. While power in the U.S. ranges from 110 to 120 volts, the rest of the world uses 200 to 240 VAC. Most power supplies are able to switch between 110 and 220 voltage. The IEC-320 plug has three holes, called hot, neutral, and ground. The hot carries electrical voltage and should output approximately 115 V in the U.S. The neutral returns electricity to the breaker panel and should have 0 V output. The ground wire returns excess electricity to the ground and should also have a 0 V output. You can use a multimeter to test voltages at the outlet.

- A multimeter, also called a volt-ohm meter (VOM), uses two probes to provide at least four measurements: AC voltage (V~), DC voltage (V with a solid line above a dashed line), continuity (whether electrons flow from one end of a wire to the other end), and resistance (whether a fuse is good or blown or whether a wire has breaks). Other AC-only testing devices are available that simply plug into the AC outlet and may display results via three light-emitting diodes (LEDs).

- A surge suppressor is an inexpensive device that protects your computer from voltage spikes. Inserted between the wall outlet and the power supply, a surge suppressor has a joule rating that measures how much electrical energy it can suppress. Be sure your surge suppressor has at least an 800 joules rating. Since telephone lines and cable connections also produce spikes, your surge suppressor should include connections for a modem, DSL, or cable modem. Make sure you purchase a surge suppressor that has the UL 1449 for 330 V rating, as this will ensure substantial protection for your system. Because surge suppressors work for only a limited time, you should check the manufacturer's recommended replacement schedules. If your surge suppressor comes with a cash guarantee, be aware that manufacturers honor it only if you follow their guidelines.

- Because the AC supply lacks consistency and actually provides power with sags and spikes, it is important that you use two devices with the computer: an uninterruptible power supply and a surge suppressor. An uninterruptible power supply (UPS) continues to supply AC power to your computer during both brownouts and blackouts via a battery that is charged from the AC current. All uninterruptible power supplies measure the amount of power or watts they supply, as well as listing the number of minutes the UPS will last with a certain voltage. You should cut the number of minutes in half for a truer estimate of the abilities of the UPS. A Smart UPS connects to your computer by a USB or serial port and comes with software that reports the UPS battery status, logs power events, and shuts down your system when a specified amount of battery time remains after power has been lost.

- The power supply converts AC into several DC voltages (5.0, 12.0, and 3.3 volts). Devices such as hard drives and CD-ROM drives require 12.0 volts while onboard electronics use 3.3- and 5.0-volt currents.

- The power supply has several standard connectors for the motherboard and interior devices. Today's motherboards have a P1 socket that uses the P1 connector from the power supply. A standard ATX power supply will have a 20-pin P1 connector while the newer ATX12V 2.0 power supplies come with a 24-pin P1 connector. Some motherboards also need a 4-, 6-, or 8-pin connector to provide an additional 12 volts of power.

- Peripherals use two or possibly three different kinds of connectors: the larger Molex connector, the smaller mini connector, and the SATA connector. Used with hard drives and CD- and DVD-media drives, the Molex has chamfers to ensure that it is connected properly. Used today only for floppy drives, the mini connector can easily be inserted incorrectly, thus destroying the floppy drive. The SATA connector is used for SATA hard drives. If you do not have enough connectors for all the devices inside your PC, you can create more connections with a splitter. Similarly, if your power supply does not have the connector needed by a device, you can purchase adapters to convert one type to another.

- The ATX power supply includes full support for power-saving functions with the modem or network interface card able to wake up the PC when there is incoming traffic. Using the soft power feature, the ATX power supply puts a 5-volt charge on the motherboard as long as there is AC from the wall socket. You can configure the ATX soft power through the Power Management section of the CMOS setup. Always unplug an ATX system before you work on it. ATX power supplies use a single P1 connector for motherboard power.

- The ATX standard has undergone several updates. ATX12V 1.3 introduced additional 4-pin (P4) and 6-pin auxiliary (AUX) connectors. ATX12V 2.0 introduced the 24-pin connector (inspired by EPS12V), dropped the AUX connector, and required SATA connectors. Additionally, ATX12V 2.0 required two, 12-volt rails for any power supply larger than 230 watts.

- The non-ATX standard EPS12V introduced a 24-pin motherboard connector and a unique 8-pin connector. It was not swappable with ATX power supplies, and while its popularity was short-lived, it introduced several features that became part of the ATX12V standard, including rails.

- The demand for smaller and quieter PCs and the introduction of the BTX motherboard form factors led to the development of niche market power supply form factors. TFX12V, SFX12V, CFX12V, and LFX12V have the same connectors as standard ATX power supplies, but differ in size or shape.

- Active power factor correction (active PFC) helps to eliminate harmonics, which can damage electrical components. Never buy a power supply that does not have active PFC.

- Power supplies are rated in watts. If you know the amount of wattage that every device in the PC needs, you can arrive at the total wattage required for all devices, and that is the minimum wattage your power supply should provide. If the power supply does not provide sufficient wattage for the PC, the computer will not work. For a new computer system, you should select at least a 400-watt power supply to have extra power for adding components in the future.

- Because converting from AC to DC may result in a significant loss of wattage, purchase a power supply that offers a high percentage of efficiency. The ATX12V 2.0 standard requires a power supply to be at least 70 percent efficient, but you can find power supplies with better then 80 percent efficiency.

Be aware that power supplies produce less wattage over time, so don't cut the wattage specification too tightly. While power supplies range from 200 to 600 watts, you should know that the more AC the power supply draws, the more heat it produces.

Key Terms

active power factor correction (active PFC) (201)
alternating current (AC) (188)
amperes (amps or A) (188)
ATX (197)
direct current (DC) (188)
IEC-320 (189)
joule (193)
mini connector (196)

Molex connector (196)
multimeter (190)
ohms (188)
P1 power connector (195)
power conditioning (193)
power supply unit (PSU) (186)
rails (200)
resistance (188)
SATA power connector (196)

smart UPS (194)
soft power (197)
surge suppressor (192)
uninterruptible power supply (UPS) (193)
volts (V) (188)
wattage (watts or W) (188)

Key Term Quiz

Use the Key Terms list to complete the sentences that follow. Not all terms will be used.

1. Supply power to the floppy drive by using the _____ from the power supply.

2. The electric company provides _____ power that the power supply converts to _____ for use by the computer components.

3. If the _____ are left off the expansion slots, the computer may overheat.

4. The _____ form factor power supply attaches to the motherboard with a _____ and supplies 5 V to the motherboard at all times.

5. Be sure your surge suppressor has a _____ rating of at least 800.

6. _____ is a measurement unit for the amount of electrons flowing past a certain point on a wire.

7. Be sure the _____ rating for your power supply is greater than the minimum required by all devices in the computer.

8. The ability to split voltage supplies into separate _____ ensures that no device will hog all the available power.

9. To supply power to an internal DVD drive, you would most likely plug in a _____ from the power supply.

10. Resistance to the flow of electrons is measured in _____.

Multiple-Choice Quiz

1. When you test voltage with a multimeter, you can assume the outlet or connector is functioning properly if the reading is within a certain percentage of the expected number. What is that maximum percentage by which the reading can vary?

A. 5 percent
B. 10 percent
C. 20 percent
D. 25 percent

2. What voltage does an ATX12V P4 connector provide for motherboards?

   A. 3.3 V

   B. 3.3 V, 5 V

   C. 5 V

   D. 12 V

3. When testing an AC outlet, what voltage should the multimeter show between the neutral and ground wires?

   A. 120 V

   B. 60 V

   C. 0 V

   D. –120 V

4. What sort of power connector does a hard drive typically use?

   A. Molex

   B. Mini

   C. Sub-mini

   D. Micro

5. Arthur installed a new motherboard in his case and connected the ATX power, but his system would not turn on. He sees an extra 4-wire port on the motherboard. What's he missing?

   A. He needs a power supply with a P2 connector for plugging in auxiliary components.

   B. He needs a power supply with a P3 connector for plugging in case fans.

   C. He needs a power supply with a P4 connector for plugging into Pentium IV and some Athlon XP motherboards.

   D. He needs a power supply with a Aux connector for plugging into a secondary power supply.

6. What is the effect of exceeding the wattage capabilities of a power supply by inserting too many devices?

   A. The system will boot normally, but some of the devices will not function properly.

   B. The system will boot normally and all of the devices will work, but only for a limited time. After an hour or so, the system will spontaneously shut down.

   C. The system will not boot or turn on at all.

   D. The system will try to boot, but the overloaded power supply will fail, burning up delicate internal capacitors.

7. Where do you put the multimeter leads when you test a Molex connector?

   A. The red lead should always touch the red wire; the black lead should touch a black ground wire.

   B. The red lead should always touch the black ground wire; the black lead should always touch the red hot wire.

   C. The red lead should always touch the yellow hot wire; the black lead should touch the red hot wire.

   D. The red lead should touch either the red or yellow hot wire; the black lead should touch a black ground wire.

8. What is the minimum PSU required for an ATX system that requires Molex, mini connectors, and SATA connectors?

   A. ATX

   B. ATX12V 1.3

   C. ATX12V 2.0

   D. EPS12V

9. Which of the following is not a PSU form factor?

   A. TFX12V

   B. SFX12V

   C. CFX12V

   D. LPX12V

10. Which statement is true?

    A. Removing the expansion slot covers on the back of your case will improve cooling by allowing hot air to escape.

    B. Shop around when purchasing a case as you will often find good deals that include a powerful PSU.

    C. Always keep the power supply plugged in to the wall outlet when working on the inside of a computer as this helps to ground it.

    D. An AC testing device is never as accurate as a multimeter.

11. Which of the following EPS12V features was incorporated into the ATX12v2.0 standard?

    A. The P4 motherboard power connector

    B. Voltage rails

    C. The 6-pin AUX connector

    D. Soft power

12. Which reading shows a good outlet voltage?

    A. Hot to Neutral 0 V

    B. Hot to Ground 0 V

    C. Neutral to Ground ~115 V

    D. Neutral to Hot ~115 V

13. Which device provides battery backup in addition to protection from electrical anomalies?

    A. Surge suppressor

    B. Power conditioner

    C. Uninterruptible power supply

    D. Active power factor correction

14. Elise needs a Molex connector for her new DVD burner, but her power supply doesn't have any more. What is her best option?

    A. Purchase a Molex splitter to create more connections

    B. Purchase a new power supply with enough connections

    C. Purchase a MiniMolex converter and use a free mini connector to power the DVD drive

    D. Return the DVD burner and purchase an external USB DVD burner

15. What feature of power supplies eliminates harmful harmonics?

    A. Power conditioning

    B. Active power factor correction

    C. Soft power

    D. Voltage rails

■ Essay Quiz

1. Jack and Denise have joined your study group. Since neither has any previous experience with basic electricity and its jargon, they want you to explain voltage, amperage, and wattage. In plain language, define these terms and explain what VA = W means.

2. Often in the computer field, advances in one area will lead to advances in another area. Do you think that improvements in the CPU and other computer devices and functions made the ATX form factor power supply necessary?

Lab Projects

• Lab Project 8.1

This chapter recommends a 400-watt power supply for a new computer. Is that the wattage that manufacturers usually offer with their computers? Check the following Web sites to see what wattage comes with a new PC:

- www.dell.com
- www.gateway.com
- www.hp.com

Do any of these companies mention a power supply upgrade with a higher wattage rating? If so, what are the wattages and what are the additional costs?

Implementing Hard Drives

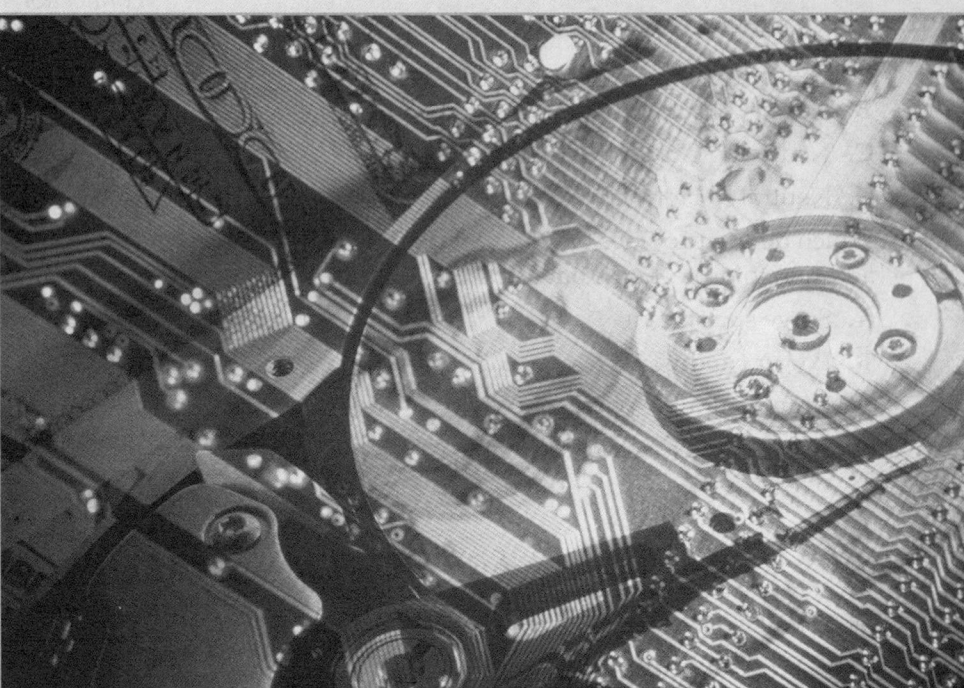

"Have you heard of the wonderful one-hoss shay, That was built in such a logical way It ran a hundred years to a day?"
"It went to pieces all at once,— All at once, and nothing first, Just as bubbles do when they burst."
—OLIVER WENDELL HOLMES, THE DEACON'S MASTERPIECE, STANZAS 1 AND 11

In this chapter, you will learn how to

- **Explain the partitions available in Windows**
- **Discuss the formatting options**
- **Partition and format hard drives**
- **Maintain and troubleshoot a hard drive**

From the standpoint of your PC, a new hard drive successfully installed is nothing more than a huge pile of sectors. CMOS sees the drive; it shows up in your autodetect screen and BIOS knows how to talk to the drive, but as far as an operating system is concerned, that drive is unreadable. Your operating system must organize that big pile of sectors so you can create two things: folders and files. This chapter covers that process.

The Essentials exam concentrates on preparing hard drives that are already installed, whereas the 220-602 (IT Technician) exam is more interested in the physical installation. Given that far more people configure already installed drives as opposed to installing drives, we can give CompTIA a bit of credit here. If you want to get into the actual installation game, check out my other book, *Mike Meyers' A+ Guide: PC Technican (Exams 220-602, 220-603, & 220-604).*

Historical/Conceptual

After you've successfully installed a hard drive, you must perform two more steps to translate a drive's geometry and circuits into something usable to the system: partitioning and formatting. *Partitioning* is the process of electronically subdividing the physical hard drive into groups of cylinders called `partitions` (or `volumes`). A hard drive must have at least one partition, and you can create multiple partitions on a single hard drive if you wish. In Windows, each of these partitions typically is assigned a drive letter such as C: or D:. After partitioning, you must *format* the drive. `Formatting` installs a `file system` onto the drive that organizes each partition in such a way that the operating system can store files and folders on the drive. Several different types of file systems are used in the Windows world. This chapter will go through them after covering partitioning.

The process of partitioning and formatting a drive is one of the few areas remaining on the software side of PC assembly that requires you to perform a series of fairly complex manual steps. The CompTIA A+ certification exams test your knowledge of *what* these processes do to make the drive work, as well as the steps needed to partition and format hard drives in Windows 2000/XP.

This chapter continues the exploration of hard drive installation by explaining partitioning and formatting and then going through the process of partitioning and formatting hard drives. The chapter wraps with a discussion on hard drive maintenance and troubleshooting issues.

■ Hard Drive Partitions

Partitions provide tremendous flexibility in hard drive organization. Partitions enable you to organize a drive in a way that suits your personal taste. For example, I partitioned my 500-GB hard drive into a 150-GB partition, where I store Windows XP and all my programs, and a 350-GB partition, where I store all my personal data. This is a matter of personal choice—in my case, it makes backups simpler because the data is stored in one partition, and that partition alone can be backed up without including the applications.

Partitioning enables a single hard drive to store more than one *operating system (OS)*. One OS could be stored in one partition and another OS stored in a second, for example. Granted, most people use only one OS, but if you want to choose to boot Windows or Linux, partitions are the key to enabling you to do so.

Essentials

Windows 2000 and XP support two different partitioning methods: the older but more universal master boot record (MBR) partitioning scheme and the newer (but proprietary to Microsoft) dynamic storage partitioning scheme. Microsoft calls a hard drive that uses the MBR partitioning scheme a `basic disk` and a drive using the dynamic storage partitioning scheme a `dynamic disk`. A single Windows system with two hard drives may have one of the drives partitioned as a basic disk and the other as a dynamic disk, and the system will run perfectly well. The bottom line? You get to learn about two totally different types of partitioning! Yay! Given that basic disks are much older, we'll start there.

Basic Disks

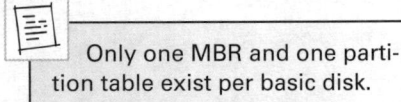

Only one MBR and one partition table exist per basic disk.

Basic disk partitioning creates two very small data structures on a drive, the `master boot record (MBR)` and a `partition table`, and stores them on the first sector of the hard drive—called the `boot sector`. The MBR is nothing more than a tiny bit of code that takes control of the boot process from the system BIOS. When the computer boots to a hard drive, BIOS automatically looks for MBR code on the boot sector. The MBR has only one job: to look in the partition table for a partition with a valid operating system (Figure 9.1).

All basic disk partition tables support up to four partitions. The partition table supports two types of partitions: primary partitions and extended partitions. `Primary partitions` are designed to support bootable operating systems. `Extended partitions` are not bootable. A single basic disk may have up to three primary partitions and one extended partition. If you do not have an extended partition, you may have up to four primary partitions.

Each partition must have some unique identifier to enable users to recognize it as an individual partition. Microsoft operating systems (DOS and Windows) traditionally assign primary partitions a drive letter from C: to Z:. Extended partitions do not get drive letters.

After you create an extended partition, you must create `logical drives` within that extended partition. A logical drive traditionally gets a drive letter from D: to Z:. (The drive letter C: is always reserved for the first primary partition in a Windows PC.)

Windows 2000 and Windows XP partitions are not limited to drive letters. With the exception of the partition that stores the boot files for Windows (which will always be C:), any other primary partitions or logical drives may get either a drive letter or a folder on a primary partition. You'll see how all of this works later in this chapter.

If a primary partition is a bootable partition, then why does a basic drive's partition table support up to four primary partitions? Remember when I said that partitioning allows multiple operating systems? This is how it works! You can install up to four different operating systems, each OS installed on its own primary partition, and boot to your choice each time you fire up the computer.

Every primary partition on a single drive has a special setting called *active* stored in the partition table. This setting is either on or off on each primary partition. At boot, the MBR uses the active setting in the partition table to determine which primary partition to choose to try to load an OS. Only one partition

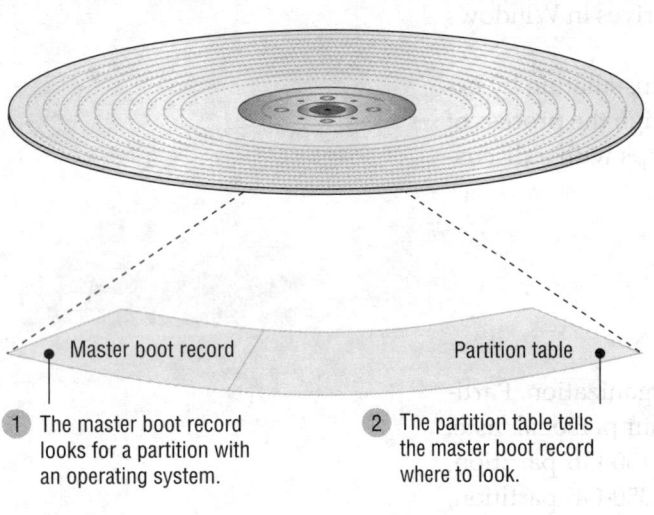

1 The master boot record looks for a partition with an operating system.

2 The partition table tells the master boot record where to look.

• **Figure 9.1**   Functions of the MBR and partition table

at a time can be the `active partition`, because you can run only one OS at a time (see Figure 9.2).

The boot sector at the beginning of the hard drive isn't the only special sector on a hard drive. The first sector of the first cylinder of each partition also has a special sector called the `volume boot sector`. While the "main" boot sector defines the partitions, the volume boot sector stores information important to its partition, such as the location of the OS boot files. Figure 9.3 shows a hard drive with two partitions. The first partition's volume boot sector contains information about the size of the partition and the code pointing to the boot files on this partition. The second volume boot sector contains information about the size of the partition.

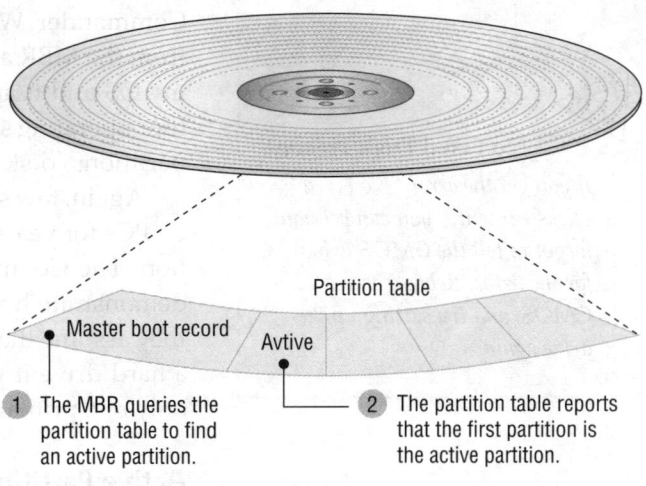

1 The MBR queries the partition table to find an active partition.

2 The partition table reports that the first partition is the active partition.

● **Figure 9.2** The MBR checks the partition table to find the active partition.

Primary Partitions

If you want to boot an operating system from a hard drive, that hard drive must have a primary partition. The MBR checks the partition table for the active primary partition (see Figure 9.4). In Windows 2000/XP, the primary partition is C:, and that cannot be changed.

Even though hard drives support up to four primary partitions, you almost never see four partitions used in the Windows world. Both Windows 2000 and Windows XP support up to four primary partitions on one drive, but how many people (other than nerdy CompTIA A+ people like you and me) really want to boot up more than one OS? We use a number of terms for this function, but `dual-boot` and *multiboot* are the most common. The system in my house, for example, uses four primary partitions, each holding one OS: Ubuntu Linux, Windows 2000, Windows XP, and Windows Vista. In other words, I chopped my drive up into four chunks and installed a different OS in each. To do multiboot, I used a third-party tool—System Commander 8 by VCOM—to set up the partitions. Windows 2000/XP and Linux come with similar tools that can do this, but I find them messy to use and prefer System

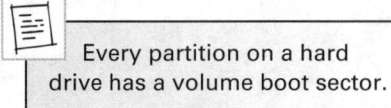

Every partition on a hard drive has a volume boot sector.

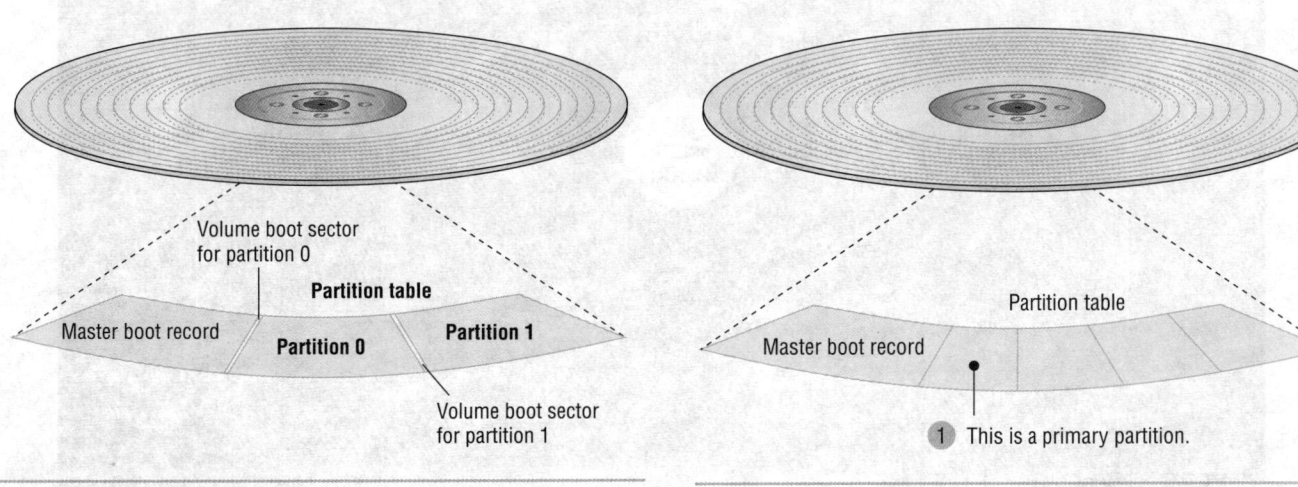

● **Figure 9.3** Volume boot sector

1 This is a primary partition.

● **Figure 9.4** The MBR checks the partition table to find a primary partition.

Commander. When my computer boots, System Commander yanks control from the MBR and asks me which OS I wish to boot (see Figure 9.5). I select my OS and it appears. As you look at this figure, you'll notice more than four operating systems. This particular system gets around the four primary partitions/disk limitation by using two hard drives.

Again, few systems use more than one primary partition. You may work on PCs for years and never see a system with more than one primary partition. The CompTIA A+ certification exams certainly don't expect you to demonstrate how to create a system with multiple primary partitions, but they assume that you know you *can* add more than one primary partition to a hard drive if you so desire. The rest of this book assumes that you want only one primary partition.

Active Partition

When you create a primary partition and decide to place an OS on that partition, you must set that partition as active. This must take place even if you use only a single primary partition. Luckily, this step is automated in the Windows installation process. Consider this: When would you want to go through the steps to define a partition as active? That would be when you install an OS on that partition! So when you install Windows on a new system,

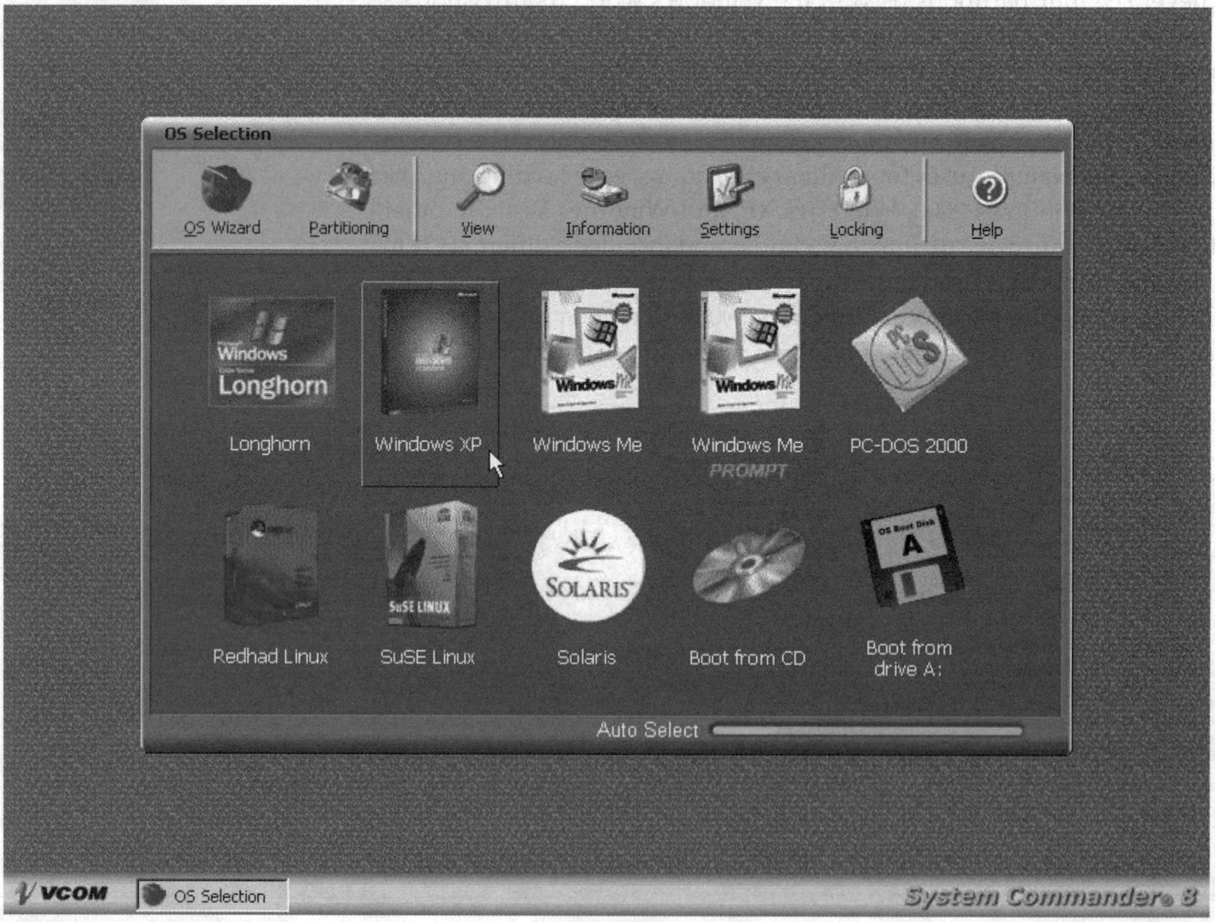

Tech Tip

No Fixed Disk Present

If you get the error "No Fixed Disks Present," you can bet you forgot to tell the CMOS to look for the drive. Reboot, access CMOS, and try setting up the drive again.

• **Figure 9.5**   System Commander's OS Selection menu

the install program automatically sets up your first primary partition as the active partition. It never actually says this in the install, it just does it for you.

So if you raise your right hand and promise to use only Microsoft Windows and make only single primary partitions on your hard drives, odds are good you'll never have to mess with manually adjusting your active partitions. Of course, since you're crazy enough to want to get into PCs, that means within a year of reading this text you're going to want to install other operating systems like Linux on your PC (and that's OK—all techs want to try this at some point). The moment you do, you'll enter the world of boot manager programs of which the just-described System Commander is only one of many, many choices. You also might use tools that enable you to change the active partition manually—exactly when and how this is done varies tremendously for each situation and is way outside the scope of the CompTIA A+ exams, but make sure you know why you might need to set a partition as active.

When my System Commander boot screen comes up, it essentially asks me, "What primary partition do you want me to make active?"

Extended Partition

Understanding the purpose of extended partitions requires a brief look at the historical PC. The first versions of the old DOS operating system to support hard drives only supported primary partitions up to 32 MB. As hard drives went past 32 MB, Microsoft needed a way to support them. Instead of rewriting DOS to handle larger drives, Microsoft developers created the idea of the extended partition. That way, if you had a hard drive larger than 32 MB, you could make a 32-MB primary partition and the rest of the drive an extended partition. Over the years, DOS and then Windows were rewritten to support large hard drives, but the extended partition is still fully supported.

The beauty of an extended partition is in the way it handles drive letters. When you create a primary partition, it gets a drive letter and that's it. But when you create an extended partition, it does not automatically get a drive letter. Instead, you then go through a second step, where you divide the extended partition into one or more logical drives. An extended partition may have as many logical drives as you wish. By default, Windows gives each logical drive in an extended partition a drive letter and most Windows users use drive letters. However, if you'd like, you may even "mount" the drive letter as a folder on any lettered drive. You can set the size of each logical drive to any size you want. You'll learn how to mount drives later in this chapter—for now, just get the idea that a partition may be mounted with a drive letter or as a folder.

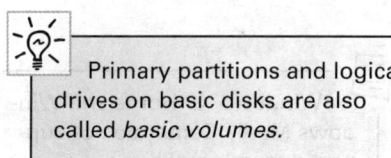
Primary partitions and logical drives on basic disks are also called *basic volumes*.

Extended partitions are completely optional; you do not have to create an extended partition on a hard drive. So, if you can't boot to an extended partition and your hard drive doesn't need an extended partition, why would you want to create one? First of all, the majority of systems do not use extended partitions. Most systems use only one hard drive and that single drive is partitioned as one big primary partition—nothing wrong with that! Some users like having an extended partition with one or more logical drives, and they use the extended partitions as a way to separate data. For example, I might store all my movie files on my G: logical drive.

Try This!

Folder Swapping

What steps would you have to go through to add a new drive to a system and remount it as the C:\STORAGE folder without losing any data in the existing C:\STORAGE folder? Don't bother telling me the tools you need, just think about the logical steps you'd need to do this.

Instead of assigning drive letters, you can mount logical drives as folders on an existing drive. It's easy to make a logical drive and call it C:\STORAGE. If the C:\STORAGE folder fills up, you could add an extra hard drive, make the entire extra drive an extended partition with one logical drive, unmount the old C:\STORAGE drive, and then mount the new huge logical drive as C:\STORAGE! It's as though you made your C: drive bigger without replacing it.

Cross Check

RAID

RAID stands for *Random Array of Independent Device* and is the process of making two or more drives look like one drive. RAID is covered in much more detail in my 602 book, but for now appreciate that there are three versions:

- **RAID 0** Data is split between two drives. Fast, but if one drive fails, all data is lost. Also called *striping*.

- **RAID 1** All data is copied to two drives, with each drive holding an exact copy of the other. Slow, but if one drive fails, the other drive has all the data. Also called *mirroring*.

- **RAID 5** Data and special recovery information are spread across three or more drives. If one drive fails, the other two drives can recover all data. Also called *striping with parity*.

Dynamic Disks

With the introduction of Windows 2000, Microsoft defined an entirely new type of partitioning called *dynamic storage partitioning*, better known as *dynamic disks*. Dynamic disks drop the word *partition* and instead use the term *volume*. There is no dynamic disk equivalent to primary vs. extended partitions. A volume is still technically a partition, but it can do things a regular partition cannot do, such as spanning. A *spanned volume* goes across more than one drive. Windows allows you to span up to 32 drives under a single volume. Dynamic disks also support RAID 0 in Windows 2000 Professional and Windows XP Professional. Windows 2000 Server and Windows Server 2003 support RAID 0, 1, and 5.

Dynamic disks use an MBR and a partition table, but these older structures are there only for backward compatibility. All of the information about a dynamic disk is stored in a hidden partition that takes up the last 1 MB of the hard drive. Every partition in a partition table holds a 2-byte value that describes the partition. For example, an extended partition gets the number 05. Windows adds a new number, 42, to the first partition on a dynamic disk. When Windows 2000 or XP reads the partition table for a dynamic disk, it sees the number 42 and immediately jumps to the 1-MB hidden partition, ignoring the old style partition table. By supporting an MBR and partition table, Windows also prevents other disk partitioning programs from messing with a dynamic disk. If a third-party partitioning program is used, it simply sees the entire hard drive as either an unformatted primary partition or a non-readable partition.

You can use five volume types with dynamic disks: simple, spanned, striped, mirrored, and RAID 5. Most folks stick with simple volumes.

Simple volumes work much like primary partitions. If you have a hard drive and you want to make half of it C: and the other half D:, you create two

Windows XP Home and Windows Media Center do not support dynamic disks.

A key thing to understand about dynamic drives is that the technology is *proprietary*. Microsoft has no intention of telling anyone exactly how dynamic disks work. Only fairly recent Microsoft operating systems (Windows 2000, XP, 2003, and Vista) can read a drive configured as a dynamic disk.

volumes on a dynamic disk. That's it—no choosing between primary and extended partitions. Remember that you were limited to four primary partitions when using basic disks. To make more than four volumes with a basic disk, you first had to create an extended partition and then make logical drives within the extended partition. Dynamic disks simplify the process by treating all partitions as volumes, so you can make as many as you need.

Spanned volumes use unallocated space on multiple drives to create a single volume. Spanned volumes are a bit risky—if any of the spanned drives fails, the entire volume is permanently lost.

Striped volumes are RAID 0 volumes. You may take any two unallocated spaces on two separate hard drives and stripe them. But again, if either drive fails, you lose all your data.

Mirrored volumes are RAID 1 volumes. You may take any two unallocated spaces on two separate hard drives and mirror them. If one of the two mirrored drives fails, the other will keep running.

RAID 5 volumes , as the name implies, are for RAID 5 arrays. A RAID 5 volume requires three or more dynamic disks with equal-sized unallocated spaces.

Other Partitions

The partition types supported by Windows are not the only partition types you may encounter—other types exist. One of the most common is called the *hidden partition*. A hidden partition is really just a primary partition that is hidden from your operating system. Only special BIOS tools may access a hidden partition. Hidden partitions are used by some PC makers to hide a backup copy of an installed OS that you can use to restore your system if you accidentally trash it—by, for example, learning about partitions and using a partitioning program incorrectly.

A *swap partition* is another special type of partition, but it is only found on Linux and BSD systems. A swap partition is an entire partition whose only job is to act like RAM when your system needs more RAM than you have installed. Windows has a similar function called a *page file* that uses a special file instead of a partition. Most OS experts believe a swap partition is a little bit faster than a page file. You'll learn all about page files and swap partitions in Chapter 12.

 Early versions of Windows (3.*x* and 9*x*/Me) called the page file a *swap file.* Most techs use the terms interchangeably today.

When to Partition

Partitioning is not a common task. The two most common situations likely to require partitioning are when you're installing an OS on a new system, and when you are adding a second drive to an existing system. When you install a new OS, the installation CD will at some point ask you how you would like to partition the drive. When you're adding a new hard drive to an existing system, every OS has a built-in tool to help you partition it.

Each version of Windows offers a different tool for partitioning hard drives. For more than 20 years, through the days of DOS and early Windows (up to Windows Me), you used a command-line program called FDISK to partition drives. Figure 9.6 shows the FDISK program. Windows 2000 and Windows XP use a graphical partitioning program called Disk Management (Figure 9.7).

```
                          Microsoft Windows 98
                       Fixed Disk Setup Program
                  (C)Copyright Microsoft Corp.  1983 - 1998

                              FDISK Options

        Current fixed disk drive: 1

        Choose one of the following:

        1. Create DOS partition or Logical DOS Drive
        2. Set active partition
        3. Delete partition or Logical DOS Drive
        4. Display partition information

        Enter choice: [1]


        Press Esc to exit FDISK
```

Figure 9.6 FDISK

This chapter explains how to partition a hard drive *before* it explains formatting, because that is the order in which you as a PC tech will actually perform those tasks. You'll learn all the specifics of the various file systems—such as FAT32 and NTFS—when I explain formatting in the next section, but until then, just accept that there are several different systems for organizing the files on a hard drive, and that part of setting up a hard drive involves choosing among them.

Linux uses a number of different tools for partitioning. The oldest is called FDISK—yup, the exact same name as the DOS/Windows version. However, that's where the similarities end, as Linux FDISK has a totally different command set. Even though every copy of Linux comes with the Linux FDISK, it's rarely used because so many better partitioning tools are available. One of the newer Linux partitioning tools is called GParted. GParted is graphical like Disk Management and is fairly easy to use (Figure 9.8). GParted is also a powerful partition management tool—so powerful that it also works with Windows partitions.

Traditionally, once a partition is made, you cannot change its size or type other than by erasing it. You might, however, want to take a hard drive partitioned as a single primary partition and change it to half primary

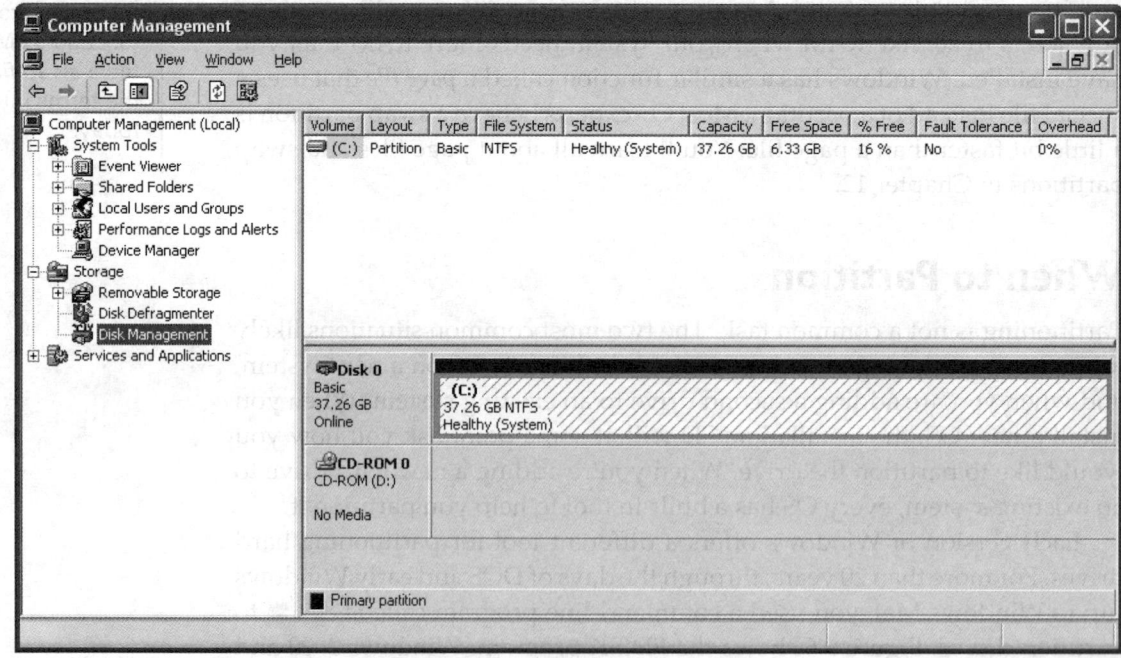

Figure 9.7 Windows XP Disk Management

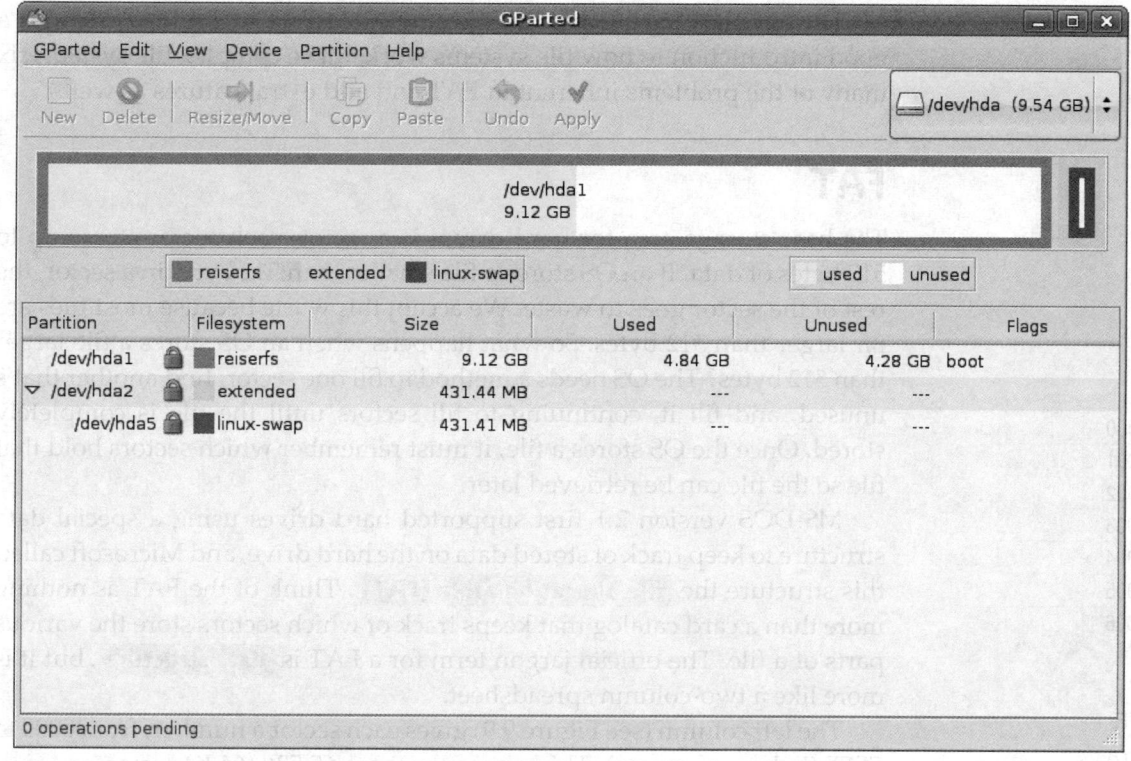

● **Figure 9.8** GParted in action

and half extended. Before Windows 2000, there was no way to do this non-destructively. As a result, a few third-party tools, led by Symantec's now famous PartitionMagic, gave techs the tools to resize partitions without losing the data they held. Windows 2000 and XP can non-destructively resize a partition to be larger but not smaller. Vista lets users non-destructively resize partitions any way they wish!

■ Hard Drive Formatting

Once a hard drive has been partitioned, there's one more step you must perform before your OS can use that drive: formatting. *Formatting* does two things: it creates a file system—like a library's card catalog—and makes the root directory in that file system. Every partition and volume you create needs to be formatted to enable it to hold data that you can easily retrieve. The various versions of Windows you're likely to encounter today can use several different file systems, so we'll look at those in detail next. The *root directory* provides the foundation upon which the OS builds files and folders.

File Systems in Windows

Every version of Windows comes with a built-in formatting utility that enables it to create one or more file systems on a partition or volume. The versions of Windows in current use support three separate Microsoft file systems: FAT16, FAT32, and NTFS.

The simplest hard drive file system, called FAT or FAT16, provides a good introduction to how file systems work. More complex file systems fix many of the problems inherent in FAT and add extra features as well.

FAT

The base storage area for hard drives is a sector; each sector stores up to 512 bytes of data. If an OS stores a file smaller than 512 bytes in a sector, the rest of the sector goes to waste. We accept this waste because most files are far larger than 512 bytes. So what happens when an OS stores a file larger than 512 bytes? The OS needs a method to fill one sector, find another that's unused, and fill it, continuing to fill sectors until the file is completely stored. Once the OS stores a file, it must remember which sectors hold that file so the file can be retrieved later.

MS-DOS version 2.1 first supported hard drives using a special data structure to keep track of stored data on the hard drive, and Microsoft called this structure the `file allocation table (FAT)`. Think of the FAT as nothing more than a card catalog that keeps track of which sectors store the various parts of a file. The official jargon term for a FAT is `data structure`, but it is more like a two-column spreadsheet.

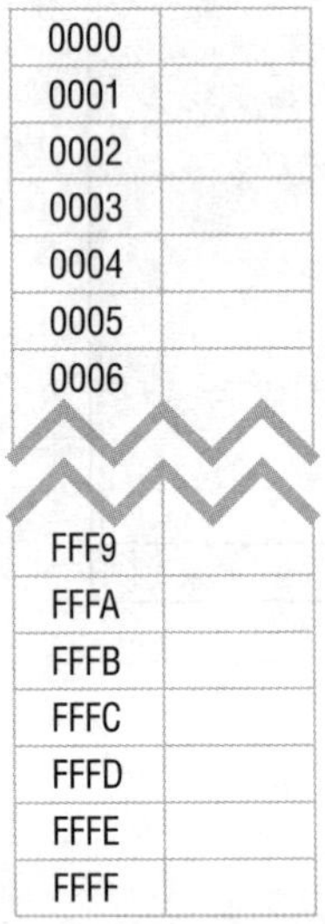

The left column (see Figure 9.9) gives each sector a number, from 0000 to FFFF (in hex, of course). This means there are 65,536 (64 K) sectors.

Notice that each value in the left column contains 16 bits. (Four hex characters make 16 bits, remember?) We call this type of FAT a *16-bit FAT* or *FAT16*. Not just hard drives have FATs. Some USB thumb drives also use FAT16. Floppy disks use FATs, but their FATs are only 12 bits since they store much less data.

The right column of the FAT contains information on the status of sectors. All hard drives, even brand-new drives fresh from the factory, contain faulty sectors that cannot store data because of imperfections in the construction of the drives. The OS must locate these bad sectors, mark them as unusable, and then prevent any files from being written to them. This mapping of bad sectors is one of the functions of `high-level formatting` (we'll talk about low-level formatting later in this chapter). After the format program creates the FAT, it proceeds through the entire partition, writing and attempting to read from each sector sequentially. If it finds a bad sector, it places a special status code (FFF7) in the sector's FAT location, indicating that sector is unavailable for use. Formatting also marks the good sectors as 0000.

Using the FAT to track sectors, however, creates a problem. The 16-bit FAT addresses a maximum of 64 K (2^{16}) locations. Therefore, the size of a hard-drive partition should be limited to 64 K × 512 bytes per sector, or 32 MB. When Microsoft first unveiled FAT16, this 32-MB limit presented no problem because most hard drives were only 5 MB to 10 MB. As hard drives grew in size, you could use FDISK to break them up into multiple partitions. You could divide a 40-MB hard drive into two partitions, for example, making each partition smaller than 32 MB. But as hard drives started to become much larger, Microsoft realized that the 32-MB limit for drives was unacceptable. We needed an improvement to the 16-bit FAT, a new and improved FAT16 that would support larger drives while still maintaining backward compatibility with the old style 16-bit FAT. This need led to the

0000	
0001	
0002	
0003	
0004	
0005	
0006	

FFF9	
FFFA	
FFFB	
FFFC	
FFFD	
FFFE	
FFFF	

• **Figure 9.9**   16-bit FAT

development of a dramatic improvement in FAT16, called *clustering*, that enabled you to format partitions larger than 32 MB (see Figure 9.10). This new FAT16 appeared way back in the DOS 4 days.

Clustering simply refers to combining a set of contiguous sectors and treating them as a single unit in the FAT. These units are called `file allocation units` or `clusters`. Each row of the FAT addressed a cluster instead of a sector. Unlike sectors, the size of a cluster is not fixed. Clusters improved FAT16, but it still only supported a maximum of 64 K storage units, so the formatting program set the number of sectors in each cluster according to the size of the partition. The larger the partition, the more sectors per cluster. This method kept clustering completely compatible with the 64-K locations in the old 16-bit FAT. The new FAT16 could support partitions up to 2 GB. (The old 16-bit FAT is so old it doesn't really even have a name—if someone says "FAT16," they mean the newer FAT16 that supports clustering.) Table 9.1 shows the number of sectors per cluster for FAT16.

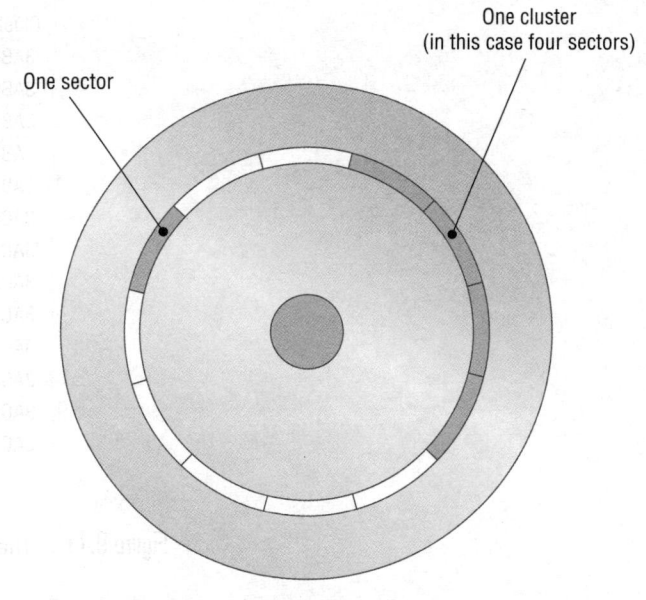

● **Figure 9.10**   Cluster versus sector

FAT16 in Action

Assume you have a copy of Windows using FAT16. When an application such as Microsoft Word tells the OS to save a file, Windows starts at the beginning of the FAT, looking for the first space marked "open for use" (0000), and begins to write to that cluster. If the entire file fits within that one cluster, Windows places the code *FFFF* (last cluster) into the cluster's status area in the FAT. Windows then goes to the folder storing the file and adds the filename and the cluster's number to the folder list. If the file requires more than one cluster, Windows searches for the next open cluster and places the number of the next cluster in the status area, filling and adding clusters until the entire file is saved. The last cluster then receives the end-of-file code (FFFF).

Let's run through an example of this process, and start by selecting an arbitrary part of the FAT: from 3ABB to 3AC7. Assume you want to save a file called MOM.TXT. Before saving the file, the FAT looks like Figure 9.11.

Table 9.1	FAT16 Cluster Sizes
If FDISK makes a partition this big:	**You'll get this many sectors/cluster:**
16 to 127.9 MB	4
128 to 255.9 MB	8
256 to 511.9 MB	16
512 to 1023.9 MB	32
1024 to 2048 MB	64

Cluster	Status
3ABB	0000
3ABC	0000
3ABD	FFF7
3ABE	0000
3ABF	0000
3AC0	0000
3AC1	0000
3AC2	0000
3AC3	0000
3AC4	0000
3AC5	0000
3AC6	0000
3AC7	0000

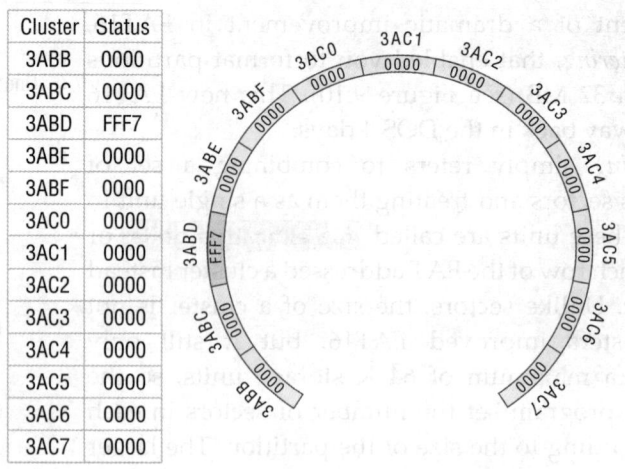

● **Figure 9.11**   The initial FAT

Windows finds the first open cluster, 3ABB, and fills it. But not all of the MOM.TXT file fits into that cluster. Needing more space, the OS goes through the FAT to find the next open cluster. It finds cluster 3ABC. Before filling 3ABC, the value *3ABC* is placed in 3ABB's status (see Figure 9.12).

Even after filling two clusters, more of the MOM.TXT file remains, so Windows must find one more cluster. The 3ABD has been marked FFF7 (bad cluster), so Windows skips over 3ABD, finding 3ABE (see Figure 9.13).

Before filling 3ABE, Windows enters the value *3ABE* in 3ABC's status. Windows does not completely fill 3ABE, signifying that the entire MOM.TXT file has been stored. Windows enters the value *FFFF* in 3ABE's status, indicating the end of file (see Figure 9.14).

After saving all the clusters, Windows now locates the file's folder (yes, folders also get stored on clusters, but they get a different set of clusters, somewhere else on the disk) and records the filename, size, date/time, and starting cluster, like this:

MOM.TXT 19234 05-19-07 2:04p 3ABB

Cluster	Status
3ABB	**3ABC** — MOM.TXT
3ABC	0000
3ABD	FFF7
3ABE	0000
3ABF	0000
3AC0	0000
3AC1	0000
3AC2	0000
3AC3	0000
3AC4	0000
3AC5	0000
3AC6	0000
3AC7	0000

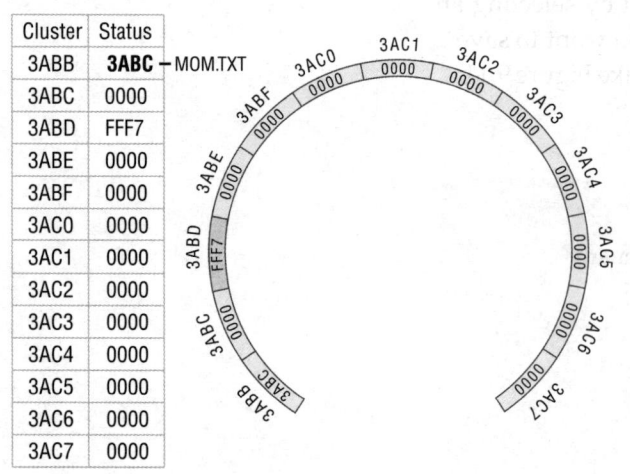

● **Figure 9.12**   The first cluster used

Cluster	Status
3ABB	3ABC
3ABC	**3ABE** — MOM.TXT
3ABD	FFF7
3ABE	0000
3ABF	0000
3AC0	0000
3AC1	0000
3AC2	0000
3AC3	0000
3AC4	0000
3AC5	0000
3AC6	0000
3AC7	0000

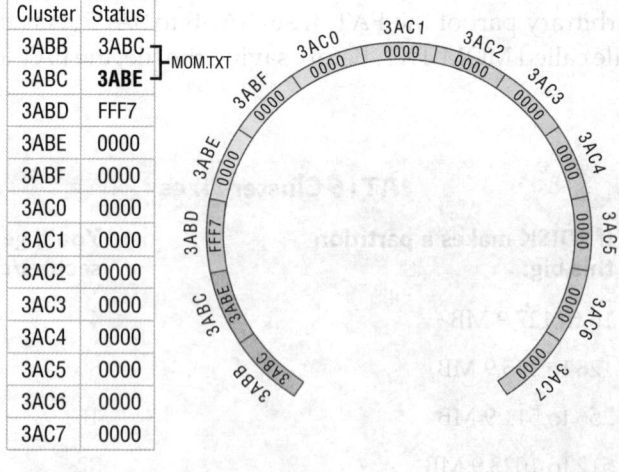

● **Figure 9.13**   The second cluster used

If a program requests that file, the process is reversed. Windows locates the folder containing the file to determine the starting cluster and then pulls a piece of the file from each cluster until it sees the end-of-file cluster. Windows then hands the reassembled file to the requesting application.

Clearly, without the FAT, Windows cannot locate files. FAT16 automatically makes two copies of the FAT. One FAT backs up the other to provide special utilities a way to recover a FAT that gets corrupted—a painfully common occurrence.

Even when FAT works perfectly, over time the files begin to separate in a process called **fragmentation**.

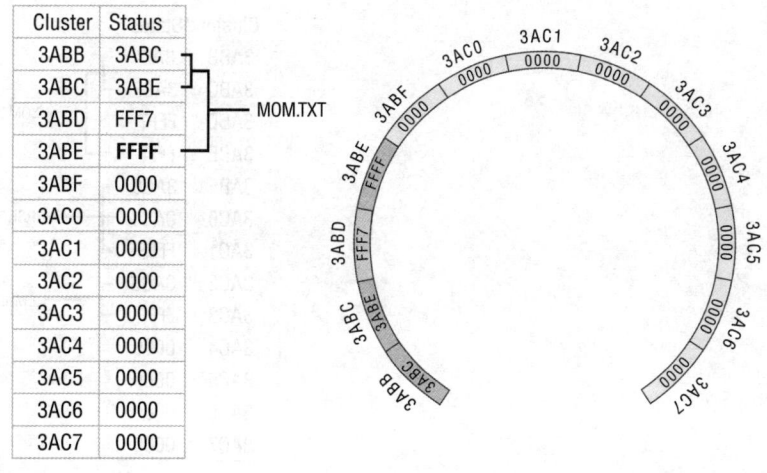

Cluster	Status
3ABB	3ABC
3ABC	3ABE
3ABD	FFF7
3ABE	**FFFF**
3ABF	0000
3AC0	0000
3AC1	0000
3AC2	0000
3AC3	0000
3AC4	0000
3AC5	0000
3AC6	0000
3AC7	0000

• **Figure 9.14**   End of file reached

Fragmentation

Continuing with the example, let's use Microsoft Word to save two more files: a letter to the IRS (IRSROB.DOC) and a letter to IBM (IBMHELP.DOC). IRSROB.DOC takes the next three clusters—3ABF, 3AC0, and 3AC1—and IBMHELP.DOC takes two clusters—3AC2 and 3AC3 (see Figure 9.15).

Now suppose you erase MOM.TXT. Windows does not delete the cluster entries for MOM.TXT when it erases a file. Windows only alters the information in the folder, simply changing the first letter of MOM.TXT to a hex code that can be translated as the Greek letter Σ (sigma). This causes the file to "disappear" as far as the OS knows. It won't show up, for example, in Windows Explorer, even though the data still resides on the hard drive for the moment (see Figure 9.16).

Note that under normal circumstances, Windows does not actually delete files when you press the DELETE key. Instead, Windows moves the files to a special hidden directory that you can access via the Recycle Bin. The files themselves are not actually deleted until you empty the Recycle Bin.

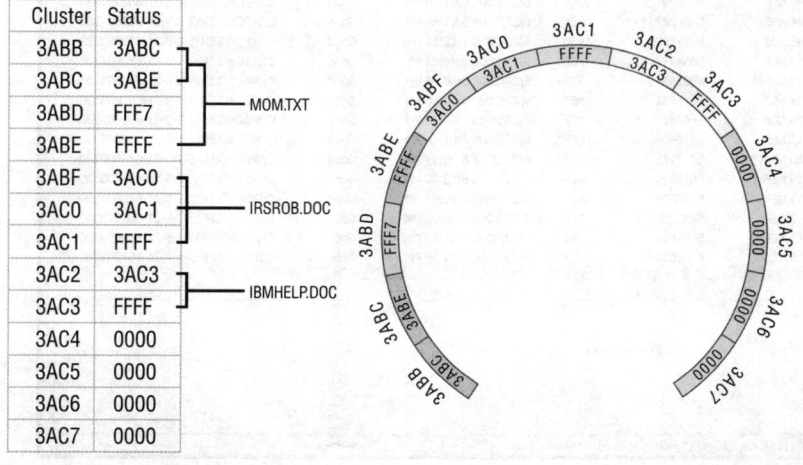

Cluster	Status
3ABB	3ABC
3ABC	3ABE
3ABD	FFF7
3ABE	FFFF
3ABF	3AC0
3AC0	3AC1
3AC1	FFFF
3AC2	3AC3
3AC3	FFFF
3AC4	0000
3AC5	0000
3AC6	0000
3AC7	0000

• **Figure 9.15**   Three files saved

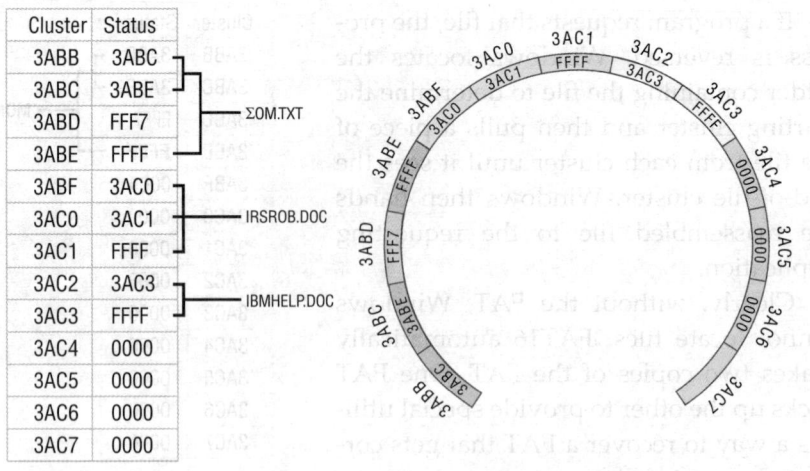

Cluster	Status
3ABB	3ABC
3ABC	3ABE
3ABD	FFF7
3ABE	FFFF
3ABF	3AC0
3AC0	3AC1
3AC1	FFFF
3AC2	3AC3
3AC3	FFFF
3AC4	0000
3AC5	0000
3AC6	0000
3AC7	0000

ΣOM.TXT

IRSROB.DOC

IBMHELP.DOC

• **Figure 9.16** MOM.TXT erased

(You can skip the Recycle Bin entirely if you wish, by highlighting a file, and then holding down the SHIFT key when you press DELETE.)

Because all the data for MOM.TXT is intact, you could use some program to change the Σ back into another letter, and thus get the document back. A number of third-party undelete tools are available. Figure 9.17 shows one such program at work. Just remember that if you want to use an

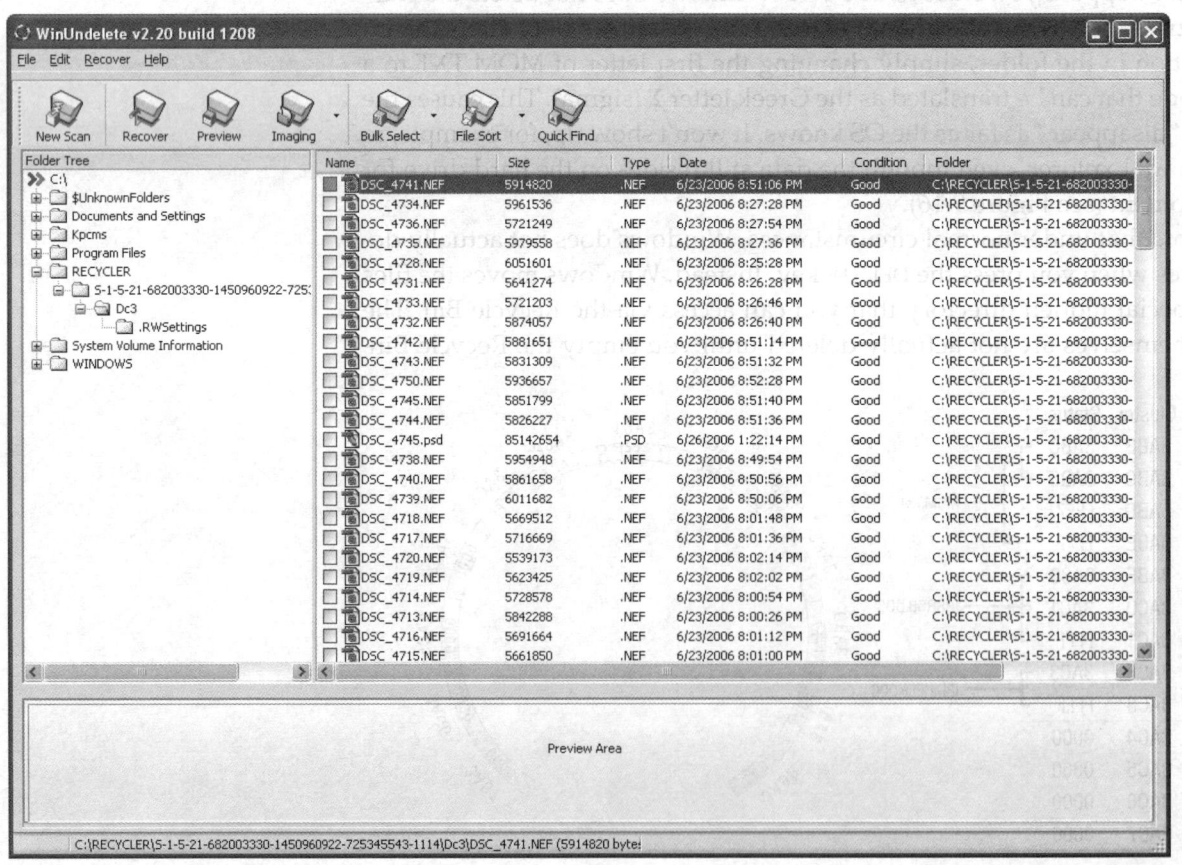

• **Figure 9.17** WinUndelete in action

undelete tool, you must use it quickly. The space allocated to your deleted file may soon be overwritten by a new file.

Let's say you just emptied your Recycle Bin. You now save one more file, TAXREC.XLS, a big spreadsheet that will take six clusters, into the same folder that once held MOM.TXT. As Windows writes the file to the drive, it overwrites the space that MOM.TXT used, but it needs three more clusters. The next three available clusters are 3AC4, 3AC5, and 3AC6 (see Figure 9.18).

Notice that TAXREC.XLS is in two pieces, thus *fragmented*. Fragmentation takes place all the time on FAT16 systems. Although the system easily negotiates a tiny fragmented file split into only two parts, excess fragmentation slows down the system during hard drive reads and writes. This example is fragmented into two pieces; in the real world, a file might fragment into hundreds of pieces, forcing the read/write heads to travel all over the hard drive to retrieve a single file. The speed at which the hard drive reads and writes files can be improved dramatically by eliminating this fragmentation.

Every version of Windows (with the exception of NT) comes with a program called Disk Defragmenter, which can rearrange the files back into neat contiguous chunks (see Figure 9.19). **Defragmentation** is crucial for ensuring the top performance of a hard drive. The "Maintaining and Troubleshooting Hard Drives" section of this chapter gives the details on working with the various Disk Defragmenters in Windows.

FAT32

When Microsoft introduced Windows 95 OSR2 (OEM Service Release 2), it also unveiled a totally new file format called **FAT32** that brought a couple of dramatic improvements. First, FAT32 supports partitions up to 2 terabytes (more than 2 trillion bytes). Second, as its name implies, FAT32 uses 32 bits to describe each cluster, which means clusters can drop to more reasonable sizes. FAT32's use of so many FAT entries gives it the power to use small clusters, making the old

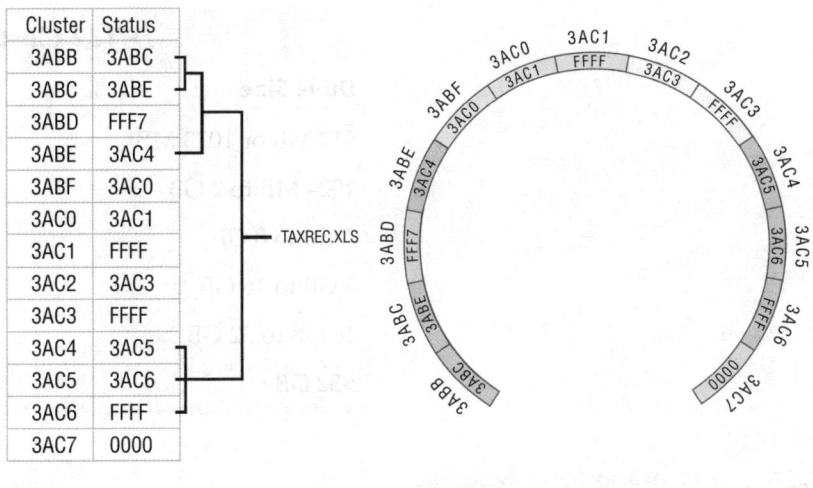

● **Figure 9.18**   TAXREC.XLS fragmented

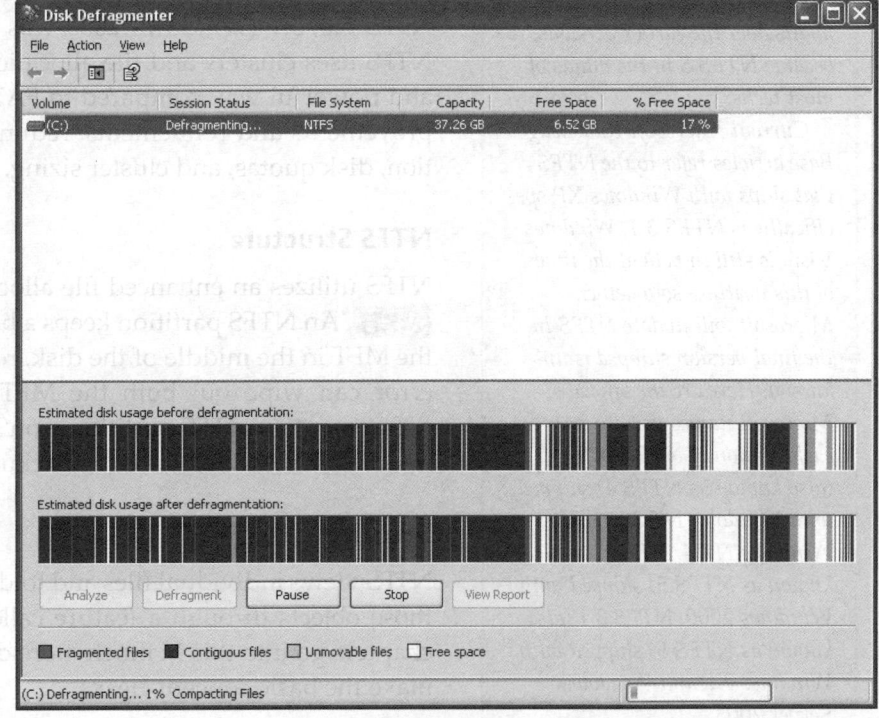

● **Figure 9.19**   Windows Disk Defragmenter

Table 9.2	FAT32 Cluster Sizes
Drive Size	Cluster Size
512 MB or 1023 MB	4 KB
1024 MB to 2 GB	4 KB
2 GB to 8 GB	4 KB
8 GB to 16 GB	8 KB
16 GB to 32 GB	16 KB
>32 GB	32 KB

Tech Tip

NTFS Naming Nightmare

Most computer writers, including those at Microsoft (until recently), label the version of NTFS that shipped with a particular version of Windows by the version number of Windows. So, the NTFS that shipped with Windows NT 4.0 is frequently called NTFS 4, although that's not technically correct. Similarly, since the NTFS that shipped with Windows 2000 offered great improvements over the earlier versions, it became NTFS 5 in the minds of most techs.

Current Microsoft Knowledge Base articles refer to the NTFS that ships with Windows XP specifically as NTFS 3.1. Windows Vista is still in beta at the time of this writing, so whether Microsoft will update NTFS in the final version shipped is unknown. Here are the official Microsoft names used to refer to each version of NTFS. NTFS 1.x (also known as NTFS 4) shipped with Windows NT 3.51 and Windows NT 4. NTFS 3.0 (also known as NTFS 5) shipped with Windows 2000. NTFS 3.1 (also known as NTFS 5) shipped with Windows XP and Windows Server 2003.

"keep your partitions small" rule obsolete. A 2-GB volume using FAT16 would use 32-KB clusters, while the same 2-GB volume using FAT32 would use 4-KB clusters. You get far more efficient use of disk space with FAT32 without the need to make multiple small partitions. FAT32 partitions still need defragmentation, however, just as often as FAT16 partitions.

Table 9.2 shows cluster sizes for FAT32 partitions.

NTFS

The Windows format of choice these days is the **NT File System (NTFS)**. NTFS came out a long time ago with the first version of Windows NT, thus the name. Over the years, NTFS has undergone a number of improvements. The version used in Windows 2000 is NTFS 3.0; the version used in Windows XP and Vista is called NTFS 3.1, although you'll see it referred to as NTFS 5.0/5.1 (Windows 2000 was unofficially Windows NT version 5). NTFS uses clusters and file allocation tables but in a much more complex and powerful way compared to FAT or FAT32. NTFS offers six major improvements and refinements: redundancy, security, compression, encryption, disk quotas, and cluster sizing.

NTFS Structure

NTFS utilizes an enhanced file allocation table called the **master file table (MFT)**. An NTFS partition keeps a backup copy of the most critical parts of the MFT in the middle of the disk, reducing the chance that a serious drive error can wipe out both the MFT and the MFT copy. Whenever you defragment an NTFS partition, you'll see a small, immovable chunk in the middle of the drive; that's the backup MFT (Figure 9.20).

Security

NTFS views individual files and folders as objects and provides security for those objects through a feature called the *access control list (ACL)*. Future chapters go into this in much more detail, but a quick example here should make the basic concept clear.

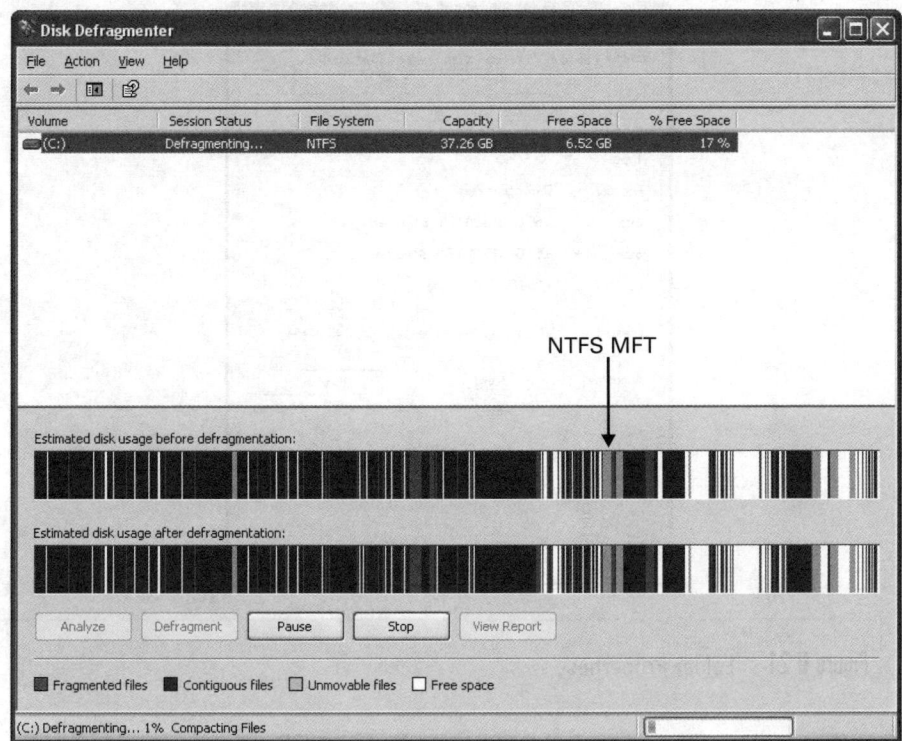

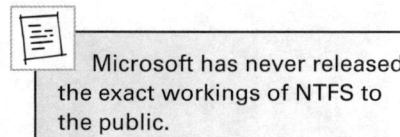
Microsoft has never released the exact workings of NTFS to the public.

All four of the CompTIA A+ exams test you on NTFS, such as when to use it, what advantages it has over FAT32, and how to lock down information. You'll also be quizzed on the tools, such as Disk Management, in all four exams. Don't skip anything in this chapter!

• **Figure 9.20**   An NTFS MFT appearing in a defragmenter program

Suppose Bill the IT Guy sets up a Windows XP PC as a workstation for three users: John, Wilma, and Felipe. John logs into the PC with his user name and password (johns and f3f2f1f0, respectively, in case you're curious) and begins to work on his project. The project folder is stored on the C: drive as C:\Projects\JohnSuperSecret. When John saves his work and gets ready to leave, he alters the permissions on his folder to deny access to anyone but him. When curious Wilma logs into the PC after John leaves, she cannot access the C:\Programs\JohnSuperSecret folder contents at all, although she can see the entry in Explorer. Without the ACL provided by NTFS, John would have no security over his files or folders at all.

Compression

NTFS enables you to compress individual files and folders to save space on a hard drive. Compression makes access time to the data slower, because the OS has to uncompress files every time you use them, but in a space-limited environment, sometimes that's what you have to do.

Encrypting File System

One of the big draws with NTFS is file encryption, the black art of making files unreadable to anybody who doesn't have the right key. You can encrypt a single file, a folder, and a folder full of files. Microsoft calls the encryption utility in NTFS the **encrypting file system (EFS)**, but it's simply an aspect of NTFS, not a standalone file system. To encrypt a file or folder, right-click it in My Computer and select Properties to open the Properties dialog box (Figure 9.21). Click the Advanced button to open the Advanced

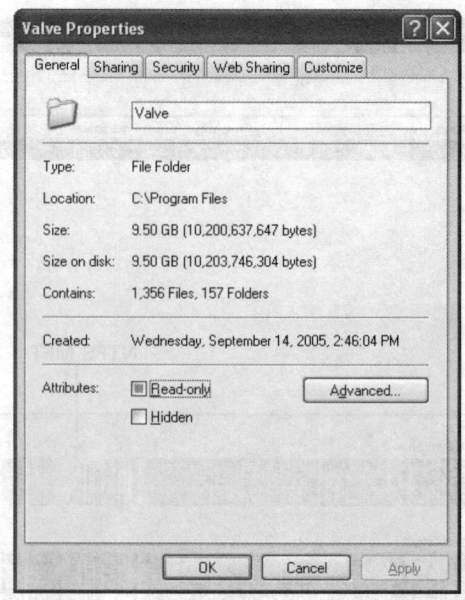

● **Figure 9.21** Folder Properties

Attributes dialog box. As you can see in Figure 9.22, encryption (and compression) is simply a selectable checkbox. Click the box next to *Encrypt contents to secure data* and then click the OK button—instantly your file is safe from prying eyes!

Encryption does not hide files; it simply makes them unreadable to other users. Figure 9.23 shows a couple of encrypted image files. Note that in addition to the pale green color of the filenames (that you can't tell are pale green in this black-and-white image), the files seem readily accessible. Windows XP can't provide a thumbnail, however, even though it can read the type of image file (JPEG) easily. Further, double-clicking the files opens the Windows Picture

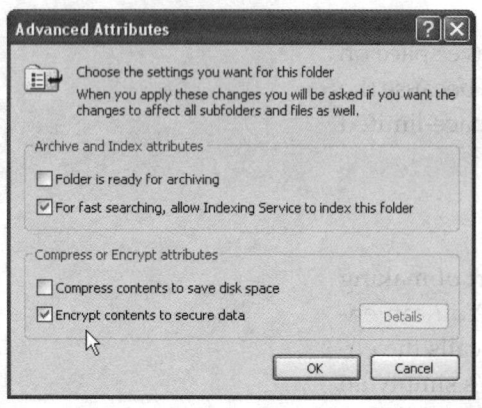

● **Figure 9.22** Options for compression and encryption

● **Figure 9.23** Encrypted files

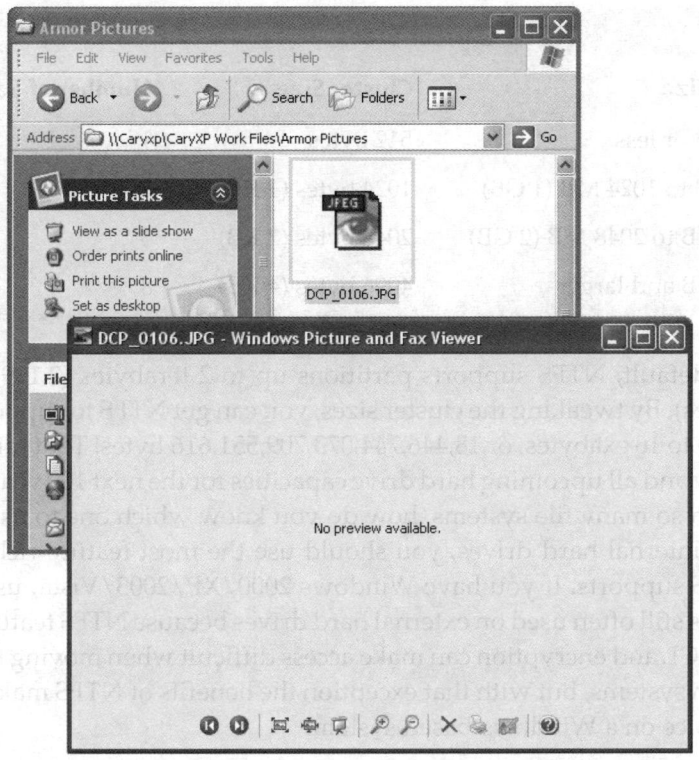

• **Figure 9.24** Windows Picture and Fax Viewer blocked by file encryption

Windows XP Home and Media Center editions do not support EFS.

Encryption protects against other users, but only if you log out. It might seem obvious, but I've had lots of users get confused by encryption, thinking that the PC *knows* who's clicking the keyboard! All protections and security are based on user accounts. If someone logs into your computer with a different account, the encrypted files will be unreadable. We'll get to user accounts, permissions, and such in later chapters in detail.

and Fax Viewer, but you still can't see the image (Figure 9.24). Better still, you can try to access the files across your network and the encryption does precisely what it's supposed to do—blocks unwanted access to sensitive data.

Remember that encryption is separate from the NTFS file security provided by the ACL—to access encrypted files, you will need both permission to access the files based on the ACL and the keys used to encrypt the files (which are stored in your user profile, typically under C:\Documents and Settings\%username%\Application Data\Microsoft\ Crypto\RSA). Fortunately, Windows makes this process transparent to the end user, automatically checking the ACL and decrypting the files as needed.

Disk Quotas

NTFS supports disk quotas , enabling administrators to set limits on drive space usage for users. To set quotas, you must log in as an Administrator, right-click the hard drive name, and select Properties. In the Drive Properties dialog box, select the Quota tab and make changes. Figure 9.25 shows configured quotas for a hard drive. While rarely used on single-user systems, setting disk quotas on multi-user systems prevents any individual user from monopolizing your hard disk space.

Cluster Sizes

Unlike FAT16 or FAT32, NTFS enables you to adjust the cluster sizes, although you'll probably rarely do so. Table 9.3 shows the default cluster sizes for NTFS.

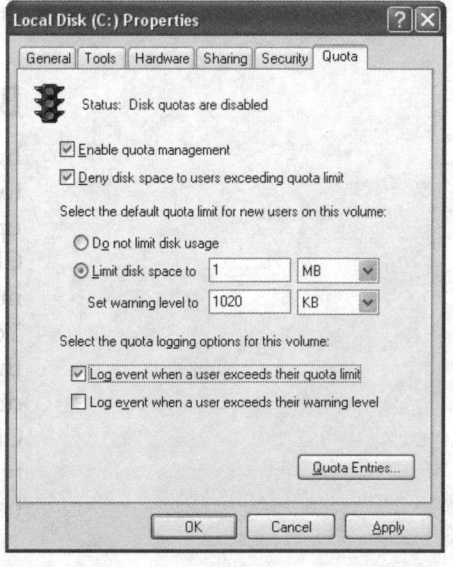

• **Figure 9.25** Hard drive quotas in Windows XP

Table 9.3	NTFS Cluster Sizes	
Drive Size	Cluster Size	Number of Sectors
512 MB or less	512 bytes	1
513 MB to 1024 MB (1 GB)	1024 bytes (1 KB)	2
1025 MB to 2048 MB (2 GB)	2048 bytes (2 KB)	4
2049 MB and larger	4096 bytes (4 KB)	8

By default, NTFS supports partitions up to 2 terabytes (2,199,023,255, 552 bytes). By tweaking the cluster sizes, you can get NTFS to support partitions up to 16 exabytes, or 18,446,744,073,709,551,616 bytes! That might support any and all upcoming hard drive capacities for the next 100 years or so.

With so many file systems, how do you know which one to use? In the case of internal hard drives, you should use the most feature-rich system your OS supports. If you have Windows 2000/XP/2003/Vista, use NTFS. FAT32 is still often used on external hard drives because NTFS features such as the ACL and encryption can make access difficult when moving the drive between systems, but with that exception the benefits of NTFS make it your best choice on a Windows-based system.

■ The Partitioning and Formatting Process

Now that you understand the concepts of formatting and partitioning, let's go through the process of setting up an installed hard drive using different partitioning and formatting tools. If you have access to a system, try following along with these descriptions. Remember, don't make any changes to a drive you want to keep, because both partitioning and formatting are destructive processes!

Bootable Disks

Imagine you've built a brand-new PC. The hard drive has no OS so you need to boot up something to set up that hard drive. Any software that can boot up a system is by definition an operating system. You need a floppy disk, CD-ROM, or USB thumb drive with a bootable OS installed. Any removable media that has a bootable OS is generically called a *boot device* or *boot disk*. Your system boots off the boot device, which then loads some kind of OS that enables you to partition, format, and install an OS on your new hard drive. Boot devices come from many sources. All Windows OS installation CDs are boot devices, as are Linux installation CDs. You can make your own bootable devices, and most techs do, because a boot device often has a number of handy tools included to do certain jobs.

In the next chapter, "Understanding Removable Media," I go through the steps to make a number of different types of boot devices for different jobs. If you want to follow along with some of the steps in this chapter, you may want to jump ahead to the next chapter to make a boot device or two and then return here.

Partitioning and Formatting with the Windows Installation CD

When you boot up a Windows installation CD and the installation program detects a hard drive that is not yet partitioned, it prompts you through a sequence of steps to partition (and format) the hard drive. Chapter 11, "Installing and Upgrading Windows," covers the entire installation process, but we'll jump ahead and dive into the partitioning part of the installation here to see how this is done, working through two examples using one, then two partitions. This example uses the Windows XP installation CD—but don't worry, this part of the Windows 2000 installation is almost identical.

Single Partition

The most common partitioning scenario involves turning a new, blank drive into a single, bootable C: drive. To accomplish this goal, you need to make the entire drive a primary partition and then make it active. Let's go through the process of partitioning and formatting a single, brand-new, 200-GB hard drive.

The Windows installation begins by booting from a Windows installation CD-ROM like the one shown in Figure 9.26. The installation program starts automatically from the CD. The installation first loads some needed files but will eventually prompt you with the screen shown in Figure 9.27. This is your clue that partitioning is about to start!

Press the ENTER key to start a new Windows installation and accept the license agreement to see the main partitioning screen (Figure 9.28). The bar that says Unpartitioned Space is the drive.

• **Figure 9.26**   Windows installation CD

```
Windows XP Professional Setup

    Welcome to Setup.

    This portion of the Setup program prepares Microsoft(R)
    Windows(R) XP to run on your computer.

        •  To set up Windows XP now, press ENTER.

        •  To repair a Windows XP installation using
           Recovery Console, press R.

        •  To quit Setup without installing Windows XP, press F3.




  ENTER=Continue    R=Repair    F3=Quit
```

• **Figure 9.27**   Welcome to Setup

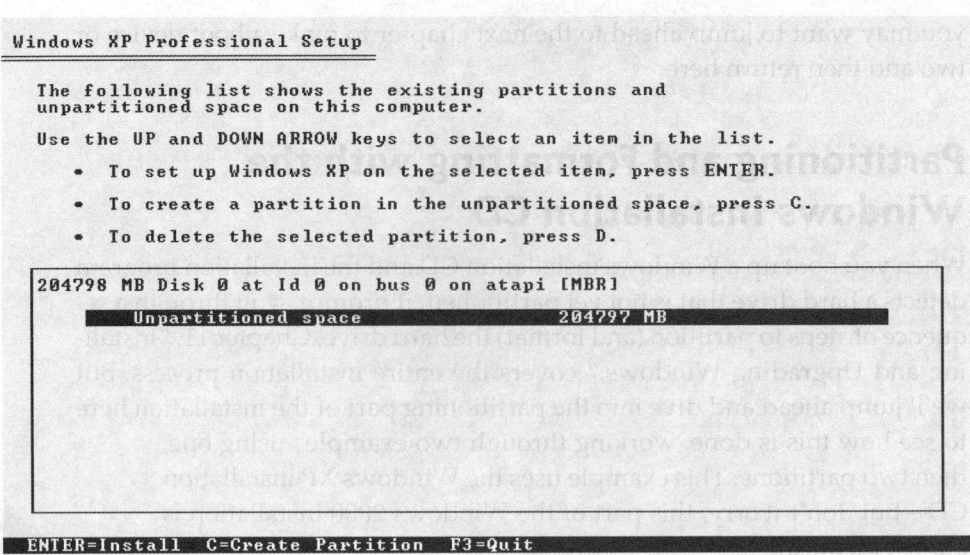

```
Windows XP Professional Setup

The following list shows the existing partitions and
unpartitioned space on this computer.

Use the UP and DOWN ARROW keys to select an item in the list.

    • To set up Windows XP on the selected item, press ENTER.

    • To create a partition in the unpartitioned space, press C.

    • To delete the selected partition, press D.

┌─────────────────────────────────────────────────────────────┐
│ 204798 MB Disk 0 at Id 0 on bus 0 on atapi [MBR]              │
│                                                               │
│     Unpartitioned space                     204797 MB         │
│                                                               │
│                                                               │
│                                                               │
│                                                               │
│                                                               │
│                                                               │
│                                                               │
└─────────────────────────────────────────────────────────────┘

 ENTER=Install    C=Create Partition    F3=Quit
```

● **Figure 9.28**   Partitioning screen

The Windows installer is pretty smart. If you press ENTER at this point, it will partition the hard drive as a single primary partition, make it active, and install Windows for you—but what fun is that? Instead, press C to create a partition. The installer then asks you how large of a partition to make (Figure 9.29). You may make the partition any size you want by typing in a number, from a minimum of 8 MB up to the size of the entire drive (in this case, 204789 MB). Let's just make the entire drive a single C: drive by pressing ENTER.

Ta-da! You just partitioned the drive! Now Windows asks you how you want to format that drive (Figure 9.30). So you might be asking—where's the basic vs. dynamic? Where do you tell Windows to make the partition primary instead of extended? Where do you set it as active?

```
Windows XP Professional Setup

You asked Setup to create a new partition on
204798 MB Disk 0 at Id 0 on bus 0 on atapi [MBR].

    • To create the new partition, enter a size below and
      press ENTER.

    • To go back to the previous screen without creating
      the partition, press ESC.

The minimum size for the new partition is       8 megabytes (MB).
The maximum size for the new partition is 204789 megabytes (MB).
Create partition of size (in MB):  204789▮




 ENTER=Create    ESC=Cancel
```

● **Figure 9.29**   Setting partition size

Mike Meyers' CompTIA A+ Guide: Essentials (Exam 220-601)

The Windows installer makes a number of assumptions for you, such as always making the first partition primary and setting it active. The installer also makes all hard drives basic disks. You'll have to convert it to dynamic later (if you even want to convert it at all).

Select NTFS for the format. Either option—quick or full—will do the job here. (Quick format is quicker, as the name would suggest, but the full option is more thorough and thus safer.) After Windows formats the drive, the installation continues, copying the new Windows installation to the C: drive.

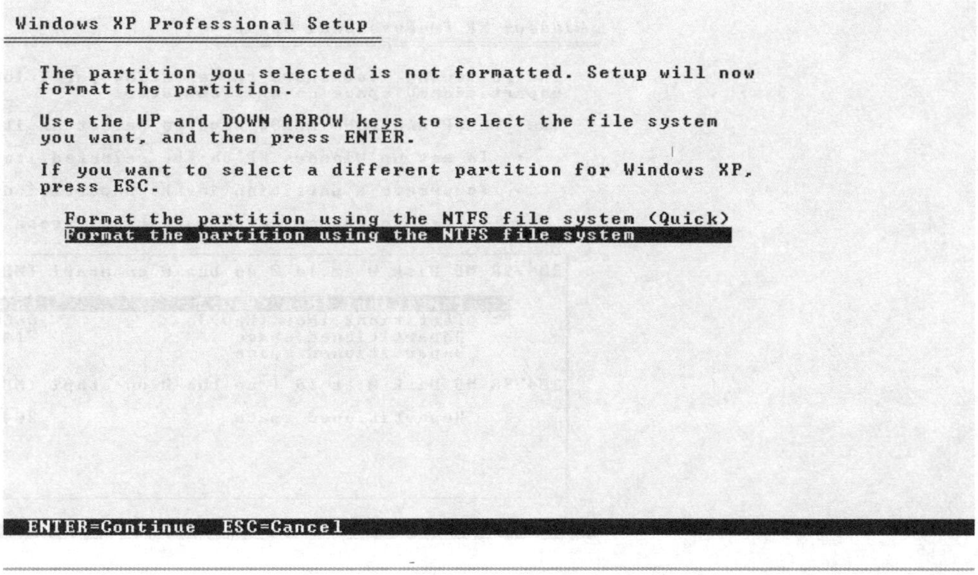

```
Windows XP Professional Setup

  The partition you selected is not formatted. Setup will now
  format the partition.

  Use the UP and DOWN ARROW keys to select the file system
  you want, and then press ENTER.

  If you want to select a different partition for Windows XP,
  press ESC.

    Format the partition using the NTFS file system (Quick)
    Format the partition using the NTFS file system

ENTER=Continue   ESC=Cancel
```

● **Figure 9.30**   Format screen

Two Partitions

Well, that was fun! So much fun that I'd like to do another new Windows install, with a bit more complex partitioning. This time, you still have the 200-GB hard drive, but you want to split the drive into three drive letters of roughly 66 GB each. That means you'll need to make a single 66-GB primary partition, then a 133-GB extended partition, and then split that extended partition into two logical drives of 66 GB each.

Back at the Windows installation main partitioning screen, first press C to make a new partition, but this time change the 204789 to 66666, which will give you a partition of about 66 GB. When you press ENTER, the partitioning screen should look like Figure 9.31. Even though the installation program doesn't tell you, the partition is primary.

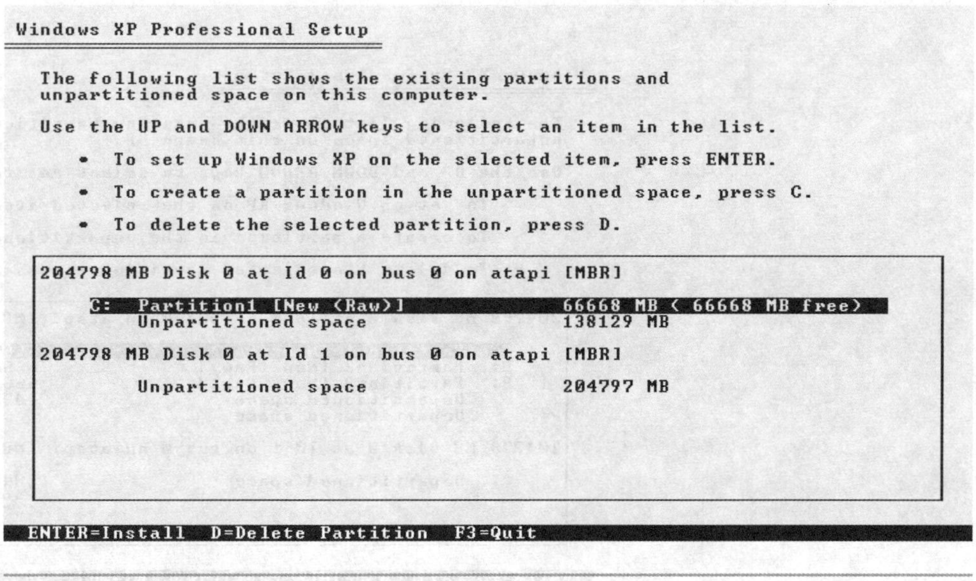

Notice that two-thirds of the drive is still unpartitioned space. Move the selection down to this option and press C to create the next partition. Once again, enter **66666** in the partition size screen and press ENTER, and you'll see something similar to Figure 9.32.

Windows will almost always adjust the number you type in for a partition size. In this case, it changed 66666 to 66668, a number that makes more sense when translated to binary. Don't worry about it!

```
Windows XP Professional Setup

  The following list shows the existing partitions and
  unpartitioned space on this computer.

  Use the UP and DOWN ARROW keys to select an item in the list.

    ● To set up Windows XP on the selected item, press ENTER.

    ● To create a partition in the unpartitioned space, press C.

    ● To delete the selected partition, press D.

  204798 MB Disk 0 at Id 0 on bus 0 on atapi [MBR]
      C:  Partition1 [New (Raw)]              66668 MB ( 66668 MB free)
          Unpartitioned space                138129 MB
  204798 MB Disk 0 at Id 1 on bus 0 on atapi [MBR]
          Unpartitioned space                204797 MB

ENTER=Install   D=Delete Partition   F3=Quit
```

● **Figure 9.31**   66-GB partition created

```
Windows XP Professional Setup

The following list shows the existing partitions and
unpartitioned space on this computer.

Use the UP and DOWN ARROW keys to select an item in the list.

    • To set up Windows XP on the selected item, press ENTER.

    • To create a partition in the unpartitioned space, press C.

    • To delete the selected partition, press D.

204798 MB Disk 0 at Id 0 on bus 0 on atapi [MBR]

      C:   Partition1 [New (Raw)]            66668 MB < 66668 MB free>
      D:   Partition2 [New (Raw)]            66668 MB < 66668 MB free>
           Unpartitioned space               71453 MB
           Unpartitioned space                   8 MB

204798 MB Disk 0 at Id 1 on bus 0 on atapi [MBR]

      Unpartitioned space                  204797 MB


ENTER=Install   D=Delete Partition   F3=Quit
```

• **Figure 9.32**   Second partition created

Create your last partition exactly as you made the other two to see your
almost-completely partitioned drive (Figure 9.33). (Note that the example is
not realistic in one respect: you would never leave any unpartitioned space
on a drive in a typical PC.)

Even though the Windows installation shows you've made three partitions, you've really made only two: the primary partition, which is C:, and
then two logical drives (D: and E:) in an extended partition. Once again, the
next step, formatting, is saved for a later section in this chapter.

You've just created three drive letters. Keep in mind that the only drive
you must partition during installation is the drive on which you install
Windows.

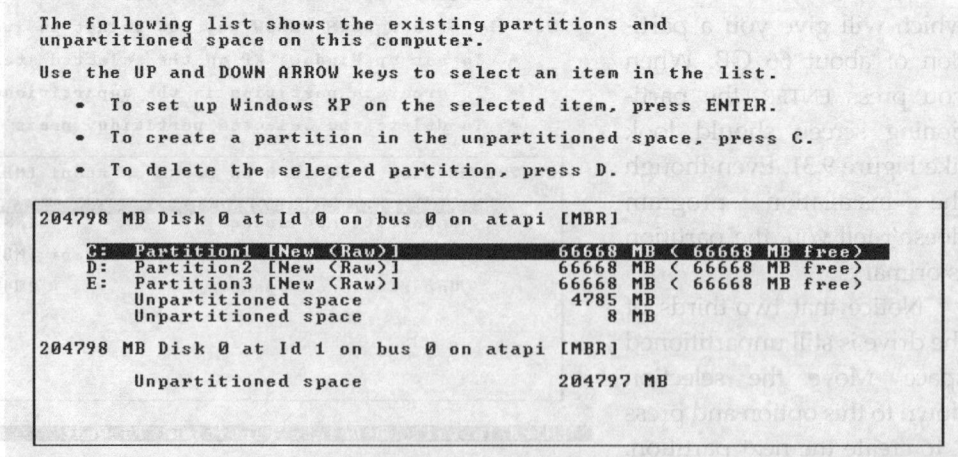

```
Windows XP Professional Setup

The following list shows the existing partitions and
unpartitioned space on this computer.

Use the UP and DOWN ARROW keys to select an item in the list.

    • To set up Windows XP on the selected item, press ENTER.

    • To create a partition in the unpartitioned space, press C.

    • To delete the selected partition, press D.

204798 MB Disk 0 at Id 0 on bus 0 on atapi [MBR]

      C:   Partition1 [New (Raw)]            66668 MB < 66668 MB free>
      D:   Partition2 [New (Raw)]            66668 MB < 66668 MB free>
      E:   Partition3 [New (Raw)]            66668 MB < 66668 MB free>
           Unpartitioned space                4785 MB
           Unpartitioned space                   8 MB

204798 MB Disk 0 at Id 1 on bus 0 on atapi [MBR]

      Unpartitioned space                  204797 MB


ENTER=Install   D=Delete Partition   F3=Quit
```

• **Figure 9.33**   Fully partitioned drive

The installation program can delete partitions just as easily as it makes them. If you use a hard drive that already has partitions, for example, you just select the partition you wish to delete and press the letter D. This will bring up a dialog where Windows gives you one last change to change your mind (Figure 9.34). Press L to kill the partition.

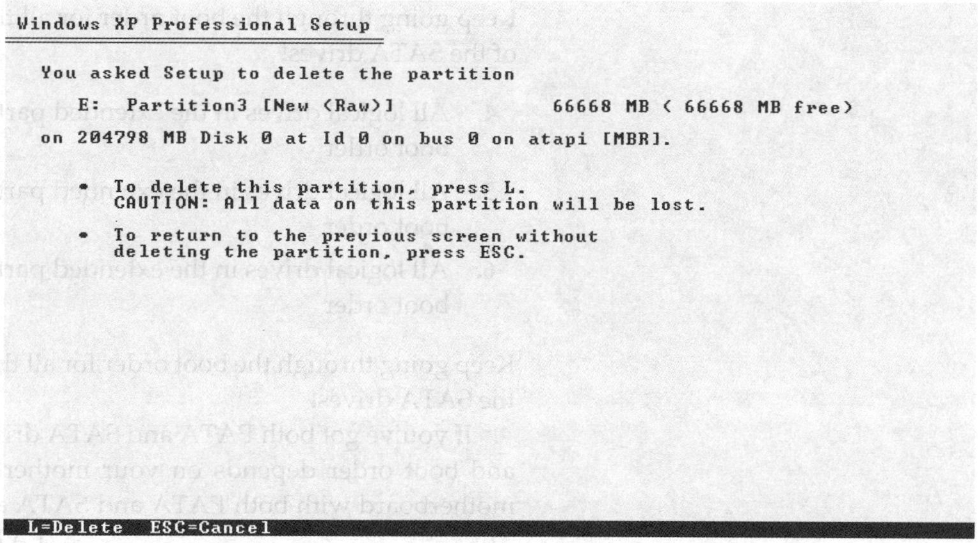

```
Windows XP Professional Setup

You asked Setup to delete the partition

    E:  Partition3 [New (Raw)]               66668 MB ( 66668 MB free)

on 204798 MB Disk 0 at Id 0 on bus 0 on atapi [MBR].

    •  To delete this partition, press L.
       CAUTION: All data on this partition will be lost.

    •  To return to the previous screen without
       deleting the partition, press ESC.




 L=Delete   ESC=Cancel
```

• Figure 9.34 Option to delete partition

Partitions and Drive Letters

Folks new to partitioning think that the drive letter gets "burned into the drive" when it is partitioned. This is untrue. The partitions receive their drive letters at every boot (but Windows will let you change any drive letter other than the C: drive, overriding the boot ordering, if you wish). If you're using PATA drives, here's the order in which hard drives receive their letters:

1. Primary partition of the primary master drive
2. Primary partition of the primary slave drive
3. Primary partition of the secondary master drive
4. Primary partition of the secondary slave drive
5. All logical drives in the extended partition of the primary master drive
6. All logical drives in the extended partition of the primary slave drive
7. All logical drives in the extended partition of the secondary master drive
8. All logical drives in the extended partition of the secondary slave drive

If you're using SATA drives, this order still exists, but given that SATA no longer uses the concept of master or slave, the drive letter is based on the order you set in CMOS:

1. Primary partition of the first drive in the boot order
2. Primary partition of the second drive in the boot order
3. Primary partition of the third drive in the boot order

Keep going through the boot order for all the primary partitions of the rest of the SATA drives!

4. All logical drives in the extended partition of the first drive in the boot order

5. All logical drives in the extended partition of the second drive in the boot order

6. All logical drives in the extended partition of the third drive in the boot order

Keep going through the boot order for all the logical partitions of the rest of the SATA drives!

If you've got both PATA and SATA drives, things get a bit complicated and boot order depends on your motherboard. The first generations of motherboard with both PATA and SATA always had you first boot to the PATA drives and then the SATA drives. Later, motherboards with both PATA and SATA will have a special setting in CMOS that shows all of the drives currently seen by the system, including hard drives, CD media, floppy drives, and even USB drives. Figure 9.35 shows a sample of this more modern CMOS.

On these systems, the boot order is determined not by whether the drives are PATA or SATA, but simply by the order of the hard drives in this list (other devices get their drive letters after the hard drives). If you have a particular drive you want to be the C: drive, just move it to the top of the list.

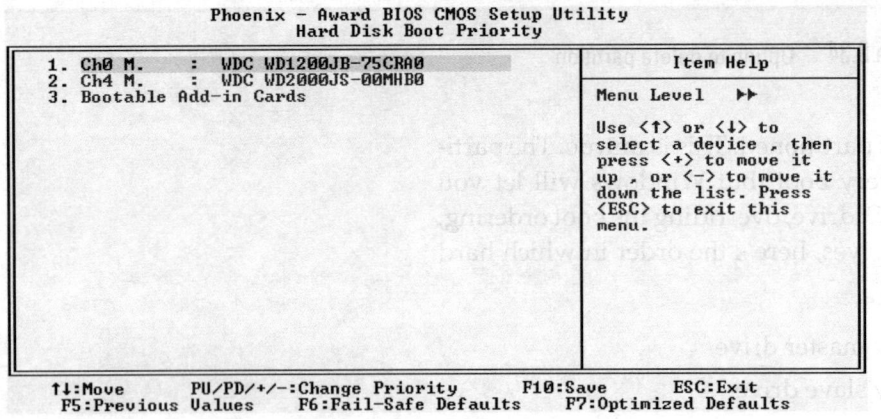

• **Figure 9.35** Modern boot order

At boot, the system uses this order to assign drive letters. If you install a single drive with one primary partition and one extended partition with one logical drive, for example, at boot the primary partition would become C: and the logical drive would become D:.

If you install a second drive, say one with a single primary partition, this changes. The system first finds the primary partition on the primary master and assigns it the letter C:, just as before. It then continues to look for any other primary partitions, finding the primary partition on the primary slave and assigning that primary partition the letter D:. Not seeing any more primary partitions, it then goes back up to the primary master drive, now looking for logical drives in extended partitions. It finds one logical drive and assigns it the letter E:. If the system had found two logical drives on the primary master, they would receive the letters E: and F:. After giving the drive letter E: to the one logical drive in the extended partition, the system continues down the list, looking for more logical drives in more extended partitions.

Disk Management

The real tool for partitioning and formatting is the Disk Management utility. Disk Management enables you to do everything you want to do to a hard drive in one handy tool. You can access Disk Management by going to the Control Panel and opening the Computer Management applet. If you're cool, you can click Start | Run, type in **diskmgmt.msc**, and press ENTER. Windows 2000, XP, and Vista come with Disk Management (Figure 9.36).

Disk Management works only within Windows, so you can't use Disk Management from a boot device. If you install Windows from an installation CD, in other words, you must use the special partitioning/formatting software built into the installation program you just saw in action.

One of the most interesting parts of Disk Management is disk initialization. Every hard drive in a Windows system has special information placed onto the drive. This initialization information includes identifiers that say "this drive belongs in this system" and other information that defines what this hard drive does in the system. If the hard drive is part of a RAID array, its RAID information is stored in the initialization. If it's part of a spanned volume, this is also stored there. All new drives must be initialized before you can use them. When you install an extra hard drive into a Windows system and start Disk Management, it notices the new drive and starts the Hard Drive Initialization Wizard. If you don't let the wizard run, the drive will be listed as unknown (Figure 9.37).

To initialize a disk, right-click the disk icon and select Initialize. Once a disk is initialized, you can see the status of the drive—a handy tool for troubleshooting.

A newly installed drive is always set as a basic disk. There's nothing wrong with using basic disks, other than that you miss out on some handy features. To create partitions, right-click the unallocated part of the drive and select New Partition. Disk Management will run the New Partition Wizard,

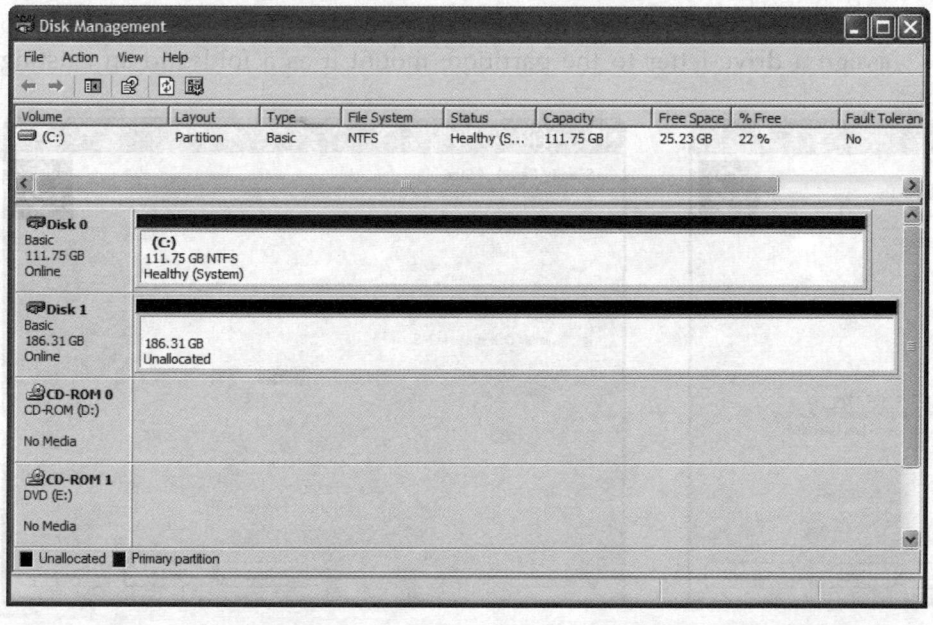

• **Figure 9.36**   Disk Management

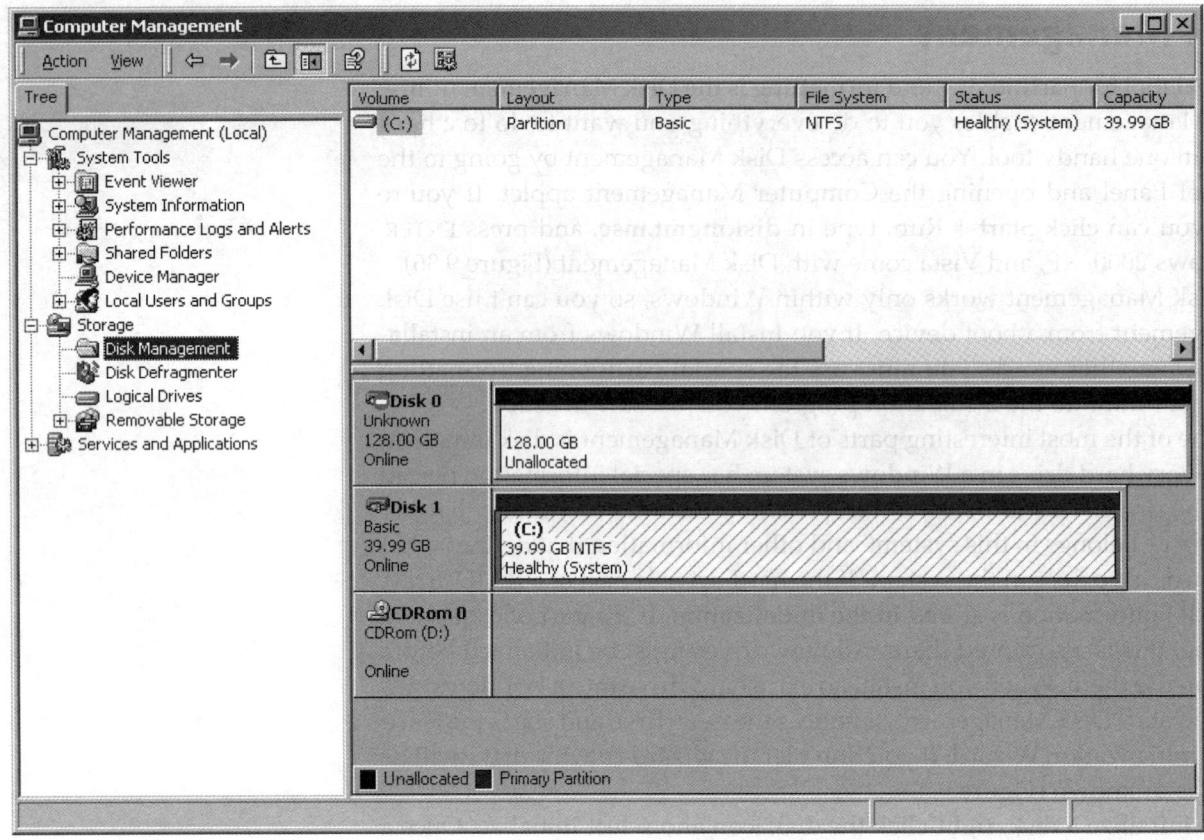

• **Figure 9.37** Unknown drive in Disk Management

enabling you to select a primary or extended partition (Figure 9.38). Afterward, you'll see a screen where you specify the size partition you prefer (Figure 9.39).

If you choose to make a primary partition, the wizard asks if you want to assign a drive letter to the partition, mount it as a folder to an existing

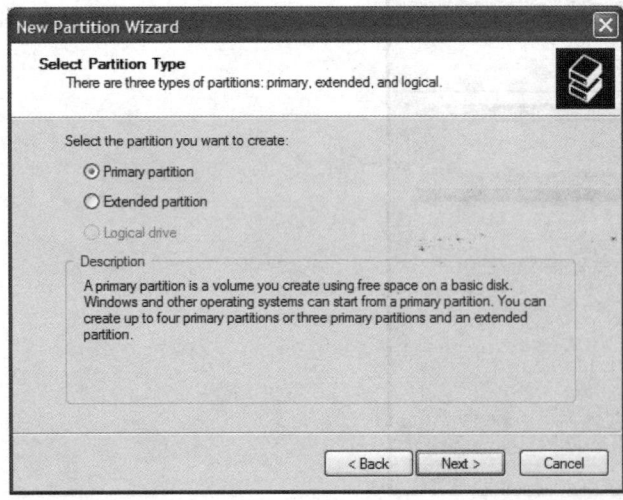

• **Figure 9.38** The New Partition Wizard

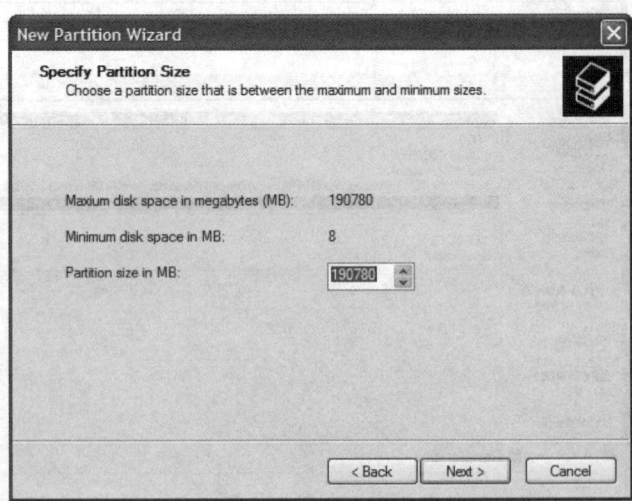

• **Figure 9.39** Specifying the partition size

partition, or do neither (Figure 9.40). (If you choose to make an extended partition, you just get a confirmation screen and you are returned to Disk Management.) In almost all cases, we give primary partitions a drive letter.

The last screen of the New Partition Wizard asks for the type of format you want to use for this partition (Figure 9.41). If your partition is 4 GB or less, you may format it as FAT, FAT32, or NTFS. If your partition is greater than 4 GB but less than 32 GB, you can make the drive FAT32 or NTFS. Windows requires NTFS on any partition greater than 32 GB. Although FAT32 supports partitions up to 2 TB, Microsoft wants you to use NTFS on larger partitions and creates this limit. In today's world of big hard drives, there's no good reason to use anything other than NTFS.

You have a few more tasks to complete at this screen. You can add a volume label if you want. You can also choose the size of your clusters (Allocation unit size). There's no reason to change the default cluster size, so leave that alone—but you can sure speed up the format if you select the Perform a quick format checkbox. This will format your drive without checking every cluster. It's fast and a bit risky, but new hard drives almost always come from the factory in perfect shape—so you must decide whether to use it or not.

Last, if you chose NTFS, you may enable file and folder compression. If you select this option, you'll be able to right-click any file or folder on this partition and compress it. To compress a file or folder, choose the one you want to compress, right-click, and select Properties. Then click the Advanced button to turn compression on or off (Figure 9.42). Compression is handy for opening up space on a hard drive that's filling up, but it also slows down disk access, so use it only when you need it.

After the drive finishes formatting, you'll go back to Disk Management and see a changed hard drive landscape. If you made a primary partition, you will see your new drive letter. If you made an extended partition,

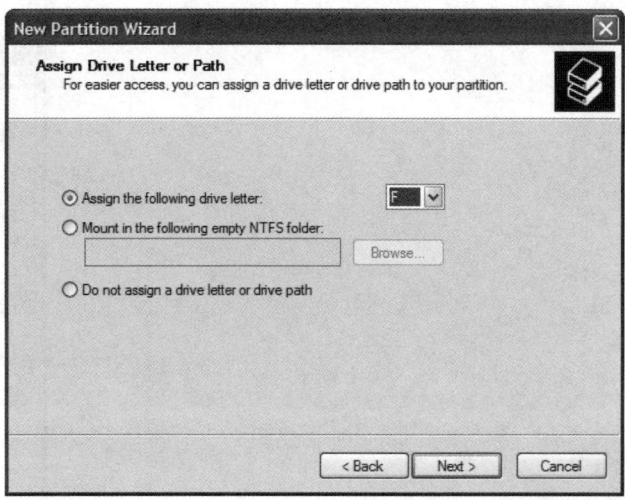

● **Figure 9.40**   Assigning a drive letter to a primary partition

 Tech Tip

Big FAT Partitions
Windows 2000, XP, and Vista read and write to FAT32 partitions larger than 32 GB; they just don't allow Disk Management to make them! If you ever stumble across a drive from a system that ran the old Windows 9x/Me that has a FAT32 partition larger than 32 GB, it will work just fine in your Windows 2000, XP, or Vista system.

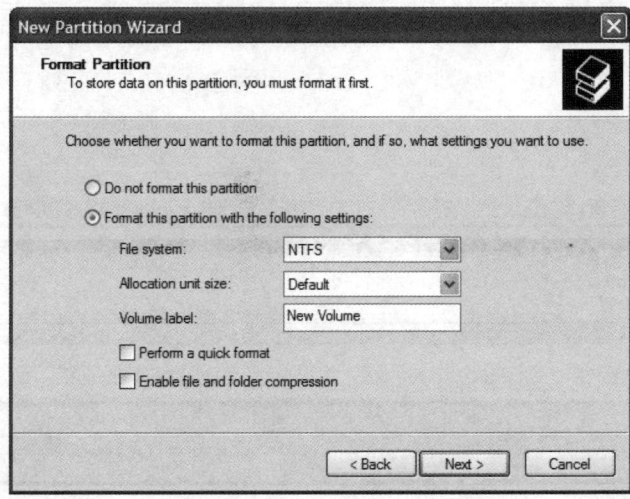

● **Figure 9.41**   Choosing a file system type

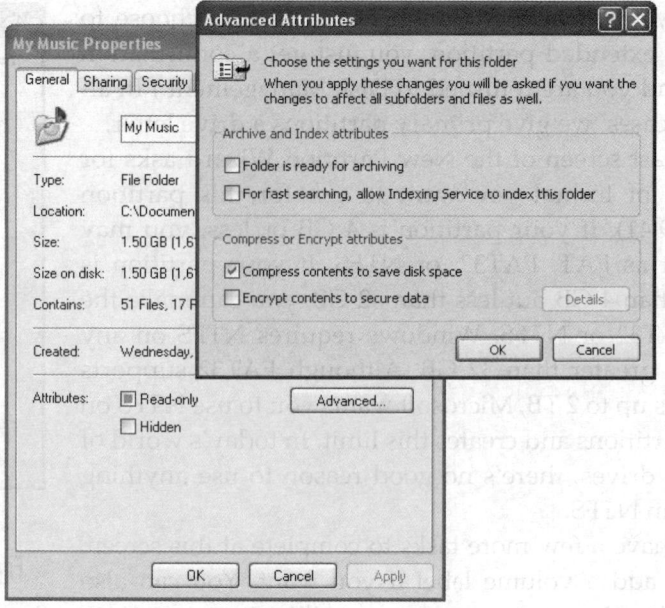

● **Figure 9.42**   Turning on compression

things will look a bit different. Figure 9.43 shows the extended partition as free space because it has no logical drive yet. As you can easily guess from Figure 9.44, to create a logical drive, simply right-click in that extended partition and choose New Logical Drive. Disk Management will fire up the New Partition Wizard again, this time with the option to create a logical drive (Figure 9.45).

When you create a logical drive, the New Partition Wizard automatically gives you the same options to format the partition using one of the

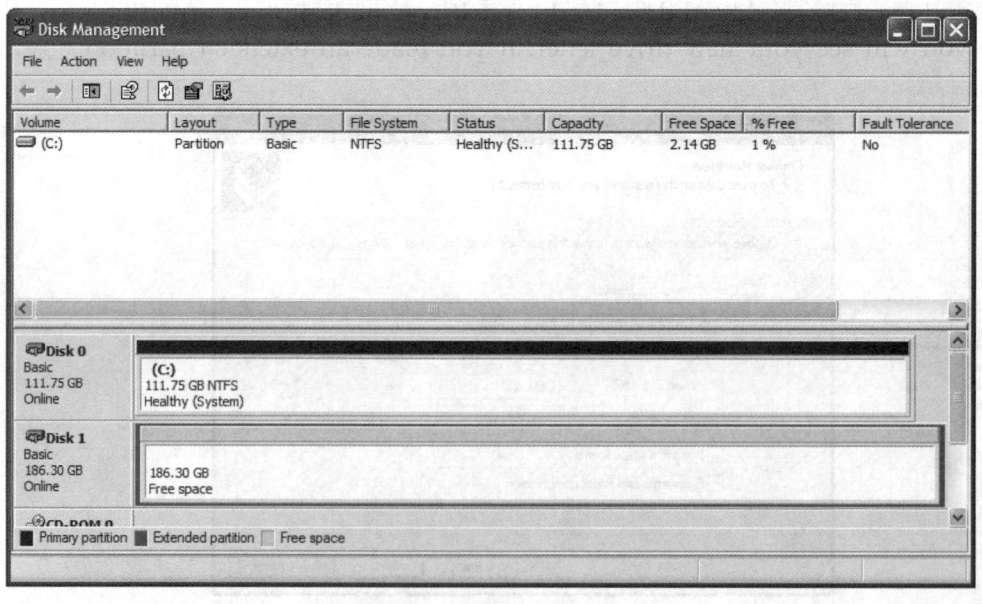

● **Figure 9.43**   Extended partition with no logical drives

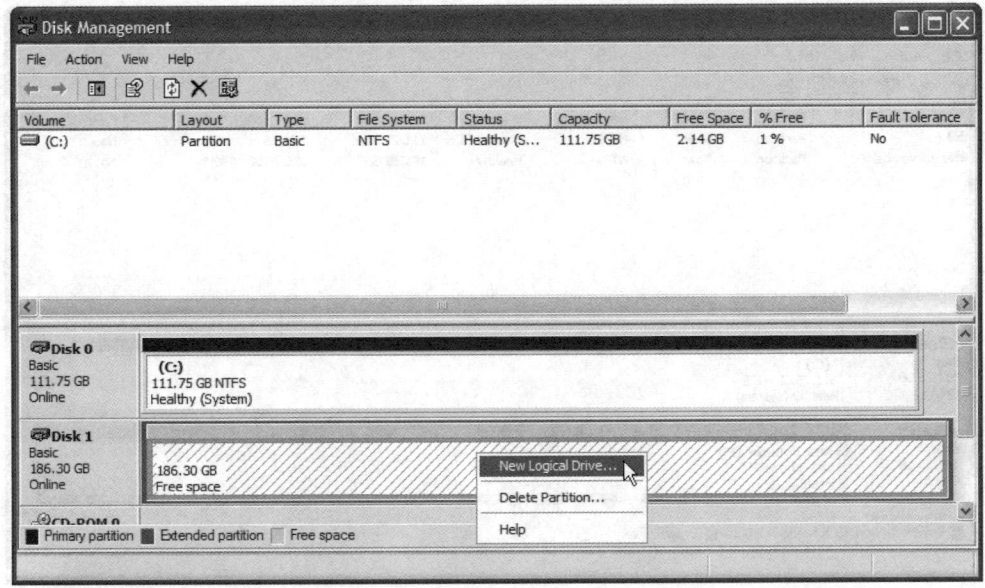

● **Figure 9.44** Creating a logical drive in the extended (free space) partition

three file systems you saw earlier with primary partitions (Figure 9.46). You'll get another confirmation screen, and then the Disk Management console will show you the newly created drive (see Figure 9.47).

One interesting aspect of Windows is the tiny (approximately 8 MB) mysterious unallocated partition that shows up on the C: drive. This is done by the Windows installation program when you first install Windows on a new system, to reserve a space Windows needs to convert the C: drive to a dynamic disk. It doesn't hurt anything and it's tiny, so just leave it alone. If you want to make a volume and format it, feel free to do so.

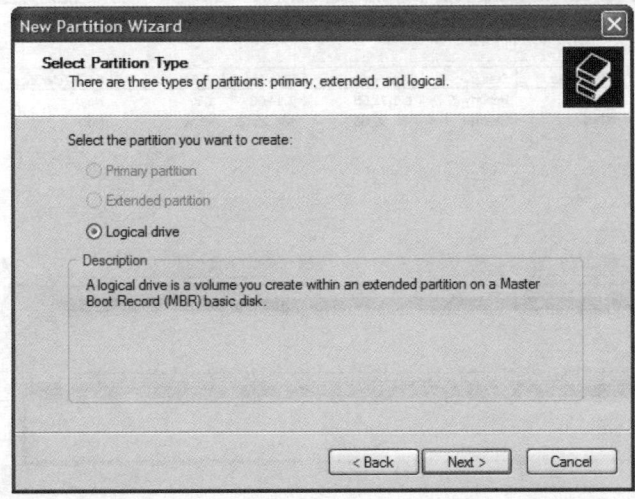

● **Figure 9.45** New Partition Wizard for logical drive

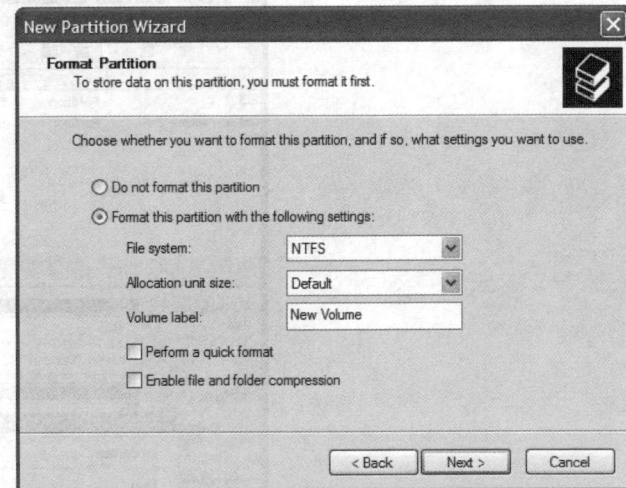

● **Figure 9.46** The New Partition Wizard offering formatting options

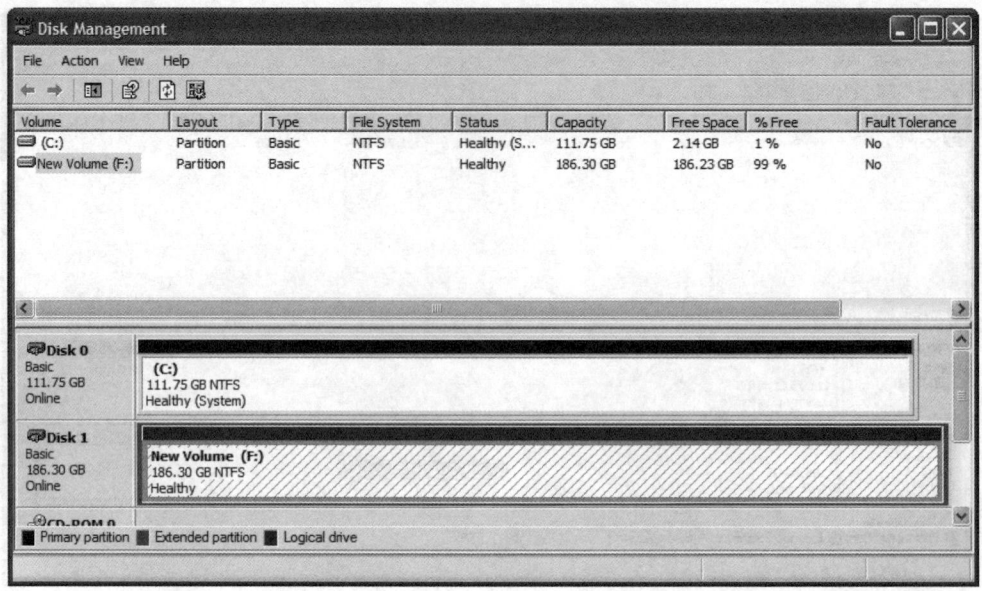

• **Figure 9.47**   The Disk Management console showing newly created logical drive

Dynamic Disks

You create dynamic disk from basic disks in Disk Management. Once you convert a drive from a basic to a dynamic disk, primary and extended partitions no longer exist; dynamic disks are divided into volumes instead of partitions.

To convert a basic disk to dynamic, just right-click the drive icon and select Convert to Dynamic Disk (Figure 9.48). The process is very quick and

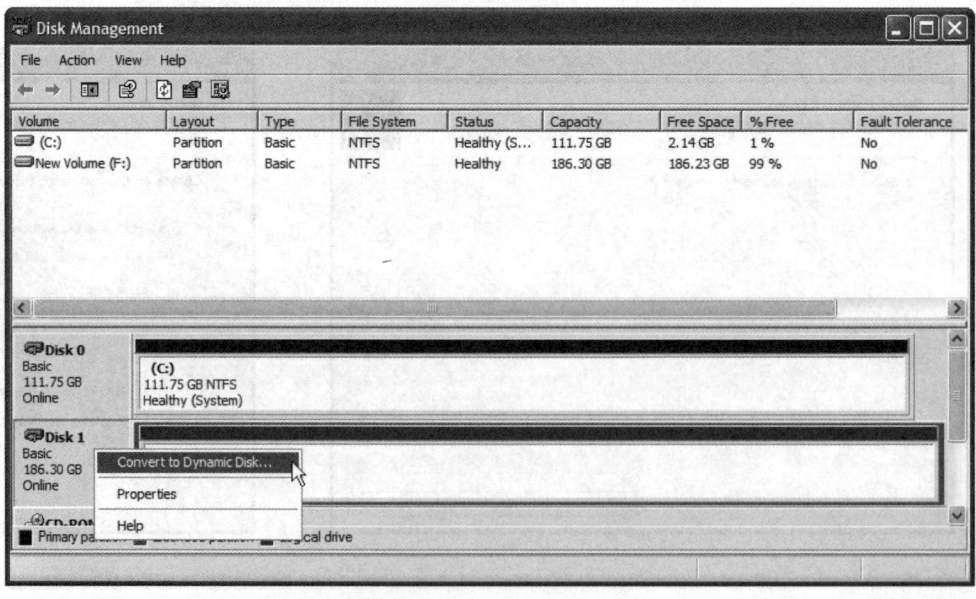

• **Figure 9.48**   Converting to a dynamic disk

safe, although the reverse is not true. The conversion from dynamic disk to basic disk first requires you to delete all partitions off the hard drive.

Once you've converted, no partitions exist, only volumes. You can make five types of volumes on a dynamic disk: simple, spanned, striped, mirrored, and RAID 5, although you'll commonly see only the first three in a Windows 2000 Professional or Windows XP Professional environment. You'll next learn how to implement the three most common volume types. The final step involves assigning a drive letter or mounting the volume as a folder.

Simple Volumes

A simple volume acts just like a primary partition. If you have only one dynamic disk in a system, it can have only a simple volume. It's important to note here that a simple volume may act like a traditional primary partition, but it is very different. If you install a hard drive partitioned as a simple volume dynamic disk into any version of Windows prior to Windows 2000, you would see no usable partition.

In Disk Management, right-click any unallocated space on the dynamic disk and choose New Volume (Figure 9.49) to run the New Volume Wizard. You'll see a series of screens that prompt you on size and file system, and then you're done. Figure 9.50 shows Disk Management with three simple volumes.

Spanning Volumes

Dynamic disks enable you to extend the size of a simple volume to any unallocated space on a dynamic disk. You can also extend the volume to grab extra space on completely different dynamic disks, creating a spanned volume. To extend or span, simply right-click the volume you want to make bigger, and choose Extend Volume from the options (Figure 9.51). This opens the Extend Volume Wizard that will prompt you for the location of free space on a dynamic disk and the increased volume size you want to

Windows XP Home does not support dynamic disks.

Tech Tip

Mirrored and Striped with Parity Volumes

Disk Management enables you to create mirrored and striped with parity volumes, but only on Windows 2000 or 2003 Server machines. The cool thing is that you can do this remotely across a network. You can sit at your Windows XP Professional workstation, in other words, and open Disk Management. Surf to a Windows 2000/2003 Server that you want to work with and poof!

You have two new options for configuring volumes. By limiting the implementation of mirroring and RAID 5 to server machines, Microsoft clearly meant to encourage small businesses to pony up for a copy of Server rather than using the less-expensive Professional OS for the company server! Both mirrored and striped with parity volumes are included here for completeness and because they show up in the Windows Help Files when you search for dynamic disks. Both are cool, but definitely way beyond CompTIA A+!

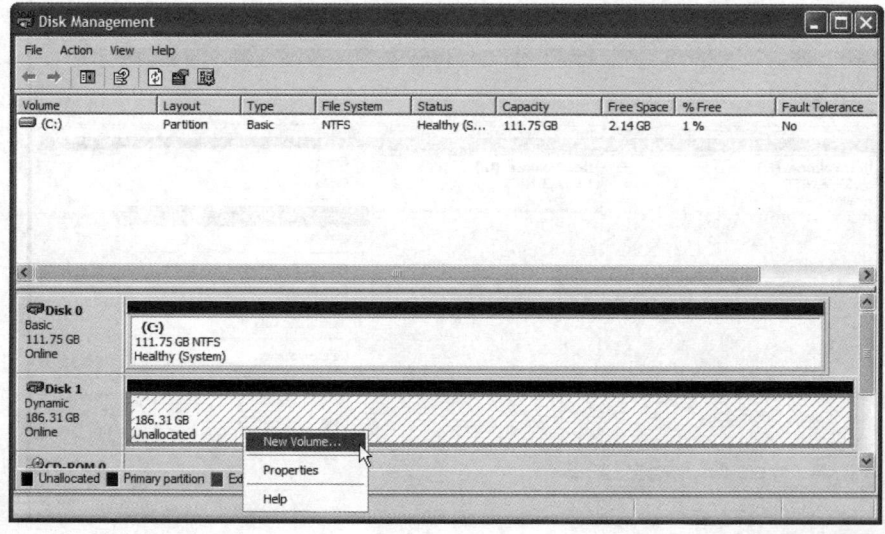

• **Figure 9.49**   Opening the New Volume Wizard

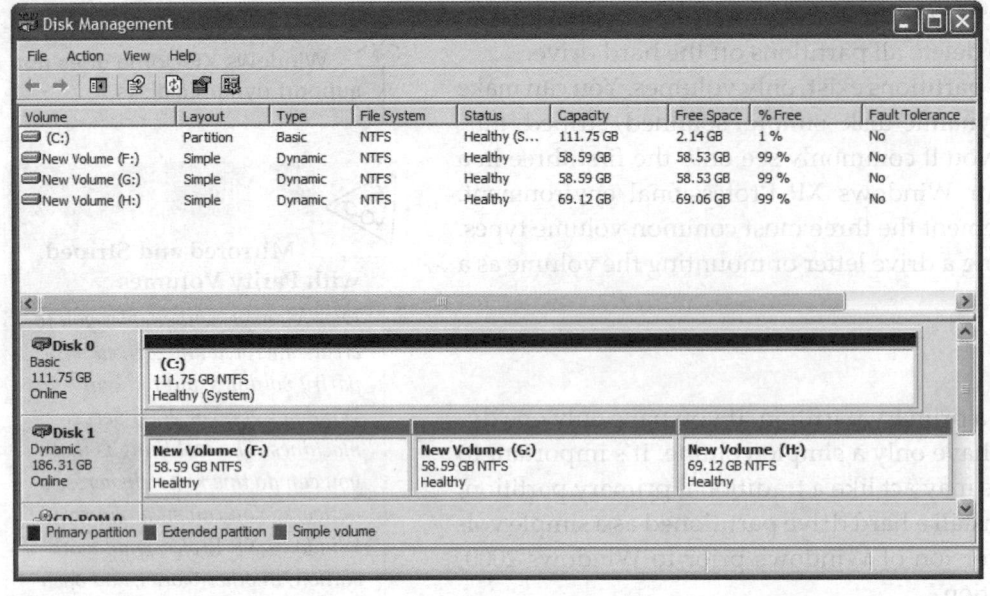

● **Figure 9.50** Simple volumes

assign (Figure 9.52). If you have multiple drives, you can span the volume just as easily to one of those drives.

The ability to extend and span volumes makes dynamic disks worth their weight in gold! If you start running out of space on a volume, you can simply add another physical hard drive to the system and span the volume to the new drive. This keeps your drive letters consistent and unchanging so your programs don't get confused, yet enables you to expand drive space when needed.

You can extend or span any simple volume on a dynamic disk, not just the "one on the end" in the Disk Management console. You simply select the volume to expand and the total volume increase you want. Figure 9.53 shows a

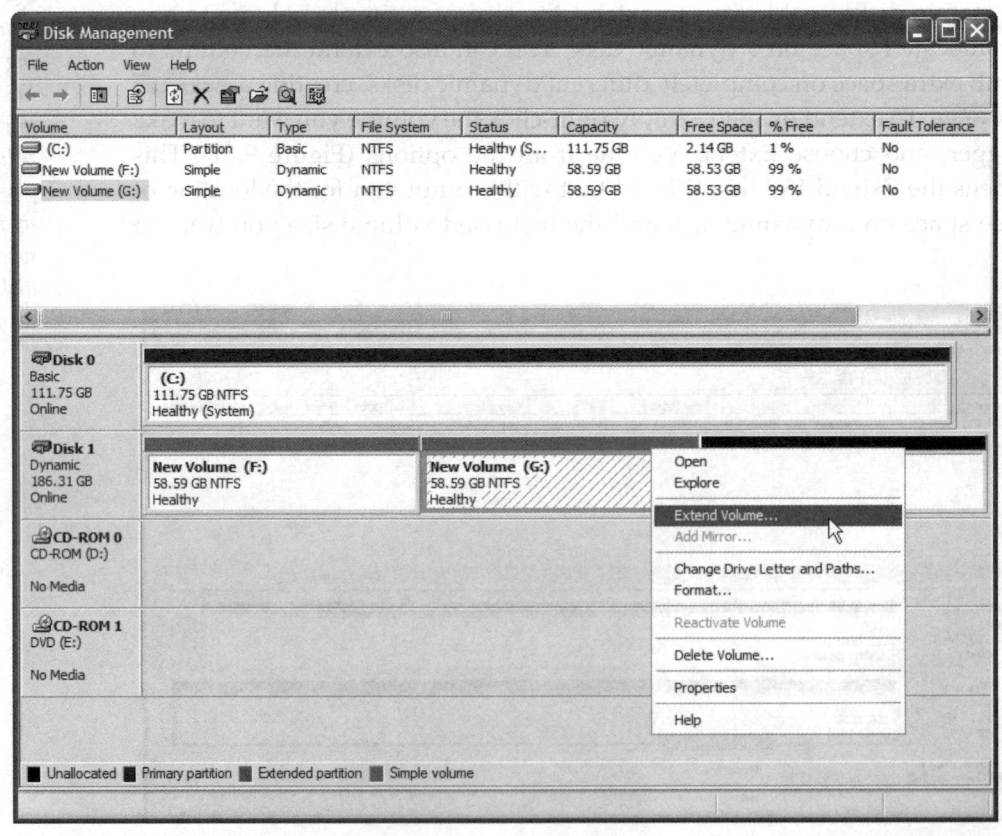

● **Figure 9.51** Selecting the Extend Volume option

simple 4-GB volume named Extended that has been enlarged an extra 7.91 GB in a portion of the hard drive, skipping the 2-GB section of unallocated space contiguous to it. This created an 11.91-GB volume. Windows has no problem skipping areas on a drive.

Striped Volumes

If you have two or more dynamic disks in a PC, Disk Management enables you to combine them into a *striped* volume. A striped volume spreads out blocks of each file across multiple disks. Using two or more drives in a group called a **stripe set**, striping writes data first to a certain number of clusters on one drive, then on the next, and so on. It speeds up data throughput because the system has to wait a much shorter time for a drive to read or write data. The drawback of striping is that if any single drive in the stripe set fails, all data in the stripe set is lost.

To create a striped volume, right-click unused space on a drive and choose New Volume, and then Striped. The wizard will ask for the other drives you want to add to the stripe, and you need to select two unallocated spaces on other dynamic disks. Select the other unallocated spaces and go through the remaining screens on sizing and formatting until you've created a new striped volume (Figure 9.54). The two stripes in Figure 9.54 seem as though they have different sizes, but if you look closely you'll see they are both 4 GB. All stripes must be the same size on each drive.

Mount Points

The one drive that can't take full advantage of being dynamic is the drive containing the operating system, your primary master C: drive. You can make it dynamic, but that still won't let you do all the cool dynamic things, like extending and spanning. So what good is the ability to allocate more space to a volume if you can't use it when you start to fill up your C: drive? If you can't add to that drive, your only option is to replace it with a new, bigger drive, right?

Not at all! Earlier we discussed the idea of mounting a drive as a folder instead of a drive letter, and here's where you get to do it. A *volume mount point* (or simply **mount point**) is a place in the directory structure of an existing volume that you can point to a volume or partition. The mounted volume will then function just like a folder, but all files stored in that segment of the directory structure will go to the mounted volume. After partitioning and formatting the drive, you don't give it a drive letter; instead, you *mount* the volume to a folder on the C: drive and make it nothing more than just

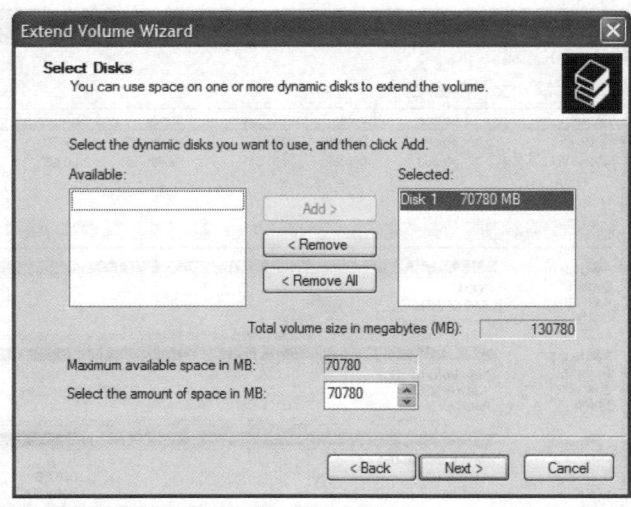

• **Figure 9.52**   The Extend Volume Wizard

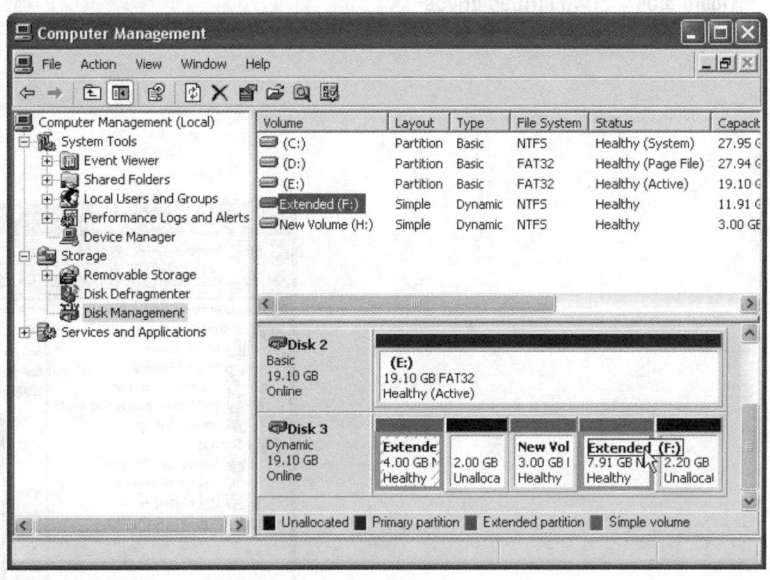

• **Figure 9.53**   Extended volume

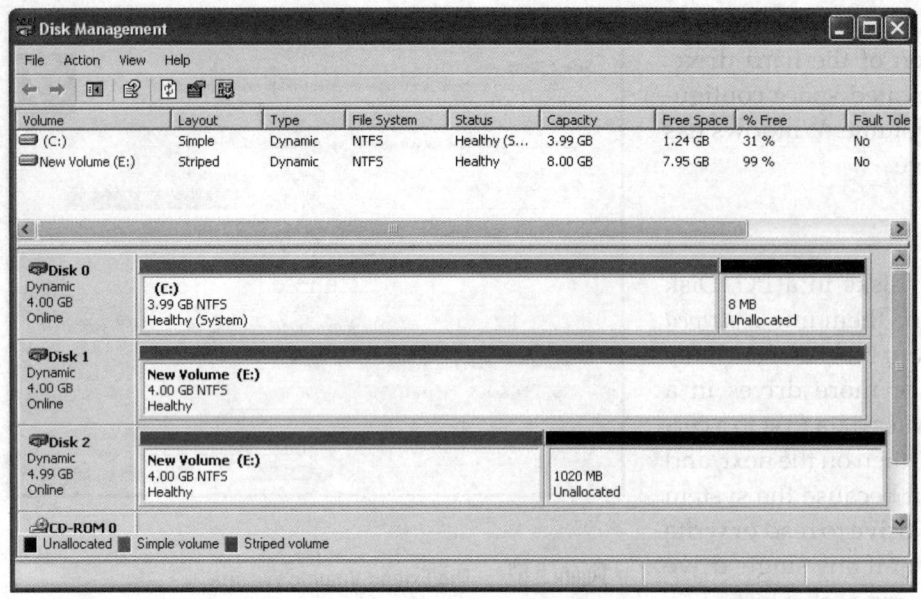

● **Figure 9.54** Two striped drives

another folder (Figure 9.55). You can load programs to that folder, just as you would to your Program Files folder. You can use it to store data files or backed-up system files. In *function*, therefore, the new hard drive simply extends the capacity of the C: drive, so neither you nor your client need ever trouble yourselves with dealing with multiple drive letters.

To create a mount point, right-click an unallocated section of a dynamic disk and choose New Volume. This opens the New Volume Wizard. In the second screen, you can select a mount point rather than a drive letter (Figure 9.56). Browse to a blank folder on an NTFS-formatted drive or create a new folder and you're in business.

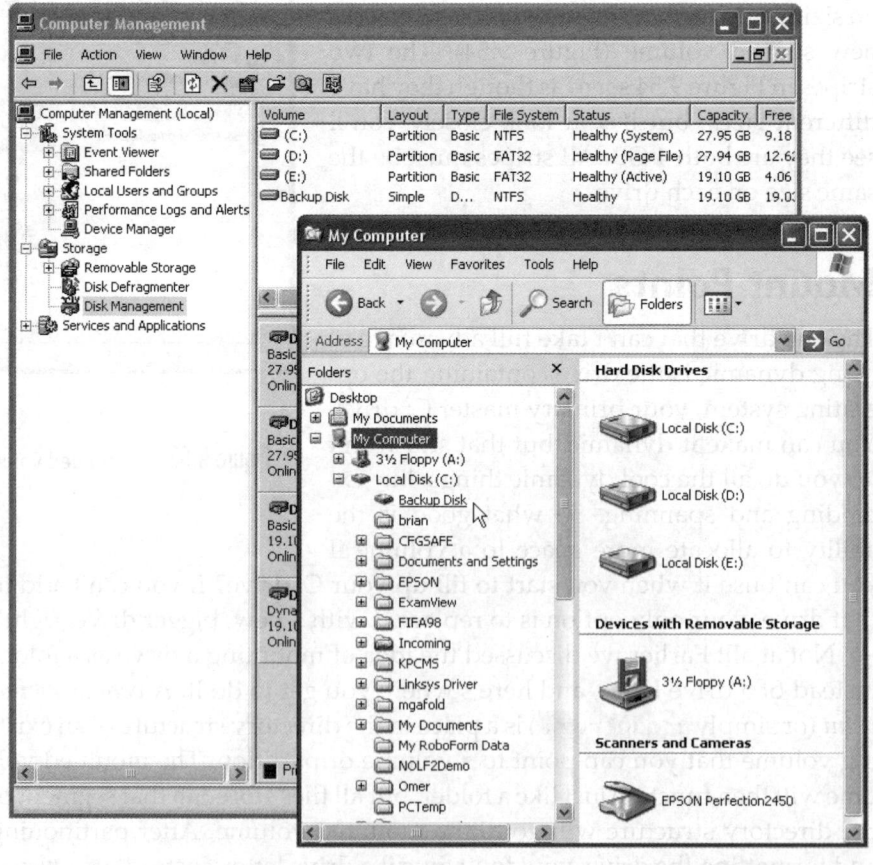

● **Figure 9.55** A drive volume mounted as a folder of drive C:

With mount points, Microsoft dramatically changed the way you can work with hard drives. You're no longer stuck in the rut of adding drive letters that mess up Windows' mapping of the CD-ROM drive. You don't have to confuse clients with multiple drive letters when they just want a little more space. You can resurrect smaller hard drives, making them a functional part of today's computer. With the Disk Management console in Windows 2000 and XP, Microsoft got it right.

Formatting a Partition

You can format any Windows partition/volume in My Computer. Just right-click the drive name and choose Format (Figure 9.57). You'll see a dialog box that asks for the type of file system you want to use, the cluster size, a place to put a volume label, and two other options. The Quick Format option tells Windows not to test the clusters and is a handy option when you're in a hurry—and feeling lucky. The Enable Compression option tells Windows to give users the ability to compress folders or files. It works well but slows down your hard drive.

Disk Management is today's preferred formatting tool for Windows 2000, XP, and Vista. When you create a new volume on a dynamic disk or a new partition on a basic disk, the New Volume Wizard will also ask you

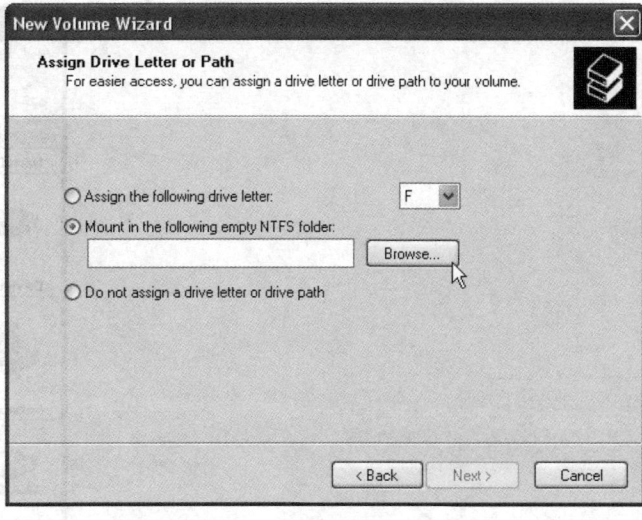

• **Figure 9.56** Choosing to create a mounted volume

Once you convert a drive to dynamic, you cannot revert it to a basic disk without losing all the data on that drive. Be prepared to back up all data before you revert.

You can mount a volume to an empty folder only on a drive formatted with NTFS 5. In theory, the mounted volume can be formatted as FAT16, FAT32, or NTFS 5, but you almost never see anything but NTFS 5.

Try This!

Working with Dynamic Drives and Mount Points

You can't begin to appreciate the ease and elegant simplicity of dynamic drives until you play with them, so Try This! Get a couple of spare drives and install them into a PC running Windows 2000 or Windows XP. Fire up the Disk Management console and try the following setups. Convert both spare drives to dynamic drives.

1. Make a mirror set.
2. Make a stripe set.
3. Make them into a single volume, spanned between both drives.
4. Make a single volume that takes up a portion of one drive, and then extend that volume onto another portion of that drive. Finally, span that volume to the other hard drive as well.
5. Create a volume of some sort—you decide—and then mount that volume to a folder on the C: drive.

You'll need to format the volumes after you create them so you see how they manifest in My Computer. (See the next section of this chapter for details on formatting.) Also, you'll need to delete volumes to create a new setup. To delete volumes, simply right-click the volume and choose Delete Volume. It's almost too easy.

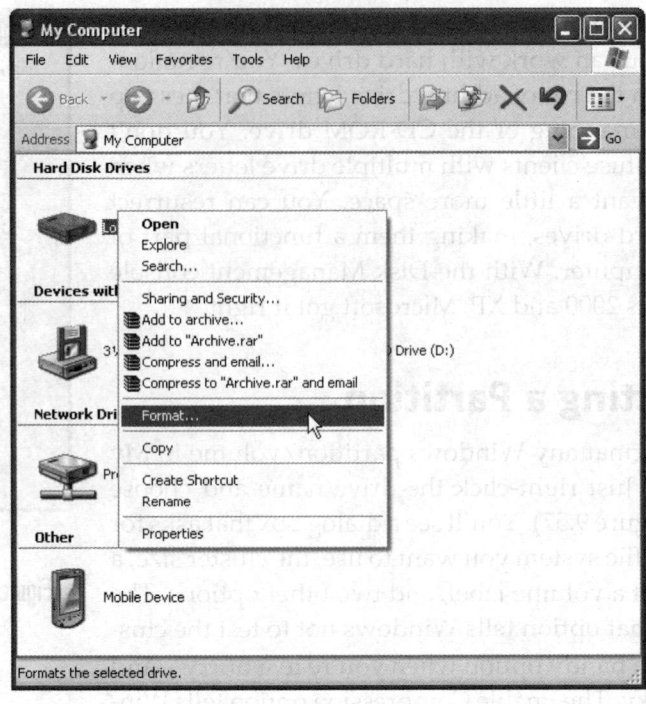

• **Figure 9.57**   Choosing Format in My Computer

what type of format you want to use. Always use NTFS unless you're that rare and strange person that wants to dual-boot Windows XP or Windows Vista with some ancient version of Windows.

All OS installation CD-ROMs will partition and format as part of the OS installation. Windows simply prompts you to partition and then format the drive. Read the screens and you'll do great.

■ Maintaining and Troubleshooting Hard Drives

Hard drives are complex mechanical and electrical devices. With platters spinning at thousands of rotations per minute, they also generate heat and vibration. All of these factors make hard drives susceptible to failure. In this section, you will learn some basic maintenance tasks that will keep your hard drives healthy, and for those inevitable instances when a hard drive fails, you will also learn what you can do to repair them.

Maintenance

Hard drive maintenance can be broken down into two distinct functions: checking the disk occasionally for failed clusters and keeping data organized on the drive so that it can be accessed quickly.

Mike Meyers' CompTIA A+ Guide: Essentials (Exam 220-601)

Error-Checking

Individual clusters on hard drives sometimes go bad. There's nothing you can do to prevent this from happening, so it's important that you check occasionally for bad clusters on drives. The tools used to perform this checking are generically called error-checking utilities, although the terms for two older Microsoft tools—**ScanDisk** and **CHKDSK** (pronounced "Checkdisk")—are often used. Microsoft calls the tool Error-checking in Windows XP. Whatever the name of the utility, each does the same job: when the tool finds bad clusters, it puts the electronic equivalent of orange cones around them so that the system won't try to place data in those bad clusters.

Most error-checking tools do far more than just check for bad clusters. They go through all of the drive's filenames, looking for invalid names and attempting to fix them. They look for clusters that have no filenames associated with them (we call these *lost chains*) and erase them. From time to time, the underlying links between parent and child folders are lost, so a good error-checking tool checks every parent and child folder. With a folder such as C:\TEST\DATA, for example, they make sure that the folder DATA is properly associated with its parent folder, C:\TEST, and that C:\TEST is properly associated with its child folder, C:\TEST\DATA.

To access Error-checking on a Windows 2000 or Windows XP system, open My Computer, right-click the drive you want to check, and choose Properties to open the drive's Properties dialog box. Select the Tools tab and click the Check Now button (Figure 9.58) to display the Check Disk dialog box, which has two options (Figure 9.59). Check the box next to *Automatically fix file system errors*, but save the option to *Scan for and attempt recovery of bad sectors* for times when you actually suspect a problem, because it takes a while on bigger hard drives.

 CompTIA A+ uses the term CHKDSK rather than Error-checking.

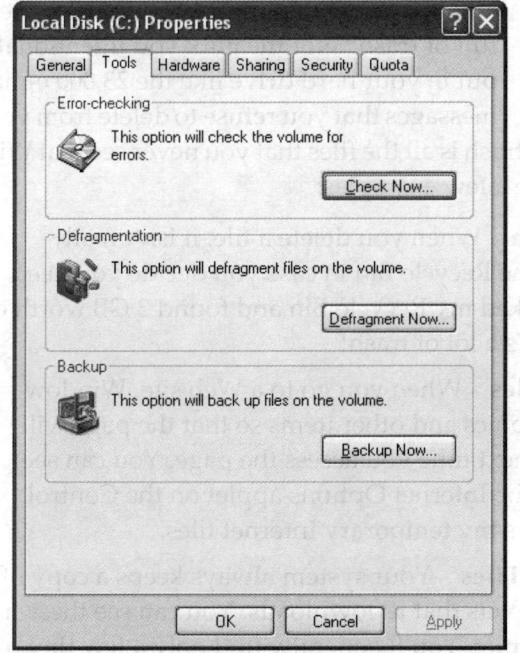

● **Figure 9.58**   The Tools tab in the Properties dialog box in Windows XP

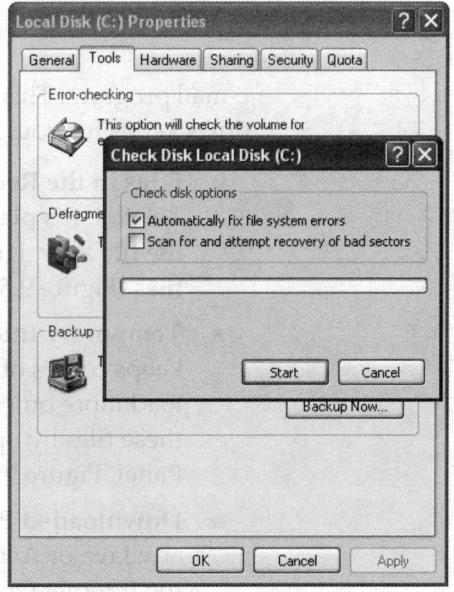

● **Figure 9.59**   The Check Disk dialog box

Now that you know how to run Error-checking, your next question should be, "How often do I run it?" A reasonable maintenance plan would include running it about once a week. Error-checking is fast (unless you use the Scan for and attempt recovery option), and it's a great tool for keeping your system in top shape.

Defragmentation

Fragmentation of clusters can make your drive access times increase dramatically. It's a good idea to defragment—or *defrag*—your drives as part of monthly maintenance. You access the defrag tool that runs with Windows 2000, XP, and Vista, called Disk Defragmenter, the same way you access Error-checking—right-click a drive in My Computer and choose Properties—except you click the Defragment Now button on the Tools tab to open the Defragmenter (Figure 9.60).

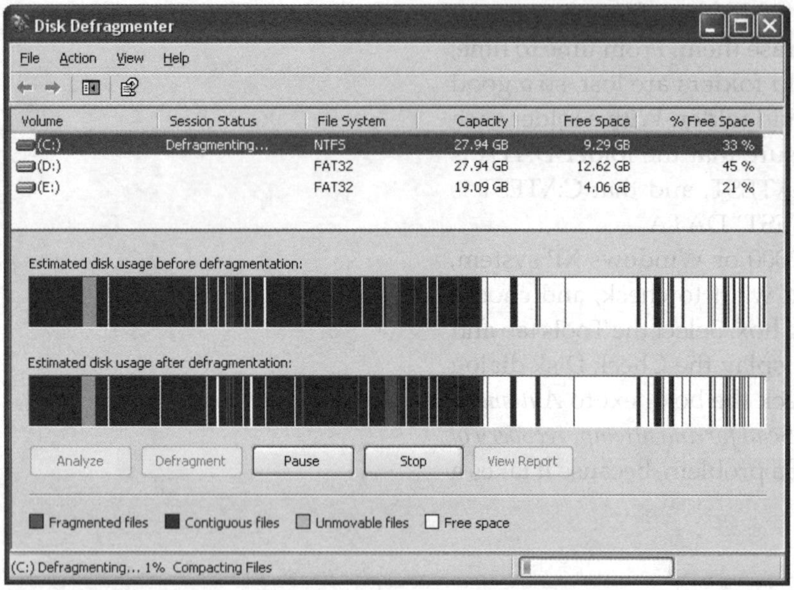

Defragmentation is interesting to watch—once. From then on, schedule it to run late at night. You should defragment your drives about once a month, although you could run it every week, and if you run it every night it takes only a few minutes. The longer you go between defrags, the longer it takes. If you don't run Disk Defragmenter, your system will run slower. If you don't run Error-checking, you may lose data.

● **Figure 9.60**   Disk Defragmenter in Windows XP

Disk Cleanup

Did you know that the average hard drive is full of trash? Not the junk you intentionally put in your hard drive like the 23,000 e-mail messages that you refuse to delete from your e-mail program. This kind of trash is all the files that you never see that Windows keeps for you. Here are a few examples:

- **Files in the Recycle Bin**   When you delete a file, it isn't really deleted. It's placed in the Recycle Bin in case you decide you need the file later. I just checked my Recycle Bin and found 3 GB worth of files (Figure 9.61). That's a lot of trash!

- **Temporary Internet Files**   When you go to a Web site, Windows keeps copies of the graphics and other items so that the page will load more quickly the next time you access the page. You can see these files by opening the Internet Options applet on the Control Panel. Figure 9.62 shows my temporary Internet files.

- **Downloaded Program Files**   Your system always keeps a copy of any Java or ActiveX applets that it downloads. You can see these in the Internet Options applet. You'll generally find only a few tiny files here.

Mike Meyers' CompTIA A+ Guide: Essentials (Exam 220-601)

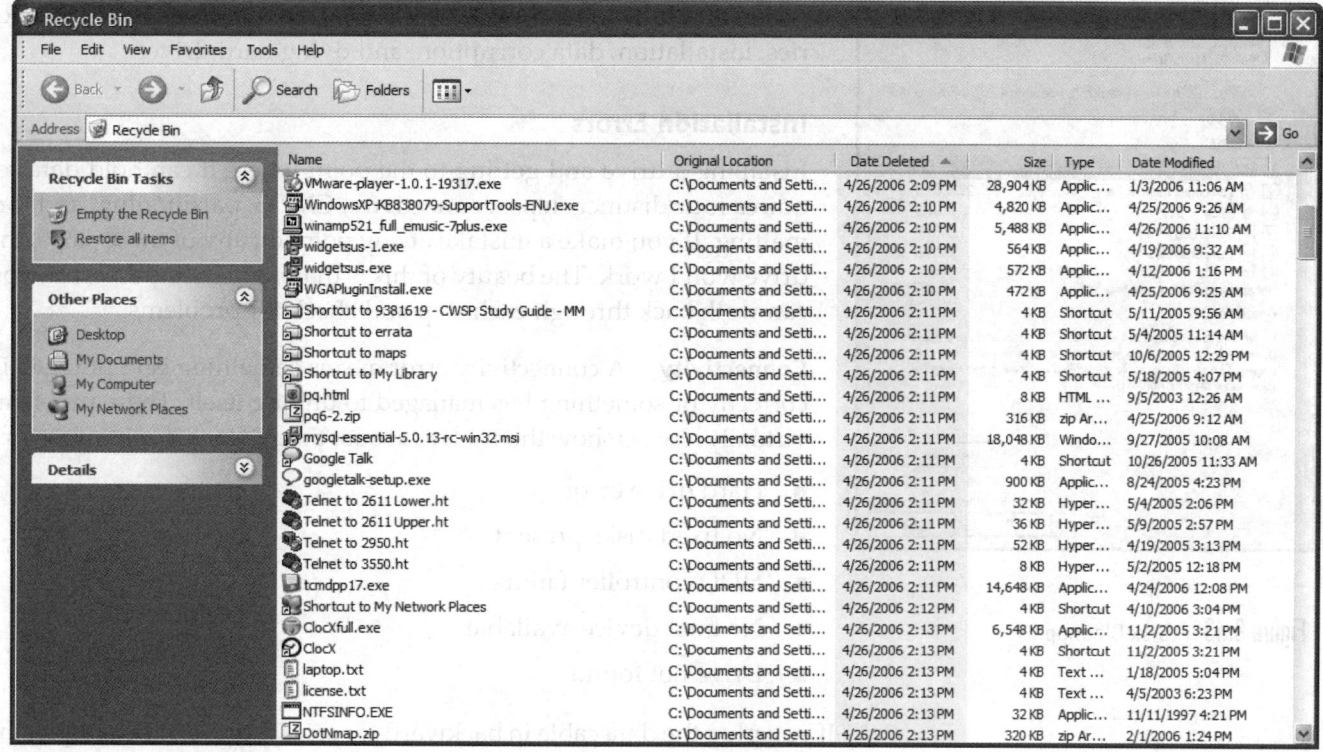

Mike's Recycle Bin

- **Temporary Files** Many applications create
temporary files that are supposed to be deleted
when the application is closed. For one reason or
another, these temporary files sometimes aren't
deleted. The location of these files varies with the
version of Windows, but they always reside in a
folder called TEMP.

Every hard drive will eventually become filled with
lots of unnecessary trash. All versions of Windows tend to
act erratically when the drives run out of unused space.
Fortunately, all versions of Windows have a powerful tool
called Disk Cleanup (Figure 9.63). You can access Disk
Cleanup in all versions of Windows by choosing Start |
Program | Accessories | System Tools | Disk Cleanup.

Disk Cleanup gets rid of the four types of files just described (and a few others). Run Disk Cleanup once a
month or so to keep plenty of space available on your hard
drive.

Troubleshooting

There's no scarier computer problem than an error that
points to trouble with a hard drive. This section looks at
some of the more common problems that occur with hard

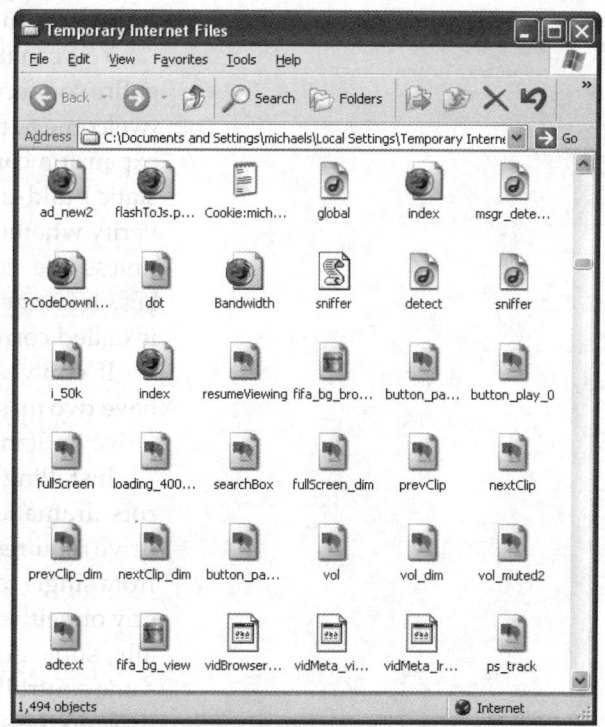

● Figure 9.62   Lots of temporary Internet files

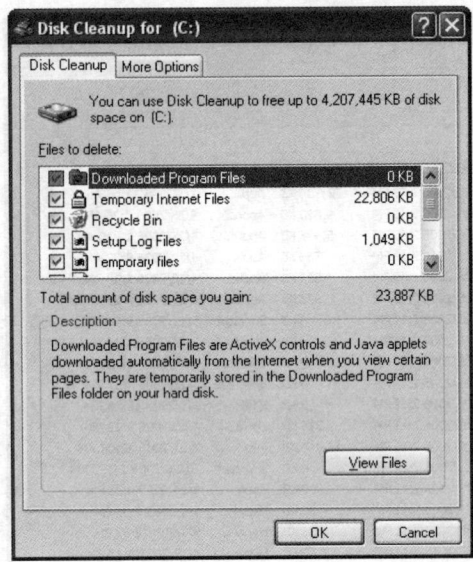

Figure 9.63   Disk Cleanup

drives and how to fix them. These issues fall into three broad categories: installation, data corruption, and dying hard drives.

Installation Errors

Installing a drive and getting to the point where it can hold data requires four distinct steps: connectivity, CMOS, partitioning, and formatting. If you make a mistake at any point on any of these steps, the drive won't work. The beauty of this is that if you make an error, you can walk back through each step and check for problems.

Connectivity   A connectivity error means something isn't plugged in correctly or something has managed to unplug itself. These problems virtually always show themselves at boot time. Here are some classics:

- Hard drive error
- No fixed disks present
- HDD controller failure
- No boot device available
- Drive not found

If you plug the data cable in backward for an IDE drive, for example, the computer simply won't see the drive—it's a famous error and everyone who has ever installed a hard drive has done it. Just reinsert the cable properly and turn the machine back on. The power connectors aren't nearly as forgiving. If you install the power cable backward, you will destroy the drive in a dazzling display of sparks and smoke. Fortunately, the chamfers on Molex connectors make this mistake difficult to do.

You can usually conquer connectivity errors by carefully inspecting the entire connection system (including electricity) and finding the silly mistake (welcome to the club). Always remove and reseat the controller (if it's on an expansion card) if you get an HDD controller failure, as they are prone to static build-up. It is also a good idea to keep an extra controller around to verify whether the controller is bad or good. Cables can go bad, but it is rare unless the cable is obviously ripped or pinched. If your BIOS has an **autodetection** function, use it. It will not detect a drive unless everything is installed correctly. It's a great, quick connectivity verifier.

If you've just installed the drive, check the jumper settings. You can't have two masters or two slaves on a single controller. And don't forget the 1 Drive or Standalone setting on some drives!

Installing two drives on the same controller increases the chances of errors dramatically. For example, adding a slave drive to an existing single drive requires you to check the first drive to see if its jumper needs to change from single to master. You need to make sure to install the slave drive properly or neither drive will work, causing the system to fail on boot. Additionally, some ATA drives are simply incompatible and will not work on the same controller. I've worked on many systems where I had to add a second drive to the secondary controller since it would not work with the existing drive.

CMOS Modern systems rarely get CMOS errors because the autodetection feature handles most drives. The errors that do occur generally fall into two groups: forgetting to run autodetect and selecting the wrong sector translation in autodetect. Two rules apply here: Always run autodetect and *always* select LBA.

Older systems could lose CMOS data for a variety of reasons, including static electricity, inserting an expansion card, and blinking with too much force. It takes nothing to do a quick CMOS check to verify that the drive's geometry is correct using autodetection. Here are some of the more common errors that might point to CMOS problems:

■ CMOS configuration mismatch

■ No boot device available

■ Drive not found

■ Missing OS

If autodetect fails to see the drive in question, it's probably a connectivity problem. Grab a screwdriver and look inside the system. This is also the one time where your hard drive's S.M.A.R.T. functions may help. Unplug the drive and make it an extra drive on a working system. Go to the hard drive manufacturer's Web site and download its diagnostic tool and run it. If you get a failure, the drive is dead and there's nothing you can do except be really happy that you back up your data all the time.

Partitioning Partitioning errors generally fall into two groups: failing to partition at all and making the wrong size or type of partition. You'll recognize the former type of error the first time you open My Computer after installing a drive. If you forgot to partition it, the drive won't even show up in My Computer, only Disk Management! If you made the partition too small, that'll become painfully obvious when you start filling it up with files.

The fix for partitioning errors is simply to open Disk Management and do the partitioning correctly. If you've added files to the wrongly sized drive, don't forget to back them up before you repartition!

Formatting Failing to format a drive makes the drive unable to hold data. Accessing the drive in Windows will result in a drive "is not accessible" error, and from a C:\ prompt, you'll get the famous "Invalid media" type error. Format the drive unless you're certain that the drive has a format already. Corrupted files can create the Invalid media type error. Check one of the sections on corrupted data later in this chapter for the fix.

Most of the time, formatting is a slow, boring process. But sometimes the drive makes "bad sounds" and you start seeing errors like the one shown in Figure 9.64 at the bottom of the screen.

An *allocation unit* is FORMAT's term for a cluster. The drive has run across a bad cluster and is trying to fix it. For years, I've told techs that seeing this error a few (610) times doesn't mean anything; every drive comes with a few bad spots. This is no longer true. Modern ATA drives actually hide a significant number of extra sectors that they use to replace bad sectors

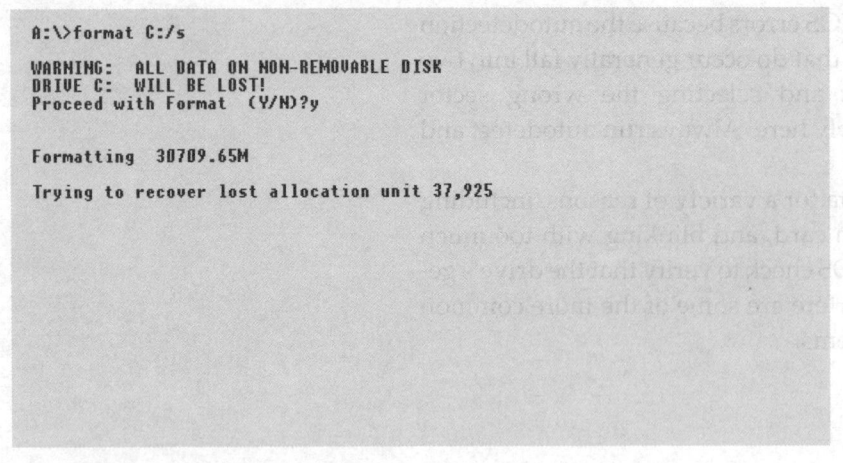

```
A:\>format C:/s

WARNING:  ALL DATA ON NON-REMOVABLE DISK
DRIVE C:  WILL BE LOST!
Proceed with Format  (Y/N)?y

Formatting  30709.65M

Trying to recover lost allocation unit 37,925
```

• **Figure 9.64**   The "Trying to recover lost allocation unit" error

automatically. If a new drive gets a lot of "Trying to recover lost allocation unit" errors, you can bet that the drive is dying and needs to be replaced. Get the hard drive maker's diagnostic to be sure. Bad clusters are reported by S.M.A.R.T.

Mental Reinstall   Focus on the fact that all of these errors share a common thread—you just installed a drive! Installation errors don't show up on a system that has been running correctly for three weeks; they show up the moment you try to do something with the drive you just installed. If a newly installed drive fails to work, do a "mental reinstall." Does the drive show up in the CMOS Autodetect? No? Then recheck the cables, master/slave settings, and power. If it does show up, did you remember to partition and format the drive? Did it need to be set to active? These are common sense questions that come to mind as you march through your mental reinstall. Even if you've installed thousands of drives over the years, you'll be amazed at how often you do things such as forget to plug in power to a drive, forget CMOS, or install a cable backward. Do the mental reinstall—it really works!

Data Corruption

All hard drives occasionally get corrupted data in individual sectors. Power surges, accidental shutdowns, corrupted installation media, and viruses, along with hundreds of other problems, can cause this corruption. In most cases, this type of error shows up while Windows is running. Figure 9.65 shows a classic example.

You may also see Windows error messages saying one of the following:

- "The following file is missing or corrupt"
- "The download location information is damaged"
- "Unable to load file"

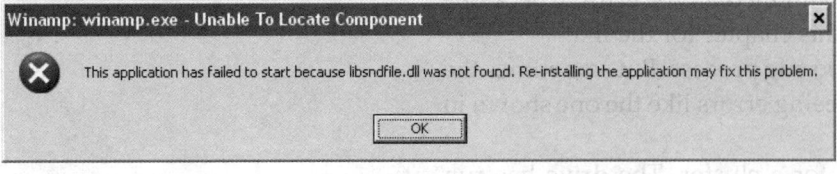

If core boot files become corrupted, you may see text errors at boot, such as the following:

- "Cannot find COMMAND.COM"
- "Error loading operating system"
- "Invalid BOOT.INI"

• **Figure 9.65**   A corrupted data error

On older programs, you may see a command prompt open with errors such as this one:

```
Sector not found reading drive C: Abort, Retry, Fail?
```

The first fix for any of these problems is to run the Error-checking utility. Error-checking will go through and mark bad clusters and hopefully move your data to a good cluster.

Extract/Expand If Error-checking fails to move a critically important file, such as a file Windows needs in order to load, you can always resort to the command line and try to extract the file from the Windows cabinet files. Most Windows programs store all files in a compressed format called CAB (which is short for cabinet file). One CAB file contains many files, and most installation disks have lots of CAB files (see Figure 9.66).

To replace a single corrupt file this way, you need to know two things: the location of the CAB file that contains the file you need, and how to get the file out so you can copy it back to its original spot. Microsoft supplies the EXPAND program to enable you to get a new copy of the missing file from the CAB files on the installation CD-ROM. Also notice how they are numbered—that's the secret to understanding these programs.

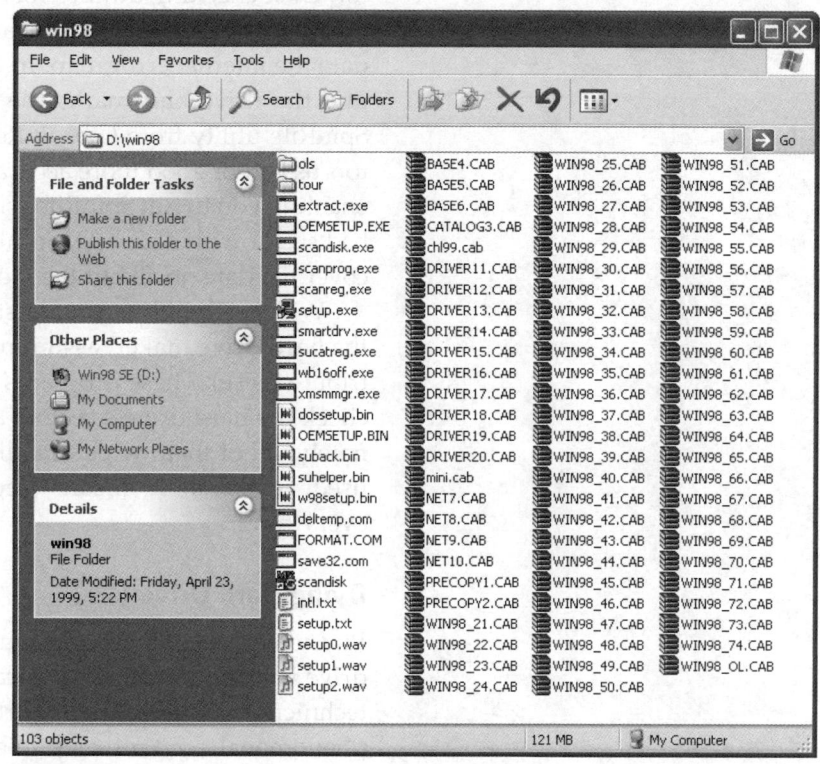

● **Figure 9.66** CAB files

In most cases, all the CAB files for a program are piled into some folder, as shown in Figure 9.66. Let's say you need a file called OLEPRO32.DLL. (I have no idea what this file does. I only know that Windows can't find it, and you need to put it back!) Get to a command prompt within Windows and tell EXPAND to check *all* the CAB files on your installation CD (drive E: in this example) with this command:

```
EXPAND e:\I386\*.CAB -F:OLEPRO32.DLL
```

EXPAND goes through all the CAB files and finds the file. If you want to see details on the EXPAND command, use Windows Help or type **EXPAND /?** at a command prompt.

The 602 exam goes into a lot of detail on using the command line.

Corrupted Data on Bad Sectors If the same errors continue to appear after running the disk-checking utility, there's a chance that the drive has bad sectors.

Almost all drives today take advantage of built-in error correction code (ECC) that constantly checks the drive for bad sectors. If the ECC detects a bad sector, it marks the sector as bad in the drive's internal error map. Don't confuse this error map with a FAT. The partitioning program creates the FAT. The drive's internal error map was created at the factory on reserved drive heads and is invisible to the system. If the ECC finds a bad sector, you will get a corrupted data error as the computer attempts to read the bad sector. Disk-checking utilities fix this problem most of the time.

Many times, the ECC thinks a bad sector is good, however, and fails to update the internal error map. In this case, you need a program that goes back into the drive and marks the sectors as bad. That's where the powerful SpinRite utility from Gibson Research comes into play. SpinRite marks sectors as bad or good more accurately than ECC and does not disturb the data, enabling you to run SpinRite without fear of losing anything. And if it finds a bad sector with data in it, SpinRite has powerful algorithms that usually recover the data on all but the most badly damaged sectors (see Figure 9.67).

Without SpinRite, you must use a low-level format program supplied by the hard drive maker, assuming you can get one (not all are willing to distribute these). These programs work like SpinRite in that they aggressively check the hard drive's sectors and update the internal error map. Unfortunately, all of them wipe out all data on the drive. At least the drive can be used, even if it means repartitioning, formatting, and reinstalling everything.

Dying Hard Drive

Physical problems are rare but devastating when they happen. If a hard drive is truly damaged physically, there is nothing that you or any service technician can do to fix it. Fortunately, hard drives are designed to take a phenomenal amount of punishment without failing. Physical problems manifest themselves in two ways: either the drive works properly but makes a lot of noise, or the drive seems to disappear.

All hard drives make noise—the hum as the platters spin and the occasional slight scratching noise as the read/write heads access sectors are normal.

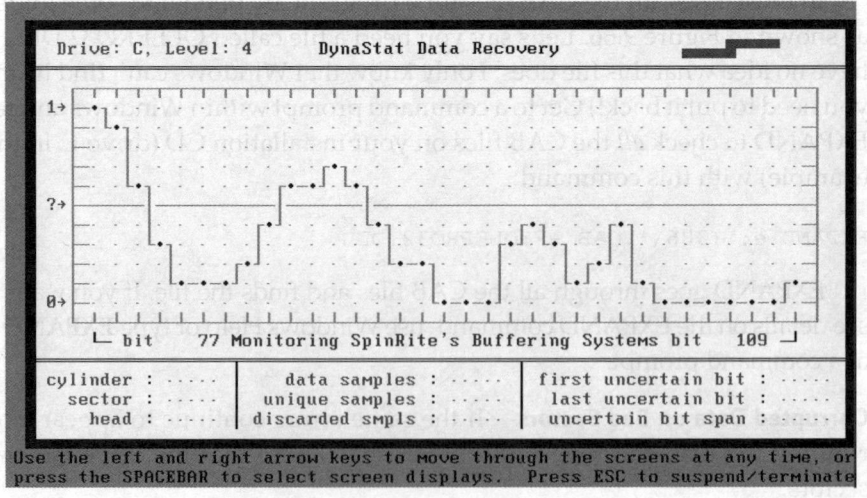

• **Figure 9.67** SpinRite at work

However, if your drive begins to make any of the following sounds, it is about to die:

- Continuous high-pitched squeal
- Series of clacks, a short pause, and then another series of clacks
- Continuous grinding or rumbling

Back up your critical data and replace the drive. Windows comes with great tools for backing up data.

You'll know when a drive simply disappears. If it's the drive that contains your operating system, the system will lock up. When you try to restart the computer, you'll see this error message:

```
No Boot Device Present
```

If it's a second drive, it will simply stop showing up in My Computer. The first thing to do in this case is to fire up the System Setup program and see if autodetect sees the drive. If it does, you do not have a physical problem with the drive. If autodetect fails, shut off the system and remove the ribbon cable, but leave the power cable attached. Restart the system and listen to the drive. If the drive spins up, you know that the drive is getting good power. In most cases, this is a clue that the drive is probably good. In that case, you need to look for more mundane problems such as an unplugged power cord or jumpers incorrectly set. If the drive doesn't spin up, try another power connector. If it still doesn't spin up and you've triple-checked the jumpers and ribbon cable, you have a problem with the onboard electronics, and the drive is dead.

Beyond A+

Modern hard drives have many other features that are worth knowing about, but that rarely impact beginning techs. A couple of the more interesting ones are spindle speed and third-party hard drive tools. If you have a burning desire to dive into hard drives in all their glory, you need not go any farther than the Storage Review, an excellent site dedicated solely to hard drives. Here's the link: www.storagereview.com.

Third-Party Partition Tools

Disk Management is a good tool, but is limited for some situations. Some really great third-party tools on the market can give you incredible flexibility and power to structure and restructure your hard drive storage to meet your changing needs. They each have interesting unique features, but in general they enable you to create, change, and delete partitions on a hard drive *without* destroying any of the programs or data stored there. Slick! These programs aren't on the CompTIA A+ exams, but all PC techs use at least one of them, so let's explore three of the most well-known examples: Symantec's PartitionMagic, VCOM's Partition Commander Professional, and the open source Linux tool, GParted.

Tech Tip

Long Warranties
Most hard drives have three-year warranties. Before you throw away a dead drive, check the hard drive maker's Web site or call them to see if the drive is still under warranty. Ask for a return material authorization (RMA). You'll be amazed how many times you get a newer, usually larger, hard drive for free! It never hurts to check!

Tech Tip

Data Rescue Specialists
If you ever lose a hard drive that contains absolutely critical information, you can turn to a company that specializes in hard drive data recovery. The job will be expensive—prices usually start around US$1000—but when you must have the data, such companies are your only hope. Do a Web search for "data recovery" or check the Yellow Pages for companies in this line of business.

● **Figure 9.68**   PartitionMagic

Probably the most well-known third-party partition tool is PartitionMagic, up to version 8 as of this writing (Figure 9.68). It supports every version of Windows and just about every other operating system, too. It enables you to create, resize, split, merge, delete, undelete, and convert partitions without destroying your data. Among the additional features it advertises are: the ability to browse, copy, or move files and folders between supported partitions; expand an NTFS partition— even if it's a system partition—without rebooting; change NTFS cluster sizes; and add new partitions for multiple OSs using a simple wizard.

VCOM offers a variety of related products, one of which is the very useful Partition Commander Professional 10. Like PartitionMagic, it supports all versions of Windows and enables you to play with your partitions without destroying your data. Among its niftier features are the ability to convert a Windows 2000/XP/2003 dynamic disk to a basic disk nondestructively (which Windows 2000/XP/2003 can't do); defrag the master file table on an NTFS partition; and move unused space from one partition to another on the same physical drive, automatically resizing the partitions based on the amount of space you tell it to move. Figure 9.69 shows the Partition Commander dialog box for moving unused space between partitions.

The only problem with PartitionMagic and Partition Commander is that they cost money. There's nothing wrong with spending money on a good product, but if you can find something that does the job for free, why not try it? If you think like I do, check out the Gnome Partition Editor, better known as GParted. You can find it at http://sourceforge.net/.

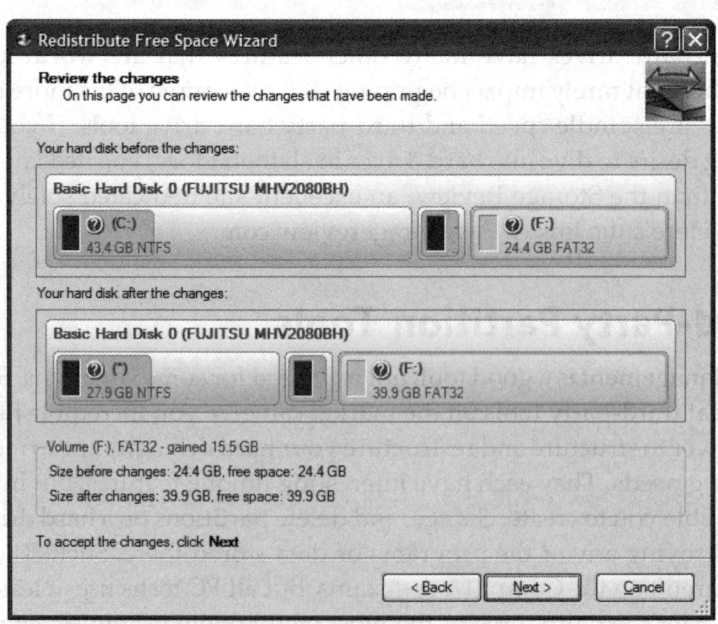

● **Figure 9.69**   Partition Commander

GParted is an incredibly powerful partition editor and does almost everything the for-pay partition editors do, but it's free. It's still in beta—which means it's constantly changing and it's got a few bugs (that are constantly being fixed)—but I use it all the time and love it. If you look closely at Figure 9.70, you'll notice that it uses strange names for the partitions such as HDA1 or HDB3. These are Linux conventions and are well documented in GParted's help screens. Take a little time and you'll love GParted, too.

The one downside to GParted is that it is a Linux program—because no Windows version exists, you need Linux to run it. So how do you run Linux on a Windows system without actually installing Linux on your hard drive? The answer is easy—the folks at GParted will give you the tools to burn a live CD that boots Linux so you can run GParted!

A live CD is a complete OS on a CD. Understand this is not an installation CD like your Windows installation disk. The OS is already installed on the CD. You boot from the live CD and the OS loads into RAM, just like the OS on your hard drive loads into RAM at boot. As the live CD boots,

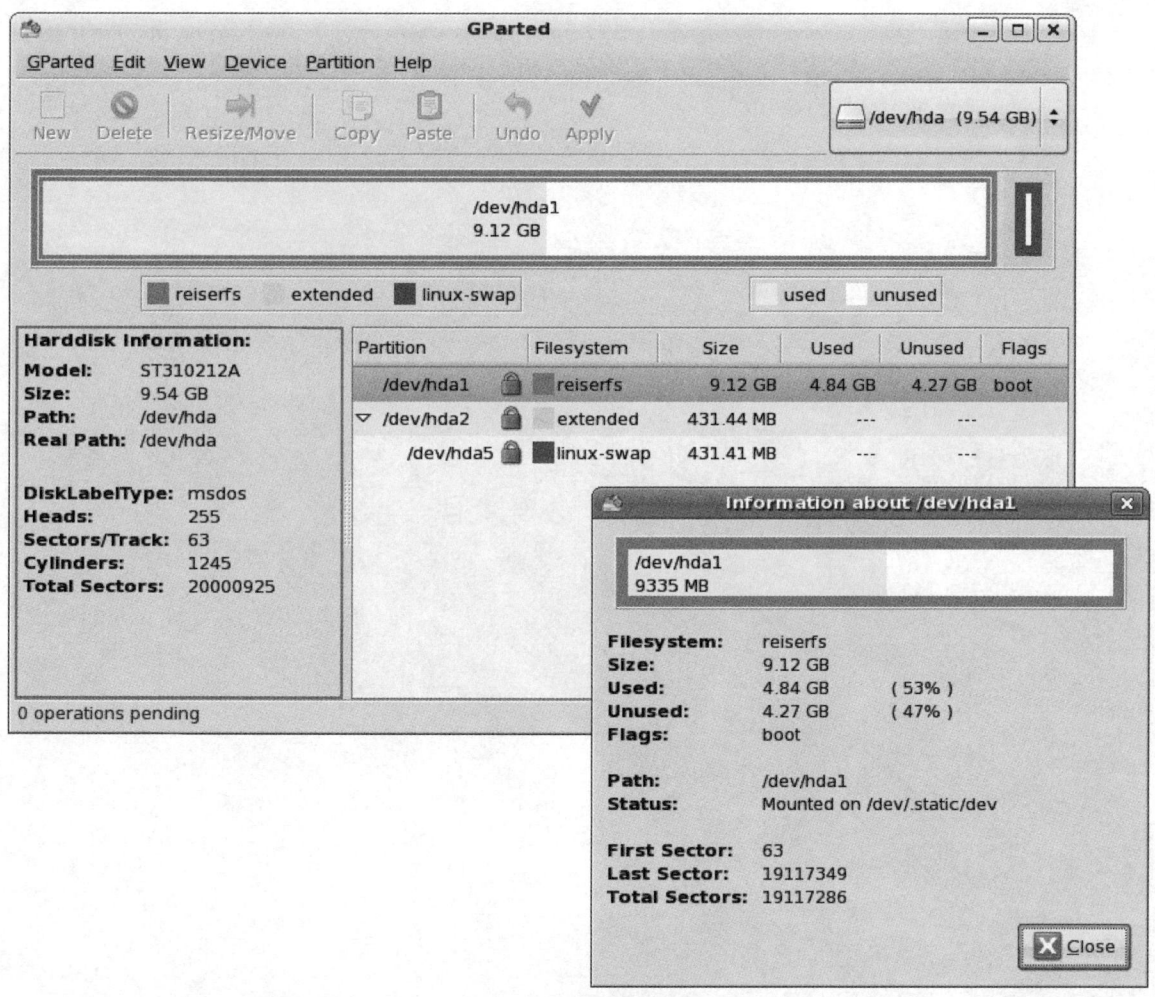

• **Figure 9.70**   GParted in action

it recognizes your hardware and loads the proper drivers into RAM so everything works. You get everything you'd expect from an OS with one big exception: a live CD does not touch your hard drive. Of course you may run programs (like GParted) that work on your hard drive, which makes live CDs popular with PC techs, because you can toss them into a cranky system and run utilities.

The truly intrepid might want to consider using The Ultimate Boot CD (UBCD), basically a huge pile of useful freeware utilities compiled by frustrated technician Ben Burrows, who couldn't find a boot disk when he needed one. His Web site is www.ultimatebootcd.com. The UBCD has more than 100 different tools, all placed on a single live CD. It has all of the low-level diagnostic tools for all of the hard drive makers, four or five different partitioning tools, S.M.A.R.T. viewers, hard drive wiping utilities, and hard drive cloning tools (nice for when you want to replace a hard drive with a larger one). Little documentation is provided, however, and many of the tools require experience way beyond the scope of the CompTIA A+ exams. I will tell you that I have a copy and I use it.

Chapter 9 Review

■ Chapter Summary

After reading this chapter and completing the exercises, you should understand the following about implementing hard drives.

Hard Drive Partitions

- Partitions are electronic subdivisions of physical hard drives into groups of cylinders. After partitioning, each partition must be formatted before it can be used to store files. Every hard drive must contain at least one partition, but many users choose to create multiple partitions on a single hard drive to make backups easier or to install another operating system for dual-boot or multiboot environments. Windows 2000 and XP support two different partitioning schemes: master boot record (MBR) and dynamic storage partitioning.

- Basic disks are those that use the master boot record (MBR) partitioning scheme. The MBR, a tiny bit of code in the first sector of a hard drive, looks for a partition in the partition table with a valid operating system. Every basic disk has one and only one MBR.

- Basic disks support primary and extended partitions. Windows limits each basic disk hard drive to a maximum of four partitions total with no more than one extended partition. Primary partitions can receive drive letters and are designed to support bootable operating systems. Extended partitions, which do not receive drive letters, exist to house logical drives. Logical drives can receive drive letters. In Windows 2000 and XP, both primary partitions and logical drives may use folder mount points instead of drive letters.

- Every partition contains a volume boot sector in its first sector. During boot up, a hard drive's MBR finds the active partition and loads the boot record code from the partition's volume boot sector. The boot record code finds and loads the operating system. Only active primary partitions can boot an operating system. Only one primary partition per hard drive can be marked as active.

- Primary partitions and logical drives may be accessed via a folder mount point rather than a drive letter. Use the administrative tool Disk Management to create mount points and change drive letters.

- Hard drives that use the dynamic storage partitioning scheme instead of an MBR are called dynamic disks by Microsoft. Dynamic disks use volumes rather than partitions and are accessible only by Windows 2000, XP, 2003, and Vista. There are no primary or extended volumes—a volume is simply a volume. Dynamic disks and volumes offer capabilities not possible with partitions, namely spanning, striping, and RAID.

- Dynamic disks support a total of five different types of volumes: simple, spanned, striped, mirrored, and RAID 5. A simple volume is similar to a primary partition in that it can store files and can receive a drive letter or be mounted to a folder. Spanned volumes combine space from several volumes and treat them as a single volume. After one volume is full, files are written to the next volume in the span. Striped volumes are similar to spanned volumes, but files are deliberately split across volumes to increase read/write access time. Neither spanned nor striped volumes are fault tolerant. RAID 1, or mirrored volumes, use exactly two volumes that are exact duplicates of each other. You suffer a slight performance hit but make up for it with fault tolerance. RAID 5, or striping with parity, requires at least three same size volumes, enjoys the speed boost of striping, and is fault tolerant.

- Other partition types include hidden and swap partitions. Hidden partitions are not visible to the operating system and are often used by PC manufacturers to store emergency restore images of the system partition. Swap partitions are used by Linux and BSD systems for virtual memory and function much the same as a Windows page file.

- Most operating systems will allow you to create partitions during the installation process. To create partitions at other times, you use a partitioning tool dedicated to that task. Older versions of Windows shipped with the command-line program FDISK (fdisk.exe) for this purpose. Windows 2000 and later versions ship with a graphical tool called Disk Management to manage partitions, convert basic disks to dynamic disks, and manage volumes. Linux uses several partitioning tools such as FDISK (same name, but different from the Windows version) and GParted.

Hard Drive Formatting

- After a disk has been partitioned, it must be formatted before it can be used. Formatting creates a file system and the root directory. You can use the Windows command-line program FORMAT (format.com) or the GUI tool Disk Management to format a partition or volume. Current versions of Windows support three file systems: FAT16, FAT32, and NTFS.

- The base storage area for hard drives is a sector, which can store up to 512 bytes of data. If a file is smaller than 512 bytes and does not fill a sector, the rest of the sector remains unused as only one file can reside in any one sector. If a file is more than 512 bytes, the file is split into pieces with each piece residing in different sectors. If the sectors containing all the pieces of a single file are not contiguous, the file is said to be fragmented.

- MS-DOS version 2.1 first supported the file allocation table (FAT). The FAT is a data structure similar to a two-column spreadsheet that tracks where data is stored on a hard drive.

- FAT comes in several variations: FAT12, FAT16, and FAT32. The number indicates how many bits are available in the left side of the FAT spreadsheet. Floppy disks use FAT12 while hard drives can use FAT16 or FAT32.

- Every version of Windows fully supports FAT16. FAT16 uses only 16 bits to address sector locations. This translates to 2^{16}, or 64 K locations. With 64 K locations of 512-byte sectors, 64 K × 512 bytes hits the ceiling at 32 MB. For this reason, FAT16 partitions were initially limited to 32 MB. FAT16 later added a feature called clustering that treats a set of contiguous sectors as a single FAT unit.

These clusters (also called file allocation units) allow a maximum partition size of 2 GB.

- Since FAT16, a cluster rather than a sector is the basic unit of storage. Unlike sectors, the size of a cluster is not fixed; it changes with the size of the partition. Because FAT16 still supported only a maximum of 64-K storage units, the formatting program set the number of sectors in each cluster according to the size of the partition.

- After the format program creates the FAT, it tests each sector and places a special status code (FFF7) in the FAT for any bad sectors so they won't be used. Good sectors are marked with 0000. When an application saves a file, the OS starts writing the file to the first available cluster marked as good. If the entire file fits in the cluster, the OS places the end-of-file marker (FFFF) in the cluster's status area. If the file does not fit entirely in a single cluster, the OS searches for the next available cluster. Once found, the location of this next available cluster is written to the status area of the preceding cluster holding a piece of the file, and the OS writes the next 512 bytes of the file in the available cluster. This continues until the file has been completely written and the final cluster in the chain receives the status code FFFF in the FAT. After saving the entire file, the OS lists the filename and starting cluster in the file's folder.

- As a file is split across multiple non-contiguous clusters, the file becomes fragmented. Fragmentation slows read/write access as the OS has to piece together the many fragments of the file. Every version of Windows, except NT, comes with a disk defragmenter program that reorganized the clusters of hard drive data so files are stored wherever possible in contiguous clusters.

- FAT32 was introduced with Windows 95 OS2. FAT32, which uses 32 bits to describe each cluster, supports partitions up to 2 terabytes. FAT32 creates smaller clusters and therefore stores files more efficiently than FAT16.

- The New Technology File System (NTFS) was introduced with Windows NT and has gone through several versions. The most recent version, used since Windows 2000, is referred to as NTFS 5. NTFS does not use a FAT like FAT16 or FAT32, but instead uses a master file table (MFT).

- NTFS offers several major improvements over FAT, including redundancy, security, compression, encryption, disk quotas, and cluster sizing. A backup copy of the most critical parts of the MFT is stored in the middle of the disk, where it is less likely to become damaged.

- With NTFS, individual files and folders can be protected by allowing only certain users or groups access to them. Individual files or folders can be compressed to save hard drive space. Files or folders can be encrypted so that they are unreadable to anyone but you. Users can be limited to the amount of disk space they use by enforcing disk quotas. Finally, cluster sizes can be adjusted to allow support of partitions up to 16 exabytes.

Partitioning and Formatting Process

- Any software that can boot up a system is called an operating system, and any removable media that contains a bootable operating system is generically called a boot device or boot disk. All Windows and Linux operating system installation CDs are boot devices. You can also make your own boot device complete with handy tech tools.

- Windows installation CDs walk you through the process of partitioning and formatting your hard drive. After accepting the license agreement, you can simply press ENTER and Windows will partition and format your drive as one large primary partition. If you prefer to partition only a portion of the hard drive, you can do so manually by pressing the letter C to create a partition, entering the desired size in MB, and pressing ENTER. Finally, you are offered several options for formatting before the installation continues. It is recommended that you choose NTFS. Note the disk is partitioned and formatted as a basic disk. Once Windows is installed, you can convert basic disks to dynamic disks with the Disk Management tool.

- Drive letters can be changed or removed with the Disk Management tool. Only the C: drive cannot be changed. Drive letters are dynamically assigned at every boot and are assigned to drives in a specific order. Drive letters may change if you install additional hard drives, so it important to plan your primary/extended partitioning scheme.

- All new disk drives must be initialized by Disk Management before you can use them. The initialization process places information on the drive identifying it as part of a particular system New drives are always initialized as basic disks but can be converted to dynamic disks by right-clicking and choosing Convert To Dynamic Disk. Creating a partition or volume is just as simple. Right-click the drive and choose Create Partition or New Volume. Remember that you must create logical drives inside an extended partition before you can format and use it to store files.

- Once a disk has been initialized and partitioned, you can format it. Microsoft requires using NTFS for any partition larger than 32 GB. Performing a Quick Format skips the checking of clusters, which results in a faster format but is risky.

- The Windows installation program creates a tiny partition on the C: drive, which is used to later convert the disk to a dynamic disk. While you can format and use that space for file storage, it is recommended that you leave it as is.

- A mount point is a folder on an NTFS drive that provides access to another drive that may or may not have a drive letter. This allows the new drive to extend the capacity of the drive providing the folder mount point. All files in the mount point folder, while looking like they are stored on the first drive, are actually stored on the additional drive. Create a mount point by first creating a folder on an NTFS drive. Then, launch Disk Management, select the additional partition/volume, right-click, and choose Change Drive Letter and Paths. From there, choose Add and browse to the mount point folder you created earlier.

- You can format any partition/volume in My Computer by right-clicking and choosing Format. Alternatively, you can format partitions/volumes from the Disk Management tool. Both methods offer you options to perform a Quick Format and enable compression.

Maintaining and Troubleshooting Hard Drives

- Hard drive maintenance can be broken down into two distinct functions: checking the disk occasionally for failed clusters and keeping data organized on the drive so that it can be accessed quickly.

- Microsoft offers Error-checking for scanning hard drives. It checks for bad clusters and, if found, marks them as bad so no data gets written to those areas of the hard drive. Additionally, it will look for invalid filenames and attempt to fix them, and it will search for and erase lost cluster chains.

- To run Error-checking in Windows 2000 or XP, right-click a drive to view its Properties window, choose the Tools tabs, and click the Check Now button. Check the box to Automatically fix file system errors, but save the option to Scan for and attempt recovery of bad sectors for times when you actually suspect a problem.

- You should run Error-checking and Disk Defragmenter once a month as preventive maintenance to keep your system running smoothly. Both are available on the Tools tab of the drive's Properties window.

- The Disk Cleanup utility will delete files from the Recycle Bin, temporary Internet files, copies of downloaded Java or ActiveX applets, and other temporary files on your hard drive. You can access Disk Cleanup in all versions of Windows by choosing Start | Programs | Accessories | System Tools | Disk Cleanup. Run Disk Cleanup once a month.

- Hard drive problems fall into three broad categories: installation, data corruption, and dying hard drives. Installation errors can happen at any of the four steps: connectivity, CMOS, partitioning, or formatting. When troubleshooting, you should always walk back through each step and check for problems.

- Usually showing up at boot time, a connectivity error indicates that something isn't plugged in correctly or something has become unplugged. Some connectivity errors are harmless, such as plugging in the data cable backward for an IDE drive, while others, such as installing the power cable backward, will destroy your drive. The IDE autodetect function of your BIOS will not detect a drive unless it is installed correctly, making it a great connectivity verifier. Some IDE drives simply will not work on the same controller.

- Because autodetect handles most drives, you rarely get CMOS errors. Those that do occur fall into two groups: forgetting to run autodetect and selecting the wrong sector translation in autodetect. Two rules apply here: Always run autodetect and always select LBA. If autodetect fails to see the drive in question, it's probably a connectivity problem.

- Partitioning errors generally fall into two groups: failing to partition at all, and making the wrong size/type of partition. If you try to access a nonpartitioned drive, you'll get an "Invalid Drive Specifications" error and you can't see the drive in anything but CMOS, FDISK, and Disk Management.

- If you try to access a drive that's not formatted, Windows will display a drive "is not accessible" error, while you'll get an "Invalid media" error from a C:\ prompt. Format the drive unless you're certain that the drive has already been formatted. Corrupted files can also create the "Invalid media" error.

- The "Trying to recover lost allocation unit" error means the drive has bad sectors. Time to replace the drive.

- If a newly installed drive fails to work, do a "mental reinstall." If the drive does not show in CMOS autodetect, recheck the cables, master/slave jumper settings, and power. If it shows up, make sure you remembered to partition and format it. Remember the drive must be marked as Active to be bootable.

- Power surges, accidental shutdowns, corrupted installation media, and viruses are among the causes of corrupted data in individual sectors. These errors usually show while Windows is running. If core boot files become corrupted, you may see text errors such as "Cannot find COMMAND.COM," "Error loading operating system," or "Invalid BOOT.INI." Older systems may generate a "sector not found" error. The first fix for any of these problems is to run an error-checking utility.

- To replace a single corrupt file, you must know the location of the numbered Windows CAB (cabinet) file that contains the file you need and how to extract the file from the CAB file. Use the EXPAND program with Windows 2000/XP to get a new copy of the desired file from the CAB file on the installation disc. EXPAND searches all CAB files to find the file you specify, and then expands it and places it in the C:\ folder.

- Almost all drives today have built-in error correction code (ECC) that constantly checks the drive for bad sectors. If it detects a bad sector, it marks the sector as bad in the drive's internal error map so that it's invisible to the system. If the ECC finds a bad sector, however, you will get a corrupted data error when the computer attempts to read the bad sector.

- The powerful SpinRite utility from Gibson Research marks sectors as bad or good more accurately than ECC and does not disturb the data. When it finds a bad sector with data in it, SpinRite uses powerful algorithms that usually recover the data on all but the most badly damaged sectors. Without SpinRite, you must use a low-level formatting program supplied by the hard drive manufacturer, which will wipe out all data on the drive.

- If a hard drive is truly physically damaged, it cannot be fixed. Physical problems manifest themselves in two ways: either the drive works properly but makes a lot of noise, or the drive seems to disappear. If you hear a continuous high-pitched squeal; a series of clacks, a short pause, and then another series of clacks; or a continuous grinding or rumbling, your hard drive is about to die. Back up your critical data and replace the drive. If the drive that contains your operating system disappears, the system will lock up or you will get the error message "No Boot Device Present" when you try to reboot. If the problem is with a second drive, it will simply stop showing up in My Computer.

- If your drive makes noise or disappears, first run the System Setup program to see if autodetect sees the drive. If it does, the drive doesn't have a physical problem. If autodetect fails, shut down the system and remove the ribbon cable, but leave the power cable attached. Restart the system and listen to the drive. If the drive spins up, the drive is getting good power, which usually means the drive is good. Next, check for an unplugged power cord or incorrectly set jumpers. If the drive doesn't spin up, try another power connector. If it still doesn't spin up and you've triple-checked the jumpers and ribbon cable, you have a problem with the onboard electronics and the drive is dead.

Key Terms

active partition *(211)*	error correction code (ECC) *(253)*	mirrored volume *(215)*
autodetection *(250)*	EXPAND *(253)*	mount point *(243)*
basic disk *(210)*	extended partition *(210)*	NT File System (NTFS) *(224)*
boot sector *(210)*	FAT32 *(223)*	partition *(209)*
CHKDSK *(247)*	FDISK *(215)*	partition table *(210)*
cluster *(219)*	file allocation table (FAT) *(218)*	primary partition *(210)*
data structure *(218)*	file allocation unit *(219)*	RAID 5 volume *(215)*
defragmentation *(223)*	file system *(209)*	ScanDisk *(247)*
Disk Cleanup *(249)*	formatting *(209)*	simple volume *(241)*
Disk Management *(215)*	fragmentation *(221)*	spanned volume *(241)*
disk quota *(227)*	high-level formatting *(218)*	stripe set *(243)*
dual-boot *(211)*	logical drive *(210)*	volume *(209)*
dynamic disk *(210)*	master boot record (MBR) *(210)*	volume boot sector *(211)*
encrypting file system (EFS) *(225)*	master file table (MFT) *(224)*	

Key Term Quiz

Use the Key Terms list to complete the sentences that follow. Not all terms will be used.

1. The MBR checks the partition table to find the _____ or bootable partition.

2. If a file is not stored in contiguous clusters, you can improve hard drive performance by using the _____ tool.

3. Instead of using a FAT, NTFS uses a(n) _____ with a backup copy placed in the middle of the disk for better security.

4. If you are installing Windows 2000 or XP, the best file system to choose is _____.

5. _____ is the tool included with Windows that attempts to fix invalid filenames, erases lost clusters, and seals off bad clusters.

6. _____ is a great way to verify that a drive is installed correctly.

7. If an operating system file has become corrupted or is missing, you can replace it by using _____ to remove a specific file from a CAB file.

8. Only a single _____ may be set to active.

9. The _____ utility is useful for purging your system of unnecessary temporary files.

10. A(n) _____ requires exactly two volumes and is extremely fault tolerant.

Multiple-Choice Quiz

1. Which is the most complete list of file systems that Windows 2000 and XP can use?
   A. FAT16, FAT32, NTFS
   B. FAT16, FAT32, FAT64, NTFS
   C. FAT16, FAT32
   D. FAT16, NTFS

2. The Disk Cleanup utility removes which types of unneeded files?
   A. Temporary Internet files
   B. Temporary files that remain when an application is closed
   C. Programs no longer in use
   D. Both A and B

3. Which of the following correctly identifies the four possible entries in a file allocation table?
   A. Filename, date, time, size
   B. Number of the starting cluster, number of the ending cluster, number of used clusters, number of available clusters
   C. An end-of-file marker, a bad sector marker, code indicating the cluster is available, the number of the cluster where the next part of the file is stored
   D. Filename, folder location, starting cluster number, ending cluster number

4. You receive an "Invalid media" error when trying to access a hard drive. What is the most likely cause of the error?
   A. The drive has not been partitioned.
   B. The drive has not been set to active.
   C. The drive has not been formatted.
   D. The drive has died.

5. Which of the following is an advantage of partitioning a hard drive into more than one partition?
   A. It enables a single hard drive to store more than one operating system.
   B. It protects against boot record viruses.
   C. It uses less power.
   D. It allows for dynamic disk RAID 5.

6. What program does Microsoft include with Windows 2000 and Windows XP to partition and format a drive?
   A. Format
   B. Disk Management console
   C. Disk Administrator console
   D. System Commander

7. What does NTFS use to provide security for individual files and folders?
   A. Dynamic disks
   B. ECC
   C. Access control list
   D. MFT

8. Which of the following statements is true about extended partitions?
   A. They are optional.
   B. They are assigned drive letters when they are created.
   C. They may be set to Active.
   D. Each drive must have at least one extended partition.

9. Adam wants to create a new simple volume in some unallocated space on his hard drive, but when he right-clicks the space in Disk Management he sees only an option to create a new partition. What is the problem?

   A. The drive has developed bad sectors.

   B. The drive is a basic disk and not a dynamic disk.

   C. The drive has less than 32 GB of unallocated space.

   D. The drive is jumpered as a slave.

10. Jaime wishes to check her hard drive for errors. What tool should she use?

   A. FDISK

   B. Format

   C. Disk Management

   D. Error-checking

11. To make your files unreadable by others, what should you use?

   A. Clustering

   B. Compression

   C. Disk quotas

   D. Encryption

12. Which of the following utilities should you run once a month to maintain the speed of your PC?

   A. Disk Defragmenter

   B. FDISK

   C. Disk Management

   D. System Commander

13. Which two terms identify a bootable partition?

   A. Master, FAT

   B. Slave, FAT

   C. Primary, Active

   D. Primary, NTFS

14. For what purpose can you use disk quotas?

   A. Limit users to a specific drive.

   B. Extend the capacity of a volume.

   C. Manage dual-boot environments.

   D. Limit users' space on a drive.

15. What is the capacity of a single sector?

   A. 256 bytes

   B. 512 bits

   C. 512 bytes

   D. 4 kilobytes

Essay Quiz

1. Your new boss is pretty old-school, having cut his teeth on Windows 3.11 and Windows 95. Accordingly, you discover that all the Windows XP computers in the office use only FAT32 for their hard drives. Write a two- to three-paragraph memo that (gently) extols the virtues and benefits of NTFS over FAT32.

2. You've been tasked by your supervisor to teach basic hard drive partitioning to a couple of new hires. Write a short essay that explains the difference between simple volumes, spanned volumes, and striped volumes. What's better? When would you use one and not the other?

3. One of your employees doesn't quite get it when it comes to computers. He keeps complaining that his hard drive is stopped up, by which he most likely means full. He installed a second hard drive using some steps he found on the Internet, but he claims it doesn't work. On closer examination, you

determine that the drive shows up in CMOS but not in Windows—he didn't partition or format the drive! Write a short essay describing partitioning and formatting, including the tools used to accomplish this task on a second hard drive.

4. Your office has a PC shared by four people to do intensive graphics work. The hard drive has about 100 GB of free space. Write a memo on how you could use disk quotas to make certain that each of the users takes no more than 25% of the free space.

5. Your office has several computers with three 20-GB drives in addition to the C: drive. Write a short essay that describes how you could use spanning and mount points to make the extra drives more easily usable for your users.

Lab Projects

• Lab Project 9.1

Grab a test system with multiple drives and experiment with the partitioning tools in Windows Disk Management. Create various partition combinations, such as all primary or all extended with logical drives. Change basic disks into dynamic disks and create volumes that span multiple drives. Add to them. You get the idea—experiment and have fun!

• Lab Project 9.2

Partitioning gets all the glory and exposure in tech classes because, frankly, it's cool to be able to do some of the things possible with Windows 2000 and Windows XP Disk Management console! But the experienced tech does not forget about the other half of drive preparation: formatting. Windows 2000 and Windows XP offer you at least two different file systems. In this lab, you'll put them through their paces.

In one or more OSs, partition a drive with two equal partitions and format one as FAT32 and the other as NTFS. Then get a couple of monster files (larger than 50 MB) and move them to those partitions. Did you notice any difference in transfer speed? Examine the drives in My Computer. Do they show the same amount of used space?

Understanding Removable Media

> "Just as a curtain is never lowered halfway through an opera, a disc should be large enough to hold all of Beethoven's Ninth Symphony."
>
> —SONY CHAIRMAN (AND PROFESSIONAL MUSICIAN) NORIO OHGA'S ARGUMENT FOR MAKING THE CD FORMAT CAPABLE OF HOLDING 75 MINUTES OF MUSIC ON ONE DISC

Removable media is any type of mass storage device that you may use in one system and then physically remove from that system and use in another. Removable media has been a part of the personal PC from its first introduction back in 1980. Granted, back then the only removable media available were floppy disks, but the ability to easily move programs and data from one machine to another was quickly established as one of the strongest points of the personal computer. Over time, higher capacity removable media technologies were introduced. Some technologies—CDs, DVDs, and thumb drives, for example—have become very common. Other technologies (that you may or may not have heard of) like the Iomega Zip drives were extremely popular for a time but faded away. The history of PCs has also left a trash heap of removable media technologies that were trumpeted in with fanfare and a lot of money but never really saw any adoption.

In this chapter, you will learn how to

- **Explain and install floppy disk drives**
- **Demonstrate the variations among flash drives and other tiny drives**
- **Identify optical-media technology**

● **Figure 10.1** Author's toolbox

Today's highly internetworked computers have reduced the need for removable media as a method of sharing programs and data, but removable media has so many other uses that this hasn't slowed things down a bit. Removable media is the perfect tool for software distribution, data archiving, and system backup. Figure 10.1 shows my software toolbox. As a PC technician, you'll not only need to install, maintain, and troubleshoot removable media on a system working for users, but you'll also find yourself turning to removable media as a way to store and run software tools to perform all types of PC support!

This chapter covers the most common types of removable media used today. For the sake of organization, all removable media are broken down into these groups:

- **Floppy drives** The traditional floppy drive

- **Flash memory** From USB thumb drives to flash memory cards

- **Optical media** Any shiny disc technology from CD-ROMs to DVDs

- **External drives** Any hard drive or optical drive that connects to a PC via an external cable

If you go by the earlier description of removable memory, then two other technologies, PC Cards and tape backups, also fit as removable media. PC Cards are a laptop-centric technology and are covered in Chapter 16, "Portable Computing," whereas tape backups are part of the big world of backups and are covered in my other book, *Mike Meyers' A+ Guide: PC Technician (Exams 220-602, 220-603, & 220-604)*.

Historical/Conceptual

■ Floppy Drives

Good old floppies! These little disks, storing a whopping 1.44 MB of data per disk, have been part of PCs from the beginning. For decades, the PC industry has made one attempt after another to replace the floppy with some higher capacity removable media, only to keep falling back to the floppy disk. Floppies were well entrenched: motherboard makers found them easy to add, all BIOS supported them, and they were almost always the first boot device, so techs loved floppies when they helped boot a system.

Only in the last few years have we finally seen systems without floppy drives due to an industry push called *legacy-free computing:* an initiative forwarded by Microsoft and Intel back in 2001 to rid computers of old technologies such as PS/2 ports, serial ports, parallel ports—and floppy drives (interesting how long it took to start getting adopted by PC makers). Thus, the venerable floppy drive will probably soon disappear from PCs. Until then, the floppy drive, that artifact from the Dark Ages of the PC world, will continue to be a viable technology you must know.

Floppy Drive Basics

If you've used computers at all, you've probably used a floppy drive. When you insert a `floppy disk` into a `floppy drive`, the protective slide on the disk opens, revealing the magnetic media inside the plastic casing. A motor-driven spindle snaps into the center of the drive to make it spin. A set of read/write heads then moves back and forth across the disk, reading or writing tracks on the disk as needed. The current floppy disks are 3½ inches wide and store 1.44 MB (Figure 10.2). You use a `3½-inch floppy drive` to access the contents of the disk.

Whenever your system accesses a floppy disk in its floppy drive, a read/write LED on the outside front of the drive will flash on. You should not try to remove the floppy disk from the drive when this light is lit! That light means that the read/writes heads are accessing the floppy drive, and pulling the disk out while the light is on can damage the floppy disk. When the light is off, you can push in the small release button on the front of the drive to eject the floppy disk.

The first PC floppy drives used a 5¼-inch floppy drive format (Figure 10.3). The 5¼-inch measurement actually described the drive, but most users also called the disks for those drives 5¼-inch disks. In the 1970s and early 1980s, before PCs became predominant, you would occasionally see an 8-inch format floppy drive in computers. Fortunately, these never saw any noticeable

 The term "floppy" comes from the fact that early floppy disks were actually floppy. You could easily bend one. Modern floppy disks come in much more robust rigid plastic casings, but the term has stuck—we still call them floppies!

• **Figure 10.2**   Floppy drive and floppy disk

• **Figure 10.3** A 5¼-inch floppy drive and disk

use in PCs. If you happen to run into an 8-inch drive or disk, keep it! Collectors of old computers pay big money for these old drives!

Around 1986, the 3½-inch drives appeared, and within a few years came to dominate the floppy world completely. If you are really interested, however, you can still purchase 5¼-inch floppy drives on the Internet!

Essentials

Installing Floppy Drives

All Windows systems reserve the drive letters A: and B: for floppy drives. You cannot name them anything other than A: or B:, but you can configure a floppy to get either drive letter. However, convention dictates that if you have only one floppy drive, you should call it A:. The second floppy drive will then be called B:.

Floppy drives connect to the computer via a **34-pin ribbon cable**. If the cable supports two floppy drives, it will have a seven-wire twist in the middle, used to differentiate electronically between the A: and B: drives (Figure 10.4). Given that the majority of users do not want two floppy drives, many system makers have dropped the twist and saved a couple of pennies on a simpler cable (Figure 10.5).

By default, almost all PCs (well, the ones that still support floppy drives) first try to boot to a floppy before any other boot device, looking for an operating system. This process enables technicians to insert a floppy disk into a sick computer to run programs when the hard drives fail. It can also enable hackers to insert bootable floppy disks into servers and do bad things. You do have a choice, however, as most systems have special

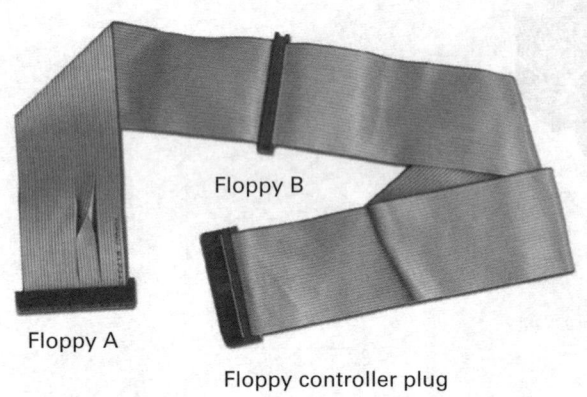

Floppy B

Floppy A

Floppy controller plug

• **Figure 10.4** Floppy cable that supports two drives

CMOS settings that enable you to change this default boot order to something other than the default drive A: and then C:; I'll show you how in a minute.

Inserting Ribbon Cables

Look at the floppy cable in Figure 10.5. Notice the connector on the left side. This connector, identical to the other connector on the same cable, plugs into the floppy controller on the motherboard, as shown in Figure 10.6. Notice how clearly the motherboard has **pin 1** marked in Figure 10.6. Not all motherboards are so clear. Make sure to orient the cable so that the colored stripe is aligned with pin 1.

● **Figure 10.5** Floppy cable for only one drive

Here are a few tips on cable orientation. By the way, these rules work for all ribbon cables, not just floppy cables! Ribbon cable connectors usually have a distinct orientation notch in the middle. If they have an orientation notch and the controller socket has a slot in which the orientation notch will fit, your job is easy (Figure 10.7).

Unfortunately, not all connectors use the orientation notch. Try looking in the motherboard book. All motherboard books provide a graphic of the motherboard showing the proper orientation position. Look at other ribbon cables on the motherboard. In almost all motherboards, all plugs orient the same way. Last of all, just guess! You will not destroy anything by inserting the cable backwards. When you boot up, the floppy drive will not work. This is not a big deal; turn off the system and try again!

After you insert the floppy ribbon cable into the floppy controller, you need to insert the ribbon cable into the floppy drive. Watch out here! You still need to orient the cable by pin 1—all the rules of ribbon cable insertion apply here, too. Before you plug in the floppy ribbon cable to the floppy drive, you need to

● **Figure 10.6** Plugging a floppy cable into a controller, pin 1 labeled at left

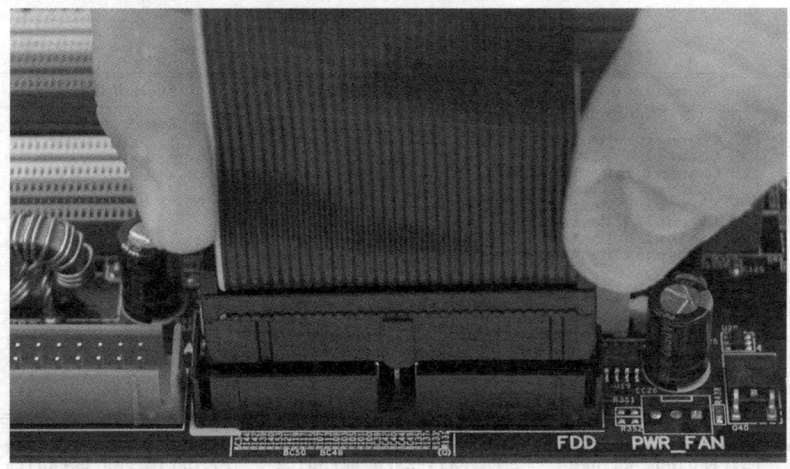

● **Figure 10.7** Floppy controller with notch

In the past, the CompTIA A+ certification exams have been very focused on the pins on cables! Know the number (34) and orientation (pin 1 to pin 1) for the pins on the floppy drive ribbon cable.

know which connector on the cable to use; it makes a big difference. The specific connector that you insert into the floppy drive determines its drive letter!

If the floppy drive is installed on the end connector, it becomes the A: drive; if the drive is installed on the middle connector, it is the B: drive (Figure 10.8). If you're installing only one floppy, make sure you install it in the A: drive position!

Power

Floppy drives need electricity in order to work, just like every other device in the PC. Modern 3½-inch floppy drives use the small **mini power connector**.

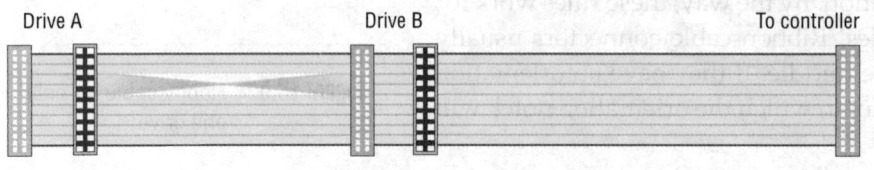

• **Figure 10.8** Cable placement determines the drive letter.

Be careful! It is easy to insert a mini connector incorrectly, and if you install it incorrectly, you'll destroy the floppy drive and make what we call "The Nasty Smell." Look at Figure 10.9, a bottom view of a properly installed mini connector—note the chamfers (beveled edges) that show correct orientation. The problem lies in the plastic used to make the connector. The plastic connector bends easily, giving even the least brawny techs the ability to put the plug in a mini backward or to hit only three of the four pins.

Great! You have installed a floppy drive! Once you have physically installed the floppy drive, it's time to go into CMOS.

CMOS

Installing *any* power connector incorrectly will destroy whatever device is unfortunate enough to be so abused. However, with the exception of minis, most power connectors are constructed so that it's almost impossible to do so unintentionally.

After the floppy drive is installed, the next step is configuring the CMOS settings, which must correspond to the capacities of the drives. Look in your CMOS for a menu called "Standard CMOS Features" (or something similar to that) to see your floppy settings. Most CMOS setups configure the A: drive by default as a 3½-inch, 1.44 MB drive, so in most cases the floppy is already configured. Simply double-check the setting in CMOS; if it's okay, exit without changing anything. Figure 10.10 shows a typical CMOS setting for a single floppy drive.

• **Figure 10.9** Properly installed mini connector

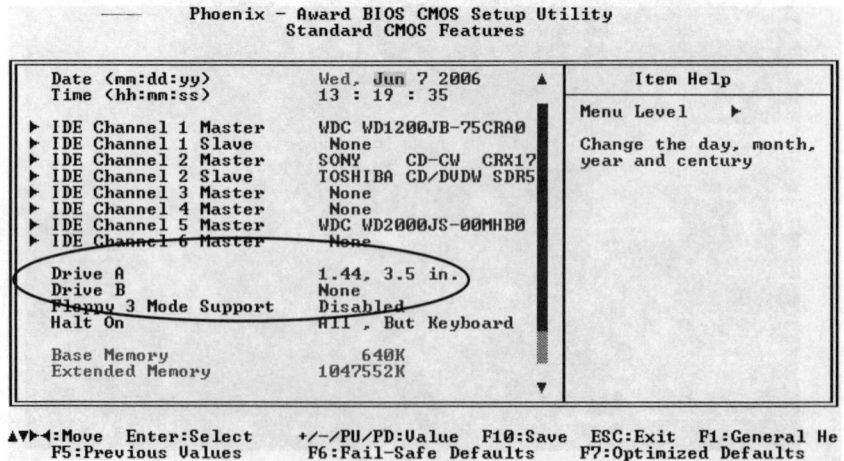

• **Figure 10.10** CMOS setting for one standard floppy drive

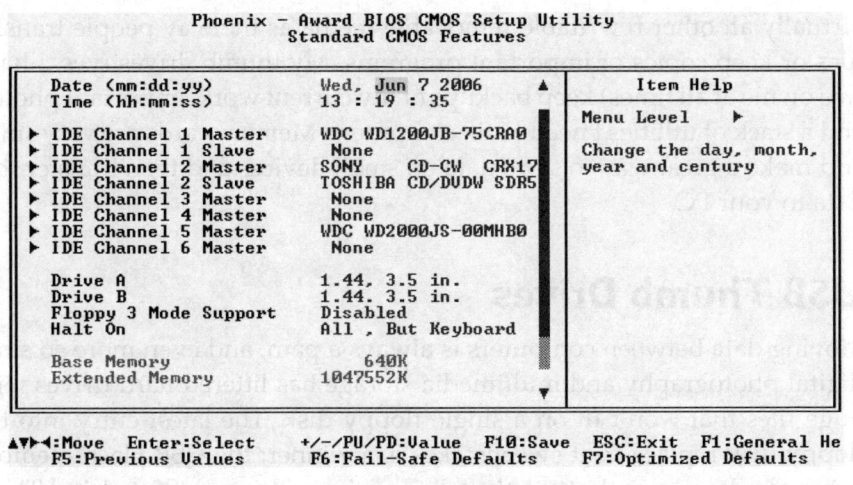

```
          Phoenix - Award BIOS CMOS Setup Utility
                   Standard CMOS Features

   Date (mm:dd:yy)        Wed, Jun 7 2006     ▲        Item Help
   Time (hh:mm:ss)        13 : 19 : 35             ┌─────────────────────
 ▶ IDE Channel 1 Master   WDC WD1200JB-75CRA0      │ Menu Level      ▶
 ▶ IDE Channel 1 Slave    None                     │
 ▶ IDE Channel 2 Master   SONY    CD-CW  CRX17      │ Change the day, month,
 ▶ IDE Channel 2 Slave    TOSHIBA CD/DVDW SDR5      │ year and century
 ▶ IDE Channel 3 Master   None                     │
 ▶ IDE Channel 4 Master   None                     │
 ▶ IDE Channel 5 Master   WDC WD2000JS-00MHB0       │
 ▶ IDE Channel 6 Master   None                      │

   Drive A                1.44, 3.5 in.
   Drive B                1.44, 3.5 in.
   Floppy 3 Mode Support  Disabled
   Halt On                All , But Keyboard

   Base Memory                 640K
   Extended Memory         1047552K             ▼

▲▼▶◀:Move  Enter:Select    +/-/PU/PD:Value  F10:Save  ESC:Exit  F1:General He
    F5:Previous Values     F6:Fail-Safe Defaults    F7:Optimized Defaults
```

● **Figure 10.11**   CMOS setting for two floppy drives

On the rare occasion that you require a different setting from the typical 3½-inch, 1.44-MB A: drive, simply select the drive (A: or B:) and enter the correct capacity. Figure 10.11 shows a CMOS with another 3½-inch floppy drive on B:.

Disabling the Boot Up Floppy Seek option tells the PC not to check the floppy disk during the POST, which isn't very handy except for slightly speeding up the boot process (Figure 10.12).

Many CMOS setup utilities have an option called Floppy 3 Mode Support. Refer to Figure 10.11 to see an example of a CMOS with this option. A Mode 3 floppy is a special 1.2-MB format used outside the United States, primarily in Japan. Unless you live in Japan and use Mode 3 floppy disks, ignore this option.

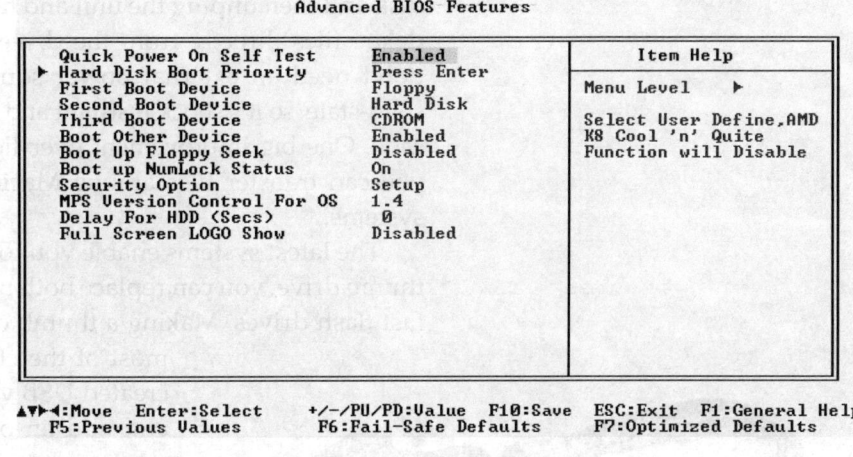

```
          Phoenix - Award BIOS CMOS Setup Utility
                   Advanced BIOS Features

   Quick Power On Self Test    Enabled           ┌─────   Item Help   ─────
 ▶ Hard Disk Boot Priority     Press Enter        │
   First Boot Device           Floppy             │ Menu Level      ▶
   Second Boot Device          Hard Disk          │
   Third Boot Device           CDROM              │ Select User Define,AMD
   Boot Other Device           Enabled            │ K8 Cool 'n' Quite
   Boot Up Floppy Seek         Disabled           │ Function will Disable
   Boot up NumLock Status      On                 │
   Security Option             Setup              │
   MPS Version Control For OS  1.4                │
   Delay For HDD (Secs)        0                  │
   Full Screen LOGO Show       Disabled           │

▲▼▶◀:Move  Enter:Select    +/-/PU/PD:Value  F10:Save  ESC:Exit  F1:General Help
    F5:Previous Values     F6:Fail-Safe Defaults    F7:Optimized Defaults
```

● **Figure 10.12**   CMOS Boot Up Floppy Seek option

■ Flash Memory

Flash memory, the same flash memory that replaced CMOS technology for your system BIOS, found another home in PCs in the form of removable mass storage devices. Flash memory comes in two different families: USB thumb drives and memory cards. *USB thumb drives* are flash devices that contain a standard USB connection. *Memory cards* is a generic term for a number of different tiny cards that are used in cameras, PDAs, and other devices. Both of these families can manifest themselves as drives in Windows, but they usually perform different jobs. USB thumb drives have replaced virtually all other rewritable removable media as the way people transfer files or keep copies of important programs. My thumb drives (yes, I have two on me at all times) keep backups of my current work, important photos, and a stack of utilities I need to fix computers. Memory cards are very small and make a great way to store data on small devices and then transfer that data to your PC.

USB Thumb Drives

Moving data between computers is always a pain, and even more so since digital photography and multimedia storage has littered hard drives with huge files that won't fit on a single floppy disk. The latest entry into the floppy disk replacement sweepstakes is a winner: the USB Flash memory drive, also known as the **USB thumb drive**, jump drive, or flash drive. These tiny new drives (Figure 10.13) are incredibly popular. For a low price in US$, you can get a 2-GB thumb drive that holds as much data as 1400 standard 3½-inch floppy disks.

The smallest thumb drives are slightly larger than an adult thumbnail, whereas others are larger and more rounded. The drives are hot-swappable in Windows 2000/XP/Vista. You simply plug one into any USB port and it will appear as a removable storage device in My Computer. After you plug the drive into a USB port, you can copy or move data to or from your hard disk and then unplug the unit and take it with you. You can read, write, and delete files directly from the drive. Because these are USB devices, they don't need an external power source. The non-volatile flash memory is solid-state, so it's shock resistant and is supposed to retain data safely for a decade. One big improvement over floppies is cross-platform compatibility—you can transfer files among Macintosh, Windows, and Linux operating systems.

The latest systems enable you to boot to a thumb drive. With a bootable thumb drive, you can replace both bootable floppies and bootable CDs with fast flash drives. Making a thumb drive bootable is a bit of a challenge, so most of the classic bootable utility CD makers have created USB versions that seek out your thumb drive and add an operating system with the utilities you wish to use. Most of these are simply versions of Linux-based live CDs. At this point, there's no single magic USB thumb drive to recommend, as bootable USB drives are still quite new and updated versions come out almost daily. If you just have to try this new technology now, check out the GParted LiveUSB at http://gparted.sourceforge.net and click on the LiveUSB link.

• **Figure 10.13**   USB thumb drives

Flash Cards

Flash cards are the way people store data on small appliances. Every digital camera, virtually every PDA, and many cell phones come with slots for some type of memory card. Memory cards come in a number of different incompatible formats, so let's start by making sure you know the more common ones.

CompactFlash

CompactFlash (CF) is the oldest, most complex, and physically largest of all removable flash media cards (Figure 10.14). Roughly one inch wide, CF cards use a simplified PCMCIA bus (see Chapter 16, "Portable Computing," for details) for interconnection. CF cards come in two sizes: CF I (3.3 mm thick) and CF II (5 mm thick). CF II cards are too thick to fit into CF I slots.

Clever manufacturers have repurposed the CF form factor to create the microdrive (Figure 10.15). Microdrives are true hard drives, using platters and read/write heads that fit into the tiny CF form factor. Microdrives are slower and use more power than flash drives but cost much less than an equivalent CF flash card. From the user's standpoint, CF flash cards and microdrives look and act exactly the same way, although the greater power consumption of microdrives makes them incompatible with some devices.

SmartMedia

SmartMedia came out as a competitor to CF cards and for a few years was quite popular in digital cameras (Figure 10.16). The introduction of SD media reduced SmartMedia's popularity, and no new devices use this media.

Secure Digital

Secure Digital (SD) cards are arguably the most common flash media format today. About the size of a small postage stamp, you'll see SD cards in just about any type of device that uses flash media. SD comes in two types: the original SD and SDIO. SD cards store only data. The more advanced SDIO (the "IO" denoting input/output rather than storage) cards also support devices such as GPS and cameras. If you want to use an SDIO device, you must have an

• **Figure 10.14** CF card

• **Figure 10.15** Microdrive

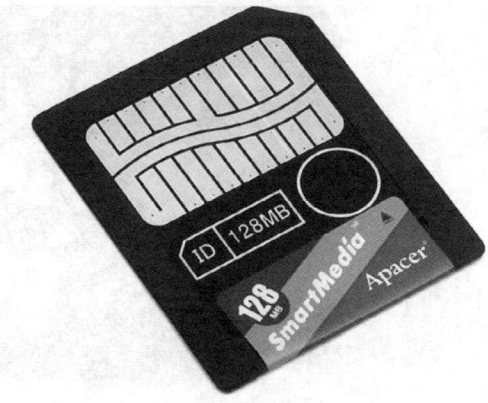

• **Figure 10.16** SmartMedia

SD cards also come in two tiny forms called *Mini Secure Digital (MiniSD)* and *Micro Secure Digital (MicroSD)* cards. They're extremely popular in cellular phones that use flash memory, but see little use in other devices. Figure 10.17 shows all three types of SD cards.

• **Figure 10.17**   SD, MiniSD, and MicroSD cards

SD cards developed out of an older, slower flash memory technology called *MultiMediaCard (MMC)*. If you happen to have an MMC card laying around, you can use it in almost any SD card slot. SD cards are a little thicker than MMC cards, though, so the reverse is not true.

Memory Stick

Sony always likes to use proprietary formats, and their `Memory Stick` flash memory is no exception. If you own something from Sony and it uses flash memory, you'll need a Memory Stick (Figure 10.18). There are several Memory Stick formats, including Standard, Pro, Duo, Pro Duo, and Micro.

xD Picture Card

The proprietary `Extreme Digital (xD) Picture Cards` (Figure 10.19) are about half the size of an SD card. They're almost exclusively used in Olympus and Fujifilm digital cameras, although Olympus (the developer of the xD technology) produces a USB housing so you can use an xD Picture Card like any other USB flash memory drive. xD Picture Cards come in three flavors: original, Standard (Type M), and Hi-Speed (Type H). The Standard cards are slower than the original cards, but offer greater storage capacity. The Hi-Speed cards are two to three times faster than the others and enable you to capture full-motion video (assuming the camera has that capability, naturally!).

Card Readers

Whatever type of flash memory you use, your PC must have a `card reader` in order to access the data on the card directly. There are a number of inexpensive USB card readers available today (Figure 10.20), and some PCs,

• **Figure 10.18**   Memory Stick

• **Figure 10.19**   xD card

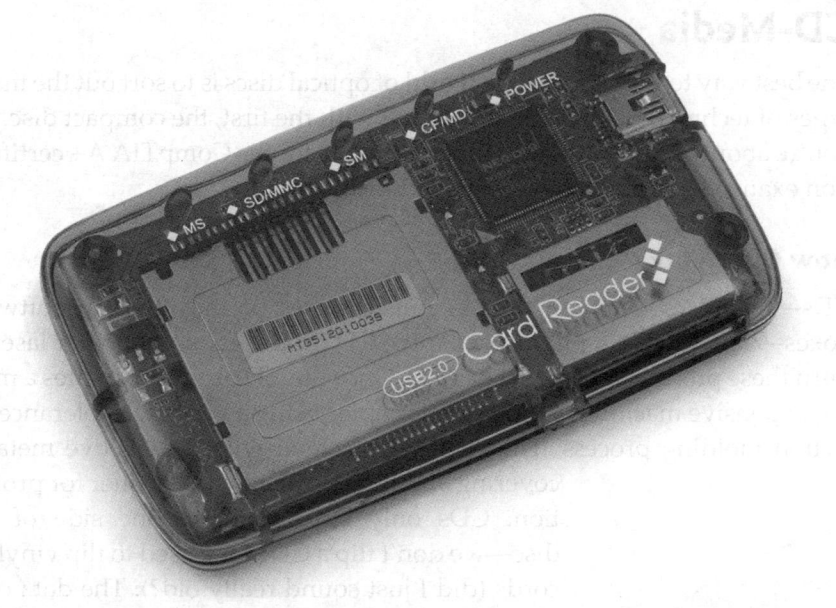

• **Figure 10.20** USB card reader

especially those tuned to home theater use, often come with built-in readers—handy to have when someone pulls out an SD card and says, "Let's look at the pictures I just took!"

Whichever type of flash memory you have, understand that it acts exactly like a hard drive. If you wish, you can format a memory card as well as copy, paste, and rename files.

Of course, if the person just happened to bring his or her camera and the usually proprietary USB cable along, you could connect the camera to the PC and pull pictures in that way. Just make sure you have spare batteries, too! Wouldn't a card reader be a more elegant solution?

Optical Drives

CD- and DVD-media discs and drives come in a variety of flavors and formats, enabling you to back up data, record music, master a home video, and much, much more. All those shiny, 12-cm-wide discs that, if you're a slob like me, collect around your PC like pizza boxes in a fraternity house, can be generically referred to as optical discs . The drives that support them are optical drives . This section examines the different types of CD-media and DVD-media.

CD stands for *compact disc,* a medium that was originally designed more than 20 years ago as a replacement for vinyl records. The CD now reigns as the primary method of long-term storage for sound and data. The digital versatile disc (DVD) first eliminated VHS cassette tapes from the commercial home movie market, but has also grown into a contender for backups and high-capacity storage. Optical media include a number of technologies with names such as CD-ROM, CD-R, CD-RW, DVD, DVD+RW, HD-DVD, and so on. Each of these technologies will be discussed in detail in this chapter. For now, understand that although *optical media* describes a number of different, exciting formats, they all basically boil down to the same physical object: that little shiny disc.

CD-Media

The best way to understand the world of optical discs is to sort out the many types of technologies available, starting with the first, the compact disc. All you're about to read is relevant and fair game for the CompTIA A+ certification exams. Let's begin by looking at how CDs work.

How CDs Work

CDs—the discs that you buy in music stores or may find in software boxes—store data via microscopic pits. CD producers use a power laser to burn these pits into a glass master CD. Once the CD producer creates a master, expensive machines create plastic copies using a very high-tolerance injection molding process. The copies are coated with a reflective metallic covering and then finished with lacquer for protection. CDs only store data on one side of the disc—we don't flip a CD as we used to flip vinyl records (did I just sound really old?). The data on a CD is near the top of the CD, where the label is located (see Figure 10.21).

Many people believe that scratching a CD on the bottom makes it unreadable. This is untrue. If you scratch a CD on the bottom (the shiny side), just polish out the scratches—assuming that they aren't too deep—and reread the CD. A number of companies sell inexpensive CD polishing kits. It's the scratches on the *top* of the disc that wreak havoc on CDs. Avoid writing on the top with anything other than a soft-tipped pen, and certainly don't scratch the top!

CD readers (like the one in your car or the one in your PC) use a laser and mirrors to read the data from the CD. The metallic covering of the CD makes a highly reflective surface—the pits create interruptions in that surface, while the non-pitted spots, called *lands*, leave it intact. The laser picks up on the reflected pattern that the pits and lands create, and the CD drive converts this pattern into binary ones and zeroes. Because the pits are so densely packed on the CD, a vast amount of data can be stored: A standard CD holds up to 5.2 billion bits, or 650 million bytes, of data.

CD Formats

The first CDs were designed for playing music and organized the music in a special format called

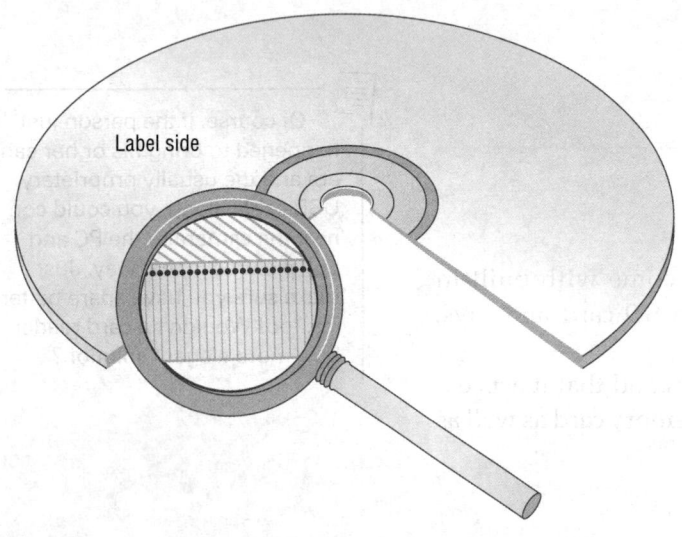

• **Figure 10.21**   Location of the data

Label side

Try This!

Repairing a CD-ROM

To revive scratched CD-ROMs and other CD-media in the comfort of your home or office, get a CD polishing kit and familiarize yourself with its operation. Try this:

1. Obtain a CD polishing kit from your local computer store, or find one online.

2. Take a CD-ROM *that you don't mind potentially ruining* and make light scratches on the bottom of the disc. Be sure not to scratch too heavily! Just try to replicate the everyday wear and tear that you've probably seen on CD-ROMs before. If you have a disc that's already lightly scratched, that's even better.

3. Use the CD polishing kit, following the provided instructions exactly.

CD-Digital Audio (CDDA), which we usually just call CD-audio. CD-audio divides the CD's data into variable-length tracks; on music CDs, each song gets one track. CD-audio is an excellent way to store music, but it lacks any error checking, file support, or directory structure, making it a terrible way to store data! For this reason, The Powers That Be created a special method for storing data on a CD, called—are you ready—**CD-ROM**. The CD-ROM format divides the CD into fixed sectors, each holding 2353 bytes.

Most CD-ROM drives also support a number of older, less known formats. You may never come across these formats—CD-I, CD-ROM/XA, and so forth—although you may see them listed among compatible formats on the packaging for a new drive (Figure 10.22). Don't let these oddball formats throw you—with few exceptions, they've pretty much fallen by the wayside. All CD-ROM drives read all of these formats, assuming that the system is loaded with the proper software.

There are two other formats called CD-R and CD-RW—perhaps you've heard of them? Well, I cover these in detail in a moment, but first I need to explain a bit more about CD-ROM. The CD-ROM format is something like a partition in the hard drive world. CD-ROM may define the sectors (and some other information), but it doesn't enable a CD-ROM disc to act like a hard drive with a file structure, directories, and such. To make CD-ROMs act like a hard drive, there's another layer of formatting that defines the file system used on the drive.

At first glance, you might think, "Why don't CD-ROMs just use a FAT or an NTFS format like hard drives?" Well, first of all, they could! There's no law of physics that prevented the CD-ROM world from adopting any file system. The problem is that the CD makers did not want CD-ROM to be tied to Microsoft's or Apple's or anyone else's file format. In addition, they wanted non-PC devices to read CDs, so they invented their own file system just for CD-ROMs, called **ISO-9660**. This format is sometimes referred by the more generic term, CD File System (CDFS). The vast majority of data CD-ROMs today use this format.

Over the years, extensions of the ISO-9660 have addressed certain limitations such as the characters used in file and directory names, filename length, and directory depth. It's important to know these ISO-9660 extensions:

- **Joliet**   Microsoft's extension of the ISO-9660. Macintosh and Linux also support Joliet formatted discs.

- **Rock Ridge**   An open standard to provide UNIX file system support for discs; rarely used outside of UNIX systems.

- **El Torito**   Added support to enable bootable CD-media. All bootable CDs use the El Torito standard, which is supported by the BIOS on all modern PCs.

- **Apple Extensions**   Apple's added support for their HFS file system. Windows systems cannot read these CDs without third-party tools.

It is important to appreciate that all of these file systems are extensions, not replacements to ISO-9660. That means a single CD/DVD can have both regular ISO-9660 information and the extension. For example, it's very common to have a CD-media that is ISO-9660 and Joliet.

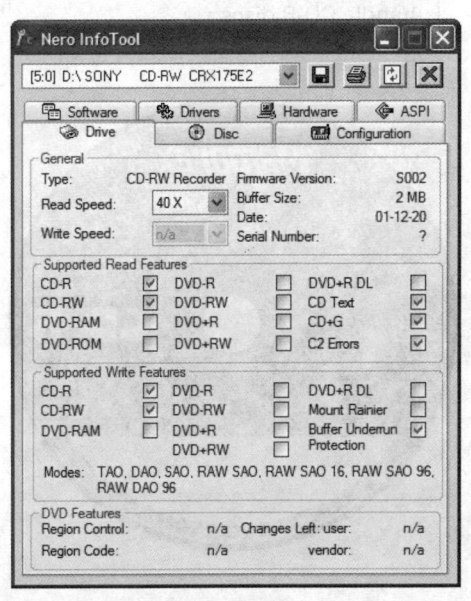

• **Figure 10.22**   Crazy CD formats

If you place the CD into a device that cannot read Joliet, it will still be able to read the ISO-9660 information.

CD-ROM Speeds

The first CD-ROM drives processed data at roughly 150,000 bytes per second (150 KBps), copying the speed from the original CD-audio format. Although this speed is excellent for listening to music, the CD-ROM industry quickly recognized that installing programs or transferring files from a CD-ROM at 150 KBps was the electronic equivalent of watching paint dry. Since the day the first CD-ROM drives for PCs hit the market, there has been a desire to speed them up to increase their data throughput. Each increase in speed is measured in multiples of the original 150 KBps drives and given an × to show speed relative to the first (1×) drives. Here's a list of the common CD-ROM speeds, including most of the early speeds that are no longer produced:

1× 150 KBps	10× 1500 KBps	40× 6000 KBps
2× 300 KBps	12× 1800 KBps	48× 7200 KBps
3× 450 KBps	16× 2400 KBps	52× 7800 KBps
4× 600 KBps	24× 3600 KBps	60× 9000 KBps
6× 900 KBps	32× 4800 KBps	72× 10800 KBps
8× 1200 KBps	36× 5400 KBps	

Keep in mind that these are maximum speeds that are rarely met in real-life operation. You can, however, count on a 32× drive reading data faster than an 8× drive. As multipliers continue to increase, so many other factors come into play that telling the difference between a 48× and a 52× drive, for example, becomes difficult. High-speed CD-ROM drives are so inexpensive, however, that most folks buy the fastest drive possible—at least installations go faster!

CD-R

Making CD-ROMs requires specialized, expensive equipment and substantial expertise, and it's done by a relatively small number of CD-ROM production companies. Yet, since the day the first CD-ROMs came to market, demand has been terrific for a way that normal PC users could make their own CDs. The CD industry made a number of attempts to create a technology that would let users record, or *burn*, their own CDs.

In the mid-1990s, the CD industry introduced the **CD-recordable (CD-R)** standard, which enables affordable CD-R drives, often referred to as *CD burners*, to add data to special CD-R discs. Any CD-ROM drive can then read the data stored on the CD-R, and all CD-R drives can read regular CD-ROMs. CD-R discs come in two varieties: a 74-minute disc that holds approximately 650 MB, and an 80-minute variety that holds approximately 700 MB (see Figure 10.23). A CD-R burner must be specifically designed to support the longer 80-minute CD-R format, but most drives you'll encounter can do this.

Some music CD players can't handle CD-R discs.

• **Figure 10.23** A CD-R disc, with its capacity clearly labeled

Mike Meyers' CompTIA A+ Guide: Essentials (Exam 220-601)

CD-R discs function similarly to regular CD-ROMs, although the chemicals used to make them produce a brightly colored recording side on almost all CD-R discs. CD-ROM discs, in contrast, have a silver recording side. CD-R technology records data using special organic dyes embedded into the disc. This dye is what gives the CD-R its distinctive bottom color. CD-R burners have a second burn laser, roughly ten times as powerful as the read laser, which heats the organic dye. This causes a change in the reflectivity of the surface, creating the functional equivalent of a CD-ROM's pits.

Once the CD-R drive burns data onto a CD-R, the data cannot be erased or changed short of destroying the disc itself. Early CD-R drives required that the entire disc be burned in one burn session, wasting any unused part of the CD-R disc. These were called single-session drives. All modern CD-R drives are **multisession drives** that enable you to go back and burn additional data onto the CD-R disc until the disc is full. Multisession drives also have the capability to "close" a partially filled CD-R so that no more data may be burned onto that disc.

CD-R drives have two speeds that matter: the record speed and the read speed, both expressed as multiples of the 150-KBps speed of the original CD-ROM drives. The record speed, which is listed first, is always equal to or slower than the read speed. For example, a CD-R drive with a specification of 8×/24× would burn at 8× and read at 24×.

CD-RW

For all their usefulness, CD-R drives have disappeared from the market. Notice that I didn't say CD-R *discs* have disappeared; more CD-R discs get burned now than ever before. Just as CD-R drives could both burn CD-R discs and read CD-ROMs, a newer type of drive called **CD-rewritable (CD-RW)** has taken over the burning market from CD-R drives. Although this drive has its own type of CD-RW discs, it also can burn to CD-R discs, which are much cheaper.

CD-RW technology enables you not only to burn a disc, but to *burn over* existing data on a CD-RW disc. This is not something you need for every disc—for example, I create CD-R archives of my completed books to store the text and graphics for posterity—this is data I want to access later, but do not need to modify. While I'm working on content for the CD that accompanies this book, however, I may decide to delete an item—I couldn't do that with a CD-R. The CD-RW format, on the other hand, essentially takes CD-media to the functional equivalent of a 650-MB floppy disk. Once again, CD-RW discs look exactly like CD-ROM discs, with the exception of a colored bottom side. Figure 10.24 shows all three formats.

A CD-RW drive works by using a laser to heat an amorphous (non-crystalline) substance that, when cooled, slowly becomes crystalline. The crystalline areas are reflective, whereas the amorphous areas are not. Because both CD-R

You can rewrite CD-RW discs a limited number of times. The number varies according to the source, but expect a maximum life of about 1000 rewrites, although in real life you'll get considerably fewer.

• **Figure 10.24**   CD-ROM, CD-R, and CD-RW discs

and CD-RW drives require a powerful laser, it was a simple process to make a drive that could burn CD-Rs and CD-RWs, making plain CD-R drives disappear almost overnight. Why buy a CD-R drive when a comparably priced CD-RW drive could burn both CD-R and CD-RW discs?

CD-RW drive specs have three multiplier values. The first shows the CD-R write speed, the second shows the CD-RW rewrite speed, and the third shows the read speed. Write, rewrite, and read speeds vary tremendously among the various brands of CD-RW drives; here are just a few representative samples: 8×4×32×, 12×10×32×, and 48×24×48×.

When CD-RWs were introduced, one of the initial goals was the idea of making a CD-RW act like a hard drive so that you could simply drag a file onto the CD-RW (or CD-R) and just as easily drag it off again. This goal was difficult for two reasons: first, the different file formats made on-the-fly conversion risky. Second, CD-RWs don't store data exactly the same way as hard drives and would quickly wear out if data was copied in the same manner.

Two developments, UDF and packet writing, enable you to treat a CD-RW just like a hard drive—with a few gotchas. The not-so-new kid in town with CD-media file formats is the **universal data format (UDF)**. UDF is a replacement for ISO-9660 and all of its various extensions, resulting in a single file format that any drive and operating system can read. UDF has already taken over the DVD world (all movie DVDs use this format) and is poised to also become the CD-media file format in the near future. UDF handles very large files and is excellent for all rewritable CD-media. UDF has been available for quite a while, but until Windows Vista came out, no version of Windows could write to UDF formatted discs. They could *read* the discs, but if you wanted to *write* to them in Windows you had to use one of a number of third-party UDF tools like Roxio's DirectCD and Nero's InCD. UDF also supports a feature called Mount Rainier, better known as packet writing, that works with UDF to enable you to copy individual files back and forth like a hard drive. With UDF and packet writing, rewritable CD-media is as easy to use as a hard drive.

Try This!

Deleting Files from a CD-RW

Windows XP comes with built-in support for CD-Rs and CD-RWs. If you have a CD-RW drive with Windows XP, copy a couple of files onto a CD-RW and burn them to the disc. Now try to delete only one file—you can't! That's because no version of Windows before Vista supports packet writing. Try installing a copy of Roxio's DirectCD or Nero's InCD and try again on a fresh CD-RW—it works! All third-party UDF tools support packet writing.

Windows and CD-Media

Virtually all optical drives are **ATAPI-compliant**, meaning they plug into the ATA controllers on the motherboard, just like a hard drive, so there's no need to install drivers. You just plug in the drive and assuming you didn't make any physical installation mistakes, the drive will appear in Windows (Figure 10.25).

Windows XP displays an optical drive in My Computer with the typical optical drive icon and assigns it a drive letter. If you want to put data onto a CD-R disc, however, you need special *burner software* to get that data onto the disc. Windows XP comes with burning support—you just drop a CD-R disc into your CD-R drive, open the drive in My Computer, drag the files you wish to copy, and click Write to Disc. This support doesn't enable you to make bootable CDs, music CDs, or other specialties. No worries, though, as almost every new CD-R drive comes with some type of burner software, so you rarely need to go out and buy your own unless you have a preference for a particular brand. Figure 10.26 shows the opening menu of one that I like, the popular Nero Express CD-burning program.

When I buy a new program on CD, the first thing I do is make a backup copy; then I stash the original under lock and key. If I break, melt, or otherwise destroy the backup, I quickly create a new one from the original. I can easily copy the disc because my system, like many, has both a regular CD-ROM and a CD-RW drive (even though CD-RW drives read CD-ROM discs). I can place a CD in the CD-ROM drive and a CD-R or CD-RW disc in the CD-RW drive. Then I run special software such as Adaptec's DiskCopy to quickly create an exact replica of the CD. CD-RW drives work great for another, bigger type of backup—not the archival "put it on the disc and stash it in the closet" type of backup, but rather the daily/weekly backups that most of us do (or should do!) on our systems. Using CD-R discs for these backups is wasteful; once a disc fills up, you throw it away at the next backup. But with CD-RW, you can use the same set of CD-RW discs time and again to perform backups.

• **Figure 10.25**   CD-media drive in Windows

Music CDs

Computers do not hold a monopoly on CD burning. Many companies offer consumer CD burners that work with your stereo system. These come in a

wide variety of formats, but they're usually dual-deck player/recorder combinations (see Figure 10.27). These recorders do not use regular CD-R or CD-RW discs. Instead, under U.S. law, these home recorders must use a slightly different disc called a Music CD-R . Makers of Music CDs pay a small royalty for each CD (and add it to your price). You can record *to* a Music CD-R or CD-RW, but you cannot record *from* one—the idea being to restrict duplication. If you decide to buy one of these burners, make sure to buy the special Music CD-Rs. Music CD-Rs are designed specifically for these types of devices and may not work well in a PC.

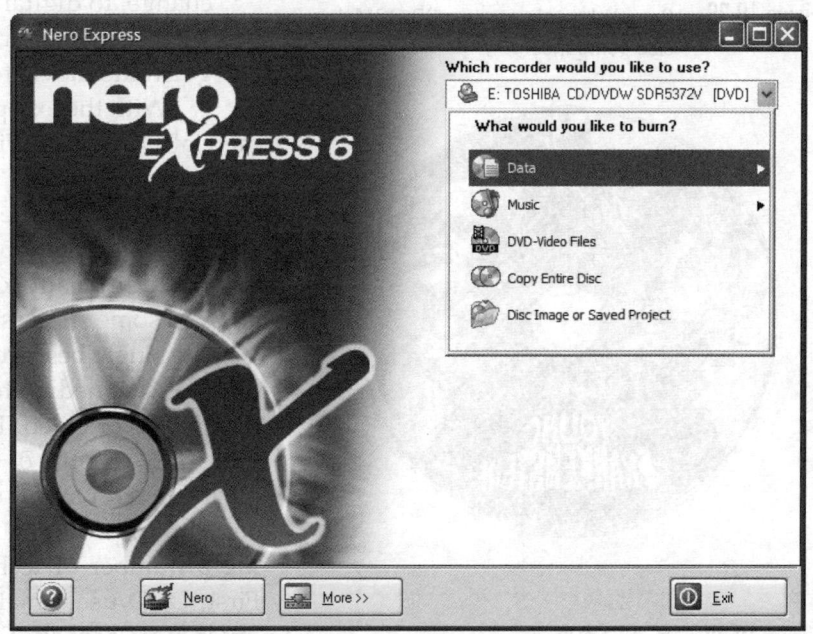

• **Figure 10.26**   Nero Express CD-burning program

● Figure 10.27   CD recorder

● Figure 10.28   Sample laserdisc with a CD-ROM disc for size comparison

● Figure 10.29   Typical DVD-video

DVD-Media

For years, the video industry tried to create an optical-media replacement for videotape. The 12-inch diameter *laserdisc* format originally introduced by Philips gained some ground in the 1980s and 1990s. But the high cost of both the discs and the players, plus various marketing factors, meant there was never a very large laserdisc market. You may still find one of them sitting around, however, or you may know someone who invested in a small collection during the laserdisc's heyday (see Figure 10.28).

The DVD was developed by a large consortium of electronics and entertainment firms during the early 1990s and released as digital *video* discs in 1995. The transformation of DVD to a data storage medium quickly required a name change, to digital *versatile* discs. You'll still hear both terms used. The industry also uses the term DVD-video to distinguish the movie format from the data formats.

With the exception of the DVD logo stamped on all commercial DVDs (see Figure 10.29), DVDs look exactly like CD-media discs; but that's pretty much where the similarities end. DVD has become the fastest growing media format in history and has completely overtaken VHS as the preferred media for video. Additionally, one variant of DVD called DVD-RAM has enjoyed some success as a mass storage medium.

The single best word to describe DVD is *capacity*. All previous optical media stored a maximum of 700 MB of data or 80 minutes of video. The lowest capacity DVD holds 4.37 GB of data, or two hours of standard definition video. The highest capacity version DVDs store roughly 16 GB of data, or more than eight hours of video! DVD achieves these amazing capacities using a number of technologies, but three are most important. First, DVD uses smaller pits than CD-media, and packs them much more densely. Second, DVD comes in both *single-sided (SS)* and *double-sided (DS)* formats. As the name implies, a DS disc holds twice the data of an SS disc, but it also requires you to flip

284

Table 10.1	DVD Versions/Capacities
DVD Version	**Capacity**
DVD-5 (12 cm, SS/SL)	4.37 GB, more than two hours of video
DVD-9 (12 cm, SS/DL)	7.95 GB, about four hours of video
DVD-10 (12 cm, DS/SL)	8.74 GB, about four and a half hours of video
DVD-18 (12 cm, DS/DL)	15.90 GB, more than eight hours of video

the disc to read the other side. Third, DVDs come in *single-layer (SL)* and *dual-layer (DL)* formats. DL formats use two pitted layers on each side, each with a slightly different reflectivity index. Table 10.1 shows the common DVD capacities.

DVD-Video

The most beautiful trait of DVD-video lies in its capability to store two hours of video on one side. You drop in a DVD-video and get to watch an entire movie without flipping it over. DVD-video supports TV-style 4:3 aspect ratio screens as well as 16:9 theater screens, but it is up to the producer to decide which to use. Many DVD-video producers distribute DVD movies on DS media with a 4:3 ratio on one side and 16:9 ratio on the other. DVD-video relies on the MPEG-2 standard of video and audio compression to reach the magic of two hours of video per side. *Moving Picture Experts Group (MPEG)* is a group of compression standards for both audio and video. The MPEG-2 standard offers resolutions of up to 1280 × 720 at 60 frames per second (fps), with full CD-quality audio (standard DVDs only offer 480 vertical resolution, the same as regular television).

DVD-ROM

DVD-ROM is the DVD equivalent of the standard CD-ROM data format except that it's capable of storing up to almost 16 GB of data. Almost all DVD-ROM drives also fully support DVD-video, as well as most CD-ROM formats. Most DVD drives sold with PCs are DVD-ROM drives.

Recordable DVD

The IT industry has no fewer than *six* distinct standards of recordable DVD-media: DVD-R for general use, DVD-R for authoring, DVD-RW, DVD+R, DVD+RW, and DVD-RAM. Both DVD-R standard discs and DVD+R discs work like CD-Rs. You can write to them but not erase or alter what's written. DVD-RW, DVD+RW, and DVD-RAM discs can be written and rewritten, just like CD-RW discs. Most DVD drives can read all formats with the exception of DVD-RAM. DVD-RAM is the only DVD format that uses a cartridge, so it requires a special drive (Figure 10.30). DVD-RAM is still around but fading away.

Although there is little if any difference in quality among the standards, the competition between corporations pushing their preferred standards has raged for years. Sony and Phillips, for example, pushed the + series, whereas other manufacturers pushed the − series. Worse, no recordable DVD drive manufactured before 2003 could write any format except

Tech Tip

MPEG Standards

Reproducing video and sound on the PC provides interesting challenges for developers. How do you take a motion picture from film, translate it into ones and zeroes that the CPU understands, process those bits, and then send high-quality video and sound to the monitor and speakers for the pleasure of the computer user? How much data do you think is required to display even a two-minute clip of a car racing through a city street, in all the minute detail of the shops, people, screeching tires, road debris, and so on? For that matter, how do you store the obviously huge amount of data required to do this?

To handle these chores, the Moving Pictures Experts Group (MPEG) has released various coding standards such as MPEG-1, MPEG-2, and MPEG-4. Each standard provides a different compression algorithm, which makes the files manageable. The standards also implement various technologies to handle movement, called motion compensation. The details of the standards matter a lot to the folks producing the movies and other video and audio content, but here's the short answer that should suffice for the purposes of a PC tech.

MPEG-1 is the standard upon which video and MP3, among other technologies, are based. The most common implementations of this standard provide a resolution of 352 × 240 at 30 fps. This video quality falls just below that of a conventional VHS video.

(Continued)

MPEG Standards (Cont.)

One very well-known subset of MPEG-1 is better known for audio than video. MPEG-1 Layer 3, better known as MP3 format, dominates the world of audio. MP3 takes an uncompressed audio file and compresses it dramatically, but the algorithm is so tight that the music that comes out of the speakers remains almost completely faithful to the original audio file. To paraphrase a catchphrase from the '80s—I want my MP3s!

MPEG-2 provides resolutions of 720 × 480 and 1280 × 720 at 60 fps (as well as others), plus CD-quality audio, making it adequate for all major TV standards, even HDTV. MPEG-2 is the standard that covers DVD-ROM technology—it can compress two hours of video into a file no larger than a few gigabytes. Although encoding video into MPEG-2 format requires a computer with some serious firepower, even a modest PC can decompress and play such a video.

The MPEG-4 standard is based on MPEG-1, MPEG-2, and Apple's QuickTime technology. MPEG-4 graphics and video files use what's known as wavelet compression to create files that are more compact than either JPEG or QuickTime files. This superior compression makes MPEG-4 popular for delivering video and images over the Web.

● **Figure 10.30** DVD-RAM disc

its own. You could plop down US$250 on a brand-new DVD+RW drive and still find yourself unable to edit a disc from your friend who used the DVD-RW format! Half of the time, the drive couldn't even *read* the competing format disc.

The situation is much better today, as DVD±RW combo drives in PCs will play just about anyone else's DVDs. The challenge is DVD players. If you want to make a DVD of your family picnic and then play it on the DVD player hooked to your television, take the time to read the documentation for your player to make sure it reads that particular DVD format—not all players read all formats.

Chapter 10 Review

■ Chapter Summary

After reading this chapter and completing the exercises, you should understand the following about floppy disk drives, flash memory, and optical-media technology.

Explain and Install Floppy Disk Drives

■ Floppy disk drives are becoming a thing of the past as Microsoft and Intel push for legacy-free computing. The small, 1.44-MB capacity floppy disks are being replaced by higher capacity removable media.

■ Floppy disks are constructed of a flexible magnetic disc housed inside a square plastic case. The case has a sliding protective cover which opens to reveal a portion of the magnetic media when inside a floppy drive. Read/write heads inside the floppy disk drive move back and forth across the media, reading or writing data as necessary.

■ During disk access, an LED on the front of the drive lights up. Never eject a floppy disk when this light is on.

■ Floppy disks have gone through several stages of improvement and have gotten smaller with each phase. Pre-PC computers used an 8-inch floppy. Early PCs used a 5¼-inch floppy. Modern floppy disks, which appeared around 1986, are 3½ inches.

■ You may have a maximum of two floppy disk drives in a system, and they must use either the drive letter A: or B:; however, a single floppy disk drive can be configured to use either drive letter. By convention, if your system has only one floppy disk drive, it should be configured as drive A:. A 34-pin ribbon data cable is used to connect the floppy disk drive to the motherboard; a 4-pin mini connector supplies power. Attaching the data cable backward won't damage anything, but the drive won't work. If you attach the power connector incorrectly, you risk damaging the drive.

■ Most floppy ribbon cables have three connectors and a twist. The end without the twist connects to the motherboard, matching the red stripe on the cable with pin 1 of the motherboard connector. The drive attached to the middle connector on the cable receives the drive letter B:. The drive attached to the other end of the cable (after the twist) is assigned the drive letter A:.

■ After connecting a floppy disk drive, configure the CMOS settings. Make sure the CMOS setting matches your floppy disk drive size/capacity. For example, 3½ inches and 1.44 MB.

Demonstrate the Variations Among Flash Drives and Other Tiny Drives

■ Flash memory includes USB thumb drives and memory cards. USB thumb drives contain a standard USB connection and have replaced many other forms of removable media as the way we transfer files. Memory cards, a generic term, are used in digital cameras, PDAs, and other devices.

■ Thumb drives store much more data than a floppy—sometimes up to the equivalent of thousands of floppy disks. They are hot-swappable in Windows 2000/XP/Vista and don't require an external power source, as they are powered directly from the USB bus. Some PCs allow you to boot from a USB thumb drive.

■ Flash cards, which are used in portable devices such as digital cameras, PDAs, and phones, come in many varieties. The most common types are CompactFlash, SmartMedia, Secure Digital, Memory Stick, and Extreme Digital (xD) Picture Card. CompactFlash cards are the oldest of these flash cards. At about 1 inch wide, they use the PCMCIA bus and come in two thicknesses: CF I at 3.3 mm thick and CF II at 5 mm thick. SmartMedia competed directly with CompactFlash and was used mainly in digital cameras. The introduction of Secure Digital has made SmartMedia all but obsolete. Secure Digital is perhaps the most popular flash card today and comes in two types: original SD and SDIO. Smaller versions of Secure Digital cards, MiniSD and MicroSD, are also available. Memory Stick, a proprietary format from Sony, comes in several different formats including Standard, Pro, Duo, Pro Duo, and Micro. xD Picture Cards, developed by Olympus, are about half the size of Secure Digital cards and are used almost exclusively in digital cameras.

- No matter what type of flash card you have, you need a card reader to access it. Some PCs have built-in card readers. External USB card readers are also available. Sometimes a device like a digital camera or PDA can double as a card reader.

Identify Optical Drives

- CDs store data using microscopic pits burned into a glass master CD with a powerful laser. Expensive machines create plastic copies of the glass master which are then coated with a reflective metallic coating. CDs store data on one side of the disc only. The CD drive reads the pits and the non-pitted areas (lands) and converts the pattern into ones and zeroes.

- CDs come in many varieties. CD-Digital Audio is for playing music, but it lacks error checking, file support, and directory structure. CD-ROM discs are for storing data. They use the ISO-9660 file system, also known as CDFS. Extensions of ISO-9660 have offered improvements to file and directory naming, filename length, and directory depth and include Joliet, Rock Ridge, El Torito, and Apple Extensions.

- CD-ROM speeds have increased substantially from the original 150 KBps. Increased speeds are measured in multiples of 150 KBps, so a 10× CD-ROM has a maximum speed of 1500 KBps.

- CD-recordable (CD-R) discs hold either 650 MB or 700 MB and can store either audio or data. Special organic dyes which give the CD-Rs their distinctive bottom color aid in the burning process. A strong laser in the CD drive heats the dye and changes the reflectivity of the CD-R's surface, resulting in a reflective/less-reflective pattern that is converted to ones and zeroes. Once data is burned to a CD-R, the data cannot be erased. Multisession drives enable you to burn data to a portion of a disc and then go back later and burn more data to the disc. CD-R discs are rated with two speeds: a write speed followed by a read speed.

- CD-rewritable (CD-RW) discs, unlike CD-Rs, enable you to erase data and burn new data. CD-RWs are rated with three speeds: write speed followed by rewrite speed followed by read speed. The UDF file format (the replacement for ISO-9660) handles large files better than CDFS. Packet writing, a feature used by UDF, allows for files to be copied back and forth to a CD-RW like a hard drive.

- Most CD drives are ATAPI compliant and do not need drivers installed for them to work. Windows XP can burn CD-Rs and CD-RWs with no additional software, but cannot burn bootable CDs. If you need to create a bootable CD you'll need a third-party application such as Ahead's Nero Express. Many companies offer standalone CD burners that attach to your stereo system instead of your PC; however, these machines use a different type of CD called a Music CD-R and are not compatible with standard CD-R or CD-RW discs.

- DVDs were released as digital video discs in 1995, but as usage evolved to include data storage, the name was changed to digital versatile disc. The lowest capacity DVD holds 4.37 GB of data. DVDs offer much higher capacities than CDs because DVDs user smaller, more densely packed pits; can be burned on both sides of the disc; and can burn two layers of pits per side for a total of four layers. DVD video uses the MPEG-2 video standard and can store two hours of video on a single side.

- DVD-ROM, the DVD equivalent of CD-ROM, can store up to 16 GB of data. Recordable DVD-media comes in many varieties: DVD-R for general purpose, DVD-R for authoring, DVD+R, DVD-RW, DVD+RW, and DVD-RAM. DVD-R and DVD+R can be written to, but not erased. DVD-RW, DVD+RW, and DVD-RAM can be burned and erased like CD-RW.

Key Terms

3½-inch floppy drive (269)	DVD-ROM (285)	MPEG-2 (285)
34-pin ribbon cable (270)	DVD-RW (285)	multisession drive (281)
ATAPI-compliant (282)	DVD-video (284)	Music CD-R (283)
card reader (276)	Extreme Digital (xD) Picture Card (276)	optical disc (277)
CD-Digital Audio (CDDA) (279)		optical drive (277)
CD-recordable (CD-R) (280)	floppy disk (269)	pin 1 (271)
CD-rewritable (CD-RW) (281)	floppy drive (269)	Secure Digital (SD) (275)
CD-ROM (279)	ISO-9660 (279)	SmartMedia (275)
CompactFlash (CF) (275)	Memory Stick (276)	universal data format (UDF) (282)
digital versatile disc (DVD) (277)	microdrives (275)	USB thumb drive (274)
DVD+RW (285)	mini power connector (272)	

Key Term Quiz

Use the Key Terms list to complete the sentences that follow. Not all terms will be used.

1. If you want to burn part of a disc and finish burning it at a later time, you need to select a(n) _____.

2. Any device that plugs into an ATA controller on the motherboard is said to be _____.

3. The first kind of CD was the _____ that is still used for music, but it is inappropriate for data because it lacks any error correction techniques.

4. A CD-ROM disc holds about 650 MB of data, whereas a(n) _____ stores from 4.37 GB to 15.9 GB, depending on the number of sides and layers used.

5. Floppy drives use a(n) _____ to connect the floppy drive to the motherboard.

6. The red stripe on a floppy drive cable must be oriented to _____ on the controller.

7. _____ is currently the most popular type of flash memory card.

8. The floppy disk is quickly being replaced by the _____ because of its large capacity and portability.

9. DVD video uses the _____ standard of video.

10. DVDs use the _____ file structure.

Multiple-Choice Quiz

1. What kind of disc must be used in a non-PC CD burner that works with your stereo system?
   A. CDDA
   B. CD-RW
   C. CD-UDF
   D. Music CD-R

2. What is the minimum capacity of a DVD?
   A. 650 MB
   B. 3.47 GB
   C. 4.37 GB
   D. 7.34 GB

3. If you have two floppy disk drives in your system, which one receives the drive letter A:?
   A. The drive jumpered for Master
   B. The drive connected to the primary floppy drive controller
   C. The drive in the middle of the floppy cable
   D. The drive at the end of the floppy cable

4. Which type of flash memory card is currently the most popular?

   A. CompactFlash

   B. Memory Stick

   C. Secure Digital

   D. SmartMedia

5. What type of device must be installed on your system in order to access data on a flash memory card?

   A. Scanner

   B. Card reader

   C. Floppy drive

   D. ZIP drive

6. Both CD and DVD drive speeds are based on multiples of the original CD-ROM drive speed. What is that speed?

   A. 100 KBps

   B. 150 KBps

   C. 100 MBps

   D. 150 MBps

7. A CD-RW has a speed rating of 12×10×32. What do the three numbers refer to, in order?

   A. Write, rewrite, read

   B. Read, write, rewrite

   C. Rewrite, read, write

   D. Write, read, rewrite

8. What type of DVD can store 15.9 GB of data or more than eight hours of video?

   A. Double-sided, single-layered

   B. Single-sided, single-layered

   C. Single-sided, dual-layered

   D. Double-sided, dual-layered

9. Which of the following kinds of discs is the best choice for performing regular backups?

   A. CD-ROM/XA

   B. CD-Interactive (CD-I)

   C. CD-R

   D. CD-RW

10. Alistair wants his new CD burner to use drive letter B:. How would you suggest he do this?

    A. Verify there is only one floppy disk drive in the system and the CD drive will automatically become drive B:.

    B. Verify there is only one floppy disk drive in the system and that it is on the end, not the middle, of the ribbon cable. The CD drive will automatically become drive B:.

    C. Disable drive letter B: in CMOS so that it will no longer be reserved for a floppy disk drive; then it will automatically be used by the CD burner.

    D. It is not possible. Drive letter B: is reserved for floppy disk drives.

11. What is the best way to properly align a ribbon cable to the floppy controller on the motherboard?

    A. Verify that the colored stripe on the cable is aligned with the pin 1 marking near one end the floppy controller.

    B. Verify that the colored stripe on the cable is opposite the pin 1 marking near one end the floppy controller.

    C. Use the orientation notch on the ribbon cable as it ensures proper alignment.

    D. Floppy cables and controllers do not need to be aligned; the cables are reversible.

12. What is the worst thing that can happen if you plug the mini power connector into a floppy disk drive incorrectly?

    A. The drive may be destroyed.

    B. The green LED on the floppy disk drive will come on and stay on. The drive will not function.

    C. The green LED on the floppy disk drive will come on and stay on. The drive will function.

    D. The drive will not function. There will be no light or any other warning.

13. What is one benefit that USB thumb drives have over floppy disks?

　A. USB thumb drives offer slower and therefore more reliable data transfer.

　B. USB thumb drives offer the ability to easily transfer files between computers with different operating systems.

　C. A USB thumb drive is less expensive than a floppy disk.

　D. No drivers are necessary for USB thumb drives.

14. What will cause the most damage to a CD?

　A. Scratching the top of the disc

　B. Scratching the bottom of the disc

　C. Fingerprints on the bottom of the disc

　D. Writing on the clear plastic in the center of the disc

15. Which ISO-9660 extension added support for bootable CDs?

　A. Joliet

　B. Rock Ridge

　C. El Torito

　D. Apple Extensions

■ Essay Quiz

1. Why do many manufacturers build computers without floppy drives? If you bought a new computer, would you still want a floppy disk on it? Write a short essay defending or attacking the floppy drive.

2. You have been tasked to provide removable media for each of the technicians in your department. One tech wants a card reader and SD cards, whereas another wants a USB thumb drive. Write a memo outlining the advantages of each technology and make a recommendation.

3. Your department is getting ready to replace the old computers, and your boss Mrs. Turner has asked you to investigate what kind of optical drives the new computers should have. Write a memo to your boss listing the device(s) you have selected and justifying your choice(s).

Lab Projects

• Lab Project 10.1

Flash media comes in many different forms. Take a trip to your local computer store, or even to a drug store that has digital picture processing, and see what sort of media or flash devices they have available. What are some of the advantages or disadvantages of one form factor over another?

• Lab Project 10.2

Use the Internet to check these sites: www.compaq.com, www.dell.com, and www.gateway.com. What kinds of optical drives do these companies offer with their new computers? Do any of the companies offer multiple optical drives? If so, which ones and what devices? What upgrades for optical drives do the companies offer and how expensive are the upgrades? If you were buying a new PC, which optical drive(s) would you want on your computer? Why?

Installing and Upgrading Windows

chapter 11

"Better still just don't install / The idiotic thing at all."

—Oompa Loompa, *Charlie and the Chocolate Factory* (2005)

In this chapter, you will learn how to

- **Identify and explain the basic functions and features of an operating system**
- **Install and upgrade Windows 2000 and Windows XP**
- **Troubleshoot installation problems**

An **operating system** provides the fundamental link between the hardware that makes up the PC and the user. Without an operating system, all the greatest, slickest PC hardware in the world is but so much copper, silicon, and gold wrapped up as a big, beige paperweight. The operating system creates the interface between human and machine, enabling you to unleash the astonishing power locked up in the sophisticated electronics of the PC to create amazing pictures, games, documents, business tools, medical miracles, and much more.

All operating systems are not created equal. They don't look the same or, on the surface, act the same. But every OS shares essential characteristics that, once you have the concepts, help lead you to answers when troubleshooting: "I know that the OS formerly known as Y must enable me to access programs; therefore, no matter how odd the interface, the option must be here!"

This chapter starts with an analysis of all operating systems, examining the functions and traits they all share. After that, we'll delve into the features common to every version of Microsoft Windows (or at least those covered on the CompTIA A+ certification exams). We'll then go through the process of installing Windows on a new system, as well as upgrading earlier versions of Windows. The chapter finishes with an in-depth examination of the core structures of Windows 2000 and XP systems. Let's get started.

■ Functions of the Operating System

An operating system (OS) is a program that performs four basic functions. First, it must communicate, or at least provide a method for other programs to communicate, with the hardware of the PC. It's up to the OS to access the hard drives, respond to the keyboard, and output data to the monitor. Second, the OS must create a user interface—a visual representation of the computer on the monitor that makes sense to the people using the computer. The OS must also take advantage of standard input devices, such as mice and keyboards, to enable users to manipulate the user interface and thereby make changes on the computer. Third, the OS, via the user interface, must enable users to determine the available installed programs and run, use, and shut down the program(s) of their choice. Fourth, the OS should enable users to add, move, and delete the installed programs and data. In a nutshell, the OS should be able to do the following:

- Communicate with hardware
- Provide a user interface
- Provide a structure for accessing applications
- Enable users to manipulate programs and data

Operating System Traits

To achieve these four functions, all operating systems share certain common traits.

First, an OS works only with a particular type of processor. For example, Microsoft Windows XP Professional 64-bit Edition only runs on systems using Intel or AMD CPUs with 64-bit support, like the AMD Athlon 64. For many years, other platforms used different CPUs that were completely incompatible with the Intel and AMD lines, such as the IBM/Motorola PowerPC CPU used inside Macintosh computers until 2005. The Macintosh OS used on those systems would not run on an Intel/AMD-based system. (This changed in 2005 when Apple switched to the Intel/AMD platform—you can now run Windows on a newer Mac with a few tweaks.) The OS must understand important aspects of the CPU, such as the amount of memory the CPU can handle, what modes of operation it is capable of performing, and the CPU commands (the codebook) needed to perform the operations. Certain OSs, such as Linux, can run on more than one type of processor, but they achieve this by having versions for each type of processor they support.

Second, an OS always starts running immediately after the PC has finished its POST, taking control of the PC. The OS continues running until the PC is rebooted or turned off. The OS cannot be turned off unless the PC is also turned off.

Third, application programs, such as word processors, spreadsheets, and Web browsers, cannot run on a PC without an OS. Therefore, programmers write application programs to function under the control of a certain OS. You cannot write one version of an application that works under

Most users and techs call application programs simply "applications."

Tech Tip

Java

The popularity of programming paradigms such as Java might make some folks want to challenge the idea that every application must come in different versions for different operating systems. Although a piece of Java code may run on any computer, each computer must have some programming installed that can interpret that Java code. That programming is OS-specific.

Table 11.1	Operating Systems and Applications
Operating System	**Application**
Mac OS X	Microsoft Office 2008
Windows XP	Microsoft Office 2007
Linux	OpenOffice

different OSs. Table 11.1 shows a selection of OSs and applications written specifically for them. The creators of an OS always provide a "rule book" that tells programmers how to write programs for a particular OS. These rule books are known as **application programming interfaces (APIs)**.

Last, an OS must have flexibility and provide some facility for using new software or hardware that might be installed. It just wouldn't do, for example, to be stuck with the same game year after year! (See Figure 11.1.)

Communicating with Hardware

In earlier chapters you learned that the system BIOS, stored on some type of non-volatile memory (ROM or Flash ROM) on the motherboard, stores programs that know how to talk to the most basic and important parts of the computer. These include the hard drives, floppy drives, keyboard, and basic video. The OS must work with the system BIOS to deal with these devices. If users want to access the hard drive to retrieve a program, the OS must take

• Figure 11.1 Progress is good: Half-Life 2 (top, the larger image) and Wolfenstein 3-D (bottom).

Mike Meyers' CompTIA A+ Guide: Essentials (Exam 220-601)

the request and pass it to the appropriate hard drive BIOS instruction that tells the drive to send the program to RAM. Plus, if for some reason the BIOS lacks the ability to perform its function, the OS should bypass the system BIOS and talk to the piece of hardware directly. Most recent operating systems, including Windows, skip the system BIOS and talk directly to almost every piece of hardware, reducing your system BIOS to little more than a relic of the past.

For the OS to take control of a new piece of hardware, it needs to communicate with that hardware. Therefore, the OS needs a method to add the programming necessary to talk to that device, preferably in some simple and flexible way. Most operating systems use *device drivers* to add this necessary code. An OS maker (such as Microsoft) tells hardware makers how to create these programs (and makes money selling the development tools) and also creates a method of adding the device driver to the OS code. Because makers of a particular piece of hardware usually supply the device drivers with the hardware, and because drivers act something like BIOS, this solution can be jokingly, although accurately, thought of as BYOB (Bring Your Own BIOS).

Because the OS handles communicating with hardware, it should provide some type of error handling, or at least error notification. If someone attempts to use a piece of hardware that isn't working properly, the OS should either try to fix the problem or at least attempt to communicate with the device a few more times. If the device continues to fail, the OS should provide an error message to notify the user of the problem.

 Cross Check

Working with BIOS

In Chapter 5, "Understanding BIOS and CMOS," you learned that all hardware needs BIOS. So turn to that chapter now and see if you can answer these questions. What are the two ways for a device to BYOB? What are the primary tools or programs for working with BIOS?

Creating a User Interface

Most users have fairly straightforward needs. First, they want to know which applications are available; second, they want easy access to those programs; and third, they want to be able to save the data they generate with some easy-to-use label by which they can retrieve it later.

A shoe store makes a good analogy for a user interface. The front of the shoe store is filled with attractive displays of shoes, organized and grouped by gender (men and women), age (adults and children), function (dress or sports), and style. Shoe sellers do this so consumers can see everything that's available and to make it much easier to select the shoes they want to purchase. If a customer wants to buy a pair of shoes, what happens? The customer points out the shoes he or she wants to try on. The salesperson looks at the inside of the shoe and disappears through a small door. Wonder why the salesperson looked in the shoe? To read an inventory code that shoe manufacturers print inside every shoe.

Have you ever seen the back of a shoe store? It's scary. All the shoes are organized, not by gender, age, function, or style, but by inventory code, and the salesperson reads the inventory code to know where to look for that

● **Figure 11.2**   Shoe display

particular shoe. Without understanding the code, no one would know where to search for a pair of shoes, but it's the best way to organize an inventory of 25,000 pairs of shoes. What a customer sees in the store is not all the shoes as they really are in the back, but a "user interface" of what's available. The front display in the store—the user interface—is a pretty, easy to use, but entirely unrealistic display of the shoes in stock (Figure 11.2).

A computer's user interface performs the same function by offering the user a display of the programs and data on the PC. The customers (users) look at the display (the user interface) and tell the salesperson (the OS) what they want, without ever really knowing how all the shoes (programs and data) are really organized.

Finishing the analogy, the shoe store's displays are not permanent. Salespeople can easily add shoes and replace old displays. They can change a rack of men's shoes into a rack of women's shoes, for example, relatively easily. Like the shoe store, a user interface should also be flexible and scalable, depending on the system in which it is installed.

Accessing and Supporting Programs

An OS must enable users to start a program. This is a simple but important concept. When a program starts, the user interface must move away from the main part of the screen and set itself to the top, bottom, or side. While the application runs, the OS must still provide whatever access to hardware the application needs, such as updating the screen, saving data, or printing. If a program loses control, the OS should have some way to stop it or at least to recognize what's happening and generate an error message. Finally, the OS should instantly return to the user interface when the application shuts down, so that the user can choose another application.

Organizing and Manipulating Programs and Data

A single PC might store hundreds of programs and thousands of separate pieces of data. Simply making all the programs and data visible would be like taking all the shoes in the back of the shoe store and setting them neatly on the display room floor. Yes, you could locate shoes in this fashion, but it would be an overly complicated mess. Much better to have some method of organizing the programs and data.

Okay, I hear you saying, I'll buy into that, but how? Let's break it down. First question: [holds up chunk of binary code] Is this a program or a piece of data used by a program? Read the label! The OS must provide a label or name for each program and each individual piece of data that identifies it as either a program or a piece of data. If it's data, there must also be some method by which the OS can identify what type of program uses it.

Next question: How can I distinguish between the various places I might store this chunk of data or program? Each floppy disk, hard drive, and optical drive needs some sort of identifier, again provided by the OS. It can be as simple as a letter of the alphabet or as complex as a fully descriptive phrase.

Third question: [picks up several more chunks of data] How can I make sure that related chunks of data or programs are stored in a way that permits efficient retrieval and alteration? Data and programs must be stored in distinct groups on each drive, and the OS user interface must enable users to interact with each of these groups individually. Users must be able to open and close these groups, and copy, move, or delete both programs and data. Finally, a good OS will have a user interface that enables users to perform these functions easily and accurately, especially in the case of deletions. Clearly, a good OS has a lot of work to do!

Essentials

Operating systems accomplish all the tasks above with two user interfaces: text-based and graphical. A text-based, command-line interface enables you to type commands directly to the OS, and, if you type them correctly, the OS responds or carries out your command. A graphical user interface (GUI) draws pictures on the screen with which you interact using a mouse or similar device. GUIs use tiny pictures called icons to represent programs and data structures. By clicking on icons and other graphical features, such as menus and buttons, you can send commands to the OS.

Today's Operating Systems

The CompTIA A+ certification concentrates almost exclusively on one operating system: Microsoft Windows. To be even more specific, CompTIA A+ certification only concentrates on two versions of Microsoft Windows: Microsoft Windows 2000 Professional and Microsoft Windows XP. That's not a bad idea on CompTIA's part, given that these two versions of Windows are easily the most common operating systems used today! Still, it's important that you understand there are a lot of operating systems available today beyond just these two, including a large number of Windows versions. You may only need to know Windows 2000 and XP in detail for the exams, but life as a tech will test you on the capabilities of others.

Microsoft Windows

Windows is the trade name for a very large family of Microsoft operating systems created over the last 20 years. The earliest versions of Windows were little more than pretty graphical front ends for the ancient DOS

The first version of Windows NT was numbered 3.1 to match up with the then-popular version of old-style Windows called 3.1.

operating system. Windows as a full-blown OS really got its start with Windows NT 3.1 way back in 1993. Windows NT was the first Microsoft product designed from the ground up to take advantage of 32-bit processing, and it included a number of important new features such as the now common NTFS file system, enhanced security, and robust network support.

Windows NT 3.1 came out in two versions: Workstation and Advanced Server. The Workstation version was for…workstations. The Advanced Server version was basically just the Workstation version with lots of extra built-in software to support servers.

Windows NT went through a number of upgrades, with each version adding improvements, such as better network support, and enhancements in NTFS. Figure 11.3 shows Windows NT version 4.0.

The only problem with NT was that it had high hardware requirements and didn't play well with older programs written for earlier versions of Windows. To keep lower-end users happy, Microsoft upgraded the old Windows into a patched-together operating system called Windows 95. Windows 95, along with its successors, Windows 98 (Figure 11.4) and the infamous Windows Me, were tasked with the difficult job of trying to be 32-bit operating systems that had virtually complete backward compatibility with every program ever written for Windows 3.x or even the old DOS. As a result, these versions of Windows (we call the entire family Windows 9x) only

• **Figure 11.3** Windows NT version 4.0

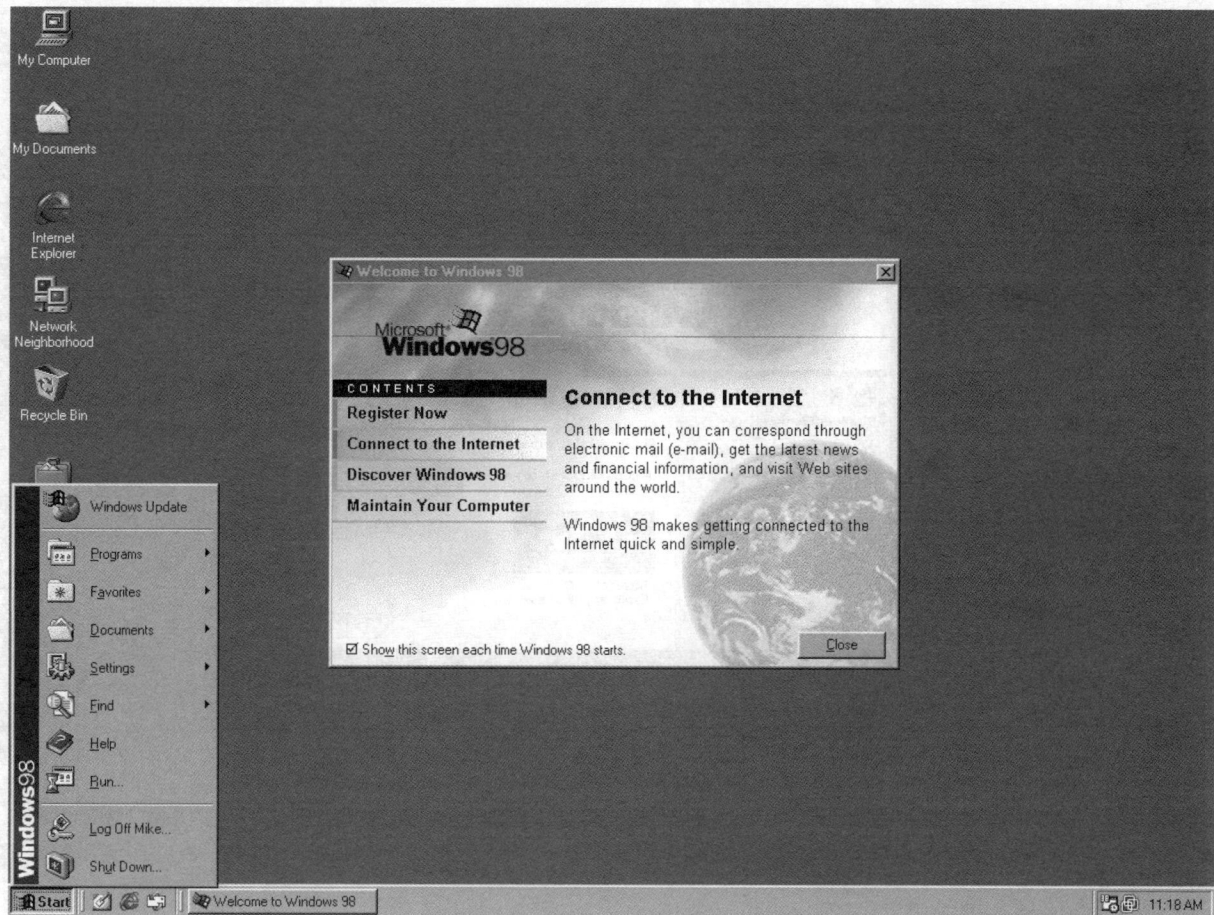

● **Figure 11.4** Windows 98

used FAT or FAT32, had a zillion little configurations files, and were prone to many problems.

Windows 2000 (Figure 11.5) was really just Windows NT with a number of very nice improvements, such as plug and play—the ability to just insert a device and have it work—and a greatly improved interface. Like NT, Windows 2000 came out in a workstation version (called Windows 2000 Professional) and a server version (called Windows 2000 Server). Microsoft kept selling Windows 9*x* versions, but a large number of users liked Windows 2000 so much that even more casual users (like home users) went to Windows 2000 Professional.

Microsoft officially ended the Windows 9*x* product line with the introduction of Windows XP in 2001. Windows XP was designed for everyone from casual home users to the heaviest workstation users. XP is based on the NT/2000 operating systems and uses NTFS. There is no server version of Windows XP, but there are five user versions. Windows XP Professional (Figure 11.6) is designed to work in Windows networks that use Active Directory (I discuss Active Directory in Chapter 19). Windows XP Home Edition is designed for single users or small networks that do not use Active Directory. Windows XP Media Center is a version of Windows XP Home Edition that comes with a Personal Video Recorder program to enable you

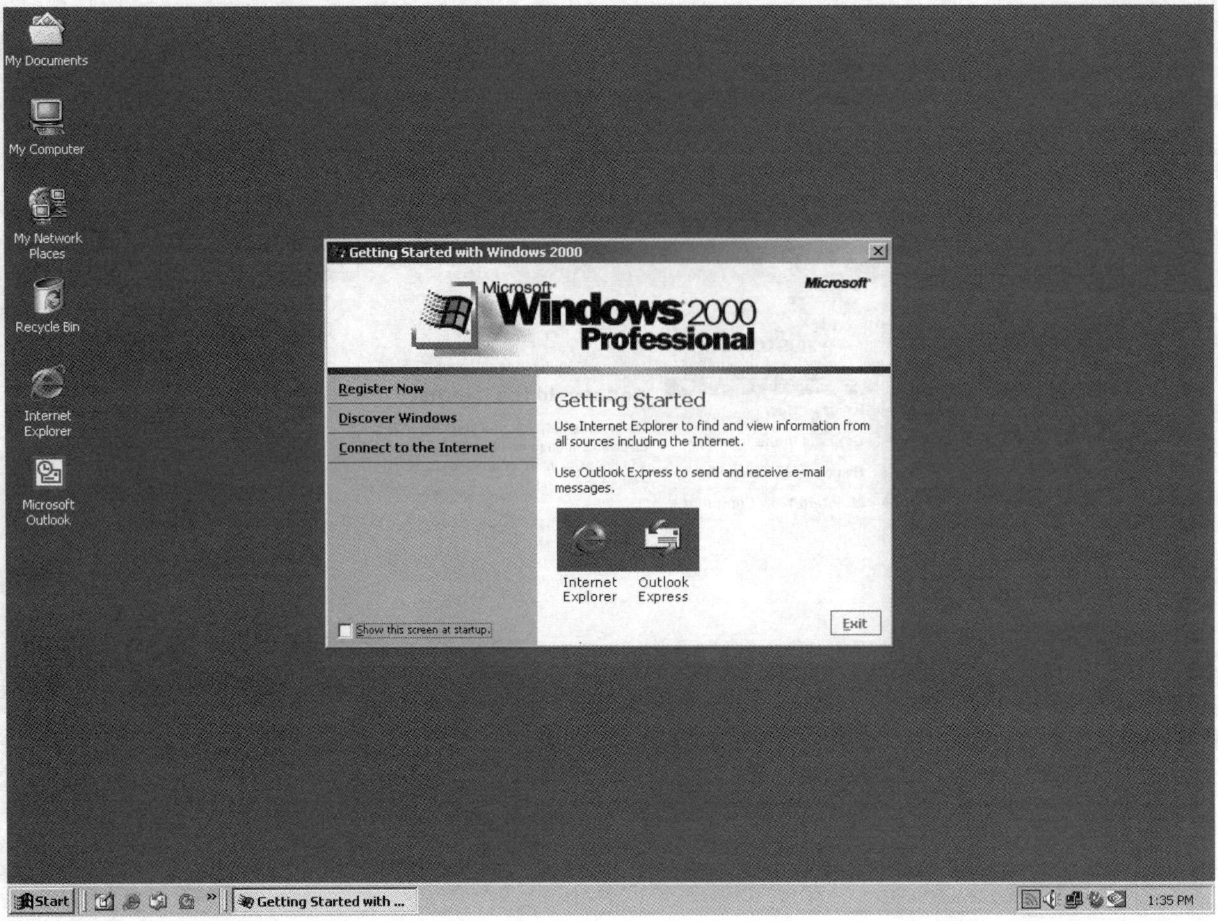

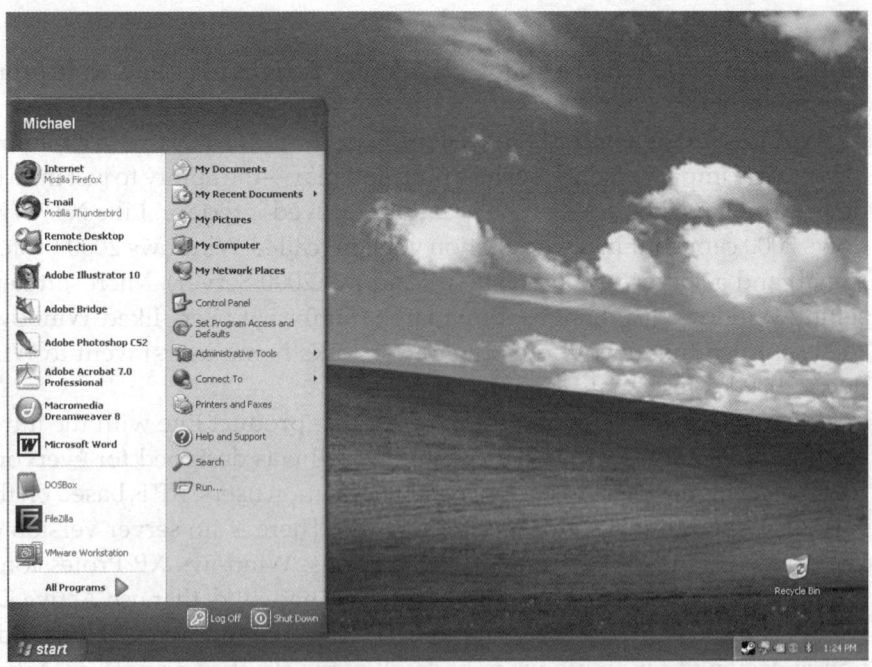

● **Figure 11.5**   Windows 2000 Professional

● **Figure 11.6**   Windows XP Professional

Mike Meyers' CompTIA A+ Guide: Essentials (Exam 220-601)

to watch television and movies. Windows XP Tablet PC Edition is a version of Windows XP Professional with additional support for tablet PCs. Finally Windows XP Professional x64 is for 64-bit CPUs.

The current server version is called Windows Server 2003 (Figure 11.7). It's very similar to Windows 2000 Server but adds a few handy extras that people who run large networks really like. Windows 2003 comes in 32-bit and 64-bit versions.

The latest version of Windows is called Windows Vista (Figure 11.8). Vista, which comes in multiple versions, is basically a rewritten Windows XP in terms of its structure and

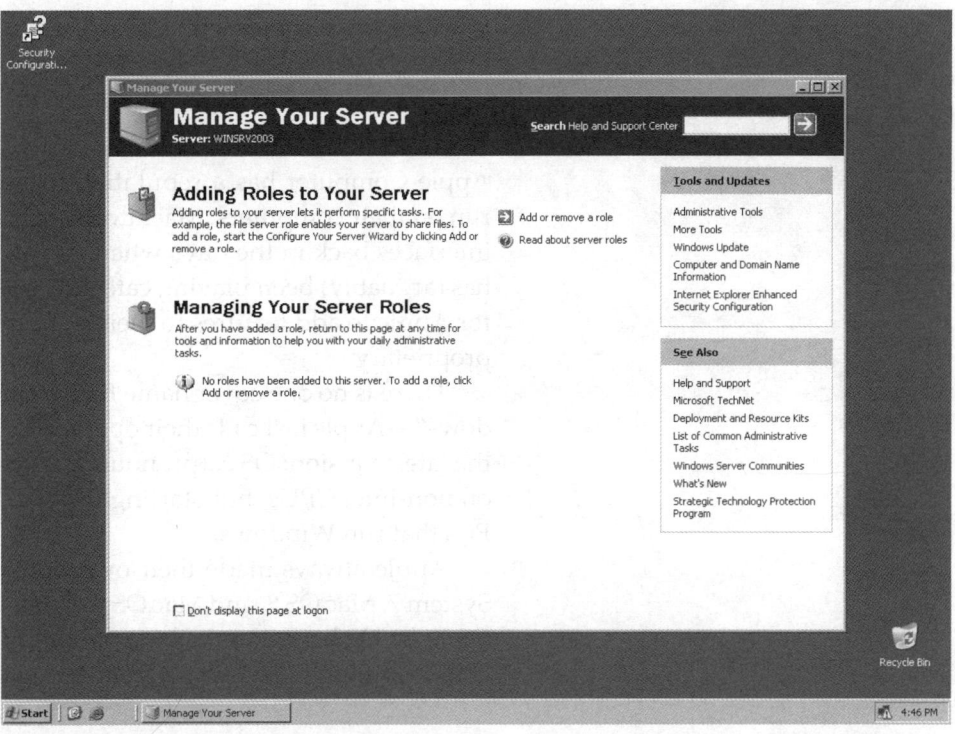

• **Figure 11.7** Windows Server 2003

• **Figure 11.8** Windows Vista

function, but it comes with a broad array of new desktop enhancements that improve usability.

Apple Macintosh

Apple Computer has a reputation for making great operating systems to run on their computers. Macintosh computers were running graphical user interfaces back in the days when PCs were still using DOS, and Microsoft has (arguably) been playing catch up with Apple ever since. It's a bit easier for Apple to add features to their computers, since all Apple computers are proprietary.

There is no one cover name for Macintosh operating systems like "Windows"—Apple just calls their operating systems Mac OS. Figure 11.9 shows the latest version: OS X (pronounced "ten," not "ex"). Originally, Macs ran on non-Intel CPUs, but starting in 2006, Macs run on Intel CPUs, just like PCs that run Windows.

Apple always made their own operating systems with names such as System 7, Mac OS 8, and Mac OS 9. However, in 2001 Apple switched to Mac OS X, an OS based on the BSD variant of UNIX. Mac OS is now a flavor of UNIX—although heavily customized by Apple.

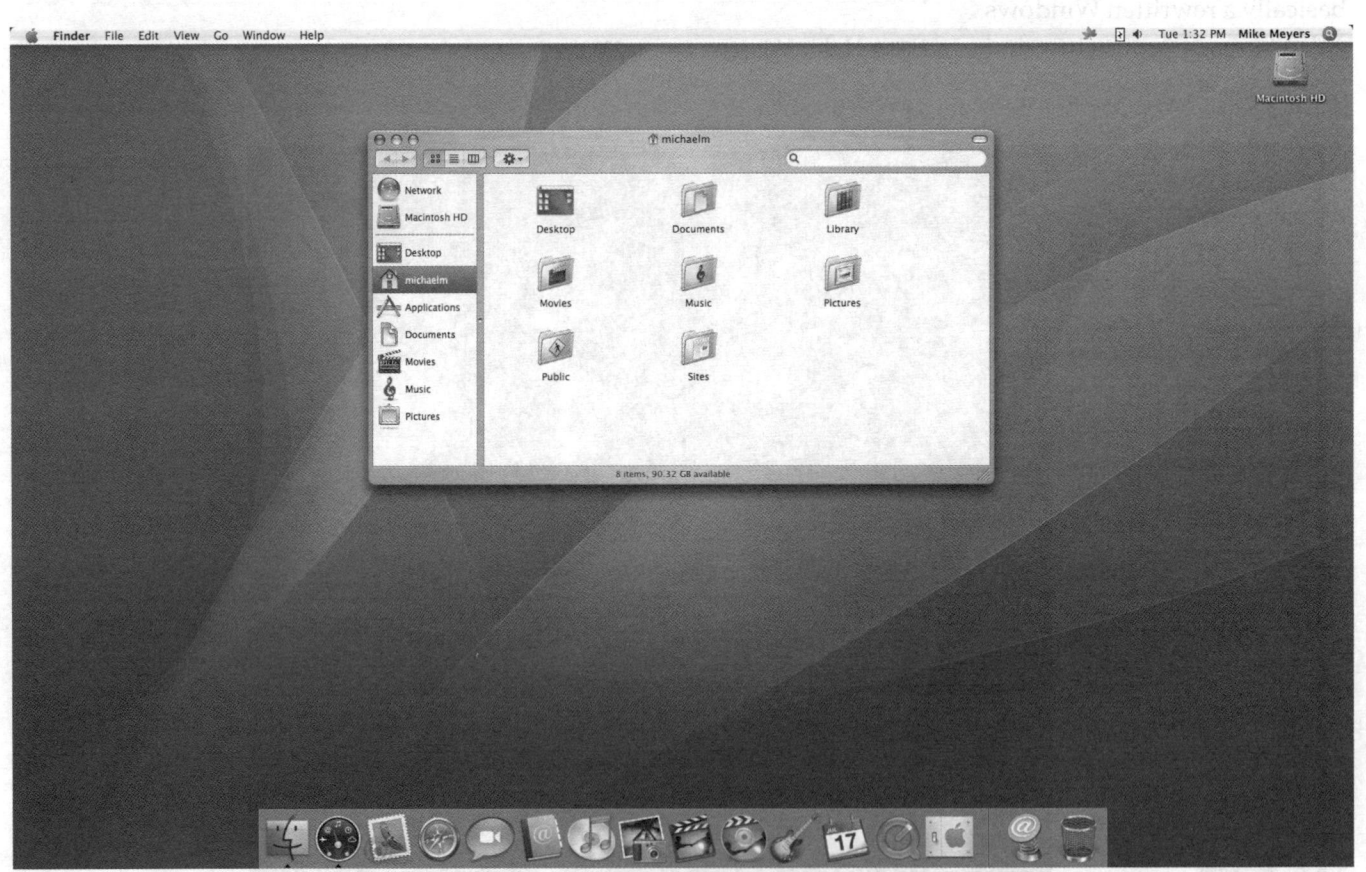

● Figure 11.9   Apple's Mac OS X

UNIX

UNIX is the oldest, most powerful, and most influential operating system ever invented. Though old, UNIX has gone through generation after generation of updates and is the operating system chosen by those geeky folks who need detailed control and raw power out of their operating system. UNIX was first developed by Bell Labs in the early 1970s and has spawned not only new versions but also entire subclasses of UNIX. It's hard to say how many variations of UNIX exist, as sometimes the variations are subtle. A good but unscientific guess would be in the area of 500 clearly defined versions!

Every popular operating system—Windows, Mac OS, even the ancient DOS—used concepts from UNIX as a starting point. Mac OS may be the leader in cool ways to make an OS user interface, but UNIX has always defined how your OS worked behind the scenes. So many things we never think about came from UNIX: hard drive volumes and tree-structured directories are just two of thousands of innovations that come from UNIX. So even if you don't use UNIX, many of the aspects of the OS you do use came from UNIX.

Linux

Linux is a UNIX clone written by a fellow named Linus Torvalds in 1991, and it has been updated constantly—almost daily—since then (Figure 11.10). Linux was designed from the beginning to run on Intel/AMD processors and has one aspect that makes it unique among popular operating systems—it's totally free. Not only is it totally free, all of the *source code* (the actual code the programmers wrote to make Linux) is also freely available to be used and changed. The only limitation to changing the source code is that you have to, in turn, make the new code available for free as well. Linux uses the **GNU general public license (GPL)**, a license that uses copyright laws to promote freely available software and keep it free, even when it's changed.

Linux comes in a variety of flavors that many companies bundle with various applications and make available for purchase or download. The Linux part of the bundle is the essential operating system software—called the *kernel*—and drivers specific to that kernel for various pieces of hardware. The bundled Linux and applications are called **Linux distributions (distros)**. Just as Microsoft bundles useful productivity applications with Windows, such as WordPad and Outlook Express, distro developers bundle all sorts of cool and useful applications with their distro, such as full-featured photo-editing software and complete office suites for word processing, presentation, and number crunching. There are quite a few Linux distributions available, but here are a few of the more famous ones:

- **Fedora Core** A popular general-purpose Linux, derived from Red Hat Linux.
- **Debian** Used for everything from individual systems to powerful servers.
- **Slackware** A favorite distro for folks who are good at Linux— flexible but not as user friendly.
- **Ubuntu** Based on Debian but designed for easy use by individual users.
- **SuSE** Another popular general-purpose distro.

The GPL is managed by the Free Software Foundation, a nonprofit organization that promotes open-source software.

Tech Tip

Linux Applications

Programmers for Linux-based applications have created a phenomenal amount of high-quality software, much of which they license under the GPL and make freely available for you to use. Here are some of my favorites.

Open Office does almost everything Microsoft Office can do, and you can save files in formats compatible with the latter as well. The popular Web browser Firefox is a quick download away and works just as well as the Windows version. The same is true of the excellent e-mail program, Thunderbird. You can download both apps from www.mozilla.org.

Beyond basic productivity apps, I use Evolution for e-mail and calendaring, the GIMP for photo manipulation, Blender for 3-D modeling, and a whole bunch more. Linux programmers are an inventive, creative crew, so you'll find new or improved applications available every day.

• **Figure 11.10**   Linux operating system

■ Installing and Upgrading Windows

Installing or upgrading an OS is like any good story: it has a beginning, a middle, and an end. In this case, the beginning is the several tasks you need to do before you actually do the installation or upgrade. If you do your homework here, the installation process is a breeze, and the post-installation tasks are minimal. In the next section, I'll give you my short list of preparation tasks, the generic procedure for installing Windows, and the tasks you need to do after the installation.

Preparing for Installation or Upgrade

Working with PCs gives us many exciting opportunities for frustrating delays and unproductive side trips! Because installing an OS can be a time-consuming task, even when everything goes right, the Windows installation process holds great potential for lost time. Nothing sets the teeth to grinding as much as encountering an indecipherable or ambiguous error message or the infamous Blue Screen of Death 55 minutes into an hour-long system installation.

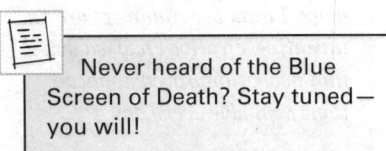
Never heard of the Blue Screen of Death? Stay tuned— you will!

Don't get discouraged at all the preparation tasks. They usually go pretty fast, and skipping them can cause you gobs of grief later when you're in the middle of installing and things blow up. Well, maybe there isn't a real explosion, but the computer might lock up and refuse to boot into anything usable. With that in mind, let's look at the nine tasks you need to complete *before* you insert that CD or DVD. Here's the list; discussion follows:

1. Identify hardware requirements.
2. Verify hardware and software compatibility.
3. Decide whether to perform a clean installation or an upgrade.
4. Determine how to back up and restore existing data, if necessary.
5. Select an installation method.
6. Determine how to partition the hard drive and what file system to use.
7. Determine your computer's network role.
8. Decide on your computer's language and locale settings.
9. Plan for post-installation tasks.

Identify Hardware Requirements

Hardware requirements help you decide whether a computer system is a reasonable host for a particular operating system. Requirements include the CPU model, the amount of RAM, the amount of free hard disk space, and the video adapter, display, and storage devices that may be required to install and run the operating system. They are stated as minimums or, more recently, as recommended minimums. Although you could install an operating system on a computer with the old minimums that Microsoft published, they were not realistic if you wanted to actually accomplish work. With the last few versions of Windows, Microsoft has published recommended minimums that are much more realistic. You will find the published minimums on the packaging and at Microsoft's Web site (www.microsoft .com). Later in this chapter, I'll also tell you what I recommend as minimums for Windows 2000 and Windows XP.

Verify Hardware and Software Compatibility

Assuming your system meets the requirements, you next need to find out how well Windows supports the brand and model of hardware and the application software you intend to use under Windows. You have two basic sources for this information: Microsoft and the manufacturer of the device or software. How do you actually access this information? Use the Web!

If you're installing Windows XP, the Setup Wizard automatically checks your hardware and software and reports any potential conflicts. But please don't wait until you are all ready to install to check this out. With any flavor of Windows, *first do your homework!*

Microsoft goes to great lengths to test any piece of hardware that might be used in a system running Windows through their Windows Marketplace (Figure 11.11). Windows Marketplace, formerly known as the *Hardware Compatibility List (HCL)*, is the definitive authority as to whether your component is compatible with the OS. Every component listed on the Windows

 You'll occasionally hear the HCL or Windows Marketplace referred to as the Windows Catalog. The Windows Catalog was a list of supported hardware Microsoft would add to the Windows installation CD. The Windows Marketplace Web site is the modern tech's best source, so use that rather than any printed resources.

Figure 11.11   Windows Marketplace

Marketplace Web site has been extensively tested to verify it works with Windows 2000 and XP and is guaranteed by Microsoft to work with your installation. The URL for Windows Marketplace is www.windowsmarketplace.com.

When you install a device that's not tested by Microsoft, a rather scary screen appears (Figure 11.12). This doesn't mean the component won't work, only that it's not been tested. Not all component makers go through the rather painful process of getting the Microsoft approval so they can list their component in the Windows Marketplace. As a rule of thumb, unless the device is more than five years old, go ahead and install it. If it still doesn't work, you can simply uninstall it later.

Don't panic if you don't see your device on the list; many supported devices aren't on it. Check the floppies or CD-ROMs that came with your hardware for proper drivers. Better yet, check the manufacturer's Web site for compatible drivers. Even when the Windows Marketplace lists a piece of hardware, I still make a point of checking the manufacturer's Web site for newer drivers.

When preparing to upgrade, check with the manufacturers of the applications already installed in the previous OS. If there are software compatibility problems with the versions

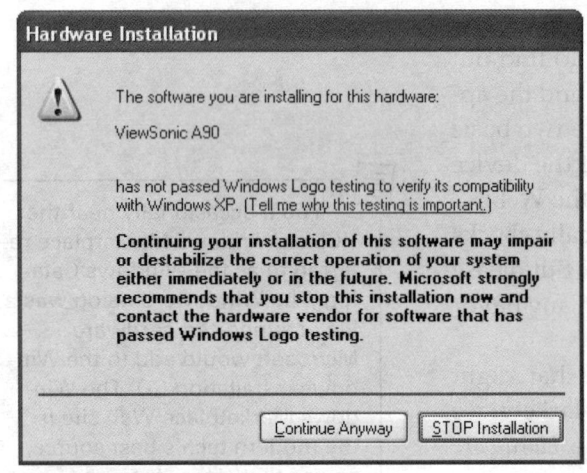

Figure 11.12   Untested device!

you have, the manufacturer should provide upgrade packs that can be installed during the Windows setup process.

Decide Whether to Perform a Clean Installation or an Upgrade

A clean installation of an OS involves installing it onto an empty hard drive with no previous OS installed. An upgrade installation is an installation of an OS on top of an earlier installed version, thus inheriting all previous hardware and software settings.

You may think the choice between doing a clean installation and an upgrade installation is simple: you do a clean installation on a brand new computer with an empty hard drive, and you do an upgrade of a preexisting installation. It isn't necessarily so! I'll tell you why as we look at this issue more closely.

Clean Installation   A clean installation usually begins with a completely empty hard disk. The advantage to doing a clean installation is that you don't carry problems from the old OS over to the new one, but the disadvantage is that all applications have to be reinstalled and the desktop and each application reconfigured to the user's preferences. You perform a clean install by resetting your CMOS to tell the system to boot from the CD-media drive before your hard drive. You then boot off a Windows 2000 or XP Installation CD-ROM, and Windows will give you the opportunity to partition and format the hard drive and then install Windows.

Upgrade Installation   In an upgrade installation, the new OS installs into the same folders as the old OS, or in tech speak, the new installs *on top of* the old. The new OS replaces the old OS but retains all saved data and inherits all the previous settings (such as font styles, desktop colors and background, and so on), hardware, and applications. You don't have to reinstall your favorite programs!

To begin the upgrade of Windows, you must run the appropriate program from the CD-ROM. This usually means inserting a Windows 2000 or Windows XP installation CD-ROM into your system while your old OS is running, which will start the install program. Then, to do an upgrade, you indicate that Windows 2000 or XP should install into a directory that already contains an installation of Windows (it will do this by default). You will be asked whether it is an upgrade or a new installation; if you select new installation, it will remove the existing OS before installing.

If for some reason the install program doesn't start automatically, go to My Computer, open the CD-ROM, and locate WINNT32.EXE. This program starts an upgrade to Windows 2000 or XP.

Multiboot Installation   A third option that you need to be aware of is dual boot or multiboot installation. Both Windows 2000 and Windows XP can install in a separate folder from your existing copy of Windows. Then every time your computer boots, you'll get a menu asking you which version of Windows you wish to boot. Multiboot sounds great, but it has lots of nasty little problems. For example, let's say you've got a system running Windows Me that you would like to upgrade to Windows XP. Windows Me must use either a FAT or a FAT32 file system; Windows XP can use these old file systems, but you'll miss out on the benefits of using NTFS.

CompTIA tests you on your ability to upgrade a Windows 9*x* or Windows NT system to Windows 2000 or Windows XP. You do not need to know about Windows 9*x* or NT for the tests, but you do need to know how to upgrade them!

Before starting an OS upgrade, make sure you have shut down all other open applications!

Tech Tip

Multiboot Configuration

When configuring a computer for multibooting, there are two basic rules: first, the system partition must be formatted in a file system that is common to all installed OSs, and second, if you're including Windows 98, you must install it first, and then install the other operating systems in order from oldest to newest.

Scripting OS and application installations is a full-time job in many organizations. There are many scripting tools and methods available from both Microsoft and third-party sources.

Other Installation Methods   In medium to large organizations, more advanced installation methods are often employed, especially when many computers need to be identically configured. A common method is to place the source files in a shared directory on a network server. Then, whenever a tech needs to install a new OS, it is a simple task of booting up the computer, connecting to the source location on the network, and starting the installation from there. This method alone has many variations, and it can be automated with special scripts that automatically select the options and components needed. The scripts can even install the necessary applications at the end of the OS installation—all without user intervention once the installation has been started.

Another type of installation that is very popular for re-creating standard configurations is an image installation . An image is a complete copy of a hard disk volume on which an operating system and, usually, all required application software have been preinstalled. Images can be on CD-media, in which case the tech runs special software on the computer that copies the image onto the local hard drive. Images can also be stored on special network servers, in which case the tech connects to the image server using special software and copies the image from the server to the local hard drive. A leader in this technology has been Norton Ghost, which is available from Symantec. Other similar programs are PowerQuest's Drive Image and Acronis's True Image.

Beginning with Windows 2000 Server, Microsoft added *Remote Installation Services (RIS)*, which can be used to initiate either a scripted installation or an installation of an image.

Determine How to Back Up and Restore Existing Data, if Necessary

Whether you are installing or upgrading, you may need to back up existing user data before installing or upgrading because things can go very wrong either way, and the data on the hard drive might be damaged. You'll need to find out where the user is currently saving data files. If they are being saved onto the local hard drive, it must be backed up before the installation or replacement takes place, in order to preserve the data. However, if all data has been saved to a network location, you are in luck because the data is safe from damage during installation.

If the user saves data locally, and the computer is connected to a network, save the data, at least temporarily, to a network location until after the upgrade or installation has taken place. If the computer is not connected to a network, but the computer has a burnable CD-media or DVD drive, copy the data to CDs or DVDs. Wherever you save the data, you will need to copy or restore any lost or damaged data back to the local hard disk after the installation.

Select an Installation Method

Once you've backed up everything important, you need to select an installation method. You have two basic choices: insert the CD-ROM disc into the drive and go, or install over a network. The latter method falls into the realm of CompTIA Network+ technicians or even network administrators, so this book assumes you'll install from disc.

Determine How to Partition the Hard Drive and What File System to Use

If you are performing a clean installation, you need to decide ahead of time how to partition the disk space on your hard disk drive, including the number and size of partitions and the file system you will use. Actually, in the decision process, the file system comes first, and then the space issue follows, as you will see.

If you are not planning a multiboot installation, use NTFS. If you are planning a multiboot configuration, the highest common denominator rule applies, at least for the system volume, and for any volumes you want usable by the oldest OS. Once you know which file system you are using, deciding the size and number of partitions will follow, because if you decide to use FAT16, you will have the size limitations of FAT16 to deal with.

Determine Your Computer's Network Role

The question of your computer's network role comes up in one form or another during a Windows installation. A Windows computer can have one of several roles relative to a network (in Microsoft terms). One role, called *standalone*, is actually a non-network role, and it simply means that the computer does not participate on a network. Any version of Windows can be installed on a standalone computer, and this is the only role that a Windows XP Home computer can play on a network. Every other modern version of Windows can be a member of either a workgroup or domain.

Decide on Your Computer's Language and Locale Settings

These settings are especially important for Windows 2000 and Windows XP, because these versions have greatly increased support for various spoken languages and locale conventions. The locale settings determine how date and time information is displayed, and which math separators and currency symbols are used for various locations.

Plan for Post-Installation Tasks

After installing Windows, you will need to install the latest service pack or update. You may also need to install updated drivers and reconfigure any settings, such as network settings, that were found not to work. You will also need to install any applications (word processor, spreadsheet, database, etc.) required by the user of the computer. Finally, don't forget to restore any data backed up before the installation or upgrade.

Performing the Installation or Upgrade

When doing a Windows installation (also called setup) you'll notice that the screen progresses from simple textual information on a plain background to a full graphical interface. During text mode, the computer is inspecting the hardware, and it will then display the **End User License Agreement (EULA)**, which must be accepted for setup to continue. It is during the text display portion of an installation that you can partition your hard disk. Also during

Windows comes in both upgrade and full versions. Make sure you use the correct CD-ROM! Some systems, particularly laptops, require a special OEM version made just for that system. Don't bother trying to use an upgrade version to install on a blank drive unless you also possess a CD-ROM with a full earlier version of Windows.

this time, the computer copies files to the local hard disk, including a base set of files for running the graphical portion of the setup.

When finished with the text part of the setup, the computer reboots, which starts the graphical portion of the installation. You are prompted to enter the product key, which is invariably located on the CD/DVD case. Most techs learn the hard way that these covers tend to disappear when you need them most, and they write the product code directly on the CD or DVD itself. (Just don't use a ballpoint pen; it'll scratch the surface of the disc.) See Figure 11.13.

Most of the installation process takes place in the graphical portion. This is where you select configuration options and choose optional Windows components.

No matter your version of Windows, the installation process always gets to the point where Windows begins to install itself on the system. I call this "The Big Copy" and use this time to catch up on my reading, eat a sandwich, or count ceiling tiles.

Post-Installation Tasks

You might think that's enough work for one day, but there are a few more things on your task list. They include updating the OS with patches and service packs, upgrading drivers, restoring user data files, and identifying installation problems (if they occur).

Identifying Installation Problems

After you install or upgrade Windows, you only need to use your powers of observation to check whether you had a serious installation problem. The worst problems show up early in the installation process, but others may show up later as you work in Windows. If your installation wasn't successful, check out the last major section of this chapter ("Troubleshooting Installation Problems"), where I will tell you about common installation problems.

• **Figure 11.13**   Product key written on the installation CD-ROM

Mike Meyers' CompTIA A+ Guide: Essentials (Exam 220-601)

Patches, Service Packs, and Updates

Someone once described an airliner as consisting of millions of parts flying in close formation. I think that's also a good description for an operating system. And we can even carry that analogy further by thinking about all the maintenance required to keep an airliner safely flying. Like an airliner, the parts (programming code) of your OS were created by different people, and some parts may even have been contracted out. Although each component is tested as much as possible, and the assembled OS is also tested, it's not possible to test for every possible combination of events. Sometimes a piece is simply found to be defective. The fix for such a problem is a corrective program called a `patch` .

In the past, Microsoft would provide patches for individual problems. They would also accumulate patches until they reached some sort of "critical mass" and then bundle them together as a `service pack` . They still do this. But they also make it easier for you to find and install the appropriate patches and service packs, which, when combined together, are called *updates*. They make these updates available at their Web site or on CD-ROM. Many organizations make the updates available for distribution from network servers. Immediately after installing Windows, install the latest updates on the computer.

Upgrading Drivers

Even if you did all your preinstallation tasks, you may decide to go with the default drivers that come with Windows, and then upgrade them to the latest drivers after the fact. In fact, this is a good strategy, because installation is a complicated task, and you can simplify it by installing old but adequate drivers. Maybe those newest drivers are just a week old—waiting until after the Windows install to install new drivers will give you a usable driver to go back to if the new driver turns out to be a lemon.

Restoring User Data Files (if Applicable)

Remember when you backed up the user data files before installation? You don't? Well, check again, because now is the time to restore that data. Your method of restoring will depend on how you backed up the files in the first place. If you used a third-party backup program, you will need to install it before you can restore those files, but if you used Windows Backup, you are in luck, because it is installed by default. If you did something simpler, like copying to CD-media or a network location, all you have to do is copy the files back to the local hard disk. Good luck!

Installing or Upgrading to Windows 2000 Professional

On the face of it, installing Windows 2000 Professional seems fairly simple. You insert the CD-ROM, access the setup routine, and go! But that conceptualization does not hold up in practice.

Hardware Requirements

The minimum specs represent what Microsoft says you need in order to install the Windows 2000 Professional OS. However, you need to take these specifications and at least double them if you want to be happy with your system's performance!

Here is a more realistic recommendation for a useful Windows 2000 Professional computer system:

Component	Minimum for a Windows 2000 Professional Computer	Recommended for a Windows 2000 Professional Computer
CPU	Intel Pentium 133 MHz	Intel Pentium II 350 MHz
Memory	64 MB	128 MB
Hard disk	2 GB with 650 MB of free space	6.4 GB with 2 GB of free space
Network	None	Modern network card
Display	Video adapter and monitor with VGA resolution	Video adapter and monitor with SVGA resolution, capable of high-color (16-bit) display
Optical drive	If you don't have an optical drive, you must use a floppy disk drive or install over a network	If you don't have an optical drive, you must use a floppy disk drive or install over a network

If your test system(s) exceeds the recommended configuration, all the better! You can never have too fast a processor or too much hard disk space.

Installing or Upgrading to Windows XP Professional

You prepare for a Windows XP installation just as you do for installing Windows 2000. Windows XP has a few different aspects to it that are worth considering as a separate issue.

Upgrade Paths

You can upgrade to Windows XP Professional from all the following versions of Windows:

- Windows 98 (all versions)
- Windows Me
- Windows NT 4.0 Workstation (Service Pack 5 and later)
- Windows 2000 Professional (including service packs)
- Windows XP Home Edition

XP Hardware Requirements

Hardware requirements for Windows XP Professional are higher than for previous versions of Windows but quite in line with even a modestly priced computer today.

Microsoft XP runs on a wide range of computers, but you need to be sure that your computer meets the minimum hardware requirements as shown here. Also shown is my recommended minimum for a system running a typical selection of business productivity software.

Component	Minimum for a Windows XP Computer	Recommended for a Windows XP Computer
CPU	Any Intel or AMD 233 MHz or higher processor	Any Intel or AMD 300 MHz or higher processor
Memory	64 MB of RAM (though Microsoft admits XP will be somewhat crippled with only this amount)	256 MB of RAM or higher
Hard disk	1.5 GB of available hard drive space	4 GB of available hard drive space
Network	None	Modern network card
Display	Video card that supports DirectX 8 with at least 800 × 600 resolution	Video card that supports DirectX 8 with at least 800 × 600 resolution
Optical drive	Any CD- or DVD-media drive	Any CD- or DVD-media drive

Hardware and Software Compatibility

You'll need to check hardware and software compatibility before installing Windows XP Professional—either as an upgrade or a new installation. Of course, if you purchase a computer with Windows XP preinstalled, you're spared this task, but you'll still need to verify that the application software you plan to add to the computer will be compatible. Luckily, Microsoft includes the Upgrade Advisor on the Windows XP CD-ROM.

Upgrade Advisor In my experience, Windows XP has supported a wide range of hardware and software, including some rather old "no name" computers, but I like to be proactive when planning an installation, especially an upgrade. You may not have the luxury of time in upgrading a computer, however. You may be asked by your boss or client to perform an upgrade *now*. Fortunately, the Upgrade Advisor is the first process that runs on the XP installation CD-ROM. It examines your hardware and installed software (in the case of an upgrade) and provides a list of devices and software that are known to have issues with XP. Be sure to follow the suggestions on this list!

The Upgrade Advisor can also be run separately from the Windows XP installation. You can run it from the Windows XP CD-ROM, or, if you want to find out about compatibility for an upgrade before purchasing Windows XP, you can download the Upgrade Advisor from Microsoft's Web site (www.microsoft.com—search for "Upgrade Advisor"). Follow the instructions in the sidebar to use the online Upgrade Advisor.

I ran the advisor on a test computer at the office that was running Windows 98. It produced a report that found only one incompatibility—an antivirus program. The details stated that the program was compatible only if installed after Windows XP was installed. Therefore, it suggested removing

Try This!

Running the Upgrade Advisor

If you have a PC with Windows XP or an older version of Windows, you should know how to run the Upgrade Advisor on your system, so try this:

1. Insert the Windows XP CD-ROM. If Autorun is enabled, the Welcome to Microsoft Windows XP screen will appear. If this does not appear, select Start | Run, enter the following, and then click OK:

   ```
   d:\SETUP.EXE
   [Where d is the drive letter for the CD-media drive.]
   ```

2. At the Welcome to Microsoft Windows XP screen, select Check System Compatibility to start the Upgrade Advisor. On the following page select Check My System Automatically.

3. In the Upgrade Advisor dialog box, select the first choice if you have an Internet connection. If you don't have an Internet connection, select No, Skip This Step and Continue Installing Windows. (Don't worry, you aren't really going to install yet.)

4. Click Next. The Upgrade Advisor will show the tasks that Dynamic Update is performing, and then it will restart Setup.

5. After Setup restarts, you'll be back at the same page in the Upgrade Advisor. This time, select No, Skip This Step and Continue Installing Windows, and click Next. The Upgrade Report page appears next. You can save the information in a file by clicking Save As and selecting a location.

6. Read the findings that the Upgrade Advisor presents. If a problem was found, click the Full Details button for instructions, and be sure to follow them. When you have recorded any necessary instructions, click Finish.

the program before installing the OS, and then reinstalling it after the OS was installed. Don't ignore the instructions provided by the Upgrade Advisor!

Booting into Windows XP Setup

The Windows XP CD-ROMs are bootable, and Microsoft no longer includes a program to create a set of setup boot disks. This should not be an issue, because PCs manufactured in the last several years have the ability to boot from the optical drive. This system BIOS setting, usually described as "boot order," is controlled through a PC's BIOS-based setup program.

In the unlikely event that your lab computer can't be made to boot from CD-media, you can create a set of six (yes!) Windows XP setup boot floppy disks using a special program you can download from Microsoft's Web site. Note that Microsoft provides separate boot disk programs for XP Home and XP Pro.

Registration Versus Activation

During setup, you will be prompted to register your product and activate it. Many people confuse activation with registration, but these are two separate operations. **Registration** tells Microsoft who the official owner or user of the product is, providing contact information such as name, address, company, phone number, e-mail address, and so on. Registration is still entirely optional. Activation is a way to combat software piracy, meaning that Microsoft wishes to ensure that each license for Windows XP is used solely on a single computer. It's more formally called **Microsoft Product Activation (MPA)**.

Mandatory Activation Within 30 Days of Installation   Activation is mandatory, but you can skip this step during installation. You will have 30 days in which to activate the product, during which time it will work normally. If you don't activate it within that time frame, it will be disabled. Don't worry about forgetting, though, because once it's installed, Windows XP frequently reminds you to activate it with a balloon message over the tray area of the taskbar. The messages even tell you how many days you have left.

Activation Mechanics Here is how product activation works. When you choose to activate, either during setup or later when XP reminds you to do it, the product ID code that you entered during installation is combined with a 50-digit value that identifies your key hardware components to create an installation ID code. You must send this code to Microsoft, either automatically if you have an Internet connection, or verbally via a phone call to Microsoft. Microsoft then returns a 42-digit product activation code. If you are activating online, you don't have to enter the activation code; it will happen automatically. If you are activating over the phone, you must read the installation ID to a representative and enter the resulting 42-digit activation code into the Activate Windows by Phone dialog box.

No personal information about you is sent as part of the activation process. Figure 11.14 shows the dialog box that will open when you start activation by clicking on the reminder message balloon.

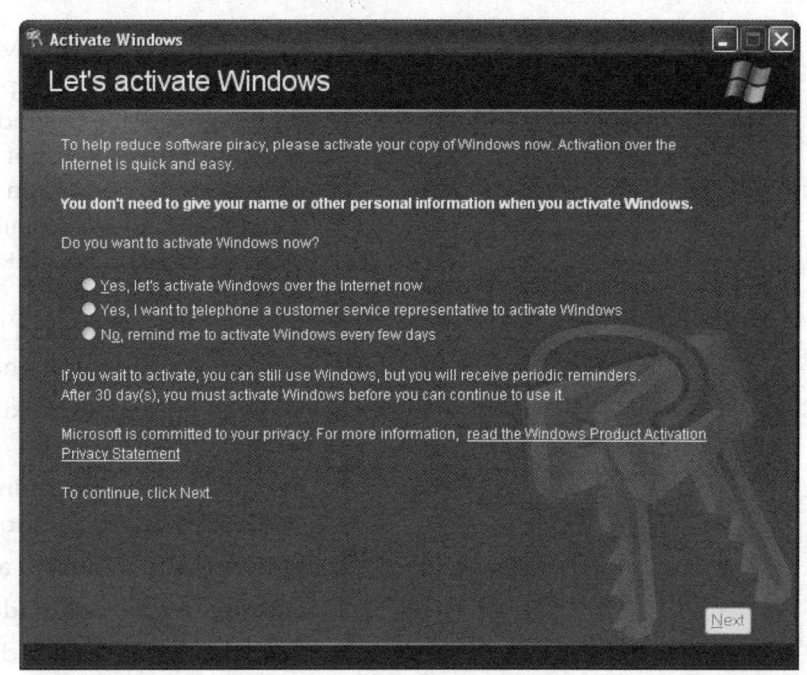

• **Figure 11.14** Activation will take just seconds with an Internet connection.

Upgrading Issues for Windows 2000 and Windows XP

Upgrading your computer system from an earlier version of Windows can be a tricky affair, with its own set of pitfalls. It is important to note that you have a somewhat higher risk of running into errors during an upgrade than you do when performing a "clean" installation.

Here are some of the issues that you should be aware of before performing an upgrade:

- You can upgrade directly to Windows 2000 Professional from Windows 95/98 (but not Windows Me) and Windows NT Workstation.

- Because of differences between Windows 9x and Windows 2000/XP, you might find that some programs that ran well under Windows 9x will not run under Windows 2000/XP. Not only does Windows 2000/XP have new hardware requirements, it also does not like a lot of Windows 9x software!

- Third-party disk compression applications are not supported by Windows 2000/XP.

- Third-party power management applications are also likely to cause problems with a Windows 2000/XP installation.

Obviously, it's worth your time to take a few extra steps before you pop in that installation CD-ROM! If you plan to upgrade rather than perform a clean installation, follow these steps first:

1. Check out the Windows Marketplace Web site or run a compatibility report using the Check Upgrade utility provided with Windows 2000 Professional or the Upgrade Advisor for Windows XP. These utilities generate a detailed list of potentially problematic devices and applications. You can run the utility in both 2000 and XP as follows: Insert the Windows Installation CD-ROM and, from your current OS, open a command prompt or use the Start Run dialog box to run the WINNT32.EXE program with the CHECKUPGRADEONLY switch turned on. The command line will look like this: `d:\i386\winnt32 / checkupgradeonly` (where `d:` is the optical drive).

2. Have an up-to-date backup of your data and configuration files handy.

3. Perform a "spring cleaning" on your system by uninstalling unused or unnecessary applications and deleting old files.

4. Perform a disk scan and a disk defragmentation.

5. Uncompress all files, folders, and partitions.

6. Perform a virus scan, and then remove or disable all virus-checking software.

7. Disable virus checking in your system CMOS.

8. Keep in mind that if worse comes to worst, you may have to start over and do a clean installation anyway. This makes step 2 exceedingly important! Back up your data!

Cross Check

Compare and Contrast

In this chapter you've learned the different installation procedures for Windows 2000 and Windows XP. It can be hard to keep them straight, but if you want to avoid being tricked on the CompTIA A+ exams, you must be able to! Review the procedures and then make sure you can identify the points of similarity and, more importantly, the differences among the two.

Not all screens in the install process are shown!

The Windows 2000/ XP Clean Install Process

The steps involved in a clean installation of Windows 2000 Professional and Windows XP are virtually identical. The only differences are the order of two steps and some of the art on the screens that appear, so we can comfortably discuss both installations at the same time.

A clean install begins with your system set to boot to your optical drive and the Windows Install CD-ROM in the drive. You start your PC, and assuming you've got the boot order right, the install program starts booting (Figure 11.15). Note at the bottom that it says to press F6 for a third-party SCSI or RAID driver. This is only done if you want to install Windows onto a strange drive and Windows does not already have the driver for that drive. Don't worry about this—Windows has a huge assortment of drivers for just about every hard drive ever made, and in the rare situation where you need a third-party driver, the folks who sell you the SCSI or RAID array will tell you ahead of time.

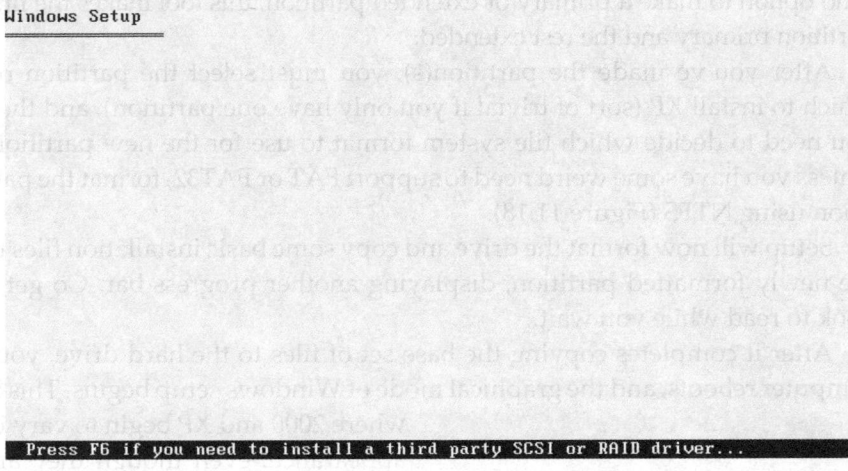

Press F6 if you need to install a third party SCSI or RAID driver...

• **Figure 11.15** Windows Setup text screen

After the system copies a number of files, you'll see the Welcome screen (Figure 11.16). This is an important screen! Techs often use the Windows installation CD-ROM as a repair tool, and this is the screen that lets you choose between installing Windows or repairing an existing installation. Since you're making a new installation, just press ENTER.

You're now prompted to read and accept the End User License Agreement (EULA). Nobody ever reads this—it just gives you a stomachache when you see what you're really agreeing to—so just press F8 and move to the next screen to start partitioning the drive (Figure 11.17).

If your hard disk is unpartitioned, you will need to create a new partition when prompted. Follow the instructions. In most cases, you can make a single partition, although you can easily make as many partitions as you wish. You can also delete partitions if you're using a hard drive that was partitioned in the past (or if you mess up your partitioning). Note that there

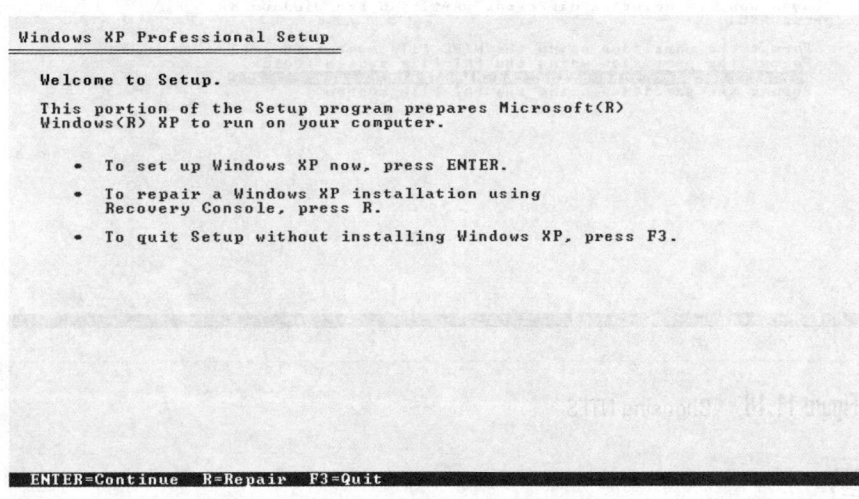

• **Figure 11.16** Welcome text screen

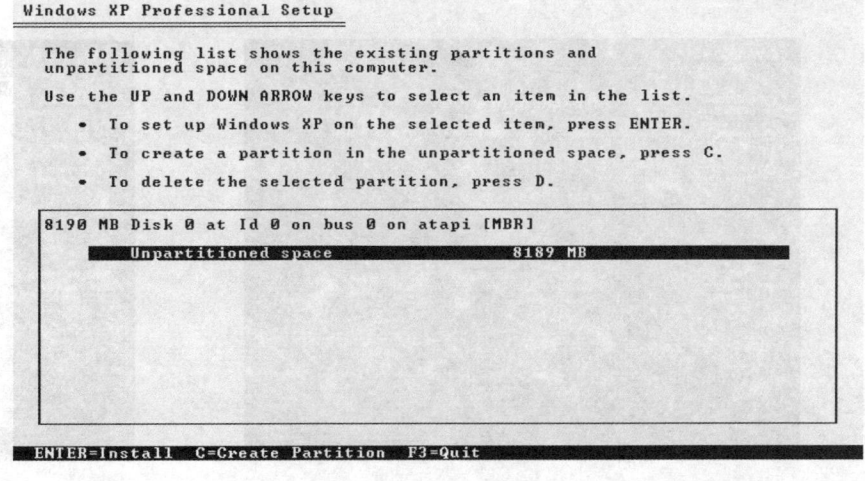

• **Figure 11.17** Partitioning text screen

Tech Tip

Save Some Space

Many techie types, at least those with big (> 100 GB) hard drives, will only partition half of their hard drive for Windows. This makes it easy for them to install an alternative OS (usually Linux) at a later date.

is no option to make a primary or extended partition; this tool makes the first partition primary and the rest extended.

After you've made the partition(s), you must select the partition on which to install XP (sort of trivial if you only have one partition), and then you need to decide which file system format to use for the new partition. Unless you have some weird need to support FAT or FAT32, format the partition using NTFS (Figure 11.18).

Setup will now format the drive and copy some basic installation files to the newly formatted partition, displaying another progress bar. Go get a book to read while you wait.

After it completes copying the base set of files to the hard drive, your computer reboots, and the graphical mode of Windows setup begins. This is where 2000 and XP begin to vary in appearance, even though they are performing the same steps. The rest of this section shows Windows XP. If you're running a Windows 2000 install, compare it to the screens you see here—it's interesting to see the different presentation doing the same job.

You will see a generic screen during the install that looks like Figure 11.19. On the left of the screen, uncompleted tasks have a white button, completed tasks have a green button, and the current task has a red button. You'll get plenty of advertising to read as you install.

The following screens ask questions about a number of things the computer needs to know. They include the desired region and language the computer will operate in, your name and organization for personalizing your computer, and a valid product key for Windows XP (Figure 11.20). Be sure to enter the product key exactly, or you will be unable to continue.

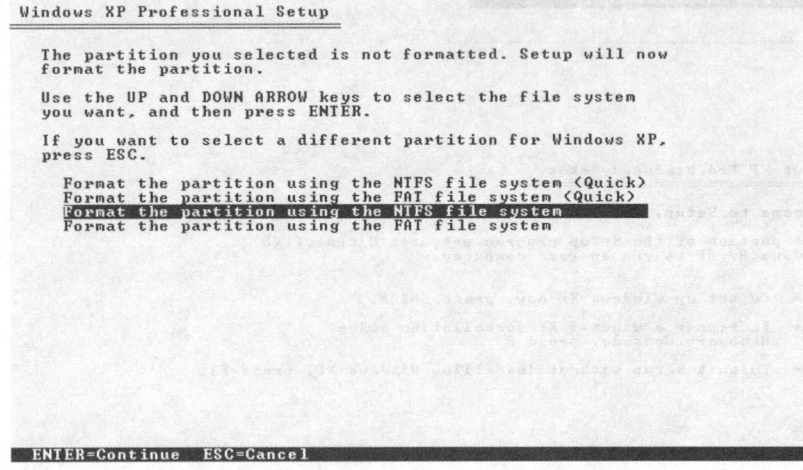

• **Figure 11.18**   Choosing NTFS

Losing your product key is a bad idea! Document it—at least write it on the install CD-ROM.

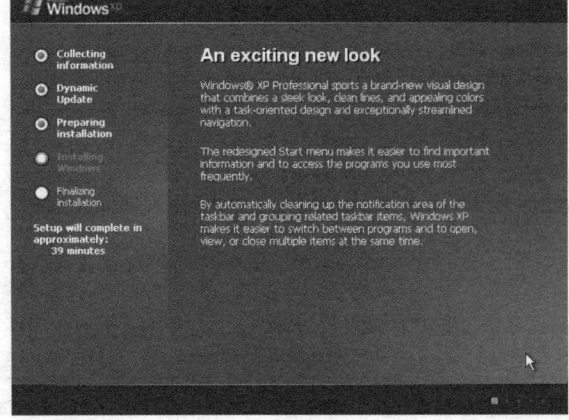

• **Figure 11.19**   Beginning of graphical mode   • **Figure 11.20**   Product key

Next, you need to give your computer a name that will identify it on a network. Check with your system administrator for an appropriate name. If you don't have a system administrator, just enter a simple name like MYPC for now—you can change this at any time—and read up on networking later in this book. You also need to create a password for the Administrator user account (Figure 11.21). Every Windows system has an Administrator user account that can do anything on the computer. Techs will need this account to modify and fix the computer in the future.

Last, you're asked for the correct date, time, and time zone. Then Windows tries to detect a network card. If a network card is detected, the network components will be installed and you'll have an opportunity to configure the network settings. Unless you know you need special settings for your network, just select the Typical Settings option (Figure 11.22). Relax; XP will do most of the work for you. Plus it's easy to change network settings after the installation.

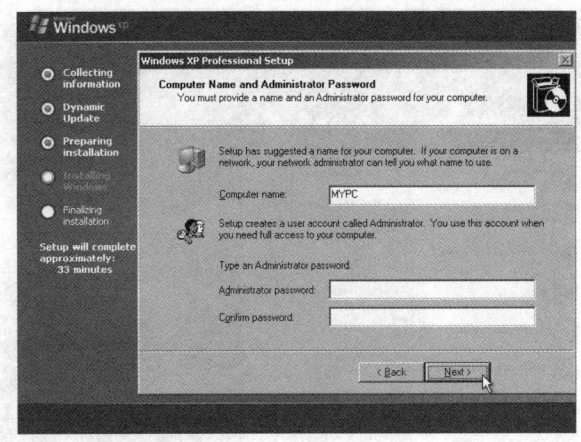

• **Figure 11.21**   Computer name and Administrator password

Even experienced techs usually select the Typical Settings option. Installation is not the time to be messing with network details unless you must.

Install now begins the big copy of files from the CD-ROM to your hard drive. This is a good time to pick your book back up, because watching the ads is boring (Figure 11.23).

After the files required for the final configuration are copied, XP will reboot again. During this reboot, XP determines your screen size and applies the appropriate resolution. This reboot can take several minutes to complete, so be patient.

Once the reboot is complete, you can log on as the Administrator. Balloon messages may appear over the tray area of the taskbar—a common message concerns the display resolution. Click the balloon and allow Windows XP to automatically adjust the display settings.

The final message in the installation process reminds you that you have 30 days left for activation. Go ahead and activate now over the Internet or by telephone. It's painless and quick. If you choose not to activate, simply click

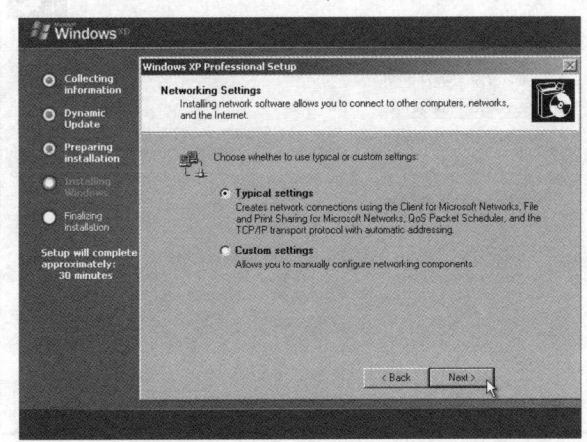

• **Figure 11.22**   Selecting typical network settings

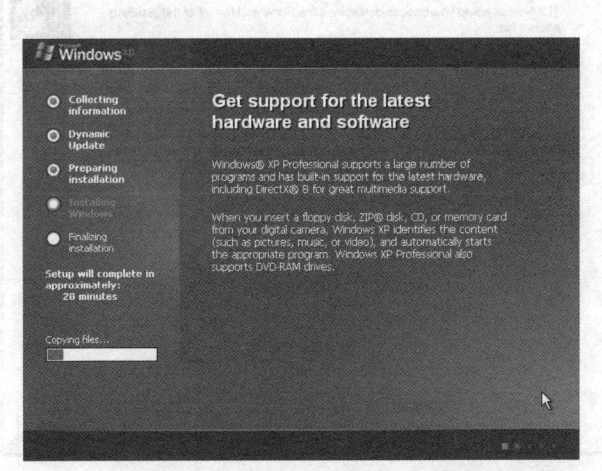

• **Figure 11.23**   The Big Copy

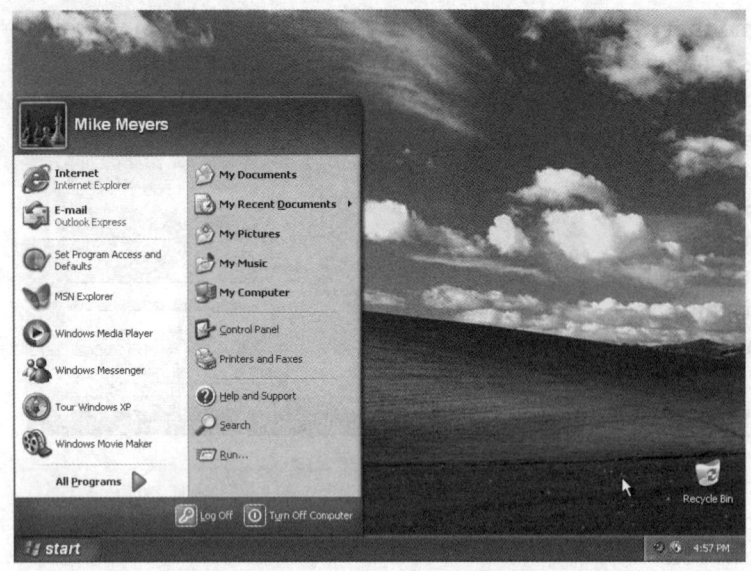

Figure 11.24 Windows XP desktop with Bliss background

the Close button on the message balloon. That's it! You have successfully installed Windows XP and should have a desktop with the default Bliss background, as shown in Figure 11.24.

Automating the Install

As you can see, you may have to sit around for quite a while. Instead of having to sit there answering questions and typing in CD keys, wouldn't it be nice just to boot up the machine and have the install process finish without any intervention on your part? Especially if you have 30 PCs that need to be ready to go tomorrow morning? Fortunately, Windows offers two good options for automating the install process: scripted installations and disk cloning.

Scripting Installations with Setup Manager

Microsoft provides *Setup Manager* to help you create a text file—called an *answer file*—containing all of your answers to the installation questions. Windows doesn't come with Setup Manager, but you can download it from the Microsoft Download Center (www.microsoft.com/downloads) as part of the Windows XP Service Pack 2 Deployment Tools. Setup Manager supports creating answer files for three different types of setups: unattended, sysprep, and Remote Installation Services (Figure 11.25). The current version of the tool create answer files for Windows XP Home Edition, Windows XP Professional, and Windows Server 2003 (Standard, Enterprise, or Web Edition). See Figure 11.26.

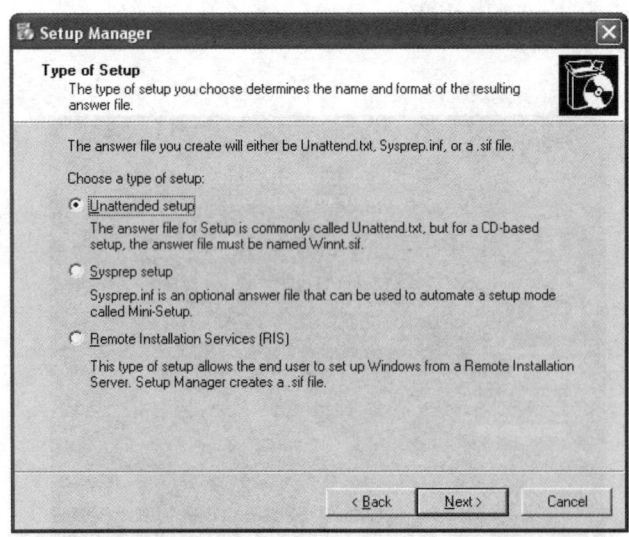

Figure 11.25 Setup Manager can create three different types of answer files.

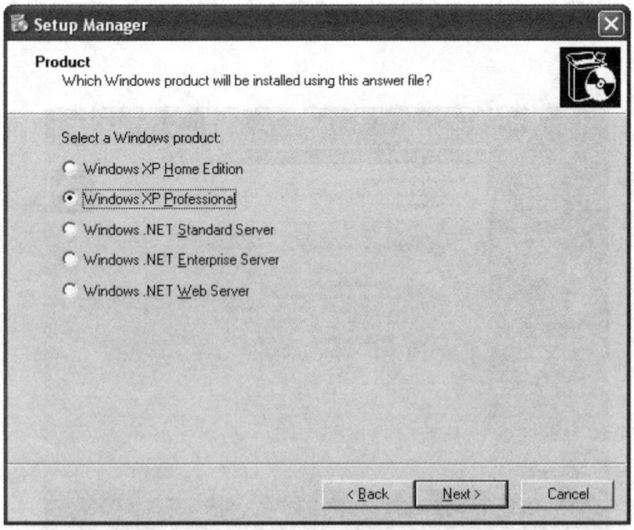

Figure 11.26 Setup Manager can create answer files for five different versions of Windows.

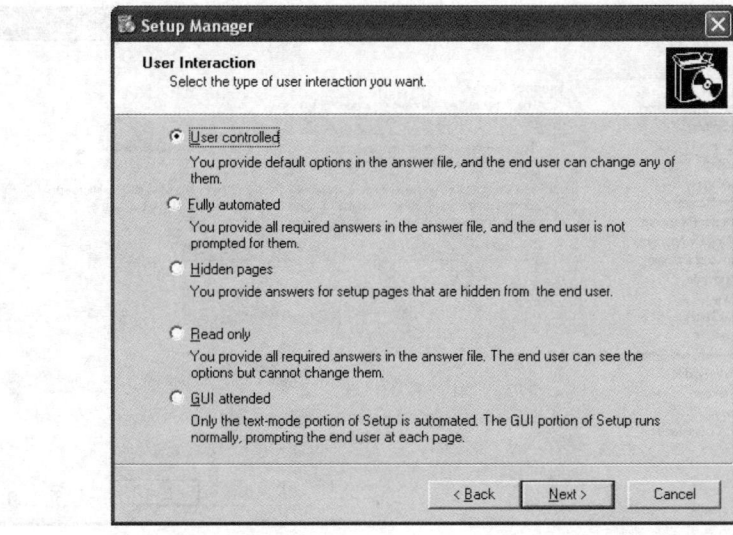

• **Figure 11.27**   Setup Manager can create several kinds of answer files.

Setup Manager can create an answer file to completely automate the process, or it can be used to set default options. You'll almost always want to create an answer file that automates the entire process (Figure 11.27).

When running a scripted install, you have to decide how to make the installation files themselves available to the PC. While you can always boot your new machine from an installation CD, you can save yourself a lot of CD swapping if you just put the install files on a network share and install your OS over the network (Figure 11.28).

When you run Setup Manager, you get to answer all those pesky questions. As always, you will also have to "Accept the Terms of the License Agreement" (Figure 11.29) and specify the product key (Figure 11.30), but at least by scripting these steps you can do it once and get it over with.

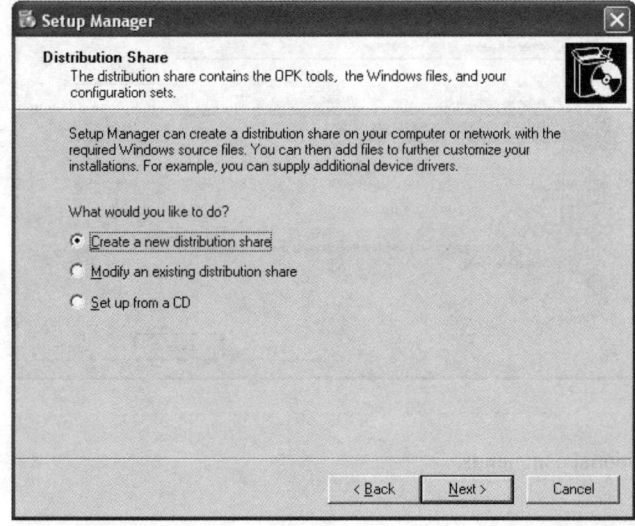

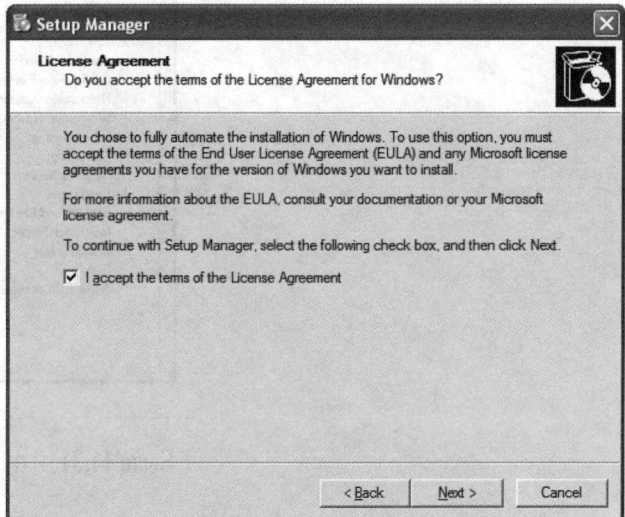

• **Figure 11.28**   Choose where to store the installation files.

• **Figure 11.29**   Don't forget to accept the license agreement!

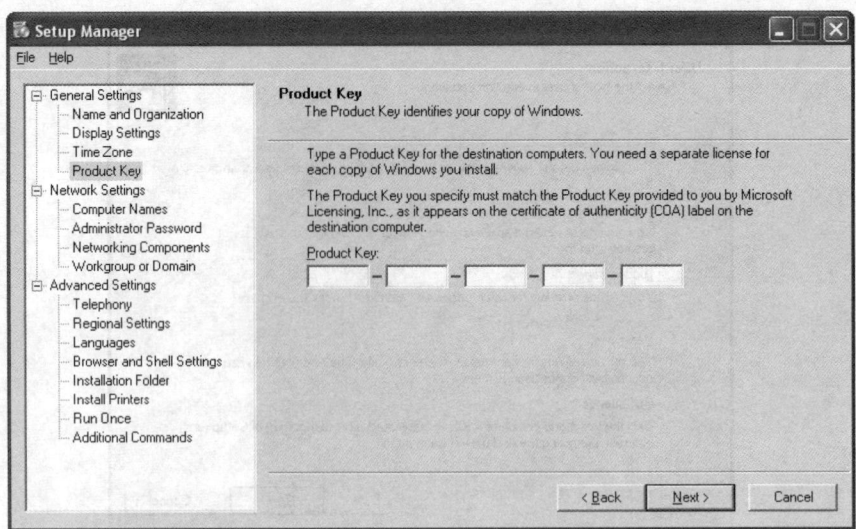

● **Figure 11.30**   Enter the product key.

Now it's time to get to the good stuff—customizing your installation. Using the graphical interface, decide what configuration options you want to use—screen resolutions, network options, browser settings, regional settings, and so on. You can even add finishing touches to the installation, installing additional programs such as Microsoft Office and Adobe Reader, by automatically running additional commands after the Windows installation finishes (Figure 11.31). You can also set programs to run once (Figure 11.32).

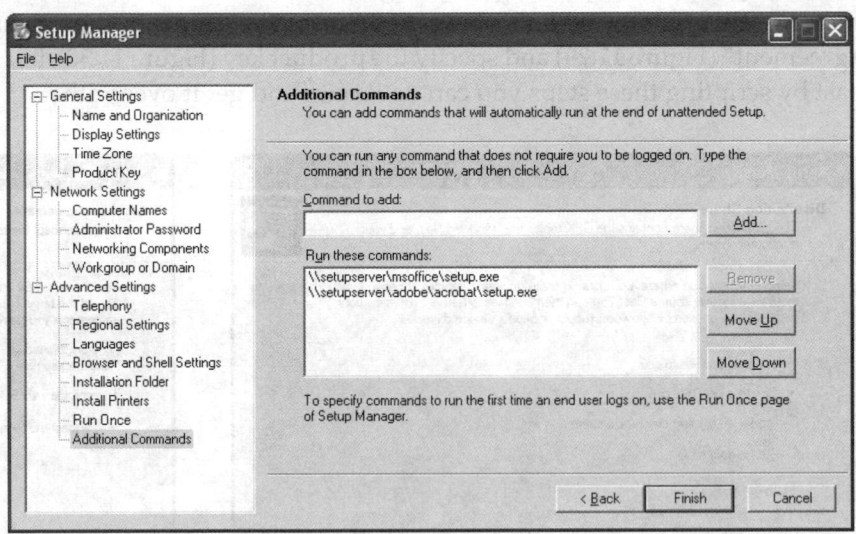

● **Figure 11.31**   Run additional commands.

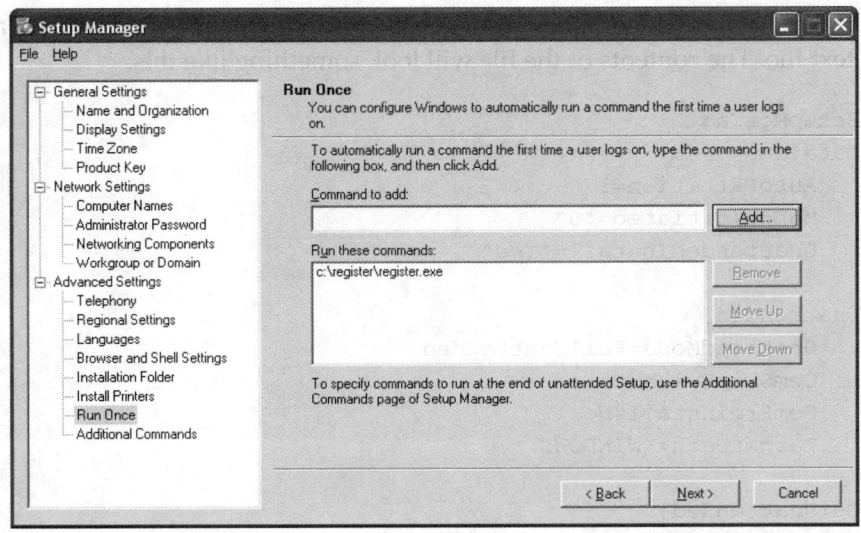

• **Figure 11.32**   Running a program once

Remember that computer names have to be unique on the network. If you're going to use the same answer files for multiple machines on the same network, you need to make sure that each one gets its own unique name. You can either provide a list of names to use, or you can have the setup program randomly generate names (Figure 11.33).

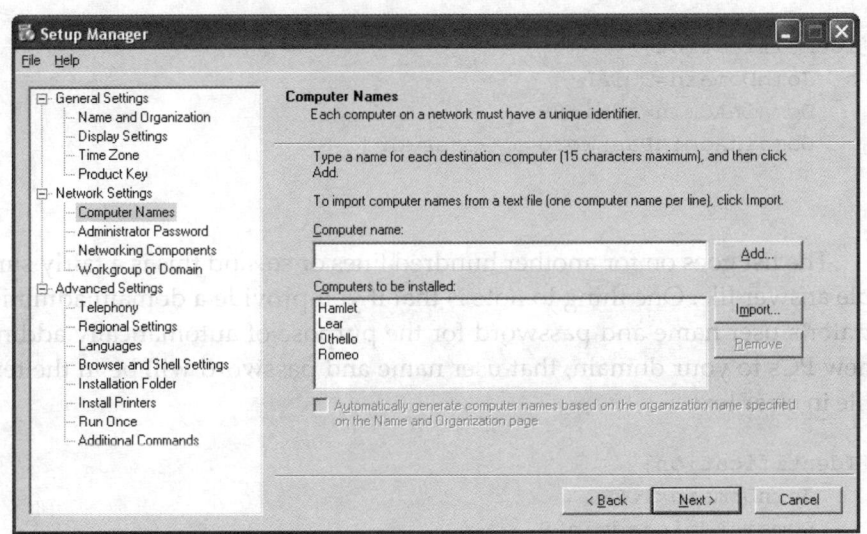

• **Figure 11.33**   Pick your computer names.

Chapter 11: Installing and Upgrading Windows

323

When you're done, Setup Manager prompts you to save your answers as a text file. The contents of the file will look something like this:

```
;SetupMgrTag
[Data]
    AutoPartition=1
    MsDosInitiated="0"
    UnattendedInstall="Yes"

[Unattended]
    UnattendMode=FullUnattended
    OemSkipEula=Yes
    OemPreinstall=No
    TargetPath=\WINDOWS

[GuiUnattended]
    AdminPassword=414c11f760b0064... [out to 64 characters]
    EncryptedAdminPassword=Yes
    OEMSkipRegional=1
    TimeZone=85
    OemSkipWelcome=1
    AutoLogon=Yes
    AutoLogonCount=1

[UserData]
    ProductKey=FFFFF-FFFFF-FFFFF-FFFFF-FFFFF
    FullName="Scott"
    OrgName="Total Seminars"
    ComputerName=*

[Identification]
    JoinDomain=TOTAL
    DomainAdmin=admin09
    DomainAdminPassword=my-password

[
```

The list goes on for another hundred lines or so, and this is a fairly simple answer file. One thing to note is that if you provide a domain administrator's user name and password for the purpose of automatically adding new PCs to your domain, that user name and password will be in the text file in clear text:

```
[Identification]
    JoinDomain=TOTAL
    DomainAdmin=admin09
    DomainAdminPassword=my-password
```

In that case, you will want to be very careful about protecting your setup files.

Once you have your answer file created, you can start your installation with this command, and go enjoy a nice cup of coffee while the installation runs:

```
D:\i386\winnt32 /s:%SetupFiles% /unattend:%AnswerFile%
```

For `%SetupFiles%`, substitute the location of your setup files—either a local path (`D:\i386` if you are installing from a CD) or a network path. If you use a network path, don't forget to create a network boot disk so that the install program can access the files. For `%AnswerFile%`, substitute the name of the text file that you created with Setup Manager (usually `unattend.txt`).

Of course, you don't have to use Setup Manager to create your answer file. Feel free to pull out your favorite text editor and write one from scratch. Most techs, however, will find it much easier to use the provided tool than to wrestle with the answer file's sometimes arcane syntax.

Scripted installations are a fine option, but they don't necessarily work well in all scenarios. Creating a fully scripted install, including the installation of all additional drivers, software updates, and applications, can be a time-consuming process involving lots of trial-and-error adjustments. Wouldn't it be easier, at least some of the time, to go ahead and take one PC, manually set it up exactly the way you want it, and then automatically create exact copies of that installation on other machines? That's where disk cloning comes into play.

Disk Cloning

Disk cloning simply takes an existing PC and makes a full copy of the drive, including all data, software, and configuration files. That copy can then be transferred to as many machines as you like, essentially creating "clones" of the original machine. In the old days, making a clone was pretty simple. You just hooked up two hard drives and copied the files from the original to the clone using something like the venerable XCOPY program (as long as the hard drive was formatted with FAT or FAT32). Today, you'll want to use a more sophisticated program, such as Norton Ghost, which enables you to make an image file that contains a copy of an entire hard drive, and then lets you copy that image either locally or over the network.

Windows complicates the process of cloning machines because each PC generates a unique security identifier, called the **SID**. Each PC must have its own SID, but if you clone a system, each clone will have the same SID, causing a variety of problems whenever two such machines interact over the network. After cloning a PC, you must somehow change the SID of each clone. The easiest way to do this is to use a utility such as Ghostwalker (included with Norton Ghost) or NewSID (available for download at www.microsoft .com/technet/sysinternals/Security/NewSid.mspx).

Sysprep

Cloning a Windows PC and changing its SID works great for some situations, but what if you need to send the same image out to machines that have slightly different hardware? What if you need the customer to go through the final steps of the Windows installation (creating a user account, accepting the license agreement, etc.)? That's when you need to combine a scripted setup and cloning by using the System Preparation Tool, **sysprep**, which can undo portions of the Windows installation process.

After installing Windows and adding any additional software (Microsoft Office, Adobe Acrobat, Yahoo Instant Messenger, etc.), run sysprep (Figure 11.34) and then create your disk image using the cloning

Tech Tip

Creating a Network-Aware Bootable Disc

If you need help creating a network boot floppy or CD, check out www.netbootdisk.com/ bootcd.htm.

Tech Tip

Slipstreaming

You can save time by modifying your installation files to include the latest patches by "slipstreaming" your installation files. See the following sites for instructions on how to merge (slipstream) Service Pack 2 into your Windows XP installation files:

www.helpwithwindows.com/ WindowsXP/ winxp-sp2-bootcd.html

www.winsupersite.com/ showcase/windowsxp_sp2_ slipstream.asp

Tech Tip

Ghosting

Norton Ghost is not the only disk imaging software out there, but it is so widely used that techs often refer to disk cloning as "ghosting the drive."

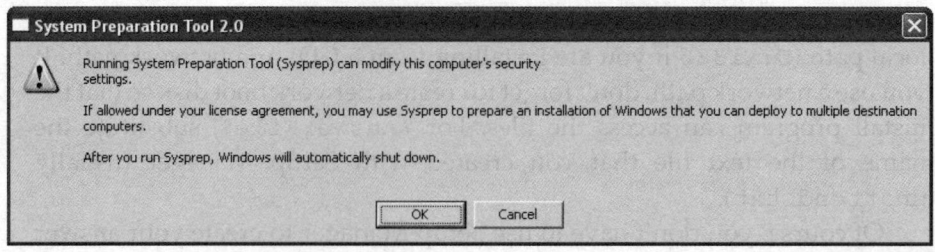

• **Figure 11.34** Sysprep, the System Preparation Tool

Tech Tip

RIS

Microsoft offers an even more advanced way of rolling out new systems: Remote Installation Services (RIS). *RIS requires Windows Server 2003 and is well beyond the scope of the CompTIA A+ exams.*

application of your choice. The first time a new system cloned from the image boots, an abbreviated version of setup, Mini-Setup, runs and completes the last few steps of the installation process: creating the new system's SID, installing drivers for hardware, prompting the user to accept the license agreement and create user accounts, and so on. Optionally, you can use Setup Manager to create an answer file to customize Mini-Setup, just as you would with a standard scripted install.

■ Troubleshooting Installation Problems

The term "installation problem" is rather deceptive. The installation process itself almost never fails. Usually, something else fails during the process that is generally interpreted as an "install failure." Let's look at some typical installation problems and how to correct them.

Text Mode Errors

If you're going to have an install problem, this is the place to get one. It's always better to have the error right off the bat, as opposed to when the installation is nearly complete. Text mode errors most often take place during clean installs and usually point to one of the following problems:

No Boot Device Present When Booting Off the Startup Disk

Either the startup disk is bad or the CMOS is not set to look at that disk drive first.

Windows Setup Requires XXXX Amount of Available Drive Space

You forgot to format the C: drive, or there's a bunch of stuff on the drive already.

Not Ready Error on Optical Drive

You probably just need to give the optical drive a moment to catch up. Press R for retry a few times. You may also have a damaged installation disc, or the optical drive may be too slow for the system.

A Stop Error (Blue Screen of Death) After the Reboot at the End of Text Mode

This is most common during a Windows 2000/XP installation and may mean that you didn't do your homework in checking hardware compatibility, especially the BIOS. If you encounter one of these errors during installation, check out the Microsoft Knowledge Base, especially article 165863, "Troubleshooting 'Stop 0x0A' Messages in Windows 2000 and Windows NT."

Graphical Mode Errors

Once the install passes the text mode and moves into graphical mode, a whole new crop of problems may arise.

Hardware Detection Errors

Failure to properly detect hardware by any version of Setup can be avoided by simply researching compatibility beforehand. Or, if you decided to skip that step, you might be lucky and only have a hardware detection error involving a non-critical hardware device. You can troubleshoot this problem at your leisure. In a sense, you are handing in your homework late, checking out compatibility and finding a proper driver after Windows is installed. Windows 2000 and Windows XP inherited the underpinnings of Windows NT. They all depend on the Setup program properly detecting the computer type (motherboard and BIOS stuff, in particular) and installing the correct hardware abstraction layer (HAL).

Can't Read CAB Files

This is probably the most common of all installation errors. **CAB (as in cabinet) files** are special compressed files, recognizable by their .cab file extension, that Microsoft uses to distribute copies of Windows. If your system can't read them, first check the CD-ROM for scratches. Then try copying all the files from the source directory on the CD (\i386) into a directory on your local hard drive. Then run Setup from there, remembering to use the correct program (WINNT32.EXE). If you can't read any of the files on the CD-ROM, you may have a defective drive.

Lockups During Install

Lockups are one of the most challenging problems that can take place during install, as they don't give you a clue as to what's causing the problem. Here are a few things to check if you get a lockup during install.

Smart Recovery, Repair Install

Most system lockups occur when Windows Setup queries the hardware. If a system locks up once during setup, turn off the computer—literally. Unplug the system! Do *not* press CTRL-ALT-DEL. Do *not* click Reset. Unplug it! Then turn the system back on, boot into Setup, and rerun the Setup program. Windows will see the partial installation and either restart the install process automatically (Smart Recovery) or prompt you for a "Repair Install." Both of these look at the installation progress and complete the installation.

Optical Drive, Hard Drive

Bad CD- or DVD-media discs, optical drives, or hard drives may cause lock-ups. Check the CD or DVD for scratches or dirt, and clean it up or replace it. Try a known good disc in the drive. If you get the same error, you may need to replace the drive.

Log Files

Windows generates a number of special text files called `log files` that track the progress of certain processes. While Windows creates a number of different log files for different purposes, two files most interest us:

- `SETUPLOG.TXT` tracks the complete installation process, logging the success or failure of file copying, Registry updates, reboots, and so on.

- `SETUPAPI.LOG` tracks each piece of hardware as it is installed. This is not an easy log file to read, as it uses Plug and Play code, but it will show you the last device installed before Windows locked up.

Windows 2000 and Windows XP store these log files in the WINNT or Windows directory (the location in which the OS is installed). These operating systems have powerful recovery options, so, honestly, the chances of your ever actually having to read a log file, understand it, and then get something fixed as a result of that understanding are pretty small. What makes log files handy is when you call Microsoft or a hardware manufacturer. They *love* to read these files, and they actually have people who understand them. Don't worry about trying to understand log files for the CompTIA A+ exams; just make sure you know the names of the log files and their location. Leave the details to the übergeeks.

No Installation Is Perfect

Even when the installation seems smooth, issues may slowly surface, especially in the case of upgrades. Be prepared to reinstall applications or deal with new functions that were absent in the previous OS. If things really fall apart, you can always go back to the previous OS.

The procedures I've laid out in this chapter may seem like a lot of work—how bad could it be to grab an installation CD-ROM, fling a copy of Windows onto a system, and as the saying goes, let the chips fall where they may? Plenty bad, is how bad. Not only is it important that you understand these procedures for the CompTIA A+ certification exams, they can save your, ah, hide, once you're a working PC tech and you're tasked to install the latest version of Windows on the boss's new computer!

Chapter 11 Review

■ Chapter Summary

After reading this chapter and completing the exercises, you should understand the following about installing and upgrading Windows.

Functions of the Operating System

■ An operating system (OS) is a program that performs four basic functions. First, it must communicate, or at least provide a method for other programs to communicate, with the hardware of the PC. Second, the OS must create a user interface—a visual representation of the computer on the monitor that makes sense to the people using the computer. Third, the OS, via the user interface, must enable users to determine the available installed programs and run, use, and shut down the program of their choice. Fourth, the OS should enable users to add, move, and delete the installed programs and data.

■ All operating systems share certain common traits. First, an OS works only with a particular type of processor. Second, an OS always starts running immediately after the PC has finished its POST, taking control of the PC until you reboot or turn off the PC. Third, application programs cannot run on a PC without an OS. Finally, an OS must have flexibility and provide some facility for using new software or hardware that might be installed.

■ The OS must work with the system BIOS to deal with the most basic and important parts of the computer: the hard drives, floppy disk and optical drives, keyboard, and basic video. Most OSs use device drivers to add programming necessary to take control of a new piece of hardware.

■ An OS must enable users to start a program. An OS must have some method of organizing the programs and data so users can access applications and store and access data.

■ Operating systems come in two basic varieties: command-line interface and graphical user interface. A command-line interface enables you to type commands directly to the OS. A GUI draws pictures on the screen with which you interact using a mouse or similar device.

■ Windows 2000 was basically Windows NT with several improvements, such as support for plug and play and an improved interface. Windows XP is based on Windows NT/2000 and supports the NTFS file system. There is no server version of Windows XP, but there are several workstation versions. Windows 2003 comes only in a server version. Windows Vista, a rewrite of Windows XP, offers many desktop improvements and comes in 32-bit and 64-bit versions.

■ Apple makes Macintosh computers, which run the Mac OS operating system. The latest version, Mac OS X, is a heavily customized version of UNIX.

■ UNIX is the oldest, most powerful, and most influential operating system ever invented. It was developed by Bell Labs in the early 1970s. Every popular operating system has borrowed from UNIX.

■ Linux is a UNIX clone partly named for its creator Linus Torvalds. It uses the GNU public license to make its code freely available to anyone who wants it. There are many versions of Linux, called distributions, freely available to download, install, and use.

Installing and Upgrading Windows

■ Identify hardware requirements, making sure that your computer meets the recommended minimums for CPU, RAM, free hard disk space, video adapter, display, and other components. Check the Windows Marketplace or the Windows Catalog at the Microsoft Web site to verify that the Windows version you're installing supports the hardware and application software you will run.

■ A clean OS installation takes place on a new hard drive or one that has been reformatted and repartitioned. You must reinstall all applications and reconfigure user preferences. In an upgrade installation, the new OS is installed in the directory where the old OS was located. The new OS retains the hardware and software settings of the old OS, including user preferences. Before you upgrade, back up any data that the user has saved on the local hard drive.

- Use the most advanced file system your version of Windows supports unless you are planning a multiboot configuration. In that case, you must use the highest common denominator for the system volume and any other volumes that the oldest OS will use. If you use FAT16, your partition size will be limited.

- A Windows installation starts in text mode, when it inspects the hardware and displays the End User License Agreement (EULA). During this portion of the install, you can partition the hard drive. After the computer copies the necessary files to the hard drive, it reboots into the graphical part of the installation and asks you to enter the product key.

- Post-installation tasks include updating the OS with patches and service packs, upgrading drivers, and restoring data files. You can get these corrective programs at the Microsoft Web site.

- Before you perform a Windows 2000 installation or upgrade, verify that your applications will run under the new OS, and use the Windows Marketplace to verify hardware compatibility. For adequate performance, your system should more than meet Microsoft's minimum system requirements.

- You can install Windows 2000 with floppy diskettes or CD-ROM. Windows XP does not create a set of setup boot disks and does not use a floppy disk by default. If you install from the CD, you must add an optical drive to your PC's boot sequence, and boot directly to the Windows 2000 or Windows XP CD-ROM. If this isn't possible in Windows XP, you can download a set of six setup boot floppy disks from the Microsoft Web site.

- During installation, you will be prompted for registration information, including your name, address, and other details. Registration is optional. Designed to prevent an XP license from being used for more than one PC, Microsoft Product Activation (MPA) is *mandatory* within 30 days of installation or the program will be disabled. You can activate the program using an Internet connection or by calling Microsoft. You give Microsoft an installation code—a 50-digit value that identifies your key hardware components—and Microsoft gives you a 42-digit product activation code.

- To do a clean install of Windows 2000/XP, boot the computer to the Windows CD-ROM, which will copy files to your hard drive. You then remove the CD-ROM, the system reboots, and Windows loads system devices and displays the Welcome to Setup screen. When prompted, accept the End User License Agreement (EULA). If necessary, create a new partition (default size or smaller). After you select the partition where Windows should be installed and the file system to use (NTFS is recommended), Setup copies files to the Windows folder and appropriate subfolders. Several reboots later and you're good to go.

Troubleshooting Installation Problems

- While the installation process itself rarely fails, you may encounter an installation failure caused by something else. Text mode errors during a clean install may range from "No Boot Device Present" (the startup disk is bad or CMOS is not set to look at the appropriate drive first), to "Drive C: does not contain a Valid FAT Partition" (there is no partition or a partition Windows cannot use), to insufficient space on the drive. If you get a "Not Ready Error on CD-ROM," it could mean you have a damaged installation disk or a slow CD-media drive that needs to catch up. A stop error (Blue Screen of Death) after the reboot at the end of the text mode points to a hardware incompatibility problem.

- Graphical mode errors indicate a different set of problems than text mode errors. Setup must be able to detect the computer type (especially the motherboard and BIOS) and install the correct Hardware Abstraction Layer (HAL). You may get a hardware detection error if Setup fails to detect a device. If it is a non-critical piece of hardware, you can work on this problem later. This error may be solved by finding the proper driver.

- Probably the most common installation problem is failure to read the compressed Windows OS distribution files called CAB files. Try copying these files to your local hard drive and running the Setup program from there.

- If the system locks up during installation, do *not* press CTRL-ALT-DEL or the Reset button to restart the installation. Instead, unplug the system and then turn it back on, so Windows will recognize a partial installation and go to the "Safe Recovery" mode where it can often complete the installation. A bad CD-ROM, optical drive, or hard drive can also cause a lockup.

- During installation, Windows creates several log files. The two files of interest are SETUPLOG.TXT, which tracks the installation process, logging success and failures, and SETUPAPI.LOG, which tracks each piece of hardware as it is installed and will show you the last device installed before Windows locked up. Windows 2000 and XP store these log files in the OS install directory (usually WINNT or Windows).

■ Key Terms

application program *(293)*
application programming interface (API) *(294)*
CAB files *(327)*
clean installation *(307)*
command-line interface *(297)*
disk cloning *(325)*
End User License Agreement (EULA) *(309)*
GNU general public license (GPL) *(303)*
graphical user interface (GUI) *(297)*

image installation *(308)*
Linux *(303)*
Linux distributions (distros) *(303)*
log files *(328)*
Mac OS X *(302)*
Microsoft Product Activation (MPA) *(314)*
multiboot installation *(307)*
operating system *(292)*
patch *(311)*
product key *(310)*
registration *(314)*

service pack *(311)*
SETUPAPI.LOG *(328)*
SETUPLOG.TXT *(328)*
SID *(325)*
sysprep *(325)*
UNIX *(303)*
Upgrade Advisor *(313)*
upgrade installation *(307)*
user interface *(295)*
Windows *(297)*
Windows Marketplace *(305)*

■ Key Term Quiz

Use the Key Terms list to complete the sentences that follow. Not all terms will be used.

1. If you do not complete the _____ within 30 days, Windows XP stops working.

2. If you have a new hard drive with nothing on it, you will likely choose to do a(n) _____.

3. A(n) _____ is a fix for a single problem with the OS while a(n) _____ is a combination of fixes.

4. If you wish to have only one OS and keep the applications and configuration of the current system, you should choose to do a(n) _____ of the new OS.

5. _____ are special compressed files that Microsoft uses to distribute copies of Windows.

6. _____ is the most recent operating system from Apple.

7. _____ is the oldest and most influential operating system around.

8. If you're not sure your system can support the new Windows XP, run the _____.

9. Windows creates _____ during the installation, which contains information about all installed hardware.

10. _____ is an operating system made freely available through the GNU general public license.

Multiple-Choice Quiz

1. Which of the following is an advantage of running Windows 2000 on NTFS as opposed to FAT32?

   A. Security

   B. Support for DOS applications

   C. Long filenames

   D. Network support

2. Ricardo's Windows XP installation has failed. What file should he check to see what files failed to copy?

   A. INSTALL.LOG

   B. SETUP.LOG

   C. SETUP.TXT

   D. SETUPLOG.TXT

3. If you do not complete the activation process for Windows XP, what will happen to your computer?

   A. Nothing. Activation is optional.

   B. The computer will work fine for 30 days and then Windows XP will be disabled.

   C. Microsoft will not know how to contact you to provide upgrade information.

   D. You will have to use a floppy disk set to boot to XP.

4. After you have completed a Windows installation and verified that the system starts and runs okay, what should you do next?

   A. Do nothing. You're through.

   B. Install World of Warcraft and enjoy.

   C. Install productivity applications and restore data.

   D. Install the latest service pack or update along with any updated drivers.

5. If Windows locks up during the installation, what should you do?

   A. Press CTRL-ALT-DEL to restart the installation process.

   B. Push the Reset button to restart the installation process.

   C. Press the ESC key to cancel the installation process.

   D. Unplug the computer and restart the installation process.

6. You can upgrade directly to Windows 2000 from which of these operating systems?

   A. Windows 3.11

   B. Windows 95

   C. Windows Me

   D. All of the above

7. If you get an error message saying that the Setup program cannot read the CAB files, what should you do?

   A. Copy the CAB files from the Windows installation CD-ROM to your local hard drive and run the Setup program from there.

   B. Skip this step since the CAB files are not necessary to install Windows successfully.

   C. Go to the Microsoft Web site and download the latest version of the CAB file wizard.

   D. Cancel the installation process and keep your old operating system, since your hardware does not meet the minimum requirements.

8. If you receive a graphical mode error saying that Windows failed to detect a non-critical piece of hardware, what should you do?

   A. You will need to remove the hardware device or replace it with one that is compatible with the OS.

   B. You can probably solve the problem after the installation is complete by finding the proper driver.

   C. You will get a "stop error" and be unable to complete the installation process.

   D. You should reboot the computer and restart the installation.

9. If you are not sure your Windows 98 system can support Windows XP, what should you do?

   A. Consult the Windows Catalog

   B. Consult the Windows Marketplace

   C. Run the XP Upgrade Advisor

   D. Install XP and hope for the best, since it will probably work

10. If you are experiencing problems with Windows Me and wish to install Windows XP, what type of installation is preferred?

    A. Clean install

    B. Upgrade install

C. Network install

D. Image install

11. Which list contains only operating systems?

    A. DOS, Windows 3.1, Windows XP

    B. Windows Me, Linux, UNIX

    C. OpenOffice, Internet Explorer, Microsoft Office

    D. Windows 2000, Microsoft Office, Mac OS X

12. Which operating system has both a workstation version and a server version?

    A. Windows 98

    B. Windows 2000

    C. Windows XP

    D. Windows 2003

13. When the text mode of Windows Setup completes and the computer reboots to continue in graphical mode, what must you enter to continue the installation?

A. Activation key

B. CPU ID

C. Registration information

D. Product key

14. The Norton Ghost software is most helpful with which method of installation?

    A. Clean installation

    B. Upgrade installation

    C. Network installation

    D. Image installation

15. Which setting affects the way currency and math separators display?

    A. Currency

    B. Language

    C. Locale

    D. Date/Time

Essay Quiz

1. You've been tasked to teach some new hires how to do a rollout of the latest version of Windows. Write a short essay that outlines what the newbies need to know to upgrade ten machines. You can assume that the network roles, language, and local settings will stay the same. Make an argument for a clean, upgrade, or multiboot installation. You can use Windows XP or, if you're feeling adventurous, Windows Vista. If you go for the latter, do a Web search for any special steps or procedures not included in this book. Check my Web site's Tech Files (www.totalsem.com) for information on Windows Vista installation.

2. The same group of newbies will need help with post-installation tasks, so write a second memo that tells them what to do after installing.

3. Your boss has decided to go higher tech on you and wants the next rollout of ten Windows machines to be automatic, rather than have techs sit through the whole process. Select one of the three methods outlined in this chapter for automating the installation process and make a case for one over the other two.

4. Your boss decided to upgrade his computer from Windows 2000 to Windows XP Professional, but Windows keeps crashing in the middle of the upgrade. Write a short note discussing what could be happening so you can walk him through the installation troubleshooting over the phone.

5. Apply the functions of a computer operating system to a device you might encounter in everyday life. For example, describe an automobile or a washing machine in terms of operating system functions. Be creative!

Lab Projects

• Lab Project 11.1

The chapter mentions a couple of alternative operating systems, including Mac OS X and Linux. Do an Internet search or a tour of your local PC superstore and compare the operating systems available. Are Mac OS X, Linux, and Windows the only operating systems out there?

• Lab Project 11.2

Search the Microsoft Knowledge Base for articles about "Stop Error 0x0A" during a Windows 2000 installation. (Hint: Use the Advanced Search feature!) Based on one of the articles you locate, prepare a five-minute report for the class about the cause of this error and the steps Microsoft recommends to solve it.

• Lab Project 11.3

You know that printers may work in Windows 2000 and not with Windows XP. Check the Windows Marketplace to determine whether the following printers are compatible with Windows XP:

- HP LaserJet 4100
- HP Photosmart 2000
- HP DeskJet 722C
- Epson Stylus Color 1160
- Canon LBP 660

If you have a different printer, check it also while you're looking at the Windows Marketplace.

Understanding Windows

"Technically, Windows is an 'operating system,' which means that it supplies your computer with the basic commands that it needs to suddenly, with no warning whatsoever, stop operating."

—DAVE BARRY

So, you've now got Windows installed and you're staring at the desktop. Pretty, eh? Well, as a tech, you need to understand Windows at a level that no regular user would dare. This chapter introduces you to and shows you the functions of some of the more powerful aspects of Windows, such as NTFS and the Registry. Not only must techs run through the standard Windows features that everyone uses every day (My Computer, Recycle Bin, and so on), they must also be comfortable drilling down underneath that user-friendly surface to get their hands a little dirty.

This chapter takes you through the Windows interface in detail, including the user interface, tech utilities, and folder structure. The second section looks in more detail at the techie aspects of Windows, including the structure of the OS, NTFS, and the boot process. The final short section runs through the many variations of Windows on the market today, going through the "Beyond A+" section to Windows Vista and non-desktop versions of Windows. Let's get started!

In this chapter, you will learn how to

- **Explain the Windows interface**
- **Identify the features and characteristics of Windows 2000 and Windows XP**
- **Describe the current versions of Windows**

■ The Windows Interface

All versions of Windows share certain characteristics, configuration files, and general look and feel. Here's some good news: you'll find the same, or nearly the same, utilities in almost all versions of Windows, and once you master one version—both GUI and command-line interface—you've pretty much got them all covered. This section covers the essentials: where to find things, how to maneuver, and what common utilities are available. Where versions of Windows differ in concept or detail, I'll point that out along the way. We'll get to the underlying structure of Windows in the subsequent two sections of this chapter. For now, let's look at the common user interface, tech-oriented utilities, and typical OS folders.

User Interface

Windows offers a set of utilities, or *interfaces,* that every user should know about—both how and why to access them. And since every user should know about them, certainly every CompTIA A+ certified tech should as well! Let's take a quick tour of the typical Windows GUI.

Login

Every version of Windows supports multiple users on a single machine, so the starting point for any tour of the Windows user interface starts with the *login screen.* Figure 12.1 shows a Windows 2000 login screen; Figure 12.2 shows a Windows XP login screen.

The login screen for Windows 9x/Me offered no security for the system—you could simply press ESC to bypass the screen and access the OS. Bowing to the home user's focus on convenience, Windows XP Home also allows users to access their accounts without requiring a login password, but by enabling password-protected individual user logins, the NT, 2000, and XP versions of Windows offer the security-conscious user a higher degree of security.

Desktop

The Windows `desktop` is your primary interface to the computer. It's always there, underneath whatever applications you have open. The desktop analogy appeals to most people—we're used to sitting down at a desk to get work done. Figure 12.3 shows a nice, clean Windows 2000 desktop; note the icons on the left and the various graphical elements across the bottom. You can add folders and files to the desktop, and customize the background to change its color or add a picture. Most people like to do so—certainly, I do! As an example, Figure 12.4 shows my desktop from my home system—a Windows XP PC.

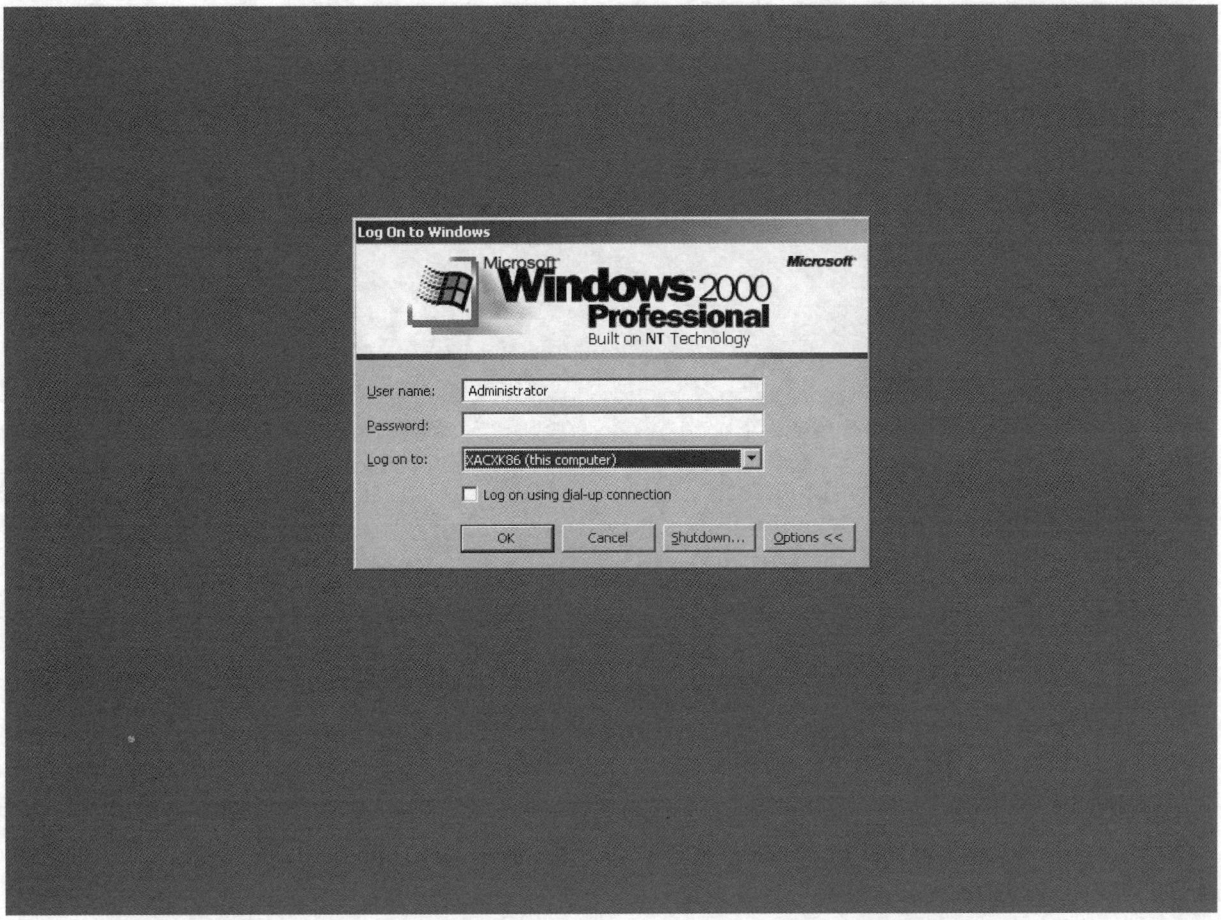

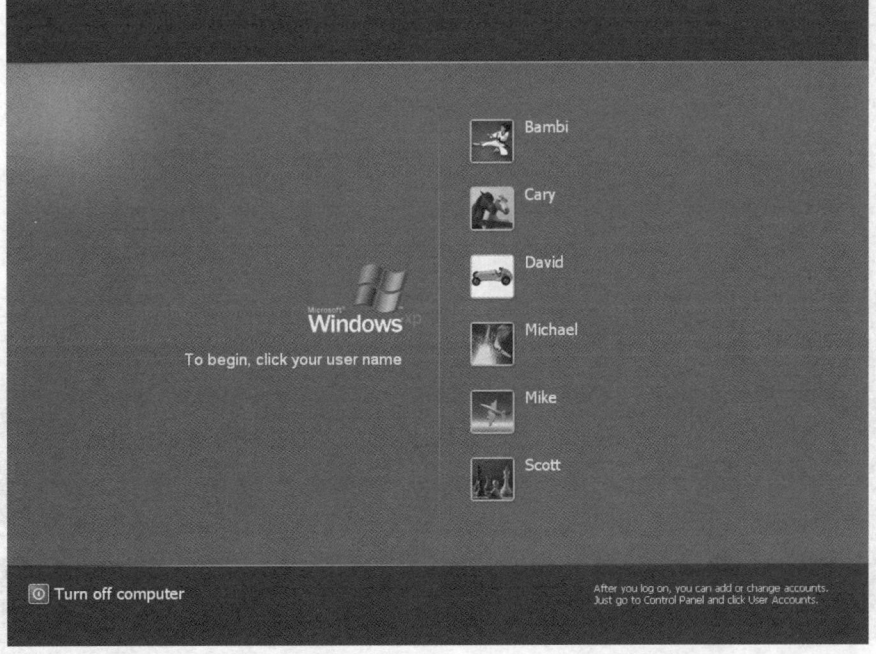

● **Figure 12.1**   Windows 2000 login screen

● **Figure 12.2**   Windows XP login screen

● **Figure 12.3** Windows 2000 desktop

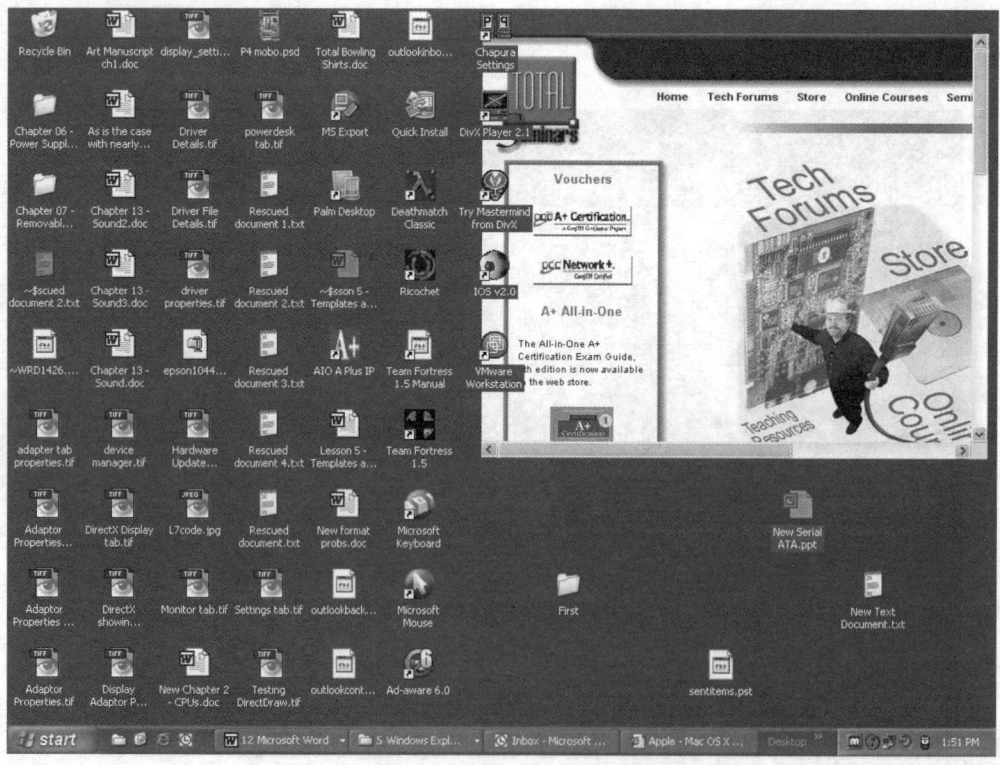

● **Figure 12.4** Mike's messy desktop

Taskbar and Start Menu

The taskbar runs along the bottom of all Windows desktops and includes up to four sections (depending on the version of Windows and your configuration). Starting at the left side, these are: the Start button, the Quick Launch toolbar, the running programs area, and the system tray. Although the taskbar by default sits at the bottom of the desktop, you can move it to either side or the top of the screen.

One of the main jobs of the taskbar is to show the Start button, probably the most clicked button on all Windows systems. You can find the Start button on the far left end of the taskbar (Figure 12.5). Click the Start button to bring up the Start menu, which enables you to see all programs loaded on the system and to start them. Now, move your mouse cursor onto All Programs. When the All Programs menu appears, move the cursor to the Accessories menu. Locate the Notepad program and click it, as shown in Figure 12.6. By default, Windows hides lesser-used menu options, so if you don't see Notepad, click the double down-arrows at the bottom of the Accessories menu. Notepad will then appear.

Great! If you opened Notepad properly, you should see something like Figure 12.7, with Notepad displaying an untitled text page. Notice how Notepad shows up on the taskbar at the bottom of the screen. Most running programs will appear on the taskbar in this way. Close the Notepad program by clicking on the button with the "X" in the upper-right corner of the Notepad window. Look again at the taskbar to see that Notepad no longer appears there.

Now look all the way to the right end of the taskbar. This part of the taskbar is known as the system tray. You will at a minimum see the current time displayed in the system tray, and on most Windows systems you'll also see a number of small icons. Figure 12.8 shows the system tray on my PC.

These icons show programs running in the background. You'll often see icons for network status, volume controls, battery state (on laptops), and PC Card status (also usually on laptops). What shows up on yours depends on your version of Windows, what hardware you use, and what programs you have loaded. For example, the icon at the far left in Figure 12.8 is my McAfee

• **Figure 12.6**   Opening Notepad in Windows XP

Tech Tip

General Rules of Clicking in Windows

You have a lot of clicking to do in this chapter, so take a moment to reflect on what I lovingly call the "General Rules of Clicking." With a few exceptions, these rules always apply, and they really help in manipulating the Windows interface to do whatever you need done:

- *Click menu items once to use them.*

- *Click icons once to select them.*

- *Click icons twice to use them.*

- *Right-click anything to see its properties.*

• **Figure 12.5**   Start button

Oddly enough, since Microsoft introduced the current Windows desktop, users and techs have called the area on the far right of the taskbar the *system tray*, but that's not the official name of that area. Microsoft calls the system tray the *notification area* in all documentation.

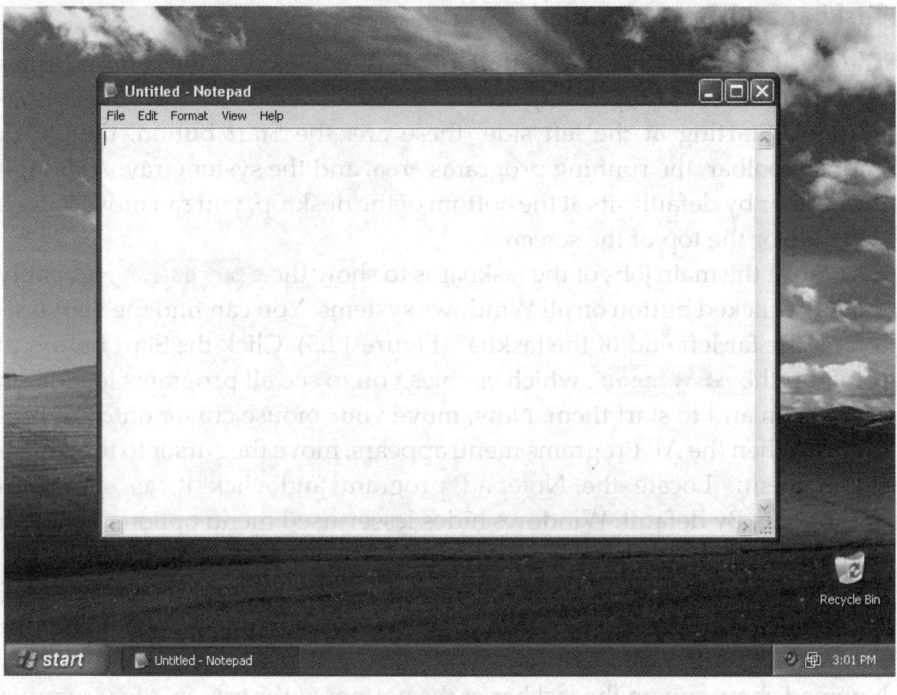

Figure 12.7 Notepad application (note the buttons in the upper-right corner)

Figure 12.8 System tray showing seven icons and the time

Figure 12.9 Quick Launch toolbar

Antivirus program, and the one at the far right is my UPS program, both humming away in the background protecting my precious data!

Near the left end of the taskbar, next to the Start button, you will find the **Quick Launch toolbar** (Figure 12.9). This handy extra enables you to select often-used programs with a single click. On Windows XP systems, the Quick Launch toolbar is not displayed on the taskbar by default, so before you can use this convenient feature, you must right-click the taskbar, select Properties, and check Show Quick Launch. To change the contents of the Quick Launch toolbar, simply drag icons onto or off of it.

My Computer

My Computer provides access to all drives, folders, and files on the system. To open My Computer, simply double-click the My Computer icon on the desktop. When you first open My Computer in Windows 2000, it displays all the drives on the system (Figure 12.10). Windows XP offers a more sophisticated My Computer, with all details and common tasks displayed in the left pane (Figure 12.11). Windows XP does not include My Computer on the desktop by default, but you can readily access it through the Start menu.

Note the interesting icons Windows XP gives for all the different devices on your computer! Most of these are storage devices, like the hard drive and optical drives—but what the heck is a scanner doing in there? The answer is that any program can add to the My Computer screen, and the folks who wrote the drivers for the scanner thought that it should go into My Computer.

340

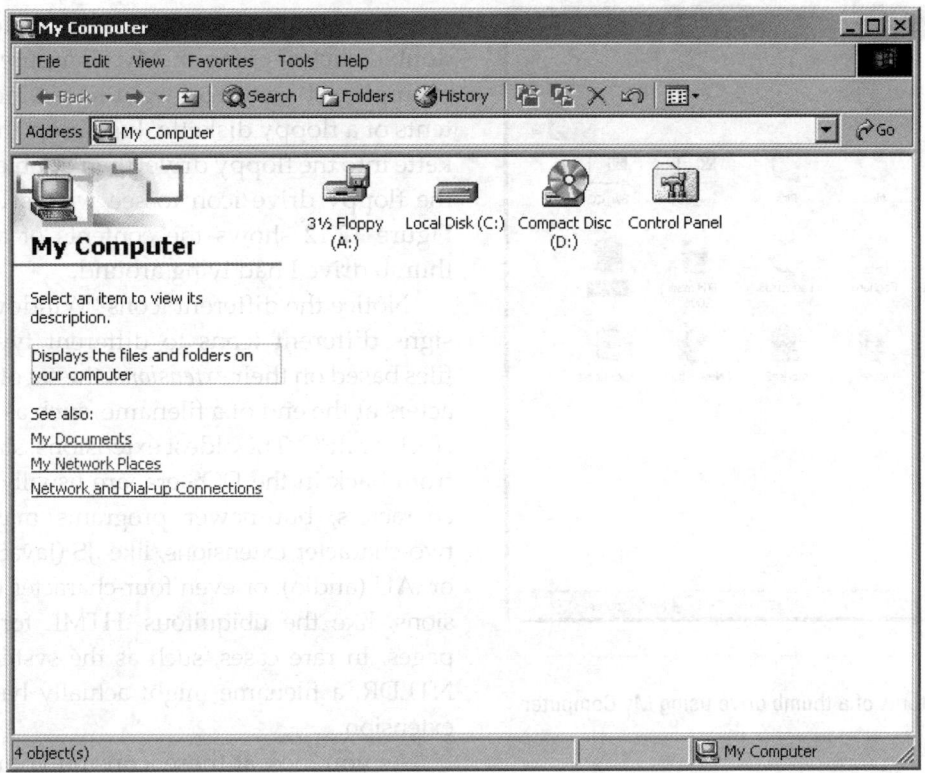

● **Figure 12.10** My Computer in Windows 2000

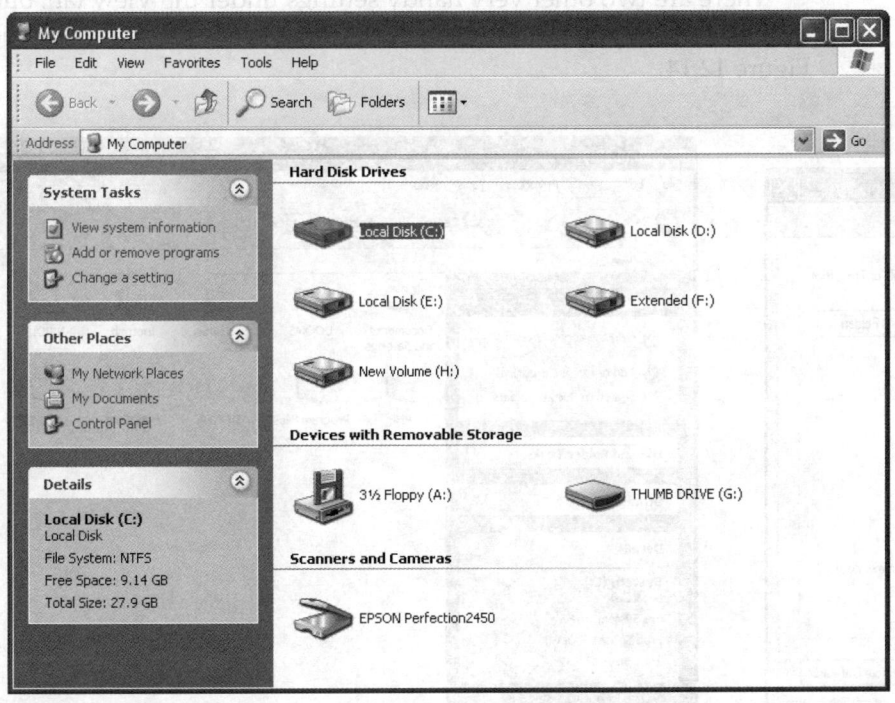

● **Figure 12.11** My Computer in Windows XP

Figure 12.12   Displaying the contents of a thumb drive using My Computer

To view the contents of any device, double-click its icon in My Computer. For example, let's say you want to see the contents of a floppy diskette. Just insert the diskette into the floppy drive, then double-click the floppy drive icon to see what's inside. Figure 12.12 shows the contents of a USB thumb drive I had lying around.

Notice the different icons? Windows assigns different icons to different types of files based on their *extensions*, the set of characters at the end of a filename, such as .EXE, .TXT, or .JPG. The oldest extensions, starting from back in the DOS era, are usually three characters, but newer programs may use two-character extensions, like .JS (JavaScript) or .AU (audio), or even four-character extensions, like the ubiquitous .HTML for Web pages. In rare cases, such as the system file NTLDR, a filename might actually have no extension.

As you look at these icons on your own screen, some of you might say, "But I don't see any extensions!" That's because Windows hides them by default. To see the extensions, select Tools | Folder Options to open the Folder Options dialog box (Figure 12.13). Click the View tab and uncheck *Hide extensions for known file types*.

There are two other very handy settings under the View tab, but to see the best results, you need to be in the C: drive of My Computer, as shown in Figure 12.14.

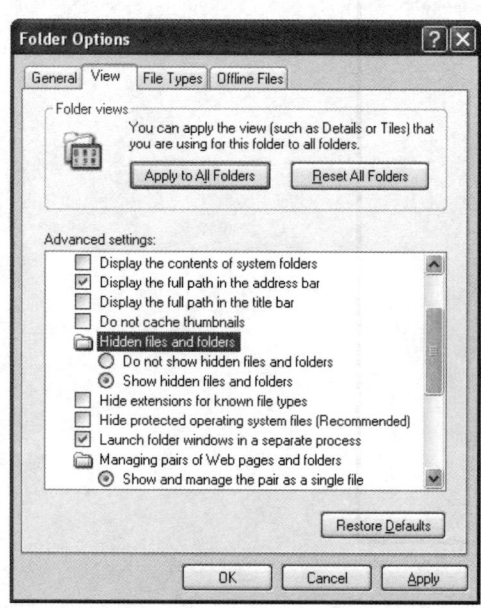

Figure 12.13   Folder Options dialog box

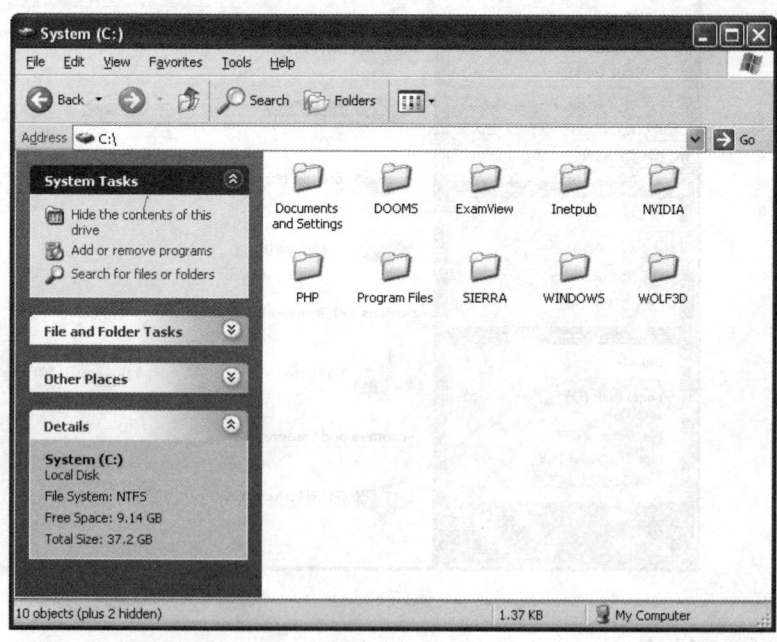

Figure 12.14   Default My Computer view

Go back into the View tab under Folder Options, click the *Show hidden files and folders* radio button, and then uncheck *Hide protected operating system files*. Click the Apply to All Folders button in Windows XP, or the Apply button (bottom right) in Windows 2000. Your C: drive should look like Figure 12.15 (it shows the Windows XP version) when you are done. As before, when you return to examining the folder contents, you will see the file extensions, and possibly some previously hidden files.

Now that those files are visible, you have the awesome responsibility of keeping them safe! In general, the less you handle your vital system files, the better. You'll learn some ways to do useful things with files that were previously hidden, but unless you really know what you're doing, it's best to leave them alone. Before you turn a PC over to someone who isn't a trained PC tech, you'll probably want to hide those system files again.

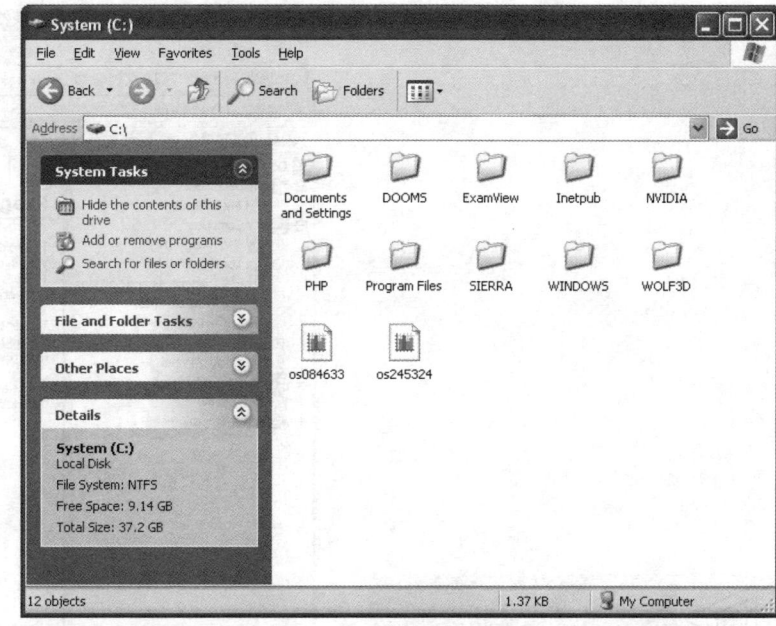

● **Figure 12.15**   My Computer displaying hidden files and folders

Windows Explorer

In every version of Windows prior to XP, **Windows Explorer** acts like a separate and distinct tool from My Computer, showing file and folder information in a double-paned fashion rather than all in a single pane (Figure 12.16). Windows XP merged the two into a single tool, but you can still get the Explorer-like interface by right-clicking a folder and selecting Explore from the options, or by clicking on the Folder button on the toolbar. Figure 12.17 shows My Computer exploring an important folder on my hard drive.

Try This!

My Computer

You should know how to get around your computer using the My Computer utility. Try this:

1. Open My Computer to look at the contents of your C: drive.

2. Pick any folder and open it. Does it contain folders as well as files? If not, find one that does. I suggest the Program Files folder.

3. When you find one, open a few of its subfolders. Keep drilling down through subfolders until you find one that contains only files.

4. Now that you can navigate through your hard drive using My Computer, close all the windows you opened.

My Documents, My [*Whatever*]

Windows provides a special folder called 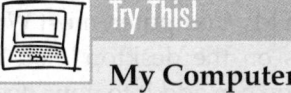. Early versions of Windows lacked a single location for users to place their files, and Microsoft discovered that users dumped their files all over the hard drive, and they often had trouble remembering where they'd put them! Microsoft recognized this issue and created My Documents as a central default storage area for all files created by applications. Many Windows programs, such as Office 2003, store their files in My Documents unless you explicitly tell them to use a different folder.

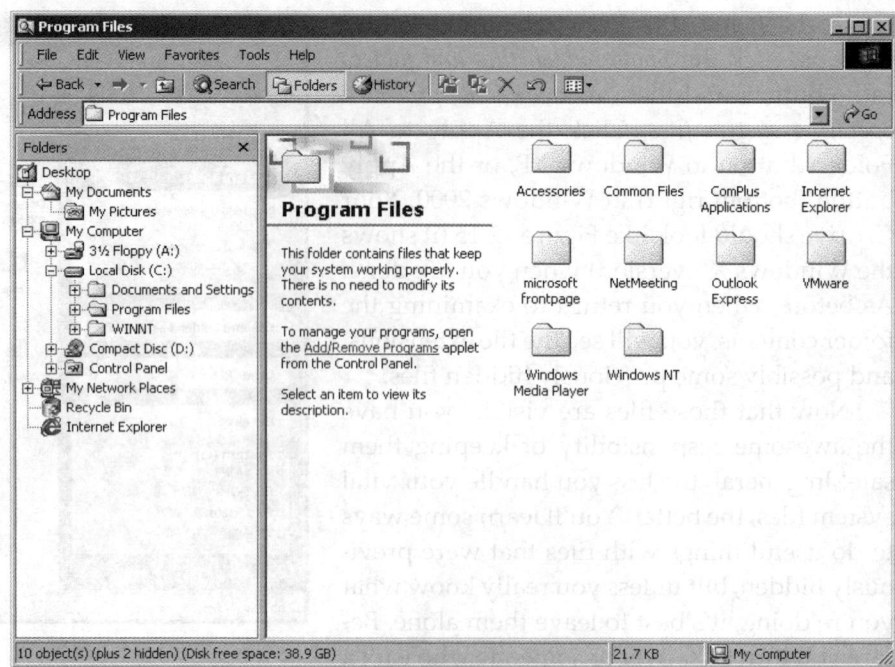

Figure 12.16 Windows Explorer in Windows 2000

Tech Tip

Right-Click Me!

As with most tools in Windows, Microsoft gives you more than one way to accomplish tasks. To make My Documents and other default folders appear on the desktop, you can right-click the icon in the Start menu and select Show on Desktop from the options. That's it!

As with My Computer, most Windows XP installations do not show My Documents on the desktop. You can access it readily through the Start menu, or you can add it to your desktop. Right-click the desktop and select Properties to open the Display Properties dialog box. Select the Desktop tab, and then click on the Customize Desktop button to open the Desktop Items dialog box (Figure 12.18). On the General tab, select the check box next to

Figure 12.17 My Computer in Windows XP masquerading as Windows Explorer

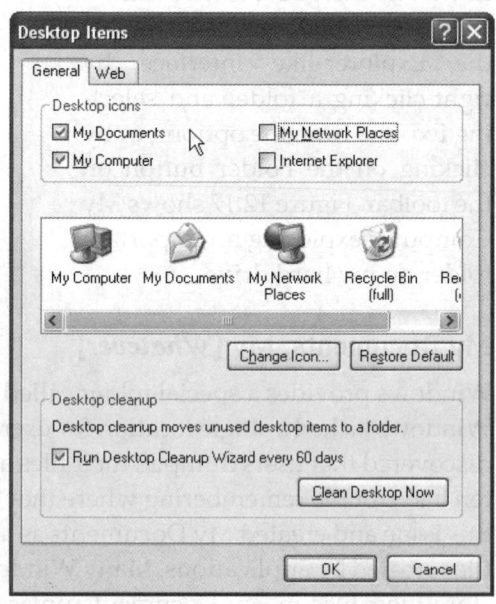

Figure 12.18 Desktop Items dialog box

344

My Documents, My Computer, or both, and then click OK to close the dialog box and make the icon(s) appear on the desktop.

Windows XP adds a number of subfolders to My Documents: My Pictures (which offers film-strip and thumbnail views of pictures you store there), My Music (which will fire up Media Player to play any file), My Videos (which, again, starts Media Player), and more. Figure 12.19 shows My Pictures, using thumbnail view. Many applications have since jumped on the bandwagon and added their own My [*Whatever*] folders in My Documents. On my PC right now, I have My eBooks, My Webs, My Received Files, My Virtual Machines…My Goodness!

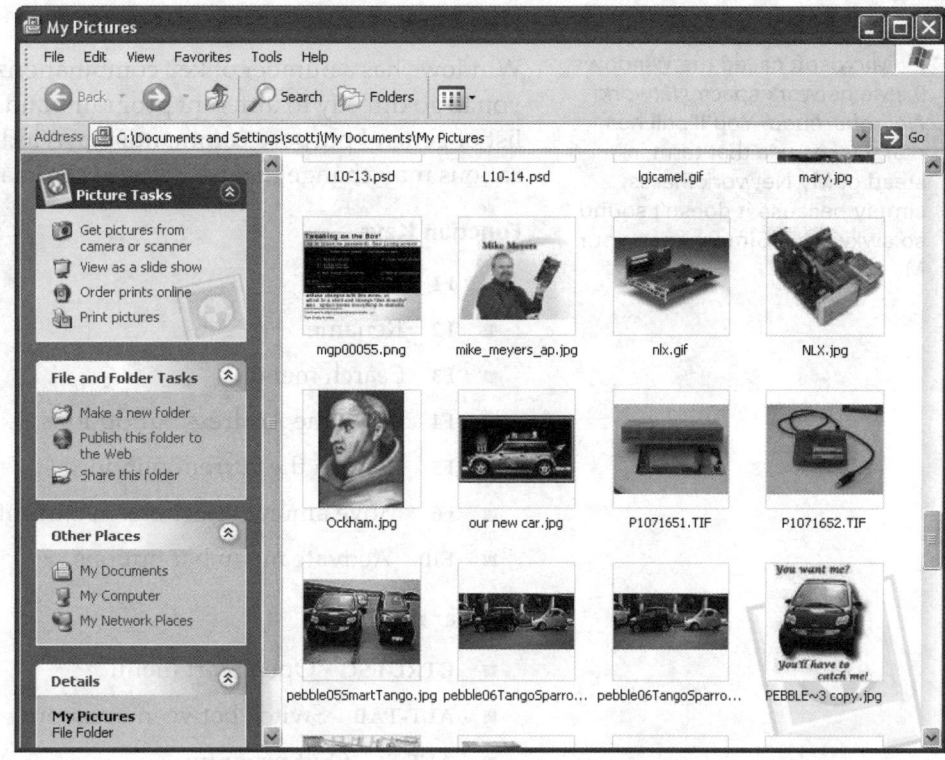

• **Figure 12.19** My Pictures subfolder in My Documents

Recycle Bin

In Windows, a file is not erased when you delete it. Windows adds a level of protection in the form of a special folder called the Recycle Bin . When you delete a file in Windows, it moves into the Recycle Bin. It stays there until you empty the Recycle Bin or restore the file, or until the Recycle Bin reaches a preset size and starts erasing its oldest contents.

To access its properties, right-click the Recycle Bin and select Properties. The Recycle Bin's properties look different in different versions of Windows, but they all work basically the same. Figure 12.20 shows the properties of a typical Windows XP Recycle Bin. Note that you set the amount of drive space to use for the Recycle Bin, 10 percent being the default amount. If a hard drive starts to run low on space, this is one of the first places to check!

My Network Places

Systems tied to a network, either via a network cable or by a modem, have a folder called My Network Places (see Figure 12.21). This shows all the current network connections available to you.

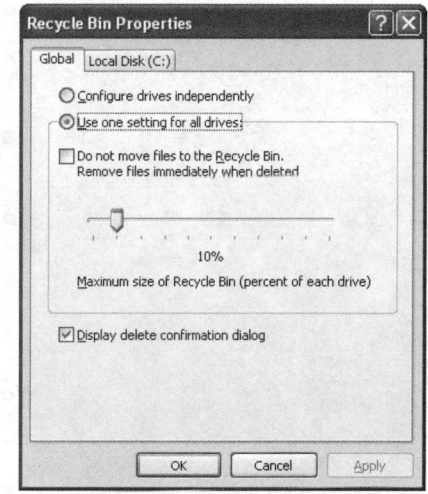

• **Figure 12.20** Windows XP Recycle Bin Properties

• **Figure 12.21** My Network Places in Windows XP

Microsoft called the Windows 9x/Me network space *Network Neighborhood.* You'll still hear many techs use that term instead of My Network Places, simply because it doesn't sound so awkward. "Simply open your My...."

Hot Keys

Windows has a number of key combinations—called hot keys—that enable you to go directly to different programs and places. Here's a fairly extensive list of general purpose commands for Windows. Be aware that some applications may change the use of these commands!

Function Keys

- **F1**   Help
- **F2**   Rename
- **F3**   Search menu
- **F4**   Open the Address Bar options
- **F5**   Refresh the current window
- **F6**   Move among selections in current windows
- **F10** Activate menu bar options

Popular Hot Keys

- **CTRL-ESC**   Open Start menu
- **ALT-TAB**   Switch between open programs
- **ALT-F4**   Quit program
- **CTRL-Z**   Undo the last command
- **CTRL-A**   Select all the items in the current window
- **SHIFT-DELETE**   Delete item permanently
- **SHIFT-F10**   Open a shortcut menu for the selected item (this is the same as right-clicking an object)
- **SHIFT**   Bypass the automatic-run feature for optical media (by pressing and holding down the SHIFT key while you insert optical media)
- **ALT-SPACE**   Display the main window's System menu (from this menu, you can restore, move, resize, minimize, maximize, or close the window)
- **ALT-ENTER**   Open the properties for the selected object

Working with Text

- **CTRL-C**   Copy
- **CTRL-X**   Cut
- **CTRL-V**   Paste
- **CTRL-Z**   Undo
- **CTRL-B**   Bold
- **CTRL-U**   Underline
- **CTRL-I**   Italic

Windows Key Shortcuts   These shortcuts use the special Windows key:

- **Windows key**   Start menu
- **Windows key-C**   Open the Control Panel

- **Windows key-D**   Show desktop
- **Windows key-E**   Windows Explorer
- **Windows key-F**   Search menu
- **Windows key-L**   Log off Windows
- **Windows key-P**   Start Print Manager
- **Windows key-R**   Run dialog box
- **Windows key-S**   Toggle CAPS LOCK
- **Windows key-V**   Open the Clipboard
- **Windows key-CTRL-F**   Find computer
- **Windows key-TAB**   Cycle through taskbar buttons
- **Windows key-BREAK**   Open the System Properties dialog box

I've covered only the most basic parts of the Windows desktop in this chapter. The typical Windows desktop will include many other parts, but for techs and for the CompTIA A+ certification exams, what you've learned here about the desktop is more than enough!

Tech Utilities

Windows offers a huge number of utilities that enable techs to configure the OS, optimize and tweak settings, install hardware, and more. The trick is to know where to go to find them. This section shows the six most common locations in Windows where you can go to access utilities: right-click, Control Panel, System Tools, command line, Administrative Tools, and the Microsoft Management Console. Note that these are locations for tools, not tools themselves, and many tools may be accessed from more than one of these locations. However, you'll see some of the utilities in many of these locations. Stay sharp in this section, as you'll need to access utilities to understand the inner workings of Windows in the next section.

Right-Click

Windows, being a graphical user interface OS, covers your monitor with windows, menus, icons, file lists—all kinds of pretty things you click on to get work done. Any single thing you see on your desktop is called an *object*. If you want to open any object in Windows, you double-click on it. If you want to change something about an object, you right-click on it.

Right-clicking on an object brings up a small menu, and it works on everything in Windows. In fact, try to place your mouse somewhere in Windows where right-clicking does *not* bring up a menu (there are a few places, but they're not easy to find). What you see on the little menu when you right-click varies dramatically, depending on the item you decide to right-click. If you right-click a running program in the running program area on the taskbar, you'll see items that relate to a window, such as move, resize, and so on (Figure 12.22). If you right-click on your desktop, you get options for changing the appearance of the desktop (Figure 12.23). Even different types of files will show different results when you right-click on them!

One menu item you'll see almost anywhere you right-click is Properties. Every object in Windows has properties. When you right-click on something and can't find what you're looking for, select Properties. Figure 12.24 shows the results of right-clicking on My Computer—not very exciting. But if you click Properties, you'll get a dialog box like the one shown in Figure 12.25.

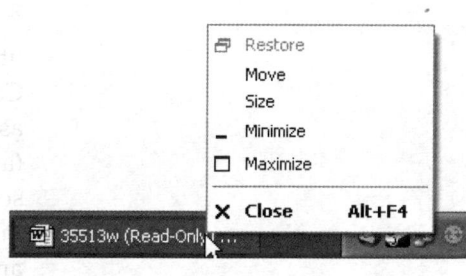

• **Figure 12.22**   Right-clicking on a program

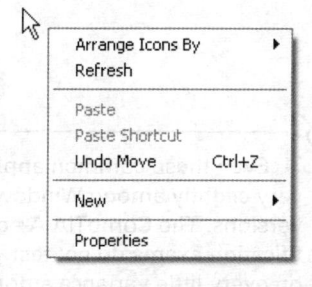

• **Figure 12.23**   Right-clicking on the desktop

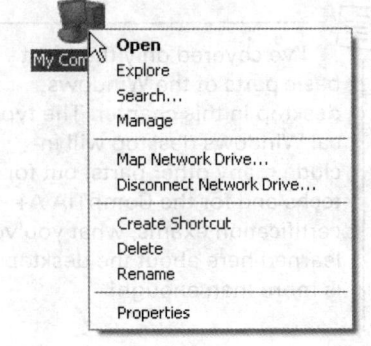

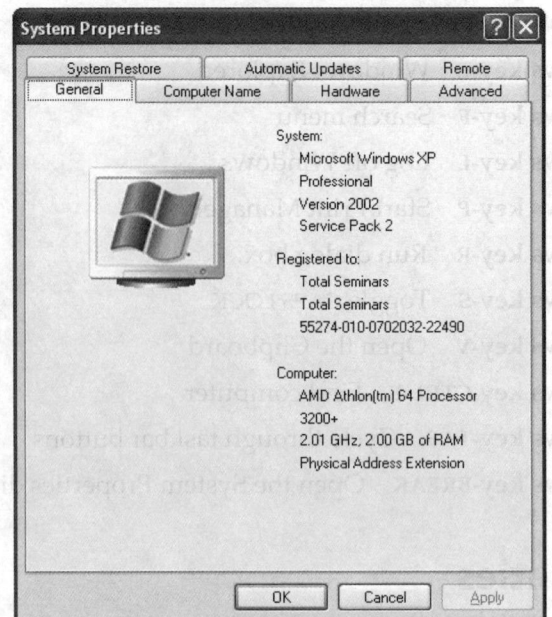

Figure 12.24 Right-clicking on My Computer

Figure 12.25 My Computer properties

Control Panel

The Control Panel handles most of the maintenance, upgrade, and configuration aspects of Windows. As such, the Control Panel is the first set of tools for every tech to explore. Select Start | Settings | Control Panel to open the Control Panel in Windows 2000. In Windows XP, it's a Start menu item.

The Control Panel in Windows 2000 opens in the traditional icon-littered view. In Windows XP and Vista, the Control Panel opens into the Category view, in which all the icons are grouped into broad categories such as "Printers and Other Hardware." This view requires an additional click (and sometimes a guess about which category includes the icon you need), so most techs use the Switch to Classic View link to get back to the icons. Figure 12.26 shows the Windows XP Control Panel in both Category (left) and Classic (right) views.

A large number of programs, called applets, populate the Control Panel. The names and selection of applets will vary depending on the version of Windows and whether any installed programs have added applets. But all versions of Windows share many of the same applets, including Display, Add or Remove Programs, and System—what I call the *Big Three* applets for techs. Display enables you to make changes to the look and feel of your Windows desktop, and to tweak your video settings. Add or Remove Programs enables you to add or remove programs. The System applet gives you access to essential system information and tools, such as the Device Manager.

Every icon you see in the Control Panel is actually a file with the extension .CPL, and any time you get an error opening the Control Panel, you can bet you have a corrupted CPL file. These are a pain to fix. You have to rename all of your CPL files with another extension (I use .CPB), and then rename them back to .CPL one at a time, each time reopening the Control Panel, until you find the CPL file that's causing the lockup.

Even these common applets vary slightly among Windows versions. The CompTIA A+ certification exams do not test you on every little variance among the same applets in different versions—just know what each applet does!

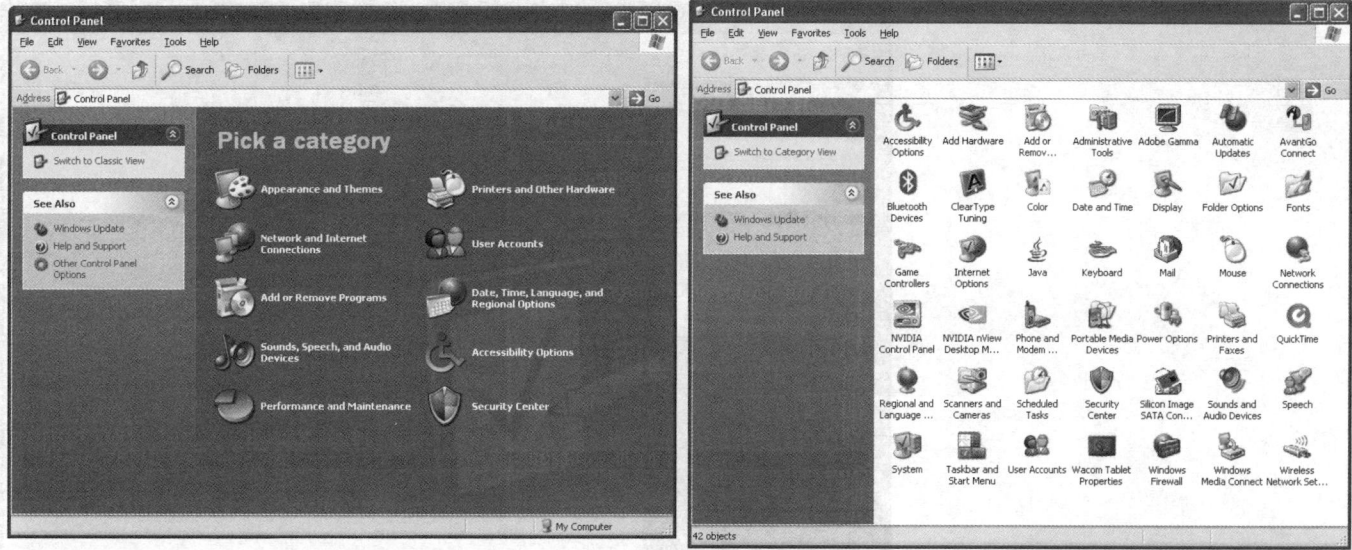

● Figure 12.26   Windows XP Control Panel—two views

The Control Panel applets enable you to do an amazing array of things to a Windows system, and each applet displays text that helps explain its functions. The Add Hardware applet (Figure 12.27), for example, says quite clearly, "Installs and troubleshoots hardware." They are all like that. Figure 12.28 shows the User Accounts applet. Can you determine its use? (If not, don't sweat it. I'll cover users in Chapter 13, "Maintaining Windows.") Each Control Panel applet relevant to the CompTIA A+ exams is discussed in detail in the relevant chapter.

Device Manager

The Device Manager enables techs to examine and configure all the hardware and drivers in a Windows PC. As you might suspect from that description, every tech spends a lot of time with this tool! You've seen it at work in several earlier chapters, and you'll work with the Device Manager many more times during the course of this book and your career as a PC tech.

There are many ways to get to the Device Manager—make sure you know all of them! The first way is to open the Control Panel and double-click the System applet icon. This brings up the System Properties dialog box. From here, you access the Device Manager by selecting the Hardware tab and then clicking the Device Manager button. Figure 12.29 shows the Hardware tab of the System Properties dialog box in Windows XP.

● Figure 12.27   Add Hardware Wizard of the Add Hardware applet

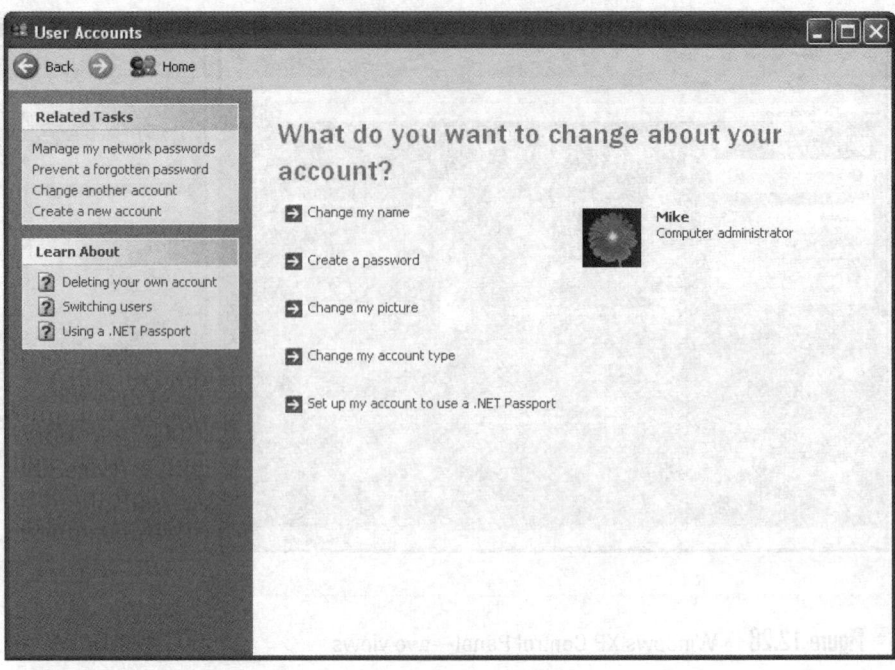

● Figure 12.28 User Accounts window of the User Accounts applet

Holding down the Windows
key and pressing the PAUSE key
is yet another way to get to the
System Properties dialog box.
Keyboard shortcuts are cool!

You can also get to the System Properties dialog box by right-clicking My Computer and selecting Properties. From there, the path to Device Manager is the same as when you access this dialog box from the Control Panel.

The second (and more streamlined) method is to right-click My Computer and select Manage (Figure 12.30). This opens a window called Computer Management, where you'll see Device Manager listed on the left side of the screen, under System Tools. Just click on Device Manager and it will open. You can also access Computer Management by opening the Administrative Tools applet in the Control Panel and then selecting Computer Management (Figure 12.31).

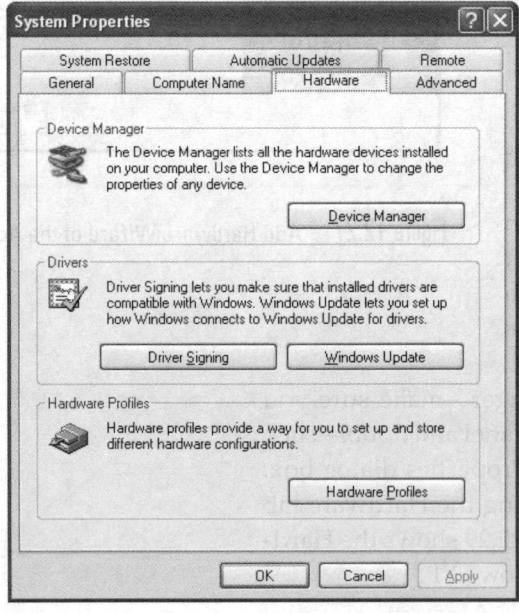

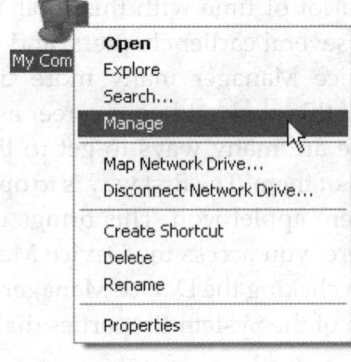

● Figure 12.29   Windows XP System applet with the
Hardware tab selected

● Figure 12.30   Right-clicking on My Computer to
select the Manage option

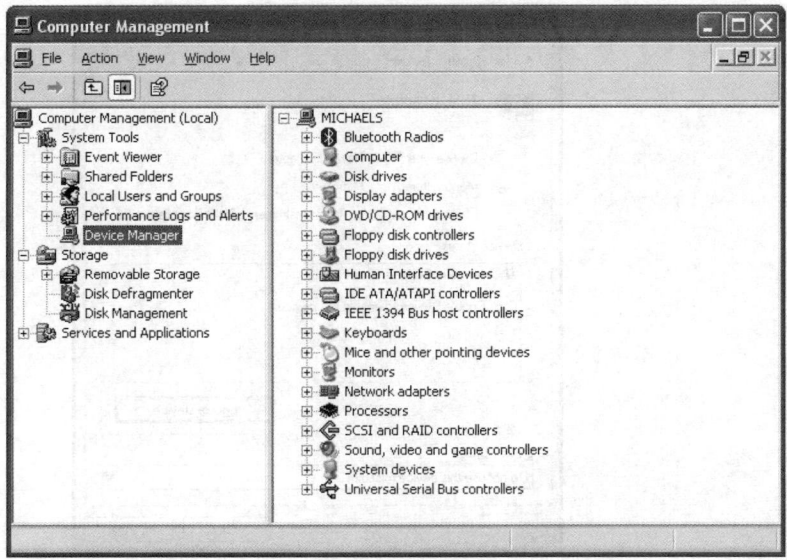

● **Figure 12.31** Device Manager in Computer Management

Why are there so many ways to open Device Manager? Well, remember that we're only looking at locations in Windows from which to open utilities, not at the actual utilities themselves. Windows wants you to get to the tools you need when you need them, and it's better to have multiple paths to a utility rather than just one.

The Device Manager displays every device that Windows recognizes, organized in special groups called *types*. All devices of the same type are grouped under the same type heading. To see the devices of a particular type, you must open that type's group. Figure 12.32 shows a typical Windows XP Device Manager screen with all installed devices in good order—which makes us techs happy. If Windows detects a problem, it shows the device with a red "X" or a yellow exclamation point, as in the case of the network adapter in Figure 12.33.

The red "X" means the device is disabled—right-click on the device to enable it. The tough one is the yellow exclamation point. If you see this, right-click on the device and select Properties; you'll see a dialog box like the one shown in Figure 12.34. Read the error code in the Device Status pane, and then look up Microsoft Knowledge Base article 310123 to see what to do. There are around 40 different errors—nobody bothers to memorize them!

The Device Manager isn't just for dealing with problems! It also enables you to update drivers with a simple click of the mouse (assuming you have a driver downloaded or on disc). Right-click a device and select Update Driver from the menu to get the process started. Figure 12.35 shows the options in Windows XP.

By double-clicking a device (or by selecting the device and clicking the Properties button) and then clicking the Resources tab, you can see the resources used by that device. Figure 12.36 shows the resources for an NVIDIA GeForce 7900 GT video card.

There is one other "problem" icon you might see on a device in Device Manager—a blue *i*. According to Microsoft, this means you turned off automatic configuration for a device. This is probably good to know for the exams, but you'll never see this error on a working machine unless you're intentionally messing with I/O address or IRQ settings for a device.

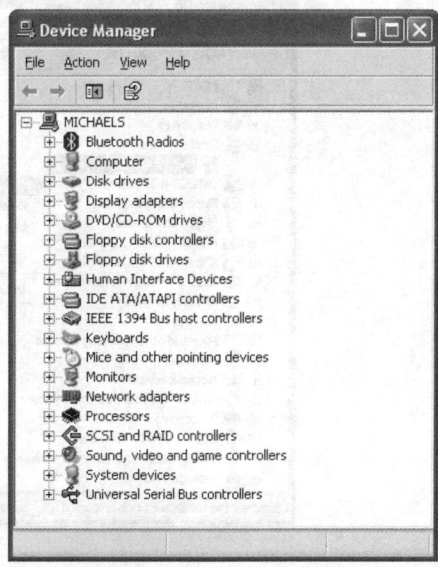

● **Figure 12.32** Happy Device Manager

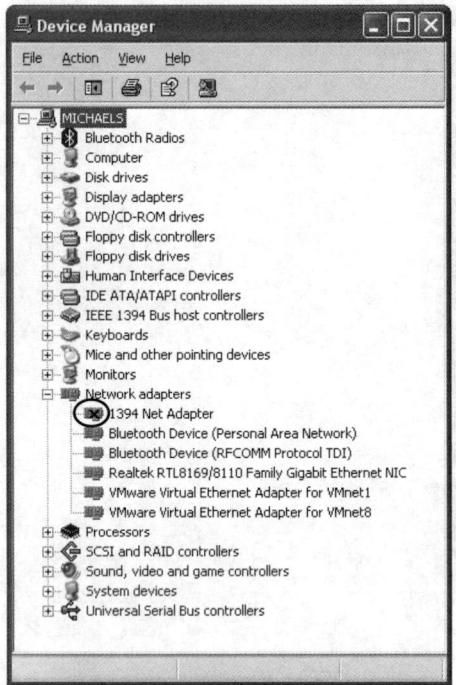

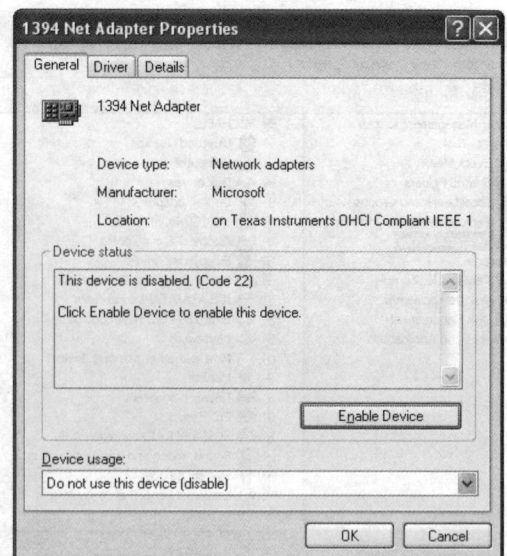

● **Figure 12.34** Problem device

● **Figure 12.33** Sad Device Manager

Make sure you can get to Device Manager! You will come back to it again and again in subsequent chapters, because it is the first tool you should access when you have a hardware problem.

System Tools

The Start menu offers a variety of tech utilities collected in one place: select Start | Programs | Accessories | System Tools. In the **System Tools** menu,

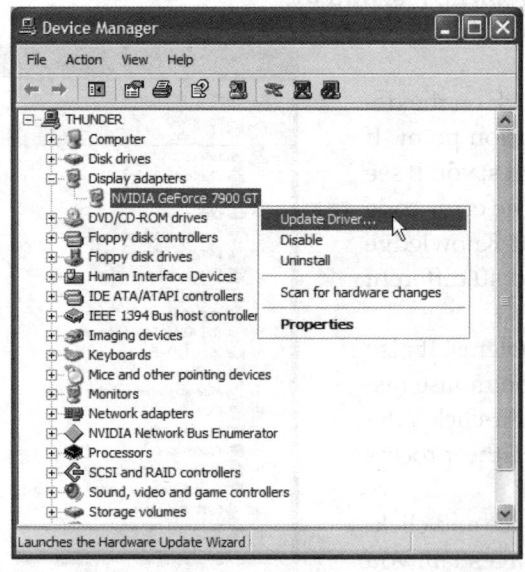

● **Figure 12.35** Selecting Update Driver in the Windows XP Device Manager

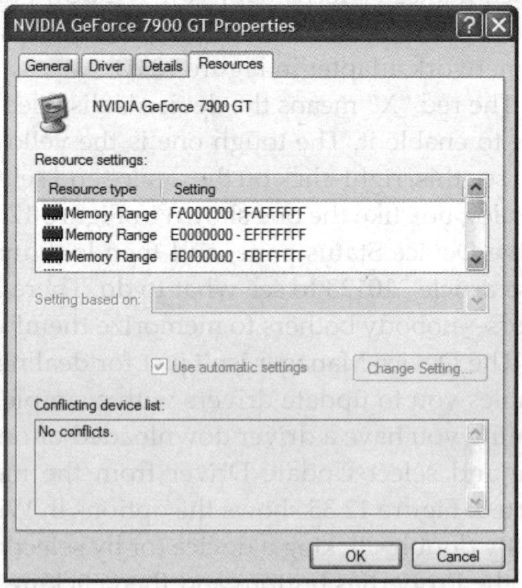

● **Figure 12.36** Resources revealed in the Windows XP Device Manager

you'll find commonly accessed tools, such as System Information and Disk Defragmenter (Figure 12.37).

Many techs overlook memorizing how to find the appropriate Windows tool to diagnose problems, but nothing hurts your credibility with a client like fumbling around, clicking a variety of menus and applets, mumbling, "I know it's around here somewhere." The CompTIA A+ certification exams therefore test you on a variety of paths to appropriate tools. One of those paths is Start | Programs | Accessories | System Tools! Windows XP has all the same tools as Windows 2000, plus a few more, so for each tool I discuss, I'll say whether the tool is in Windows 2000 or only in XP.

Activate Windows (XP only) Windows XP unveiled a copy protection scheme called *Product Activation*, or simply *activation*, that you learned about in the Windows installation process in Chapter 11. Activation is a process where your computer sends Microsoft a unique code generated on your machine based on the installation CD's product key and a number of hardware features, such as the amount of RAM, the CPU processor model, and other ones and zeroes in your PC. Normally, activation is done at install time, but if you choose not to activate at install or if you make "substantial" changes to the hardware, you'll need to use the Activate Windows utility (Figure 12.38). The Activate Windows utility enables you to activate over the Internet or over the telephone.

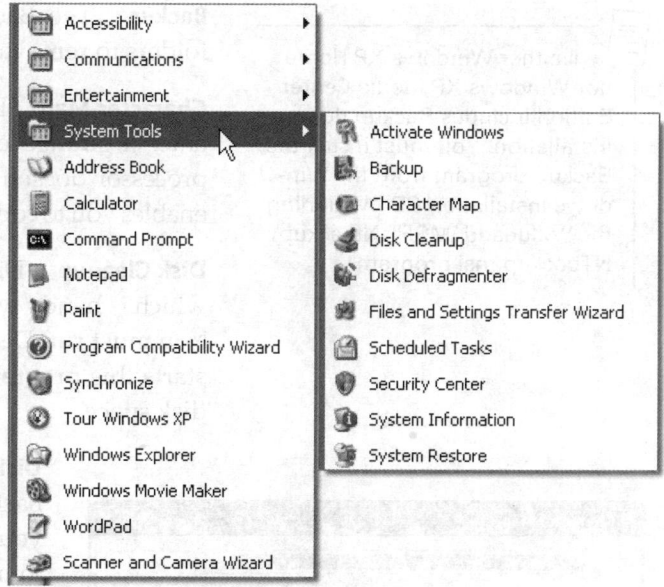

● **Figure 12.37** System Tools menu options

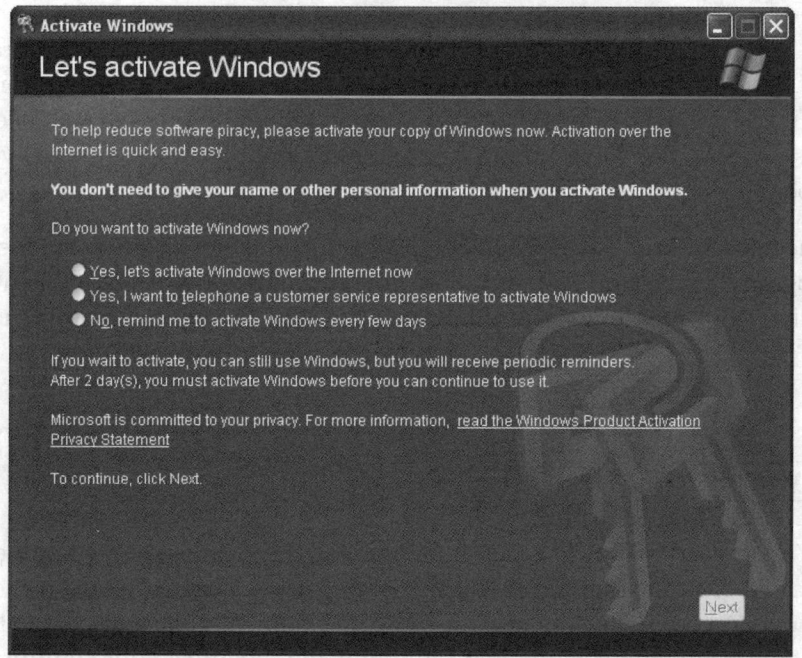

● **Figure 12.38** Activate Windows

Neither Windows XP Home nor Windows XP Media Center Edition includes Backup during installation. You must install the Backup program from the Windows installation CD by running the \Valueadd\MSFT\Ntbackup\NTbackup.msi program.

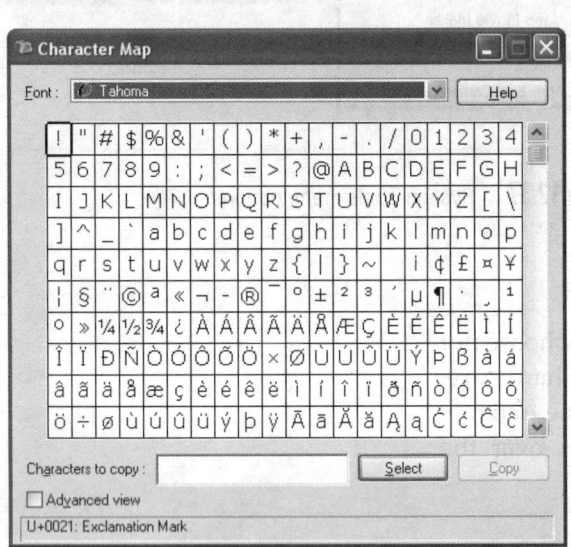

Figure 12.39 Character Map

Backup The Backup utility enables you to back up selected files and folders to removable media like tape drives.

Character Map Ever been using a program only to discover you need to enter a strange character such as the euro character ( ) but your word processor doesn't support it? That's when you need the Character Map. It enables you to copy any Unicode character into the Clipboard (Figure 12.39).

Disk Cleanup Disk Cleanup looks for unneeded files on your computer, which is handy when your hard drive starts to get full and you need space! You must run Disk Cleanup manually in Windows 2000, but Windows XP starts this program whenever your hard drive gets below 200 MB of free disk space.

Disk Defragmenter We first discussed Disk Defragmenter back in Chapter 9. You can access this utility in the same way you access the Device Manager; Disk Defragmenter is also found in the Computer Management console. A simpler method is to select Start | Programs | Accessories | System Tools—you'll find Disk Defragmenter listed there. You can also right-click on any drive in My Computer, select Properties, and click the Tools tab, where you'll find a convenient Defragment Now button.

Files and Settings Transfer Wizard (XP Only) Suppose you have an old computer full of files and settings, and you just got yourself a brand-new computer. You want to copy everything from your old computer onto your new computer—what to do? Microsoft touts the Files and Settings Transfer Wizard (Figure 12.40) as just the tool you need. This utility copies your desktop files and folders, and most conveniently, your settings from Internet Explorer and Outlook Express; however, it won't copy over your programs, not even the Microsoft ones, and it won't copy settings for any programs other than IE and Outlook Express. If you need to copy everything from an old computer to a new one, you'll probably want to use a disk imaging tool like Norton Ghost.

Scheduled Tasks The Scheduled Tasks utility enables you to schedule any program to start and stop any time you wish. The only trick to this utility is that you must enter the program you want to run as a command on

 Cross Check

Fragmentation

You learned about Disk Defragmenter and the problem of file fragmentation back in Chapter 9, "Implementing Hard Drives," so turn there now and see if you can answer these questions. What causes file to become fragmented? How does file fragmentation affect your computer? How often should you defragment your hard drives?

● **Figure 12.40**   Files and Settings Transfer Wizard

the command line, with all the proper switches. Figure 12.41 shows the configuration line for running the Disk Defragmenter program.

Don't know anything about the command line or switches? Don't worry, my book for the 602 course has an entire chapter on the command line.

Security Center (XP Only)   The ▐Security Center▐ is a one-stop location for configuring many security features on your computer. All of these security features, and many more, are discussed in detail in their related chapters.

System Information   System Information is one of those tools that everyone (including the CompTIA A+ exams) likes to talk about, but it's uncommon to meet techs who say they actually use this tool. System Information shows tons of information about the hardware and software on your PC (Figure 12.42). You can also use it as a launch point for a number of programs by clicking on the Tools menu.

System Restore (XP Only)   System Restore is not only handy, it's also arguably the most important single utility you'll ever use in Windows when it comes to fixing a broken system. ▐System Restore▐ enables you to take a "snapshot"—a copy of a number of critical files and settings—and return to that state later (Figure 12.43). System Restore holds multiple snapshots, any of which you may restore to in the future.

Imagine you're installing some new device in your PC, or maybe a piece of software. Before you actually install, you take a snapshot and call it "Before Install." You install the device, and now something starts acting weird. You go back into System Restore and reload the previous snapshot, and the problem goes away.

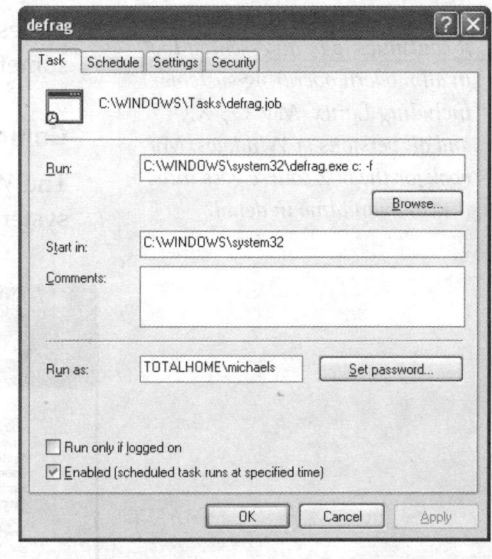

● **Figure 12.41**   Task Scheduler

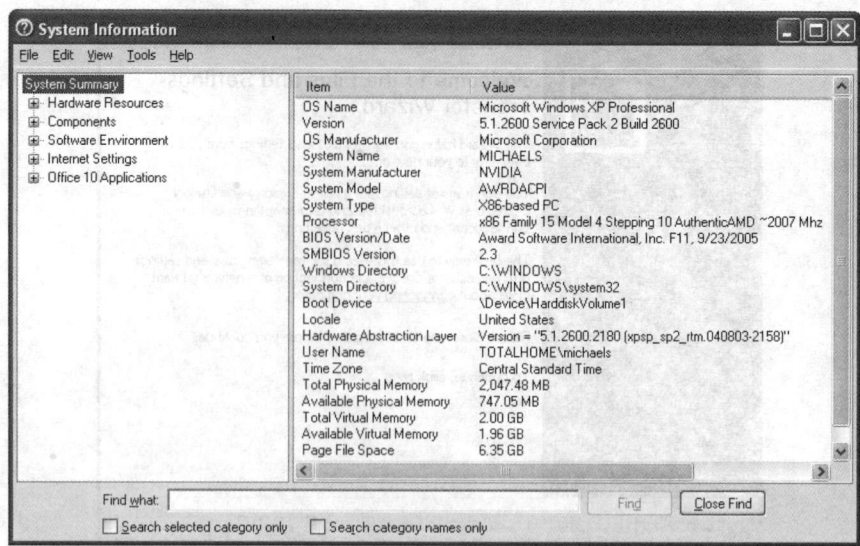

• **Figure 12.42**   System Information

Tech Tip

Command Line

The command line goes back to the early days of computing, but it continues to be an essential tool in all modern operating systems, including Linux, Mac OS X, and all versions of Windows. My book for the 602 course goes into the command line in detail.

System Restore isn't perfect. It only backs up a few critical items, and it's useless if the computer won't boot, but it's usually the first thing to try when something goes wrong—assuming, of course, you made a snapshot!

Command Line

The Windows command line is a throwback to how Microsoft operating systems worked a long, long time ago, when text commands were entered at

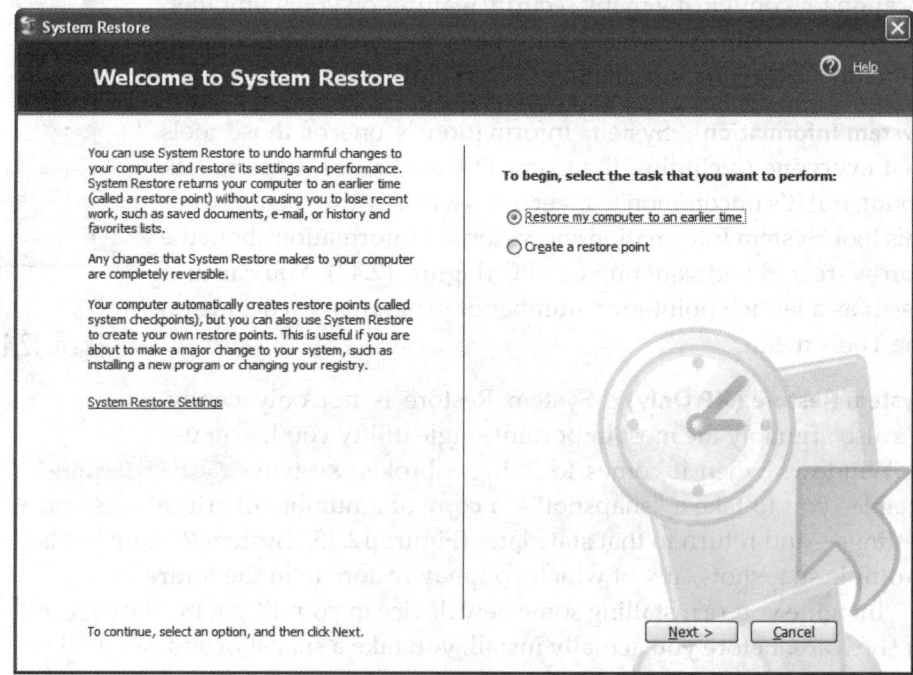

• **Figure 12.43**   System Restore

```
C:\>ver

MS-DOS Version 6.00

C:\>_
```

● **Figure 12.44** DOS command prompt

a command prompt. Figure 12.44 shows the command prompt from DOS, the first operating system commonly used in PCs.

DOS is dead, but the command prompt is alive and well in Windows—including Vista. Every good tech knows how to access and use the command prompt. It is a lifesaver when the GUI part of Windows doesn't work, and it is often faster than using a mouse, if you're skilled at using it. To access a command prompt from within Windows. Select Start | Run, and type **cmd** in the dialog box. Click OK and you'll get to a command prompt (Figure 12.45).

```
C:\WINDOWS\system32\cmd.exe                              _ □ X
08/31/2006   09:19 AM            112,128 CSERHelper.dll
08/31/2006   09:19 AM            489,984 dbghelp.dll
08/31/2006   09:20 AM    <DIR>           friends
09/14/2005   02:46 PM              2,482 INSTALL.LOG
05/08/2006   09:03 AM    <DIR>           Public
06/01/2006   08:55 AM    <DIR>           resource
08/31/2006   09:20 AM    <DIR>           servers
09/14/2005   02:46 PM    <DIR>           skins
09/16/2005   03:02 PM    <DIR>           steam
08/31/2006   09:19 AM          3,174,400 Steam.dll
09/14/2005   02:46 PM          1,249,280 Steam.exe
09/14/2006   09:06 AM            449,270 Steam.log
07/07/2006   12:34 PM    <DIR>           SteamApps
08/31/2006   09:19 AM            970,752 steamclient.dll
09/14/2006   09:07 AM    <DIR>           SteamLogs
08/31/2006   09:19 AM          3,379,200 SteamUI.dll
08/31/2006   09:19 AM             11,191 SteamUI_193.mst
09/14/2005   02:46 PM                 14 Steam_14.mst
08/31/2006   09:19 AM             61,440 Steam_api.dll
08/31/2006   09:19 AM            241,664 tier0_s.dll
07/26/2002   05:02 PM            153,088 UNWISE.EXE
08/31/2006   09:19 AM            229,376 vstdlib_s.dll
08/31/2006   09:19 AM            245,760 WriteMiniDump.exe
               17 File(s)    11,520,608 bytes
               14 Dir(s)  7,037,157,376 bytes free

C:\Program Files\Valve\Steam>
```

● **Figure 12.45** Command prompt in Windows XP

Microsoft Management Console

One of the biggest complaints about earlier versions of Windows was the wide dispersal of the many utilities needed for administration and troubleshooting. Despite years of research, Microsoft could never find a place for all the utilities that would please even a small minority of support people. In a moment of sheer genius, Microsoft determined that the ultimate utility was one that the support person made for herself! This brought on the creation of the amazing Microsoft Management Console.

The Microsoft Management Console (MMC) is simply a shell program in Windows 2000 and XP that holds individual utilities called snap-ins. You can start the MMC by selecting Start | Run and typing in **MMC** to get a blank MMC. Blank MMCs aren't much to look at (Figure 12.46).

The CompTIA A+ Essentials exam expects you to know about the MMC and other tools discussed in the rest of this chapter, so don't skip it!

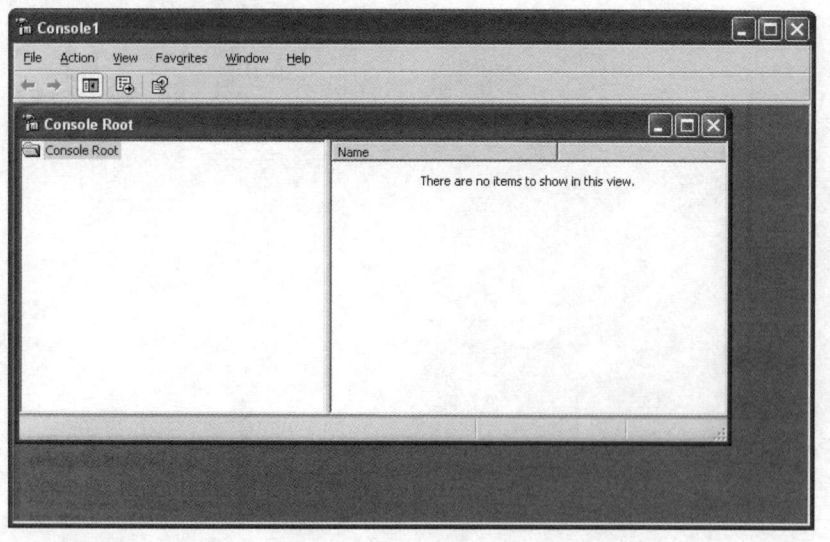

• **Figure 12.46** Blank MMC

You make a blank MMC console useful by adding snap-ins, and most of the utilities you use in Windows are really snap-ins. Even the good old Device Manager is a snap-in. You can add as many snap-ins as you like, and there are many to choose from. Many companies sell third-party utilities as MMC snap-ins.

For example, to add the Device Manager snap-in, open the blank MMC, select File (Console in Windows 2000) | Add/Remove Snap-in, and then click the Add button to open the Add Standalone Snap-in dialog box. Here you will see a list of available snap-ins (Figure 12.47). Select Device Manager and click the Add button to open a dialog box that prompts you to choose the local or a remote PC for the snap-in to work with. Choose Local Computer for this exercise, and click the Finish button. Click the Close button to close the Add Standalone Snap-in dialog box, and then click OK to close the Add/Remove Snap-in dialog box.

You should see Device Manager listed in the console. Click it. Hey, that looks kind of familiar, doesn't it? (See Figure 12.48.)

Once you've added the snap-ins you want, just save the console under any name, anywhere you want. I'll save this console as Device Manager,

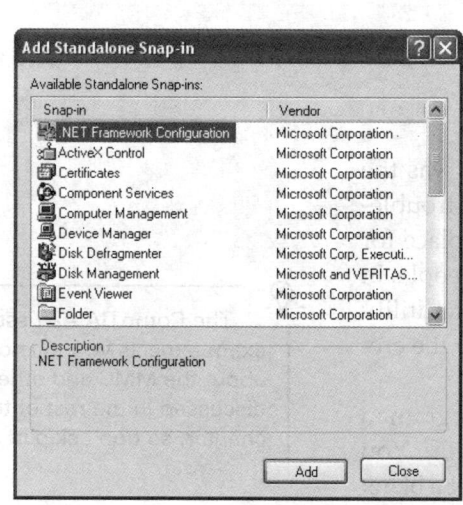

• **Figure 12.47** Available snap-ins

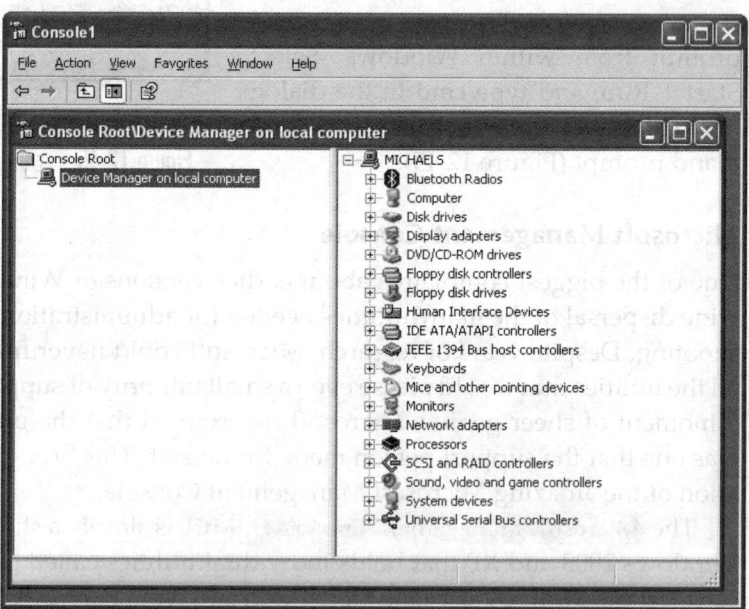

• **Figure 12.48** Device Manager as a snap-in

Creating a Custom MMC

You'll work with the MMC many times in the chapters ahead, and the CompTIA A+ certification exams expect you to know the tool fairly well. Nothing beats doing it to learn how to use something, so try this!

Open a blank MMC, as discussed previously, and then add some snap-ins to create a custom MMC. Need some suggestions?

1. You've used Disk Defragmenter, so add it.
2. Since you played extensively with Disk Management, add it, too.
3. Finally, add Device Manager—well, just because.
4. Now experiment with the MMC to see how useful it can be to have one custom-made!

for example, and drop it on my desktop (see Figure 12.49). I'm now just a double-click away from the Device Manager!

Administrative Tools

Windows 2000 and XP have combined almost all of the snap-ins into an applet in the Control Panel called **Administrative Tools**. Open the Control Panel and open Administrative Tools (Figure 12.50).

Administrative Tools is really just a folder that stores a number of premade consoles. As you poke through these, you'll notice that many of the consoles share some of the same snap-ins—nothing wrong with that. Of the consoles in a standard Administrative Tools collection, the ones you'll spend the most time with are Computer Management, Event Viewer, Performance, and Services.

● **Figure 12.49** The Device Manager shortcut on the desktop

> The CompTIA A+ certification exams have little interest in some of these snap-ins, so this book won't cover them all. If I don't mention it, it's almost certainly not on the exams!

● **Figure 12.50** Administrative Tools

Cross Check

Disk Management

You spent a lot of time in Disk Management in Chapter 9, so turn back there now and see if you can answer these questions. What types of RAID can you implement on a Windows XP Professional computer? Can you boot to your Windows CD (a given) and run Disk Management from the Recovery Console? Can you use Disk Management to make a volume that spans multiple disks, or do you need to use a third-party utility?

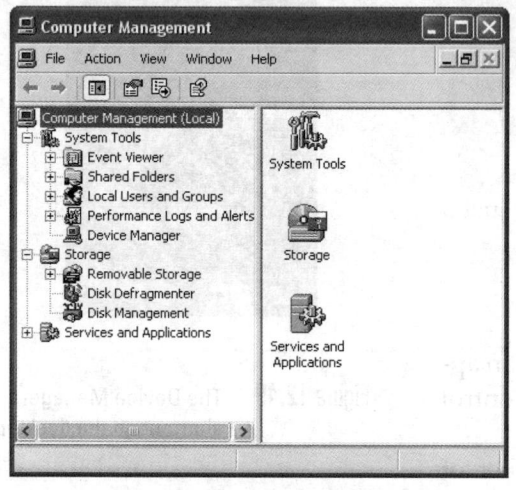

• **Figure 12.51**   Computer Management applet

Computer Management   The Computer Management applet is a tech's best buddy, or at least a place where you'll spend a lot of time when building or maintaining a system (Figure 12.51). You've already spent considerable time with two of its components, System Tools and Storage. System Tools offers System Information, Performance Logs and Alerts, Device Manager, and more. Storage is where you'll find Disk Management.

Event Viewer   Event Viewer enables you to tell at a glance what has happened in the last day, week, or more, including when people logged in and when the PC had problems (Figure 12.52).

Performance   The Performance console consists of two snap-ins: System Monitor and Performance Logs and Alerts. You can use these for reading *logs*—files that record information over time. The System Monitor can also monitor real-time data (Figure 12.53).

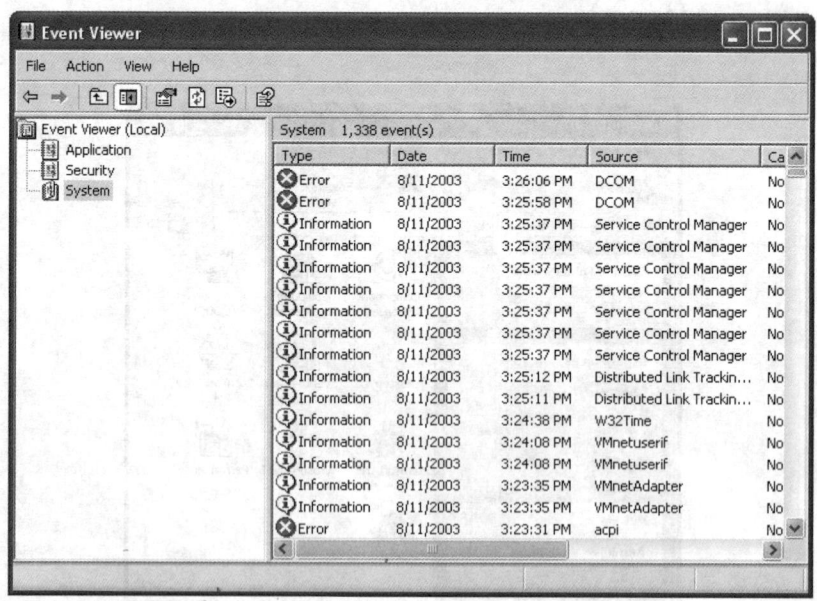

• **Figure 12.52**   Event Viewer reporting system errors

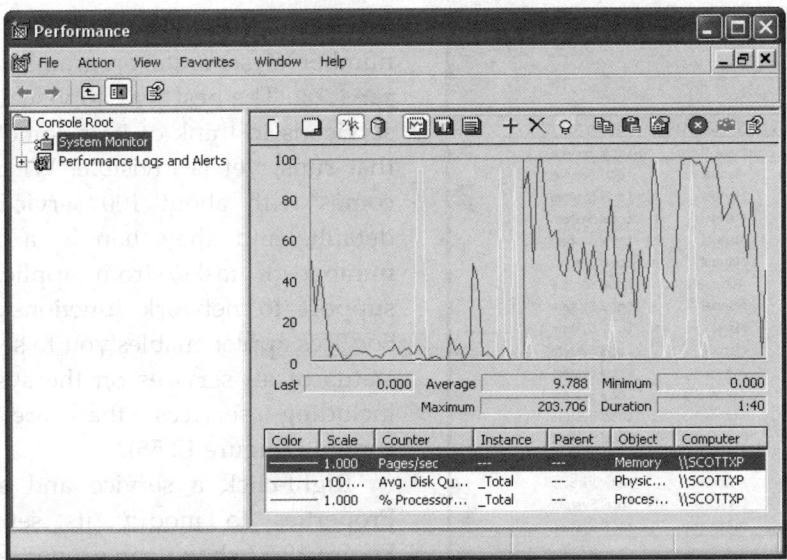

• **Figure 12.53** System Monitor in action

Suppose you just got a new cable modem and you want to know just how fast you can download data. Click the plus sign (+) on the toolbar to add a counter. Click the *Use local computer counters* radio button, and then choose Network Interface from the Performance Object pull-down menu. Make sure the Select Counters from List radio button is selected. Last, select Bytes Received/sec. The dialog box should look like Figure 12.54.

Click Add, and then click Close—probably not much is happening. Go to a Web site, preferably one where you can download a huge file. Start downloading and watch the chart jump; that's the real throughput (Figure 12.55).

You'll learn more about the Performance console in Chapter 13.

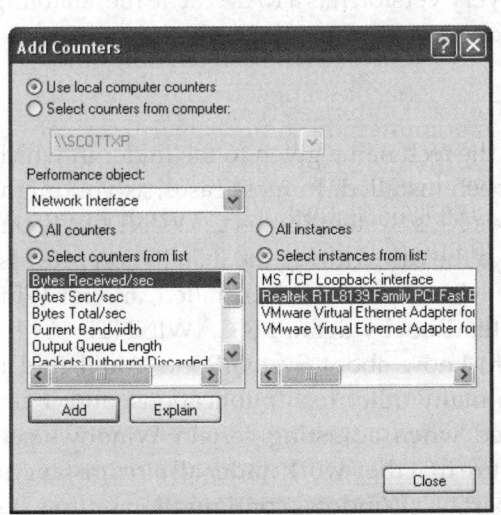

• **Figure 12.54** Setting up a throughput test

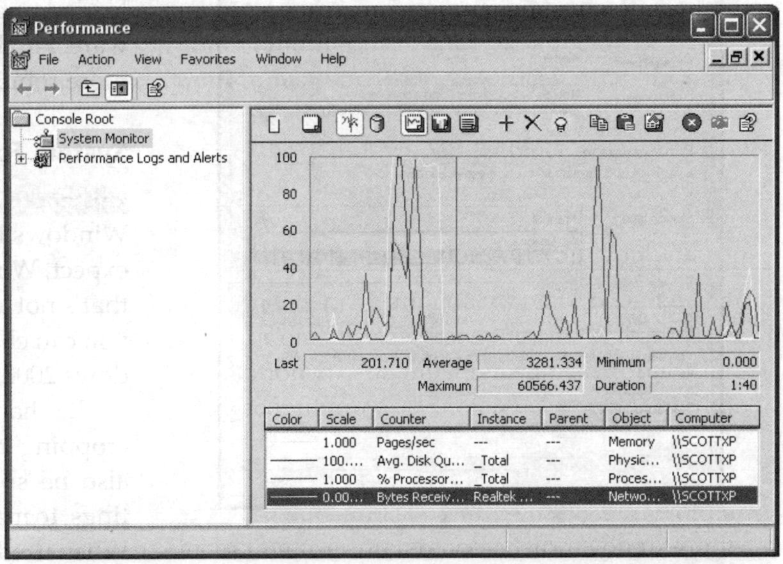

• **Figure 12.55** Downloading with blazing speed

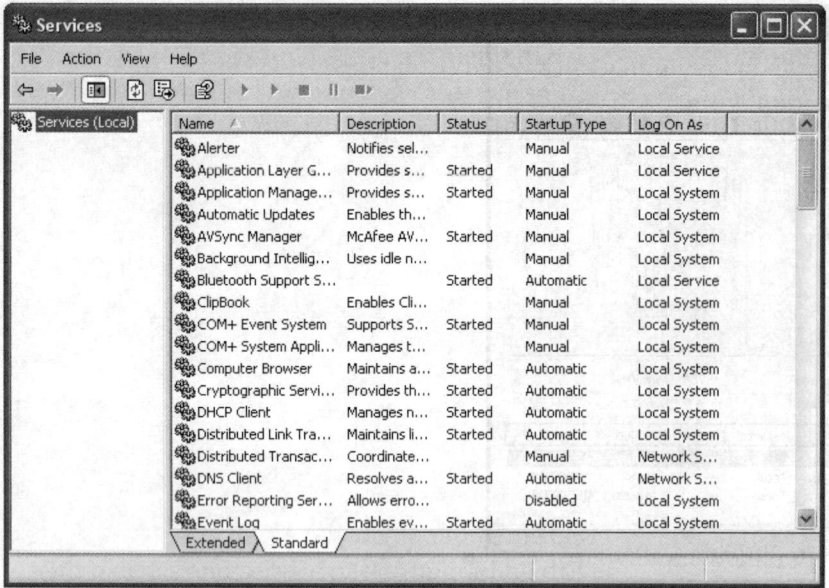

Services Windows runs a large number of separate programs called **services** . The best way to visualize a service is to think of it as something that runs, yet is invisible. Windows comes with about 100 services by default, and they handle a huge number of tasks, from application support to network functions. The Services applet enables you to see the status of all services on the system, including services that are not running (Figure 12.56).

Right-click a service and select Properties to modify its settings. Figure 12.57 shows the properties for the Alerter service. See the Startup type pull-down menu? It shows three options: Automatic, Manual, and Disabled. Automatic means it starts when the system starts, Manual

● **Figure 12.56** Services applet

The CompTIA A+ certification exams are not interested in having you memorize all of these services—just make sure you can manipulate them!

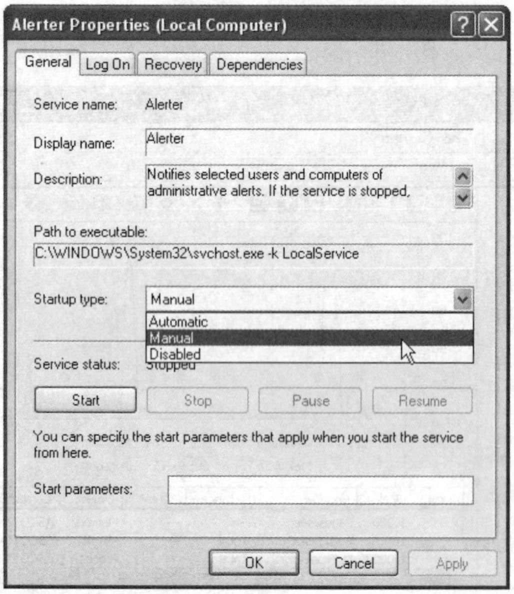

means you have to come to this tab to start it, and Disabled prevents anything from starting it. Make sure you know these three settings, and also make sure you understand how to start, stop, pause, and resume services (note the four buttons underneath Startup Type).

OS Folders

Each modern version of Windows organizes essential files and folders in a similar fashion. All have a primary system folder for storing most Windows internal tools and files. All use the Registry to keep track of all the hardware loaded and the drivers that enable you to use that hardware. Finally, every version has a RAM cache file, enabling more robust access to programs and utilities.

System Folder

SystemRoot is the tech name given to the folder in which Windows has been installed. In most cases, as you might expect, Windows XP's SystemRoot is C:\WINDOWS, but that's not always the case; during the installation process, you can change where Windows is installed, and for Windows 2000, SystemRoot by default is C:\WINNT.

It's handy to know about SystemRoot. You'll find it cropping up in many other tech publications, and it can also be specified when adjusting certain Windows settings, to make sure that they work under all circumstances. When used as part of a Windows configuration setting, it's often written as %SystemRoot%.

● **Figure 12.57** Alerter service properties

Finding the SystemRoot Folder

If you don't know where Windows is installed on a particular system, here's a handy trick. Try this:

Go to a command prompt, type **cd %systemroot%**, and press ENTER. The prompt will change to the directory in which the Windows OS files are stored. Slick!

Other Important Folders

Windows has a number of important folders other than the system folder. Here's a list of the ones you'll most likely encounter. For simplicity, let's assume the system root is C:\WINNT.

Windows XP has more system folders than Windows 2000. This list only contains folders common to both Windows 2000 and XP.

- **C:\Program Files**   This is the default location for all of the installed programs.

- **C:\Documents and Settings**   This is where all of the personal settings for each user are stored. Every user has their own subfolder in Documents and Settings. In each user folder, you'll find another level of folders with familiar names such as Desktop, My Documents, and Start Menu. These folders hold the actual contents of these items.

- **C:\WINNT**   The SystemRoot has a number of critical subfolders, but surprisingly holds no critical files in the folder itself. About the most interesting file found here is good old notepad.exe. Remember that this is C:\WINDOWS on a Windows XP system!

- **C:\WINNT\FONTS**   All of the fonts installed in Windows live here.

- **C:\WINNT\SYSTEM32**   This is the *real* Windows! All of the most critical programs that make Windows run are stored here.

Registry

The Registry is a huge database that stores everything about your PC, including information on all the hardware in the PC, network information, user preferences, file types, and virtually anything else you might run into with Windows. Almost any form of configuration done to a Windows system involves editing the Registry. In Windows 2000/XP, the numerous Registry files (called *hives*) are in the \%SystemRoot%\System32\config folder. Fortunately, you rarely have to access these massive files directly. Instead, you can use a set of relatively user-friendly applications to edit the Registry.

The CompTIA A+ certification exams do not expect you to memorize every aspect of the Windows Registry. You should, however, understand the basic components of the Registry, know how to edit the Registry manually, and know the best way to locate a particular setting.

Accessing the Registry   Before we look in the Registry, let's look at how you access the Registry directly using a Registry editor. Once you know that, you can open the Registry on your machine and compare what you see to the examples in this chapter.

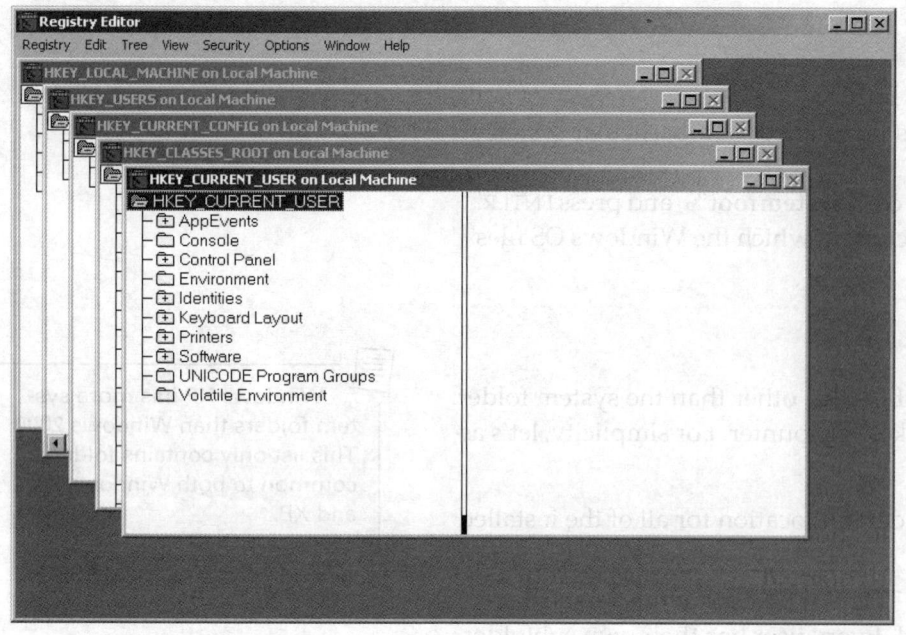

• Figure 12.58   REGEDT32 in Windows 2000

Windows 2000 comes with two Registry editors: REGEDT32.EXE, shown in Figure 12.58, and the much older REGEDIT.EXE (Figure 12.59). You start either of these programs by going to a command prompt and typing its name.

The reason for having two different Registry editors is long and boring, and explaining it would require a very dull 15-minute monologue (preferably with an angelic chorus singing in the background) about how the Registry worked in Windows 9x and Windows NT. Suffice it to say that in Windows 2000 only REGEDT32 is safe to use for actual editing, but you can use the older REGEDIT to perform searches, because REGEDT32's search capabilities are not very good.

Windows XP and Vista have eliminated the entire two-Registry-editor nonsense by creating a new **Registry Editor** that includes strong search functions. No longer are there two separate programs, but interestingly, entering either REGEDIT or REGEDT32 at a command prompt will bring up the

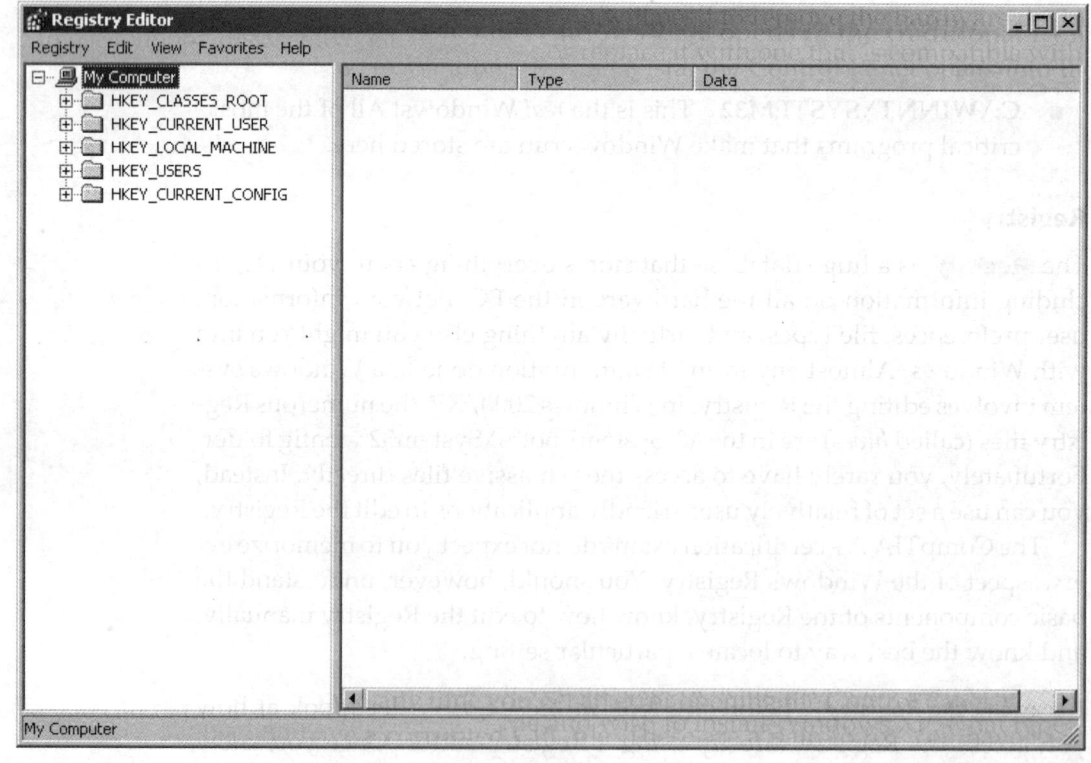

• Figure 12.59   REGEDIT in Windows 2000

same program, so feel free to use either program name. Figure 12.60 shows the Registry Editor on a typical Windows XP system.

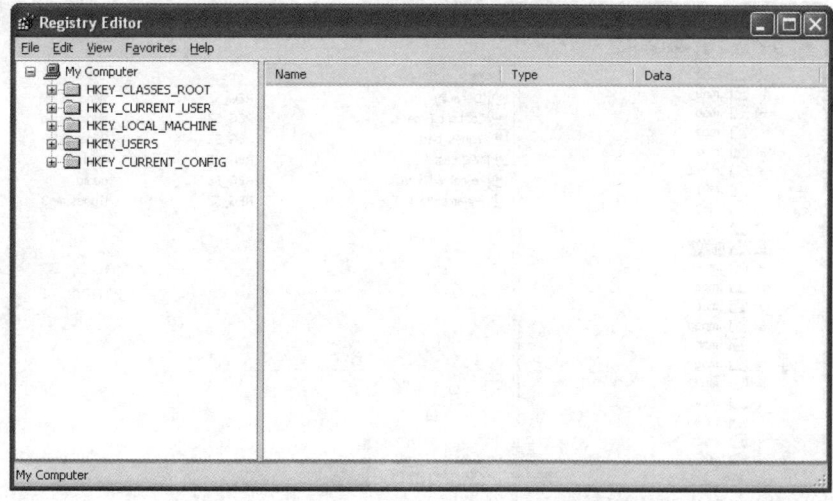

Registry Components The Registry is organized in a tree structure similar to the folders in the PC. Once you open the Registry Editor in Windows, you will see five main subgroups, or *root keys*:

- HKEY_CLASSES_ROOT
- HKEY_CURRENT_USER
- HKEY_USERS
- HKEY_LOCAL_MACHINE
- HKEY_CURRENT_CONFIG

• **Figure 12.60** Registry Editor in Windows XP

Try opening one of these root keys by clicking on the plus sign to its left; note that more subkeys are listed underneath. A subkey also has other subkeys, or *values*. Figure 12.61 shows an example of a subkey with some values. Notice that REGEDIT shows keys on the left and values on the right, just as Windows Explorer shows directories on the left and files on the right.

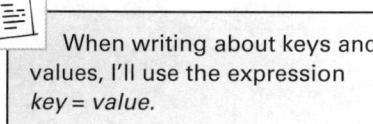

When writing about keys and values, I'll use the expression *key = value.*

The secret to understanding the Registry is to understand the function of the six root keys first. Each of these root keys has a specific function, so let's take a look at them individually.

HKEY_CLASSES_ROOT This root key defines the standard *class objects* used by Windows. A class object is a named group of functions that define what you can do with the object it represents. Pretty much everything that has to do with files on the system is defined by a class object. For example,

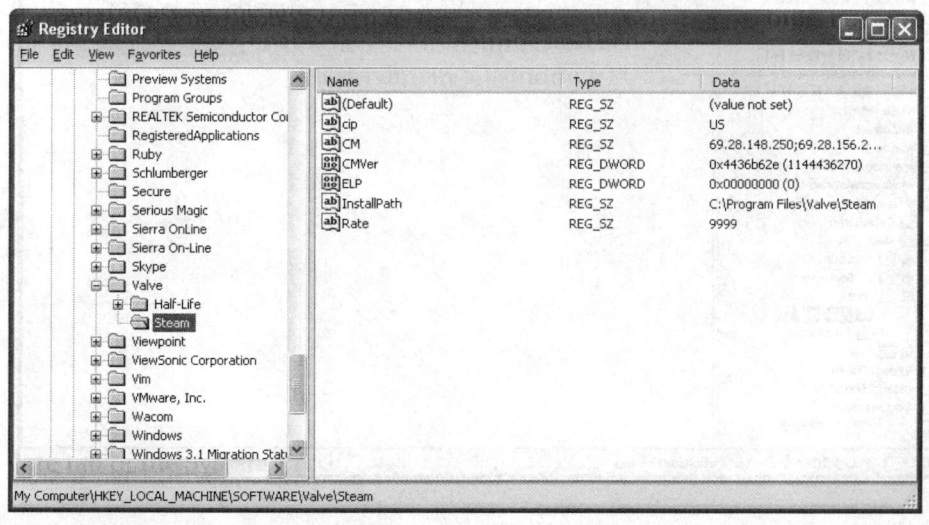

• **Figure 12.61** Typical Registry keys and values

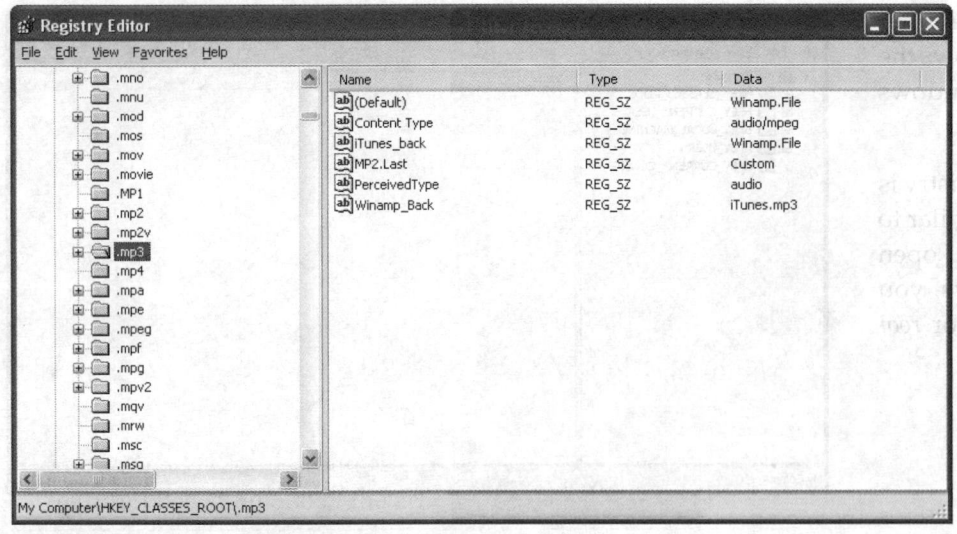

● **Figure 12.62**   Association of .MP3 with Winamp

the Registry defines the popular MP3 sound file using two class objects. If you search the Registry for the .MP3 file extension, you will find the first class object, which associates the .MP3 file extension with the name "Winamp.File" on this computer (Figure 12.62).

Ah, but what are the properties of Winamp.File? That's what the HKEY_CLASSES_ROOT root key is designed to handle. Search this section again for "Winamp.File" (or whatever it said in the value for your MP3 file) and look for a subkey called "open." This variable determines the **file association** (Figure 12.63), which is the Windows term for what program to use to open a particular type of file.

This subkey tells the system everything it needs to know about a particular software item, from which program to use to open a file, to the type of icon used to show the file, to what to show when you right-click on that file type. Although it is possible to change most of these settings via the Registry Editor, the normal way is to choose more user-friendly methods. For example, in Windows XP you can right-click on a file and select Properties, and then click the Change button next to Open With (Figure 12.64).

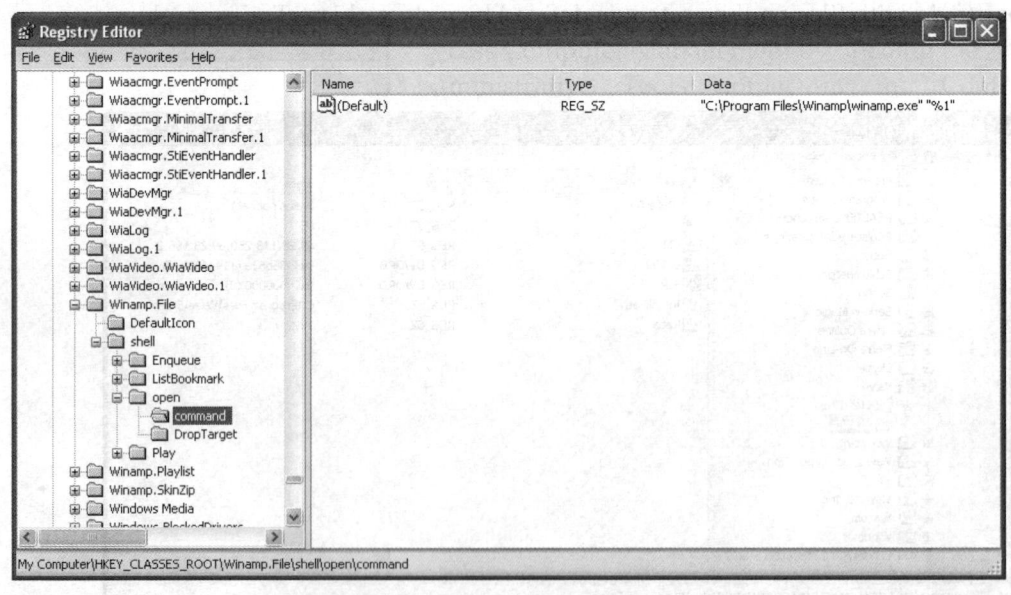

● **Figure 12.63**   Winamp file settings

HKEY_CURRENT_USER and HKEY_USERS Windows is designed to support more than one user on the same PC, storing personalized information such as desktop colors, screen savers, and the contents of the desktop for every user that has an account on the system. HKEY_CURRENT_USER stores the current user settings, and HKEY_USERS stores all of the personalized information for all users on a PC. While you certainly can change items like the screen saver here, the better way is to right-click on the desktop and select Properties!

HKEY_LOCAL_MACHINE This root key contains all the data for a system's non-user-specific configurations. This encompasses every device and every program in your PC. For example, Figure 12.65 shows the description of a CD-ROM drive.

HKEY_CURRENT_CONFIG If the values in HKEY_LOCAL_MACHINE have more than one option, such as two different monitors, this root key defines which one is currently being used. Because most people have only one type of monitor and similar equipment, this area is almost never touched.

Swap File or Page File

Windows uses a portion of the hard drive as an extension of system RAM, through what's called a *RAM cache*. A RAM cache is a block of cylinders on a hard drive set aside as what's called a **swap file**, **page file**, or **virtual memory**. When the PC starts running out of real RAM because you've loaded too many programs, the system swaps programs from RAM to the swap file, opening more space for programs currently active. All versions of Windows use a swap file, so let's look at how one works.

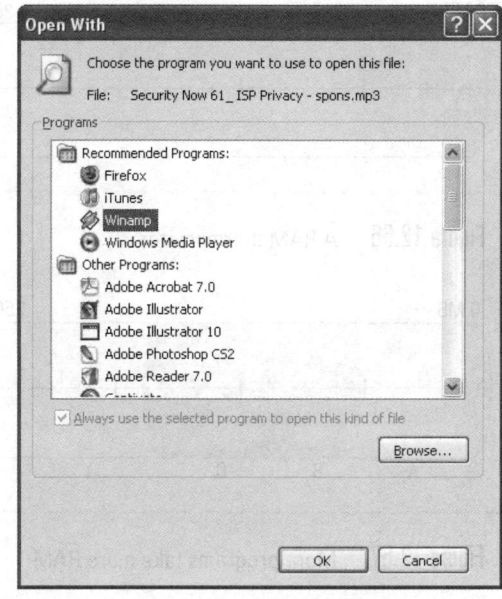

● **Figure 12.64** Changing the file association the easy way

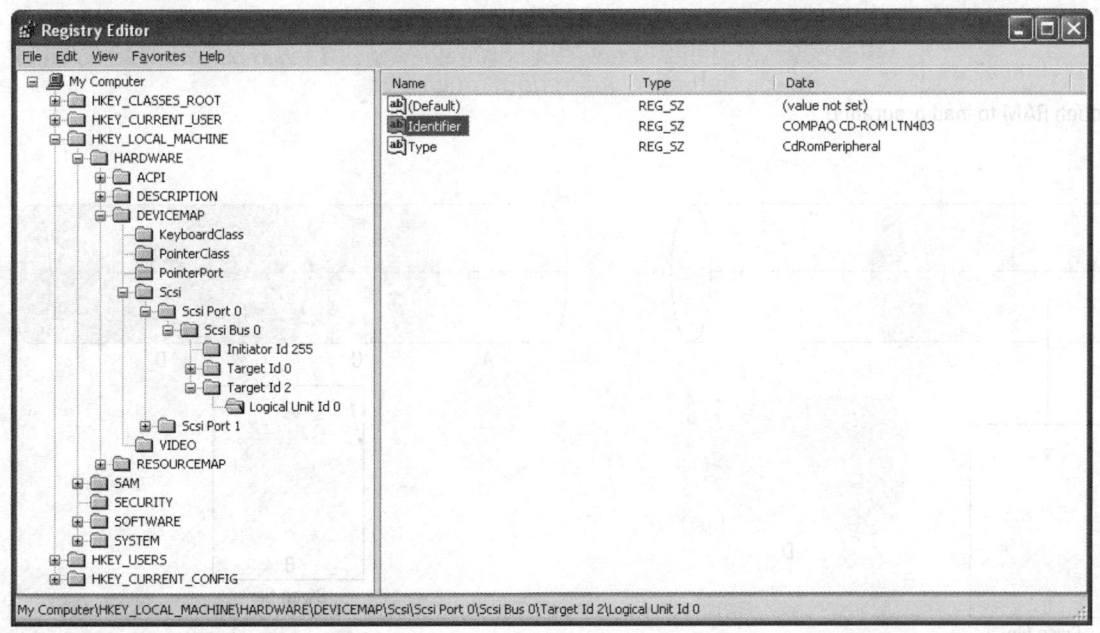

● **Figure 12.65** Registry information for a CD-ROM drive

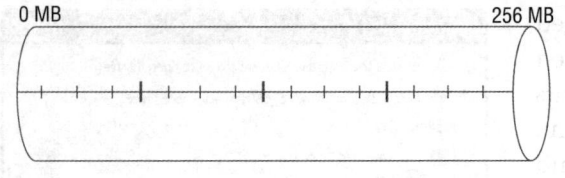

● **Figure 12.66** A RAM thermometer

Let's assume you have a PC with 256 MB of RAM. Figure 12.66 shows the system RAM as a thermometer with gradients from 0 to 256 MB. As programs load, they take up RAM, and as more and more programs are loaded (labeled A, B, and C in the figure), more RAM is used (Figure 12.67).

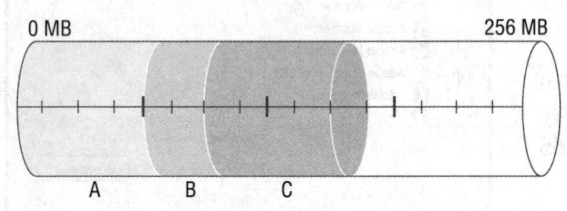

● **Figure 12.67** More programs take more RAM

At a certain point, you won't have enough RAM to run any more programs (Figure 12.68). Sure, you could close one or more programs to make room for yet another program, but you can't keep all the programs running simultaneously. This is where virtual memory comes into play. Windows' virtual memory starts by creating a swap file that resides somewhere on your hard drive. The swap file works like a temporary storage box. Windows removes running programs temporarily from RAM into the swap file so other programs can load and run. If you have enough RAM to run all your programs, Windows does not need to use the swap file—Windows brings the swap file into play only when insufficient RAM is available to run all open programs.

> Virtual memory is a fully automated process and does not require any user intervention. Tech intervention is another story!

To load, Program D needs a certain amount of free RAM. Clearly, this requires that some other program (or programs) be unloaded from RAM without actually closing the program(s). Windows looks at all running programs, in this case A, B, and C, and decides which program is the least used. That program is then cut out of or swapped from RAM and copied into the swap file. In this case, Windows has chosen Program B (Figure 12.69). Unloading Program B from RAM provides enough RAM to load Program D (Figure 12.70).

It is important to understand that none of this activity is visible on the screen! Program B's window is still visible along with those of all the other running programs. Nothing tells the user that Program B is no longer in RAM (Figure 12.71).

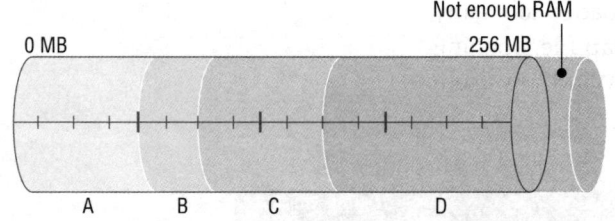

● **Figure 12.68** Not enough RAM to load program D

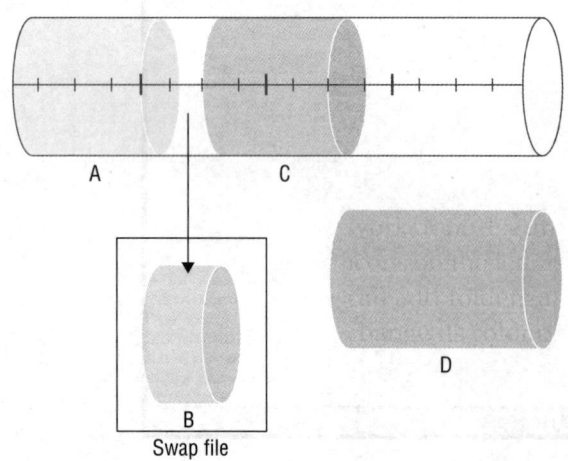

● **Figure 12.69** Program B being unloaded from memory

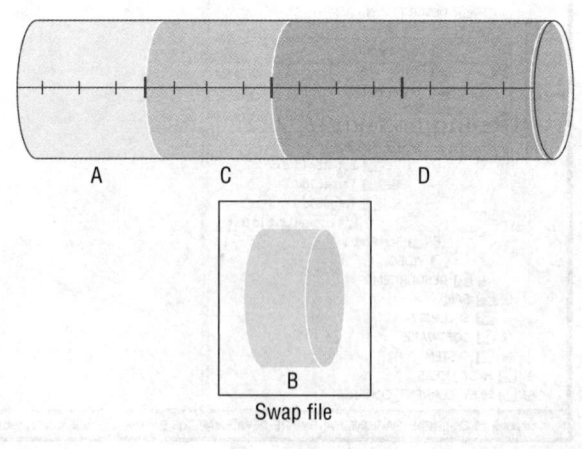

● **Figure 12.70** Program B stored in the swap file—room is made for Program D

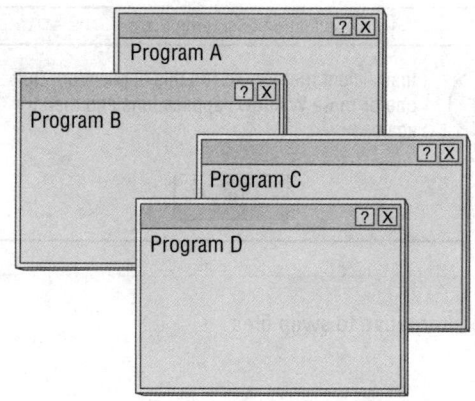

● **Figure 12.71**   You can't tell whether a program is swapped or not.

So what happens if you click on Program B's window to bring it to the front? The program can't actually run from the swap file; it must be reloaded back into RAM. First, Windows decides which program must be removed from RAM, and this time Windows chooses Program C (Figure 12.72). Then it loads Program B into RAM (Figure 12.73).

Swapping programs to and from the swap file and RAM takes time. Although no visual clues suggest that a swap is taking place, the machine will slow down quite noticeably as Windows performs the swaps. However, the alternative (Figure 12.74) is far less acceptable. Swap files are a crucial aspect of Windows operation.

Windows handles swap files automatically, but occasionally you'll run into problems and need to change the size of the swap file or delete it and let Windows re-create it automatically. The swap file, or page file in Windows 2000 and XP, is PAGEFILE.SYS. You can often find it in the root directory of the C: drive, but again, that can be changed. Wherever it is, the swap file will be a hidden system file, which means in practice that you'll have to play with your folder viewing options to see it.

Moving the Page File in Windows 2000/XP

If you have a second hard drive installed in your PC, you can often get a small performance boost by moving your page file from the C: drive (the default) to the second drive. To move your page file, go to the Control Panel | System applet and select the Advanced tab. In the Performance section, click the Settings button to open the Performance Options dialog box. Select the Advanced tab, and then click the Change button in the Virtual Memory section. Select a drive from the list and give it a size or range, and you're ready to go!

Just don't turn virtual memory off completely. Although Windows can run without virtual memory, you will definitely take a performance hit.

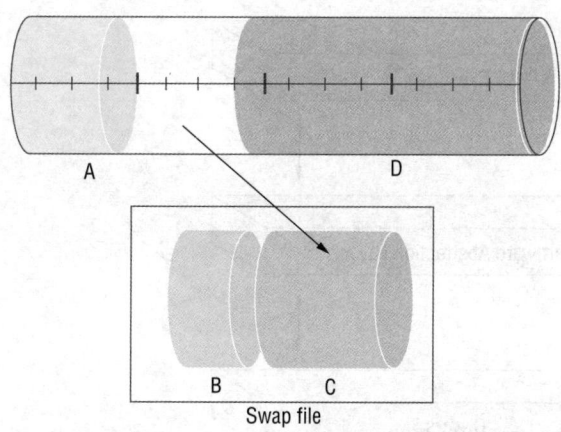

● **Figure 12.72**   Program C is swapped to the swap file.

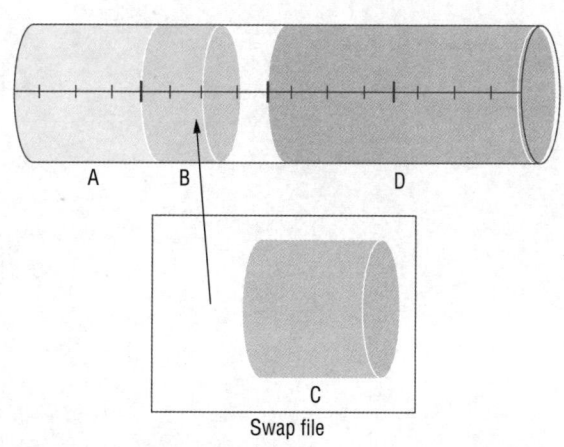

● **Figure 12.73**   Program B is swapped back into RAM.

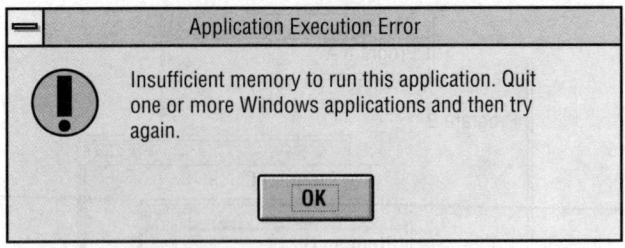

• **Figure 12.74**   The alternative to swap files

■ Features and Characteristics of Windows 2000/XP

Microsoft Windows 2000 and XP are stable, high-performance operating systems that offer scalability and, above all else, security. Windows 2000 and Windows XP share the same core structure, files, and features, so the discussion that follows applies to both operating systems. Let's cover both in detail and then discuss the differences between the two OSs.

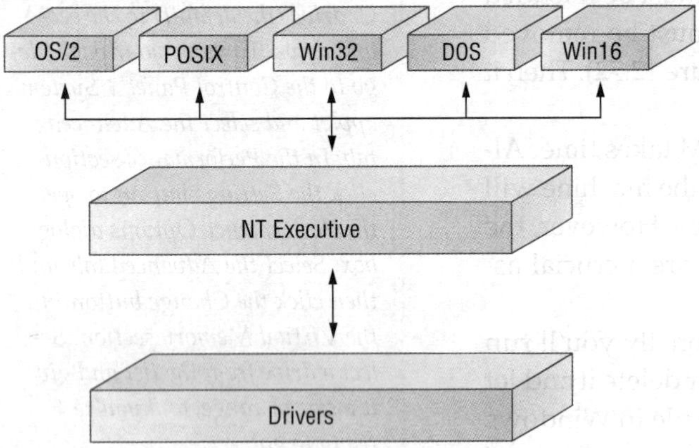

OS Organization

Three words best describe Windows 2000/XP organization: robust, scalable, and cross-platform. Microsoft takes an object-oriented approach to the OS, separating it into three distinct parts: the drivers, the NT Executive, and the subsystems (Figure 12.75).

The **NT Executive** is the core power of the Windows 2000/XP OS, handling all of the memory management and multitasking. The NT Executive uses a hardware abstraction layer (HAL) to separate the system-specific device drivers from the rest of the operating system (Figure 12.76).

• **Figure 12.75**   Windows NT organization

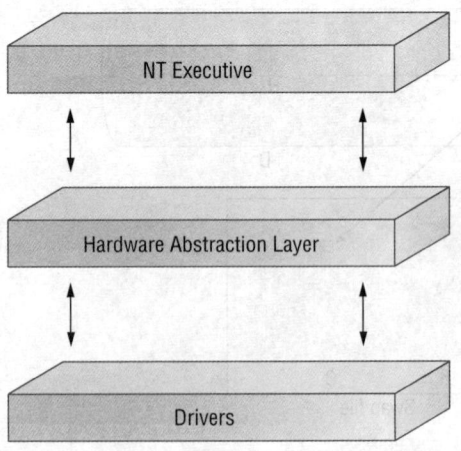

• **Figure 12.76**   NT Executive and the HAL

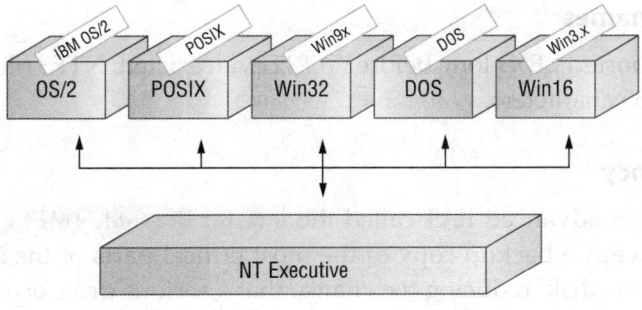

● **Figure 12.77**   NT Executive can handle a lot of different OSs.

Windows 2000/XP's robustness comes from the separation of running processes into a myriad of subsystems. Each of these subsystems supports different types of applications in separate areas; that way, if one program locks up, it won't cause the entire system to lock up. Windows supports DOS and older programs designed for earlier versions of Windows, as well as current Windows applications, via these numerous subsystems (Figure 12.77).

 **Cross Check**

Multicore CPUs

You learned about multicore CPUs, such as the Athlon X2 and the Core 2 Duo, way back in Chapter 3, "Understanding CPUs," so turn there now and see if you can answer these questions. How does a multicore processor manifest in a computer? What advantages do multicore processors offer over single core processors? Would Microsoft's earlier operating systems that didn't support SMP, such as Windows 98, be able to handle multicore processors? Or, more specifically, would they be able to use them to their full potential? (The last question isn't in Chapter 3, but just something for class discussion!)

Windows 2000/XP's scalability makes them the only modern Microsoft operating systems to support **symmetric multiprocessing (SMP)**, providing support for systems with up to 32 CPUs. Yee hah! The server versions of Windows go beyond SMP by adding the power of clustering, enabling multiple computers to share redundant data for ultimate protection. (Say that three times fast—I dare you!) If one system goes down, the other systems continue to run.

 For those of you who are a little weak on networking, take a moment to read through Chapter 18. You need to understand basic networking to appreciate Windows 2000/XP.

NT File System (NTFS)

From the beginning, Microsoft designed and optimized every aspect of Windows 2000/XP for multi-user, networked environments. This is most evident in the NT file system. Whereas all previous Microsoft OSs used either FAT16 or FAT32, Windows 2000 and XP use a far more powerful and robust file system, appropriately called **NT File System (NTFS)**.

Chapter 9 contains a good basic description of NTFS, but let's go into a bit more detail. NTFS offers the following excellent features:

- Long filenames (LFNs)
- Redundancy
- Backward compatibility
- Recoverability
- Security

Long Filenames

NTFS supported LFNs long before FAT32 even existed. NTFS filenames can be up to 255 characters.

Redundancy

NTFS has an advanced FAT called the **master file table (MFT)**. An NTFS partition keeps a backup copy of the most critical parts of the MFT in the middle of the disk, reducing the chance that a serious drive error can wipe out both the MFT and the MFT copy. Whenever you defrag an NTFS partition, you'll see a small, immovable "chunk" in the middle of the drive; that's the backup MFT.

Backward Compatibility

For all its power, NTFS is amazingly backward compatible. You can copy DOS or Windows 9x/Me programs to an NTFS partition—Windows will even keep the LFNs.

Recoverability

Accidental system shutdowns, reboots, and lockups in the midst of a file save or retrieval wreak havoc on most systems. NTFS avoids this with *transaction logging*. Transaction logging identifies incomplete file transactions and restores the file to the original format automatically and invisibly.

Security

NTFS truly shines with its powerful security functions. When most people hear the term "security," they tend to think about networks, and NTFS security works perfectly in a networked environment, but it works equally well on single systems that support multiple users. Let's look at three major features of NTFS security: accounts, groups, and permissions.

Accounts   To use a Windows 2000/XP system, you must have a valid account (and, frequently, a password). Without an account, you cannot use the system (Figure 12.78).

Every Windows 2000/XP system has a "super" account called **administrator**. Remember when you saw the installation of Windows and it prompted you for a password for the administrator account? As you might imagine, this account has access to everything—a dangerous thing in the wrong hands!

Groups   The administrator creates user accounts with a special program called Users and Passwords in Windows 2000 (Figure 12.79) and User Accounts in Windows XP. Note that the account list has three columns: User Name, Domain, and Group. To understand domains requires an extensive networking discussion, so

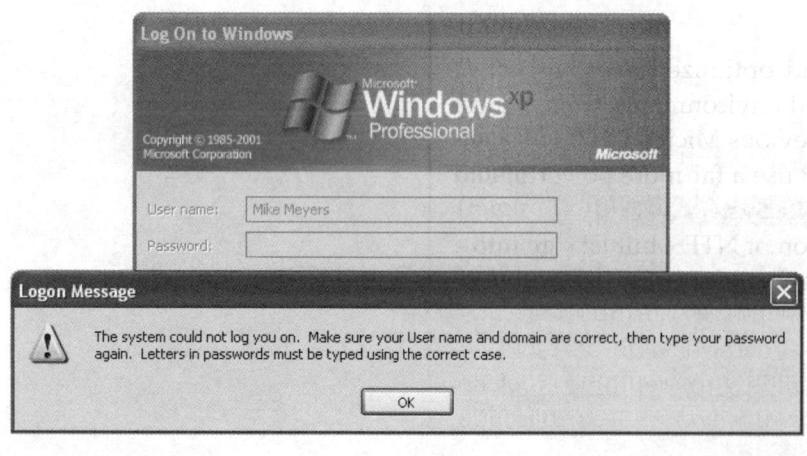

● **Figure 12.78**   Login failure

we'll leave that for Chapter 18, "Understanding Networking." We'll instead focus here on user names and groups. A **user name** defines an account for a person who has access to the PC. A **group** is simply a collection of accounts that share the same access capabilities. A single account can be a member of multiple groups.

Groups make Windows administration much easier in two ways. First, you can assign a certain level of access for a file or folder to a group, instead of to just a single user account. For example, you can make a group called Accounting and put all the accounting user accounts in that group. If a person quits, you don't need to worry about assigning all the proper access levels when you create a new account for her replacement. After you make an account for the new person, you just add the new account to the appropriate access group!

Second, Windows provides seven built-in groups: Administrators, Power Users, Users, Backup Operators, Replicator, Everyone, and Guests. These built-in groups have a number of preset abilities. You cannot delete these groups.

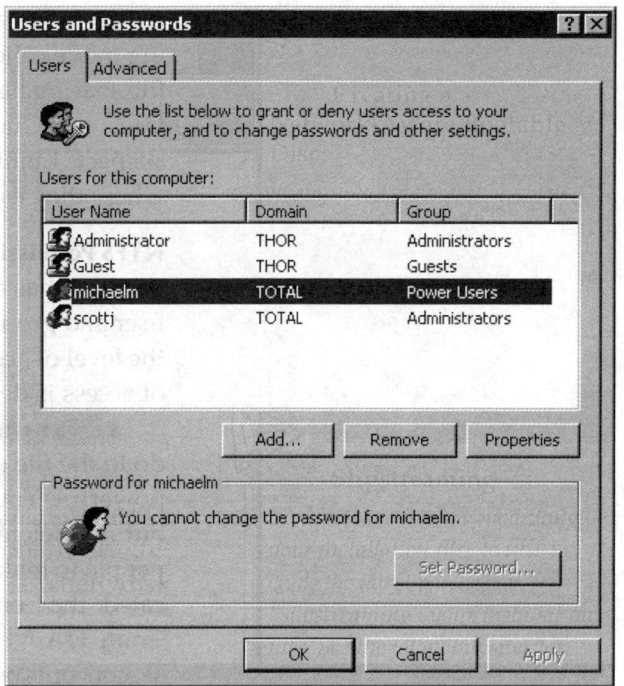

• **Figure 12.79** Users and Passwords dialog box in Windows 2000

- **Administrators**   Any account that is a member of this group has complete administrator privileges. It is common for the primary user of a Windows 2000/XP system to have his or her account in the Administrators group.

- **Power Users**   Power users are almost as powerful as administrators, but they cannot install new devices or access other users' files or folders unless the files or folders specifically provide them access.

- **Users**   Users cannot edit the Registry or access critical system files. They can create groups but can manage only those they create.

- **Backup Operators**   Backup operators have the same rights as users, except that they can run backup programs that access any file or folder—for backup purposes only.

- **Replicator**   Members of the Replicator group can replicate files and folders in a domain.

- **Everyone**   This group applies to any user who can log onto the system. You cannot edit this group.

- **Guests**   Someone who does not have an account on the system can log on using a Guest account if the system has been set up to enable that option. This group is useful in certain network situations.

Windows XP diverges a lot from Windows 2000 on user accounts. If you're running XP Professional and you are on a Windows domain, XP offers all the accounts listed above, but it adds four other specialized types, including Help Services Group and Remote Desktop Users. Windows XP Home and XP Professional, when it's installed as a standalone PC or connected to a workgroup but not a domain, run in a specialized networking mode called simple file sharing. A Windows XP system running simple file sharing has only three account types: Computer Administrator, Limited User, and Guest. Computer Administrators can do anything, as you might suspect. Limited Users can access only certain things and have limits on where they can save files on the PC.

NTFS Permissions In the 2000/XP world, every folder and file on an NTFS partition has a list that contains two sets of data. First, the list details every user and group that has access to that file or folder. Second, the list specifies the level of access that each user or group has to that file or folder. The level of access is defined by a set of restrictions called NTFS permissions.

NTFS permissions define exactly what a particular account can or cannot do to the file or folder on an NTFS volume and are thus quite detailed and powerful. You can make it possible, for example, for a person to edit a file but not delete it. You can let someone create a folder and not allow other people to make subfolders. NTFS file and folder permissions are so complicated that entire books have been written on them! Fortunately, the CompTIA A+ certification exams test your understanding of only a few basic concepts of NTFS permissions: Ownership, Take Ownership permission, Change permissions, Folder permissions, and File permissions.

- **Ownership** When you create a new file or folder on an NTFS partition, you become the *owner* of that file or folder. A newly created file or folder by default gives everyone full permission to access, delete, and otherwise manipulate that file or folder. Owners can do anything they want to the files or folders they own, including changing the permissions to prevent anybody, even administrators, from accessing them.

- **Take Ownership permission** This special permission enables anyone with the permission to seize control of a file or folder. Administrator accounts have Take Ownership permission for everything. Note the difference here between owning a file and accessing a file. If you own a file, you can prevent anyone from accessing that file. An administrator who you have blocked, however, can take that ownership away from you and *then* access that file!

- **Change permissions** Another important permission for all NTFS files and folders is the Change permission. An account with this permission can give or take away permissions for other accounts.

- **Folder permissions** Let's look at a typical folder in my Windows XP system to see how this one works. My E: drive is formatted as NTFS, and on it I created a folder called E:\MIKE. In My Computer, it looks like Figure 12.80. I set the permissions for the E:\MIKE folder by accessing the folder's properties and clicking the Security tab (see Figure 12.81).

- **File permissions** File permissions are similar to Folder permissions. We'll talk about File permissions right after we cover Folder permissions.

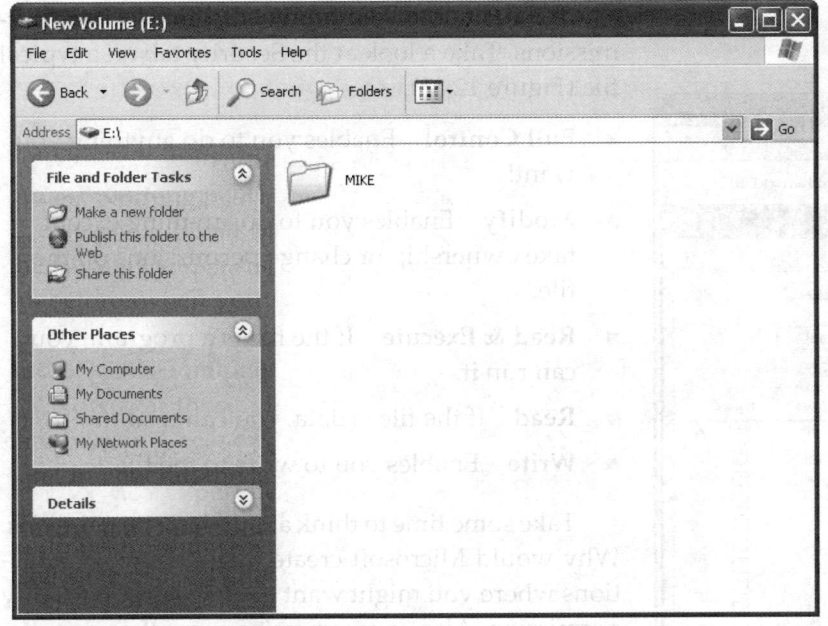

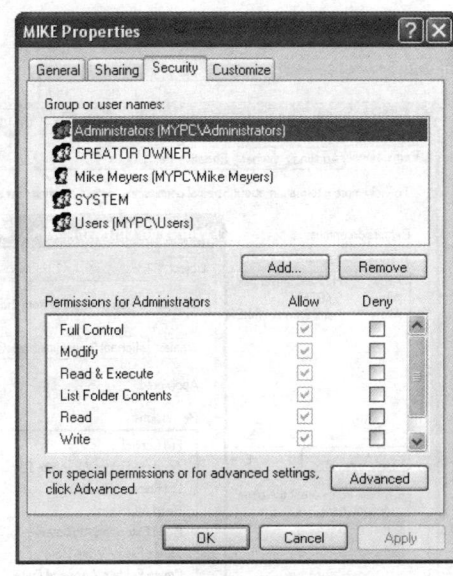

Figure 12.80   My E:\MIKE folder—isn't it lovely?

Figure 12.81   The Security tab lets you set permissions.

In Windows 2000/XP, just about everything in the computer has a Security tab in its properties, and every Security tab contains two main areas. The top area shows the list of accounts that have permissions for that resource. The lower area shows exactly what permissions have been assigned to the selected account.

Here are the standard permissions for a folder:

- **Full Control**   Enables you to do anything you want!

- **Modify**   Enables you to do anything except delete files or subfolders.

- **Read & Execute**   Enables you to see the contents of the folder and any subfolders.

- **List Folder Contents**   Enables you to see the contents of the folder and any subfolders. (This permission seems the same as the Read & Execute permission, but it is only inherited by folders.)

- **Read**   Enables you to read any file in the folder.

- **Write**   Enables you to write to files and create new files and folders.

If you look at the bottom of the Security tab in Windows 2000, you'll see a little check box that says Allow Inheritable Permissions from Parent to Propagate to This Object. In other words, any files or subfolders created in this folder get the same permissions for the same users/groups that the folder has. Unchecking this option enables you to stop a user from getting a specific permission via inheritance. Windows XP has the same feature, only it's accessed through the Advanced button in the Security tab. Windows also provides explicit Deny functions for each option (Figure 12.82). Deny overrules inheritance.

Don't panic about memorizing special permissions; just appreciate that they exist and that the permissions you see in the Security tab cover the vast majority of our needs.

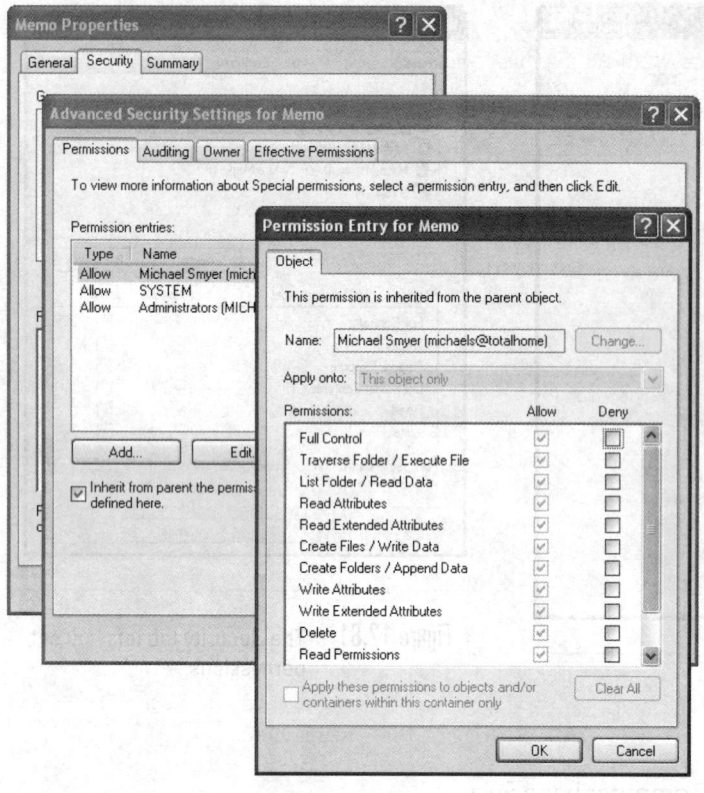

File permissions are quite similar to folder permissions. Take a look at the Security tab on a typical file (Figure 12.83).

- **Full Control**   Enables you to do anything you want!

- **Modify**   Enables you to do anything except take ownership or change permissions on the file.

- **Read & Execute**   If the file is a program, you can run it.

- **Read**   If the file is data, you can read it.

- **Write**   Enables you to write to the file.

Take some time to think about these permissions. Why would Microsoft create them? Think of situations where you might want to give a group Modify permission. Also, you can assign more than one permission. In many situations, we like to give users both the Read as well as the Write permission.

Permissions are cumulative. If you have Full Control on a folder and only Read permission on a file in the folder, you get Full Control permission on the file.

Techs and Permissions   Techs, as a rule, hate NTFS permissions. You must have administrative privileges to do almost anything on a Windows 2000/XP machine, and most administrators hate giving out administrative permissions (for obvious

● **Figure 12.82**   Special permissions

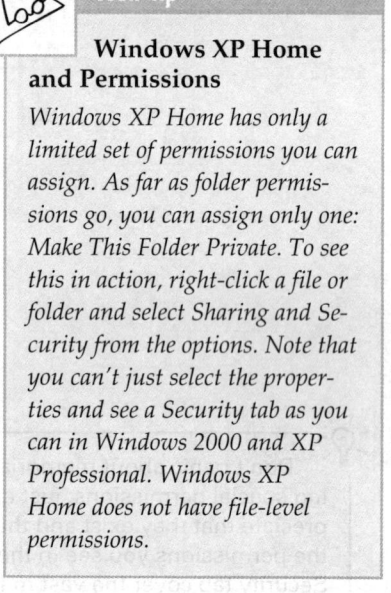

Tech Tip

Windows XP Home and Permissions

Windows XP Home has only a limited set of permissions you can assign. As far as folder permissions go, you can assign only one: Make This Folder Private. To see this in action, right-click a file or folder and select Sharing and Security from the options. Note that you can't just select the properties and see a Security tab as you can in Windows 2000 and XP Professional. Windows XP Home does not have file-level permissions.

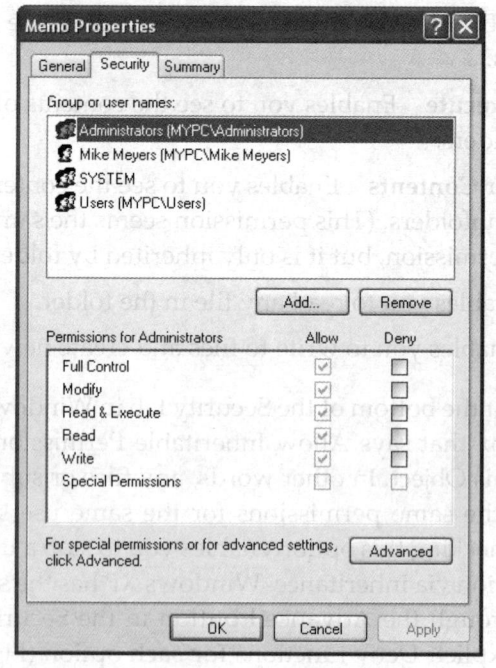

● **Figure 12.83**   Security tab

reasons). If one does give you administrative permission for a PC, and something goes wrong with that system while you're working on it, you immediately become the primary suspect!

If you're working on an 2000/XP system administered by someone else, make sure he or she understands what you are doing and how long you think it will take. Have the administrator create a new account for you with administrator privileges. Never ask for the password for a permanent administrator account! That way, you won't be blamed if anything goes wrong on that system: "Well, I told Janet the password when she installed the new hard drive…maybe she did it!" When you have fixed the system, make sure that the administrator deletes the account you used.

This "protect yourself from passwords" attitude transcends just Windows 2000/XP. PC support folks get lots of passwords, scan cards, keys, and ID tags. Most newer techs tend to get an "I can go anywhere and access anything" attitude, and this is dangerous. I've seen many jobs lost and friendships ruined when a tape backup suddenly disappears or a critical file gets erased. Everybody points to the support tech in these situations. In physical security situations, make other people unlock doors for you. In some cases, I've literally made the administrator or system owner sit behind me reading a magazine, jumping up and punching in passwords as needed. What you don't have access to can't hurt you.

The Boot Process

Windows 2000 and XP distinguish between the files that start the operating system (often called the system files or Windows startup files) and the rest of the operating system files (usually in the \WINDOWS or \WINNT folders). The system files (memorize these!) consist of three required files: NTLDR, BOOT.INI, and NTDETECT.COM. If you're using a SCSI hard drive, there's a fourth file called NTBOOTDD.SYS. NTLDR (pronounced *NT loader*) begins the boot process.

You know from earlier chapters that to make a drive bootable requires an active, primary partition, right? Let's look at the process in a PC with a hard drive partitioned as C: and D:. Ready?

The CPU wakes up and runs the system BIOS, and then the BIOS sends out a routine looking for a valid operating system in the boot sector of the primary, master hard drive. The MFT lives in the boot sector of the C: partition. It points to the location of the Windows 2000/XP system files, also on the C: drive, because that's the bootable drive. Windows calls the primary, active partition the system partition or the system volume (if it's a dynamic disk).

The Windows 2000/XP boot files consist of NTOSKRNL.EXE (the Windows kernel), the \WINNT\SYSTEM32\CONFIG\SYSTEM file (which controls the loading of device drivers), and the device drivers. Even though these files are the core of the Windows 2000/XP OS, they are not capable of booting, or starting, the system. For that feat, they require NTLDR, NTDETECT.COM, and BOOT.INI—the system files.

The system files start the PC and then, at the end of that process, point the CPU to the location of the boot files. The CPU goes over and chats with NTOSKRNL, and the GUI starts to load. The operating system is then up and running, and you're able to do work.

The odd part about all this is that Microsoft decided to make the OS files mobile. *The Windows operating system files can reside on any partition or volume in the PC.* The \WINDOWS folder, for example, could very well be on drive D:, not drive C:. Whichever drive holds the core OS files is called the **boot partition**. This can lead to a little confusion when you say the system files are on my C: drive, but Windows is on my D: drive, but that's just the way it is. The vast majority of Windows 2000/XP systems have the system partition and the boot partition both on the same big C: partition.

You've got the process now in general, so let's look more specifically at the makeup and function of the individual files involved in the boot process.

System Partition Files

Windows 2000 and XP require the three system files in the root directory of the system partition:

- NTLDR
- BOOT.INI
- NTDETECT.COM

To see these files, go into My Computer and open the C: drive. Then open Folder Options, as shown in the "My Computer" section earlier in the chapter. Click on the *Show hidden files and folders* radio button, uncheck the *Hide protected operating system files (Recommended)* option, and click OK. Now when you return to viewing the folder in My Computer, you will see certain critical files that Windows otherwise hides from you, so you don't accidentally move, delete, or change them in some unintended way (Figure 12.84).

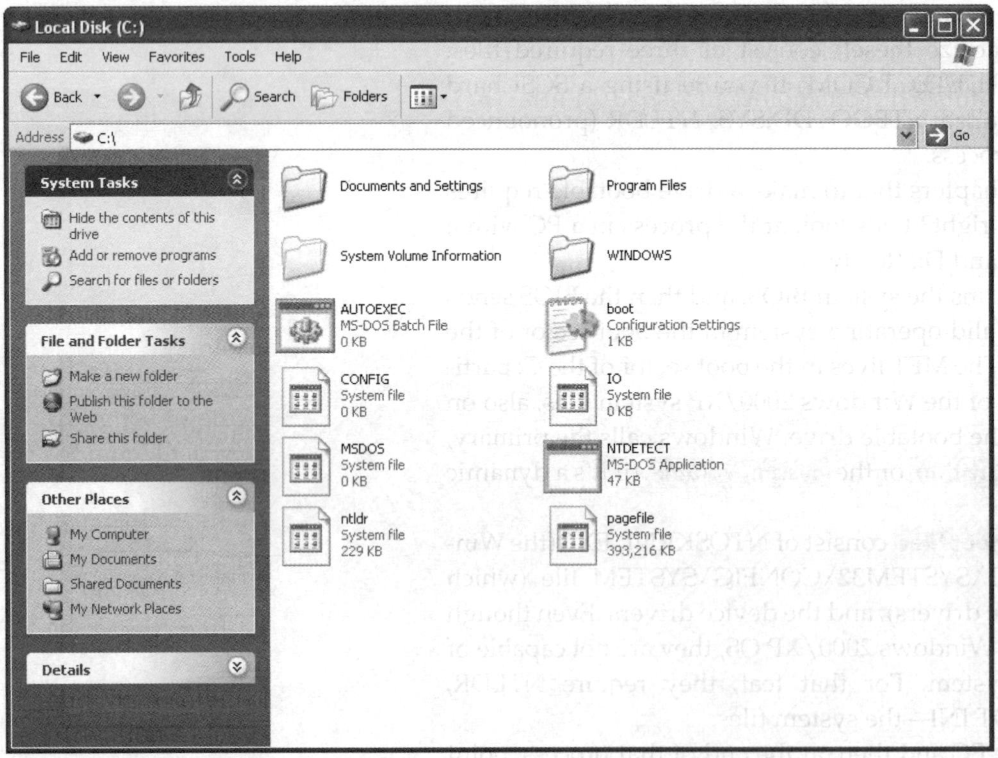

NTLDR

When the system boots up, the master boot record (MBR) or MFT on the hard drive starts the **NTLDR** program. The NTLDR program then launches Windows 2000/XP or another OS. To find the available operating systems, the NTLDR program must read the BOOT.INI configuration file, and to do so it loads its own minimal file system, which enables it to read the BOOT.INI file off the system partition.

● **Figure 12.84**   My Computer showing the system files

BOOT.INI File

The **BOOT.INI** file is a text file that lists the operating systems available to NTLDR and tells NTLDR where to find the boot partition (where the OS is stored) for each of them. The BOOT.INI file has sections defined by headings enclosed in brackets. A basic BOOT.INI in Windows XP looks like this:

```
[boot loader]
timeout=30
default=multi(0)disk(0)rdisk(0)partition(1)\WINDOWS
[operating systems]
multi(0)disk(0)rdisk(0)partition(1)\WINDOWS="Microsoft Windows XP
Professional" /fastdetect
```

A more complex BOOT.INI may look like this:

```
[boot loader]
timeout=30
default=multi(0)disk(0)rdisk(0)partition(1)\WINDOWS
[operating systems]
multi(0)disk(0)rdisk(0)partition(1)\WINDOWS="Microsoft Windows XP
Professional" /fastdetect
multi(0)disk(0)rdisk(0)partition(1)\WINNT="Microsoft Windows 2000
Professional" /fastdetect
```

Such a BOOT.INI would result in the boot menu that appears in Figure 12.85.

This crazy `multi(0)disk(0)rdisk(0)partition(1)` is an example of the **ARC naming system**. It's a system that's designed to enable your PC to use any hard drive, including removable devices, to boot Windows. Let's take a quick peek at each ARC setting to see how it works.

> ARC stands for *advanced RISC computing*, but because that means very little to techs, most folks simply call it *ARC* as a name rather than an acronym.

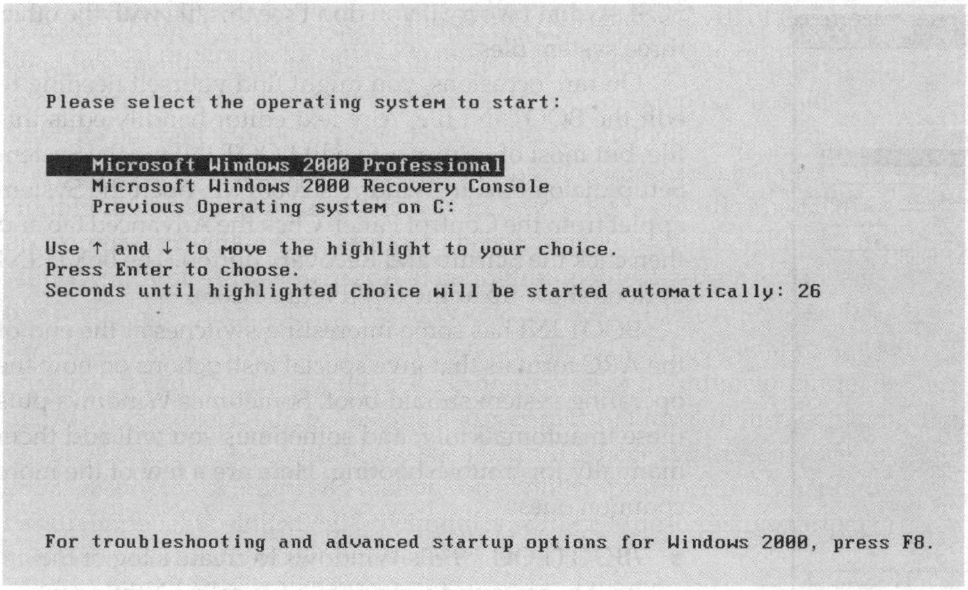

```
Please select the operating system to start:

    Microsoft Windows 2000 Professional
    Microsoft Windows 2000 Recovery Console
    Previous Operating system on C:

Use ↑ and ↓ to move the highlight to your choice.
Press Enter to choose.
Seconds until highlighted choice will be started automatically: 26

For troubleshooting and advanced startup options for Windows 2000, press F8.
```

• **Figure 12.85** Boot loader in Windows 2000 with System Recovery Console

`Multi(x)` is the number of the adapter and always starts with 0. The adapter is determined by how you set the boot order in your CMOS setting. For example, if you have a single PATA controller and a SATA controller, and you set the system to boot first from the PATA, any drive on that controller will get the value `multi(0)` placed in their ARC format. Any SATA drive will get `multi(1)`.

`Disk(x)` is only used for SCSI drives, but the value is required in the ARC format, so with ATA systems it's always set to `disk(0)`.

`Rdisk(x)` specifies the number of the disk on the adapter. On a PATA drive, the master is `rdisk(0)` and the slave is `rdisk(1)`. On SATA drives, the order is usually based on the number of the SATA connection printed on the motherboard, though some systems allow you to change this in CMOS.

`Partition(x)` is the number of the partition or logical drive in an extended partition. The numbering starts at 1, so the first partition is `partition(1)`, the second is `partition(2)`, and so on.

The `\WINDOWS` is the name of the folder that holds the boot files. This is important to appreciate! The ARC format looks at the folder, so there's no problem running different versions of Windows on a single partition. You can simply install them in different folders. Of course, you have other limitations, such as file system type, but in general, multibooting in Windows is pretty trivial. Better yet, this is all handled during the install process.

ARC format can get far more complicated. SCSI drives get a slightly different ARC format. For example, if you installed Windows on a SCSI drive, you might see this ARC setting in your BOOT.INI:

```
scsi(0)disk(1)rdisk(0)partition(1)
```

If you want to boot to a SCSI drive, Windows will add a fourth file to your system files called NTBOOTDD.SYS. This file will only exist if you want to boot to a SCSI drive. Most people don't boot to a SCSI, so don't worry if you don't see this file with the other three system files.

On rare occasions, you might find yourself needing to edit the BOOT.INI file. Any text editor handily edits this file, but most of us prefer to edit BOOT.INI via the System Setup dialog box. In Windows 2000/XP, open the System applet from the Control Panel. Click the Advanced tab and then click the Startup and Recovery button. The BOOT.INI options show up at the top (Figure 12.86).

BOOT.INI has some interesting switches at the end of the ARC formats that give special instructions on how the operating system should boot. Sometimes Windows puts these in automatically, and sometimes you will add them manually for troubleshooting. Here are a few of the more common ones:

- **/BOOTLOG** Tells Windows to create a log of the boot process and write it to a file called Ntbtlog.txt.

- **/CMDCONS** Tells Windows to start the Recovery Console (see Chapter 13).

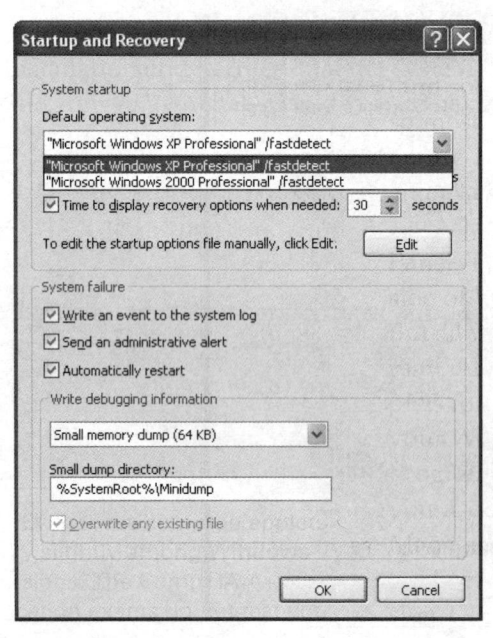

• **Figure 12.86** BOOT.INI options

- **/LASTKNOWNGOOD**   Tells Windows to boot the Last Known Good set of files.

- **/NOEXECUTE**   Newer CPUs come with Data Execute Protection (DEP) to prevent unruly programs from causing system lockups. The setting for this, /NOEXECUTE=OPTIN, is the default on Windows systems.

NTDETECT.COM

If the NTLDR determines that you have chosen to start Windows 2000/XP, it boots the system into protected mode and then calls on **NTDETECT.COM** to detect the installed hardware on the system. NTLDR then refers to the BOOT.INI file to locate the Windows boot files.

Critical Boot Files

Naming all of the critical boot files for Windows 2000/XP is akin to naming every muscle in the human body—completely possible, but time-consuming and without any real benefit. However, a few of the *most* important files certainly deserve a short mention.

Once NTLDR finishes detections, it loads NTOSKRNL.EXE, HAL.DLL, some of the Registry, and some basic device drivers; then it passes control to the NTOSKRNL.EXE file. NTOSKRNL.EXE completes the Registry loading, initializes all device drivers, and starts the WINLOGON.EXE program, which displays the Windows 2000/XP logon screen (Figure 12.87).

Take the time to memorize the primary boot files and the boot process for Windows 2000/XP. Most boot errors are easily repaired if you know which files are used for booting and in which order they load.

• **Figure 12.87**   Where do you want to go today?

■ Windows Versions

Up to this point, we've been talking about two different versions of Windows: Windows 2000 Professional and Windows XP Professional. This is a great way to look at the big picture with Windows operating systems, but if you want to get detailed—and we need to get detailed—Windows 2000 and Windows XP are really families of Windows operating systems. In this section, we'll look at every version of Windows 2000 and XP, as well as a few other versions of Windows, and see the differences in detail.

Before Windows XP came along, Windows was in a bit of a mess. Microsoft had two totally different operating systems—each called Windows—that it sold for two different markets. Microsoft sold the old Windows 9x series (Windows 95, Windows 98, and Windows Me) for the home user and small office, and the much more powerful Windows NT was for corporate environments. The Windows 9x operating systems were little more than upgrades from the old DOS operating system, still tied to old 8088 programs (we call these 16-bit programs), unable to use the powerful NTFS file system and generally unstable for any serious work. Windows NT had all the power and security we love in Windows 2000 and XP, but it lacked a powerful interface and many other little niceties we expect in our Windows today.

Windows 2000 was the first step towards changing this mess. It was based on the old Windows NT, but for the first time it included a great interface, support for dang near any program, and was generally substantially easier to use than the old Windows NT. Microsoft originally presented Windows 2000 as a replacement for Windows NT, but its stability and ease of use motivated many knowledgeable Windows 9x users to upgrade. Windows 2000 is still very popular today, even with Windows XP and Windows Vista now available.

Windows 2000 comes in two versions: Professional and Server. Every description of Windows 2000 thus far has referred to the Professional version, so let's talk about Server. If you were to look at the Windows 2000 Server desktop, you'd be hard-pressed to see any obvious differences from Windows 2000. Windows 2000 Server (Figure 12.88) is the heavy-duty version, loaded with extra software and features that make it superb for running an office server. Windows 2000 Server is also extremely expensive, costing on average around US$200 per computer that accesses the server.

Windows XP was designed to be the one-stop OS for everyone. And because Microsoft sees three types of users—professionals, home users, and

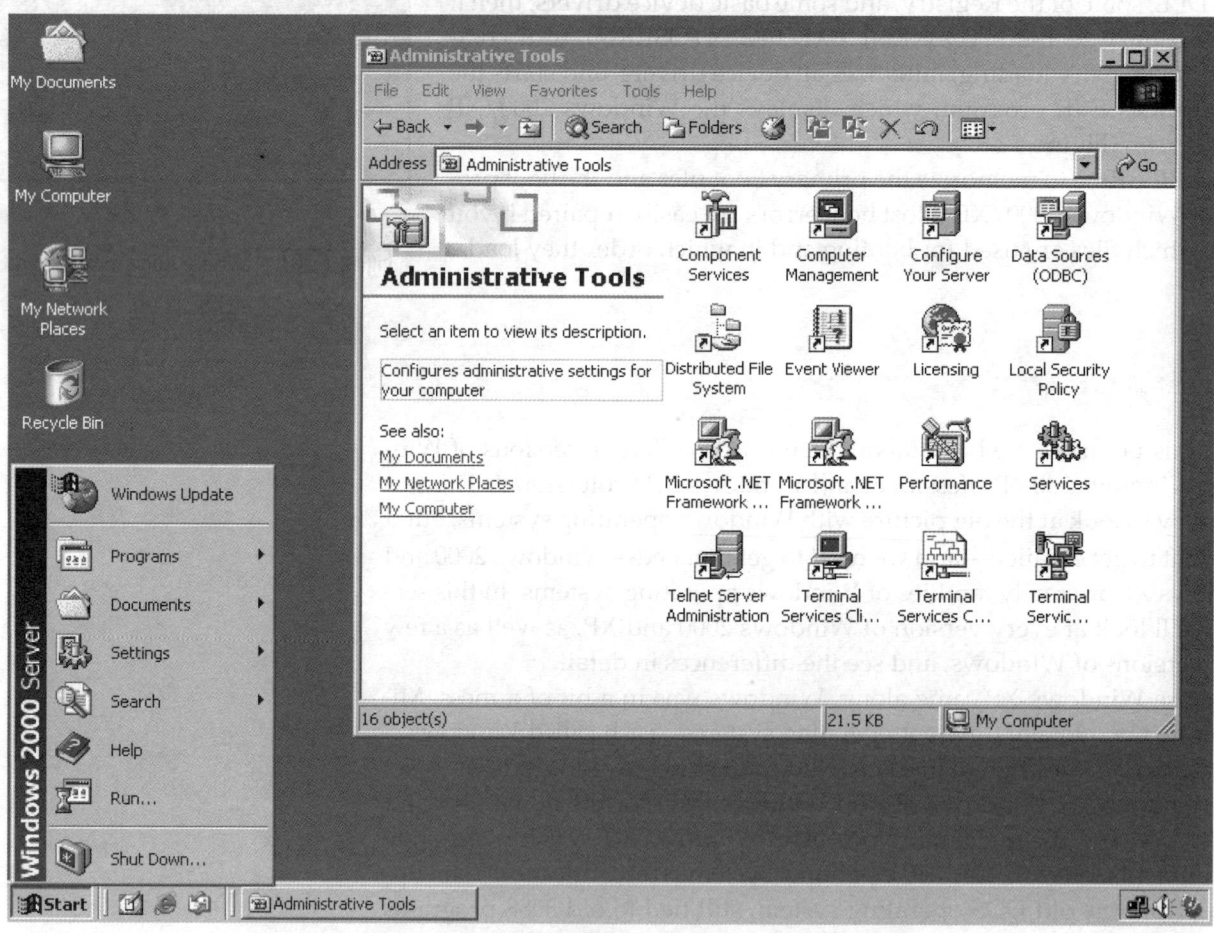

● Figure 12.88   Windows 2000 Server

media junkies—Windows XP comes in three different versions: Windows XP Professional, Windows XP Home, and Windows XP Media Center. There is no official server version of Windows XP.

Windows Server 2003 is not an official XP version, but it is the server Microsoft likes folks to use with Windows XP.

Windows XP Professional

Microsoft Windows XP Professional offers a complete computing solution, tuned for office environments that support multiple users. It provides full-blown data security, and it is the only version of Windows with the capability of logging into a special Windows Server–controlled network called a *domain*. (Windows domains are discussed in detail in Chapter 18, "Understanding Networking.")

Windows XP Home

As its name implies, Windows XP Home is designed for the home and small office user. The best way to describe Windows XP Home is to list the Windows XP Professional features that Windows XP Home lacks. Windows XP Home does *not* have:

- **The ability to log on to a Windows domain**   A Windows Home PC may log into any single Windows server, but you must have a user name and password on every single server. With a domain, you can have one user name and password that works on all computers that are members of the domain.

- **Encrypted File System**   With Windows XP Professional you can encrypt a file so that only you can read it.

- **Support for multiple processors**   Windows XP Home does not support more than one CPU. Surprisingly, it does support dual-core CPUs!

- **Support for Remote Desktop**   A Windows XP Professional PC may be remotely accessed from another computer using the Remote Desktop (Figure 12.89). You cannot access a Windows XP Home system in this fashion.

- **Support for NTFS Access Control**   Remember all those neato NTFS permissions like Full Control, Modify, and Read & Execute? Well, Windows XP Home doesn't give you the ability to control these NTFS permissions individually. When you look at the properties of a file or folder in Windows XP Home, you'll notice that there is no Security Tab. Instead, Windows XP Home's Sharing Tab (Figure 12.90) shows that only one folder, the Shared Documents folder, is open for sharing—very different from XP Professional!

- **Support for group policies**   Do you need to keep users from using a certain program? Do you want to prevent them from changing the screensaver? What do you want to do if they try to log in three times unsuccessfully? That's the job of group polices. Well, if you want this level of control on your system, get Windows XP Professional as XP Home doesn't support them. Group policies are discussed in detail in Chapter 19, "Computer Security."

Figure 12.89   Remote Desktop

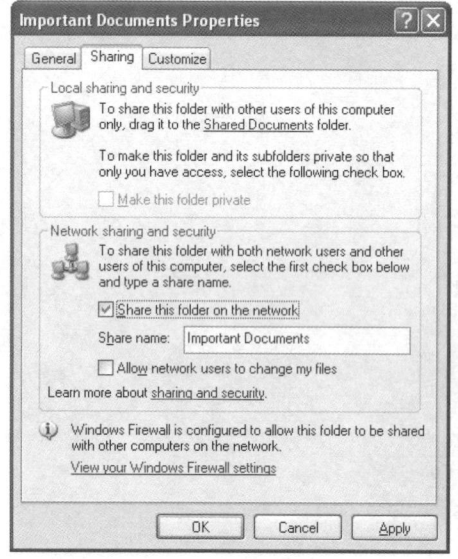

Figure 12.90   Windows XP Home Sharing tab

There are a few more differences between Windows XP Professional and XP Home, but these are the ones you're most likely to run into. Basically, if you want serious control of the folders, files, users, and network, you need XP Professional.

Windows XP Media Center

Microsoft Media Center is a specialized XP version that includes the very handy Windows Media Center program (Figure 12.91). Media Center is a powerful Personal Video Recorder (PVR) program that enables you to watch and record television (you'll need a TV tuner card) and organize all of your media, from photos to music.

On the Microsoft Media Center Web site, Microsoft declares that the Windows XP Microsoft Media Center edition is based on Windows XP Professional; however, other than the Media Center program, Windows XP Media Center's capabilities are identical to those of Windows XP Home.

Windows 64-Bit Versions

Microsoft has multiple versions of Windows designed to support 64-bit CPUs. If you remember from the CPU chapter, there are two families of 64-bit CPUs: the ones that don't support 32-bit processors (like the Intel Itanium2) and ones that can run both 64-bit and 32-bit (like the Intel Core 2). The 64-bit-only version of Windows is called Windows XP 64-bit Edition (apparently Microsoft decided not to get cute when naming that one). Given that it only works on Intel Itanium processors, the chance of you seeing this operating system is pretty small unless you decide to work in a place with powerful server needs. The Windows XP Professional x64 Edition is much more common, as it runs on any AMD or Intel processor that supports both 32 and 64 bits (Figure 12.92).

Windows XP 64-bit versions have had some impact, as they were the first stable Windows versions that truly supported 64-bit processing, but it was the introduction of Microsoft Vista that really started the move into the 64-bit world.

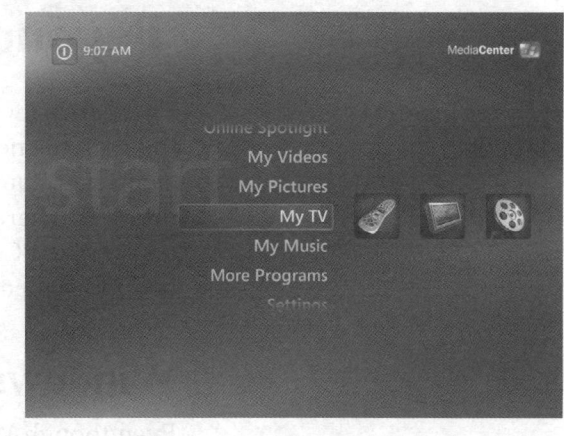

• **Figure 12.91**   Microsoft Media Center

Windows Server 2003 also has a 64-bit version.

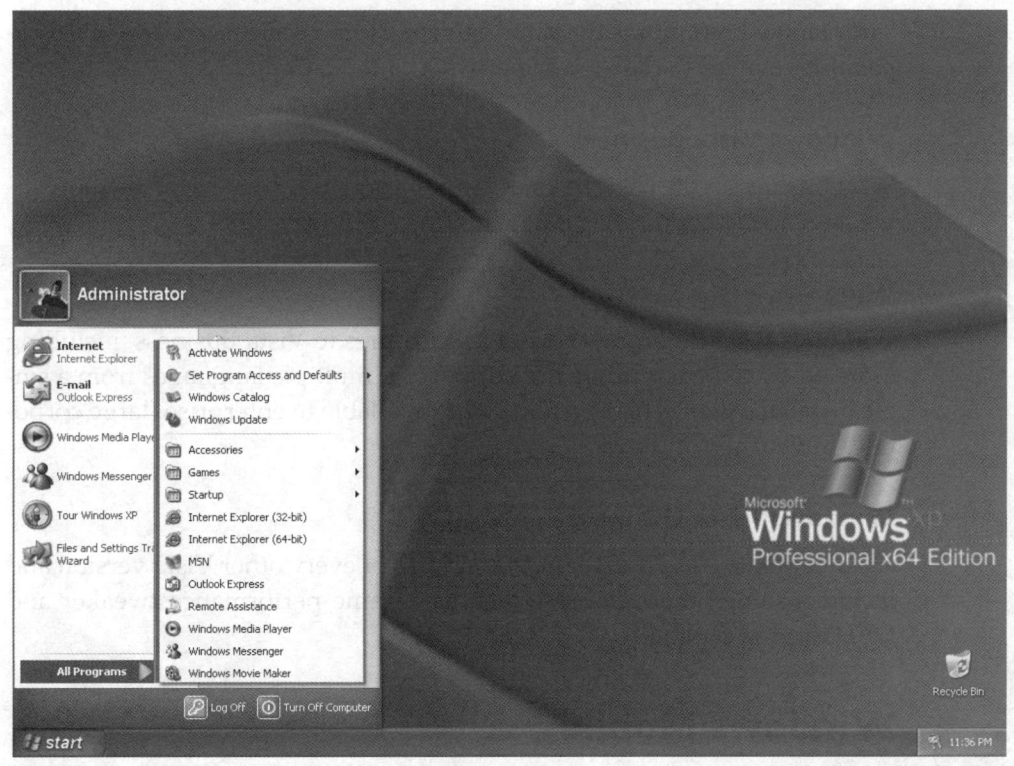

• **Figure 12.92**   Windows XP Professional x64 Edition

Beyond A+

There are a few more versions of Windows you should know about, starting with the newest version, Windows Vista. It's not on the CompTIA A+ exam (yet), but if you're working as a PC tech, you'll soon start encountering it. There are also several specialized versions that you won't find on regular PCs but that are very popular on PDAs, tablet PCs, and embedded systems.

Windows Vista

Even though Windows Vista is not a part of the current CompTIA A+ exams, it's important to at least recognize what Vista is, and know what choices you have when deciding which version of Vista you need for a particular PC. Windows has a number of different versions of Vista, each geared toward a particular market segment. Let's look at the different version of Vista.

Windows Vista Home Basic

Vista Home Basic is roughly equivalent to XP Home. Microsoft gears it to home users not needing more advanced multimedia support.

Windows Vista Home Premium

Vista Home Premium is the same as Vista Home Basic, but it adds PVR capabilities similar to those of Windows XP Media Center.

Windows Vista Business

Vista Business is the basic business version and has all the security, file sharing, and access controls seen in Windows XP Professional.

Windows Vista Enterprise

Windows Vista Enterprise adds a few features to Vista Business, including more advanced encryption and support for multiple languages from a single install location. This version is only available to enterprise (large corporate) buyers of Windows.

Windows Vista Ultimate

Vista Ultimate combines all of the features of every other Vista version and includes some other features, such as a game performance tweaker and DVD ripping capability.

Windows Mobile

Windows Mobile is a very small version of Windows designed for PDAs and phones. Windows Mobile is only available as an Original Equipment Manufacturer (OEM) product, which means you buy the device and it comes with Windows Mobile—you can't buy some PDA or phone and then buy Windows Mobile separately.

Windows XP Tablet PC

A tablet PC is a laptop with a built-in touch screen (Figure 12.93). The idea behind a tablet PC is to reduce drastically, if not totally eliminate, the use of a keyboard. Tablet PCs have become quite popular in several roles, such as teaching and health care. Windows XP Tablet PC edition is Microsoft's operating solution for tablet PCs. Tablet PC is still Windows XP, but it adds special drivers and applications to support the tablet.

You'll see more of Windows XP Tablet PC Edition in Chapter 16, "Portable Computing."

Windows Embedded

The world is filled with PCs in the most unlikely places. Everything from cash registers to the F-22 Raptor fighting plane contain some number of tiny PCs. These aren't the PCs you're used to seeing, though. They almost never have mice, monitors, keyboards, and the usual I/O you'd expect to see, but they are truly PCs, with a CPU, RAM, BIOS, and storage.

These tiny PCs need operating systems just like any other PC, and there are a number of different companies that make specialized OSs for embedded PCs. Microsoft makes Windows Embedded just for these specialized embedded PCs.

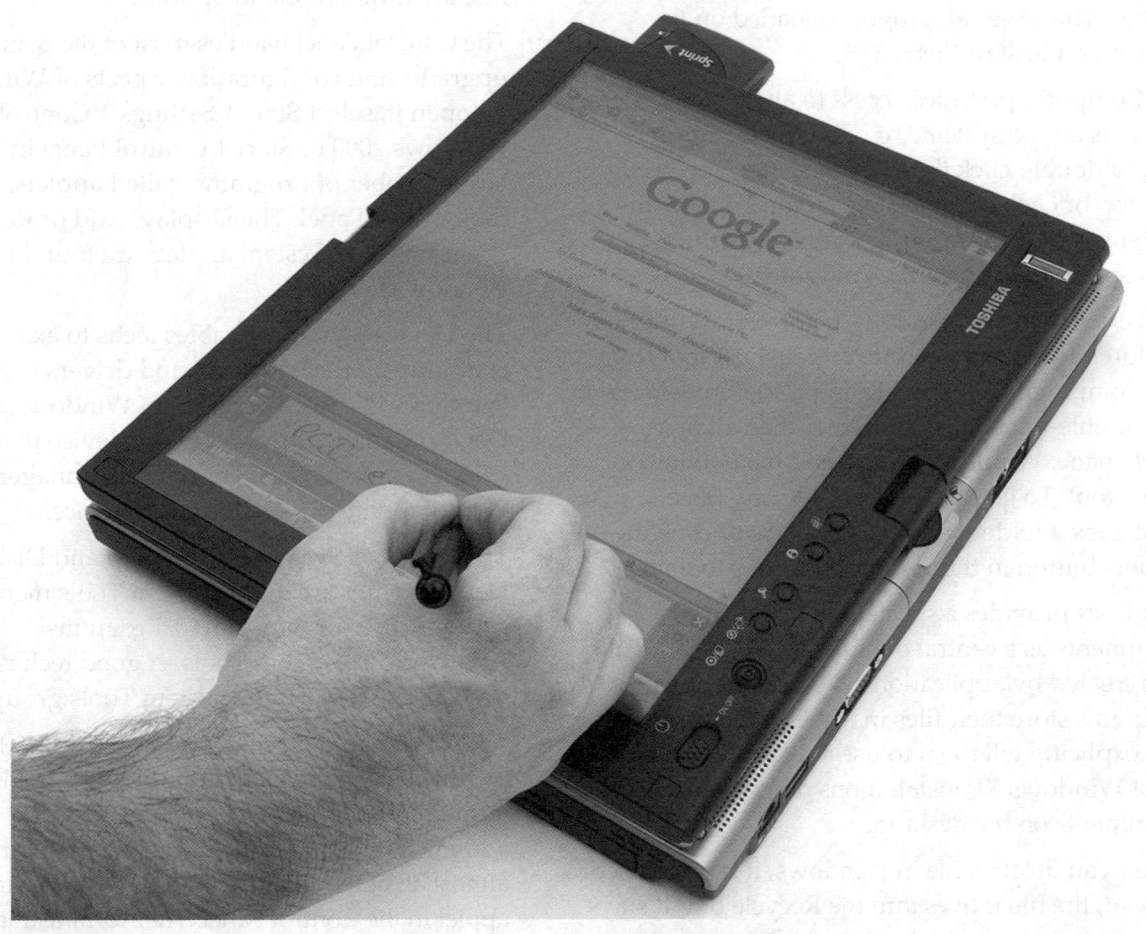

• **Figure 12.93**   Tablet PC

Chapter 12 Review

■ Chapter Summary

After reading this chapter and completing the exercises, you should understand the following about Windows.

The Windows Interface

■ Every version of Windows supports multiple users on a single machine, and thus the starting point for any tour of the Windows user interface starts with the login screen. Logging in displays the Windows desktop, the primary interface to the computer. It contains icons and various graphical elements.

■ The taskbar, by default, runs along the bottom of the Windows desktop and has up to four sections (depending on the version of Windows and your configuration): Start button, Quick Launch toolbar, running programs area, and system tray. Clicking the Start button opens the Start menu, which enables you to see all programs loaded on the system and to start them.

■ My Computer provides access to all drives, folders, and files on the system. To open My Computer, simply double-click the My Computer icon on the desktop or click it in the Start menu. To view the contents of a drive or disk, double-click the corresponding icon in My Computer.

■ In every version of Windows before XP, Windows Explorer acts like a separate and distinct tool from My Computer, showing file and folder information in a double-paned fashion rather than all in a single pane. Windows XP merged the two into a single tool. To get the Explorer-like interface, right-click a folder and select Explore or click the Folders button in the Standard Buttons toolbar.

■ Windows provides a special folder called My Documents as a central default storage area for all files created by applications. Newer Windows programs store their files in My Documents unless you explicitly tell them to use a different folder. Most Windows XP installations do not show My Documents on the desktop.

■ When you delete a file in Windows, it is not erased. Instead, the file moves into the Recycle Bin. It stays there until you empty the Recycle Bin or restore the folder or file, or until the Recycle Bin grows larger than a preset amount. To access the Recycle Bin's

settings, right-click on the Recycle Bin and select Properties.

■ Systems tied to a network, either via a network cable or by a modem, have a folder called My Network Places. This shows all the current network connections available to you.

■ Windows offers six locations where techs can access utilities to configure the OS, optimize and tweak settings, install hardware, and more: right-click menu, Control Panel, System Tools, command line, Administrative Tools, and the Microsoft Management Console.

■ Right-clicking an object brings up a context menu offering commands to deal with the object on which you clicked. Different types of files will display different menu options.

■ The Control Panel handles most of the maintenance, upgrade, and configuration aspects of Windows. To open it, select Start | Settings | Control Panel in Windows 2000 or Start | Control Panel in XP. A large number of programs, called applets, populate the Control Panel. The Display, Add or Remove Programs, and System applets are found in all Windows versions.

■ The Device Manager enables techs to examine and configure all the hardware and drivers in a Windows PC. In all versions of Windows, the Device Manager displays every device that Windows recognizes. The Device Manager enables you to update drivers for listed devices.

■ Tools such as System Information and Disk Defragmenter are in the System Tools menu, accessed by choosing Start | Programs | Accessories | System Tools. A good tech is familiar with all the tools in the System Tools group.

■ The Microsoft Management Console (MMC) is a shell program in Windows 2000 and XP that holds individual utilities, called *snap-ins*, used for administration and troubleshooting. You can find almost all of the snap-ins in the Administrative Tools applet in the Control Panel. The Administrative Tools most used by techs are Computer Management, Event Viewer, Performance, and Services.

- The Computer Management applet's components include System Tools and Storage. System Tools offers System Information, Performance Logs and Alerts, the Device Manager, and more. Storage is where you'll find Disk Management.

- Event Viewer enables you to tell at a glance what has happened in the last day, week, or more, including when people have logged in and when the PC had problems.

- The Performance console consists of two snap-ins: System Monitor and Performance Logs and Alerts. You can use these for reading logs—files that record information over time. The System Monitor can also monitor real-time data.

- Windows comes with about 100 separate programs called services that run invisibly in the background. The Services applet enables you to see the status of all services on the system, including services that are not running. Right-click a service and select Properties to modify its settings.

- The Registry stores everything about your PC, including information on all the hardware in the PC, network information, user preferences, and file types. Almost any form of configuration done to a Windows system involves editing the Registry. In Windows 2000/XP, the numerous Registry files (called *hives*) are in the \%SystemRoot%\System32\config folder.

- The main way to access the Registry is through the Control Panel. You can open the Control Panel by selecting Start | Settings | Control Panel. The main function of the Control Panel applets is to update the Registry via fairly intuitive interfaces.

- When you want to access the Registry directly, you must use the Registry Editor. In Windows 2000, there were two similar tools: REGEDIT.EXE and REGEDT32.EXE. Windows XP has combined these into a single tool. To start the Registry Editor, choose Start | Run and type **REGEDIT** or **REGEDT32** (Windows 2000 will open the tool you specify, while Windows XP will open the unified tool no matter which you type).

- The Registry is organized in a tree structure similar to the folders in the PC. The Registry has five main subgroups or root keys: HKEY_CLASSES_ROOT, HKEY_CURRENT_USER, HKEY_LOCAL_MACHINE, HKEY_USERS, and HKEY_CURRENT_CONFIG. Each of the root keys has a specific function, and subkeys are listed underneath them. A subkey also has other subkeys or values. REGEDIT shows keys on the left and values on the right, just as Windows Explorer shows directories on the left and files on the right.

- All versions of Windows can use a portion of the hard drive as an extension of system RAM by using a RAM cache. A RAM cache is a block of cylinders set aside on a hard drive as what's called a swap file, page file, or virtual memory, called PAGEFILE.SYS in Windows 2000/XP. When the PC starts running out of real RAM because you've loaded too many programs, the system swaps programs from RAM to the swap file, opening more space for programs currently active.

Features and Characteristics of Windows 2000/XP

- Windows 2000/XP takes an object-oriented approach, separating the OS into three distinct parts: the drivers, the NT Executive, and the subsystems. The NT Executive uses the HAL to separate the system-specific device drivers from the rest of the system. Windows' robustness comes from separating running processes into subsystems.

- Microsoft designed and optimized every aspect of Windows 2000/XP for multiuser, networked environments. This is most evident in the file system—2000 and XP use a powerful and robust file system called NTFS.

- NTFS offers the following excellent features: long filenames, redundancy, backward compatibility, recoverability, and security. NTFS filenames can be up to 255 characters. NTFS has a very advanced FAT called the MFT. An NTFS partition keeps a backup copy of the most critical parts of the MFT in the middle of the disk, reducing the chance that a serious drive error can wipe out both the MFT and the MFT copy.

- NTFS has powerful security functions. The three major features of NTFS security are accounts, groups, and permissions. To use a Windows 2000/XP system, you must have a valid account and password. Every Windows 2000/XP system has a "super" account called administrator that has access to everything. When you first install a Windows 2000/XP system, it prompts you for a password for the administrator account.

- The administrator creates user accounts with a special program called Users and Passwords in Windows 2000 and User Accounts in Windows XP. A user name defines an account for a person who has access to the PC. A group is a collection of accounts that share the same access capabilities, and a single account can be a member of multiple groups. An administrator can assign a certain level of access for a file or folder to a group instead of an account.

- In the Windows 2000/XP world, every folder and file on an NTFS partition has a list that contains two sets of data: every user and group that has access to that file or folder, and the level of access that each user or group has to that file or folder. A set of detailed and powerful restrictions called permissions define exactly what a particular account can or cannot do to the file or folder.

- When you create a new file or folder on an NTFS partition, you become the owner of that file or folder, which means you can do anything you want to it, including changing the permissions to prevent anybody, even administrators, from accessing it.

- In Windows 2000/XP, just about everything in the computer has a Security tab in its properties (provided the hard drive is NTFS). Every Security tab contains a list of accounts that have permissions for that resource, and the permissions assigned to those accounts. The standard permissions for a folder are Full Control, Modify, Read & Execute, List Folder Contents, Read, and Write. The standard File permissions are Full Control, Modify, Read & Execute, Read, and Write. Permissions are cumulative.

- Windows 2000 and XP separate the startup or system files from the rest of the operating system files. The system files—NTLDR, NTDETECT.COM, BOOT.INI, and sometimes NTBOOTDD.SYS— must be on the system partition, but the rest of the operating system files can be anywhere. The system files begin the startup process and the boot files—NTOSKRNL.EXE, SYSTEM—load drivers and the GUI. The boot files are located on the boot

partition, right along with the rest of the operating system files.

- When the system starts up, the master boot record (MBR) on the hard drive starts the NTLDR program. The NTLDR program then launches either Windows 2000/XP or another OS. To find the available OSs, the NTLDR program must read the BOOT.INI configuration file.

- NTLDR boots the system into protected mode and then calls on NTDETECT.COM to detect the installed hardware on the system. Once NTLDR finishes detections, it loads NTOSKRNL.EXE, HAL.DLL, some of the Registry, and some basic device drivers, and then it passes control to the NTOSKRNL.EXE file. NTOSKRNL.EXE completes the Registry loading, initializes all devices drivers, and starts the WINLOGON.EXE program, which displays the famous Windows logon screen.

Windows Versions

- Windows 9*x* includes Windows 95, 98, and Me. Windows NT, 2000, XP, 2003, and Vista are all based on Windows NT and offer substantial benefits over Windows 9*x* editions.

- Windows 2000 comes in two basic varieties: Professional and Server. Professional was aimed at the business workstation user while Server was meant for servers. There are several different versions of Windows 2000 Server.

- Windows XP comes as a workstation OS only— there is no XP Server. The two main versions of XP are XP Home, designed for the home user, and XP Professional, designed for business environments and power users. XP Professional contains several features not available in XP Home, including Remote Desktop, Encrypted File System, the ability to join a Windows domain, and support for multiple processors.

- Other versions of Windows XP are aimed at specialty markets: XP Media Center Edition, XP 64-bit Edition, and XP Tablet PC Edition.

- The newest version of Windows is Windows Vista. It comes in five varieties, each targeting a different type of user.

Key Terms

Administrative Tools (359)
administrator (372)
ARC naming system (379)
applets (348)
boot files (377)
boot partition (378)
BOOT.INI (379)
class object (365)
Computer Management (360)
Control Panel (348)
desktop (336)
Device Manager (349)
Event Viewer (360)
Files and Settings Transfer Wizard (354)
file association (366)
group (373)
hot keys (346)
master file table (MFT) (372)

Microsoft Management Console (MMC) (357)
My Computer (340)
My Documents (343)
My Network Places (345)
NT Executive (370)
NT File System (NTFS) (371)
NTDETECT.COM (381)
NTFS permissions (374)
NTLDR (378)
page file (367)
Quick Launch toolbar (340)
Recycle Bin (345)
Registry (363)
Registry Editor (364)
Scheduled Tasks (354)
Security Center (355)
services (362)
simple file sharing (374)

snap-in (357)
Start button (339)
Start menu (339)
swap file (367)
symmetric multiprocessing (SMP) (371)
system files (377)
system partition (377)
System Restore (355)
system tools (352)
system tray (339)
system volume (377)
SystemRoot (362)
taskbar (339)
user name (373)
virtual memory (367)
Windows Explorer (343)
Windows startup files (377)

Key Term Quiz

Use the Key Terms list to complete the sentences that follow. Not all terms will be used.

1. You can readily see programs running in the background by looking at the _____.

2. The _____ stores information about all the hardware, drivers, and applications on a Windows system.

3. The first place you should look on a PC with malfunctioning hardware is _____.

4. Most tech tools in Windows can be found in _____.

5. In Windows XP, _____ starts the boot process.

6. The _____ in Windows offers a great spot for accessing favorite programs without resorting to the Start menu or cluttering your desktop with program shortcuts.

7. Jill accidentally deleted a critical file. Winona the tech assures her that the file is no doubt in the _____ and not lost forever.

8. Windows uses the _____ or swap file for virtual memory.

9. On a system that has a dynamic disk for a C: drive, the Windows startup files can be found in the _____.

10. The BOOT.INI file uses the _____ notation to locate the operating system.

Multiple-Choice Quiz

1. What is the best way to access the Registry editor in Windows XP?

   A. Start | Programs | DOS prompt icon. Type **EDIT**.

   B. Start | Programs | Registry Editor.

   C. Start | Run. Type **REGEDIT32** and click OK.

   D. Start | Run. Type **REGEDT32** and click OK.

2. Which of the following files is necessary for *all* Windows 2000/XP systems?

   A. NTLDR

   B. NTBOOTDD.SYS

C. BOOT.INF

D. CONFIG.SYS

3. Windows XP provides a number of ready-made MMC snap-ins stored in the _____ applet in the Control Panel.

A. System

B. Network

C. Administrative Tools

D. MMC

4. Which feature of Windows enables you to revive a PC that crashes hard after installing some new application?

A. Command-line interface

B. Driver Rollback

C. System Recovery

D. System Restore

5. Which of the following are part of the Windows desktop?

A. Services, command line, applications

B. Right-click, drag and drop, point and click

C. Quick Launch toolbar, system tray, taskbar

D. CPU, RAM, hard drive

6. Turning off automatic configuration of a device results in Device Manager displaying what icon?

A. Red "X"

B. Yellow "!"

C. Blue "i"

D. Green "a"

7. The Disk Cleanup utility keeps starting automatically on your Windows XP system. Why might this happen?

A. Your disk is more than 20 percent fragmented.

B. Windows Update has installed a security patch.

C. Security Center has detected a virus.

D. You have less than 200 MB of free disk space.

8. The Microsoft Management Console holds individual utilities called what?

A. Built-ins

B. Snap-ins

C. Applets

D. MMCs

9. The folder in which Windows is installed is known generically as what?

A. RootFolder

B. WinRoot

C. SystemRoot

D. System32

10. Windows 2000 and Windows XP default to installing into which folders respectively?

A. WINNT, Windows

B. Windows, WINNT

C. Windows, Windows

D. WINNT, WINNT

11. What is the name of the virtual memory file in Windows 2000/XP?

A. SWAP.SYS

B. CACHE.VM

C. SYSTEM.RAM

D. PAGEFILE.SYS

12. Which component handles the memory management and multitasking of Windows?

A. NTLDR

B. NT Executive

C. Hardware abstraction layer (HAL)

D. NT file system

13. Which built-in group is the most powerful in Windows?

A. Administrators

B. Root

C. Power Users

D. Replicators

14. If you were booting from the first controller, the first hard drive, and the first partition, what would the ARC path look like in BOOT.INI?

A. multi(0)disk(0)rdisk(0)partition(0)

B. multi(0)disk(0)rdisk(0)partition(1)

C. multi(0)disk(1)rdisk(0)partition(0)

D. multi(0)disk(1)rdisk(0)partition(1)

15. Which Windows OS has only desktop editions and no server edition?

A. 2000

B. 2003

C. XP

D. Both A and B

Essay Quiz

1. Your department just got four new interns who will share two PCs running Windows XP. Your boss has decided that you're the person who should take the newbies under your wing and teach them about Windows. Write a brief essay on some essential Windows folders and interfaces that every *user* should know.

2. Your boss just got off the phone with the corporate headquarters and is in somewhat of a panic. She doesn't know the first thing about the Microsoft Management Console, but now every tech is going to be issued a custom MMC. Write a brief essay explaining the function of the MMC to help allay her worries.

3. A colleague has approached you with a serious problem. He was on tech support for his home PC, and the support person told him the only way to fix the problem he was having on his Windows XP Home PC was to edit the Registry manually. Then the tech scared him, saying that if he messed up, he could destroy his PC forever. Write a short essay discussing the Registry and the tools for editing it.

4. As part of your promotion, it is your responsibility to train the new techs your boss just hired. Write a brief essay describing the tools in the System Tools folder group.

5. A friend has just upgraded from Windows 98 to Windows XP. She was familiar with right-clicking My Computer and choosing Properties in Windows 98 to get to the System Properties dialog box, but she has questions about the Manage option in Windows XP. Write a brief essay explaining the differences between the windows that appear when choosing Properties versus Manage when right-clicking My Computer.

Lab Projects

• Lab Project 12.1

Create your own MMC loaded with the snap-ins you use the most, or that you would like to experiment with. Add at least three snap-ins. Save the MMC on your desktop and give it an appropriate name.

• Lab Project 12.2

In a couple of places in the chapter, you got a taste of working with some of the more complex tools in Windows 2000/XP, such as the Event Viewer and Performance console. Go back through the text and reread those sections, and then do an Internet search for a "how-to" article. Then work with the tools.

Maintaining Windows

chapter 13

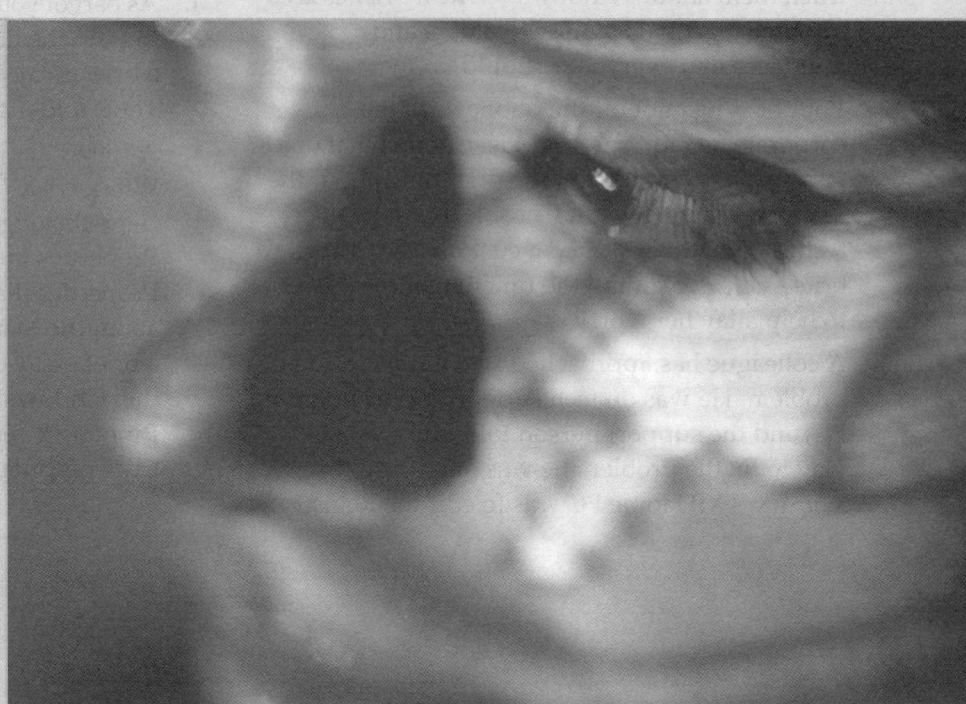

"I am not interested in excuses. Fix it."

—Colonel Tigh,
Battlestar Galactica

In this chapter, you will learn how to

- **Maintain Windows 2000/XP**
- **Optimize Windows 2000/XP**

An installed Windows operating system needs occasional optimization, ongoing maintenance, and troubleshooting when it doesn't work correctly. Not that long ago, Windows had a bit of a bad rap as being difficult to maintain and challenging to troubleshoot problems. Microsoft used its 20-plus years of experience with operating systems searching for ways to make the tasks of maintaining and troubleshooting less onerous. They've done such a good job with the latest versions of Windows that, out of the box, they are easy to optimize and maintain, although troubleshooting—and all operating systems share this—is still a bit of a challenge.

The chapter covers optimization and maintenance, so let's make sure you know what these two terms mean. CompTIA sees optimization as jobs you do to your Windows system to make it better—a good example is adding RAM. Maintenance means jobs you do from time to time to keep Windows running well, such as running hard drive utilities. This chapter covers the standard maintenance and optimization activities performed on Windows and the tools techs use to perform them.

Essentials

■ Maintaining Windows

Maintaining Windows can be compared to maintaining a new automobile. Of course, a new automobile comes with a warranty, so most of us just take it to the dealer to get work done. In this case, *you* are the mechanic, so you need to think as an auto mechanic would think. First, an auto mechanic needs to apply recalls when the automaker finds a serious problem. For a PC Tech, that means keeping the system patches announced by Microsoft up to date. You also need to check on the parts that wear down over time. On a car that might mean changing the oil or rotating the tires. In a Windows system that includes keeping the hard drive and Registry organized and uncluttered.

Patches, Updates, and Service Packs

Updating Windows has been an important, but often neglected, task for computer users. Typically, Microsoft finds and corrects problems with its software in a timely fashion. Because earlier versions of Windows let users decide when, if ever, to update their computers, the net result could be disastrous. The Blaster worm hammered computers all over the world in the summer of 2003, causing thousands of computers to start rebooting spontaneously—no small feat for a tiny piece of programming! Blaster exploited a flaw in Windows 2000/XP and spread like wildfire, but Microsoft had *already corrected* the flaw with a security update weeks earlier. If users had simply updated their computers, the virus would not have caused such widespread damage.

The Internet has enabled Microsoft to make updates available, and the Windows Update program can grab those updates and patch user systems easily and automatically. Even if you don't want to allow Windows Update to patch your computer automatically, it'll still nag you about updates until you patch your system. Microsoft provides the Windows Update utility in Windows 2000 and Windows XP.

Once Microsoft released Service Pack 2 for Windows XP, it began pushing for wholesale acceptance of automatic updates from Windows Update. You can also start Windows Update manually. When your computer is connected to the Internet, start the utility in Windows 2000 by selecting Start | Windows Update. In Windows XP, you will find it at Start | All Programs | Windows Update. When you run Windows Update manually, the software connects to the Microsoft Web site and scans your computer to determine what updates may be needed. Within a few seconds or minutes, depending on your connection speed, you'll get a straightforward screen, like the one shown in Figure 13.1.

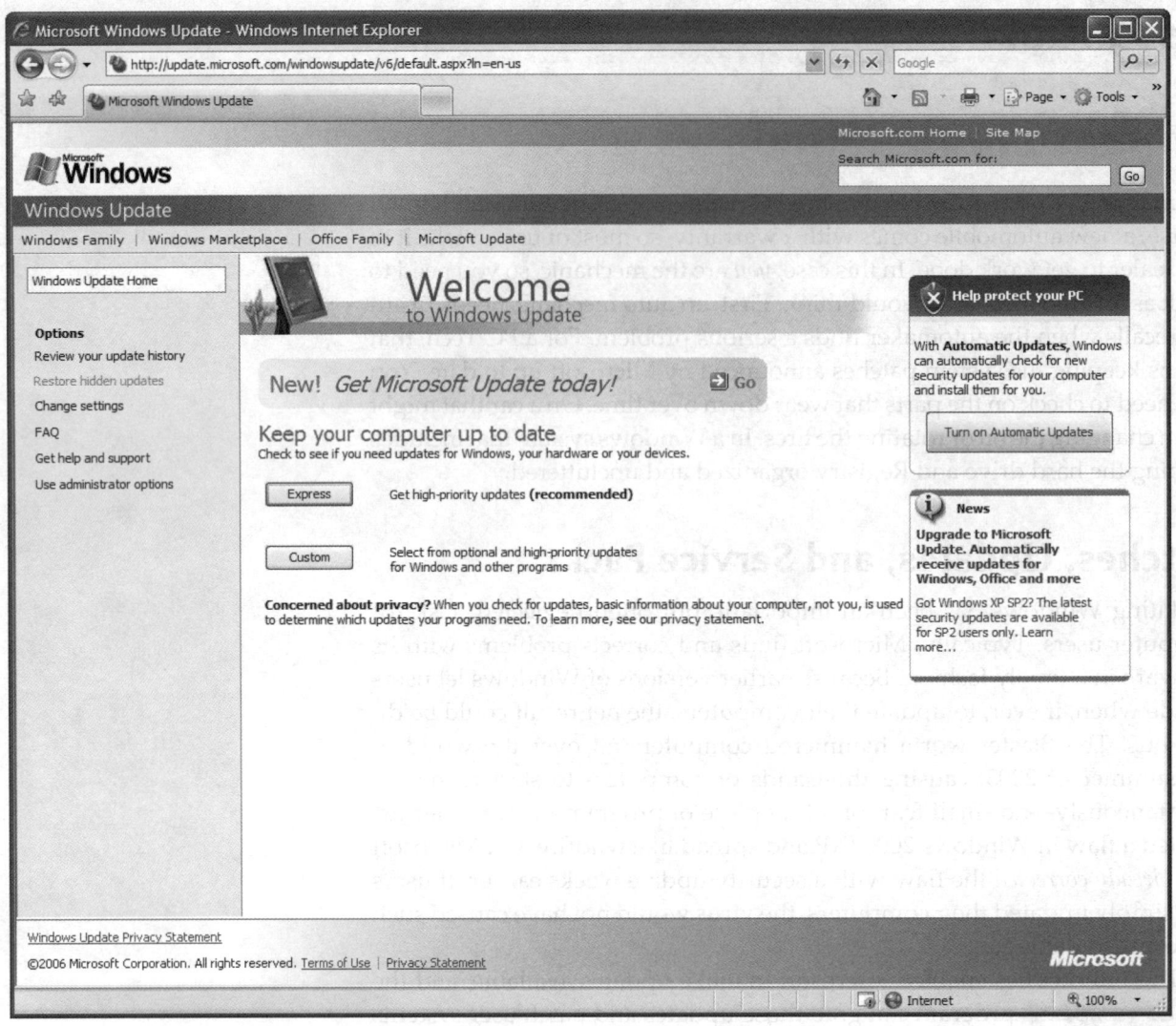

● **Figure 13.1** Microsoft Windows Update page

You have several choices here, although two are most obvious. If you click the Express button, Windows Update will grab any high-priority updates—these are security patches—and install them on your computer. If you click the Custom button, you can select from a list of optional updates.

Figure 13.2 shows the updater with a list of patches and security updates. You can scroll through the list and review the description of each update. You can deselect the checkbox next to a patch or update, and Windows Update will not download or install it. If you click the Clear All button, as you might suspect, all the updates will be removed from the list. When you click Install Updates, all the updates remaining in the list will be installed. A dialog box like the one in Figure 13.3 appears during the copying and installing phases.

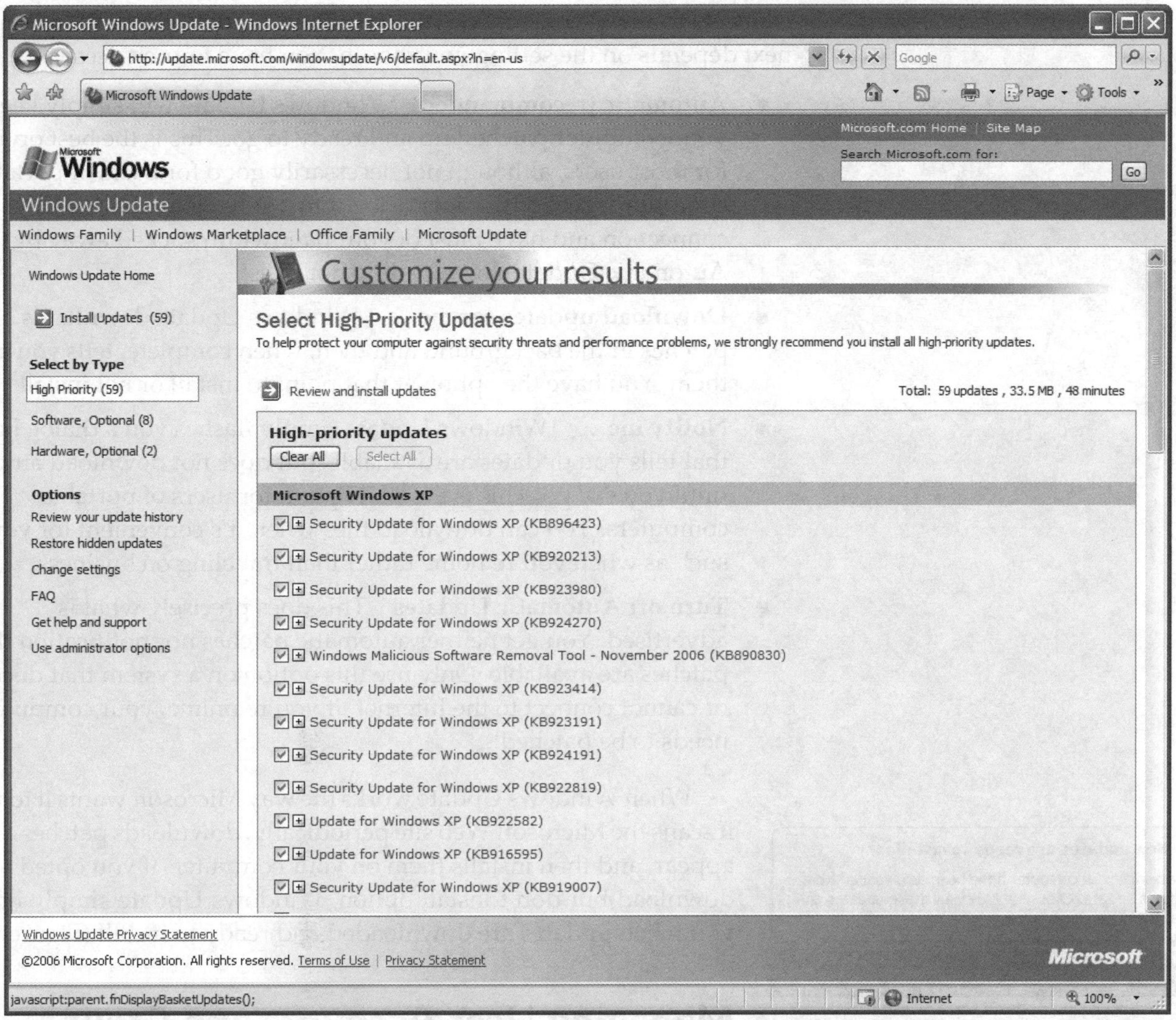

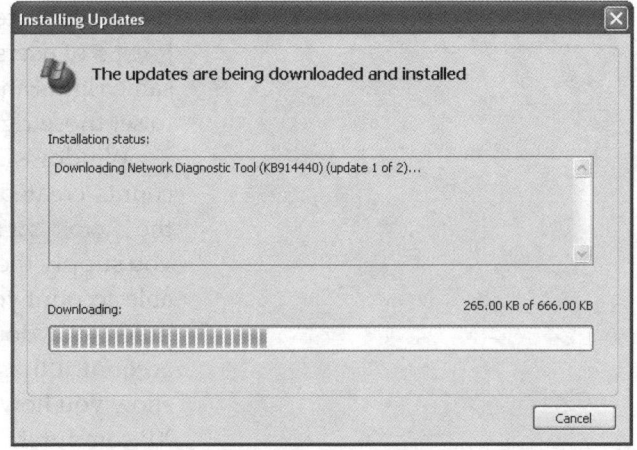

Figure 13.2 showing Microsoft Windows Update browser window with the following content:

Microsoft Windows Update - Windows Internet Explorer

http://update.microsoft.com/windowsupdate/v6/default.aspx?ln=en-us

Google

Microsoft Windows Update

Page ▼ Tools ▼

Microsoft.com Home | Site Map

Search Microsoft.com for:

Go

Windows

Windows Update

Windows Family | Windows Marketplace | Office Family | Microsoft Update

Windows Update Home

Install Updates (59)

Select by Type

High Priority (59)

Software, Optional (8)

Hardware, Optional (2)

Options

Review your update history

Restore hidden updates

Change settings

FAQ

Get help and support

Use administrator options

Customize your results

Select High-Priority Updates
To help protect your computer against security threats and performance problems, we strongly recommend you install all high-priority updates.

Review and install updates   Total: 59 updates , 33.5 MB , 48 minutes

High-priority updates

[Clear All] [Select All]

Microsoft Windows XP

☑ Security Update for Windows XP (KB896423)

☑ Security Update for Windows XP (KB920213)

☑ Security Update for Windows XP (KB923980)

☑ Security Update for Windows XP (KB924270)

☑ Windows Malicious Software Removal Tool - November 2006 (KB890830)

☑ Security Update for Windows XP (KB923414)

☑ Security Update for Windows XP (KB923191)

☑ Security Update for Windows XP (KB924191)

☑ Security Update for Windows XP (KB922819)

☑ Update for Windows XP (KB922582)

☑ Update for Windows XP (KB916595)

☑ Security Update for Windows XP (KB919007)

Windows Update Privacy Statement

©2006 Microsoft Corporation. All rights reserved. Terms of Use | Privacy Statement

Microsoft

javascript:parent.fnDisplayBasketUpdates();   Internet   100%

● Figure 13.2   Choose updates to be installed

Automatic Updates

Updates are so important that Microsoft gives you the option to update Windows automatically through the **Automatic Updates** feature. Actually, it nags you about it! Soon after installing XP (a day or two, in my experience), a message balloon will pop up from the taskbar suggesting that you automate updates. If you click this balloon, the Automatic Updates Setup Wizard will run, enabling you to configure the update program. You say you've never seen this message balloon, but would like to automate the update process? No problem—simply right-click My Computer (on the Start menu), select Properties, click the Automatic Updates tab, and select Automatic Update options. Alternatively, open the Control Panel and double- click the Automatic Updates icon. Then, whenever your computer

Installing Updates

The updates are being downloaded and installed

Installation status:

Downloading Network Diagnostic Tool (KB914440) (update 1 of 2)...

Downloading: 265.00 KB of 666.00 KB

Cancel

● Figure 13.3   Installing Updates dialog box

connects to the Web, it checks the Windows Update page. What happens next depends on the setting you choose. You have four choices:

- **Automatic (recommended)**   Windows Update will simply keep your computer patched up and ready to go. This is the best option for most users, although not necessarily good for users of portable computers. Nobody wants to log into a slow hotel dial-up connection and have most of your bandwidth sucked away by Automatic Update downloading hot fixes!

- **Download updates for me...**   Windows Update downloads all patches in the background and then, when complete, tells you about them. You have the option at that point to install or not install.

- **Notify me...**   Windows Update simply flashes you a dialog box that tells you updates are available, but does not download anything until you say go. This is the best option for users of portable computers. You can download files when it's convenient for you, such as when you're home rather than traveling on business.

- **Turn off Automatic Updates**   This does precisely what is advertised. You get neither automatic patches nor notification that patches are available. Only use this option on a system that does not or cannot connect to the Internet. If you're online, your computer needs to be patched!

When Windows Update works the way Microsoft wants it to work, it scans the Microsoft Web site periodically, downloads patches as they appear, and then installs them on your computer. If you opted for the download but don't install option, Windows Update simply notifies you when updates are downloaded and ready to install (Figure 13.4).

Managing User Accounts and Groups

The most basic element of Windows security is the `user account`. Each user must present a valid user name and the password of a user account in order to log on to a Windows computer. There are ways to make this logon highly simplified, even invisible in some cases, but there is no exception to this rule. Each user is also a member of one or more `groups` of users. Groups enable the system administrator to easily assign the same rights and permissions to all members of the group without the need to set those rights and permissions individually.

Windows 2000 and XP have several built-in groups and two user accounts created during installation—Administrator and Guest—with only the `Administrator account` enabled by default. When you install Windows, you supply the password for the Administrator account. This is the only usable account you have to log on to the computer, unless you joined the computer to a domain (a Chapter 18 topic) or until you create a new user account. I'll assume that your computer doesn't belong to a domain and show you how to create local accounts on your Windows 2000 or Windows XP computer.

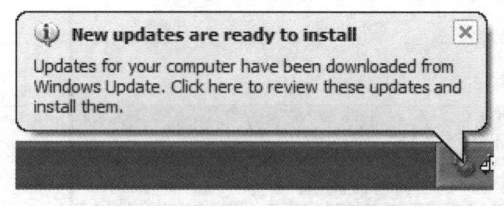

• **Figure 13.4**   Windows Update balloon message

You can manage users and groups using the `Local Users and Groups` node in the Computer Management console, accessed by right-clicking on My Computer and selecting Manage. (I'll show you more in Chapter 18.) Local Users and Groups can also be used on standalone computers, but Microsoft includes simpler GUI tools for that purpose in Windows 2000 and Windows XP. In Windows XP, Microsoft made significant changes in the GUI tools for managing users and groups, so I'll break up this discussion between these two operating systems.

Using the Users and Passwords Applet in Windows 2000

When you install Windows 2000 Professional, assuming your computer is not made a member of a domain, you may choose to let the OS assume that you are the only user of the computer and do not want to see the logon dialog box. You can check this setting after installation by opening the `Users and Passwords applet` in Control Panel to see the setting for *Users must enter a user name and password to use this computer*. Figure 13.5 shows this choice selected, which means that you will see a logon box every time you restart your computer. Also notice that the only user is Administrator. That's the account you're using to log on!

Using the Administrator account is just fine when you're doing administrative tasks such as installing updates, adding printers, adding and removing programs and Windows components, and creating users and groups. Best practice for the workplace is to create one or more user accounts and only log in with the user accounts, not the Administrator account. This gives you a lot more control over who or what happens to the computer.

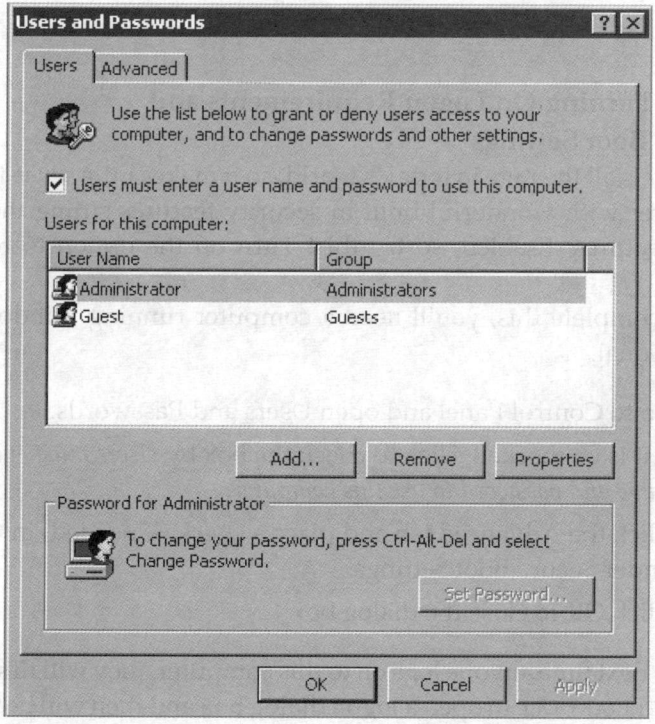

• **Figure 13.5** Security begins with turning on *Users must enter a user name and password to use this computer.*

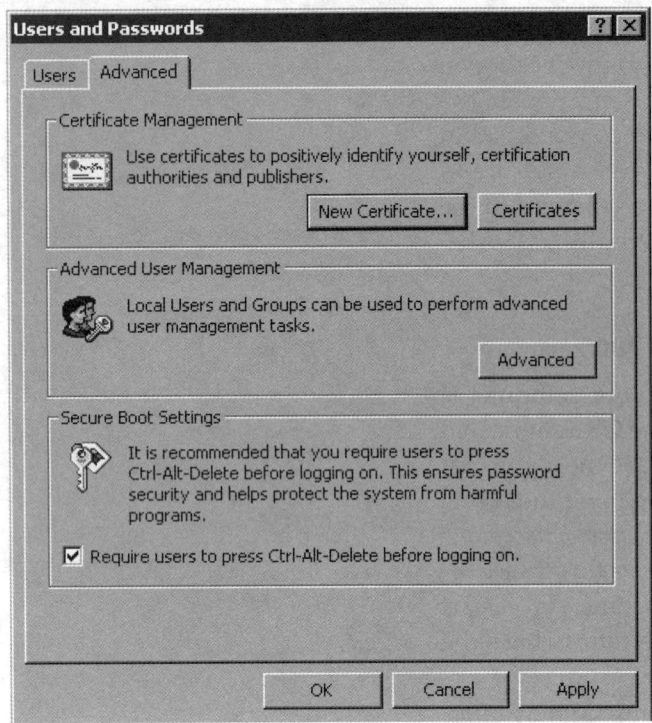

Users and Passwords

Users | Advanced

Certificate Management

Use certificates to positively identify yourself, certification authorities and publishers.

New Certificate...   Certificates

Advanced User Management

Local Users and Groups can be used to perform advanced user management tasks.

Advanced

Secure Boot Settings

It is recommended that you require users to press Ctrl-Alt-Delete before logging on. This ensures password security and helps protect the system from harmful programs.

☑ Require users to press Ctrl-Alt-Delete before logging on.

OK   Cancel   Apply

• **Figure 13.6**   Make your computer more secure by enabling Secure Boot Settings.

There's a second setting in Users and Passwords that's important to enable for the sake of security—the setting on the Advanced Tab under Secure Boot Settings. If checked, as shown in Figure 13.6, it requires users to press CTRL-ALT-DEL before logging on. This setting is a defense against certain viruses that try to capture your user name and password, sometimes by presenting a fake logon prompt. Pressing CTRL-ALT-DEL will remove a program like that from memory and allow the actual logon dialog box to appear.

Creating a New User in Windows 2000

Creating a new user account enables that user to log on with a user name and password. This enables an administrator to set the rights and permissions for the user as well as to audit access to certain network resources. For that reason, it is good practice to create users on a desktop computer. You are working with the same concepts on a small scale that an administrator must work with in a domain. Let's review the steps in this procedure for Windows 2000.

If you're logged on in Windows 2000 as the Administrator or a member of the local Administrators group, open the Users and Passwords applet from Control Panel and click the Add button. This opens the Add New User Wizard (Figure 13.7). Enter the user name that the user will

If the password requirement is turned off and you have user accounts that aren't password protected in Windows 2000 (or XP, for that matter), anyone with physical access to your computer can turn it on and use it by pressing the power button. This is potentially a very bad thing!

To create and manage users, you must be logged on as the Administrator, be a member of the Administrators group, or have an Administrator account (in Windows XP). Assign a password to the Administrator account so that only authorized users can access this all-powerful account.

Try This!

Turning On Logon Requirements and Secure Boot Settings

Security is all the rage in today's world, so it makes little sense to have a computer with wonderful built-in security features sitting there with those features disabled, so try this! Turn on the option to require a logon.

To complete this, you'll need a computer running Windows 2000 Professional.

1. Go to Control Panel and open Users and Passwords.
2. If it is unchecked, click to check the box by *Users must enter a user name and password to use this computer.*
3. Click the Advanced tab and place a check (if needed) in the box under Secure Boot Settings.
4. Click OK to close the dialog box.

The next time anyone logs on to this computer, they will first have to press CTRL-ALT-DEL to open a logon dialog box and then will be required to provide a user name and password.

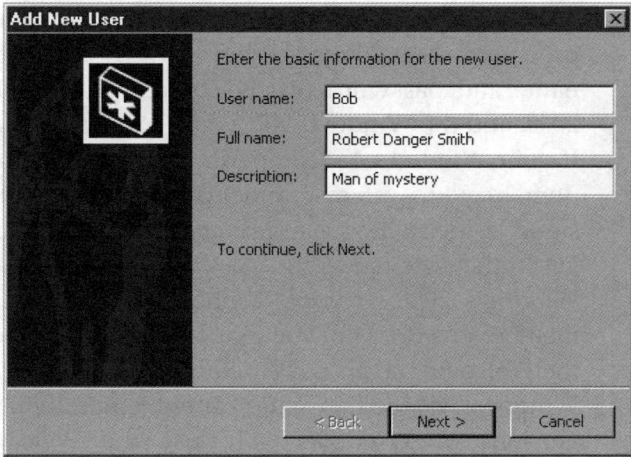

● **Figure 13.7**   Adding a new user

use to log on. Enter the user's first and last names in the Full name field, and if you wish, enter some text that describes this person in the Description field. If this is at work, enter a job description in this field. The Full name and Description fields are optional.

After entering the user information, click the Next button to continue. This opens a password dialog box (Figure 13.8) where you can enter and confirm the initial password for this new user. Click the Next button to continue.

Now you get to decide what groups the new user should belong to. Select one of the two suggested options—Standard User or Restricted User—or select the Other option button and choose a group from the drop-down list. Select Standard User, which on a Windows 2000 Professional desktop makes this person a member of the local Power Users group as well as the Local Users group. Click the Finish button to close the dialog box. You should see your new user listed in the Users and Passwords dialog box. While you're there, note how easy it is for an administrator to change a user's password. Simply select a user from the list, and then click on the Set Password button. Enter and confirm the new password in the Set Password dialog box. Figure 13.9 shows the Set Password dialog box with the Users and Passwords dialog box in the background.

Now let's say you want to change a password. Select the new user in the *Users for this computer* list on the Users page. Then click the Set Password button on the Users page. Enter and confirm the new password, and then click the OK button to apply the changes.

> ⚠ Blank passwords or those that are easily visible on a sticky note provide *no security.* Always insist on non-blank passwords, and do not let anyone leave a password sitting out in the open.

Managing Users in Windows XP

Although Windows XP has essentially the same type of accounts database as Windows 2000, the **User Accounts applet** in the Control Panel replaces the Users and Passwords applet and further simplifies user management tasks.

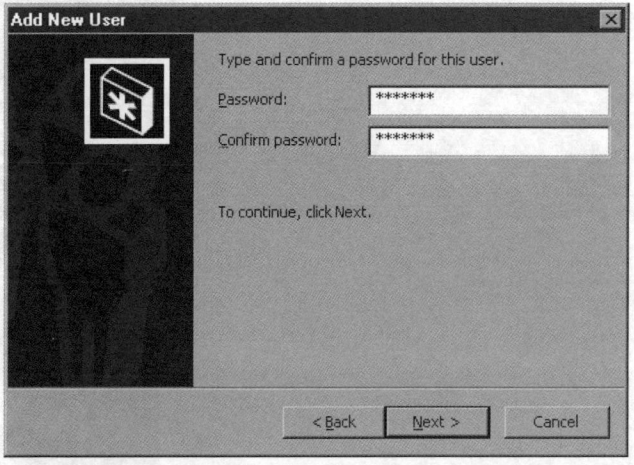

● **Figure 13.8**   Create user password

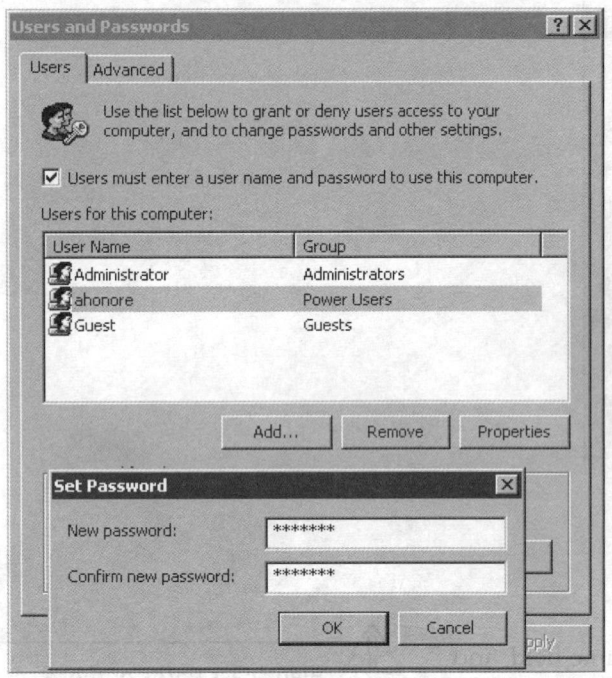

● **Figure 13.9**   Set Password dialog box

Windows XP has two very different ways to deal with user accounts and how you log on to a system: the blank user name and password text boxes, reminiscent of Windows 2000, and the Windows XP **Welcome screen** (Figure 13.10). If your Windows XP computer is a member of a Windows domain, your system automatically uses the Windows Classic style, including the requirement to press CTRL-ALT-DEL to get to the user name and password text boxes, just like in Windows 2000. If your Windows XP computer is not a member of a domain, you may use either method, although the Welcome screen is the default. Windows XP Home and Windows XP Media Center cannot join a domain, so these versions of Windows only use the Welcome screen. Windows Tablet PC Edition functions just like Windows XP Professional.

Assuming that your Windows XP system is *not* a member of a domain, I'll concentrate on the XP Welcome screen and some of the options you'll see in the User Accounts Control Panel applet.

The User Accounts applet is very different from the old Users and Passwords applet in Windows 2000. User Accounts hides the complete list of users, using a simplistic reference to account types that is actually a reference to its group membership. An account that is a member of the local Administrators group is said to be a Computer Administrator; an account that only belongs to the Local Users group is said to be a **Limited account**. Which users the applet displays depends on which type of user is currently logged on (see Figure 13.11). When an Administrator is

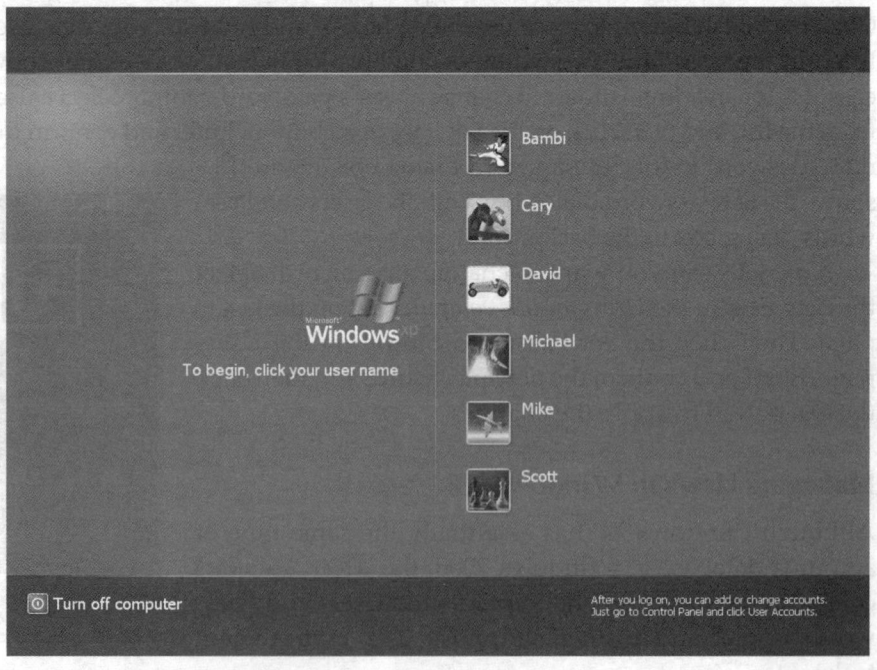

● **Figure 13.10**   Windows XP Welcome screen

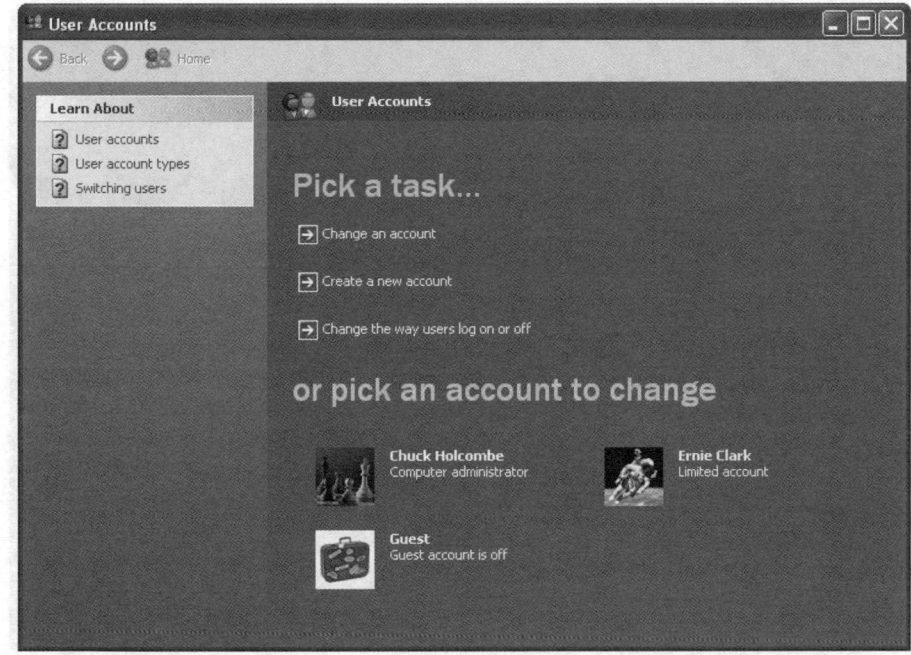

● **Figure 13.11**   User Accounts dialog box showing a Computer Administrator, a Limited account, and the Guest account (disabled)

logged on, she will see both types of accounts and the Guest account. A Limited user will only see his or her own account in User Accounts.

Windows requires you to create a second account that is a member of the Administrators group during the initial Windows installation. This is for

simple redundancy—if one administrator is not available or is not able to log on to the computer, another one can.

Creating users is a straightforward process. You need to provide a user name (a password can be added later), and you need to know which type of account to create: Computer Administrator or Limited. To create a new user in Windows XP, open the User Accounts applet from the Control Panel and click *Create a new account*. On the *Pick an account type* page (Figure 13.12), you can create either type of account. Simply follow the prompts on the screen. After you have created your local accounts, you'll see them listed when you open the User Accounts applet. It will look something like Figure 13.13.

If you upgrade from Windows NT, Windows 2000, or a Windows 9*x* installation in which user accounts were enabled, Setup will migrate the existing accounts to Windows XP.

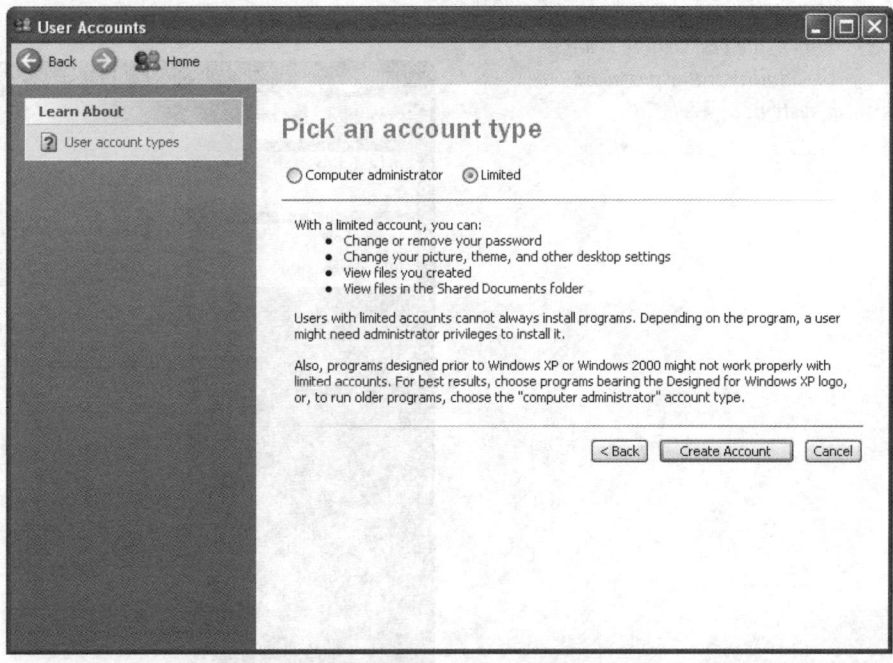

● **Figure 13.12**   The *Pick an account type* page showing both options available

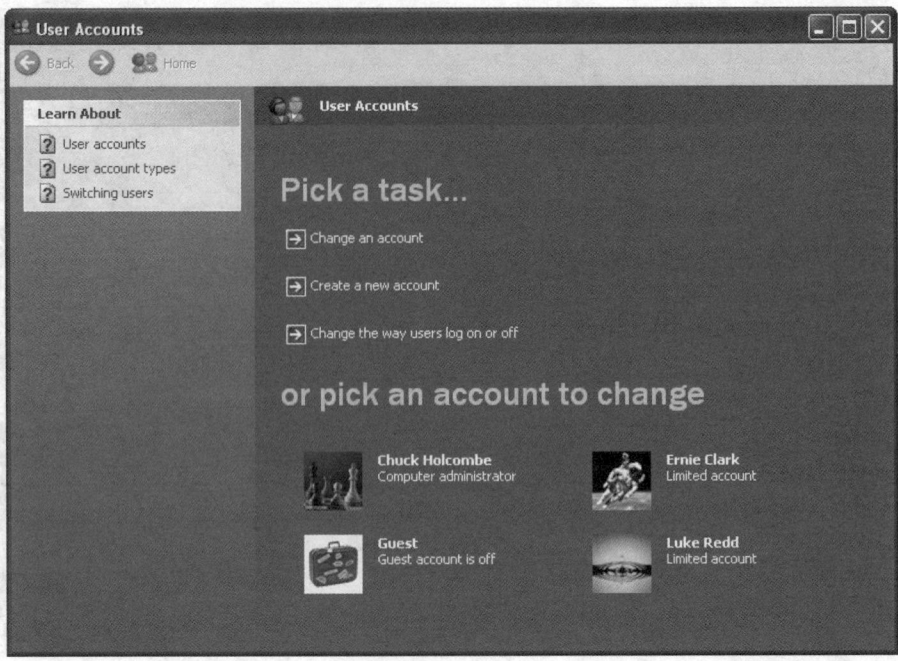

● **Figure 13.13**   New Limited account listed in User Accounts

Tech Tip

Going Retro

The old Users and Passwords Control Panel applet is still in every version of Windows XP. If you're on a Windows XP Professional or Windows XP Tablet PC Edition system and your system is part of a domain, the old program comes up automatically when you click the User Accounts applet. If you're running Window XP Professional or Windows XP Tablet PC Edition but not on a domain, or if you're running XP Home or Media Center, go to a command prompt and type the following:

`control userpasswords2`

This will bring up the old applet. This is the best way to change the administrator password on a system.

Head back to the User Accounts applet and look at the *Change the way users log on and off* option. Select it; you will see two checkboxes (Figure 13.14). If you select the Use the Welcome screen checkbox, Windows will bring up the friendly Welcome screen shown in Figure 13.15 each time users log in.

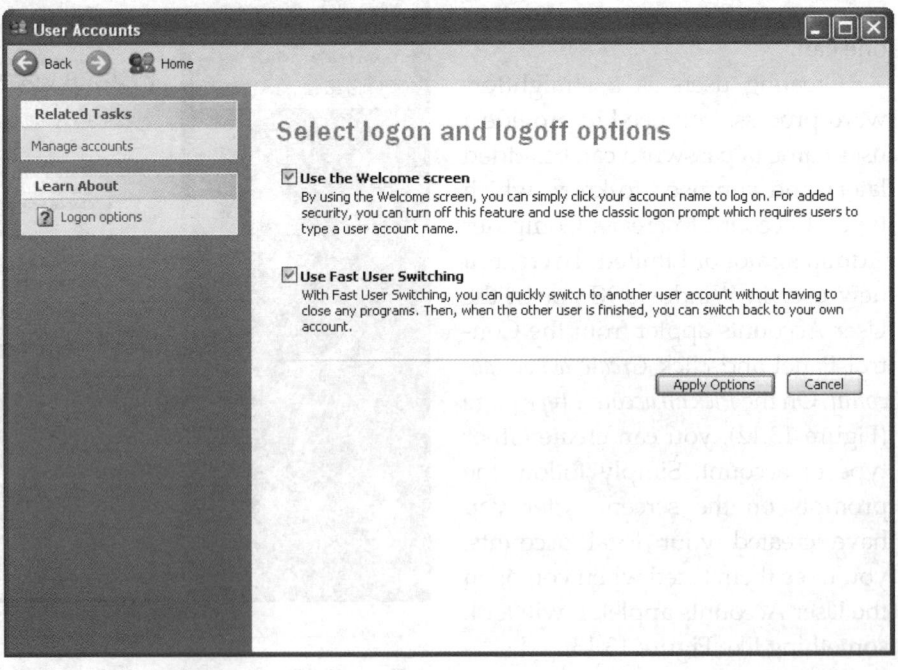

● **Figure 13.14**   Select logon and logoff options

● **Figure 13.15** Single account logon screen

If this box is unchecked, you'll have to enter a user name and password (Figure 13.16).

The second option, Use Fast User Switching, enables you to switch to another user without logging off the currently running user. This is a handy option when two people actively share a system, or when someone wants to borrow your system for a moment but you don't want to close all your programs. This option is only active if you have the Use the Welcome screen checkbox enabled. If Fast User Switching is enabled, when you click on the Log Off button on the Start menu, you get the option to switch users shown in Figure 13.17.

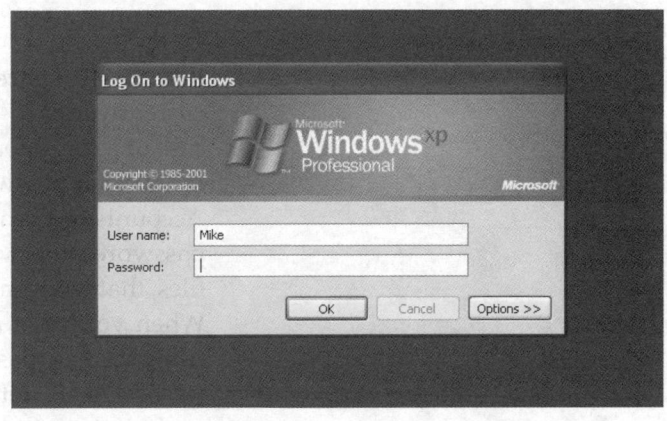

● **Figure 13.16** Classic Logon screen, XP style

Passwords

Passwords are the ultimate key to protecting your computers. A user account with a valid password will get you into any system. Even if the user account only has limited permissions, you still have a security breach. Remember: for a hacker, just getting into the network is half the battle.

Protect your passwords. Never give out passwords over the phone. If a user loses a password, an administrator should reset the password to a complex combination of letters and numbers, and then allow the user to change the password to something they want. All of the stronger operating systems have this capability.

Make your users choose good passwords. I once attended a security seminar, and the speaker had everyone stand up. She then

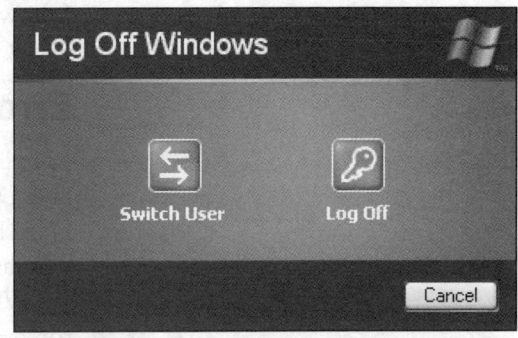

● **Figure 13.17** Switch User option

Using non-alphanumeric characters makes any password much more difficult to crack for two reasons. First, adding non-alphanumeric characters forces the hacker to consider many more possible characters than just letters and numbers. Second, most password crackers use combinations of common words and numbers to try to hack a password.

Because non-alphanumeric characters don't fit into common words or numbers, including a character such as an exclamation point will defeat these common-word hacks. Not all serving systems allow you to use characters such as @, $, %, or \, however, so you need to experiment to see if a particular server will accept them.

began to ask questions about our passwords—if we responded yes to the question we were to sit down. She began to ask questions such as

"Do you use the name of your spouse as a password?" and

"Do you use your pet's name?"

By the time she was done asking about 15 questions, only 6 people out of some 300 were still standing! The reality is that most of us choose passwords that are amazingly easy to hack. Make sure you use strong passwords: at least six to eight characters in length, including letters, numbers, and punctuation symbols.

Once you've forced your users to choose strong passwords, you should make them change passwords at regular intervals. While this concept sounds good on paper, in the real world it is a hard policy to maintain. For starters, users tend to forget passwords when they change a lot. This can lead to an even bigger security problem because users start writing passwords down!

If your organization forces you to change passwords often, one way to remember the password is to use a numbering system. I worked at a company that required me to change my password at the beginning of each month, so I did something very simple. I took a root password—let's say it was "m3y3rs5"—and simply added a number to the end representing the current month. So when June rolled around, for example, I would change my password to "m3y3rs56." It worked pretty well!

Resetting Forgotten Passwords in Windows XP   Windows XP allows the currently logged-on user to create a `password reset disk` that can be used in case of a forgotten password. This is very important to have because if you forget your password, and an administrator resets the password using User Accounts or Local Users and Groups, then when you log on using the new password, you will discover that you cannot access some items, including files that you encrypted when logged on with the forgotten password. When you reset a password with a password reset disk, you can log on using the new password and still have access to previously encrypted files.

Best of all, with the password reset disk, users have the power to fix their own passwords. Encourage your users to create this disk; you only have this power if you remember to create a password reset disk *before* you forget the password! If you need to create a password reset disk for a computer on a network (domain), search the Help system for "password reset disk" and follow the instructions for password reset disks for a computer on a domain.

Error-Checking and Disk Defragmentation

Keeping drives healthy and happy is a key task for every tech. Error-checking and Disk Defragmenter, discussed way back in Chapter 9, "Implementing Hard Drives," are the key Windows maintenance tools you use to accomplish this task.

When you can't find a software reason (and there are many possible ones) for a problem like a system freezing on shutdown, the problem might be the actual physical hard drive. The tool to investigate that is Error-checking. Error-checking can be done from a command line or the Start | Run dialog box using the CHKDSK command. You can also access the tool through the GUI by opening My Computer, right-clicking on the drive you want to check, selecting Properties, and then clicking the Tools tab. Click Check Now to have Error-checking scan the drive for bad sectors, lost clusters, and similar problems, and repair them if possible.

Run the Disk Defragmenter (Figure 13.18) on a regular basis to keep your system from slowing down due to files being scattered in pieces on your hard drive. Before you click the Defragment button, click the Analyze button to have Windows analyze the disk and determine if defragmentation is actually necessary.

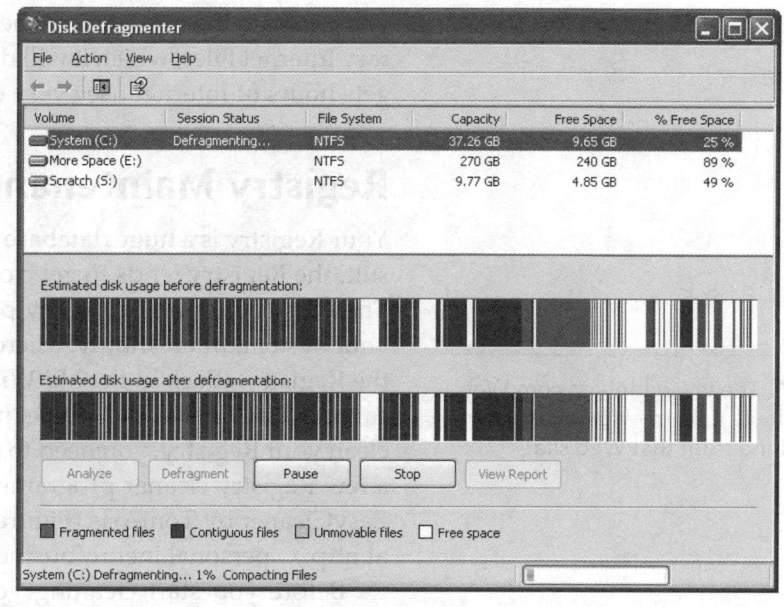

• Figure 13.18   Disk Defragmenter

Temporary File Management with Disk Cleanup

Before you defrag a drive, you should run the Disk Cleanup utility to make sure you've cleared out the junk files that accumulate from daily use. All that late-night Web surfing doesn't just use up time, it uses up disk space, leaving behind hundreds of temporary Internet files. Those, and other bits and pieces such as those "deleted" files still hanging around in your Recycle Bin, can add up to a lot of wasted disk space if you don't periodically clean them out.

You can reach this tool through the Start menu (Start | All Programs | Accessories | System Tools), or you can open My Computer, right-click the drive you want to clean up, select Properties, and right there in the middle of the General tab you'll find the Disk Cleanup button. Disk Cleanup calculates the space you will be able to free up and then displays the Disk Cleanup dialog box (Figure 13.19), which tells you how much disk space it can free up—the total amount possible as well as the amount you'll get from each of the different categories of files it checks. In Figure 13.19, the list of Files to delete only has a few categories checked, and the actual amount of disk space to be gained by allowing Disk Cleanup to delete these files is much smaller than the estimate. As you select and deselect choices, watch the value for this total change.

If you scroll down through the list, you will see a choice to compress old files. What do you know, Disk Cleanup does more than just delete files. In fact, this file compression trick is where Disk Cleanup really, uh, cleans up. This is one of the few choices where

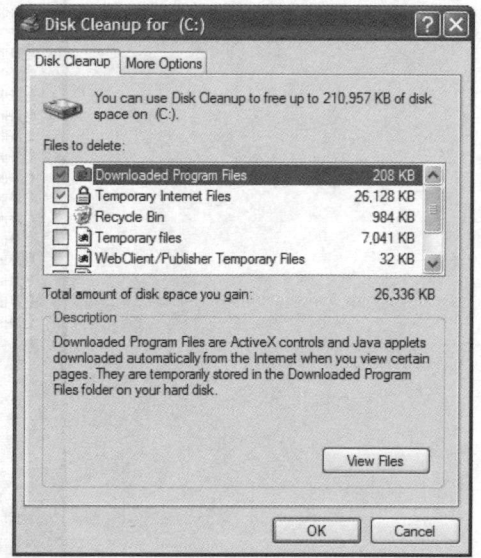

• Figure 13.19   Disk Cleanup dialog box

you will gain the most space. The other big heavyweight category is Temporary Internet Files, which it will delete. Try Disk Cleanup on a computer that gets hours of Internet use every day and you'll be pleased with the results.

Registry Maintenance

Your Registry is a huge database that Windows constantly updates. As a result, the Registry tends to get clogged with entries that are no longer valid. These usually don't cause any problems directly, but they can slow down your system. Interestingly, Microsoft does not provide a utility to clean up the Registry. (Back in the old Windows 9*x* days, there was a Microsoft tool called REGCLEAN, but it was never updated for Windows 2000/XP.) To clean your Registry, you need to turn to a third-party utility. There are quite a few Registry cleaner programs out there, but my favorite is the freeware EasyCleaner by ToniArts (Figure 13.20). You can download the latest copy at http://personal.inet.fi/business/toniarts/ecleane.htm.

Before you start cleaning your Registry with wild abandon, keep in mind that all Registry cleaners are risky in that there is a chance that it may delete something you want in the Registry. I've used EasyCleaner for a while and it has worked well for me—your experience may differ! Always use EasyCleaner's handy undo feature so that you can restore what you deleted.

EasyCleaner is a powerful optimization tool that does far more than just clean your Registry. Check out the file duplicate finder, space usage, and other tools that come with this package. If you like this program, go to the Web site and donate some money to Toni.

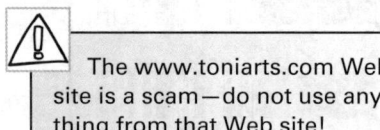

The www.toniarts.com Web site is a scam—do not use anything from that Web site!

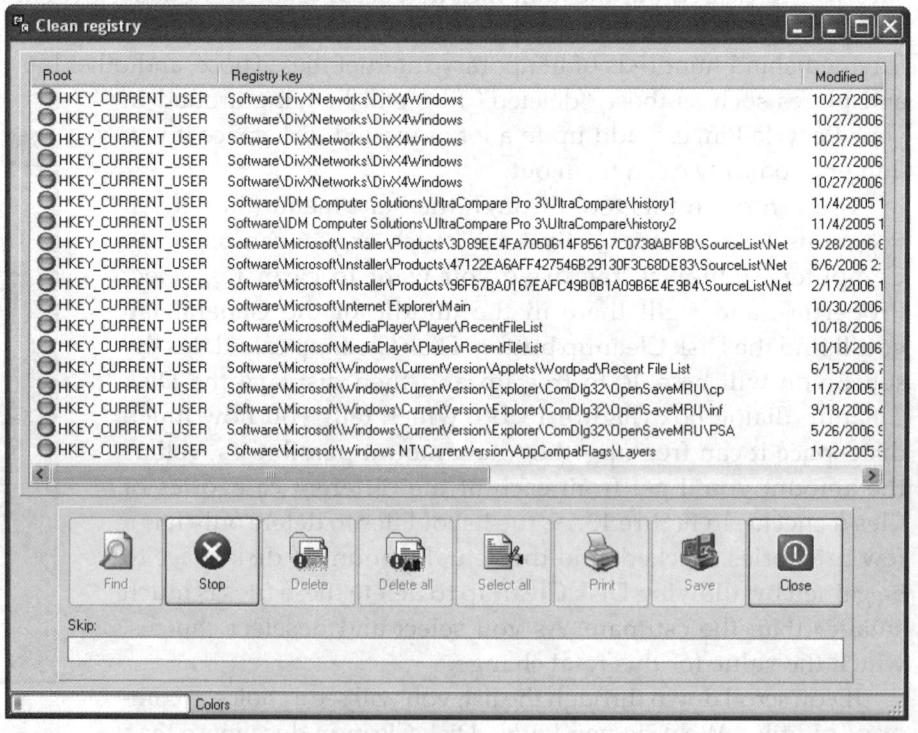

• **Figure 13.20**   EasyCleaner

Security: Spyware/Antivirus/Firewall

You simply cannot run a computer today without a large number of security programs to protect you from malicious attacks from spyware, malware, viruses, and hacking. In fact, the installation, monitoring, and updating of these programs (and possibly even hardware) is so important that they get their own chapter. Head to Chapter 19, "Computer Security," for a complete discussion of how to keep your computer safe!

■ Optimizing Windows

Maintenance is about keeping Windows' performance from degrading with time and use. Of course, we don't just want to keep trouble at bay—we want to make our systems better, stronger, faster! Anything you do that makes Windows better than it was before, such as adding a piece of software or hardware to make something run better, is an optimization.

Installing and Removing Software

The most common optimization performed on any PC is probably adding and removing applications. Installing and removing software is part of the normal life of any PC. Each time you add or remove software, you are making changes and decisions that can affect the system beyond whatever the program does, so it pays to know how to do it right.

Installing Software

Most application programs are distributed on CD-ROMs. Luckily, Windows supports **Autorun**, a feature that enables it to look for and read a special file called—wait for it—Autorun immediately after a CD-ROM is inserted, and then run whatever program is listed in AUTORUN.INF. Most application programs distributed on CD-ROM have an Autorun file that calls up the installation program.

Sometimes, however, it is necessary to institute the installation sequence yourself. Perhaps the installation CD lacks an Autorun installation program, or perhaps Windows is configured so that programs on a CD-ROM must be started manually. In some cases, a CD-ROM may contain more than one program, and you must choose which of them to install. Regardless of the reason, beginning the installation manually is a simple and straightforward process using the **Add or Remove Programs applet** in the Control Panel. (Windows 2000 calls the applet Add/Remove Programs.) Click the Add New Programs button (Figure 13.21), follow the prompts, and provide the disk or location of the files.

As long as you have sufficient permissions to install an application— your account is a member of the Administrators group in Windows 2000, for example, or is an Administrator Account in Windows XP—the application will begin its install routine. If you don't have sufficient permissions to install an application, Windows will stop the installation.

Assuming all is well, you typically first must accept the terms of a software license before you are allowed to install an application. These steps

Programs keep getting bigger and bigger, and distributors have started using DVD discs for applications. Expect that trend to continue in a big way. Apple switched over to DVD for OS X some time ago, and Microsoft has followed suit with Windows Vista. Autorun works with DVDs just fine.

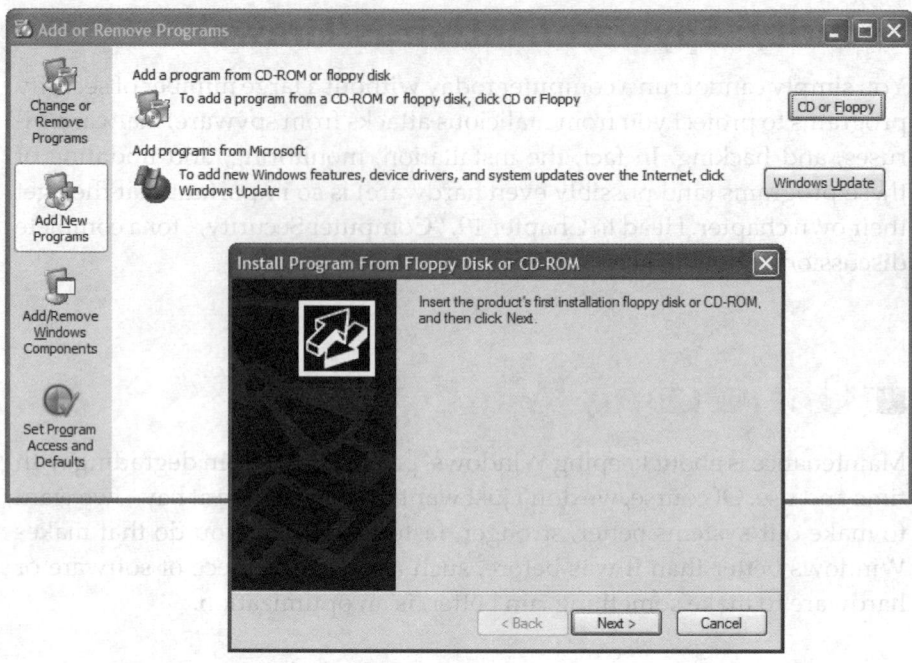

● **Figure 13.21**　Add New Programs

are not optional—the installation simply won't proceed until you accept all terms the software manufacturer requires, and in many cases enter a correct code. You may also be asked to make several decisions during the installation process. For example, you may be asked where you would like to install the program and if you would like certain optional components installed. Generally speaking, it is best to accept the suggested settings unless you have a very specific reason for changing the defaults.

Removing Software

Each installed application program takes up space on your computer's hard drive, and programs that you no longer need simply waste space that could be used for other purposes. Removing unnecessary programs can be an important piece of optimization.

You remove a program from a Windows PC in much the same manner as you install it. That is, you use the application's own uninstall program, when possible. You normally find the uninstall program listed under the application's icon on the Start Menu, as shown in Figure 13.22.

If an uninstall program is not available, then use Windows' Add or Remove Programs applet from Control Panel. Figure 13.23 shows this applet. You select the program you want to remove and click the Change/Remove button. You should not be surprised by now to hear that it does

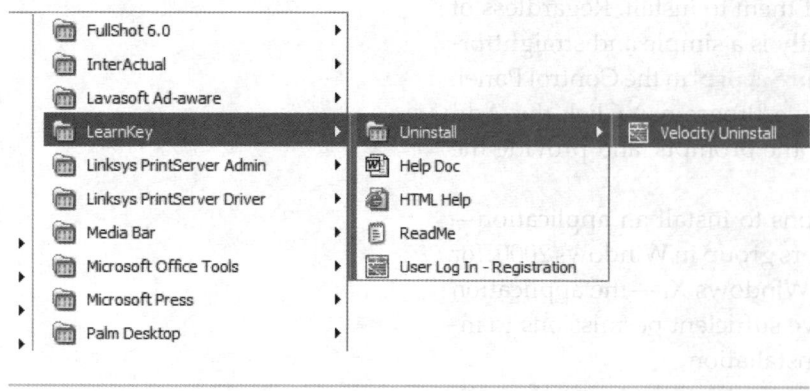

● **Figure 13.22**　Uninstall me!

not disappear in a flash. First, you'll see a message warning you that the program will be permanently removed from your PC. If you're certain you want to continue, click Yes.

You may then see a message telling you that a shared file that appears to no longer be in use is about to be deleted, and asking your approval. Generally speaking, it's safe to delete such files. If you do not delete them, they will likely be orphaned and remain unused on your hard disk forever. In some cases, clicking the Change/Remove button will start the application's install program (the one you couldn't find before) so that you can modify the installed features. This is a function of the program you're attempting to remove. The end result should be the removal of the application and all of its pieces and parts, including files and Registry entries.

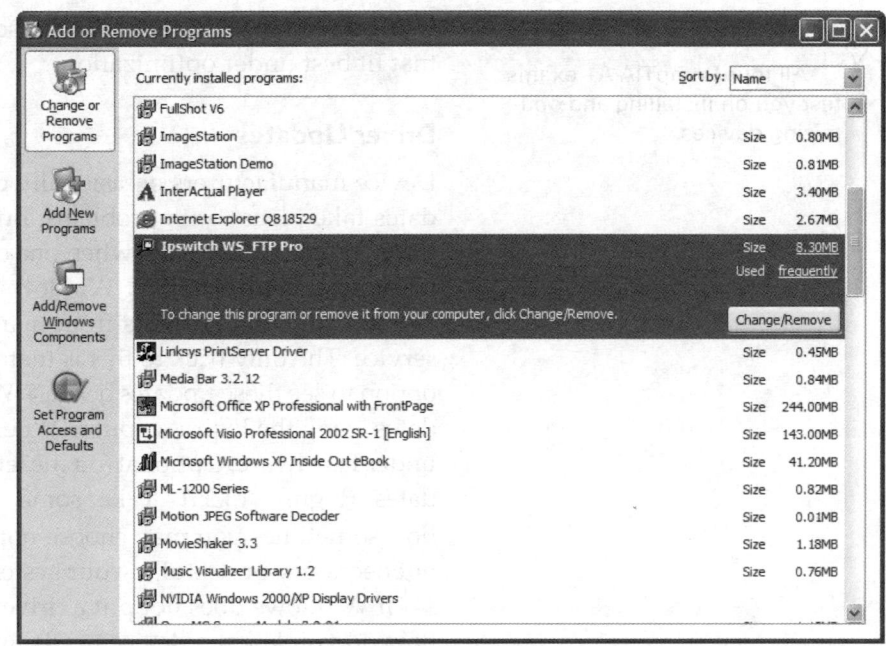

• Figure 13.23   Add or Remove Programs applet

Adding or Removing Windows Components

When you installed Windows, it tried to guess which optional Windows components you would need. It installed Notepad, modem support, and games on your computer. These Windows components can be removed from your system if you like, and other components can be added as well. If you're adding components, you'll need a copy of your Windows CD, or another location where the Windows source files are stored. This task really hasn't changed from previous versions of Windows.

To add or remove a Windows component, open the Add or Remove Programs applet in the Control Panel (Add/Remove Programs in Windows 2000). From here, select Add/Remove Windows Components, which opens the Windows Components Wizard (Figure 13.24). You can select an installed program; see how frequently it is used, how much disk space it uses, and (sometimes) the last time it was used.

Installing/Optimizing a Device

The processes for optimizing hardware in Windows 2000 and Windows XP are absolutely identical, even down to the troubleshooting and backup utilities, and are very similar to the steps for installing a new device. The install process is covered in every chapter of this book that deals

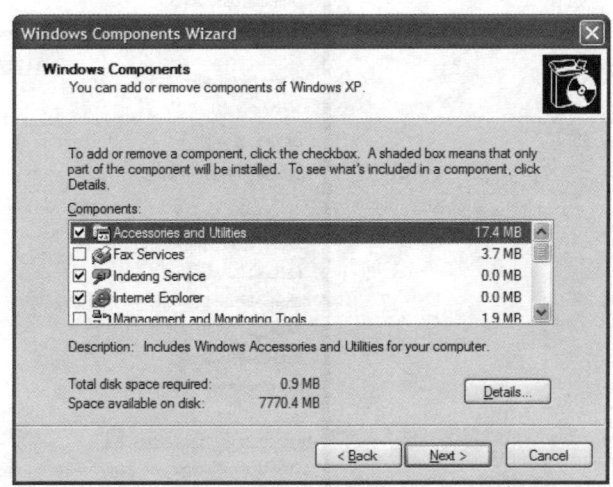

• Figure 13.24   Windows Components Wizard

All four CompTIA A+ exams test you on installing and optimizing devices.

with one type of device or another, so this section concentrates on the issues that fit best under optimization.

Driver Updates

Device manufacturers occasionally update their drivers. Most of these updates take place to fix problems, but many updates incorporate new features. Whatever the case, when one of your devices gets an updated driver, it's your job to install it. Windows/Microsoft Update provides an easy method to update drivers from manufacturers that take advantage of the service. The only trick to this is that you usually need to select the Custom option to see these updates because Windows only installs high-priority updates using the Express option. When you click on the Custom option, look under Hardware, Optional (on the left) to see if Windows has any driver updates (Figure 13.25). Take some time and read what these updates do—sometimes you may choose not to install a driver update because it's not necessary or useful to your system.

If Windows does not put a driver update in the Windows Update tool, how do you know a device needs updating? The trick is to know your devices. Video card manufacturers update drivers quite often. Get in the habit

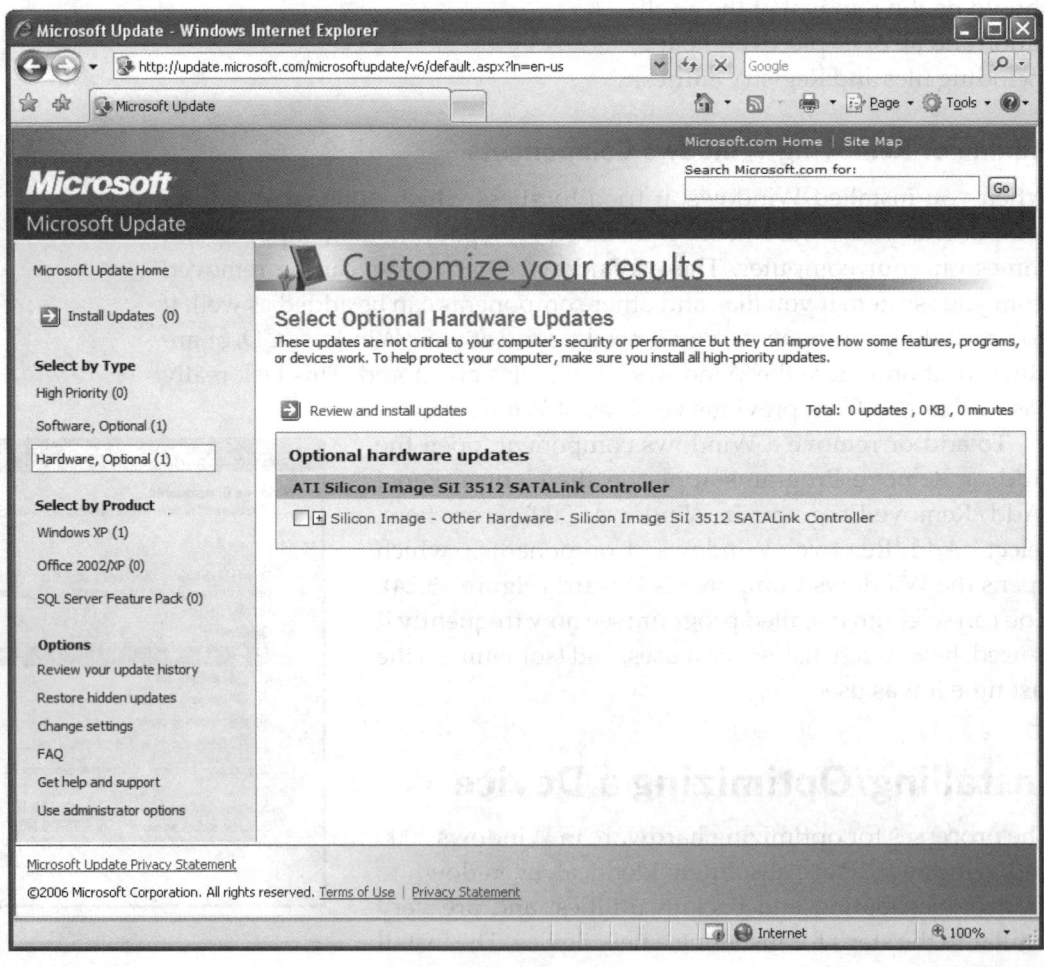

• **Figure 13.25**   Hardware, Optional

of registering your video card with the manufacturer to stay up to date. Any very new device is also a good candidate for an update. When you buy that new cool toy for your system, make a point to head over to the manufacturer's Web site and see if any updates have come out since it was packaged for sale. That happens more often than you might think!

Driver Signing

Device drivers become part of the operating system and thus have the potential to cause lots of problems if they're written poorly. To protect Windows systems from bad device drivers, Microsoft uses **driver signing**, which means that each driver has a digital signature. Any drivers included on the Windows CD-ROM or at the Windows Update Web site are digitally signed. Once you have installed a driver, you can look at its Properties to confirm that it was digitally signed. Figure 13.26 shows a digitally signed network card driver.

When an unsigned driver is detected during hardware installation, you'll see the message in Figure 13.27 offering you the choice to stop or continue the installation. Signed drivers are more or less a sure thing, but that doesn't mean unsigned ones are a problem—just consider the source of the driver and ensure that your device works properly after installation.

You can control how Windows behaves when drivers are being installed. Click the Driver Signing button on the Hardware tab of the System Properties dialog box to display the Driver Signing Options dialog box shown in Figure 13.28. If you select Ignore, Windows will install an unsigned driver without warning you. If you select Warn, you will be prompted when Windows detects an unsigned driver during driver installation, and you will be given the opportunity to either stop or continue the installation. Choosing Block will prevent the installation of unsigned drivers.

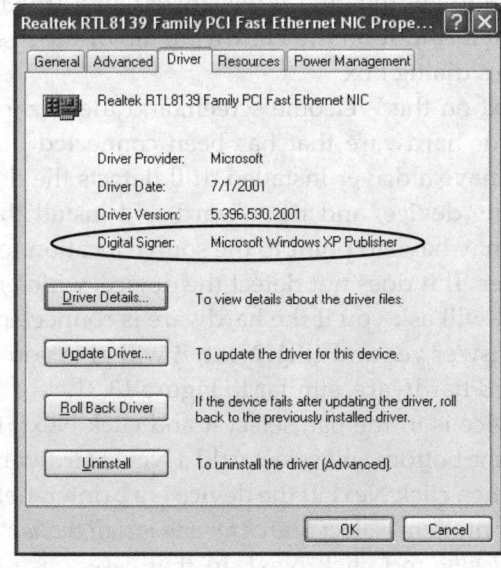

• **Figure 13.26**   A digitally signed driver

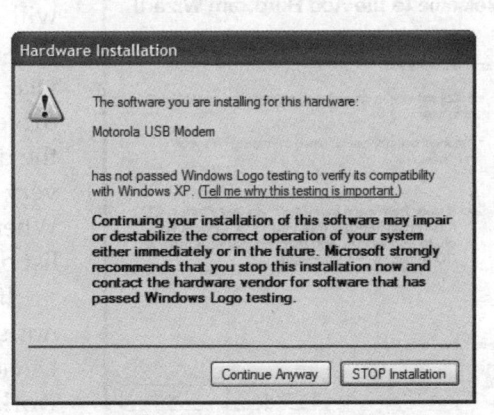

• **Figure 13.27**   Stop or continue installation of an unsigned driver

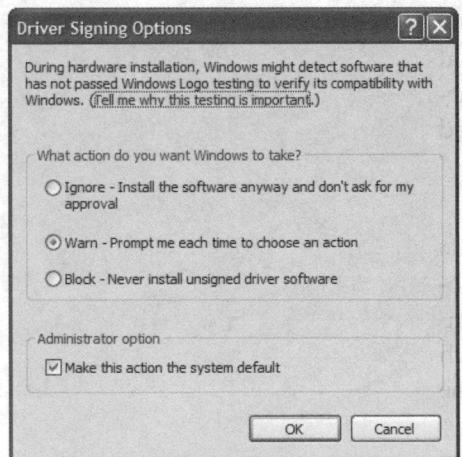

Figure 13.28 Driver Signing Options dialog box

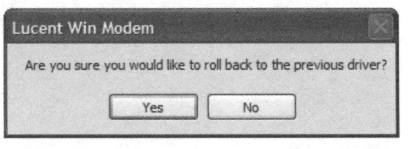

Figure 13.29 Rollback

The default Driver Signing setting is Warn. This also is the default setting during installation, so you will always be warned when Windows detects an unsigned driver during Windows installation. This is no problem for an standard installation, when you are sitting at the computer, responding to all prompts—but it is a problem for automated, unattended installations. This is a good reason to check out all your device drivers before installing Windows.

Device Manager

You've worked with the **Device Manager** in other chapters when installing and troubleshooting devices; it's also the tool to use when optimizing device drivers. Right-click on a device in Device Manager to display the context menu. From here, you can update or uninstall the driver, disable the device, scan for hardware changes, or display the Properties dialog box. When you open the Properties dialog box, you'll see several tabs that vary according to the specific device. Most have General, Driver, Details, and Resources. The tab that matters most for optimization is the Driver tab.

The Driver tab has buttons labeled Driver Details, Update Driver, Roll Back Driver, and Uninstall. Driver Details lists the driver files and their locations on disk. Update Driver opens the Hardware Update Wizard—not very useful given that the install programs for almost all drivers do this automatically. The Roll Back Driver option is a different story. It enables you to remove an updated driver, thus rolling back to the previous driver version. Rollback (Figure 13.29) is a lifesaver when you install a new driver and suddenly discover it's worse than the driver it replaced! Uninstall removes the driver.

Adding a New Device

Windows should automatically detect any new device you install in your system. If Windows does not detect a newly connected device, use the Add Hardware Wizard (Figure 13.30) to get the device recognized and drivers installed. You'll find it on the Hardware tab of the System Properties dialog box.

Click Next on the Welcome screen, and the wizard will search for hardware that has been connected but does not yet have a driver installed. If it detects the device, select the device, and the wizard will install the driver. You may have to point to the source location for the driver files. If it does not detect the device, which is very likely, it will ask you if the hardware is connected. When you answer yes and click Next, it will give you a list of installed hardware, similar to Figure 13.31.

If the device is in the list, select it and click Next. If not, scroll to the bottom and select Add a New Hardware Device, and then click Next. If the device is a printer, network card, or modem, select *Search for and install the hardware automatically* and click Next. In that case, once it detects the device and installs the driver, you're done. If you do see your device on the list, your best hope is to

Figure 13.30 Add Hardware Wizard

select *Install the hardware that I manually select from a list.* In the subsequent screens, select the appropriate device category, select the device manufacturer and the correct model, and respond to the prompts from the Add Hardware Wizard to complete the installation.

Performance Options

One optimization you can perform on both Windows 2000 and Windows XP is setting Performance Options. **Performance Options** are used to configure CPU, RAM, and virtual memory (page file) settings. To access these options, right-click My Computer and select Properties, click the Advanced tab, and click the Options button (Windows 2000) or Settings button (Windows XP) in the Performance section of that tab. The Performance Options dialog box differs between the two families of operating systems.

In Windows 2000, the Performance Options dialog box shows a pair of radio buttons called Applications and Background Services. These radio buttons set how processor time is divided between the foreground application and all other background tasks. Set this to Applications if you run applications that need more processor time. Set it to Background Services to give all running programs the same processor usage. You can also adjust the size of the page file in this dialog box, but in most cases I don't mess with these settings and instead leave control of the page file to Windows.

The Windows XP Performance Options dialog box has three tabs: Visual Effects, Advanced, and Data Execution Prevention (Figure 13.32). The Visual Effects tab enables you to adjust visual effects that impact performance. Try clicking the top three choices in turn and watch the list of settings. Notice the tiny difference between the first two choices. The third choice, *Adjust for best performance*, turns off all visual effects, and the fourth option is an invitation to make your own adjustments. If you're on a computer that barely supports Windows XP, turning off visual effects can make a huge difference in the responsiveness of the computer. For the most part, though, just leave these settings alone.

The Advanced tab, shown in Figure 13.33, has three sections: Processor scheduling, Memory usage, and Virtual memory. Under the Processor scheduling section, you can choose to adjust for best performance of either Programs or Background services. The Memory usage settings enable you to allocate a greater share of memory to programs or to the system cache. Finally, the Virtual memory section of this page enables you to modify the size and location of the page file.

Microsoft introduced *Data Execution Prevention (DEP)* with Windows XP Service Pack 2. DEP works in the background to stop viruses and other malware from taking over programs loaded in system memory. It doesn't prevent viruses from being installed on your computer, but makes them less effective. By default, DEP monitors only critical operating system files in RAM, but the Data Execution Prevention tab enables you to have DEP monitor all running programs. It works, but you'll take

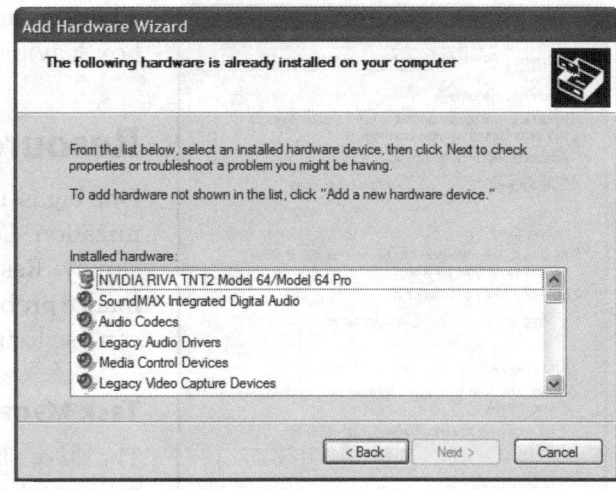

● **Figure 13.31** List of installed hardware

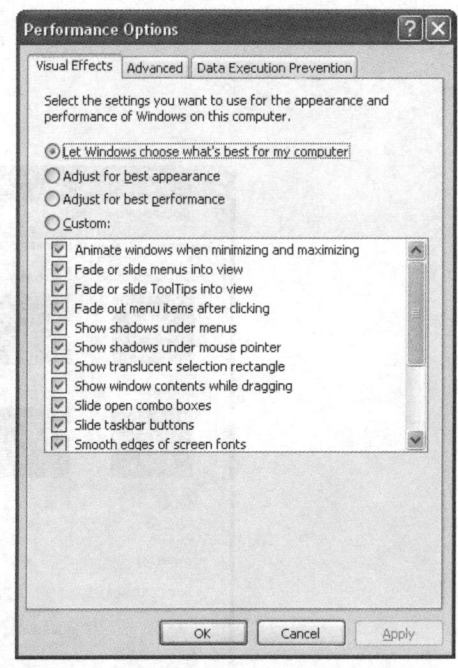

● **Figure 13.32** Windows XP Performance Options dialog box

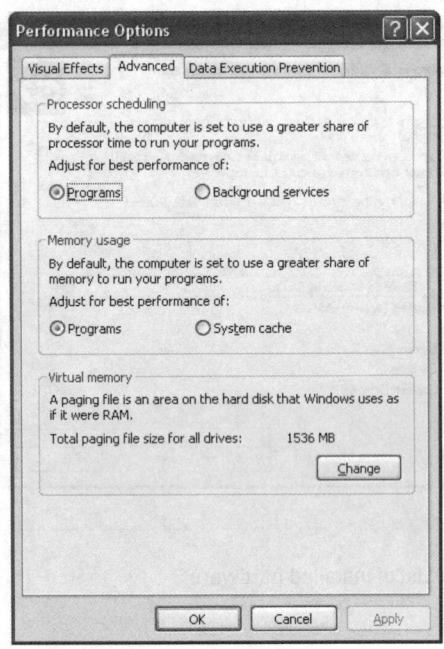

• **Figure 13.33**   Advanced tab of
                    Performance Options

a performance hit. Like other options in the Performance Options dialog box, leaving the DEP settings as default is the best option most of the time.

Resource Tracking

One big issue with optimization is knowing when something needs optimization. Let's say your Windows computer seems to be running more slowly. Resource tracking is very important for identifying the performance problem. Task Manager and the Performance console are tools you can use to figure out what (if anything) has become a bottleneck.

Task Manager

The Task Manager has many uses. Most users are only aware of the Applications tab, used to shut down a troublesome program. For optimization purposes, Task Manager is a great tool for investigating how hard your RAM and CPU are working at any given moment and why. The quick way to open the Task Manager is to press CTRL-SHIFT-ESC. Click the Performance tab to reveal a handy screen with the most commonly used information: CPU usage, available physical memory, the size of the disk cache, commit charge (memory for programs), and kernel memory (memory used by Windows). Figure 13.34 shows a system with a dual-core processor, which is why you see two screens under CPU Usage History. A system with a single-core processor would have a single screen.

Not only does Task Manager tell you how much CPU and RAM usage is taking place, it also tells you what program is using those resources. Let's say your system is running slowly. You open up Task Manager and see that your CPU usage is at 100 percent. You then click on the Processes tab to see all the processes running on your system. Click on the CPU column to sort all processes by CPU usage to see who's hogging the CPU (Figure 13.35)! To shut off a process, just right-click on the process and select End Process.

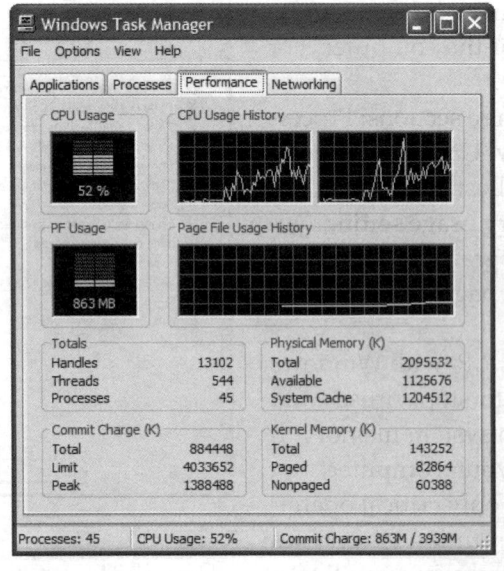

• **Figure 13.34**   Task Manager

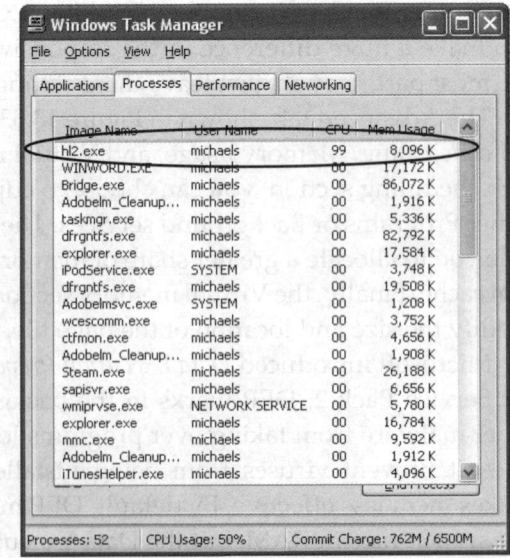

• **Figure 13.35**   CPU usage

Many times, a single process will open many other processes. If you want to be thorough, click on End Process Tree to turn off not only the one process, but also any other processes it started.

Task Manager is also a great tool for turning off processes that are hogging memory. Let's say you're experiencing a slowdown, but this time you also notice your hard drive light is flickering nonstop—a clear sign that you've run out of memory and the page file is now in use. You go into Task Manager and see that there is no available system memory—now you *know* the page file is in use! In order to make the PC run faster, you have got to start unloading programs—but which ones? By going into the Processes tab in Task Manager, you can see exactly which processes are using the most memory. Just be careful not to shut down processes you don't recognize; they might be something the computer needs!

Every program that runs on your system is composed of one or more processes.

Performance Console

Task Manager is good for identifying current problems, but what about problems that happen when you're not around? What if your system is always running at a CPU utilization of 20 percent—is that good or bad? Windows provides a tool called the **Performance console** that is used to log resource usage so that you can track items such as CPU and RAM usage over time. Performance is an MMC console file, PERFMON.MSC, so you call it from Start | Run or through the Performance icon in Administrative Tools. Use either method to open the Performance console (Figure 13.36). As you can see, there are two nodes, System Monitor and Performance Logs and Alerts.

Objects and Counters   To begin working with the Performance console, you need to understand two terms: object and counter. An **object** is a system component that is given a set of characteristics and can be managed by the operating system as a single entity. A **counter** tracks specific information about an object. For example, the Processor object has a counter, %Processor Time, which tracks the percentage of elapsed time the processor uses to execute a non-idle thread. There can be many counters associated with an object.

System Monitor   **System Monitor** gathers real-time data on objects such as memory, physical disk, processor, and network, and displays this data as a graph (line graph), histogram (bar graph), or a simple report. Think of System Monitor as a more detailed, customizable Task Manager. When you first open the Performance console, the System Monitor shows data in graph form. The data displayed is from the set of three counters listed below the chart. If you want to add counters, click the Add button (the one that looks like a plus sign) or press CTRL-I to open the Add Counters dialog box. Click the Performance object drop-down list and select one of the many different objects you can monitor. The Add Counters dialog box includes a helpful feature; you can select a counter and click the Explain button to learn about the counter, just like Figure 13.37. Try that now.

Even with just three counters selected, the graph can get a little busy. That's where one of my favorite System Monitor features shines. If you want the line of charted data from just one counter to stand out, select the counter in the list below the graph, and then press CTRL-H. See how this trick makes

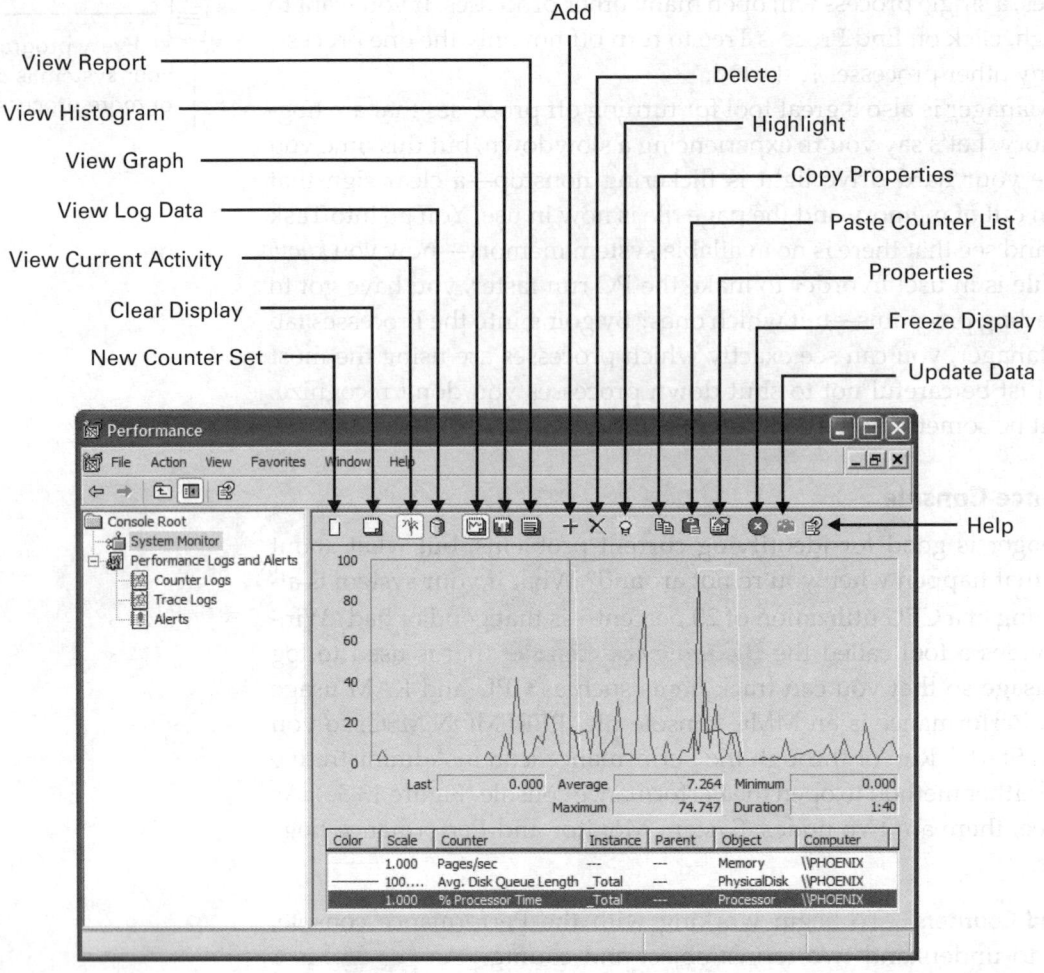

View Report
View Histogram
View Graph
View Log Data
View Current Activity
Clear Display
New Counter Set

Add
Delete
Highlight
Copy Properties
Paste Counter List
Properties
Freeze Display
Update Data

Help

● **Figure 13.36**   Performance console

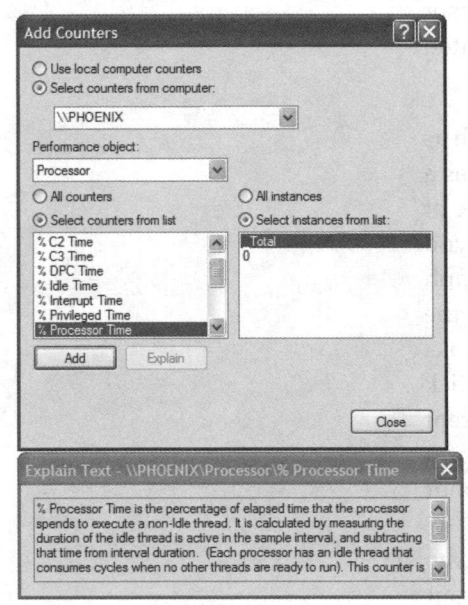

● **Figure 13.37**   Add Counters dialog box

the %Processor Time line stand out in Figure 13.38? Imagine how useful that is when you are monitoring a dozen counters.

Performance Logs and Alerts   The **Performance Logs and Alerts** snap-in enables Windows 2000/XP to create a written record of just about anything that happens on your system. Do you want to know if someone is trying to log onto your system when you're not around? The following procedure is specific to Windows XP, but the steps are nearly identical in Windows 2000.

To create the new event log, right-click Counter Logs and select New Log Settings. Give the new log a name—in this example, "Unauthorized Accesses." Click OK, and a properties box for the new log will open, similar to that in Figure 13.39.

To select counters for the log, click Add Counters, and then select the *Use local computer counters* radio button. Select Server from the Performance object pull-down menu, then select Errors Logon from the list of counters; click Add, and then Close.

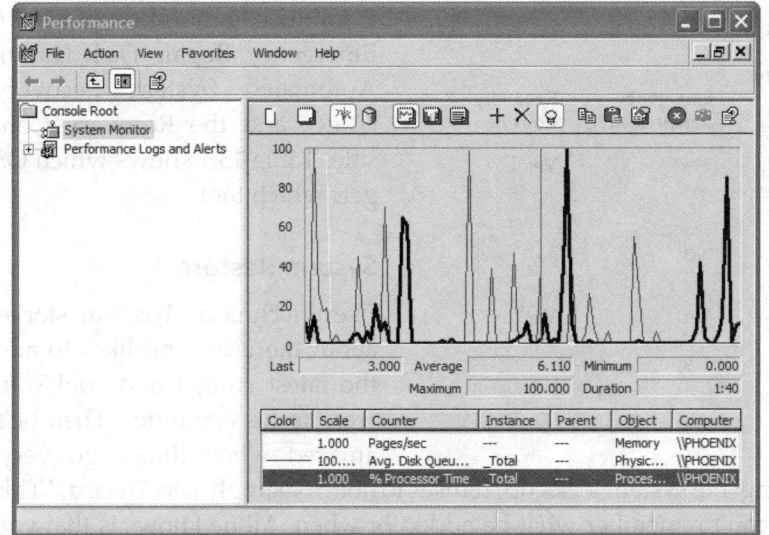

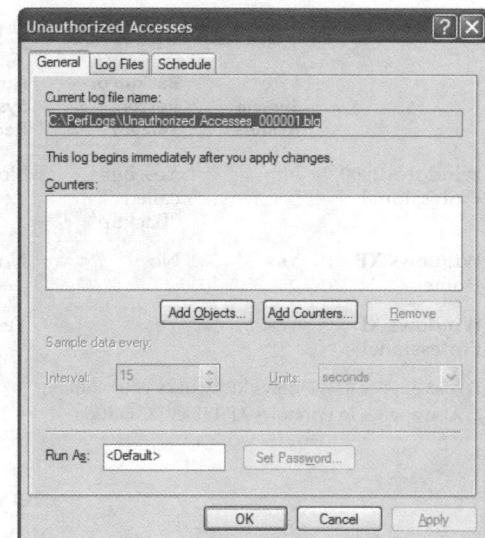

• **Figure 13.38** CTRL-H makes one set of data stand out.

• **Figure 13.39** Creating a new performance log

Back in the properties box for your new log, click the Schedule tab and set up when you want this thing to start running—probably at the end of the workday today. Then select when it should stop logging—probably tomorrow morning when you start work. Click the Log Files tab to see where the log file will be saved—probably C:\PerfLogs—and make a note of the file name. The file name will consist of the name you gave the log and a number. In this example, I named the new performance log "Unauthorized Accesses," so the file name is Unauthorized Accesses_000001.blg.

When you come back in the morning, open the Performance console, select Performance Logs and Alerts, and then select Counter Logs. Your log should be listed on the right. The icon by the log name will be green if the log is still running or red if it has stopped. If it has not stopped, select it and click the stop button (the one with the black square). See Figure 13.40.

To view the log, open the Performance console, select System Monitor, change to Report view, and load the file as a new source using the Properties box.

Preparing for Problems

The secret to troubleshooting Windows is preparation. You must have critical system files and data backed up and tools in place for the inevitable glitches. The various versions of Windows offer five different tools for the job, although none offer them all: System Restore, the Backup or Restore Wizard (called NTBackup if you want to run it

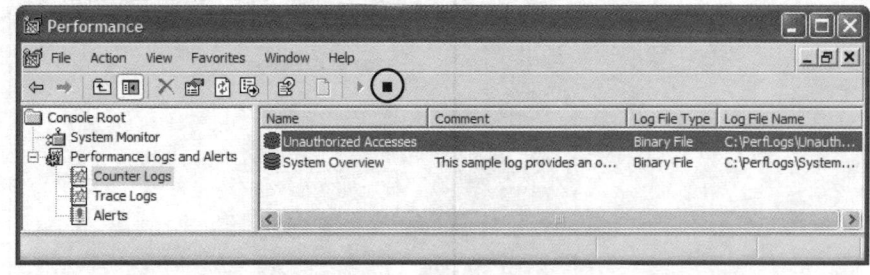

• **Figure 13.40** Stopping the performance log

Table 13.1	Backup and Recovery Tools in Windows				
	System Restore	Backup or Restore Wizard	Automated System Recovery	Emergency Repair Disk	Recovery Console
Windows 2000 Professional	No	Yes, but called "Backup"	No	Yes	Yes
Windows XP Home[1]	Yes	No	No	No	No
Windows XP Professional[2]	Yes	Yes	Yes	No	Yes

1. Also applies to Windows XP Media Center Edition
2. Also applies to Windows XP Tablet PC Edition

from the command prompt), the Emergency Repair Disk (ERD), Automated System Recovery (ASR), and the Recovery Console. Table 13.1 shows which OS gets which tool.

System Restore

Every technician has war stories about the user who likes to add the latest gadget and cool software to his computer. Then he's amazed when things go very, very wrong: the system locks up, refuses to boot, or simply acts "weird." This guy also can't remember what he added or when. All he knows is that you should be able to fix it—fast.

This is not news to the folks at Microsoft, and they have a solution to this problem. It's called System Restore, and they first introduced it in Windows Me, with further refinements in Windows XP. The System Restore tool enables you to create a restore point, a copy of your computer's configuration at a specific point in time. If you later crash or have a corrupted OS, you can restore the system to its previous state.

To create a restore point, go to Start | All Programs | Accessories | System Tools | System Restore. When the tool opens, select Create a restore point, and then click Next (Figure 13.41). Type in a description on the next screen. There's no need to include the date and time because the System Restore adds them automatically. Click Create and you're done.

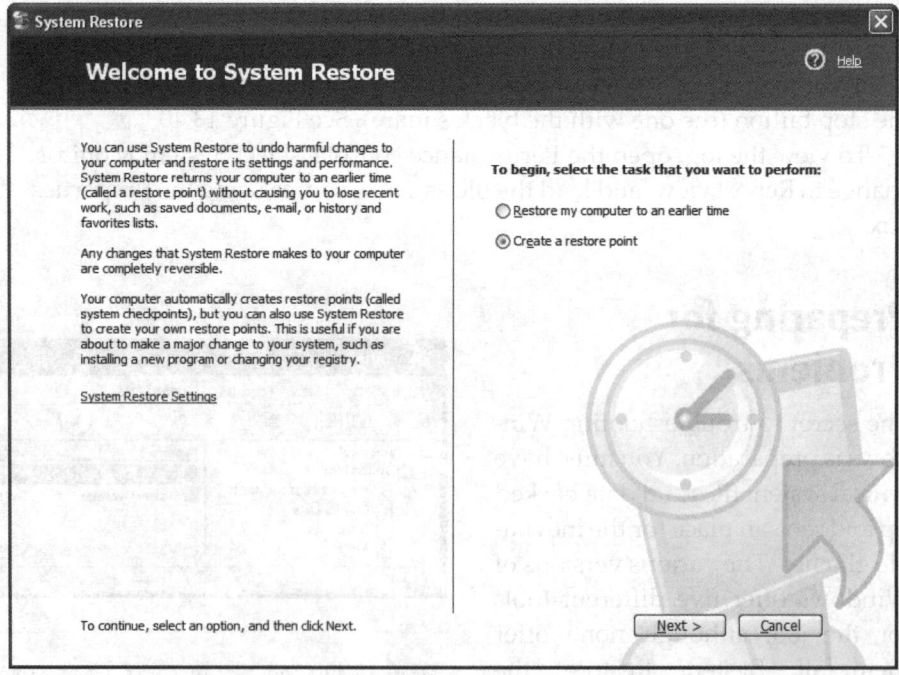

• Figure 13.41 Create a restore point

Mike Meyers' CompTIA A+ Guide: Essentials (Exam 220-601)

The System Restore tool creates some of the restore points in time automatically. For instance, by default, every time you install new software, XP creates a restore point. Thus, if installation of a program causes your computer to malfunction, simply restore the system to a time point prior to that installation, and the computer should work again.

During the restore process, only settings and programs are changed. No data is lost. Your computer will include all programs and settings as of the restore date. This feature is absolutely invaluable for overworked techs. A simple restore will fix many user-generated problems.

To restore to a previous time point, start the System Restore Wizard by choosing Start | All Programs | Accessories | System Tools | System Restore. Select the first radio button, Restore my computer to an earlier time, and then click Next. Figure 13.42 shows a calendar with restore points. Any day with a boldface date has at least one restore point. These points are created after you add or remove software or install Windows updates and during the normal shutdown of your computer. Select a date on the calendar; then select a restore point from the list on the right and click Next.

The last screen before the system is restored shows a warning. It advises you to close all open programs and reminds you that Windows will shut down during the restore process. It also states that the restore operation is completely reversible. Thus, if you go too far back in time, you can restore to a more recent date.

You don't have to count on the automatic creation of restore points. You can open System Restore at any time and simply select Create a restore point. Consider doing this before making changes that might not trigger an automatic restore point, such as directly editing the Registry.

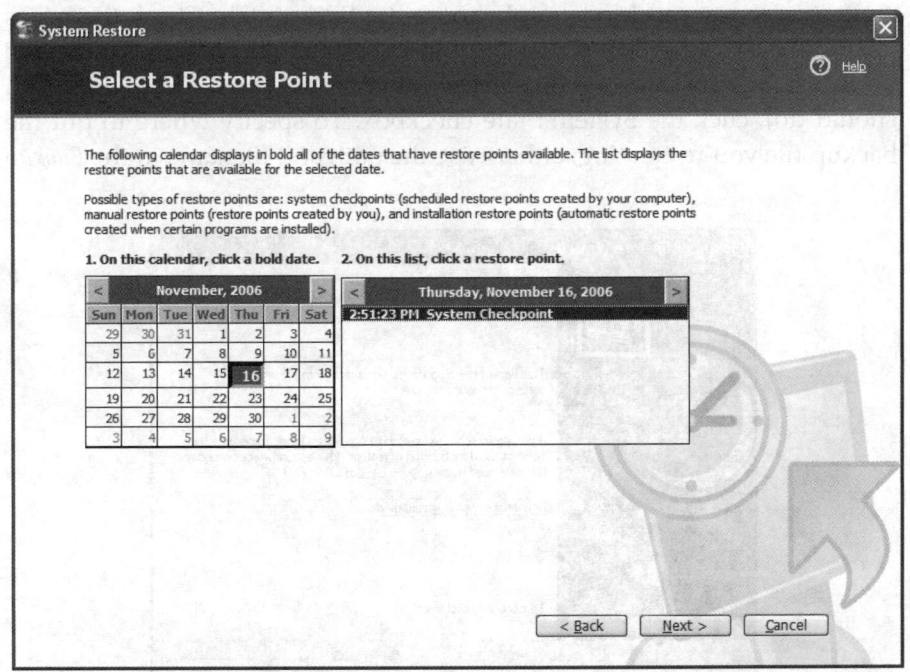

• **Figure 13.42** Calendar of restore points

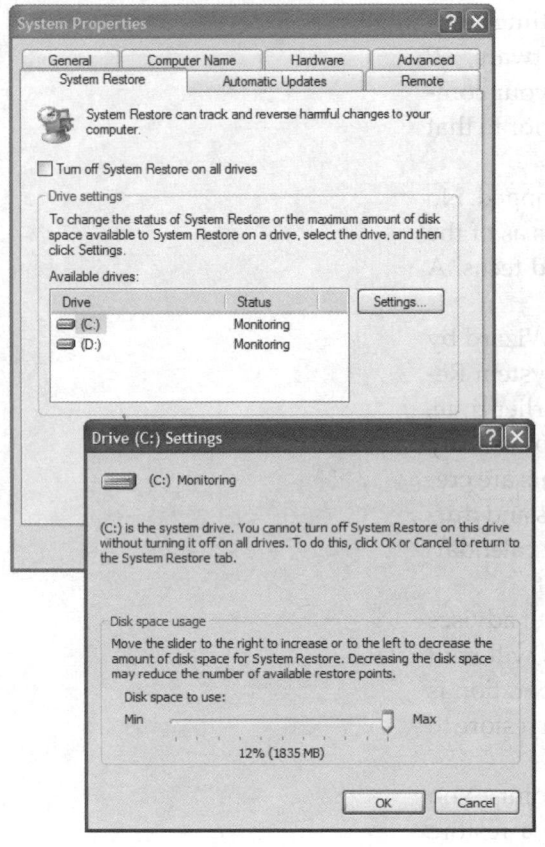

● **Figure 13.43** System Restore tab in System
Properties applet

📄 The Backup Utility is not included in the default installation
of Windows XP Home. You must
install it manually from the
Windows CD-ROM.

System Restore is turned on by default and uses some of
your disk space to save information on restore points. To turn
System Restore off or change the disk space usage, open the
System Properties applet in Control Panel and select the System Restore tab (Figure 13.43).

Backup Utility (NTBackup)

Windows 2000 Backup and Windows XP **Backup Utility** provide almost all the tools you need to back up files and folders.
It has come a long way from its origins in Windows NT. It
supports a greater variety of devices, enabling you to back up
to network drives, logical drives, tape, and removable disks
(but not optical discs). Most folks, however, still turn to
third-party utilities to create system, e-mail, browser, and
personal data backups.

You can start Backup by navigating the Start menu to
Accessories | System Tools, or by clicking the Backup Now
button on the Tools page of the local disk properties box. I prefer
to start it from Start | Run with the command NTBACKUP.
Click the Backup Wizard button to run the Backup Wizard. This
technique works in both Windows 2000 and Windows XP. To
use the Windows XP version in Advanced Mode (Figure 13.44),
click Advanced Mode on the opening screen. To have it always
open in Advanced Mode, uncheck the *Always start in wizard
mode* checkbox. If the program is in Advanced Mode and you
want to run it as a wizard, click the Wizard Mode link to open
the Backup or Restore Wizard.

To create a backup, start the Backup Utility, click Advanced Mode, and choose the Backup tab. Check the boxes
next to the drives and files you want to include in the backup. To include
your system state information, such as Registry and boot files (which you
should do), click the System State checkbox. To specify where to put the
backup file you're creating, either type the path and filename in the *Backup*

● **Figure 13.44** Advanced Mode

media or file name box or click Browse, select a location, type the filename, and click Save. Click Start Backup. Choose whether you want to append this backup to a previous one or overwrite it. Click Advanced to open the Advanced Backup Options dialog box, select *Verify data after backup*, and click OK. Click Start Backup again. A dialog box will show you the utility's progress. When it's done, click Close, and then close the Backup Utility.

Both versions of Backup give you three choices after you click Advanced Mode: Backup Wizard (Advanced), Restore Wizard (Advanced), and a third choice that is very important. The third option in Windows 2000 is the Emergency Repair Disk. As you can see in Figure 13.45, the third option in Windows XP is the Automated System Recovery Wizard.

Windows 2000 Emergency Repair Disk (ERD)   Let's first consider the Windows 2000 Emergency Repair Disk (ERD) . This disk saves critical boot files and partition information and is your main tool for fixing boot problems in Windows 2000. It is not a bootable disk, nor does it store very much information; the ERD does not replace a good system backup! It works with a special folder called \WINNT\REPAIR to store a copy of your Registry. It's not perfect, but it gets you out of most startup problems. It's good practice to make a new ERD before you install a new device or program. Then the ERD is ready if you need it.

So, you have this great Emergency Repair Disk that'll take care of all of your system repair problems; you just pop it in the floppy drive and go, right?

Not just yet. As I mentioned, the ERD itself is not a bootable disk. To use the ERD, you must first boot the system using the Windows installation CD-ROM. Follow these steps to repair a system using the ERD:

1.   Boot the system using either your set of boot diskettes or installation CD-ROM.

2.   In the Welcome to Setup dialog box, press the R key to select the option to repair a Windows 2000 installation.

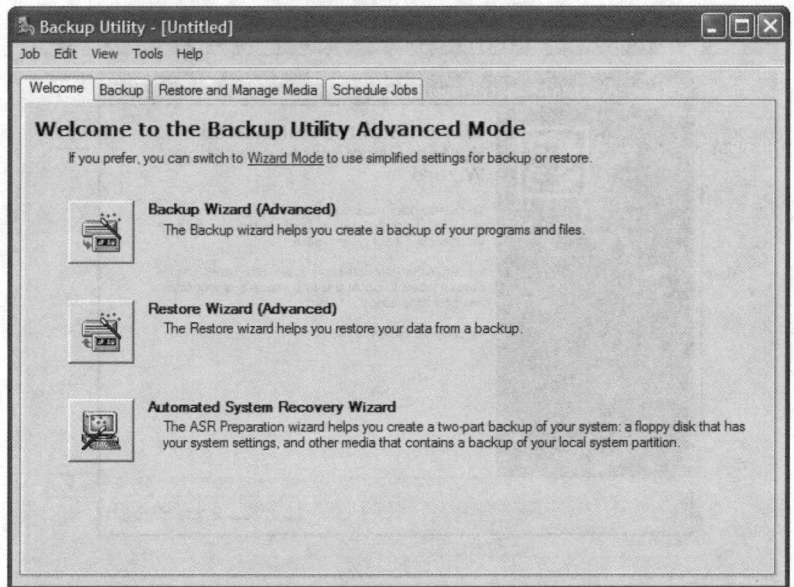

Backup Program Naming Nightmare

Microsoft has been dreadfully inconsistent on the naming of the backup programs that it bundles with Windows. Here's the scoop in a nutshell. In Windows 2000, the official name of the backup program is Microsoft Windows Backup, *but the dialog box that opens is simply called* Backup. *The wizard interface is called the* Backup Wizard. *The quick command-line command you run to get to the utility is* NTBACKUP. *Are you with me?*

The backup program in Windows XP has a similar slew of names. The official name of the program is Backup Utility for Windows. *The Advanced Mode dialog box is called* Backup Utility, *but the wizard interface differs, depending on whether you run the utility in Wizard Mode or click the Backup Wizard button in the Advanced Mode dialog box. The former runs the* Backup or Restore Wizard; *the latter runs the* Backup Wizard. *These wizards offer different options, with the Backup or Restore Wizard providing the simpler, consumer-oriented interface. Both wizards are only different faces for the Backup Utility. Got it? Oh, and NTBACKUP is the command-line command to run the program in Windows XP, so Microsoft provides at least a nod at naming consistency.*

Most seasoned techs call the backup programs in Windows 2000 and Windows XP Backup *or* NTBackup. *You need to know the variety of names, however, to provide proper customer support. This is especially true in a help desk environment.*

• **Figure 13.45**   Windows XP Backup Utility options

Chapter 13: Maintaining Windows

3. The Windows 2000 Repair Options menu appears. You have the option of either entering the Recovery Console or using the Emergency Repair Disk.

4. Press the R key to select the option to repair Windows 2000 using the emergency repair process.

5. The next screen offers the choice of Manual or Fast repair.

   ■ Manual repair lets you select the following repair options: inspect the startup environment, verify the system files, and inspect the boot sector.

   ■ Fast repair doesn't ask for any further input.

6. Follow the on-screen instructions and insert the ERD when prompted.

7. Your system will be inspected and, if possible, restored. When finished, the system will restart.

Windows XP Automated System Recovery (ASR)   The   Windows   XP   Automated System Recovery (ASR) looks and acts very similar to the Windows 2000 ERD. The ASR Wizard lets you create a backup of your system. This backup includes a floppy disk and backup media (tape or CD-R) containing the system partition and disks containing operating system components (Figure 13.46).

The restore side of ASR involves a complete reinstall of the operating system, preferably on a new partition. This is something you do when all is lost. Run Setup and press F2 when prompted during the text-mode portion of Setup. Follow the prompts on the screen, which will first ask for the floppy disk and then for the backup media.

Backup Wizard   Data files are not backed up by the ERD or by the ASR. Therefore, you have to back up data files. If you run the Backup Wizard and

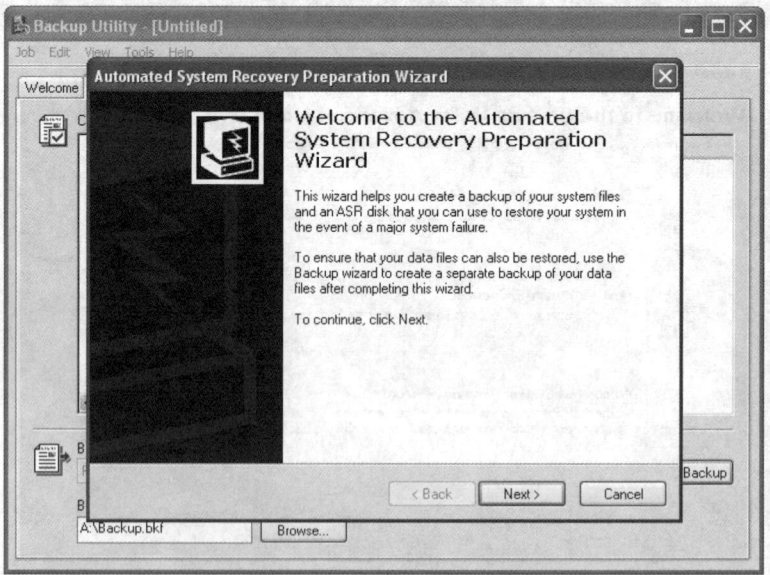

• **Figure 13.46**   Creating an ASR backup

click the Next button on the Welcome screen, you'll open the dialog box in Figure 13.47. You have three options here. The first two are fairly self-explanatory: You can back up everything or just selected drives and files.

The third option needs some explanation. The *Only back up the System State data* radio button enables you to save "other" system-critical files, but with Windows 2000/XP, it's not much more than making an ERD with the Registry backup. This option really makes sense for Windows 2000 Server and Windows Server 2003 systems because it saves Active Directory information (which your Windows 2000/XP systems do not store) as well as other critical, server-specific functions. (More on these topics in Chapter 19.) But the CompTIA A+ certification exams may still expect you to know about it!

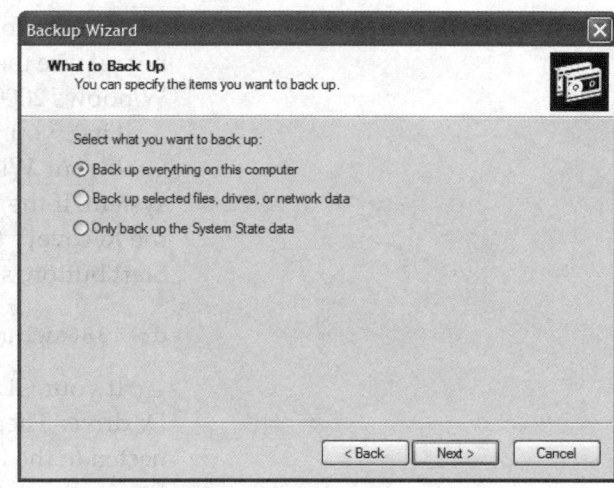

• Figure 13.47   Backup Wizard options

Tape Backup   The odd fact that Microsoft has not updated the Backup or Restore Wizard to enable you to back up to optical media of any sort has kept alive the practice of tape backups. Tape drives connect to the ATA or SCSI bus, just like optical drives, but rather than using a shiny CD-R or DVD+R disc, you have to back up to magnetic tape (Figure 13.48).

Tape drive manufacturers have done pretty much everything they can do to make tape backups as fast as possible, but the technology suffers from two huge drawbacks. First, it's tape, which means all data must be stored and restored in sequential access. The drive has to go through Files 1 and 2 before reaching File 3, in other words. Second, tape is painfully slow in comparison to hard drives, optical drives, or Flash- media drives.

The only great benefit to tape is that it's relatively cheap to buy multiple tapes with a lot of storage capacity. With hard drive and recordable DVD prices at rock bottom today, however, tape's days are numbered.

• Figure 13.48   Backup tapes

Installing Recovery Console

When things get really bad on a Windows system, you need to turn to the Recovery Console. The Recovery Console is a text-based startup of Windows that gets you to a command prompt similar to the Windows command prompt.

If you have the Windows 2000/XP CD-ROM, you can start the Recovery Console by running Setup, selecting Repair, and then selecting Recovery Console. If you like to be proactive, however, you can install the Recovery

Console on your hard drive so that it is one of your startup options and does not require the Windows 2000 or XP CD-ROM to run. The steps to do this in Windows 2000 and Windows XP are very nearly identical.

First, you need to log into the system with the Administrator account. Grab your Windows 2000 or XP installation CD-ROM and drop it in your system. If the Autorun function kicks in, just click the No button. To install the Recovery Console and make it a part of your startup options, click the Start button, select Run, and type the following:

```
d:\i386\winnt32 /cmdcons
```

If your CD-ROM drive uses a different drive letter, substitute it for the D: drive. Then just follow the instructions on the screen. If you are connected to the Internet, allow the Setup program to download updated files. From now on, every time the system boots, the OS selection menu will show your Windows OS (Windows 2000 Professional or Windows XP) and the Microsoft Windows Recovery Console. It may also show other choices if yours is a multi-boot computer.

Chapter 13 Review

Chapter Summary

After reading this chapter and completing the exercises, you should understand the following about maintaining and optimizing Windows 2000/XP.

Maintaining Windows

- It is important to keep Windows updated with the latest security patches from Microsoft. You can perform a manual update via the Windows Update utility found in Start | Windows Update (Windows 2000) or Start | All Programs | Windows Update (Windows XP). After launching the utility and scanning your computer, you are presented with a list of recommended updates. Clicking the Install button will begin the update procedure.

- Automatic Updates are configurable in Windows XP through the My Computer Properties window's Automatic Updates tab or the Automatic Updates Control Panel applet. You can choose to automatically download and install updates at a certain time, download updates automatically but be prompted to install them, or be prompted to download updates. The default setting will download updates automatically, and then prompt you to install them.

- Each Windows 2000/XP computer user must log on with a valid user name and password. The logon process can be configured to be invisible to the user (although this is not recommended, for security reasons), but there is no exception to the rule that users must log on. Each user account is a member of at least one group. Groups make it easier for computer administrators to manage permissions and security. Built-in user accounts include the Administrator and Guest accounts. The Guest account is disabled by default.

- Users and groups are managed differently, depending on if your computer is a member of a Windows domain or not. For non-domain accounts, manage users and groups through the Local Users and Groups node in the Computer Management console. Alternatively, use the Users and Passwords applet (Windows 2000) or User Accounts applet (Windows XP) in the Control Panel.

- User accounts enable a system administrator to set permissions for the user and to audit their access to files and network resources. Administrators can create users in Windows 2000 via the Add New User Wizard from the Users and Passwords applet in the Control Panel. Although blank passwords are possible, they are not recommended, as they offer no security. If a new user account is created as a Standard User, the account is made a member of the local Power Users group. An existing user's password can be changed in the Users and Passwords applet by selecting the user and clicking the Set Password button.

- The Windows XP User Accounts applet shows all accounts that are members of the Administrators group as Computer Administrators and all other accounts as Limited accounts. Administrators will see all user accounts in the applet, whereas a Limited account user will see only their own account. Windows XP requires you to create two administrator accounts for redundancy.

- If a Windows XP computer is a member of a domain, it uses the Windows 2000 Classic–style logon screen that requires the pressing of CTRL-ALT-DEL. If the computer is not a domain member, it defaults to the Welcome screen for logons. You can change the type of logon screen users see in Windows XP if the computer is not on a domain. In the User Accounts applet, select *Change the way users log on and off* to view the available options.

- Passwords are the ultimate key to protecting your computers. A user account with a valid password will get you into any system. Protect your passwords and make users choose good passwords that mix letters and numbers. Windows XP allows a currently logged-on user to create a password reset disk that can be used to recover forgotten passwords. If the administrator resets the password instead, you may lose access to some items, including files encrypted with the forgotten password.

- To check a physical hard drive for problems (bad sectors, lost clusters, and similar problems), use the Error-checking tool available from the CHKDSK command line or from the Tools tab on a drive's Properties dialog box. Use Disk Defragmenter regularly to keep your system from slowing down due to fragmented files. Click the Analyze button before defragmenting to make sure defragmentation is necessary.

- Before defragmenting a drive, run the Disk Cleanup utility. To run it, click the Disk Cleanup button on the Properties dialog box for any drive. Disk Cleanup offers a projected summary of how much space will be freed up by running the tool and deleting files from certain categories. In addition to deleting files, the utility can compress files that are rarely used. File compression is where you are likely to regain the most hard drive storage space.

- To clean the registry for Windows 2000/XP, you'll need to use a third-party tool, such as the freeware EasyCleaner by ToniArts. The utility can be downloaded from http://personal.inet.fi/business/toniarts/ecleane.htm. Do not use anything from http://www.toniarts.com, as that site is a scam!

Optimizing Windows

- Most applications have an Autorun file on the CD that calls up the installation program if Windows is configured for Autorun. If the CD does not have an Autorun file, you can begin the software installation process manually by using the Add or Remove Programs applet. After accepting the terms of the software license, you may be asked to make decisions about which components to install. Usually, it is best to accept the suggested settings.

- Removing applications that are no longer needed is an important piece of housekeeping. When possible, use the uninstall program that came with the application. Be prepared to provide the application CD-ROM if prompted for it. If an uninstall program did not come with the application, use the Add or Remove Program applet from the Windows Control Panel. If prompted to remove shared files that no longer seem needed, you should agree. If you leave them, they become orphaned and take up hard disk space forever. It is necessary to use an uninstall

program to remove all remnants of a program, including Registry entries.

- You can also add or remove Windows components as needed. From the Add or Remove Program applet, simply select Add/Remove Windows Components. You should have your Windows CD handy. You will be prompted for it when you add a component. When you select a program that is already installed, the wizard will show you how much disk space it occupies and how often it is used.

- Installing the proper driver for a hardware device is essential. Although Windows includes generic device drivers for many devices, it is best to use the specialized driver software designed for a specific device. You can find the driver on the discs that come with the device, on Microsoft's Web site, or on the Web site of the device manufacturer.

- To protect Windows systems from bad device drivers, Microsoft uses driver signing, which means that each driver has a digital signature. Any drivers included on the Windows CD-ROM or at the Windows Update Web site are digitally signed. Once you have installed a driver, you can look at its Properties to confirm that it was digitally signed. Often unsigned drivers work fine. If not, you can use the System Restore tool to restore the computer to its previous state. You can also configure the Driver Signing Options for Windows to install an unsigned driver without warning you or to block all unsigned drivers.

- The Device Manager is one of the most important tools for checking hardware, drivers, and resources. Open the Properties for My Computer and select the Hardware tab to find the Device Manager button. By right-clicking on a device, you will see the context menu from which you can update or install the driver, disable the device, scan for hardware changes, or display the Properties dialog box. Windows XP also includes the Roll Back Driver feature that will remove an updated driver and roll back to a previous version.

- Performance Options differs between Windows 2000 and Windows XP, but both versions enable you to set how processor time is divided between applications and background services. You can also adjust the size of the page file, but it is best to let Windows control this feature.

- Resource tracking can help solve performance problems. The Task Manager and Performance tools help identify bottlenecks. To access the Task Manager, press CTRL-SHIFT-ESC, and then click the Performance tab. This program tracks CPU usage, available memory, size of disk cache, and other resources or operations such as handles, threads, and processes. It also displays the applications and processes that are running and the computer resources they are using.

- If an application hangs, use the Task Manager to end the program. It can also be used to switch between applications or to shut down the computer. The Task Manager can also shut down locked-up processes.

- The Performance console includes the System Monitor node and the Performance Logs and Alerts node. System Monitor gathers real-time data about objects and displays them in a graph, histogram, or report. You can add additional counters. The Performance Logs and Alerts counters track a variety of system statistics. You can determine when the tool will monitor performance and what the log file will be named.

- Preparation is the key to troubleshooting Windows 2000 and XP. Five different tools prepare for possible problems: System Restore, the Backup Utility, Emergency Repair Disk, Automated System Recovery, and Recovery Console.

- First introduced with Windows Me, System Restore enables you to create a restore point or configuration at a specific time. If the computer crashes or becomes corrupted, you can restore the system settings and programs. Data is not lost with System Restore. Although the OS itself creates a restore point when you install new software, you can designate other restore points.

- Although many choose third-party backup utilities, Windows 2000 and XP include a full-featured backup program that works with network drives, logical drives, tape, and removable disks. Both Windows 2000 and XP offer choices of Backup and Restore. With Windows 2000, the third choice is Emergency Repair Disk (ERD); Windows XP offers the Automated System Recovery Wizard. The ERD saves critical boot files and partition information. Although it is not a bootable disk, it works with the \WINNT\REPAIR folder to store a copy of the Registry. Windows XP uses the ASR Wizard to create a backup of the system. It uses a floppy disk and a backup medium such as tape. The restore capability of ASR involves a complete reinstall of the operating system, preferably on a new partition.

- Neither the ERD nor the ASR backs up data files. You should use the Backup Wizard to back up everything or just system-critical files. A third option involves System State data that involves little more than an ERD with a Registry backup.

- The Windows 2000/XP Recovery Console is a text-based startup of Windows. To start this utility, run Setup and select Repair. If you wish, you can install the Recovery Console on the hard drive as one of the startup options.

■ Key Terms

Add or Remove Programs applet (409)

Administrator account (398)

Automated System Recovery (ASR) (424)

Automatic Updates (397)

Autorun (409)

Backup Utility (422)

counter (417)

Device Manager (414)

Disk Cleanup (407)

driver signing (413)

Emergency Repair Disk (ERD) (423)

groups (398)

Limited account (402)

Local Users and Groups (398)

object (417)

password reset disk (406)

Performance console (417)

Performance Logs and Alerts (418)

Performance Options (415)

Recovery Console (425)

restore point (420)

System Monitor (417)

System Restore (420)

Task Manager (416)

user account (398)

User Accounts applet (401)

Users and Passwords applet (399)

Welcome screen (402)

Windows Update (395)

Key Term Quiz

Use the Key Terms list to complete the sentences that follow. Not all terms will be used.

1. A(n) _____ is a system component with a set of characteristics that is managed by the OS as a single entity.

2. You can use the _____ utility to manually create a restore point for disaster recovery.

3. If an administrator resets the password, you may lose access to some items; but if you use a _____, you will still have access to everything.

4. Windows XP uses the _____ to create a backup of the system using both a floppy diskette and a backup medium such as tape; restoring involves completely reinstalling the operating system.

5. Although not bootable, the _____ works with the \WINNT\REPAIR folder to store a copy of the Windows 2000 Registry.

6. System Monitor gathers real-time data about objects and places them in a(n) _____ that may be a graph, histogram, or report.

7. With Windows XP, an account that belongs only to the Local Users group is said to be a(n) _____.

8. The _____, accessed by pressing CTRL-ALT-DEL once, enables you to see all applications or programs currently running or to close an application that has stopped working.

9. Fast User Switching is only available in Windows XP if you have enabled the use of the _____.

10. You can set up a user account in Windows XP using the Local Users and Groups or the _____.

Multiple-Choice Quiz

1. Which of the following commands would you use to install the Recovery Console?

   A. Start | Run; then type **d:\i386\winnt32 /cmdcons**.

   B. Start | Run; then type **d:\i386\winnt32 /rc**.

   C. Start | Run; then type **d:\i386\winnt32 /cmd:command_line**.

   D. Start | Run; then type **d:\i386\winnt32 /copydir:recovery_console**.

2. Which tool in Windows XP Home, loaded by default, can you use to back up essential system files?

   A. Emergency Repair Disk

   B. Backup and Recovery Wizard

   C. System Restore

   D. Recovery Console

3. Mark loaded a new video card on his system, but now everything looks very bad. What should he do first?

   A. Go to Event Viewer and check the log.

   B. Go to Device Manager.

   C. Go to the printed manual.

   D. Call tech support.

4. Anthony sets up a new Windows XP Professional PC for his client in an insecure, networked environment. What's his first step for making the data safe?

   A. Make sure the user shuts the machine off every night.

   B. Require the user to log in with a password.

   C. Require the user to log in with a password composed of alphanumeric characters.

   D. Nothing. Anybody with a floppy disk can access the data on the PC.

5. Which of the following should be your first choice to remove an application that you no longer need?

   A. Delete the program files.

   B. Use the uninstall program that came with the application.

   C. Use the Add or Remove Programs applet.

   D. Use the Registry Editor to remove references to the application.

6. Which utility is useful in identifying a program that is hogging the processor?

A. Task Manager

B. Device Manager

C. System Monitor

D. System Information

7. You've just installed a software update, rebooted, and now your system experiences random crashes. Which utility should you use first to try to fix the problem?

A. Automated System Restore

B. Device Manager

C. System Restore

D. Recovery Console

8. What program can you use to keep your systems patched and up to date?

A. Windows Dispatcher

B. Windows Patcher

C. Windows Update

D. Windows Upgrade

9. Wendy wants to create two user accounts on a Windows 2000 Professional computer. What tools could she use? (Select two.)

A. Local Users and Groups

B. Passwords and Accounts

C. User Accounts

D. Users and Passwords

10. Diane complains that her system seems sluggish and she keeps running out of disk space. What tool can she use to get rid of unnecessary files and compress older files? (Select the best answer.)

A. Disk Cleanup

B. Disk Doctor

C. File Manager

D. Registry Cleaner

11. Alberto installs a video card into a Windows XP computer; it seems to work just fine until he tries to run a game. Then he gets low-end graphics and it just doesn't look right. What might he try to fix the problem? Select the best answer.

A. Check the video card manufacturer's Web site and download updated drivers.

B. Check the video card manufacturer's Web site and download the FAQ.

C. Run the Driver Update utility.

D. Reinstall Windows.

12. Janet thinks that someone is logging into her computer after she leaves work. What tool could you use to track who logs on and off the computer?

A. Log Monitor snap-in

B. Performance Logs and Alerts snap-in

C. System Monitor

D. Task Manager

13. Which user accounts are created during installation? (Choose all that apply.)

A. Administrator

B. Guest

C. Root

D. User

14. In Windows 2000 Professional, a Standard User account is a member of which built-in group?

A. Administrators

B. Power Users

C. Guests

D. Limited Accounts

15. Lily is busy typing a report on her Windows XP computer, but Clayton needs to check his e-mail. What can Lily do to let Clayton log in with his user account, but keep her word processor running with her document open?

A. Log off

B. Standby

C. Switch user

D. Hibernate

Essay Quiz

1. A colleague of yours is about to set up the PCs for a new office in Boston. The office will have 16 computer stations for the 32 employees to share, and all the PCs will run Windows XP Professional in the same workgroup. What advice would you give your colleague about setting up the user accounts?

2. Your boss wants you to write a brief essay on how your users should back up their data for protection against accidental loss. Half the users have Windows 2000 PCs; the other half are running Windows XP Professional. Keep in mind that your target audience is users, not trained technicians, so you should go for the user-level tools.

3. You've been tasked with organizing the standard maintenance routines for the Boston office of 16 Windows XP Professional PCs. Write a couple of paragraphs describing the tools available and how often each should be run.

4. Your friend Steve got a new Windows XP Home computer, but it's so loaded with trial-version software from the manufacturer that it confuses him. He wants to unload some of these useless programs, but he doesn't want to trash his new PC. Write a brief essay describing the tool(s) he needs to use to uninstall the programs and clean up afterward.

Lab Projects

• Lab Project 13.1

You learned that restore points are copies of your system's configuration at a specific point in time. You know that Windows automatically creates some restore points. But there may be situations when you would like to have a copy of the current system configuration. That's why Microsoft also allows users to create a restore point at any time. Review the process, decide on a description for a new restore point, and then create a restore point. Note that it automatically includes the date and time when you created it.

If you are using Windows 2000, another prevention tool is the Emergency Repair Disk. Review the process for creating an ERD. Then create one and store it in a safe place in case of an emergency. (Note that Windows XP does not include the ERD option.)

Input/Output

*"I do not understand this
'mouse-magic' that makes me do
your bidding."*
—EDWIN, BALDUR'S GATE (1998)

In Chapter 2, you learned how to recognize and connect a number of common devices and the ports they use. Because these devices and their ports sometimes fail, it is important that you learn how they work and how to troubleshoot them when problems arise. This chapter reviews some of the major types of input ports, discusses a number of common and not-so-common input/output (I/O) devices, and deals with some of the troubleshooting issues you may encounter with I/O devices and their ports.

The CompTIA A+ certification exams split the domains of computer I/O devices into three groups: common, multimedia, and specialty. Common I/O devices, such as keyboards and mice, are found on virtually every PC. Multimedia I/O devices support video and sound functions. Specialty I/O devices run the gamut from common (touch screens) to rare (biometric devices). In fact, the exams deal with an entire set of I/O devices—networking devices—as completely distinct technologies. This book dedicates entire chapters to printing, video, and networking, providing details about dealing with these types of devices and the ports they use. This chapter concentrates on two of the I/O device groups: the common devices and the specialty devices. You'll learn how to identify and support both the most common and some of the most unusual I/O devices used in today's PCs.

In this chapter, you will learn how to

- **Explain how to support common input/output ports**
- **Identify certain common input/output devices on a PC**
- **Describe how certain specialty input/output devices work on a PC**

Essentials

This entire chapter shows up in the CompTIA A+ certification Essentials exam, but that does *not* mean that none of these topics appear on the three CompTIA A+ specialty exams! All four CompTIA A+ exams test you on certain aspects of I/O devices, ports, configuration, and so on.

Having trouble finding a PC with serial ports? Try a laptop—almost all laptops come with built-in modems.

Serial ports might be dead on PCs, but they're still alive and cooking in other computer hardware. The standard way to make the initial configuration on most routers—the machines that form the backbone of many networks, including the Internet—is by connecting through a serial port. To get around the lack of traditional serial ports, networking people use a USB-to-serial dongle.

Tech Tip

Serial Ports Are RS-232 Ports

Speaking of standardization, all serial ports on PCs use the RS-232 standard. Many old techs will look at a serial port and say "That's an RS-232 port!" Since all physical serial ports are standardized on RS-232, they're right.

■ Supporting Common I/O Ports

Whenever you're dealing with an I/O device that isn't playing nice, you need to remember that you're never dealing with just a device—you're dealing with a device and the port to which it is connected. Before you start looking at I/O devices, you need to take a look into the issues and technologies of some of the more common I/O ports and see what needs to be done to keep them running well.

Serial Ports

It's difficult to find a new PC with a real serial port, because devices that traditionally used serial ports have for the most part moved on to better interfaces, in particular USB. Physical serial ports may be getting hard to find on new PC cases, but many devices, in particular the modems many people still use to access the Internet, continue to use built-in serial ports.

In Chapter 6, you learned that COM ports are nothing more than preset I/O addresses and interrupt request lines (IRQs) for serial ports. Want to see a built-in serial port? Open Device Manager on a system and see if you have an icon for Ports (COM and LPT). If you do, click the plus (+) sign to the left of the icon to open it and see the ports on your system—don't be surprised if you have COM ports on your PC. Even if you don't see any physical serial ports on your PC, the serial ports are really there; they're simply built into some other device, probably a modem.

Your PC's expansion bus uses parallel communication—multiple data wires, each one sending one bit of data at a time between your devices. Many I/O devices use serial communication—one wire to send data and another wire to receive data. The job of a **serial port** is to convert data moving between parallel and serial devices. A traditional serial port consists of two pieces: the physical, 9-pin DB connector (Figure 14.1), and a chip that actually does the conversion between the serial data and parallel data, called the

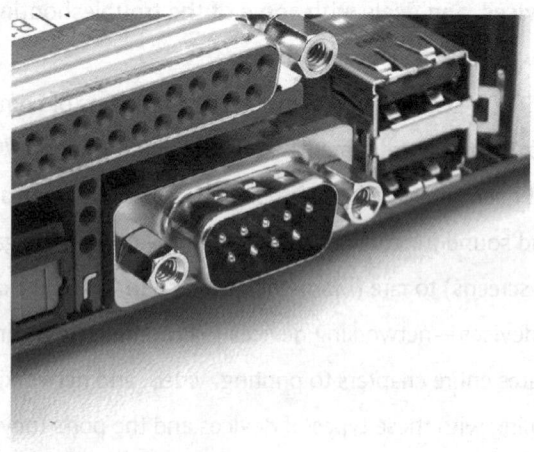

• **Figure 14.1** Serial port

universal asynchronous receiver/transmitter (UART) chip. If you want to be completely accurate, the UART *is* the serial port. The port on the back of your PC is nothing more than a standardized connector that enables different serial devices to use the serial port. The UART holds all the smarts that make the true serial port.

RS-232 is a very old standard that defines everything about serial ports: how fast they communicate, the "language" they use, even how the connectors should look. The RS-232 standard specifies that two serial devices must talk to each other in 8-bit chunks of data, but it also allows flexibility in other areas, such as speed and error-checking. Serial came out back in the days when devices were configured manually, and the RS-232 standard has never been updated for automatic configuration. Serial ports are a throwback to the old days of computer maintenance and are the last manually configured port you'll find on a PC.

So what type of settings do you need to configure on a serial port? Find a PC with a real serial port (a real 9-pin connector on the back of the PC). Right-click the COM port and choose Properties to see the properties of that port in Device Manager. Open the Port Settings tab and click the Advanced button to see a dialog box that looks like Figure 14.2.

Devices such as modems that have built-in serial ports don't have COM port icons in Device Manager, because there's nothing to change. Can you see why? Even though these devices are using a COM port, that port is never going to connect to anything other than the device it's soldered onto, so all the settings are fixed and unchangeable—thank goodness!

When you are configuring a serial port, the first thing you need to set is its speed in bits per second. A serial port may run as slowly as 75 bps up to a maximum speed of 128,000 bps. Next, you should set the parameters of the data "chunks": serial data moves up and down the cable connecting the serial device to your serial port in either 7- or 8-bit chunks, and it may or may not use a special "stop" bit to identify the end of each chunk. Serial ports use parity for error-checking and flow control to ensure that the sending device doesn't overload the receiving device with data. The convenient part about all this is that when you get a new serial device to plug into your serial port, the instructions will tell you what settings to use. Figure 14.3 shows an instruction sheet for a Cisco switch.

Tech Tip

UARTs and COM Ports

Every UART in a system is assigned a COM port value. An internal modem snaps right into your expansion bus, so every internal modem has a built-in UART. Therefore, even though a modem doesn't have a physical serial connection, it most certainly has a serial port—a built-in one.

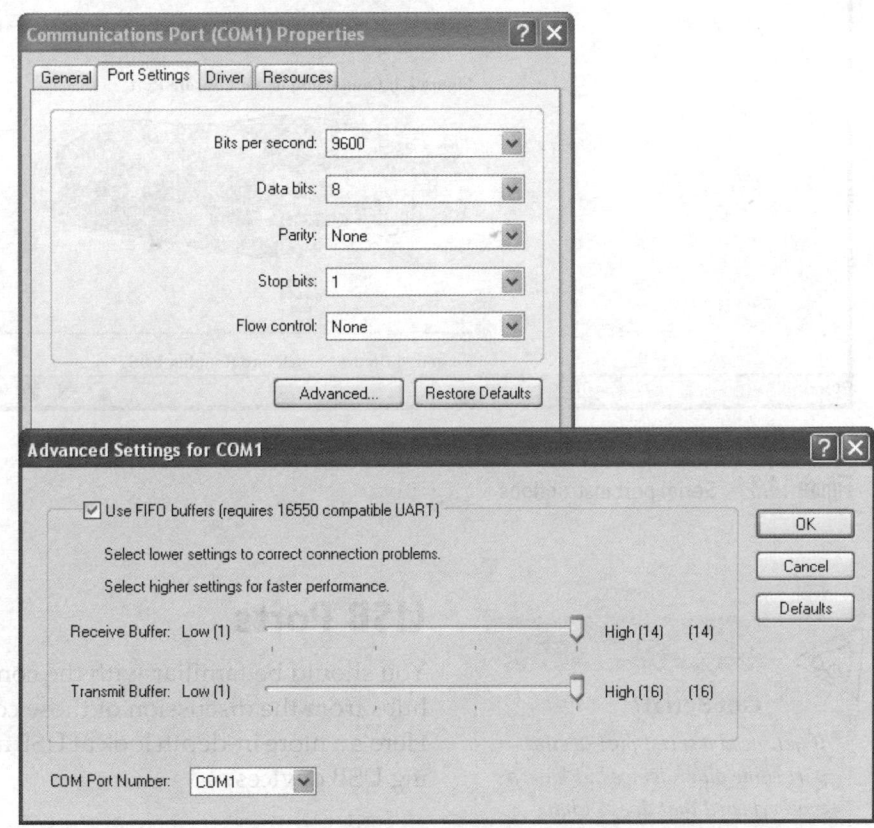

• **Figure 14.2** Serial port settings

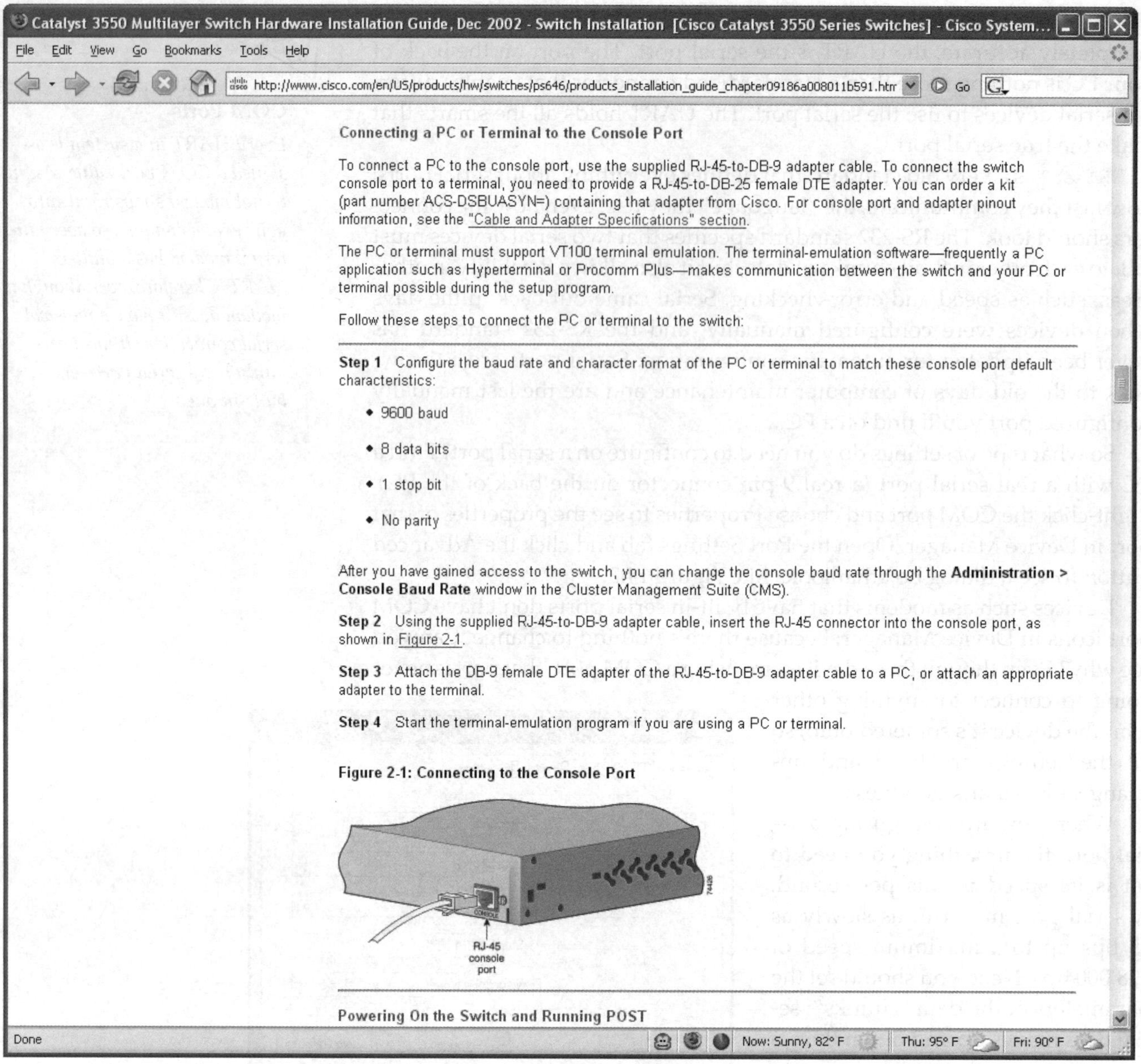

Catalyst 3550 Multilayer Switch Hardware Installation Guide, Dec 2002 - Switch Installation [Cisco Catalyst 3550 Series Switches] - Cisco System...

File   Edit   View   Go   Bookmarks   Tools   Help

http://www.cisco.com/en/US/products/hw/switches/ps646/products_installation_guide_chapter09186a008011b591.htm   Go

Connecting a PC or Terminal to the Console Port

To connect a PC to the console port, use the supplied RJ-45-to-DB-9 adapter cable. To connect the switch console port to a terminal, you need to provide a RJ-45-to-DB-25 female DTE adapter. You can order a kit (part number ACS-DSBUASYN=) containing that adapter from Cisco. For console port and adapter pinout information, see the "Cable and Adapter Specifications" section.

The PC or terminal must support VT100 terminal emulation. The terminal-emulation software—frequently a PC application such as Hyperterminal or Procomm Plus—makes communication between the switch and your PC or terminal possible during the setup program.

Follow these steps to connect the PC or terminal to the switch:

Step 1   Configure the baud rate and character format of the PC or terminal to match these console port default characteristics:

  ♦ 9600 baud

  ♦ 8 data bits

  ♦ 1 stop bit

  ♦ No parity

After you have gained access to the switch, you can change the console baud rate through the **Administration > Console Baud Rate** window in the Cluster Management Suite (CMS).

Step 2   Using the supplied RJ-45-to-DB-9 adapter cable, insert the RJ-45 connector into the console port, as shown in Figure 2-1.

Step 3   Attach the DB-9 female DTE adapter of the RJ-45-to-DB-9 adapter cable to a PC, or attach an appropriate adapter to the terminal.

Step 4   Start the terminal-emulation program if you are using a PC or terminal.

Figure 2-1: Connecting to the Console Port

RJ-45
console
port

Powering On the Switch and Running POST

Done   Now: Sunny, 82° F   Thu: 95° F   Fri: 90° F

● **Figure 14.3**   Serial port instructions

Tech Tip

Got Serial?

If you need a serial port to support some older device but have a motherboard that doesn't have one, don't fret. You can always get a PCI expansion card with classic, 9-pin serial ports.

USB Ports

You should be familiar with the concept of USB, USB connectors, and USB hubs from the discussion of those concepts in Chapter 2, "The Visible PC." Here's a more in-depth look at USB and some of the issues involved with using USB devices.

Understanding USB

The cornerstone of a USB connection is the USB host controller, an integrated circuit that is usually built into the chipset, which controls every USB device that connects to it. Inside the host controller is a USB root hub—the part of the host controller that makes the physical connection to the USB ports. Every USB root hub is really just a bus—similar in many ways to an expansion bus. Figure 14.4 shows a diagram of the relationship between the host controller, root hub, and USB ports.

No rule says how many USB ports a single host adapter may use. Early USB host adapters had two USB ports. The most recent ones support up to ten. Even if a host adapter supports a certain number of ports, there's no guarantee that the motherboard maker will supply that many ports. To give a common example, a host adapter might support eight ports while the motherboard maker only supplies four adapters.

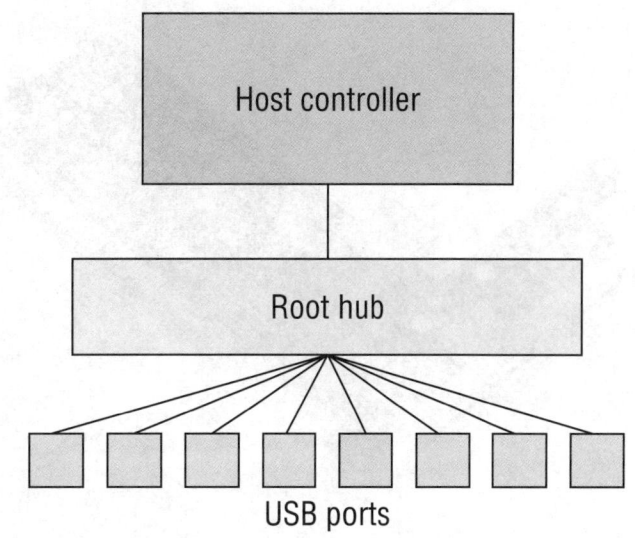

● **Figure 14.4**   Host controller, root hub, and USB ports

The most important point to remember about this is that every USB device connected to a single host adapter/root hub *shares* that USB bus with every other device connected to it. The more devices you place on a single host adapter, the more the total USB bus slows down and the more power they use. These issues are two of the biggest headaches that take place with USB devices in the real world.

USB devices, like any electrical device, need power to run, but not all take care of their own power needs. A powered USB device comes with its own electrical cord that is usually connected in turn to an AC adapter. *Bus-powered* USB devices take power from the USB bus itself; they don't bring any AC or DC power with them. When too many bus-powered devices take too much power from the USB bus, bad things happen—devices that work only some of the time and devices that lock up. You'll also often get a simple message from Windows saying that the hub power has been exceeded and it just won't work.

Every USB device is designed to run at one of three different speeds. The first USB standard, version 1.1, defined two speeds: **Low-Speed USB**, running at a maximum of 1.5 Mbps (plenty for keyboards and mice), and **Full-Speed USB**, running up to 12 Mbps. Later, the USB 2.0 standard introduced **Hi-Speed USB** running at a whopping 480 Mbps. The industry sometimes refers to Low-Speed and Full-Speed USB as USB 1.1 and Hi-Speed as USB 2.0, respectively.

In addition to a much faster transfer rate, Hi-Speed USB is fully backward compatible with devices that operate under the slower USB standards. Those old devices won't run any faster than they used to, however. To take advantage of the fastest USB speed, you must connect Hi-Speed USB devices to Hi-Speed USB ports using Hi-Speed USB cables. Hi-Speed USB devices will function when plugged into Full-Speed USB ports, but they will run at only 12 Mbps. While backward compatibility at least allows you to use the newer USB device with an older port, a quick bit of math will tell you

USB 2.0 defined more than just a new speed. Many Low-Speed and Full-Speed USB devices are also under the USB 2.0 standard.

 The USB Implementers Forum (USB-IF) does not officially use Low-Speed and Full-Speed to describe 1.5-Mbps and 12-Mbps devices, calling both of them simply "USB." On the CompTIA A+ certification exams, however, you'll see the marketplace-standard nomenclature.

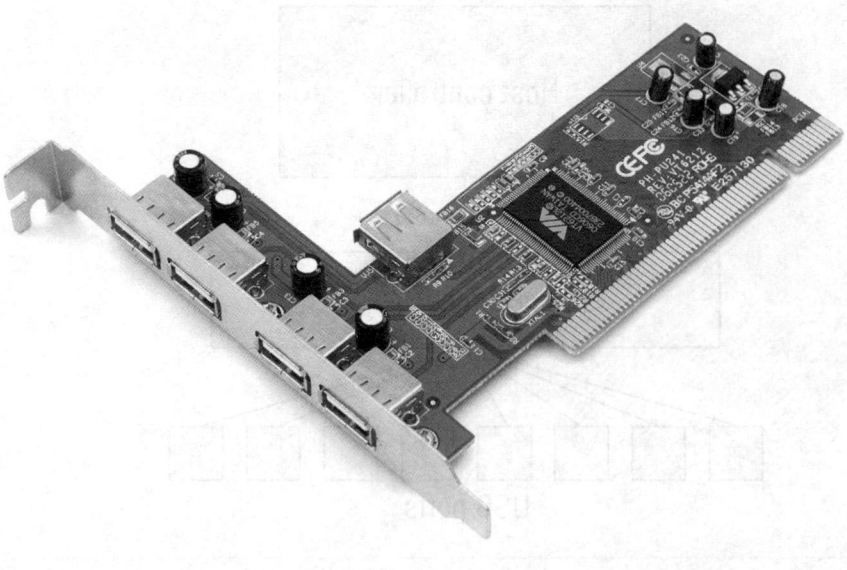

• **Figure 14.5**   USB adapter card

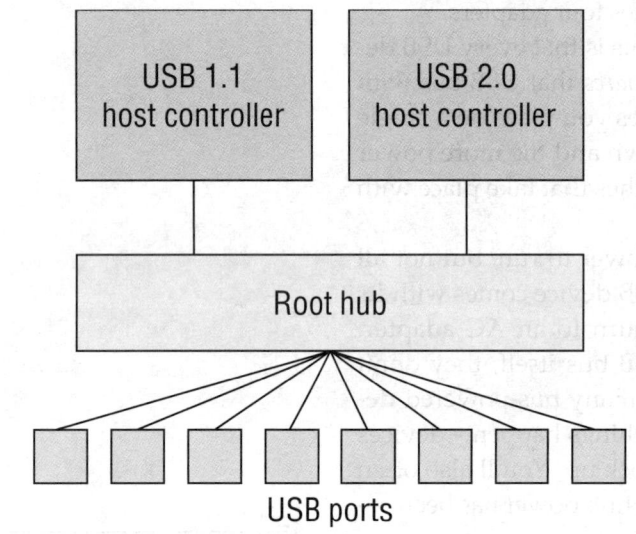

• **Figure 14.6**   Shared USB ports

how much time you're sacrificing when you're transferring a 240-MB file at 12 Mbps instead of 480 Mbps!

When USB 2.0 came out in 2001, folks scrambled to buy USB 2.0 controllers so their new Hi-Speed devices would work at their designed speeds. Of the variety of different solutions people came up with, the most popular early on was to add a USB 2.0 adapter card like the one shown in Figure 14.5.

Motherboard makers quickly added a second USB 2.0 host controller—and they did it in a clever way. Instead of making the USB 2.0 host controller separate from the USB 1.1 host controller, they designed things so that both controllers share all of the connected USB ports (Figure 14.6). That way, no matter which USB port you choose, if you plug in a Low-Speed or Full-Speed device, the 1.1 host controller takes over, and if you plug in a Hi-Speed device, the USB 2.0 host controller takes over. Clever, and convenient!

USB Hubs and Cables

Each USB host controller supports up to 127 USB devices, but as mentioned earlier, most motherboard makers provide only six to eight real USB ports. So what do you do when you need to add more USB devices than the motherboard provides ports? You can add more host controllers (in the form of internal cards), or you can use a USB hub. A **USB hub** is a device that extends a single USB connection to two or more USB ports, almost always directly from one of the USB ports connected to the root hub. Figure 14.7 shows a typical USB hub. USB hubs are

 Try This!

What Speed Is Your USB?
Using a PC running Windows 2000 or later, open the Device Manager and locate two controllers under the Universal Serial Bus icon. The one named Standard Enhanced Host Controller is the Hi-Speed controller. The Standard OpenHCD Host Controller is the Low- and Full-Speed controller.

● **Figure 14.7** USB hub

sometime embedded into peripherals. The keyboard in Figure 14.8 comes with a built-in USB hub—very handy!

USB hubs are one of those parts of a PC that tend not to work nearly as well in the real world as they do on paper. (Sorry, USB folks, but it's true!) USB hubs have a speed just like any other USB device; for example, the hub in the keyboard in Figure 14.8 runs at Full-Speed. This becomes a problem when someone decides to insert a Hi-Speed USB device into one of those ports, as it forces the Hi-Speed device to crawl along at only 12 Mbps. Windows XP is nice and will at least warn you of this problem with a bubble over the system tray like the one shown in Figure 14.9.

● **Figure 14.8** USB keyboard with built-in hub

Hubs also come in powered and bus-powered versions. If you choose to use a general purpose USB hub like the one shown in Figure 14.7, try to find a powered one, as too many devices on a single USB root hub will draw too much power and create problems.

Cable length is an important limitation to keep in mind with USB. USB specifications allow for a maximum cable length of 5 meters, although you may add a powered USB hub every 5 meters to extend this distance. Although most USB devices never get near this maximum, some devices, such as digital cameras, can come with cables at or near the maximum 5-meter cable length. Because USB is a two-way (bi-directional) connection, as the cable grows longer, even a standard, well-shielded, 20-gauge, twisted-pair USB cable begins to suffer from electrical interference. To avoid these problems, I stick to cables that are no more than about 2 meters long.

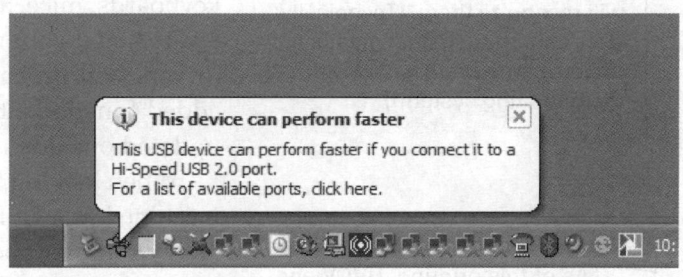

● **Figure 14.9** Windows XP speed warning

If you really want to play it safe, spend a few extra dollars and get a high-quality USB 2.0 cable like the one shown in Figure 14.10. These cables come with extra shielding and improved electrical performance to make sure your USB data gets from the device to your computer safely.

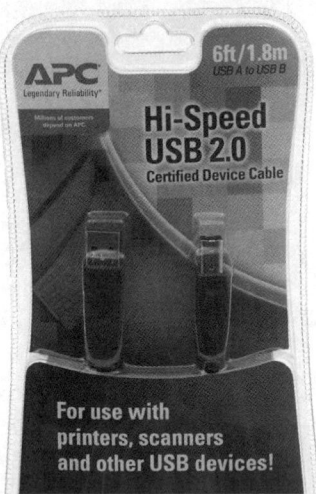

Figure 14.10 USB 2.0 cable

There are exceptions to the "install the driver first" rule. USB thumb drives, for example, as you will recall from Chapter 10, don't need extra drivers at all. Just plug them in and Windows will recognize them. (Technically speaking, though, that means the drivers came *preinstalled* with the operating system!)

As of this printing, UVCView may be found at www .microsoft.com/whdc/device/ stream/vidcap/UVCView .mspx—but keep in mind Microsoft does change URLs rather frequently!

Cross Check

USB Cable Connectors

You read about USB cables and connectors way back in Chapter 2, "The Visible PC," so turn there now and see if you can answer these questions. What are the three types of connectors found on USB cables? Which connector plugs into the PC or hub rather than the device? What does downstream and upstream mean in terms of connectivity for USB?

USB Configuration

The biggest troubleshooting challenge you encounter with USB is a direct result of its widespread adoption and ease of use. Pretty much every modern PC with multiple USB ports, and it's easy for anyone to pick up a cool new USB device at the local computer store. The problems arise when all this USB installation activity gets out of control, with too many devices using the wrong types of ports or pulling too much power. Happily, by following a few easy steps, you can avoid or eliminate these issues.

The first and often-ignored rule of USB installation is this: Always install the device driver for a new USB device *before* you plug it into the USB port. Once you've installed the device and you know the ports are active (running properly in Device Manager), feel free to plug in the new device and hot swap to your heart's content. USB device installation really is a breeze as long as you follow this rule!

Windows 2000 and XP have a large number of built-in drivers for USB devices. You can count on Windows 2000 and Windows XP to recognize keyboards, mice, and other basic devices with their built-in drivers. Just be aware that if your new mouse or keyboard has some extras, the default USB drivers will probably not support them. To be sure I'm not missing any added functionality, I always install the driver that with the device or an updated one downloaded from the manufacturer's Web site.

When looking to add a new USB device to a system, first make sure your machine has a USB port that supports the speed you need for the USB device. On more modern PCs, this is more likely to be a non-issue, but even then if you start adding hubs and such you can end up with devices that either won't run at all or, worse yet, exhibit strange behaviors. Your best tool for a quick check of your ports is the free Microsoft Utility UVCView. UVCView works on all versions of Windows. Do a Web search for "UVCView.exe" to locate a copy and download it; it's a single .EXE file that requires no installation. When you run UVCView, you see something like Figure 14.11, which shows an AMD64 system using only the onboard USB host controllers.

UVCView is a very powerful tool used by USB professionals to test USB devices; as such, it has a number of features that are not of interest to the typical PC tech. Nevertheless, two features make it worth the download. UVCView quickly answers the questions, "What and where are all the USB devices plugged into my system right now?" and "What speed is this USB device?" Figure 14.12 shows UVCView finding a number of installed USB devices, including a keyboard with a built-in hub. Look on the left side to see how easy it is to locate the USB hub and the thumb drive installed on that hub. Note that a USB thumb drive is selected. Look on the upper-right side of the program, where the details of the device are shown, to see that the thumb drive is a Hi-Speed USB device.

The last and toughest issue is power. A mismatch between available and required power for USB devices can result in non-functioning or malfunctioning USB devices. If you're pulling too much power, you must take devices off that root hub until the error goes away. Buy an add-in USB hub card if you need to use more devices than your current USB hub supports.

To check the USB power usage in Windows, open Device Manager and locate any USB hub under the Universal Serial Bus Controller icon. Right-click the hub and select Properties, and then select the Power tab. This will show you the current use for each of the devices connected to that root hub (Figure 14.13).

Most root hubs provide 500 mA per port—more than enough for any USB device. Most power problems take place when you start adding hubs, especially bus-powered hubs, and then you add too many devices to them. Figure 14.14 shows the Power tab for a bus-powered hub—note that it provides a maximum of 100 mA per port.

There's one more problem with USB power: sometimes USB devices go to sleep and don't wake up. Actually, the system is telling them to sleep, to save power. You can suspect this problem if you try to access a USB device that was working earlier, but that suddenly no longer appears in Device

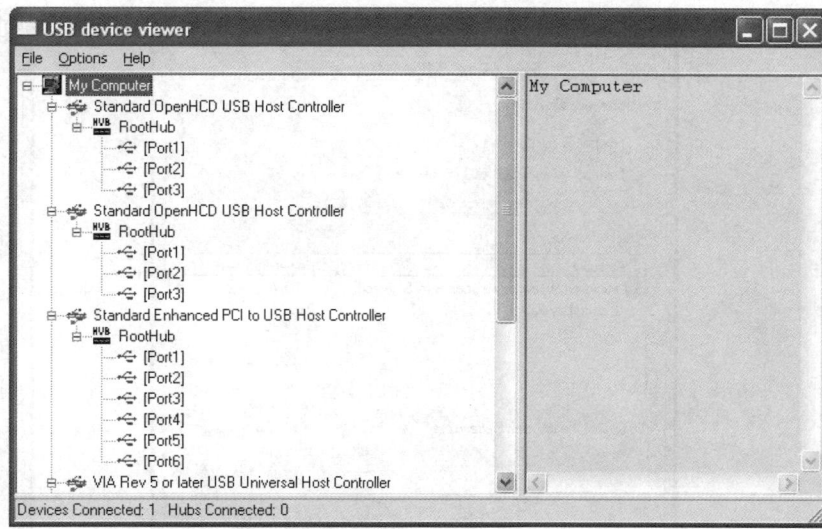

• **Figure 14.11** UVCView in action

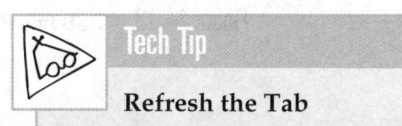

Tech Tip

Refresh the Tab

The USB Hub Power Properties tab shows you the power usage only for a given moment, so to ensure that you keep getting accurate readings, you must click the Refresh button to update its display. Make sure your USB device works, and then refresh to see the maximum power used.

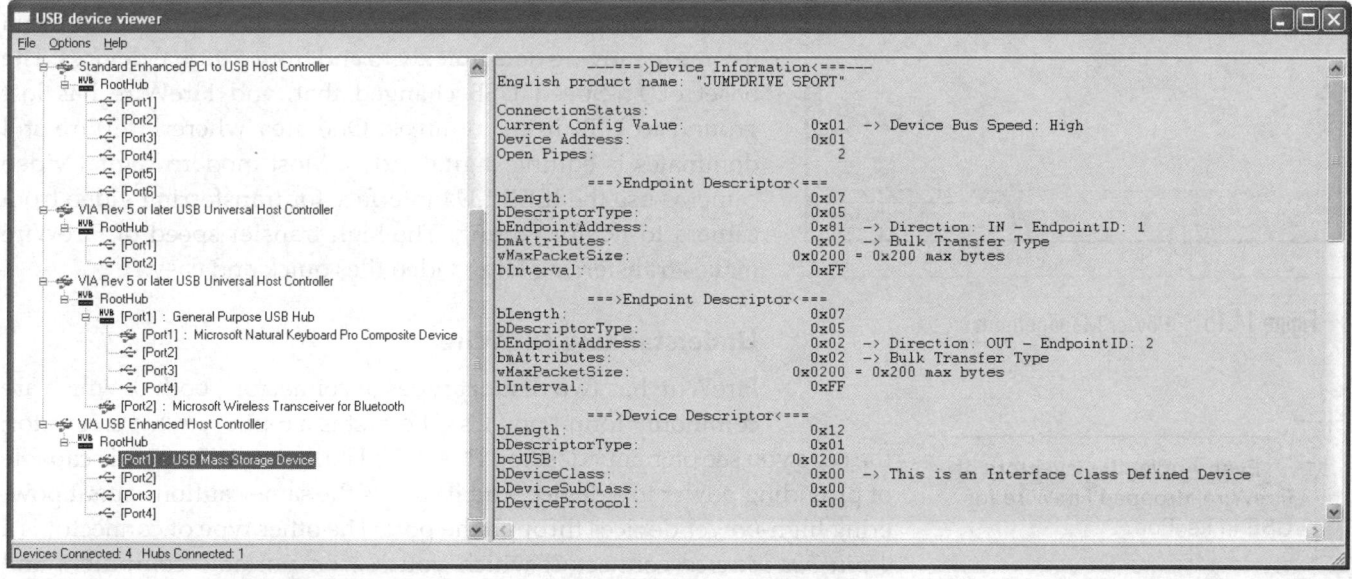

• **Figure 14.12** UVCView details

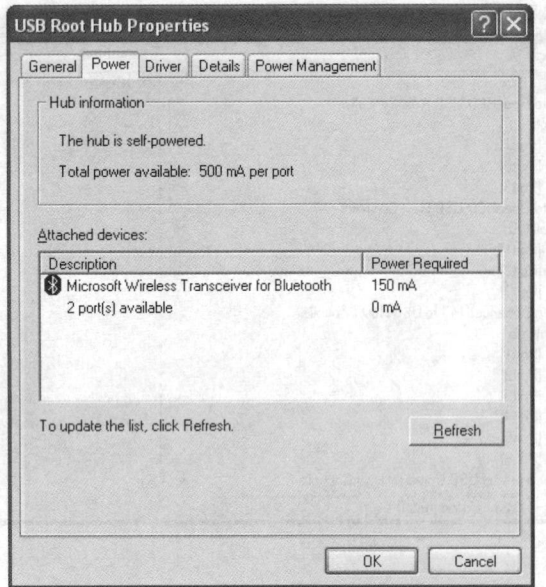

• **Figure 14.13**   USB hub Power tab

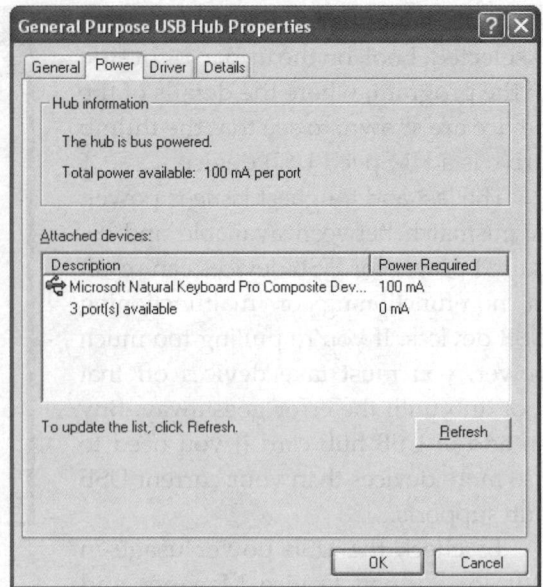

• **Figure 14.14**   General purpose bus-powered hub

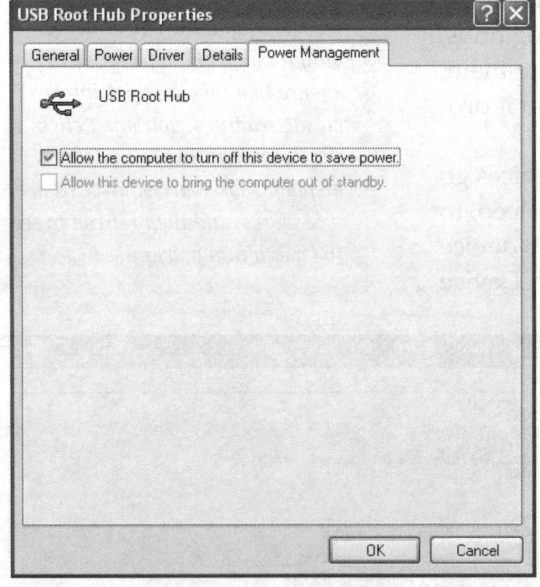

• **Figure 14.15**   Power Management

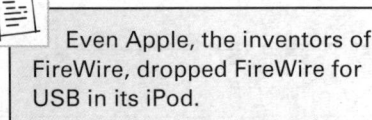
Even Apple, the inventors of FireWire, dropped FireWire for USB in its iPod.

Manager. To fix this, head back in to Device Manager to inspect the hub's Properties, but this time open the Power Management tab and uncheck the *Allow the computer to turn off this device to save power* check box, as shown in Figure 14.15.

FireWire Ports

At first glance, FireWire , also known as IEEE 1394, looks and acts much like USB. FireWire has all the same features of USB, but it uses different connectors and is actually the older of the two technologies. For years, FireWire had the upper hand when it came to moving data quickly to and from external devices. The onset of Hi-Speed USB changed that, and FireWire has lost ground to USB in many areas. One area where FireWire still dominates is editing digital video. Most modern digital video cameras use the IEEE 1394 interface for transferring video from camera to PC for editing. The high transfer speed of FireWire makes transferring large video files quick and easy.

Understanding FireWire

FireWire has two distinct types of connectors, both of which are commonly found on PCs. The first is a 6-pin *powered* connector, the type you see on many desktop PCs. Like USB, a FireWire port is capable of providing power to a device, and it carries the same cautions about powering high-power devices through the port. The other type of connector is a 4-pin *bus-powered* connector, which you see on portable computers and some FireWire devices such as cameras. This type of connector does not provide power to a device, so you will need to find another method of powering the external device.

FireWire comes in two speeds: IEEE 1394a, which runs at 400 Mbps, and IEEE 1394b, which runs at 800 Mbps. FireWire devices can also take advantage of bus mastering, enabling two FireWire devices—such as a digital video camera and an external FireWire hard drive—to communicate directly with each other. When it comes to raw speed, FireWire 800—that would be 1394b, naturally—is much faster than Hi-Speed USB.

FireWire does have differences from USB other than just speed and a different-looking connector. First, a USB device must connect directly to a hub, but a FireWire device may use either a hub or daisy-chaining. Figure 14.16 shows the difference between hubbed connections and daisy-chaining. Second, FireWire supports a maximum of 63 devices, compared to USB's 127. Third, each cable in a FireWire daisy chain has a maximum length of 4.5 meters, as opposed to USB's 5 meters.

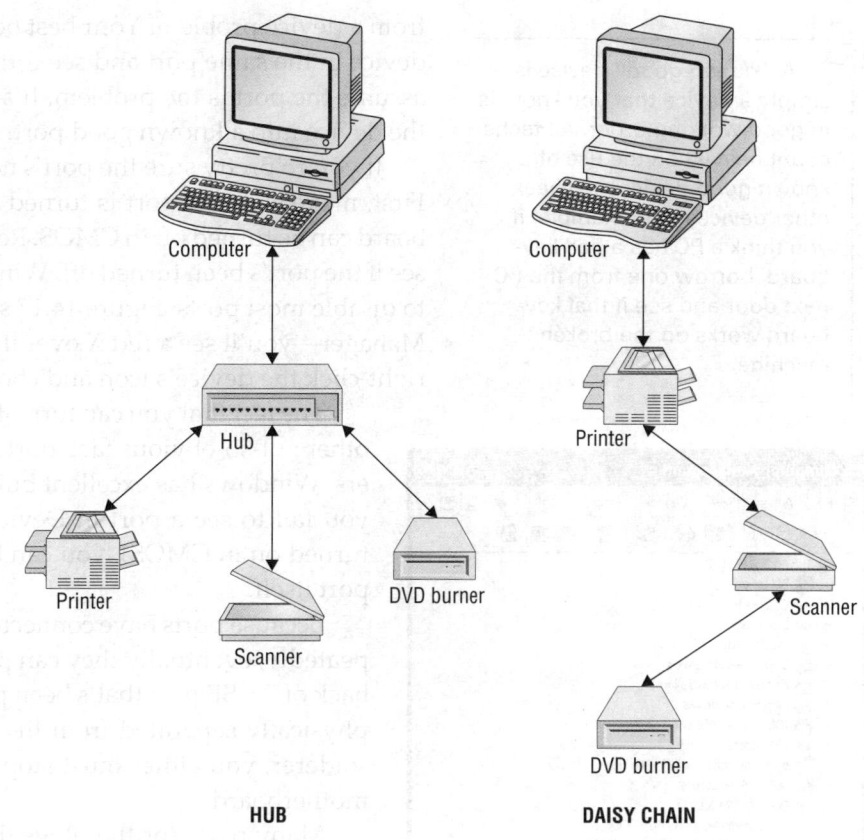

• Figure 14.16   Hubbed versus daisy-chain connections

Configuring FireWire

FireWire was invented and is still controlled to a degree by Apple Computer. This single source of control makes FireWire more stable and more interchangeable than USB—in plain language, FireWire is ridiculously easy to use. In a Windows environment, FireWire is subject to many of the same issues as USB, such as the need to pre-install drivers, verify that onboard devices are active, and so on. But none of these issues is nearly as crucial with a FireWire connection. For example, as with USB, you really should install a FireWire device driver before attaching the device, but given that 95 percent of the FireWire devices used in PCs are either external hard drives or digital video connections, the pre-installed Windows drivers almost always work perfectly. FireWire devices do use much more power than USB devices, but the FireWire controllers are designed to handle higher voltages, and they'll warn you on the rare chance your FireWire devices pull too much power.

General Port Issues

No matter what type of port you use, if it's not working, you should always check out a few issues. First of all, make sure you can tell a port problem

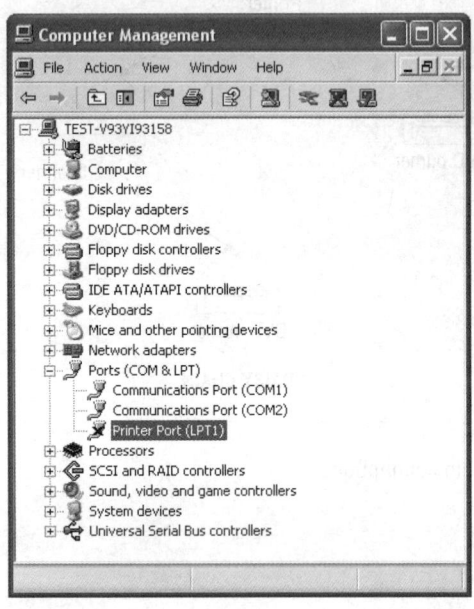

A "known good" device is simply a device that you know is in good working order. All techs count heavily on the use of known good devices to check other devices. For example, if you think a PC has a bad keyboard, borrow one from the PC next door and see if that keyboard works on the broken machine.

• **Figure 14.17** An X marks a disabled parallel port in Device Manager.

from a device problem. Your best bet here is to try a second "known good" device in the same port and see if that device works. If it does *not*, you can assume the port is the problem. It's not a bad idea to reverse this and plug the device into a known good port.

If you're pretty sure the port's not working, you can check three things: First, make sure the port is turned on. Almost any I/O port on a motherboard can be turned off in CMOS. Reboot the system and find the device and see if the port's been turned off. Windows Device Manager also enables you to disable most ports. Figure 14.17 shows a disabled parallel port in Device Manager—you'll see a red *X* over the device icon. To turn the port back on, right-click the device's icon and choose Enable.

The fact that you can turn off a port in Device Manager points to another not-so-obvious fact: ports need drivers just as devices need drivers. Windows has excellent built-in drivers for all common ports, so if you fail to see a port in Device Manager (and you know the port is turned on in CMOS), you can bet there's a physical problem with the port itself.

Because ports have connectors inserted and removed from them repeatedly, eventually they can physically break. Figure 14.18 shows the back of a USB port that's been pushed on too hard for too long and has physically separated from the motherboard. Unless you're an expert solderer, you either must stop using those ports or replace the entire motherboard.

Many ports (or the plugs that fit into those ports) use tiny pins or relatively delicate metal casings that are susceptible to damage. PS/2 plugs are some of the worst for bent pins or misshaped casings. Figure 14.19 shows what happened to a PS/2 plug when I was in a hurry and thought that force was an alternative to lining up the plug properly. Replacement plugs are available—but again, unless you're excellent at soldering, they're not a viable alternative. Still, if you're patient, you might be able to save the plug. Using needle-nose pliers and a pair of scissors, I was able to reshape the plug so that it once again fit in the PS/2 port.

• **Figure 14.18** Broken USB port

• **Figure 14.19** Badly bent PS/2 plug

■ Common I/O Devices

So what is a "common" I/O device? I'm hoping you immediately thought of the mouse and the keyboard, two of the most basic, necessary, and abused I/O devices on a computer. Another fairly common input device that's been around a long time is the scanner. To these oldsters, you can add relative newcomers to the world of common devices: digital cameras and Web cameras.

Keyboards

Keyboards are both the oldest and still the primary way you input data into a PC. Windows comes with perfectly good drivers for any keyboard, although some fancier keyboards may come with specialized keys that require a special driver be installed to operate properly. About the only issue that might affect keyboard installation is if you're using a USB keyboard: make sure that the USB Keyboard Support option is enabled in your CMOS (Figure 14.20). Other than that, any keyboard installation issue you're likely to encounter is covered in the general port issues sections at the beginning of this chapter.

There's not much to do to configure a standard keyboard. The only configuration tool you might need is the Keyboard Control Panel applet. This tool enables you to change the repeat delay (the amount of time you must hold down a key before the keyboard starts repeating the character), the repeat rate (how quickly the character is repeated after the repeat delay), and the default cursor blink rate. Figure 14.21 shows the default Windows Keyboard Properties window—some keyboard makers provide drivers that add extra tabs.

Keyboards might be easy to install, but they do fail occasionally. Given their location—right in front of you—the three issues that cause the most keyboard problems stem from spills, physical damage, and dirt.

If you want to get picky, these five common I/O devices enable a user only to *input* data; they don't provide any output at all.

Tech Tip

Wireless Keyboards and Batteries
Wireless keyboards are a wonderful convenience, as they remove the cable between you and the PC, but make sure that you keep a complete set of spare batteries around.

```
OnChip USB              U1.1+2.0
- USB Keyboard Support   Enabled
- USB Mouse Support      Enabled
```

● **Figure 14.20** CMOS USB Keyboard Support option

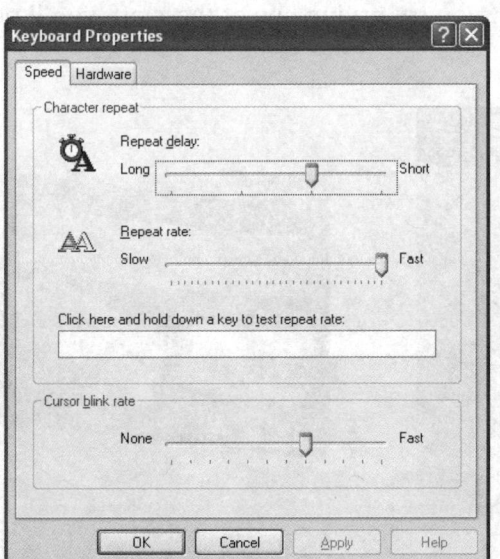

● **Figure 14.21** Keyboard Control Panel applet

● Figure 14.22 Cleaning keys

Spilling a soda onto your keyboard can make for a really bad day. If you're quick and unplug the keyboard from the PC before the liquid hits the electrical components, you might be able to save the keyboard. It'll take some cleaning, though (keep reading for cleaning tips). More often than not, you'll get a sticky, ill-performing keyboard, which is not worth the hassle—just replace it!

Other common physical damage comes from dropping objects onto the keyboard, such as a heavy book (like the one in your hands). This can have bad results! Most keyboards are pretty resilient, though, and can bounce back from the hit.

Clean dirt and grime off the keys using a cloth dampened with a little water, or if the water alone doesn't do the job, use a bit of isopropyl alcohol on a cloth (Figure 14.22).

Dirty keys might be unsightly, but dirt under the keys might cause the keyboard to stop working completely. When your keys start to stick, grab a bottle of compressed air and shoot some air under the keys. Do this outside or over a trash can—you'll be amazed how much junk gets caught under the keys! If you really mess up a keyboard by dumping a chocolate milkshake on the keys, you're probably going to need to dismantle the keyboard to clean it. This is pretty easy as long as you keep track of where all the parts go. Keyboards are made of layers of plastic that create the electrical connections when you press a key. Unscrew the keyboard (keep track of the screws!) and gently peel away the plastic layers, using a damp cloth to clean each layer (Figure 14.23). Allow the sheets to dry and then reassemble the keyboard.

Sometimes dirt or foreign objects get under individual keys, requiring you to remove the key to get to the dirt or object. Removing individual keys from a keyboard is risky business, as keyboards are set up in many different ways. Most manufacturers use a process in which keys are placed on a single plastic post. In that case, you may use a screwdriver or other flat tool to safely pop off the key (Figure 14.24). Be careful! You'll need to use a good amount of force and the key will fly across the room. Other keyboard makers (mainly on laptops) use tiny plastic pins shaped like scissors. In that case, beware—if you try prying one of these off, you'll permanently break the key!

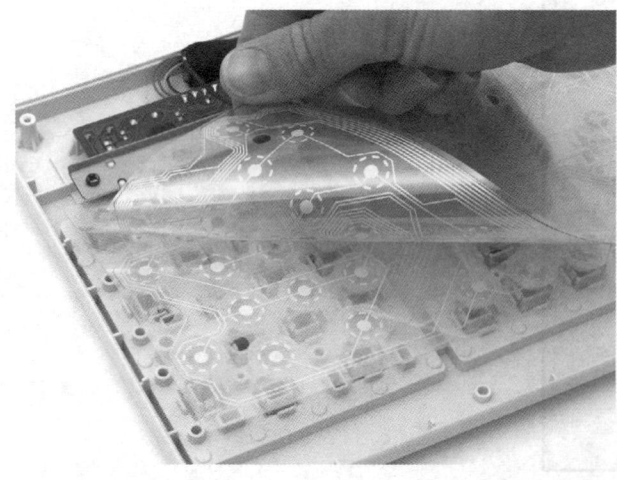

● Figure 14.23 Serious keyboard surgery

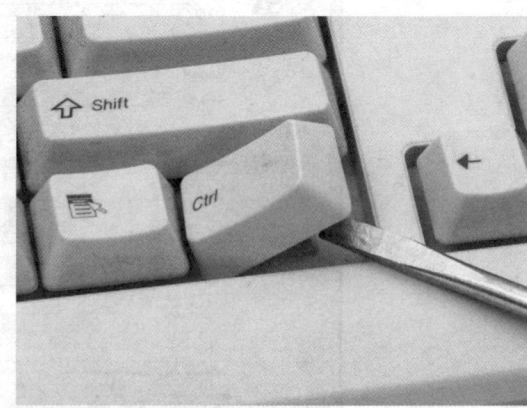

● Figure 14.24 Prying off a key

The bottom line when it comes to stuck keys is that the keyboard's probably useless with the stuck key, so you might as well try to clean it. Worse comes to worst, you can always buy another keyboard.

Mice

Have you ever tried to use Windows without a mouse? It's not fun, but it can be done. All techs eventually learn the Windows navigation hot keys for those times when mice fail, but all in all we do love our mice. Like keyboards, Windows comes with excellent drivers for all standard mice; the exception you're likely to encounter is the more advanced mice that come with extra buttons. Conveniently, the built-in Windows drivers consider a mouse's scroll wheel to be standard equipment and will support it.

You can adjust your mouse settings through the Mouse Control Panel applet. Figure 14.25 shows the Windows 2000 version. Be aware that the Mouse Properties window in Windows 2000 uses a different layout than that of Windows XP (Figure 14.26).

All the settings you need for adjusting your mouse can be found in the Mouse Properties window. In particular, make sure to adjust the mouse speed, double-click speed, and acceleration to fit your preferences. Mouse speed and double-click speed are obvious, but mouse acceleration needs a bit of explaining as it has changed from Windows 2000 to Windows XP. Originally, mouse *acceleration* referred to a feature that caused the mouse speed to increase when the mouse moved a relatively large distance across the screen. The Windows 2000 Mouse Properties window included a Motion tab where you could set the mouse speed and acceleration. Windows XP dropped the Motion tab in favor of an Enhance Pointer Precision

Tech Tip

A Clean Mouse Is a Happy Mouse!

As with keyboards, the biggest troublemaker for mice is dirt. Whenever a mouse stops working or begins to act erratically, always check first for dirt.

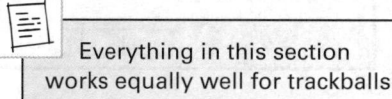

Everything in this section works equally well for trackballs.

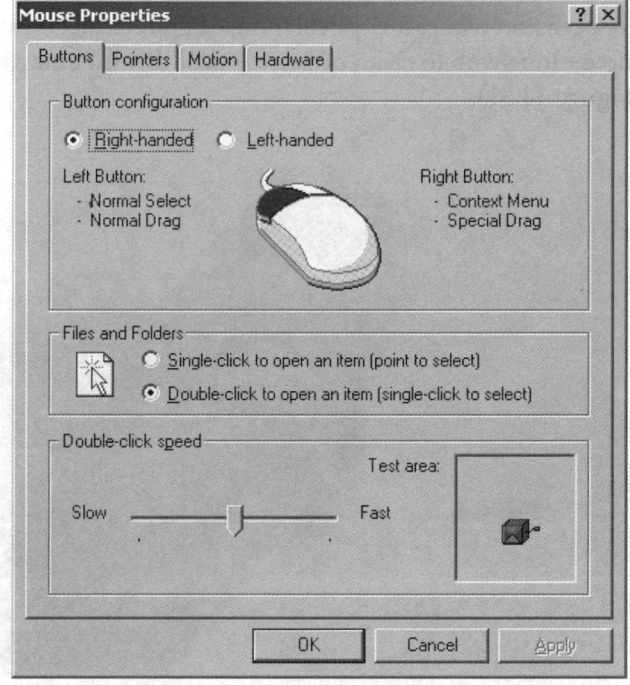

• **Figure 14.25**   Windows 2000 Mouse Control Panel applet

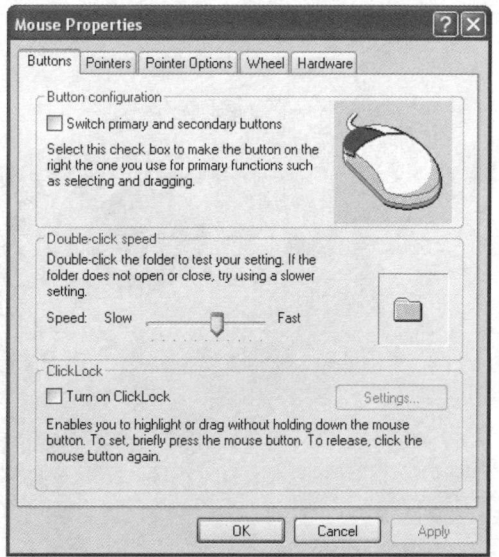

• **Figure 14.26**   Windows XP Mouse Control Panel applet

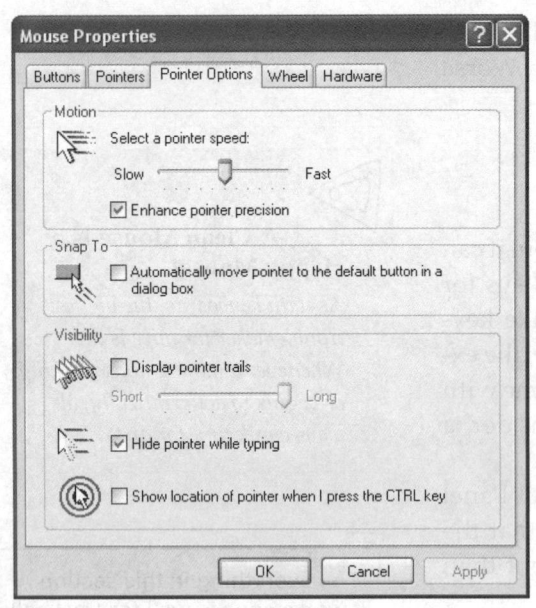

Figure 14.27 Enhance pointer precision checkbox on the Pointer Options tab

check box on the Pointer Options tab (Figure 14.27). Enhance pointer precision is a much more advanced form of automatic acceleration. While it works well, it can cause erratic mouse movements in some applications.

Currently, two types of mouse technologies dominate the market: ball mice and optical mice. Ball mice use a small round ball, whereas optical mice use LEDs or lasers and a camera to track their movements and thus move the mouse pointer across the screen. The problem with ball mice is that the ball inside the mouse picks up dirt over time and deposits the dirt on internal rollers that contact the ball. Dirt builds up to the point that the mouse stops responding smoothly. If you are struggling with your mouse to point at objects on your screen, you need to clean the mouse (Figure 14.28). Few mice manufacturers still make ball mice, as they tend to require far more maintenance than optical mice.

To access the internals of a ball mouse, turn it over and remove the protective cover over the mouse ball. The process of removing the cover varies, but it usually involves rotating the collar that surrounds the ball until the collar pops out (Figure 14.29). Be careful—without the collar, the mouse ball will drop out the instant you turn it upright.

Use any non-metallic tool to scrape the dirt from the roller without scratching or gouging the device. Although you could use a commercial "Mouse cleaning kit," I find that a fingernail or a pencil eraser will clean the rollers quite nicely and at much less expense (Figure 14.30). Clean a ball mouse in this way at least every two or three months.

Optical mice require little maintenance and almost never need cleaning, as the optics that make them work are never in contact with the grimy outside world. On the rare occasion where an optical mouse begins to act erratically, try using a damp cotton swab to clean out any bits of dirt that may be blocking the optics (Figure 14.31).

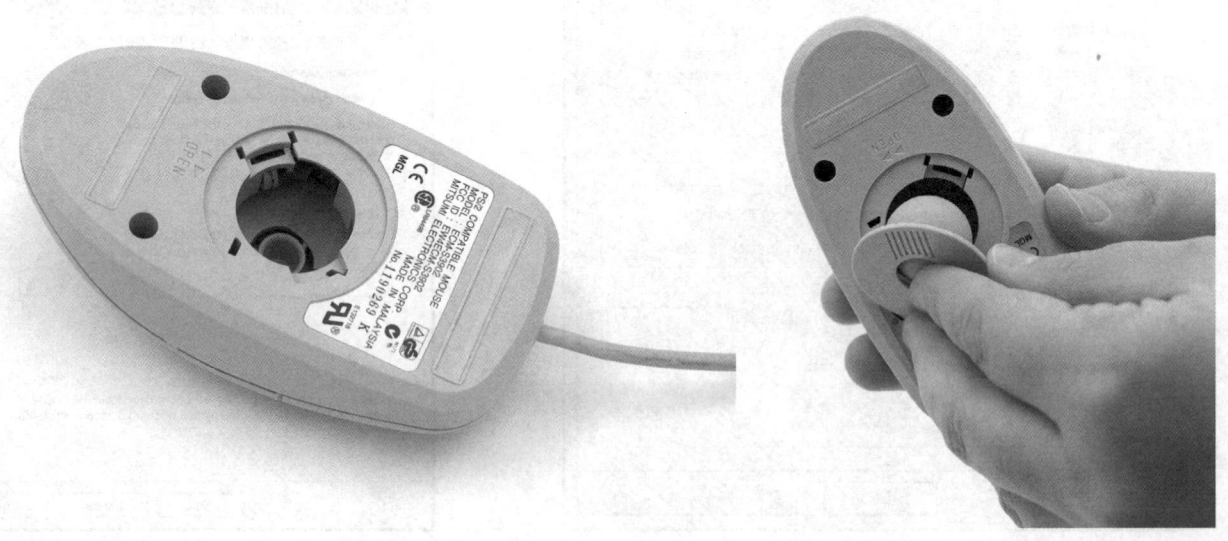

Figure 14.28 Dirty mouse internals

Figure 14.29 Removing the collar

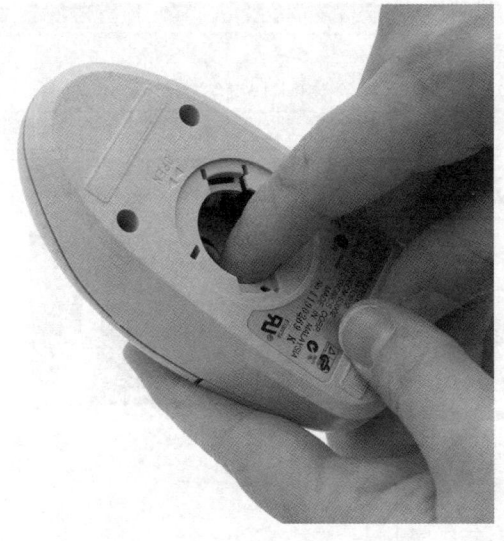

• **Figure 14.30**   Cleaning the rollers

• **Figure 14.31**   Cleaning the optics

Scanners

A scanner enables you to make digital copies of existing paper photos, documents, drawings, and more. Better scanners give you the option of copying directly from a photographic negative or slide, providing images of stunning visual quality—assuming the original photo was halfway decent, of course! In this section, you'll look at how scanners work and then turn to what you need to know to select the correct scanner for you or your clients.

How Scanners Work

All consumer-level scanners—called `flatbed scanners` —work the same way. You place a photo or other object facedown on the glass, close the lid, and then use software to initiate the scan. The scanner runs a bright light along the length of the glass tray once or more to capture the image. Figure 14.32 shows an open scanner.

The scanning software that controls the hardware can be manifested in a variety of ways. Nearly every manufacturer will have some sort of drivers and other software to create an interface between your computer and the scanner. When you push the front button on the Epson Perfection scanner in Figure 14.33, for example, the Epson software opens the Photoshop program as well as its own interface.

You can also open your favorite image-editing software first, and then choose to acquire a file from a scanner. Figure 14.34 shows the process of acquiring an image from a scanner in the popular shareware image-editing

• **Figure 14.32**   Scanner open with photograph facedown

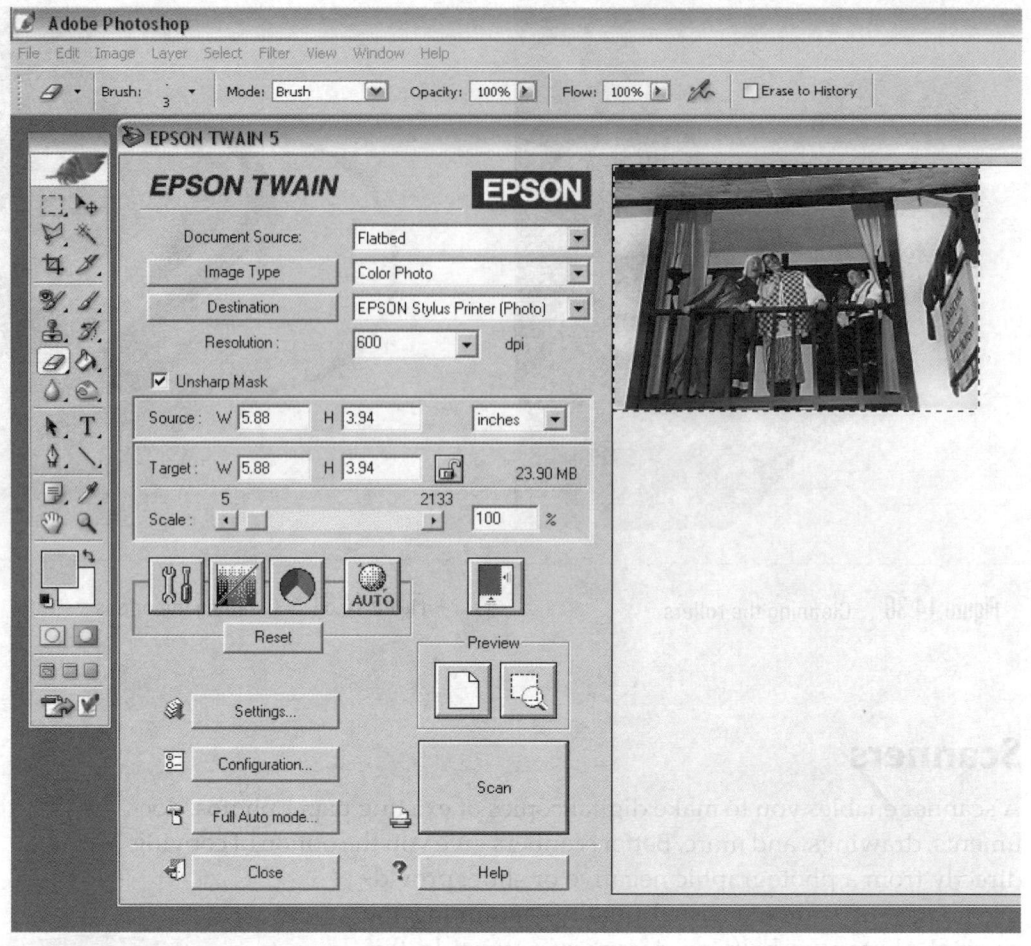

● **Figure 14.33** Epson software with Photoshop open in the background

software, Paint Shop Pro. As in most such software, you choose File | Import and then select a source. In this case, the scanner uses the traditional TWAIN drivers. **TWAIN** stands for *Technology Without an Interesting Name*—I'm not making this up!—and has been the default driver type for scanners for a long time.

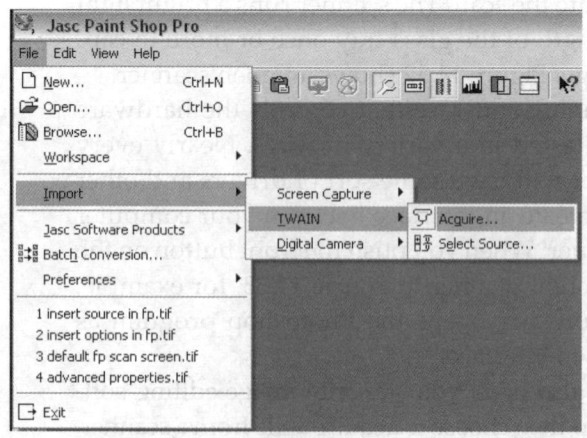

● **Figure 14.34** Acquiring an image in Paint Shop Pro

At this point, the drivers and other software controlling the scanner pop up, providing an interface with the scanner (as shown in Figure 14.33). Here, you can set the resolution of the image as well as many other options.

How to Choose a Scanner

You must consider five primary variables when choosing a scanner: resolution, color depth, grayscale depth, connection, and scan speed. You can and will adjust the first three during the scanning process, although probably only down from their maximum. You need to decide on the connection before you buy. The scan speed relates to all four of the other variables, and the maximum speed is hard-coded into the scanner.

Configurable Variables Scanners convert the scanned image into a grid of dots. The maximum number of dots determines how well you can capture an image and how the image will look when scaled up in size. Most folks use the term *resolution* to define the grid size. As you might imagine, the higher the resolution, the better the scanned image will look and scale.

Older scanners can create images of only 600 × 600 dots per inch (dpi), while newer models commonly achieve four times that density and high-end machines do much more. Manufacturers cite *two* sets of numbers for a scanner's resolution: the resolution it achieves mechanically—called the optical resolution—and the enhanced resolution it can achieve with assistance from some onboard software.

The enhanced resolution numbers are useless. I recommend at least 2400 × 2400 dpi optical resolution or better, although you can get by with a lower resolution for purely Web-destined images.

The color depth of a scan defines the number of bits of information the scanner can use to describe each individual dot. This number determines color, shade, hue, and so forth, so a higher number makes a dramatic difference in your picture quality. With binary numbers, each extra bit of information *doubles* the quality. An 8-bit scan, for example, can save up to 256 color variations per dot. A 16-bit scan, in contrast, can save up to 65,536 variations, not the 512 that you might expect!

Modern scanners come in 24-bit, 36-bit, and 48-bit variations. These days, 48-bit scanners are common enough that you shouldn't have to settle for less, even on a budget. Figures 14.35, 14.36, and 14.37 show pretty clearly the difference resolution makes when scanning.

Tech Tip

Optical Character Recognition

In addition to loading pictures into your computer, many scanners offer a feature called optical character recognition (OCR), *a way to scan a document and have the computer turn the picture into text that you can manipulate using a word processing program. Many scanners come with OCR software, such as ABBYY FineReader.*

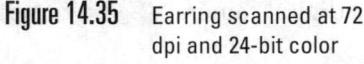

• **Figure 14.35** Earring scanned at 72 dpi and 24-bit color

• **Figure 14.36** Same earring, scanned at 300 dpi and 24-bit color

• **Figure 14.37** Same earring, scanned at 1200 dpi and 24-bit color

Scanners differ a lot in grayscale depth , a number that defines how many shades of gray the scanner can save per dot. This matters if you work with black-and-white images in any significant way, because grayscale depth is usually a much lower number than color depth. Current consumer-level scanners come in 8-bit, 12-bit, and 16-bit grayscale varieties. I recommend 16-bit or better.

Connection   Almost all modern scanners plug into the USB port on your PC, although some high-end models offer FireWire as well. Older scanners come in SCSI and parallel varieties.

Scanning Speed   Scanners have a maximum scanning speed defined by the manufacturer. The time required to complete a scan is also affected by the parameters you set—the time increases as you increase the amount of detail captured. A typical low-end scanner, for example, takes upwards of 30 seconds to scan a 4 × 6-inch photo at 300 dpi. A faster scanner, in contrast, can crank out the same scan in 10 seconds.

Raise the resolution of the scan to 600 dpi at 48-bit resolution, and that faster scanner can take a full minute to complete the scan. Adjust your scanning settings to optimize for your project. Don't always go for the highest possible scan if you don't need the resolution.

Connections matter as well. A good Hi-Speed USB scanner can scan an 8 × 10-inch image in about 12 seconds at 300 dpi. I made the mistake of taking the scanner to a friend's house to scan some of her jewelry, but she had only a Full-Speed USB port. I plugged the scanner into her PC and it took about 45 seconds to scan each 8 × 10-inch image. We were up all night finishing the project!

Installing and Scanning Tips

Most USB and FireWire devices require you to install the software drivers before you plug in the device for the first time. I have run into exceptions, though, so I strongly suggest you read the scanner's documentation before you install.

As a general rule, you should obtain the highest quality scan you can manage, and then play with the size and image quality when it's time to include it in a Web site or an e-mail. The amount of RAM in your system—and to a lesser extent, the processor speed—dictates how big a file you can handle.

For example, don't do 8 × 10-inch scans at 600 dpi if you have only 128 MB of RAM, because the image file alone weighs in at over 93 MB. Because your operating system, scanner software, image-editing program, and a lot of other things are taking up plenty of that RAM already, your system will likely crash.

If you travel a lot, you'll want to make sure to use the locking mechanism for the scanner light assembly. Just be sure to unlock before you try to use it or you'll get a light that's stuck in one position. That won't make for very good scans!

Digital Cameras

Another option available for those not-yet-taken pictures is to put away your point-and-shoot film camera and use a digital camera. Digital cameras electronically simulate older film technology and provide a wonderful tool for capturing a moment and then sending it to friends and relatives.

In a short period of time, digital camera prices have gone from levels that made them the province of a few wealthy technogeeks to being competitive with a wide range of electronic consumer goods. Because digital cameras interface with computers, CompTIA A+ certified techs need to know the basics.

Storage Media—Digital Film for Your Camera

Every consumer-grade camera saves the pictures it takes onto some type of *removable storage media*. Think of it as your digital film. Probably the most common removable storage media used in modern digital cameras (and probably your best choice) is the Secure Digital (SD) card (Figure 14.38). About the size of a Wheat Thin (roughly an inch square), you can find these tiny cards with capacities ranging from 64 MB to more than 1 GB. They are among the fastest of the various media types at transferring data to and from a PC, and they're quite sturdy.

Cross Check

Flash Media

You learned all about the many types of flash media and micro drives back in Chapter 10, "Removable Media," so go there now and answer these questions. What's the difference between a thumb drive and an SD card? Can you make a bootable flash-media drive?

Connection

These days, almost all digital cameras plug directly into a USB port (Figure 14.39). Another common option, though, is to connect only the camera's storage media to the computer, using one of the many digital media readers available.

You can find readers designed specifically for SD cards, as well as other types. Plenty of readers can handle multiple media formats. Many computers come with a decent built-in digital media reader (Figure 14.40).

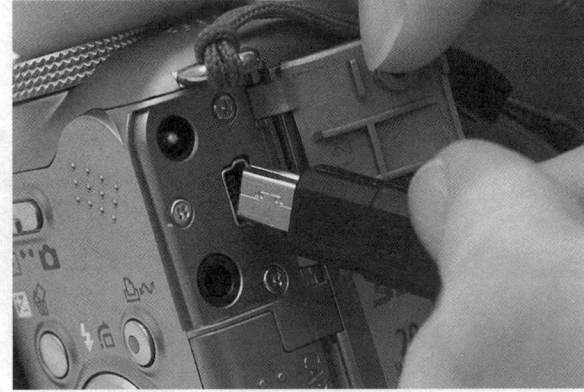

• **Figure 14.38** Secure Digital card

• **Figure 14.39** Camera connecting to USB port

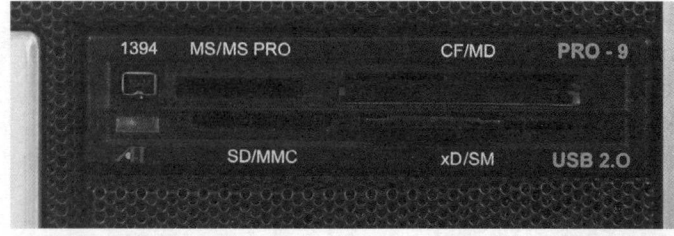

• **Figure 14.40** Digital media reader built into computer

Quality

As with scanners, you should consider the amount of information a particular model of camera can capture, which in the digital camera world is expressed as some number of **megapixels**. Instead of light-sensitive film, digital cameras have one CCD (charged coupled device) or CMOS (complementary metal-oxide semiconductor) sensor covered with photosensitive pixels (called *photosites*) to capture the image; the more pixels on the sensor, the higher the resolution of the images it captures.

Not so long ago, a 1-megapixel digital camera was the bleeding edge of digital photographic technology, but now you can find cameras with ten times that resolution for a few hundred dollars. As a basis of reference, a 2-megapixel camera will produce snapshot-sized (4 × 6 inch) pictures with print photograph quality, whereas a 5-megapixel unit can produce a high-quality 8 × 10-inch print.

Another feature of most digital cameras is the ability to zoom in on your subject. The way you ideally want to do this is the way film cameras do it, using the camera's optics—that's the lens. Most cameras above the basic level have some **optical zoom**—meaning the zoom is physically built into the lens of the camera, but almost all models include multiple levels of **digital zoom**, accomplished by some very clever software in the camera. Choose your camera based on optical zoom—3× at a minimum, or better if you can afford it. Digital zoom is useless.

Form Factor

As was the case with film cameras, size matters on digital cameras. Digital cameras come in several form factors. They range from tiny, ultra compact models that readily fit in a shirt pocket to monster cameras with huge lenses. Although it's not universally true, the bigger the camera the more features and sensors it can have. Thus, bigger is usually better in terms of quality. In shape, they come in a rectangular package, in which the lens retracts into the body, or as an SLR-type, with a lens that sticks out of the body. Figure 14.41 shows both styles.

• **Figure 14.41** Typical digital cameras

Web Cameras

PC cameras, often called webcams because their most common use is for Internet video communication, are fairly new to the world of common I/O devices. Too many people run out and buy the cheapest one, not appreciating the vast difference between a discount webcam and more expensive models; nor do they take the time to configure the webcam properly. Let's consider some of the features you should look for when buying webcams and some of the problems you can run into when using them.

The biggest issue with webcams is the image quality. Webcams measure their resolution in pixels. You can find webcams with resolutions of as few as 100,000 pixels, and webcams with millions of pixels. Most people who use webcams agree that 1.3 million pixels (megapixels) is pretty much the highest resolution quality you can use before your video becomes so large it will bog down even a broadband connection.

The next issue with webcams is the frame rate; that is, the number of times the camera "takes your picture" each second. Higher frame rates make for smoother video; 30 frames per second is considered the best. A good camera with a high megapixel resolution and fast frame rate will provide you with excellent video conferencing capabilities. Figure 14.42 shows the author using his headset to chat via webcam using Skype software.

Most people who use online video will also want a microphone. Many cameras come with microphones, or you can use your own. Those who do a lot of video chatting may prefer to get a camera without a microphone, and then buy a good quality headset with which to speak and listen.

Many cameras now have the ability to track you when you move, to keep your face in the picture—a very handy feature for fidgety folks using video conferencing! This interesting technology recognizes a human face with little or no "training" and rotates its position to keep your face in the picture. Some companies even add funny extras which, while not very productive, are good for a laugh (Figure 14.43).

Configuring Webcams

Almost all webcams use USB connections. Windows comes with a limited set of webcam drivers, so always make sure to install the drivers supplied with the camera before you plug it in. Most webcams use Hi-Speed USB, so make sure you're plugging your webcam into a Hi-Speed USB port.

Once the camera's plugged in, you'll need to test it. All cameras come with some type of program, but finding the program can be a challenge. Some brands put the program in the system tray, some place it in My

• **Figure 14.42**   Video chatting by webcam with Skype

Read more about pixels in Chapter 15, "Video."

• **Figure 14.43**   This webcam program's animated character mirrors your movements as you conference with friends or co-workers.

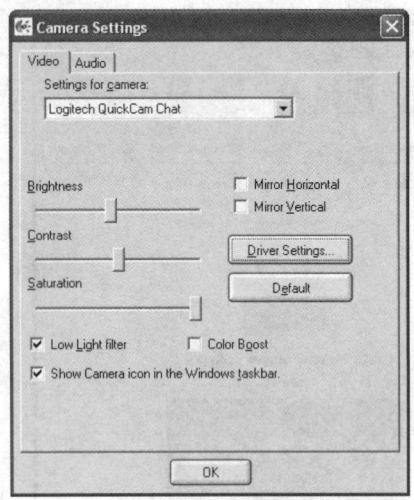

● **Figure 14.44** Camera Settings applet

Computer, and others put it in the Control Panel—and some do all three! Figure 14.44 shows the Control Panel applet that appeared when I installed the webcam driver.

The biggest challenge to using webcams is getting your webcam applications to recognize that your webcam is available and configured for use. Every program does this differently, but conceptually the steps are basically the same (with plenty of exceptions):

1. Tell the program you want to use a camera.
2. Tell the program whether you want the camera to turn on automatically when you chat.
3. Configure the image quality.
4. Test the camera.

If you're having problems with a camera, always go through the general I/O problems first, as this will clear up most problems. If you're still having problems getting the camera to work in a program, be sure to turn off all other programs that may also be using the camera. Windows allows only one program at a time to use a webcam.

■ Specialty I/O Devices

The CompTIA A+ certification exams want to make sure you're aware of two other types of I/O devices: biometric scanners and touch screens. Let's look at these fairly specialized devices.

Biometric Devices

If you look up *biometrics* on the popular Wikipedia Web site, you'll get the following definition: "**Biometrics** (ancient Greek: *bios* ='life,' *metron* ='measure') is the study of automated methods for uniquely recognizing humans based upon one or more intrinsic physical or behavioral traits." The field of biometrics also encompasses a number of security devices, such as door locks and security cameras, that don't really fit into the world of PCs. This section concentrates on the types of biometrics that you can actually buy and use on your PC. Within the realm of computers, biometrics includes a huge number of technologies, from thumb drives that read fingerprints, to software that does voice recognition.

PCs use biometrics for security. Biometric devices scan and remember unique aspects of various body parts such as your retina, iris, head image, or fingerprint, using some form of sensing device such as a retinal scanner. This information is used as a key to prevent unauthorized people from accessing whatever the biometric device is securing. Most biometric devices currently used in PCs secure only themselves. The USB thumb drive in Figure 14.45 has a tiny fingerprint scanner. You slide your finger (any finger, you choose) over the drive to unlock the contents of the thumb drive.

Less common are biometric security devices that secure entire computers. The Microsoft fingerprint scanner is a USB device that replaces standard user name and password security. Figure 14.46 shows the scanner built into a keyboard. When a program or Web site asks for a user name and password, you simply press your finger against the fingerprint scanner. It will confirm your identity (assuming your fingerprint matches), and then special software that comes with the scanner will supply the program or Web site with your stored user name and password.

Biometric devices are also used for recognition. Recognition is different from security in that the biometric device doesn't care who you are, it just wants to know what you're doing. The best example of this is voice recognition. Voice recognition programs convert human voice input into commands or text. Voice recognition for PCs has been around for some time. While it has never achieved enough accuracy to replace a keyboard completely, voice recognition is common in devices that have a limited number of commands to interpret, such as cell phones and PDAs. If you speak the words "Call Mike Meyers" into your PocketPC PDA/phone (Figure 14.47), your phone knows what to do—at least, *my* phone does!

No matter what biometric device you use, you use the same steps to make it work:

1. Install the device.

2. Register your identity with the device by sticking your eye, finger, or other unique body part (why are you snickering?) into the device so it can scan you.

3. Configure its software to tell the device what to do when it recognizes your scanned identity.

Bar Code Readers

Bar code readers are designed to read standard Universal Product Code (UPC) bar codes (Figure 14.48). We read bar codes for only one reason—to track inventory. Bar code readers enable easy updating of inventory databases stored on PCs. Bar code readers are just about the oldest "specialty" I/O device used with PCs.

Two types of bar code readers are commonly found with PCs: pen scanners and hand scanners. Pen scanners (Figure 14.49) look like an ink pen and must be swiped across the bar code. Hand scanners are held in front of the UPC code while a button is pressed to scan. All bar code readers emit a tone to let you know the scan was successful.

Older bar code readers used serial ports, but all of the newer readers use either PS/2 or USB ports. No configuration is usually necessary, other than making sure that the particular bar code reader works with whatever database/point-of-sale software you use. When in doubt, most people find the PS/2-style bar code readers work best, as they simply act like a keyboard. You plug the reader into your keyboard port and then plug your keyboard into the reader. Then all you need is software that accepts keyboard input (and what one doesn't!), and it will work.

● **Figure 14.45** USB thumb drive with fingerprint scanner *(courtesy of Lexar Media, Inc.)*

● **Figure 14.46** Microsoft fingerprint scanner on a keyboard

Figure 14.47 Using voice recognition to dial a phone number

Touch Screens

A touch screen is a monitor with some type of sensing device across its face that detects the location and duration of contact, usually by a finger or stylus. All touch screens then supply this contact information to the PC as though it were a click event from a mouse. Touch screens are used in situations for which conventional mouse/keyboard input is either impossible or impractical. Here are a few places you'll see touch screens at work:

- Information kiosks
- PDAs
- Point-of-sale systems
- Tablet PCs

Touch screens can be separated into two groups: built-in screens like the ones in PDAs, and standalone touch-screen monitors like those used in many point-of-sale systems. From a technician's standpoint, you can think of a standalone touch screen as a monitor with a built-in mouse. All touch screens will have a separate USB or PS/2 port for the "mouse" part of the device, along with drivers that you install just as you would for any USB mouse.

Neo HE430

0 761345 284301

Figure 14.48   Typical UPC code

Figure 14.49   Pen scanner *(courtesy of Wasp Barcode Technologies)*

Chapter 14 Review

■ Chapter Summary

After reading this chapter and completing the exercises, you should understand the following about input/output.

Supporting common input/output ports

■ Many new computers do not come with serial ports, as other high-speed ports such as USB have replaced them. You can tell if you have serial ports by checking for the Ports icon (COM and LPT) in Device Manager.

■ The UART chip, which comprises the serial port, converts data moving between the parallel expansion bus on a PC and the serial bus used by many I/O devices. Most serial port connectors consist of a 9-pin, DB-style connector. The connector on the PC or device itself (not the cable) is male. Serial ports are also known as RS-232, which is the standard that describes how serial ports work.

■ The USB host controller (sometimes called a host adapter) controls every USB device connected to it. The host controller includes a root hub which provides the physical connection for devices. Host controllers support many ports, but the number of USB ports a system has is usually dependent on what the motherboard manufacturer decided to supply. The host controller is shared by every device plugged into it, so speed and power is reduced with each new device.

■ Powered USB devices require their own power cord, and thus do not pull power from the USB bus itself. Bus-powered devices draw their power directly from the USB bus and do not require a separate power cord. Too many bus-powered devices may result in system lockups, device lockups, or devices that just don't work. To solve the power problem, unplugging a device or two will lower the demand for bus power. Alternatively, you can purchase and install a USB expansion card, which will provide another USB host controller with its own set of connection ports.

■ There are three flavors of USB in use today: Low-Speed USB that runs at 1.5 Mbps, Full-Speed USB that runs at 12 Mbps, and Hi-Speed USB that runs at 480 Mbps. Many people refer to the Low-Speed and Full-Speed devices as USB 1.1, although that's not correct. All three speeds are part of the USB 2.0 specification. You can plug a Hi-Speed device into a Low-Speed host, or *vice versa*, and the device will work just fine, but at the lower speed.

■ In theory, the USB interface can support up to 127 devices on a single USB port; in reality, too many devices on a single USB chain will overtax its power capabilities. USB specifications allow for a maximum cable length of 5 meters, although you may add a powered USB hub every 5 meters to extend this distance.

■ USB hubs extend the number of USB devices you can connect to a single port. Make sure you get a powered Hi-Speed USB hub so it will support the fastest speed and not draw power away from other devices.

■ Normally, you install the device driver before connecting the USB device to the system. Although this is the norm, it is not carved in stone. Be sure to read the manual that came with your device for instructions on installation. For example, many USB devices, such as flash drives, do not need a separate driver installed and work fine if simply plugged in (they can use the generic driver provided by Windows 2000/XP).

■ The high transfer speed of FireWire makes transferring large video files quick and easy. Most modern digital video cameras use the IEEE 1394 interface for transferring video from camera to PC for editing. FireWire has two distinct types of connectors: a 6-pin powered connector and a 4-pin bus-powered connector. IEEE 1394a runs at 400 Mbps, and IEEE 1394b runs at 800 Mbps.

■ FireWire devices must connect directly to a root hub, but may be daisy-chained to support up to 63 devices. Similar to USB devices, drivers should be installed before connecting the device, but most devices can use the generic Windows driver so they can be plugged in immediately.

- When troubleshooting problems, first determine if the issue is a port problem or a device problem. Swap out the troubled device for a known good device (one that works in another computer). If a known good device fails, you can safely assume you have a port problem. If a known good device functions properly, the problem is most likely a device problem. For device problems, replace the device. For port problems, verify the port is enabled, make sure you have the drive installed for the port itself, and check the condition of the cables and physical connectors.

Common input/output devices

- Keyboards are the oldest type of input device and still the primary way users input data. Although a keyboard will work without the installation of additional drivers, you need to install drivers for specialty keyboards, such as keyboards with fancy buttons or other programmable features. If you're using a USB keyboard, make sure to enable USB keyboard support in CMOS.

- Configure basic keyboard settings in the Keyboard Control Panel applet. You can change the repeat delay, repeat rate, and cursor blink rate.

- Clean dirty keys with a damp cloth or isopropyl alcohol. Compressed air works well to dislodge hair, dust, and other small objects from the keys. With most keyboards, you can pop off individual keys to do some deep cleaning. Some keyboards (like those on laptops) are not meant to have keys removed, and doing so might permanently damage the keyboard.

- Mice work with the generic Windows drivers. You only need to install mouse drivers if your mouse has special programmable features, like additional buttons. Various mouse settings can be configured via the Mouse Control Panel applet. Configurable settings include mouse speed, double-click speed, and acceleration.

- A ball mouse needs the internal rubber ball cleaned every few months. Rotate the collar on the underside of the mouse to release the rubber ball. Optical mice, which use LEDs or lasers to track movement, may occasionally need their lenses wiped free of grime, but overall outperform and outlive ball mice.

- Flatbed scanners have a hinged lid and flat glass surface where you place material to be scanned. Most scanners come with software to control the hardware and to control the scanning process itself. The scan software enables users to select the color mode and resolution of the scanned document. Scanners use a traditional TWAIN driver to transfer digital images to the PC. Some scanners offer additional features such as OCR capabilities.

- When choosing a scanner, consider the scanner's optical resolution (ignore the enhanced resolution), color depth, grayscale depth, connection type, and scan speed. The higher these numbers, the better quality the scanned images will be. Shoot for a minimum of 2400 × 2400 dpi optical resolution, 48-bit color depth, 16-bit grayscale depth, and a Hi-Speed USB or FireWire connection.

- Most digital cameras store images on removable media, such as SD cards. Photos can be transferred to a PC by connecting the camera directly to a USB or FireWire port. Alternatively, if the PC is equipped with a media card reader, the flash memory card can be removed from the camera and inserted directly into the PC's card reader.

- A 2-megapixel camera will produce 4 × 6-inch pictures with print photograph quality, whereas a 5-megapixel camera will produce 8 × 10-inch pictures with print photograph quality. The more sensors a camera has, the better the image quality, so you'll find that physically larger cameras take better pictures than tiny ones. Look for a camera with at least 3× optical zoom and ignore the digital zoom that is advertised.

- Webcams are often used for Internet video communication. A 1.3-megapixel webcam delivers a decent resolution video without bogging down a broadband connection. Look for a webcam that has a frame rate of about 30 frames per second. Some webcams come with built-in microphones, but if you want high quality audio without feedback or echo, invest in a microphone headset. After installing the driver and connecting a webcam, be sure to configure it properly so your Internet chat software knows to use the webcam.

Specialty input/output devices

- Biometric devices scan various body parts, such as fingerprints or retinas, for authentication, security, and recognition. Some biometric devices control access to an entire PC; some small devices such as USB thumb drives have biometric fingerprint scanners built in to control access to the single device. Voice recognition enables users to speak commands to the computer, such as "Call Mike Meyers" to dial the phone via a modem.

- Bar code readers read the standard Universal Product Code (UPC) bar code. The two types of bar code readers are pen scanners and hand scanners.

Pen scanners look like ink pens and must be swiped across the bar code. Hand scanners are aimed at the bar code and scan it when a button or trigger is pressed. All bar code scanners produce an audible tone to verify the bar code has been read. Old bar code readers used serial ports, but newer ones use either USB or PS/2 connections.

- Tablet PCs feature touch screens, as do information kiosks, PDAs, and point-of-sale systems. Touch screens can be operated with either a finger or stylus. Some devices, like PDAs, have built-in touch screens, whereas a point-of-sale system may use a standalone touch-screen monitor.

■ Key Terms

ball mice *(448)*
bar code reader *(457)*
biometric device *(456)*
color depth *(451)*
digital camera *(452)*
digital zoom *(454)*
FireWire *(442)*
flatbed scanner *(449)*
Full-Speed USB *(437)*
grayscale depth *(452)*

Hi-Speed USB *(437)*
IEEE 1394a *(443)*
IEEE 1394b *(443)*
Low-Speed USB *(437)*
megapixel *(454)*
optical mice *(448)*
optical resolution *(451)*
optical zoom *(454)*
RS-232 *(435)*
serial port *(434)*

touch screen *(458)*
TWAIN *(450)*
universal asynchronous receiver/ transmitter (UART) *(435)*
Universal Product Code (UPC) *(457)*
USB host controller *(436)*
USB hub *(438)*
USB root hub *(436)*
webcam *(455)*

■ Key Term Quiz

Use the Key Terms list to complete the sentences that follow. Not all terms will be used.

1. Serial ports are defined by the _____ standard.

2. A(n) _____ is useful when scanning a page from a book, whereas a _____ is useful when scanning the price of retail items at a store.

3. A(n) _____ device transfers data at up to 12 Mbps on the universal serial bus.

4. A(n) _____ FireWire device transfers data at up to 800 Mbps.

5. A(n) _____ captures digital images on removable media, whereas a _____

transmits digital images across the Internet for video communication.

6. The amount of information a digital camera can capture is measured in a unit called a(n) _____.

7. A scanner's ability to produce color, hue, and shade is defined by its _____.

8. The _____ contains the logic to convert data moving between parallel and serial devices.

9. When comparing digital cameras and their zoom capabilities, pay attention to the _____, and ignore the _____.

10. For moving the mouse pointer, most people prefer _____ over _____ because the former is much easier to keep clean.

■ Multiple-Choice Quiz

1. How many devices can a single USB host controller support?

    A. 2

    B. 4

    C. 63

    D. 127

2. What is the maximum USB cable length as defined by the USB specifications?

    A. 4.5 feet

    B. 4.5 meters

    C. 5 feet

    D. 5 meters

3. Malfunctioning USB devices may be caused by which of the following?

    A. Too many USB devices attached to the host controller

    B. Improper IRQ settings for the device

    C. Device plugged in upside-down

    D. USB 1.1 device plugged into USB 2.0 port

4. FireWire dominates USB in which area?

    A. Keyboards and mice

    B. Digital video editing

    C. MP3 players

    D. Biometric devices

5. Which FireWire standard is properly matched with its speed?

    A. IEEE 1394a, 400 Mbps

    B. IEEE 1394a, 480 Mbps

    C. IEEE 1394b, 400 Mbps

    D. IEEE 1394b, 480 Mbps

6. FireWire supports a maximum of how many devices?

    A. 2

    B. 4

    C. 63

    D. 127

7. What icon does Device Manager display over disabled devices?

    A. Yellow triangle

    B. Red X

C. Blue I

D. Green D

8. A user reports that his mouse is jittery. What is the most likely cause?

    A. His optical mouse has the wrong driver installed.

    B. His wireless mouse has a dead battery.

    C. His ball mouse has acquired dirt in the rollers.

    D. He had one too many cups of coffee that morning.

9. Which specifications describe a high quality webcam?

    A. 5 megapixels at 15 frames per second

    B. 1.3 megapixels at 15 frames per second

    C. 5 megapixels at 40 frames per second

    D. 1.3 megapixels at 30 frames per second

10. Which device is a biometric device?

    A. Bar code reader

    B. Optical mouse

    C. Retinal scanner

    D. Flatbed scanner

11. What measurement describes how many shades of gray per dot that a scanner can save?

    A. Resolution

    B. DPI

    C. Color depth

    D. Grayscale depth

12. If you are scanning at a color depth of 16 bits, how many color variations per dot can the scan store?

    A. 16

    B. 32

    C. 512

    D. 65,536

13. List these technologies in order from slowest to fastest.

    A. Serial, Full-Speed USB, Hi-Speed USB, IEEE 1394a, IEEE 1394b

    B. Serial, Full-Speed USB, IEEE 1394a, Hi-Speed USB, IEEE 1394b

C. Full-Speed USB, Serial, Hi-Speed USB, IEEE 1394a, IEEE 1394b

D. Low-Speed USB, Serial, IEEE 1394a, Hi-Speed USB, IEEE 1394b

14. What benefit does FireWire offer over USB?

A. FireWire devices consume less power.

B. FireWire devices run at faster speeds.

C. FireWire supports more devices per host controller.

D. FireWire devices are hot-swappable.

15. What do serial ports use to ensure that the sending device doesn't overload the receiving device with data?

A. Flow control

B. Parity

C. Stop bits

D. 7-bit chunking

Essay Quiz

1. A friend at the local film school needs a new keyboard and external hard drive. What advice can you give her regarding the connection style for each of these devices?

2. Dylan is excited because he just got a new USB digital camera. He tried to install it on his laptop, but the computer doesn't recognize it. He's called you for help. What will you tell him?

3. Ken asks for your help because he is always forgetting his Windows password. What can you recommend to make logons easier for him?

4. Sandra is having trouble with her modem and suspects her port settings may be off. She vaguely remembers reading in the manual that the stop bit should be set to 1. Explain to Sandra where she can verify this setting.

5. The new head of sales is frustrated because when she tries to use her keyboard, letters repeat across the screen, even if she quickly taps a key only once, resulting in messages that llllooooooookkkk lllliiiiikkkkeeee tttthhhhiiiissss. How can you walk her through fixing this problem over the phone?

Lab Projects

• Lab Project 14.1

Many personal computers do not normally include FireWire ports. Check the following three Web sites: www.dell.com, www.hp.com, and www.apple.com. Is a FireWire port standard built-in equipment on

their new computers? If so, how many FireWire ports are included? If not, do the sites offer FireWire as an optional add-on?

• Lab Project 14.2

Explore the Keyboard and Mouse Control Panel applets. Change the settings and try to use the devices. Which settings caused the most frustration?

Were there any changes you made that you preferred over the original settings?

• Lab Project 14.3

Grab a lab partner and a stopwatch. How many input devices can you each name in 30 seconds? Reset the timer. How many output devices can you

each name in 30 seconds? Are there any devices that are considered to be both input and output devices?

Understanding Video

chapter 15

Jimmy: "But Dad, all my friends are going."
Mr. Neutron: "I know, son, but if all your friends were named Cliff, would you jump off them? I don't think so."

—JIMMY NEUTRON AND MR. NEUTRON, *JIMMY NEUTRON: BOY GENIUS* (2001)

In this chapter, you will learn how to

- **Explain how video displays work**
- **Define pixels, resolution, and bandwidth**
- **Discuss the different types of monitor technologies**
- **Differentiate between different types of video cards**

The term *video* encompasses a complex interaction among numerous parts of the PC, all designed to put a picture on the screen. The monitor or video display shows you what's going on with your programs and operating system. It's the primary output device for the PC. The video card or display adapter handles all of the communication between the CPU and the monitor (see Figure 15.1). The operating system needs to know how to handle communication between the CPU and the display adapter, which requires drivers specific for each card and proper setup within Windows. Finally, each application needs to be able to interact with the rest of the video system.

Let's begin with the video display and then move to the video card.

■ Video Displays

To understand displays, you need a good grasp of each component and how they work together to make a beautiful (or not so beautiful) picture on the screen. Different types of displays use different methods and technologies to accomplish this task. Video displays for PCs come in three varieties: CRT, LCD, and projectors. The first two you'll see on the desktop or laptop; the last you'll find in boardrooms and classrooms, splashing a picture onto a screen.

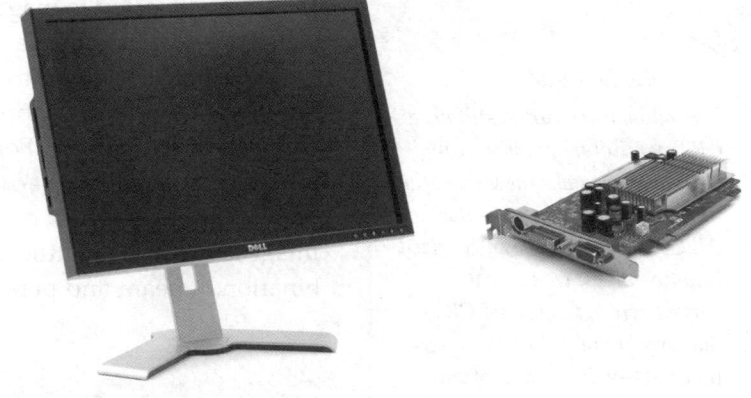

● **Figure 15.1** Typical monitor and video card

Historical/Conceptual

CRT Monitors

Cathode ray tube (CRT) monitors were the original computer monitors—those heavy, boxy monitors that take up half your desk. Although for the most part they've been replaced by LCD technology on new systems, there are plenty of CRT monitors still chugging away in the field. As the name implies, this type of display contains a large cathode ray tube, a type of airtight vacuum tube. One end of this tube is a slender cylinder that contains three electron guns. The other end of the tube, which is fatter and wider, is the display screen.

The inside of the display screen has a phosphor coating. When power is applied to one or more of the electron guns, a stream of electrons shoots toward the display end of the CRT (see Figure 15.2). Along the way, this

Before we begin in earnest, I want to give you a note of warning about the inside of a traditional monitor. I will discuss what can be repaired and what requires more specialized expertise. Make no mistake—the interior of a monitor might appear similar to the interior of a PC because of the printed circuit boards and related components, but that is where the similarity ends. No PC has voltages exceeding 15,000 to 30,000 V, but most monitors do. So let's get one thing perfectly clear: Opening up a monitor can kill you! Even when the power is disconnected, certain components retain a substantial voltage for an extended period of time. You can inadvertently short one of the components and fry yourself—to death. Given this risk, certain aspects of monitor repair lie outside the necessary skill set for a normal PC support person and definitely outside the CompTIA A+ certification exam domains! I will show you how to address the problems you can fix safely and make sure you understand the ones you need to hand over to a monitor shop.

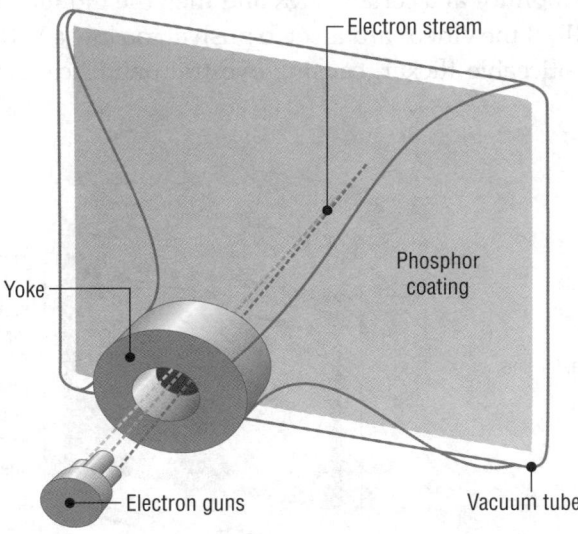

Electron stream

Phosphor coating

Yoke

Electron guns

Vacuum tube

● **Figure 15.2** Electron stream in the CRT

Tech Tip

Perfect Flat

Several manufacturers still make CRT monitors, but only a couple of companies make the CRT—the tube inside the monitor—itself. All CRT tubes can be categorized into two types: traditional curved-screen CRTs and CRTs that are often referred to as per-fect flat—using a kind of vac-uum tube that has a completely flat screen and no bending around the edges. The perfect flat screens offer a wider viewing an-gle than standard CRT screens. About the only negative to the perfect flat screens is that they tend to lack true black, so pictures seem just shy of a natural richness of color and contrast.

stream is subjected to magnetic fields generated by a ring of electromagnets called a *yoke* that controls the electron beam's point of impact.

When struck by a stream of electrons, a phosphor quickly releases a burst of energy. This happens far too quickly for the human eye and brain connection to register. Fortunately, the phosphors on the display screen have a quality called persistence , which means the phosphors continue to glow after being struck by the electron beam. Too much persistence and the image is smeary; too little and the image appears to flicker. The perfect com-bination of beam and persistence creates the illusion of a solid picture.

Essentials

Refresh Rate

The monitor displays video data as the electron guns make a series of hori-zontal sweeps across the screen, energizing the appropriate areas of the phosphorous coating. The sweeps start at the upper-left corner of the moni-tor and move across and down to the lower-right corner. The screen is "painted" only in one direction; then the electron guns turn and retrace their path across the screen, to be ready for the next sweep. These sweeps are called raster lines (see Figure 15.3).

The speed at which the electron beam moves across the screen is known as the horizontal refresh rate (HRR) , as shown in Figure 15.4. The monitor draws a number of lines across the screen, eventually covering the screen with glowing phosphors. The number of lines is not fixed, unlike television screens, which have a set number of lines. After the guns reach the lower-right corner of the screen, they turn off and point back to the up-per-left corner. The amount of time it takes to draw the entire screen and get the electron guns back to the upper-left corner is called the vertical refresh rate (VRR) , shown in Figure 15.5.

The monitor does not determine the HRR or VRR; the video card "pushes" the monitor at a certain VRR and then the monitor sets the corre-sponding HRR. If the video card is set to push at too low a VRR, the monitor produces a noticeable flicker, causing eyestrain and headaches for users.

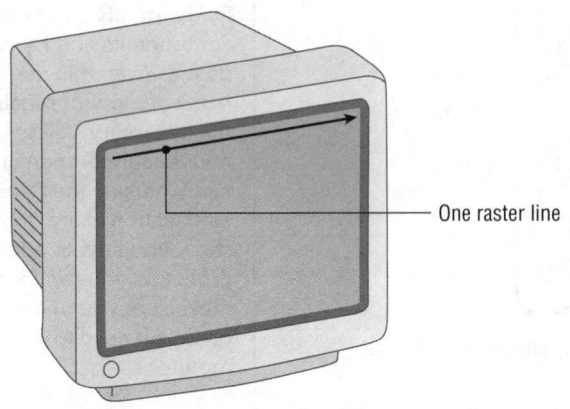

One raster line

The time it takes to draw one line across screen and be ready for the next is called the horizontal refresh rate (HRR). This is measured in KHz (thousands of lines per second).

• **Figure 15.3** Electron guns sweep from left to right.

• **Figure 15.4** Horizontal refresh rate

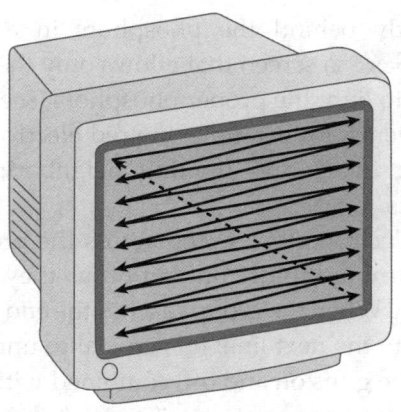

The number of times per second the electron guns can draw the entire screen and then return to the upper left-hand corner is called the vertical refresh rate (VRR). This is measured in Hz (screens per second).

• **Figure 15.5**   Vertical refresh rate

Pushing the monitor at too high of a VRR, however, causes a definite distortion of the screen image and will damage the circuitry of the monitor and eventually destroy it. The number one killer of monitors is improper VRR settings, and the number one reason your office is filled with crabby workers is due to the VRR being set too low. All good PC support techs understand this and take substantial time tweaking the VRR to ensure that the video card pushes the monitor at the highest VRR without damaging the monitor—this is the Holy Grail of monitor support!

 Try This!

Discovering Your Refresh Rate

You should know the refresh rate for all CRTs you service. Setting up monitors incorrectly can cause havoc in the workplace, so Try This!

1. Most PCs have two places where you can discover the current refresh rate of the monitor. Many monitors offer a menu button for adjusting the display. Often it will show the refresh rate when pushed once.

2. If that doesn't work, go to the Control Panel and open the Display applet. Select the Settings tab and then click the Advanced button. Select the Monitor tab in the Monitor Properties dialog box.

3. Write down your refresh rate. How does it compare with that of your classmates?

Phosphors and Shadow Mask

All CRT monitors contain dots of phosphorous or some other light-sensitive compound that glows *red, green,* or *blue* (RGB) when an electron gun sweeps over it. These phosphors are evenly distributed across the front of the monitor (see Figure 15.6).

A normal CRT has three electron guns: one for the red phosphors, one for the blue phosphors, and one for the green phosphors. It is important to understand that the electron guns do not fire colored light; they simply fire electrons at different intensities, which then make the phosphors glow. The higher the intensity of the electron stream, the brighter the color produced by the glowing phosphor.

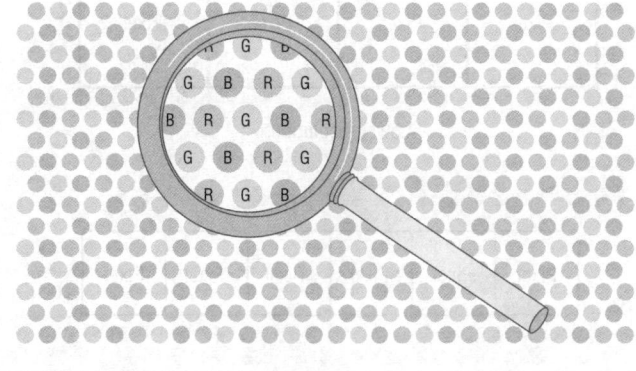

• **Figure 15.6**   A monitor is a grid of red, green, and blue phosphors.

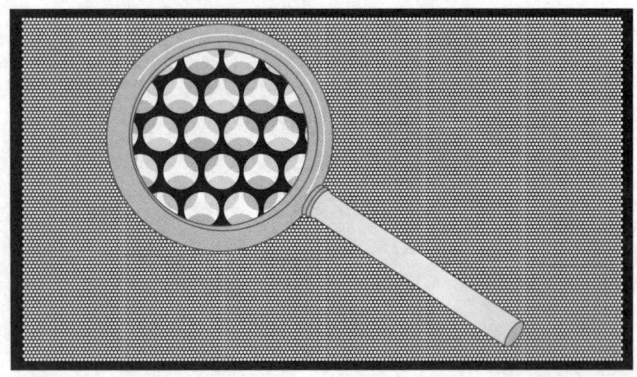

● **Figure 15.7**   Shadow mask

Tech Tip

Trinitron

Not all CRT monitors use dots. The popular Sony Trinitron line of CRT monitors uses bars of red, green, and blue instead of dots. The holes in the shadow mask have a rectangular shape. Many people feel this makes the monitor's image much crisper and clearer. Some consumers must agree because the Trinitron enjoys tremendous popularity. Even though the phosphors and shadow mask have a different shape, everything you learn here applies to Trinitrons also.

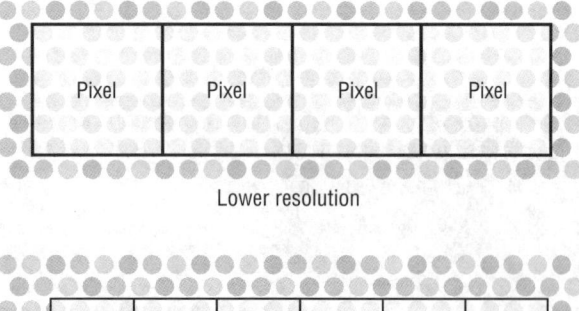

● **Figure 15.8**   Resolution versus pixel size

Directly behind the phosphors in a CRT is the shadow mask, a screen that allows only the proper electron gun to light the proper phosphors (see Figure 15.7). This prevents, for example, the red electron beam from "bleeding over" and lighting neighboring blue and green dots.

The electron guns sweep across the phosphors as a group, turning rapidly on and off as they move across the screen. When the group reaches the end of the screen, it moves to the next line. It is crucial to understand that turning the guns on and off, combined with moving the guns to new lines, creates a "mosaic" that is the image you see on the screen. The number of times the guns turn on and off, combined with the number of lines drawn on the screen, determines the number of mosaic pieces used to create the image. These individual "pieces" are called pixels, from the term *picture elements.* You can't hold a pixel in your hand; it's just the area of phosphors lit at one instant when the group of guns is turned on. The size of pixels can change, depending on the number of times the group of guns is turned on and off and the number of lines drawn.

Resolution

Monitor resolution is always shown as the number of horizontal pixels times the number of vertical pixels. A resolution of 640 × 480, therefore, indicates a horizontal resolution of 640 pixels and a vertical resolution of 480 pixels. If you multiply the values together, you can see how many pixels are on each screen: 640 × 480 = 307,200 pixels per screen. An example of resolution affecting the pixel size is shown in Figure 15.8.

Some common resolutions are 640 × 480, 800 × 600, 1024 × 768, 1280 × 960, 1280 × 1024, and 1600 × 1200. Notice that most of these resolutions match a 4:3 ratio. This is called the aspect ratio. Many monitors are shaped like television screens, with a 4:3 aspect ratio, so most resolutions are designed to match—or at least be close to—that shape. Many monitors, generically called *wide-screen monitors,* have a 16:9 or 16:10 ratio. Two of the common resolutions you'll see with these monitors are 1366 × 768 and 1920 × 1200.

The last important issue is to determine the maximum possible resolution for a monitor. In other words, how small can one pixel be? Well, the answer lies in the phosphors. A pixel must be made up of at least one red, one green, and one blue phosphor to make any color, so the smallest theoretical pixel would consist of one group of red, green, and blue phosphors: a triad (see Figure 15.9). Various limitations in screens, controlling electronics, and electron gun technology make the maximum resolution much bigger than one triad.

Dot Pitch

The resolution of a monitor is defined by the maximum amount of detail the monitor can render. The dot pitch of the monitor ultimately limits this resolution. The **dot pitch** defines the diagonal distance between phosphorous dots of the same color, and is measured in *millimeters (mm)*. Because a lower dot pitch means more dots on the screen, it usually produces a sharper, more defined image (see Figure 15.10). Dot pitch works in tandem with the maximum number of lines the monitor can support in order to determine the greatest working resolution of the monitor. It might be possible to place an image at 1600 × 1200 on a 15-inch monitor with a dot pitch of 0.31 mm, but it would not be very readable.

The dot pitch can range from as high as 0.39 mm to as low as 0.18 mm. For most Windows-based applications on a 17-inch monitor, many people find that 0.28 mm is the maximum usable dot pitch that still produces a clear picture.

Bandwidth

Bandwidth defines the maximum number of times the electron gun can be turned on and off per second. Bandwidth is measured in *megahertz (MHz)*. In essence, bandwidth tells us how fast the monitor can put an image on the screen. A typical value for a better-quality 17-inch color monitor would be around 150 MHz, which means that the electron beam can be turned on and off 150 million times per second. The value for a monitor's bandwidth determines the maximum VRR the video card should push the monitor for any given resolution. It reads as follows:

maximum VRR = bandwidth ÷ pixels per page

For example, what is the maximum VRR that a 17-inch monitor with a bandwidth of 100 MHz and a resolution of 1024 × 768 can support? The answer is

maximum VRR = 100,000,000 ÷ (1024 × 768) = 127 Hz

That's a pretty good monitor, as most video cards do not push beyond 120 Hz! At a resolution of 1200 × 1024, the vertical refresh would be

100,000,000 ÷ (1200 × 1024) = 81 Hz

So, we would make sure to set the video card's VRR to 80 Hz or less. If you had a monitor with a bandwidth of only 75 MHz, the maximum VRR at a 1200 × 1024 resolution would be only 61 Hz.

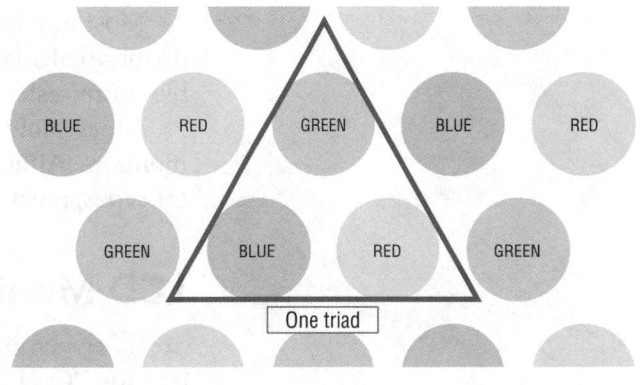

● **Figure 15.9**   One triad

   **Try This!**

Determine the Dot Pitch of Your Monitor

Have you ever wondered what the dot pitch measurement of a CRT monitor is? Well, let's try to figure it out. First, take note of the manufacturer and model name/number of your monitor or of any CRT. You might need this information in a second.

Now, doing your best contortionist pose, try to take a look at the back of your monitor. Normally, there is a small metal plate back there that indicates information such as the model number and serial number of your monitor. Sometimes this plate also lists a few monitor specifications, including dot pitch. Did you find it? No? Well then, crawl down off your desk, slowly, and fire up your favorite Web browser.

Search for the Web site of your monitor's manufacturer. See if you can find the technical specifications for your monitor listed on the Web site. Use the manufacturer, model name, and model number information that you wrote down earlier.

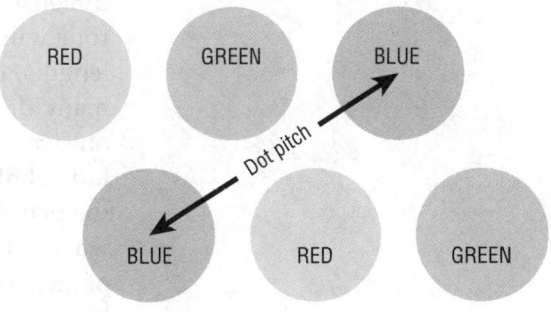

● **Figure 15.10**   Measuring dot pitch

Most monitor makers know that people aren't going to take the time to do these calculations. Instead, they do the calculations for you and create tables of refresh rates at certain resolutions to show what a monitor can do.

Great! Now that you have the basics of CRT monitors, let's turn to LCD monitors. Although the technology differs dramatically between the monitor types, most of the terms used for CRTs also apply to LCD functions.

LCD Monitors

Liquid crystal displays (LCDs) are the most common type of display technology for PCs. LCD monitors have many advantages over CRTs. They are thinner and lighter, use much less power, are virtually flicker free, and don't emit potentially harmful radiation. LCDs still have resolution, refresh rates, and bandwidth, but LCDs also come with their own family of abbreviations, jargon, and terms that you need to understand in order to install, maintain, and support LCDs.

How LCDs Work

The secret to understanding LCD panels is to understand the concept of the polarity of light. Anyone who played with a prism in sixth grade or has looked at a rainbow knows that light travels in waves (no quantum mechanics here, please!) and the wavelength of the light determines the color. What you might not appreciate is the fact that light waves emanate from a light source in three dimensions. It's impossible to draw a clear diagram of three-dimensional waves, so instead, let's use an analogy. To visualize this, think of light emanating from a flashlight. Now think of the light emanating from that flashlight as though someone was shaking a jump rope. This is not a rhythmic shaking, back and forth or up and down; it's more as if a person went crazy and was shaking the jump rope all over the place—up, down, left, right—constantly changing the speed.

That's how light really acts. Well, I guess we could take the analogy one step further by saying the person has an infinite number of arms, each holding a jump rope shooting out in every direction to show the three-dimensionality of light waves, but (a) I can't draw that and (b) one jump rope will suffice to explain LCD panels. The different speeds create wavelengths, from very short to very long. When light comes into your eyes at many different wavelengths, you see white light. If the light came in only one wavelength, you would see only that color. Light flowing through a polarized filter (like sunglasses) is like putting a picket fence between you and the people shaking the ropes. You see all of the wavelengths, but only the waves of similar orientation. You would still see all of the colors, just fewer of them because you only see the waves of the same orientation, making the image darker. That's why many sunglasses use polarizing filters.

Now, what would happen if we added another picket fence but put the slats in a horizontal direction? This would effectively cancel out all of the waves. This is what happens when two polarizing filters are combined at a 90-degree angle—no light passes through.

What would happen if a third fence was added between the two fences with the slats at a 45-degree angle? Well, it would sort of "twist" some of the shakes in the rope so that the waves could then get through. The same thing is true with the polarizing filters. The third filter twists some of the light so that it gets through. If you're really feeling scientific, go to any teacher's supply store and pick up three polarizing filters for about US$3 each and try it. It works.

Liquid crystals take advantage of the property of polarization. Liquid crystals are composed of a specially formulated liquid full of long, thin crystals that always want to orient themselves in the same direction, as shown in Figure 15.11. This substance acts exactly like a liquid polarized filter. If you poured a thin film of this stuff between two sheets of glass, you'd get a darn good pair of sunglasses.

Imagine cutting extremely fine grooves on one side of one of those sheets of glass. When you place this liquid in contact with a finely grooved surface, the molecules naturally line up with the grooves in the surface (see Figure 15.12).

If you place another finely grooved surface, with the grooves at a 90-degree orientation to the other surface, opposite the first one, the molecules in contact with that side will attempt to line up with it. The molecules in between, in trying to line up with both sides, will immediately line up in a nice twist (see Figure 15.13). If two perpendicular polarizing filters are then placed on either side of the liquid crystal, the liquid crystal will twist the light and enable it to pass (see Figure 15.14).

If you expose the liquid crystal to an electrical potential, however, the crystals will change their orientation to match the direction of the electrical field. The twist goes away and no light passes through (see Figure 15.15).

A color LCD screen is composed of a large number of tiny liquid crystal molecules (called sub-pixels) arranged in rows and columns between polarizing filters. Each tiny distinct group of three sub-pixels—one red, one green, and one blue—form a physical pixel, as shown in Figure 15.16.

Once all the pixels are laid out, how do you charge the right spots to make an image? Early LCDs didn't use rectangular pixels. Instead, images were composed of different-shaped elements, each electrically separate

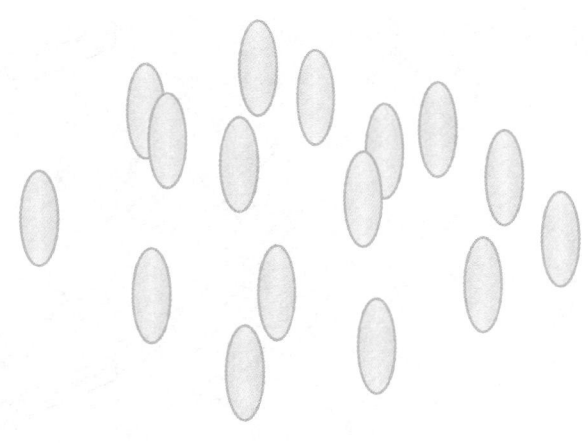

• **Figure 15.11**   Waves of similar orientation

LCD pixels are very different from the pixels in a CRT. A CRT pixel's size will change depending on the resolution. The pixels in an LCD panel are fixed and cannot be changed. See the "LCD Resolution" section later in the chapter for the scoop.

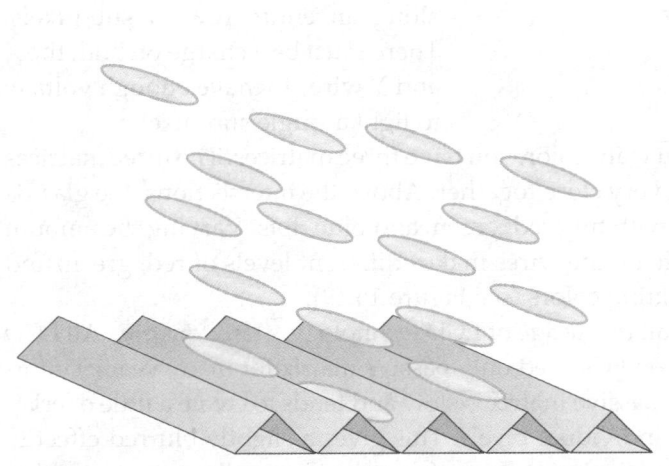

• **Figure 15.12**   Liquid crystal molecules tend to line up together.

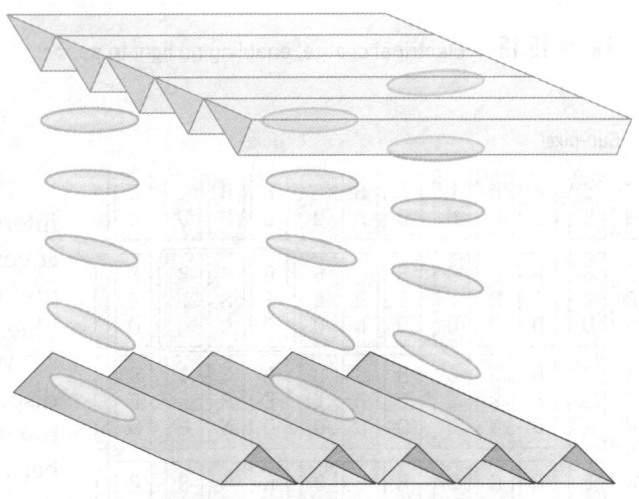

• **Figure 15.13**   Liquid crystal molecules twisting

Chapter 15: Understanding Video

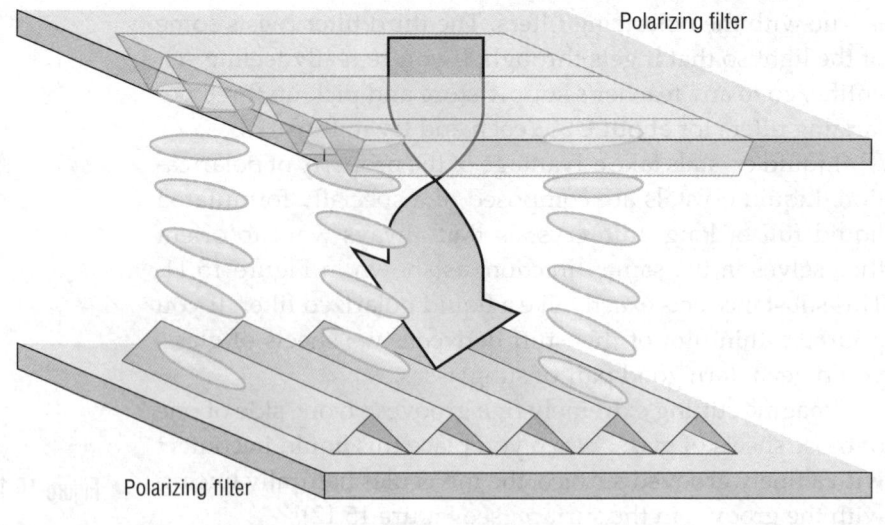

● **Figure 15.14**   No charge, enabling light to pass

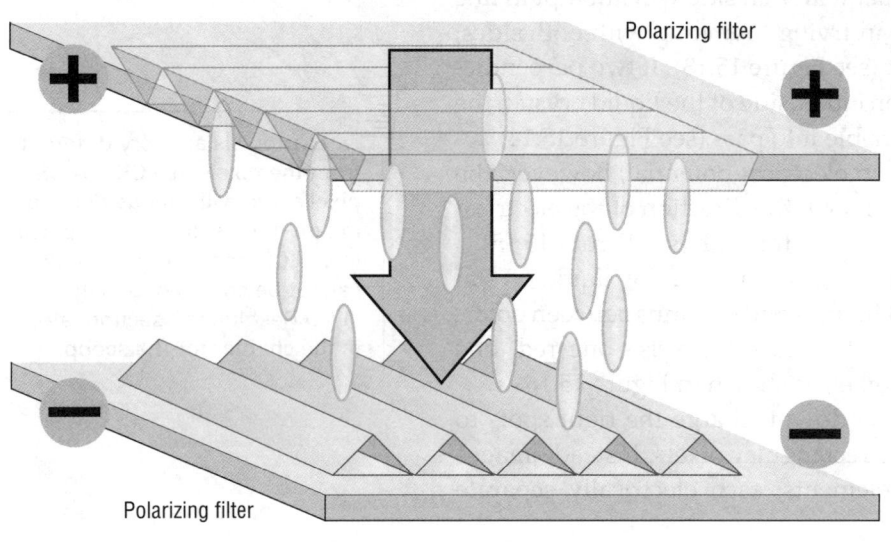

● **Figure 15.15**   Electrical charge, enabling no light to pass

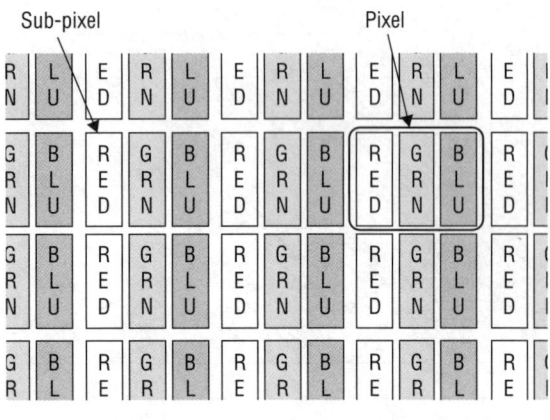

● **Figure 15.16**   LCD pixels

from the others. To create an image, each area was charged at the same time. Figure 15.17 shows the number zero, a display made possible by charging six areas to make an ellipse of sorts. This process, called *static charging*, is still quite popular in more basic numeric displays such as calculators.

The static method would not work in PCs due to its inherent inflexibility. Instead, LCD screens use a matrix of wires (see Figure 15.18). The vertical wires, the Y wires, run to every sub-pixel in the column. The horizontal wires, the X wires, run along an entire row of sub-pixels. There must be a charge on both the X and Y wires to make enough voltage to light a single sub-pixel.

If you want color, you have three matrices. The three matrices intersect very close together. Above the intersections, the glass is covered with tiny red, green, and blue dots. Varying the amount of voltage on the wires makes different levels of red, green, and blue, creating colors (see Figure 15.19).

We call this usage of LCD technology **passive matrix**. All LCD displays on PCs used only passive matrix for many years. Unfortunately, passive matrix is slow and tends to create a little overlap between individual pixels. This gives a slightly blurred effect to the image displayed. Manufacturers eventually came up with a speedier method of display, called **dual-scan passive matrix**, in which the screen refreshed two lines at a time. Although other

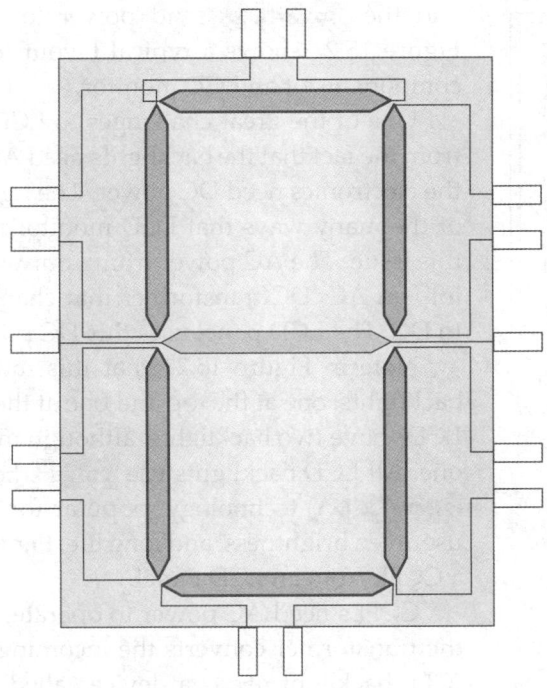

● **Figure 15.17**   Single character for static LCD numeric display

LCD technologies have since appeared, dual-scan continues to show up on some lower-end LCD panels.

Thin Film Transistor

A vast improvement over dual scan is called `active matrix` or `thin film transistor (TFT)`. Instead of using X and Y wires, one or more tiny transistors control each color dot, providing faster picture display, crisp definition, and much tighter color control. TFT is the LCD of choice today, even though it is much more expensive than passive matrix (see Figure 15.20).

LCD Components

The typical LCD projector is composed of three main components: the LCD panel, the backlight(s), and the inverters. The LCD panel creates the image, the `backlights` illuminate the image so you can see it,

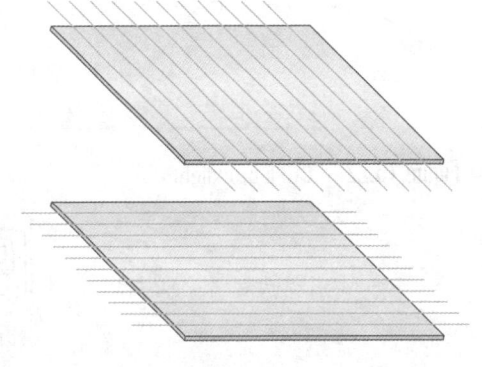

● **Figure 15.18**   An LCD matrix of wires

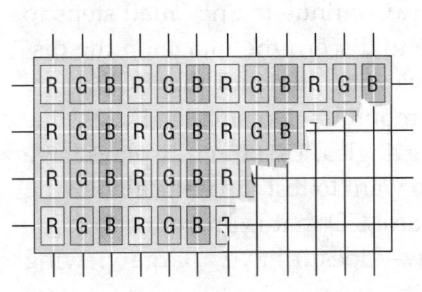

● **Figure 15.19**   Passive matrix display

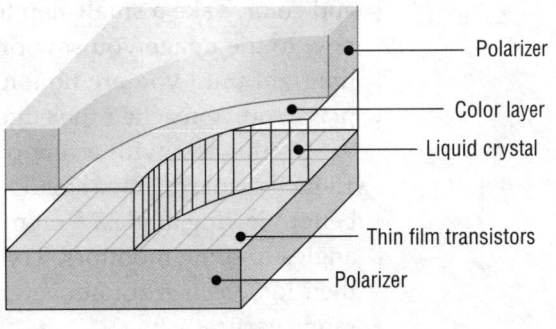

Polarizer
Color layer
Liquid crystal
Thin film transistors
Polarizer

● **Figure 15.20**   Active matrix display

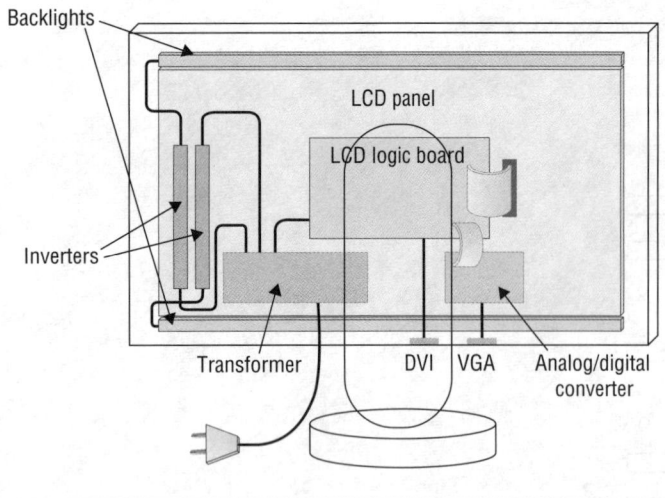

Backlights

LCD panel

LCD logic board

Inverters

Transformer   DVI VGA   Analog/digital
converter

● **Figure 15.21**   LCD internals

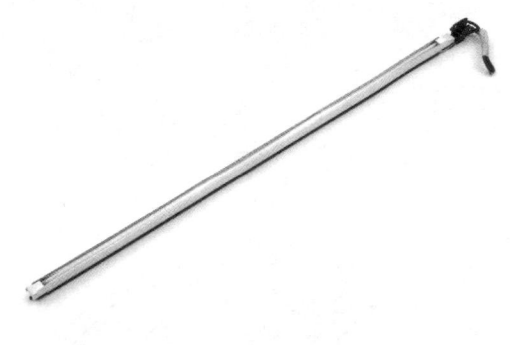

● **Figure 15.22**   CCFL backlight

and the **inverters** send power to the backlights. Figure 15.21 shows a typical layout for the internal components of an LCD monitor.

One of the great challenges to LCD power stems from the fact that the backlights need AC power while the electronics need DC power. The figure shows one of the many ways that LCD monitor makers handle this issue. The AC power from your wall socket goes into an AC/DC transformer that changes the power to DC. The LCD panel uses this DC power.

Note in Figure 15.21 that this monitor has two backlights: one at the top and one at the bottom. Most LCDs have two backlights, although many only have one. All LCD backlights use **cold cathode fluorescent lamp (CCFL)** technology, popular for its low power use, even brightness, and long life. Figure 15.22 shows a CCFL from an LCD panel.

CCFLs need AC power to operate, but given that the transformer converts the incoming AC power to DC, each CCFL backlight needs a device called an inverter to convert the DC power back into AC. Figure 15.23 shows a typical inverter used in an LCD.

Looking once again at Figure 15.21, note the DVI and VGA inputs. DVI is a digital signal, so it connects directly to the LCD's logic circuitry. The VGA goes to an analog to digital converter before reaching the LCD logic board.

Keep in mind that Figure 15.21 is a generic illustration. The actual location and interconnections of the different components are as variable as the number of LCD panels available today!

Try This!

Test the Viewing Angle of LCDs

Take a trip to your local computer store to look at LCD displays. Don't get distracted looking at all the latest graphics cards, sound cards, CPUs, motherboards, and RAM—well, actually, it's okay to look at those things. Just don't forget to look at LCDs!

Stand about two feet in front of an LCD display. Look directly at the image on the screen and consider the image quality, screen brightness, and color. Take a small step to your right. Compare the image you see now to the image you saw previously. Continue taking small steps to the right until you are no longer able to discern the image on the display. You've reached the edge of the viewing angle for that LCD.

Do this test with a few different monitors. Do smaller LCDs, like 15-inch displays, have smaller viewing angles? Do larger displays have better viewing angles? You might also want to test the vertical viewing angles of some monitors. Try to find an LCD that is on your eye level; then look at it from above and below—does it have a large viewing range vertically?

Two LCD panels that have the same physical size may have different native resolutions.

• **Figure 15.23**   Inverter

LCD Resolution

All LCD monitors have a native resolution, such as 1680 × 1050, that enables them to display the sharpest picture possible. As mentioned earlier, the pixels are fixed. You simply cannot run an LCD monitor at a resolution higher than the native one. Worse, because LCDs have no equivalent to a shadow mask, they can't run at a *lower* than native resolution without severely degrading image quality. A CRT can simply use more dots and the filtering and smoothing of the shadow mask to make a picture at a lower resolution look as good and crisp as the same picture at a higher resolution, but an LCD cannot. The LCD has to use an edge-blurring technique called anti-aliasing to soften the jagged corners of the pixels when running at lower than native resolution, which simply does not look as good. The bottom line? Always set the LCD at native resolution!

Brightness

The strength of an LCD monitor's backlights determines the brightness of the monitor. The brightness is measured in nits. LCD panels vary from 100 nits on the low end to over 1000 nits or more on the high end. Average LCD panels are around 300 nits, which most monitor authorities consider excellent brightness.

Response Rate

An LCD panel's response rate is the amount of time it takes for all of the sub-pixels on the panel to go from pure black to pure white and back again. This is roughly the same concept as the CRT refresh rate, but with one important difference. Once the electron gun on a CRT lights a phosphor, that phosphor begins to fade until it is lit again. Individual LCD sub-pixels hold their intensity until the LCD circuitry changes that sub-pixel, making the problem of flicker nonexistent on LCDs.

   Manufacturers measure LCD response rates in milliseconds, with lower being better. A typical lower-end or older LCD will have a response rate of 20–25 ms. The screens look fine, but you'll get some ghosting if you try to watch a movie or play a fast-paced video game. In recent years, manufacturers have figured out how to overcome this issue, and you can find many LCD monitors with a response rate of 6–8 ms.

Tech Tip

Dealing with High Resolution LCDs

The hard-wired nature of LCD resolution creates a problem for techs and consumers when dealing with bigger, better-quality monitors. A typical 15-inch LCD has a 1024 × 768 resolution, but a 17-inch usually has 1280 × 1024 or higher. These high resolutions make the menus and fonts on a monitor super tiny, a problem for people with less-than-stellar vision. Many folks throw in the towel and run these high-end LCDs at lower resolution and just live with the lower quality picture, but that's not the best way to resolve this problem.

   With Windows XP (and to a lesser extent with the earlier versions of Windows), Microsoft allows incredible customizing of the interface. You can change the font size, shape, and color. You can resize the icons, toolbars, and more. You can even change the number of dots per inch (DPI) for the full screen, making everything bigger or smaller!

   For basic customizing, start at the Control Panel | Display applet | Appearance tab. To change the DPI for the display, go to the Settings tab and click the Advanced button. Your clients will thank you!

One nit equals one candela/m². One candela is roughly equal to the amount of light created by a candle.

Contrast Ratio

A big drawback of LCD monitors is that they don't have nearly the color saturation or richness of contrast of a good CRT monitor—although LCD technology continues to improve every year. A good contrast ratio—the difference between the darkest and lightest spots that the monitor can display—is 450:1, although a quick trip to a computer store will reveal LCDs with lower levels (250:1) and higher levels (1000:1).

• **Figure 15.24**   Rear-view projector *(photo courtesy of Samsung)*

📄 Another type of technology that's seen in projectors but is outside the scope of the CompTIA A+ exams is called digital light processing (DLP).

Projectors

Projectors are a third option for displaying your computer images and the best choice when displaying to an audience or in a classroom. There are two ways to project an image on a screen: rear-view and front-view. As the name would suggest, a **rear-view projector** (Figure 15.24) shoots an image onto a screen from the rear. Rear-view projectors are always self-enclosed and very popular for televisions, but are virtually unheard of in the PC world.

A **front-view projector** shoots the image out the front and counts on you to put a screen in front at the proper distance. Front-view projectors connected to PCs running Microsoft PowerPoint have been the cornerstone of every meeting almost everywhere for at least the last ten years (Figure 15.25). This section deals exclusively with front-view projectors that connect to PCs.

Projector Technologies

Projectors that connect to PCs have been in existence for almost as long as PCs themselves. Given all that time, there have been a number of technologies used in projectors. The first generation of projectors used CRTs. Each color used a separate CRT that projected the image onto a screen (Figure 15.26). CRT projectors create beautiful images but are expensive, large, and very heavy, and have for the most part been abandoned for more recent technologies.

Given that light shines through an LCD panel, LCD projectors are a natural fit for front projection. LCD projectors are light and very inexpensive compared to CRTs, but lack the image quality. LCD projectors are so light that almost all portable projectors use LCD (Figure 15.27).

All projectors share the same issues of their equivalent technology monitors. LCD projectors have a specific native resolution, for example. In addition, you need to understand three concepts specific to projectors: lumens, throw, and lamps.

• **Figure 15.25**   Front-view projector *(photo courtesy of Dell Inc.)*

Lumens

The brightness of a projector is measured in lumens. A `lumen` is the amount of light given off by a light source from a certain angle that is perceived by the human eye. The greater the lumen rating of a projector, the brighter the projector will be. The best lumen rating depends on the size of the room and the amount of light in the room. There's no single answer for "the right lumen rating" for a projector, but use this as a rough guide. If you use a projector in a small, darkened room, 1000 to 1500 lumens will work well. If you use a projector in a mid-sized room with typical lighting, in contrast, you'll need at least 2000 lumens. Projectors for large rooms have ratings over 10,000 lumens and are very expensive.

Throw

A projector's `throw` is the size of the image at a certain distance from the screen. All projectors have a recommended minimum and maximum throw distance that you need to take into consideration. A typical throw would be expressed as follows. A projector with a 16:9 image aspect ratio needs to be 11 to 12 feet away from the projection surface to create a 100-inch diagonal screen. A *long throw lens* has about a 1:2 ratio of screen size to distance, so to display a 4-foot screen, you'd have to put the projector 8 feet away. Some *short throw lenses* drop that ratio down as low as 1:1!

• **Figure 15.26**   CRT projector

Lamps

The bane of every projector is the lamp. Lamps work hard in your projector, as they must generate a tremendous amount of light. As a result, they generate quite a bit of heat, and all projectors come with a fan to keep the lamp from overheating. When you turn off a projector, the fan will continue to run until the lamp is fully cooled. Lamps are also very expensive, usually in the range of a few hundred dollars (U.S.), which comes as a nasty shock to someone who's not prepared for that price when their lamp dies!

• **Figure 15.27**   LCD projector *(photo courtesy of ViewSonic)*

Common Features

CRT or LCD, all monitors share a number of characteristics that you need to know for purchase, installation, maintenance, and troubleshooting.

Size

You need to take care when buying CRT monitors. CRT monitors come in a large number of sizes, all measured in inches (although most metric

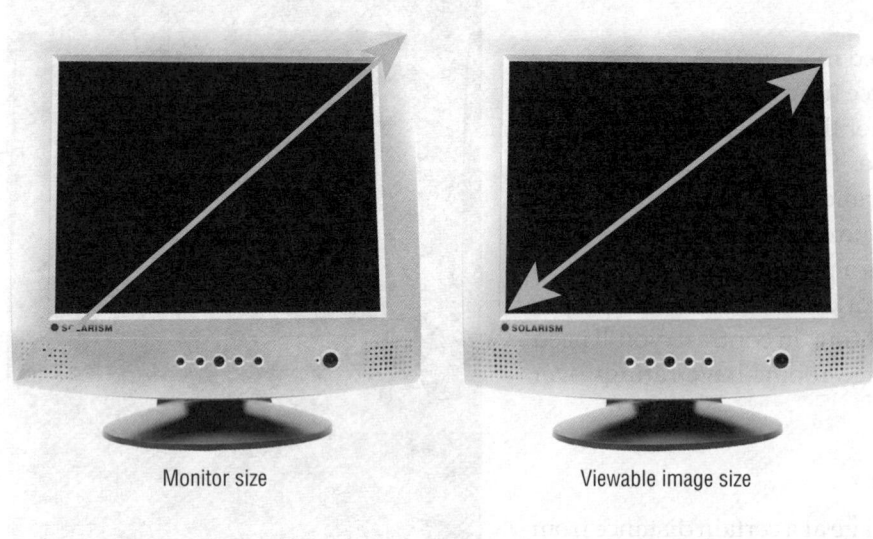

Monitor size Viewable image size

• **Figure 15.28** Viewable image size of a CRT

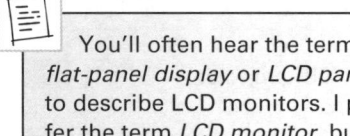

You'll often hear the terms *flat-panel display* or *LCD panels* to describe LCD monitors. I prefer the term *LCD monitor*, but you should be prepared to hear it a few different ways.

• **Figure 15.29** A traditional CRT connection

countries provide the metric equivalent value). All monitors provide two numbers: the monitor size and the actual size of the screen. The monitor size measures from two opposite diagonal corners. The actual screen is measured from one edge of the screen to the opposite diagonal side. This latter measurement is often referred to as the **viewable image size (VIS)**; see Figure 15.28. You will commonly see a size difference of one to two inches between the two measurements. A 17-inch CRT monitor, for example, might have a 15.5-inch VIS.

LCD monitors dispense with the two values and simply express the VIS value. You must consider this issue when comparing LCDs to CRTs. A 15-inch LCD monitor will have about the same viewing area as a 17-inch CRT.

Connections

CRT monitors for PCs all use the famous 15-pin, three-row, DB-type connector (see Figure 15.29) and a power plug. Larger or multipurpose monitors may have a few other connectors, but as far as the CRT is concerned, these are the only two you need for video.

Unlike the analog CRTs, LCD monitors need a digital signal. This creates somewhat of an issue. The video information stored on a video card's RAM is clearly digital. All VGA and better video cards include a special chip (or function embedded into a chip that does several other jobs) called the **random access memory digital-to-analog converter (RAMDAC)**. As the name implies, RAMDAC takes the digital signal from the video card and turns it into an analog signal for the analog CRT (see Figure 15.30). The RAMDAC really defines the bandwidth that the video card outputs.

Well, RAMDACs certainly make sense for analog CRT monitors. However, if you want to plug your LCD monitor into a regular video card, you need circuitry on the LCD monitor to convert the signal from analog to digital (see Figure 15.31).

Many LCD monitors use exactly this process. These are called *analog LCD monitors*. The monitor really isn't analog; it's digital, but it takes a standard VGA input. These monitors have one advantage: You may use any standard VGA video card. But these monitors require adjustment of the analog timing signal to the digital clock inside the monitor. This used to be a fairly painful process, but most analog LCD monitors now include intelligent circuitry to make this process either automatic or very easy.

Why convert the signal from digital to analog and then back to digital? Well, many monitor and video card people agree. We now see quite a few digital LCD monitors and digital video cards. They use a completely different connector than the old 15-pin DB connector used on analog video cards and monitors. After a few false starts with connection standards, under names like P&D and DFP, the digital LCD world, with a few holdouts, moved to the **digital video interface (DVI)** standard. DVI is actually three different connectors that look very much alike: DVI-D is for digital, DVI-A is for analog (for backward compatibility if the monitor maker so desires), and the DVI-A/D or DVI-I (interchangeable) accepts either a DVI-D or DVI-A. DVI-D and DVI-A are keyed so that they will not connect.

DVI-D and DVI-I connectors come in two varieties, single link and dual link. *Single-link DVI* has a maximum bandwidth of 165 MHz, which, translated into practical terms, limits the maximum resolution of a monitor to 1920 × 1080 at 60 Hz or 1280 × 1024 at 85 Hz. *Dual-link DVI* uses more pins to double throughput and

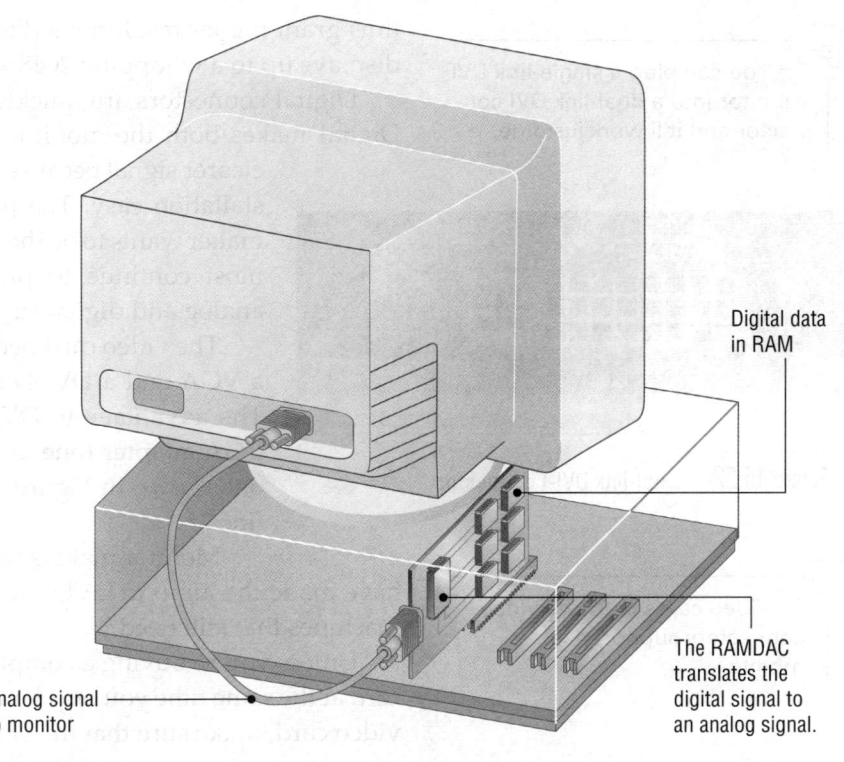

Digital data in RAM

The RAMDAC translates the digital signal to an analog signal.

Analog signal to monitor

● **Figure 15.30**   An analog signal sent to a CRT monitor

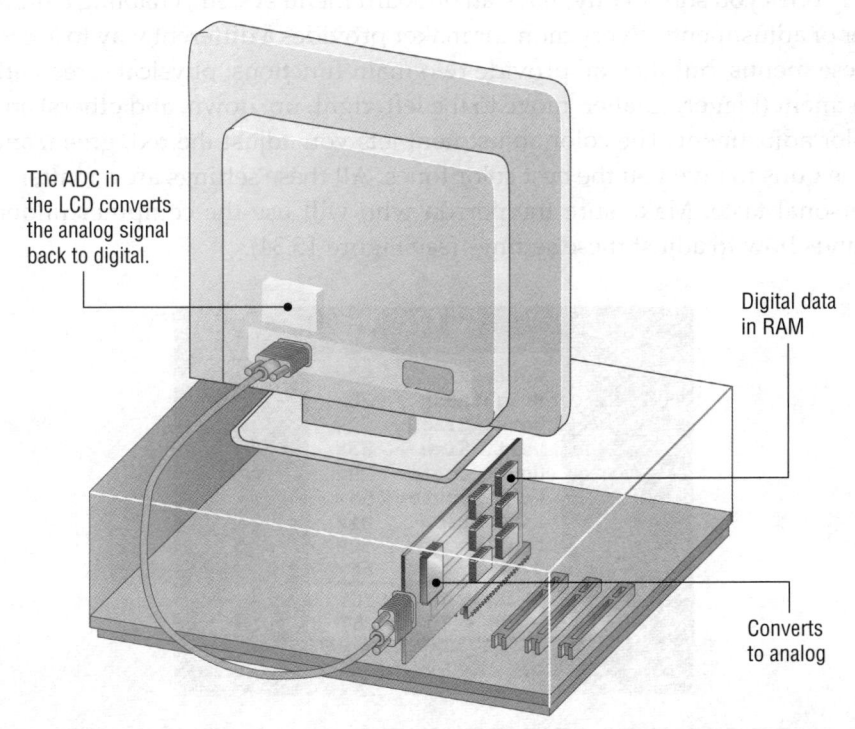

The ADC in the LCD converts the analog signal back to digital.

Digital data in RAM

Converts to analog

● **Figure 15.31**   Converting analog back to digital on the LCD

You can plug a single-link DVI monitor into a dual-link DVI connector and it'll work just fine.

Figure 15.32   Dual-link DVI-I connector

Video cards with two video connectors support dual monitors.

Figure 15.33   DVI to VGA adapter

thus grant higher resolutions (Figure 15.32). With dual link, you can have displays up to a whopping 2048 × 1536 at 60 Hz!

Digital connectors are quickly replacing analog in the monitor world. Digital makes both the monitor and the video card cheaper, provides a clearer signal because no conversion is necessary, and makes installation easy. The problem is that no video card or monitor maker wants to be the first to go all digital, so to hedge their bets, most continue to produce display products that offer both analog and digital support.

The video card people have it easy. They either include both a VGA and a DVI-D connector or they use a DVI-I connector. The advantage to DVI-I is that you can add a cheap DVI-I to VGA adapter (one usually comes with the video card) like the one shown in Figure 15.33 and connect an analog monitor just fine.

Monitor makers have it tougher. Most LCD monitor makers have made the jump to DVI, but many include a VGA connector for those machines that still need it.

Unless you're buying a complete new system, you'll rarely buy a video card at the same time you buy a monitor. When you're buying a monitor or a video card, make sure that the new device will connect to the other!

Adjustments

Most adjustments to the monitor take place at installation, but for now, let's just make sure you know what they are and where they are located. Clearly, all monitors have an On/Off button or switch. Also, see if you can locate the Brightness and Contrast buttons. Beyond that, most monitors (at least the only ones you should buy) have an onboard menu system, enabling a number of adjustments. Every monitor maker provides a different way to access these menus, but they all provide two main functions: physical screen adjustment (bigger, smaller, move to the left, right, up, down, and others) and color adjustment. The color adjustment lets you adjust the red, green, and blue guns to give you the best color tones. All these settings are a matter of personal taste. Make sure the person who will use the computer understands how to adjust these settings (see Figure 15.34).

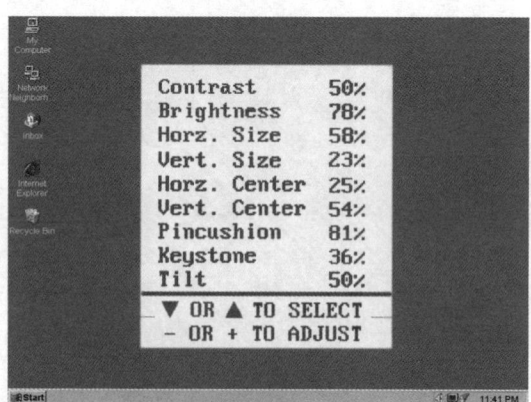

Figure 15.34   Typical menu controls

Power Conservation

CRT and LCD monitors differ greatly in the amount of electricity they require. The bottom line is that CRTs use a lot and LCDs use a lot less. Here's the scoop.

Approximately half the power required to run a desktop PC is consumed by the CRT monitor. Monitors that meet the Video Electronics Standards Association (VESA) specification for display power-management signaling (DPMS) can reduce monitor power consumption by roughly 75 percent. This is accomplished by reducing or eliminating the signals sent by the video card to the monitor during idle periods. By eliminating these pulses, the monitor essentially takes catnaps. The advantage over simply shutting the monitor off is in the time it takes to restore the display.

A typical CRT monitor consumes approximately 120 watts. During a catnap or power-down mode, the energy consumption is reduced to below 25 watts, while enabling the screen to return to use in less than ten seconds. Full shutoff is accomplished by eliminating all clocking pulses to the monitor. Although this reduces power consumption to below 15 watts, it also requires anywhere from 15 to 30 seconds to restore a usable display.

A typical LCD monitor, in contrast, uses less than half the electricity that a CRT uses. A 19-inch, 4:3 aspect-ratio flat panel, for example, uses around 33 watts at peak usage and less than 2 watts in DPMS mode. Larger LCDs use more power at peak usage than smaller ones. A 21-inch wide-screen model, for example, might draw approximately 75 watts at peak, but still drop down to less than 2 watts in DPMS mode. Swapping out CRTs with LCDs is a great way to save on your electric bill!

Tech Tip

Power Switch versus DPMS

Turning off the monitor with the power switch is the most basic form of power management. The downside to this is the wear and tear on the CRT. The CRT is the most expensive component of a monitor, and turning it on and off frequently can damage the CRT. When using a non-DPMS monitor or video card, it is best to turn the monitor on once during the day and then turn it off only when you are finished for the day. This on-off cycle must be balanced against the life of the CRT display phosphors. The typical monitor will lose about half its original brightness after roughly 10,000 to 15,000 hours of display time. Leaving the monitor on all the time will bring a noticeable decrease in brightness in just over a year (8766 hours). The only way around this is enabling the DPMS features of the monitor or taking care to turn the monitor off.

■ Video Cards

The video card, or display adapter, handles the video chores within the PC, processing information from the CPU and sending it out to the monitor. The video card is composed of two major pieces: the video RAM and the video processor circuitry. The video RAM stores the video image. On the first video cards, this RAM was good old dynamic RAM (DRAM), just like the RAM on the motherboard. Today's video cards often have better RAM than your system has! The video processing circuitry takes the information on the video RAM and shoots it out to the monitor. While early video processing circuitry was little more than an intermediary between the CPU and the video RAM, modern video processors are more powerful than all but the latest CPUs! It's not at all uncommon to see video cards that need fans to cool their onboard processors (see Figure 15.35).

• **Figure 15.35**   Video card with a cooling fan

The trick to understanding video cards is to appreciate the beginnings and evolution of video. Video output to computers was around long before PCs were created. At the time PCs became popular, video was almost exclusively text-based, meaning that the only image the video card could place on the monitor was one of the 256 ASCII characters. These characters were made up of patterns of pixels that were stored in the system BIOS. When a program wanted to make a character, it talked to DOS or to the BIOS, which stored the image of that character in the video memory. The character then appeared on the screen.

The beauty of text video cards was that they were simple to use and cheap to make. The simplicity was based on the fact that only 256 characters existed, and no color choices were available—just monochrome text (see Figure 15.36).

You could, however, choose to make the character bright, dim, normal, underlined, or blinking. It was easy to position the characters, as space on the screen allowed for only 80 characters per row and 24 rows of characters.

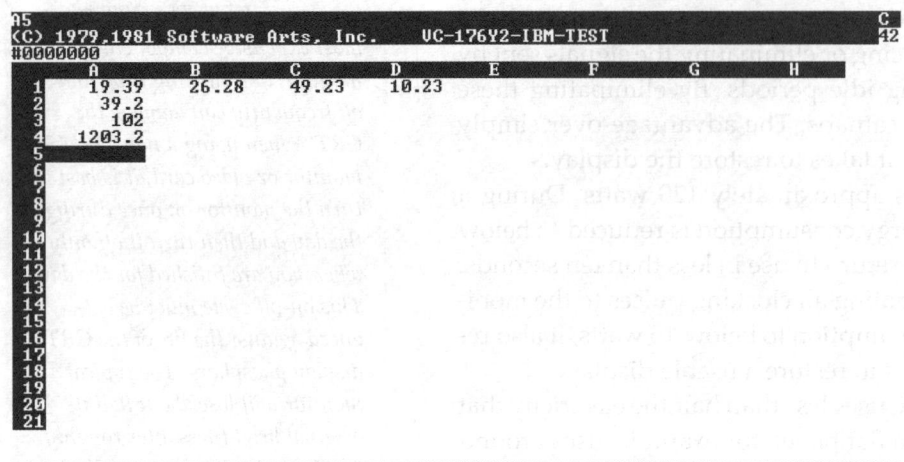

• **Figure 15.36** Text mode

Long ago, RAM was very expensive, so video card makers were interested in using the absolute least amount of RAM possible. Making a monochrome text video card was a great way to keep down RAM costs. Let's consider this for a minute. First, the video RAM is where the contents of the screen are located. You need enough video RAM to hold all the necessary information for a completely full screen. Each ASCII character needs eight bits (by definition), so a monitor with 80 characters/row and 24 rows will need

80 characters × 24 rows = 1920 characters = 15,360 bits or 1920 bytes

The video card would need less than 2000 bytes of memory, which isn't much, not even in 1981 when the PC first came out. Now, be warned that I'm glossing over a few things—where you store the information about underlines, blinking, and so on. The bottom line is that the tiny amount of necessary RAM kept monochrome text video cards cheap.

Very early on in the life of PCs, a new type of video, called a *graphics video card*, was invented. It was quite similar to a text card. The text card, however, was limited to the 256 ASCII characters, whereas a graphics video card enabled programs to turn any pixel on the screen on or off. It was still monochrome, but programs could access any individual pixel, enabling much more creative control of the screen. Of course, it took more video RAM. The first graphics cards ran at 320 × 200 pixels. One bit was needed for each pixel (on or off), so

320 × 200 = 64,000 bits or 8000 bytes

That's a lot more RAM than what was needed for text, but it was still a pretty low amount of RAM—even in the old days. As resolutions increased, however, the amount of video RAM needed to store this information also increased.

Once monochrome video was invented, it was a relatively easy step to move into color for both text and graphics video cards. The only question was how to store color information for each character (text cards) or pixel (graphics cards). This was easy—just set aside a few more bits for each pixel or character. So now the question becomes, "How many bits do you set aside?" Well, that depends on how many colors you want. Basically, the number of colors determines the number of bits. For example, if you wanted four colors, you need two bits (two bits per pixel). Then, you could do something like this

00 = black	01 = cyan (blue)
10 = magenta (reddish pink)	11 = white

So if you set aside two bits, you could get four colors. If you want 16 colors, set aside four bits, which would make 16 different combinations. Nobody ever invented a text mode that used more than 16 colors, so let's start thinking in terms of only graphics mode and bits per pixels. To get 256 colors, each pixel would have to be represented with eight bits. In PCs, the number of colors is always a power of 2: 4, 16, 256, 64 K, and so on. Note that as more colors are added, more video RAM is needed to store the information. Here are the most common color depths and the number of bits necessary to store the color information per pixel:

2 colors = 1 bit (mono)
4 colors = 2 bits
16 colors = 4 bits
256 colors = 8 bits
64 K colors = 16 bits
16.7 million colors = 24 bits

Most technicians won't say, for example, "I set my video card to show over 16 million colors." Instead, they'll say, "I set my color depth to 24 bits." Talk in terms of bits, not colors. It is assumed that you know the number of colors for any color depth.

You can set the color depth for a Windows 2000 or Windows XP computer in the Display Properties applet on the Settings tab (Figure 15.37). If you set up a typical Windows XP computer, you'll notice that Windows offers you 32-bit color quality, which might make you assume you're about to crank out more than 4 billion colors, but that's simply not the case. The 32-bit color setting offers 24-bit color plus an 8-bit alpha channel. An alpha channel controls the opacity of a particular color. By using an alpha channel, Windows can more effectively blend colors to create the effect of semi-transparent images. In Windows XP you see this in the drop shadow under a menu; in Windows Vista almost every screen element can be semi-transparent (Figure 15.38).

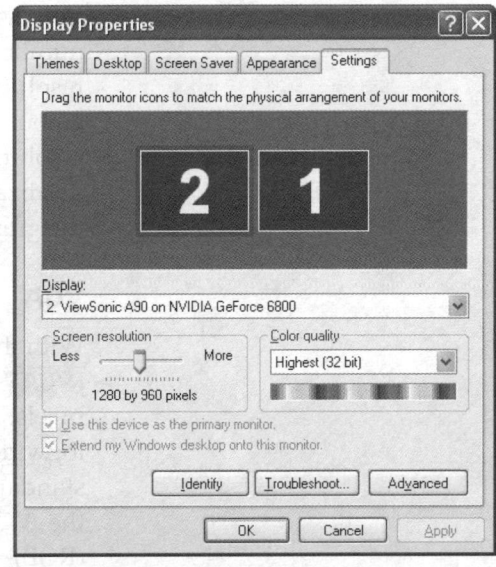

• **Figure 15.37** Adjusting color settings in Windows XP

• **Figure 15.38**   Semi-transparency in Windows Vista

Modes

Your video card and monitor are capable of showing Windows in a fixed number of different resolutions and color depths. The choices depend on the resolutions and color depths the video card can push to the monitor and the amount of bandwidth your monitor can support. Any single combination of resolution and color depth you set for your system is called a *mode*. For standardization, VESA defines a certain number of resolutions, all derived from the granddaddy of video modes: VGA.

VGA

With the introduction of the PS/2, IBM introduced the **video graphics array (VGA)** standard. This standard offered 16 colors at a resolution of 640 × 480 pixels. VGA supported such an amazing variety of colors by using an analog video signal instead of a digital one, as was the case prior to the VGA standard. A digital signal is either all on or all off. By using an analog signal, the VGA standard can provide 64 distinct levels for the three colors (RGB)—that is, 64^3 or 262,144 possible colors—although only 16 or 256 can be seen at a time. For most purposes, 640 × 480 and 16 colors defines VGA mode. This is typically the display resolution and color depth referred to on many software packages as a minimum display requirement. Every video card made in the last 15 years can output as VGA, but VGA-only cards are now obsolete.

Beyond VGA

The 1980s were a strange time for video. Until the very late 1980s, VGA was the highest mode defined by VESA, but demand grew for modes that went beyond VGA. This motivated VESA to introduce (over time) a number of new modes with names such as SVGA, XGA, and many others. Even today, new modes are being released! Table 15.1 shows the more common modes.

Motherboard Connection

Using more color depth slows down video functions. Data moving from the video card to the display has to go through the video card's memory chips and the expansion bus, and this can happen only so quickly. The standard PCI slots used in almost all systems are limited to 32-bit transfers at roughly

Table 15.1	Typical Display Modes		
Video Mode	**Resolution**	**Aspect Ratio**	**Typical Device**
QVGA "Quarter" VGA	320 × 240	4:3	PDAs and small video players
WVGA	800 × 480	5:3	Car navigation systems and ultra mobile PCs
SVGA	800 × 600	4:3	Small monitors
XGA	1024 × 768	4:3	Monitors and portable projectors
WXGA	1280 × 800	16:10	Small widescreen laptops
HDTV 720p	1280 × 720	16:9	Lowest resolution that can be called HDTV
SXGA	1280 × 1024	5:4	Native resolution for many desktop LCD monitors
WSXGA	1440 × 900	16:10	Widescreen laptops
SXGA+	1400 × 1050	4:3	Laptop monitors and high-end projectors
WSXGA+	1680 × 1050	16:10	Large laptops and 20" widescreen monitors
UXGA	1600 × 1200	4:3	Larger CRT monitors
HDTV 1080p	1920 × 1080	16:9	Full HDTV resolution
WUXGA	1920 × 1200	16:10	Big 24" widescreen monitors
WQUXGA	2560 × 1600	16:10	Big 30" widescreen monitors; requires dual-link DVI connector

33 MHz, yielding a maximum bandwidth of 132 MBps. This sounds like a lot until you start using higher resolutions, high color depths, and higher refresh rates.

For example, take a typical display at 800 × 600 with a fairly low refresh of 70 Hz. The 70 Hz means the display screen is being redrawn 70 times per second. If you use a low color depth of 256 colors, which is 8 bits ($2^8 = 256$), you can multiply all the values together to see how much data per second has to be sent to the display:

$$800 \times 600 \times 1 \text{ byte} \times 70 = 33.6 \text{ MBps}$$

If you use the same example at 16 million (24-bit) colors, the figure jumps to 100.8 MBps. You might say, "Well, if PCI runs at 132 MBps, it can handle that!" That statement would be true if the PCI bus had nothing else to do but tend to the video card, but almost every system has more than one PCI device, each requiring part of that throughput. The PCI bus simply cannot handle the needs of many current systems.

• Figure 15.39   AGP

AGP

Intel answered the desire for video bandwidth even higher than PCI with the Accelerated Graphics Port (AGP). AGP is a single, special port, similar to a PCI slot, which is dedicated to video. You will never see a motherboard with two AGP slots. Figure 15.39 shows an early-generation AGP. AGP is derived from the 66-MHz, 32-bit PCI 2.1 specification. AGP uses a function called *strobing* that increases the signals two, four, and eight times for each clock cycle.

Simply describing AGP as a faster PCI would seriously misrepresent the power of AGP. AGP has several technological advantages over PCI, including the bus, internal operations, and the capability to handle 3-D texturing.

First, AGP currently resides alone on its own personal data bus, connected directly to the Northbridge (see Figure 15.40). This is very important because more advanced versions of AGP outperform every bus on the system except the frontside bus!

Second, AGP takes advantage of pipelining commands, similar to the way CPUs pipeline. Third, AGP has a feature called sidebanding—basically a second data bus that enables the video card to send more commands to the Northbridge while receiving other commands at the same time.

☑ **Cross Check**

Multiple Actions per Clock Cycle

You've run into devices in the PC that can handle multiple actions during a single clock cycle, right? Refer back to Chapters 3 and 4 and cross check your memory. Which CPUs can clock double? What advantages does that bring to the PC? Which types of RAM run faster than the system clock? What chip or chips enable the PC to benefit from multi- action CPUs and RAM?

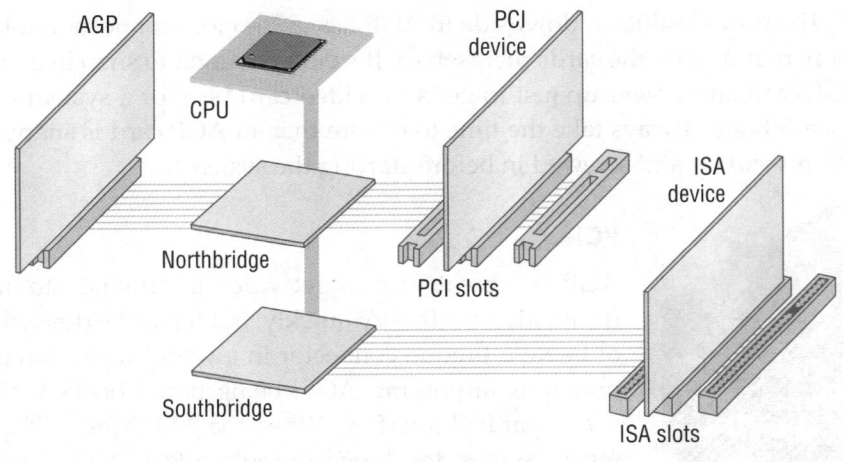

• **Figure 15.40**   An AGP bus

Video cards do all kinds of neat stuff with their RAM; for example, video cards store copies of individual windows so that they can display the windows at different points on the screen very quickly. Demanding applications can quickly max out the onboard RAM on a video card, so AGP provides a pathway so that the AGP card may "steal" chunks of the regular system memory to store video information, especially textures. This is generically called a *system memory access* and is quite popular.

AGP has gone through three sets of specifications (AGP1.0, AGP2.0, and AGP3.0), but the official names tend to be ignored. Most techs and consumers refer to the various cards by their strobe multiplier, such as AGP 1×, 2×, 4×, and 8×. The only problem with blurring the distinctions between the specifications comes from the fact that many new motherboards simply don't support the older AGP cards because the older cards require a different physical connection than the new ones.

Some motherboards support multiple types of AGP. Figure 15.41 shows an AGP slot that accommodates everything up to 8×, even the very rare AGP Pro cards. Note that the tab on the slot covers the extra pins required for AGP Pro.

Because many AGP cards will run on older AGP motherboards, you can get away with mixing AGP specifications. To get the best, most stable performance possible, you should use an AGP card that's fully supported by the motherboard.

Tech Tip

GART and AGP Aperture

Intel couldn't quite bring itself to call AGP's system memory access …err… system memory access, so they use a couple of different terms. The video processor maps out a portion of system memory using the Graphics Address Remapping Table (GART). *The size of the remapped region is called the AGP aperture. A typical AGP aperture is 32 MB or 64 MB.*

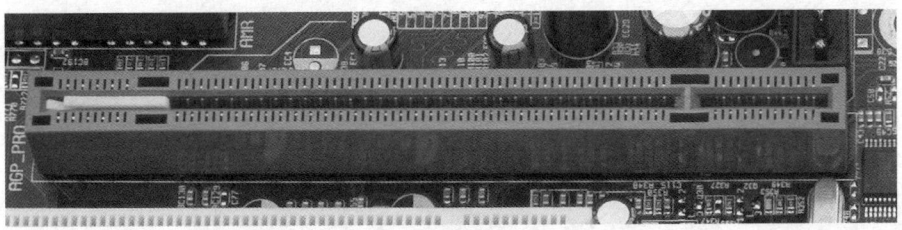

• **Figure 15.41**   AGP 8× slot

The only significant downside to AGP lies in the close connection tolerances required by the cards themselves. It's very common to snap in a new AGP card and power up just to get a no-video-card beep or a system that doesn't boot. Always take the time to ensure that an AGP card is snapped down securely and screwed in before starting the system.

• Figure 15.42   PCIe video card connected in PCIe slot

PCIe

AGP is a great way to get video information to and from video cards very quickly, but it has the downside of being a unique connector in a world where saving money is important. AGP, being based on PCI, also uses a parallel interface. When the **PCI Express (PCIe)** interface was developed to replace PCI, the PCIe designers also worked hard to make sure it would replace AGP too. PCIe is a natural evolution for video as it is incredibly fast, using a serial communication method. Also, because PCIe is a true expansion bus designed to talk to the CPU and RAM, it also supports all the little extras found in AGP such as sidebanding and system memory access. All PCIe video cards use the PCIe ×16 connector (Figure 15.42).

Chapter 15 Review

■ Chapter Summary

After reading this chapter and completing the exercises, you should understand the following about video.

Video Displays

- The term *video* encompasses a complex interaction among numerous parts of the PC, all designed to put a picture on the screen. The monitor shows you what's going on with your programs and operating system. It's the primary output device for the PC. The video card or display adapter handles all of the communication between the CPU and the monitor. Video displays come in three varieties: CRT, LCD, and projectors.

- CRT monitors have a tube that contains three electron guns at the slender end and a display screen coated with phosphor at the wide end. The speed of the electron beam across the screen is the horizontal refresh rate (HRR), more commonly referred to as the refresh rate. The vertical refresh rate (VRR) is the time it takes to draw the entire screen and return the electron guns to the upper-left corner.

- Monitors do not determine the HRR or VRR. The video card "pushes" the monitor at a certain VRR that, in turn, determines the HRR. Setting the VRR too low results in screen flicker, which causes headaches and eyestrain. Setting the VRR too high results in image distortion and damage to the monitor's circuitry. The monitor's bandwidth dictates the maximum VRR.

- A monitor is a grid of red, green, and blue light-sensitive dots called phosphors. Normal CRT monitors have three electron guns that fire electrons of different intensities (not color) at the colored phosphors. A shadow mask ensures that the electrons from any of the three guns hit only their own colored phosphors. The area of phosphors lit at one instant is a pixel and must consist of at least one red, one green, and one blue phosphor; therefore, the smallest pixel, a triad, would consist of three phosphors.

- Resolution is the number of horizontal pixels times the number of vertical pixels. A resolution of 640 × 480 means 640 pixels across and 480 pixels down,

for a total of 307,200 pixels total. Many monitors have a resolution that matches a 4:3 aspect ratio. Widescreen monitors have an aspect ratio of 16:9 or 16:10.

- Dot pitch, measured in millimeters (mm), defines the diagonal distance between phosphorous dots of the same color.

- Liquid crystal displays are the most common type of display for PCs. They offer many advantages over CRTs. An LCD monitor is thinner and lighter, uses less power, is virtually flicker free, and does not emit potentially harmful radiation.

- An LCD screen is composed of tiny liquid crystal molecules called sub-pixels. Although dual-scan passive matrix may still be found on some low-end LCD panels, most of today's LCD panels use active matrix or thin film transistor (TFT) technology.

- The typical LCD projector is composed of the LCD panel, backlights, and inverters. The backlights require AC power, but the electronics require DC. The AC/DC transformer changes the AC wall current into DC that the LCD panel can use. All LCD backlights use cold cathode fluorescent lamp (CCFL) technology. CCFLs require AC power, so inverters convert the DC back to AC.

- LCD monitors, unlike CRTs, have a native resolution and a fixed pixel size. LCDs cannot run at a resolution higher than their native resolution, and running a lower resolution results in degraded image quality. Anti-aliasing softens the edges of jagged pixel corners when running at lower resolutions, but because the image quality degrades, you should use the native resolution.

- An LCD monitor's brightness is determined by its backlights and is measured in nits. An average LCD measures around 300 nits, with higher numbers being brighter and better.

- The time it takes for sub-pixels to go from pure black to pure white and back again is the LCD's response rate. Response rate is measured in milliseconds, with lower numbers being faster and better. An excellent LCD monitor will have a response rate somewhere between 6–8 ms.

- LCD monitors lack the color saturation and contrast of a CRT, making CRT the choice for graphic artists. Look for an LCD monitor with a contrast ratio of 450:1 or higher.

- Projectors come in two main varieties: rear-view and front-view. Rear-view projectors shoot an image onto a screen from the back and are almost always self enclosed. They are a popular choice for televisions, but not for PCs. Front-view projectors shoot an image from the front and are widely used during computer presentations.

- LCD projectors, like LCD monitors, have a native resolution and are lightweight, but lack the image quality of a CRT. Projector brightness is measured in lumens. Larger numbers are brighter and better, with 1500 lumens being sufficient for a small dark room. The size of the projected image at a certain distance from the screen is the projector's *throw*. LCD projectors come with internal fans, which cool the lamp. Lamps are very costly to replace and are considered consumable (meaning you can expect to replace them periodically).

- Measured from two opposite diagonal corners, size for CRT monitors is not usually the same as the viewable image size. A 17-inch CRT monitor might have only a 15.5-inch VIS. Because LCD monitors report only VIS, a 15-inch LCD monitor may have approximately the same viewing area as a 17-inch CRT.

- CRT monitors require two connectors: a 15-pin, 3-row DB connector and a power plug. Video cards use a RAMDAC that takes the digital signal from the video card and turns it into an analog signal for the CRT. LCD monitors require a digital signal. Analog LCD monitors reverse the effects of the RAMDAC and allow you to plug your LCD monitor into the 15-pin VGA connector on the video card.

- The DVI standard enables an LCD monitor to use the digital signal from a PC without any digital-to-analog-and-back-to-digital conversion. The DVI standard includes DVI-D, DVI-A, and DVI-I. DVI-D and DVI-I come in single-link and dual-link varieties, with dual-link offering significantly higher resolutions.

- Monitors have adjustment controls for brightness, contrast, image size and position, and color adjustment. These controls are usually accessed via an onboard menu system rather than hardware knobs or dials.

- A CRT monitor accounts for about half of the power consumption of a desktop PC. Monitors using the VESA specification for display power-management signaling can cut monitor power consumption by about 75 percent. An LCD monitor uses less than half the electricity that a CRT uses.

Video Cards

- The video card has two major pieces: the video RAM and the video processing circuitry. The video RAM stores the video image; the processing circuitry is similar to that of your computer's CPU.

- The combination of a specific resolution and color depth is referred to as a mode. The VGA mode is defined by a resolution of 640 × 480 and 4-bit color depth (16 colors). Modern video cards and monitors are capable of supporting many modes.

- Using more color depth slows down video functions. PCI slots maxed out at a bandwidth of 132 MBps. The Accelerated Graphics Port (AGP) is better suited for video than PCI because it resides alone on its own bus, pipelines commands, and supports sidebanding and system memory access.

- AGP cards are normally referred to by their strobe multiplier. Although you can mix some AGP specifications, it is best to use an AGP card that is fully supported by your motherboard. Make sure AGP cards are properly and fully inserted in the AGP port, as they require a close connection between card and port.

- PCI Express video cards are becoming more popular and may soon replace AGP on all new systems. Like AGP, PCIe supports sidebanding and system memory access; however, PCIe uses a faster serial communication method than AGP's parallel communication method.

Key Terms

Accelerated Graphics Port (AGP) *(486)*

active matrix *(473)*

anti-aliasing *(475)*

aspect ratio *(468)*

backlights *(473)*

bandwidth *(469)*

cathode ray tube (CRT) *(465)*

cold cathode fluorescent lighting (CCFL) *(474)*

digital video interface (DVI) *(479)*

display adapter *(464)*

display power-management signaling (DPMS) *(481)*

dot pitch *(469)*

dual-scan passive matrix *(472)*

front-view projector *(476)*

horizontal refresh rate (HRR) *(466)*

inverter *(474)*

liquid crystal display (LCD) *(470)*

lumen *(477)*

monitor *(464)*

native resolution *(475)*

nit *(475)*

passive matrix *(472)*

PCI Express (PCIe) *(488)*

persistence *(466)*

phosphors *(467)*

pixel *(468)*

projector *(476)*

random access memory digital-to-analog converter (RAMDAC) *(478)*

raster lines *(466)*

rear-view projector *(476)*

resolution *(468)*

response rate *(475)*

shadow mask *(468)*

sidebanding *(486)*

sub-pixels *(471)*

thin film transistor (TFT) *(473)*

throw *(477)*

triad *(468)*

vertical refresh rate (VRR) *(466)*

video display *(464)*

video graphics array (VGA) *(484)*

viewable image size (VIS) *(478)*

Key Term Quiz

Use the Key Terms list to complete the sentences that follow. Not all terms will be used.

1. Perhaps the most important value of a CRT monitor, _____ defines the maximum number of times the electron gun can turn on and off per second.

2. On a CRT screen, a(n) _____ consists of one red, one green, and one blue phosphor; in theory, the smallest pixel a monitor can display.

3. Using an aspect ratio of 4:3, the _____ refers to the number of horizontal pixels times the number of vertical pixels.

4. The _____ bus, designed specifically for video cards, connects directly to the Northbridge, but is being phased out in favor of the _____ bus.

5. The number of sweeps or raster lines that the electron guns make across the screen is called the _____; the time it takes to draw the entire screen is called the _____.

6. Measured in millimeters, where the lower the number means the clearer the picture, _____ is the diagonal distance between phosphors of the same color.

7. The size of a projected image at a specific distance from the screen is defined as the projector's _____.

8. The phosphors in a CRT continue to glow after being struck by the electron beam because of their _____.

9. The _____ ensures that only the proper electron beam lights the intended color phosphor, without bleeding over to the other color phosphors.

10. The _____ converts the digital signal from the video card to an analog signal for the CRT.

Multiple-Choice Quiz

1. Which of the following resolutions will produce the best quality picture on the monitor (assuming the monitor is capable of displaying the resolutions well)?

   A. 640 × 480

   B. 800 × 600

   C. 1024 × 768

   D. 1280 × 1024

2. CRT monitors attach to the video card using a _____ connector.

   A. 9-pin, 2-row, DB

   B. 36-pin Centronics

   C. 15-pin, 3-row, DB

   D. 25-pin, 2-row, DB

3. Which of these dot pitch numbers indicates a better quality monitor?

   A. .39

   B. .31

   C. .28

   D. .23

4. Which of the following statements best describes the electron guns in a CRT monitor?

   A. A single gun shoots electrons at the phosphors on the screen.

   B. Three electron guns, one each for red, green, and blue phosphors, paint the screen.

   C. The electron guns stay on all the time to shoot electrons that produce the solid image on the screen.

   D. One electron gun shoots red phosphors, another shoots green phosphors, and the third shoots blue phosphors at the screen.

5. What advantages do LCD monitors offer over CRT monitors?

   A. Better color and more contrast

   B. Energy efficiency and no emission of potentially harmful radiation

   C. Electron guns fire CMYK instead of RGB

   D. Both A and B

6. Which projector will produce the brightest image?

   A. One with the longest throw lens

   B. One with the largest lamp

   C. One with the largest degaussing coil

   D. One with the highest lumen rating

7. Which statement best describes pixels?

   A. Pixels consist of exactly one red, one green, and one blue phosphor.

   B. Pixels on a CRT are always the same size.

   C. Higher resolutions result in more pixels per row.

   D. LCDs don't use pixels.

8. A user wishes to display millions of colors. What is the minimum color depth they must set in their adapter settings?

   A. 4-bit

   B. 8-bit

   C. 16-bit

   D. 24-bit

9. The same user calls back almost immediately and complains that the icons and screen elements are bigger, but now everything is fuzzy. What's most likely the problem?

   A. She has an LCD and set the resolution lower than the native resolution.

   B. She has an LCD and set the resolution higher than the native resolution.

   C. She has a CRT and set the resolution lower than the native resolution.

   D. She has a CRT and set the resolution higher than the native resolution.

10. Why should you never work on the inside of a CRT?

    A. The phosphors are sticky and difficult to clean from your fingers.

    B. You risk cracking the glass.

    C. It requires a specialized screwdriver that most computers techs don't own.

    D. You can be electrocuted.

11. What benefit do perfect flat CRT screens offer that traditional CRTs do not?

   A. They have a wider viewing angle.

   B. They are able to represent blacker blacks and whiter whites for better contrast.

   C. They use 40 percent less power.

   D. They do not emit potential harmful radiation.

12. What is true about HRR and VRR?

   A. Both the HRR and VRR are determined by the monitor.

   B. Both the HRR and VRR are determined by the video card.

   C. The video card is configured for a certain VRR and then the monitor determines the appropriate HRR.

   D. The video card is configured for a certain HRR and then the monitor determines the appropriate VRR.

13. What is the aspect ratio of most wide-screen monitors?

   A. 4:3

   B. 16:9

   C. 800 × 600

   D. 1900 × 1200

14. What would produce the best picture?

   A. Low dot pitch, low contrast, low resolution

   B. High dot pitch, high contrast, high resolution

   C. Low dot pitch, high contrast, high resolution

   D. High dot pitch, low contrast, low resolution

15. What is true about the brightness of a projector?

   A. Higher lumens are always better.

   B. Lower lumens are always better.

   C. Projectors rated at 1000–1500 lumens outperform those rated at 1500–2000 lumens

   D. The larger the room, the more lumens you need.

■ Essay Quiz

1. Your company is getting ready to replace all their computers and monitors. Write a memo to your boss that discusses the advantages and disadvantages of LCD monitors versus CRT monitors. Then make a recommendation of which type of monitor your company should purchase.

2. William's new PC supports a variety of screen resolutions and color depths. William is unfamiliar with the settings and how they relate to his video card's memory. Explain to him the relationship between resolution, color depth, and video RAM, using an example of 800 × 600 resolution and millions of colors.

Lab Projects

• Lab Project 15.1

If you just got a $500 bonus and decided to buy a new video system for your computer, what would you select? Go to the local computer store or to Web sites such as www.newegg.com and pick out the best combination of monitor and video card that you can buy with your bonus. Now imagine that you also received a $200 birthday gift and have decided to purchase an even better graphics card and monitor. Which ones will you select now that you have $700 to spend?

Portable Computing

"The great thing about a computer notebook is that no matter how much you stuff into it, it doesn't get bigger or heavier."

—BILL GATES, *BUSINESS @ THE SPEED OF THOUGHT*

In this chapter, you will learn how to

- **Describe the many types of portable computing devices available**
- **Enhance and upgrade portable computers**
- **Manage and maintain portable computers**
- **Troubleshoot portable computers**

There are times when the walls close in, when you need a change of scenery to get that elusive spark that inspires greatness...or sometimes you just need to get away from your coworkers for a few hours because they're driving you nuts! For many occupations, that's difficult to do. You've got to have access to your documents and spreadsheets; you can't function without e-mail or the Internet. In short, you need a computer to get your job done.

Portable computing devices combine mobility with accessibility to bring you the best of both worlds; put more simply, portables let you take some or even all of your computing abilities with you when you go. Some portable computers feature Windows XP systems with all the bells and whistles and all your Microsoft Office apps for a seamless transition from desk to café table. Even the smallest portable devices enable you to check your appointments and address book, or play Solitaire during the endless wait at the doctor's office. This chapter takes an in-depth look at portables, first going through the major variations you'll run into and then hitting the tech-specific topics of enhancing, upgrading, managing, and maintaining portable computers. Let's get started!

Essentials

■ Portable Computing Devices

All portable devices share certain features. For output, they have LCD screens, although these vary from 20-inch behemoths to microscopic 2-inch screens. Portable computing devices employ sound of varying quality, from simple beeps to fairly nice music reproductions. All of them run on DC electricity stored in batteries, although several different technologies offer a range of battery life, lifespan, and cost. Other than screen, sound, and battery, portable computing devices come in an amazing variety of shapes, sizes, and intended uses.

 If you look at the CompTIA A+ exam objectives for the Essentials, IT Technician, and Depot Technician exams, you'll notice that the objectives covered in this chapter are, for all intents and purposes, virtually the same for each exam. CompTIA has not differentiated the questions for each exam covered by this domain, so we have used the same chapter for the Essentials and IT Technician exams.

LCD Screens

Laptops come in a variety of sizes and at varying costs. One major contributor to the overall cost of a laptop is the size of the LCD screen. Most laptops offer a range between 12-inch to 17-inch screens (measured diagonally), while a few offer just over 20-inch screens. Not only are screens getting larger, but also wider screens are becoming the status quo. Many manufacturers are phasing out the standard 4:3 aspect ratio screen in favor of the widescreen format. Aspect ratio is the comparison of the screen width to the screen height. Depending on screen resolution, widescreens can have varying aspect ratios of 10:6, 16:9, 16:9.5, or 16:10. The 16:9 aspect ratio is the standard for widescreen movies while 16:10 is the standard for 17-inch LCD screens.

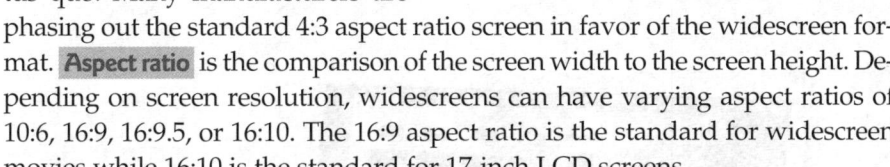

Cross Check

LCD Monitors

Stretching back to the early days of mobile computing, almost every make and model of portable device has used an LCD monitor of some shape or size. You know all about LCD monitors from Chapter 15, "Understanding Video." Everything that applies to desktop LCDs applies to screens designed for portable devices as well, so turn to Chapter 15 and cross check your knowledge. What are the variations of LCD screen you'll find today? Which technology offers the best picture? What connectors do you find with LCDs?

 Note that this chapter does not have an Historical/Conceptual section. Everything in here is on the CompTIA A+ certification exams, so pay attention!

Laptop LCD screens come in a variety of supported resolutions, described with acronyms such as XGA, WXGA, WSXGA, and more. The *W* in front of the letters indicates widescreen. Table 16.1 lists commonly supported laptop display resolutions.

Table 16.1	Screen Resolutions	
Acronym	**Name**	**Native Resolution**
XGA	eXtended Graphics Array	1024 × 768
SXGA	Super eXtended Graphics Array	1280 × 1024
SXGA+	Super eXtended Graphics Array Plus	1400 × 1050
WSXGA+	Widescreen SXGA Plus	1680 × 1050
UXGA	Ultra eXtended Graphics Array	1600 × 1200
WUXGA	Widescreen UXGA	1920 × 1200

Laptop screens come with two types of finish: matte and high gloss . The matte finish was the industry standard for many years and offers a good trade-off between richness of colors and reflection or glare. The better screens have a wide viewing angle and decent response time. The major drawback for matte-finished laptop screens is that they wash out a lot in bright light. Using such a laptop at an outdoor café, for example, is almost hopeless during daylight.

Manufacturers released high-gloss laptop screens in 2006, and they've rapidly taken over many store shelves. The high-gloss finish offers sharper contrast, richer colors, and wider viewing angles when compared to the matte screens. Each manufacturer has a different name for high-gloss coatings. Dell calls theirs TrueLife; Acer calls theirs CrystalBrite; and HP calls theirs BrightView. The drawback to the high-gloss screens is that, contrary to what the manufacturers' claim, they pick up lots of reflection from nearby objects, including the user! So while they're usable outside during the day, you'll need to contend with increased reflection as well.

Desktop Replacements

When asked about portable computing devices, most folks describe the traditional clamshell laptop computer, such as the one in Figure 16.1, with built-in LCD monitor, keyboard, and input device (a *touchpad*, in this case). A typical laptop computer functions as a fully standalone PC, potentially even replacing the desktop. The one in Figure 16.1, for example, has all of the features you expect the modern PC to have, such as a fast CPU, lots of RAM, a high-capacity hard drive, CD-RW and DVD drives, an excellent sound system, and a functioning copy of Windows XP. Attach it to a

Tech Tip

What's in a Name?

There's no industry standard naming for the vast majority of styles of portable computing devices, so manufacturers let their marketing folks have fun with naming. What's the difference between a portable, a laptop, and a notebook? Nothing. One manufacturer might call its four-pound portable system with 12-inch LCD a notebook, while another manufacturer might call its much larger desktop-replacement portable a notebook as well. A laptop refers in general to the clamshell, keyboard-on-the-bottom and LCD-screen-at-the-top design that is considered the shape of mobile PCs.

• **Figure 16.1** A notebook PC

network and you can browse the Internet and send e-mail. Considering it weighs almost as much as a mini-tower PC (or at least it feels like it does when I'm lugging it through the airport!), such a portable can be considered a desktop replacement, because it does everything that most people want to do with a desktop PC and doesn't compromise performance just to make the laptop a few pounds lighter or the battery last an extra hour.

For input devices, desktop replacements (and other portables) used trackballs in the early days, often plugged in like a mouse and clipped to the side of the case. Other models with trackballs placed them in front of the keyboard at the edge of the case nearest the user, or behind the keyboard at the edge nearest the screen.

The next wave to hit the laptop market was IBM's TrackPoint device, a pencil eraser–sized joystick situated in the center of the keyboard. The TrackPoint enables you to move the pointer around without taking your fingers away from the "home" typing position. You use a forefinger to push the joystick around, and click or right-click using two buttons below the spacebar. This type of pointing device has since been licensed for use by other manufacturers, and it continues to appear on laptops today.

But by far the most common laptop pointing device found today is the touchpad (Figure 16.2)—a flat, touch-sensitive pad just in front of the keyboard. To operate a touchpad, you simply glide your finger across its surface to move the pointer, and tap the surface once or twice to single- or double-click. You can also click using buttons just below the pad. Most people get the hang of this technique after just a few minutes of practice. The main advantage of the touchpad over previous laptop pointing devices is that it uses no moving parts—a fact that can really extend the life of a hard-working laptop. Some modern laptops actually provide both a TrackPoint-type device and a touchpad, to give the user a choice.

● **Figure 16.2**   Touchpad on a laptop

Desktop Extenders

Manufacturers offer desktop extender portable devices that don't replace the desktop, but rather extend it by giving you a subset of features of the typical desktop that you can take away from the desk. Figure 16.3 shows a portable with a good but small 13.3-inch-wide screen. The system has 512 MB of RAM, a 2-GHz processor, a 60-GB hard drive, and a battery that enables you to do work on it for more than five hours while disconnected from the wall socket. Even though it plays music and has a couple of decent, tiny speakers, you can't game on this

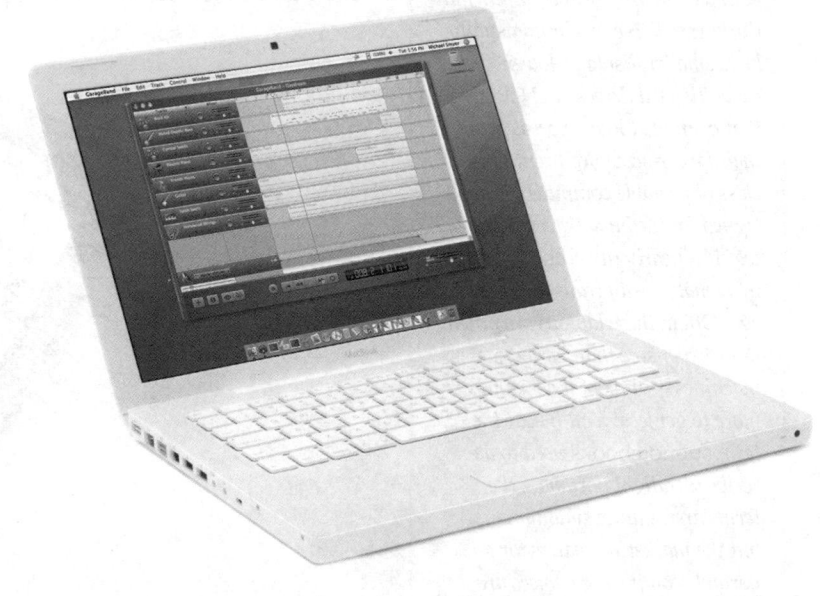

● **Figure 16.3**   Excellent mid-sized portable computer

Tech Tip

Spin the Weight

Manufacturers advertise the weight of portable PCs, for the most part, without the weight of the battery or the removable drives. Although this deception is deplorable, it's pretty much universal in the industry because no manufacturer wants to be the first to say that their desktop-replacement portable, including battery and DVD-RW drive, weighs 15 pounds when their competitor advertises the same kind of machine at 7.5 pounds! They'd lose market share quickly.

When you shop or recommend portable PCs, take the real weight into consideration. By the time you fill your laptop bag with a power adapter, an external mouse, a spare battery, and all the extra accessories, you'll definitely be carrying more than the advertised 5–6 pounds.

Tech Tip

Ultralights

Ultralight portables are computers that normally weigh less than three pounds and are less than an inch in thickness. These machines usually have smaller displays, lower-capacity hard drives, and CPUs that operate at lower speeds than their larger-sized brethren. This class of portable computers is designed for the busy traveler who wants a nearly full-featured laptop in a small, easily transported package. Often, these laptops are much more expensive than larger, faster machines—think of it as paying more to get less! You'll hear the term subnotebooks used to describe ultralight portables; the terms aren't quite synonymous, but the marketing waters for all portable computing devices are pretty muddy.

computer (Solitaire, perhaps, but definitely not Half-Life 2!). But it weighs only five pounds, nearly half the weight of the typical desktop replacement portable.

Desktop extenders enable you to go mobile. When I'm on a roll writing, for example, I don't want to stop. But sometimes I do want to take a break from the office and stroll over to my favorite café for a latté or a pint of fine ale. At moments like these, I don't need a fully featured laptop with a monster 15-inch or 17-inch screen, but just a good word processing system—and perhaps the ability to surf the Internet on the café's wireless network so I can research other important topics once I finish my project for the day. A lightweight laptop with a 12-inch or 13-inch screen, a reasonably fast processor, and gobs of RAM does nicely.

PDAs

Having a few computing essentials on hand at all times eases the day and makes planning and scheduling much more likely to succeed. Several companies, such as Palm, Sony, Toshiba, Hewlett-Packard, Dell, and Microsoft, manufacture tiny handheld portable computing devices that hold data such as your address book, personal notes, appointment schedules, and more. Such machines are called **personal digital assistants (PDAs)**. All modern PDAs have many applications, such as word processors for jotting down notes or shopping lists, expense reports, and even image viewers. Figure 16.4 shows a Palm Zire 71 PDA.

PDAs don't run Windows XP or even 98, but rather require specialized OSs such as Windows CE, PocketPC, PalmOS, and Linux. All of these OSs provide a GUI that enables you to interact with the device by touching the screen directly. Many of today's PDAs use handwriting recognition combined with modified mouse functions, usually in the form of a pen-like **stylus** to make a type of input called **pen-based computing**. To make an application load, for example, you would slide the stylus out of its holder in the PDA case and touch the appropriate icon with the stylus tip.

• **Figure 16.4**   Palm Zire 71 displaying a to-do list

HotSync

PDAs make excellent pocket companions because you can quickly add a client's address or telephone number, check the day's schedule before going to your next meeting, and modify your calendar entries when something unexpected arises. Best of all, you can then update all the equivalent features on your desktop PC automatically! PDAs synchronize with your primary PC so you have the same essential data on both machines. Many PDAs come with a cradle, a place to rest your PDA and recharge its battery. The cradle connects to the PC most often through a USB port. You can run special software to synchronize the data between the PDA and the main PC. Setting up the Zire 71 featured previously, for example, requires you to install a portion of the Palm desktop for Windows. This software handles all the synchronization chores. You simply place the PDA in the properly connected cradle and click the button to synchronize. Figure 16.5 shows a PDA in the middle of a HotSync operation, PalmOS's term for the process of synchronizing.

• **Figure 16.5**   HotSync in progress

Beaming

Just about every PDA comes with an infrared port that enables you to transfer data from one PDA to another, a process called beaming . For example, you can readily exchange business information when at a conference or swap pictures that you carry around in your PDA. The process is usually as simple as clicking a drop-down list and selecting Beam or Beaming from the menu. The PDA searches the nearby area—infrared has a very limited range—to discover any PDA nearby. The receiving PDA flashes a message to its owner asking permission to receive. Once that's granted, you simply stand there and wait for a moment while the PDAs transfer data. Slick!

PDA Memory

Almost every PDA has both internal flash ROM memory of 1 MB or more, and some sort of removable and upgradeable storage medium. Secure Digital (SD) technology has the strongest market share among the many competing standards, but you'll find a bunch of different memory card types out there. SD cards come in a variety of physical sizes (SD, Mini SD, and Micro SD) and fit in a special SD slot. Other popular media include CompactFlash (CF) cards and Sony's proprietary Memory Stick. You'll find capacities for all the standards ranging from 128 MB up to 8 GB—on a card the size of a postage stamp! Figure 16.6 shows some typical memory cards.

> ### Tech Tip
>
> #### Memory Cards
>
> *Memory cards of all stripes made the leap in 2003 from the exclusive realm of tiny devices such as PDAs and digital photographic cameras to full-featured portable PCs and even desktop models. Some Panasonic PCs sport SD card slots, for example, and you can expect nearly every Sony PC—portable or otherwise—made in 2003 and later to offer a Memory Stick port.*

• **Figure 16.6**   SD, Mini SD, and Micro SD *(photos courtesy of SanDisk)*

Tablet PCs

Tablet PCs combine the handwriting benefits of PDAs with the full-fledged power of a traditional portable PC to create a machine that perfectly meets the needs of many professions. Unlike PDAs, tablet PCs use a full-featured PC operating system such as Microsoft Windows XP Tablet PC Edition 2005. Instead of (or in addition to) a keyboard and mouse, tablet PCs provide a screen that doubles as an input device. With a special pen, called a *stylus*, you can actually write on the screen (Figure 16.7). Just make sure you don't grab your fancy Cross ball-point pen accidentally and start writing on the screen! Unlike many PDA screens, most tablet PC screens are not pressure sensitive—you have to use the stylus to write on the screen. Tablet PCs come in two main form factors: *convertibles*, which include a keyboard that can be folded out of the way, and *slates*, which do away with the keyboard entirely. The convertible tablet PC in Figure 16.7, for example, looks and functions just like the typical clamshell laptop shown back in Figure 16.1. But here it's shown with the screen rotated 180 degrees and snapped flat so it functions as a slate. Pretty slick!

In applications that aren't "tablet-aware," the stylus acts just like a mouse, enabling you to select items, double-click, right-click, and so on. To input text with the stylus, you can either tap keys on a virtual keyboard (shown in Figure 16.8), write in the writing utility (shown in Figure 16.9), or use speech recognition software. With a little practice, most users will find the computer's accuracy in recognizing their handwriting to be sufficient for most text input, although speedy touch-typists will probably still want to use a keyboard when typing longer documents.

Tablet PCs work well when you have limited space or have to walk around and use a laptop. Anyone who has ever tried to type with one hand, while walking around the factory floor holding the laptop with the other hand, will immediately appreciate the beauty of a tablet PC. In this scenario, tablet PCs are most effective when combined with applications designed to

Tech Tip

Power Corrupts, but in This Case, It's Good

Handwriting recognition and speech recognition are two technologies that benefit greatly from increased CPU power. As multicore CPUs become more common, get ready to see more widespread adoption of these technologies!

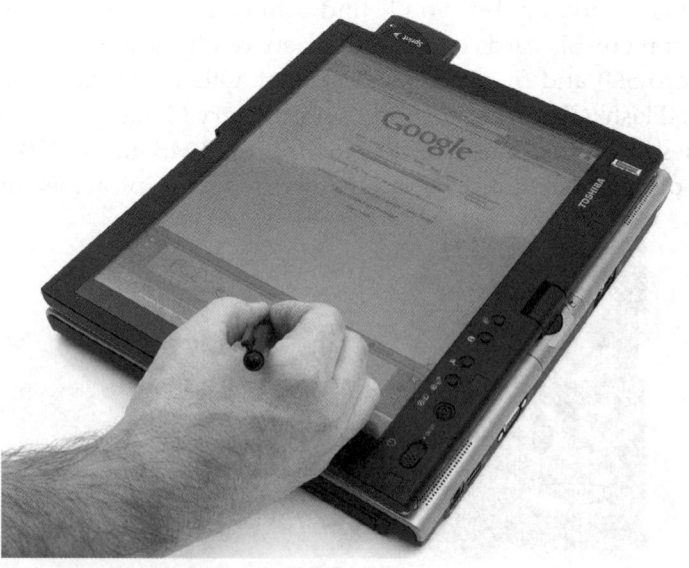

• **Figure 16.7**   A tablet PC

The quick brown fox j

● **Figure 16.8** The virtual keyboard

be used with a stylus instead of a keyboard. An inventory control program, for example, might present drop-down lists and radio buttons to the user, making a stylus the perfect input tool. With the right custom application, tablet PCs become an indispensable tool.

Microsoft encourages software developers to take advantage of a feature they call *digital ink,* which allows applications to accept pen strokes as input without first converting the pen strokes into text or mouse-clicks. Microsoft Journal (Figure 16.10), which comes with Windows-based tablet PCs, allows you to write on the screen just as though you were writing on a

● **Figure 16.9** The writing pad

paper legal pad. Many other applications, including Microsoft Office, allow users to add ink annotations. Imagine sitting on an airplane reviewing a Microsoft Word document and simply scribbling your comments on the screen (Figure 16.11). No more printing out hard copy and breaking out the red pen for me! Imagine running a PowerPoint presentation and being able to annotate your presentation as you go. In the future, look for more applications to support Microsoft's digital ink.

There are many useful third-party applications designed specifically to take advantage of the tablet PC form factor. In fields such as law and medicine where tablet PCs have been especially popular, the choices are endless. One handy free utility that anyone who spends time in front of an audience

● **Figure 16.10** Microsoft Journal preserves pen strokes as digital ink.

(teachers, salespeople, cult leaders, and so on) will appreciate is InkyBoard (http://www.cfcassidy.com/Inkyboard/). Inkyboard provides a virtual dry-erase board, eliminating the need to find a flip chart or dry-erase board when holding meetings. Ever wished you could have a record of everything that was written on the chalkboard in a class (or at a business meeting)? If the professor had used Inkyboard, creating and distributing a copy would be a snap.

Portable Computer Device Types

Sorting through all the variations of portable computing devices out there would take entirely too much ink (and go well beyond CompTIA A+). Table 16.2 lists the seven most common styles of portable computing devices, some of their key features, and the intended use or audience for the product. This table is in no way conclusive, but lists the highlights.

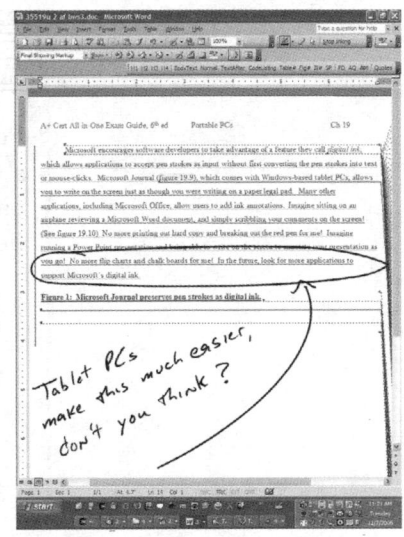

• **Figure 16.11**   Microsoft Office supports digital ink.

Table 16.2	Portable Computing Devices			
	Screen Size	**Weight**	**Features**	**Uses**
Desktop replacements	14–20 inch+	8–12+ lbs	Everything on a desktop	Mobile multimedia editing, presentations, mobile gaming
Desktop extenders	10–14 inch	4–7 lbs	Almost everything you'll find on a desktop; better battery life than desktop replacements	Presentations, note-taking in class or meetings, traveling companion for business folks
Ultralights	6–12 inch	2–3 lbs	Ultimate mobility without sacrificing full PC status; excellent battery life; few have internal optical drives	Long-term traveling companion, in the purse or pack for writing or doing e-mail on the road, coolness factor
Tablet PCs	10–12 inch	4 lbs	Pen-based interface enables you to use them like a paper notepad; no optical drives, but integrated wireless networking	Niche market for people who need handwritten notes that have to be transcribed to the PC
Ultra-Mobile PCs	4–7 inch	1–2 lbs	A variation of tablet PCs, UMPCs run Windows XP (Tablet or Home edition); pen-based interface and no optical drives	More of a niche market than tablet PCs, but similar audience; see the "Beyond A+" section for details
PDAs	3–4 inch	1 lbs	Light, multifunction devices that carry address book and scheduler; many offer other features, such as MP3 and video playback	Helps busy people get/stay organized, fun, can carry many electronic books (e-books) so you're never caught waiting in line and being bored
PDA phones	2 inch	< 1 lbs	Tiny PDA built into a cell phone; some offer e-mail and other Internet connectivity	Reduces the number of gadgets some folks carry

Try This!

Variations

Portables come in such a dizzying variety of sizes, styles, features, and shapes that a simple table in a book cannot do justice to the ingenuity and engineering of the manufacturers of these devices. Only a hands-on field trip can bring home the point for you, so try this!

1. Visit your local computer or electronics store and tour the portable computing devices.

2. How many variations of laptops are there? Do any offer funky features, such as a swivel screen or a portrait-to-landscape mode?

3. How many variations of PDA are displayed? What operating systems do they run?

4. What other devices do you find? What about tablet PCs?

5. If you want to wander into the realm of extremes, check out www.dynamism.com. This company specializes in bringing Japanese-only products to the English-speaking market. You'll find the hottest desktop replacement laptops and the sleekest subnotebooks at the site, with all the details beautifully converted from native Japanese to English.

■ Enhance and Upgrade the Portable PC

In the dark ages of mobile computing, you had to shell out top dollar for any device that would unplug, and what you purchased was what you got. Upgrade a laptop? Add functions to your desktop replacement? You had few if any options, so you simply paid for a device that would be way behind the technology curve within a year and functionally obsolete within two.

Portable PCs today offer many ways to enhance their capabilities. Internal and external expansion buses enable you to add completely new functions to portables, such as attaching a scanner or mobile printer or both! You can take advantage of the latest wireless technology breakthrough simply by slipping a card into the appropriate slot on the laptop. Further, modern portables offer a modular interior. You can add or change RAM, for example— the first upgrade that almost every laptop owner wants to make. You can increase the hard drive storage space and, at least with some models, swap out the CPU, video card, sound card, and more. Gone forever are the days of buying guaranteed obsolescence! Let's look at four specific areas of technology that laptops use to enhance functions and upgrade components: PC Cards, single- and multiple-function expansion ports, and modular components.

PC Cards

The *Personal Computer Memory Card International Association (PCMCIA)* establishes standards involving portable computers, especially when it comes to expansion cards, which are generically called PC Cards. **PC Cards** are roughly credit card–sized devices that enhance and extend the functions of a portable PC. PC Cards are as standard on today's mobile computers as the hard drive. PC Cards are easy to use, inexpensive, and convenient. Figure 16.12 shows a typical PC Card.

Almost every portable PC has one or two PC Card slots, into which you insert a PC Card. Each card will have at least one function, but many have two, three, or more! You can buy a PC Card that offers connections for removable media, for example, such as combination SD and CF card readers. You can also find PC Cards that enable you to plug into multiple types of networks. All PC Cards are hot-swappable, meaning you can plug them in without powering down the PC.

The PCMCIA has established two versions of PC Cards, one using a parallel bus and the other using a serial bus. Each version, in turn, offers two technology variations as well as several physical varieties. This might sound complicated at first, but here's the map to sort it all out.

Parallel PC Cards

Parallel PC Cards come in two flavors, **16-bit** and **CardBus**, and each flavor comes in three different physical sizes, called Type I, Type II, and Type III. The 16-bit PC Cards, as the name suggests, are 16-bit, 5-V cards that can have up to two distinct functions or devices, such as a modem/network card combination. CardBus PC Cards are 32-bit, 3.3-V cards that can have up to eight (!) different functions on a single card. Regular PC Cards will fit into and work in CardBus slots, but the reverse is not true. CardBus totally dominates the current PC Card landscape, but you might still run into older 16-bit PC Cards.

Type I, II, and III cards differ only in the thickness of the card (Type I being the thinnest, and Type III the thickest). All PC Cards share the same 68-pin interface, so any PC Card will work in any slot that's high enough to accept that card type. Type II cards are by far the most common of PC Cards. Therefore, most laptops will have two Type II slots, one above the other, to enable the computer to accept two Type I or II cards or one Type III card (Figure 16.13).

Although PCMCIA doesn't require that certain sizes perform certain functions, most PC Cards follow their recommendations. Table 16.3 lists the sizes and typical uses of each type of PC Card.

ExpressCard

ExpressCard, the high-performance serial version of the PC Card, has begun to replace PC Card slots on

CompTIA uses the older term PCMCIA cards to describe PC Cards. Don't be shocked if you get that as an option on your exams! You'll hear many techs use the phrase as well, though the PCMCIA trade group has not used it for many years.

Many manufacturers use the term *hot-pluggable* rather than hot-swappable to describe the ability to plug in and replace PC Cards on the fly. Look for either term on the exams.

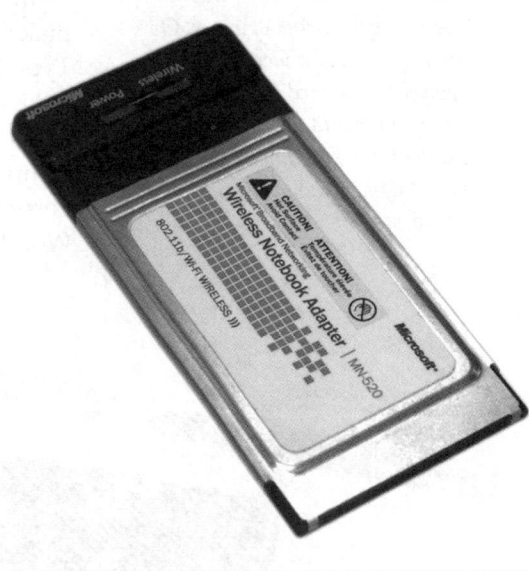
• **Figure 16.12**   PC Card

• **Figure 16.13**   PC Card slots

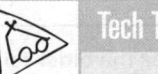

Tech Tip

Keeping Your PC Cards Healthy

Most PC Cards normally come with a hard plastic storage case. Always be sure to use this case to store the cards when you're not using them. If dust, dirt, or grime gets into the array of contacts at the end of the card, the card won't work when you try to use it next. Also, be careful when using PC Cards that extend out of the PC Card slot past the edge of your laptop. One dark night I set my laptop on the floor with a PC Card NIC sticking out of it while I went to get a drink of water. On my way back, I accidentally stepped on the card sticking out of my laptop and nearly snapped it in half. Luckily, my laptop wasn't damaged, but the card was toast!

Table 16.3	PC Card Types and Their Typical Uses			
Type	**Length**	**Width**	**Thickness**	**Typical Use**
Type I	85.6 mm	54.0 mm	3.3 mm	Flash memory
Type II	85.6 mm	54.0 mm	5.0 mm	I/O (Modem, NIC, and so on)
Type III	85.6 mm	54.0 mm	10.5 mm	Hard drives

newer laptop PCs. While ExpressCard offers significant performance benefits, keep in mind that ExpressCard and PC Cards are incompatible. You cannot use your PC Card in your new laptop's ExpressCard socket. The PC Card has had a remarkably long life in portable PCs, and you can still find it on some new laptops, but get ready to replace all your PC Card devices. ExpressCard comes in two widths: 54 mm and 34 mm. Figure 16.14 shows a 34-mm ExpressCard. Both cards are 75-mm long and 5-mm thick, which makes them shorter than all previous PC Cards and the same thickness as a Type II PC Card.

ExpressCards connect to either the Hi-Speed USB 2.0 bus or a PCI Express bus. These differ phenomenally in speed. The amazingly slow-in-comparison USB version has a maximum throughput of 480 Mbps. The PCIe version, in contrast, roars in at 2.5 Gbps in unidirectional communication. Woot!

Table 16.4 shows the throughput and variations for the parallel and serial PC Cards currently or soon to be on the market.

Software Support for PC Cards

The PCMCIA standard defines two levels of software drivers to support PC Cards. The first, lower level is known as socket services. Socket services are device drivers that support the PC Card socket, enabling the system to detect when a PC Card has been inserted or removed, and providing the necessary I/O to the device. The second, higher level is known as card services. The card services level recognizes the

© 2003 PCMCIA
www.expresscard.org

• **Figure 16.14** 34-mm ExpressCard *(photo courtesy of PCMCIA)*

Table 16.4	PC Card Speeds
Standard	**Maximum Theoretical Throughput**
PC Card using 16-bit bus	160 Mbps
CardBus PC Card using PCI bus	1056 Mbps
ExpressCard using USB 2.0 bus	480 Mbps
ExpressCard using PCIe bus	2.5 Gbps

function of a particular PC Card and provides the specialized drivers necessary to make the card work.

In today's laptops, the socket services are standardized and are handled by the system BIOS. Windows itself handles all card services and has a large preinstalled base of PC Card device drivers, although most PC Cards come with their own drivers.

ExpressCards don't require either socket or card services, at least not in the way PC Cards do. The ExpressCard modules automatically configure the software on your computer, which makes them truly plug and play.

Limited-Function Ports

All portable PCs and many PDAs come with one or more single-function ports, such as an analog VGA connection for hooking up an external monitor and a PS/2 port for a keyboard or mouse. Note that contrary to the setup on desktop PCs, the single PS/2 port on most laptops supports both keyboards and pointing devices. Most portable computing devices have a speaker port, and this includes modern PDAs. My Compaq iPAQ doubles as an excellent MP3 player, by the way, a feature now included with most PDAs. Some portables have line-in and microphone jacks as well. Finally, most current portable PCs come with built-in NICs or modems for networking support. (See the section "The Modular Laptop" later in this chapter for more on networking capabilities.)

All limited-function ports work the same way on portable PCs as they do on desktop models. You plug in a device to a particular port and, as long as Windows has the proper drivers, you will have a functioning device when you boot. The only port that requires any extra effort is the video port.

Most laptops support a second monitor via an analog VGA port or a digital DVI port in the back of the box. With a second monitor attached, you can display Windows on only the laptop LCD, only the external monitor, or both simultaneously. Not all portables can do all variations, but they're more common than not. Most portables have a special Function (FN) key on the keyboard that, when pressed, adds an additional option to certain keys on the keyboard. Figure 16.15 shows a close-up of a typical keyboard with the Function key; note the other options that can be accessed with the Function key such as indicated on the F5 key. To engage the second monitor or to cycle through the modes, hold the Function key and press F5.

Although many laptops use the Function key method to cycle the monitor selections, that's not always the case. You might have to pop into the Display applet in the Control Panel to click a checkbox. Just be assured that if the laptop has a VGA or DVI port, you can cycle through monitor choices!

General-Purpose Ports

Sometimes the laptop doesn't come with all of the hardware you want. Today's laptops usually include several USB ports and a selection of the legacy general-purpose expansion ports (PS/2, RS-232 serial ports, and so on) for installing peripheral hardware. If you're lucky, you might even get a FireWire port so you can plug in your fancy new digital video camera. If you're really lucky, you might even

Figure 16.15 Laptop keyboard with Function (FN) key that enables you to access additional key options, as on the F5 key

Cross Check

USB and FireWire

You explored USB and FireWire back in Chapter 14, "Input/Output." What kind of connectors do USB and FireWire use? What cable length limitations are there? How many devices can each support?

Tech Tip

USB and Handheld Computing Devices

Almost all PDAs and other handheld devices—such as iPod music players—connect to PCs through USB ports. Most come with a USB cable that has a standard connector on one end and a proprietary connector on the other. Don't lose the cable!

Although portable PCs most often connect to port replicators via USB ports, some manufacturers have proprietary connections for proprietary port replicators. As long as such a portable PC has a USB port, you can use either the proprietary hardware or the more flexible USB devices.

have a docking station or port replicator so you don't have to plug in all of your peripheral devices one at a time.

USB and FireWire

Universal serial bus (USB) and FireWire (or more properly, IEEE 1394) are two technologies that have their roots in desktop computer technology, but have also found widespread use in portable PCs. Both types of connections feature an easy-to-use connector and give the user the ability to insert a device into a system while the PC is running—you won't have to reboot a system in order to install a new peripheral. With USB and FireWire, just plug the device in and go! Because portable PCs don't have multiple internal expansion capabilities like desktops, USB and FireWire are two of the more popular methods for attaching peripherals to laptops (see Figure 16.16).

Port Replicators

A port replicator plugs into a single port on the portable computer— often a USB port, but sometimes a proprietary port—and offers common PC ports, such as serial, parallel, USB, network, and PS/2. By plugging the port replicator into your notebook computer, you can instantly connect it to non-portable components such as a printer, scanner, monitor, or a full-sized keyboard. Port replicators are typically used at home or in the office with the non-portable equipment already connected. Figure 16.17 shows an Dell Inspiron laptop connected to a port replicator.

Once connected to the port replicator, the computer can access any devices attached to it; there's no need to connect each individual device to the PC. As a side bonus, port replicators enable you to attach legacy devices, such as parallel printers, to a new laptop that only has modern

● **Figure 16.16**   Devices attached to USB or FireWire connector on portable PC

multifunction ports such as USB and FireWire, and not parallel or serial ports.

Docking Stations

Docking stations (see Figure 16.18) resemble port replicators in many ways, offering legacy and modern single-function and multifunction ports. The typical docking station uses a proprietary connection, but has extra features built in, such as a DVD drive or PC Card slot for extra enhancements. You can find docking stations for most laptop models, but you'll find them used most frequently with the desktop extender and ultralight models. Many ultralights have no internal CD or DVD media drive (because the drives weigh too much), and so must rely on external drives for full PC functionality. Docking stations make an excellent companion to such portables.

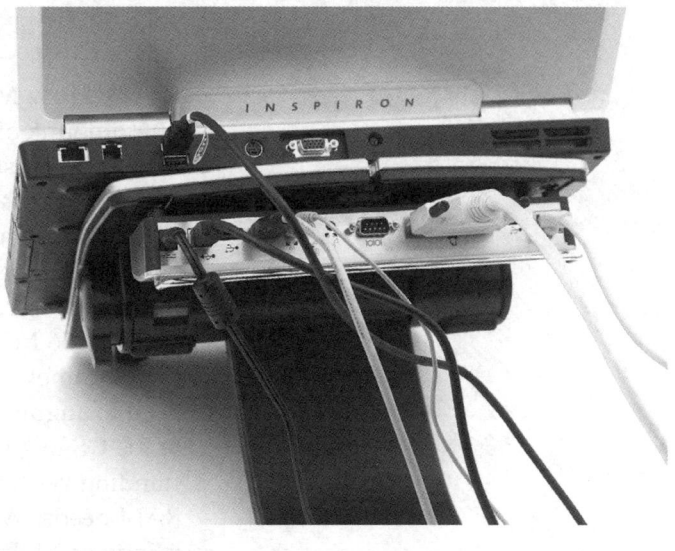

● **Figure 16.17**   Port replicator for a Dell portable computer

The Modular Laptop

For years, portable PC makers required completely proprietary components for each system model they developed. For the most part, this proprietary attitude still prevails, but manufacturers have added some modularity to today's portable PCs, enabling you to make basic replacements and upgrades without going back to the manufacturer for expensive, proprietary components. You need to surf the Web for companies that sell the components, because very few storefronts stock them. The most common modular components are RAM, hard drives, CPUs, video cards, optical drives, and network cards.

RAM

Stock factory portable PCs almost always come with a minimal amount of RAM, so one of the first laptop upgrades you'll be called on to do is to add more RAM. Economy laptops running Windows XP Home routinely sit on

● **Figure 16.18**   Docking station

Cross Check

How Much RAM is Enough?

The amount of RAM needed to run a PC—portable or otherwise—smoothly and stably depends on both the type of applications that it will run and the needs of the OS. When making a recommendation to a client about upgrading a laptop's memory, you should ask the basic questions, such as what he or she plans to do on the laptop. If the laptop will be used for e-mail, word processing, and Web surfing, a medium level of RAM, such as 256 MB, might be adequate. If the user travels, uses a high-end digital camera, and wants to use Photoshop to edit huge images, you'll need to augment the RAM accordingly. Then you need to add the needs of the OS to give a good recommendation. Turn to Chapter 12, "Understanding Windows," and cross check your knowledge about specific OS RAM needs. What's a good minimum for Windows 2000? What about Windows XP Professional?

store shelves and go home to consumers with as little 256 MB of RAM, an amount guaranteed to limit the use and performance of the laptop. The OS alone will consume more than half of the RAM! Luckily, every decent laptop has upgradeable RAM slots. Laptops use one of four types of RAM. Most older laptops use either 72-pin or 144-pin SO-DIMMs with SDRAM technology (Figure 16.19). DDR and DDR2 systems primarily use 200-pin SO-DIMMs although some laptops use micro-DIMMs.

How to Add or Replace RAM Upgrading the RAM in a portable PC requires a couple of steps. First, you need to get the correct RAM. Many older portable PCs use proprietary RAM solutions, which means you need to order directly from Dell, HP, or Sony and pay exorbitant prices for the precious extra megabytes. Most manufacturers have taken pity on consumers in recent years and use standard SO-DIMMs or micro-DIMMs. Refer to the manufacturer's Web site or to the manual (if any) that came with the portable for the specific RAM needed.

Second, every portable PC offers a unique challenge to the tech who wants to upgrade the RAM because there's no standard for RAM placement in portables. More often than not, you need to unscrew or pop open a panel on the underside of the portable (Figure 16.20). Then you press out on the restraining clips and the RAM stick will pop up (Figure 16.21). Gently remove the old stick of RAM and insert the new one by reversing the steps.

• **Figure 16.19**   72-pin SO-DIMM stick (front and back)

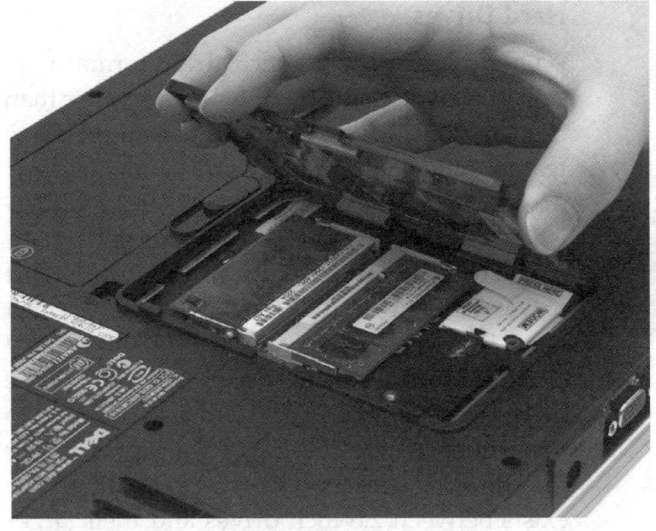

● **Figure 16.20**   Removing a RAM panel

● **Figure 16.21**   Releasing the RAM

Shared Memory   Some laptops (and desktops) support shared memory . Shared memory is a means of reducing the cost of video cards by reducing the amount of memory on the video card itself. Instead of a video card with 256 MB of RAM, it might have only 64 MB of RAM but can borrow 192 MB of RAM from the system. This equates to a 256-MB video card. The video card uses regular system RAM to make up for the loss.

The obvious benefit of shared memory is a less expensive video card with performance comparable to its mega-memory alternative. The downside is your overall system performance will suffer because a portion of the system RAM is no longer available to programs. (The term *shared* is a bit misleading because the video card takes control of a portion of RAM. The video portion of system RAM is *not* shared back and forth between the video card processor and the CPU.) Shared memory technologies include TurboCache (developed by NVIDIA) and HyperMemory (developed by ATI).

Some systems give you control over the amount of shared memory while others simply allow you to turn shared memory on or off. The settings are found in CMOS setup and only on systems that support shared memory. Shared memory is not reported to Windows so don't panic if you've got 1 GB of RAM in your laptop, but Windows only sees 924 MB—the missing memory is used for video!

Adding more system RAM to a laptop with shared memory will improve laptop performance. Although it might appear to improve video performance, that doesn't tell the true story. It'll improve overall performance because the OS and CPU get more RAM to work with. On some laptops, you can improve video performance as well, but that depends on the CMOS setup. If the shared memory is not set to maximum by default, increasing the overall memory and upping the portion reserved for video will improve video performance specifically.

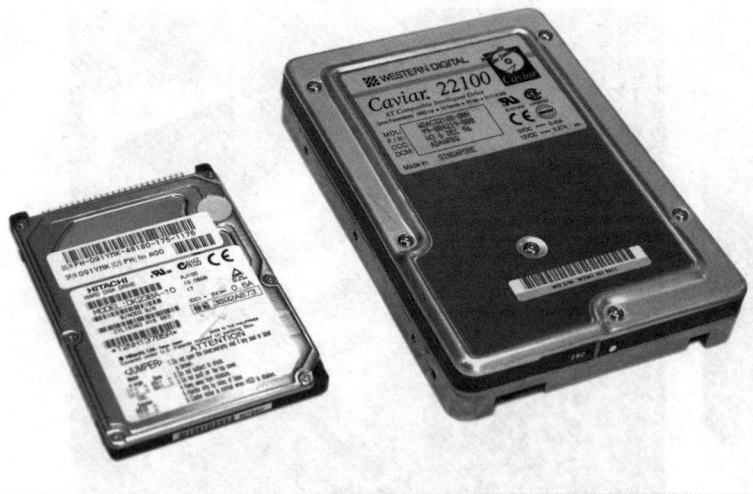

Hard Drives

ATA drives in the 2.5-inch drive format now rule in all laptops. Although much smaller than regular ATA drives, they still use all the same features and configurations. These smaller hard drives have suffered, however, from diminished storage capacity compared to their 3.5-inch brothers. Currently, large 2.5-inch hard drives hold up to 120 GB, while the 3.5-inch hard drives can hold more than 750 GB of data! Some manufacturers may require you to set the drive to use a cable select setting as opposed to master or slave, so check with the laptop maker for any special issues. Otherwise, no difference exists between 2.5-inch drives and their larger 3.5-inch brethren (Figure 16.22).

• **Figure 16.22**   The 2.5-inch and 3.5-inch drives are mostly the same.

Tech Tip

Going Inside

To reach most modular components on a laptop, you need to do more than remove an exterior panel. You need to go inside to get access to devices directly connected to the motherboard. Many laptops have an easily removable keyboard that, once removed, gives you access to a metal heat spreader (just a plate that sits over the motherboard) and a half-dozen or more tiny screws. You'll need a special screwdriver to avoid stripping the screws— check a watch or eyeglass shop if your local hardware store doesn't carry anything appropriate.

You need to take major precautions when you remove the keyboard and heat spreader. The keyboard will be attached to a small cable that can easily disconnect if you pull hard. Don't forget to check this connection before you reinsert the keyboard at the end of the procedure! Avoid ESD like you would with any other PC, and definitely unplug the laptop from the wall and remove the battery *before you do any work inside!*

Modular CPUs

You know from Chapter 3, "Understanding CPUs," that both AMD and Intel make specialized CPUs for laptops that produce less heat and consume less power, yet only now are folks realizing that they can easily upgrade many systems by removing the old CPU and replacing it with a new one. Be very careful to follow manufacturer's specifications! You should keep in mind, however, that replacing the CPU in a laptop often requires that you disassemble the entire machine. This can be a daunting task, even for professionals. If you want to upgrade the CPU in your laptop, it's often best to let the professionals take care of it.

Video Cards

Some video card makers make modular video cards for laptops. Although no single standard works in all systems, a quick phone call to the tech support department of the laptop maker often reveals upgrade options (if any). Modular video cards are the least standardized of all modular components, but as manufacturers adopt more industry-wide standards, we'll be able to replace video cards in laptops more readily.

Modular Drives

In order to add functionality to laptops, manufacturers include "modular drives" with their machines. CD-ROM, DVD-ROM, CD-R/RW, and CD-RW/DVD-ROM drives are the most common modular drives that are included with portables. The beauty of modular drives is that you can swap easily back and forth between different types of drives. Need more storage space? Pull out the CD-ROM drive and put in another hard drive. Many laptops enable you to replace a drive with a second battery, which obviously can extend the time you can go before you have to plug the laptop into an AC outlet.

I have a laptop that allows me to swap out my CD-ROM drive for a second battery. If I don't need to access any CDs and don't need super-extended battery life, I just take out the component that's currently installed and put a blank faceplate into the empty slot. Traveling with an empty bay makes my hefty laptop weigh a little bit less, and every little bit helps!

Most modular drives are truly hot-swappable, enabling you to remove and insert devices without any special software. Many still require you to use the Hardware Removal Tool (also known as Safely Remove Hardware) located in the system tray or notification area (Figure 16.23). When in doubt, always remove modular devices using this tool. Figure 16.24 shows the Safely Remove Hardware dialog box. To remove a device, highlight it and click the Stop button. Windows will shut down the device and tell you when it's safe to remove the device.

● **Figure 16.23**   Hardware Removal Tool in system tray

Mobile NICs and Mini PCI

Every laptop made in the last few years comes with networking capabilities built in. They have modems for dial-up and Ethernet ports for plugging into a wired network. Because they run Windows, OS X, or some Linux distro, laptops have all the networking software ready to go, just like their desk-bound cousins.

> See Chapter 18, "Understanding Networks," for the scoop on dial-up networking and Ethernet.

Many laptops now come with integrated wireless networking support by way of a built-in Wi-Fi adapter usually installed in a Mini PCI slot on the laptop motherboard. The **Mini PCI** bus is an adaptation of the standard PCI bus and was developed specifically for integrated communications peripherals such as modems and network adapters. Built-in networking support means you don't need an additional PC Card to provide a network adapter. The Mini PCI bus also provides support for other integrated devices such as Bluetooth, modems, audio, or hard drive controllers. One great aspect of Mini PCI is that if some new technology eclipses the current wireless technology or some other technology that uses the bus, you can upgrade by swapping a card.

Officially released in 1999, Mini PCI is a 32-bit 33-MHz bus and is basically PCI v2.2 with a different form factor. Like PCI, it supports bus mastering and DMA. Mini PCI cards are about a quarter the size of a regular PCI card and can be as small as 2.75 inches by 1.81 inches by .22 inches. They can be found in small products such as laptops, printers, and set-top boxes.

● **Figure 16.24**   Safely Remove Hardware dialog box

> A typical reason to upgrade a Mini PCI Wi-Fi NIC is to gain access to improved security options such as better encryption.

To extend battery life, built-in communication devices such as Wi-Fi and Bluetooth adapters can be toggled on and off without powering down the computer. Many laptops come with a physical switch along the front or side edge allowing you to power on or off the communications adapter. Similarly, you can often use a keyboard shortcut for this, generally by pressing the Function (FN) key along with some other key. The FN key, when pressed, allows other keys to accomplish specific tasks. For example, on my laptop pressing FN-F2 toggles my Wi-Fi adapter on and off; pressing FN-F10 ejects my CD-ROM drive.

■ Managing and Maintaining Portable Computers

Most portable PCs come from the factory solidly built and configured. Manufacturers know that few techs outside their factories know enough to work on them, so they don't cut corners. From a tech's standpoint, your most common work on managing and maintaining portables involves taking care of the batteries and extending the battery life through proper power management, keeping the machine clean, and avoiding excessive heat.

Everything you normally do to maintain a PC applies to portable PCs. You need to keep current on Windows patches and Service Packs, and use stable, recent drivers. Run Check Disk with some frequency, and definitely defragment the hard drive. Disk Cleanup is a must if the laptop runs Windows XP. That said, let's look at issues specifically involving portables.

Batteries

Manufacturers use three different types of batteries for portable PCs and each battery type has its own special needs and quirks. Once you've got a clear understanding of the quirks, you can *usually* spot and fix battery problems. The three types of batteries commonly used in mobile PCs are Nickel-Cadmium (Ni-Cd), Nickel-Metal Hydride (Ni-MH), and Lithium-Ion (Li-Ion) batteries. Manufacturers have also started working with fuel cell batteries, although most of that work is experimental at this writing.

Nickel-Cadmium

Ni-Cds were the first batteries commonly used in mobile PCs, which means the technology was full of little problems. Probably most irritating was a little thing called battery memory, or the tendency of a Ni-Cd battery to lose a significant amount of its rechargeability if it was charged repeatedly without being totally discharged. A battery that originally kept a laptop running for two hours would eventually only keep that same laptop going for 30 minutes or less. Figure 16.25 shows a typical Ni-Cd battery.

To prevent memory problems, a Ni-Cd battery had to be discharged completely before each recharging. Recharging was tricky as well, because Ni-Cd batteries disliked being overcharged. Unfortunately, there was no way to verify when a battery was fully charged without an expensive charging machine, which none of us had. As a result, most Ni-Cd batteries lasted an extremely short time and had to be replaced. A quick fix was to purchase a conditioning charger. These chargers would first totally discharge the Ni-Cd battery, and then generate a special "reverse" current that, in a way, "cleaned" internal parts of the battery so that it could be recharged more often and would run longer on each recharge. Ni-Cd batteries would, at best, last for 1000 charges, and far fewer with poor treatment. Ni-Cds

● **Figure 16.25**   Ni-Cd battery

were extremely susceptible to heat and would self-discharge over time if not used. Leaving a Ni-Cd in the car in the summer was guaranteed to result in a fully discharged battery in next to no time!

But Ni-Cd batteries didn't stop causing trouble after they died. The highly toxic metals inside the battery made it unacceptable simply to throw them in the trash. Ni-Cd batteries should be disposed of via specialized disposal companies. This is very important! Even though Ni-Cd batteries aren't used in PCs very often anymore, many devices, such as cellular and cordless phones, still use Ni-Cd batteries. Don't trash the environment by tossing Ni-Cds in a landfill. Turn them in at the closest special disposal site; most recycling centers are glad to take them. Also, many battery manufacturers/distributors will take them. The environment you help preserve just might be yours—or your kids'!

> You *must* use disposal companies or battery recycling services to dispose of the highly toxic Ni-Cd batteries.

Nickel-Metal Hydride

Ni-MH batteries were the next generation of mobile PC batteries and are still quite common today. Basically, Ni-MH batteries are Ni-Cd batteries without most of the headaches. Ni-MH batteries are much less susceptible to memory problems, can better tolerate overcharging, can take more recharging, and last longer between rechargings. Like Ni-Cds, Ni-MH batteries are still susceptible to heat, but at least they are considered less toxic to the environment. It's still a good idea to do a special disposal. Unlike a Ni-Cd, it's usually better to recharge a Ni-MH with shallow recharges as opposed to a complete discharge/recharge. Ni-MH is a popular replacement battery for Ni-Cd systems (Figure 16.26).

Lithium Ion

The most common type battery used today is Li-Ion. Li-Ion batteries are very powerful, completely immune to memory problems, and last at least twice as long as comparable Ni-MH batteries on one charge. Sadly, they can't handle as many charges as Ni-MH types, but today's users are usually more than glad to give up total battery lifespan in return for longer periods between charges. Li-Ion batteries will explode if they are overcharged, so all Li-Ion batteries sold with PCs have built-in circuitry to prevent accidental overcharging. Lithium batteries can only be used on systems designed to use them. They can't be used as replacement batteries (Figure 16.27).

● **Figure 16.26**   Ni-MH battery

Other Portable Power Sources

In an attempt to provide better maintenance for laptop batteries, manufacturers have developed a new type of battery called the smart battery . Smart batteries tell the computer when they need to be charged, conditioned, or replaced.

Portable computer manufacturers are also looking at other potential power sources, especially ones that don't have the shortcomings of current batteries. The most promising of these new technologies is fuel cells . The technology behind fuel cells is very complex, but to summarize, fuel cells produce electrical power as a result of a chemical reaction between the hydrogen

● **Figure 16.27**   Li-Ion battery

and oxygen contained in the fuel cell. It is estimated that a small fuel cell could power a laptop for up to 40 hours before it needs to be replaced or refilled. This technology is still a year or two from making it to the consumer market, but it's an exciting trend!

Try This!

Recycling Old Portable PC Batteries

Got an old portable PC battery lying around? Well, you've got to get rid of it, and since there are some pretty nasty chemicals in that battery, you can't just throw it in the trash. Sooner or later, you'll probably need to deal with such a battery, so try this:

1. Do an online search to find the battery recycling center nearest to you.

2. Sometimes, you can take old laptop batteries to an auto parts store that disposes of old car batteries—I know it sounds odd, but it's true! See if you can find one in your area that will do this.

3. Many cities offer a hazardous materials disposal or recycling service. Check to see if and how your local government will help you dispose of your old batteries.

The Care and Feeding of Batteries

In general, keep in mind the following basics. First, always store batteries in a cool place. Although a freezer is in concept an excellent storage place, the moisture, metal racks, and food make it a bad idea. Second, condition your Ni-Cd and Ni-MH batteries by using a charger that also conditions the battery; they'll last longer. Third, keep battery contacts clean with a little alcohol or just a dry cloth. Fourth, *never* handle a battery that has ruptured or broken; battery chemicals are very dangerous. Finally, always recycle old batteries.

Power Management

Many different parts are included in the typical laptop, and each part uses power. The problem with early laptops was that every one of these parts used power continuously, whether or not the system needed that device at that time. For example, the hard drive would continue to spin whether or not it was being accessed, and the LCD panel would continue to display, even when the user walked away from the machine.

The optimal situation would be a system where the user could instruct the PC to shut down unused devices selectively, preferably by defining a maximum period of inactivity that, when reached, would trigger the PC to shut down the inactive device. Longer periods of inactivity would eventually enable the entire system to shut itself down, leaving critical information loaded in RAM, ready to restart if a wake-up event (such as moving the mouse or pressing a key) would tell the system to restart. The system would have to be sensitive to potential hazards, such as shutting down in the middle of writing to a drive, and so on. Also, this feature could not add significantly to the cost of the PC. Clearly, a machine that could perform these functions would need specialized hardware, BIOS, and operating system to operate properly. This process of cooperation among the hardware, the BIOS, and the OS to reduce power use is known generically as *power management*.

System Management Mode (SMM)

Intel began the process of power management with a series of new features built into the 386SX CPU. These new features enabled the CPU to slow down or stop its clock without erasing the register information, as well as enabling power saving in peripherals. These features were collectively called System Management Mode (SMM) . All modern CPUs have SMM. Although a power-saving CPU was okay, power management was relegated to special "sleep" or "doze" buttons that would stop the CPU and all of the peripherals on the laptop. To take real advantage of SMM, the system needed a specialized BIOS and OS to go with the SMM CPU. To this end, Intel put forward the Advanced Power Management (APM) specification in 1992 and the Advanced Configuration and Power Interface (ACPI) standard in 1996.

Requirements for APM/ACPI

APM and ACPI require a number of items in order to function fully. First is an SMM-capable CPU. As virtually all CPUs are SMM-capable, this is easy. Second is an APM-compliant BIOS, which enables the CPU to shut off the peripherals when desired. The third requirement is devices that will accept being shut off. These devices are usually called "Energy Star" devices, which signals their compliance with the EPA's Energy Star standard. To be an Energy Star device, a peripheral must have the ability to shut down without actually turning off and show that they use much less power than the non–Energy Star equivalent. Last, the system's OS must know how to request that a particular device be shut down, and the CPU's clock must be slowed down or stopped.

ACPI goes beyond the APM standard by supplying support for hot-swappable devices—always a huge problem with APM. This feature aside, it is a challenge to tell the difference between an APM system and an ACPI system at first glance.

Don't limit your perception of APM, ACPI, and Energy Star just to laptops! Virtually all desktop systems also use the power management functions.

APM/ACPI Levels

APM defines four different power-usage operating levels for a system. These levels are intentionally fuzzy to give manufacturers considerable leeway in their use; the only real difference among them is the amount of time each takes to return to normal usage. These levels are as follows:

- **Full On**   Everything in the system is running at full power. There is no power management.

- **APM Enabled**   CPU and RAM are running at full power. Power management is enabled. An unused device may or may not be shut down.

- **APM Standby**   CPU is stopped. RAM still stores all programs. All peripherals are shut down, although configuration options are still stored. (In other words, to get back to APM Enabled, you won't have to reinitialize the devices.)

- **APM Suspend**   Everything in the PC is shut down or at its lowest power-consumption setting. Many systems use a special type of Suspend called hibernation , where critical configuration information is written to the hard drive. Upon a wake-up event, the system is reinitialized, and the data is read from the drive to return the system to the APM Enabled mode. Clearly, the recovery time between Suspend and Enabled will be much longer than the time between Standby and Enabled.

ACPI handles all these levels plus a few more, such as "soft power on/off," which enables you to define the function of the power button.

Configuration of APM/ACPI

You configure APM/ACPI via CMOS settings or through Windows. Windows settings will override CMOS settings. Although the APM/ACPI standards permit a great deal of flexibility, which can create some confusion among different implementations, certain settings apply generally to CMOS configuration. First is the ability to initialize power management; this enables the system to enter the APM Enabled mode. Often CMOS will then present time frames for entering Standby and Suspend mode, as well as settings to determine which events take place in each of these modes. Also, many CMOS versions will present settings to determine wake-up events, such as directing the system to monitor a modem or a particular IRQ (Figure 16.28). A true ACPI-compliant CMOS provides an ACPI setup option. Figure 16.29 shows a typical modern BIOS that provides this setting.

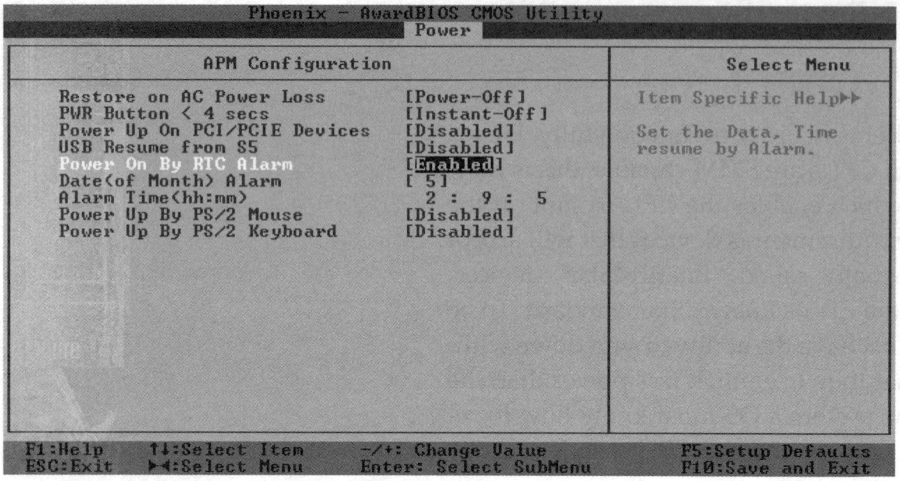

● **Figure 16.28**   Setting a wake-up event in CMOS

> You can also access your Power Options by right-clicking on the Desktop, selecting Properties, and then clicking the Power button on the Screen Saver tab.

APM/ACPI settings can be found in the Windows 2000/XP control panel applet Power Options. The Power Options applet has several built-in *power schemes* such as Home/Office and Max Battery that put the system into standby or suspend after a certain interval (Figure 16.30). You can also require the system to go into standby after a set period of time or turn off the monitor or hard drive after a time, thus creating your own custom power scheme.

Another feature, Hibernate mode, takes everything in active memory and stores it on the hard drive just before the system powers down. When the PC comes out of hibernation, Windows reloads all the files and applications into RAM. Figure 16.31 shows the Power Options Properties applet in Windows XP.

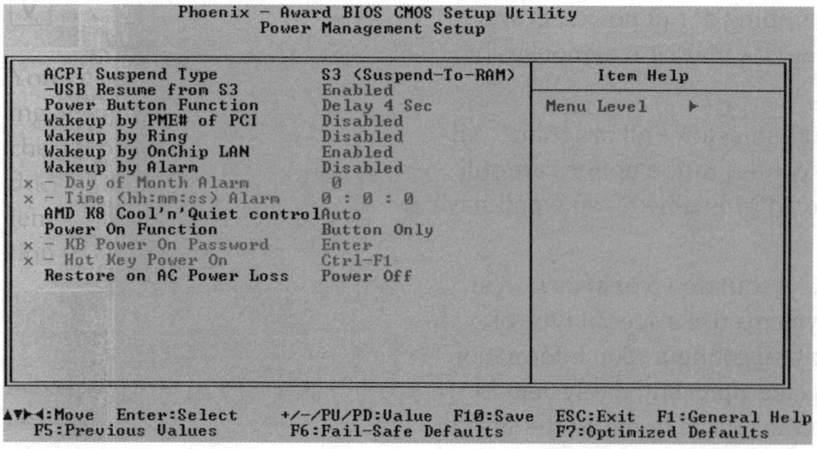

Cleaning

Most portable PCs take substantially more abuse than a corresponding desktop model. Constant handling, travel, airport food on the run, and so on can

● **Figure 16.29**   CMOS with ACPI setup option

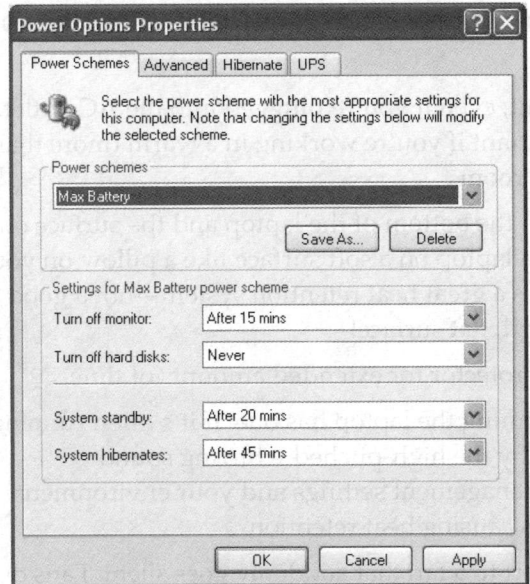

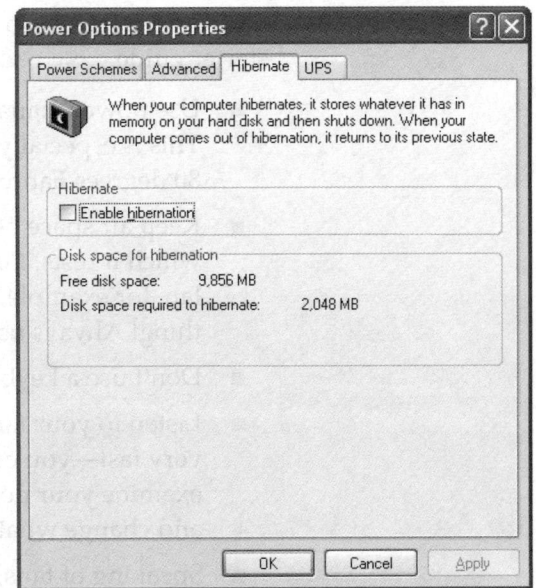

- **Figure 16.30** The Power Options applet's Power Schemes tab

- **Figure 16.31** Hibernation settings in the Power Options applet

radically shorten the life of a portable if you don't take action. One of the most important things you should do is clean the laptop regularly. Use an appropriate screen cleaner (not a glass cleaner!) to remove fingerprints and dust from the fragile LCD panel.

If you've had the laptop in a smoky or dusty environment where the air quality alone causes problems, try compressed air for cleaning. Compressed air works great for blowing out the dust and crumbs from the keyboard and for keeping PC Card sockets clear. Don't use water on your keyboard! Even a minor amount of moisture inside the portable can toast a component.

 **Try This!**

Adjusting Your System's Power Management

Go into the Power Options applet and take a look at the various settings. What is the current power scheme for your computer? If you're using a laptop, is your system still using the Home/Office Desktop power scheme? If this is the case, go ahead and change the power scheme to Portable/Laptop.

Try changing the individual settings for each power scheme. For instance, set a new value for the System Standby setting—try making your computer go into standby after five minutes. Don't worry, you aren't going to hurt anything if you fiddle with these settings.

Heat

To manage and maintain a healthy portable PC, you need to deal with issues of heat. Every portable has a stack of electronic components crammed into a very small space. Unlike their desktop brethren, portables don't have lots of freely-moving air space that enables fans to cool everything down. Even with lots of low-power-consumption devices inside, portable PCs still crank out a good deal of heat. Excessive heat can cause system lockups and hardware failures, so you should handle the issue wisely. Try this as a starter guide.

- Use power management, even if you're plugged into the AC outlet. This is especially important if you're working in a warm (more than 80 degrees Fahrenheit) room.

- Keep air space between the bottom of the laptop and the surface on which it rests. Putting a laptop on a soft surface like a pillow on your lap, for example, creates a great heat retention system—not a good thing! Always use a hard, flat surface!

- Don't use a keyboard protector for extended amounts of time.

- Listen to your fan, assuming the laptop has one. If it's often running very fast—you can tell by the high-pitched whirring sound— examine your power management settings and your environment and change whatever is causing heat retention.

- Speaking of fans, be alert to a fan that suddenly goes silent. Fans do fail on laptops, causing overheating and failure. All laptop fans can be replaced easily.

Protect the Machine

While prices continue to drop for basic laptops, a fully loaded system is still pricey. To protect your investment, you'll want to adhere to certain best practices. You've already read tips in this chapter to deal with cleaning and heat, so let's look at the "portable" part of portable computers.

Tripping

Pay attention to where you run the power cord when you plug in a laptop. One of the primary causes of laptop destruction is people tripping over the power cord and knocking the laptop off a desk. This is especially true if you plug in at a public place such as a café or airport. Remember, the life you save could be your portable PC's!

Storage

If your laptop or PDA isn't going to be used for a while, storing it safely will go a long way toward keeping it operable when you do power it up again. It's worth the extra few dollars to invest in a quality case also—preferably one with ample padding. Smaller devices such as PDAs are well protected inside small shock-resistant aluminum cases that clip on to your belt while laptops do fine in well-padded cases or backpacks. Not only will this protect your system on a daily basis when transporting it from home to office, but it will keep dust and pet hair away as well. Lastly, remove the battery if you'll be storing your device for an extended period of time to protect from battery leakage.

Travel

If traveling with a laptop, take care to protect yourself from theft. If possible, use a case that doesn't look like a computer case. A well-padded backpack makes a great travel bag for a laptop and appears less tempting to would-be thieves. Don't forget to pack any accessories you might need, like modular devices, spare batteries, and AC adapters. Make sure to remove any disks, such as CD/DVD or floppies, from their drives. Most importantly—back up any important data before you leave!

Make sure to have at least a little battery power available. Heightened security at airports means you might have to power on your system to prove it's really a computer and not a transport case for questionable materials. And never let your laptop out of your sight. If going through an x-ray machine, request a manual search. The x-ray won't harm your computer like a metal detector will, but if the laptop gets through the line at security before you do, someone else might walk away with it. If flying, keep your laptop out of the overhead bins and under the seat in front of you where you can keep an eye on it.

If you travel to a foreign country, be very careful about the electricity. North America uses ~115-V power outlets, but the most of the rest of the world uses ~230-V outlets. Many portable computers have **auto-switching power supplies**, meaning they detect the voltage at the outlet and adjust accordingly. For these portables, a simple plug converter will do the trick. Other portable computers, however, have *fixed-input power supplies*, which means they run only on ~115-V or ~230-V power. For these portables, you need a full-blown electricity converting device, either a step-down or step-up *transformer*. You can find converters and transformers at electrical parts stores, such as Radio Shack in the U.S.

Shipping

Much of the storage and travel advice can be applied to shipping. Remove batteries and CD/DVD/floppies from their drives. Pack the laptop well and disguise the container as best you can. Back up any data and verify the warranty coverage. Ship with a reputable carrier and always request a tracking number and, if possible, delivery signature. It's also worth the extra couple of bucks to pay for the shipping insurance. And when the clerk asks what's in the box, it's safer to say "electronics" rather than "a new 20-inch laptop computer."

Security

The fact is, if someone really wants to steal your laptop, they'll find a way. There are, however, some things you can do to make yourself, and your equipment, a less desirable target. As you've already learned, disguise is a good idea. While you don't need to camouflage your laptop or carry it in a brown grocery bag on a daily basis, an inconspicuous carrying case will draw less attention.

Another physical deterrent is a laptop lock. Similar to a steel bicycle cable, there is a loop on one end and a lock on the other. The idea is to loop the cable around a solid object, like a bed frame, and secure the lock to the small security hole on the side of the laptop. Again, if someone really wants to steal your computer, they'll find a way. They'll dismantle the bed frame if they're desperate. The best protection is to be vigilant and not let the computer out of your sight.

An alternative to physically securing a laptop with a lock is to use a software tracking system. Software makers, such as Computer Security Products, Inc. at www.computersecurity.com, offer tracking software that transmits a signal to a central office if the laptop is stolen and connected to a phone line or the Internet. The location of the stolen PC can be tracked, and sensitive files can even be deleted automatically with the aid of the stealth signal.

■ Troubleshooting Portable Computers

Many of the troubleshooting techniques you learned about for desktop systems can be applied to laptops. Additionally, there are some laptop-specific procedures to try.

Laptop Won't Power On

- Verify AC power by plugging another electronic device into the wall outlet. If the other device receives power, the outlet is good.

- If the outlet is good, connect the laptop to the wall outlet and try to power on. If no LEDs light up, you may have a bad AC adapter. Swap it out with a known-good power adapter.

- A faulty peripheral device might keep the laptop from powering up. Remove any peripherals such as USB or FireWire devices.

Screen Doesn't Come On Properly

- If the laptop is booting (you hear the beeps and the drives), first make sure the display is on. Press the FN key and the key to activate the screen a number of times until the laptop display comes on.

- If the laptop display is very dim, you may have lost an inverter. The clue here is that inverters never go quietly. They can make a nasty hum as they are about to die and an equally nasty popping noise when they actually fail. Failure often occurs when you plug in the laptop's AC adapter, as the inverters take power directly from the AC adapter.

Wireless Networking Doesn't Work

- Check for a physical switch along the front, rear, or side edges of the laptop that toggles the internal wireless adapter on and off.

- Try the special key combination for your laptop to toggle the wireless adapter. You usually press the FN key in combination with another key.

- You might simply be out of range. Physically walk the laptop over to the wireless router or access point to ensure there are no "out of range" issues.

Tech Tip

Battery Won't Charge

If you have a laptop with a battery that won't charge, it could be one of two things: the battery is cooked or the AC adapter isn't doing its job. To troubleshoot, replace the battery with a known good battery. If the new battery works, then you've found the problem. Just replace the battery. Alternatively, remove the battery and run the laptop on AC only. If that works, you know the AC adapter is good. If it doesn't, then replace the AC adapter.

Handwriting Is Not Recognized

- If your PDA or tablet PC no longer recognizes your handwriting or stylus, you may need to retrain the digitizer. Look for an option in your PDA OS settings to "align the screen." On Windows tablet PCs, you will find a similar option under Start | Settings | Control Panel.

Keypad Doesn't Work

- If none of the keys work on your laptop, there's a good chance you've unseated the keypad connector. These connectors are quite fragile and are prone to unseating from any physical stress on the laptop. Check the manufacturer's disassembly procedures to locate and reseat the keypad.

- If you're getting numbers when you're expecting to get letters, the number lock (NUMLOCK) function key is turned on. Turn it off.

Touchpad Doesn't Work

- A shot of compressed air does wonders for cleaning pet hair out of the touchpad sensors. You'll get a cleaner shot if you remove the keyboard before using the compressed air. Remember to be gentle when lifting off the keyboard and make sure to follow the manufacturer's instructions.

- The touchpad driver might need to be reconfigured. Try the various options in the Control Panel | Mouse applet.

Beyond A+

Centrino Technology

As mentioned previously in this chapter, consumers have always, and will always, demand better performance, more features, and longer battery life from their portable PCs. Intel, for example, promotes a combination of three components—extremely low-power, yet speedy, CPUs; integrated wireless networking technology; and an Intel chipset—that, when combined, produce portable PCs that not only are exceptionally powerful, but also boast an extremely long battery life!

Origami—Ultra-Mobile PCs

Microsoft started pushing the Ultra-Mobile PC (UMPC) standard in 2005 and has started to get some traction in the industry. UMPCs are a small form-factor tablet PC, designed to fill the spot between PDAs and tablet PCs. Most of the versions use a 7-inch widescreen, touch-enabled LCD (although at least one model on the market has a 4.3-inch widescreen LCD) and feature everything you would expect to find in their bigger

 Microsoft initially called the UMPC project "Origami." The name has stuck, even though Microsoft has since shifted over to the more generic UMPC name.

cousins, with the exception of optical drives. They have internal 30–80 GB hard drives, 512 MB to 1 GB of RAM, built-in Wi-Fi and Bluetooth for connectivity, and more. Some even have USB and FireWire ports! All weigh under 2 pounds and come in at under 1 inch thick.

The feature that most distinguishes UMPCs from PDAs is that the former runs a fully featured version of Windows XP, just like your desktop and laptop PCs. Most UMPCs run Windows Tablet PC edition, although a few devices run Windows XP Home or Windows Vista. (A few übergeeks have even installed versions of Linux on UMPCs!) Figure 16.32 shows a Sony VAIO UX UMPC.

• **Figure 16.32**   Sony VAIO UX *(photo courtesy of Sony Electronics)*

Chapter 16 Review

Chapter Summary

After reading this chapter and completing the exercises, you should understand the following about portable computers.

Portable Computing Devices

- All portable devices share certain features: video output using LCD screens, some kind of PC sound, and DC battery power. There's no industry standard naming for the vast majority of styles of portable computing devices.

- A laptop refers in general to the clamshell, keyboard-on-the-bottom, and LCD-screen-at-the-top design that is considered the shape of mobile PCs. The traditional clamshell laptop computer features a built-in LCD monitor, keyboard, and input device, and functions as a fully standalone PC. A portable PC can be considered a desktop replacement if it does everything that most people want to do with a desktop PC.

- Desktop extender portable devices don't replace the desktop, but rather extend it by giving you a subset of features of the typical desktop that you can take away from the desk. They are usually smaller and lighter than desktop replacement portables. Ultralight portables (sometimes called subnotebooks, although the terms aren't necessarily synonymous) normally weigh less than three pounds and are less than an inch in thickness. These machines usually have smaller displays, lower-capacity hard drives, and CPUs that operate at lower speeds than their more full-sized brethren.

- Personal digital assistants (PDAs) are handheld portable computing devices that hold data such as your address book and appointment schedules. PDAs require specialized OSs such as Windows CE, PocketPC, PalmOS, or Linux. All of these OSs provide a GUI that enables you to interact with the device by touching the screen directly. PDAs synchronize with your PC, most often using a cradle and USB port, so you have the same essential data on both machines.

- Over the years, input devices for portables have ranged from trackballs that clipped to the case or were built in near the keyboard to IBM's TrackPoint pencil eraser–sized joystick embedded in the keyboard. The most common laptop pointing device found today, the touchpad, is a flat, touch-sensitive pad that you slide your finger across to move the cursor or pointer around the screen, and tap on to perform "mouse clicks."

Enhance and Upgrade the Portable PC

- PC Cards are roughly credit card–sized devices that enhance and extend the functions of a portable PC. Still commonly known by their older name, PCMCIA cards, PC Cards are as standard on today's mobile computers as the hard drive. Almost every portable PC has one or two PC Card slots. All PC Cards are hot-swappable.

- Parallel PC Cards come in two flavors, 16-bit and CardBus, and each flavor comes in three different physical sizes called Type I, Type II, and Type III. Type I, II, and III cards differ only in the thickness of the card (Type I being the thinnest, and Type III the thickest). Type II cards are by far the most common. All parallel PC Cards share the same 68-pin interface. The 16-bit PC Cards are 16-bit, 5-V cards that can have up to two distinct functions or devices, such as a modem/network card combination. CardBus PC Cards are 32-bit, 3.3-V cards that can have up to eight different functions on a single card. The 16-bit PC Cards will fit into and work in CardBus slots, but the reverse is not true.

- The serial ExpressCard comes in two widths: 54 mm and 34 mm. Both cards are 75 mm long and 5 mm thick, which makes them shorter than all previous PC Cards and the same thickness as a Type II PC Card. ExpressCards connect to either the Hi-Speed USB 2.0 bus (480 Mbps) or a PCI Express bus (2.5 Gbps).

- The PCMCIA standard defines two levels of software drivers to support PC Cards. The first, lower level is known as socket services. Socket services are device drivers that support the PC Card socket, enabling the system to detect when a PC Card has been inserted or removed, and providing the necessary I/O to the device. The second, higher level is known as card services. The card-services level recognizes the function of a particular PC Card and provides the specialized drivers necessary to make the card work. In today's laptops, the socket services are standardized and are handled by the system BIOS. Windows itself handles all card services and has a large preinstalled base of PC Card device drivers, although most PC Cards come with their own drivers.

- Every portable PC and many PDAs come with one or more single-function ports, such as an analog VGA connection for hooking up an external monitor and a PS/2 port for a keyboard or mouse. The single PS/2 port on most laptops supports both keyboards and pointing devices. Most portable computing devices have a speaker port, and some have line-in and microphone jacks as well. Most current portable PCs come with built-in NICs or modems for networking support. Simply plug a device into a particular port and, as long as Windows has the proper drivers, you will have a functioning device when you boot. The only port that requires any extra effort is the video port.

- Most laptops support a second monitor, giving the user the option to display Windows on the laptop only, the external monitor only, or both simultaneously. Usually, a special function key on the keyboard cycles through the different monitor configurations.

- Most portable PCs have one or more general-purpose expansion ports that enable you to plug in many different types of devices. Older portables sport RS-232 serial and IEEE 1284 parallel ports for mice, modems, printers, scanners, external CD-media drives, and more. USB and FireWire are popular and widespread methods for attaching peripherals to laptops. Both have easy-to-use connectors and can be hot-swapped.

- Port replicators are devices that plug into a single port (usually USB, but sometimes proprietary) and offer common PC ports, such as serial, parallel, USB, network, and PS/2. Docking stations resemble port replicators in many ways, offering legacy and modern single-function and multifunction ports, but have extra features built in, such as DVD drives or PC Card slots.

- In the past, manufacturers required proprietary components for portable PCs, but today's portable PCs offer some modularity, making it possible to do basic replacements and upgrades without buying expensive proprietary components from the manufacturer. These replaceable components include RAM, hard drives, video cards, floppy drives, and CD-media devices. Modular video cards are the least standardized of all modular components, but manufacturers are beginning to adopt industry-wide standards. Many manufacturers use modular floppy disk drives and CD-media devices, even allowing users to swap easily between different types of drives.

- Laptops use one of four types of RAM. Most older laptops use either 72-pin or 144-pin SO-DIMMs with SDRAM technology. DDR SDRAM systems primarily use 200-pin SO-DIMMs, although you'll also find 172-pin micro-DIMMs. Every decent laptop has upgradeable RAM slots. Get the correct RAM; many portable PC makers use proprietary RAM solutions. No standard exists for RAM placement in portables. More often than not, you need to unscrew or pop open a panel on the underside of the portable and press out on the restraining clips to make the RAM stick pop up so that you can remove and replace it.

- Laptops that support shared memory benefit from more affordable video cards. The video card has less built-in RAM and uses a portion of the computer's system RAM to make up the difference. This results in a lower cost, but system performance suffers because RAM that is shared with the video card is not available to programs. Shared memory technologies include TurboCache (by NVIDIA) and HyperMemory (by ATI).

- ATA drives in the 2.5-inch drive format now rule in all laptops. Currently, the larger 2.5-inch hard drives holds up to 120 GB while the larger 3.5-inch hard drives hold more than 750 GB.

- Both Intel and AMD have long sold specialized, modular CPUs for laptops; however, replacing the CPU in a laptop often requires disassembling the entire machine.

- To add functionality to laptops, manufacturers include modular drives with their machines. Modular drive bays can accommodate various optical drives, hard drives, or batteries. Most modular drives are truly hot-swappable, enabling you to remove and insert devices without any special software.

- Many laptops now come with integrated wireless networking support by way of a built-in Wi-Fi adapter usually installed in a Mini PCI slot on the laptop motherboard. The Mini PCI bus is an adaptation of the standard PCI bus and was developed specifically for integrated communications peripherals such as modems and network adapters. To extend battery life, built-in communication devices such as Wi-Fi and Bluetooth adapters can be toggled on and off without powering down the computer.

Managing and Maintaining Portable Computers

- Portable computers use three different types of batteries: Nickel-Cadmium (Ni-Cd), Nickel-Metal Hydride (Ni-MH), and Lithium-Ion (Li-Ion).

- The first batteries used in mobile PCs were Nickel-Cadmium (Ni-Cd). If a Ni-Cd battery was not completely discharged before each recharge, it would lose a significant amount of its rechargeability, a condition referred to as battery memory. At best, Ni-Cd batteries would last for 1000 charges, but they were very susceptible to heat. Because of the toxic metals inside these batteries, they had to be disposed of via specialty disposal companies. Although no longer used in PCs, Ni-Cd batteries are still found in cellular and cordless phones.

- The second generation of mobile PC batteries, the Nickel-Metal Hydride (Ni-MH) batteries are less susceptible to memory problems, tolerate overcharging better, take more recharging, and last longer between rechargings, but they are still susceptible to heat.

- Although some portable PCs still use Ni-MH batteries, Lithium-Ion (Li-Ion) is more common today. This third-generation battery takes fewer charges than Ni-MH, but it lasts longer between charges. Li-Ion batteries can explode if they are overcharged, so they have circuitry to prevent overcharging.

- A new type of battery called the smart battery tells the computer when it needs to be charged, conditioned, or replaced.

- Research continues on other power sources, with the most promising technology being fuel cells that produce electrical power as a result of a chemical reaction between hydrogen and oxygen. A small fuel cell may be able to power a laptop for up to 40 hours before it needs to be replaced or refilled.

- Batteries should be stored in a cool place, but not in the freezer because of moisture, metal racks, and food. Condition Ni-Cd and Ni-MH batteries to make them last longer. You can clean battery contacts with alcohol or a dry cloth. Batteries contain dangerous chemicals; never handle one that has ruptured. Always recycle old batteries rather than disposing of them in the trash.

- The process of cooperation among the hardware, the BIOS, and the OS to reduce power use is known generically as power management. Early laptops used power continuously, regardless of whether the system was using the device at the time or not. With power management features, today's laptops can automatically turn off unused devices or can shut down the entire system, leaving the information in RAM ready for a restart.

- Starting with the 386SX, Intel introduced System Management Mode (SMM), a power management system that would make the CPU and all peripherals go to "sleep." In 1992, Intel introduced the improved Advanced Power Management (APM) specification, followed by the Advanced Configuration and Power Interface (ACPI) standard in 1996.

- To use APM or ACPI, the computer must have an SMM-capable CPU, an APM-compliant BIOS, and devices that can be shut off. Referred to as "Energy Star" devices, these peripherals can shut down without actually turning off. The OS must also know how to request that a particular device be shut down. ACPI extends power-saving to include hot-swappable devices.

- Virtually all laptops and desktops use power management functions. APM defines four power-usage levels, including Full On, APM Enabled, APM Standby, and APM Suspend.

- Configure APM/ACPI through CMOS or through the Power Options Control Panel applet in Windows 2000/XP, with Windows settings overriding CMOS settings. Many CMOS versions enable configuration of wake-up events, such as having the system monitor a modem or particular IRQ.

- Hibernation writes information from RAM to the hard drive. Upon waking up, the data is returned to RAM, and programs and files are in the same state as when the computer entered hibernation.

- Use an appropriate screen cleaner (not glass cleaner) to clean the LCD screen. Use compressed air around the keyboard and PC card sockets. Never use water around the keyboard.

- To combat the inevitable heat produced by a portable computer, always use power management, keep an air space between the bottom of the laptop and the surface on which it rests, don't use a keyboard protector for an extended period of time, and be aware of your fan.

- Store your portable computer in a quality case when traveling. Laptops benefit from a cushy carrying case; hard aluminum cases keep your PDA from getting banged up. Well-padded backpacks not only keep your laptop protected, but make your system less appealing to would-be thieves. When traveling, don't forget accessories like AC power cords, additional batteries, or modular devices. Remove all discs from drives and make sure you have enough battery power to boot up for security personnel. If shipping your computer, go with a reputable carrier, keep your tracking number, and request a delivery signature. Use a laptop lock or a software tracking system to protect your laptop when traveling.

Troubleshooting Portable Computers

- If your laptop won't power on, try a different wall outlet. If it still fails to power up, remove all peripheral devices and try again.

- If the screen doesn't come on properly, verify the laptop is configured to use the built-in LCD screen by pressing the appropriate key to cycle through the internal and external monitors. If you hear a popping sound, you may have blown an inverter.

- If wireless networking is not working, check for the physical switch that toggles the internal wireless adapter on and off. If your laptop doesn't have a switch, check for a key combination that toggles the wireless adapter. You also may be out of range. Physically walk the laptop closer to the wireless router or access point.

- If your PDA or tablet PC fails to recognize handwriting, retrain the digitizer. PDAs often have a setting to align the screen; tablet PC users can check the Control Panel for the appropriate applet.

- If the keypad or touchpad doesn't work, try a shot of compressed air, reseat the physical internal connection, or reconfigure the driver settings through the Keyboard or Mouse Control Panel applets.

Key Terms

16-bit (505)

Advanced Configuration and Power Interface (ACPI) (517)

Advanced Power Management (APM) (517)

aspect ratio (495)

auto-switching power supply (521)

battery memory (514)

beaming (499)

card services (506)

CardBus (505)

conditioning charger (514)

desktop extender (497)

desktop replacement (497)

docking station (509)

ExpressCard (505)

fuel cell (515)

hibernation (517)

high gloss (496)

HotSync (499)

laptop (496)

Lithium-Ion (Li-Ion) (514)

matte (496)

Mini PCI (513)

Nickel-Cadmium (Ni-Cd) (514)

Nickel-Metal Hydride (Ni-MH) (514)

PC Card (505)

pen-based computing (498)

personal digital assistant (PDA) (498)

port replicator (508)

shared memory (511)

smart battery (515)

socket services (506)

stylus (498)

System Management Mode (SMM) (517)

Tablet PC (500)

touchpad (497)

TrackPoint (497)

Key Term Quiz

Use the Key Terms list to complete the sentences that follow. Not all terms will be used.

1. PC Cards require two levels of software drivers: _____ to allow the laptop to detect when a PC Card has been inserted or removed and _____ to provide drivers to make the card work.

2. Although _____ were the first batteries for mobile PCs, they are limited now to cellular and cordless phones because of their problems with battery memory.

3. The _____ tells the computer when it needs to be charged, conditioned, or replaced.

4. John read an ad recently for a _____ portable PC that had everything he could possibly want on a PC, desktop or portable!

5. Small, reduced-function portable computing devices, called _____, use cut-down operating systems such as Windows CE or Palm OS.

6. Using a chemical reaction between hydrogen and oxygen, _____ may in a few years be able to provide laptops with electrical power for up to 40 hours.

7. With the 386SX, Intel introduced _____, the first power management system with the ability to make the CPU and all peripherals go to sleep.

8. Many newer laptops feature _____ screens offering richer color, higher contrast, and wider viewing angles.

9. Laptops using _____ are less expensive, as the video card has less built-in memory, but the RAM it borrows from the system results in less memory available to programs.

10. A(n) _____ combines the best of PDAs and fully featured laptops.

Multiple-Choice Quiz

1. What infrared process enables you to transfer data from one PDA to another wirelessly?
   A. Beaming
   B. Flashing
   C. Panning
   D. Sending

2. Which of the following statements best describes hard drives typically found in laptops?
   A. They are 2.5-inch ATA drives, but they do not hold as much data as the 3.5-inch hard drives found in desktop PCs.
   B. They are 3.5-inch ATA drives just like those found in desktop PCs, but they usually require "cable select" settings rather than master or slave.
   C. They are 3.5-inch ATA drives that hold more data than the 2.5-inch hard drives found in desktop PCs.
   D. They are 2.5-inch PCMCIA drives while desktops usually have 3.5-inch SCSI drives.

3. Which of the following APM power levels writes information from RAM to the hard drive and then copies the data back to RAM when the computer is activated again?
   A. Full On
   B. APM Enabled
   C. APM Standby
   D. Hibernation

4. Portable PCs typically use which of the following kinds of upgradeable RAM?
   A. 68-pin and 72-pin RIMMs
   B. 30-pin and 72-pin SIMMs
   C. 72-pin and 144-pin SO-DIMMs
   D. 30-pin and 72-pin SO-RIMMs

5. Where do you configure APM/ACPI in Windows XP? (Select all that apply.)
   A. The Power Options applet in the Control Panel
   B. The Display applet in the Control Panel

C. The Power Management applet in the Control Panel

D. The Power and Devices applet in the Control Panel

6. Which of the following kinds of PC Cards is the most commonly used, especially for I/O functions?

   A. Type I

   B. Type II

   C. Type III

   D. Type IV

7. Which of the following input devices will you most likely find on a portable PC?

   A. TrackPoint

   B. Touchpad

   C. Trackball

   D. Mouse

8. When a new USB mouse is plugged in, the laptop does not recognize that a device has been added. What is the most likely cause of this problem?

   A. The device was plugged in while the system was running.

   B. The device was plugged in while the system was off and then booted.

   C. The system is running Windows 98.

   D. The system does not yet have the proper drivers loaded.

9. How should you remove a modular drive?

   A. Use the Hardware Removal Tool in the System Tray.

   B. Shut down, remove the drive, and power back on.

   C. Simply remove the drive with no additional actions.

   D. Use Device Manager to uninstall the device.

10. Which buses do ExpressCards use?

   A. Hi-Speed USB and FireWire

   B. Hi-Speed USB and PCI Express

   C. PCI and PCI Express

   D. Mini PCI and Parallel

11. Convertibles and slates describe what type of device?

   A. Multicore processor

   B. Clamshell laptop computer

   C. PDA

   D. Tablet PC

12. If wireless networking is not working, what should you check?

   A. Check the switch on the side of the laptop that toggles power to the network card.

   B. Make sure the Ethernet cable is plugged into the laptop.

   C. Make sure the digitizer has been trained.

   D. Make sure Power Management is enabled.

13. Which bus was developed specifically for integrated communications peripherals such as modems and network adapters?

   A. FireWire

   B. Mini PCI

   C. PCI

   D. USB

14. Erin has an older laptop with a switch on the back that says 115/230. What does this indicate?

   A. The laptop has an auto-switching power supply.

   B. The laptop has a fixed-input power supply.

   C. The laptop has a step-down transforming power supply.

   D. The laptop has a step-up transforming power supply.

15. John's PDA suddenly stopped recognizing his handwriting. What's a likely fix for this problem?

   A. Replace the stylus.

   B. Retrain the digitizer.

   C. Replace the digitizer.

   D. Retrain the stylus.

Essay Quiz

1. At the upcoming training seminar for new techs, your boss wants to make sure they understand and use power management settings. You've been asked to prepare a short presentation showing the range of power management settings available in Windows 2000 and XP and demonstrating how to set them. What will you include in your presentation?

2. You've been tasked to advise your group on current portable computer technology so they can purchase ten new laptops by the end of the quarter. In a short essay, weigh the pros and cons of getting desktop replacements versus smaller laptops that would come with docking stations.

3. Your boss has a new portable computer and is planning to take it with him on a business trip to Paris. He's not all that tech-savvy or much of a traveler, so write a memo that tells him what to do or avoid while traveling, especially overseas.

4. Norm wants to upgrade his laptop's hard drive, CPU, and RAM. He's upgraded all of these components on his desktop, so he doesn't think that he'll run into much trouble. What advice will you give him about selecting the components and upgrading the laptop?

5. Monica just received her aunt's old laptop. It uses a Ni-Cd battery, but no matter how long she charges it, it only runs her PC for about 30 minutes before it dies. She can't understand why the battery runs out so fast, but she figures she needs a new battery. The local computer store has two kinds of batteries, Ni-MH and Li-Ion, both of which will physically fit into her computer. She's not sure which of these to buy or whether either of them will work with her PC. She's asked you whether her old battery is indeed bad and to help her select a new battery. What will you tell her?

Lab Projects

• Lab Project 16.1

This chapter mentioned that, although they are more expensive, portable PCs typically provide less processing power, have smaller hard drives, and in general are not as full-featured as desktop computers. Use the Internet to check sites such as www.ibm.com, www.gateway.com, www.dell.com, and www.hp.com to compare the best equipped, most powerful laptop you can find with the best equipped, most powerful desktop computer you can find. How do their features and prices compare? Now find a less expensive laptop and try to find a desktop computer that is as similar as possible in terms of capabilities, and compare their prices.

• Lab Project 16.2

A local company just donated ten laptops to your school library. They are IBM ThinkPad 600x PIII 500-Mhz laptops with 128 MB of RAM and two Type II PC slots. The school would like to let distance education students check out these computers, but the laptops do not have modems. Your hardware class has been asked to select PC Card modems for these laptops. What features will you look for in selecting the right modem? Either go to the local computer store or search the Internet to find the modem cards you will recommend.

Understanding Printing

"People believe almost anything they see in print."

—CHARLOTTE, *CHARLOTTE'S WEB* BY E. B. WHITE

In this chapter, you will learn how to

- **Describe current printer technologies**

- **Explain how printers communicate with PCs**

- **List the different ways that printers may be connected to PCs**

Despite all of the talk about the "paperless office," printers continue to be a vital part of the typical office. In many cases, PCs are used exclusively for the purpose of producing paper documents. Many people simply prefer dealing with a hard copy. Programmers cater to this preference by using metaphors such as *page, workbook,* and *binder* in their applications. The CompTIA A+ certification strongly stresses the area of printing and expects a high degree of technical knowledge of the function, components, maintenance, and repair of all types of printers.

■ Printer Technologies

No other piece of your computer system is available in a wider range of styles, configurations, and feature sets than a printer, or at such a wide price variation. What a printer can and can't do is largely determined by the type of printer technology it uses—that is, how it gets the image onto the paper. Modern printers can be categorized into several broad types: impact, inkjet, dye-sublimation, thermal, laser, and solid ink.

Impact Printers

Printers that create an image on paper by physically striking an ink ribbon against the paper's surface are known as **impact printers**. While *daisy-wheel* printers (essentially an electric typewriter attached to the PC instead of directly to a keyboard) have largely disappeared, their cousins, **dot-matrix printers**, still soldier on in many offices. While dot-matrix printers don't deliver what most home users want—high-quality and flexibility at a low cost—they're still widely found in businesses for two reasons: dot-matrix printers have a large installed base in businesses, and they can be used for multipart forms because they actually strike the paper. Impact printers tend to be relatively slow and noisy, but when speed, flexibility, and print quality are not critical, they provide acceptable results. PCs used for printing multipart forms, such as *point of sale (POS)* machines that need to print receipts in duplicate, triplicate, or more, represent the major market for new impact printers, although many older dot-matrix printers remain in use.

Dot-matrix printers (Figure 17.1) use a grid, or matrix, of tiny pins, also known as **printwires**, to strike an inked printer ribbon and produce images on paper. The case that holds the printwires is called a **printhead**. Using either 9 or 24 pins, dot-matrix printers treat each page as a picture broken up into a dot-based raster image. The 9-pin dot-matrix printers are generically called *draft quality*, while the 24-pin printers are known as *letter quality* or **near-letter quality (NLQ)**. The BIOS for the printer (either built into the printer or a printer driver) interprets the raster image in the same way that a monitor does, "painting" the image as individual dots. Naturally, the more pins, the

Figure 17.1 An Epson FX-880+ dot-matrix printer *(photo courtesy of Epson America, Inc.)*

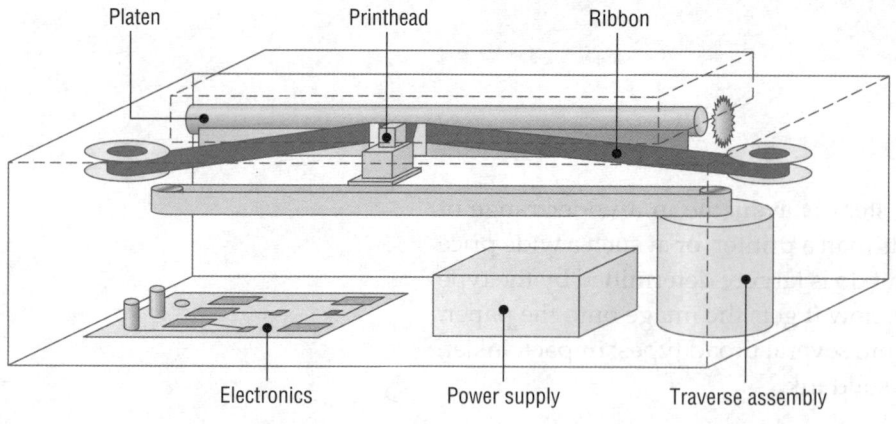

Platen   Printhead   Ribbon

Electronics   Power supply   Traverse assembly

• **Figure 17.2**   Inside a dot-matrix printer

higher the resolution. Figure 17.2 illustrates the components common to dot-matrix printers.

Inkjet Printers

Inkjet printers (also called *ink-dispersion printers*) like the one in Figure 17.3 are relatively simple devices consisting of a printhead mechanism, support electronics, a transfer mechanism to move the printhead back and forth, and a paper feed component to drag, move, and eject paper (Figure 17.4). They work by ejecting ink through tiny tubes. Most inkjet printers use heat to move the ink, while a few use a mechanical method. The heat-method printers use tiny resistors or electroconductive plates at the end of each tube (Figure 17.5), which literally boil the ink; this creates a tiny air bubble that ejects a droplet of ink onto the paper, thus creating portions of the image.

The ink is stored in special small containers called **ink cartridges**. Older inkjet printers had two cartridges: one for black ink and another for colored ink. The color cartridge had separate compartments for cyan (blue), magenta (red), and yellow ink, to print colors using a method known as CMYK (you'll read more about CMYK later in this chapter). If your color cartridge ran out of one of the colors, you had to purchase a whole new color cartridge or deal with a messy refill kit.

Printer manufacturers began to separate the ink colors into three separate cartridges, so that printers

• **Figure 17.3**   Typical inkjet printer

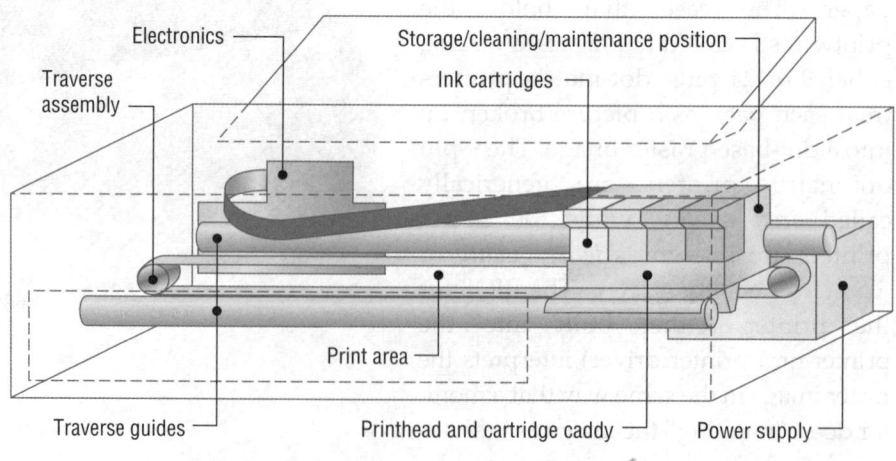

Electronics   Storage/cleaning/maintenance position

Traverse assembly   Ink cartridges

Print area

Traverse guides   Printhead and cartridge caddy   Power supply

• **Figure 17.4**   Inside an inkjet printer

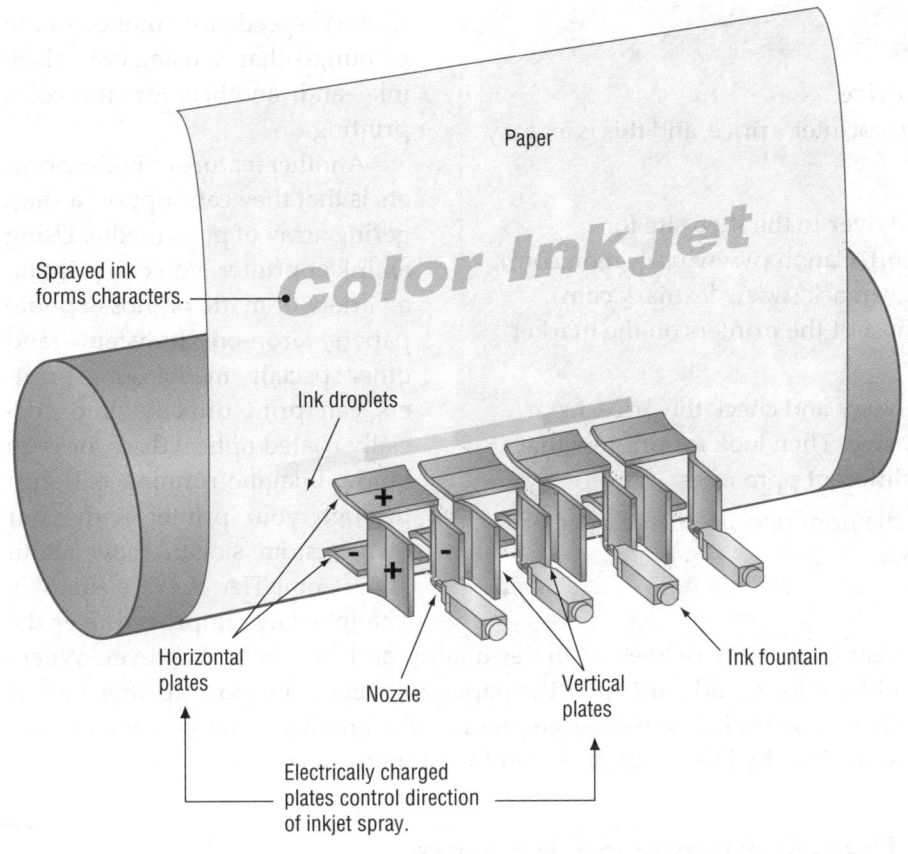

Paper

Sprayed ink
forms characters.

Ink droplets

+

+

-

-

Horizontal
plates

Nozzle

Vertical
plates

Ink fountain

Electrically charged
plates control direction
of inkjet spray.

• **Figure 17.5**   Detail of the inkjet printhead

came with four cartridges: one for each color and a fourth for black (Figure 17.6). This not only was more cost-effective for the user, but it also resulted in higher quality printouts. Today you can find color inkjet printers with six, eight, or more color cartridges. In addition to the basic CMYK inks, the other cartridges provide for green, blue, gray, light cyan, dark cyan, and more. Typically, the more ink cartridges a printer uses, the higher the quality of the printed image—and the higher the cost of the printer.

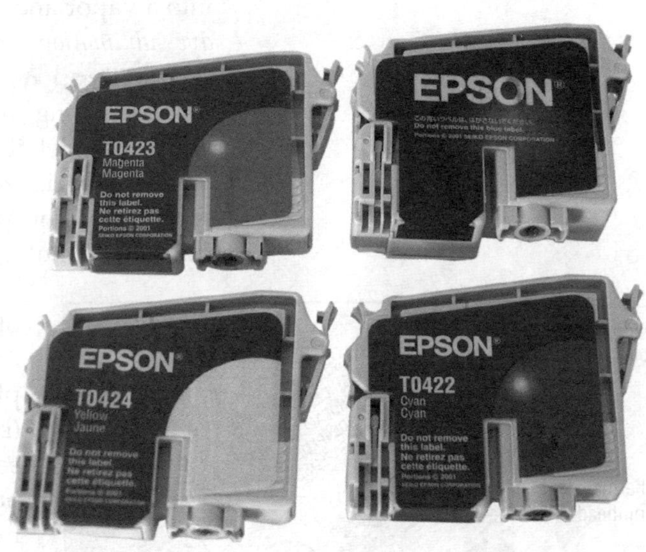

The two key features of an inkjet printer are the **print resolution**—that is, the density of ink, which affects print quality—and the print speed. Resolution is measured in **dots per inch (dpi)** ; higher numbers mean that the ink dots on the page are closer together, so your printed documents will look better. Resolution is most important when you're printing complex images such as full-color photos, or when you're printing for duplication and you care that your printouts look good. Print speed is measured in **pages per minute (ppm)** , and this specification is normally indicated right on the printer's box. Most printers have one

• **Figure 17.6**   Inkjet ink cartridges

Try This!

Pages per Minute versus Price

Printer speed is a key determinant of a printer's price, and this is an easy assertion to prove. Try this:

1. Fire up your browser and head over to the Web site for Hewlett-Packard (www.hp.com), Canon (www.usa.canon.com), Epson (www.epson.com), or Lexmark (www.lexmark.com). These four companies make most of the printers on the market today.

2. Pick a particular printer technology and check the price, from the cheapest to the most expensive. Then look for printers that have the same resolution but different ppm rates.

3. Check the prices and see how the ppm rate affects the price of two otherwise identical printers.

(faster) speed for monochrome printing—that is, using only black ink—and another for full-color printing.

Another feature of inkjet printers is that they can support a staggering array of print media. Using an inkjet printer, you can print on a variety of matte or glossy photo papers, iron-on transfers, and other specialty media; some printers can print directly onto specially coated optical discs, or even fabric. Imagine running a T-shirt through your printer with your own custom slogan (how about "I'm CompTIA A+ Certified!"). The inks have improved over the years, too, now delivering better quality and longevity than ever. Where older inks would smudge if the paper got wet or start to fade after a short time, modern inks are smudge proof and of archival quality—for example, some inks by Epson are projected to last up to 200 years.

Dye-Sublimation Printers

The term *sublimation* means to cause something to change from a solid form into a vapor and then back into a solid. This is exactly the process behind *dye-sublimation printing*, sometimes called *thermal dye transfer* printing. **Dye-sublimation printers** are used mainly for photo printing, high-end desktop publishing, medical and scientific imaging, or other applications for which fine detail and rich color are more important than cost and speed. Smaller, specialized printers called *snapshot* printers use dye-sublimation specifically for printing photos at a reduced cost compared to their full-sized counterparts.

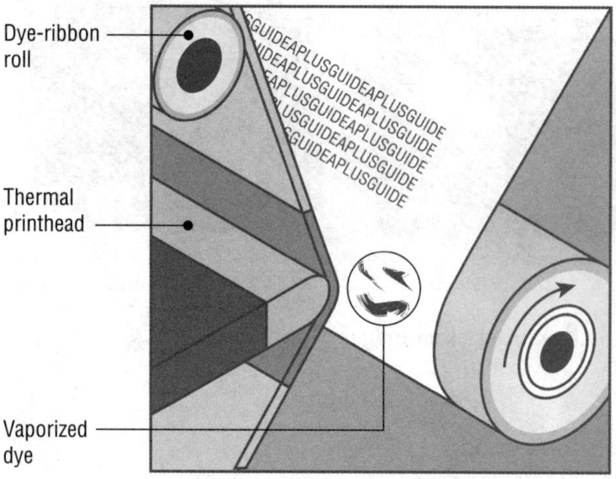

The dye-sublimation printing technique is an example of the so-called CMYK (**c**yan, **m**agenta, **y**ellow, blac**k**) method of color printing. It uses a roll of heat-sensitive plastic film embedded with page-sized sections of cyan (blue), magenta (red), and yellow dye; many also have a section of black dye. A print head containing thousands of heating elements, capable of precise temperature control, moves across the film, vaporizing the dyes and causing them to soak into specially-coated paper underneath before cooling and reverting to a solid form. This process requires one pass per page for each color. Some printers also use a final finishing pass that applies a protective laminate coating to the page. Figure 17.7 shows how a dye-sublimation printer works.

Documents printed through the dye-sublimation process display *continuous tone* images, meaning that the printed image is not constructed of pixel dots, but is a

Dye-ribbon roll

Thermal printhead

Vaporized dye

• **Figure 17.7**   The dye-sublimation printing process

continuous blend of overlaid differing dye colors. This is in contrast to other print technologies' *dithered* images, which use closely packed, single-color dots to simulate blended colors. Dye-sublimation printers produce high-quality color output that rivals professional photo lab processing.

Thermal Printers

Thermal printers use a heated printhead to create a high-quality image on special or plain paper. You'll see two kinds of thermal printers in use. The first is the *direct thermal* printer, and the other is the *thermal wax transfer* printer. Direct thermal printers burn dots into the surface of special heat-sensitive paper. If you remember the first generation of fax machines, you're already familiar with this type of printer. It is still used as a receipt printer in many retail businesses. Thermal wax printers work similarly to dye-sublimation printers, except that instead of using rolls of dye-embedded film, the film is coated with colored wax. The thermal print head passes over the film ribbon and melts the wax onto the paper. Thermal wax printers don't require special papers like dye-sublimation printers, so they're more flexible and somewhat cheaper to use, but their output isn't quite as good because they use color dithering.

Laser Printers

Using a process called *electro-photographic imaging*, laser printers produce high-quality and high-speed output of both text and graphics. Figure 17.8 shows a typical laser printer. Laser printers rely on the photoconductive properties of certain organic compounds. *Photoconductive* means that particles of these compounds, when exposed to light (that's the "photo" part), will *conduct* electricity. Laser printers usually use lasers as a light source because of their precision. Some lower-cost printers use LED arrays instead.

• **Figure 17.8** Typical laser printer

Tech Tip

Hidden Costs

Some printers use consumables—such as ink—at a much faster rate than others, prompting the industry to rank printers in terms of their cost per page. Using an inexpensive printer (laser or inkjet) costs around 4 cents per page, while an expensive printer can cost more than 20 cents per page—a huge difference if you do any volume of printing. This hidden cost is particularly pernicious in the sub-US$100 inkjet printers on the market. Their low prices often entice buyers, who then discover that the cost of consumables is outrageous—these days, a single set of color and black inkjet cartridges can cost as much as the printer itself, if not more!

The first laser printers created only monochrome images. Today, you can also buy a color laser printer, although the vast majority of laser printers produced today are still monochrome. Although a color laser printer can produce complex full-color images such as photographs, they really shine for printing what's known as *spot color*—for example, eye-catching headings, lines, charts, or other graphical elements that dress up an otherwise plain printed presentation.

Critical Components of the Laser Printer

The CompTIA A+ certification exams take a keen interest in the particulars of the laser printing process, so it pays to know your way around a laser printer. Let's take a look at the many components of a laser printer and their functions (Figure 17.9).

Toner Cartridge   The toner cartridge in a laser printer (Figure 17.10) is so named because of its most obvious activity—supplying the toner that creates the image on the page. To reduce maintenance costs, however, many other laser printer parts, especially those that suffer the most wear and tear, have been incorporated into the toner cartridge. Although this makes replacement of individual parts nearly impossible, it greatly reduces the need for replacement; those parts that are most likely to break are replaced every time you replace the toner cartridge.

Photosensitive Drum   The photosensitive drum is an aluminum cylinder coated with particles of photosensitive compounds. The drum itself is grounded to the power supply, but the coating is not. When light hits these particles, whatever electrical charge they may have had "drains" out through the grounded cylinder.

Erase Lamp   The erase lamp exposes the entire surface of the photosensitive drum to light, making the photosensitive coating conductive. Any electrical charge present in the particles bleeds away into the grounded drum, leaving the surface particles electrically neutral.

Primary Corona   The primary corona wire, located close to the photosensitive drum, never touches the drum. When the primary corona is

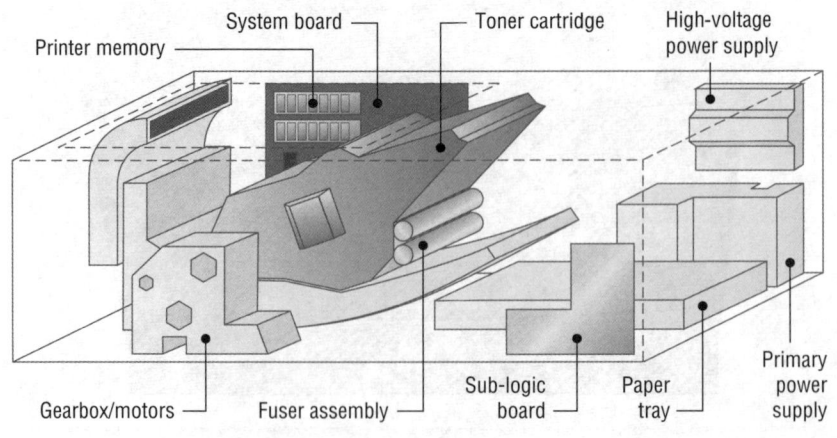

• Figure 17.9   Components inside a laser printer

charged with an extremely high voltage, an electric field (or corona) forms, enabling voltage to pass to the drum and charge the photosensitive particles on its surface. The *primary grid* regulates the transfer of voltage, ensuring that the surface of the drum receives a uniform negative voltage of between ~600 and ~1000 volts.

● **Figure 17.10**   Laser printer's toner cartridge

Laser   The laser acts as the writing mechanism of the printer. Any particle on the drum struck by the laser becomes conductive, enabling its charge to be drained away into the grounded core of the drum. The entire surface of the drum has a uniform negative charge of between ~600 and ~1000 volts following its charging by the primary corona wire. When particles are struck by the laser, they are discharged and left with a ~100 volt negative charge. Using the laser, we can "write" an image onto the drum. Note that the laser writes a positive image to the drum.

Toner   The toner in a laser printer is a fine powder made up of plastic particles bonded to iron particles. The *toner cylinder* charges the toner with a negative charge of between ~200 and ~500 volts. Because that charge falls between the original uniform negative charge of the photosensitive drum (~600 to ~1000 volts) and the charge of the particles on the drum's surface hit by the laser (~100 volts), particles of toner are attracted to the areas of the photosensitive drum that have been hit by the laser (that is, areas that have a *relatively* positive charge with reference to the toner particles).

Transfer Corona   To transfer the image from the photosensitive drum to the paper, the paper must be given a charge that will attract the toner particles off of the drum and onto the paper. The transfer corona is a thin wire, usually protected by other thin wires, that applies a positive charge to the paper, drawing the negatively charged toner particles to the paper. The paper, with its positive charge, is also attracted to the negatively charged drum. To prevent the paper from wrapping around the drum, a static charge eliminator removes the charge from the paper.

In most laser printers, the transfer corona is outside the toner cartridge, especially in large commercial grade machines. The transfer corona is prone to a build-up of dirt, toner, and debris through electrostatic attraction, and it must be cleaned. It is also quite fragile—usually finer than a human hair. Most printers with an exposed transfer corona will provide a special tool to clean it, but you can also—very delicately—use a cotton swab soaked in 90 percent denatured alcohol (don't use rubbing alcohol because it contains emollients). As always, never service any printer without first turning it off and unplugging it from its power source.

Fuser Assembly   The fuser assembly is almost always separate from the toner cartridge. It is usually quite easy to locate as it will be close to the bottom of the toner cartridge and will usually have two rollers to fuse the toner. Sometimes the fuser is somewhat enclosed and difficult to recognize, because the rollers are hidden from view. To help you determine the location of the fuser, think about the data path of the paper and the fact that fusing is the final step of printing.

The toner is merely resting on top of the paper after the static charge eliminator has removed the paper's static charge. The toner must be permanently attached to the paper to make the image permanent. Two rollers, a pressure roller and a heated roller, are used to fuse the toner to the paper. The pressure roller presses against the bottom of the page while the heated roller presses down on the top of the page, melting the toner into the paper. The heated roller has a nonstick coating such as Teflon to prevent the toner from sticking to the heated roller.

Power Supplies   All laser printers have at least two separate power supplies. The first power supply is called the "primary power supply" or sometimes just the "power supply." This power supply, which may actually be more than one power supply, provides power to the motors that move the paper, the system electronics, the laser, and the transfer corona. The high-voltage power supply usually provides power only to the primary corona. The extremely high voltage of the high-voltage power supply makes it one of the most dangerous devices in the world of PCs! Before opening a printer to insert a new toner cartridge, it is imperative that you *always turn off* a laser printer!

 Cross Check

High Voltage—Keep Away!

The power supply inside a laser printer is not the only dangerous high-voltage toy in the world of PC equipment. You've learned about two other potentially hazardous electrical components that you should approach with caution.

1.   What are they?
2.   Which of these three items is potentially the most deadly?

To refresh your memory, check out Chapter 8, "Understanding PC Power," and Chapter 15, "Understanding Video."

Turning Gears   A laser printer has many mechanical functions. First, the paper must be picked up, printed upon, and kicked out of the printer. Next, the photosensitive roller must be turned and the laser, or a mirror, must be moved from left to right. Finally, the toner must be evenly distributed, and the fuser assembly must squish the toner into the paper. All these functions are served by complex gear systems. In most laser printers, these gear systems are packed together in discrete units generically called *gear packs* or *gearboxes*. Most laser printers will have two or three gearboxes that a tech can remove relatively easily in the rare case when one of them fails. Most gearboxes also have their own motor or solenoid to move the gears.

System Board   Every laser printer contains at least one electronic board. On this board is the main processor, the printer's ROM, and RAM used to store the image before it is printed. Many printers divide these functions among two or three boards dispersed around the printer. An older printer may also have an extra ROM chip and/or a special slot where you can install an extra ROM chip, usually for special functions such as PostScript.

On some printer models you can upgrade the contents of these ROM chips (the *firmware*) by performing a process called *flashing* the ROM. Flashing is a lot like upgrading the system BIOS, which you learned about in Chapter 5, "Understanding BIOS and CMOS." Upgrading the firmware can help fix bugs, add new features, or update the fonts in the printer.

Of particular importance is the printer's RAM. When the printer doesn't have enough RAM to store the image before it prints, you get a memory overflow problem. Also, some printers will store other information in the RAM, including fonts or special commands. Adding RAM is usually a simple job—just snapping in a SIMM or DIMM stick or two—but getting the *right* RAM is important. Call or check the printer manufacturer's Web site to see what type of RAM you need. Although most printer companies will happily sell you their expensive RAM, most printers can use generic DRAM like the kind you use in a PC.

Ozone Filter The coronas inside laser printers generate ozone (O_3). Although not harmful to humans in small amounts, even tiny concentrations of ozone will cause damage to printer components. To counter this problem, most laser printers have a special ozone filter that needs to be vacuumed or replaced periodically.

Sensors and Switches Every laser printer has a large number of sensors and switches spread throughout the machine. The sensors are used to detect a broad range of conditions such as paper jams, empty paper trays, or low toner levels. Many of these sensors are really tiny switches that detect open doors and so on. Most of the time these sensors/switches work reliably. Yet occasionally, they can become dirty or broken, sending a false signal to the printer. Simple inspection is usually sufficient to determine if a problem is real or just the result of a faulty sensor/switch.

Solid Ink

Solid ink printers use just what you'd expect—solid inks. The technology was originally developed by Tektronix, a company that was acquired by Xerox. Solid ink printers use solid sticks of non-toxic "ink" that produce more vibrant color than other print methods. The solid ink is melted and absorbed into the paper fibers; it then solidifies, producing a continuous tone output. Unlike dye-sublimation printers, all colors are applied to the media in a single pass, reducing the chances of misalignment. Solid ink sticks do not rely on containers like ink for inkjet printers and can be "topped off" midway through a print job by inserting additional color sticks without taking the printer offline.

These printers are fast, too! A full-color print job outputs the first page in about six seconds. Of course, all that speed and quality comes at a price. Xerox's base model starts at about twice the cost of a laser printer, with the expensive model selling for about six times the cost! Solid ink printers become a bit more affordable when you factor in the cost of consumables. A single stick of ink costs about as much as an inkjet cartridge, for example, but with a print capacity of 1000 pages, that completely beats the cost of inkjet cartridges over time.

Printer Languages

Now that you've learned about the different types of print devices and techniques, it's time to take a look at how they communicate with the PC. How do you tell a printer to make a letter *A* or to print a picture of your pet iguana? Printers are designed to accept predefined printer languages that handle both characters and graphics. Your software must use the proper language when communicating with your printer so that your printer can output your documents onto a piece of paper. Following are the more common printer languages.

ASCII

You might think of the **American Standard Code for Information Interchange (ASCII)** language as nothing more than a standard set of characters, the basic alphabet in upper and lowercase with a few strange symbols thrown in. ASCII actually contains a variety of control codes for transferring data, some of which can be used to control printers. For example, ASCII code 10 (or 0A in hex) means "Line Feed," and ASCII code 12 (0C) means "Form Feed." These commands have been standard since before the creation of IBM PCs, and all printers respond to them. If they did not, the PRT SCR (print screen) key would not work with every printer. Being highly standardized has advantages, but the control codes are extremely limited. Printing high-end graphics and a wide variety of fonts requires more advanced languages.

PostScript

Adobe Systems developed the **PostScript** page description language in the early 1980s as a device-independent printer language capable of high-resolution graphics and scalable fonts. PostScript interpreters are embedded in the printing device. Because PostScript is understood by printers at a hardware level, the majority of the image processing is done by the printer and not the PC's CPU, so PostScript printers print fast. PostScript defines the page as a single raster image; this makes PostScript files extremely portable—they can be created on one machine or platform and reliably printed out on another machine or platform (including, for example, high-end typesetters).

Hewlett Packard Printer Control Language (PCL)

Hewlett Packard developed its **printer control language (PCL)** as a more advanced printer language to supersede simple ASCII codes. PCL features a set of printer commands greatly expanded from ASCII. Hewlett Packard designed PCL with text-based output in mind; it does not support advanced graphical functions. The most recent version of PCL, PCL6 features scalable fonts and additional line drawing commands. Unlike PostScript, however, PCL is not a true page description language; it uses a series of commands to define the characters on the page. Those commands must be supported by each individual printer model, making PCL files less portable than PostScript files.

Windows GDI

Windows 2000/XP use the graphical device interface (GDI) component of the operating system to handle print functions. Although you *can* use an external printer language such as PostScript, most users simply install printer drivers and let Windows do all the work. The GDI uses the CPU rather than the printer to process a print job and then sends the completed job to the printer. When you print a letter with a TrueType font in Windows, for example, the GDI processes the print job and then sends bitmapped images of each page to the printer. Therefore, the printer sees a page of TrueType text as a picture, not as text. As long as the printer has a capable enough raster image processor and plenty of RAM, you don't need to worry about the printer language in most situations.

Printer Connectivity

Most printers connect to one of two ports on the PC: a DB-25 parallel port or a USB port. The parallel connection is the classic way to plug in a printer, but most printers today use USB. You'll need to know how to support the more obscure parallel ports, cables, and connections as well as the plug-and-play USB connections.

Parallel Communication and Ports

The parallel port was included in the original IBM PC as a faster alternative to serial communication. The IBM engineers considered serial communication, limited to 1 bit at a time, to be too slow for the "high-speed" devices of the day (for example, dot-matrix printers). The standard parallel port has been kept around for backward compatibility despite several obvious weaknesses.

Parallel ports may be far faster than serial ports, but they are slow by modern standards. The maximum data transfer rate of a standard parallel port is still only approximately 150 kilobytes per second (KBps). Standard parallel communication on the PC also relies heavily on software, eating up a considerable amount of CPU time that could be better used.

Parallel ports are hindered by their lack of true bidirectional capability. One-way communication was acceptable for simple line printers and dot-matrix printers, but parallel communication became popular for a wide

Although the phrase "Centronics standard" was commonly used in the heyday of parallel ports, no such animal actually existed. Prior to the development of IEEE 1284, a very loose set of "standards" were adopted by manufacturers in an attempt to reduce incompatibility issues somewhat.

Many techs confuse the concept of duplex printing—a process that requires special printers capable of printing on both sides of a sheet of paper—with bidirectional printing. They are two different things!

Cross Check

LPT Port Resources

In Chapter 6, "Understanding the Expansion Bus," you learned about LPT ports, which come into play when you need to connect a printer to a parallel port.

1. Do you remember the chart of LPT and COM port system resources?

2. Can you name the IRQ and I/O base address assignments for LPT1 and LPT2?

range of external devices that required two-way communication. Although it is possible to get two-way communication out of a standard parallel port, the performance is not impressive.

IEEE 1284 Standard

In 1991, a group of printer manufacturers proposed to the *Institute of Electrical and Electronics Engineers (IEEE)* that a committee be formed to propose a standard for a backward-compatible, high-speed, bidirectional parallel port for the PC. The committee was the IEEE 1284 committee (hence the name of the standard).

The **IEEE 1284 standard** requires the following:

- Support for five distinct modes of operation: *compatibility mode, nibble mode, byte mode, EPP,* and *ECP*
- A standard method of negotiation for determining which modes are supported both by the host PC and by the peripheral device
- A standard physical interface (that is, the cables and connectors)
- A standard electrical interface (that is, termination, impedance, and so on)

Because only one set of data wires exists, all data transfer modes included in the IEEE 1284 standard are half-duplex: Data is transferred in only one direction at a time.

Tech Tip

IEEE 1284 Transfer Modes

The five modes of operation for parallel printing specified in the IEEE 1284 standard (compatibility, nibble, byte, EPP, ECP) are inching closer to obsolescence as USB printers take over the market. You can look up these modes by name using various Web search tools, if you find yourself needing to optimize the performance of a legacy parallel printer.

Parallel Connections, Cabling, and Electricity

Although no true standard exists, "standard parallel cable" usually refers to a printer cable with the previously-mentioned male **DB-25 connector** on one end and a 36-pin **Centronics connector** on the other (Figure 17.11). The shielding (or lack thereof) of the internal wiring and other electrical characteristics of a standard parallel printer cable are largely undefined except by custom. In practice, these standard cables are acceptable for transferring data at 150 KBps, and for distances of less than 6 feet, but they would be dangerously unreliable for some transfer modes.

For more reliability at distances up to 32 feet (10 meters), use proper IEEE 1284–compliant cabling. The transfer speed drops with the longer cables, but it does work, and sometimes the trade-off between speed and distance is worth it.

Installing a parallel cable is a snap. Just insert the DB-25 connector into the parallel port on the back of the PC and insert the Centronics connector into the printer's Centronics port, and you're ready to go to press!

• **Figure 17.11**   Standard parallel cable with 36-pin Centronics connector on one end and DB-25 connector on the other

Some printers come with both USB and parallel connections, but this is becoming increasingly rare. If you need a parallel printer for a system, be sure to confirm that the particular model you want will work with your system!

USB Printers

New printers now use USB connections that can be plugged into any USB port on your computer. USB printers don't usually come with a USB cable, so you need to purchase one at the time you purchase a printer. (It's quite a disappointment to come home with your new printer only to find you can't connect it because it didn't come with a USB cable.) Most printers use the standard USB type A connector on one end and the smaller USB type B connector on the other end, although some use two type A connectors. Whichever configuration your USB printer has, just plug in the USB cable—it's literally that easy!

 In almost all cases, you must install drivers before you plug a USB printer into your computer.

FireWire Printers

Some printers offer FireWire connections in addition to or instead of USB connections. A FireWire printer is just as easy to connect as a USB printer, as FireWire is also hot-swappable and hot-pluggable. Again, make sure you have the proper cable, as most printers don't come with one. If your printer has both connections, which one should you use? The answer is easy if your PC has only USB and not FireWire. If you have a choice, either connection is just as good as the other, and the speeds are comparable. If you already have many USB devices, you may want to use the FireWire printer connection, to leave a USB port free for another device.

Network Printers

Connecting a printer to a network isn't just for offices anymore. More and more homes and home offices are enjoying the benefits of network printing. It used to be that to share a printer on a network—that is, to make it available to all network users—you would physically connect the printer to a single computer and then share the printer on the network. The downside to this was that the computer to which the printer was connected had to be left on for others to use the printer.

Today, the typical network printer comes with its own onboard network adapter that uses a standard RJ-45 Ethernet cable to connect the printer directly to the network by way of a router. The printer can typically be assigned a static IP address, or it can acquire one dynamically from a DHCP server. (Don't know what a router, IP address, or DHCP server is? Take a look at Chapter 18, "Understanding Networking.") Once connected to the network, the printer acts independently of any single PC. Some of the more costly network printers come with a built-in Wi-Fi adapter to connect to the network wirelessly. Alternatively, some printers offer Bluetooth interfaces for networking.

Even if a printer does not come with built-in Ethernet, Wi-Fi, or Bluetooth, you can purchase a standalone network device known as a *print server* to connect your printer to the network. These print servers, which can be Ethernet or Wi-Fi, enable one or several printers to attach via parallel port or USB. So take that ancient ImageWriter dot-matrix printer and network it—I dare you!

 See Appendix A, "Installing and Troubleshooting Printers," for more details on the laser printing process and installing and troubleshooting printers. The Essentials exam expects you to know the basic concepts of installing and troubleshooting printers, but these concepts receive much more emphasis in the 220-602 (IT Technician) and 220-604 (Depot Technician) exams.

Other Printers

Plenty of other connection types are available for printers. We've focused mainly on parallel, USB, FireWire, and networked connections. Be aware that you may run into an old serial port printer or a SCSI printer. While this is unlikely, know that it's a possibility.

Chapter 17 Review

■ Chapter Summary

After reading this chapter and completing the exercises, you should understand the following aspects of printers.

Printer Technologies

■ Impact printers create an image on paper by physically striking an ink ribbon against the paper's surface. The most commonly-used impact printer technology is dot matrix. Dot-matrix printers have a large installed base in businesses, and they can be used for multipart forms because they actually strike the paper. Dot-matrix printers use a grid, or matrix, of tiny pins, also known as printwires, to strike an inked printer ribbon and produce images on paper. The case that holds the printwires is called a printhead. Dot-matrix printers come in two varieties: 9-pin (draft quality) and 24-pin (letter quality).

■ Inkjet printers include a printhead mechanism, support electronics, a transfer mechanism to move the printhead back and forth, and a paper feed component to drag, move, and eject paper. They eject ink through tiny tubes. The heat or pressure used to move the ink is created by tiny resistors or electroconductive plates at the end of each tube.

■ Ink is stored in ink cartridges. Older color printers used two cartridges: one for black and one for cyan, magenta, and yellow. Newer printers come with four, six, eight, or more cartridges.

■ The quality of a print image is called the print resolution. The resolution is measured in dots per inch (dpi), which has two values: horizontal and vertical (for example, 600 × 600 dpi). Printing speed is measured in pages per minute (ppm). Modern inkjet printers can print on a variety of media, including glossy photo paper, optical discs, or fabric.

■ Dye-sublimation printers are used to achieve excellent print quality, especially in color, but they're expensive. Documents printed through the dye-sublimation process display continuous tone

images, meaning that each pixel dot is a blend of the different dye colors. This is in contrast to other print technologies' dithered images, which use closely packed, single-color dots to simulate blended colors.

■ Two kinds of thermal printers create either quick, one-color printouts (direct thermal), such as faxes or store receipts, or higher-quality (thermal wax transfer) color prints.

■ Using a process called electro-photographic imaging, laser printers produce high-quality and high-speed output. Laser printers usually use lasers as a light source because of their precision, but some lower-cost printers may use LED arrays instead. The toner cartridge in a laser printer supplies the toner that creates the image on the page; many other laser printer parts, especially those that suffer the most wear and tear, have been incorporated into the toner cartridge. Although the majority of laser printers are monochrome, you can find color laser printers capable of printing photographs.

■ Be aware of the cost of consumables when purchasing a printer. Some less expensive printers may seem like a good deal, but ink or toner cartridge replacements can cost as much as the entire printer.

■ The photosensitive drum in a laser printer is an aluminum cylinder coated with particles of photosensitive compounds. The erase lamp exposes the entire surface of the photosensitive drum to light, making the photosensitive coating conductive and leaving the surface particles electrically neutral. When the primary corona is charged with an extremely high voltage, an electric field (or corona) forms, enabling voltage to pass to the drum and charge the photosensitive particles on its surface; the surface of the drum receives a uniform negative voltage of between ~600 and ~1000 volts.

- The laser acts as the writing mechanism of the printer. When particles are struck by the laser, they are discharged and left with a ~100-volt negative charge. The toner in a laser printer is a fine powder made up of plastic particles bonded to iron particles. The toner cylinder charges the toner with a negative charge of between ~200 and ~500 volts. Because that charge falls between the original uniform negative charge of the photosensitive drum (~600 to ~1000 volts) and the charge of the particles on the drum's surface hit by the laser (~100 volts), particles of toner are attracted to the areas of the photosensitive drum that have been hit by the laser. The transfer corona applies a positive charge to the paper, drawing the negatively charged toner particles on the drum to the paper. A static charge eliminator removes the paper's static charge. Two rollers, a pressure roller and a heated roller, are used to fuse the toner to the paper.

- All laser printers have at least two separate power supplies. The primary power supply, which may actually be more than one power supply, provides power to the motors that move the paper, the system electronics, the laser, and the transfer corona. The high-voltage power supply usually only provides power to the primary corona; it is one of the most dangerous devices in the world of PCs. Always unplug a laser printer before opening it up.

- A laser printer's mechanical functions are served by complex gear systems packed together in discrete units, generically called gear packs or gearboxes. Most laser printers have two or three. Every laser printer has sensors that detect a broad range of conditions such as paper jams, empty paper trays, or low toner levels.

- Every laser printer contains at least one electronic system board (many have two or three) that contains the main processor, the printer's ROM, and RAM used to store the image before it is printed. When the printer doesn't have enough RAM to store the image before it prints, you get a memory overflow problem. Most printers can use generic DRAM like the kind you use in your PC, but check with the manufacturer to be sure.

- Because even tiny concentrations of ozone (O_3) will cause damage to printer components, most laser printers have a special ozone filter that needs to be vacuumed or replaced periodically.

- Solid ink printers use sticks of solid ink to produce extremely vibrant color. The ink is melted and absorbed into the paper fibers, and then it solidifies, producing continuous tone output in a single pass.

- ASCII contains a variety of control codes for transferring data, some of which can be used to control printers; ASCII code 10 (or 0A in hex) means "Line Feed," and ASCII code 12 (0C) means "Form Feed." These commands have been standard since before the creation of IBM PCs, and all printers respond to them; however, the control codes are extremely limited. Utilizing high-end graphics and a wide variety of fonts requires more advanced languages.

- Adobe Systems' PostScript page description language is a device-independent printer language capable of high-resolution graphics and scalable fonts. PostScript is understood by printers at a hardware level, so the majority of the image processing is done by the printer, not the PC's CPU—so PostScript printers print fast. PostScript defines the page as a single raster image; this makes PostScript files extremely portable.

- Hewlett Packard's printer control language (PCL) features a set of printer commands greatly expanded from ASCII, but it does not support advanced graphical functions. PCL6 features scalable fonts and additional line drawing commands. PCL uses a series of commands to define the characters on the page, rather than defining the page as a single raster image.

- Windows 2000/XP use the graphical device interface (GDI) component of the operating system to handle print functions. The GDI uses the CPU rather than the printer to process a print job and then sends the completed job to the printer. As long as the printer has a capable-enough raster image processor (RIP) and plenty of RAM, you don't need to worry about the printer language at all in most situations.

- Most printers connect to one of two ports on the PC: a DB-25 parallel port or a USB port. The parallel connection is the classic way to plug in a printer, but most new printers use USB. The parallel port was included in the original IBM PC as a faster alternative to serial communication, and has been kept around for backward compatibility. Parallel ports are slow by modern standards, with a maximum data transfer rate of 150 KBps. Parallel ports lack true bidirectional capability. A standard parallel connection usually consists of a female DB-25 connector on the PC and a corresponding male connector on the printer cable. Eight wires are used as grounds, four for control signals, five for status signals, and eight for data signals going from the PC to the device. The parallel connector on the printer side is called a Centronics connector.

- IEEE 1284 was developed as a standard for a backward-compatible, high-speed, bidirectional parallel port for the PC. It requires support for compatibility mode, nibble mode, byte mode, EPP, and ECP; a standard method of negotiating compatible modes between printer and PC; standard cables and connectors; and a standard electrical interface.

- USB is the most popular type of printer connection today. USB printers rarely come with the necessary USB cable, so you may need to purchase one at the same time you purchase the printer. FireWire printers are less prevalent than USB, but offer easy connectivity, high speed, and hot-swapping capability.

- Network printers come with their own network card and connect directly to a network. This can be an RJ-45 port for an actual cable, or a wireless network card. Some printers offer Bluetooth adapters for networking. To connect a printer with a network card directly to a network, use a print server.

Key Terms

American Standard Code for Information Interchange (ASCII) (542)
Centronics connector (544)
DB-25 connector (544)
dot-matrix printer (533)
dots per inch (dpi) (535)
dye-sublimation printer (536)
erase lamp (538)
fuser assembly (539)
graphical device interface (GDI) (543)
IEEE 1284 standard (544)

impact printer (533)
ink cartridge (534)
inkjet printer (534)
laser (539)
laser printer (537)
near-letter quality (NLQ) (533)
network printer (545)
pages per minute (ppm) (535)
parallel port (543)
photosensitive drum (538)
PostScript (542)
primary corona (538)

printhead (533)
print resolution (535)
printwires (533)
printer control language (PCL) (542)
solid ink printer (541)
static charge eliminator (539)
thermal printer (537)
toner (539)
toner cartridge (538)
transfer corona (539)

Key Term Quiz

Use the Key Terms list to complete the sentences that follow. Not all terms will be used.

1. The _____ requires support for compatibility mode, nibble mode, byte mode, EPP, and ECP.

2. A standard parallel printer cable normally has a male _____ on one end and a 36-pin _____ on the other.

3. A printer that creates an image on paper by physically striking an ink ribbon against the paper's surface is known as a(n) _____.

4. Laser printers use lasers to create the print image on the _____.

5. The _____ on a standard laser printer contains a pressure roller and a heated roller.

6. Adobe's _____ is a device-independent printer language capable of high-resolution graphics and scalable fonts.

7. Windows 2000/XP use the _____ component of the operating system to handle print functions.

8. The resolution of a printer is measured in _____.

9. A printer's speed is rated in _____.

10. The _____ is responsible for cleaning the photosensitive drum of electrical charge.

Multiple-Choice Quiz

1. Which part of a laser printer applies a positive charge to the paper that attracts the toner particles to it?
   A. Erase lamp
   B. Transfer corona
   C. Laser
   D. Primary corona

2. What is the approximate maximum data transfer rate of a standard parallel port?
   A. 50 KBps
   B. 150 KBps
   C. 500 KBps
   D. 2 MBps

3. The dye-sublimation printing technique is an example of what method of color printing?
   A. CMYK
   B. Thermal wax transfer
   C. RGB
   D. Direct thermal

4. What is the best way to make a printer available to everyone on your network and maintain the highest level of availability?
   A. Use a FireWire printer connected to a user's PC and share that printer on the network.
   B. Use a USB printer connected to a user's PC and share that printer on the network.
   C. Use a network printer connected directly to the network.
   D. Use a mechanical switch box with the printer.

5. Sheila in accounting needs to print receipts in duplicate. The white copy stays with accounting and the pink copy goes to the customer. What type of printer should you install?
   A. Inkjet
   B. Impact
   C. LaserJet
   D. Thermal wax transfer

6. Which statement about inkjet printers is true?
   A. All modern inkjet printers use four cartridges consisting of cyan, magenta, yellow, and black ink.
   B. An inkjet printer's resolution is measured in ppm.
   C. Inkjet printers create continuous-tone images.
   D. Inkjet printers eject ink through tiny tubes.

7. Ron's inkjet printer uses four cartridges—cyan, magenta, yellow, and black. To produce a particular shade of green, tiny dots of cyan and yellow are packed closely together on the paper. What is this simulation of color blending called?
   A. Blending
   B. Dithering
   C. Rasterizing
   D. Sublimation

8. What is the maximum length supported by IEEE 1284–compliant cabling?
   A. 6 feet
   B. 10 feet
   C. 15 feet
   D. 32 feet

9. Which statement about laser printers is true?

   A. All laser printers use lasers.

   B. Laser printers do not print color.

   C. Replacing the toner cartridge when the laser printer is powered on is dangerous.

   D. The transfer corona can be cleaned with a cotton swab and rubbing alcohol.

10. Which comparison is true about solid-ink printers and dye-sublimation printers?

   A. Solid-ink printers can output continuous tone, producing a higher quality image than dye-sublimation.

   B. Solid-ink printers produce output in a single pass, unlike dye-sublimation printers which require multiple passes of the paper. Therefore, solid-ink printers suffer less from misalignment.

   C. Solid-ink printers can produce multi-page forms, such as invoices in triplicate. Dye-sublimation printers cannot.

   D. Solid-ink printers vaporize the solid ink into a gas, which then solidifies on the paper. This is the same process used in dye-sublimation.

11. Which of the following is *not* a printer language?

   A. ASCII

   B. Hexcode

   C. PCL

   D. PostScript

12. Which type of printer can produce continuous tone?

   A. Impact

   B. Inkjet

   C. Dye-sublimation

   D. Direct thermal

13. What connectors are on the ends of an IEEE 1284 parallel printer cable? (Choose two.)

   A. DB-25

   B. DB-36

   C. 25-pin Centronics

   D. 36-pin Centronics

14. What port can be used to connect a printer to a PC? (Choose all that apply.)

   A. Parallel port

   B. USB

   C. FireWire

   D. Ethernet

15. Which printer description language was developed by Hewlett Packard?

   A. GDI

   B. PCI

   C. PCL

   D. PostScript

Essay Quiz

1. Your department needs a number of color inkjet printers. At your organization, however, all purchases are handled through professional buyers. Sadly, they know nothing about color inkjet printers. You need to submit a Criteria for Purchase form to your buyers. This is the standard form that your organization gives to buyers so they know what to look for in the products they buy. What are the top three purchasing criteria that you think they need to consider? Write the criteria as simply and clearly as possible.

2. Interview a person who uses a computer for work. Ask the person about the tasks they normally do during then day, and then write a short description of the type of printer that would most suit that person's needs. Explain why this printer would be the best choice.

3. You have been tasked to make a recommendation for a printer purchase for a busy office of ten people. Make a case for purchasing either an inkjet or laser printer (choose the technology that you did not select for Essay Question #2), providing enough information to compare the two technologies.

4. Write a short essay comparing and contrasting inkjet printers with the three less-common print technologies: dye-sublimation, thermal, and solid ink.

Lab Project 17.1

Select a laser printer (preferably one that you actually have on hand) and then locate and compile, on paper, all of the following information about your printer:

- User's guide
- List of error codes

- Troubleshooting guides
- Location of the latest drivers for Windows XP

Understanding Networking

"Since you cannot do good to all, you are to pay special attention to those who, by accidents of time, or place, or circumstance, are brought into closer connection to you."

—Saint Augustine

In this chapter, you will learn how to

- **Explain network technologies**
- **Explain network operating systems**
- **Install and configure wired networks**

Networks dominate the modern computing environment. A vast percentage of businesses have PCs connected in a small local area network (LAN), and big businesses simply can't survive with connecting their many offices into a single wide area network (WAN). Even the operating systems of today demand networks. Windows XP and Windows Vista, for example, come out of the box *assuming* you'll attach them to a network of some sort just to make them work past 30 days (Product Activation), and they get all indignant if you don't.

Because networks are so common today, every good tech needs to know the basics of networking technology. Accordingly, this chapter teaches you how to build and configure a basic network.

■ Networking Technologies

When the first network designers sat down at a café to figure out a way to enable two or more PCs to share data and peripherals, they had to write a lot of details on little white napkins to answer even the most basic questions. The first big question was: *How?* It's easy to say, "Well, just run a wire between them!" Although most networks do manifest themselves via some type of cable, this barely touches the thousands of questions that come into play here. Here are a few of the *big* questions:

- How will each computer be identified? If two or more computers want to talk at the same time, how do you ensure all conversations are understood?

- What kind of wire? What gauge? How many wires in the cable? Which wires do which things? How long can the cable be? What type of connectors?

- If more than one PC accesses the same file, how can they be prevented from destroying each other's changes to that file?

- How can access to data and peripherals be controlled?

Clearly, making a modern PC network entails a lot more than just stringing up some cable! Most commonly, you have a `client` machine, a PC that requests information or services. It needs a `network interface card (NIC)` that defines or labels the client on the network. A NIC also helps break files into smaller data units, called `packets`, to send across the network, and it helps reassemble the packets it receives into whole files. Second, you need some medium for delivering the packets between two or more PCs—most often this is a wire that can carry electrical pulses; sometimes it's radio waves or other wireless methods. Third, your PC's operating system has to be able to communicate with its own networking hardware and with other machines on the network. Finally, modern PC networks often employ a `server` machine that provides information or services. Figure 18.1 shows a typical network layout.

This section of the chapter looks at the inventive ways network engineers found to handle the first two of

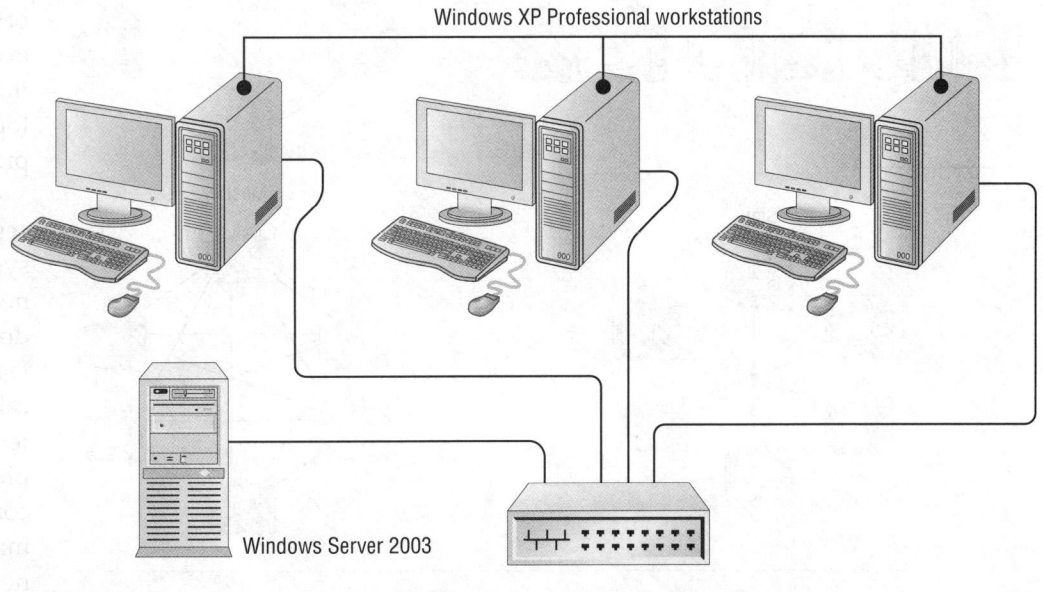

Windows XP Professional workstations

Windows Server 2003

● **Figure 18.1** A typical network

the four issues. After a brief look at core technology, the chapter dives into four specific types of networks.

Topology

If a bunch of computers connect together to make a network, some logic or order must influence the way that they connect. Perhaps each computer connects to a single main line that snakes around the office. Each computer might have its own cable, with all the cables coming together to a central point. Or maybe all the cables from all the computers connect to a main loop that moves data along a track, picking up and dropping off data like a circular subway line.

A network's *topology* describes the way that computers connect to each other in that network. The most common network topologies are called *bus, ring, star,* and *mesh.* Figure 18.2 shows the four types: a **bus topology** , where all computers connect to the network via a main line called a *bus cable*; a **ring topology** , where all computers on the network attach to a central ring of cable; a **star topology** , where the computers on the network connect to a central wiring point (usually called a *hub*); and a **mesh topology** , where each computer has a dedicated line to every other computer. Make sure you know these four topologies!

If you're looking at Figure 18.2 and thinking that a mesh topology looks amazingly resilient and robust, it is—at least on paper. Because every computer physically connects to every other computer on the network, even if half the PCs crash, the network still functions as well as ever (for the survivors). In a practical sense, however, implementing a true mesh topology network would be an expensive mess. For example, even for a tiny network with only 10 PCs, you would need *45* separate and distinct pieces of cable to connect every PC to every other PC. What a mesh mess! Because of this, mesh topologies have never been practical in a cabled network.

While a topology describes the method by which systems in a network connect, the topology alone doesn't describe all of the features necessary to make a cabling system work. The term *bus topology,* for example, describes a network that consists of some number of machines connected to the network via the same piece of cable. Notice that this

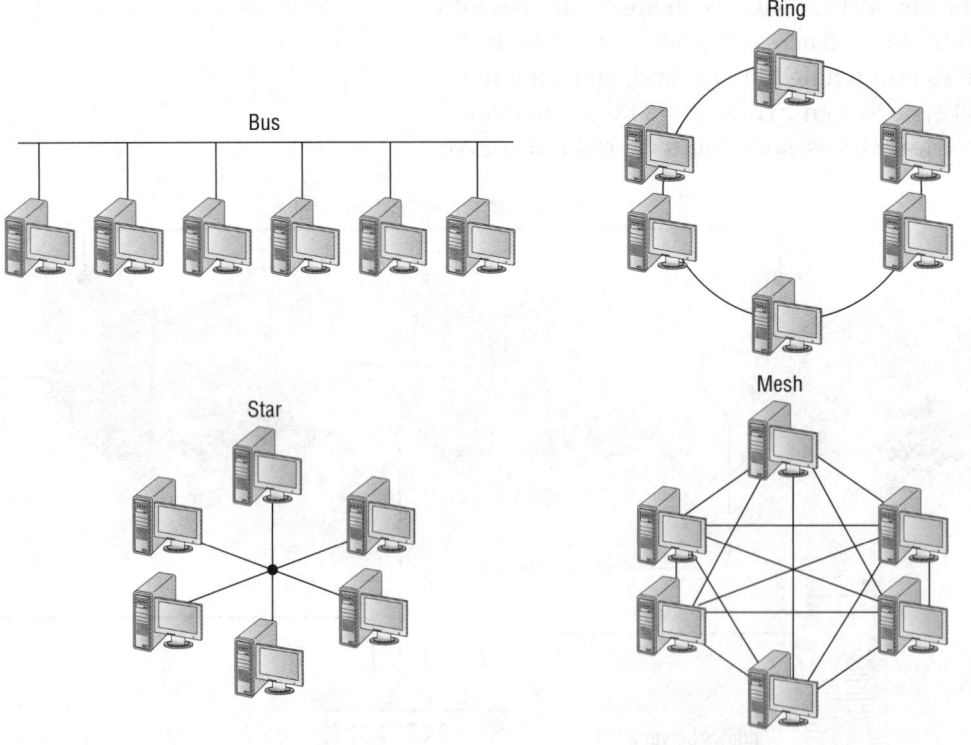

definition leaves a lot of questions unanswered. What is the cable made of? How long can it be? How do the machines decide which machine should send data at a specific moment? A network based on a bus topology can answer these questions in a number of different ways.

Most techs make a clear distinction between the *logical topology* of a network—how the network is laid out on paper, with nice straight lines and boxes—and the physical topology. The *physical topology* describes the typically messy computer network, with cables running diagonally through the ceiling space or snaking their way through walls. If someone describes the topology of a particular network, make sure you understand whether they're talking about the logical or physical topology.

Over the years, manufacturers and standards bodies created several specific network technologies based on different topologies. A *network technology* is a practical application of a topology and other critical technologies to provide a method to get data from one computer to another on a network. These network technologies have names like Ethernet and Token Ring, which will be discussed later in this chapter.

Essentials

Packets/Frames and NICs

Data is moved from one PC to another in discrete chunks called *packets* or *frames.* The terms *packet* and *frame* are interchangeable. Every NIC in the world has a built-in identifier, a binary address unique to that single network card, called a **media access control (MAC) address**. You read that right—every network card in the world has its own unique MAC address! The MAC address is 48 bits long, providing more than 281 *trillion* MAC addresses, so there are plenty of MAC addresses to go around. MAC addresses may be binary, but we represent them using 12 hexadecimal characters. These MAC addresses are burned into every NIC, and some NIC makers print the MAC address on the card. Figure 18.3 shows the System Information utility description of a NIC, with the MAC address highlighted.

Hey! I thought we were talking about packets? Well, we are, but you need to understand MAC addresses to understand packets. All the many varieties of packets share certain common features (Figure 18.4). First, packets contain the MAC address of the network card to which the data is being sent. Second, they have the MAC address of the network card that sent the data. Third is the data itself (at this point, we have no

> Even though MAC addresses are embedded into the NIC, some NICs will allow you to change the MAC address on the NIC. This is rarely done.

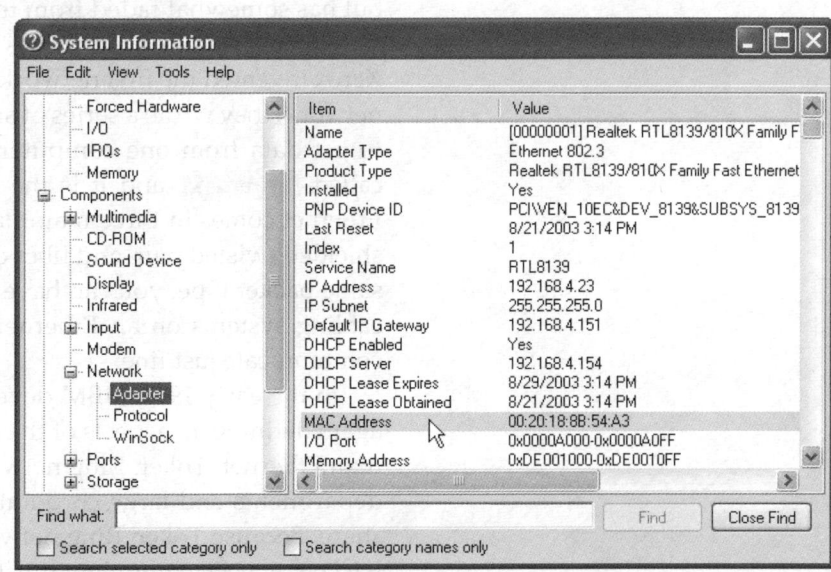

• **Figure 18.3**   MAC address

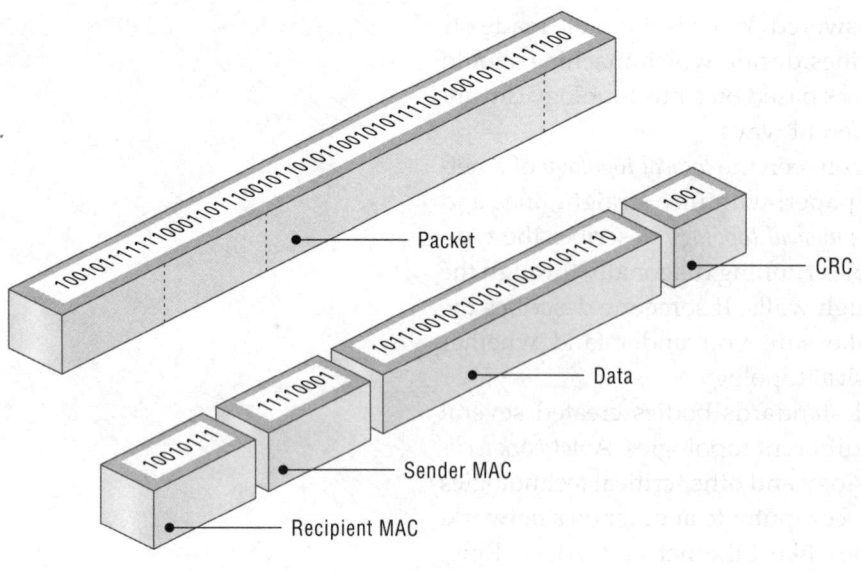

Packet

CRC

Data

Sender MAC

Recipient MAC

• **Figure 18.4**   Generic packet/frame

idea what the data is—certain software handles that question), which can vary in size depending on the type of frame. Finally, some type of data check—such as a **cyclic redundancy check (CRC)**—is performed and information is stored in the packet to enable the receiving network card to verify if the data was received in good order.

This discussion of packets raises the question, how big is the packet? Or more specifically, how much data do you put into each packet? How do you ensure that the receiving PC understands the *way* that the data was broken down by the sending machine and can thus put the pieces back together? The problem in answering these questions is that they encompass so many items. When the first networks were created, *everything* from the frames to the connectors to the type of cable had to be invented from scratch.

To make a successful network, you need the sending and receiving PCs to use the same hardware protocol. A **hardware protocol** defines many aspects of a network, from the topology, to the packet type, to the cabling and connectors used. A hardware protocol defines everything necessary to get data from one computer to another. Over the years, many hardware protocols have been implemented, with names like Token Ring, FDDI, and ARCnet, but one hardware protocol dominates the modern PC computing landscape: Ethernet. Token Ring contended with Ethernet for many years but has somewhat faded from the mainstream.

A consortium of companies centered on Digital Equipment, Intel, and Xerox invented the first network in the mid-1970s. More than just creating a network, they wrote a series of standards that defined everything necessary to get data from one computer to another. This series of standards was called **Ethernet**, and it is the dominant standard for today's networks. Ethernet comes in three main flavors defined by cabling type: coaxial, unshielded twisted pair, and fiber optic. Because all flavors of Ethernet use the same packet type, you can have any combination of hardware devices and cabling systems on an Ethernet network and all the PCs will be able to communicate just fine.

In the early 1980s, IBM developed the **Token Ring** network standard, again defining all aspects of the network but using radically different ideas than Ethernet. Token Ring networks continue to exist in some government departments and large corporations, but Ethernet has a far larger market share. Because Token Ring networks use a different structure for their data packets, special equipment must be used when connecting Token Ring and Ethernet networks. You'll read about Token Ring later in this chapter; focus on Ethernet for the moment.

Coaxial Ethernet

The earliest Ethernet networks connected using coaxial cable . By definition, coaxial cable (*coax* for short) is a cable within a cable—two cables that share the same center or axis. Coax consists of a center cable (core) surrounded by insulation. This in turn is covered with a *shield* of braided cable. The inner core actually carries the signal. The shield effectively eliminates outside interference. The entire cable is then surrounded by a protective insulating cover.

You've seen coaxial cable before, most likely, although perhaps not in a networking situation. Your cable TV and antenna cables are coaxial, usually RG-59 or the highly shielded RG-6. Watch out for questions on the exams dealing specifically with networking hardware protocols, trying to trip you up with television-grade coaxial answers!

Thick Ethernet—10Base5

The original Xerox Ethernet specification that eventually became known as *10Base5* defined a very specific type of coaxial cabling for the first Ethernet networks, called *Thick Ethernet*. (In fact, the name for the cable became synonymous with the 10Base5 specification.) Thick Ethernet, also known as Thicknet , was a very thick (about half an inch in diameter) type of coaxial called RG-8 . *RG* stands for Radio Grade, an industry standard for measuring coaxial cables. The *10* in 10Base5 refers to the fact that data could move through an RG-8 cable at up to 10 Mbps with this Ethernet standard.

Every PC in a 10Base5 network connected to a single cable, called a *segment* or *bus*. Thicknet supported attaching up to 100 devices to one segment. The maximum length of a Thicknet segment was 500 meters—that's what the *5* in *10Base5* meant (Figure 18.5). Networks like 10Base5 are laid out in a bus topology.

Bus Topology The Ethernet bus topology works like a big telephone party line—before any device can send a packet, devices on the bus must first determine that no other device is sending a packet on the cable (Figure 18.6). When a device sends its packet out over the bus, every other network card on the bus sees and reads the packet. Ethernet's scheme of having devices communicate like they were in a chat room is called carrier sense multiple access/collision detection (CSMA/CD) . Sometimes two cards talk (send packets) at the same time. This creates a collision, and the cards themselves arbitrate to decide which one will resend its packet first (Figure 18.7).

All PCs on a bus network share a common wire, which also means they share the data transfer capacity of that wire—or, in tech terms, they

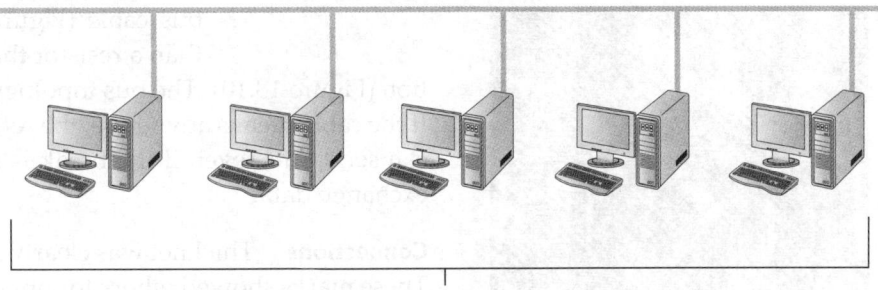

10Base5
Max. 100 PCs on one segment

Max. segment length is 500 meters

● **Figure 18.5**   10Base5

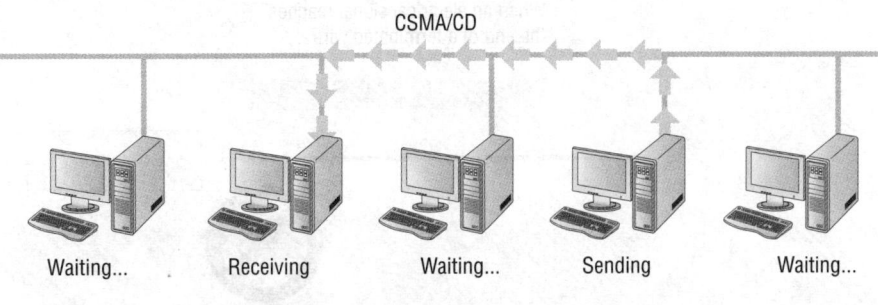

CSMA/CD

Waiting...   Receiving   Waiting...   Sending   Waiting...

● **Figure 18.6**   Devices can't send packets while others are talking.

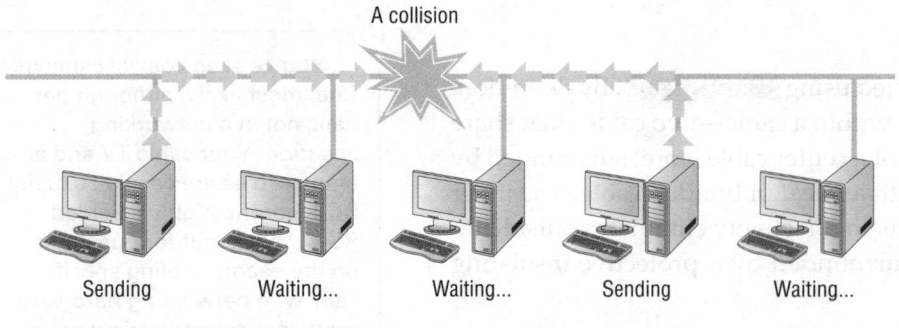

A collision

Sending   Waiting...   Waiting...   Sending   Waiting...

Figure 18.7   Collisions result when two devices send simultaneously.

When an electrical signal reaches the end of a wire...

some of the signal is reflected back.

Figure 18.8   Reflection

Figure 18.9   Terminator on back of PC

share its *bandwidth*. This creates an interesting effect. Ten PCs chatting on a bus each get to use a much higher proportion of its total bandwidth than, for instance, 100 PCs on the same bus (in this case, one-tenth compared to one-hundredth). The more PCs on a bus, the more likely you'll have a communication traffic jam. This problem does not get solved until you get beyond coaxial Ethernet.

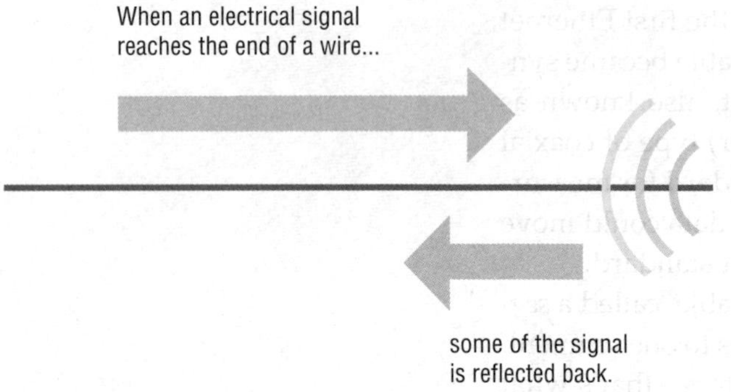

Reflection and Termination   The ends of the bus present a bit of a problem for the signal moving along the wire. Any time a device sends voltage along a wire, some voltage bounces back, or *reflects*, when it reaches the end of the wire (Figure 18.8). Network cables are no exception. Because of CSMA/CD, these packets reflecting back and forth on the cable would bring the network down. The NICs that want to send data would wait for no reason because they would misinterpret the reflections as a "busy signal." After a short while, the bus will get so full of reflecting packets that no other card can send data.

To prevent packets from being reflected, a device called a **terminator** must be plugged into the end of the bus cable (Figure 18.9). A terminator is nothing more than a resistor that absorbs the signal, preventing reflection (Figure 18.10). The bus topology's need for termination is a weak spot. If the cable breaks anywhere, the reflections quickly build up and no device can send data, even if the break is not between the devices attempting to exchange data.

Connections   Thicknet was clearly marked every 2.5 meters (Figure 18.11). These marks showed where to connect devices to the cable. All devices on a Thicknet connected at these marks to ensure that all devices were some multiple of 2.5 meters apart.

Devices are connected to Thicknet by means of a *vampire connector*. A vampire connector was so named because it actually pierces the cable to

When an electrical signal reaches the end of a terminated wire...

Terminator

there is no reflection.

Figure 18.10   No reflection with a terminator

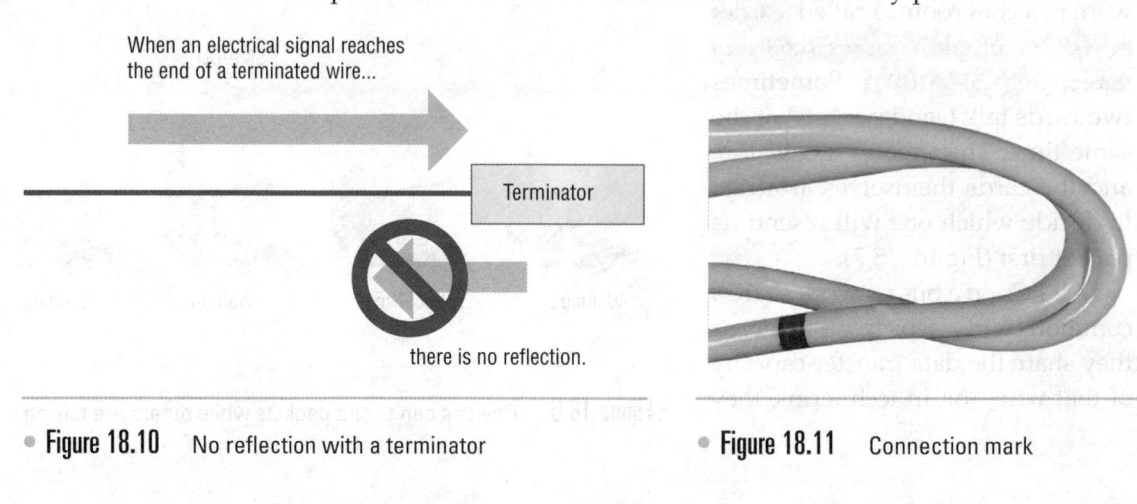

Figure 18.11   Connection mark

create the connection (Figure 18.12). A vampire connector was part of a transceiver—the device that both receives and sends data. Transceivers enable connections between the networked devices and the common cable and detect when collisions take place. Actually, all networks use transceivers, but Thicknet used an external transceiver—often referred to as an *access unit interface (AUI)*. The cable from the vampire connector/transceiver to the device had to be no more than 50 meters in length.

Thick Ethernet used a bus topology so it needed terminators. A very specific 50-ohm terminator was made just for Thicknet. It had to be placed on each end of the segment. Thicknet connected to a PC's network card via a 15-pin DB type connector. This connector was called the AUI or sometimes the *Digital, Intel, Xerox (DIX)* connector. Figure 18.13 shows the corresponding AUI port.

Thick Ethernet is on the way out or completely dead. Bus topology is always risky, because one break in the cable will cause the entire network to fail. In addition, Thicknet was expensive and hard to work with. The cable, transceivers, and terminators cost far more than those in any other network.

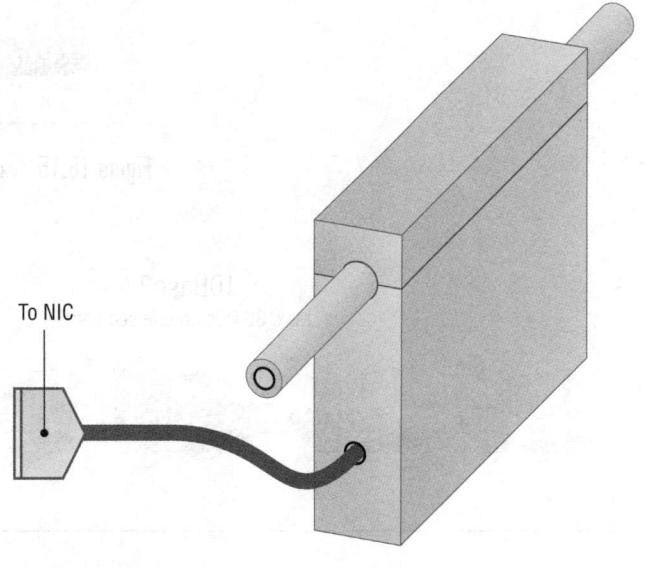

To NIC

● **Figure 18.12**   10Base5 transceiver (vampire connector)

The vast majority of 10Base5 networks have gone away, so it's unlikely you'll ever encounter one in the field. The CompTIA A+ certification exams like using older or obscure technology for incorrect answers, though, so watch out for references to 10Base5, AUI, DIX, and Thicknet as wrong answers on exam questions.

Thin Ethernet—10Base2

Thin Ethernet, also known as **Thinnet** or *Cheapernet*, was invented as a cheap alternative to Thicknet. Thinnet used a specific type of coax called **RG-58** (Figure 18.14). This type of coax looked like a skinny version of the RG-59 or RG-6 coax used by your cable television, but it was quite different. The RG rating was clearly marked on the cable. If it was not, the cable would say something like "Thinnet" or "802.3" to let you know you had the right cable (Figure 18.15).

Although Thin Ethernet also ran at 10 Mbps, it had several big limitations compared to Thick Ethernet. Thin Ethernet supported only 30 devices per segment, and each segment could be no more than 185 meters long (Figure 18.16). The 2 in 10Base2 originally meant 200 meters, but practical experience forced the standard down to 185 meters.

● **Figure 18.13**   DIX or AUI port

● **Figure 18.14**   RG-58 coaxial

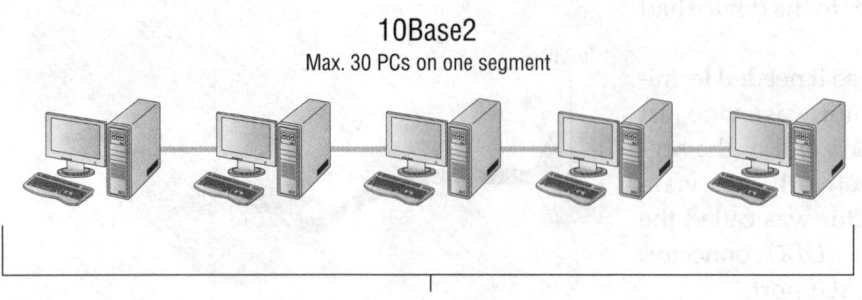

• Figure 18.15   Cable markings

10Base2
Max. 30 PCs on one segment

Max. segment length is 185 meters.

• Figure 18.16   10Base2

• Figure 18.17   T connector

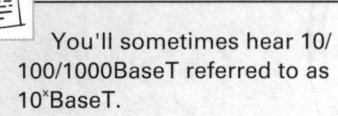

You'll sometimes hear 10/100/1000BaseT referred to as 10ˣBaseT.

On the plus side, cabling with Thinnet was a snap compared to Thicknet. The cable was much thinner and more flexible than Thicknet. In addition, the transceiver was built into the Thinnet network card, so Thinnet did not require an external transceiver. Each Thinnet network card was simply connected to the bus cable with a T connector (Figure 18.17).

The Thinnet cable had twist-on connectors, called *BNC connectors,* that attached to the T connector to form the network. Termination was handled by twisting small, specialized terminators onto the unused ends of the T connector on the machines at the ends of the chain. When installing Thinnet, it was important that one of the terminators be grounded. Special terminators could be grounded to the case of the PC. The PC also had to be grounded. You *had to* use a T connector! To add another PC to a Thinnet network, you simply removed the terminator from the last PC, added another piece of cable with another T connector, and added the terminator on the new end. It was also very easy to add a PC between two systems by unhooking one side of a T connector and inserting another PC and cable.

Thinnet, like its hefty cousin 10Base5, is on its way out or already dead. Very popular for a time in *small office/home office (SOHO)* networks, the fact that it used a bus topology where any wire break meant the whole network went down made 10Base2 unacceptable in a modern network.

UTP Ethernet (10/100/1000BaseT)

Most modern Ethernet networks employ one of three technologies (and sometimes all three), 10BaseT , 100BaseT , or 1000BaseT . As the numbers in the names would suggest, 10BaseT networks run at 10 Mbps, 100BaseT networks run at 100 Mbps, and 1000BaseT networks—called Gigabit Ethernet—run at 1000 Mbps, or 1 Gbps. All three technologies—sometimes referred to collectively as *10/100/1000BaseT*—use a *star bus* topology and connect via a type of cable called unshielded twisted pair (UTP) .

Star Bus

Imagine taking a bus network and shrinking the bus down so it will fit inside a box. Then, instead of attaching each PC directly to the wire, you attach them via cables to special ports on the box (Figure 18.18). The box with the bus takes care of termination and all those other tedious details required by

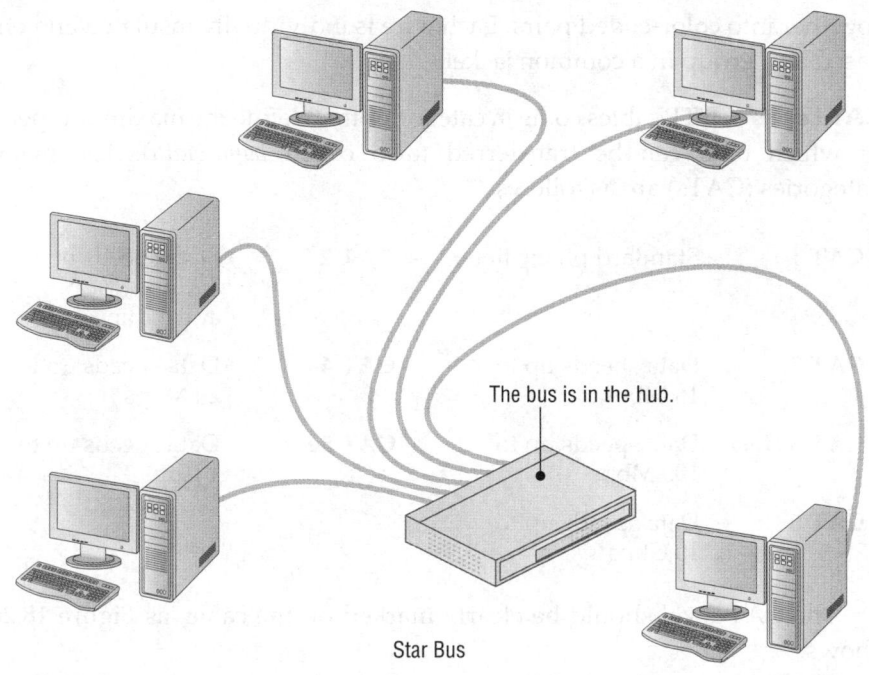

The bus is in the hub.

Star Bus

• **Figure 18.18**   Star bus

a bus network. The bus topology would look a lot like a star topology, wouldn't it?

The central box with the bus is called a hub or switch. The **hub** provides a common point for connection for network devices. Hubs can have a wide variety of ports. Most consumer-level hubs have 4 or 8, but business-level hubs can have 32 or more ports. A hub is the old style device, still in use in many networks. A **switch** is a newer, far superior version of a hub. Figure 18.19 shows a typical consumer-level switch.

A hub provides no cure for the bandwidth-sharing problem of Ethernet networks. If you put 32 PCs on a 32-port 100BaseT hub, you have 32 PCs sharing the 100 Mbps bandwidth. A switch addresses that problem by making each port a separate Ethernet network. Each PC gets to use the full bandwidth available, because a switch stops most collisions. Bottom line? Swap out your old hubs for newer switches and you'll dramatically improve your network performance.

• **Figure 18.19**   A switch

Cheap and centralized, a star bus network does not go down if a cable breaks. True, the network would go down if the hub itself failed, but that is very rare. Even if a hub fails, replacing a hub in a closet is much easier than tracing a bus running through walls and ceilings trying to find a break!

Unshielded Twisted Pair

UTP cabling is the specified cabling for 10/100/1000BaseT and is the predominant cabling system used today. Many different types of twisted pair cabling are available, and the type used depends on the needs of the network. Twisted pair cabling consists of AWG 22–26 gauge wire twisted together into color-coded pairs. Each wire is individually insulated and encased as a group in a common jacket.

CAT Levels UTP cables come in categories that define the maximum speed at which data can be transferred (also called *bandwidth*). The major categories (CATs) are as follows:

CAT 1	Standard phone line	CAT 2	Data speeds up to 4 Mbps (ISDN and T1 lines)
CAT 3	Data speeds up to 16 Mbps	CAT 4	Data speeds up to 20 Mbps
CAT 5	Data speeds up to 100 Mbps	CAT 5e	Data speeds up to 1 Gbps
CAT 6	Data speeds up to 10 Gbps		

The CAT level should be clearly marked on the cable, as Figure 18.20 shows.

The *Telecommunication Industry Association/Electronics Industries Alliance (TIA/EIA)* establishes the UTP categories, which fall under the TIA/EIA 568 specification. Currently, most installers use CAT 5e or CAT 6 cable. Although many networks run at 10 Mbps, the industry standard has shifted to networks designed to run at 100 Mbps and faster. Because only CAT 5 or better handles these speeds, just about everyone is installing the higher rated cabling, even if they are running at speeds that CAT 3 or CAT 4 would do. Consequently, it is becoming more difficult to get anything but CAT 5, CAT 5e, or CAT 6 cables.

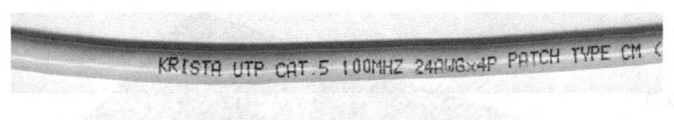

● **Figure 18.20** Cable markings for CAT level

Implementing 10/100/1000BaseT

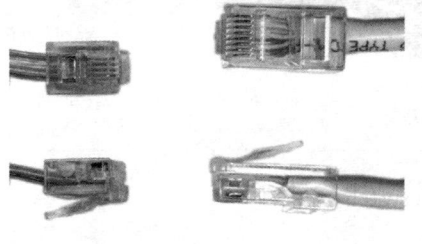

● **Figure 18.21** RJ-11 and RJ-45

The 10BaseT, 100BaseT, and 1000BaseT cabling standards require two pairs of wires: a pair for sending and a pair for receiving. 10BaseT runs on CAT 3, CAT 4, or CAT 5 cable. 100BaseT requires at least CAT 5 to run. 1000BaseT is a special case because it needs all four pairs of wires in a CAT 5e or CAT 6 cable. These cables use a connector called an **RJ-45** connector. The *RJ* designation was invented by Ma Bell (the phone company, for you youngsters) years ago and is still used today. Currently, only two types of RJ connectors are used for networking: RJ-11 and RJ-45 (Figure 18.21). **RJ-11** is the connector that hooks your telephone to the telephone jack. It supports up to two pairs of wires, though most phone lines use only one pair. The other pair is used to support a second phone line. RJ-11 connectors are primarily used for telephones and are not used in any common LAN installation, although a few weird (and out of business) "network in a box"–type companies used them. RJ-45 is the standard for UTP connectors. RJ-45 has connections for up to four pairs and is visibly much wider than RJ-11. Figure 18.22 shows the position of the #1 and #8 pins on an RJ-45 jack.

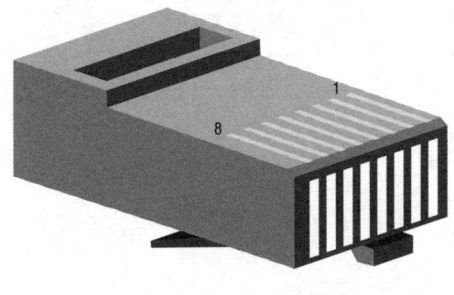

● **Figure 18.22** RJ-45 pin numbers

The TIA/EIA has two standards for connecting the RJ-45 connector to the UTP cable: the TIA/EIA 568A and the TIA/EIA 568B. Both are acceptable. You do not have to follow any standard as long as you use the same pairings on each end of the cable; however, you will make your life simpler if you choose a standard. Make sure that all of your cabling uses the same standard and you will save a great deal of work in the end. Most importantly, *keep records!*

Like all wires, the wires in UTP are numbered. However, a number does not appear on each wire. Instead, each wire has a standardized color. Table 18.1 shows the official TIA/EIA Standard Color Chart for UTP.

Table 18.1	UTP Cabling Color Chart				
Pin	568A	568B	Pin	568A	568B
1	White/Green	White/Orange	5	White/Blue	White/Blue
2	Green	Orange	6	Orange	Green
3	White/Orange	White/Green	7	White/Brown	White/Brown
4	Blue	Blue	8	Brown	Brown

Combo Cards All Ethernet networks share the same language, so you can easily have mixed or combined networks. All it takes is a network card capable of running at multiple speeds or even over multiple cables. Most NICs built into motherboards (Figure 18.23), for example, are 10/100 auto-sensing cards. If you plug into a 10BaseT network, they automatically run at 10 Mbps. If you log into a 100 Mbps network, they'll quickly ramp up and run at 100 Mbps. You might find older cards that have both an RJ-45 port and a BNC connector for 10Base2. These sorts of cards can connect to either a 10BaseT or 10Base2 network (Figure 18.24).

Hubs and Switches In a 10/100/1000BaseT network, each PC is connected to a 10/100/1000BaseT hub or switch, as mentioned earlier. To add a device to the network, simply plug another cable into the hub or switch (Figure 18.25). Remember that 10/100/1000BaseT uses the star bus topology. The hub holds the actual bus and allows access to the bus through the ports. Using a star bus topology creates a robust network; the failure of a single PC will not bring down the entire network.

Tech Tip

Plenum versus PVC Cabling

Most workplace installations of network cable go up above the ceiling and then drop down through the walls to present a nice port in the wall. The space in the ceiling, under the floors, and in the walls through which cable runs is called the plenum space. The potential problem with this cabling running through the plenum space is that the protective sheathing for networking cables, called the jacket, is made from plastic, and if you get any plastic hot enough, it will create smoke and noxious fumes. Standard network cables usually use PVC (poly-vinyl chloride) for the jacket, but PVC produces noxious fumes when burned. Fumes from cables burning in the plenum space can quickly spread throughout the building, so you want to use a more fire-retardant cable in the plenum space. Plenum-grade cable is simply network cabling with a fire-retardant jacket and is required for cables that go in the plenum space. Plenum-grade cable costs about three to five times more than PVC, but you should use it whenever you install cable in a plenum space.

• Figure 18.23 NIC built into motherboard

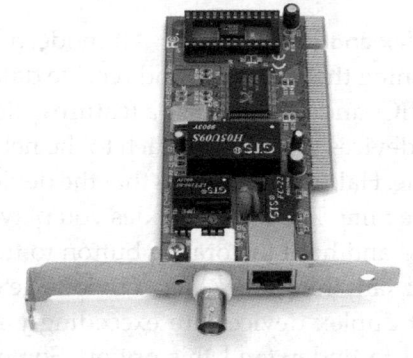

• Figure 18.24 Ethernet 10Base2/10BaseT combo card

● **Figure 18.25**   Typical switch with several cables connected

10/100/1000BaseT
Max. one PC on each segment

Max. segment length is 100 meters.
Max. 1024 PCs per hub or switch.

● **Figure 18.26**   10/100/1000BaseT

Tech Tip

Crossover Cables

*You can actually hook two 10/
100/1000BaseT network cards together without a hub by using a
special UTP cable called a* crossover cable . *A crossover cable is a
standard UTP cable but with one
RJ-45 connector using the 568A
standard and the other using the
568B. This reverses the signal between sending and receiving wires
and thus does the job of a hub or
switch. Crossover cables work great
as a quick way to network two PCs.
You can purchase a crossover cable
at any computer store.*

In a 10/100/1000BaseT network, the maximum distance from
the hub to any device is 100 meters.
No more than one PC can be attached to each segment, and the
maximum number of PCs that can
be attached to any one hub is
1024—although you will be hard
pressed to find a hub with that
many connectors (Figure 18.26).
Most hubs come with 4, 8, 16, or 24
ports. 10/100/1000BaseT hubs act
as repeaters, turning received signals into binary data and then
re-creating a new signal to send out
to devices connected to other ports. They need power, so make sure that the
hubs are plugged into a good power source.

Duplex and Half-Duplex   All modern NICs can run in full-duplex mode,
meaning they can send and receive data at the same time. The vast majority
of NICs and switches use a feature called *auto-sensing* to accommodate very
old devices that might attach to the network and need to run in half-duplex
mode. Half-duplex means that the device can send and receive but not at the
same time. The walkie-talkies you played with as a kid that required you to
press and hold the orange button to transmit—at which time you couldn't
hear anything—are an obvious example of a half-duplex device.
Half-duplex devices are exceedingly rare in modern computers, but you
need to understand this option. Some NICs just can't handle full-duplex
communication when you plug them directly to another NIC using a
crossover cable—that is, no switch. Dropping both NICs down from
full-duplex or auto-sensing can sometimes enable these odd NICs to
communicate.

Fiber Optic Ethernet

Fiber optic cable is a very attractive way to transmit Ethernet network packets. First, because it uses light instead of electricity, fiber optic cable is immune to electrical problems such as lightning, short circuits, and static. Second, fiber optic signals travel much farther, up to 2000 meters (compared with 100 meters for 10/100/1000BaseT) with some standards. Most fiber Ethernet networks use *62.5/125 multimode* fiber optic cable. All fiber Ethernet networks that use these cables require two cables. Figure 18.27 shows three of the more common connectors used in fiber optic networks. Square *SC* connectors are shown in the middle and on the right, and the round *ST* connector is on the left.

Like many other fiber optic connectors, the SC and ST connectors are half-duplex, meaning data flows only one way—hence the need for two cables in a fiber installation. Other half-duplex connectors you might run into are FC/PC, SMA, D4, MU, and LC. They look similar to SC and ST connectors but offer variations in size and connection. Newer and higher end fiber installations use full-duplex connectors, such as the MT-RJ connectors.

The two most common fiber optic standards are called 10BaseFL and 100BaseFX. As you can guess by the names, the major difference is the speed of the network (there are some important differences in the way hubs are interconnected, and so on). Fiber optic cabling is delicate, expensive, and difficult to use, so it is usually reserved for use in data centers and is rarely used to connect desktop PCs.

Token Ring

Token Ring remains Ethernet's most significant competitor for connecting desktop PCs to the network, but its market share has continued to shrink in recent years. Developed by IBM, Token Ring uses a combination of ring and star topologies. Because Token Ring has its own packet structure, you need special equipment to connect a Token Ring to an Ethernet network.

Ring Topology

A ring topology connects all the PCs together on a single cable that forms a ring (Figure 18.28). Ring topologies use a transmission method called *token passing*. In token passing, a mini-packet called a *token* constantly passes from one NIC to the next in one direction around the ring (see Figure 18.29). A PC wanting to send a packet must wait until it gets the token. The PC's NIC then attaches data to the token and sends the packet back out to the ring. If another PC wants to send data, it must wait until a free token (one that doesn't have an attached packet) comes around.

Implementing Token Ring

The CompTIA A+ certification has a very old-school view of Token Ring networks, focusing on the traditional rather than the current iterations. As such, you'll find the exams test you only on the ancient 4 Mbps or 16 Mbps networks, which depended on the type of Token Ring network cards you

● **Figure 18.27**   Typical fiber optic cables with connectors

 Tech Tip

Multimode and Single Mode
Light can be sent down a fiber optic cable as regular light or as laser light. Each type of light requires totally different fiber optic cables. Most network technologies that use fiber optics use light emitting diodes (LEDs) to send light signals. These use multimode fiber optic cabling. Multimode fiber transmits multiple light signals at the same time, each using a different reflection angle within the core of the cable. The multiple reflection angles tend to disperse over long distances, so multimode fiber optic cables are used for relatively short distances.

Network technologies that use laser light use single-mode fiber optic cabling. Using laser light and single-mode fiber optic cables allows for phenomenally high transfer rates over long distances. Except for long-distance links, single-mode is currently quite rare; if you see fiber optic cabling, you can be relatively sure that it is multimode.

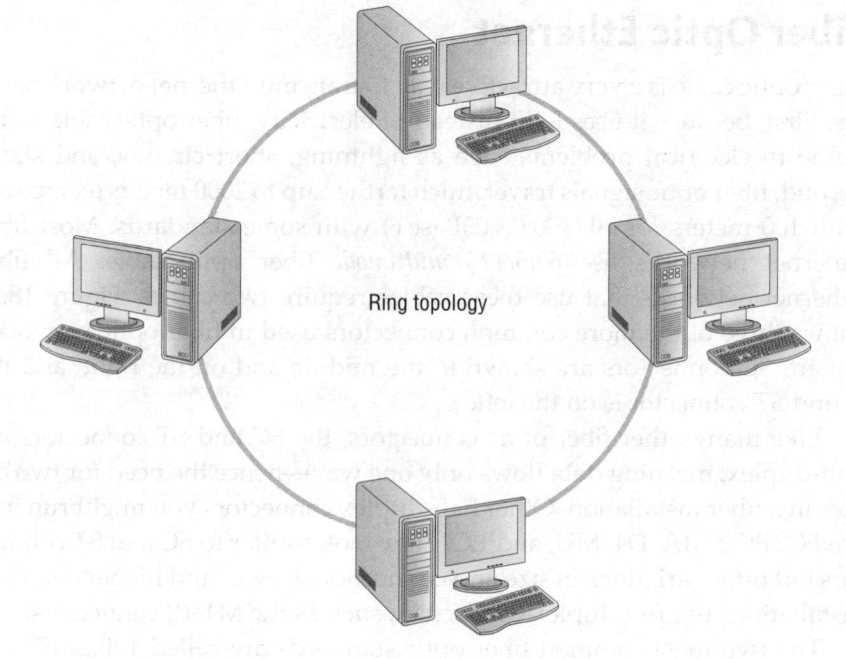

Ring topology

● **Figure 18.28** Ring topology

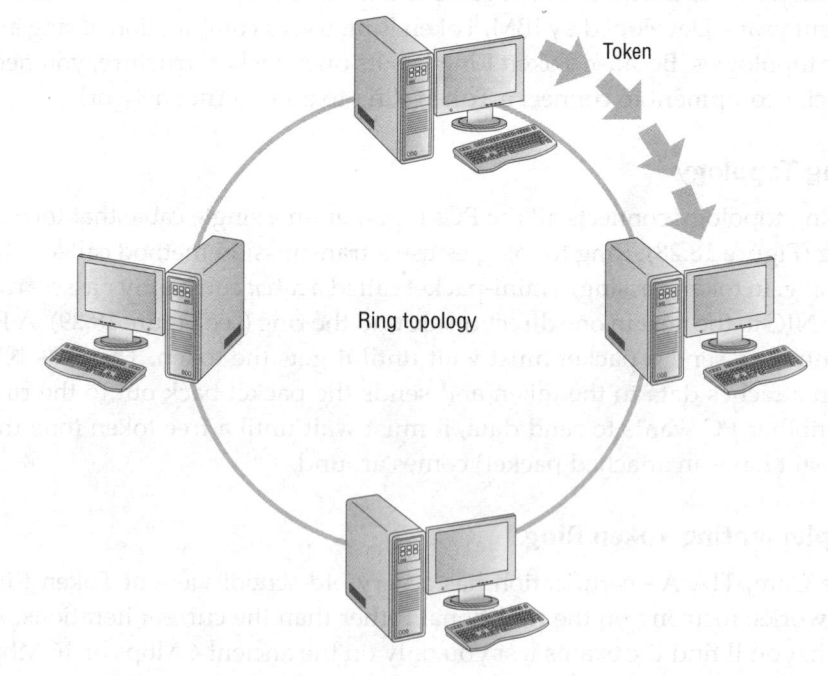

Tech Tip

Modern Token Ring Networks

Token Ring manufacturers have not rolled over and given in to the pressure of Ethernet standards, but rather have continued to adapt and innovate. Modern IEEE 802.5t Token Ring networks run at 100 Mbps or faster and, because the ring technology does not suffer from the overhead of CSMA/CD, you get phenomenally faster performance from High Speed Token Ring (HSTR) networks than on comparably speedy Ethernet. Check them out here: www.token-ring.com.

bought. Token Ring was originally based around the IBM Type 1 cable. Type 1 cable is a two-pair, **shielded twisted pair (STP)** cable designed to handle speeds up to 20 Mbps (Figure 18.30). Today, Token Ring topologies can use either STP or UTP cables, and UTP cabling is far more common.

Token

Ring topology

● **Figure 18.29** Token passing

STP Types STP cables have certain categories. These are called types and are defined by IBM. The most common types are the following:

- **Type 1** Standard STP with two pairs—the most common STP cable
- **Type 2** Standard STP plus two pairs of voice wires
- **Type 3** Standard STP with four pairs
- **Type 6** Patch cable—used for connecting hubs
- **Type 8** Flat STP for under carpets
- **Type 9** STP with two pairs—Plenum grade

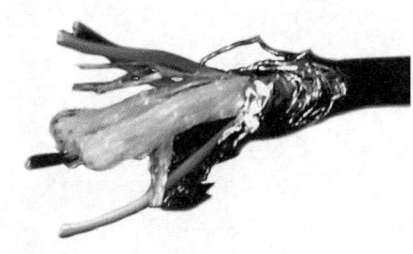

• **Figure 18.30** Type 1 STP Token Ring cable

Token Ring Connectors The Type 1 Token Ring connectors are not RJ-45. Instead, IBM designed a unique *hermaphroditic* connector called either an IBM-type Data Connector (IDC) or Universal Data Connector (UDC). These connectors are neither male nor female; they are designed to plug into each other (Figure 18.31). Token Ring network cards use a 9-pin female connector. A standard Token Ring cable has a hermaphroditic connector on one end and a 9-pin connector on the other.

Token Ring can also be used with CAT 3, 4, 5, 5e, and 6 UTP. When combined with UTP, Token Ring uses an RJ-45 connector, so from a cabling standpoint, Token Ring UTP and Ethernet UTP look the same. Many Token Ring network cards are combo cards, which means they come with both a 0-pin connection for STP and an RJ-45 connection for UTP.

As discussed earlier, Token Ring uses a star ring topology. The central connecting device, or concentrator, is sometimes called a hub, but the proper term is multistation access unit (MAU or MSAU). Token Ring MAUs and Ethernet hubs look similar but are *not* interchangeable. Each Token Ring MAU can support up to 260 PCs using STP and up to 72 PCs using UTP. Using UTP, the maximum distance from any MAU to a PC is 45 meters. Using STP, the maximum distance from any MAU to a PC is 100 meters (Figure 18.32). Token Ring can also uses repeaters, but the repeaters can be used only between MAUs. With a repeater, the functional distance between two MAUs increases to 360 meters (with UTP) and 720 meters (with STP).

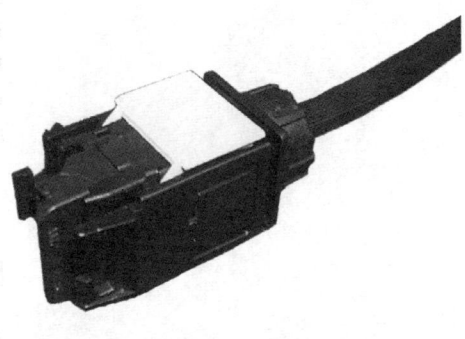

• **Figure 18.31** IDC/UDC connector

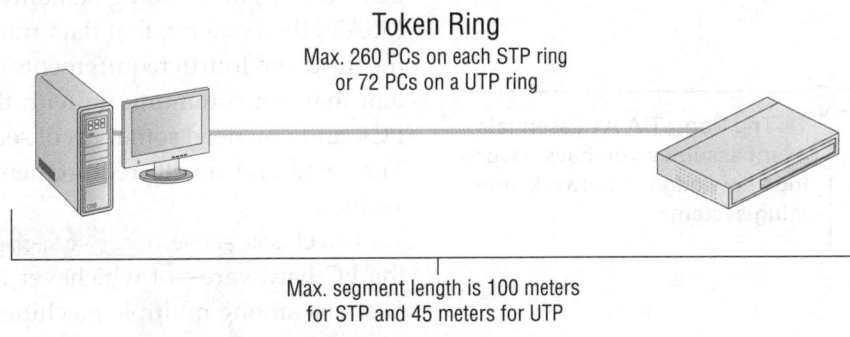

Token Ring
Max. 260 PCs on each STP ring
or 72 PCs on a UTP ring

Max. segment length is 100 meters
for STP and 45 meters for UTP

• **Figure 18.32** Token Ring specifications

Parallel/Serial

It would be unfair not to give at least a token nod to the possibility of making direct cable connections using the parallel or serial ports on a pair of PCs. All versions of Windows have complete support for allowing two, and no more than two, systems to network together using either parallel or serial cables. You need crossover versions of IEEE1284 cables for parallel and RS-232 cables for serial. These should be considered only as a last resort option, given the incredibly slow speeds of parallel and especially serial cable transmission compared to that of Ethernet and Token Ring. Direct cable connections should never be used unless no other viable alternative exists.

FireWire

You can connect two computers together using FireWire cables. Apple designed FireWire to be network aware, so the two machines will simply recognize each other and, assuming they're configured to share files and folders, you're up and running.

USB

You can also connect two computers using USB, but it's not quite as elegant as FireWire. You can use several options. The most common way is to plug a USB NIC into each PC and then run a UTP crossover cable between the Ethernet ports. You can buy a special USB crossover cable to connect the two machines. Finally, at least one company makes a product that enables you to connect with a normal USB cable, called USB Duet.

■ Network Operating Systems

At this point in the discussion of networking, you've covered two of the four main requirements for making a network work. Through Ethernet or Token Ring hardware protocols, you have a NIC for the PC that handles splitting data into packets and putting the packets back together at the destination PC. You've got a cabling standard to connect the NIC to a hub/switch or MSAU, thus making that data transfer possible. Now it's time to dive into the third and fourth requirements for a network. You need an operating system that can communicate with the hardware and with other networked PCs, and you need some sort of server machine to give out data or services. The third and fourth requirements are handled by a network operating system.

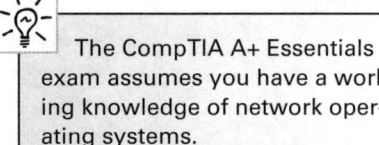

The CompTIA A+ Essentials exam assumes you have a working knowledge of network operating systems.

In a classic sense, a network operating system (NOS) communicates with the PC hardware—of whichever hardware protocol—and makes the connections among multiple machines on a network. The NOS enables one or more PCs to act as a server machine and share data and services over a network—to share resources, in other words. You then need to run software on client computers to enable those computers to access the shared resources on the server machine.

Every Windows OS is an NOS and enables the PC to share resources and access shared resources. But it doesn't come out of the box ready to work on all networks! You need to configure Windows to handle all three tasks to make all this work: install a network protocol to communicate with hardware, enable server software to share resources, and install client software to enable the PC to access shared resources.

All NOSs are not alike, even among Windows. Before you can share resources across a network, you must answer a number of questions. How do you make that happen? Can everyone share his or her hard drives with everyone else? Should you place limits on sharing? If everyone needs access to a particular file, where will it be stored? What about security? Can anyone access the file? What if someone erases it accidentally? How are backups to be handled? Different NOSs answer these questions differently. Let's look at network organization and then turn to protocols, client software, and server software.

Network Organization

All NOSs can be broken into three basic organizational groups: client/server, peer-to-peer, and domain-based. All Windows PCs can function as network clients and servers, so this muddies the waters a bit. Let's take a look at traditional network organization.

Client/Server

In a client/server network , one machine is dedicated as a resource to be shared over the network. This machine will have a dedicated NOS optimized for sharing files. This special OS includes powerful caching software that enables high-speed file access. It will have extremely high levels of protection and an organization that permits extensive control of the data. This machine is called a *dedicated server*. All of the other machines that use the data are called *clients* (because it's what they usually are) or *workstations*.

The client/server system dedicates one machine to act as a "server." Its only function is to serve up resources to the other machines on the network. These servers do not run Windows 9*x* or Windows XP. They use highly sophisticated and expensive NOSs that are optimized for the sharing and administration of network resources. Dedicated server operating systems include Windows 2003 Server, Novell NetWare, and some versions of Linux.

Novell NetWare servers provide the purest example of a dedicated server. A NetWare server doesn't provide a user environment for running any applications except for tools and utilities. It just *serves* shared resources; it does not *run* programs such as Excel or CorelDraw. Many network administrators will even remove the keyboard and monitor from a NetWare server to keep people from trying to use it. NetWare has its own commands and requires substantial training to use, but in return, you get an amazingly powerful NOS! While Linux and Windows 2003 server machines can technically run client applications such as word processors, they have been optimized to function as servers and you don't typically use them to run end-user applications.

 The terms *client* and *server* are, to say the least, freely used in the Windows world. Keep in mind that a *client* generally refers to any process (or in this context, computer system) that can request a resource or service, and a *server* is any process (or system) that can fulfill the request.

 Cross Check

NTFS Permissions

NTFS permissions enable strong data security, even when sharing files and folders across a network, so now is a good time to revisit Chapter 9 and refresh your memory on NTFS.

1. How do you access the permissions for a file or folder?

2. Which permission would stop someone from modifying a file on your server, but still enable him or her to read the contents of that file?

3. What's up with Windows XP Home and permissions, anyway?

Novell NetWare provides excellent security for shared resources. Its security permissions are similar to Microsoft NTFS permissions.

Peer-to-Peer

Some networks do not require dedicated servers—every computer can perform both server and client functions. A **peer-to-peer network** enables any or all of the machines on the network to act as a server. Peer-to-peer networks are much cheaper than client/server networks, because the software costs less and does not require that you purchase a high-end machine to act as the dedicated server. The most popular peer-to-peer NOSs today are Windows 2000/XP and Macintosh OS X.

The biggest limiting factor to peer-to-peer networking is that it's simply not designed for a large number of computers. Windows has a built-in limit (10) to the number of users who can concurrently access a shared file or folder. Microsoft recommends that peer-to-peer workgroups not exceed 15 PCs. Beyond that, creating a domain-based network makes more sense.

Security is the other big weakness of peer-to-peer networks. Each system on a peer-to-peer network maintains its own security.

Windows 2000 Professional and Windows XP Professional enable you to tighten security by setting NTFS permissions locally, but you are still required to place a local account on every system for any user who's going to access resources. So, even though you get better security in a Windows 2000 Professional or Windows XP Professional peer-to-peer network, system administration entails a lot of running around to individual systems to create and delete local users every time someone joins or leaves the network. In a word: bleh.

Peer-to-peer workgroups are little more than a pretty way to organize systems to make navigating through My Network Places a little easier (Figure 18.33). In reality, workgroups have no security value. Still, if your networking needs are limited—such as a small home network—peer-to-peer networking is an easy and cheap solution.

Domain-Based

One of the similarities between the client/server network model and peer-to-peer networks is that each PC in the network maintains its own list of user accounts. If you want to access a server, you must log on. When only one server exists, the logon process takes only a second and works very well. The trouble comes when your network contains multiple servers. In that case, every time you access a different server, you must repeat the logon process (Figure 18.34). In larger networks containing many servers, this becomes a time-consuming nightmare not only for the user, but also for the network administrator.

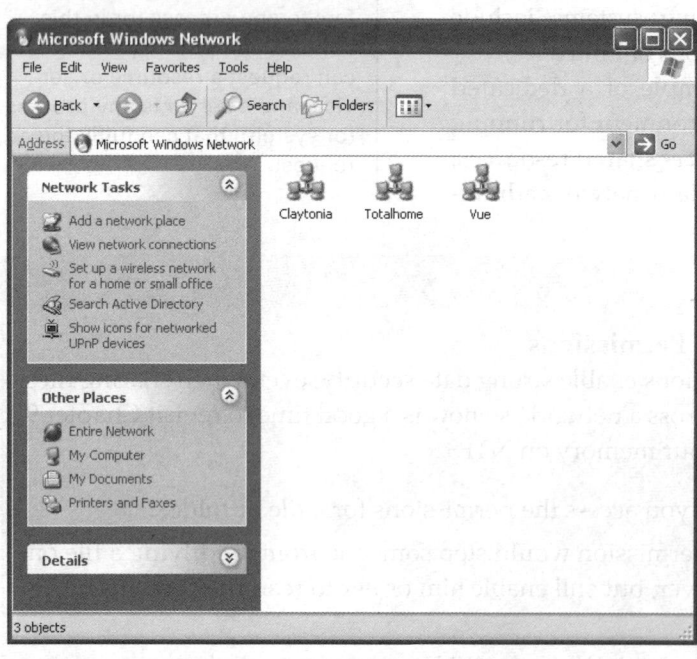

• **Figure 18.33**   Multiple workgroups in a network

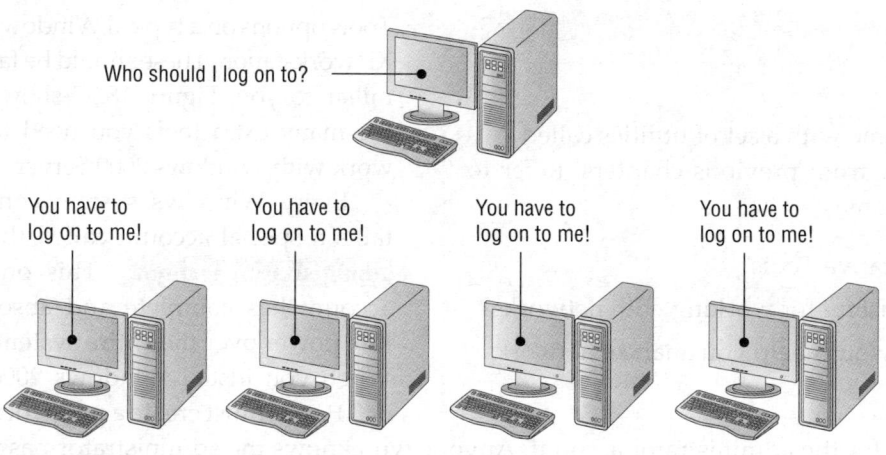

Who should I log on to?

You have to log on to me!   You have to log on to me!   You have to log on to me!   You have to log on to me!

● **Figure 18.34**   Multiple logins in a peer-to-peer network

A **domain-based network** provides an excellent solution for the problem of multiple logins. In a domain-based environment, one or more dedicated servers called *domain controllers* hold the security database for all systems. This database holds a list of all users and passwords in the domain. When you log on to your computer or to any computer, the logon request goes to an available domain controller, to verify the account and password (Figure 18.35).

Modern domain-based networks use what is called a **directory service** to store user and computer account information. Current versions of Novell NetWare move from the strict client/server model described to a directory service-based model implementing the appropriately named *NetWare Directory Service (NDS)*. Large Microsoft-based networks use the *Active Directory (AD)* directory service. Think of a directory service as a big, centralized index, similar to a telephone book, that each PC accesses to locate resources in the domain.

Server versions of Microsoft Windows look and act similar to the workstation versions, but they come with extra networking capabilities, services, and tools to enable them to take on the role of domain controller, file server, *remote access services (RAS)* server, application server, Web server, and so on. A quick glance at the options you have in Administrative Tools shows how much more full-featured the server versions are compared to the workstation versions of Windows. Figure 18.36 shows the Administrative

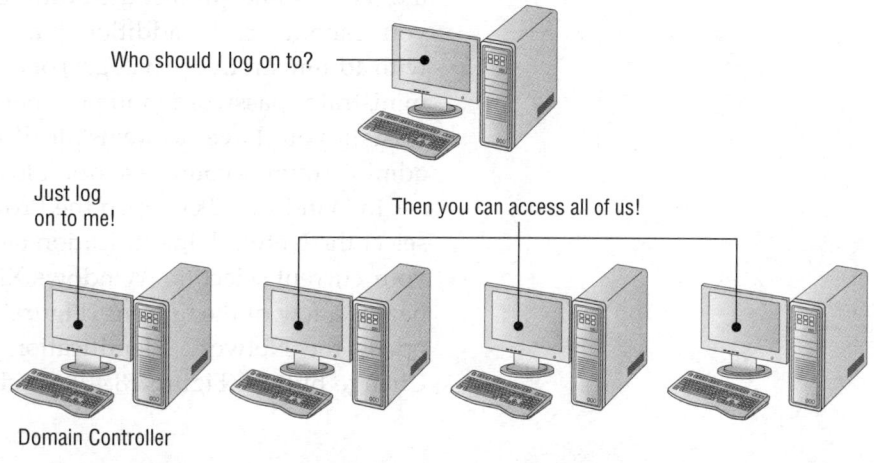

Who should I log on to?

Just log on to me!   Then you can access all of us!

Domain Controller

● **Figure 18.35**   A domain controller eliminates the need for multiple logins.

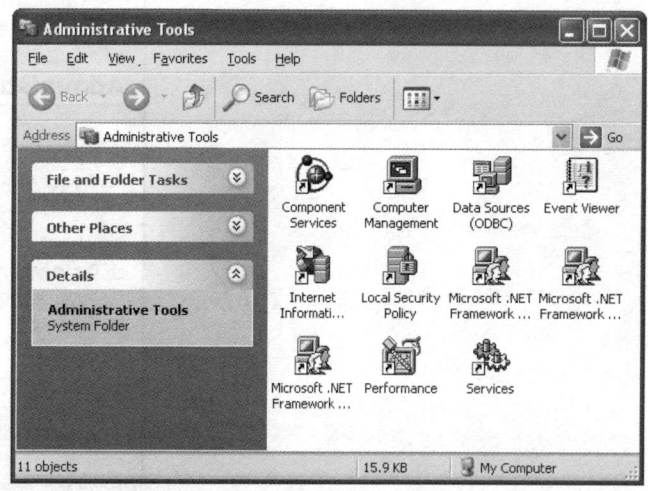

● **Figure 18.36**   Administrative Tools in Windows XP Professional

Cross Check

Administrative Tools

Windows 2000 and Windows XP come with a set of utilities called Administrative Tools, as you know from previous chapters. Refer to Chapter 12 and answer these questions.

1. How do you access Administrative Tools?

2. Which tool or tools might be useful for working with networks?

3. More specifically, which tool would help you analyze network performance?

Tools options on a typical Windows XP workstation. These should be familiar to you. Figure 18.37 shows the many extra tools you need to work with Windows 2000 Server.

Every Windows system contains a special account called the **administrator account**. This one account has complete and absolute power over the entire system. When you install Windows 2000 or XP, you must create a password for the administrator account. Anyone who knows the administrator password has the ability to install/delete any program, read/change/delete any file, run any program, and change any system setting. As you might imagine, you should protect the administrator password carefully. Without it, you cannot create additional accounts (including additional accounts with administrative privileges) or change system settings. If you lose the administrator password (and no other account with administrative privileges exists), you have to reinstall Windows completely to create a new administrator account—so don't lose it!

In Windows 2000, open the Properties window for My Computer, and select the Network Identification tab, as shown in Figure 18.38. This shows your current selection. Windows XP calls the tab Computer Name and renames a few of the buttons (Figure 18.39). Clicking the Network ID button opens the Network Identification Wizard, but most techs just use the Change button (Figure 18.40). Clicking the Change button does the same

• **Figure 18.37** Administrative Tools in Windows 2000 Server

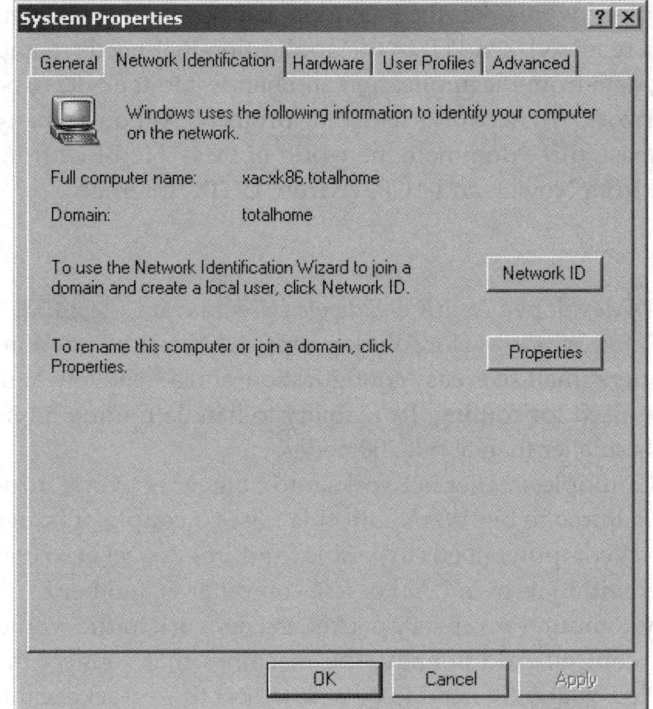

• **Figure 18.38** Network Identification tab in Windows 2000

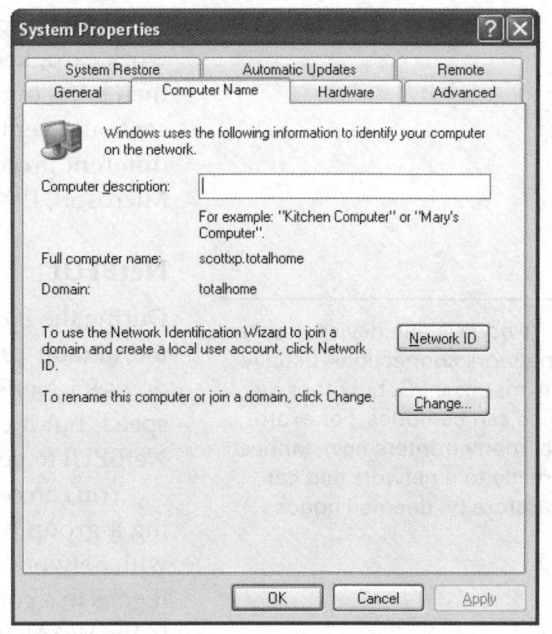

• **Figure 18.39** Computer Name tab in Windows XP

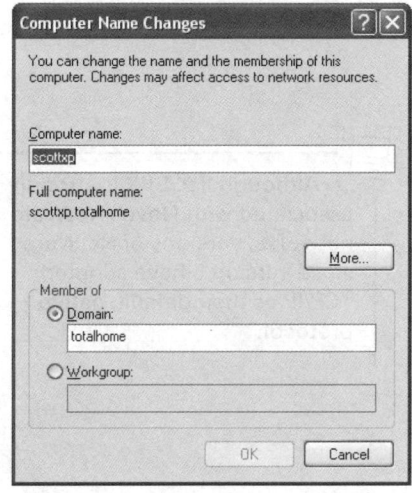

• **Figure 18.40** Using the Change button

thing as clicking the Network ID button, but the wizard does a lot of explaining that you don't need if you know what you want to do. Make sure you have a valid domain account or you won't be able to log in to a domain.

At this point, you've prepared the OS to network in general, but now you need to talk to the specific hardware. For that, you need to load protocols.

Protocols

Simply moving data from one machine to another is hardly sufficient to make a complete network; many other functions need to be handled. For example, if a file is being copied from one machine to another, something must keep track of all the packets so that the file can be properly reassembled. If many machines are talking to the same machine at once, that machine must somehow keep track of which packets it sends to or receives from each of the other PCs.

Another issue arises if one of the machines in the network has its network card replaced. Up to this point, the only way to distinguish one machine from another was by the MAC address on the network card. To solve this, each machine must have a name, an identifier for the network, which is "above" the MAC address. Each machine, or at least one of them, needs to keep a list of all the MAC addresses on the network and the names of the machines, so that packets and names can be correlated. That way, if a PC's network card is replaced, the network, after some special queries, can update the list to associate the name of the PC with its new network card's MAC address.

Network protocol software takes the incoming data received by the network card, keeps it organized, sends it to the application that needs it, and then takes outgoing data from the application and hands it to the NIC to be sent out over the network. All networks use some protocol. Although many different protocols exist, three dominate the world of PCs—NetBEUI from Microsoft, IPX/SPX from Novell, and TCP/IP from UNIX/Internet.

NetBEUI

During the 1980s, IBM developed *NetBIOS Extended User Interface* (**NetBEUI**), the default protocol for Windows for Workgroups, LANtastic, and Windows 95. NetBEUI offers small size, easy configuration, and a relatively high speed, but it can't be used for routing. Its inability to handle routing limits NetBEUI to networks smaller than about 200 nodes.

You can connect multiple smaller networks into a bigger network, turning a group of LANs into one big WAN, but this raises a couple of issues with network traffic. A computer needs to be able to address a packet so that it goes to a computer within its own LAN or to a computer in another LAN in the WAN. If every computer saw every packet, the network traffic would quickly spin out of control! Additionally, the machines that connect the LANs together—called **routers**—need to be able to sort those packets and send them along to the proper LAN. This process, called *routing,* requires a routing-capable protocol and routers to be able to function correctly.

NetBEUI was great for a LAN, but it lacked the extra addressing capabilities needed for a WAN. A new protocol was needed, one that could handle routing.

IPX/SPX

Novell developed the *Internetwork Packet Exchange/Sequenced Packet Exchange* (**IPX/SPX**) protocol exclusively for its NetWare products. The IPX/SPX protocol is speedy, works well with routers, and takes up relatively little RAM when loaded. Microsoft implements a version of IPX/SPX called **NWLink** .

TCP/IP

Transmission Control Protocol/Internet Protocol (**TCP/IP**) was originally developed for the Internet's progenitor, the *Advanced Research Projects Agency Network (ARPANET)* of the U.S. Department of Defense. In 1983, TCP/IP became the built-in protocol for the popular BSD UNIX, and other flavors of UNIX quickly adopted it as well. TCP/IP is the best protocol for larger (more than 200 nodes) networks. The biggest network of all, the Internet, uses TCP/IP as its protocol. Windows NT also uses TCP/IP as its default protocol. TCP/IP lacks speed and takes up a large amount of memory when loaded, but it is robust, well understood, and universally supported.

AppleTalk

AppleTalk is the proprietary Apple protocol. Similar to IPX, it is small and relatively fast. The only reason to use the AppleTalk protocol is to communicate with older Apple computers on a network. Apple Macintosh OS X

A *node* is any device that has a network connection—usually this means a PC, but other devices can be nodes. For example, many printers now connect directly to a network and can therefore be deemed nodes.

Although IPX/SPX is strongly associated with Novell NetWare networks, versions of NetWare since version 5 have adopted TCP/IP as their default, native protocol.

uses TCP/IP natively, so you won't need AppleTalk to plug a modern Mac into a Windows network.

Client Software

To access data or resources across a network, a Windows PC needs to have client software installed for every kind of server that you want to access. When you install a network card and drivers, Windows installs at least one set of client software, called Client for Microsoft Networks (Figure 18.41). This client enables your machine to do the obvious: connect to a Microsoft network! To connect to a NetWare network, you'd need to add Client Service for NetWare. Internet-based services work the same way. You need a Web client (such as Internet Explorer) to access a Web server.

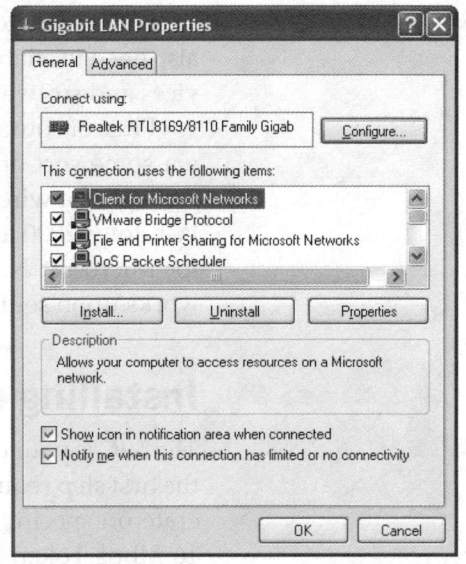

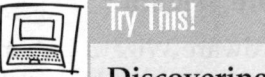 **Figure 18.41** LAN Properties window showing Client for Microsoft Networks installed (along with other network software)

Server Software

You can turn any Windows PC into a server, simply by enabling the sharing of files, folders, and printers. Windows 2000 and XP have File and Printer Sharing installed but not activated by default, but activating it requires nothing more than a click on a checkbox next to the *File and Printer Sharing for Microsoft Networks* option, as you can see in Figure 18.41.

> **Try This!**
>
> ### Discovering Protocols and Clients
>
> If you have a network card installed in your PC, chances are extremely high that you already have one or more protocols or clients installed. Try This!
>
> 1. Right-click My Network Places and select Properties. Then double-click on the Local Area Connection icon.
>
> 2. Which protocols or clients are loaded? If you have a classmate running through the same exercise, compare protocols. Can your two machines connect and swap data?

■ Installing and Configuring a Wired Network

We're finally getting to the good stuff—installing and configuring a network! To have network connectivity, you need to have three things in place:

- **NIC** The physical hardware that connects the computer system to the network media.

- **Protocol** The language that the computer systems use to communicate.

- **Network client** The interface that allows the computer system to speak to the protocol.

If you want to share resources on your PC with other network users, you also need to enable Microsoft's File and Printer Sharing. This installs the services and software that turns a Windows PC into a server.

Plus, of course, you need to connect the PC to the network hub or switch via some sort of cable (preferably CAT 6 with Gigabit Ethernet cranking through the wires, but that's just me!). When you install a NIC, by default, Windows 2000 and XP Professional install the TCP/IP protocol, the Client for Microsoft Networks, and File and Printer Sharing for Microsoft Networks upon setup.

Installing a NIC

The NIC is your computer system's link to the network, and installing one is the first step required to connect to a network. NICs are manufactured to operate on specific media and network types, such as 100BaseT Ethernet or 16 Mbps Token Ring. Follow the manufacturer's instructions for installation. If your NIC is of recent vintage, it will be detected, installed, and configured automatically by Windows 2000 or Windows XP. You might need a driver disc or a driver download from the manufacturer's Web site if you install the latest and greatest Gigabit Ethernet card.

Add Hardware Wizard

If you have the option, you should save yourself potential headaches and troubleshooting woes by acquiring new, name-brand NICs for your Windows installation.

The Add Hardware Wizard automates installation of non–plug-and-play devices, or plug-and-play devices that were not detected correctly. Start the wizard by clicking Start | Settings | Control Panel, and double-clicking the icon for the Add Hardware applet. (Note that Windows 2000 calls this the Add/Remove Hardware applet.) Click the Next button to select the hardware task you wish to perform, and follow the prompts to complete the wizard.

Configuring a Network Client

To establish network connectivity, you need a network client installed and configured properly. You need a client for every type of server NOS to which you plan to connect on the network. Let's look at the two most used for Microsoft and Novell networks.

Client for Microsoft Networks

Installed as part of the OS installation, the Client for Microsoft Networks rarely needs configuration, and, in fact, few configuration options are available. To start it in Windows XP, click Start, and then right-click My Network Places and select Properties. In Windows 2000, click Start | Settings | Network and Dial-up Connections.

In all versions of Windows, your next step is to double-click the Local Area Connection icon, click the Properties button, highlight Client for Microsoft Networks, and click the Properties button. Note that there's not much to do here. Unless told to do something by a network administrator, just leave this alone.

Client Service for NetWare

Microsoft's Client Service for NetWare provides access to file and print resources on NetWare 3.*x* and 4.*x* servers. Client Service for NetWare supports some NetWare utilities and NetWare-aware applications. To connect Microsoft client workstations to NetWare servers running NDS also requires the Microsoft Service for NetWare Directory Services (NDS). Once installed, Client Service for NetWare offers no configuration options.

 Client Service for NetWare does not support the IP protocol used in NetWare 5.*x* and more recent versions of NetWare.

Configuring Simple Protocols

Protocols come in many different flavors and perform different functions on the network. Some, such as NetBEUI, lack elements that allow their signals to travel through routers, making them non-routable (essentially, this protocol is unsuitable for a large network that uses routers to re-transmit data). The network protocols supported by Windows include NetBEUI, NWLink (IPX/SPX), and TCP/IP, although Windows XP drops support for NetBEUI. This section looks at installing and configuring the simple protocols used by Windows 2000: NetBEUI and NWLink.

NetBEUI

NetBEUI is easy to configure, since no network addresses are needed. Generally, all you need to establish a connection between computer systems using NetBEUI is a NetBIOS computer name. NetBIOS names must be unique and contain 15 or fewer characters, but other than that there isn't much to it. To install the NetBEUI protocol in any version of Windows except XP, follow these steps:

1. In Windows 2000, click Start | Settings | Network and Dial-up Connections. Double-click the Local Area Connection icon to bring up the Local Area Connection Status dialog box (Figure 18.42).

2. Click the Properties button to bring up the Local Area Connection Properties dialog box (Figure 18.43).

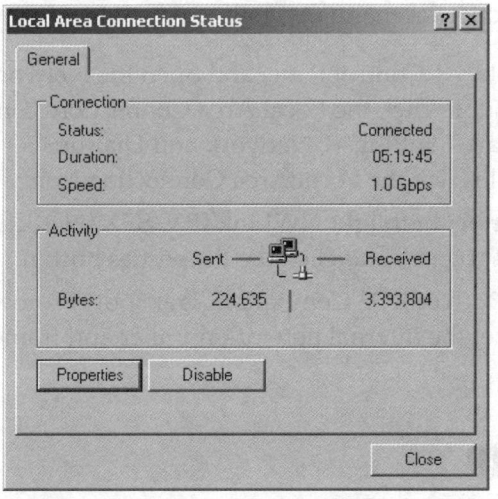

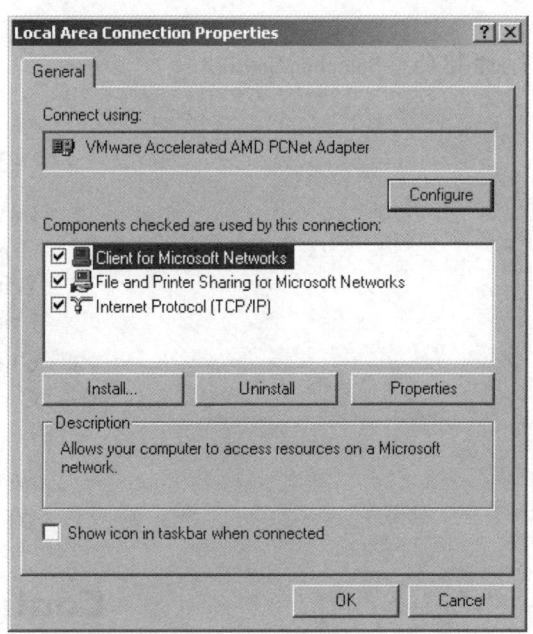

• **Figure 18.42** LAN Status dialog box in Windows 2000

• **Figure 18.43** LAN Properties dialog box in Windows 2000

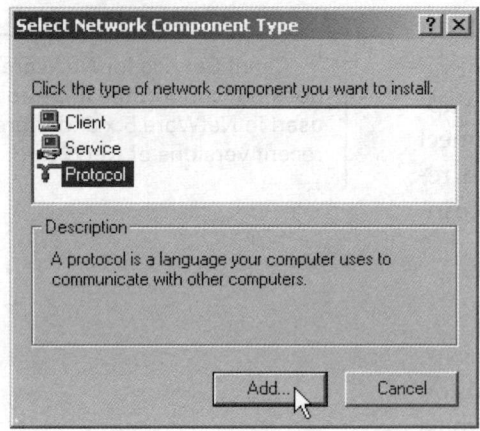

3. Click the Install button. In the Select Network Component Type dialog box, highlight Protocol and click the Add button (Figure 18.44).

4. In the Select Network Protocol dialog box, select NetBEUI Protocol (Figure 18.45), and click the OK button. You will be prompted to reboot the system to make the changes take effect.

NWLink (IPX/SPX)

As mentioned, NWLink is Microsoft's implementation of the IPX/SPX protocol. The Microsoft version of NWLink provides the same level of functionality as the Novell protocol and also includes an element for resolving NetBIOS names. NWLink packages data to be compatible with client/server services on NetWare networks, but it does not provide access to NetWare File and Print Services. For this, you also need to install the Client Service for NetWare, as noted earlier.

● **Figure 18.44**   Adding a protocol

Follow the same steps used to install NetBEUI to install NWLink, except choose NWLink rather than NetBEUI when you make your final selection. You'll be prompted to reboot after adding the protocol.

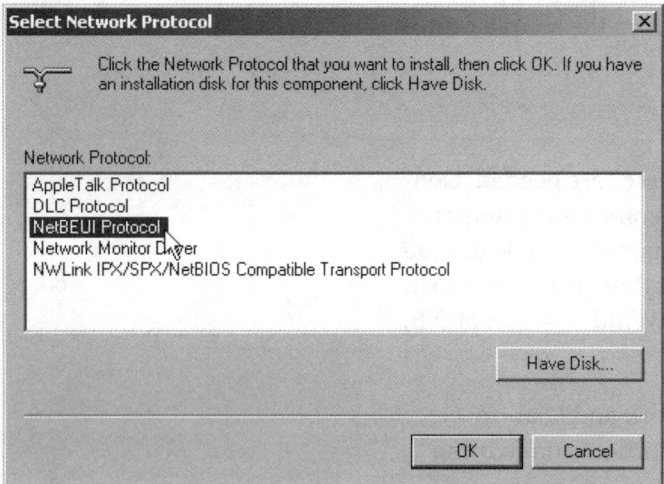

● **Figure 18.45**   Selecting NetBEUI

NWLink is a relatively easy protocol to configure. Normally, the only settings you may need to specify are the internal network number and frame type (usually, however, the default values are sufficient). The internal network number is used by the network for routing purposes. The frame type specifies how the data is packaged for transport over the network. For computers to communicate by NWLink, they must have the same frame types. By default, the frame type is set to Auto Detect.

To configure NWLink properties manually, follow these steps:

1. In Windows XP, click Start | Control Panel and open the Network Connections applet. Double-click the Local Area Connection icon. In Windows 2000, click Start | Settings | Network and Dial-up Connections, and double-click the Local Area Connection icon.

2. Click the Properties button, highlight NWLink IPX/SPX/NetBIOS Compatible Transport Protocol, and click the Properties button.

3. In the NWLink IPX/SPX/NetBIOS Compatible Transport Protocol properties dialog box, set the internal network number and frame type (Figure 18.46).

Configuring TCP/IP

This final section on protocols covers TCP/IP, the primary protocol of most modern networks, including the Internet. For a PC to access the Internet, it

Try This!

Adding a Simple Protocol

Knowing how to access and change protocols in a PC is an essential skill in today's wired world, and nothing beats doing something to reinforce what you learn, so Try This!

1. Access the LAN Properties and, using the steps outlined earlier, add a simple protocol to your PC. If you have Windows XP, you're limited to NWLink, but earlier versions of Windows offer more choices.

2. If you're plugged into a network, what effect do you notice when you reboot and have a new protocol installed?

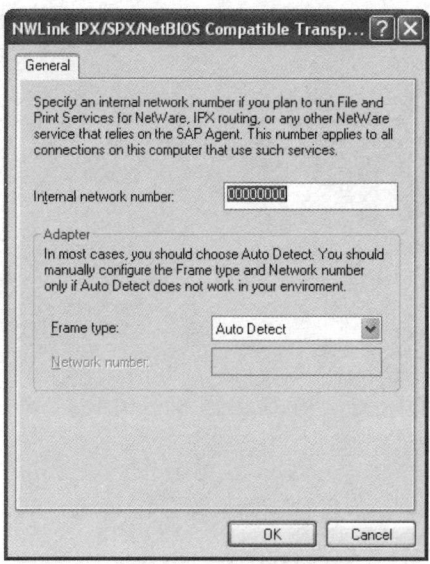

• **Figure 18.46**   Configuring NWLink

must have TCP/IP loaded and configured properly. TCP/IP has become so predominant that most network folks use it even on networks that do not connect to the Internet. Although TCP/IP is very powerful, it is also a bit of a challenge to set up. So whether you are installing a modem for a dial-up connection to the Internet or setting up 500 computers on their own private *intranet*, you must understand some TCP/IP basics. You'll go through the following basic sections of the protocol and then you'll look at specific steps to install and configure TCP/IP.

Network Addressing

Any network address must provide two pieces of information: it must uniquely identify the machine and it must locate that machine within the larger network. In a TCP/IP network, the IP address identifies the PC and the network on which it resides.

IP Addresses   In a TCP/IP network, the systems don't have names but rather use IP addresses. The **IP address** is the unique identification number for your system on the network. Part of the address identifies the network, and part identifies the local computer (host) address on the network. IP addresses consist of four sets of eight binary numbers (octets), each set separated by a period. This is called *dotted-decimal notation*. So, instead of a computer being called SERVER1, it gets an address like so:

```
202.34.16.11
```

Written in binary form, the address would look like this:

```
11110010.00000101.00000000.00001010
```

But the TCP/IP folks decided to write the decimal equivalents:

```
00000000 = 0
00000001 = 1
00000010 = 2
...
11111111 = 255
```

IP addresses are divided into class licenses, which correspond with the potential size of the network: Class A, Class B, and Class C. Class A licenses were intended for huge companies and organizations, such as major multinational corporations, universities, and governmental agencies. Class B licenses were assigned to medium-size companies, and Class C licenses were designated for smaller LANs. Class A networks use the first octet to identify the network address and the remaining three octets to identify the host. Class B networks use the first two octets to identify the network address and the remaining two octets to identify the host. Class C networks use the first three octets to identify the network address and the last octet to identify the host. Table 18.2 lists range (class) assignments.

You'll note that the IP address ranges listed above skip from 126.x.x.x to 128.x.x.x. That's because the 127 address range (i.e., 127.0.0.1–127.255.255.255) is reserved for network testing (loopback) operations. (We usually just use the address 127.0.0.1 for loopback purposes, and call it the *localhost* address, but any address that starts off with *127* will work just as well.) That's not the only reserved range, either! Each network class has a specific IP address range reserved for *private* networks—traffic from these networks doesn't get routed to the Internet at large. Class A's private range goes from 10.0.0.1 to 10.255.255.254. Class B's private range is 172.16.0.1 up to 172.16.255.254. Class C has two private addresses ranges: 192.168.0.0 to 192.168.255.254 for manually configured addresses, and 169.254.0.1 to 169.254.255.254 to accommodate the Automatic Private IP Addressing (APIPA) function.

Subnet Mask The subnet mask is a value that distinguishes which part of the IP address is the network address and which part of the address is the host address. The subnet mask blocks out (or "masks") the network portions (octets) of an IP address. Certain subnet masks are applied by default. The default subnet mask for Class A addresses is 255.0.0.0; for Class B, it's 255.255.0.0; and for Class C, 255.255.255.0. For example, in the Class B IP address 131.190.4.121 with a subnet mask of 255.255.0.0, the first two octets (131.190) make up the network address, and the last two (4.121) make up the host address.

TCP/IP Services

TCP/IP is a very different type of protocol. Although it supports File and Printer Sharing, it adds a number of special sharing functions unique only to it, lumped together under the umbrella term *TCP/IP services*. The most famous TCP/IP service is called *Hypertext Transfer Protocol (HTTP)*, the language of the

Pinging the loopback is the best way to test if a NIC is working properly. To test a NIC's loopback, the other end of the cable must be in a working switch or you must use a loopback device.

The CompTIA A+ certification exams do not require you to break down IP addresses and subnet masks into their binary equivalents or to deal with non-standard subnet masks like 255.255.240.0, but you should know what IP addresses and subnet masks are and how to configure your PC to connect to a TCP/IP network.

Table 18.2	Class A, B, and C Addresses		
Network Class	Address Range	No. of Network Addresses Available	No. of Host Nodes (Computers) Supported
A	1–126	129	16,777,214
B	128–191	16,384	65,534
C	192–223	2,097,152	254

World Wide Web. If you want to surf the Web, you must have TCP/IP. But TCP/IP supplies many other services beyond just HTTP. Using a service called Telnet, for example, you can access a remote system as though you were actually in front of that machine.

Another example is a handy utility called *Ping*. Ping enables one machine to check whether it can communicate with another machine. Figure 18.47 shows an example of Ping running on a Windows 2000 system. Isn't it interesting that many TCP/IP services run from a command prompt? Good thing you know how to access one! I'll show you other services in a moment.

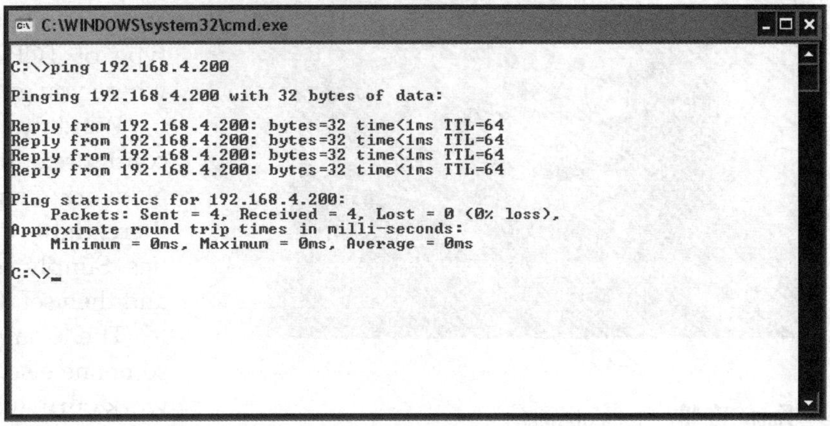

```
C:\WINDOWS\system32\cmd.exe

C:\>ping 192.168.4.200

Pinging 192.168.4.200 with 32 bytes of data:

Reply from 192.168.4.200: bytes=32 time<1ms TTL=64
Reply from 192.168.4.200: bytes=32 time<1ms TTL=64
Reply from 192.168.4.200: bytes=32 time<1ms TTL=64
Reply from 192.168.4.200: bytes=32 time<1ms TTL=64

Ping statistics for 192.168.4.200:
    Packets: Sent = 4, Received = 4, Lost = 0 (0% loss),
Approximate round trip times in milli-seconds:
    Minimum = 0ms, Maximum = 0ms, Average = 0ms

C:\>_
```

The goal of TCP/IP is to link any two hosts (remember, a host is just a computer in TCP/IP lingo), whether the two computers are on the same LAN or on some other network within the WAN. The LANs within the WAN are linked together with a variety of different types of connections, ranging from basic dial-ups to dedicated, high-speed (and expensive) data lines (Figure 18.48). To move traffic between networks, you use routers (Figure 18.49). Each host will send traffic to the router only when that data is destined for a remote network, cutting down on traffic across the more expensive WAN links. The host makes these decisions based on the destination IP address of each packet. Routers are most commonly used in TCP/IP networks, but other protocols also use them, especially IPX/SPX.

• **Figure 18.47**   Ping in action

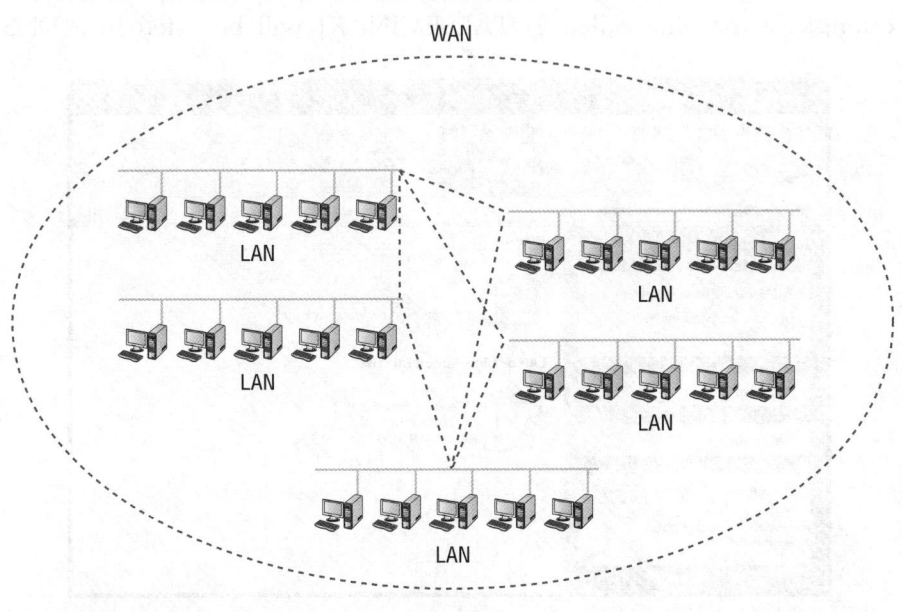

• **Figure 18.48**   WAN concept

● **Figure 18.49**   Typical router

The CompTIA A+ certification exams have a rather strange view of what you should know about networking. Take a lot of time practicing how to get to certain network configuration screens. Be ready for questions that ask, "Which of the following steps will enable you to change a particular value?"

TCP/IP Settings

TCP/IP has a number of unique settings that you must set up correctly to ensure proper network functioning. Unfortunately, these settings can be quite confusing, and there are quite a few of them. Not all settings are used for every type of TCP/IP network, and it's not always obvious where you go to set them.

Windows 2000/XP make this fairly easy by letting you configure both dial-up and network connections using the Network Connections dialog box (Figure 18.50). To get there, right-click on My Network Places and select Properties. Simply select the connection you wish to configure, and then set its TCP/IP properties.

The CompTIA A+ certification exams assume that someone else, such as a tech support person or some network guru, will tell you the correct TCP/IP settings for the network. Your only job is to understand roughly what they do and to know where to enter them so the system works. Following are some of the most common TCP/IP settings.

Default Gateway   A computer that wants to send data to another machine outside its LAN is not expected to know exactly how to reach every other computer on the Internet. Instead, all IP hosts know the address of at least one router to which they pass all the data packets they need to send outside the LAN. This router is called the default gateway, which is just another way of saying "the local router" (Figure 18.51).

Domain Name Service (DNS)   Knowing that users were not going to be able to remember lots of IP addresses, early Internet pioneers came up with a way to correlate those numbers with more human-friendly computer designations. Special computers, called domain name service (DNS) servers, keep databases of IP addresses and their corresponding names. For example, a machine called TOTALSEMINAR1 will be listed in a DNS

● **Figure 18.50**   Network Connections dialog box showing Dial-up and LAN connections

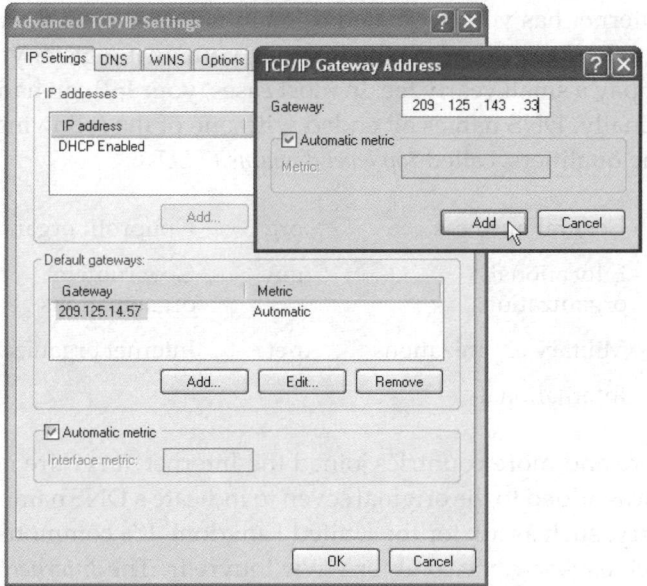

Figure 18.51 Setting a default gateway

directory with a corresponding IP address, such as 209.34.45.163. So instead of accessing the \\209.34.45.163\FREDC share to copy a file, you can ask to see \\TOTALSEMINAR1\FREDC. Your system will then query the DNS server to get TOTALSEMINAR1's IP address and use that to find the right machine. Unless you want to type in IP addresses all the time, a TCP/IP network will need at least one DNS server (Figure 18.52).

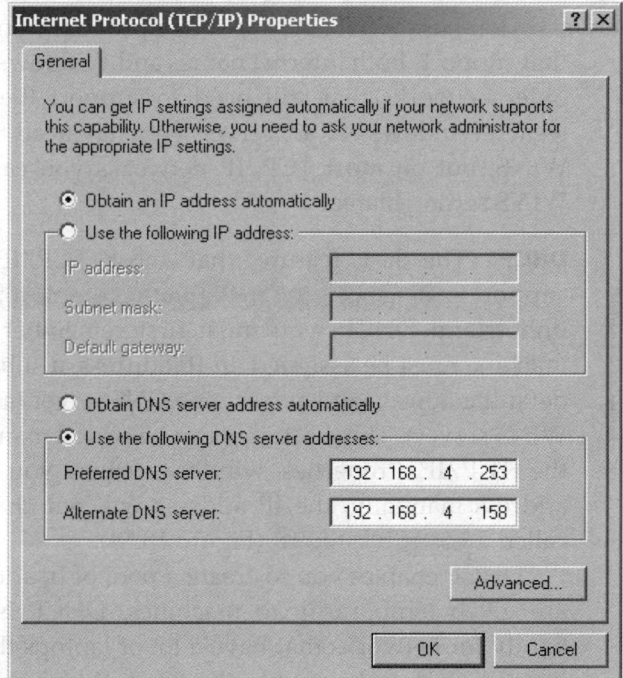

Figure 18.52 Adding two DNS servers in Windows 2000

The Internet has very regulated domain names. If you want a domain name that others can access on the Internet, you must register your domain name and pay a small yearly fee. In most cases, your ISP can handle this for you. Originally, DNS names all ended with one of the following seven domain name qualifiers, called *top level domains (TLDs)*:

.com	General business	.org	Nonprofit organizations
.edu	Educational organizations	.gov	Government organizations
.mil	Military organizations	.net	Internet organizations
.int	International		

As more and more countries joined the Internet, an entire new level of domains was added to the original seven to indicate a DNS name in a particular country, such as .uk for the United Kingdom. It's common to see DNS names such as www.bbc.co.uk or www.louvre.fr. The *Internet Corporation for Assigned Names and Numbers (ICANN)* announced the creation of several more new domains, including .name, .biz, .info, and others. Given the explosive growth of the Internet, these are unlikely to be the last ones! For the latest developments, check ICANN's Web site at www.icann.org.

WINS Before Microsoft came fully on board with Internet standards such as TCP/IP, the company implemented its own type of name server: *Windows Internet Name Server (WINS)*. WINS enables Windows network names such as SERVER1 to be correlated to IP addresses, just as DNS does, except these names are *Windows* network names such as SERVER1, not Internet names such as server1.example.com. Assuming that a WINS server exists on your network, all you have to do to set up WINS on your PC is type in the IP address for the WINS server (Figure 18.53). Many Windows 2000/XP–based networks don't use WINS; they use an improved "dynamic" DNS that supports both Internet names and Windows names. On older networks that still need to support the occasional legacy Windows NT 4.0 server, you may need to configure WINS, but on most TCP/IP networks you can leave the WINS setting blank.

DHCP The last feature that most TCP/IP networks support is dynamic host configuration protocol (DHCP). To understand DHCP, you must first remember that every machine must be assigned an IP address, a subnet mask, a default gateway, and at least one DNS server (and maybe a WINS server). These settings can be added manually using the TCP/IP Properties window. When you set the IP address manually, the IP address will not change and is called a static IP address (Figure 18.54).

DHCP enables you to create a pool of IP addresses that are given temporarily to machines. DHCP is especially handy for networks that have a lot of laptops that join and leave the network on a regular basis. Why give a machine that is on the network for only a few hours a day a static IP address? For that reason, DHCP is quite popular. If you add

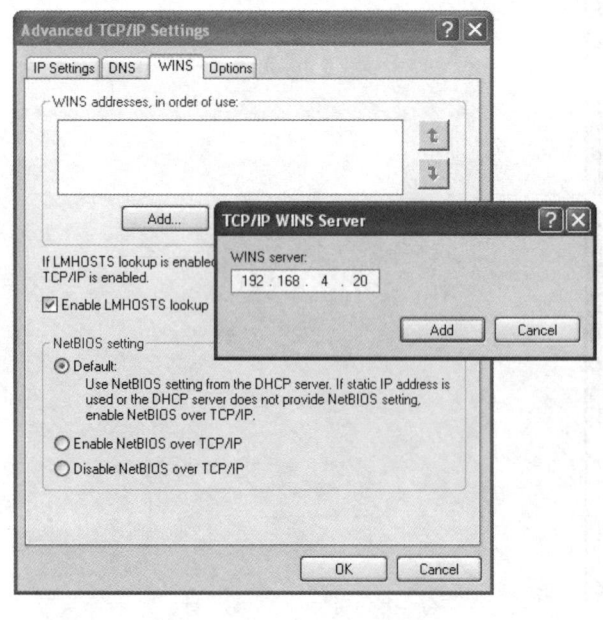

• **Figure 18.53**   Setting up WINS to use DHCP

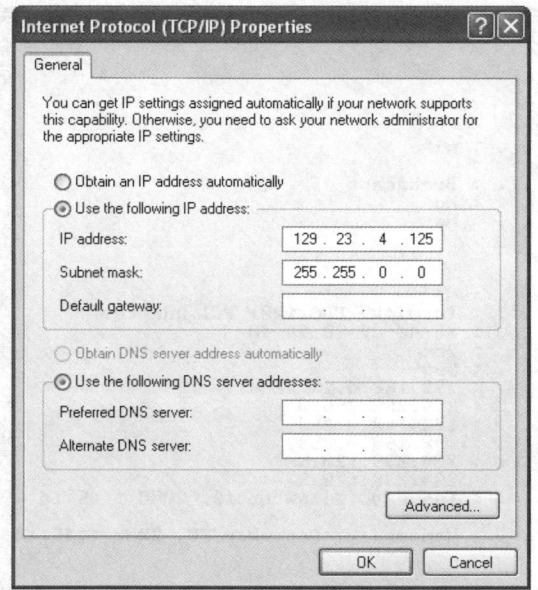

• **Figure 18.54** Setting a static IP address

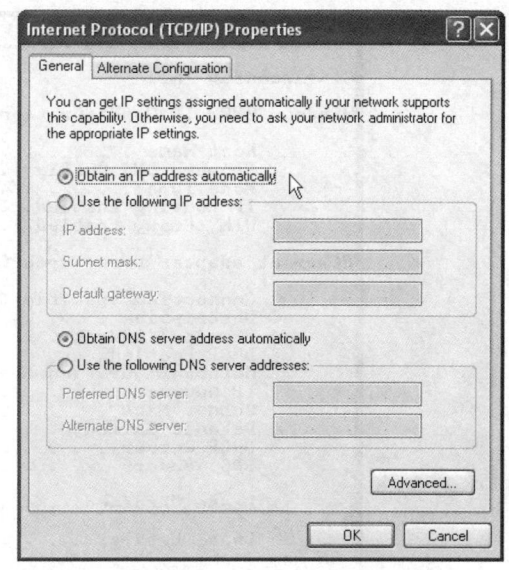

• **Figure 18.55** Automatically obtain an IP address

a NIC to a Windows system, the default TCP/IP settings are set to use DHCP. When you accept those automatic settings, you're really telling the machine to use DHCP (Figure 18.55).

TCP/IP Tools

All versions of Windows come with handy tools to test TCP/IP. Those that you're most likely to use in the field are Ping, IPCONFIG, NSLOOKUP, and TRACERT. All of these programs are command prompt utilities! Open a command prompt to run them—if you just place these commands in the Run command, you'll see the command prompt window open for a moment and then quickly close!

Ping   You've already seen ` Ping `, a really great way to find out if you can talk to another system. Here's how it works. Get to a command prompt and type **ping** followed by an IP address or by a DNS name, such as **ping www.chivalry.com.** Press the ENTER key on your keyboard and away it goes! Figure 18.56 shows the common syntax for Ping.

IPCONFIG   Windows 2000/XP offer the command-line tool ` IPCONFIG ` for a quick glance at your network settings. Click Start | Run and type **CMD** to get a command prompt. From the prompt, type **IPCONFIG / ALL** to see all of your TCP/IP settings (Figure 18.57).

```
C:\WINDOWS\System32\cmd.exe

C:\Documents and Settings\scottj>ping /?

Usage: ping [-t] [-a] [-n count] [-l size] [-f] [-i TTL] [-v TOS]
            [-r count] [-s count] [[-j host-list] | [-k host-list]]
            [-w timeout] target_name

Options:
    -t             Ping the specified host until stopped.
                   To see statistics and continue - type Control-Break;
                   To stop - type Control-C.
    -a             Resolve addresses to hostnames.
    -n count       Number of echo requests to send.
    -l size        Send buffer size.
    -f             Set Don't Fragment flag in packet.
    -i TTL         Time To Live.
    -v TOS         Type Of Service.
    -r count       Record route for count hops.
    -s count       Timestamp for count hops.
    -j host-list   Loose source route along host-list.
    -k host-list   Strict source route along host-list.
    -w timeout     Timeout in milliseconds to wait for each reply.

C:\Documents and Settings\scottj>_
```

• **Figure 18.56** Ping syntax

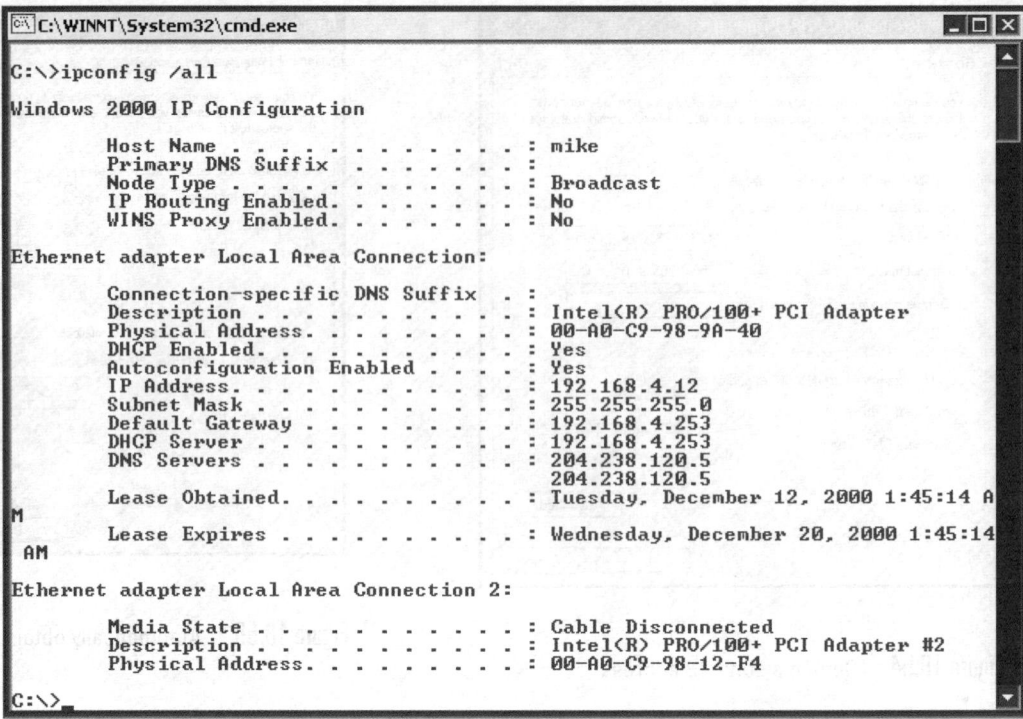

C:\WINNT\System32\cmd.exe

```
C:\>ipconfig /all

Windows 2000 IP Configuration

        Host Name . . . . . . . . . . . . : mike
        Primary DNS Suffix  . . . . . . . :
        Node Type . . . . . . . . . . . . : Broadcast
        IP Routing Enabled. . . . . . . . : No
        WINS Proxy Enabled. . . . . . . . : No

Ethernet adapter Local Area Connection:

        Connection-specific DNS Suffix  . :
        Description . . . . . . . . . . . : Intel(R) PRO/100+ PCI Adapter
        Physical Address. . . . . . . . . : 00-A0-C9-98-9A-40
        DHCP Enabled. . . . . . . . . . . : Yes
        Autoconfiguration Enabled . . . . : Yes
        IP Address. . . . . . . . . . . . : 192.168.4.12
        Subnet Mask . . . . . . . . . . . : 255.255.255.0
        Default Gateway . . . . . . . . . : 192.168.4.253
        DHCP Server . . . . . . . . . . . : 192.168.4.253
        DNS Servers . . . . . . . . . . . : 204.238.120.5
                                            204.238.120.5
        Lease Obtained. . . . . . . . . . : Tuesday, December 12, 2000 1:45:14 A
M
        Lease Expires . . . . . . . . . . : Wednesday, December 20, 2000 1:45:14
 AM

Ethernet adapter Local Area Connection 2:

        Media State . . . . . . . . . . . : Cable Disconnected
        Description . . . . . . . . . . . : Intel(R) PRO/100+ PCI Adapter #2
        Physical Address. . . . . . . . . : 00-A0-C9-98-12-F4

C:\>
```

• **Figure 18.57**   IPCONFIG /ALL on Windows 2000

When you have a static IP address, IPCONFIG does little beyond reporting your current IP settings, including your IP address, subnet mask, default gateway, DNS servers, and WINS servers. When using DHCP, however, IPCONFIG is also the primary tool for releasing and renewing your IP address. Just type **ipconfig /renew** to get a new IP address or **ipconfig /release** to give up the IP address you currently have.

NSLOOKUP   **NSLOOKUP** is a powerful command-line program that enables you to determine exactly what information the DNS server is giving you about a specific host name. Every version of Windows makes NSLOOKUP available when you install TCP/IP. To run the program, type **NSLOOKUP** from the command line and press the ENTER key (Figure 18.58). Note that this gives you a little information, but that the prompt has changed. That's because you're running the application. Type **exit** and press the ENTER key to return to the command prompt.

TRACERT   The **TRACERT** utility shows the route that a packet takes to get to its destination. From a command line, type **TRACERT** followed by a space and an IP address. The output describes the route from your machine to the destination machine, including all devices it passes through and how long each hop takes (Figure 18.59). TRACERT can come in handy when you have to troubleshoot bottlenecks. When users complain that it's difficult to reach a particular destination using TCP/IP, you can run this utility to determine whether the problem exists on a machine or connection over which you have control, or if it is a problem on another machine or router. Similarly, if a destination is completely

You can do some cool stuff with NSLOOKUP, and consequently some techs absolutely love the tool. It's way outside the scope of CompTIA A+ certification, but if you want to play with it, type **HELP** at the NSLOOKUP prompt and press ENTER to see a list of common commands and syntax.

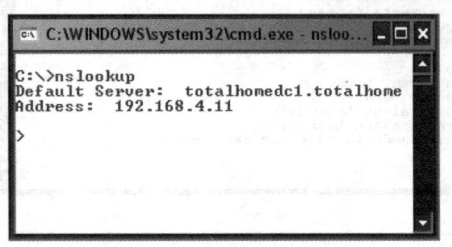

C:\WINDOWS\system32\cmd.exe - nsloo...

```
C:\>nslookup
Default Server:  totalhomedc1.totalhome
Address:  192.168.4.11

>
```

• **Figure 18.58**   NSLOOKUP in action

```
Command Prompt                                                       _ □ ✕

C:\>tracert www.chivalry.com

Tracing route to chivalry.com [65.18.214.130]
over a maximum of 30 hops:

  1     2 ms     1 ms     1 ms  192.168.4.151
  2    20 ms    19 ms    21 ms  adsl-208-190-121-38.dsl.hstntx.swbell.net [208.1
90.121.38]
  3    22 ms    19 ms    19 ms  dist1-vlan50.hstntx.swbell.net [151.164.11.126]

  4    20 ms    19 ms    19 ms  bb1-g1-0.hstntx.swbell.net [151.164.11.230]
  5    22 ms    22 ms    23 ms  core1-p6-0.crhstx.sbcglobal.net [151.164.188.1]

  6    25 ms    26 ms    26 ms  core3-p3-0.crdltx.sbcglobal.net [151.164.240.189
]
  7    27 ms    26 ms    26 ms  core2-p8-0.crdltx.sbcglobal.net [151.164.242.113
]
  8    26 ms    26 ms    25 ms  bb1-p14-3.dllstx.sbcglobal.net [151.164.240.97]

  9    28 ms    26 ms    26 ms  bb2-p15-0.dllstx.sbcglobal.net [151.164.243.150]

 10    27 ms    29 ms    29 ms  sl-gw40-fw-3-0.sprintlink.net [144.228.39.225]
 11    29 ms    29 ms    29 ms  sl-bb22-fw-4-3.sprintlink.net [144.232.8.249]
 12    28 ms    29 ms    29 ms  sl-st20-dal-14-1.sprintlink.net [144.232.20.138]

 13    29 ms    29 ms    29 ms  so-1-1-1.edge1.Dallas1.Level3.net [64.158.168.73
]
```

• **Figure 18.59**   TRACERT in action

unreachable, TRACERT can again determine whether the problem is on a machine or router over which you have control.

Configuring TCP/IP

By default, TCP/IP is configured to receive an IP address automatically from a DHCP server on the network (and automatically assign a corresponding subnet mask). As far as the CompTIA A+ certification exams are concerned, Network+ techs and administrators give you the IP address, subnet mask, and default gateway information and you plug them into the PC. That's about it, so here's how to do it manually:

 Try This!

Running TRACERT

Ever wonder why your e-mail takes *years* to get to some people but arrives instantly for others? Or why some Web sites are slower to load than others? Part of the blame could lie with how many hops away your connection is to the target server. You can use TRACERT to run a quick check of how many hops it takes to get to somewhere on a network, so Try This!

1. Run TRACERT on some known source, such as www.microsoft.com or www.totalsem.com.

2. How many hops did it take? Did your TRACERT time out or make it all the way to the server? Try a TRACERT to a local address. If you're in a university town, run a TRACERT on the campus Web site, such as www.rice.edu for folks in Houston, or www.ucla.edu for those of you in Los Angeles. Did you get fewer hops with a local site?

1. In Windows XP, open the Control Panel and double-click the Network Connections applet. Double-click the Local Area Connection icon. In Windows 2000, click Start | Settings | Network and Dial-up Connections, and double-click the Local Area Connection icon.

2. Click the Properties button, highlight Internet Protocol (TCP/IP), and click the Properties button.

3. In the dialog box, click the *Use the following IP address* radio button.

4. Enter the IP address in the appropriate fields.

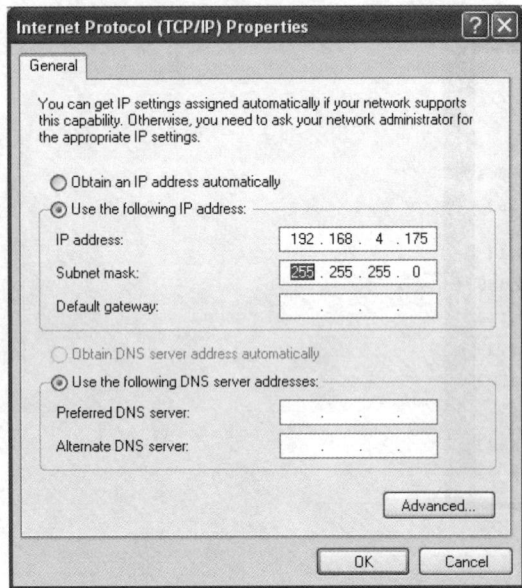

Figure 18.60 Setting up IP

> A computer system on a network with an active DHCP server that has an IP address in this range usually indicates that there is a problem connecting to the DHCP server.

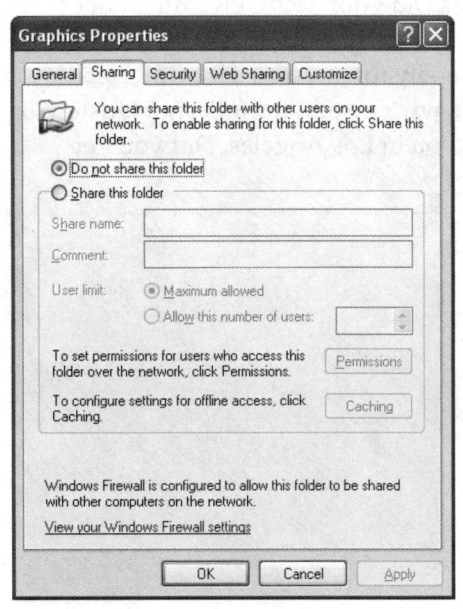

Figure 18.61 Windows Sharing tab on NTFS volume

5. Press the TAB key to skip down to the Subnet mask field. Note that the subnet mask is entered automatically (you can type over this if you want to enter a different subnet mask). See Figure 18.60.

6. Optionally, enter the IP address for a default gateway (router, or another computer system that will forward transmissions beyond your network).

7. Optionally, enter the IP address of a primary and secondary DNS server.

8. Click the OK button to close the dialog box.

9. Click the Close button to exit the Local Area Connection Status dialog box.

10. Windows will alert you that you must restart the system for the changes to take effect.

Automatic Private IP Addressing

Windows 2000 and XP support a feature called Automatic Private IP Addressing (APIPA) that automatically assigns an IP address to the system when the client cannot obtain an IP address automatically. The Internet Assigned Numbers Authority, the non-profit corporation responsible for assigning IP addresses and managing root servers, has set aside the range of addresses from 169.254.0.0 to 169.254.255.254 for this purpose.

If the computer system cannot contact a DHCP server, the computer randomly chooses an address in the form of 169.254.$x.y$ (where $x.y$ is the computer's identifier) and a 16-bit subnet mask (255.255.0.0) and broadcasts it on the network segment (subnet). If no other computer responds to the address, the system assigns this address to itself. When using APIPA, the system can communicate only with other computers on the same subnet that also use the 169.254.$x.y$ range with a 16-bit mask. APIPA is enabled by default if your system is configured to obtain an IP address automatically.

Sharing and Security

Windows systems can share all kinds of resources: files, folders, entire drives, printers, faxes, Internet connections, and much more. Conveniently for you, the CompTIA A+ certification exams limit their interests to folders, printers, and Internet connections. You'll see how to share folders and printers now; Internet connection sharing is discussed in my other book, *Mike Meyers' CompTIA A+ Guide: PC Technician (Exams 220-602, 220-603, & 220-604)*.

Sharing Drives and Folders

All versions of Windows share drives and folders in basically the same manner. Simply right-click any drive or folder and choose Properties. Select the Sharing tab (Figure 18.61). Select *Share this folder*, add something in the Comment or User Limit fields if you wish (they're not required), and click Permissions (Figure 18.62).

Hey! Doesn't NTFS have all those wild permissions like Read, Execute, Take Ownership, and all that? Yes, it does, but NTFS permissions and network permissions are totally separate beasties. Microsoft wanted Windows 2000 and XP to support many different types of partitions (NTFS, FAT16, FAT32), old and new. Network permissions are Microsoft's way of enabling you to administer file sharing on any type of partition supported by Windows, no matter how ancient. Sure, your options will be pretty limited if you are working with an older partition type, but you *can* do it.

The beauty of Windows 2000/XP is that they provide another tool—NTFS permissions—that can do much more. NTFS is where the power lies, but power always comes with a price: You have to configure two separate sets of permissions. If you are sharing a folder on an NTFS drive, as you normally are these days, you must set *both* the network permissions and the NTFS permissions to let others access your shared resources. Some good news: This is actually no big deal! Just set the network permissions to give everyone full control, and then use the NTFS permissions to exercise more precise control over *who* accesses the shared resources and *how* they access them. Open the Security tab to set the NTFS permissions.

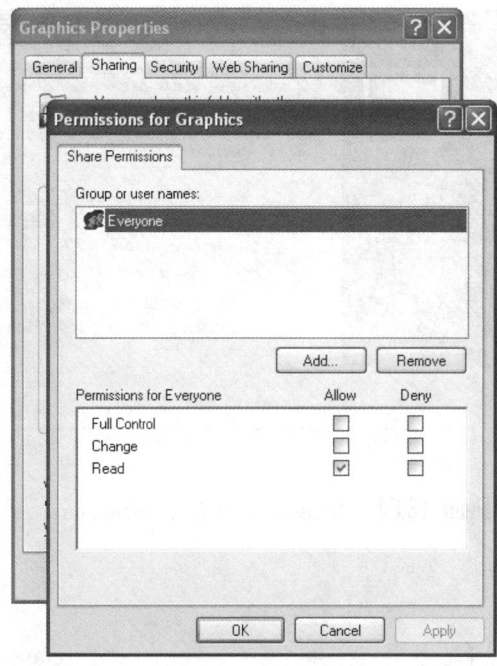

● **Figure 18.62**   Network permissions

Accessing Shared Drives/Directories

Once you have set up a drive or directory to be shared, the final step is to access that shared drive or directory from another machine. Windows 2000 and XP use My Network Places, although you'll need to do a little clicking to get to the shared resources (Figure 18.63).

> Windows 2000/XP offer two types of sharing: network permissions and NTFS permissions.

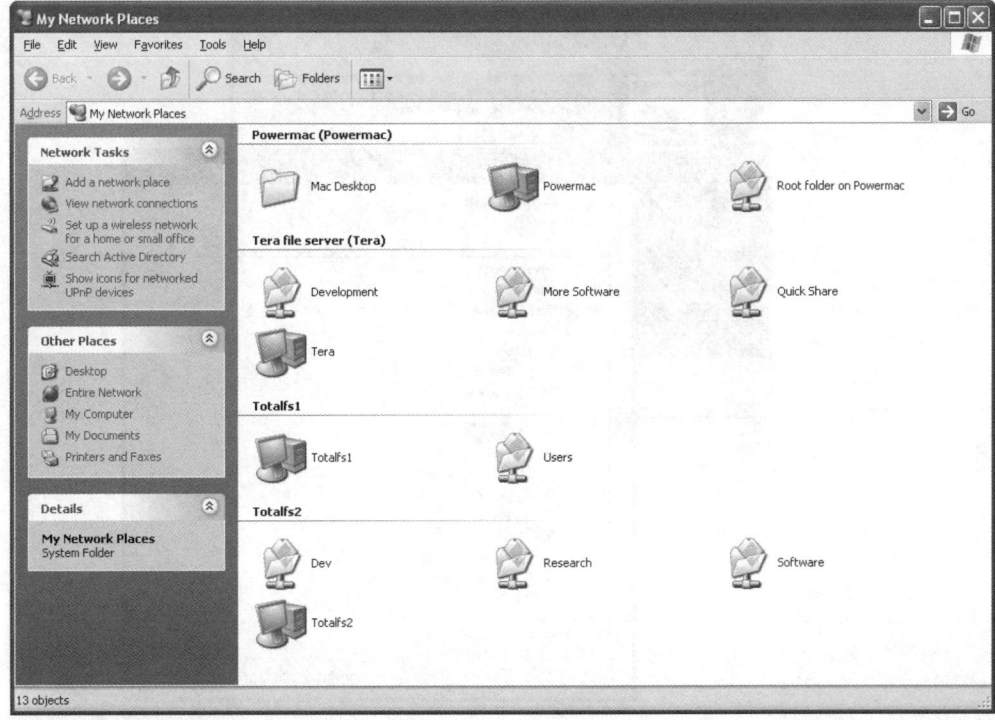

● **Figure 18.63**   Shared resources in My Network Places

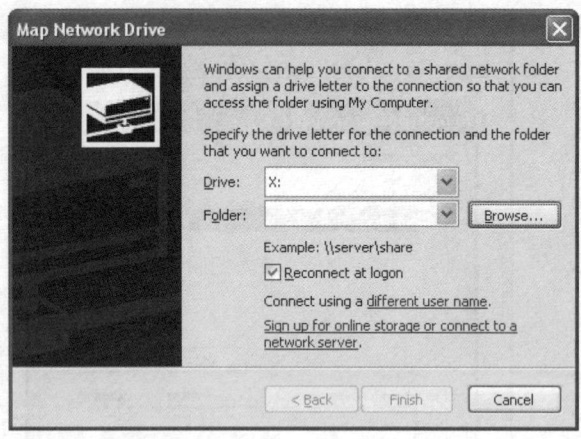

● **Figure 18.64** Map Network Drive dialog box

All shared resources should show up in My Network Places. If a shared resource fails to show up, make sure you check the basics first: Is File and Printer Sharing activated? Is the device shared? Don't let silly errors fool you!

Network resources can also be "mapped" to a local resource name. For example, the FREDC share can be mapped to be a local hard drive such as E: or F:. From within any My Computer/Explorer window (such as My Documents or My Network Places), choose Tools | Map Network Drive to open the Map Network Drive dialog box (Figure 18.64). Click the Browse button to check out the neighborhood and find a shared drive (Figure 18.65).

In Windows 2000, you can also use the handy Add Network Place icon in My Network Places to add network locations you frequently access without using up drive letters. Windows XP removed the icon but added the menu option in its context bar on the left. Here's how it looks on a Windows 2000 system (Figure 18.66).

Mapping shared network drives is a common practice, as it makes a remote network share look like just another drive on the local system. The only downside to drive mapping stems from the fact that users tend to forget they are on a network. A classic example is the user who always accesses a particular folder or file on the network and then suddenly gets a "file not found" error when the workstation gets disconnected from the network. Instead of recognizing this as a network error, the user often imagines the problem as a missing or corrupted file.

UNC

All computers that share must have a network name, and all of the resources they share must also have network names. Any resource on a network can

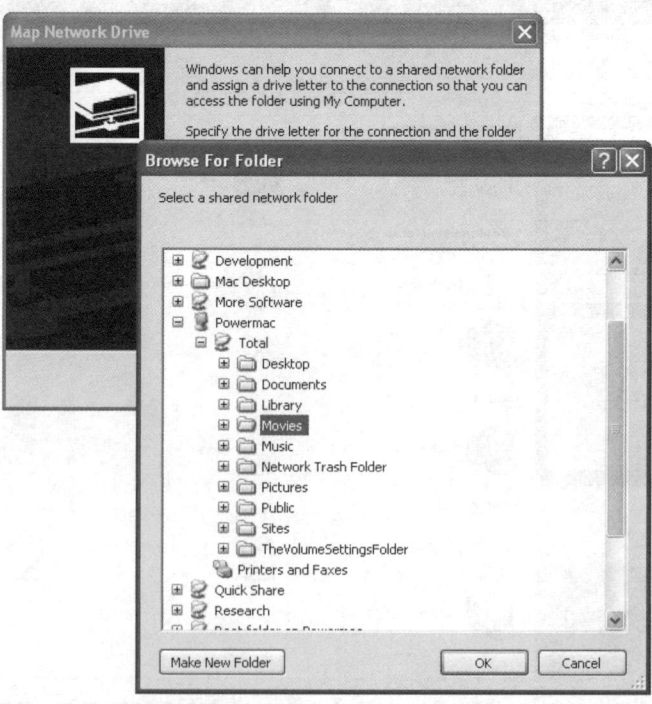

● **Figure 18.65** Browsing for shared folders

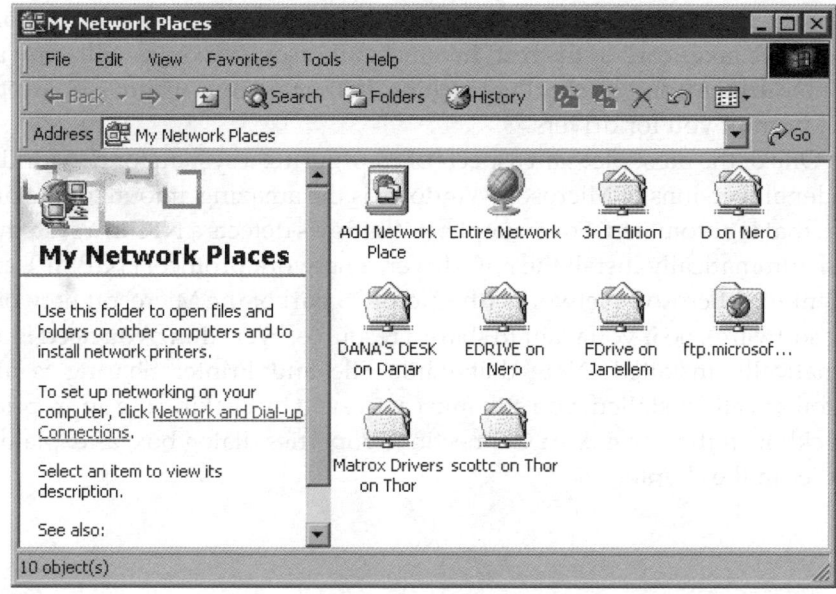

● Figure 18.66   My Network Places

be described by combining the names of the resource being shared and the system sharing. If a machine called SERVER1 is sharing its C: drive as FREDC, for example, the complete name would look like this:

```
\\SERVER1\FREDC
```

This is called the **universal naming convention (UNC)**. The UNC is distinguished by its use of double backslashes in front of the sharing system's name, and a single backslash in front of the shared resource's name. A UNC name can also point directly to a specific file or folder:

```
\\SERVER1\FREDC\INSTALL-FILES\SETUP.EXE
```

In this example, INSTALL-FILES is a subdirectory in the shared folder FREDC (which may or may not be called FREDC on the server), and SETUP.EXE is a specific file.

Sharing Printers

Sharing printers in Windows is just as easy as sharing drives and directories. Assuming that the system has printer sharing services loaded, just go to the Printers folder in the Control Panel and right-click the printer you wish to share. Select Properties, go to the Sharing tab, click Share this printer, and give it a name (see Figure 18.67).

To access a shared printer in any version of Windows, simply click the Add Printer icon in the Printers folder. When asked if the printer is Local or Network,

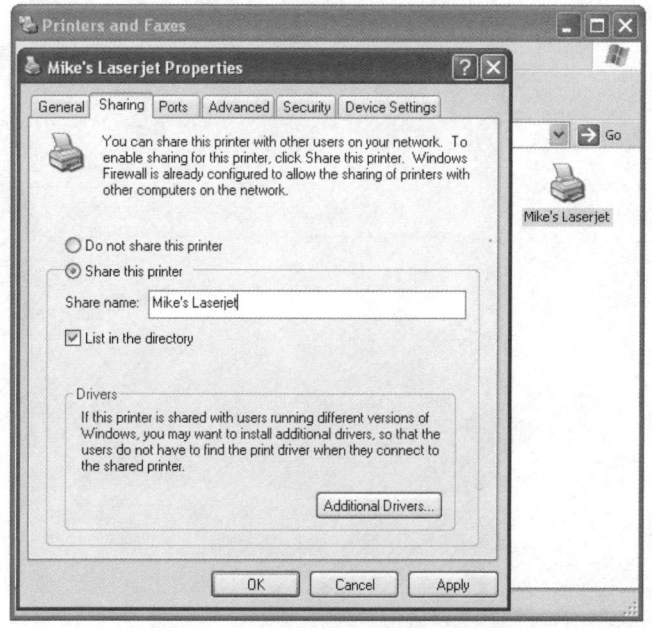

● Figure 18.67   Giving a name to a shared printer

select Network; browse the network for the printer you wish to access, and Windows takes care of the rest! In almost all cases, Windows will copy the printer driver from the sharing machine. In the rare case where it doesn't, it will prompt you for drivers.

One of the most pleasant aspects of configuring a system for networking under all versions of Microsoft Windows is the amazing amount of the process that is automated. For example, if Windows detects a NIC in a system, it will automatically install the NIC driver, a network protocol (TCP/IP), and Client for Microsoft Networks (the NetBIOS part of the Microsoft networking software). So if you want to share a resource, everything you need is automatically installed. Note that while File and Printer Sharing is also automatically installed, you still must activate it by clicking the appropriate checkbox in the Local Area Connection Properties dialog box, as explained earlier in the chapter.

Chapter 18 Review

■ Chapter Summary

After reading this chapter and completing the exercises, you should understand the following about networking.

Networking Technologies

■ A PC connected to a network, called a client machine, must have a NIC. The PC must be able to initiate and carry out the exchange of data, using either a cable or some type of wireless transmission method, with other client machines and with one or more server machines.

■ The most common network topologies include bus, ring, star, and mesh. Logical topology refers to how the network is laid out on paper. Physical topology refers to the actual hardware (clients, servers, cables).

■ Data is sent in discrete chunks called packets or frames. The built-in 48-bit MAC address, unique to each NIC, is vital to the creation and function of data packets. Each data packet includes certain vital elements: the MAC of the recipient's NIC, the MAC of the sender's NIC, the data itself, and a CRC that enables the recipient to verify that the data arrives intact.

■ A hardware protocol defines many aspects of a network, from the packet type to the cabling and connectors used—in short, everything necessary to get data from one computer to another. The hardware protocol that dominates the modern computing landscape is Ethernet.

■ The three main types of Ethernet are based on the cable type: coaxial, UTP, and fiber optic. All Ethernet uses the same packet type, so any combination of hardware devices and cabling systems can work on an Ethernet network.

■ The 10Base5 coaxial Ethernet specification used Thick Ethernet, or Thicknet, cabling, more technically known as RG-8. The *10* in 10Base5 indicates a maximum data speed of 10 Mbps, and the *5* indicates a maximum segment length of 500 meters. Up to 100 devices can be attached per segment.

■ 10Base5 used a bus topology, so only one device could use the cable at a time. To prevent data

reflection and a resulting network deadlock, the ends of the main cable had to be terminated. Ethernet networks use CSMA/CD to handle data communication and packet collision.

■ 10Base2 used thinner RG-58 coaxial cable and cable lengths were limited to a maximum of 185 meters. Thinnet NICs connected to the main bus cable using T connectors and BNC connectors.

■ Most modern Ethernet networks use either 10BaseT, 100Base T, or 1000BaseT, all of which use UTP cable. 10BaseT runs at 10 Mbps; 100BaseT runs at 100 Mbps; 1000BaseT runs at 1000 Mbps (or 1 Gbps). These three technologies, known collectively as 10/100/1000BaseT, use a star bus topology, which employs hubs or switches to make termination simpler and avoid the vulnerabilities of a bus topology.

■ UTP cables come in different categories intended for different uses. CAT 1 cable is standard phone wire. Most UTP networks today use CAT 5e (maximum speed 1 Gbps) or CAT 6 cable (maximum speed 10 Gbps). 100BaseT requires a minimum of CAT 5 (maximum speed 100 Mbps) to run, while 1000BaseT requires a minimum of CAT 5e.

■ UTP cables use the RJ-45 connector, which is essentially a wider version of the familiar RJ-11 phone connector. Two TIA/EIA standards, 568A and 568B, dictate acceptable ways to arrange the eight UTP cable wires in an RJ-45 jack. You should choose a wiring standard and stick with it to avoid network headaches.

■ Standard network cables use PVC for the jacket, which emits toxic fumes when burned. Plenum-grade cables use a fire-retardant jacket and should be used when cables are installed in a plenum space.

■ In a 10/100/1000BaseT network, each PC connects to a hub or switch via one of the hub's or switch's ports. The maximum distance from the hub or switch to a connected device is 100 meters. Hubs and switches act as repeaters, boosting signals as they pass on data, so they require a reliable power source.

- Fiber optic Ethernet transmits light instead of electricity, achieving much greater maximum distances than other forms of Ethernet. Most fiber networks use LEDs to send light signals and use multimode fiber optic cabling. Networks that use laser light use single-mode fiber optic cabling. Laser light and single-mode cabling are used most often for very long distance connections.

- Most fiber optic cables use one of two connectors: the square SC type and the round ST type. The two most common fiber optic standards are 10BaseFL and 100BaseFX.

- Token Ring networks use a ring topology, most often a star ring. The Token Ring version of the network hub or switch is called a MAU. A UTP Token Ring cable uses RJ-45 connectors, just like an Ethernet cable.

Network Operating Systems

- An NOS communicates with the PC hardware to make connections between machines. At least one machine on a network must play the server role, sharing data and services, while client machines access these shared resources. To make Windows networking happen, you have to install a network protocol, set up server software to share resources, and set up client software to access shared resources.

- There are three types of network organization: client/server, peer-to-peer, and domain-based. All Windows PCs can function as network clients and servers.

- A client/server network dedicates one machine to act as a server. The server will have a dedicated NOS optimized for sharing files, with powerful caching software that enables high-speed file access, extremely high levels of protection, and an organization that permits extensive control of the data.

- A peer-to-peer network enables any or all of the machines on the network to act as a server. Every computer can perform both server and client functions. A peer-to-peer network comprising only Windows 2000 and Windows XP machines requires you to place a local account on every system, which the system administrator must add and delete individually.

- In a domain-based network environment, the security database for all systems is centralized on one or more servers called domain controllers. This database holds a single list of all users and passwords. When you log on to any computer in the network, the logon request goes to an available domain controller for verification.

- Every Windows system contains a very special account called administrator that has complete and absolute power over the entire system. When you install Windows 2000/XP, you must create a password for the administrator account. Anyone who knows the administrator password has the ability to read any file and run any program.

- Network protocol software takes the incoming data received by the network card, keeps it organized, sends it to the application that needs it, and then takes outgoing data from the application and hands it to the NIC to be sent out over the network. All networks use some protocol, such as NetBEUI (Microsoft), IPX/SPX (Novell), and TCP/IP (UNIX/Internet).

- IBM developed NetBEUI, the default protocol for Windows for Workgroups, LANtastic, and Windows 95. NetBEUI was small and relatively high speed, but it couldn't be used for routing. Novell invented IPX/SPX protocol and built all versions of its NetWare software around it. TCP/IP is the best protocol for larger (more than 200 nodes) networks. The Internet uses TCP/IP as its default protocol.

- To access data or resources across a network, a Windows PC needs to have client software installed for every kind of server that you want to access. When you install a network card and drivers, Windows installs at least one set of client software, called Client for Microsoft Networks, which enables your system to connect to a Microsoft network.

- You can turn any Windows PC into a server simply by enabling File and Print Sharing to share files, folders, and printers. Windows 2000 and XP installations come with this feature, but it is not activated by default. Activating takes only a click in a check box.

Installing and Configuring a Wired Network

■ When you install a NIC, by default, Windows 2000 and XP Professional install the TCP/IP protocol (configured for Dynamic DHCP), the Client for Microsoft Networks, and File and Printer Sharing for Microsoft Networks upon setup.

■ To establish network connectivity, you need a network client installed and configured properly. The Client for Microsoft Networks is installed as part of the OS installation.

■ Generally, all that is needed to establish a connection between computer systems using NetBEUI is a NetBIOS computer name.

■ NWLink is Microsoft's implementation of IPX/SPX protocol, which includes an element for resolving NetBIOS names.

■ Systems in a TCP/IP network use IP addresses rather than names. IP addresses are four sets of eight binary numbers (octets) separated by a period (dotted-octet notation). The first part of the address identifies the network; the second part identifies the local computer (host) address. The subnet mask is a value that distinguishes which part of the IP address is the network address and which part is the host address. The subnet mask blocks out (or "masks") the network portions (octets) of an IP address.

■ A traditional TCP/IP network divides IP addresses into classes, which correspond with the potential size of the network: Class A, Class B, and Class C. Class A networks use the first octet to identify the network address, and the remaining three octets to identify the host. Class B networks use two and two. Class C networks use three and one.

■ TCP/IP not only supports File and Print Sharing, it adds a number of special sharing functions unique only to it, called TCP/IP services, such as HTTP, the language of the World Wide Web. Another example is Telnet, which enables you to access a remote system as though you were actually in front of that machine.

■ The goal of TCP/IP is to link together multiple LANs to make a WAN. You use routers to move traffic between networks. Each host will send traffic to the router only when that data is destined for a remote network, cutting down on traffic across the more expensive WAN links.

■ On a Windows 2000/XP system, you can configure both dial-up and network connections using the Network Connections dialog box. Simply select the connection you wish to configure, and then set its TCP/IP properties.

■ A computer that wants to send data to another machine outside its LAN is not expected to know all the IP addresses of all the computers on the Internet. Instead, all IP machines know the name of one computer, called the default gateway, to which they pass all the data they need to send outside the LAN. The default gateway is the local router.

■ DNS servers keep databases of IP addresses and their corresponding names. Virtually all TCP/IP networks require you to set up DNS server names.

■ If you want an Internet domain name that others can access on the Internet, you must register your domain name and pay a small yearly fee. Originally, DNS names all ended with one of the following top level domains: .com, .org, .edu, .gov, .mil, .net, and .int.

■ DHCP automatically assigns IP address settings (including IP, subnet mask, default gateway, DNS servers, and WINS server, if necessary). If you add a NIC to a Windows system, the TCP/IP settings are set to use DHCP. A manually assigned IP address is known as a static IP address.

■ All versions of Windows come with handy tools to test TCP/IP. The four you're most likely to use in the field are Ping, IPCONFIG, NSLOOKUP, and TRACERT. IPCONFIG can both display your current IP address settings and be used to renew and release your DHCP-assigned settings. NSLOOKUP is a powerful command-line program that enables you to determine the name of a DNS server, among many other things. The TRACERT utility shows the route that a packet takes to get to its destination.

■ By default, TCP/IP is configured to receive an IP address automatically from a DHCP server, but you can assign a static IP address. Use the Network Connections applet in the Control Panel for Windows XP; Network and Dial-up Connections from the Start menu in Windows 2000.

- Windows supports Automatic Private IP Addressing (APIPA). APIPA automatically assigns an IP address to the system when the client cannot obtain an IP address automatically. If your PC gets an address with 169.254.x.y, you know the PC is not connecting to your DHCP server. Check your connection!

- All versions of Windows share drives and folders in basically the same manner. Simply right-click any drive or folder, choose Properties, and then select the Sharing tab. Click the Share this folder radio button and type a share name.

- When sharing a folder on an NTFS drive, you must set the network permissions to give everyone full control, and then use the NTFS permissions (on the Security tab) to exercise more precise control over who accesses the shared resources and how they access them.

- Network resources can be mapped to a local resource name. This can be done from Windows Explorer or by right-clicking a share in My Network Places and choosing Map Network Drive.

- All computers that share must have a share name, and all the resources they share must also have names. Any resource on a network can be described by combining the names of the resource being shared and the system that is sharing. The complete UNC name of the FREDC share on SERVER1, for example, would be \\SERVER1\FREDC.

- To share a printer in Windows, open the Printers folder in the Control Panel and right-click the printer you want to share. Select Properties and go to the Sharing tab; then click Shared as and give it a name. To access a shared printer in any version of Windows, simply click the Add Printer icon in the Printers folder.

■ Key Terms

10BaseT *(560)*

100BaseT *(560)*

1000BaseT *(560)*

administrator account *(572)*

Automatic Private IP Addressing (APIPA) *(580)*

bus topology *(554)*

carrier sense multiple access/ collision detection (CSMA/CD) *(557)*

client *(553)*

client/server network *(569)*

coaxial cable *(557)*

crossover cable *(564)*

cyclic redundancy check (CRC) *(556)*

default gateway *(582)*

directory service *(571)*

domain name service (DNS) *(582)*

domain-based network *(571)*

dynamic host configuration protocol (DHCP) *(584)*

Ethernet *(556)*

full-duplex *(564)*

hardware protocol *(556)*

hub *(561)*

IP address *(579)*

IPCONFIG *(585)*

IPX/SPX *(574)*

media access control (MAC) address *(555)*

mesh topology *(554)*

multistation access unit (MAU) *(567)*

NetBEUI *(574)*

network interface card (NIC) *(553)*

network operating system (NOS) *(568)*

NSLOOKUP *(586)*

NWLink *(574)*

packets *(553)*

peer-to-peer network *(570)*

Ping *(585)*

resources *(568)*

RG-8 *(557)*

RG-58 *(559)*

ring topology *(554)*

RJ-11 *(562)*

RJ-45 *(562)*

router *(574)*

server *(553)*

shielded twisted pair (STP) *(566)*

star topology *(554)*

static IP address *(584)*

subnet mask *(580)*

switch *(561)*

TCP/IP *(574)*

terminator *(558)*

Thicknet *(557)*

Thinnet *(559)*

Token Ring *(556)*

TRACERT *(586)*

universal naming convention (UNC) *(591)*

unshielded twisted pair (UTP) *(560)*

Key Term Quiz

Use the Key Terms list to complete the sentences that follow. Not all terms will be used.

1. Every network card has a unique built-in identifier called a(n) _____.

2. The _____ hardware protocol dominates the modern computing landscape.

3. A(n) _____ enables a PC to act as a server and share data and services over a network.

4. The _____ is a value that distinguishes which part of an IP address is the network address and which part is the host address.

5. HTTP and TELNET are both examples of special sharing functions called _____ services.

6. A(n) _____ helps break files into packets to send across the network and reassemble packets it receives into whole files.

7. The command-line utility called _____ enables one machine to check whether it can communicate with another machine.

8. _____ consists of a center cable surrounded by insulation and covered with a shield of braided cable.

9. The _____ connector is the standard connector used for UTP Ethernet installations.

10. A person logged into the _____ on a Windows XP system has the ability to read any file and run any program on the system.

Multiple-Choice Quiz

1. Simon's Windows 2000 system can't contact a DHCP server to obtain an IP address automatically, but he can still communicate with other systems on his subnet. What feature of Windows 2000 makes this possible?

   A. Subnet masking

   B. WINS

   C. APIPA

   D. Client for Microsoft Networks

2. Which of the following are true of NetBEUI? (Select two.)

   A. No logical addresses required

   B. Supported only on Microsoft network systems

   C. Supports routing

   D. Supported by all versions of Windows through XP

3. James needs to connect his Windows XP system to a Windows 2000 network domain. Which of the following will get him to the screen he needs?

   A. Control Panel | Client for Microsoft Networks | Log on to Windows NT domain

   B. Right-click My Computer | Properties | Client for Microsoft Networks | Network ID

   C. Control Panel | Network Connections | Network Identification | Log on to Windows NT domain

   D. Right-click My Computer | Properties | Computer Name | Network ID

4. What is the meaning of the networking term *topology*?

   A. The choice of network protocol

   B. The cabling specification of a network

   C. The physical layout of a network

   D. A network that uses hubs

5. What transmits the sender's MAC address, recipient's MAC address, data, and CRC when two computers communicate across a network?

   A. Packet

   B. IP unit

   C. CSMA

   D. Token

6. You need to check the status of the local area connection of a Windows XP machine on your Microsoft network. How do you get to the screen where you can perform this task? (Select all that apply.)

    A. Start | right-click My Network Places | Properties | Local Area Connection

    B. Start | Settings | Network and Dial-up Connections | Local Area Connection

    C. Start | Control Panel | Network Connections | Local Area Connection

    D. Right-click My Computer | Properties | Network Connections | Local Area Connection

7. What *minimum* level of cabling must be used to support Gigabit networks?

    A. CAT 3

    B. CAT 5

    C. CAT 5e

    D. CAT 6

8. Computers that connect directly to a central hub are said to be part of what topology?

    A. Bus

    B. Mesh

    C. Ring

    D. Star

9. What uniquely identifies every network card in the world?

    A. 32-bit IP address

    B. 48-bit MAC address

    C. 24-bit WEP key

    D. 16-bit APIPA address

10. What is an example of a hardware protocol?

    A. Token Ring

    B. CAT 5e

    C. Bus topology

    D. TCP/IP

11. What kind of cable must be installed in the space above a drop ceiling?

    A. CAT 5e or higher

    B. Plenum

    C. PVC

    D. Ethernet

12. How can you connect two PCs directly to each other without using a hub?

    A. Use CAT 6 cable.

    B. Use a crossover cable.

    C. Use STP cable.

    D. It is not possible to connect two PCs without a hub.

13. What is the recommended maximum number of PCs for a peer-to-peer network?

    A. 10

    B. 15

    C. 20

    D. 25

14. Which protocol must be installed and properly configured on any PC connecting to the Internet?

    A. AppleTalk

    B. NetBEUI

    C. IPX/SPX

    D. TCP/IP

15. You have connected a new PC to a network running NWLink, but you can't connect to any network computers. What is most likely the problem?

    A. Your PC has an APIPA address.

    B. You set the incorrect frame type.

    C. You used CAT 3 cable, but the rest of the network is running CAT 5e.

    D. You forgot to install IPX/SPX.

Essay Quiz

1. Your office has recently received a box of networking equipment that's a mix of 10BaseT, 100BaseT, and 10Base2 NICs and hubs. Your boss wants you to network the office machines using all the equipment. Write out a short essay describing the differences between the various standards and what you would need to make such a mixed network work.

2. A client wants to implement a network in her building, but she can't decide on the technology to use. She inherited the building with some networking stuff in place, namely CAT 5e strung through the walls and the ceiling to a central wiring area. All the offices have RJ-45 outlets for workstations. Write an essay detailing the technologies she could install using the existing equipment and why she might select one over the other(s). Include an explanation of the equipment she has already installed.

3. You get a late-night telephone call from a senior network tech with a crisis on her hands. "I need help getting 20 PCs networked within 24 hours, and your boss told me you might be able to assist me. I'll buy all the pizza you can eat and when the project's over, the beer is on me. Do you know the basics of a network? What must you do to get a PC ready to network?" Write a short essay responding to her question. (Hint: Discuss four things in response to her last question.)

4. The network tech is gone for the day, and your boss has a serious problem: he can't access the file server. Tag. You're it. Write a brief essay describing what you would need to know about your network and your boss to begin troubleshooting; describe the tool(s) you might use if your network uses TCP/IP.

Lab Projects

• Lab Project 18.1

This chapter described simple network protocols as almost interchangeable and that you could install NetBEUI on some networked PCs and it would enable them to communicate. Experiment with this idea. If you have a network of Windows 2000 PCs that you can play with, install and enable just NetBEUI or IPX/SPX, but make sure TCP/IP is disabled. Try to share resources and access shared resources on other machines in the lab. Once you've tried that, install a different simple protocol and try it again.

• Lab Project 18.2

The PC is not the only device that can connect to an Ethernet network. Do an Internet search or a run to your local computer store and come back with a list of network devices. What did you find? How would they be used?

Computer Security

"First, secure the data."

—TECH VERSION OF THE OATH
ATTRIBUTED TO GALEN AND OFTEN
ASSOCIATED WITH PHYSICIANS: "PRIMUM
NON NOCERE" ("FIRST, DO NO HARM")

In this chapter, you will learn how to

- **Explain the threats to your computers and data**
- **Describe how to control the local computing environment**
- **Explain how to protect computers from network threats**

Your PC is under siege. Through your PC, a malicious person can gain valuable information about you and your habits. He can steal your files. He can run programs that log your keystrokes and thus gain account names and passwords, credit card information, and more. He can run software that takes over much of your computer processing time and use it to send spam or steal from others. The threat is real and right now. Worse, he's doing one or more of these things to your clients as I write these words. You need to secure your computer and your users from these attacks.

But what does computer security mean? Is it an antivirus program? Is it big, complex passwords? Sure, it's both of these things, but what about the fact that your laptop can be stolen easily? Before you run out in a panic to buy security applications, let's take a moment to understand the threat to your computers, see what needs to be protected, and how to do so.

■ Analyzing the Threat

Threats to your data and PC come from two directions: accidents and malicious people. All sorts of things can go wrong with your computer, from a user getting access to a folder he or she shouldn't see to a virus striking and deleting folders. Files can get deleted, renamed, or simply lost. Hard drives can die, and optical discs get scratched and rendered unreadable. Accidents happen, and even well-meaning people can make mistakes.

Unfortunately, there are a lot of people out there who intend to do you harm. Add that intent together with a talent for computers, and you've got a deadly combination. Let's look at the following issues:

- Unauthorized access
- Data destruction, accidental or deliberate
- Administrative access
- Catastrophic hardware failures
- Viruses/spyware

 If you look at the CompTIA A+ exam objectives for the Essentials, IT Technician, and specialization exams, you'll notice that the objectives covered in this chapter are, for all intents and purposes, virtually the same for each exam. CompTIA has not differentiated the questions for each exam covered by this domain, so we have used the same chapter for the Essentials exam and the IT Technician and specialization exams.

Historical/Conceptual

Unauthorized Access

Unauthorized access occurs when a user accesses resources in an unauthorized way. Resources in this case mean data, applications, and hardware. A user can alter or delete data; access sensitive information, such as financial data, personnel files, or e-mail messages; or use a computer for purposes the owner did not intend.

Not all unauthorized access is malicious—often this problem arises when users who are randomly poking around in a computer discover that they can access resources in a fashion the primary user did not intend. Unauthorized access can sometimes be very malicious when outsiders knowingly and intentionally take advantage of weaknesses in your security to gain information, use resources, or destroy data!

Data Destruction

Often an extension of unauthorized access, data destruction means more than just intentionally or accidentally erasing or corrupting data. It's easy to imagine some evil hacker accessing your network and deleting all your important files, but consider the case where authorized users access certain data, but what they do to that data goes beyond what they are authorized to do. A good example is the person who legitimately accesses a Microsoft Access product database to modify the product descriptions, only to discover he or she can change the prices of the products, too.

This type of threat is particularly dangerous when users are not clearly informed about the extent to which they are authorized to make changes. A fellow tech once told me about a user who managed to mangle an important database due to someone giving them incorrect access. When confronted, the user said: "If I wasn't allowed to change it, the system wouldn't let me do it!" Many users believe that systems are configured in a paternalistic way that wouldn't allow them to do anything inappropriate. As a result, users will often assume they're authorized to make any changes they believe are necessary when working on a piece of data they know they're authorized to access.

Administrative Access

Every operating system enables you to create user accounts and grant those accounts a certain level of access to files and folders in that computer. As an administrator, supervisor, or root user, you have full control over just about every aspect of the computer. Windows XP, in particular, makes it entirely too easy to give users administrative access to the computer, especially Windows XP Home because it allows only two kinds of users, administrators and limited users. Because you can't do much as a limited user, most home and small office systems simply use multiple administrator accounts. If you need to control access, you really need to use Windows 2000 or XP Professional.

System Crash/Hardware Failure

Like any technology, computers can and will fail—usually when you can least afford for it to happen. Hard drives crash, the power fails—it's all part of the joy of working in the computing business. You need to create redundancy in areas prone to failure (like installing backup power in case of electrical failure) and perform those all-important data backups. Chapter 13, "Maintaining Windows," goes into detail about using Microsoft Backup and other issues involved in creating a stable and reliable system.

Virus/Spyware

Networks are without a doubt the fastest and most efficient vehicles for transferring computer viruses among systems. News reports focus attention on the many virus attacks from the Internet, but a huge number of viruses still come from users who bring in programs on floppy disks, writable optical discs, and USB drives. This chapter describes the various methods of virus infection, and what you need to do to prevent virus infection of your networked systems in the "Network Security" section.

Essentials

■ Local Control

To create a secure computing environment, you need to establish control over local resources. You need to back up data and make sure that retired hard drives and optical discs have no sensitive data on them. You should recognize security issues and be able to respond properly. You need to implement good access control policies, such as having all computers in your care locked down with proper passwords or other devices that recognize who should have access. Finally, you need to be able to implement methods for tracking computer usage. If someone is doing something wrong, you and the network or computer administrator should be able to catch him or her!

To mimic the physician's oath, here's the technician's oath: "Technician, first, secure your data." You need to back up data on machines in your care properly. Also, techs need to follow correct practices when retiring or donating old equipment. Let's take a look.

What to Back Up

Systems in your care should have regular backups performed of essential operating system files and, most importantly, data files. Chapter 13, "Maintaining Windows," covers the process of backing up data, such as running the Backup or Restore Wizard in Windows 2000 and Windows XP, so the mechanics aren't covered here. Instead, this chapter looks more critically at what files to back up and how to protect those files.

Essential Data

By default, the Backup or Restore Wizard in Windows XP offers to back up your Documents and Settings folder (Figure 19.1). You also have options to back up everyone's documents and settings. That takes care of most, but not all, of your critical data. There are other issues to consider.

First, if you use Microsoft Outlook for your e-mail, the saved e-mail messages—both received and sent—will not be backed up. Neither will your address book. If you don't care about such things, then that's fine, but if you share a computer with multiple users, you need to make certain that you or the users back up both their mail and address book manually and then put

 Windows 2000 and 2003 open the Backup Wizard with somewhat different settings. You are prompted to back up the entire drive initially, for example, rather than just Documents and Settings. This is also the case when you run the wizard in Windows XP in Advanced Mode.

• **Figure 19.1** Backup or Restore Wizard

Chapter 19: Computer Security

603

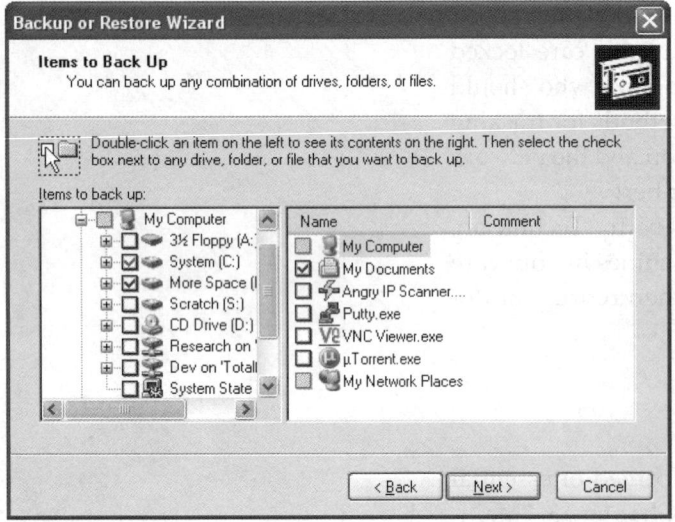

Figure 19.2   Selecting items to back up

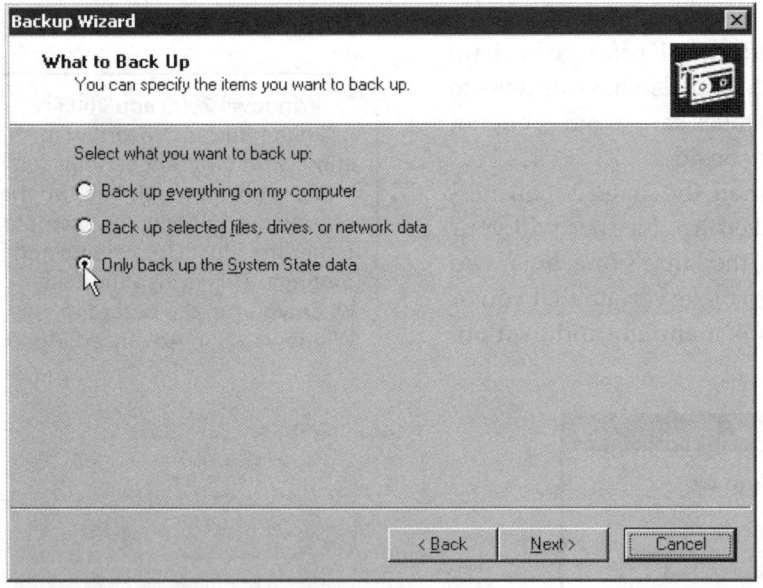

Figure 19.3   Backup Wizard

> The CompTIA A+ certification exams most likely *won't* ask you about off-site storage, but in today's world, anything less would be illogical.

the backed-up files in the Documents and Settings folder! That way, the Backup or Restore Wizard will grab those files.

Second, if you or others on the computer use any folders outside the Documents and Settings environment, then you need to select the *Let me choose what to back up* option from the Backup or Restore Wizard when prompted. This opens the Items to Back Up dialog where you can select individual files and folders to back up (Figure 19.2).

Server Environments

If you work in an environment that requires you to back up Windows 2000 Server or Windows Server 2003 computers, you need to back up some extra data. This is especially true if you have a Windows network running. Windows networking features **Active Directory**, a system that enables you to share files easily within the network, yet still maintain rock-solid security. A user only has to log in once to an Active Directory server and then they have access to resources throughout the Active Directory network (assuming, of course, that the user has permission to access those resources).

To back up the extra data, you need to run the Backup Wizard and select the radio button that says *Only back up the System State data* (Figure 19.3). The **System State data** takes care of most of the registry, security settings, the desktop files and folders, and the default user.

If you want to back up more than that, close the wizard and select the Backup tab in the Backup dialog box. Check the box next to System State and then check off any other file or folder that you want backed up (Figure 19.4). From this same dialog box, you can select where to back up the data, such as to a tape drive or external hard drive.

Off-Site Storage

Backing up your data and other important information enables you to restore easily in case of a system crash or malicious data destruction, but to ensure proper security, you need to store your backups somewhere other than your office. **Off-site storage** means that you take the tape or portable hard drive that contains your backup and lock it in a briefcase. Take it home and put it in your home safe, if you have one. This way, if the building burns down or some major flood renders your office inaccessible, your company can be up and running very quickly from a secondary location.

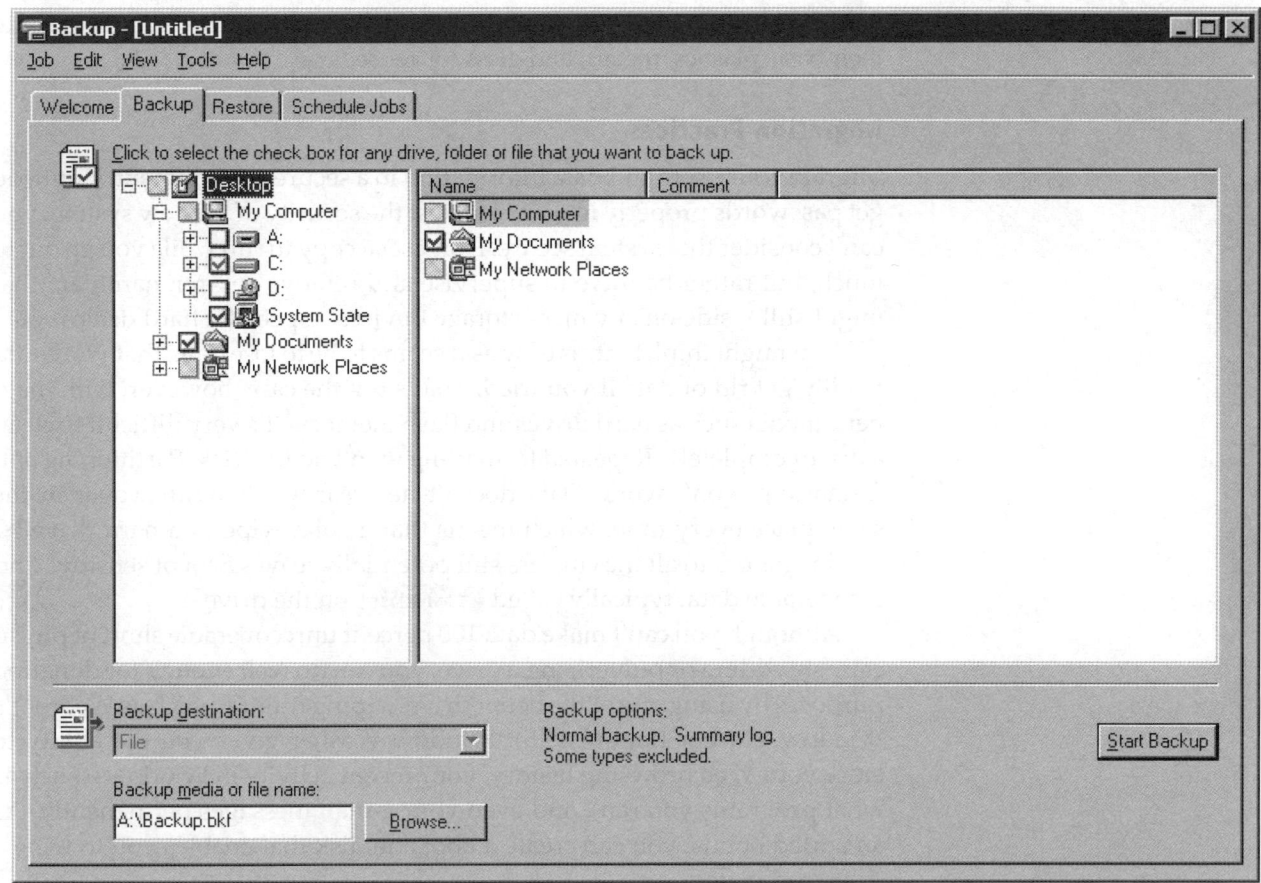

● **Figure 19.4**   Backup tab in the Backup dialog box with System State and My Documents selected

Migrating and Retiring

Seasons change and so does the state of the art in computing. At a certain point in a computer's life, you'll need to retire an old system. This means you must migrate the data and users to a new system or at least a new hard drive—a process called **migration**—and then safely dispose of the old system. When talking about migration or retirement in terms of security, you need to answer one question: what do you do with the old system or drive?

All but the most vanilla new installations have sensitive data on them, even if it's simply e-mail messages or notes-to-self that would cause embarrassment if discovered. Most PCs, especially in a work environment, contain a lot of sensitive data. You can't just format C: and hand over the drive.

Follow three principles when migrating or retiring a computer. First, migrate your users and data information in a secure environment. Until you get passwords properly in place and test the security of the new system, you can't consider that system secure. Second, remove data remnants from hard drives that you store or give to charity. Third, recycle the older equipment; don't throw it in the trash. PC recyclers go through a process of deconstructing hardware, breaking system units, keyboards, printers, and even monitors into their basic plastics, metals, and glass for reuse.

Migration Practices

Migrate your users and data information in a secure environment. Until you get passwords properly in place and test the security of the new system, you can't consider that system secure. Don't set a copy to run while you go out to lunch, but rather be there to supervise and remove any remnant data that might still reside on any mass storage devices, especially hard drives.

You might think that, as easy as it seems to be to lose data, that you could readily get rid of data if you tried. That's not the case, however, with magnetic media such as hard drives and flash memory. It's very difficult to clean a drive completely. Repeated formatting won't do the trick. Partitioning and formatting won't work. Data doesn't necessarily get written over in the same place every time, which means that a solid wipe of a hard drive by writing zeroes to all the clusters still potentially leaves a lot of sensitive and recoverable data, typically called **remnants**, on the drive.

Although you can't make data 100 percent unrecoverable short of physically shredding or pulverizing a drive, you can do well enough for donation purposes by using one of the better drive-wiping utilities, such as Webroot's Window Washer (Figure 19.5). Window Washer gives you the ability to erase your Web browsing history, your recent activity in Windows (such as what programs you ran), and even your e-mail messages permanently. As an added bonus, you can create a bootable disk that enables you to wipe a drive completely.

Recycle

An important and relatively easy way to be an environmentally conscious computer user is to *recycle*. Recycling products such as paper and printer cartridges not only keeps them out of overcrowded landfills, but also ensures that the more toxic products are disposed of in the right way. Safely disposing of hardware containing hazardous materials, such as computer monitors, protects both people and the environment.

Anyone who's ever tried to sell a computer more than three or four years old learns a hard lesson—they're not worth much if anything at all. It's a real temptation to take that old computer and just toss it in the garbage, but never do that!

First of all, many parts of your computer—such as your computer monitor—contain hazardous materials that pollute the environment. Luckily, thousands of companies now specialize in computer recycling and will gladly accept your old computer. If you have enough computers, they might even pick them up. If you can't find a recycler, call your local municipality's waste authority to see where to drop off your system.

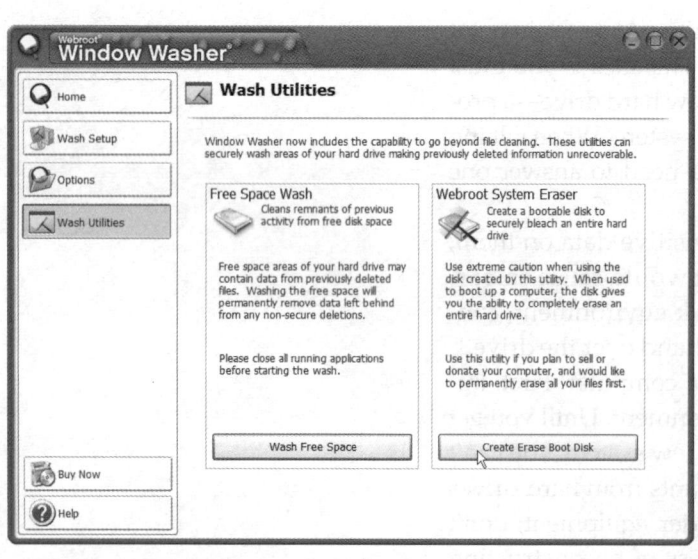

• **Figure 19.5** Webroot Window Washer security software

An even better alternative for your old computer is donation. Many organizations actively look for old computers to refurbish and to donate to schools and other organizations. Just keep in mind that the computer can be too old—not even a school wants a computer more than five or six years old.

Social Engineering

Although you're more likely to lose data through accident, the acts of malicious users get the vast majority of headlines. Most of these attacks come under the heading of social engineering —the process of using or manipulating people inside the networking environment to gain access to that network from the outside. The term "social engineering" covers the many ways humans can use other humans to gain unauthorized information. This unauthorized information may be a network login, a credit card number, company customer data—almost anything you might imagine that one person or organization may not want a person outside of that organization to access.

Social engineering attacks aren't hacking—at least in the classic sense of the word—although the goals are the same. Social engineering is where people attack an organization through the people in the organization or physically access the organization to get the information they need. Here are a few of the more classic types of social engineering attacks.

 It's common for social engineering attacks to be used together, so if you discover one of them being used against your organization, it's a good idea to look for others.

Infiltration

Hackers can physically enter your building under the guise of someone who might have a legitimate reason for being there, such as cleaning personnel, repair technicians, or messengers. They then snoop around desks, looking for whatever they can find. They might talk with people inside the organization, gathering names, office numbers, department names—little things in and of themselves, but powerful tools when combined later with other social engineering attacks.

Telephone Scams

 Telephone scams are probably the most common social engineering attack. In this case, the attacker makes a phone call to someone in the organization to gain information. The attacker attempts to come across as someone inside the organization and uses this to get the desired information. Probably the most famous of these scams is the "I forgot my user name and password" scam. In this gambit, the attacker first learns the account name of a legitimate person in the organization, usually using the infiltration method. The attacker then calls someone in the organization, usually the help desk, in an attempt to gather information, in this case a password.

Hacker: "Hi, this is John Anderson in accounting. I forgot my password. Can you reset it please?"
Help Desk : "Sure, what's your user name?"
Hacker: "j_w_Anderson"
Help Desk: "OK, I reset it to e34rd3."

Certainly telephone scams aren't limited to attempts to get network access. There are documented telephone scams against organizations aimed at getting cash, blackmail material, or other valuables.

Dumpster Diving

Dumpster diving is the generic term for anytime a hacker goes through your refuse, looking for information. The amount of sensitive information that makes it into any organization's trash bin boggles the mind! Years ago, I worked with an IT security guru who gave me and a few other IT people a tour of our office's trash. In one 20-minute tour of the personal wastebaskets of one office area, we had enough information to access the network easily, as well as to embarrass seriously more than a few people. When it comes to getting information, the trash is the place to look!

Physical Theft

I once had a fellow network geek challenge me to try to bring down his newly installed network. He had just installed a powerful and expensive firewall router and was convinced that I couldn't get to a test server he added to his network just for me to try to access. After a few attempts to hack in over the Internet, I saw that I wasn't going to get anywhere that way. So I jumped in my car and drove to his office, having first outfitted myself in a techy-looking jumpsuit and an ancient ID badge I just happened to have in my sock drawer. I smiled sweetly at the receptionist and walked right by my friend's office (I noticed he was smugly monitoring incoming IP traffic using some neato packet-sniffing program) to his new server. I quickly pulled the wires out of the back of his precious server, picked it up, and walked out the door. The receptionist was too busy trying to figure out why her e-mail wasn't working to notice me as I whisked by her carrying the 65-pound server box. I stopped in the hall and called him from my cell phone.

> **Me (cheerily):** "Dude, I got all your data!"
> **Him (not cheerily):** "You rebooted my server! How did you do it?"
> **Me (smiling):** "I didn't reboot it—go over and look at it!"
> **Him (really mad now):** "YOU <EXPLETIVE> THIEF! YOU STOLE MY SERVER!"
> **Me (cordially):** "Why, yes. Yes, I did. Give me two days to hack your password in the comfort of my home, and I'll see everything! Bye!"

I immediately walked back in and handed him the test server. It was fun. The moral here is simple—never forget that the best network software security measures can be rendered useless if you fail to protect your systems physically!

Access Control

Access is the key. If you can control access to the data, programs, and other computing resources, you've secured your system. **Access control** is composed of five interlinked areas that a good, security-minded tech should think about: physical security, authentication, the file system, users and

Tech Tip

Spoofing

Some sophisticated hackers alter the identifying labels or addresses of their computers to appear as if they're someone or something else. This process is called spoofing. An e-mail message that appears to be from a friend but is actually spam is an example of simple spoofing.

Mike Meyers' CompTIA A+ Guide: Essentials (Exam 220-601)

groups, and security policies. Much of this you know from previous chapters, but this section should help tie it all together as a security topic.

Secure Physical Area and Lock Down Your System

The first order of security is to block access to the physical hardware from people who shouldn't have access. This isn't rocket science. Lock the door. Don't leave a PC unattended when logged in. In fact, don't ever leave a system logged in, even as a limited user. God help you if you walk away from a server still logged in as an administrator. You're tempting fate.

For that matter, when you see a user's computer logged in and unattended, do the user and your company a huge favor and lock the computer. Just walk up and press CTRL-L on the keyboard to lock the system. It works in Windows 2000 and all versions of Windows XP and Windows Vista.

Authentication

Security starts with properly implemented **authentication**, which means in essence, how the computer determines who can or should access it. And, once accessed, what that user can do. A computer can authenticate users through software or hardware, or a combination of both.

Software Authentication: Proper Passwords   It's still rather shocking to me to power up a friend's computer and go straight to his or her desktop; or with my married-with-kids friends, to click one of the parent's user account icons and not get prompted for a password. This is just wrong! I'm always tempted to assign passwords right then and there—and not tell them the passwords, of course—so they'll see the error of their ways when they try to log in next. I don't do it, but always try to explain gently the importance of good passwords.

You know about passwords from Chapter 13, "Maintaining Windows," so I won't belabor the point here. Suffice it to say that you need to make certain that all your users have proper passwords. Don't let them write passwords down or tape them to the underside of their mouse pads either!

It's not just access to Windows that you need to think about. If you have computers running in a public location, there's always the temptation for people to hack the system and do mean things, like change CMOS settings to render the computer inoperable to the casual user until a tech can undo the damage. All modern CMOS setup utilities come with an access password protection scheme (Figure 19.6).

Hardware Authentication   Smart cards and biometric devices enable modern systems to authenticate users with more authority than mere passwords. **Smart cards** are credit card–sized cards with circuitry that can be used to identify the bearer of the card. Smart cards are relatively common for tasks such as authenticating users for mass transit systems, for example, but fairly

Cross Check

Proper Passwords

So, what goes into making a good password? Based on what you learned in Chapter 13, see if you can answer these questions. What sorts of characters should make up a password? Should you ask for a user's password when working on his or her PC? Why or why not? If you're in a secure environment and know you'll have to reboot several times, is it okay to ask for a password then? What should you do?

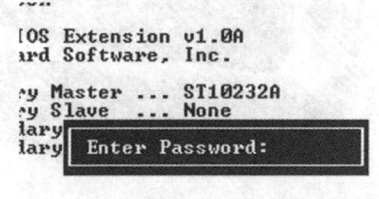

• **Figure 19.6**   CMOS access password request

● **Figure 19.7** Keyboard-mounted smart card reader being used for a commercial application (*photo courtesy of Cherry Corp.*)

Full disclosure time. Microsoft does not claim that the keyboard in Figure 19.8 offers any security at all. In fact, the documentation specifically claims that the fingerprint reader is an accessibility tool, not a security device. Because it enables a person to log onto a local machine, though, I think it falls into the category of authentication devices.

uncommon in computers. Figure 19.7 shows a smart card and keyboard combination.

People can guess or discover passwords, but it's a lot harder to forge someone's fingerprints. The keyboard in Figure 19.8 authenticates users on a local machine using fingerprints. Other devices that will do the trick are key fobs, retinal scanners, and PC cards for laptop computers. Devices that require some sort of physical, flesh-and-blood authentication are called biometric devices.

Clever manufacturers have developed key fobs and smart cards that use radio frequency identification (RFID) to transmit authentication information, so users don't have to insert something into a computer or card reader. The Prevarius plusID combines, for example, a biometric fingerprint fob with an RFID tag that makes security as easy as opening a garage door remotely! Figure 19.9 shows a plusID device.

NTFS, not FAT32!

The file system on a hard drive matters a lot when it comes to security. On a Windows machine with multiple users, you simply must use NTFS, or you have no security at all. Not just primary drives, but any secondary drives in computers in your care should be formatted as NTFS, with the exception of removable drives, such as the one you use to back up your system.

When you run into a multiple-drive system that has a second or third drive formatted as FAT32, you can use the CONVERT command-line utility to go from FAT to NTFS. The syntax is pretty straightforward. To convert a D: drive from FAT or FAT32 to NTFS, for example, you'd type the following:

```
CONVERT D: /FS:NTFS
```

● **Figure 19.8** Microsoft keyboard with fingerprint accessibility

plusID

PRIVARIS

● **Figure 19.9** plusID (*photo courtesy of Privaris, Inc.*)

Mike Meyers' CompTIA A+ Guide: Essentials (Exam 220-601)

You can substitute a mount name in place of the drive letter in case you have a mounted volume. The command has a few extra switches as well, so at the command prompt, type **a** /? after the CONVERT command to see all your options.

Users and Groups

Windows uses user accounts and groups as the bedrock of access control. A user account gets assigned to a group, such as Users, Power Users, or Administrators, and by association gets certain permissions on the computer. Using NTFS enables the highest level of control over data resources.

Assigning users to groups is a great first step in controlling a local machine, but this feature really shines once you go to a networked environment. Let's go there now.

■ Network Security

The vast majority of protective strategies related to internal threats are based on policies rather than technology. Even the smallest network will have a number of user accounts and groups scattered about with different levels of rights/permissions. Every time you give a user access to a resource, you create potential loopholes that can leave your network vulnerable to unauthorized access, data destruction, and other administrative nightmares. To protect your network from internal threats, you need to implement the correct controls over user accounts, permissions, and policies.

Networks are under threat from the outside as well, so this section looks at issues involving Internet-borne attacks, firewalls, and wireless networking. The section finishes with discussion of the tools you need to track computer and network activity and, if necessary, lock down your systems.

User Account Control Through Groups

Access to user accounts should be restricted to the assigned individuals, and those accounts should have permission to access only the resources they need, no more. Tight control of user accounts is critical to preventing unauthorized access. Disabling unused accounts is an important part of this strategy, but good user account control goes far deeper than that. One of your best tools for user account control is groups. Instead of giving permissions/rights to individual user accounts, give them to groups; this makes keeping track of the permissions assigned to individual user accounts much easier. Figure 19.10 shows me giving permissions to a group for a folder in Windows 2000. Once a group is created and its permissions set, you can then add user accounts to that group as needed. Any user account that becomes a member of a group

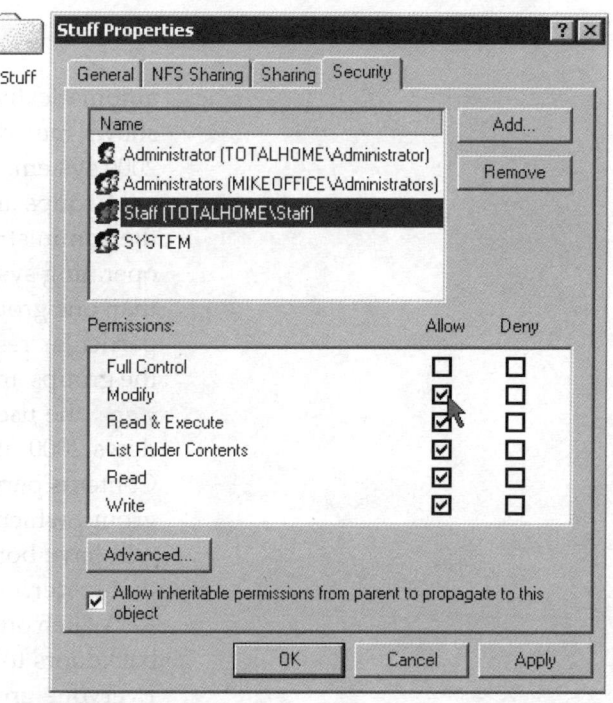

● **Figure 19.10** Giving a group permissions for a folder in Windows 2000

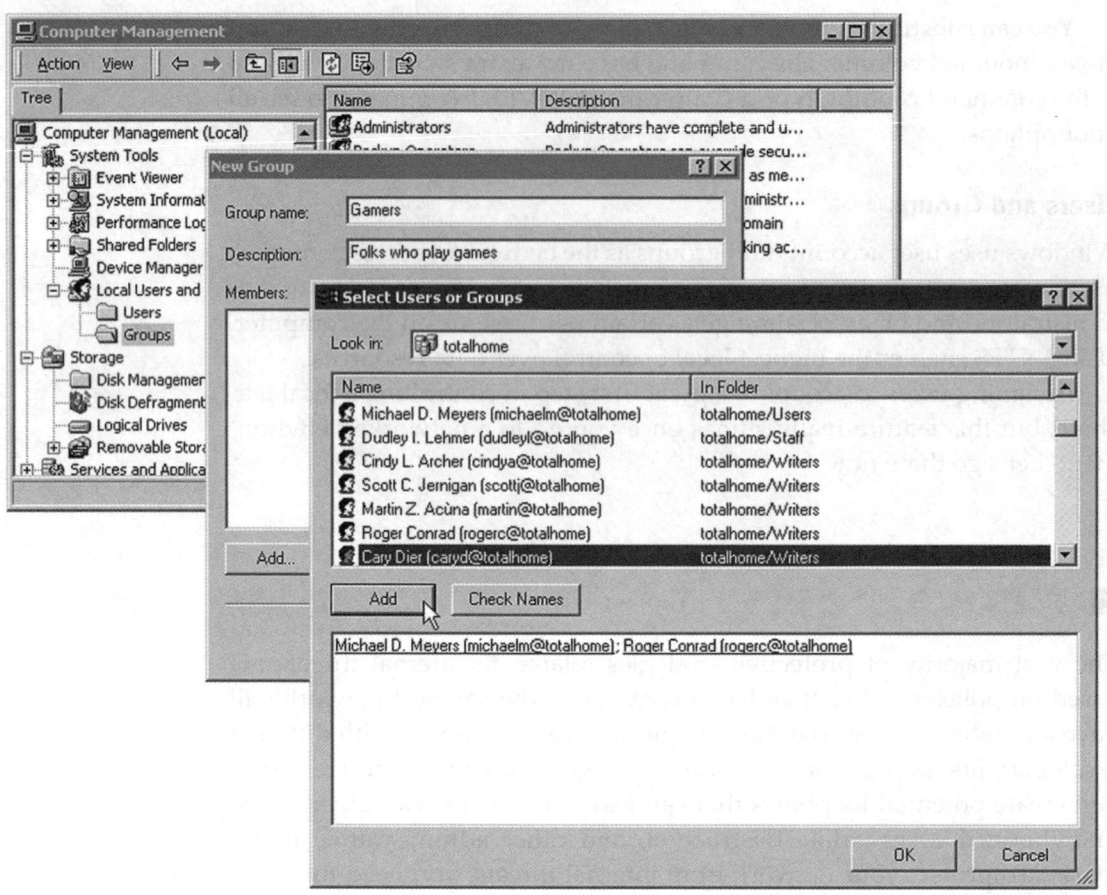

● **Figure 19.11** Adding a user to a newly created group in Windows 2000

automatically gets the permissions assigned to that group. Figure 19.11 shows me adding a user to a newly created group in the same Windows 2000 system.

Groups are a great way to get increased complexity without increasing the administrative burden on network administrators, because all network operating systems combine permissions. When a user is a member of more than one group, which permissions does he or she have with respect to any particular resource? In all network operating systems, the permissions of the groups are *combined*, and the result is what you call the effective permissions the user has to access the resource. Let's use an example from Windows 2000. If Rita is a member of the Sales group, which has List Folder Contents permission to a folder, and she is also a member of the Managers group, which has Read and Execute permissions to the same folder, Rita will have both List Folder Contents *and* Read and Execute permissions to that folder.

Watch out for *default* user accounts and groups—they can become secret backdoors to your network! All network operating systems have a default Everyone group, and it can be used to sneak into shared resources easily. This Everyone group, as its name implies, literally includes anyone who connects to that resource. Windows 2000 gives full control to the Everyone group by default, for example, so make sure you know to lock this down!

All of the default groups—Everyone, Guest, Users—define broad groups of users. Never use them unless you intend to permit all those folks to access a resource. If you use one of the default groups, remember to configure them with the proper permissions to prevent users from doing things you don't want them to do with a shared resource!

All of these groups and organizational units only do one thing for you: They let you keep track of your user accounts, so you know they are only available for those who need them, and they only access the resources you want them to use.

Security Policies

While permissions control how users access shared resources, there are other functions you should control that are outside the scope of resources. For example, do you want users to be able to access a command prompt on their Windows system? Do you want users to be able to install software? Would you like to control what systems or what time of day a user can log in? All network operating systems provide you with some capability to control these and literally hundreds of other security parameters, under what Windows calls *policies*. I like to think of policies as permissions for activities as opposed to true permissions, which control access to resources.

A policy is usually applied to a user account, a computer, or a group. Let's use the example of a network composed of Windows XP Professional systems with a Windows 2003 Server system. Every Windows XP system has its own local policies program, which enables policies to be placed on that system only. Figure 19.12 shows the tool you use to set local policies on an individual system, called **Local Security Settings**, being used to deny the user account Danar the capability to log on locally.

Local policies work great for individual systems, but they can be a pain to configure if you want to apply the same settings to more than one PC on your network. If you want to apply policy settings *en masse*, then you need to step up to Windows Active Directory domain-based **Group Policy**. Using Group Policy, you can exercise deity-like—Microsoft prefers to use the term *granular*—control over your network clients.

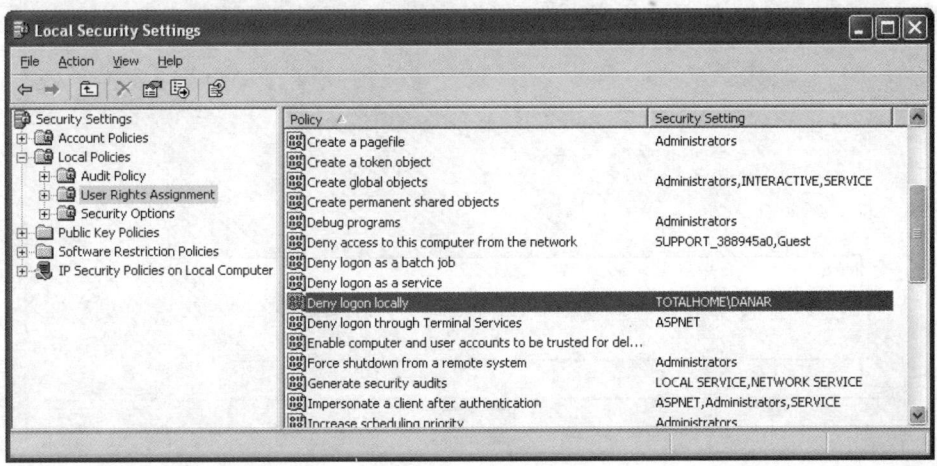

• **Figure 19.12** Local Security Settings

Tech Tip

Linux and Policies

Linux doesn't provide a single application that you open to set up policies, like Windows does. In fact, Linux doesn't even use the name "policies." Instead, Linux relies on individual applications to set up policies for whatever they're doing. This is in keeping with the Linux paradigm of having lots of little programs that do one thing well, as opposed to the Windows paradigm of having one program try to be all things for all applications.

Want to set default wallpaper for every PC in your domain? Group Policy can do that. Want to make certain tools inaccessible to everyone except authorized users? Group Policy can do that, too. Want to control access to the Internet, redirect home folders, run scripts, deploy software, or just remind folks that unauthorized access to the network will get them nowhere fast? Group Policy is the answer. Figure 19.13 shows Group Policy; I'm about to change the default title on every instance of Internet Explorer on every computer in my domain!

That's just one simple example of the types of settings you can configure using Group Policy. There are literally hundreds of "tweaks" you can apply through Group Policy, from the great to the small, but don't worry too much about familiarizing yourself with each and every one. Group Policy settings are a big topic in the Microsoft Certified Systems Administrator (MCSA) and Microsoft Certified Systems Engineer (MCSE) certification tracks, but for the purposes of the CompTIA A+ exams, you simply have to be comfortable with the concept behind Group Policy.

Although I could never list every possible policy you can enable on a Windows system, here's a list of some of those more commonly used:

■ **Prevent Registry Edits** If you try to edit the Registry, you get a failure message.

■ **Prevent Access to the Command Prompt** This policy keeps users from getting to the command prompt by turning off the Run command and the MS-DOS Prompt shortcut.

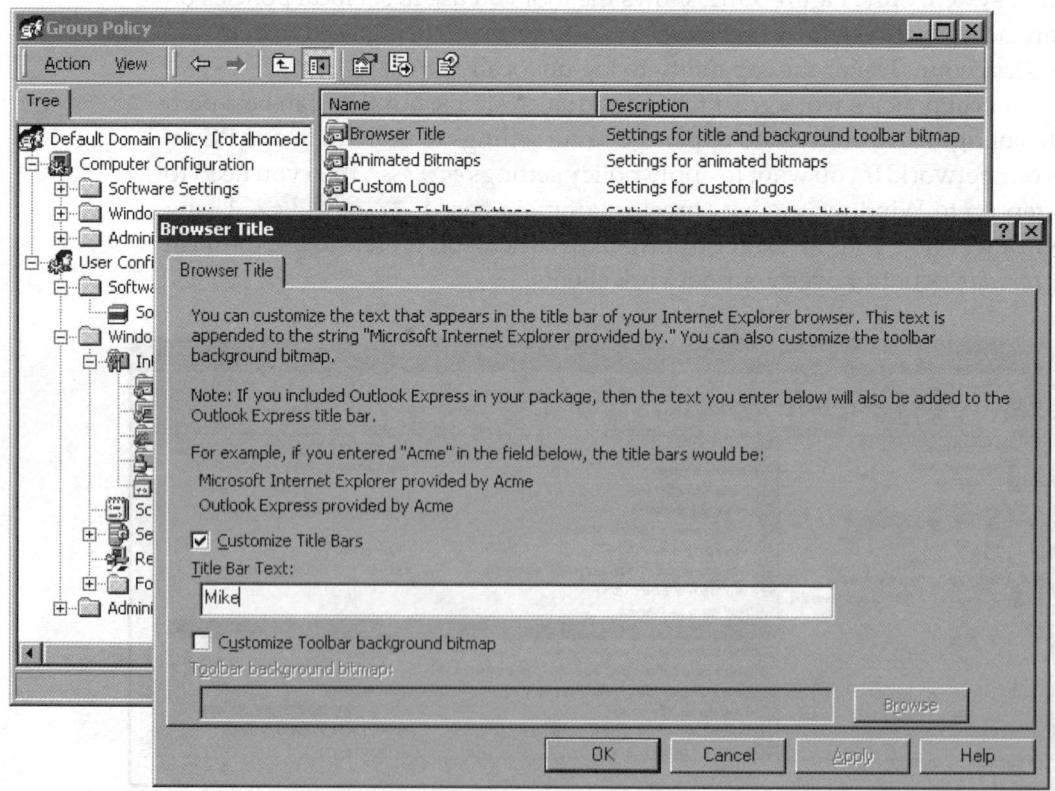

• **Figure 19.13** Using Group Policy to make IE title say "provided by Mike!"

- **Log on Locally**   This policy defines who may log on to the system locally.

- **Shut Down System**   This policy defines who may shut down the system.

- **Minimum Password Length**   This policy forces a minimum password length.

- **Account Lockout Threshold**   This policy sets the maximum number of logon attempts a person can make before they are locked out of the account.

- **Disable Windows Installer**   This policy prevents users from installing software.

- **Printer Browsing**   This policy enables users to browse for printers on the network, as opposed to using only assigned printers.

While the CompTIA A+ exams don't expect you to know how to implement policies on any type of network, you are expected to understand that policies exist, especially on Windows networks, and that they can do amazing things in terms of controlling what users can do on their systems. If you ever try to get to a command prompt on a Windows system, only to discover the Run command is grayed out, blame it on a policy, not the computer!

Malicious Software

The beauty of the Internet is the ease of accessing resources just about anywhere on the globe, all from the comfort of your favorite chair. This connection, however, runs both ways, and people from all over the world can potentially access your computer from the comfort of their evil lairs. The Internet is awash with malicious software—*malware*—that is even at this moment trying to infect your systems. Malware consists of computer programs designed to break into computers or cause havoc on computers. The most common types of malware are viruses, worms, spyware, Trojan horses, adware, and grayware. You need to understand the different types of malware so you can combat them for you and your users successfully.

Viruses

Just as a biological virus gets passed from person to person, a computer virus is a piece of malicious software that gets passed from computer to computer (Figure 19.14). A computer virus is designed to attach itself to a program on your computer. It could be your e-mail program, your word processor, or even a game. Whenever you use the infected program, the virus goes into action and does whatever it was designed to do. It can wipe out your e-mail or even erase your entire hard drive! Viruses are also sometimes used to steal information or send spam e-mails to everyone in your address book.

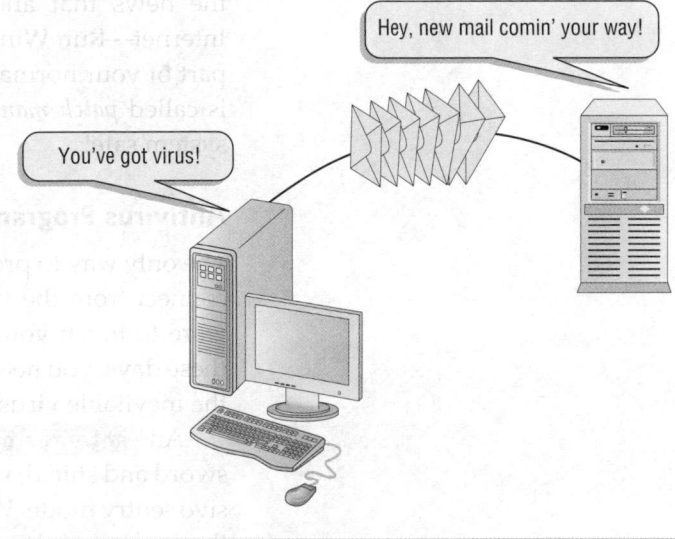

• **Figure 19.14**   You've got mail!

Trojans

Trojans are true, freestanding programs that do something other than what the person who runs the program thinks they will do. An example of a *Trojan virus* is a program that a person thinks is a game but is actually a CMOS eraser. Some Trojans are quite sophisticated. It might be a game that works perfectly well, but when the user quits the game, it causes some type of damage.

Worms

Similar to a Trojan, a worm is a complete program that travels from machine to machine, usually through computer networks. Most worms are designed to take advantage of security problems in operating systems and install themselves on vulnerable machines. They can copy themselves over and over again on infected networks, and can create so much activity that they overload the network, in worst cases even bringing chunks of the entire Internet to a halt.

There are several things you can do to protect yourself and your data against these threats. First, make sure you are running up-to-date virus software—especially if you connect to the Internet via an always-on broadband connection. You should also be protected by a firewall, either as part of your network hardware or by means of a software program. (See the sections on antivirus programs and firewalls later in this chapter.)

Since worms most commonly infect systems because of security flaws in operating systems, the next defense against them is to make sure you have the most current version possible of your operating system and to check regularly for security patches. A *security patch* is an addition to the operating system to patch a hole in the operating system code. You can download security patches from the software vendor's Web site (Figure 19.15).

Microsoft's Windows Update tool is handy for Windows users as it provides a simple method to ensure that your version's security is up to date. The one downside is that not everyone remembers to run Windows Update. Don't wait until something goes wrong on your computer, or you hear on the news that another nasty program is running rampant across the Internet—Run Windows Update weekly (or even better automatically) as a part of your normal system maintenance. Keeping your patches up to date is called *patch management,* and it goes a long way toward keeping your system safe!

Antivirus Programs

The only way to protect your PC permanently from getting a virus is to disconnect from the Internet and never permit any potentially infected software to touch your precious computer. Because neither scenario is likely these days, you need to use a specialized antivirus program to help stave off the inevitable virus assaults.

An antivirus program protects your PC in two ways. It can be both sword and shield, working in an active seek-and-destroy mode and in a passive sentry mode. When ordered to seek and destroy, the program will scan the computer's boot sector and files for viruses, and if it finds any, present you with the available options for removing or disabling them. Antivirus programs can also operate as virus shields that passively monitor your

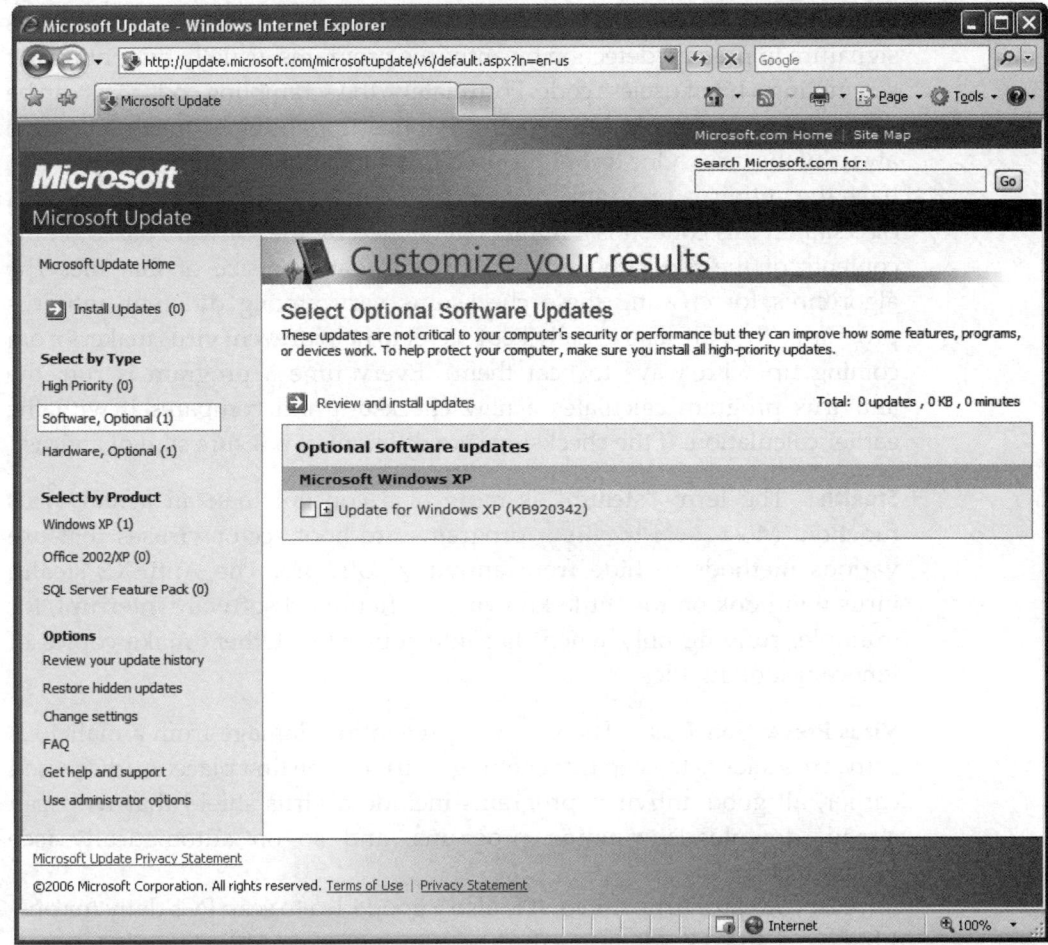

● **Figure 19.15**   Microsoft Update

computer's activity, checking for viruses only when certain events occur, such as a program executing or a file being downloaded.

Antivirus programs use different techniques to combat different types of viruses. They detect boot sector viruses simply by comparing the drive's boot sector to a standard boot sector. This works because most boot sectors are basically the same. Some antivirus programs make a backup copy of the boot sector. If they detect a virus, the programs will use that backup copy to replace the infected boot sector. Executable viruses are a little more difficult to find because they can be on any file in the drive. To detect executable viruses, the antivirus program uses a library of signatures. A **signature** is the code pattern of a known virus. The antivirus program compares an executable file to its library of signatures. There have been instances where a perfectly clean program coincidentally held a virus signature. Usually the antivirus program's creator will provide a patch to prevent further alarms. Antivirus programs detect macro viruses through the presence of virus signatures or certain macro commands that indicate a known macro virus. Now that we understand the types of viruses and how antivirus programs try to protect against them, let's review a few terms that are often used when describing certain traits of viruses.

Polymorphics/Polymorphs A polymorph virus attempts to change its signature to prevent detection by antivirus programs, usually by continually scrambling a bit of useless code. Fortunately, the scrambling code itself can be identified and used as the signature—once the antivirus makers become aware of the virus. One technique used to combat unknown polymorphs is to have the antivirus program create a checksum on every file in the drive. A *checksum* in this context is a number generated by the software based on the contents of the file rather than the name, date, or size of that file. The algorithms for creating these checksums vary among different antivirus programs (they are also usually kept secret to help prevent virus makers from coming up with ways to beat them). Every time a program is run, the antivirus program calculates a new checksum and compares it with the earlier calculation. If the checksums are different, it is a sure sign of a virus.

Stealth The term "stealth" is more of a concept than an actual virus function. Most stealth virus programs are boot sector viruses that use various methods to hide from antivirus software. The AntiEXE stealth virus will hook on to a little-known but often-used software interrupt, for example, running only when that interrupt runs. Others make copies of innocent-looking files.

Virus Prevention Tips The secret to preventing damage from a malicious software attack is to keep from getting a virus in the first place. As discussed earlier, all good antivirus programs include a virus shield that will scan e-mail, downloads, running programs, and so on automatically (see Figure 19.16).

Use your antivirus shield. It is also a good idea to scan PCs daily for possible virus attacks. All antivirus programs include terminate-and-stay resident programs (TSRs) that will run every time the PC is booted. Last but not least, know the source of any software before you load it. While the chance of commercial, shrink-wrapped software having a virus is virtually nil (there have been a couple of well-publicized exceptions), that illegal copy of Unreal Tournament you borrowed from a local hacker should definitely be inspected with care.

Keep your antivirus program updated. New viruses appear daily, and your program needs to know about them. The list of viruses your antivirus program can recognize is called the definition file, and you must keep that definition file up to date. Fortunately, most antivirus programs will update themselves automatically.

Get into the habit of keeping around an antivirus CD-R—a bootable, CD-R disc with a copy of an antivirus program. If you suspect a virus, use the disc, even if your antivirus program claims to have eliminated the virus. Turn off the PC and reboot it from

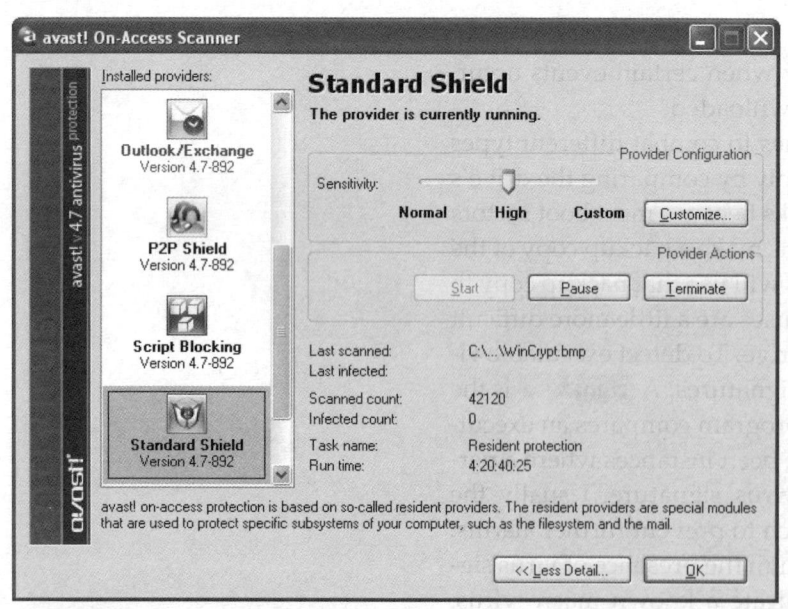

• **Figure 19.16** A virus shield in action

the antivirus disc. (You might have to change CMOS settings to boot to optical media.) Run your antivirus program's most comprehensive virus scan. Then check all removable media that were exposed to the system, and any other machine that might have received data from it or that is networked to the cleaned machine. A virus or other malicious program can often lie dormant for months before anyone knows of its presence.

E-mail is still a common source of viruses, and opening infected e-mails is a common way to get infected. If you view an e-mail in a preview window, that opens the e-mail message and exposes your computer to some viruses. Download files only from sites you know to be safe, and of course the less reputable corners of the Internet are the most likely places to pick up computer infections.

Viruses are not, however, the only malicious software lurking in e-mail. Sometimes the e-mail itself is the problem.

Spam

E-mail that comes into your Inbox from a source that's not a friend, family member, or colleague, and that you didn't ask for, can create huge problems for your computer and you. This unsolicited e-mail, called **spam**, accounts for a huge percentage of traffic on the Internet. Spam comes in many flavors, from legitimate businesses trying to sell you products to scammers who just want to take your money. Hoaxes, pornography, and get-rich-quick schemes pour into the Inboxes of most e-mail users. They waste your time and can easily offend.

You can use several options to cope with the flood of spam. The first option is defense. Never post your e-mail address on the Internet. One study tested this theory and found that *over 97 percent* of the spam received during the study went to e-mail addresses they had posted on the public Internet.

Filters and filtering software can block spam at your mail server and at your computer. AOL implemented blocking schemes in 2004, for example, that dropped the average spam received by its subscribers by a large percentage, perhaps as much as 50 percent. You can set most e-mail programs to block e-mail from specific people—good to use if someone is harassing you—or to specific people. You can block by subject line or keywords. Most people use a third-party anti-spam program instead of using the filters in their e-mail program.

Pop-ups, Spyware, and Adware

On most systems, the Internet Web browser client is the most often used piece of software. Over the years, Web sites have come up with more and more ways to try to get you to see what they want you to see: their advertising. When the Web first got underway, we were forced to look at an occasional banner ad. In the last few years, Web site designers have become

The Center for Democracy and Technology conducted the 2003 study entitled "Why Am I Getting All This Spam? Unsolicited Commercial E-mail Research Six Month Report." Here's the Web link if you're curious: www.cdt.org/speech/spam/030319spamreport.shtml.

Try This!

Fight Spam Right!

Spam filtering software that you purchase and put on your computer can help, but you have to do some research to see which software offers the best performance. You want to avoid software that causes *false positives*—mislabeling acceptable e-mail as spam—because then you miss legitimate e-mail messages from family and friends. So, time to fire up your trusty Web browser and do some searching.

Start by going to Google and searching for **anti-spam software reviews**. One of the first sites that should come up takes you to *PC Magazine*'s review list, which is kept up to date. What's the current Editor's Choice? What other options do you have?

much more sophisticated, creating a number of intrusive and irritating ways to get you to part with your money in one form or another.

There are basically three irritating Web browser problems: pop-ups, spyware, and adware. `Pop-ups` are those surprise browser windows that appear automatically when you visit a Web site, proving themselves irritating and unwanted and nothing else. `Spyware`, meanwhile, defines a family of programs that run in the background on your PC, sending information about your browsing habits to the company that installed it on your system. `Adware` is not generally as malicious as spyware, but it works similarly to display ads on your system. As such, these programs download new ads and generate undesirable network traffic. Of the three, spyware is much less noticeable but far more nefarious. At its worst, spyware can fire up pop-up windows of competing products on the Web site you're currently viewing. For example, you might be perusing a bookseller's Web site only to have a pop-up from a competitor's site appear.

Pop-Ups   Getting rid of pop-ups is actually rather tricky. You've probably noticed that most of these pop-up browser windows don't look like browser windows at all. There's no menu bar, button bar, or address window, yet they are each separate browser windows. HTML coding permits Web site and advertising designers to remove the usual navigation aids from a browser window so all you're left with is the content. In fact, as I'll describe in a minute, some pop-up browser windows are deliberately designed to mimic similar pop-up alerts from the Windows OS. They might even have buttons similar to Windows' own exit buttons, but you might find that when you click them, you wind up with more pop-up windows instead! What to do?

The first thing you need to know when dealing with pop-ups is how to close them without actually having to risk clicking them. As I said, most pop-ups have removed all navigation aids, and many are also configured to appear on your monitor screen in a position that places the browser window's exit button—the little X button in the upper right-hand corner—outside of your visible screen area. Some even pop up behind the active browser window and wait there in the background. Most annoying! To remedy this, use alternate means to close the pop-up browser window. For instance, you can right-click the browser window's taskbar icon to generate a pop-up menu of your own. Select Close, and the window should go away. You can also bring the browser window in question to the forefront by pressing ALT-TAB until it becomes visible, and then press ALT-F4 to close it.

Most Web browsers have features to prevent pop-up ads in the first place, but I've found that these types of applications are sometimes *too* thorough. That is, they tend to prevent *all* new browser windows from opening, even those you want to view. Still, they're free to try, so have a look to see if they suit your needs. Applications such as AdSubtract control a variety of Internet annoyances, including pop-up windows, cookies, and Java applets, and are more configurable—you can specify what you want to allow on any particular domain address—but the fully functional versions usually cost at least something, and that much control is too confusing for most novice-level users.

Dealing with Spyware   Some types of spyware go considerably beyond this level of intrusion. They can use your computer's resources to run *distributed computing* applications, capture your keystrokes to steal passwords, reconfigure your dial-up settings to use a different phone number at a much higher connection charge, or even use your Internet connection and e-mail address list to propagate itself to other computers in a virus-like fashion! Are you concerned yet?

Setting aside the legal and ethical issues, and there are many, you should at least appreciate that spyware can seriously impact your PC's performance and cause problems with your Internet connection. The threat is real, so what practical steps can you take to protect yourself? Let's look at how to prevent spyware installation, and how to detect and remove any installed spyware.

Preventing Spyware Installation   How does this spyware get into your system in the first place? Obviously, a sensible person doesn't download and install something that they know is going to compromise their computer. Makers of spyware know this, so they bundle their software with some other program or utility that purports to give you some benefit.

What kind of benefit? How about free access to MP3 music files? A popular program called Kazaa does that. How about a handy *e-wallet* utility that remembers your many screen names, passwords, and even your credit card numbers to make online purchases easier and faster? A program called Gator does that, and many other functions as well. How about browser enhancements, performance boosters, custom cursor effects, search utilities, buddy lists, file savers, or media players? The list goes on and on, yet they all share one thing—they're simply window-dressing for the *real* purpose of the software. So you see, for the most part spyware doesn't need to force its way into your PC. Instead they saunter calmly through the front door. If the graphic in Figure 19.17 looks familiar, you might have installed some of this software yourself.

Some spyware makers use more aggressive means to get you to install their software. Instead of offering you some sort of attractive utility, they instead use fear tactics and deception to try to trick you into installing their software. One popular method is to use pop-up browser windows crudely disguised as Windows' own system warnings (Figure 19.18). When clicked, these may trigger a flood of other browser windows, or may even start a file download.

The lesson here is simple—*don't install these programs!* Careful reading of the software's license agreement before you install a program is a good idea, but realistically, it does little to protect your PC. With that in mind, here are a couple of preventive measures you can take to keep parasitic software off of your system.

If you visit a Web site and are prompted to install a third-party application or plug-in that you've never heard of, *don't install it.* Well-known and reputable plug-ins, such as Adobe's *Shockwave* or *Flash*, are safe, but be suspicious of any others. Don't click

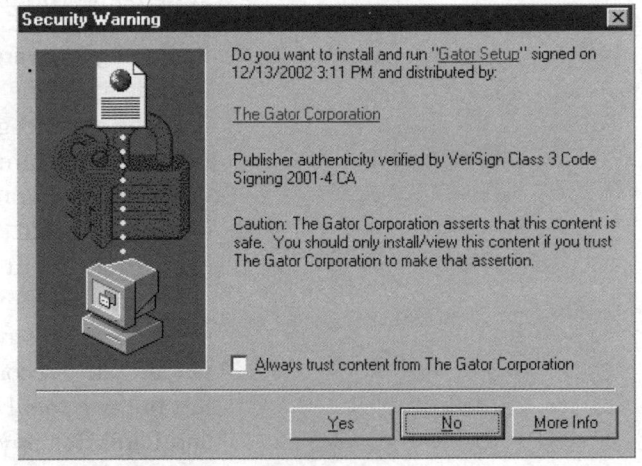

● **Figure 19.17**   Gator Corporation's acknowledgment warning

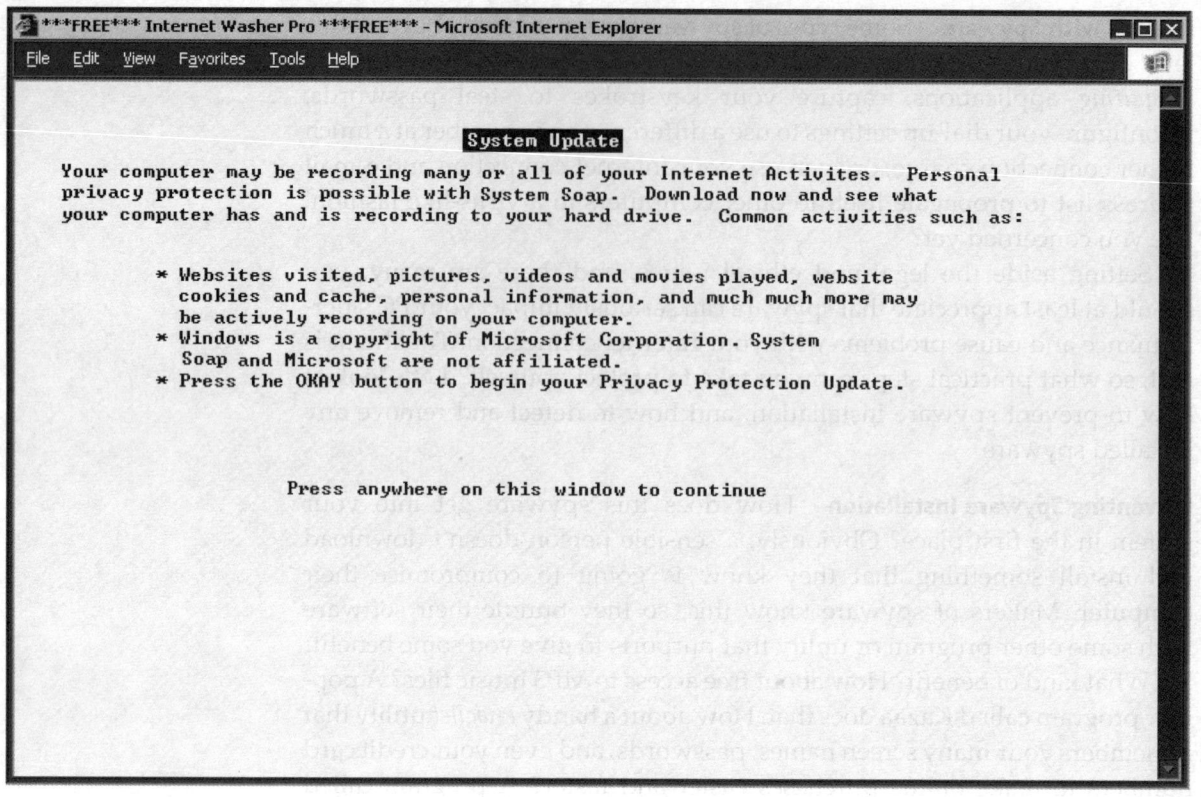

FREE Internet Washer Pro ***FREE*** - Microsoft Internet Explorer

File   Edit   View   Favorites   Tools   Help

System Update

Your computer may be recording many or all of your Internet Activites. Personal
privacy protection is possible with System Soap. Download now and see what
your computer has and is recording to your hard drive. Common activities such as:

* Websites visited, pictures, videos and movies played, website
  cookies and cache, personal information, and much much more may
  be actively recording on your computer.
* Windows is a copyright of Microsoft Corporation. System
  Soap and Microsoft are not affiliated.
* Press the OKAY button to begin your Privacy Protection Update.

Press anywhere on this window to continue

• Figure 19.18   A spyware pop-up browser window, disguised as a Windows alert

anywhere inside of a pop-up browser window, even if it looks just like a Windows alert window or DOS command-line prompt—as I just mentioned, it's probably fake and the Close button is likely a hyperlink. Instead, use other means to close the window, such as pressing ALT-F4 or right-clicking the browser window's icon on the taskbar and selecting Close.

You can also install spyware detection and removal software on your system and run it regularly. Let's look at how to do that.

Removing Spyware   Some spyware makers are reputable enough to include a routine for uninstalling their software. Gator, for instance, makes it fairly easy to get rid of their programs—just use the Windows Add/ Remove Programs applet in the Control Panel. Others, however, aren't quite so cooperative. In fact, because spyware is so—well, *sneaky*—it's entirely possible that your system already has some installed that you don't even know about. How do you find out?

Windows comes with Windows Defender, a fine tool for catching most spyware but it's not perfect. The better solution is to back up Windows Defender with a second spyware removal program. There are several on the market, but two that I highly recommend are Lavasoft's Ad-Aware (Figure 19.19) and PepiMK's Spybot Search & Destroy.

Both of these applications work exactly as advertised. They detect and delete spyware of all sorts—hidden files and folders, cookies, registry keys and values, you name it. Ad-Aware is free for personal use, while Spybot

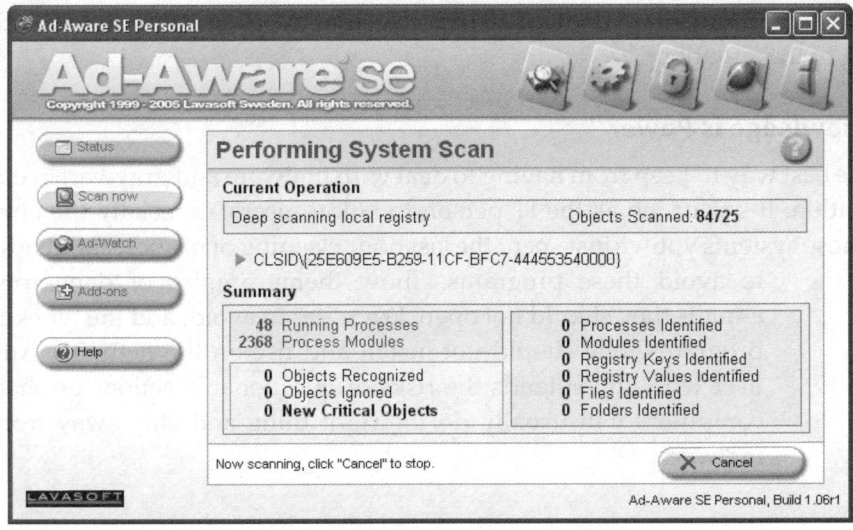

● **Figure 19.19** Lavasoft's Ad-Aware

Search & Destroy is shareware (Figure 19.20). Many times I've used both programs at the same time because one tends to catch what the other misses.

Grayware

Some programs, called grayware, are not destructive in and of themselves, but they leach bandwidth in networks and can turn a speedy machine into a doddering shell of a modern computer. These programs are called grayware because some people consider them beneficial. They might even be beneficial in the right setting. The primary example of grayware is the highly popular peer-to-peer file-sharing programs, such as Bittorrent. Peer-to-peer file-sharing programs enable a lot of users to upload portions of files on demand so that other users can download them. By splitting the load to many computers, the overall demand on a single computer is light.

The problem is that if you have a tight network with lots of traffic and suddenly you have a bunch of that bandwidth hogged by uploading and downloading files, then your network performance can degrade badly overall. So, is the grayware bad? Only in

> ### Try This!
> #### Spybot
> If you haven't done this already, do it now. Go to www.spybot.info and download the latest copy of Spybot Search & Destroy. Install it on your computer and run it. Did it find any spyware that slipped in past your defenses?

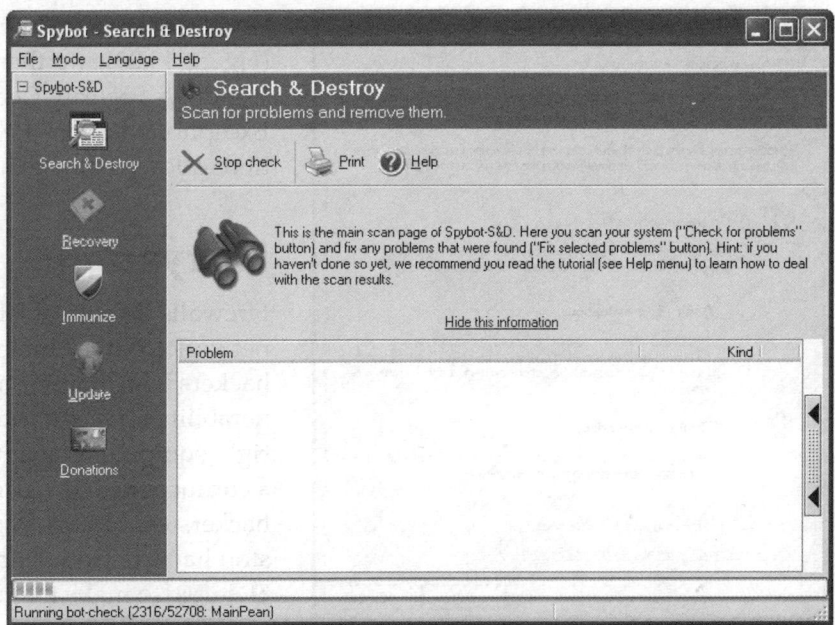

● **Figure 19.20** Spybot Search & Destroy

some environments. You need to judge each network or computer according to the situation.

Knowledge is Power

The best way to keep from having to deal with malware and grayware is education. It's your job as the IT person to talk to users, especially the ones whose systems you've just spent the last hour cleaning of nasties, about how to avoid these programs. Show them samples of dangerous e-mails they should not open, Web sites to avoid, and the types of programs they should not install and use on the network. Any user who understands the risks of questionable actions on their computers will usually do the right thing and stay away from malware.

● **Figure 19.21**   Linksys router as a firewall

Firewalls

Firewalls are an essential tool in the fight against malicious programs on the Internet. Firewalls are devices or software that protect an internal network from unauthorized access to and from the Internet at large. Hardware firewalls protect networks using a number of methods, such as hiding IP addresses and blocking TCP/IP ports. Most SOHO networks use a hardware firewall, such as the Linksys router in Figure 19.21. These devices do a great job.

Windows XP comes with an excellent software firewall, called the Windows Firewall (Figure 19.22). It can also handle the heavy lifting of port blocking, security logging, and more.

You can access the Windows Firewall by opening the Windows Firewall applet in the Control Panel. If you're running the Control Panel in Category view, click the Security Center icon (Figure 19.23), and then click the Windows Firewall option in the Windows Security Center dialog box. Figure 19.24 illustrates the Exceptions tab on the Windows Firewall, showing the applications allowed to use the TCP/IP ports on my computer.

Encryption

Firewalls do a great job controlling traffic coming into or out of a network from the Internet, but they do nothing to stop interceptor hackers who monitor traffic on the public Internet looking for vulnerabilities. Once a packet is on the Internet itself, anyone with the right equipment can intercept and inspect it. Inspected packets are a cornucopia of passwords, account names, and other tidbits that hackers can use to intrude into your network. Because we can't stop hackers from inspecting these packets, we must turn to encryption to make them unreadable.

Network encryption occurs at many different levels and is in no way limited to Internet-based activities. Not only are there many levels of network encryption, but each encryption level provides multiple standards and options, making encryption one of

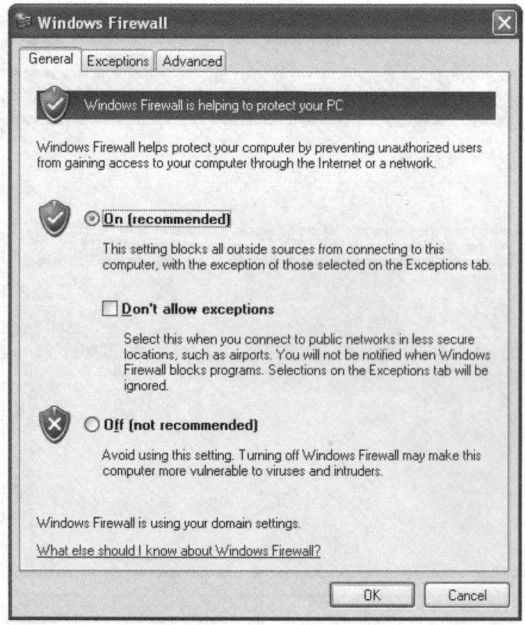

● **Figure 19.22**   Windows Firewall

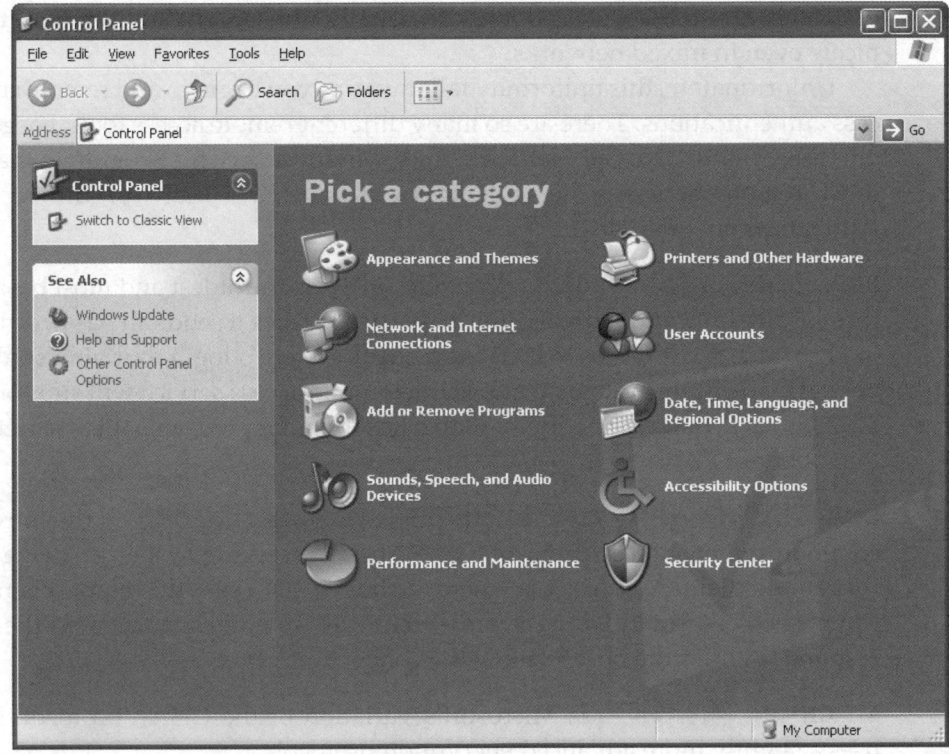

● **Figure 19.23**   Control Panel, Category view

the most complicated of all networking issues. You need to understand where encryption comes into play, what options are available, and what you can use to protect your network.

Network Authentication

Have you ever considered the process that takes place each time a person types in a user name and password to access a network, rather than just a local machine? What happens when this *network* authentication is requested? If you're thinking that when a user types in a user name and password, that information is sent to a server of some sort to be authenticated, you're right—but do you know how the user name and password get to the serving system? That's where encryption becomes important in authentication.

In a local network, encryption is usually handled by the NOS. Because NOS makers usually control software development of both the client and the server, they can create their own proprietary encryptions. However, in today's increasingly interconnected and diverse networking environment, there is a motivation to enable different network operating systems to authenticate any client system from any other NOS. Modern network operating systems such as Windows NT/2000/XP/2003 and NetWare 4.x/5.x/6.x use standard authentication encryptions like MIT's Kerberos , enabling multiple brands of servers to authenticate multiple brands

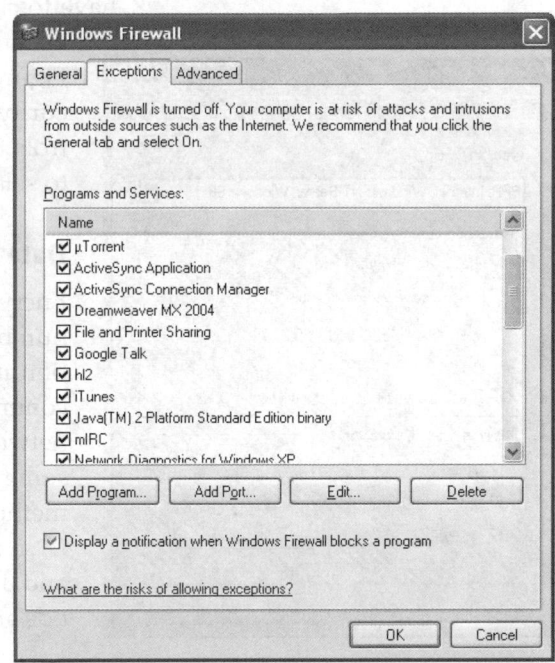

● **Figure 19.24**   Essential programs (doesn't everyone need to run Half-Life 2?)

of clients. These LAN encryptions are usually transparent and work quite nicely even in mixed networks.

Unfortunately, this uniformity falls away as you begin to add remote access authentications. There are so many different remote access tools, based on UNIX/Linux, Novell NetWare, and Windows serving programs, that most remote access systems have to support a variety of different authentication methods.

PAP Password Authentication Protocol (PAP) is the oldest and most basic form of authentication. It's also the least safe, because it sends all passwords in clear text. No NOS uses PAP for a client system's login, but almost all network operating systems that provide remote access service will support PAP for backward compatibility with a host of older programs (like Telnet) that only use PAP.

CHAP Challenge Handshake Authentication Protocol (CHAP) is the most common remote access protocol. CHAP has the serving system challenge the remote client. A *challenge* is where the host system asks the remote client some secret—usually a password—that the remote client must then respond with for the host to allow the connection.

MS-CHAP MS-CHAP is Microsoft's variation of the CHAP protocol. It uses a slightly more advanced encryption protocol.

Configuring Dial-up Encryption

It's the server not the client that controls the choice of dial-up encryption. Microsoft clients can handle a broad selection of authentication encryption methods, including no authentication at all. On the rare occasion when you have to change your client's default encryption settings for a dial-up connection, you'll need to journey deep into the bowels of its properties. Figure 19.25 shows the Windows 2000 dialog box, called Advanced Security Settings, where you configure encryption. The person who controls the server's configuration will tell you which encryption method to select here.

Data Encryption

Encryption methods don't stop at the authentication level. There are a number of ways to encrypt network *data* as well. The choice of encryption method is dictated to a large degree by the method used by the communicating systems to connect. Many networks consist of multiple networks linked together by some sort of private connection, usually some kind of telephone line like ISDN or T1. Microsoft's encryption method of choice for this type of network is called **IPSec** (derived from *IP security*). IPSec provides transparent encryption between the server and the client. IPSec will also work in VPNs, but other encryption methods are more commonly used in those situations.

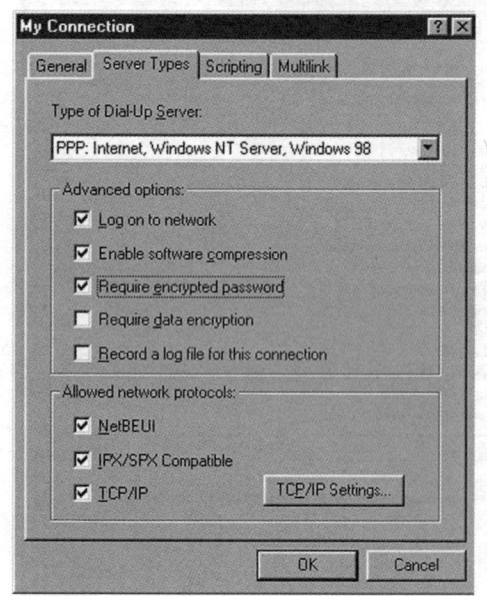

• **Figure 19.25** Setting dial-up encryption in the Windows 2000 Advanced Security Settings dialog box

Application Encryption

When it comes to encryption, even TCP/IP applications can get into the swing of things. The most famous of all application encryptions is Netscape's Secure Sockets Layer (SSL) security protocol, which is used to create secure Web sites. Microsoft incorporates SSL into its more far-reaching **HTTPS** (HTTP over SSL) protocol. These protocols make it possible to create the secure Web sites used to make purchases over the Internet. HTTPS Web sites can be identified by the *HTTPS://* included in their URL (see Figure 19.26).

To make a secure connection, your Web browser and the Web server must encrypt their data. That means there must be a way for both the Web server and your browser to encrypt and decrypt each other's data. This is done by the server sending a public key to your Web browser so the browser knows how to decrypt the incoming data. These public keys are sent in the form of a **digital certificate**. This certificate not only provides the public key but also is signed by a trusted authority that guarantees the public key you are about to get is actually from the Web server and not from some evil person trying to pretend to be the Web server. There are a number of companies that issue digital certificates to Web sites; probably the most famous is VeriSign, Inc.

Your Web browser has a built-in list of trusted authorities. If a certificate comes in from a Web site that uses one of these highly respected companies, you won't see anything happen in your browser; you'll just go to the secure Web page and a small lock will appear in the corner of your browser. Figure 19.27 shows the list of trusted authorities built into the Firefox Web browser.

● **Figure 19.26**   A secure Web site

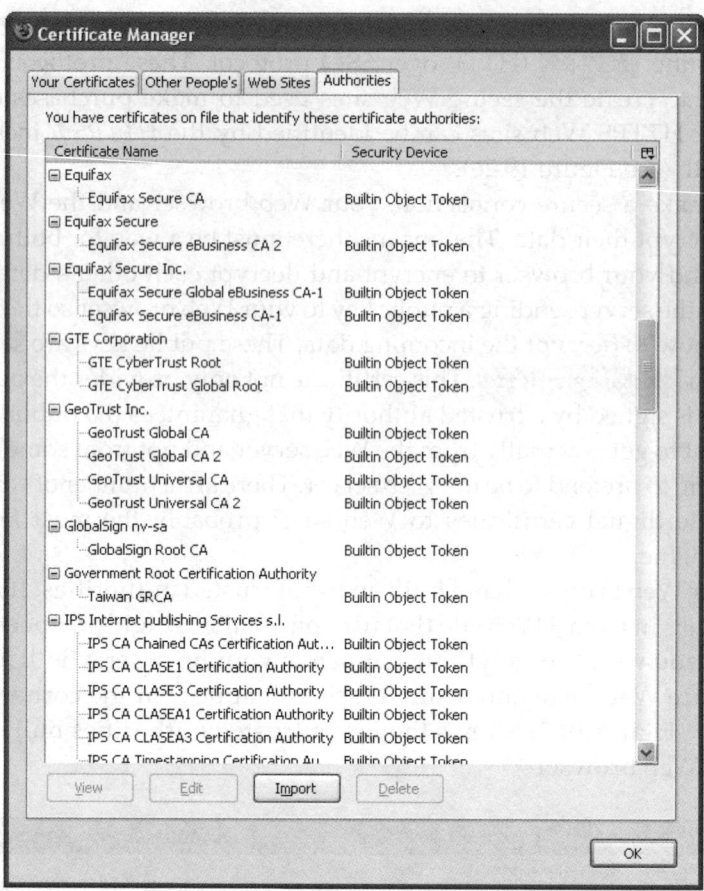

● **Figure 19.27**   Trusted authorities

However, if you receive a certificate from someone *not* listed in your browser, the browser will warn you and ask if you wish to accept the certificate, as shown in Figure 19.28.

What you do here is up to you. Do you wish to trust this certificate? In most cases, you simply say yes, and this certificate is added to your SSL cache of certificates. However, there are occasions where an accepted certificate becomes invalid, usually due to something boring, for instance, it goes out of date or the public key changes. This never happens with the "big name" certificates built into your browser—you'll see this more often

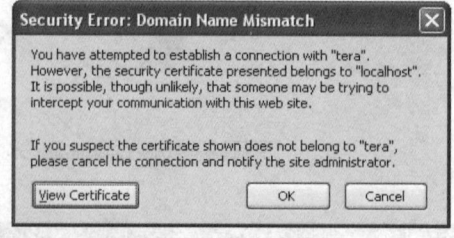

● **Figure 19.28**   Incoming certificate

when a certificate is used, for example, in-house on a company intranet and the administrator forgets to update their certificates. If a certificate goes bad, your browser issues a warning the next time you visit that site. To clear invalid certificates, you need to clear the SSL cache. The process varies on every browser, but on Internet Explorer, go to the Content tab under Internet Options and click the Clear SSL state button (Figure 19.29).

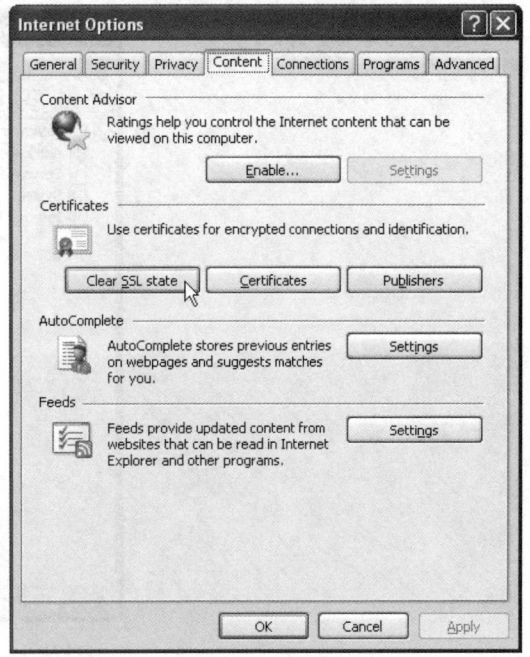

● **Figure 19.29** The Internet Options Content tab

Wireless Issues

Wireless networks add a whole level of additional security headaches for techs to face. Some of the points to remember or to go back and look up are as follows:

- Set up wireless encryption—at least WEP, but preferably WPA or the more secure WPA2—and configure clients to use them.

- Disable DHCP and require your wireless clients to use a static IP address.

- If you need to use DHCP, only allot enough DHCP addresses to meet the needs of your network to avoid unused wireless connections.

- Change the WAP's SSID from default and disable SSID broadcast.

- Filter by MAC address to allow only known clients on the network.

- Change the default user name and password. Every hacker has memorized the default user names and passwords.

- Update the firmware as needed.

- If available, make sure the WAP's firewall settings are turned on.

Reporting

As a final weapon in your security arsenal, you need to report any security issues so a network administrator or technician can take steps to make them go away. You can set up two tools within Windows so that the OS reports problems to you: Event Viewer and Auditing. You can then do your work and report those problems. Let's take a look.

Event Viewer

Event Viewer is Window's default tattletale program, spilling the beans about many things that happen on the system. You can find Event Viewer in Administrative Tools in the Control Panel. By default, Event Viewer has three sections, Application, Security, and System, and if you've downloaded Internet Explorer 7, you'll see a fourth option for the browser,

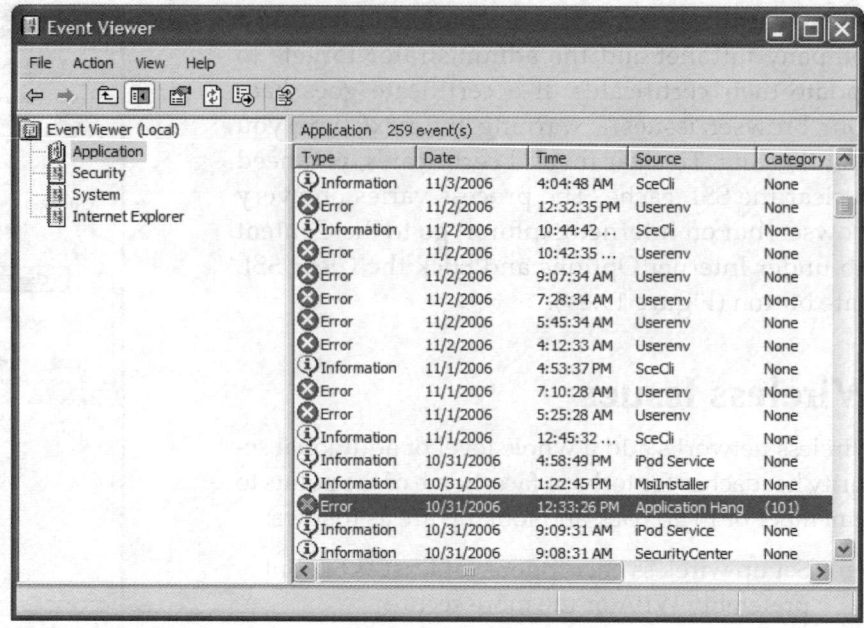

● Figure 19.30   Event Viewer

Internet Explorer (Figure 19.30). The most common use for Event Viewer is to view application or system errors for troubleshooting (Figure 19.31).

One very cool feature of Event Viewer is that you can click the link to take you to the online Help and Support Center at Microsoft.com, and the software reports your error (Figure 19.32), checks the online database, and comes back with a more or less useful explanation (Figure 19.33).

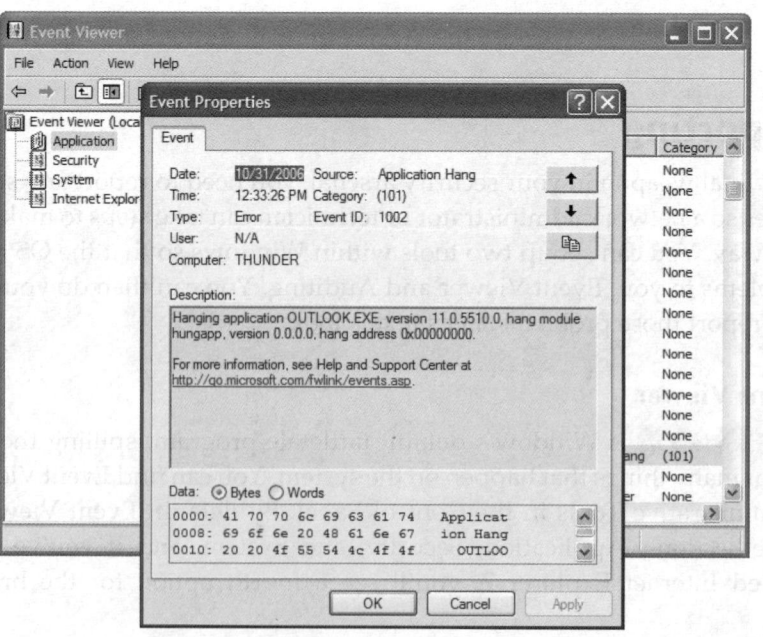

● Figure 19.31   Typical application error message

Auditing

The Security section of Event Viewer doesn't show you anything by default. To unlock the full potential of Event Viewer, you need to set up auditing. *Auditing* in the security sense means to tell Windows to create an entry in the Security Log when certain events happen, for example, a user logs on—called event auditing —or tries to access a certain file or folder—called object access auditing . Figure 19.34 shows Event Viewer tracking logon and logoff events.

The CompTIA A+ certification exams don't test you on creating a brilliant auditing policy for your office—that's what network administrators do. You simply need to know what auditing does and how to turn it on or off so that you can provide support for the network administrators in the field. To turn on auditing at a local level, go to Local Security Settings in Administrative Tools. Select Local Policies and then click Audit Policies. Double-click one of the policy options and select one or both of the

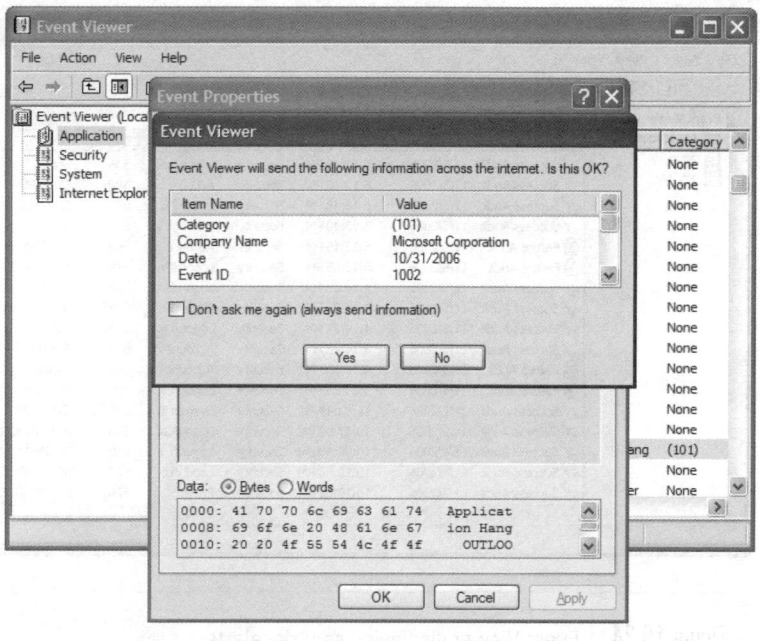

● **Figure 19.32**   Details about to be sent

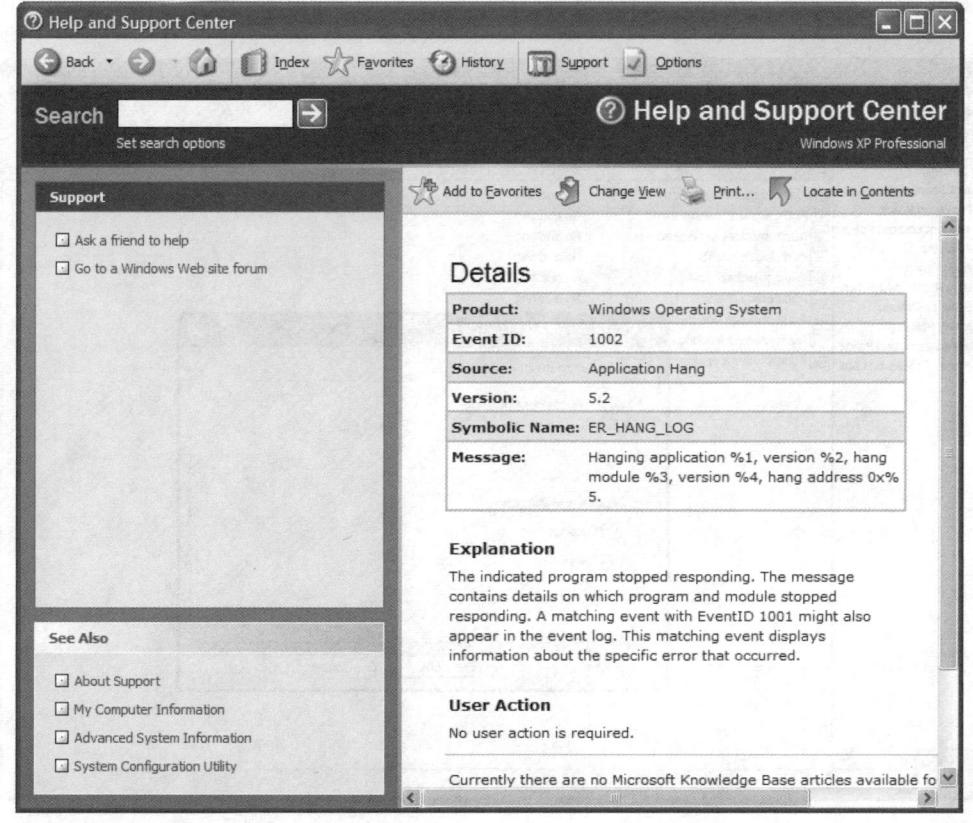

● **Figure 19.33**   Help and Support Center being helpful

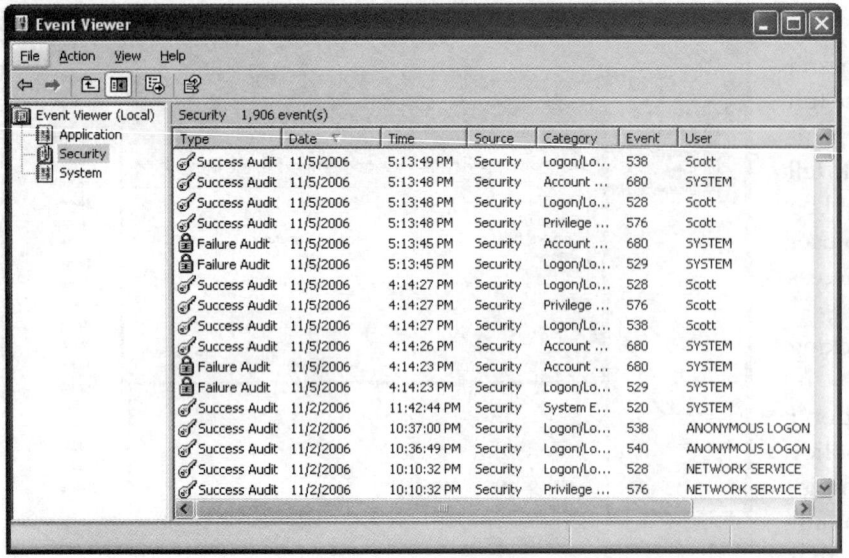

● **Figure 19.34**   Event Viewer displaying security alerts

checkboxes. Figure 19.35 shows the Audit object access dialog box.

Incidence Reporting

Once you've gathered data about a particular system or you've dealt with a computer or network problem, you need to complete the mission by telling your supervisor. This is called **incidence reporting**. Many companies have pre-made forms that you simply fill out and submit. Other places are less formal. Regardless, you need to do this!

Incidence reporting does a couple of things for you. First, it provides a record of work you've done and accomplished. Second, it provides a piece of information that, when combined with other information that you might or might not know, reveals a pattern or bigger problem to someone higher up the chain. A seemingly innocuous security audit report, for example, might match other such events in numerous places in the building at the same time and thus show conscious, coordinated action rather than a glitch was at work.

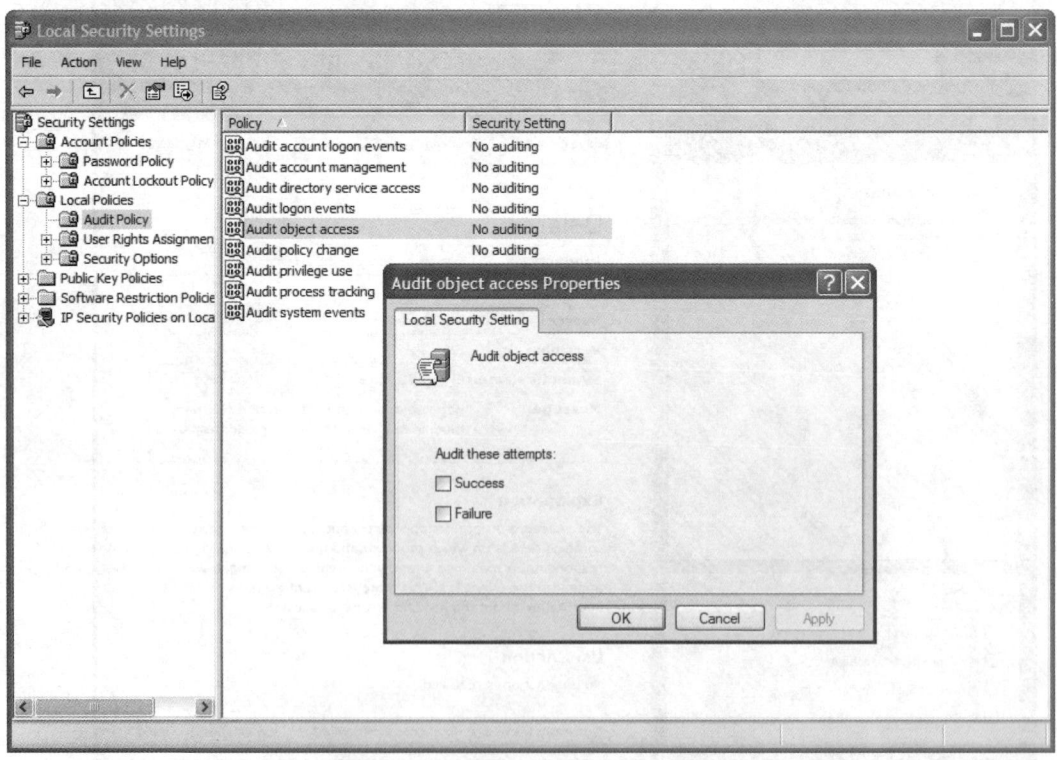

● **Figure 19.35**   Audit object access with the Local Security Settings dialog box open in the background

Beyond A+

Security in Windows Vista

With Windows Vista, Microsoft offers great security features, including tight control over user accounts and actions, a centralized security dialog, and parental controls over content. And these just scratch the surface!

User Account Control

Windows XP made it too easy—and in fact almost necessary—to make your primary account on a computer an Administrator account. Because Limited Users can't do common tasks such as run certain programs, install applications, update applications, update Windows, and so on, most users simply created an Administrator-level account and logged in. Because such accounts have full control over the computer, malware that slipped in with that account could do a lot more harm.

Microsoft addressed this problem with the *User Account Control (UAC)*. This feature enables standard users to do common tasks and provides a permissions dialog (Figure 19.36) when standard users *and* administrators do certain things that could potentially harm the computer (such as attempt to install a program). Vista user accounts now function much more like user accounts in Linux and Mac OS X.

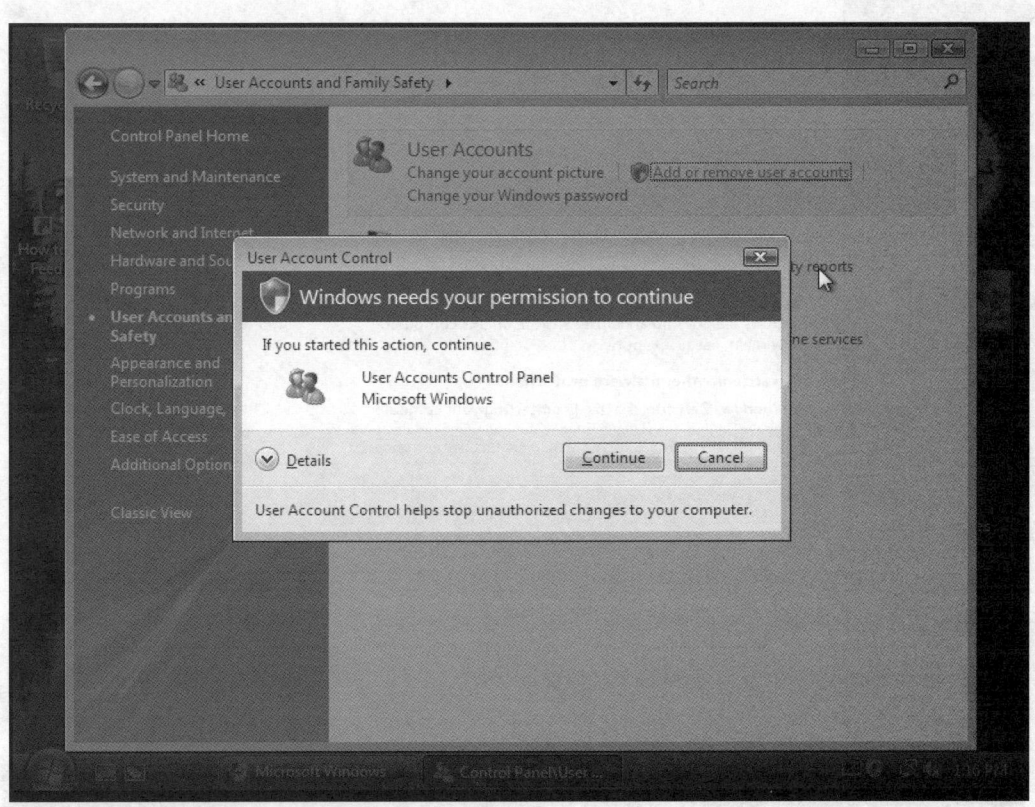

• Figure 19.36   Prompting for permission

Security Center

Microsoft has buffed up the *Windows Security Center (WSC)* for Windows Vista to provide a one-stop shop for users to get information about critical security issues (Figure 19.37). First introduced with Windows XP SP2, WSC provides information about whether or not the Windows Firewall, Automatic Updates, and an antivirus program are turned on. That's just a start; the WSC in Vista goes beyond to monitor other malware solutions, such as the spyware- and adware-crushing Windows Defender. The WSC shows Internet security settings and the status of UAC. It even shows third-party security solutions installed, monitors whether they're engaged, and provides an Update Now button so you can download the latest updates to their signatures.

Parental Controls

With Parental Controls, you can monitor and limit the activities of any Standard User in Windows Vista, a feature that gives parents and managers an excellent level of control over the content their children and employees can access (Figure 19.38). Activity Reporting logs applications run or attempted to run, Web sites visited or attempted to visit, any kind of files downloaded, and more. You can block various Web sites by type or specific URL, or you can allow only certain Web sites, a far more powerful option.

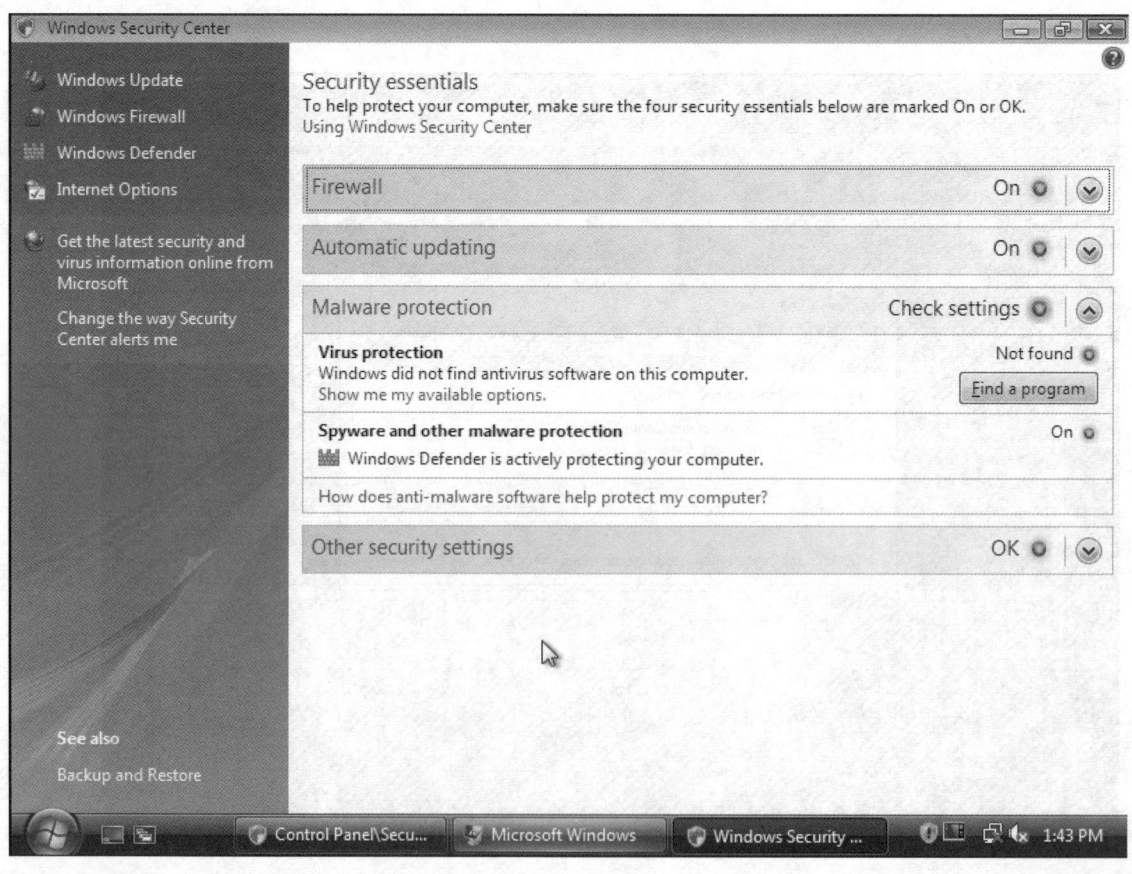

● **Figure 19.37**   Windows Security Center in Vista

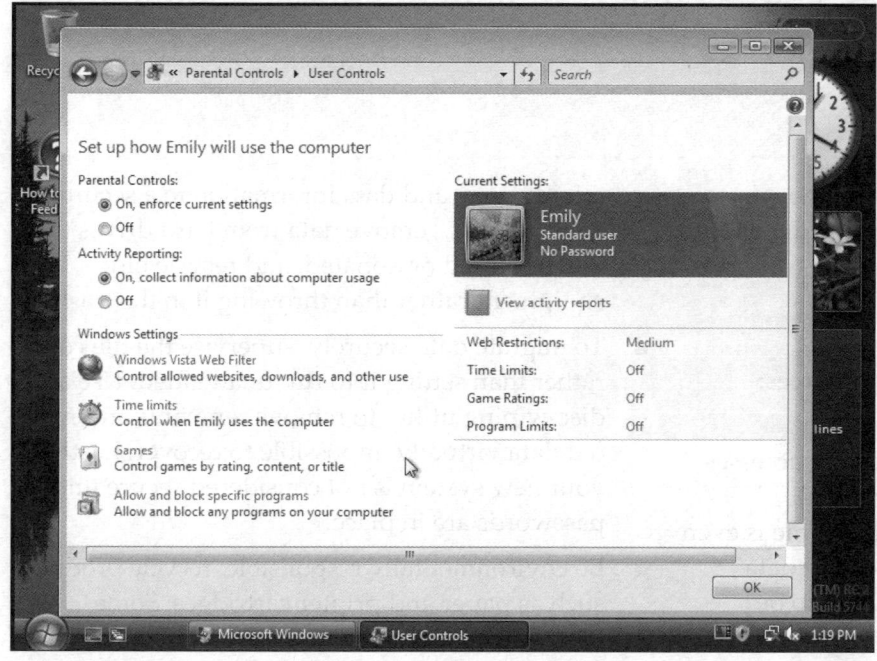

● Figure 19.38 Parental Controls

Parental Controls enable you to limit the time that Standard Users can spend logged in. You can specify acceptable and unacceptable times of day when Standard Users can log in. You can restrict access to types of games and specific applications. For example, if you like playing rather gruesome games filled with monsters and blood that you don't want your kids to play, you can simply block any games with certain ESRB ratings, such as T for teen.

Other Security Features

Vista offers many other security features that you may or may not encounter, such as improved hard drive encryption. In a corporate environment, you might run into Vista machines that completely block USB thumb drives. Underneath all these security features runs an OS that protects essential system files with far greater robustness than Windows XP or Windows 2000.

Chapter 19 Review

Chapter Summary

After reading this chapter and completing the exercises, you should understand the following about computer security.

Analyzing the Threat

- Threats to your data come from two sources: accidents and malicious people.

- Unauthorized access occurs when a user accesses resources in an unauthorized way. Not all unauthorized access is malicious, and some is even accidental. Authorized access can lead to data destruction by users who do not intend to be malicious. When users have access to a file or database, they typically believe the system won't let them make any changes they are not authorized to make.

- Windows XP Home has only two types of user accounts: administrative and limited. If you need to control access, you are better off using Windows XP Professional or Windows 2000.

- Computers, hard drives, and power all fail. As a tech, you need to plan for redundancy in these areas. You also need to protect your computers against viruses distributed through the network and removable media. You should back up data, make sure retired hard drives and optical discs don't have sensitive data, implement good access policies, and implement methods for tracking computer usage.

Local Control

- In addition to backing up everyone's Document and Settings folders, make sure to back up files users have stored outside their Documents and Settings folder. In server environments, be sure to back up the System State data, which includes portions of the Registry, security settings, desktop files and folders, and the default user. Backups should be stored off-site.

- When retiring a system and migrating the data to a new machine, three principles should be followed:

migrate user and data information in a secure environment, remove data from hard drives that will be stored or donated, and recycle old equipment rather than throwing it in the trash.

- To migrate data securely, supervise the file copy rather than setting it to run unattended. Use a disc-wiping utility to remove remnants and make old data virtually impossible to recover. Lastly, your new system is not considered secure until all passwords are in place.

- Be environmentally responsible: recycle products such as paper and printer cartridges. Some hardware, such as a computer monitor, contains toxic or hazardous materials. Donate these items to an organization that will use them, or contact a company that specializes in the disposal of hazardous materials or computer components.

- Most computer attacks are accomplished through social engineering rather than hacking. Telephone scams are one of the most common social engineering tactics. Dumpster driving involves physically going through an organization's trash looking for documents that might reveal user names, passwords, or other sensitive information. Be sure to secure your computer equipment in a locked room to prevent physical theft.

- Controlling access to programs, data, and other computing resources is the key to securing your system. Access control includes five interlinked areas: physical security, authentication, file system, users and groups, and security policies.

- Store computers with sensitive data in a locked room, and never walk away from your computer while logged in. Log out, or lock the computer by pressing CTRL-L.

- For software authentication, every user account should have a password to protect against unauthorized access. Additionally, CMOS setup should have a password for any computer in a public place.

- For hardware authentication, try smart cards or biometric devices. Smart cards are the size of credit cards and contain circuitry that can be used to identify the card holder. Biometric devices identify users by physical characteristics such as fingerprints or retinal scans. Some smart cards use radio frequency identification to transmit authentication information, so users don't have to insert something into a computer or card reader.

- All hard drives should be formatted with NTFS, not FAT32. Use the CONVERT command-line utility to convert a drive from FAT to NTFS without losing data.

- Windows controls access with user accounts and groups. Users are assigned user accounts, user accounts are assigned to a group or groups, and groups are granted permission to resources. Using NTFS enables the highest level of control over local data resources.

Network Security

- Accounts should be given permissions to access only what they need, no more. Unused accounts should be disabled.

- When a user account is a member of several groups, and permissions have been granted to groups, the user account will have a set of combined permissions that may conflict. The resulting permissions that ultimately control access are referred to as the effective permissions.

- Make sure to lock down the default Everyone group, as all users are automatically members of this group. Windows 2000 gives full control to the Everyone group by default. Never use the default Everyone or Users groups or the default Guest account unless you intend to permit all those accounts access to resources.

- Policies control permissions for activities, such as installing software, access to a command prompt, or time of day a user can log on. A policy is usually applied to a user account, computer account, or a group. Use the Local Security Settings tool to manage policies for an individual computer.

- Group Policy enables you to control such things as setting each computer in a domain to use the same wallpaper or deploy software. Commonly used policies include Prevent Registry Edits, Prevent Access to the Command Prompt, Log On Locally, and Minimum Password Length.

- Malware includes viruses, worms, Trojan horses, adware, and grayware—all of which can wreak havoc on your system.

- A virus is a piece of malicious software that gets passed from computer to computer and is designed to attach itself to another program on your computer. Trojans are freestanding programs that do something other than what the user expects it to do when run, such as expecting a game to run but erasing CMOS Settings instead. A worm is a freestanding program that takes advantage of security flaws and copies itself over and over again, thereby bogging down a network.

- To help protect a computer from malware, make sure to run up-to-date antivirus software, use a firewall, and apply all security patches for your software and operating system. Run Windows Update automatically, or at least weekly if you choose to configure it for manual updates.

- Antivirus software works in active mode to scan your file system for viruses and in passive mode by monitoring your computer's activity and checking for viruses in response to an action, such as running a program or downloading a file. Antivirus software detects boot-sector viruses by comparing the drive's boot sector to a standard boot sector. To detect executable viruses, a library of virus signatures is used. Macro viruses are detected through virus signatures or the presence of certain macro commands that are known macro viruses.

- Polymorph viruses attempt to change their signature to prevent detection by antivirus software. Fortunately, the scrambled code itself can be used as a signature. A checksum, based on file contents, can be created for every file on the drive. If the checksum changes, it is a sign of a virus infection. Most stealth viruses are boot sector viruses that hide from antivirus software.

- The best way to prevent damage from a virus is to keep from getting a virus in the first place. Use your passive antivirus shield, scan the PC daily, know where software has come from before you load it, and keep your antivirus definitions updated. Don't view e-mail messages in a preview pane, and only download files from sites you know to be safe.

- Unsolicited e-mail is called spam. Never post your e-mail address on the Internet, as over 97 percent of spam comes from e-mail addresses posted online. Spam filters can block spam at the mail server or at your computer. You can set most e-mail programs to block e-mail sent from specific people or to a specific person.

- Irritating Web browser problems include pop-ups, spyware, and adware. Many pop-ups remove the navigation aids from the browser window or mimic Windows dialog boxes. To safely close a pop-up, right-click the pop-up's Taskbar icon and choose Close, or press ALT-TAB until the pop-up window is active, and then press ALT-F4 to close it.

- Spyware can use your computer's resources to run distributed computing applications, capture keystrokes to steal passwords, or worse. Spyware typically disguises itself as useful utilities, so be vigilant about what you install. Some spyware can be removed via Add/Remove Programs, but for stubborn spyware use a third-party tool such as Lavasoft's Ad-Aware or PepiMK's Spybot Search & Destroy.

- Grayware leaches network bandwidth, although some consider the programs beneficial. Peer-to-peer file-sharing programs that enable a lot of users to upload portions of files on demand might seem useful to someone, but these programs can eat up a significant portion of the network bandwidth, causing other users or programs to respond slowly to network or Internet applications.

- Hardware firewalls protect networks by hiding IP addresses and blocking TCP/IP ports. Windows XP comes with a built-in software firewall that is accessible from the Control Panel Security Center applet.

- Encryption makes network packets unreadable by hackers who intercept network traffic. You are especially vulnerable when using the Internet over a public network. Modern operating systems use Kerberos to encrypt authentication credentials over a local network.

- PAP sends passwords in clear text, so it is not very safe. CHAP is the most common remote access protocol, in which the serving system challenges the remote system with a secret, like a password. MS-CHAP is Microsoft's version of CHAP and uses a more advanced encryption protocol.

- Network data can be encrypted similar to authentication credentials. Microsoft's encryption method of choice is called IPSec. Netscape's Secure Sockets Layer (SSL) creates secure Web sites. Microsoft's HTTPS protocol incorporates SSL into HTTP. Web sites whose URL begins with HTTPS:// are used to encrypt credit card purchases.

- To secure a wireless network, use wireless encryption and disable DHCP. Require wireless clients to use a static IP address or allot only enough DHCP addresses to meet the needs of your network. Definitely change the default administrator user name and password on the WAP.

- Use Event Viewer to track activity on your system. Event Viewer offers three sections: Application, Security, and System. The Security section doesn't show you everything by default, so it is good practice to enable event auditing and object auditing. Event auditing creates an entry in the Security Log when certain events happen, like a user logging on. Object Auditing creates entries in response to object access, like someone trying to access a certain file or folder.

- Incidence reporting means telling your supervisor about the data you've gathered regarding a computer or network problem. This provides a record of what you've done and accomplished. It also provides information that, when combined with other information you may or may not know, may reveal a pattern or bigger problem to someone higher up the chain.

Key Terms

access control (608)
Active Directory (604)
adware (620)
antivirus program (616)
authentication (609)
biometric devices (610)
Challenge Handshake
   Authentication Protocol
   (CHAP) (626)
CONVERT (610)
definition file (618)
digital certificate (627)
dumpster diving (608)
effective permissions (612)
encryption (624)
event auditing (631)
Event Viewer (629)

firewall (624)
grayware (623)
Group Policy (613)
HTTPS (627)
incidence reporting (632)
IPSec (626)
Kerberos (625)
Local Security Settings (613)
migration (605)
MS-CHAP (626)
object access auditing (631)
off-site storage (604)
Password Authentication Protocol
   (PAP) (626)
polymorph virus (618)
pop-up (620)

remnants (606)
Secure Sockets Layer (SSL) (626)
signature (617)
smart card (609)
social engineering (607)
spam (619)
spyware (620)
stealth virus (618)
System State data (604)
telephone scams (607)
Trojan (616)
unauthorized access (601)
virus (615)
virus shield (616)
worm (616)

Key Term Quiz

Use the Key Terms list to complete the sentences that follow. Not all terms will be used.

1. Use the _____ command-line tool to convert a FAT drive to NTFS without losing data.

2. A(n) _____ masquerades as a legitimate program, yet does something different than what is expected when executed.

3. Antivirus software uses an updatable _____ to identify viruses by their _____.

4. Enable _____ to create Event Viewer entries when a specific file is accessed.

5. Not all _____ is malicious, but it can lead to data destruction.

6. Most attacks on computer data are accomplished through _____.

7. A(n) _____ protects against unauthorized access from the Internet.

8. _____ is the most common remote authentication protocol.

9. Before making a credit card purchase on the Internet, be sure the Web site uses the _____ security protocol, which can be verified by checking for the _____ protocol in the address bar.

10. A(n) _____ changes its signature to prevent detection.

Multiple-Choice Quiz

1. Which of the following would you select if you need to back up an Active Directory server?

   A. Registry

   B. System State data

   C. My Computer

   D. My Server

2. Johan migrated his server data to a bigger, faster hard drive. At the end of the process, he partitioned and formatted the older hard drive before removing it to donate to charity. How secure is his company's data?

   A. Completely secured. The drive is blank after partitioning and formatting.

   B. Mostly secured. Only super-skilled professionals have the tools to recover data after partitioning and formatting.

   C. Very unsecured. Simple software tools can recover a lot of data, even after partitioning and formatting.

   D. Completely unsecured. The data on the drive will show up in the Recycle Bin as soon as someone installs it into a system.

3. What is the process of using or manipulating people to gain access to network resources?

   A. Cracking

   B. Hacking

   C. Network engineering

   D. Social engineering

4. Which of the following might offer good hardware authentication?

   A. Strong password

   B. Encrypted password

   C. NTFS

   D. Smart card

5. Randall needs to change the file system on his second hard drive (currently the D: drive) from FAT32 to NTFS. Which of the following commands would do the trick?

   A. CONVERT D: /FS:NTFS

   B. CONVERT D: NTFS

   C. NTFS D:

   D. NTFS D: /FAT32

6. Which of the following tools would enable you to stop a user from logging on to a local machine, but still enable him to log on to the domain?

   A. AD Policy

   B. Group Policy

   C. Local Security Settings

   D. User Settings

7. Which type of encryption offers the most security?

   A. MS-CHAP

   B. PAP

   C. POP3

   D. SMTP

8. Zander downloaded a game off the Internet and installed it, but as soon as he started to play, he got a Blue Screen of Death. Upon rebooting, he discovered that his My Documents folder had been erased. What happened?

   A. He installed spyware.

   B. He installed a Trojan.

   C. He broke the Group Policy.

   D. He broke the Local Security Settings.

9. Which of the following should Mary set up on her Wi-Fi router to make it the most secure?

   A. NTFS

   B. WEP

   C. WPA

   D. WPA2

10. A few of your fellow techs are arguing about backup policies for a new network server. Who is right?

    A. Andalyn recommends backing up data to a removable hard drive and then storing the hard drive off-site.

    B. Bart recommends backing up data to a removable hard drive, storing it in the server room so it is easily accessible and restorations can get started quickly.

    C. Carthic recommends backing up files across the network to another computer to save money on additional media.

    D. Dianthus recommends backing up files to another hard drive in the server to keep everything self-contained.

11. What single folder on a standalone PC can be backed up to secure all users' My Documents folders?

    A. All Users folder

    B. Documents and Settings folder

    C. System32 folder

    D. Windows folder

12. A user account is a member of several groups, and the groups have conflicting rights and permissions to several network resources. The culminating permissions that ultimately affect the user's access are referred to as what?

A. Effective permissions

B. Culminating rights

C. Last rights

D. Persistent permissions

13. What is true about virus shields?

A. They automatically scan e-mails, downloads, and running programs.

B. They protect against spyware and adware.

C. They are effective in stopping pop-ups.

D. They can reduce the amount of spam by 97 percent.

14. What does Windows use to encrypt the user authentication process over a LAN?

A. PAP

B. MS-CHAP

C. HTTPS

D. Kerberos

15. Which threats are categorized as social engineering? Choose all that apply.

A. Telephone scams

B. Dumpster diving

C. Trojans

D. Spyware

Essay Quiz

1. Your boss is considering getting an Internet connection for the office so employees can have access to e-mail, but she is concerned about hackers getting into the company server. What can you tell your boss about safeguards you will implement to keep the server safe?

2. A coworker complains that he is receiving a high amount of spam on his home computer through his personal e-mail account. What advice can you give him to alleviate his junk mail?

3. An intern in your IT department has asked for your help in understanding the differences between a virus, worm, and Trojan horse. What advice can you offer?

4. The boss's assistant has been asked to purchase a new coffee machine for the break room, but is nervous about shopping online with the company credit card. What can you tell her about secure online purchases?

5. You've been tasked to upgrade five computers in your office, replacing hard drives and video cards. Write a short essay describing the steps you'll need to take to migrate the users, secure the company data, and dispose of the excess hardware.

Lab Projects

Lab Project 19.1

You have learned a little bit about the local security policy in Windows. Fire up your Web browser and do a search for local security policy. Make a list of at least five changes you might consider making to your personal computer using the Local Security Settings tool. Be sure to include what the policy is, what it does, and where in the tool it can be configured.

• Lab Project 19.2

You know you must run antivirus and antispyware software on any computer connected to the Internet, and there are many companies that will sell you good, bad, and indifferent software. Using the Internet, find a free antivirus and free antispyware program. Make sure that these are legitimate and reputable programs, not spyware masquerading as legitimate programs! What free antivirus did you find? What free antispyware did you find? How do you know these are reputable? Would you install these on your own personal computer? Why or why not?

The Complete PC Tech

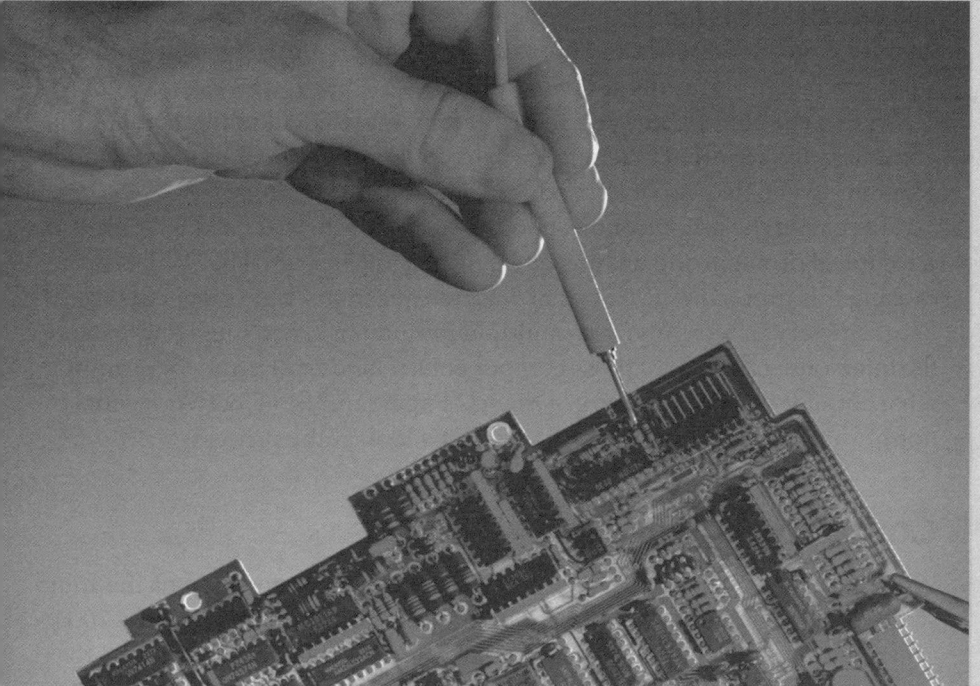

> *"I'm going to give you a little advice. There's a force in the universe that makes things happen. And all you have to do is get in touch with it, stop thinking, let things happen, and be the ball."*
>
> —TY WEBB, *CADDYSHACK* (1980)

When a mission-critical computer goes down, regardless of the industry, people get upset. Workers can't work, so they feel guilty. Employers can't get product out on time, so they feel anxious. Supervisors blame employees for fouling things up, or at least the employees fear such blame, even if they did not break the machine.

Into this charged atmosphere comes the tech, ready to fix the computer and move on to the next challenge. Accomplishing this task, however, requires three things: First, a good tech must know the broken machine inside and out—how it's *supposed* to work when working properly. Second, the tech has to calm the workers and supervisors, and get answers to questions to gain relevant information about the problem. Third, the tech must troubleshoot the problem and fix the machine.

This chapter starts with an overview of how computers work and then dives into a section on dealing with customers and how to get them to tell you what you need to know and smile about it. The chapter wraps up with a proven troubleshooting methodology to help you figure out the source of problems and point you to the fix quickly.

In this chapter, you will learn how to

- **Describe how computers work**
- **Explain the nuances of dealing with customers**
- **Implement a troubleshooting methodology**

If you look at the CompTIA A+ exam objectives for the Essentials, IT Technician, and specialization exams, you'll notice that the objectives covered in this chapter are, for all intents and purposes, virtually the same for each exam. CompTIA has not differentiated the questions for each exam covered by this domain, so we have used the same chapter for the Essentials exam and the IT Technician and specialization exams.

Essentials

■ How Computers Work

You've spent a lot of time going through this book, reading about technologies and components in great detail. Each chapter contained information and methodologies for the components contained in that chapter. With each chapter, you added more and more information about the pieces that make up the personal computer today.

In this chapter, I want you to distill that knowledge, to think about the computer as a coherent machine. Each of the computer's components works together to enable people to produce some amazing things.

To master the art of troubleshooting as a PC tech, you need to approach a technical problem and answer one question: "What can it be? What can be causing this problem?" (Okay, that was two questions, but you get the idea.) Because every process involves multiple components, you must understand the interconnectedness of those components. If Jane can't print, for example, what could it be? Connectivity? Drivers? Paper jam? Slow network connection? Frozen application? Solar flares? Let's look at the process.

Computing Process

When you run a program, your computer goes through three of the four stages of the **computing process**: input, processing, and output (Figure 20.1).

Input requires specific devices, such as the keyboard and mouse, that enable you to tell the computer to do something, such as open a program or type a word. The operating system (OS) provides an interface and tools so that the microprocessor and other chips can process your request. The image on the monitor or sound from the speakers effectively tell you that the computer has interpreted your command and spit out the result. The fourth stage, storage, comes into play when you want to save a document and when you first open programs and other files.

Making this process work, though, requires the complex interaction of many components, including multiple pieces of hardware and layers of software. As a tech, you need to understand all the components and how they work together so when something doesn't

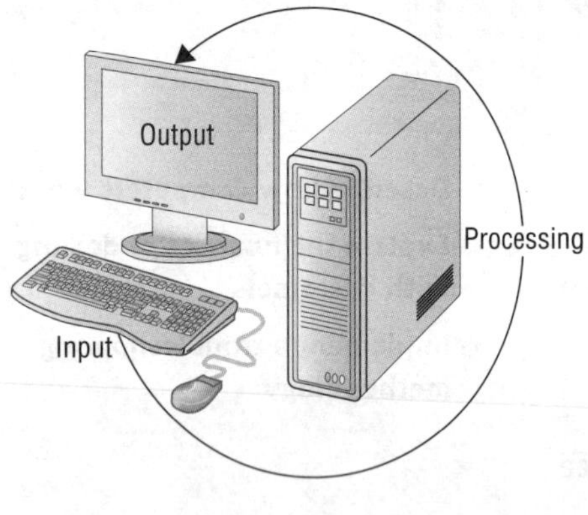

● **Figure 20.1** Input, processing, and output

Cross Check

Printing Process

You learned all about the printing process in Chapter 17, "Understanding Printing," but now think in terms of the computing process. Does the computing process translate when applied to printers? How? If a user can't print, how does knowledge of the computing process help you troubleshoot the printing process?

work right, you can track down the source and fix it. A look at a modern program reveals that even a relatively simple-seeming action or change on the screen requires many things to happen within the computer.

Games such as Second Life (Figure 20.2) are huge, taking up multiple gigabytes of space on an Internet server. They simply won't fit into the RAM in most computers, so developers have figured out ways to minimize RAM usage.

In Second Life, for example, you move through the online world in a series of more or less seamlessly connected areas. Crossing a bridge from one island to another triggers the game to update the information you're about to see on the new island quickly, so you won't be out of the action and the illusion of being in the game world remains intact. Here's what happens when you press the W key on your keyboard and your character steps across the invisible zone line.

The keyboard controller reads the grid of your keyboard and, on discovering your input, sends the information to the CPU through the wires of the motherboard (Figure 20.3). The CPU understands the keyboard controller because of a small program it loaded into RAM from the system BIOS stored

Second Life is a massively multiplayer online role-playing game (MMORPG) that offers a unique twist on the genre. You can create just about anything you can imagine, as far as your time and talent can take you. Second Life has a functioning economy that spills out into the real world, meaning you can buy and sell things within the game and turn that into real US dollars, although the more common scenario is to spend real money to get virtual possessions.

Figure 20.2 Second Life

Cross Check

Input Process

You learned about keyboards and many other input devices in Chapter 14, "Input/Output," but now apply the computing process to input devices for troubleshooting purposes. Obviously, keyboards do the "input" part of the computing process, but what can the problem be if you press a key and nothing happens? What other input devices can you recall from Chapter 14? If they seem not to work, where in the computing process could the problem lie?

on the system ROM chip on the motherboard when you first booted the computer.

The CPU and the application determine what should happen in the game, and on discovering that your character is about to cross the zone line, they trigger a whole series of actions. The application sends the signal to the OS that it needs a specific area loaded into RAM. The OS sends a signal to the CPU that it needs data stored on the hard drive plus information stored on the Second Life servers. The CPU then sends the commands to the hard drive controller for it to grab the proper stored data and send it to RAM, while at the same time sending a command to the NIC to download the updated information (Figure 20.4).

The hard drive controller tells the hard drive to cough up the data—megabytes worth—and then sends that data through the motherboard to the memory controller, which puts it into RAM and communicates with the CPU when it's finished. The network card and network

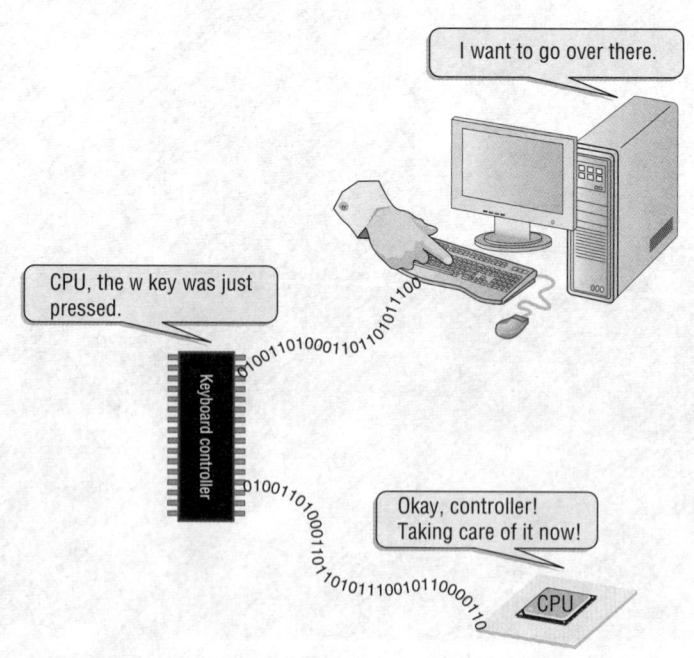

• **Figure 20.3**   Keyboard to CPU

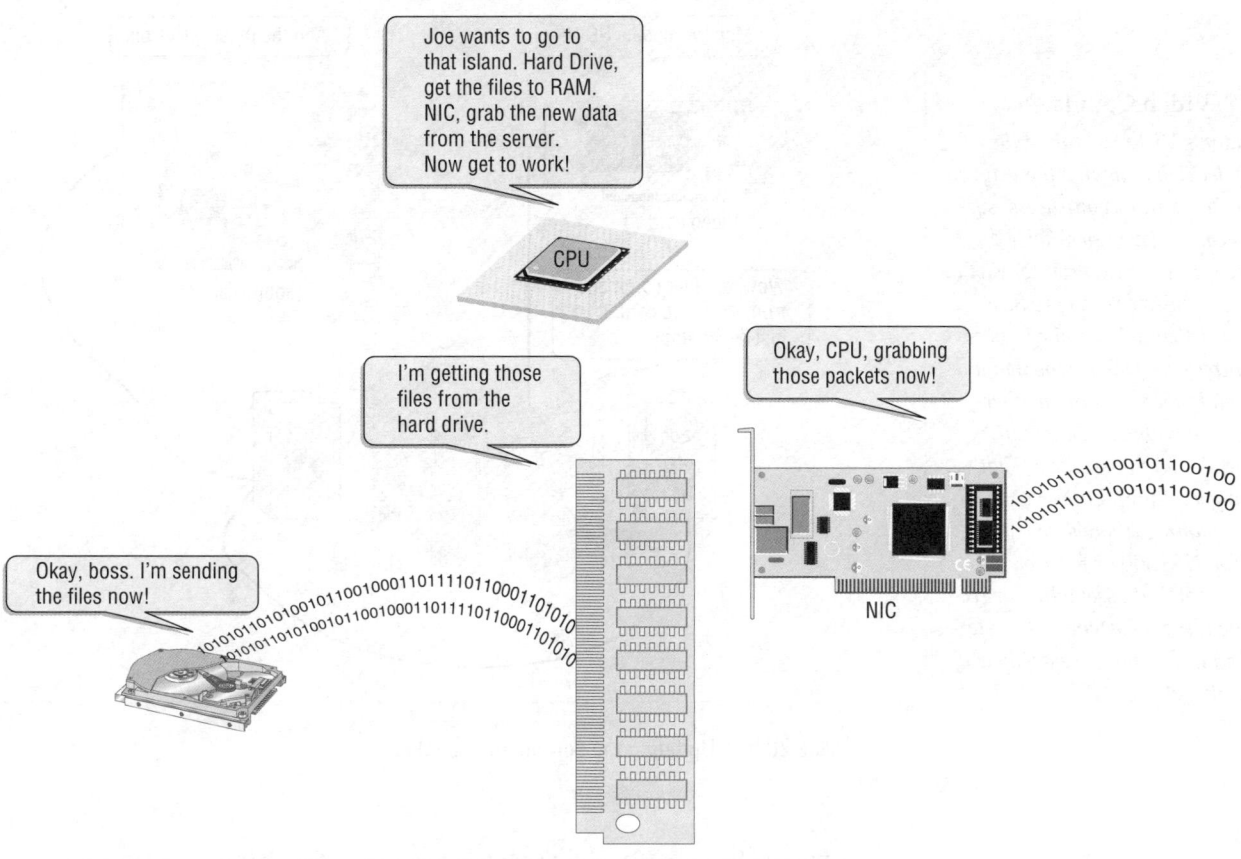

• **Figure 20.4** CPU to hard drive and NIC

operating system communicate with the Second Life servers and download the necessary updated information. The CPU then uses the application and OS to process the new data, sending video data to the video card and sound data to the sound card, again through the wires on the motherboard (Figure 20.5).

The video card processor puts the incoming data into its RAM, processes the data, and then sends out commands to the monitor to update the screen. The sound card processor likewise processes the data and sends out commands to the speakers to play a new sound (Figure 20.6).

For all of this to work, the PC has to have electricity, so the direct current (DC) provided by the power supply and the alternating current (AC) provided to the power supply must both be the proper voltage and amperage.

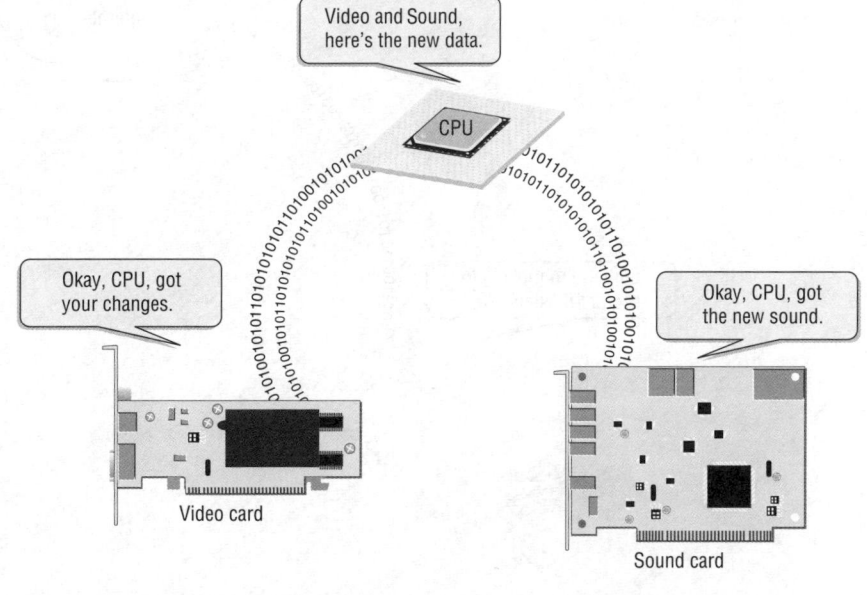

• **Figure 20.5** CPU to video card and sound card

Tech Tip

Video Counts

Windows Vista has raised the bar on video demands in a big way, so the video card in your users' systems can make a remarkable difference on their experience. Vista uses the video card to produce many of the cool visual effects of the interface. This means that a low-end video card in an otherwise serviceable machine can cause Vista to misbehave. That's not a good thing. Unless your client is gaming, there's no reason to drop US$300 or more on a video card, but assembling or recommending a system with yesterday's video is not necessarily a good thing!

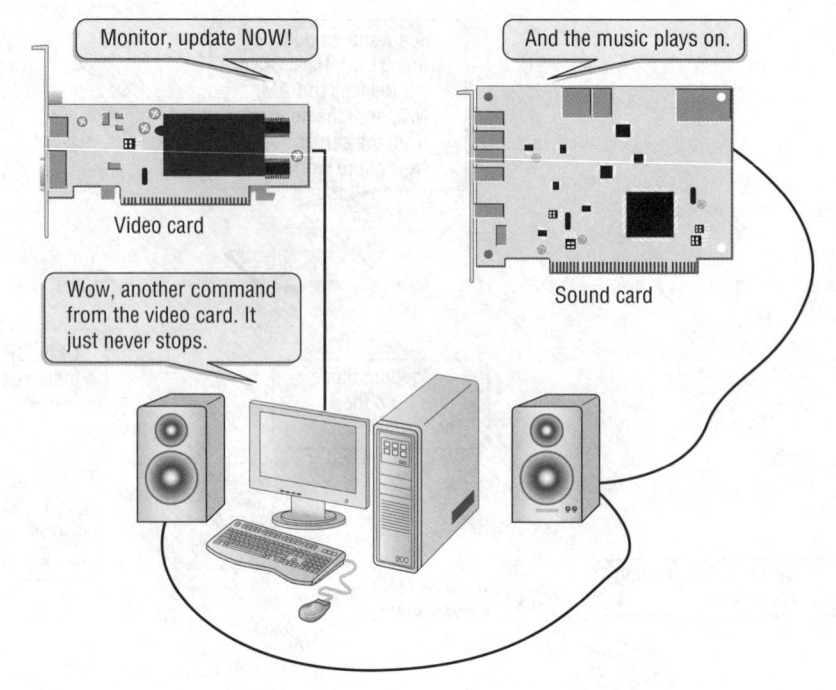

● **Figure 20.6**   Updating the screen and speakers

Finally, because Second Life is a network application, the OS has to send information through the NIC and onto the Internet to update everyone else's computer. That way, the other characters in the game world see you move forward a step (Figure 20.7).

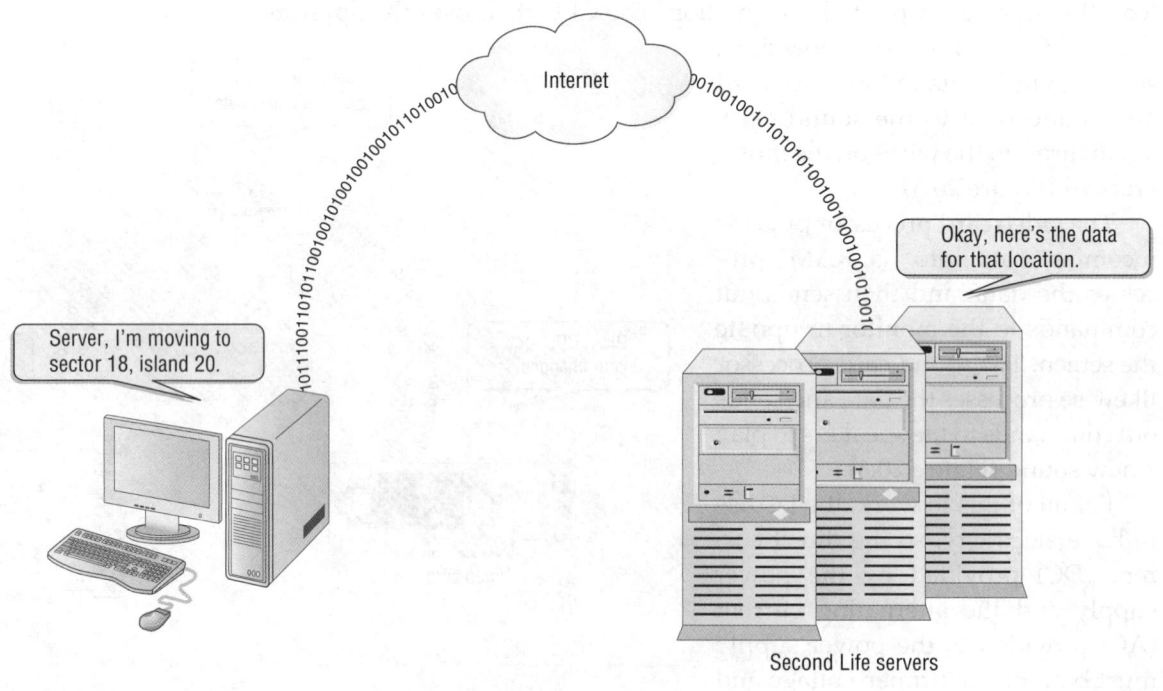

● **Figure 20.7**   PC to Second Life servers

What do you see or hear with all these electrons zipping all over the place? Out of a seemingly blank vista (Figure 20.8), a castle begins to appear, building itself piece by piece as your computer processes the new information and updates the video screen. You hear music begin to play from your speakers. Within a few seconds, with the data describing the new island fully downloaded and processed, the world on your monitor looks very different (Figure 20.9). That's when all goes well. Many megabytes of data have flowed from your hard drive and across the Internet, been processed by multiple processors, and sent to the monitor and the speakers.

To keep the action continuous and unbroken, Second Life, like many current online games, uses a process of continuous or **stream loading** : your computer constantly downloads updated information and data from the Second Life servers, so the world you see changes with every step you take. When done right, stream loading can do some amazing things. In the GameCube game Zelda, for example, the game anticipates where you will go next and loads that new area into RAM before you take the step. You can be in one area and use a telescope to zoom in on another fully developed

Figure 20.8   New area loading

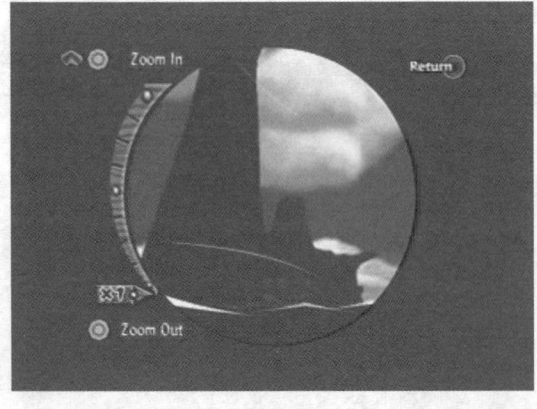

● **Figure 20.9**   Castle completed

● **Figure 20.10**   Zelda zoomed

area (Figure 20.10), making the experience amazingly seamless, just like real life.

Troubleshooting

Good techs understand the components involved in inputting, processing, and outputting data, including the devices that store data, such as hard drives. That's because if something doesn't work properly, you can start answering the ultimate troubleshooting question—what can it be?—accurately. If your screen freezes or the sound goes wonky, where in the process is the problem located?

As you go into any troubleshooting scenario, always keep the computing process in mind. This helps you sort through possibilities quickly and accurately. If you know all the stages, you won't miss a simple step, such as figuring out that a user can't print because the cleaning service accidentally turned off the print server

Try This!

Analyze Your Apps

What applications do you use on your computer? What applications do your clients or potential clients use? Analyzing them in terms of the computing process can help elevate your troubleshooting game by a huge factor. Take for example Microsoft Excel, a program designed to let you take numbers and turn them into charts, among other things. When you sit down to work in Excel, you load it from the hard drive into memory; then you input information via the keyboard and columns with the mouse. Every click requires the CPU to analyze and update RAM and the video card information.

the night before, or waste time reinstalling printer drivers when the real issue is a stalled print job in the print queue.

Dealing with Customers

When you deal with users, managers, and owners who are frustrated and upset because a computer or network is down and they can't work, your job requires you to take on the roles of detective and psychologist. It takes skill to talk with frazzled and confused people and get answers to questions about how the PC got into the state it's in. It's important to be able to communicate clearly and effectively. Plus, you need to follow the rules of tech-person decorum, acting with personal integrity and respect for the customer. Finally, use assertive communication to empathize with and educate the user. Great techs spend the time needed to develop these essential skills.

Eliciting Answers

Your job as a tech is to get the computer fixed, and the best way to start that process is to determine what the computer is doing or not doing. You must start by talking to the customer. Allow the customer to explain the problem fully while you record the information. Once the person has described the situation, you must then ask questions. This process is called `eliciting answers`.

Although each person is different, most users with a malfunctioning computer or peripheral will be afraid and often defensive about the problem. To overcome this initial attitude, you need to ask the right questions *and* listen to the customer's answers. Then ask the proper follow-up questions.

Always avoid accusatory questions because they won't help you in the least. "What did you do?" generally gets a confused or defensive "Nothing" in reply, which doesn't get you closer to solving the problem. First, ask questions that help clarify the situation. Repeat what you think is the problem after you've listened all the way through the user's story.

Follow up with fact-seeking questions. "When did it last work?" "Has it ever worked in this way?" "Has any software changed recently?" "Any new hardware?"

By keeping your questions friendly and factual, you show the user that you won't accuse them or judge their actions. You also show them that you're there to help them. After the initial tension drops away, you'll often get more information, for instance, a recitation of something the user might have tried or changed. These clues can help lead to a quick resolution of the problem.

It's important to remember that you may know all about computer technology, but the user probably does not. This means they will often use vague and/or incorrect terms to describe a particular computer component or function. That's just the way it works, so don't bother to correct the user. Wherever possible, avoid using jargon, acronyms, or abbreviations specific to computers. They simply confuse the already upset user. Just ask direct, factual questions in a friendly tone using simple, non-jargon language to zero in on what the user was trying to accomplish and what happened when things went wrong. Point at the machine or go to a working PC to have the user show what went wrong or what he or she did or tried to do.

Although you don't want to overwhelm them, people do usually want to get a handle on what you are doing—although in a simplified way. Don't be afraid to use simple analogies or concepts to give them an idea of what is happening. If you have the time (and the skills), use drawings, equipment, and other visual aids to make technical concepts more clear. If a customer is a "closet tech" and is really digging for answers—to the point that it's affecting your ability to do your job—compliment their initiative and then direct them to outside training opportunities. Better yet, tell them where they can get a copy of this book!

Integrity

A computer tech must bring integrity to his or her job, just like any other service professional. Treat anything said to you as a personal confidence, not to be repeated to coworkers or bosses. Respect the privacy and property of the user.

You have a lot of power when you sit in front of someone's computer. You can readily read private e-mail, discover Web sites surfed, and more. With a click of the Start button, you can know the last five programs the user ran, including Word and Solitaire, and the last few documents he or she worked on. Don't do this. You really don't want to know! Plus, if you get caught violating a customer's privacy, you'll not only lose credibility and respect, you could lose your job.

Passwords are a big issue for techs. We have to reboot computers and access shares and other jobs that require passwords. The rule here is to *avoid learning other folks' passwords at all costs*. If you know a password to access a mission-critical machine, and that machine ends up compromised or with data missing, who might be blamed? You, that's who, so avoid learning passwords! If you only need a password once, let the user type it in for you. If you anticipate accessing something multiple times (the more usual situation), ask the user to change his or her password temporarily.

It's funny, but people assume ownership of things they use at work. John in accounting doesn't call the computer he uses anything but "my PC." The phone on Susie's desk isn't the company phone, it's "Susie's phone." Regardless of the logic or illogic involved with this sense of ownership, a tech needs to respect that feeling. You'll never go wrong if you follow the Golden Rule or the `ethic of reciprocity` : "Do unto others as you would have them do unto you." In a tech's life, this can translate as "treat people's things as you would have other people treat yours." Don't use or touch anything—keyboard, printer, laptop, monitor, mouse, phone, pen, paper, or cube toy—without first asking permission. Follow this rule at all times, even when the customer isn't looking!

Beyond basic manners, never assume that just because you are comfortable with friendly or casual behavior, the customer will be, too. Even an apparently casual user will still expect you to behave with professional decorum. On the flip side, don't allow a user to put you in an awkward or even potentially dangerous or illegal situation. Never socialize with customers while on the clock. Never do work outside the scope of your assigned duties without the prior approval of your supervisor (when possible in such cases, try to direct users to someone who *can* help them). You are not a babysitter—never volunteer to "watch the kids" while the customer leaves the job site, or tolerate a potentially unsafe situation if a customer isn't properly supervising a child. Concentrate on doing your job safely and efficiently, and maintain professional integrity.

Respect

The final key in communicating with the user revolves around `respect` . You don't do his or her job, but should respect that job and person as an essential cog in your organization. Communicate with users the way you would like them to communicate with you were the roles reversed. Again, this follows the ethic of reciprocity.

Generally, IT folks are there to support the people doing a company's main business. You are there to serve their needs, and all things being equal, to do so at their convenience, not yours.

Don't assume the world stops the moment you walk in the door and that you may immediately interrupt their work to do yours. Although most customers are thrilled and motivated to help you the moment you arrive, this may not always be the case. Ask the magic question, "May I start working on the problem now?" Give your customer a chance to wrap up, shut down, or do anything else necessary to finish his or her business and make it safe for you to do yours.

Engage the user with the standard rules of civil conversation. Take the time to listen. Don't interrupt a story, but rather let it play out. You might hear something that leads to resolving the problem. Use an even, non-accusatory tone, and although it's okay to try to explain a problem if the user asks, never condescend, and never argue.

Remain positive in the face of adversity. Don't get defensive if you can't figure something out quickly and the user starts hassling you. Remember that an angry customer isn't really angry with you—he's just frustrated—so don't take his anger personally. Take it in stride; smile and assure him that computer troubleshooting sometimes takes awhile!

Avoid letting outside interruptions take your focus away from the user and his or her computer problem. Things that break your concentration slow down the troubleshooting process immensely. Plus, customers will feel insulted if you start chatting on your cell phone with your significant other about a movie date later that night when you're supposed to be fixing their computers! You're not being paid to socialize, so turn those cell phones and pagers to vibrate. That's why the technogods created voicemail. Never take any call except one that is potentially urgent. If a call is potentially urgent, explain the urgency to the customer, step away, and deal with the call as quickly as possible.

If you discover that the user caused the problem, either through ignorance or by accident, don't minimize the importance of the problem, but don't be judgmental or insulting about the cause. We all screw up sometimes, and these kinds of mistakes are your job security! *You get paid because people make mistakes and machines break.* Chances are you'll be back at that workstation six months or a year later, fixing something else. By becoming the user's advocate and go-to person, you create a better work environment. If it's a mistaken action that caused the problem, explain in a positive and supportive way how to do the task correctly and then have the user go through the process while you are there to reinforce what you said.

Assertive Communication

In many cases, a PC problem is due to user error or neglect. As a technician, you must show users the error of their ways without creating anger or conflict. You do this by using assertive communication. Assertive communication is a technique that isn't pushy or bossy, but it's also not the language of a pushover. Assertive communication first requires you show the other person that you understand and appreciate the importance of his or her feelings. Use statements such as "I know how frustrating it feels to lose data" or "I understand how infuriating it is when the network goes out and you can't get your job done." Statements like these cool off the situation and let the customer know you are on his or her side.

The second part of assertive communication is making sure the problem is clearly stated—without accusing the user directly: "Not keeping up with defragmenting your hard drive slows it down" or "Help me understand how the network cable keeps getting unplugged during your lunch hour." Lastly, tell the user what you need from them to prevent this error in the future: "Please call me whenever you hear that buzzing sound" or "Please check the company's approved software list before installing anything." Always use "I" and "me," and never make judgments. "I can't promise the keyboard will work well if it's always getting dirty" is much better than "Stop eating cookies over the keyboard, you slob!"

■ Troubleshooting Methodology

Following a sound troubleshooting methodology helps you figure out and fix problems quickly. But because troubleshooting is as much art as science, I can't give you a step-by-step list of things to try in a particular order. You've got to be flexible.

First, make sure you have the proper tools for the job. Second, back up everything important before doing repair work. And third, analyze the problem, test your solution, and complete your troubleshooting.

Tech Toolkit

Way back in Chapter 2, "The Visible PC," you learned the basic parts of a tech toolkit (Figure 20.11): a Phillips-head screwdriver and a few other useful tools, such as a Torx wrench and a pair of tweezers. You also should carry some computer components.

Always carry several field replaceable units (FRUs)—a fancy way to say *spare parts*—when going to a job site or workstation. Having several known good components on hand enables you to swap out a potentially bad piece of hardware to see if that's the problem. Different technicians will have different FRUs. A printer specialist might carry a number of different fusers, for example. Your employer will also have a big effect on what is an FRU and what is not. I generally carry a couple of RAM sticks (DDR and DDR2), a PCI video card, a NIC, and a 300-watt power supply.

Backup

In many troubleshooting situations, it's important to back up critical files before making changes to a system. To some extent, this is a matter of proper ongoing maintenance. If you're in charge of a set of machines for your company, for example, make sure they're set to back up critical files automatically on a regular basis.

If you run into a partially functional system, where you might have to reinstall the OS but can access the hard drive, then you should definitely back up essential data, such as e-mail, browser favorites, important documents, and any data not stored on a regularly backed-up server. Because you can always boot to a copy of Windows and go to the Recovery Console, you should never lose essential data, barring full-blown hard drive death.

Steps

Troubleshooting a computer problem can create a great day for a computer tech—if he or she goes about solving it systematically and logically. Too many techs get into a rut, thinking that when symptom A occurs, the problem must be caused by problem A and require solution A. They might even be right nine times out of ten, but if you think this way, you're in trouble

Tech Tip

Why PCI?

I keep a PCI video card in my kit because every computer made in the past ten years has PCI slots. If you run into a system with video problems, you can almost always simply slap in the PCI video card and discover quickly whether or not the AGP or PCIe video card or card slot is a problem. If the computer boots up with the PCI video card but fails on the AGP card, for example, you know that either the AGP card or slot is causing the problem.

The CompTIA A+ certification exams assume that all techs should back up systems *every time* before working on them, even though that's not how it works in the real world.

Dead hard drives retain their data, so you can recover it—if you're willing to pay a lot of money. Having a good backup in place makes a lot more economic sense!

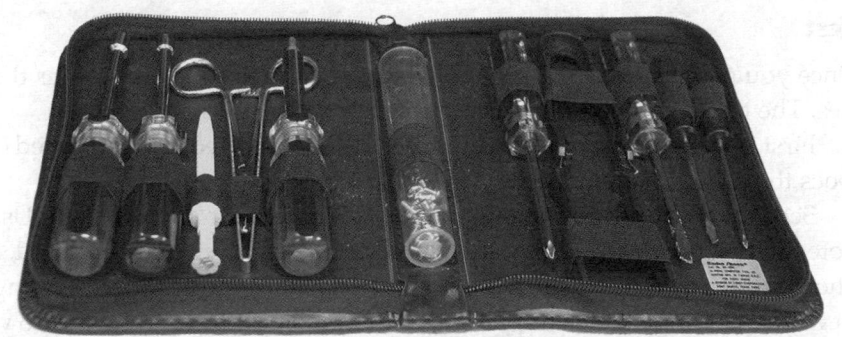

when the problem is really Z and requires a completely different solution. What do you do when the fix doesn't work and you're sure it's got to be problem A? Your customer won't be happy, you'll end up frustrated or embarrassed, and you still won't have the problem fixed. Follow the right methodology: analyze, test, and complete your task.

Analyze

Everything starts with analyzing the problem. Because you know how the process should work, when you run into a computer problem, the first question you should ask is, "What can it be?" Don't limit yourself in the initial analysis, but examine all possibilities.

Make sure you understand the nature of the problem first. A big portion of the initial fact-finding involves talking to the user with your newly-honed customer communication skills. Practice asking friendly, factual questions to get the results you want.

When you run into big problems, such as a completely dead PC, or some weird issue that involves networking as well as a local machine, break the problem down into smaller parts. For a dead PC, for example, organize your inquiry into categories, like this:

- **Power**   Check the AC connections and power switches on the power supply and UPS or surge suppressor.

- **Connectivity**   Check inside the box to make sure nothing is unplugged.

- **CMOS**   If you've got power (you see an LED lit up, for example), then check CMOS to see if the hard drive shows up.

- **Operating system**   If you have some life in the PC, but get no boot option, then try booting to the CD and running the recovery console. Check to see if you can access the hard drive. If you have a boot option, then try booting to Safe mode or Last Known Good Configuration.

By breaking the problem into discrete chunks, you make a big problem more manageable. You can determine whether the problem is caused by a hardware failure, connection problem, or perhaps an issue with the operating system or other software.

Test

Once you determine what might have caused the problem, test your theories. The testing procedure follows a simple set of rules:

First, check the easy stuff. Is the failed device plugged in? Is it turned on? Does the printer have paper?

Second, use a process of elimination to home in on the problem. Use a notepad to write down what you've tried and what effect that effort had. Do one thing at a time. If you go into CMOS and make a whole series of changes to various settings, for example, and then the computer works, how do you know what was wrong? You can't know when you make multiple changes. Worse yet, you risk breaking something else while fixing the first problem!

Third, if hardware seems to be the problem, swap out the suspect parts with known good parts from your stash of FRUs. With a dead or dying piece of hardware, you can generally get almost immediate results. A fried stick of RAM, for example, can create a dead PC. Pop in a good stick, and you'll have a functional machine.

Complete

Once you finish the testing phase, you can complete the troubleshooting process with four more steps: evaluate, escalate, clean up, and document.

First, evaluate the results of your actions. Run the system through its paces; don't just get it working and walk away. Make certain the user can accomplish his or her primary tasks before you consider a job complete. If you can't get the computer or peripheral working in a fairly short period of time, take the second step and escalate the problem—in other words, call for help. Because you've taken notes on the symptoms and each troubleshooting step you've tried, you can very quickly get a more senior tech up to speed on the problem and get suggestions for where you might go next.

Third, clean up the work environment. If you installed a drive, for example, do the right thing and tie off the ribbon cables. If you see a mess of cables coming out of the back of the PC or running across the floor, take a moment to tie them off. Good cable management does more than leave your clients with a nice-looking computer and workstation area, it also helps prevent accidents.

Finally, document your results. Many companies have specific forms for you to use to describe the problem and its resolution. If not, then make some for yourself and other techs in your workplace. Documenting problems helps you track the troubleshooting history of a machine over time, enabling you to make longer-term determinations about retiring it or changing out more parts. If you and fellow techs fix a specific problem with Mary's machine several times, for example, you might decide to swap out her whole system rather than fix it a fourth time.

Documenting helps fellow techs if they have to follow up on a task you didn't finish or troubleshoot a machine that you've worked on previously. The reverse is also true. If you get a call about Frank's computer, for example, and check the records to find other service calls on his computer, you might find that the fix for a particular problem is already documented. This is especially true for user-generated problems. Having documentation of what you did also means you don't have to rely on your memory when your coworker asks what you did to fix the weird problem with Jane's computer a year ago!

Documenting also comes into play when you or a user has an accident on site. If your colleague Joe drops a monitor on his foot and broke both the monitor and his foot, for example, you need to fill out an *incident report*, just like you would with any kind of accident—electrical, chemical, or physical. An incident report should detail what happened and where it happened. This helps your supervisors take the appropriate actions quickly and efficiently.

 The power supply provides the only exception to the instant gratification rule of part swapping. If you have a wonky computer that has intermittent problems, swap out the power supply and leave your FRU in the computer for a half day or longer. You need the user to road test the PC and report if he or she has the same problems.

 Know the four steps for completing troubleshooting: evaluate, escalate, clean up, and document.

Chapter 20 Review

■ Chapter Summary

After reading this chapter and completing the exercises, you should understand the following about working as a tech.

How Computers Work

■ Good techs must know how their systems are supposed to work when working properly, must be able to calm workers and supervisors and get answers to relevant questions, and must be able to troubleshoot and fix computer problems. A question you must be able to answer is "What can be causing this problem?"

■ When you run a program, computers work through three stages of the four-stage computing process: input, processing, and output. Input requires special input devices such as a keyboard or mouse. The operating system provides the interface and tools so that the CPU and other chips can process requests. The output devices, such as the monitor, speakers, or printer, tell you the computer has interpreted your commands. For all this to work, the PC must have electricity and proper AC/DC voltage and amperage.

■ When a keyboard key is pressed, the keyboard controller reads the grid of your keyboard and discovers your input, and then sends the information to the CPU. The CPU understands the keyboard controller because of a small program that was loaded into RAM from the ROM BIOS on the motherboard when the PC booted up.

■ Good techs understand the components involved in inputting, processing, and outputting, including the devices that store data, such as hard drives.

Dealing with Customers

■ The first step in fixing a computer problem is talking to the client. To determine what the computer is doing or not doing, first allow the client to describe the situation; then ask leading questions to elicit answers.

■ Most people feel defensive when asked to explain computer problems, so it is your job to put them at ease by asking the right kinds of questions. Questions like "What did you do?" generally aren't much help.

A better question might be, "When did it last work?" By taking the user explicitly out of the question, you show that you aren't accusing or judging.

■ Refrain from using computer jargon, acronyms, or abbreviations, as a user is unlikely to be familiar with them and may get confused. Ask simple questions that don't use technical lingo. Have the user physically demonstrate what is happening or what is not happening.

■ Treat every incident with integrity. Respect the confidentiality of what a user said to you and don't repeat it to coworkers. Don't abuse your power as a tech. Although you could read private e-mail, see the last several programs someone used, or see the last few documents someone worked on, don't do it. Your credibility may be damaged beyond repair.

■ Avoid learning other people's passwords. Have the user type in any passwords for you. If you'll need the same password entered many times, have the user temporarily change their password for you to use, and then have them change it back when you are done working.

■ People are protective of their things. Don't touch anything unless necessary—that means the keyboard, printer, monitor, phone, pen, stapler, or anything else.

■ Don't allow yourself to be put in a questionable situation. You're a tech, not a babysitter.

■ Don't assume the customer is ready for you to begin upon your arrival. Ask the customer if it is okay for you to start work, and allow them to close any files and exit any programs. Don't interrupt customers. Let them finish their story. Although you may think it is irrelevant, there may be important information.

■ Stay positive, don't get defensive, and don't take a customer's anger personally. Remind the customer that troubleshooting takes time. Avoid letting outside interruptions take your focus away from the job; set your cell phone and pager to vibrate. While working with a customer, only take phone calls that are urgent. Explain the urgency to your customer and deal with the call as quickly as possible.

- If you determine the problem was caused by the user, don't be judgmental or insulting. Explain to the user how to do the task they wanted to accomplish, and have the user go through the process while you supervise to reinforce what you said.

- Use assertive, but not pushy or bossy, communication. Show the person you understand his or her feelings and appreciate their importance. Make sure the problem is clearly stated without accusing the user directly. Tell the user what you need from them to prevent this error in the future. Use "I" statements rather than accusatory statements.

Troubleshooting Methodology

- Troubleshooting is more art than science, and as such, there is no step-by-step list of actions to follow. You need to be flexible.

- Carry a well-stocked tech toolkit. You should also carry several FRUs. The FRUs you carry will depend on what kind of tech you are, but in general, most techs should carry a few sticks each of DDR and DDR2 RAM, a PCI video card, a NIC, and a 300-watt power supply.

- Be sure to back up critical files before making changes to a system. Back up e-mail, favorites, personal documents, and any data not stored on a regularly backed-up server.

- Begin troubleshooting by analyzing the problem. Make sure you understand the problem. Talk to the client and use your communication skills to gather facts.

- It is helpful to break down large problems into smaller categories. For example, if a PC is completely dead or there is an issue involving both the network and the local machine, organize your inquiry into smaller categories including power, connectivity, CMOS, and operating system.

- Once you determine what might have caused the problem, test your theories. First, check the easy stuff, like is the device plugged in and powered on. Second, use the process of elimination to narrow in on the problem. Third, swap out parts with known good parts from your stash of FRUs. Swapping out bad hardware for good hardware almost immediately yields results. The exception to this rule is the power supply, which should be road tested for half a day or longer.

- Complete the troubleshooting process by testing the results of your actions and running the PC through its paces. If the problem persists, call a senior tech for help. Your notes should get a senior tech up to speed on the problem. Finally, document your results.

Key Terms

assertive communication (654)	**ethic of reciprocity** (653)	**respect** (653)
clean up (657)	**evaluate** (657)	**stream loading** (649)
computing process (644)	**field replaceable unit (FRU)** (655)	**tech toolkit** (655)
document (657)	**incident report** (657)	**troubleshooting**
eliciting answers (651)	**integrity** (652)	**methodology** (654)
escalate (657)	**passwords** (652)	

Key Term Quiz

Use the Key Terms list to complete the sentences that follow. Not all terms will be used.

1. _____ are commonly known as spare parts and at a minimum include extra sticks of RAM and a video card.

2. A few screwdrivers and an anti-static wrist strap should be in your _____.

3. Understanding the _____ enables you to troubleshoot problems more efficiently.

4. An effective use of _____ means clearly stating a problem without accusing the user of creating that problem.

5. Better online applications use _____ to download updated information and data constantly.

6. An accomplished computer tech should treat anything said to him or her as a personal confidence, not to be repeated to coworkers or bosses. The tech brings _____ to his or her job.

7. You should avoid learning _____ to other folks' computers so you don't get blamed if something happens to those computers.

8. If you can't solve a troubleshooting problem, the next step is to _____ the problem to a higher-level tech.

9. Treating other people how you want to be treated is an example of the _____.

10. A(n) _____ gives the details about an accident on the job site.

■ Multiple-Choice Quiz

1. While troubleshooting a fairly routine printing problem, the customer explains in great detail precisely what he was trying to do, what happened when he tried to print, and what he had attempted as a fix for the problem. At what point should you interrupt him?

   A. After he describes the first problem

   B. As soon as you understand the problem

   C. As soon as you have a solution

   D. Never

2. While manning the help desk, you get a call from a distraught user who says she has a blank screen. What would be a useful follow-up question?

   A. Is the monitor turned on?

   B. Did you reboot?

   C. What did you do?

   D. What's your password?

3. While manning the help desk, you get a call from Sharon in accounting. She's lost a file that she knows she saved to her hard drive. Which of the following statements would direct Sharon to open her My Documents folder in the most efficient and professional manner?

   A. Sharon, check My Documents.

   B. Sharon, a lot of programs save files to a default folder, often to a folder called My Documents. Let's look there first. Click on the Start button and move the mouse until the cursor hovers over My Documents. Then click the left mouse button and tell me what you see when My Documents opens.

   C. Probably just defaulted to My Docs. Why don't you open Excel or whatever program you used to make the file, and then open a document, and point it to My Documents.

   D. Look Sharon, I know you're a clueless noob when it comes to computers, but how could somebody lose a file? Just open up My Documents, and look there for the file.

4. What tool should be in every technician's toolkit?

   A. Pliers

   B. Hammer

   C. Straight-slot screwdriver

   D. Phillips-head screwdriver

5. Al in marketing calls in for tech support, complaining that he has a dead PC. What is a good first question to begin troubleshooting the problem?

   A. Did the computer ever work?

   B. When did the computer last work?

   C. When you say "dead," what do you mean? What happens when you press the power button?

   D. What did you do?

6. While manning the help desk, you get a call from Bryce in Sales complaining that he can't print, and every time he clicks on the network shared drive, his computer stops and freezes. He says he thinks it's his hard driver. What would be a good follow-up question or statement?

   A. Bryce, you're an idiot. Don't touch anything. I'll be there in five minutes.

   B. Okay, let's take this one step at a time. You seem to have two problems: one with printing and the second with the network shared drive, right?

C. First, it's not a hard *driver,* but a hard *drive.* It doesn't have anything to do with the network share or printing, so that's just not right.

D. When could you last print?

7. When troubleshooting a software problem on Phoebe's computer and listening to her describe the problem, your beeper goes off. It's your boss. What would be an acceptable action for you to make?

A. Excuse yourself, walk out of the cube, and use a cell phone to call your boss.

B. Pick up Phoebe's phone and dial your boss's number.

C. Wait until Phoebe finishes her description and then ask to use her phone to call your boss.

D. Wait until Phoebe finishes her description and run through any simple fixes; then explain that you need to call your boss on your cell phone.

8. You've just installed new printer drivers into Roland's computer for the big networked laser printer. What should you do to complete the assignment?

A. Document that you installed new printer drivers.

B. Tell Roland to print a test page.

C. Print a test page and go to the printer to verify the results. Assuming everything works, you're done.

D. Print a test page and go to the printer to verify the results. Document that you installed new printer drivers successfully.

9. While fixing a printing problem on Paul's computer, you notice several personal e-mails he has sent sitting in his Sent Items mail folder. Using the company computer for personal e-mail is against regulations. What should you do?

A. Leave the e-mails on the computer and notify your boss.

B. Delete the e-mails from the computer and notify your boss.

C. Delete the e-mails from the computer and remind Paul of the workplace regulations.

D. You shouldn't be looking in his e-mail folders at all, as it compromises your integrity.

10. Upon responding to a coworker's request for help, you find her away from her desk, and Microsoft Excel is on the screen with a spreadsheet open. How do you proceed?

A. Go find the coworker and ask her to exit her applications before touching her computer.

B. Exit Excel, saving changes to the document, and begin troubleshooting the computer.

C. Exit Excel without saving changes to the document and begin troubleshooting the computer.

D. Use the Save As command to save the file with a new name, exit Excel, and begin troubleshooting the computer.

11. You are solving a problem on Kate's computer, which requires you to reboot several times. Upon each reboot, the logon screen appears and prompts you for a user name and password before you can continue working. Kate has gone to another office to continue her work on another computer. How do you proceed?

A. Call Kate, ask her for her password, type it in, and continue working on the problem.

B. Insist that Kate stay with you and have her type the password each time it is needed.

C. Call Kate and have her come in to type the password each time it is needed.

D. Have Kate temporarily change her password for you to use as you work; then have her change it back when you are through.

12. You are working in a customer's home, and his five-year-old child is screaming and kicking the back of your chair. What do you do?

A. Ignore the child and finish your work as quickly as you can.

B. Discipline the child as you see fit.

C. Politely ask your client to please remove the child from your work area.

D. Tell your client you refuse to work under such conditions and leave the premises with the job half done.

13. After replacing a keyboard a user has spilled coffee on for the fifth time, what should you say to the user?

   A. I can't guarantee the new keyboard will work if it gets dirty.

   B. I can't guarantee the new keyboard will work if you continue to spill coffee on it.

   C. These keyboards are expensive. Next time we replace one because you spilled coffee, it's coming out of your paycheck.

   D. You need to be more careful with your coffee.

14. When is it appropriate to yell at a user?

   A. When he screws up the second time

   B. When he interrupts your troubleshooting

   C. When he screws up the fifth time

   D. Never

15. Once you figure out what can be causing a computer to malfunction, what's your next step?

   A. Escalate the problem to a higher-level tech.

   B. Talk to the user about stream loading and other geeky topics because your knowledge will put him or her at ease.

   C. Test your theory by checking for power and connectivity.

   D. Write an incident report to document the problem.

Essay Quiz

1. A friend is considering turning his computer hobby into a career and has asked your advice on outfitting himself as a freelance computer technician. What tools can you recommend to your friend?

2. A user phones you at your desk and reports that, after pressing the power button on his computer and hearing the hard drive spin up, his screen remains blank. What questions can you ask to determine the problem?

3. Briefly explain the three steps in a troubleshooting methodology.

Lab Projects

• Lab Project 20.1

Think of items you would like to always have on hand as FRUs. Using the Internet, find prices for these items. Make a list of your items and their individual costs, and then find the total cost for your equipment.

• Lab Project 20.2

Visit your local computer store or hardware store and purchase the items for a hardware tech toolkit. You may want to include a variety of screwdrivers, an anti-static wrist strap, tweezers, or other items.

• Lab Project 20.3

Create a software tech toolkit on CD or a USB flash drive loaded with a variety of drivers for NICs and video cards. Include free/open-source antivirus software, antispyware software, and any other software tools you think might be useful.

Installing and Troubleshooting Printers

Printers are a complex technology, with their own sets of parts, processes, troubleshooting steps, and repair requirements. In fact, printers are the one component of the PC system that still supports an entire subgroup of specialists—many techs make a healthy living doing nothing more than working on printers. In this appendix, I cover the laser printing process in detail to give you a greater understanding of the most common printer you'll encounter in office environments. Then you will learn to install and troubleshoot printers. This reference won't turn you into a PC printer specialist, but it does cover the more common issues that the generalist PC tech will encounter in the day-to-day world of printer support.

■ The Laser Printing Process

The laser printing process can be broken down into six steps, and the CompTIA A+ exams expect you to know them all. As a tech, you should be familiar with these phases, as this can help you troubleshoot printing problems. For example, if an odd line is printed down the middle of every page, you know there's a problem with the photosensitive drum or cleaning mechanism and the toner cartridge needs to be replaced.

You'll look into the physical steps that occur each time a laser printer revs up and prints a page; then you'll see what happens electronically to ensure that the data is processed properly into flawless, smooth text and graphics.

The Physical Side of the Process

Most laser printers perform the printing process in a series of six steps. Keep in mind that some brands of laser printers may depart somewhat from this process, although most work in exactly this order:

1. Clean
2. Charge
3. Write
4. Develop
5. Transfer
6. Fuse

Clean the Drum

The printing process begins with the physical and electrical cleaning of the photosensitive drum (Figure A.1). Before printing each new page, the drum must be returned to a clean, fresh condition. All residual toner left over from printing the previous page must be removed, usually by scraping the surface of the drum with a rubber cleaning blade. If residual particles remain on the drum, they will appear as random black spots and streaks

Be sure that you know the order of a laser printer's printing process! Here's a mnemonic to help: Clarence Carefully Wrote Down The Facts.

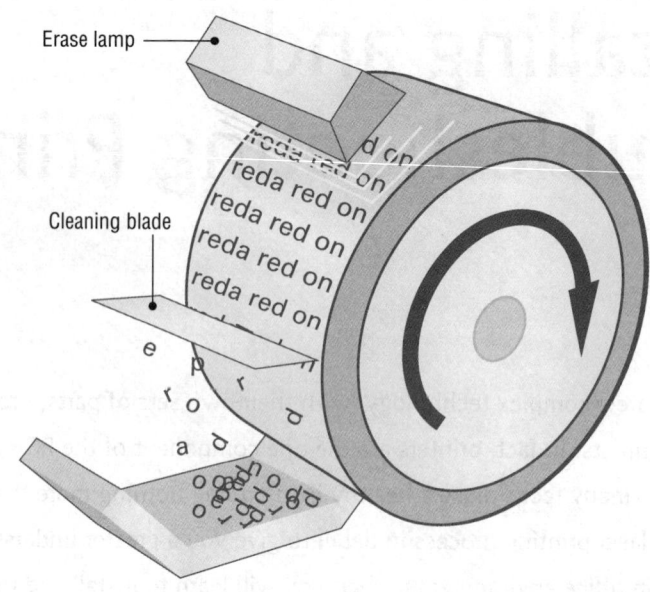

Erase lamp

Cleaning blade

- **Figure A.1** Cleaning and erasing the drum

on the next page. The physical cleaning mechanism either deposits the residual toner in a debris cavity or recycles it by returning it to the toner supply in the toner cartridge. The physical cleaning must be done carefully. Damage to the drum will cause a permanent mark to be printed on every page.

The printer must also be electrically cleaned. One or more erase lamps bombard the surface of the drum with the appropriate wavelengths of light, causing the surface particles to discharge into the grounded drum. After the cleaning process, the drum should be completely free of toner and have a neutral charge.

Charge the Drum

Primary corona

To make the drum receptive to new images, it must be charged (Figure A.2). Using the primary corona wire, a uniform negative charge is applied to the entire surface of the drum (usually between ~600 and ~1000 volts).

Write and Develop the Image

A laser is used to write a positive image on the surface of the drum. Every particle on the drum hit by the laser will release most of its negative charge into the drum. Those particles with a lesser negative charge will be positively charged relative to the toner particles and will attract them, creating a developed image (Figure A.3).

Transfer the Image

The printer must transfer the image from the drum onto the paper. The transfer corona is used to give the paper a positive charge. Once the paper has a positive charge, the negatively charged toner particles leap from the drum to the paper.

- **Figure A.2** Charging the drum with a uniform negative charge

Mike Meyers' CompTIA A+ Guide: Essentials (Exam 220-601)

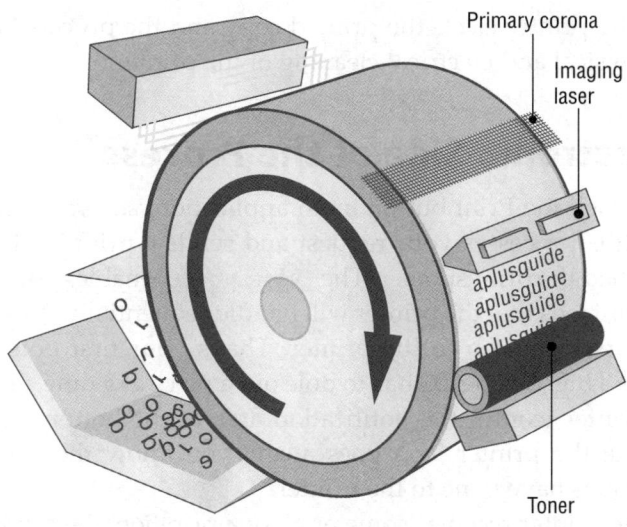

Primary corona

Imaging laser

Toner

• **Figure A.3**   Writing the image and applying the toner

At this point, the particles are merely resting on the paper. They must still be permanently fused to the paper.

Fuse the Image

The particles have been attracted to the paper because of the paper's positive charge, but if the process stopped here, the toner particles would fall off the page as soon as the page was lifted. Because the toner particles are mostly composed of plastic, they can be melted to the page. Two rollers—a heated roller coated in a nonstick material and a pressure roller—melt the toner to the paper, permanently affixing it. Finally, a static charge eliminator removes the paper's positive charge (Figure A.4). Once the page is

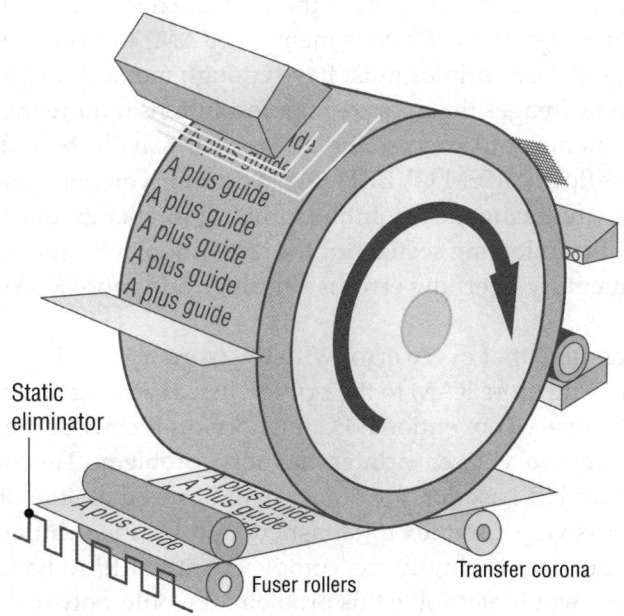

Static eliminator

Fuser rollers

Transfer corona

• **Figure A.4**   Transferring the image to the paper and fusing the final image

Tech Tip

Laser Printing in Color

Color laser printers use four different colors of toner (cyan, magenta, yellow, and black) to create their printouts. Most models put each page through four different passes, adding one color at each pass to create the needed results, while others place all the colors onto a special belt and then transfer them to the page in one pass. In some cases, the printer uses four separate toner cartridges and four lasers for the four toner colors, and in others the printer simply lays down one color after the other on the same drum, cleaning after each of four passes per page.

The heated roller produces enough heat to melt some types of plastic media, particularly overhead transparency materials. This could damage your laser printer (and void your warranty), so make sure you're printing on transparencies designed for laser printers!

complete, the printer ejects the printed copy and the process begins again with the physical and electrical cleaning of the printer.

The Electronic Side of the Process

When you click the Print button in an application, several things happen. First, the CPU processes your request and sends a print job to an area of memory called the print spooler. The print spooler enables you to queue up multiple print jobs that the printer will handle sequentially. Next, Windows sends the first print job to the printer. That's your first potential bottleneck—if it's a big job, the OS has to dole out a piece at a time, and you'll see the little printer icon in the notification area at the bottom right of your screen. Once the printer icon goes away, you know the print queue is empty—all jobs have gone to the printer.

Once the printer receives some or all of a print job, the hardware of the printer takes over and processes the image. That's your second potential bottleneck, and it has multiple components.

Raster Images

Impact printers transfer data to the printer one character or one line at a time, whereas laser printers transfer entire pages at a time to the printer. A laser printer generates a raster image (a pattern of dots) of the page representing what the final product should look like. It uses a device (the laser) to "paint" a raster image on the photosensitive drum. Because a laser printer has to paint the entire surface of the photosensitive drum before it can begin to transfer the image to paper, it processes the image one page at a time.

A laser printer uses a chip called the raster image processor (RIP) to translate the raster image sent to the printer into commands to the laser. The RIP takes the digital information about fonts and graphics and converts it to a rasterized image made up of dots that can then be printed. An inkjet printer also has a RIP, but it's part of the software driver instead of onboard hardware circuitry. The RIP needs memory (RAM) to store the data that it must process. A laser printer must have enough memory to process an entire page. Some images that require high resolutions require more memory. Insufficient memory to process the image will usually be indicated by a memory overflow ("MEM OVERFLOW") error. If you get a memory overflow error, try reducing the resolution, printing smaller graphics, or turning off RET (see the following section for the last option). Of course, the best solution to a memory overflow error is simply to add more RAM to the laser printer.

Do not assume that every error with the word *memory* in it can be fixed simply by adding more RAM to the printer. Just as adding more RAM chips will not solve every conventional PC memory problem, adding more RAM will not solve every laser printer memory problem. The message "21 ERROR" on an HP LaserJet, for example, indicates that "the printer is unable to process very complex data fast enough for the print engine." This means that the data is simply too complex for the RIP to handle. Adding more memory would *not* solve this problem; it would only make your wallet lighter. The only answer in this case is to reduce the complexity of the

Tech Tip

Inkjet RIPs

Inkjet printers use RIPs as well, but they're written into the device drivers instead of the onboard programming. You can also buy third-party RIPs that can improve the image quality of your printouts; for an example, see www.colorbytesoftware.com.

page image (that is, fewer fonts, less formatting, reduced graphics resolution, and so on).

Resolution

Laser printers can print at different resolutions, just as monitors can display different resolutions. The maximum resolution that a laser printer can handle is determined by its physical characteristics. Laser printer resolution is expressed in dots per inch (dpi). Common resolutions are 600 × 600 dpi or 1200 × 1200 dpi. The first number, the horizontal resolution, is determined by how fine a focus can be achieved by the laser. The second number is determined by the smallest increment by which the drum can be turned. Higher resolutions produce higher quality output, but keep in mind that higher resolutions also require more memory. In some instances, complex images can be printed only at lower resolutions because of their high-memory demands. Even printing at 300 dpi, laser printers produce far better quality than dot-matrix printers because of resolution enhancement technology (RET).

RET enables the printer to insert smaller dots among the characters, smoothing out the jagged curves that are typical of printers that do not use RET (Figure A.5). Using RET enables laser printers to output high-quality print jobs, but it also requires a portion of the printer's RAM. If you get a MEM OVERFLOW error, sometimes disabling RET will free up enough memory to complete the print job.

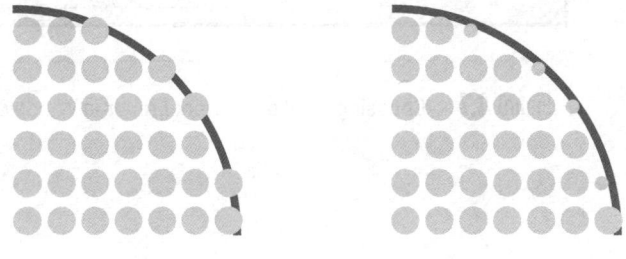

● **Figure A.5** RET fills in gaps with smaller dots to smooth out jagged characters.

■ Installing a Printer in Windows

You need to take a moment to understand how Windows 2000 and Windows XP handle printing, and then you'll see how to install, configure, and troubleshoot printers in these operating systems.

To Windows 2000/XP, a "printer" is not a physical device; it is a *program* that controls one or more physical printers. The *physical* printer is called a "print device" to Windows (although I continue to use the term "printer" for most purposes, just like almost every tech on the planet). Printer drivers and a spooler are still present, but in Windows 2000/XP they are integrated into the printer itself (Figure A.6). This arrangement gives Windows 2000/XP amazing flexibility. For example, one printer can support multiple print devices, enabling a system to act as a print server. If one print device goes down, the printer automatically redirects the output to a working print device.

The general installation, configuration, and troubleshooting issues are basically identical in Windows 2000 and Windows XP. Here's a review of a typical Windows printer installation. I'll mention the trivial differences between Windows 2000 and XP as I go along.

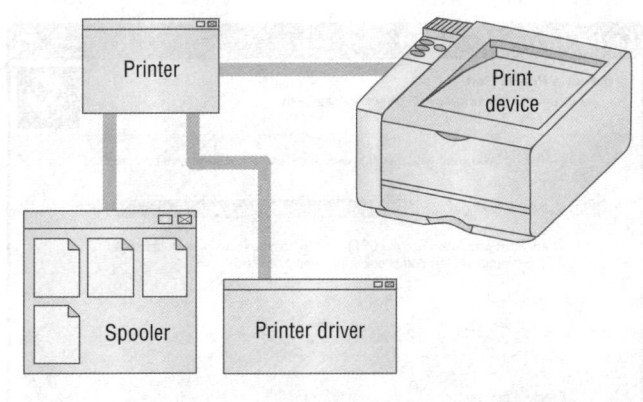

● **Figure A.6** Printer driver and spooler in Windows 2000/XP

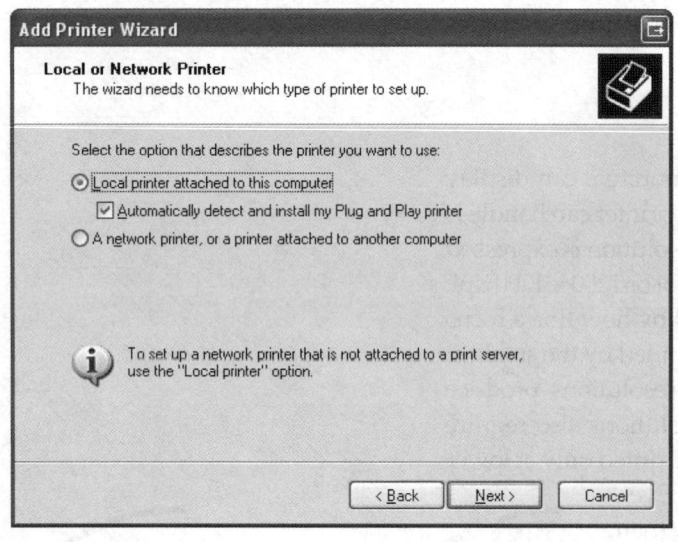

Figure A.7 Choosing local or network printer in Windows XP

Setting Up Printers

Setting up a printer is so easy that it's almost scary. Most printers are plug and play, so installing a printer is reduced to simply plugging it in and loading the driver if needed. If the system does not detect the printer or if the printer is not plug and play, click Start | Printers and Faxes in Windows XP to open the Printers applet; in Windows 2000, click Start | Settings | Printers. The icon for this applet can also be found in the Control Panel.

As you might guess, you install a new printer by clicking the Add Printer icon (somehow Microsoft has managed to leave the name of this applet unchanged through all Windows versions since 9*x*). This starts the Add Printer Wizard. After a pleasant intro screen, you must choose to install either a printer plugged directly into your system or a network printer (Figure A.7). You also have the *Automatically detect and install my Plug and Play printer* option, which you can use in many cases when installing a USB printer.

If you choose a local printer, the applet next asks you to select a port (Figure A.8); select the one where you installed the new printer. Once you select the port, Windows asks you to specify the type of printer, either by selecting the type from the list or using the Have Disk option, just as you would for any other device (Figure A.9). Note the handy Windows Update button, which you can use to get the latest printer driver from the Internet. When you click Next on this screen, Windows installs the printer.

Figure A.10 shows a typical Windows XP Printers and Faxes screen on a system with one printer installed. Note the small check mark in the icon's corner; this shows that the device is the default printer. If you have multiple

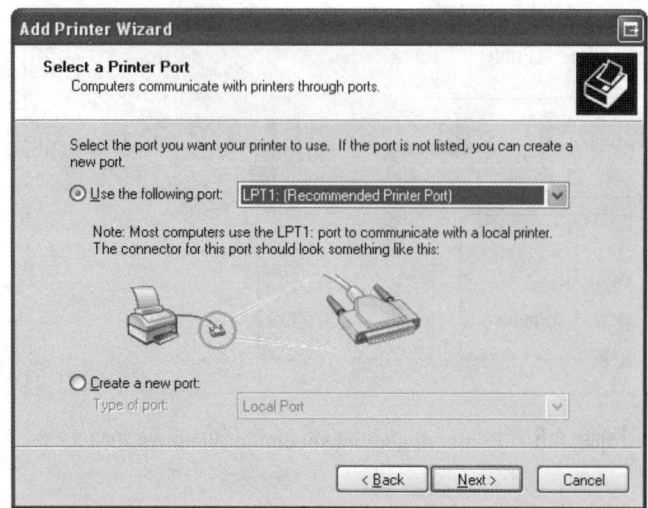

Figure A.8 Selecting a port in Windows XP

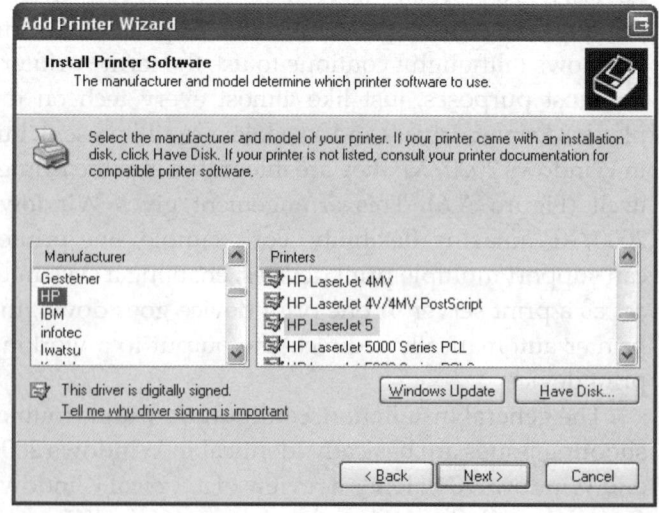

Figure A.9 Selecting a printer model/driver in Windows XP

printers, you can change the default printer by selecting the printer's properties and checking Make Default Printer.

In addition to the regular driver installation outlined previously, some installations use printer emulation. *Printer emulation* simply means using a substitute printer driver for a printer, as opposed to using one made exclusively for that printer. You'll run into printer emulation in two circumstances. First, some new printers do not come with their own drivers. They instead emulate a well-known printer (such as an HP LaserJet 4) and run perfectly well on that printer driver. Second, you may see emulation in the "I don't have the right driver!" scenario. I keep about three different HP LaserJet and Epson inkjet printers installed on my PC as I know that with these printer drivers, I can print to almost any printer. Some printers may require you to set them into an *emulation mode* to handle a driver other than their native one.

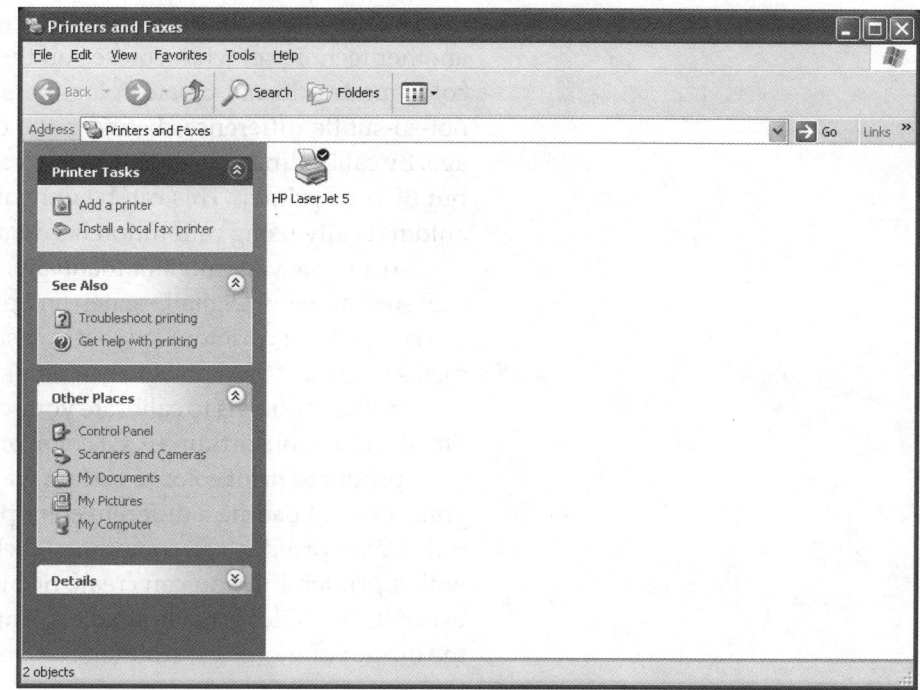

● **Figure A.10**   Installed default printer in the Printers and Faxes applet

Optimizing Print Performance

Although a quality printer is the first step toward quality output, your output relies on factors other than the printer itself. What you see on the screen may not match what comes out of the printer, so calibration is important. Using the wrong type of paper can result in less than acceptable printed documents. Configuring the printer driver and spool settings can also affect your print jobs.

Calibration

If you've ever tweaked that digital photograph so it looks perfect on screen, only to discover that the final printout was darker than you had hoped, consider calibrating your monitor. Calibration matches the print output of your printer to the visual output on your monitor and governs that through software. All three parts need to be set up properly for you to print what you see consistently.

Computer monitors output in RGB—that is, they compose colors using red, green, and blue pixels, as discussed in Chapter 15, "Understanding Video"—while printers mix their colors differently to arrive at their output. For example, the CMYK method composes colors from cyan (blue), magenta (red), yellow, and black.

Tech Tip

Readme Files

You've seen how to get your system to recognize a printer, but what do you do when you add a brand-new printer? Like most peripherals, the printer will include an installation CD-ROM that contains various useful files. One of the most important, but least used, tools on this CD-ROM is the Readme file. This file, generally in TXT format, contains the absolute latest information on any idiosyncrasies, problems, or incompatibilities related to your printer or printer driver. Usually, you can find it in the root folder of the installation CD-ROM, although many printer drivers install the Readme file on your hard drive, so you can access it from the Start menu. The rule here is read first to avoid a headache later!

The upshot of all this is that the printer tries to output using CMYK (or another technique) what you see on the screen using RGB. Because the two color modes do not create color the same way, you see color shifts and not-so-subtle differences between the onscreen image and the printed image. By calibrating your monitor, you can adjust the setting to match the output of your printer. This can be done manually through "eyeballing" it or automatically using calibration hardware.

To calibrate your monitor manually, obtain a test image from the Web (try sites such as www.DigitalDog.net) and print it out. If you have a good eye, you can compare this printout to what you see on the screen and make the adjustments manually through your monitor's controls or display settings.

Another option is to calibrate your printer through the use of an International Color Consortium (ICC) color profile, a preference file that instructs your printer to print colors a certain way—for example, to match what is on your screen. Loading a different color profile results in a different color output. Color profiles are sometimes included on the installation CD-ROM with a printer, but you can create or purchase custom profiles as well. The use of ICC profiles is not limited to printers; you can also use them to control the output of monitors, scanners, or even digital cameras.

■ Troubleshooting Printers

As easy as printers are to set up, they are equally robust at running, assuming that you install the proper drivers and keep the printer well maintained. But printer errors do occasionally develop. Take a look at the most common print problems with Windows 2000/XP as well as problems that crop up with specific printer types.

General Troubleshooting Issues

Printers of all stripes share some common problems, such as print jobs that don't go, strangely sized prints, and misalignment. Other issues include consumables, sharing multiple printers, and crashing on power-up. Let's take a look at these general troubleshooting issues, but start with a recap of the tools of the trade.

Tools of the Trade

Before you jump in and start to work on a printer that's giving you fits, you'll need some tools. You can use the standard computer tech tools in your toolkit, plus a couple of printer-specific devices. Here are some that will come in handy:

- A multimeter for troubleshooting electrical problems such as faulty wall outlets

- Various cleaning solutions, such as denatured alcohol

- An extension magnet for grabbing loose screws in tight spaces and cleaning up iron-based toner

- An optical disc or USB thumb drive with test patterns for checking print quality

- Your trusty screwdriver—both a Phillips-head and flat-head because if you bring just one kind, it's a sure bet that you'll need the other

Print Job Never Prints

If you click Print but nothing comes out of the printer, first check all the obvious possibilities. Is the printer on? Is it connected? Is it online? Does it have paper? Assuming the printer is in good order, it's time to look at the spooler. You can see the spooler status either by double-clicking the printer's icon in the Printers applet or by double-clicking the tiny printer icon in the notification area if it's present. If you're having a problem, the printer icon will almost always be there. Figure A.11 shows the print spooler open.

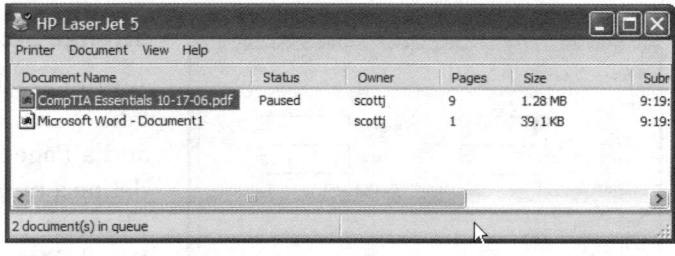

● **Figure A.11**   Print spooler

Print spoolers can easily overflow or become corrupt due to a lack of disk space, too many print jobs, or one of a thousand other factors. The status window shows all of the pending print jobs and enables you to delete, start, or pause jobs. I usually just delete the affected print job(s) and try again.

Print spoolers are handy. If the printer goes down, you can just leave the print jobs in the spooler until the printer comes back online. Some versions of Windows require you to select Resume Printing manually, but others will automatically continue the print job(s). If you have a printer that isn't coming on anytime soon, you can simply delete the print job in the spooler window and try another printer.

If you have problems with the print spooler, you can get around it by changing your print spool settings. Go into the Printers and Faxes applet, right-click the icon of the printer in question, and choose Properties. In the resulting Properties window (see Figure A.12), choose the *Print directly to the printer* radio button and click OK; then try sending your print job again. Note that this window also offers you the choice of printing immediately—that is, starting to print pages as soon as the spooler has enough information to feed to the printer—or holding off on printing until the entire job is spooled.

Another possible cause for a stalled print job is that the printer is simply waiting for the correct paper! Laser printers in particular have settings that tell them what size paper is in their standard paper tray or trays. If the application sending a print job specifies a different paper size—for example, it wants to print a standard No. 10 envelope, or perhaps a legal sheet, but the standard paper tray holds only 8.5 × 11 letter paper—the printer will usually pause and hold up the queue until someone switches out the tray or manually feeds the type of paper that's required for this print job. You can usually override this by pressing the OK or GO button on the printer or by manually feeding any size paper you want just to clear out the print queue, but the printer is doing its best to print the job properly.

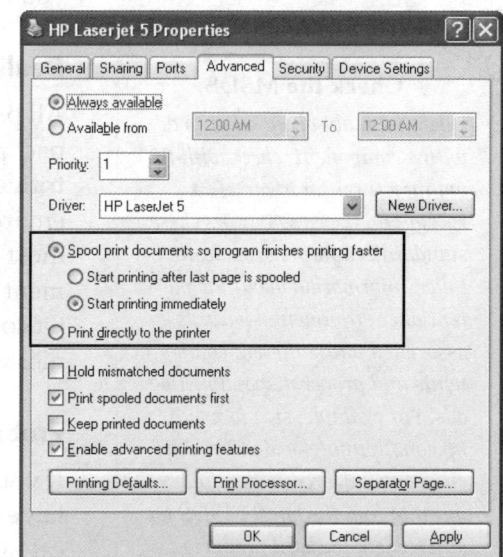

● **Figure A.12**   Print spool settings

The printer's default paper tray and paper size options will differ greatly depending on the printer type and model. To find these settings, go into the printer's Properties window from the Printers and Faxes applet, and then select the Device Settings tab. This list of settings includes Form To Tray Assignment, where you can specify which tray (in the case of a printer with multiple paper trays) holds which size paper.

Strange Sizes

A print job that comes out a strange size usually points to a user mistake in setting up the print job. All applications have a Print command and a Page Setup interface. The Page Setup interface enables you to define a number of print options, which vary from application to application. Figure A.13 shows the Page Setup options for Microsoft Word. Make sure the page is set up properly before you blame the printer for a problem.

If you know the page is set up correctly, recheck the printer drivers. If necessary, uninstall and reinstall the printer drivers. If the problem persists, you may have a serious problem with the printer's print engine, but that comes up as a likely answer only when you continually get the same strangely sized printouts using a number of different applications.

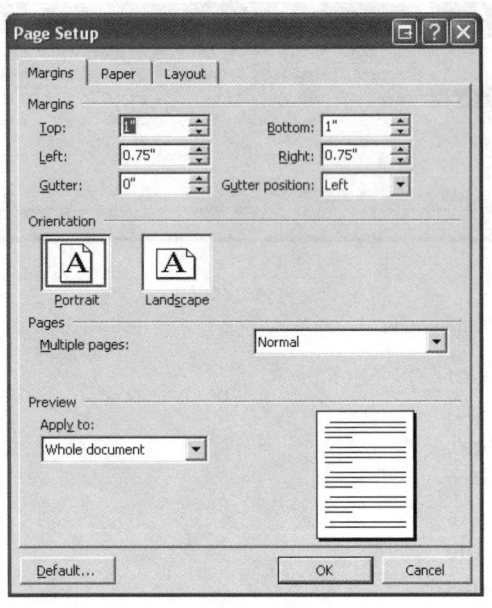

● **Figure A.13** Page Setup options for Microsoft Word

Misaligned or Garbage Prints

Misaligned or garbage printouts invariably point to a corrupted or incorrect driver. Make sure you're using the right driver (it's hard to mess this up, but not impossible) and then uninstall and reinstall the printer driver. If the problem persists, you may be asking the printer to do something it cannot do. For example, you may be printing to a PostScript printer with a PCL driver. Check the printer type to verify that you haven't installed the wrong type of driver for that printer!

Dealing with Consumables

All printers tend to generate a lot of trash in the form of consumables. Impact printers use paper and ribbons, inkjet printers use paper and ink cartridges, and laser printers use paper and toner cartridges. In today's environmentally sensitive world, many laws regulate the proper disposal of most printer components. Be sure to check with the local sanitation department or disposal services company before throwing away any component. Of course, you should never throw away toner cartridges—certain companies will *pay* for used cartridges!

Problems Sharing Multiple Printers

If you want to use multiple printers attached to the same parallel port, you have to use a switch box. Laser printers should never be used with mechanical switch boxes. Mechanical switch boxes create power surges that can damage your printer. If you must use a switch box, use a box that switches between printers electronically and has built-in surge protection.

Tech Tip

Check the MSDS

When in doubt about what to do with a component, check with the manufacturer for a material safety data sheet (MSDS) *. These standardized forms provide detailed information about the potential environmental hazards associated with different components and proper disposal methods. For example, surf to www.hp.com/hpinfo/globalcitizenship/environment/productdata/index.html to find the latest MSDS for all Hewlett-Packard products. This isn't just a printer issue—you can find an MSDS for most PC components.*

Crashes on Power-up

Both laser printers and PCs require more power during their initial power-up (the POST on a PC and the warm-up on a laser printer) than once they are running. Hewlett Packard recommends a *reverse power-up*. Turn on the laser printer first and allow it to finish its warm-up before turning on the PC. This avoids having two devices drawing their peak loads simultaneously.

Troubleshooting Dot-Matrix Printers

Impact printers require regular maintenance but will run forever as long as you're diligent. Keep the platen (the roller or plate on which the pins impact) clean and the printhead clean with denatured alcohol. Be sure to lubricate gears and pulleys according to the manufacturer's specifications. Never lubricate the printhead, however, because the lubricant will smear and stain the paper.

Bad-Looking Text

White bars going through the text point to a dirty or damaged printhead. Try cleaning the printhead with a little denatured alcohol. If the problem persists, replace the printhead. Printheads for most printers are readily available from the manufacturer or from companies that rebuild them. If the characters look chopped off at the top or bottom, the printhead probably needs to be adjusted. Refer to the manufacturer's instructions for proper adjustment.

Bad-Looking Page

If the page is covered with dots and small smudges—the "pepper look"—the platen is dirty. Clean the platen with denatured alcohol. If the image is faded, and you know the ribbon is good, try adjusting the printhead closer to the platen. If the image is okay on one side of the paper but fades as you move to the other, the platen is out of adjustment. Platens are generally difficult to adjust, so your best plan is to take it to the manufacturer's local warranty/repair center.

Troubleshooting Inkjet Printers

Inkjet printers are reliable devices that require little maintenance as long as they are used within their design parameters (high-use machines will require more intensive maintenance). Because of the low price of these printers, manufacturers know that people don't want to spend a lot of money keeping them running. If you perform even the most basic maintenance tasks, they will soldier on for years without a whimper. Inkjets generally have built-in maintenance programs that you should run from time to time to keep your inkjet in good operating order.

Inkjet Printer Maintenance

Inkjet printers don't get nearly as dirty as laser printers, and most manufacturers do not recommend periodic cleaning. Unless your manufacturer explicitly tells you to do so, don't vacuum an inkjet. Inkjets generally do not have maintenance kits, but most inkjet printers come with extensive

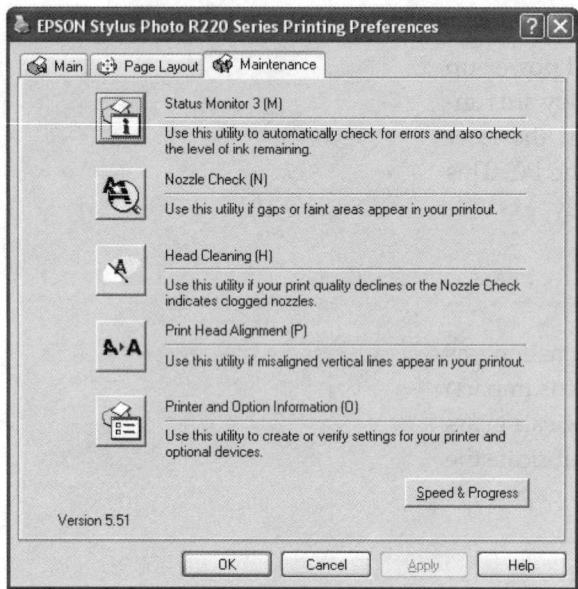

• **Figure A.14**   Inkjet printer maintenance screen

All inkjet inks are water-based, so water works better than alcohol to clean them up.

Cleaning the heads on an inkjet printer is sometimes necessary, but I don't recommend that you do it on a regular basis as preventive maintenance. The head-cleaning process uses up a lot of that very expensive inkjet ink—so do this only when a printing problem seems to indicate clogged or dirty print heads!

Before you service a laser printer, always, *always* turn it off and unplug it! Don't expose yourself to the very dangerous high voltages found inside these machines.

maintenance software (Figure A.14). Usually, the hardest part of using this software is finding it in the first place. Look for an option in Printing Preferences, a selection on the Start menu, or an icon on your desktop. Don't worry—it's there!

When you first set up an inkjet printer, it normally instructs you to perform a routine to align the printheads properly, wherein you print out a page and select from sets of numbered lines. If this isn't done, the print quality will show it, but the good news is that you can perform this procedure at any time. If a printer is moved or dropped or it's just been working away untended for a while, it's often worth running the alignment routine.

Inkjet Problems

Did I say that you never should clean an inkjet? Well, that may be true for the printer itself, but there is one part of your printer that will benefit from an occasional cleaning: the inkjet's printer head nozzles. The nozzles are the tiny pipes that squirt the ink onto the paper. A common problem with inkjet printers is the tendency for the ink inside the nozzles to dry out when not used even for a relatively short time, blocking any ink from exiting. If your printer is telling Windows that it's printing and it's feeding paper through, but either nothing is coming out (usually the case if you're just printing black text), or only certain colors are printing, the culprit is almost certainly dried ink clogging the nozzles.

Every inkjet has a different procedure for cleaning the printhead nozzles. On older inkjets, you usually have to press buttons on the printer to start a maintenance program. On more modern inkjets, you can access the head-cleaning maintenance program from Windows.

Another problem that sometimes arises is the dreaded multi-sheet paper grab. This is often not actually your printer's fault—humidity can cause sheets of paper to cling to each other—but sometimes the culprit is an overheated printer, so if you've been cranking out a lot of documents without stopping, try giving the printer a bit of a coffee break. Also, fan the sheets of the paper stack before inserting it into the paper tray.

Finally, in the maintenance area where the printheads park is usually a small tank or tray to catch excess ink from the cleaning process. If the printer has one, check to see how full it is. If this tray overflows onto the main board or even the power supply, it will kill your printer. If you discover that it's about to overflow, you can remove excess ink by inserting a twisted paper towel into the tank to soak up some of the ink. It is advisable to wear latex or vinyl gloves while doing this. Clean up any spilled ink with a paper towel dampened with distilled water.

Troubleshooting Laser Printers

Quite a few problems can arise with laser printers, but before getting into those details, you need to review some recommended procedures for *avoiding* those problems.

Laser Printer Maintenance

Unlike PC maintenance, laser printer maintenance follows a fairly well established procedure. Follow these steps to ensure a long, healthy life for your system.

Keep It Clean Laser printers are quite robust as a rule. A good cleaning every time you replace the toner cartridge will help that printer last for many years. I know of many examples of original HP LaserJet I printers continuing to run perfectly after a dozen or more years of operation. The secret is that they were kept immaculately clean.

Your laser printer gets dirty in two ways: Excess toner, over time, will slowly coat the entire printer. Paper dust, sometimes called *paper dander,* tends to build up where the paper is bent around rollers or where pickup rollers grab paper. Unlike (black) toner, paper dust is easy to see and is usually a good indicator that a printer needs to be cleaned. Usually, a thorough cleaning using a can of pressurized air to blow out the printer is the best cleaning you can do. It's best to do this outdoors, or you may end up looking like one of those chimney sweeps from *Mary Poppins*! If you must clean a printer indoors, use a special low-static vacuum designed especially for electronic components (Figure A.15).

● **Figure A.15** Low-static vacuum

Every laser printer has its own unique cleaning method, but one little area tends to be skipped in the included cleaning instructions. Every laser printer has a number of rubber guide rollers through which the paper is run during the print process. These little rollers tend to pick up dirt and paper dust over time, making them slip and jam paper. They are easily cleaned with a small amount of 90 percent or better alcohol on a fibrous cleaning towel. The alcohol will remove the debris and any dead rubber. You can also give the rollers and separator pads a textured surface that will restore their feeding properties by rubbing them with a little alcohol on a non-metallic scouring pad.

If you're ready to get specific, get the printer's service manual. Almost every printer manufacturer sells these; they are a key source for information on how to keep a printer clean and running. Sadly, not all printer manufacturers provide these, but most do. While you're at it, see if the manufacturer has a Quick Reference Guide; these can be very handy for most printer problems!

Finally, be aware that Hewlett Packard sells maintenance kits for most of its laser printers. These are sets of replacement parts for the parts most likely to wear out on each particular type of HP LaserJet. Although their use is not required to maintain warranty coverage, using these kits when prescribed by HP helps to assure the continuing reliability of your LaserJet.

> ⚠ The photosensitive drum, usually contained in the toner cartridge, can be wiped clean if it becomes dirty, but be very careful if you do so! If the drum becomes scratched, the scratch will appear on every page printed from that point on. The only repair in the event of a scratch is to replace the toner cartridge.

Periodic Maintenance Although keeping the printer clean is critical to its health and well being, every laser printer has certain components that will need to be replaced periodically. Your ultimate source for determining the parts that need to be replaced (and when to replace them) is the printer manufacturer. Following the manufacturer's maintenance guidelines will help to ensure years of trouble-free, dependable printing from your laser printer.

Failure of the thermal fuse (used to keep the fuser from overheating) can necessitate replacing the fuser assembly. Some machines contain more than one thermal fuse. As always, follow the manufacturer's recommendations. Many manufacturers have kits that alert you to replace the fuser unit and key rollers and guides at predetermined page counts with an alarm code.

⚠ The fuser assembly operates at 200 to 300 degrees Fahrenheit, so always allow time for this component to cool down before you attempt to clean it.

Some ozone filters may be cleaned with a vacuum and some can only be replaced—follow the manufacturer's recommendation. The fuser assembly may be cleaned with 90 percent or better denatured alcohol. Check the heat roller (the Teflon coated one with the light bulb inside) for pits and scratches. If you see surface damage on the rollers, replace the fuser unit.

Most printers will give you an error code when the fuser is damaged or overheating and needs to be replaced; others will produce the error code at a preset copy count as a preventive maintenance measure. Again, follow the manufacturer's recommendations.

The transfer corona can be cleaned with a 90 percent denatured alcohol solution on a cotton swab. If the wire is broken, you can replace it; many just snap in or are held in by a couple of screws. Paper guides can also be cleaned with alcohol on a fibrous towel.

Laser Printer Problems

Laser printers usually manifest problems by creating poor output. One of the most important tests you can do on any printer, not just a laser printer, is called a *diagnostic print page* or an *engine test page*. This is done by either holding down the On Line button as the printer is started or using the printer's maintenance software.

Blank Paper   Blank sheets of paper usually mean the printer is out of toner. If the printer does have toner and nothing prints, print a diagnostic print page. If that is also blank, remove the toner cartridge and look at the imaging drum inside. If the image is still there, you know the transfer corona or the high-voltage power supply has failed. Check the printer's maintenance guide to see how to focus on the bad part and replace it.

Dirty Printouts   If the fusing mechanism gets dirty in a laser printer, it will leave a light dusting of toner all over the paper, particularly on the back of the page. When you see toner speckles on your printouts, you should get the printer cleaned.

Ghosting   Ghost images sometimes appear at regular intervals on the printed page. This can be caused either because the imaging drum has not fully discharged (and is picking up toner from a previous image) or because a previous image has used up so much toner that either the supply of charged toner is insufficient or the toner has not been adequately charged. Sometimes it can also be caused by a worn-out cleaning blade that isn't removing the toner from the drum.

Light Ghosting versus Dark Ghosting   A variety of problems can cause both light and dark ghosting, but the most common source of light ghosting is "developer starvation." If you ask a laser printer to print an extremely dark or complex image, it can use up so much toner that the toner cartridge will not be able to charge enough toner to print the next image. The proper solution is to use less toner. You can fix ghosting problems in the following ways:

- Lower the resolution of the page (print at 300 dpi instead of 600 dpi).
- Use a different pattern.
- Avoid 50 percent grayscale and "dot-on/dot-off patterns."

- Change the layout so that grayscale patterns do not follow black areas.
- Make dark patterns lighter and light patterns darker.
- Print in landscape orientation.
- Adjust print density and RET settings.
- Print a completely blank page immediately prior to the page with the ghosting image, as part of the same print job.

In addition to these possibilities, low temperature and low humidity can aggravate ghosting problems. Check your users' manual for environmental recommendations. Dark ghosting can sometimes be caused by a damaged drum. It may be fixed by replacing the toner cartridge. Light ghosting would *not* be solved in this way. Switching other components will not usually affect ghosting problems because they are a side effect of the entire printing process.

Vertical White Lines   Vertical white lines are usually due to a clogged toner preventing the proper dispersion of toner on the drum. Try shaking the toner cartridge to dislodge the clog. If that doesn't work, replace the toner cartridge.

Blotchy Print   This is most commonly due to uneven dispersion of toner, especially if the toner is low. Try shaking the toner from side to side and then try to print. Also be sure that the printer is sitting level. Finally, make sure the paper is not wet in spots. If the blotches are in a regular order, check the fusing rollers and the photosensitive drum for any foreign objects.

Spotty Print   If the spots appear at regular intervals, the drum may be damaged or some toner may be stuck to the fuser rollers. Try wiping off the fuser rollers. Check the drum for damage. If the drum is damaged, get a new toner cartridge.

Embossed Effect   If your prints are getting an embossed effect (like putting a penny under a piece of paper and rubbing it with a lead pencil), there is almost certainly a foreign object on a roller. Use 90 percent denatured alcohol or regular water with a soft cloth to try to remove it. If the foreign object is on the photosensitive drum, you're going to have to use a new toner cartridge. An embossed effect can also be caused by the contrast control being set too high. The contrast control is actually a knob on the inside of the unit (sometimes accessible from the outside, on older models). Check your manual for the specific location.

Incomplete Characters   Incompletely printed characters on laser-printed transparencies can sometimes be corrected by adjusting the print density. Be extremely careful to use only materials approved for use in laser printers.

Creased Pages   Laser printers have up to four rollers. In addition to the heat and pressure rollers of the fuser assembly, other rollers move the paper from the source tray to the output tray. These rollers crease the paper to avoid curling that would cause paper jams in the printer. If the creases are noticeable, try using a different paper type. Cotton bond paper is usually more susceptible to noticeable creasing than other bonds. You might also try sending the output to the face-up tray, which avoids one roller. There is no hardware solution to this problem; it is simply a side effect of the process.

Paper Jams   Every printer jams now and then. If you get a jam, always refer first to the manufacturer's jam removal procedure. It is simply too easy to damage a printer by pulling on the jammed paper! If the printer reports a jam but there's no paper inside, you've almost certainly got a problem with one of the many jam sensors or paper feed sensors inside the printer, and you'll need to take it to a repair center.

Pulling Multiple Sheets   If the printer grabs multiple sheets at a time, first try opening a new ream of paper and loading that in the printer. If that works, you've got a humidity problem. If the new paper angle doesn't work, check the separation pad on the printer. The separation pad is a small piece of cork or rubber that separates the sheets as they are pulled from the paper feed tray. A worn separation pad will look shiny and, well, *worn!* Most separation pads are easy to replace. Check out www.printerworks .com to see if you can replace yours.

Warped, Overprinted, or Poorly Formed Characters   Poorly formed characters can indicate either a problem with the paper (or other media) or a problem with the hardware.

Incorrect media cause a number of these types of problems. Avoid paper that is too rough or too smooth. Paper that is too rough interferes with the fusing of characters and their initial definition. If the paper is too smooth (like some coated papers, for example), it may feed improperly, causing distorted or overwritten characters. Even though you can purchase laser printer–specific paper, all laser printers will print acceptably on standard photocopy paper. Try to keep the paper from becoming too wet. Don't open a ream of paper until it is loaded into the printer. Always fan the paper before loading it into the printer, especially if the paper has been left out of the package for more than just a few days.

The durability of a well-maintained laser printer makes hardware a much rarer source of character printing problems, but you should be aware of the possibility. Fortunately, it is fairly easy to check the hardware. Most laser printers have a self-test function—often combined with a diagnostic printout but sometimes as a separate process. This self-test shows whether the laser printer can properly develop an image without actually having to send print commands from the PC. The self-test is quite handy to verify the question, "Is it the printer or is it the computer?" Run the self-test to check for connectivity and configuration problems.

Possible solutions include replacing the toner cartridge, especially if you hear popping noises; checking the cabling; and replacing the data cable, especially if it has bends or crimps, or if objects are resting on the cable. If you have a front menu panel, turn off advanced functions and high-speed settings to determine whether the advanced functions are either not working properly or not supported by your current software configuration (check your manuals for configuration information). If these solutions do not work, the problem may not be user serviceable. Contact an authorized service center.

%Systemroot%   The folder where the Windows boot files are located. This is by default the C:\Windows or C:\WINNT folder.

1.44 MB   The storage capacity of a typical 3.5-inch floppy disk.

10BaseT   An Ethernet LAN designed to run on UTP cabling. 10BaseT runs at 10 megabits per second. The maximum length for the cabling between the NIC and the hub (or switch, repeater, etc.) is 100 meters. It uses baseband signaling. No industry standard spelling exists, so sometimes written 10BASE-T or 10Base-T.

100BaseFX   An Ethernet LAN designed to run on fiber-optic cabling. It runs at 100 megabits per second and uses baseband signaling. No industry standard spelling exists, so sometimes written 100BASE-FX or 100Base-FX.

100BaseT   A generic term for an Ethernet cabling system designed to run at 100 megabits per second on UTP cabling. It uses baseband signaling. No industry standard spelling exists, so sometimes written 100BASE-T or 100Base-T.

1000BaseT   Gigabit Ethernet on UTP.

16-bit   Able to process 16 bits of data at a time.

16-bit ISA bus   Also called the **AT bus**. A bus technology introduced with the first AT computers.

2.1   Speaker setup consisting of two stereo speakers combined with a subwoofer.

24-bit color   Referred to as 24-bit or true color, using 3 bytes per pixel to represent a color image in a PC display. The 24 bits enable up to 16,777,216 colors to be stored and displayed.

286   Also called **80286.** Intel's second-generation processor. The 286 has a 16-bit external data bus and a 24-bit address bus. It was the first Intel processor to achieve 286 protected mode.

3.5-inch floppy drive format   All modern floppy disk drives are of this size; the format was introduced in 1986 and is one of the longest surviving pieces of computer hardware.

30-pin SIMM   An obsolete memory package that utilized 30 contacts to connect to the motherboard and required a whole bank to be filled before the memory was recognized.

34-pin ribbon cable   This type of cable is used by floppy disk drives.

386   Also called **80386**. Intel's third-generation processor. The 386 has a 32-bit external data bus and 32-bit address bus. It was Intel's first true 32-bit processor.

3-D sound   A generic term for making sounds emanate from all directions—i.e., *surround sound*—and for making sounds realistic. Popular in 3-D games and home theaters.

4.1   Four speakers and a subwoofer.

40-pin ribbon cable   This type of cable is used to attached EIDE devices (such as hard drives) or ATAPI devices (such as CD-ROMs) to a system.

486   Intel's fourth-generation CPU. Essentially an 80386 with a built-in cache and math coprocessor.

5.1   Four satellite speakers plus a center speaker and a subwoofer.

5.25-inch floppy drive format   The predecessor to the modern 3.5-inch floppy drive format; very rarely used currently.

50-pin ribbon cable   Also called a **Type A cable**. A type of ribbon cable used for connecting SCSI-1 and SCSI-2 devices.

68-pin ribbon cable   Also called a **P type cable**. There are two types of 68-pin ribbon cables: an obsolete Type B used in conjunction with a 50-pin Type A cable to connect early SCSI-2 devices and a P type that can be used singularly.

72-pin SIMM   An obsolete memory package that utilized 72 contacts to connect to the motherboard, replacing 30-pin SIMMs and eliminating some of the issues with banking.

8.3 naming system   A file naming convention that specified a maximum of eight characters for a filename, followed by a 3-character file extension. Has been replaced by LFN (Long Filename) support.

802.11b   A wireless networking standard that operates in the 2.4-GHz band with a theoretical maximum throughput of 11 Mbps.

8086/8088   The first generation of Intel processor used in IBM PCs. The 8086 and 8088 were identical with the exception of the external data bus—the 8086 had a 16-bit bus whereas the 8088 had an 8-bit bus.

80-wire cable   Also called a **D type cable**. Special type of cable used with some SCSI-3 devices that allows for devices to be hot-swapped. Alternatively, a ribbon cable used to connect ATA-66/100/133 hard drives to an ATA controller.

AC (alternating current)   A type of electricity in which the flow of electrons alternates direction, back and forth, in a circuit.

Access speed   The amount of time needed for the DRAM to supply the Northbridge with any requested data.

ACPI (advanced configuration and power interface)   A power management specification that far surpasses its predecessor, APM, by providing support for hot-swappable devices and better control of power modes.

Activation   The processes of confirming that an installed copy of a Microsoft product (most commonly Windows or a Microsoft Office application) is legitimate. Usually done at the end of software installation.

Active Directory   A form of directory service used in networks with Windows 2000 Server and Windows Server 2003 servers.

Active matrix   Also called **TFT (thin film transistor)**. A type of liquid crystal display that replaced the passive matrix technology used in most portable computer displays.

Active PFC (power factor correction)   Circuitry built into PC power supplies to reduce harmonics.

Active termination   A method for terminating fast/wide SCSI that uses voltage regulators in lieu of resistors.

ActiveSync (synchronization)   A term used to describe the synchronizing of files between a PDA and a desktop computer. ActiveSync is the name of the synchronization program that is used by Windows OS–based PDAs.

Address bus   The wires leading from the CPU to the memory controller chip (usually the Northbridge) that enable the CPU to address RAM. Also used by the CPU for I/O addressing. An internal electronic channel from the microprocessor to random access memory, along which the addresses of memory storage locations are transmitted. Like a post office box, each memory location has a distinct number or address; the address bus provides the means by which the microprocessor can access every location in memory.

Address space   The total amount of memory addresses that an address bus can contain.

Administrative Tools   A group of Control Panel applets, including Computer Management, Event Viewer, and Performance.

Administrator account   A user account, created when the OS is first installed, that is allowed complete, unfettered access to the system without restriction.

ADSL (asymmetric digital subscriber line)   A fully digital, dedicated connection to the telephone system that provides download speeds up to 9 Mbps and upload speeds of up to 1 Mbps.

Advanced Startup Options menu   A menu that can be reached during the boot process that offers advanced OS startup options, such as boot in Safe mode or boot into Last Known Good Configuration.

AGP (accelerated graphics port)   A 32/64-bit expansion slot designed by Intel specifically for video that runs at 66 MHz and yields a throughput of at least 254 Mbps. Later versions (2×, 4×, 8×) give substantially higher throughput.

AIX (Advanced Interactive Executive)   IBM's version of UNIX, which runs on 386 or better PCs.

Algorithm   A set of rules for solving a problem in a given number of steps.

ALU (arithmetic logic unit) The CPU logic circuits that perform basic arithmetic (add, subtract, multiply, and divide).

AMD (Advanced Micro Devices) CPU and chipset manufacturer that competes with Intel. Produces the popular Athlon and Duron processors.

AMI (American Megatrends, Inc) Major producer of BIOS software for motherboards, as well as many other computer-related components and software.

Amperes (amps or A) The unit of measure for amperage, or electrical current.

Amplifier A device that strengthens electrical signals, enabling them to travel further.

AMR (audio/modem riser) A proprietary slot used on some motherboards to provide a sound inference–free connection for modems, sound cards, and NICs.

Analog An analog device uses a physical quantity, such as length or voltage, to represent the value of a number. By contrast, digital storage relies on a coding system of numeric units.

Analog video Picture signals represented by a number of smooth transitions between video levels. Television signals are analog, as opposed to digital video signals, which assign a finite set of levels. Because computer signals are digital, analog video must be converted into a digital form before it can be shown on a computer screen.

ANSI (American National Standards Institute) Body responsible for standards such as ASCII.

ANSI character set The ANSI-standard character set, which defines 256 characters. The first 128 are ASCII, and the second group of 128 contain math and language symbols.

Anti-aliasing In computer imaging, a blending effect that smoothes sharp contrasts between two regions—e.g., jagged lines or different colors. This reduces the jagged edges of text or objects. In voice signal processing, it refers to the process of removing or smoothing out spurious frequencies from waveforms produced by converting digital signals back to analog.

Anti-static bag A bag made of anti-static plastic into which electronics are placed for temporary or long-term storage. Used to prevent electrostatic discharge.

Anti-static mat A special surface upon which electronics are laid. These mats come with a grounding connection designed to equalize electrical potential between a workbench and one or more electronic devices. Used to prevent electrostatic discharge.

Anti-static wrist strap A special device worn around the wrist with a grounding connection designed to equalize electrical potential between a technician and an electronic device. Used to prevent electrostatic discharge.

API (application programming interface) A software definition that describes operating system calls for application software; conventions defining how a service is invoked.

APM (advanced power management) The BIOS routines that enable the CPU to turn on and off selected peripherals.

Archive attribute An attribute of a file that shows whether the file has been backed up since the last change. Each time a file is opened, changed, or saved, the archive bit is turned on. Some types of backups will turn off this archive bit to indicate that a good backup of the file exists on tape.

Archive To copy programs and data onto a relatively inexpensive storage medium (disk, tape, etc.) for long-term retention.

ARP (address resolution protocol) A protocol in the TCP/IP suite used with the command-line utility of the same name to determine the MAC address that corresponds to a particular IP address.

ASCII (American Standard Code for Information Interchange) The industry-standard 8-bit characters used to define text characters, consisting of 96 upper and lowercase letters, plus 32 non-printing control characters, each of which is numbered. These numbers were designed to achieve uniformity among different computer devices for printing and the exchange of simple text documents.

ASD (Automatic Skip Driver) A utility for preventing "bad" drivers from running the next time that you boot your computer. This utility examines startup log files and removes problematic drivers from the boot process.

Aspect ratio   The ratio of width to height of an object. Standard television has a 4:3 aspect ratio.

ASR (Automated System Recovery)   A Windows XP tool designed to recover a badly corrupted Windows system; similar to ERD.

Asynchronous   Communication whereby the receiving devices must send an acknowledgment, or "ACK," to the sending unit to verify a piece of data has been sent.

AT (advanced technology)   The model name of the second-generation, 80286-based IBM computer. Many aspects of the AT, such as the BIOS, CMOS, and expansion bus, have become *de facto* standards in the PC industry. The physical organization of the components on the motherboard is called the AT form factor.

ATA (AT attachment)   A type of hard drive and controller. ATA was designed to replace the earlier ST506 and ESDI drives without requiring replacement of the AT BIOS—hence, AT attachment. These drives are more popularly known as IDE drives. (*See* IDE.) The **ATA/33** standard has drive transfer speeds up to 33 MBps; the **ATA/66** up to 66 MBps; the **ATA/100** up to 100 MBps; and the **ATA/133** up to 133 MBps. (*See* Ultra DMA.)

ATAPI (ATA packet interface)   A series of standards that enable mass storage devices other than hard drives to use the IDE/ATA controllers. Extremely popular with CD-ROM drives and removable media drives like the Iomega Zip drive. (*See* EIDE.)

Athlon   Name used for a popular series of CPUs manufactured by AMD.

ATTRIB.EXE   A command used to view the specific properties of a file; can also be used to modify or remove file properties, such as Read-Only, System, or Archive.

ATX (AT eXtended)   The popular motherboard form factor, which generally replaced the AT form factor.

ATX12V   A series of improvements to the original ATX standard for power supplies, including extra power connections and an increase of the ATX P1 power connector size from 20 pins to 24 pins.

Autodetection   The process through which new disks are automatically recognized by the BIOS.

AUTORUN.INF   A file included on some CD-ROMs that automatically launches a program or installation routine when the CD-ROM is inserted into a CD-ROM drive.

Award Software   Major producer of BIOS software for motherboards.

Back up   To save important data in a secondary location as a safety against loss of the primary data.

Backside bus   The set of wires that connect the CPU to Level 2 cache. First appearing in the Pentium Pro, most modern CPUs have a special backside bus. Some buses, such as that in the later Celeron processors (300A and beyond), run at the full speed of the CPU, whereas others run at a fraction. Earlier Pentium IIs, for example, had backside buses running at half the speed of the processor. *See also* frontside bus and EDB (external data bus).

Backup or Restore Wizard   A utility contained within Windows that allows a user to create system backups and set system restore points.

Bandwidth   A piece of the spectrum occupied by some form of signal, such as television, voice, fax data, etc. Signals require a certain size and location of bandwidth in order to be transmitted. The higher the bandwidth, the faster the signal transmission, allowing for a more complex signal such as audio or video. Because bandwidth is a limited space, when one user is occupying it, others must wait their turn. Bandwidth is also the capacity of a network to transmit a given amount of data during a given period.

Bank   The total number of SIMMs or DIMMs that can be accessed simultaneously by the chipset. The "width" of the external data bus divided by the "width" of the SIMM or DIMM sticks.

Baseband   Digital signaling that has only one signal (a single signal) on the cable at a time. The signals can only be in one of three states at one time: one, zero, and idle.

Baseline   Static image of a system's (or network's) performance when all elements are known to be working properly.

Basic disks   A hard drive partitioned in the "classic" way with a master boot record (MBR) and partition table. *See also* dynamic disks.

Baud   One analog cycle on a telephone line. In the early days of telephone data transmission, the baud rate was often analogous to bits per second. Due to advanced modulation of baud cycles as well as data compression, this is no longer true.

Beep codes   A series of audible tones produced by a motherboard during the POST. These tones identify whether the POST has completed successfully or whether some piece of system hardware is not working properly. Consult the manual for your particular motherboard for a specific list of beep codes.

Binary numbers   A number system with a base of 2, unlike the number systems most of us use which have bases of 10 (decimal numbers), 12 (measurement in feet and inches), and 60 (time). Binary numbers are preferred for computers for precision and economy. An electronic circuit that can detect the difference between two states (on–off, 0–1) is easier and more inexpensive to build than one that could detect the differences among ten states (0–9).

Biometric device   Hardware device used to support authentication, which works by scanning and remembering unique aspects of a user's various body parts (e.g., retina, iris, face, or fingerprint) using some form of sensing device such as a retinal scanner.

BIOS (basic input/output system)   Classically, the software routines burned onto the system ROM of a PC. More commonly seen as any software that directly controls a particular piece of hardware. A set of programs encoded in Read-Only Memory (ROM) on computers. These programs handle startup operations and low-level control of hardware such as disk drives, the keyboard, and monitor.

Bit   A bit is a single binary digit. Any device that can be in an on or off state.

Bit depth   The number of colors a video card is capable of producing. Common bit depths are 16-bit and 32-bit, representing 65,536 colors and 16.7 million colors, respectively.

Blu-ray Disc   An optical disc format that stores 25 or 50 GB of data, designed to be the replacement media for DVD. Competes with HD DVD.

Boot   To initiate an automatic routine that clears the memory, loads the operating system, and prepares the computer for use. The term is derived from "pull yourself up by your bootstraps." PCs must do that because RAM doesn't retain program instructions when power is turned off. A *cold boot* occurs when the PC is physically switched on. A *warm boot* loads a fresh OS without turning off the computer, lessening the strain on the electronic circuitry. To do a *warm* boot, press the CTRL-ALT-DELETE keys at the same time twice in rapid succession (the three-fingered salute).

Boot sector   The first sector on an PC hard drive or floppy disk, track 0. The boot-up software in ROM tells the computer to load whatever program is found there. If a system disk is read, the program in the boot record directs the computer to the root directory to load the operating system.

BOOT.INI   A text file used during the boot process that provides a list of all OSs currently installed and available for NTLDR. Also tells where each OS is located on the system.

Bootable disk   A disk that contains a functional operating system; can also be a floppy disk or CD-ROM.

BOOTLOG.TXT   A text file where information concerning the boot process is logged; useful when troubleshooting system boot errors and problems.

Bootstrap loader   A segment of code in a system's BIOS that scans for an operating system, looks specifically for a valid boot sector, and, when one is found, hands control over to the boot sector; then the bootstrap loader removes itself from memory.

bps (bits per second)   Measurement of how fast data is moved from one place to another. A 56K modem can move 56,000 bits per second.

Bridge   A device that connects two networks and passes traffic between them based only on the node address, so that traffic between nodes on one network does not appear on the other network. For example, an Ethernet bridge only looks at the Ethernet address. Bridges filter and forward packets based on MAC addresses and operate at Level 2 (Data Link layer) of the OSI seven-layer model.

Broadband   A type of signaling that sends multiple signals (channels) over the cable at the same time. The best example of broadband signaling is cable television. The zero, one, and idle states (*see* baseband) exist on multiple channels on the same cable. Also, broadband refers to high-speed, always-on communication links such as cable modems and DSL.

Broadcast A broadcast is a packet addressed to all machines. In TCP/IP, the general broadcast address is 255.255.255.255.

Browser A program specifically designed to retrieve, interpret, and display Web pages.

BSoD (Blue Screen of Death) The infamous error screen that appears when Windows encounters an unrecoverable error.

BTX A motherboard form factor designed as an improvement over ATX.

Buffer Electronic storage, usually DRAM, that holds data moving between two devices. Buffers are used in situations where one device may send or receive data faster or slower than the other device with which it is in communication.

Buffer underrun The inability of a source device to provide a CD-burner with a constant stream of data while burning a CD-R or CD-RW.

Bug A programming error that causes a program or a computer system to perform erratically, produce incorrect results, or crash. The term was coined when a real bug was found in one of the circuits of one of the first ENIAC computers.

Burn The process of writing data to a writable CD or DVD.

Bus A series of wires connecting two or more separate electronic devices, enabling those devices to communicate.

Bus topology A configuration wherein all computers connect to the network via a central bus cable.

Byte A unit of eight bits, the fundamental data unit of personal computers. Storing the equivalent of one character, the byte is also the basic unit of measurement for computer storage.

CAB files Short for cabinet files. These files are compressed and most commonly used during OS installation to store many smaller files, such as device drivers.

Cable modem A network device that enables a PC to connect to the Internet using RG-6 coaxial cabling (i.e., the same coax used for cable television). Capable of download speeds up to 1.5 megabits per second.

Cable tester Device that tests the continuity of cables. Some testers also test for electrical shorts, crossed wires, or other electrical characteristics.

Cache (disk) A special area of RAM that stores the data most frequently accessed from the hard drive. Cache memory can optimize the use of your systems.

Cache memory A special section of fast memory, usually built into the CPU, used by the onboard logic to store information most frequently accessed from RAM.

Caching The act of holding data in cache memory for faster access and use.

Card Generic term for anything that you can snap into an expansion slot.

Card services The uppermost level of PCMCIA services. The card services level recognizes the function of a particular PC Card and provides the specialized drivers necessary to make the card work.

CardBus 32-bit PC Cards that can support up to eight devices on each card. Electrically incompatible with earlier PC Cards (3.3 V versus 5 V).

Case The metal or plastic enclosure for the system unit.

CAT 3 Category 3 wire; a TIA/EIA standard for UTP wiring that can operate up to 20 megabits per second.

CAT 5 Category 5 wire; a TIA/EIA standard for UTP wiring that can operate up to 100 megabits per second.

CAT 5e Category 5e wire; a TIA/EIA standard for UTP wiring that can operate up to 1 gigabit per second.

CAT 6 Category 6 wire; a TIA/EIA standard for UTP wiring that can operate up to 10 gigabits per second.

Catastrophic failure Occurs when a component or whole system will not boot; usually related to a manufacturing defect of a component. Could also be caused by overheating and physical damage to computer components.

CCFL (cold cathode fluorescent lamp) A light technology used in LCDs and flatbed scanners. CCFLs use relatively little power for the amount of light they provide.

CD quality   CD-quality audio has a sample rate of 44.4 KHz and a bit rate of 128 bits.

CD-DA (CD-digital audio)   A special format used for early CD-ROMs and all audio CDs; divides data into variable length tracks. A good format to use for audio tracks but terrible for data due to lack of error checking.

CD-I   CD Interactive "green disk" format by Philips; designed to play compressed movies.

CD-R (compact disc recordable)   A type of CD technology that accepts a single "burn" but cannot be erased after that one burn.

CD-ROM (compact disc/read only memory)   A read-only compact storage disk for audio or video data. Recordable devices, such as CD-Rs, are updated versions of the older CD-ROM players. CD-ROMs are read using *CD-ROM drives*.

CD-RW (compact disc rewritable)   A type of CD technology that accepts multiple reads/writes like a hard drive.

Celeron   A lower-cost CPU based on Intel's Pentium CPUs.

Centronics connector   A connector commonly used with printers.

Chipset   Electronic chips, specially designed to work together, that handle all of the low-level functions of a PC. In the original PC the chipset consisted of close to 30 different chips; today, chipsets usually consist of one, two, or three separate chips embedded into a motherboard.

CHS (cylinder/heads/sectors per track)   The initials for the combination of the three critical geometries used to determine the size of a hard drive—cylinders, heads, and sectors per track.

Clean installation   An operating system installed on a fresh drive, following a reformat of that drive. A clean install is often the only way to correct a problem with a system when many of the crucial operating system files have become corrupted.

Cleaning kit   A set of tools used to clean a device or piece of media.

Client   A computer program that uses the services of another computer program. Software that extracts information from a server; your auto-dial phone is a client, and the phone company is its server. Also a machine that accesses shared resources on a server.

Client/server   A relationship in which client software obtains services from a server on behalf of a person.

Client/server application   An application that performs some or all of its processing on an application server rather than on the client. The client usually only receives the result of the processing.

Client/server network   A network that has dedicated server machines and client machines.

Clock cycle   A single charge to the clock wire of a CPU.

Clock multiplying CPU   A CPU that takes the incoming clock signal and multiples it inside the CPU to let the internal circuitry of the CPU run faster.

Clock speed   The speed at which a CPU executes instructions, measured in MHz or GHz. In modern CPUs, the internal speed is generally a multiple of the external speed. *See also* clock multiplying CPU.

Clock   An electronic circuit that uses a quartz crystal to generate evenly-spaced pulses at speeds of millions of cycles per second. These pulses are used to synchronize the flow of information through the computer's internal communication channels.

Cluster   The basic unit of storage on a floppy or hard disk. Two or more sectors are contained in a cluster. When Windows stores a file on disk, it writes those files into dozens or even hundreds of contiguous clusters. If there aren't enough contiguous open clusters available, the operating system finds the next open cluster and writes there, continuing this process until the entire file is saved. The FAT tracks how the files are distributed among the clusters on the disk.

CMD.COM   In Windows, the file that contains the command processor. Usually located in the C:\WINNT\system32 folder on a Windows PC.

CMOS (complementary metal-oxide semiconductor)   Originally, the type of non-volatile RAM that held information about the most basic parts of your PC such as hard drives, floppies, and amount of DRAM. Today, actual CMOS chips have been replaced by Flash-type non-volatile RAM. The information is the same, however, and is still called CMOS—even though it is now almost always stored on Flash RAM.

CNR (Communications and Network Riser)   A proprietary slot used on some motherboards to provide a sound inference–free connection for modems, sound cards, and NICs.

Coaxial cable   Cabling in which an internal conductor is surrounded by another, outer conductor, thus sharing the same axis.

Code   A set of symbols representing characters (e.g., ASCII code) or instructions in a computer program (a programmer writes *source* code, which must be translated into *executable* or *machine* code for the computer to use). Used colloquially as a verb, *to code* is to write computer code; and as a noun, "He writes clean/sloppy/bad code."

Codec (compressor/decompressor)   Software that compresses or decompresses media streams.

Collision   The result of two nodes transmitting at the same time on a multiple access network such as Ethernet. Both packets may be lost, or partial packets may result.

Collision domain   A set of Ethernet segments that receive all traffic generated by any node within those segments. Repeaters, amplifiers, and hubs do not create separate collision domains, but bridges, routers, and switches do.

COM port(s)   A system name that refers to the serial communications ports available on your computer. When used as a program extension, .COM indicates an executable program file limited to 64 KB.

Command   A request, typed from a terminal or embedded in a file, to perform an operation or to execute a particular program.

Command processor   The part of the operating system that accepts input from the user and displays any messages, such as confirmation and error messages.

Command prompt   A text prompt for entering commands.

Command-line interface   A user interface for an OS devoid of all graphical trappings; interfaces directly with the OS.

Communications program   A program that makes a computer act as a terminal to another computer.

Communications programs usually provide for file transfer between microcomputers and mainframes.

Compact Flash (CF)   One of the older but still popular flash media formats. Its interface uses a simplified PC Card bus, so it also supports I/O devices.

Component failure   Occurs when a system device fails due to manufacturing or some other type of defect.

Compression   The process of squeezing data to eliminate redundancies, allowing files to be stored or transmitted using less space.

Conditioning charger   A battery charger that contains intelligent circuitry that prevents portable computer batteries from being overcharged and damaged.

Connectionless protocol   A protocol that does not establish and verify a connection between the hosts before sending data—it just sends it and hopes for the best. This is faster than connection-oriented protocols. UDP is an example of a connectionless protocol.

Connection-oriented protocol   A protocol that establishes a connection between two hosts before transmitting data, and verifies receipt before closing the connection between the hosts. TCP is an example of a connection-oriented protocol.

Connectors   Small receptacles that are used to attach cables to a system. Common types of connectors include USB, PS/2, and DB-25.

Control Panel   A collection of Windows applets, or small programs, that can be used to configure various pieces of hardware and software in a system.

Controller card   A card adapter that connects devices, like a disk drive, to the main computer bus/motherboard.

Convergence   A measure of how sharply a single pixel appears on a CRT; a monitor with poor convergence would produce images that are not sharply defined.

Copy backup   A type of backup similar to Normal or Full, in that all selected files on a system are backed up. This type of backup *does not* change the archive bit of the files being backed up.

Core Name used for the family of Intel CPUs that succeeded the Pentium 4.

Counter Used to track data about a particular object when using the Performance console.

CPU (central processing unit) The "brain" of the computer. The microprocessor that handles the primary calculations for the computer. CPUs are known by names such as Pentium 4 and Athlon.

CPU fan The cooling unit that sits directly on and cools the CPU.

CPUID Information stored in a CPU that gives very detailed information about every aspect of the CPU including vendor, speed, and model. Many programs access and display this information.

CRC (cyclic redundancy check) A very accurate mathematical method that is used to check for errors in long streams of transmitted data. Before data is sent, the main computer uses the data to calculate a CRC value from the data's contents. If the receiver calculates a different CRC value from the received data, the data was corrupted during transmission and is resent. Ethernet packets have a CRC code.

C-RIMM (continuity RIMM) A passive device added to populate unused banks in a system that uses RAMBUS RIMMs.

Crossover cable Special UTP cable used to connect hubs or to connect network cards without a hub. Crossover cables reverse the sending and receiving wire pairs from one end to the other.

Crossover port Special port in a hub that crosses the sending and receiving wires, thus removing the need for a crossover cable to connect the hubs.

CRT (cathode ray tube) The tube of a monitor in which rays of electrons are beamed onto a phosphorescent screen to produce images. Also a shorthand way to describe a monitor that uses CRT rather than LCD technology.

CSMA/CD (carrier sense multiple access with collision detection) The access method Ethernet systems use in local area networking technologies enabling packets of data information to flow through the network ultimately to reach address locations.

Cylinder A single track on all the platters in a hard drive. Imagine a hard drive as a series of metal cans, nested one inside another; a single can would represent a cylinder.

Cyrix Company that made CPUs in direct competition with Intel and AMD. Bought by Via Technologies in 2000.

Daily backup Also called **daily copy backup**. A backup of all files that have been changed on that day without changing the archive bits of those files.

Daisy-chaining A method of connecting together several devices along a bus and managing the signals for each device.

DAT (digital audio tape) Higher storage capacity tape recording system that uses digital recording methods. Used for digital audio and video as well as data backups.

Data structure A term that is used interchangeably with the term "file system." *See also* file system.

DB connectors D-shaped connectors used for a variety of connections in the PC and networking world. Can be male (with prongs) or female (with holes) and have a varying number of pins or sockets. Also called D-sub or D-subminiature connectors.

DB-15 A two- or three-row DB connector (female) used for 10Base5 networks, MIDI/joysticks, and analog video.

DB-25 connector DB connector (female), commonly referred to as a parallel port connector.

DC (direct current) A type of electricity in which the flow of electrons is in a complete circle in one direction.

DDR SDRAM (double data rate SDRAM) A type of DRAM that makes two processes for every clock cycle. *See also* DRAM.

DDR2 SDRAM A type of SDRAM that sends four bits of data in every clock cycle. *See* double data rate SDRAM.

Debug To detect, trace, and eliminate errors in computer programs.

Decoder A tool used to decode data that has been encoded; for instance, a DVD decoder breaks down the code used to encrypt the data on a piece of DVD Video media.

Dedicated circuit   Circuit that runs from a breaker box to specific outlets.

Dedicated server   A machine that is not used for any client functions, only server functions.

Dedicated telephone line   A telephone line on a circuit that is always open, or connected. Dedicated telephone lines usually are not assigned numbers.

Default   A software function or operation which occurs automatically unless the user specifies something else.

Default gateway   In a TCP/IP network, the nearest router to a particular host. This router's IP address is part of the necessary TCP/IP configuration for communicating with multiple networks using IP.

Defragmentation (DEFRAG)   A procedure in which all the files on a hard disk are rewritten on disk so that all parts of each file reside in contiguous clusters. The result is an improvement of up to 75 percent of the disk's speed during retrieval operations.

Degauss   The procedure used to break up the electromagnetic fields that can build up on the cathode ray tube of a monitor; involves running a current through a wire loop. Most monitors feature a manual degaussing tool.

Desktop   A user's primary interface to the Windows operating system.

Desktop extenders   A type of portable computer that offers some of the features of a full-fledged desktop computer, but with a much smaller footprint and lower weight.

Desktop replacement   A type of portable computer that offers the same performance of a full-fledged desktop computer; these systems are normally very heavy to carry and often cost much more than the desktop systems they replace.

Detlog.txt   A log file created during the initial operating system installation that tracks the detection, query, and installation of all devices.

Device driver   A program used by the operating system to control communications between the computer and peripherals.

Device Manager   A utility that allows techs to examine and configure all the hardware and drivers in a Windows PC.

DHCP (dynamic host configuration protocol)   A protocol that enables a DHCP server to set TCP/IP settings automatically for a DHCP client.

Differential backup   Similar to an incremental backup. Backs up the files that have been changed since the last backup. This type of backup does not change the state of the archive bit.

Digitally signed driver   All drivers designed specifically for Windows 2000 and Windows XP are digitally signed, meaning they are tested to work stably with these operating systems.

DIMM (dual inline memory module)   A 32- or 64-bit type of DRAM packaging, similar to SIMMs, with the distinction that each side of each tab inserted into the system performs a separate function. DIMMs come in a variety of sizes, with 184- and 240-pin being the most common on desktop computers.

DIPP (dual inline pin package)   An early type of RAM package that featured two rows of exposed connecting pins; very fragile and difficult to install. DIPPs were replaced first with SIPPs and later with SIMMs and DIMMs.

DIR command   A command used in the command-line interface that displays the entire contents of the current working directory.

Directory   Another name for a folder.

DirectX   A set of APIs enabling programs to control multimedia, such as sound, video, and graphics. Used in Windows Vista to draw the Aero desktop.

Disk cache   A piece of DRAM, often integrated into a disk drive, that is used to store frequently accessed data in order to speed up access times.

Disk Cleanup   A series of utilities, built into Windows, that can help a user clean up their disks by removing temporary Internet files, deleting unused program files, and more.

Disk drive controller   The circuitry that controls the physical operations of the floppy disks and/or hard disks connected to a computer.

Disk Management   A snap-in available with the Microsoft Management Console that allows a user to configure the various disks installed in a system; available from the Administrative Tools area of the Control Panel.

Disk mirroring   Process by which data is written simultaneously to two or more disk drives. Read and write speed is decreased but redundancy in case of catastrophe is increased.

Disk striping   Process by which data is spread among multiple (at least two) drives. It increases speed for both reads and writes of data. Considered RAID level 0, because it does *not* provide fault tolerance.

Disk striping with parity   A method for providing fault tolerance by writing data across multiple drives and then including an additional drive, called a *parity drive*, that stores information to rebuild the data contained on the other drives. Requires at least three physical disks: two for the data and a third for the parity drive. This provides data redundancy at RAID levels 3–5 with different options.

Disk thrashing   A term used to describe a hard drive that is constantly being accessed due to lack of available system memory. When system memory runs low, a Windows system utilizes hard disk space as "virtual" memory, thus causing an unusual amount of hard drive access.

Distro   Shortened form of "distribution," most commonly used to describe the many different delivered packages for Linux operating systems and applications.

Dithering   A technique for smoothing out digitized images; using alternating colors in a pattern to produce perceived color detail.

DMA (direct memory access)   A technique that some PC hardware devices use to transfer data to and from the memory without using the CPU.

DNS (domain name system)   A TCP/IP name resolution system that translates a host name into an IP address.

DNS domain   A specific branch of the DNS name space. First-level DNS domains include .COM, .GOV, and .EDU.

Documentation   A collection of organized documents or the information recorded in documents. In the computer world, instructional material specifying the inputs, operations, and outputs of a computer program or system; for example, a manual and Getting Started card.

Dolby Digital   A technology for sound reductions and channeling methods.

Domain   Term used to describe groupings of users, computers, or networks. In Microsoft networking, a domain is a group of computers and users that share a common account database, called a SAM, and a common security policy. On the Internet, a domain is a group of computers that share a common element in their hierarchical name. Other types of domains exist—e.g., collision domain, etc.

Domain controller   A Microsoft Windows NT machine that stores the user and server account information for its domain in a database called a SAM (security accounts manager) database.

DOS (Disk Operating System)   The first popular operating system available for PCs. It was a text-based, single-tasking operating system that was not completely replaced until the introduction of Windows 95.

DOS prompt   A symbol, usually a letter representing the disk drive followed by the greater-than sign (>), which tells you that the operating system is ready to receive a command. Windows systems use the term *command prompt* rather than DOS prompt.

DOSKEY   A DOS utility that enables you to type more than one command on a line, store and retrieve previously used command-line commands, create stored macros, and customize all commands. DOSKEY is still supported in Windows XP.

Dot pitch   A value relating to CRTs, showing the diagonal distance between phosphors measured in millimeters.

Dot-matrix printer   A printer that creates each character from an array of dots. Pins striking a ribbon against the paper, one pin for each dot position, form the dots. The printer may be a serial printer (printing one character at a time) or a line printer.

Double word   A unit of 32 binary digits; four bytes.

Double-side high density   A type of floppy disk that is capable of holding 1.2 MB on a 5.25-inch disk and 1.44 MB on a 3.5-inch disk. This format can be read in all modern floppy disk drives.

Double-sided RAM   A RAM stick with RAM chips soldered to both sides of the stick. May only be used with motherboards designed to accept double-sided RAM. Very common.

Downstream   A term used to define the part of a USB connection that plugs into a USB device.

DPI (dots per inch)   A measure of printer resolution that counts the dots the device can produce per linear (horizontal) inch.

DRAM (dynamic random access memory or dynamic RAM)   The memory used to store data in most personal computers. DRAM stores each bit in a "cell" composed of a transistor and a capacitor. Because the capacitor in a DRAM cell can only hold a charge for a few milliseconds, DRAM must be continually refreshed, or rewritten, to retain its data.

DS3D (DirectSound3D)   Introduced with DirectX 3.0, DS3D is a command set used to create positional audio, or sounds that appear to come from in front, in back, or to the side of a user. *See also* DirectX.

DSL (digital subscriber line)   A high-speed Internet connection technology that uses a regular telephone line for connectivity. DSL comes in several varieties, including Asynchronous (ADSL) and Synchronous (SDSL), and many speeds. Typical home-user DSL connections are ADSL with a download speed of up to 1.5 Mbps and an upload speed of 384 Kbps.

DSP (digital signal processor)   A specialized microprocessor-like device that processes digital signals at the expense of other abilities, much as the FPU is optimized for math functions. DSPs are used in such specialized hardware as high-speed modems, multimedia sound cards, MIDI equipment, and real-time video capture and compression.

DTS (Digital Theatre Systems)   A technology for sound reductions and channeling methods, similar to Dolby Digital.

Dual boot   Refers to a computer with two operating systems installed, enabling a user to choose which operating system to load on boot. Can also refer to kicking a device a second time just in case the first time didn't work.

Dual-channel memory   A form of DDR and DDR2 memory access used by many motherboards that requires two identical sticks of DDR or DDR2 RAM.

Duplexing   Also called **disk duplexing** or **drive duplexing**. Similar to mirroring in that data is written to and read from two physical drives, for fault tolerance. Separate controllers are used for each drive, both for additional fault tolerance and additional speed. Considered RAID level 1.

Duron   A lower-cost version of AMD's Athlon series of CPUs.

DVD (digital versatile disc)   An optical media format that provides for 4–17 GB of video or data storage.

DVD Multi   A description given to DVD drives that are capable of reading all six DVD formats.

DVD+RW   A type of rewritable DVD media.

DVD-RAM   A type of rewritable DVD media that uses a cartridge.

DVD-ROM   The DVD-ROM is the DVD equivalent of the standard CD-ROM.

DVD-RW   A type of rewritable DVD media.

DVD-Video   A DVD format used exclusively to store digital video; capable of storing over 2 hours of high-quality video on a single DVD.

DVI (digital video interface)   A special video connector designed for digital-to-digital connections; most commonly seen on PC video cards and LCD monitors. Some versions also support analog signals with a special adapter.

Dynamic disks   A special feature of Windows 2000 and Windows XP that allows a user to span a single volume across two or more drives. Dynamic disks do not have partitions; they have volumes. Dynamic disks can be striped, mirrored, and striped or mirrored with parity.

EAX   3-D sound technology developed by Creative Labs, but now supported by most sound cards.

ECC (error correction code) Special software, embedded on hard drives, that constantly scans the drives for bad sectors.

ECC DRAM (error correction code DRAM) A type of RAM that uses special chips to detect and fix memory errors. This type of RAM is commonly used in high-end servers where data integrity is crucial.

EDB (external data bus) The primary data highway of all computers. Everything in your computer is tied either directly or indirectly to the external data bus. *See also* frontside bus and backside bus.

EDO DRAM (enhanced data out DRAM) An improvement on FPM DRAM in that more data can be read before the RAM must be refreshed.

EEPROM (electrically erasable programmable read-only memory) A type of ROM chip that can be erased and reprogrammed electrically. EEPROMs were the most common storage device for BIOS before the advent of Flash ROM.

EFS (encrypting file system) The encryption tool found in NTFS 5.

EIA/TIA *See* TIA/EIA.

EIDE (enhanced IDE) A marketing concept of hard drive–maker Western Digital, encompassing four improvements for IDE drives. These improvements included drives larger than 528 MB, four devices, increase in drive throughput, and non–hard drive devices. (*See* ATAPI, PIO.)

EISA (enhanced ISA) An improved expansion bus, based on the ISA bus, with a top speed of 8.33 MHz, a 32-bit data path, and a high degree of self-configuration. Backward compatible with legacy ISA cards.

E-mail, email (electronic mail) Messages, usually text, sent from one person to another via computer. E-mail can also be sent automatically to a group of addresses (mailing list).

EMI (electro-magnetic interference) EMI is electrical interference from one device to another, resulting in poor performance of the device being interfered with. An example is having static on your TV while running a blow dryer, or placing two monitors too close together and getting a "shaky" screen.

EPROM (erasable programmable read-only memory) A special form of ROM that can be erased by high-intensity ultraviolet light and then rewritten (reprogrammed).

ERD (emergency repair disk) This disk saves critical boot files and partition information and is the main tool for fixing boot problems in Windows 2000.

ESD (electrostatic discharge) The movement of electrons from one body to another. ESD is a real menace to PCs, as it can cause permanent damage to semiconductors.

Ethernet Name coined by Xerox for the first standard of network cabling and protocols. Ethernet is based on a bus topology.

EULA (end user license agreement) An agreement that accompanies a piece of software, which the user must agree to in order to use the software. This agreement outlines the terms of use for software and also lists any actions on the part of the user that violate the agreement.

Event Viewer A utility made available as an MMC snap-in that allows a user to monitor various system events, including network bandwidth usage and CPU utilization.

EXPAND A CAB file utility program included with Windows 2000. Usage of EXPAND is similar to usage of EXTRACT. *See also* EXTRACT.

Expansion bus crystal The crystal that controls the speed of the expansion bus.

Expansion bus Set of wires going to the CPU, governed by the expansion bus crystal, directly connected to expansion slots of varying types (PCI, AGP, PCIe, etc.). Depending on the type of slots, the expansion bus runs at a percentage of the main system speed (8.33–133 MHz).

Expansion slots Connectors on a motherboard that enable a user to add optional components to a system. *See also* AGP (accelerated graphics port) and PCI (peripheral components interconnect).

ExpressCard A serial PC Card designed to replace CardBus PC Cards. ExpressCards connect to either a Hi-Speed USB (480 Mbps) or PCI Express (2.5 Gbps) bus.

Extended partition A type of hard disk partition. Extended partitions are not bootable and you may only have one extended partition per disk. The purpose of an extended partition is to divide a large disk into smaller partitions, each with a separate drive letter.

Extension The three or four letters that follow a filename; an extension identifies the type of file. Common file extensions are .ZIP, .EXE, and .DOC.

EXTRACT A program native to Windows 9*x*/Me that can be used to extract data from compressed CAB files. *See also* EXPAND.

Fast Ethernet Any of several flavors of Ethernet that operate at 100 megabits/second.

FAT (file allocation table) A hidden table of every cluster on a hard disk. The FAT records how files are stored in distinct clusters. The address of the first cluster of the file is stored in the directory file. In the FAT entry for the first cluster is the address of the second cluster used to store that file. In the entry for the second cluster for that file is the address for the third cluster, and so on until the final cluster, which gets a special "end of file" code. This table is the only way DOS knows where to access files. There are two FATs, mirror images of each other, in case one is destroyed or damaged.

FAT16 File allocation table that uses 16 bits for addressing clusters. Commonly used with DOS and Windows 95 systems.

FAT32 File allocation table that uses 32 bits for addressing clusters. Commonly used with Windows 98 and Windows Me systems. Some Windows 2000 Professional and Windows XP systems also use FAT32, although most use the more robust NTFS.

FDISK A disk partitioning utility included with Windows.

Fiber optics A high-speed channel for transmitting data, made of high-purity glass sealed within an opaque tube. Much faster than conventional copper wire such as coaxial cable.

File A collection of any form of data that is stored beyond the time of execution of a single job. A file may contain program instructions or data, which may be numerical, textual, or graphical information.

File allocation unit Another term for cluster. *See also* cluster.

File format The way information is encoded in a file. Two primary types are binary (pictures) and ASCII (text), but within those there are many formats, such as BMP and GIF for pictures. Commonly represented by a suffix at the end of the filename—for example, .txt for a text file or .exe for an executable.

File fragmentation The allocation of a file in a non-contiguous sector on a disk. Fragmentation occurs because of multiple deletions and write operations.

File server A computer designated to store software, courseware, administrative tools, and other data on a local- or wide-area network. It "serves" this information to other computers via the network when users enter their personal access codes.

File system A scheme that directs how an OS stores and retrieves data on and off a drive; FAT32 and NTFS are both file systems.

Filename A name assigned to a file when the file is first written on a disk. Every file on a disk within the same folder must have a unique name. Filenames can contain any character (including spaces), except the following: \ / : * ? " < > |

Firewall A device that restricts traffic between a local network and the Internet.

FireWire (IEEE 1394) An IEEE 1394 interconnection standard to send wide-band signals over a serialized, physically thin connector system. This serial bus developed by Apple and Texas Instruments enables connection of 60 devices at speeds up to 800 megabits per second.

Firmware Embedded programs or code that is stored on a ROM chip. Firmware is generally OS-independent, thus allowing devices to operate in a wide variety of circumstances without direct OS support. The system BIOS is firmware.

Flash ROM A type of ROM technology that can be electrically reprogrammed while still in the PC. Flash is the overwhelmingly most common storage medium of BIOS in PCs today, as it can be upgraded without even having to open the computer on most systems.

FlexATX A motherboard form factor. Motherboards built in accordance with the FlexATX form factor are very small, much smaller than microATX motherboards.

Flexing Condition that can result when components are installed on a motherboard after it has been installed into a computer case. Excessive flexing can cause damage to the motherboard itself.

Floppy disk A type of removable storage media that can hold between 720 KB and 1.44 MB of data.

Floppy drive A piece of system hardware that uses removable 3.5-inch disks as storage media.

Flux reversal The point at which a read/write head detects a change in magnetic polarity.

FM synthesis A method for producing sound that used electronic emulation of various instruments to more or less produce music and other sound effects.

Form factor A standard for the physical organization of motherboard components and motherboard size. The most common form factors are ATX, BTX, and NLX.

Formatting The process of magnetically mapping a disk to provide a structure for storing data; can be done to any type of disk, including a floppy disk, hard disk, or other type of removable disk.

FPM (fast page mode) DRAM that uses a "paging" function to increase access speed and to lower production costs. Virtually all DRAMs are FPM DRAM. The name FPM is also used to describe older style, non-EDO DRAM.

FPT (forced perfect termination) A method for terminating SCSI devices that uses diodes instead of resistors.

FPU (floating point unit) A formal term for the math coprocessor (also called a *numeric processor*) circuitry inside a CPU. A math coprocessor calculates using floating point math (which allows for decimals). Before the Intel 80486, FPUs were separate chips from the CPU.

Fragmentation Occurs when files and directories get jumbled on a fixed disk and are no longer contiguous. Fragmentation can significantly slow down hard drive access times and can be repaired by using the DEFRAG utility that is included with each version of Windows. *See also* defragmentation (DEFRAG), file fragmentation.

Freeware Software that is distributed for free, with no license fee.

Frontside bus Name for the wires that connect the CPU to the main system RAM. Generally running at speeds of 66–133 MHz. Distinct from the expansion bus and the backside bus, though it shares wires with the former.

FRU (field replaceable unit) Any part of a PC that is considered to be replaceable "in the field," i.e., a customer location. There is no official list of FRUs—it is usually a matter of policy by the repair center.

FTP (file transfer protocol) A set of rules that enables two computers to talk to one another as a file transfer is carried out. This is the protocol used when you transfer a file from one computer to another across the Internet.

Fuel cells A type of power source that uses chemical reactions to produce electricity. Lightweight, compact, and stable, these devices are expected to replace batteries as the primary power source for portable PCs.

Full-duplex Describes any device that can send and receive data simultaneously.

Function key A keyboard key that gives an instruction to a computer, as opposed to keys that produce letters, numbers, marks of punctuation, etc.

Fuser assembly A mechanism, found in laser printers, that uses two rollers to fuse toner to paper during the print process.

Gateway The technical meaning is a hardware or software setup that translates between two dissimilar protocols. For example, Prodigy has a gateway that translates between its internal, proprietary e-mail format and Internet e-mail format. Another, less technical meaning of gateway is any mechanism for providing access to another system, e.g., AOL might be called a gateway to the Internet. *See* default gateway.

General-purpose registers The registers that handle the most common CPU calculations. *See* register.

Giga- The prefix for the quantity 1,073,741,824 or for 1 billion. One gigabyte would be 1,073,741,824 bytes, except for with hard drive labeling, where it means 1 billion bytes. One gigahertz is 1 billion hertz.

Gigabyte   1024 megabytes.

Green PC   A computer system designed to operate in an energy-efficient manner.

Guest   Very limited built-in account type for Windows.

GUI (graphical user interface)   An interface is the method by which a computer and a user interact. Early interfaces were text-based; that is, the user "talked" to the computer by typing and the computer responded with text on a CRT. A GUI (pronounced "gooey"), on the other hand, enables the user to interact with the computer graphically, by manipulating icons that represent programs or documents with a mouse or other pointing device.

HAL (hardware abstraction layer)   A part of the Windows OS that separates system-specific device drivers from the rest of the NT system.

Half-duplex   Any device that at any given moment can either send or receive data, but not both. Most Ethernet transmissions are half-duplex.

Handshaking   A procedure performed by modems, terminals, and computers to verify that communication has been correctly established.

Hang   When a computer freezes so that it does not respond to keyboard commands, it is said to "hang" or to have "hung."

Hang time   The number of seconds a too-often-hung computer is airborne after you have thrown it out a second-story window.

Hard drive   A data-recording system using solid disks of magnetic material turning at high speeds to store and retrieve programs and data in a computer.

Hardware   Physical computer equipment such as electrical, electronic, magnetic, and mechanical devices. Anything in the computer world that you can hold in your hand. A floppy drive is hardware; Microsoft Word is not.

Hardware profile   A list of devices that Windows automatically enables or disables in the Device Manager, depending on what devices the system detects.

Hardware protocol   A hardware protocol defines many aspects of a network, from the packet type to the cabling and connectors used.

Hayes command set   A standardized set of instructions used to control modems.

HCL (Hardware Compatibility List)   Now part of Windows Marketplace, a list that is maintained by Microsoft that lists all the hardware that is supported by an operating system. This list is helpful to use when upgrading a system; with a quick glance, you can make sure that support is available for all the devices in a system before you begin the upgrade.

HD (Hi-Definition)   A multimedia transmission standard that defines high-resolution images and 5.1 sound.

HD DVD   An optical disc format that stores 15 or 30 GB of data, designed to be the replacement media for DVD. Competes with Blu-ray Disc.

HDMI (hi-definition multimedia interface)   A single multimedia connection that includes both high-definition video and audio. HDMI also contains copy protection features.

Hex (hexadecimal)   A base-16 numbering system using 10 digits (0 through 9) and six letters (A through F). Used in the computer world as a shorthand way to write binary numbers, by substituting one hex digit for a four-digit binary number (e.g., hex 9 = binary 1001).

Hibernation   A power management setting in which all data from RAM is written to the hard drive before going to sleep. Upon waking up, all information is retrieved from the hard drive and returned to RAM.

Hidden attribute   A file attribute that, when used, does not allow a file to be seen when using the DIR command.

Hierarchical directory tree   The method by which Windows organizes files into a series of folders, called directories, under the root directory. *See also* Root directory.

High-level formatting   A type of format that sets up a file system on a drive.

High-voltage anode   A component in a CRT monitor. The high-voltage anode has very high voltages of electricity flowing through it.

Host   A single device (usually a computer) on a TCP/IP network that has an IP address—any device that can be the source or destination of a data packet. Also, in the mainframe world, a computer that is made available for use by multiple people simultaneously.

Host adapter   An expansion card that serves as a host to a particular device; for instance, you can install a SCSI host adapter into a system to allow for SCSI functionality even if SCSI hardware was not originally included with the machine.

Host ID   The portion of an IP address that defines a specific machine.

Hot-swappable   A term used for any type of hardware that may be attached to or removed from a PC without interrupting the PC's normal processing.

HotSync (synchronization)   A term used to describe the synchronizing of files between a PDA and a desktop computer. HotSync is the name of the synchronization program that is used by PalmOS-based PDAs.

HRR (horizontal refresh rate)   The amount of time it takes for a CRT to draw one horizontal line of pixels on a display.

HTML (Hypertext Markup Language)   An ASCII-based, script-like language for creating hypertext documents like those on the World Wide Web.

HTTP (Hypertext Transfer Protocol)   Extremely fast protocol used for network file transfers in the WWW environment.

HTTPS (HTTP over Secure Sockets Layer)   A secure form of HTTP, used commonly for Internet business transactions or any time when a secure connection is required. *See also* HTTP.

Hub   An electronic device that sits at the center of a star topology network, providing a common point for the connection of network devices. Hubs repeat all information out to all ports and have been replaced by switches, although the term is still commonly used.

HVD (high-voltage differential)   A rare type of SCSI device that uses two wires for each bit of information: one wire for data and one for the inverse of this data. The inverse signal takes the place of the ground wire in the single-ended cable. By taking the difference of the two signals, the device can reject the common-mode noise in the data stream.

Hyperthreading   A CPU feature that enables a single pipeline to run more than one thread at once.

I/O (input/output)   A general term for reading and writing data to a computer. The term "input" includes data from a keyboard, pointing device (such as a mouse), or loading a file from a disk. "Output" includes writing information to a disk, viewing it on a CRT, or printing it to a printer.

I/O addressing   The process of using the address bus to talk to system devices.

ICF (Internet Connection Firewall)   A software firewall built into Windows XP that protects your system from unauthorized access from the Internet.

ICH (I/O controller hub)   The official name for the Southbridge chip found in Intel's chipsets.

Icon   A small image or graphic, most commonly found on a system's desktop, that launches a program when selected.

ICS (Internet Connection Sharing)   A method for allowing a single network connection to be shared among several machines. ICS was first introduced with Windows 98.

IDE (intelligent drive electronics)   Also known as **integrated drive electronics**. A PC specification for small- to medium-sized hard drives in which the controlling electronics for the drive are part of the drive itself, speeding up transfer rates and leaving only a simple adapter (or "paddle"). IDE only supported two drives per system of no more than 504 megabytes each, and has been completely supplanted by Enhanced IDE. EIDE supports four drives of over 8 gigabytes each and more than doubles the transfer rate. The more common name for PATA drives. (*See* PATA.)

IEC-320   Type of connector used to connect the cable supplying AC power from a wall outlet into the power supply.

IEEE (Institute of Electronic and Electrical Engineers) IEEE is the leading standards-setting group in the United States.

IEEE 1284 The IEEE standard governing parallel communication.

IEEE 1394 The IEEE standard governing FireWire communication. *See also* FireWire (IEEE 1394).

IFCONFIG A command-line utility for Linux servers and workstations that displays the current TCP/IP configuration of the machine, similar to Windows' IPCONFIG.

Image file A bit-by-bit image of the data to be burned on the CD or DVD—from one file to an entire disc—stored as a single file on a hard drive. Image files are particularly handy when copying from CD to CD or DVD to DVD.

Image installation An operating system installation that uses a complete image of a hard drive as an installation media. This is a helpful technique to use when installing an operation system on a large number of identical PCs.

Impact printer A type of printer that uses pins and inked ribbons to print text or images on a piece of paper.

Impedance The amount of resistance to an electrical signal on a wire. It is used as a relative measure of the amount of data a cable can handle.

Incremental backup A type of backup that backs up all files that have their archive bits turned on, meaning that they have been changed since the last backup. This type of backup turns the archive bits off after the files have been backed up.

INF file A Windows driver file.

Inkjet printer A type of printer that uses liquid ink, sprayed through a series of tiny jets, to print text or images on a piece of paper.

Instruction set All of the machine-language commands that a particular CPU is designed to understand.

Interlaced TV/video systems in which the electron beam writes every other line; then retraces itself to make a second pass to complete the final framed image. Originally, this reduced magnetic line paring, but took twice as long to paint, which added some flicker in graphic images.

InterNIC Organization run by Network Solutions, Inc. (NSI) and AT&T that provides several services to Internet users, the most prominent being the registration of domain names and assignment of IP addresses.

Interrupt A suspension of a process, such as the execution of a computer program, caused by an event external to the computer and performed in such a way that the process can be resumed. Events of this kind include sensors monitoring laboratory equipment or a user pressing an interrupt key.

Interrupt 13 (INT13) extensions An improved type of BIOS that accepts EIDE drives up to 137 GB.

Intranet A private network inside a company or organization that uses the same kinds of software that you find on the public Internet, but that is only for internal use.

Inverter A device used to convert DC current into AC. Commonly used with CCFLs in laptops and flatbed scanners.

IP (Internet protocol) The Internet standard protocol that provides a common layer over dissimilar networks used to move packets among host computers and through gateways if necessary. Part of the TCP/IP protocol suite.

IP address Also called **Internet address**. The numeric address of a computer connected to the Internet. The IP address is made up of octets of 8-bit binary numbers that are translated into their shorthand numeric values. The IP address can be broken down into a network ID and a host ID.

IPCONFIG A command-line utility for Windows NT servers and workstations that displays the current TCP/IP configuration of the machine, similar to WINIPCFG and IFCONFIG.

IPX/SPX (Internetwork Packet Exchange/Sequence Packet Exchange) Protocol suite developed by Novell, primarily for supporting Novell NetWare-based networks.

IRC (Internet Relay Chat) The Internet Relay Chat, or just Chat, is an online group discussion.

IRQ (interrupt request)   A signal from a hardware device, such as a modem or a mouse, indicating that it needs the CPU's attention. In PCs, IRQs are sent along specific IRQ channels associated with a particular device. IRQ conflicts were a common problem in the past when adding expansion boards, but the plug-and-play specification has removed this headache in most cases.

ISA (industry standard architecture)   The Industry Standard Architecture design was found in the original IBM PC for the slots on the motherboard that allowed additional hardware to be connected to the computer's motherboard. An 8-bit, 8.33-MHz expansion bus was designed by IBM for its AT computer and released to the public domain. An improved 16-bit bus was also released to the public domain. Replaced by PCI in the mid-1990s.

ISDN (integrated services digital network)   The CCITT (Comité Consultatif Internationale de Télégraphie et Téléphonie) standard that defines a digital method for communications to replace the current analog telephone system. ISDN is superior to POTS (see POTS) telephone lines because it supports up to 128 Kbps transfer rate for sending information from computer to computer. It also allows data and voice to share a common phone line. DSL reduced demand for ISDN substantially.

ISO 9660   CD format to support PC file systems on CD media. Supplanted by the Joliet format.

ISP (Internet service provider)   A company that provides access to the Internet, usually for money.

Jack (physical connection)   The part of a connector into which a plug is inserted. Jacks are also referred to as ports.

Joliet   An extension of the ISO 9660 format. The most popular CD format to support PC file systems on CD media.

Joystick   A peripheral often used while playing computer games; originally intended as a multipurpose input device.

Jumper   A pair of small pins that can be shorted with a "shunt" to configure many different aspects of PCs. Usually used in configurations that are rarely changed, such as master/slave settings on IDE drives.

K   Most commonly used as the suffix for the binary quantity 1024 (2^{10}). Just to add some extra confusion to the IT industry, K is often spoken as "kilo," the metric value for 1000. 10 KB, for example, spoken as "10 kilobytes," actually means 10,240 bytes rather than 10,000 bytes.

Kbps (kilobits per second)   Data transfer rate.

Kernel   The core portion of the program that resides in memory and performs the most essential operating system tasks.

Keyboard   An input device. There are two common types of keyboards—those that use a mini-DIN (PS/2) connection and those that use a USB connection.

KHz (kilohertz)   A unit of measure that equals a frequency of one thousand cycles per second.

Knowledge Base   A large collection of documents and FAQs that is maintained by Microsoft. Found on Microsoft's Web site, the Knowledge Base is an excellent place to search for assistance on most operating system problems.

LAN (local area network)   A group of PCs connected together via cabling, radio, or infrared that use this connectivity to share resources such as printers and mass storage.

Laser   A single-wavelength, in-phase light source that is sometimes strapped to the head of sharks by bad guys. Note to henchmen: lasers should never be used with sea bass, no matter how ill-tempered they might be.

Laser printer   An electro-photographic printer in which a laser is used as the light source.

Last Known Good Configuration   An option on the Advanced Startup Options menu that allows your system to revert to a previous configuration in order to troubleshoot and repair any major system problems.

Latency   The amount of delay before a device may respond to a request; most commonly used in reference to RAM.

Layer   In the communications field, a grouping of related tasks involving the transfer of information. Also, a level of the OSI reference model used for networking computers. In graphics work, images can be created in layers, which can be manipulated separately and then flattened into a single image.

Layer 2 Switch   Also called a **bridge**. Filters and forwards data packets based on the MAC addresses of the sending and receiving machines.

Layer 3 Switch   Also called a **router**. Filters and forwards data packets based on the network addresses of the sending and receiving machines.

LBA (logical block addressing)   A translation (algorithm) of IDE drives promoted by Western Digital as a standardized method for breaking the 504-MB limit in IDE drives. Subsequently universally adopted by the PC industry and is standard on all EIDE drives.

LCD (liquid crystal display)   A display technology that relies on polarized light passing through a liquid medium rather than on electron beams striking a phosphorescent surface.

LED (light-emitting diode)   Solid-state device that vibrates at luminous frequencies when current is applied.

Legacy device   Any device that is not plug-and-play compatible.

Level 1 (L1) cache   The first RAM cache accessed by the CPU, which stores only the absolute most-accessed programming and data used by currently running threads. This is always the smallest and fastest cache on the CPU.

Level 2 (L2) cache   The second RAM cache accessed by the CPU, which is much larger and often slower than the L1 cache; accessed only if the requested program/data is not in the L1 cache.

Level 3 (L3) cache   The third RAM cache accessed by the CPU, which is much larger and slower than the L1 and L2 cache; accessed only if the requested program/data is not in the L2 cache. Seen only on high-end CPUs.

Li-Ion (lithium ion)   A type of battery commonly used in portable PCs. Li-Ion batteries don't suffer from the memory effects of NiCd batteries and provide much more power for a great length of time.

Limited account   A type of user account in Windows XP that has limited access to a system. Accounts of this type cannot alter system files, cannot install new programs, and cannot edit settings using the Control Panel.

Linux   Open source UNIX-clone operating system.

Local bus   A high-speed data path that directly links the computer's CPU with one or more slots on the expansion bus. This direct link means signals from an adapter do not have to travel through the computer expansion bus, which is significantly slower.

Localhost   An alias for the loopback address of 127.0.0.1, referring to the current machine.

Logical address   An address that describes both a specific network and a specific machine on that network.

Logical drives   Sections of a hard drive that are formatted and assigned a drive letter, each of which is presented to the user as if it were a separate drive.

Loopback address   A reserved IP address for internal testing: 127.0.0.1.

Low-level format   Defining the physical location of magnetic tracks and sectors on a disk.

LPT port   Commonly referred to as a printer port; usually associated with a local parallel port.

Lumens   A unit of measure for the amount of brightness on a projector or other light source.

Luminescence   The part of the video signal that controls the luminance/brightness of the picture. Also known as the "Y" portion of the component signal.

LUNs (logical unit numbers)   A specialized SCSI configuration that allows for multiple devices to share a single SCSI ID. This type of arrangement is found most commonly in high-end servers that have large hard disk arrays.

LVD (low voltage differential)   A type of differential SCSI. LVD SCSI requires less power than HVD and is compatible with existing SE SCSI controllers and devices. LVD devices can sense the type of SCSI and then work accordingly. If you plug an LVD device into an SE chain, it will act as an SE device. If you plug an LVD device into LVD, it will run as LVD. LVD SCSI chains can be up to 12 meters in length.

Mac   Also **Macintosh**. Apple Computers' flagship operating system, currently up to OS X and running on Intel-based hardware.

MAC (Media Access Control) address   Unique 48-bit address assigned to each network card. IEEE assigns blocks of possible addresses to various NIC manufacturers to help ensure that the address is always unique. The Data Link layer of the OSI model uses MAC addresses for locating machines.

Machine language   The binary instruction code that is understood by the CPU.

Mass storage   Hard drives, CD-ROMs, removable media drives, etc.

Math coprocessor   Also called **math unit** or **floating point unit (FPU)**. A secondary microprocessor whose function is the handling of floating point arithmetic. Although originally a physically separate chip, math coprocessors are now built into today's CPUs.

MB (megabyte)   1,048,576 bytes.

MBR (master boot record)   A tiny bit of code that takes control of the boot process from the system BIOS.

MCA (Micro Channel architecture)   Expansion bus architecture developed by IBM as the (unsuccessful) successor to ISA. MCA had a full 32-bit design as well as being self-configuring.

MCC (memory controller chip)   The chip that handles memory requests from the CPU. Although once a special chip, it has been integrated into the chipset on all PCs today.

Mega-   A prefix that usually stands for the binary quantity 1,048,576 (2^{20}). One megabyte is 1,048,576 bytes. One megahertz, however, is a million hertz. Sometimes shortened to **Meg**, as in "a 286 has an address space of 16 Megs."

Memory   A device or medium for temporary storage of programs and data during program execution. The term is synonymous with storage, although it is most frequently used for referring to the internal storage of a computer that can be directly addressed by operating instructions. A computer's temporary storage capacity is measured in kilobytes (KB) or megabytes (MB) of RAM (random-access memory). Long-term data storage on disks is also measured in kilobytes, megabytes, gigabytes, and terabytes.

Memory Stick   Sony's flash memory card format; rarely seen outside of Sony devices.

MFT (master file table)   An enhanced file allocation table used by NTFS. *See also* FAT (file allocation Table).

MHz (megahertz)   A unit of measure that equals a frequency of one million cycles per second.

Micro ATX   A smaller size of ATX motherboard and case, which uses the ATX power supply.

Micro DIMM   A type of memory used in portable PCs because of its small size.

MicroATX   A variation of the ATX form factor. MicroATX motherboards are generally smaller than their ATX counterparts, but retain all the same functionality.

Microcomputer   A computer system in which the central processing unit is built as a single, tiny semiconductor chip or as a small number of chips.

Microprocessor   Also called **CPU**. The "brain" of a computer. The primary computer chip that determines the relative speed and capabilities of the computer.

MIDI (musical instrument digital interface)   MIDI is a standard that describes the interface between a computer and a device for simulating musical instruments. Rather than sending large sound samples, a computer can simply send "instructions" to the instrument describing pitch, tone, and duration of a sound. MIDI files are therefore very efficient. Because a MIDI file is made up of a set of instructions rather than a copy of the sound, it is easy to modify each component of the file. Additionally, it is possible to program many channels, or "voices," of music to be played simultaneously, creating symphonic sound.

MIME (Multipurpose Internet Mail Extensions)   MIME is a standard for attaching binary files (such as executables and images) to the Internet's text-based mail (24-Kbps packet size). The first packet of information received contains information about the file.

Mini audio connector   A very popular, 1/8-inch diameter connector used to transmit two audio signals; perfect for stereo sound.

Mini PCI   A specialized form of PCI designed for use in laptops.

Mini power connector   A type of connector used to provide power to floppy disk drives.

Mini-DIN   A very popular small connection most commonly used for keyboards and mice.

MIPS (millions of instructions per second)   Used for processor benchmarks.

Mirrored volume   A volume that is mirrored on another volume. *See also* mirroring.

Mirroring   Also called **drive mirroring**. Reading and writing data at the same time to two drives for fault tolerance purposes. Considered RAID level 1.

MMC (Microsoft Management Console)   A new means of managing a system, introduced by Microsoft with Windows 2000. The MMC allows an Administrator to customize management tools by picking and choosing from a list of snap-ins. Some snap-ins that are available are the Device Manager, Users and Groups, and Computer Management.

MMU (memory management unit)   A chip or circuit that translates virtual memory addresses into physical addresses and may implement memory protection.

MMX (multimedia extensions)   A set of specific CPU instructions that enables a CPU to handle many multimedia functions, such as digital signal processing. Introduced with the Pentium CPU, these instructions are now used on all ×86 CPUs.

Mobile CPU   A CPU designed for use in portable computers that uses much less power than a normal, desktop CPU.

Modem (modulator/demodulator)   A device that converts a digital bit stream into an analog signal (modulation) and converts incoming analog signals back into digital signals (demodulation). The analog communications channel is typically a telephone line, and the analog signals are typically sounds.

Molex connector   A type of computer power connector. CD-ROM drives, hard drives, and case fans all use this type of connector. A Molex connector is keyed to prevent it from being inserted into a power port improperly.

Motherboard   A flat piece of circuit board that resides inside your computer case. The motherboard has a number of connectors on it; you can use these connectors to attach a variety of devices to your system, including hard drives, CD-ROM drives, floppy disk drives, and sound cards.

Motherboard book   A valuable resource when installing a new motherboard. The motherboard book normally lists all the specifications about a motherboard, including the type of memory and type of CPU that should be used with the motherboard.

Mount point   A drive that functions like a folder mounted into another drive.

Mouse   An input device that enables a user to manipulate a cursor on the screen in order to select items.

MP3   Short for MPEG, Layer 3. MP3 is a type of compression used specifically for turning high-quality digital audio files into much smaller, yet similar sounding, files.

MPA (Microsoft Product Activation)   Introduced by Microsoft with the release on Windows XP, Microsoft Product Activation prevents unauthorized use of Microsoft's software by requiring a user to activate the software.

MSCONFIG   The executable file that runs the System Configuration Utility, a utility found in Windows that enables a user to configure a system's boot files and critical system files. Often used for the name of the utility, as in "just run MSCONFIG."

MS-DOS (Microsoft Disk Operating System)   The first operating system released by Microsoft.

Multiboot   A type of OS installation in which multiple operating systems are installed on a single machine. Can also refer to kicking a device several times in frustration.

Multimeter   A device that is used to measure voltage, amperage, and resistance.

Multiplexer   A device that merges information from multiple input channels to a single output channel.

MultiRead   The ability of most modern CD-ROM drives to read a wide variety of discs is called MultiRead. Modern CD-ROMs can read CD-ROM, CD-R, and CD-RW discs.

Multisession drive   A recordable CD drive that is capable of burning multiple sessions onto a single recordable disc. A multisession drive also has the ability to "close" a CD-R so that no further tracks can be written to it.

Multitasking   The process of running multiple programs or tasks on the same computer at the same time.

My Computer   An applet that allows a user to access a complete listing of all fixed and removable drives contained within a system.

My Documents   Introduced with Windows 98, the My Documents folder provides a convenient place for a user to store their documents, log files, and any other type of files.

Native resolution   The resolution on an LCD monitor that matches the physical pixels on the screen. CRTs do not have fixed pixels and therefore do not have a native resolution.

NBTSTAT   A command-line utility used to check the current NetBIOS name cache on a particular machine. The utility compares NetBIOS names to their corresponding IP addresses.

NDS (Novell Directory Services)   The default security and directory system for Novell NetWare 4.*x* and 5.*x*. Organizes users, servers, and groups into a hierarchical tree.

NetBEUI (NetBIOS Extended User Interface)   A protocol supplied with all Microsoft networking products that operates at the Transport layer. Also a protocol suite that includes NetBIOS. NetBEUI does not support routing.

NetBIOS (network basic input/output system)   A protocol that operates at the Session layer of the OSI seven-layer model. This protocol creates and manages connections based on the names of the computers involved.

NetBIOS name   A computer name that identifies both the specific machine and the functions that machine performs. A NetBIOS name consists of 16 characters: 15 characters of a name, with a 16th character that is a special suffix that identifies the role the machine plays.

NETSTAT   A command-line utility used to examine the sockets-based connections open on a given host.

Network   A collection of two or more computers interconnected by telephone lines, coaxial cables, satellite links, radio, and/or some other communication technique. A computer network is a group of computers that are connected together and that communicate with one another for a common purpose.

Network ID   A number that identifies the network on which a device or machine exists. This number exists in both IP and IPX protocol suites.

Newsgroup   The name for discussion groups on Usenet.

Nibble   A unit of four bits.

NIC (network interface card)   An expansion card that enables a PC to physically link to a network.

NiCd (nickel-cadmium)   A type of battery that was used in the first portable PCs. Heavy and inefficient, these batteries also suffered from a memory effect that could drastically shorten the overall life of the battery. *See also* NiMH (nickel metal hydride), Li-Ion (lithium ion).

NiMH (nickel metal hydride)   A type of battery used in portable PCs. NiMH batteries had fewer issues with the "memory" effect than NiCd batteries. NiMH batteries have been replaced by lithium-ion batteries. *See also* NiCd (nickel-cadmium), Li-Ion (lithium ion).

Nit   A value used to measure the brightness of an LCD displays. A typical LCD display has a brightness of between 100 and 400 nits.

Node   A member of a network or a point where one or more functional units interconnect transmission lines.

Noise   Undesirable signals bearing no desired information and frequently capable of introducing errors into the communication process.

Non-system disk or disk error   An error that occurs during the boot process. Common causes for this error are leaving a non-bootable floppy disk in the floppy disk drive while the computer is booting.

Non-volatile   A type of memory that retains data even if power is removed.

Normal backup   A full backup of every selected file on a system. This type of backup turns off the archive bit after the backup.

Northbridge   The chip that connects a CPU to memory, the PCI bus, Level 2 cache, and AGP activities; it communicates with the CPU through the FSB. Newer Athlon 64-bit CPUs feature an integrated Northbridge.

NOS (network operating system)   An NOS is a standalone operating system or part of an operating system that provides basic file and supervisory services over a network. Although each computer attached to the network will have its own OS, the NOS describes which actions are allowed by each user and coordinates distribution of networked files to the user who requests them.

Notification area   Located by default at the right edge of the Windows taskbar, the notification area contains icons representing background processes, and also contains the system clock and volume control. Most users call this area the System Tray.

Ns (nanosecond)   A billionth of a second. Light travels 11 inches in one nanosecond.

NTBOOTDD.SYS   A critical Windows system file only for PCs booting to SCSI drives.

NTDETECT.COM   One of the critical Windows startup files.

NTFS (NT File System)   A robust and secure file system that was introduced by Microsoft with Windows NT. NTFS provides an amazing array of configuration options for user access and security. Users can be granted access to data on a file-by-file basis. NTFS enables object-level security, long filename support, compression, and encryption.

NTFS permissions   A set of restrictions that determine the amount of access given to a particular user on a system using NTFS.

NTLDR   A Windows NT/2000/XP boot file. Launched by the MBR or MFT, NTLDR looks at the BOOT.INI configuration file for any installed operating systems.

NVIDIA   A company that is one of the foremost manufacturers of graphics cards and chipsets.

NWLink   Also called **IPX/SPX-Compatible Protocol.** Microsoft's implementation of IPX/SPX. *See also* IPX/SPX.

Object   A system component that is given a set of characteristics and can be managed by the operating system as a single entity.

Ohm(s)   Electronic measurement of a cable's impedance.

OS (operating system)   A series of programs and code that create an interface so that a user can interact with a system's hardware, for example, DOS, Windows, and Linux.

OS X   Pronounced "ten" rather than "ex;" the current operating system on Apple Macintosh computers. Based on a Unix core, early versions of OS X ran on Motorola-based hardware; current versions run on Intel-based hardware.

OSI (Open Systems Interconnect)   An international standard suite of protocols, defined by the International Organization for Standardization (ISO), that implements the OSI reference model for network communications between computers.

OSI seven-layer model   An architecture model based on the OSI protocol suite that defines and standardizes the flow of data between computers. The seven layers are:

Layer 1   The **Physical layer** defines hardware connections and turns binary into physical pulses (electrical or light). Repeaters and hubs operate at the Physical layer.

Layer 2   The **Data Link layer** identifies devices on the Physical layer. MAC addresses are part of the Data Link layer. Bridges operate at the Data Link layer.

Layer 3   The **Network layer** moves packets between computers on different networks. Routers operate at the Network layer. IP and IPX operate at the Network layer.

Layer 4   The **Transport layer** breaks data down into manageable chunks. TCP, UDP, SPX, and NetBEUI operate at the Transport layer.

Layer 5   The **Session layer** manages connections between machines. NetBIOS and Sockets operate at the Session layer.

Layer 6   The **Presentation layer,** which can also manage data encryption, hides the differences between various types of computer systems.

Layer 7   The Application layer provides tools for programs to use to access the network (and the lower layers). HTTP, FTP, SMTP, and POP3 are all examples of protocols that operate at the Application layer.

Overclocking   To run a CPU or video processor faster than its rated speed.

P1 connector   A type of connector used to provide power to ATX motherboards.

P4 12V connector   A type of connector used to provide additional 12-volt power to motherboards that support Pentium 4 and later processors.

P8 and P9 connectors   A type of connector used to provide power to AT-style motherboards.

Packet   Basic component of communication over a network. A group of bits of fixed maximum size and well-defined format that is switched and transmitted as a single entity through a network. It contains source and destination address, data, and control information.

Paragraph   A unit of 64 binary bits; eight bytes. Not a commonly used term.

Parallel port   A connection for the synchronous, high-speed flow of data along parallel lines to a device, usually a printer.

Parity   A method of error detection where a small group of bits being transferred are compared to a single "parity" bit that is set to make the total bits odd or even. The receiving device reads the parity bit and determines if the data is valid based on the oddness or evenness of the parity bit.

Partition   A section of the storage area of a hard disk. A partition is created during initial preparation of the hard disk, before the disk is formatted.

Partition table   A table located in the boot sector of a hard drive that lists every partition on the disk that contains a valid operating system.

Password reset disk   A special type of floppy disk that can enable a user to recover a lost password without losing access to any encrypted, or password-protected, data.

PATA (parallel ATA)   A disk drive implementation that integrates the controller on the disk drive itself. *See also* ATA, IDE, SATA.

Patch   A small piece of software released by a software manufacturer that is used to correct a flaw or problem with a particular piece of software.

Patch cables   Short (2–5 foot) UTP cables that connect patch panels to hubs.

Patch panel   A panel containing a row of female connectors (ports) that terminate the horizontal cabling in the equipment room. Patch panels facilitate cabling organization and provide protection to horizontal cabling.

Path   The route the operating system must follow to find an executable program stored in a subdirectory.

PC Card   Credit card-sized adapter cards that add functionality in many notebook computers, PDAs, and other computer devices. PC Cards come in 16-bit and CardBus parallel format and ExpressCard serial format. *See also* PCMCIA.

PCI (peripheral component interconnect)   A design architecture for the expansion bus on the computer motherboard, which enables system components to be added to the computer. PCI is a "local bus" standard, meaning that devices added to a computer through this port will use the processor at the motherboard's full speed (up to 33 MHz), rather than at the slower 8 MHz speed of the regular bus. In addition to moving data at a faster rate, PCI moves data 32 or 64 bits at a time, rather than the 8 or 16 bits that the older ISA buses supported.

PCIe (PCI Express)   The serialized successor to PCI and AGP, which uses the concept of individual data paths called lanes. A PCIe slot may use any number of lanes, although single lanes (×1) and 16 lanes (×16) are the most common on motherboards.

PCL   A printer control language created by Hewlett-Packard and used on a broad cross-section of printers.

PCMCIA (Personal Computer Memory Card International Association)   A consortium of computer manufacturers who devised the PC Card standard for credit card–sized adapter cards that add functionality in many notebook computers, PDAs, and other computer devices.

PDA (personal digital assistant) A handheld computer that blurs the line between the calculator and computer. Early PDAs were calculators that enabled the user to program in such information as addresses and appointments. Modern PDAs, such as the Palm and PocketPC, are fully programmable computers. Most PDAs use a pen/stylus for input rather than a keyboard. A few of the larger PDAs have a tiny keyboard in addition to the stylus.

Peer-to-peer networks A network in which each machine can act as both a client and a server.

Pentium Name given to the fifth and later generations of Intel microprocessors; has a 32-bit address bus, 64-bit external data bus, and dual pipelining. Also used for subsequent generations of Intel processors—the Pentium Pro, Pentium II, Pentium III, and Pentium 4. The Pentium name was retired after the introduction of the Intel Core CPUs.

Peripheral Any device that connects to the system unit.

PGA (pin grid array) A popular CPU package where a CPU is packaged in a ceramic material and a large number of pins extend from the bottom of the package. There are many variations on PGA.

Phoenix Technologies Major producer of BIOS software for motherboards.

Phosphor An electro-fluorescent material used to coat the inside face of a cathode ray tube (CRT). After being hit with an electron, it glows for a fraction of a second.

Photo CD A compressed image format developed by Kodak that allows for many photos to be stored on a single CD-ROM.

Photosensitive drum An aluminum cylinder coated with particles of photosensitive compounds that is used in a laser printer. The photosensitive drum is usually contained within the toner cartridge.

Physical address Defines a specific machine without any reference to its location or network. A MAC address is an example of a physical address.

Pin 1 A designator used to ensure proper alignment of floppy disk drive and hard drive connectors.

Ping (packet Internet groper) Slang term for a small network message (ICMP ECHO) sent by a computer to check for the presence and aliveness of another. Used to verify the presence of another system. Also the command used at a prompt to ping a computer.

PIO (programmable input/output) Using the address bus to send communication to a peripheral. The most common way for the CPU to communicate with peripherals.

PIO mode A series of speed standards created by the Small Form Factor committee for the use of PIO by hard drives. The PIO modes range from PIO mode 0 to PIO mode 4.

Pipeline A processing methodology where multiple calculations take place simultaneously by being broken into a series of steps. Often used in CPUs and video processors.

Pixel (picture element) In computer graphics, the smallest element of a display space that can be independently assigned color or intensity.

Platen The cylinder that guides paper through an impact printer and provides a backing surface for the paper when images are impressed onto the page.

Platform Hardware environment that supports the running of a computer system.

Plug A hardware connection with some sort of projection, which connects to a port.

Plug and play (PnP) A combination of smart PCs, smart devices, and smart operating systems that automatically configure all the necessary system resources and ports when you install a new peripheral device.

POP3 (Post Office Protocol) Also called **point of presence**. Refers to the way e-mail software such as Eudora gets mail from a mail server. When you obtain a SLIP, PPP, or shell account you almost always get a POP account with it; and it is this POP account that you tell your e-mail software to use to get your mail.

Port (input/output) A predefined combination of I/O address and IRQ assigned to a physical serial or parallel port. They have names that start with "COM" for serial ports and "LPT" for parallel ports. For example, COM1, one of the preset designations for serial ports, is defined as I/O address 3F8 with IRQ 4.

Port (physical connection) The part of a connector into which a plug is inserted. Physical ports are also referred to as jacks.

Port or port number In networking, the number used to identify the requested service (such as SMTP or FTP) when connecting to a TCP/IP host. Some example port numbers include 80 (HTTP), 20 (FTP), 69 (TFTP), 25 (SMTP), and 110 (POP3).

Port replicator A device that plugs into a USB port or other specialized port that offers common PC ports, such as serial, parallel, USB, network, and PS/2. By plugging your notebook computer into the port replicator, you can instantly connect it to non-portable components such as a printer, scanner, monitor, or a full-sized keyboard. Port replicators are typically used at home or in the office with the non-portable equipment already connected.

POST (power-on self test) A basic diagnostic routine completed by a system at the beginning of the boot process. The POST checks to make sure that a display adapter is installed and that a system's memory is installed; then it searches for an operating system before handing over control of the machine to an operating system, if one is found.

POST cards A diagnostic tool used to identify problems that occur during the POST. These cards usually fit into a PCI slot and have a series of LED indicators to indicate any problems that occur during the POST. *See also* POST (power-on self test).

PostScript A language defined by Adobe Systems, Inc. for describing how to create an image on a page. The description is independent of the resolution of the device that will actually create the image. It includes a technology for defining the shape of a font and creating a raster image at many different resolutions and sizes.

POTS (plain old telephone service) *See* PSTN.

Power conditioning The process of ensuring and adjusting incoming AC wall power to as close to standard as possible. Most UPS devices provide power conditioning.

Power supply A device that provides the electrical power for a PC. A power supply converts standard AC power into various voltages of DC electricity in a PC.

Power supply fan A small fan located in a system power supply that draws warm air from inside the power supply and exhausts it to the outside.

Power User(s) The second most powerful account and group type in Windows after Administrator/Administrators.

ppm (pages per minute) A measure of the speed of a printer.

PPP (Point-to-Point Protocol) A protocol that enables a computer to connect to the Internet through a dial-in connection and enjoy most of the benefits of a direct connection. PPP is considered to be superior to SLIP because of its error detection and data compression features, which SLIP lacks, and the ability to use dynamic IP addresses.

PPTP (Point-to-Point Tunneling Protocol) Protocol that works with PPP to provide a secure data link between computers using encryption.

Primary corona A wire, located near the photo-sensitive drum in a laser printer, that is charged with extremely high voltage in order to form an electric field, enabling voltage to pass to the photosensitive drum, thus charging the photosensitive particles on the surface of the drum.

Primary partition The partition on a Windows hard drive designated to store the operating system.

Print resolution The quality of a print image.

Printer An output device that can print text or illustrations on paper. Microsoft uses the term to refer to the software that controls the physical print device.

Program, programming A series of binary electronic commands sent to a CPU to get work done.

Promiscuous mode A mode of operation for a network interface card where the NIC processes all packets that it sees on the cable.

Prompt A character or message provided by an operating system or program to indicate that it is ready to accept input.

Proprietary Technology unique to a particular vendor.

Protected mode The operating mode of a CPU allowing more than one program to be run while ensuring that no program can corrupt another program currently running.

Protocol   An agreement that governs the procedures used to exchange information between cooperating entities; usually includes how much information is to be sent, how often it is sent, how to recover from transmission errors, and who is to receive the information.

Protocol stack   The actual software that implements the protocol suite on a particular operating system.

Protocol suite   A set of protocols that are commonly used together and operate at different levels of the OSI seven-layer model.

Proxy server   A device that fetches Internet resources for a client without exposing that client directly to the Internet. Most proxy servers accept requests for HTTP, FTP, POP3, and SMTP resources. The proxy server will often cache, or store, a copy of the requested resource for later use. A common security feature in the corporate world.

PSTN (public switched telephone network)   Also called **POTS (plain old telephone service)**. Most common type of phone connection that takes your sounds—translated into an analog waveform by the microphone—and transmits them to another phone.

QIC (quarter inch cassette or cartridge)   Tape backup cartridges that use quarter-inch tape.

Queue   The area where objects wait their turn to be processed. Example: the printer queue, where print jobs wait until it is their turn to be printed.

Quick Launch menu   A toolbar that enables you to launch commonly-used programs with a single click.

QVGA   Video display mode of 320 × 240.

RAID (redundant array of inexpensive devices)   A way of creating a fault-tolerant storage system. There are six levels. Level 0 uses byte-level striping and provides no fault tolerance. Level 1 uses mirroring or duplexing. Level 2 uses bit-level striping. Level 3 stores error-correcting information (such as parity) on a separate disk, and uses data striping on the remaining drives. Level 4 is level 3 with block-level striping. Level 5 uses block level and parity data striping.

RAID-5 volume   A striped set with parity. *See also* RAID (redundant array of inexpensive devices).

RAM (random access memory)   Memory that can be accessed at random, that is, in which any memory address can be written to or read from without touching the preceding address. This term is often used to mean a computer's main memory.

RAMDAC (random access memory digital-to-analog converter)   The circuitry used on video cards that support analog monitors to convert the digital video data to analog.

Raster   The horizontal pattern of lines that form an image on the monitor screen.

RDRAM (Rambus DRAM)   A patented RAM technology that uses accelerated clocks to provide very high-speed memory.

Read-only attribute   A file attribute that does not allow a file to be altered or modified. This is helpful when protecting system files that should not be edited.

Real-time   The processing of transactions as they occur rather than batching them. Pertains to an application in which response to input is fast enough to affect subsequent inputs and guide the process, and in which records are updated immediately. The lag from input time to output time must be sufficiently small for acceptable timeliness. Timeliness is a function of the total system: missile guidance requires output within a few milliseconds of input, scheduling of steamships requires response time in days. Real-time systems respond in milliseconds, interactive systems in seconds, and batch systems in hours or days.

Recovery Console   A command-line interface boot mode for Windows that is used to repair a Windows 2000 or Windows XP system that is suffering from massive OS corruption or other problems.

Recycle Bin   When files are "deleted" from a modern Windows system, they are moved to the Recycle Bin. To permanently remove files from a system, they must be emptied from the Recycle Bin.

Refresh   The process of repainting the CRT screen, causing the phosphors to remain lit (or change).

REGEDIT.EXE   A program used to edit the Windows registry.

REGEDT32.EXE A program used to edit the Windows registry. REGEDT32.EXE is available in Windows 2000 and XP only.

Register A storage area inside the CPU used by the onboard logic to perform calculations. CPUs have many registers to perform different functions.

Registry A complex binary file used to store configuration data about a particular system. To edit the Registry, a user can use the applets found in the Control Panel or REGEDIT.EXE or REGEDT32.EXE.

Remote access The ability to access a computer from outside of the building in which it is housed. Remote access requires communications hardware, software, and actual physical links.

Remote Desktop Connection The Windows XP tool to enable a local system to graphically access the desktop of a remote system.

Repeater A device that takes all of the data packets it receives on one Ethernet segment and re-creates them on another Ethernet segment. This allows for longer cables or more computers on a segment. Repeaters operate at Level 1 (Physical) of the OSI seven-layer model.

Resistor Any material or device that impedes the flow of electrons. Electronic resistors measure their resistance (impedance) in Ohms. (*See* Ohm(s).)

Resolution A measurement for CRTs and printers expressed in horizontal and vertical dots or pixels. Higher resolutions provide sharper details and thus display better-looking images.

Restore point A system snapshot created by the System Restore utility that is used to restore a malfunctioning system. *See also* system restore.

RG-58 Coaxial cabling used for 10Base2 networks.

RIMM (not an abbreviation) An individual stick of Rambus RAM.

RIS (Remote Installation Services) A tool introduced with Windows 2000 that can be used to initiate either a scripted installation or an installation of an image of an operating system onto a PC.

Riser card A special adapter card, usually inserted into a special slot on a motherboard, that changes the orientation of expansion cards relative to the motherboard. Riser cards are used extensively in slimline computers to keep total depth and height of the system to a minimum.

RJ (registered jack) UTP cable connectors, used for both telephone and network connections. **RJ-11** is a connector for four-wire UTP; usually found in telephone connections. **RJ-45** is a connector for eight-wire UTP; usually found in network connections.

RJ-11 *See* RJ (registered jack).

RJ-45 *See* RJ (registered jack).

ROM (read-only memory) The generic term for non-volatile memory that can be read from but not written to. This means that code and data stored in ROM cannot be corrupted by accidental erasure. Additionally, ROM retains its data when power is removed, which makes it the perfect medium for storing BIOS data or information such as scientific constants.

Root directory The directory that contains all other directories.

Router A device connecting separate networks that forwards a packet from one network to another based on the network address for the protocol being used. For example, an IP router looks only at the IP network number. Routers operate at Layer 3 (Network) of the OSI seven-layer model.

RS-232C A standard port recommended by the Electronics Industry Association for serial devices.

Run dialog box A command box designed to enable users to enter the name of a particular program to run; an alternative to locating the icon in Windows.

S.M.A.R.T. (Self-Monitoring, Analysis, and Reporting Technology) A monitoring system built into hard drives.

S/PDIF (Sony/Philips Digital Interface Format) A digital audio connector found on many high-end sound cards. This connector enables a user to connect their computer directly to a 5.1 speaker system or receiver. S/PDIF comes in both a coaxial and an optical version.

Safe mode An important diagnostic boot mode for Windows that causes Windows to start only running very basic drivers and turning off virtual memory.

Sampling The process of capturing sound waves in electronic format.

SATA (serial ATA) A serialized version of the ATA standard that offers many advantages over PATA (parallel ATA) technology, including new, thinner cabling, keyed connectors, and lower power requirements.

ScanDisk A utility included with Windows designed to detect and repair bad sectors on a hard disk.

SCSI (small computer system interface) A powerful and flexible peripheral interface popularized on the Macintosh and used to connect hard drives, CD-ROM drives, tape drives, scanners, and other devices to PCs of all kinds. Because SCSI is less efficient at handling small drives than IDE, it did not become popular on IBM-compatible computers until price reductions made these large drives affordable. Normal SCSI enables up to seven devices to be connected through a single bus connection, whereas Wide SCSI can handle 15 devices attached to a single controller.

SCSI chain A series of SCSI devices working together through a host adapter.

SCSI ID A unique identifier used by SCSI devices. No two SCSI devices may have the same SCSI ID.

SCSI-1 The first official SCSI standard. SCSI-1 is defined as an 8-bit, 5-MHz bus capable of supporting eight SCSI devices.

SCSI-2 Another SCSI standard that was the first SCSI standard to address all aspects of SCSI in detail. SCSI-2 defined a common command set that allowed all SCSI devices to communicate with one another.

SCSI-3 The latest SCSI standard that offers transfer rates up to 320 MBps.

SD (Secure Digital) A very popular format for flash media cards; also supports I/O devices.

SDRAM (synchronous DRAM) A type of DRAM that is synchronous, or tied to the system clock. This type of RAM is used in all modern systems.

SDRAM (synchronous DRAM) DRAM that is tied to the system clock and thus runs much faster than traditional FPM and EDO RAM.

SE (single-ended) A term used to describe SCSI-1 devices that used only one wire to communicate a single bit of information. Single-ended SCSI devices are vulnerable to common-mode noise when used in conjunction with SCSI cables over 6 meters in length.

SEC (single-edge cartridge) A radical CPU package where the CPU was contained in a cartridge that snapped into a special slot on the motherboard called *Slot 1*.

Sector A segment of one of the concentric tracks encoded on the disk during a low-level format. A sector holds 512 bytes of data.

Sector translation The translation of logical geometry into physical geometry by the onboard circuitry of a hard drive.

Segment The bus cable to which the computers on an Ethernet network connect.

Serial port A common connector on a PC used to connect input devices (such as a mouse) or communications devices (such as a modem).

Server A computer that shares its resources, such as printers and files, with other computers on a network. An example of this is a Network File System Server that shares its disk space with a workstation that does not have a disk drive of its own.

Service pack A collection of software patches released at one time by a software manufacturer.

Services Background programs running in Windows that provide a myriad of different functions such as printer spooling and wireless networking.

Setuplog.txt A log file that tracks the complete installation process, logging the success or failure of file copying, Registry updates, and reboots.

Share-level security Security system in which each resource has a password assigned to it; access to the resource is based on knowing the password.

Shareware A program protected by copyright; holder allows (encourages!) you to make and distribute copies under the condition that those who adopt the software after preview pay a fee to the holder of the copyright. Derivative works are not allowed, although you may make an archival copy.

Shell   A term that generally refers to the user interface of an operating system. A shell is the command processor that is the actual interface between the kernel and the user.

Shunt   A tiny connector of metal enclosed in plastic that creates an electrical connection between two posts of a jumper.

SIMM (single in-line memory module)   A type of DRAM packaging distinguished by having a number of small tabs that install into a special connector. Each side of each tab is the same signal. SIMMs come in two common sizes: 30-pin and 72-pin.

Simple volume   A type of volume created when setting up dynamic disks. A simple volume acts like a primary partition on a dynamic disk.

Single-session drive   An early type of CD-R drive that required a disc to be burned in a single session. This type of drive has been replaced by multisession drives. *See also* multisession drive.

Slimline   A motherboard form factor used to create PCs that were very thin. NLX and LPX were two examples of this form factor.

Slot covers   Metal plates that cover up unused expansion slots on the back of a PC. These items are useful in maintaining proper airflow through a computer case.

Smart battery   A new type of portable PC battery that tells the computer when it needs to be charged, conditioned, or replaced.

SmartMedia   A format for flash media cards; no longer used with new devices.

SMM (System Management Mode)   A special CPU mode that enables the CPU to reduce power consumption via the selective shutdown of peripherals.

SMTP (Simple Mail Transport Protocol)   The main protocol used to send electronic mail on the Internet.

Snap-ins   Small utilities that can be used with the Microsoft Management Console.

SNMP (Simple Network Management Protocol)   A set of standards for communication with devices connected to a TCP/IP network. Examples of these devices include routers, hubs, and switches.

SO DIMM (small outline DIMM)   A type of memory used in portable PCs because of its small size.

Social engineering   The process of using or manipulating people inside the networking environment to gain access to that network from the outside.

Socket   A combination of a port number and an IP address that uniquely identifies a connection. Also a mounting area for an electronic chip.

Soft power   A characteristic of ATX motherboards. They can use software to turn the PC on and off. The physical manifestation of soft power is the power switch. Instead of the thick power cord used in AT systems, an ATX power switch is little more than a pair of small wires leading to the motherboard.

Soft-off by PWRBTN   A value found in the BIOS of most ATX motherboards. This value controls the length of time that the power button must be depressed in order for an ATX computer to turn off. If the on/off switch is set for a four-second delay, you must hold down the switch for four seconds before the computer cuts off.

Software   A single group of programs designed to do a particular job; always stored on mass storage devices.

Sound card   An expansion card that can produce audible tones when connected to a set of speakers.

Sounds and Audio Devices   A Control Panel applet used to configure audio hardware and software in Windows XP.

Southbridge   The Southbridge is part of a motherboard chipset. It handles all the inputs and outputs to the many devices in the PC.

Spanned volume   A volume that uses space on multiple dynamic disks.

SPD (serial presence detect)   Information stored on a RAM chip that describes the speed, capacity, and other aspects of the RAM chip.

Spool   A scheme that enables multiple devices to write output simultaneously to the same device, such as multiple computers printing to the same printer at the same time. The data is actually written to temporary files while a program called a *spooler* sends the files to the device one at a time.

SPS (standby power supply or **system)** A device that supplies continuous clean power to a computer system immediately following a power failure. *See also* UPS (uninterruptible power supply).

SRAM (static RAM) A type of RAM that uses a flip-flop type circuit rather than the typical transistor/capacitor of DRAM to hold a bit of information. SRAM does not need to be refreshed and is faster than regular DRAM. Used primarily for cache.

Standard account A type of user account in Windows Vista that has limited access to a system. Accounts of this type cannot alter system files, cannot install new programs, and cannot edit some settings using the Control Panel without supplying an administrator password. Replaces the Limited accounts in Windows XP.

Standouts Small connectors that screw into a computer case. A motherboard is then placed on top of the standouts, and small screws are used to secure the motherboard to the standouts.

Start menu A menu that can be accessed by clicking the Start button on the Windows taskbar. This menu enables you to see all programs loaded on the system and to start them.

Startup disk A bootable floppy disk that contains just enough files to perform basic troubleshooting from an A:\ prompt.

Stick The generic name for a single physical SIMM, RIMM, or DIMM.

STP (shielded twisted pair) A popular cabling for networks composed of pairs of wires twisted around each other at specific intervals. The twists serve to reduce interference (also called *crosstalk*). The more twists, the less interference. The cable has metallic shielding to protect the wires from external interference. Token Ring networks are the only common network technology that uses STP, although Token Ring more often now uses UTP.

Stripe set Two or more drives in a group that are used for a striped volume.

Subdirectories A directory that resides inside of another directory.

Subnet In a TCP/IP internetwork, each independent network is referred to as a subnet.

Subnet mask The value used in TCP/IP settings to divide the IP address of a host into its component parts: network ID and host ID.

Subwoofer A powerful speaker capable of producing extremely low-frequency sounds.

Super I/O chip A chip specially designed to control low-speed, legacy devices such as the keyboard, mouse, and serial and parallel ports.

Superuser Default, all-powerful account in UNIX/Linux.

Surge suppressor An inexpensive device that protects your computer from voltage spikes.

SVGA (super video graphics array) Video display mode of 800 × 600.

Swap file A name for the large file used by virtual memory.

Switch A device that filters and forwards traffic based on some criteria. A bridge and a router are both examples of switches.

SXGA Video display mode of 1280 × 1024.

SXGA+ Video display mode of 1400 × 1050.

Synchronous Describes a connection between two electronic devices where neither must acknowledge ("ACK") when receiving data.

System attribute A file attribute used to designate important system files, like CONFIG.SYS or WIN.INI.

System BIOS The primary set of BIOS stored on an EPROM or Flash chip on the motherboard. Defines the BIOS for all the assumed hardware on the motherboard, such as keyboard controller, floppy drive, basic video, RAM, etc.

System bus speed The speed at which the CPU and the rest of the PC operates; set by the system crystal.

System crystal The crystal that provides the speed signals for the CPU and the rest of the system.

System fan The name of any fan controlled by the motherboard but not directly attached to the CPU.

System Monitor A utility that can be used to evaluate and monitor system resources, like CPU usage and memory usage.

System resources   System resources are I/O addresses, IRQs, DMA channels, and memory addresses.

System Restore   A utility in Windows Me that enables you to return your PC to a recent working configuration when something goes wrong. System Restore returns your computer's system settings to the way they were the last time you remember your system working correctly—all without affecting your personal files or e-mail.

System ROM   The ROM chip that stores the system BIOS.

System Tools menu   A menu that can be accessed by selecting Start | Accessories | System Tools. In this menu, you can access tools like System Information and Disk Defragmenter.

System Tray   Located by default at the right edge of the Windows taskbar, the system tray contains icons representing background processes, and also contains the system clock. Accurately called the "notification area."

System unit   The main component of the PC in which the CPU, RAM, CD-ROM, and hard drive reside. All other devices like the keyboard, mouse, and monitor connect to the system unit.

Tablet PC   A small portable computer distinguished by the use of a touch screen with stylus and handwriting recognition as the primary mode of input. Also the name of the Windows operating system designed to run on such systems.

Task Manager   The Task Manager shows all running programs, including hidden ones. You access the Task Manager by pressing CTRL-ALT-DEL. You can use it to shut down an unresponsive application that refuses to close normally.

Taskbar   Located by default at the bottom of the desktop, the taskbar contains the Start button, the system tray, the Quick Launch bar, and buttons for running applications.

TCP (Transmission Control Protocol)   Part of the TCP/IP protocol suite, TCP operates at Layer 4 (the Transport layer) of the OSI seven-layer model. TCP is a connection-oriented protocol.

TCP/IP (Transmission Control Protocol/Internet Protocol)   A set of communication protocols developed by the U.S. Department of Defense that enables dissimilar computers to share information over a network.

TCP/IP services   A set of special sharing functions unique to TCP/IP. The most famous is Hypertext Transfer Protocol (HTTP), the language of the World Wide Web. Telnet and Ping are two other widely-used TCP/IP services.

Tera-   A prefix that usually stands for the binary number 1,099,511,627,776 (2^{40}). When used for mass storage, often shorthand usage for a trillion bytes.

Terabyte   1,099,551,627,776 bytes.

Terminal emulation   Software that enables a PC to communicate with another computer or network as if the PC were a specific type of hardware terminal.

Terminal   A "dumb" device connected to a mainframe or computer network that acts as a point for entry or retrieval of information.

Termination   The use of terminating resistors to prevent packet reflection on a network cable.

Terminator   A resistor that is plugged into the end of a bus cable to absorb the excess electrical signal, preventing it from bouncing back when it reaches the end of the wire. Terminators are used with coaxial cable and on the ends of SCSI chains. RG-58 coaxial cable requires resistors with a 50-Ohm impedance.

Text mode   During a Windows installation, the period when the computer displays simple textual information on a plain background, before switching to full graphical screens. During this part of the installation, the system inspects the hardware, displays the EULA for you to accept, enables you to partition the hard drive, and copies files to the hard drive, including a base set of files for running the graphical portion of the OS.

TFT (thin film transistor)   A type of LCD screen. *See also* active matrix.

Thermal compound   Also called **heat dope**. A paste-like material with very high heat transfer properties; applied between the CPU and the cooling device, it ensures the best possible dispersal of heat from the CPU.

Thread The smallest logical division of a single program.

TIA/EIA (Telecommunications Industry Association, Electronics Industry Association) The standards body that defines most of the standards for computer network cabling. Most of these standards are defined under the TIA/EIA 568 standard.

Toner cartridge The object used to store the toner in a laser printer. *See also* laser printer, toner.

Toner The toner in a laser printer is a fine powder made up of plastic particles bonded to iron particles, used to create the text and images during the printing process.

TRACERT Also called **TRACEROUTE**. A command-line utility used to follow the path a packet takes between two hosts.

Traces Small electrical connections embedded in a circuit board.

Trackball A pointing device distinguished by a ball that is rolled with the fingers.

Transfer corona A thin wire, usually protected by other thin wires, that applies a positive charge to the paper during the laser printing process, drawing the negatively charged toner particles off of the drum and onto the paper.

Triad A group of three phosphors—red, green, blue—in a CRT.

TWAIN (technology without an interesting name) A programming interface that enables a graphics application, such as a desktop publishing program, to activate a scanner, frame grabber, or other image-capturing device.

UAC (User Account Control) A feature in Windows Vista that enables Standard accounts to do common tasks and provides a permissions dialog when Standard *and* Administrator accounts do certain things that could potentially harm the computer (such as attempt to install a program).

UART (universal asynchronous receiver/transmitter) A UART is a device that turns serial data into parallel data. The cornerstone of serial ports and modems.

UDP (User Datagram Protocol) Part of the TCP/IP protocol suite, UDP is an alternative to TCP. UDP is a connectionless protocol.

Ultra DMA A hard drive technology that enables drives to use direct memory addressing. Ultra DMA mode 3 drives—called ATA/33—have data transfer speeds up to 33 MBps. Mode 4 and 5 drives—called ATA/66 and ATA/100, respectively—transfer data at up to 66 MBps for mode 4 and 100 MBps for mode 5. Both modes 4 and 5 require an 80-wire cable and a compatible controller in order to achieve these data transfer rates.

Unattended install A method to install Windows without user interaction.

Unintentional install An installation of a USB device before installing the drivers, creating a nightmare of uninstalling and reinstalling software.

UNIX A popular computer software operating system developed by and for programmers at Bell Labs in the early 1970s, used on many Internet host systems because of its portability across different platforms.

Upgrade Advisor The first process that runs on the XP installation CD. It examines your hardware and installed software (in the case of an upgrade) and provides a list of devices and software that are known to have issues with XP. It can also be run separately from the Windows XP installation, from the Windows XP CD.

Upgrade installation An installation of Windows on top of an earlier installed version, thus inheriting all previous hardware and software settings.

UPS (uninterruptible power supply) A device that supplies continuous clean power to a computer system the whole time the computer is on. Protects against power outages and sags. The term UPS is often used mistakenly when people mean SPS (Stand-by Power Supply).

Upstream A term used to define the part of a USB connection that plugs into a USB hub.

URL (uniform resource locator) An address that defines the location of a resource on the Internet. URLs are used most often in conjunction with HTML and the World Wide Web.

USB (universal serial bus) A general-purpose serial interconnect for keyboards, printers, joysticks, and many other devices. Enables hot-swapping and daisy-chaining devices.

User account A container that identifies a user to an application, operating system, or network, including name, password, user name, groups to which the user belongs, and other information based on the user and the OS or NOS being used. Usually defines the rights and roles a user plays on a system.

User interface A visual representation of the computer on the monitor that makes sense to the people using the computer, through which the user can interact with the computer.

User level security A security system in which each user has an account and access to resources is based on user identity.

User profiles A collection of settings that correspond to a specific user account and may follow the user regardless of the computer at which he or she logs on. These settings enable the user to have customized environment and security settings.

UTP (unshielded twisted pair) A popular type of cabling for telephone and networks, composed of pairs of wires twisted around each other at specific intervals. The twists serve to reduce interference (also called *crosstalk*). The more twists, the less interference. The cable has *no* metallic shielding to protect the wires from external interference, unlike its cousin, STP. 10BaseT uses UTP, as do many other networking technologies. UTP is available in a variety of grades, called *categories*, as follows:

Category 1 UTP Regular analog phone lines—not used for data communications.

Category 2 UTP Supports speeds up to 4 megabits per second.

Category 3 UTP Supports speeds up to 16 megabits per second.

Category 4 UTP Supports speeds up to 20 megabits per second.

Category 5 UTP Supports speeds up to 100 megabits per second.

V standards Standards established by CCITT for modem manufacturers to follow (voluntarily) to ensure compatible speeds, compression, and error correction.

VESA (Video Electronics Standards Association) A consortium of computer manufacturers that standardized improvements to common IBM PC components. VESA is responsible for the Super VGA video standard and the VLB bus architecture.

VGA (Video Graphics Array) The standard for the video graphics adapter that was built into IBM's PS/2 computer. It supports 16 colors in a 640 × 480 pixel video display, and quickly replaced the older CGA (Color Graphics Adapter) and EGA (Extended Graphics Adapter) standards.

VIA Technologies Major manufacturer of chipsets for motherboards. Also produces Socket 370 CPUs through its subsidiary Cyrix that compete directly with Intel.

Video card An expansion card that works with the CPU to produce the images that are displayed on your computer's display.

Virtual Pertaining to a device or facility that does not physically exist, yet behaves as if it does. For example, a system with 4 MB of virtual memory may have only 1 MB of physical memory plus additional (slower and cheaper) auxiliary memory. Yet programs written as if 4 MB of physical memory were available will run correctly.

Virtual memory A section of a system's hard drive that is set aside to be used when physical memory is unavailable or completely in use.

Virus A program that can make a copy of itself without you necessarily being aware of it; some viruses can destroy or damage files, and generally the best protection is always to maintain backups of your files.

Virus definition or **data file** These files are also called signature files depending on the virus protection software in use. These files enable the virus protection software to recognize the viruses on your system and clean them. These files should be updated often.

VIS (viewable image size) A measurement of the viewable image that is displayed by a CRT rather than a measurement of the CRT itself.

Voice coil motor A type of motor used to spin hard drive platters.

Volatile   Memory that must have constant electricity in order to retain data. Alternatively, any programmer six hours before deadline after a non-stop, 48-hour coding session, running on nothing but caffeine and sugar.

Volts (V)   The pressure of the electrons passing through a wire is called voltage and is measured in units called volts (V).

Volume boot sector   The first sector of the first cylinder of each partition has a boot sector called the volume boot sector, which stores information important to its partition, such as the location of the operating system boot files.

Volume   A physical unit of a storage medium, such as tape reel or disk pack, that is capable of having data recorded on it and subsequently read. Also refers to a contiguous collection of cylinders or blocks on a disk that are treated as a separate unit.

VRAM (video RAM)   A type of memory in a video display adapter that's used to create the image appearing on the CRT screen. VRAM uses dual-ported memory, which enables simultaneous reads and writes, making it much quicker than DRAM.

VRM (voltage regulator module)   A small card supplied with some CPUs to ensure that the CPU gets correct voltage. This type of card, which must be used with a motherboard specially designed to accept it, is not commonly seen today.

VRR (vertical refresh rate)   A measurement of the amount of time it takes for a CRT to completely draw a complete screen. This value is measured in hertz, or cycles per second. Most modern CRTs have a VRR of 60 Hz or better.

VxD (virtual device driver)   A special type of driver file used to support older Windows programs. Windows protection errors take place when VxDs fail to load or unload. This usually occurs when a device somehow gets a device driver in both CONFIG.SYS and SYSTEM.INI or the Registry.

WAN (wide area network)   A geographically dispersed network created by linking various computers and local-area networks over long distances, generally using leased phone lines. There is no firm dividing line between a WAN and a LAN.

Warm boot   A system restart performed after the system has been powered and operating. This clears and resets the memory, but does not stop and start the hard drive.

Wattage (watts or W)   The amount of amps and volts needed by a particular device to function is expressed as how much wattage (watts or W) that device needs.

WAV (Windows Audio Format)   The default sound format for Windows.

Wave table synthesis   A technique that supplanted FM synthesis, wherein recordings of actual instruments or other sounds are embedded in the sound card as WAV files. When a particular note from a particular instrument or voice is requested, the sound processor grabs the appropriate prerecorded WAV file from its memory and adjusts it to match the specific sound and timing requested.

Wildcard   A character used during a search to represent search criteria. For instance, searching for "*.doc" will return a list of all files with a .doc extension, regardless of the filename. "*" is the wildcard in that search.

Windows 2000   The Windows version that succeeded Windows NT; it came in both Professional and Server versions.

Windows 9x   A term used collectively for Windows 95, Windows 98, and Windows Me.

Windows NT   The precursor to Windows 2000, XP, and Vista, which introduced many important features (such as HAL and NTFS) used in all later versions of Windows.

Windows Vista   The latest version of Windows; comes in many different versions for home and office use, but does not have a Server version.

Windows XP   The version of Windows that replaced both the entire Windows 9x line and Windows 2000; does not have a Server version.

WINS (Windows Internet Name Service)   A name resolution service that resolves NetBIOS names to IP addresses.

Word   A unit of 16 binary digits or two bytes.

Worm A worm is a very special form of virus. Unlike other viruses, a worm does not infect other files on the computer. Instead, it replicates by making copies of itself on other systems on a network by taking advantage of security weaknesses in networking protocols.

WQUXGA Video display mode of 2560 × 1600.

WS (wait state) A microprocessor clock cycle in which nothing happens.

WSXGA Video display mode of 1440 × 900.

WSXGA+ Video display mode of 1680 × 1050.

WUXGA Video display mode of 1920 × 1200.

WVGA Video display mode of 800 × 480.

WWW (World Wide Web) A system of Internet servers that support documents formatted in HTML and related protocols. The Web can be accessed using Gopher, FTP, HTTP, Telnet, and other tools.

WXGA Video display mode of 1280 × 800.

xD (Extreme Digital) A very small flash media card format.

Xeon A line of Intel CPUs designed for servers.

XGA (extended graphics array) Video display mode of 1024 × 768.

XMS (extended memory services) The RAM above 1 MB that is installed directly on the motherboard, and is directly accessible to the microprocessor. Usually shortened to simply "extended memory."

ZIF (zero insertion force) socket A socket for CPUs that enables insertion of a chip without the need to apply pressure. Intel promoted this socket with its overdrive upgrades. The chip drops effortlessly into the socket's holes, and a small lever locks it in.

INDEX

▪ Numbers

1-byte vs. 2-byte commands, RAM, 107–108
10/100/1000BaseT. *See* UTP Ethernet (10/100/1000BaseT)
100BaseFX, 565
10BaseFL, 565
16-bit PC Cards, 505
16-bit programs, DOS, 381
32-bit processing
    CPUs, 69–70
    RAM form factors and, 110
34-pin ribbon cable, 270
36-pin Centronics connectors, 544
64-bit processing
    CPUs, 92
    PCI bus and, 152
    RAM form factors, 110
    Windows OS, 385
8086 processor, 108
8088 processor
    1-byte vs. 2-byte commands, 108
    16-bit programs, 381
    AX–DX worktables in, 55
    frontside bus, 107
    Intel and AMD and, 66
    machine language example, 56
    PC bus and, 150

▪ A

A (amperes), 188
A connectors, USB, 27
AC (alternating current)
    computing process and, 647
    multimeter for measuring, 190–192
    overview of, 188
    supplying, 189, 193–195
    surge suppressors and, 192–193
    testing AC outlets, 191
    testing AC voltage, 190, 192
    UPS (uninterruptible power supply) and, 193–195
AC adapters, 191
Accelerated Graphics Port (AGP), 153, 486–488

access control, 608–611
    authentication, 609–610
    NFTS vs. FAT, 610–611
    overview of, 608–609
    physical security, 609
    unauthorized access and, 601
    users and groups and, 611
    in Windows XP Home, 383
access control lists (ACLs), 224
access unit interface (AUI), in Thicknet networks, 559
account lockout policies, 615
accounts. *See also* groups; user accounts
ACLs (access control lists), 224
acronyms list, on CD-ROM accompanying this book, 680
activation, Windows XP, 314–315, 353
Active Directory. *See* AD (Active Directory)
active matrix, LCDs, 473
active partitions
    defined, 211
    making primary partition active, 212–213
active PFC (active power factor correction), 201
AD (Active Directory)
    backing up, 604
    directory services in domain-based networks, 571
    Group Policy, 613–614
Ad-Aware, from Lavasoft, 622–623
adapters, SATA power connectors, 197
Add Hardware Wizard
    in Control Panel, 349
    devices, 414–415
    NICs, 576
Add or Remove Programs applet
    Control Panel applets, 348
    software installation, 409
    software removal, 410–411
    Windows components, adding/removing, 411
Add/Remove Hardware applet, Windows 2000, 576

address bus, 61–64
    address space, 63
    chipset for extending, 126
    defined, 62
    devices connecting to, 127
    frontside bus and, 78
    as link between external data bus and RAM, 61
address space, 63
adjustments, display, 480
administrative access, threats and, 602
Administrative Tools
    Computer Management, 360
    Event Viewer, 360, 629
    Performance console, 360
    Windows OS tech utilities, 359, 571–572
Administrator account
    built-in accounts, 398
    creating and managing users, 400
    logon options, 399–400
    password for, 572
    software installation and, 409
    in Windows 2000/XP, 372
Administrators group, 373, 409
Advanced Backup, in Backup Utility, 423
Advanced BIOS Features, CMOS, 138
Advanced Chipset Features, CMOS, 138
Advanced Micro Devices. *See* AMD (Advanced Micro Devices)
Advanced Power Management/ Advanced Configuration and Power Interface. *See* APM/ACPI (Advanced Power Management/ Advanced Configuration and Power Interface)
Advanced Research Projects Agency Network (ARPANET), 574
Advanced tab, Performance Options, 415
Advanced Technology Attachment Packet Interface. *See* ATAPI (Advanced Technology Attachment Packet Interface)

AGP (Accelerated Graphics Port), 153, 486–488
airflow, 84, 520. *See also* fans
allocation units, 251
alpha channels, 483
alternating current. *See* AC (alternating current)
ALU (arithmetic logic unit), 64, 71. *See also* integer unit; man-in-the-box analogy
AMBIOS, BIOS manufacturers, 134
AMD (Advanced Micro Devices), 65–66
    chipset manufacturers, 39, 178
    collaboration with Intel in manufacture of 8088 processor, 66
    competition with Intel, 65
AMD processors
    64-bit processing, 92
    Athlon, 83
    Athlon 64, 95–96
    Athlon 64 (dual core), 97–98
    Athlon Duron, 85–86
    Athlon Thunderbird, 84–85
    Athlon XP (Palomino and Thoroughbred), 87
    Athlon XP (Thorton and Barton), 89
    K5, 76–77
    K6, 81
    mobile versions, 90
    Opteron, 94–95
    pipelining and, 71
    PowerNow (throttling), 91
    Sempron, 96
    Windows XP and, 293
American Standard Code for Information Interchange (ASCII), 542
amperes (A), 188
AMR (audio modem riser), 181
analog LCD monitors, 478
analysis stage, of troubleshooting methodology, 656
answer files, Setup Manager, 320–325
anti-aliasing, LCDs, 475
anti-static tools, 22–24
    anti-static bags, 24
    anti-static mats, 23
    anti-static wrist straps, 23–24

    options for, 24
    potential of static electricity and, 22
antivirus programs, 409, 616–617
APIPA (Automatic Private IP Addressing), 580, 588
APIs (application programming interfaces), 294
APM/ACPI (Advanced Power Management/Advanced Configuration and Power Interface), 517–518
    configuring, 518
    levels of, 517–518
    requirements for, 517
Apple Computer
    FireWire developed by, 442–443
    Macintosh. *See* Macintosh computers
Apple Extensions, ISO-9660, 279
AppleTalk, 574–575
applets, Control Panel, 348
application encryption, 626–629
application programming interfaces (APIs), 294
applications
    accessing and supporting, 296
    analyzing, 651
    Linux, 303
    organizing and manipulating, 297
    OSs and, 293–294
    types of programming applications, 18
ARC naming system, 379
arithmetic logic unit (ALU), 64, 71. *See also* integer unit; man-in-the-box analogy
ARPANET (Advanced Research Projects Agency Network), 574
ASCII (American Standard Code for Information Interchange), 542
aspect ratio
    CRTs, 468
    LCDs, 495
ASR (Automated System Recovery), 424–426
AT Attachment drives. *See* ATA (AT Attachment) drives
AT bus, 150–151
AT motherboards, 170–172
ATA (AT Attachment) drives
    hard drive capacity and, 43
    in portables, 512

ATAPI (Advanced Technology Attachment Packet Interface), 282
Athlon processors
    Athlon, 83
    Athlon 64, 95–96
    Athlon 64 (dual core), 97–98
    Athlon Duron, 85–86
    Athlon Thunderbird, 84–85
    Athlon XP (Palomino and Thoroughbred), 87
    Athlon XP (Thorton and Barton), 89
ATI, chipset manufacturers, 178
ATI video cards, 511
ATX motherboards, 172–174
ATX power supplies
    ATX12V 1.3, 198–199
    ATX12V 2.0, 200
    soft power feature, 197–198
audio connectors, 29–30
audio jacks, 32
audio modem riser (AMR), 181
audits, Event Viewer, 631–632
AUI (access unit interface), in Thicknet networks, 559
authentication
    hardware authentication, 609–610
    network authentication, 625–626
    software authentication, 609
auto-sensing, NICs and switches and, 564
auto-switching power supplies, 521
autodetection, hard drives, 250
Automated System Recovery (ASR), 424–426
Automatic Private IP Addressing (APIPA), 580, 588
Automatic Updates, Windows 2000/XP, 397–398
automating installation, Windows OSs, 320
Autorun, Windows software, 409
Award BIOS, Phoenix, 135–139
AX–DX worktables, in 8088 processor, 55

B

B connectors, USB, 27
backlight, LCD components, 473
backside bus, 78
Backup Operators group, 373

Backup or Restore Wizard, 423,
603–604
Backup Utility (NT Backup), 354,
422–423
Backup, Windows 2000, 422
Backup Wizard, 423, 424–425
backups, 603–605
backing up/restoring data in
Windows installation, 308
essential data, 603–604
making changes to system
and, 655
naming conventions for
Windows backup
programs, 423
off-site storage and,
604–605
overview of, 603
in server environments, 604
tape backups, 425
backward compatibility, NTFS
and, 372
Balanced Technology eXtended (BTX)
motherboards, 175–176
ball mice, 448
bandwidth
CAT levels and, 562
CRT displays, 469–470
sharing, 557
banks, of DIMMs, 112
bar code readers, 457
basic disks, 210–214
active partitions, 212–213
converting basic disks to
dynamic disks, 240–241
extended partitions, 213–214
overview of, 210–211
primary partitions, 211–212
reverting dynamic disks to
basic, 245
basic input/output services. See BIOS
(basic input/output services)
basic volumes, 213
batteries
Li-Ion, 515
Ni-Cd, 514–515
NiMH, 515
portable computing and,
514–516
battery memory, 514
beaming, between PDAs, 499
betamaxed, slang for obsolete, 113
bidirectional printing, 543

binary system
communication in 1s and 0s, 54
converting to/from
hexadecimal, 157–158
biometric devices, 456–457, 609–610
BIOS (basic input/output services),
126–130. See also CMOS
(complementary metal-oxide
semiconductor)
accessing CMOS setup, 135
autodetection of hard
drives, 250
BYOB (Bring Your Own
BIOS), 140
CPU communication with
components, 125–126
CPU communication with
keyboard, 126–130
device drivers and, 141
function of, 130
hardware support, 132
key terms, 144
lab projects, 146
Option ROM, 140
OSs and, 294–295
quizzes, 144–146
review and summary, 142–143
ROM chips and, 131–132
bits, of memory, 60
Blue Screen of Death. See BSoD (Blue
Screen of Death)
Bluetooth
network printers and, 545
wireless networking in
laptops, 513
BNC connectors, in Thinnet
networks, 560
boot devices. See boot disks
boot disks
overview of, 228–229
text mode errors, 326
boot files, 377, 381
boot partition, 378
boot process
booting into XP setup, 314
Windows 2000/XP, 377–378
boot sectors, basic disks, 210
bootable discs. See boot disks
BOOT.INI, 379–381
branch prediction, Pentiums, 72
branch statements, in programs, 60
brightness
LCD displays, 475
measuring in lumens, 477

Bring Your Own BIOS. See BYOB
(Bring Your Own BIOS)
BSoD (Blue Screen of Death), 327
BTX (Balanced Technology eXtended)
motherboards, 175–176
buffered/registered DRAM, 118–119
burner software, 282
bus cable, 554, 557
bus mastering, 163
bus topology, 554, 557
BYOB (Bring Your Own BIOS)
device drivers and, 141, 295
Option ROM, 140
overview of, 140
bytes
1-byte vs. 2-byte commands in
DRAM, 107–108
bits of memory and, 60
hard drive capacity and, 43
RAM capacity and, 39, 111

C

CAB (cabinet) files
EXPAND program, 253
graphical mode errors in
Windows 2000/XP
installation, 327
cables. See also connections/
connectors
parallel cables for printers, 544
USB, 439–440
cables, drive
CD and DVD drives, 44
floppy drives, 42, 270–272
hard drives, 43
cables, networking
coaxial cable, 557, 559
fiber optic, 565
IEEE 1284 cables for parallel
networks, 567
RG-58 for Thinnet, 559
RG-8 for Thicknet, 557
RS-232 cables for serial
networks, 567
STP, 566–567
UTP (unshielded twisted pair),
561–562
cache
CPU, 72–74
RAM, 367–369
SRAM, 73
cameras
digital, 452–454
webcams, 455–456

card readers, USB, 276–277
card services, PC Cards, 506
CardBus, 505
carrier sense multiple access/
    collision detection (CSM/CD),
    557, 566
CAs (certificate authorities),
    627–628
CAS (column array strobe), 117
cases, 37–38. *See also* system unit
CAT levels
    RJ-45 connectors and, 562
    Token Ring cable and, 567
    UTP cable and, 562
CCFL (cold cathode fluorescent
    lamp), 474
CCIE (Cisco Certified Internetwork
    Engineer), 2
CCNA (Cisco Certified Network
    Associate), 4, 5
CCNP (Cisco Certified Networking
    Professional), 4, 5
CD drives. *See also* optical drives
    CD burners, 280
    CD-R drives, 280
    CD-R/RW modular drives for
        laptops, 512
    CD recorders, 284
    overview of, 277
CD-media, 278–284. *See also* optical
    media
    burners, 280
    CD-ROMs, 280
    CD-Rs, 280–281
    CD-RWs, 281–282
    formats, 278–280
    how they work, 278
    music CDs, 283
    recorders for, 284
    types of, 44–45
    Windows OSs and, 282–283
CD-ROM, accompanying this book
    accessing PDF documents
        on, 680
    LearnKey online training,
        680–681
    overview of features on, 679
    shareware and freeware
        on, 680
    system requirements for
        software on, 679
    technical support, 681
    Total Tester on, 679–680

CD-ROMs
    CD-ROM format, 279
    installation discs, 141
    ISO-9660 and, 279
    modular drives for laptops, 512
    PATA technology used by, 44
    repairing, 278
    speeds, 280
    types of optical media, 44
CD-Rs (CD-recordable)
    CD-R format, 279
    CD-R modular drives for
        laptops, 512
    overview of, 280–281
    types of optical media, 44
CD-RWs (CD-rewritable)
    CD-RW format, 279
    CD-RW modular drives for
        laptops, 512
    deleting files from, 282
    overview of, 281–282
    types of optical media, 45
CDDA (CD-Digital Audio), 279
Celeron processors, 81–83
central processing units. *See* CPUs
    (central processing units)
Centrino technology, 90, 523
Centronics connectors (36-pin), 544
certificate authorities (CAs), 627–628
certificates, digital, 627–629
certifications
    CompTIA A+ certification. *See*
        CompTIA A+ certification
    concept of, 1–2
    importance of, 2
    other than CompTIA A+, 3–4
Certified Novell Engineer (CNE), 2
CF (CompactFlash), 275, 499
CFX12V power supply, 201
Challenge Handshake Authentication
    Protocol (CHAP), 626
Change permissions, NTFS, 374
CHAP (Challenge Handshake
    Authentication Protocol), 626
Character Map, in System Tools, 354
Cheapernet. *See* Thin Ethernet
    (10Base2)
chipsets, 176–181
    comparison chart, 180
    device drivers and, 177–178
    manufacturers, 178
    Northbridge and Southbridge
        on, 126, 176–177
    overview of, 169

    schematic of, 179
    Super I/O chip, 177
CHKDSK command, for
    Error-checking, 247–248, 407
circuit breakers, 188
Cisco Certified Internetwork Engineer
    (CCIE), 2
Cisco Certified Network Associate
    (CCNA), 5
Cisco Certified Networking
    Professional (CCNP), 5
Cisco routers, 4
CL2, CL3, RAM latency, 117
class objects, Windows OSs, 365
classes, IP address, 580
clean install
    vs. upgrade, 307
    Windows 2000/XP, 316–320
clean up, in troubleshooting
    methodology, 657
cleaning
    keyboards, 446
    mice, 448–449
    portable computers, 518–519
clicking, in Windows OSs, 339
Client for Microsoft Networks, 576
Client for NetWare, 576
client/server networks
    client configuration, 576–577
    client software, 575
    clients and servers defined, 553
    overview of, 569–570
    server software, 575
clients
    client software, 575
    configuring, 576–577
    defined, 553, 569
    network connectivity
        and, 575
CLK wire, 56, 149
clock, CPU
    CLK wire, 56, 149
    cycle and speed, 57
    system crystal and, 58
clock cycle, in CPU clock, 57
clock doubling, 74
clock-multiplying CPUs, 74
clock speed
    Athlon 64, 95
    in CPU clock, 58
    dual-core processors and, 96
    Intel processors, 74–75
    of later Pentiums, 80
    SDRAM, 112

clusters
    FAT16, 219
    FAT32, 224
    NTFS, 227–228
CMD command, 357
CMOS (complementary metal-oxide semiconductor). *See also* BIOS (basic input/output services)
    accessing CMOS setup, 135
    Advanced BIOS Features, 138
    Advanced Chipset Features, 138
    APM/ACPI configuration, 518
    Features screen, 136
    floppy drive settings, 272–273
    functions of, 134
    hard drive settings, 251
    Integrated Peripherals screen, 138
    key terms, 144
    lab projects, 146
    laser printer settings, 541
    Main screen, 135–136
    "No Fixed Disks Present," 212
    other settings, 139–140
    overview of, 133
    PnP/PCI setting, 139
    Power Management settings, 139
    quizzes, 144–146
    review and summary, 142–143
    setup program, 133–134
    shared memory settings in, 511
    Soft menu, 137
    soft power feature, 197–198
    USB Keyboard Support option in, 445
CMYK (**c**yan, **m**agenta, **y**ellow, and blac**k**)
    dye-sublimation printing and, 536
    inkjet printers and, 534–535
CNE (Certified Novell Engineer), 2
CNR (communications and networking riser), 181
coaxial cable
    RG-58 for Thinnet, 559
    RG-8 for Thicknet, 557
coaxial Ethernet
    overview of, 557
    Thick Ethernet (10Base5), 557–559
    Thin Ethernet (10Base2), 559–560
cold cathode fluorescent lamp (CCFL), 474

color depth, scanners, 451
column array strobe (CAS), 117
COM ports
    serial ports and, 434
    system resources, 161
    UART and, 435
combo cards, UTP Ethernet, 563
COMMAND (CMD) command, 357
command-line interface
    operating systems and, 356–357
    types of user interfaces, 297
command prompt, protecting access to, 614
communications and networking riser (CNR), 181
CompactFlash (CF), 275, 499
compatibility, backward compatibility in NTFS, 372
complementary metal-oxide semiconductor. *See* CMOS (complementary metal-oxide semiconductor)
compression, NTFS, 225
CompTIA 220-602 (IT Technician), 5
CompTIA 220-603 (Help Desk Technician), 5
CompTIA 220-604 (Depot Technician), 5
CompTIA A+ certification
    adaptive exams and, 6
    changes to exams, 5
    cost of exams, 8
    deciding which exams to take, 7–8
    Essentials exam, 6–7
    exam track options, 5–6
    how to become certified, 4–5, 14–15
    how to pass exams, 8–11
    how to take exams, 8
    importance of, 2, 14
    key terms, 15
    path to certifications other than, 3–4
    quizzes, 15–16
    summary/review, 14–15
    what it is, 2–3
CompTIA A+ Certified Service Technicians, 5
CompTIA A+ Essentials
    exam tracks, 5
    subject matter (domains) covered by, 6–7
CompTIA (Computing Technology Industry Association), 3–4

CompTIA Network+ certification, 4
computer components, in CompTIA A+ Essentials exam, 6–7
Computer Management, 350–351, 360
computer security
    access control and, 608–611
    administrative access, 602
    audits, 631–632
    backups and, 603–605
    data destruction, 601–602
    encryption, 624–629
    Event Viewer reports, 629–630
    firewalls, 624
    grayware, 623–624
    groups for controlling user accounts, 611–613
    incidence reports, 632
    key terms, 639
    lab projects, 641–642
    local control of resources and, 602–603
    malware. *See* malware
    migration to new system/ retiring old, 605–607
    network authentication, 625–626
    network security, 611
    overview of, 600
    policies, 613–615
    quizzes, 639–641
    reports, 629
    social engineering attacks, 607–608
    summary/review, 636–638
    system crash/hardware failures, 602
    threat analysis, 601
    unauthorized access, 601
    viruses and spyware, 602
    Vista features, 633–635
    wireless issues, 629
Computer Security Products, Inc., 522
computers/computing process
    how computers work, 644
    input, 646
    interaction of components in, 644–645
    Second Life game as example of, 645
    stages of computing process, 19–20, 644
Computing Technology Industry Association. *See* CompTIA (Computing Technology Industry Association)

conditioning chargers, Ni-Cd batteries and, 514
connections
  displays, 478–480
  video cards to motherboard, 485–486
connections/connectors. *See also* cables
  audio, 29–30, 32–33
  DB connectors. *See* DB connectors
  defined, 26
  device connectors, 30
  digital cameras, 453
  expansion cards, 147
  external connections on PCs, 25–26
  FireWire, 28, 442
  floppy drives, 272
  front connections on PCs, 36
  identifying on system unit, 46
  joysticks, 35–36
  keyboards, 31
  mice, 33–34
  mini connectors, 196, 272
  mini-DIN connectors, 26
  modems, 34
  molex connectors, 196–197
  monitors, 31–32
  motherboard power connectors (P1), 195
  parallel, 161
  PCIe connector, 200
  power connectors, 42, 195–197
  power supplies, 189
  RJ connectors, 29
  scanners, 452
  serial, 154, 161
  sound devices, 32–33
  splitters and adapters, 197
  USB, 27–28, 440
  video, 31–32
connections, network, 33. *See also* cables, networking
  fiber optic Ethernet, 565
  Thicknet, 558–559
  Thinnet, 559–560
  Token Ring, 567
  UTP Ethernet, 561
connections, printer, 543–545
  FireWire, 545
  IEEE 1284 and, 544

network printers, 545
other options, 545
parallel, 35, 543–544
USB, 544–545
connectivity errors, hard drives, 250
continuity RIMMs (CRIMMs), 113
continuous tone images, 536–537
contrast ratio, LCD displays, 476
Control Panel
  Add Hardware Wizard, 349, 576
  Add or Remove Programs, 409
  Administrative Tools, 629
  applets, 349
  Display, 349
  Firewall applet, 624
  Mouse applet, 447
  Power Options, 518–519
  System, 349
  User Accounts applet, 401–405
controllers
  DMA, 162
  floppy drive, 42
  keyboard, 127–130
CONVERT command, 610–611
convertibles, tablet PCs, 500
cooling, challenges to CPU manufacturers, 84
coronas, laser printers
  ozone filters and, 541
  primary, 538
  transfer, 539
counters, System Monitor, 361, 417–418
.CPL extension, 348
CPU cache, 72–74
CPU code names, 84
CPUID (CPU Identifier), 75
CPUs (central processing units)
  64-bit processors, 92
  address bus and, 61–64
  AMD processors. *See* AMD processors
  clock, 56–58
  code names, 84
  communicating with components, 125–126
  communicating with keyboards, 126–130
  comparing, 99
  core components, 52
  dual core, 96
  ESD (electrostatic discharge) and, 40

external data bus and, 58
input process and, 646
Intel. *See* Intel processors
key terms, 101
lab projects, 104
man-in-the-box analogy, 52–54
manufacturers, 64–66
memory and, 58–59
mobile processors, 90–91
multicore, 371
multiple processor support in XP Home edition, 383
OSs and, 293
overview of, 38–39, 51
packages, 66–68
for portable computers, 512
processing and wattage, 84
quizzes, 102–104
RAM and, 60–61
registers, 54–56
review and summary, 100–101
Task Manager for viewing CPU usage, 416
CRC (cyclic redundancy check), 556
CRIMMs (continuity RIMMs), 113
crossover cables, UTP, 564
CRTs (cathode ray tubes), 465–470
  bandwidth, 469–470
  connections, 478–480
  dot pitch, 468–469
  flat vs. traditional, 466
  overview of, 465–466
  phosphors and shadow mask, 467–468
  power conservation, 481
  refresh rates, 466–467
  resolution, 468
  size options, 477–478
CSMA/CD (carrier sense multiple access/collision detection), 557, 566
customer relations, 651–654
  assertive communication and, 654
  eliciting answers from customers, 651–652
  integrity and, 652–653
  overview of, 651
  respect and, 653–654
cyan, **m**agenta, **y**ellow, and blac**k**. *See* CMYK (**c**yan, **m**agenta, **y**ellow, and blac**k**)
cyclic redundancy check (CRC), 556

D

D-sub (D-subminiature)
  connectors, 28
daisy-wheel printers, 533. *See also*
  impact printers
data
      backing up essential, 603–604
      OSs, organizing and
        manipulating, 296–297
data destruction, threat analysis
  and, 601–602
data encryption, 626. *See also*
  encryption
data errors, hard drives, 252–254
Data Execution Prevention (DEP),
  415–416
data files
      backing up/restoring data in
        Windows installation, 308
      restoring, 311
data structures, FAT, 218
DB connectors
      CRTs, 478
      DB-25 parallel cables, 544
      joysticks, 35
      overview of, 28–29
      sound devices and, 32
DC (direct current)
      computing process and, 647
      overview of, 188
      supplying DC power, 195
      testing DC voltage, 190
DDR-SDRAM (double data rate
  SDRAM)
      DDR2-SDRAM, 116
      dual-channel architecture,
        115–116
      fully buffered, 118
      overview of, 114
      speeds, 115
Debian, Linux distributions
  (distros), 303
dedicated servers. *See* servers
default gateways, TCP/IP, 582
definition files, antivirus
  programs, 618
defragmentation, 223. *See also* Disk
  Defragmenter
DEP (Data Execution Prevention),
  415–416
Depot Technician (220-604), 7–8

desktop
      showing folders on, 344–345
      Windows OS, 336, 338
desktop extenders, portable
  computers, 497–498, 503
desktop replacements, portable
  computers, 95, 496–497, 503
device drivers
      BYOB (Bring Your Own BIOS)
        and, 141
      chipset features supported
        by, 177
      defined, 130
      installing before/after
        devices?, 440
      optimizing, 414
      OSs and, 295
      signing, 413–414
      TWAIN drivers for
        scanners, 450
      updating, 351, 412–413
      upgrading, 311
Device Manager, 349–352
      accessing, 349–350
      device driver management, 141
      device drivers, optimizing, 414
      devices, adding, 414–415
      devices, displaying by type, 351
      devices, viewing by I/O
        addresses, 157–158
      DMA resources, viewing, 163
      IRQ management, 159
      as MMC snap-in, 358
      ports, disabling, 444
      serial ports, viewing, 434
      USB speeds, viewing, 438
      working with, 351–352
devices. *See also* hardware
      adding new, 414–415
      connecting, to address bus, 127
      connectors, 30
      controllers on Southbridge and
        Northbridge chipset, 128
      CPUs communicating with, 126
      installing/optimizing, 411–412
      "known good," 444
      My Computer for viewing
        device content, 342
      PCs and, 125
      system resources used by, 156
      Windows Marketplace for
        testing compatibility, 305–307

devices, I/O
      bar code readers, 457
      biometric devices, 456–457
      digital cameras, 452–454
      keyboards, 445–447
      mice, 447–449
      overview of, 445
      scanners, 449–452
      specialty devices, 456
      touch screens, 458
      webcams, 455–456
DHCP (dynamic host configuration
  protocol), 584–585
dial-up encryption, 626
digital cameras, 452–454
      connections, 453
      form factors, 454
      overview of, 452–453
      quality, 454
      as removable storage
        media, 453
digital certificates, 627–629
digital ink, 501
digital LCD monitors, 478–480
digital light processing (DLP), 476
digital multimeter (DMM), 190
digital versatile disc. *See* DVD-media
digital video interface (DVI), 31,
  479–480, 507
digital zoom, 454
DIMMs (dual inline memory
  modules)
      banks, 112
      DDR-SDRAM, 114
      double-sided DIMMs,
        116–117
      laser printers, 541
      RAM sticks, 40
      SDRAM and, 111–112
direct current. *See* DC (direct current)
direct thermal printers, 537
directories, accessing shared, 589
directory services, in domain-based
  networks, 571
Disk Cleanup
      maintaining hard drives,
        248–249
      managing temporary files,
        407–408
      System Tools, 354
disk cloning, Windows OS
  installation, 325–326

Disk Defragmenter
  maintaining hard drives
    and, 248
  regular use of, 406–407
  System Tools, 354
Disk Management (diskmgmt.msc)
  converting basic disks to
    dynamic disks, 240–241
  mirrored volumes and striped
    volumes with parity, 241
  partitioning and formatting
    with, 235–240
  for partitioning drives, 215–216
  simple volumes, 241
  spanned volumes, 241–243
  striped volumes, 243
disk quotas, NTFS, 227
disk space, cleaning up, 354
display adapter. *See* video cards
Display, Control Panel applets, 348
display power-management signaling
  (DPMS), 481
Display properties, Windows
  2000/XP, 483
displays
  adjustments, 480
  basic peripherals, 25
  connections, 478–480
  connectors, 31–32
  Display applet, 349
  external monitors on
    portables, 507
  high voltage hazards and, 465
  LCD, 495–496
  overview of, 465
  power conservation, 481
  size options, 477–478
  summary/review, 489–490
  touch screens, 458
  troubleshooting laptops, 522
dithered images, 536–537
DIX (Digital, Intel, Xerox) connectors,
  in Thicknet networks, 559
DL (dual-layer) DVDs, 285
DLP (digital light processing), 476
DMA (direct memory access), 161–163
  controllers, 162
DMM (digital multimeter), 190
DNS (Domain Name Service),
  582–584
docking stations, laptops, 508–509
documentation, in troubleshooting
  methodology, 657

Documents and Settings
  Documents and Settings
    Transfer Wizard, 605
  Windows folders, 363
domain-based networks, 570–573
domain controllers, in domain-based
  networks, 571
Domain Name Service (DNS), 582–584
domain names, 584
domains (subject matter), CompTIA
  exams, 6
dongles
  USB/FireWire, 181
  USB-to-serial, 434
DOS
  16-bit programs, 381
  early Windows OSs and, 297
dot-matrix printers. *See also* impact
  printers
  overview of, 533
dot pitch, CRT displays, 468–469
dots per inch (dpi), print
  resolution, 535
dotted-decimal notation,
  IP addresses, 579
double data rate SDRAM. *See*
  DDR-SDRAM (double data rate
  SDRAM)
double-pumped frontside bus, in
  Athlon Thunderbird, 85
double-sided DIMMs, 116–117
double-sided (DS) DVD, 284–285
double words, bits of memory and, 60
downloaded program files, Disk
  Cleanup and, 248
dpi (dots per inch), print
  resolution, 535
DPMS (display power-management
  signaling), 481
draft quality, dot-matrix printers, 533
DRAM (dynamic RAM), 61
  1-byte vs. 2-byte commands
    and, 107–108
  buffered/registered, 118–119
  conventions regarding RAM
    capacity, 110
  defined, 106
  ECC (error correction code)
    RAM, 118
  history/development of, 106–107
  organization on RAM
    sticks, 107
  sticks, 108–109

drive letters, partitions, 233–234
driver signing, 413–414
drives
  accessing shared, 589–590
  DVD. *See* DVD drives
  floppy. *See* floppy drives
  hard. *See* hard drives
  modular for laptops, 512
  optical. *See* optical drives
  remnants, 606
  sharing over networks, 588–590
  USB thumb drives. *See* USB
    thumb drives
DS (double-sided) DVD, 284–285
DTR (desktop replacement). *See*
  desktop replacements, portable
  computers
dual-boot operating systems, 211
dual-channel architecture, in RAM
  development, 115
dual-core processors, 96
dual inline memory modules.
  See DIMMs (dual inline memory
  modules)
dual-layer (DL) DVDs, 285
dual-scan passive matrix, LCDs,
  472–473
dumpster diving, social engineering
  attacks, 608
duplex printing, 543
DVD drives
  modular drives for laptops, 512
  PATA technology used by, 44
DVD-media
  defined, 277
  DVD-R, 285–286
  DVD-ROM, 285
  DVD-RW, 285–286
  DVD-video, 284–285
  formats, 45
  modular drives for
    laptops, 512
  overview of, 284–285
  PATA technology used by, 44
  as a type of optical media, 44
DVD-R, 285–286
DVD-ROM, 285
DVD-RW, 285–286
DVD-video, 284–285
DVI (digital video interface), 31,
  479–480, 507
dye-sublimation printers,
  536–537

Mike Meyers' CompTIA A+ Guide: Essentials (Exam 220-601)

dynamic disks, 214–215
    converting basic disks to, 240–241
    defined, 210
    reverting to basic, 245
    simple volumes, 241
    spanned volumes, 241–243
    working with, 245
dynamic host configuration protocol (DHCP), 584–585
dynamic RAM. *See* DRAM (dynamic RAM)
dynamic storage partitioning. *See* dynamic disks

■ E

e-mail, as source of viruses, 619
e-wallet, 621
EasyCleaner, by ToniArts, 408
ECC (error correction code), 253–254
ECC (error correction code) RAM, 118
EDB (external data bus)
    address bus for extending, 61
    chipset for extending, 126
    communication mechanism in man-in-the-box analogy, 53–54
    exercise applying, 58
    frontside bus and, 78
    stages, 70
effective permissions, 612
EFS (encrypting file system)
    NTFS and, 225–227
    in Windows XP Home, 383
EIDE (enhanced IDE). *See also* ATA (AT Attachment) drives
EISA (Extended ISA) bus, 152
El Torito, ISO-9660 extension, 279
electricity, 187–189
electro-photographic imaging, 537. *See also* laser printers
electrostatic discharge. *See* ESD (electrostatic discharge)
electron guns, CRTs, 466–468
embedded PCs, Windows Embedded, 387
Emergency Repair Disk (ERD), 423–424
enclosure. *See* cases
encrypting file system (EFS)
    NTFS and, 225–227
    in Windows XP Home, 383

encryption, 624–629
    application encryption, 626–629
    data encryption, 626
    dial-up encryption, 626
    EFS (encrypting file system), 225–227, 383
    network authentication and, 625–626
    overview of, 624–625
End User License Agreement (EULA), 310–311, 318
enhanced IDE (EIDE). *See also* ATA (AT Attachment) drives
EPS12V, power supplies, 199–200
erase lamp, laser printers, 538
ERD (Emergency Repair Disk), 423–424
Error-checking, hard drives, 247–248
Error-checking, Windows 2000/XP, 406–407
error correction code (ECC), 253–254
error correction code RAM (ECC RAM), 118
errors
    CMOS, 251
    CMOS errors, "No Fixed Disks Present," 212
    connectivity, 250
    data corruption, 252–254
    device error codes, 351
    graphical mode errors, 329
    partitioning and formatting errors, 251–252
    text mode errors, 327–328
escalation, in troubleshooting methodology, 657
ESD (electrostatic discharge)
    anti-static tools, 22–24
    avoiding, 46
    CPUs and RAM vulnerable to, 40
    overview of, 22
Essentials exam. *See* CompTIA A+ Essentials
Essentials, sections in this book, 11
Ethernet
    coaxial Ethernet, 557–560
    fiber optic Ethernet, 565
    standards, 556
    UTP Ethernet (10/100/ 1000BaseT), 560–564
ethic of reciprocity, customer relations, 653

EULA (End User License Agreement), 309–310, 317
evaluation, in troubleshooting methodology, 657
Event Viewer, 360
    auditing with, 631–632
    Help and Support Center (Microsoft.com), 630–631
    incidence reports, 632
Everyone group, 373
exams, CompTIA A+
    changes to exams, 5
    cost of, 8
    deciding which exams to take, 7–8
    Essentials, 6–7
    exam objectives on CD-ROM accompanying this book, 680
    exam tracks, 5–6
    how to pass, 8–11
    how to take, 8
    naming system for, 6
    quizzes, 15–16
    summary/review, 14–15
    Total Tester for preparation, 679–680
EXPAND program, 253
expansion bus, 147–177
    crystal, 149
    ISA bus, 150–151
    key terms, 165
    lab projects, 167
    limitations of EISA, MCA, and VL bus, 152
    modern versions, 151
    overview of, 147–148
    PC bus, 150
    PCI bus, 152–155
    quizzes, 165–167
    review and summary, 164–165
    structure and function of, 148–150
    system resources. *See* system resources
expansion cards. *See* PC Cards
expansion slots. *See also* PC Cards
    device connections on PCs, 30
    more than one type per motherboard, 152
ExpressCard, 505–507
Extended ISA (EISA) bus, 152
extended partitions, 210, 213–214
extensions, file, 342

external connections, PC ports, 25–26
external data bus. *See* EDB (external data bus)
external drives, types of removable media, 268

■ F

F (function) keys (F1, F2, etc.), 346
false positives, antispam programs and, 619
fans
    CPUs and, 38–39
    heat in laptops and, 520
fast page mode (FPM) RAM, 112
Fast User Switching, Windows XP, 405
FAT (file allocation table)
    FAT16, 219–221
    FAT32, 223–224
    fragmentation and, 221–223
    history of Windows OSs, 298–299
    NTFS vs. FAT32 for access control, 610–611
    overview of, 218–219
FDISK
    Linux, 215
    Windows, 215
Features screen, CMOS, 136
Fedora Core, Linux distributions (distros), 303
fiber optic Ethernet, 565
field replaceable units (FRUs), 187, 655
file allocation table. *See* FAT (file allocation table)
file allocation units, 219
File and Printer Sharing, Windows 2000/XP, 575
file association, 366
file extensions, 342
file extensions, icons assigned according to file type, 342
file sharing, 374
file systems
    FAT, 218–219
    FAT16, 219–223
    FAT32, 223–224
    formatting hard drives, 209
    NTFS, 224–228
    overview of, 217–218
    Windows OS installation and, 309

files and folders
    compression and, 225
    hide/unhide file extensions, 342
    NTFS permissions, 374–375
    revealing hidden, 343
    root directory and, 217
    sharing folders over networks, 588–590
    showing folders on desktop, 344–345
    Windows folders, 362–363
Files and Settings Transfer Wizard, System Tools, 354
filters, spam, 619
Firefox, Mozilla, 627–628
firewalls
    need for, 409
    overview of, 624
FireWire
    configuring, 443
    connectors, 28
    laptop ports, 507
    laptops and, 508
    motherboards and, 179–181
    networks, 568
    overview of, 442–443
    printers, 545
    speeds (IEEE 1394a and IEEE 1394b), 443
firmware, ROM chips and, 132
flash cards, 274–276
    CompactFlash (CF), 275
    digital cameras, 453
    Memory Stick, 276
    overview of, 274–275
    Secure Digital (SD), 275–276
    SmartMedia, 275
    xD Picture Card, 276
flash memory, 273–277
    card readers, 276–277
    flash cards, 274–276
    overview of, 273–274
    types of removable media, 268
    USB thumb drives, 274
flash ROM
    laser printers, 541
    motherboards use of, 131
    PDAs and, 499
flatbed scanners, 449. *See also* scanners
FlexATX motherboards, 174
floating point unit (FPU), 71
floppy drives, 268–273
    CMOS settings, 272–273
    controllers, 42

    installing, 270–271
    overview of, 42, 269–270
    power supply for, 272
    ribbon cables for connecting, 271–272
    types of removable media, 268
Folder Options
    hide/unhide file extensions, 342
    revealing hidden files and folders, 343
Folder permissions, NTFS, 374
folders. *See* files and folders
fonts, Windows folders, 363
form factors, 169–172
    32-bit and 64-bit RAM, 110
    AT, 170–172
    ATX drive, 172–174
    ATX power supply, 197–200
    BTX, 175–176
    digital cameras, 454
    niche market power supply form factors, 201
    overview of, 169
    SO-DIMMs for laptops, 112
    tablet PCs, 500
formats
    CD-media, 278–280
    DVD-media, 45
formatting hard drives
    bootable discs, 228–229
    defined, 209
    with Disk Management, 235–240
    errors, 251–252
    FAT16, 219–223
    FAT32, 223–224
    NTFS, 224–228
    overview of, 217
    partitions, 229, 245–246
    Windows file systems, 217–218
    with Windows installation CD, 229
FPM (fast page mode) RAM, 112
FPU (floating point unit), 71
fragmentation
    Disk Defragmenter, 354–355
    FAT (file allocation table) and, 221–223
frames. *See* packets
Free Software Foundation, 303
freeware, on CD-ROM accompanying this book, 680
front connections, on PCs, 36
front-view projectors, 476

frontside bus
    8088 processor, 107
    double-pumped, 85
    increasing clock speed of, 113
    overview of, 78
    quad-pumped, 86
FRUs (field replaceable units), 187, 655
fuel cells, as power source for portables, 515
Full Control, file and folder permissions, 375
full-duplex mode
    fiber optic Ethernet, 565
    UTP Ethernet, 564
Full-Speed USB, 437
fully buffered DDR-SDRAM, 118
function key (FN) on laptops, 507
function keys (F1, F2, etc.), 346
fuser assembly, laser printers, 539–540
fuses, electrical, 188

G

games, Second Life example, 645–650
GART (Graphics Address Remapping Table), 487
Gator, 621
GB (gigabyte)
    defined, 63
    hard drive capacity and, 43
    RAM capacity, 39
GDI (graphical device interface), 543
general public license (GPL), 305
Ghost, Norton, 326
Ghosting, disk imaging with, 325
Gibson Research, SpinRite utility, 254
gigabyte. See GB (gigabyte)
glossary, accessing on CD-ROM accompanying this book, 680
GNU general public license, 303
GParted, Linux partitioning tools, 216, 256–258
GPL (general public license), 303
graphical device interface (GDI), 543
graphical mode errors, Windows OS installation and, 327
graphical user interface. See GUI (graphical user interface)
Graphics Address Remapping Table (GART), 487
graphics video cards, 482
grayware, 623–624
grid-array packages, 67

group policies
    security and, 613–614
    in Windows XP Home, 383
groups
    access control and, 611
    assigning new users to, 401
    for controlling user accounts, 611–613
    default or built in, 398–399
    Local Users and Groups for managing, 399
    NTFS, 373–374
    security and, 398
Guest account, 398
Guests group, 373
GUI (graphical user interface), 297

H

HAL (hardware abstraction layer), 370
half-duplex mode
    fiber optic Ethernet, 565
    UTP Ethernet, 564
handwriting recognition
    CPU power and, 500
    troubleshooting laptops, 523
hard drives
    ATA. See ATA (AT Attachment) drives
    controllers, 646
    costs of data recovery, 655
    lockups and, 328
    overview of, 42–44
    partitioning, 309
    PATA. See PATA (parallel ATA)
    portable computing, 512
    RAID protections. See RAID (redundant array of independent devices)
    SATA. See SATA (serial ATA)
    warranties, 255
hard drives, implementing, 208–266
    basic disk partitioning, 210–214
    bootable discs, 228–229
    converting basic disks to dynamic disks, 240–241
    drive letters, 233–234
    dynamic disk volumes, 214–215
    FAT16, 219–223
    FAT32, 223–224
    formatting drives, 217
    formatting partitions, 245–246
    hidden partitions and swap partitions, 215

key terms, 263
lab projects, 266
mount points, 243–245
NTFS, 224–228
overview of, 209
partitioning and formatting with Disk Management, 235–240
partitioning and formatting with Windows installation CD, 229
partitions, 209–210
quizzes, 263–265
simple volumes, 241
single partition, 229–231
spanned volumes, 241–243
summary/review, 259–261
third-party partition tools, 255–258
two partitions, 231–233
when to partition, 215–217
Windows file systems, 217–218
hard drives, maintaining, 246–249
    Disk Cleanup, 248–249
    Disk Defragmenter, 248
    Error-checking, 247–248
    key terms, 263
    lab projects, 266
    overview of, 246–247
    quizzes, 263–265
    summary/review, 261–263
hard drives, troubleshooting
    CMOS errors, 251
    connectivity errors, 250
    data corruption errors, 252–254
    data rescue specialists, 255
    dying hard drive, 254–255
    key terms, 263
    lab projects, 266
    overview of, 249–250
    partitioning and formatting errors, 251–252
    performing "mental reinstall," 252
    quizzes, 263–265
    summary/review, 261–263
hardware. See also devices
    Add Hardware Wizard, 414–415
    detection errors, 327
    failure and threat analysis, 602
    installing/optimizing, 411–412

hardware (*continued*)
    OS communication with,
        294–295
    system BIOS support, 132
hardware abstraction layer (HAL), 370
hardware compatibility list (HCL), 307
hardware firewalls, 624
hardware protocols, 556
Hardware Removal Tool, 513
hardware requirements
    Windows 2000, 312
    Windows OSs, 305
    Windows XP, 312–313
Hardware tab, System Properties, 349
HCL (hardware compatibility list), 305
HDMI (High-Definition Multimedia
    Interface), 32
headphones, 25
heat, portables and, 519–520
heat sinks
    in BTX motherboards, 175
    CPU and, 38–39
Help and Support Center
    (Microsoft.com), 630–631
Help Desk Technician (220-603), 7–8
hermaphroditic connectors, for Token
    Ring, 567
hexadecimal format, for I/O
    addresses, 157–158
Hi-Speed USB, 437
Hibernate mode, Power Options, 518
hidden partitions, 215
High-Definition Multimedia Interface
    (HDMI), 32
high-gloss finish, LCD monitors, 496
high-level formatting, FAT file
    system, 218
High Speed Token Ring (HSTR), 566
Historical/Conceptual sections, in this
    book, 11
hives, Registry, 363
HKEY_CLASSES_ROOT, 365–366
HKEY_CURRENT_CONFIG, 367
HKEY_CURRENT_USER, 367
HKEY_LOCAL_MACHINE, 367
HKEY_USERS, 367
Home edition, Windows XP, 383–384.
    See also Windows 2000/XP;
    Windows XP
horizontal refresh rate (HRR),
    CRTs, 466
hot keys, 346–347
    function keys (F1, F2, etc.), 346
    for text, 346
    Windows shortcuts, 346–347

hot-swappable devices
    FireWire, 28
    modular drives in laptops, 513
    printers, 545
    USB, 27
HotSync, PDAs, 499
HRR (horizontal refresh rate),
    CRTs, 466
HSTR (High Speed Token Ring), 566
HTTP (Hypertext Transfer Protocol),
    580–581
HTTPS (HTTP over Secure Sockets
    Layer), 627
hubs
    implementing UTP Ethernet
        and, 563–564
    overview of, 561
    in star topology, 554
    USB, 438–439
HyperMemory, from ATI, 511
Hypertext Transfer Protocol (HTTP),
    580–581
hyperthreading, in Pentium 4
    (Northwood and Prescott), 87–88

I

I/O addresses
    COM ports and LPT ports
        and, 161
    system resources and,
        156–158
I/O Advanced Programmable
    Interrupt Controller (IOAPIC),
    159–160
I/O base address, 158
I/O Controller Hub (ICH), Intel
    chipsets, 178
I/O (input/output)
    bar code readers, 457
    biometric devices, 456–457
    devices, 445
    digital cameras, 452–454
    FireWire ports, 442–443
    key terms, 461
    keyboards, 445–447
    lab projects, 463
    mice, 447–449
    overview of, 433
    port issues, 444
    ports, 434
    quizzes, 461–463
    scanners, 449–452
    serial ports, 434–436
    specialty devices, 456

summary/review, 459–461
    touch screens, 458
    USB ports. *See* USB (universal
        serial bus)
    webcams, 455–456
IBM
    IDC (IBM-type Data Connector)
        for, 567
    PC bus and, 150
    PowerPC, 293
ICANN (Internet Corporation for
    Assigned Names and
    Numbers), 584
ICH (I/O Controller Hub), Intel
    chipsets, 178
icons, assigned by file extension, 342
IDC (IBM-type Data Connector), 567
IDE (integrated drive electronics). *See
    also* ATA (AT Attachment) drives
IEC-320 connectors, power
    supplies, 189
IEEE 1284
    cables for parallel networks, 567
    standard for printers, 544
IEEE 1394 (FireWire). *See* FireWire
IEEE 802.11 standards, 592
IEEE 802.5t, Token Ring standard, 566
IF statements, in programs, 60
image installations, Windows
    OSs, 308
impact printers, 533–534
incidence reports
    Event Viewer, 632
    in troubleshooting
        methodology, 657
Industry Standard Architecture (ISA)
    bus, 150–151
infiltration, social engineering
    attacks, 607
information technology (IT), 1
ink cartridges, 534
ink-dispersion printers. *See* inkjet
    printers
inkjet printers, 534–536
input. *See also* I/O (input/output)
    computing process and, 646
    stages of PC operation, 19–20
input/output or memory (IO/MEM),
    wire, 156–157
installation
    device drivers, 440
    devices, 411–412
    floppy drives, 270–271
    keyboards, 445
    NICs, 576

Mike Meyers' CompTIA A+ Guide: Essentials (Exam 220-601)

scanners, 452
software, 409–410
Windows OS. *See* Windows
    OSs, installing and upgrading
Windows OSs, installing and
    upgrading, 309–310
installation discs, CD-ROMs, 141
instruction set, machine language, 56
INT wire, 158
integer unit, 71
integrated drive electronics (IDE). *See
also* ATA (AT Attachment) drives
Integrated Peripherals screen,
    CMOS, 138
integrity, PC techs and, 652–653
Intel Corporation
    as chipset manufacturer, 178
    collaboration with AMD in
        manufacture of 8088
        processor, 66
    competition with AMD, 65
    as CPU manufacturer, 39
    on numbering scheme for Intel
        processors, 88
    overview of, 65
Intel processors
    32-bit processing, 69–70
    64-bit processing, 92
    Celeron, 81
    clock speed and multipliers,
        74–75
    CPU cache, 72–74
    CPU voltages, 75–76
    early Pentiums, 76
    Intel core, 98–99
    Itanium, 92–94
    later Pentiums, 79–80
    man-in-the-box analogy, 69
    mobile versions, 90
    numbering scheme for Intel
        processors, 88
    Pentium 4 (Northwood and
        Prescott), 87–89
    Pentium 4 (Willamette), 86
    Pentium D, 96–97
    Pentium II, 80–82
    Pentium III, 82–83
    Pentium IV Extreme Edition,
        89–90
    Pentium Pro, 77–79
    pipelining, 70–72
    SpeedStep (throttling), 91

Windows XP and, 293
    Xeon, 91–92
Internet Corporation for Assigned
    Names and Numbers (ICANN), 584
Internetwork Packet Exchange/
    Sequenced Packet Exchange
    (IPX/SPX), 574, 578
interrupt requests (IRQs), 159–161, 434
interruption mechanism, 158
inverters, LCD components, 474
IO/MEM (input/output or memory),
    wire, 156–157
IOAPIC (I/O Advanced
    Programmable Interrupt
    Controller), 159–160
IP addresses
    APIPA (Automatic Private IP
        Addressing), 580
    overview of, 579–580
    static IP addresses, 584–585
    subnet masks and, 580
iPAQ, from Compaq, MP3 player, 507
IPCONFIG, 585–586
IPSec, 626
IPX/SPX (Internetwork Packet
    Exchange/Sequenced Packet
    Exchange), 574, 578
IRQs (interrupt requests), 159–161, 434
ISA (Industry Standard Architecture)
    bus, 150–151
ISO-9660
    CD-ROMs, 279
    UDF as replacement for, 282
IT (information technology), 1
IT Technician (220-602)
    deciding which exams to take
        and in what sequence, 7–8
    hard drive installation, 208
Itanium processor, 92–94

J

jacks, defined, 26
Java code, 294
Joliet, 279
joules, of electrical energy, 193
joystick connector, 35–36

K

K5, AMD processors, 76–77
K6, AMD processors, 81
KB (kilobyte), 63

Kerberos, 625–626
keyboard controllers
    8043 as convention for, 128
    overview of, 127–128
    scan code, 128–130
keyboard shortcuts, 350
keyboards, 445–447
    basic peripherals, 25
    configuring/installing, 445
    connectors, 31
    controllers, 127
    keyboard reader, 610
    laptop ports, 507
    on laptops, 496
    mini-DIN connectors and, 26
    troubleshooting, 445–447
keypads, troubleshooting laptops, 523
kilobyte (KB), 63
"known good devices"
    (hardware), 444

L

L1, L2, L3 cache, on Pentium Pro,
    73–74, 78
lamps, projectors, 477
land-grid array (LGA), in Pentium 4
    (Prescott), 88
language settings, Windows OS, 309
languages, printer, 542–543
LANs (local area networks), 552, 581.
    See also networks
laptops. *See also* portable computing
    desktop extenders, 497–498
    desktop replacements, 496–497
    overview of, 496
laser, 539
laser printers
    components of, 538–541
    overview of, 537–538
    printing process, 663–667
laserdiscs, 284
latency, RAM, 117
Lavasoft Ad-Aware, 622–623
LCDs (liquid crystal displays),
    470–476
    brightness, 475
    components, 473–474
    connections, 478–480
    contrast ratio, 476
    high resolution issues, 475
    how they work, 470–473
    overview of, 470

LCDs (liquid crystal displays)
(*continued*)
 portable computing and,
  495–496
 power conservation, 481
 resolution, 475
 response rate, 475
 size options, 478
 testing viewing angle of, 474
 TFT, 473
LearnKey
 online training, 680–681
 technical support, 681
legacy-free computing, 269
letter quality, dot-matrix printers, 533
LFN (long file names), 372
LFX12V power supply, 201
LGA (land-grid array), in Pentium 4
 (Prescott), 88
Li-Ion batteries, 515
licenses, Windows OSs, 409–410
lines of code. *See* machine language
Linux
 applications, 294
 distributions (distros), 303
 partitioning tools, 215–217
 policies, 614
 servers, 569
List Folder Contents, folder
 permissions, 375
local area networks (LANs), 552, 581.
 See also networks
Local Security Settings,
 Windows XP, 613
Local Users and Groups, 399
locale settings, Windows OSs, 309
lockup, during Windows install,
 327–328
logical drives, 210
logical topology, compared with
 physical topology, 555
login screen, Windows OSs, 336–337
logon policies, 615
logs
 creating event logs, 418
 Performance console and, 360
 transaction logging in NTFS, 372
 viewing event logs, 419
 Windows 2000/XP installation
  and, 328
long file names (LFN), 372
Low-Speed USB, 437

LPT ports
 converting data moving
  between serial and parallel
  devices, 434
 printer connectivity and, 543–544
 system resources and, 161
LPX form factor, 171
lumens, projectors, 477

■ M

MAC (media access control), 555
Mac OSs
 peer-to-peer networking in Mac
  OS X, 570
 UNIX basis of, 302
machine language
 1-byte vs. 2-byte commands in
  DRAM, 108
 lines of code in programs, 59
 registers and, 55–56
Macintosh computers
 applications, 294
 PowerPC CPU, 293
Macromedia Certified Professional, 19
Main screen, CMOS, 135–136
maintenance, hard drives. *See* hard
 drives, maintaining
maintenance, Windows 2000/XP. *See*
 Windows 2000/XP, maintaining
malware, 615–623
 antivirus programs, 616–617
 overview of, 615
 polymorph viruses, 617
 pop-ups, 619–620
 spam, 619
 spyware, 621–623
 stealth viruses, 617
 Trojans, 616
 virus prevention, 617–618
 viruses, 615
 worms, 616
man-in-the-box analogy, 52–54, 64, 69
manufacturers
 chipsets, 178
 CPUs, 64–66
mass storage devices. *See* removable
 media
massively multiplayer online role-
 playing game (MMORPG), 645–650
master file table (MFT)
 NTFS and, 224, 372
 NTLDR and, 378

matte finish, LCD monitors, 496
MAU (multistation access unit), 567
MB (megabyte)
 defined, 63
 hard drive capacity and, 43
 RAM capacity, 39
MBR (master boot record). *See also*
 basic disks
 on basic disks, 210
 dynamic disks and, 214
 NTLDR and, 378
 partitioning schemes, 209–210
MCA (Micro Channel Architecture)
 bus, 152
MCC (memory controller chip)
 CAS (column array strobe) and
  RAS (row array strobe), 117
 CPU and, 107
 defined, 62
 knowing location of DRAM, 110
MCH (Memory Controller Hub), Intel
 chipsets, 178
MCP (Microsoft Certified
 Professional), 4
MCSE (Microsoft Certified System
 Engineer)
 value of, 4
 vendor-specific certifications, 2
media access control (MAC), 555
Media Center. *See* Windows Media
 Center
megabyte. *See* MB (megabyte)
megahertz (MHz), measuring
 bandwidth, 469
megapixels, 454
memory
 CPUs and, 58–59
 defined, 106
memory addresses, 163
memory cards, 273, 499
Memory Stick, 276, 499
"mental reinstall," of hard drives, 252
mesh topology, 554
MFT (master file table)
 NTFS and, 224, 372
 NTLDR and, 378
MHz (megahertz), measuring
 bandwidth, 469
mice, 447–449
 basic peripherals, 25
 cleaning/maintaining, 448–449
 configuring, 447–448
 connections, 33–34

laptop ports, 507
   mini-DIN connectors and, 26
   types of, 448
micro-DIMMs, 112, 114, 510
microATX motherboards, 174
microBTX motherboards, 175
microprocessors. *See* CPUs (central
   processing units)
Microsoft
   Help and Support Center
      (Microsoft.com), 630–631
   vendor-specific certifications, 2
Microsoft Journal, 501–502
Microsoft Management Console. *See*
   MMC (Microsoft Management
   Console)
Microsoft Office, 501
Microsoft Office Specialist
   (MOS), 19
Microsoft Outlook, 603
Microsoft PowerPoint, 501
Microsoft Product Activation (MPA),
   315–316
Microsoft Vista. *See* Vista
Microsoft Windows. *See*
   Windows OSs
Microsoft Word, 501
migration, to new system/retiring old,
   605–607
*Mike Meyers' A+ Guide: PC Technician
   (Exams 220-602, 220-603,
   & 220-604)*, 208
mini-ATX motherboards, 174
mini-audio connectors, 29–30
mini-B connectors, USB, 27
mini connectors, 195–196, 272
mini-DIN connectors, 26, 32
mini-PCI bus, 153–154, 513
mirrored volumes, 215, 241
mirroring, RAID support on
   motherboards, 181
MMC (Microsoft Management
   Console)
   Administrative Tools, 359
   Computer Management, 360
   creating custom snap-ins, 359
   Event Viewer, 360
   overview of, 357–359
   Performance console,
      360–361, 417
   services, 362
MMORPG (massively multiplayer
   online role-playing game), 645–650

MMX (multimedia extensions), 79
mobile processors, 90–91
modems (MOdulator/DEmodulators)
   connectors, 34
   external modems connecting via
      serial ports, 34–35
modes, video cards, 484
Modify, file and folder
   permissions, 375
modular laptops
   components, 512
   drives, 512–513
   overview of, 509
MOdulator/DEmodulators. *See*
   modems (MOdulator/
   DEmodulators)
modules, of RAM. *See* RAM sticks
molex connectors, 196–197
monitors. *See* displays
MOS (Microsoft Office Specialist), 19
motherboards, 168–185
   AMR/CNR, 181
   ATX form factor, 172–174
   BTX form factor, 175–176
   chipsets, 176–181
   components, 179–181
   CPU clock speed, 58
   expansion slots, 152
   flash ROM and, 131
   form factors, 169–172
   how they work, 169
   key terms, 183
   lab projects, 185
   overview of, 40–41, 168
   P1 power connector, 195
   power supply for, 195
   proprietary form factors, 176
   quizzes, 183–185
   RAID, 181
   review and summary, 182–183
   sound chips, 181
   speed of, 149
   USB/FireWire, 179–181
   USB host controllers on, 438
   video card connections, 485–486
   voltage and multiplier CMOS
      settings, 137
Motorola PowerPC, 293
mount points, volume, 243–245
mouse. *See* mice
mouse acceleration, 447
Mouse applet, Control Panel, 447

Moving Pictures Experts Group. *See*
   MPEG (Moving Pictures Experts
   Group)
Mozilla, Firefox, 627–628
MP3s (MPEG-1 Layer 3), 507
MPA (Microsoft Product Activation),
   314–315
MPEG (Moving Pictures Experts
   Group)
   MPEG-1 Layer 3 (MP3s), 507
   MPEG-2, 285
   standards, 285–286
MS-CHAP, 626
MSAU. *See* MAU (multistation
   access unit)
MT-RJ connectors, fiber optic
   cable, 565
multiboot installations, Windows
   OSs, 307
multiboot operating systems, 211
multimedia extensions (MMX), 79
multimeters, for measuring electrical
   current, 190–192
multimode fiber optic cable, 565
multipliers
   changing CMOS settings
      for, 138
   clock-multiplying CPUs, 74–75
   features of later Pentiums, 80
multisession drives, CD-Rs, 281
multistation access unit (MAU), 567
music CDs, 283
music, My Music, 345
My Computer, 340–343
My Documents, My [Whatever],
   343–345
My Music, 345
My Network Places
   accessing shared drives/
      directories, 589–590
   overview of, 345
   peer-to-peer networking
      and, 570
My Pictures, 345
My Videos, 345

■ N

native resolution, LCDs, 475
NDS (NetWare Directory
   Services), 571
near-letter quality (NLQ), dot-matrix
   printers, 533

NetBEUI (NetBIOS Extended User Interface)
    configuring for wired networks, 577–578
    as network protocol, 574
Netburst, in Pentium IV Willamette, 86
NetWare client, 576
NetWare Directory Services (NDS), 571
NetWare servers, 569
network addressing, 579–580
network authentication, 625–626
Network Identification tab, Windows 2000, 572–573
Network Neighborhood, Windows 9x, 346
network operating system (NOS), 568–570
network printers, 545
network protocols. *See* protocols, networking
network security, 611
network technicians, CompTIA Network+ certification and, 4
network topologies, 554–555
networking role, Windows OS installation and, 309
networks
    client/server organization, 569–570
    client software, 575
    coaxial Ethernet, 557
    connections (RJ-45), 33
    domain-based organization, 570–573
    fiber optic Ethernet, 565
    installing/configuring wired network. *See* wired networks, installing and configuring
    IT (information technology) and, 1
    key terms, 596
    lab projects, 599
    My Network Places, 345
    Network Neighborhood, 346
    NOS (network operating system), 568–569
    overview of, 552
    packets/frames and NICs, 555–556
    parallel/serial options, 567–568

peer-to-peer organization, 570
    protocols, 573–575
    quizzes, 597–599
    server software, 575
    summary/review, 593–596
    technologies, 553–554
    Thick Ethernet, 557–559
    Thin Ethernet, 559–560
    Token Ring, 565–567
    topologies, 554–555
    USB and FireWire, 568
    UTP Ethernet, 560–564
Ni-Cd batteries, 514–515
nibbles, bits of memory and, 60
NICs (network interface cards)
    full-duplex and half-duplex modes, 564
    functions of, 553
    installing for wired networks, 576
    MAC addresses and, 555–556
    network connectivity and, 33, 555–556, 575
    portable computing and, 507, 513
NiMH batteries, 515
nits, of brightness in LCDs, 475
NLQ (near-letter quality), dot-matrix printers, 533
NLX form factor, 171
"No Fixed Disks Present," CMOS errors, 212
non-volatile memory, ROM chips, 131
Northbridge
    on chipsets, 176–177
    device controllers and, 128
    expansion card connections, 147
    function of, 126
Norton, Ghost, 325
NOS (network operating system), 568–570
notification area, 339. *See also* system tray
Novell certification, 2
Novell NetWare
    client, 576
    directory services, 571
    servers, 569
NSLOOKUP, 586
NT Executive, Windows 2000/XP, 370
NTDETECT.COM, Windows 2000/XP, 381

NTFS (NT File System), 224–228, 371–377
    accounts, 372
    cluster sizes, 227–228
    compression and, 225
    disk quotas, 227
    EFS (encrypting file system), 225–227
    vs. FAT32 for access control, 610–611
    features, 371–372
    groups, 373–374
    overview of, 224
    security of, 224–225
    structure of, 224
NTFS permissions
    file sharing and, 569
    overview of, 374–377
    sharing resources and, 589
NTLDR, 378
NTOSKRNL.EXE, 377
NVIDIA Corporation, 178
NVIDIA video cards, 511
NWLink (IPX/SPX), 578

◼ O

objects
    auditing access to, 631
    desktop, 347
    Performance console, 417
    Windows class objects, 365
OEM (Original Equipment Manufacturer), 386
off-site storage, of backups, 604–605
ohms (Ω), 188
online gaming, stream loading and, 649
Opteron, AMD processors, 94–95
optical drives. *See also* CD drives
    ATAPI-compliance, 282
    lockups and, 328
    not ready errors, 326
    overview of, 277
optical media, 277–301. *See also* CD-media
    CD-media. *See* CD-media
    DVD-media. *See* DVD-media
    overview of, 277
    types of removable media, 268
optical mice, 448
optical resolution, scanners, 451
optical zoom, in digital cameras, 454

Option ROM, 140, 163
Origami UMPC project, 523
Original Equipment Manufacturer (OEM), 386
OSs (operating systems)
    accessing and supporting programs (applications), 296
    Apple Macintosh. *See* Mac OSs
    applications and, 18–19
    common traits, 293–294
    communication with hardware, 294–295
    in computing process, 644
    functions of, 293
    Linux, 303
    Microsoft Windows. *See* Windows OSs
    organizing and manipulating programs and data, 297
    overview of, 292
    partitioning for using more than one, 209
    UNIX, 303
    user interface, 295–296
out-of-order processing/speculative execution, Pentium Pro, 77–78
outlets, electrical, 191
Outlook, Microsoft, 603
output. *See also* I/O (input/output)
    stages of PC operation, 20
overclocking CPUs, 58
Ownership permission, NTFS, 374
ozone filters, laser printers, 541

■ P

P1 power connector, motherboards, 195
P8/P9 sockets, motherboards, 170
PAC (pin array cartridge), in Intel Itanium processors, 92
packages, CPUs, 66–68
packets
    data transfer via, 555–556
    NICs breaking files into, 553
page files. *See* swap files
PAGEFILE.SYS, 369
pages per minute (ppm), 535–536
PAP (Password Authentication Protocol), 626
paperless office, 532
paragraphs, bits of memory and, 60

parallel ATA. *See* PATA (parallel ATA)
parallel connections
    LPT ports, 161
    parallel ports, 35
parallel devices, 434
parallel networking, 567–568
parallel PC Cards, 505
parallel ports
    I/O addresses and, 161
    LPT ports, 543–544
    printers, 35
Parental Controls, in Vista, 634–635
parity RAM, 118
Partition Commander Professional, from VCOM, 256
partition tables
    basic disks, 210
    dynamic disks, 214
partitioning
    with Disk Management, 235–240
    drive letters and, 233–234
    errors, 251–252
    simple volumes, 241
    single partition, 229–231
    spanned volumes, 241–243
    third-party tools for, 255–258
    two partitions, 231–233
    when to partition, 215–217
    with Windows installation CD, 229
PartitionMagic, from Symantec, 256
partitions
    basic disks, 210–214
    defined, 209
    dynamic disks, 214–215
    formatting, 245–246
    hidden partitions and swap partitions, 215
    overview of, 209–210
    system partition, 377, 378
    Windows OS installation and, 309, 318
passive matrix, LCDs, 472–473
Password Authentication Protocol (PAP), 626
password reset disks, 406
passwords
    authentication and, 609
    CMOS, 139
    creating user password, 401

dangers of blank or easily visible, 401
    PC tech integrity and, 652
    resetting forgotten, 406
    security policies for, 615
    strong passwords, 405–406
    Windows 2000/XP installation and, 319
PATA (parallel ATA)
    drive letters and, 234
    hard drive capacity and, 43
patches
    maintaining Windows 2000/XP, 394–397
    overview of, 311
    security patches, 616
PC bus, 150
PC Cards, 505–507
    expansion slots on PCs, 30–31
    ExpressCard, 505–506
    NICs (network interface cards), 33
    overview of, 505
    parallel PC Cards, 505
    protecting, 506
    software support for, 506–507
PC techs, 643–662
    anti-static tools, 22–24
    art of, 21
    avoiding electrostatic discharge, 22
    backing up before changing system, 655
    certification of, 2
    computing process and, 644–650
    customer relations, 651–654
    how computers work, 644
    key terms, 15, 617, 659
    lab projects, 620, 662
    overview of, 1, 643
    quizzes, 15–16, 617–620, 659–662
    review/summary, 658–659
    step-based systematic approach to problem solving, 655–657
    summary/review, 14–15, 616–617
    tools of, 21–22, 655
    troubleshooting, 650–651
    troubleshooting methodology, 654

PCBs (printed circuit boards). *See also*
  motherboards
    magnifiers for reading, 22
    overview of, 169
PCI Express (PCIe), 488
PCI (peripheral component
  interconnect), 152–155
    AGP bus, 153
    CMOS settings, 139–140
    mini-PCI, 153–154
    overview of, 152
    PCI card in tech toolkit, 655
PCI-X bus, 153
PCIe (PCI Express), 488
    connector, 200
    video cards and, 154–155
PCL (printer control language), 542
PCMCIA (Personal Computer
  Memory Card International
  Association), 505–506. *See also*
  PC Cards
PCs (personal computers), 17–30
    art of PC techs and, 21
    audio connectors, 29–30
    case, 36–38
    components and peripherals, 25
    CPU, 38–39
    DB connectors, 28–29
    devices and device
      connectors, 30
    expansion cards, 30–31
    external connections, 25–26
    FireWire connectors, 28
    floppy drives, 42
    AT form factor and, 170
    hard drives, 42–44
    how they work, 18–19
    input, 19–20
    joysticks, 35–36
    key terms, 47
    keyboards, 31
    lab projects, 50
    mini-DIN connectors, 26
    modems, 34
    monitors, 31–32
    motherboard, 40–41
    mouse connections, 33–34
    network connections, 33
    optical media, 44–45
    output, 20
    overview of, 17–18
    plugs, ports, jacks, and
      connectors, 26
    power supply and connectors,
      41–42

printers, 35
processing, 20
quizzes, 47–49
RAM, 39–40
range of people who use, 1
review and summary, 46–47
RJ connectors, 29
serial ports, 34–35
sound devices, 32–33
storage, 20
system unit, 36
tools of PC techs, 21–22
USB connectors, 27–28
PDAs (personal digital assistants), 503
    overview of, 498–499
    touch screens, 458
    Windows Mobile for, 386
PDF documents, on CD-ROM
  accompanying this book, 680
Pearson/VUE, 9
peer-to-peer networks, 570
pen-based computing,
  in PDAs, 498
Pentiums
    32-bit processing, 69–70
    clock speed and multipliers,
      74–75
    CPU cache, 72–74
    CPU voltages, 75–76
    early Pentiums, 76
    later Pentiums, 79–80
    man-in-the-box analogy, 69
    Pentium D, 96–97
    Pentium II, 80–82
    Pentium III, 82–83
    Pentium IV Extreme Edition,
      89–90
    Pentium IV (Northwood and
      Prescott), 87–89
    Pentium IV Willamette, 86
    Pentium Pro, 77–79
    pipelining, 70–72
PepiMK, Spybot Search & Destroy,
  622–623
Performance console
    overview of, 417
    Performance Logs and Alerts,
      418–419
    System Monitor, 417
    as tech utility, 360–361
Performance Logs and Alerts,
  418–419
Performance Options, Windows
  2000/XP, 415–416

performance rating (PR), in AMD
  Athlon XP processors, 87
peripherals
    defined, 25
    power connectors for, 195–196
    power supply for, 195–197
permissions
    access control and, 383
    assigning to groups, 611–612
    file sharing and, 569
    NTFS, 374–377
    software installation, 409
persistence, CRT images, 466
Personal Computer Memory Card
  International Association
  (PCMCIA), 505–506. *See also*
  PC Cards
personal computers. *See* PCs (personal
  computers)
personal digital assistants. *See* PDAs
  (personal digital assistants)
Personal Video Recorder (PVR), 384
PGA (pin-grid array)
    CPU packages, 39
    as example of grid array
      packaging, 67
Phoenix Technologies, BIOS
  manufacturers, 134
phosphors, CRT displays, 467
photoconductivity, in laser
  printers, 537
photosensitive drum, laser printer
  components, 538
photosites, 454
physical security, access control
  and, 609
physical theft, social engineering
  attacks and, 608
physical topology, compared with
  logical topology, 555
pico BTX motherboards, 175
picture elements (pixels), 468
pictures, My Pictures, 345
pin 1, floppy drive cables, 271
pin array cartridge (PAC), in Intel
  Itanium processors, 92
pin-grid array. *See* PGA
  (pin-grid array)
Ping
    checking communication
      between machines, 581
    how it works and syntax
      for, 585
pipeline stalls, 70, 73
pipelining, CPUs, 70–72

Mike Meyers' CompTIA A+ Guide: Essentials (Exam 220-601)

pixels (picture elements)
CRT images, 468
LCD vs. CRT, 471
plenum, network cabling, 563
Plug and Play, CMOS settings, 139
plug-ins, 621
plugs, 26
plusID devices, 610
PnP (plug and play), CMOS
settings, 139
point-of-sale systems, touch screens
and, 458
Pointer Options, mice, 448
polarizing filters, LCDs and, 470–471
policies, security, 613–615
account lockout, 615
command prompt, 614
group policies, 383, 613–614
Linux, 614
logon/shut down, 615
passwords, 615
Registry, 614
poly-vinyl chloride (PVC), wiring
conduit, 563
polymorph viruses, 617
pop-ups, protection against,
619–620
port replicators, laptops, 508–509
portable computing
APM/ACPI, 517–518
batteries, 514–516
Centrino technology and, 523
cleaning, 518–519
CPUs, 512
desktop extenders, 497–498
desktop replacements, 496–497
hard drives, 512
heat and, 519–520
key terms, 528
lab projects, 531
LCDs, 495–496
modular drives, 512–513
modular laptops, 509
NICs and Mini PCI bus, 513
overview of, 494
PC Cards, 505–507
PDAs (personal digital
assistants), 498–499
portable power sources,
515–516
ports, 507–509
power management, 516
protecting portables, 520–522

quizzes, 529–531
RAM (random access memory),
509–510
shared memory, 511
SMM (System Management
Model), 516–517
summary/review, 525–528
table of devices and
features, 503
tablet PCs, 500–503
troubleshooting, 522–523
UMPC (Ultra-Mobile PC),
523–524
upgrades, 504
video cards, 512
weight of portable PCs, 498
ports, 137
common issues, 444
defined, 26
FireWire, 442–443
laptops, 507–509
overview of I/O ports, 434
parallel (LPT). See parallel ports
serial (COM). See serial ports
USB. See USB (universal
serial bus)
POS (point of sale) machines, 533
PostScript, 542
post-installation tasks, Windows
OSs, 309–311
potential, of static electricity, 22
power conditioning, 193
power conservation, 481
displays, 481
power management
APM/ACPI, 517–518
CMOS settings, 139
heat and, 520
in laptops, 516
SMM (System Management
Model), 516–517
Power Options, in Control Panel,
518–519
power requirements, USB devices, 441
power schemes, Power Options, 518
power supplies, 186–218
AC power, 189
active PFC, 201
ATX power supply, 197–200
auto-switching power
supplies, 521
connectors, 42
DC power, 195

EPS12V, 199
for floppy drives, 272
key terms, 205
lab projects, 207
laser printers, 540
for motherboard, 195
multimeter for measuring
electrical current, 190–192
niche market form factors, 201
overview of, 41–42, 186–187
for peripherals, 195–197
portable power sources, 515–516
quizzes, 205–207
review and summary, 203–205
surge suppressors, 192–193
testing AC voltage, 192
troubleshooting laptops, 522
understanding electricity and,
187–189
UPS (uninterruptible power
supply), 193–195
versus AC adapters, 191
wattage requirements, 202
Power Users group, 373
PowerNow (throttling), AMD
processors, 91
PowerPC, Motorola, 293
ppm (pages per minute), 535–536
PR (performance rating), in AMD
Athlon XP processors, 87
primary corona, laser printers, 538
primary grid, in laser printers, 539
primary partitions
basic disks and, 210
number of primary partitions
supported, 211–212
print media, 536
print resolution, in inkjet printers, 535
print servers, 545
printed circuit boards. See PCBs
(printed circuit boards)
printer control language (PCL), 542
printers
basic peripherals, 25
connectivity, 543–545
dye-sublimation printers,
536–537
hidden costs, 538
impact printers, 533–534
inkjet printers, 534–536
installing in Windows, 667–670
key terms, 548
lab projects, 551

printers (*continued*)
    languages, 542–543
    laser printers, 537–541
    laser printing process, 663–667
    overview of, 532–533
    parallel port connection for, 35
    quizzes, 548–550
    sharing over networks, 591–592
    solid ink printers, 541
    summary/review, 546–548
    thermal printers, 537
    troubleshooting, 670–678
printwires, dot-matrix printers, 533
processes, Task Manager for turning
    off resource hogs, 417
processing, stages of PC operation,
    20, 84
processors. *See also* CPUs (central
    processing units)
    laser printers, 540
product activation, 314–315, 353
product key
    OS installation and, 310
    scripted installation and, 322
    Windows 2000/XP installation
        and, 318
Professional edition, Windows XP, 383
Program Files, Windows folders, 363
programming, computers consisting
    of, 18
programs. *See also* applications
    lines of code in, 59
    OSs organizing and
        manipulating, 297
    threads of, 72
projectors, 476–477
    lamps, 477
    lumens, 477
    overview of, 476
    throw, 477
Prometric, 8, 9
properties
    Recycle Bin, 345
    right-click for viewing object
        properties, 347
protocols, networking, 573–575
    adding simple protocol, 579
    AppleTalk, 574–575
    IPX/SPX, 574
    NetBEUI, 574
    NetBEUI configuration, 577–578
    network connectivity and, 575
    overview of, 573–574

TCP/IP. *See* TCP/IP
    (Transmission Control
    Protocol/Internet Protocol)
PS/2 ports, 507
PSU (power supply unit). *See* power
    supplies
PVC (poly-vinyl chloride), wiring
    conduit, 563
PVR (Personal Video Recorder), 384

Q

quad-pumped frontside bus, 86
quads, bits of memory and, 60
Quick Launch toolbar, Windows
    OSs, 340

R

radio frequency identification
    (RFID), 610
RAID (redundant array of
    independent devices)
    motherboards and, 181
    RAID 5 (disk striping with
        distributed parity), 215
rails, in EPS 12V power supply,
    199–200
RAM cache, 367–369
RAM interface, 78
RAM (random access memory),
    105–124
    1-byte vs. 2-byte commands
        and, 107–108
    adding/replacing in
        portables, 510
    address space and, 62–63
    buffered/registered DRAM,
        118–119
    compared with ROM, 131
    computing process and, 646–647
    conventions regarding RAM
        capacity, 110
    DDR-SDRAM, 114–116
    defined, 106
    DRAM (dynamic RAM), 61
    as an electronic spreadsheet,
        60–61
    ESD (electrostatic discharge)
        and, 40
    FPM (fast page mode)
        RAM, 112
    history/development of
        DRAM, 106–107

    key terms, 121
    lab projects, 124
    laser printers, 540–541
    latency and, 117
    notation on address bus, 64
    organization of DRAM, 107
    overview of, 39–40, 105–106
    parity and ECC, 118
    portable PCs and, 509–510
    quizzes, 121–123
    RDRAM, 112–113
    review and summary, 120–121
    SDRAM, 111–112
    single- and double-sided RAM
        sticks, 116–117
    sticks, 108–109
    Task Manager for viewing RAM
        usage, 416
    types of, 110
    variations, 116
    video cards and, 481–482
    working with older RAM, 110
RAM sticks
    DIMMs, 39–40
    DRAM, 108–109
    laser printers, 541
    parity RAM and ECC RAM
        and, 118
    single- and double-sided,
        116–117
rambus DRAM (RDRAM), 112–113
RAMDAC (random access memory
    digital-to-analog converter), 478
random access memory. *See* RAM
    (random access memory)
random access memory
    digital-to-analog converter
    (RAMDAC), 478
RAS (remote access services), 571
RAS (row array strobe), 117
raster lines, in CRT display, 466
RDRAM (rambus DRAM), 112–113
Read & Execute, file and folder
    permissions, 375
Read, file and folder permissions, 375
read-only memory chip. *See* ROM
    (read-only memory) chips
rear-view projectors, 476
recoverability, in NTFS, 372
Recovery Console
    installing, 425–426
    Windows 2000 Repair Options
        menu, 424

Recycle Bin
  Disk Cleanup and, 248
  overview of, 345
recycling, old computers, 606–607
red, green, blue (RGB), CRT
  phosphors, 467
redundancy, MFT (master file table)
  and, 372
redundant array of independent
  devices (RAID)
    motherboards and, 181
    RAID 5 (disk striping with
      distributed parity), 215
reflection, in 10Base5 networks, 558
refresh rates, CRTs, 466–467
REGCLEAN, 408
REGEDIT.EXE, 364
REGEDT32.EXE, 364
registers, 54–56
  16-bit vs. 32-bit, 69
  exercise applying, 58
  general purpose, 55
  machine language and, 55–56
  as worktables in man-in-the-box
    analogy, 54
registration, Windows XP, 314
Registry, 363–369
  accessing, 363–364
  maintaining, 408
  overview of, 363
  protecting with security
    policies, 614
  Registry Editor, 364–365
  root keys, 365–367
  swap files, 367–370
  types of information stored
    in, 141
Registry Editor, 364–365
remnants, drives, 606
remote access services (RAS), 571
Remote Desktop, Windows XP, 383
Remote Installation Services (RIS)
  rolling out new systems, 327
  Windows 2000 Server, 309
removable media
  boot disks, 228
  digital cameras and, 453
  flash memory, 273–277
  floppy drives. See floppy drives
  key terms, 289
  lab projects, 291
  optical drives. See optical drives
  overview of, 267–268
  quizzes, 289–291
  review and summary, 287–288

Repair Options menu, Windows
  2000, 424
Replicator group, 373
reports, computer security, 629
resistance
  measured in ohms, 188
  testing with multimeter, 190
resistors, in anti-static straps, 24
resolution
  CRT displays, 468
  high resolution issues in
    LCDs, 475
  LCD displays, 475
resolution, LCD monitors, 495
resolution, print, 535
resources
  sharing over networks, 568–569
  viewing resources used by
    devices, 351
resources, tracking
  overview of, 416
  Performance console, 417–419
  Task Manager, 416–417
response rate, LCD displays, 475
restore
  backing up/restoring data in
    Windows installation, 308
  data files, 311
  System Restore, 355–356
restore points, System Restore,
  421–422
Restore Wizard, in Backup Utility, 423
RFID (radio frequency
  identification), 610
RG-58 connectors, 559
RG-8 connectors, 557
RGB (red, green, blue), CRT
  phosphors, 467
ribbon cable
  for CD and DVD drives, 44
  for floppy drives, 42, 270–272
  for hard drives, 43
right-click
  general rules for clicking in
    Windows OSs, 339
  My Computer, 348
  object properties, 347–348
RIMMs, 113
ring topology, 554, 565
RIS (Remote Installation Services)
  rolling out new systems, 326
  Windows 2000 Server, 308
riser cards, on slimline form factor
  motherboards, 171

RJ-11 connectors
  modems, 34
  overview of, 29
  telephones, 562
RJ-45 connectors
  CAT 5e and CAT 6 and, 562
  crossover cables and, 564
  network connections, 33
  overview of, 29
RJ connectors, 29
Rock Ridge, ISO-9660 extension, 279
ROM (read-only memory) chips,
  131–132
  firmware and, 132
  laser printers, 540–541
  overview of, 131
root directory, files and folders
  and, 217
root hub, USB, 436–437
root keys
  HKEY_CLASSES_ROOT,
    365–366
  HKEY_CURRENT_CONFIG,
    367
  HKEY_CURRENT_USER and
    HKEY_USERS, 367
  HKEY_LOCAL_MACHINE,
    367
  overview of, 365
routers
  Cisco, 5
  default gateway, 582
  defined, 4
row array strobe (RAS), 117
RS-232
  laptop ports, 507
  serial cables, 567
  serial ports, 434–435

S

S/PDIF (Sony/Philips Digital
  Interface Format), 32–33
S-video, 32
Safely Remove Hardware, in system
  tray, 513
SATA (serial ATA)
  drive letters and, 234
  hard drive capacity and, 43
  power connectors, 196–197
SC connectors, 565
scan code, keyboard controllers,
  128–129
ScanDisk, 247–248

scanners, 449–452
    color depth, 451
    how they work, 449–451
    how to choose, 451–452
    installing and using, 452
    overview of, 449
Scheduled Tasks, System Tools,
    354–355
scripts, scripting installations with
    Setup Manager, 320–325
SCSI (small computer system
    interface), 43
SD (Secure Digital)
    for digital cameras, 453
    PDA memory cards, 499
    types of flash cards, 275–276
SDR SDRAM (single data rate
    SDRAM), 114
SDRAM (synchronous DRAM),
    111–112. *See also* DDR-SDRAM
    (double data rate SDRAM)
SEC (single edge cartridge)
    Pentium II features, 80
    Slot A package in AMD Athlon
        processors, 83
sectors, hard drives, 253–254
Secure Boot Settings, 400
Secure Digital. *See* SD (Secure Digital)
Secure Sockets Layer (SSL),
    626–627
security. *See also* computer security
    laptop theft and, 521–522
    NTFS (NT File System),
        224–225, 372–373
    patches, 616
    peer-to-peer networking
        and, 570
    spyware, antivirus programs,
        and firewalls, 409
Security Center, System Tools,
    354–355
segments, 10Base5 networks, 557
Sempron, 96
sensors, laser printers, 541
SEP (single edge processor), features
    of Celeron processors, 81–82
serial ATA. *See* SATA (serial ATA)
serial connections, PCIe bus, 154
serial devices, data conversion
    and, 434

serial networks, 567–568
serial ports, 434–436
    COM ports, 161
    configuring, 435–436
    function of, 434
    overview of, 34–35
    RS-232 standard, 435
servers
    backing up in server
        environment, 604
    client software, 575
    defined, 553, 569
    Windows OSs, 571
Service Pack 2, Windows XP, 394
service packs
    maintaining Windows 2000/XP,
        394–397
    overview of, 311
services. *See also* device drivers
    TCP/IP, 580–581
    Windows OS, 362
settings, TCP/IP, 582
    default gateways, 582
    DHCP (dynamic host
        configuration protocol),
        584–585
    DNS servers, 582–584
    WINS servers, 584
Setup Manager, 320–325
setup program, CMOS. *See also* CMOS
    (complementary metal-oxide
    semiconductor)
    accessing, 135
    Advanced BIOS Features, 138
    Advanced Chipset Features, 138
    Features screen, 136
    Integrated Peripherals
        screen, 138
    Main screen, 135–136
    other settings, 139–140
    overview of, 133–134
    PnP/PCI settings, 139
    Power Management, 139
    Soft menu, 137
SETUPAPI.LOG, 328
SETUPLOGL.TXT, 328
SFX12V power supply, 201
shadow mask, CRT displays, 468
shareware, on CD-ROM
    accompanying this book, 680

sharing resources
    drives and folders, 588–590
    laptops and desktops support
        for shared memory, 511
    over networks, 568–569
    printers, 591–592
    simple file sharing, 374
shield, coaxial cable, 557
shielded twisted pair (STP) cable,
    566, 567
shortcuts, Windows shortcut keys,
    346–347
shut down policies, 615
sidebanding, AGP and, 486
signatures, of viruses, 617
SIMMs (single inline memory modules)
    example of, 109–110
    laser printers, 541
simple file sharing, 374
simple volumes
    dynamic disks, 241
    overview of, 214–215
single data rate SDRAM (SDR
    DRAM), 114
single edge cartridge (SEC)
    Pentium II features, 80
    Slot A package in AMD Athlon
        processors, 83
single edge processor (SEP), features
    of Celeron processors, 81–82
single inline memory modules. *See*
    SIMMs (single inline memory
    modules)
single-layer (SL) DVDs, 285
single partition, 229–231
single-sided (SS) DVD, 284–285
size options
    CRT displays, 477–478
    LCD displays, 478
skill levels
    form for analyzing, 10
    troubleshooting and managing
        PCs and, 14
SL (single-layer) DVDs, 285
Slackware, Linux distributions
    (distros), 303
slates, tablet PCs, 500
slimline form factor, 171
slipstreaming installation files, 325

Slot A package, 83
small computer system interface. *See* SCSI (small computer system interface)
small office/home office (SOHO) networks, 560
small outline DIMMs (SO-DIMMs), 112, 510
smart batteries, for laptops, 515
smart cards, hardware authentication, 609–610
smart UPS, 194
SmartMedia, flash cards, 275
SMM (System Management Model), 90, 516–517
SMP (symmetric multiprocessing), 371
snap-ins, MMC (Microsoft Management Console), 358
snapshot printers, 536
SO-DIMMs (small outline DIMMs), 112, 510
SO-RIMMs, 113
social engineering attacks, 607–608
    dumpster diving, 608
    infiltration, 607
    overview of, 607
    physical theft, 608
    telephone scams, 607–608
Socket A package, Athlon Thunderbird, 84
socket services, PC Cards, 506
Soft menu, CMOS setup program, 137
soft power feature
    on ATX motherboards, 172
    overview of, 197–198
software
    client/server, 575
    compatibility, Windows OSs, 305–307, 313–314
    consisting of operating systems and applications, 19
    installing, 409–410
    for PC Cards, 506–507
    removing, 410–411
software firewalls, 624
software tracking systems, for laptops, 522
SOHO (small office/home office) networks, 560
solid ink printers, 541
Sony/Philips Digital Interface Format. *See* S/PDIF (Sony/Philips Digital Interface Format)

sound chips, onboard, 181
sound connectors, 32–33
Southbridge
    on chipsets, 176–177
    in CMOS, 134
        device controllers and, 128
        expansion card connections, 147
        function of, 126
        as keyboard controller, 127–130
spam, 619
spanned volumes
    defined, 214
    dynamic disks, 241–243
    overview of, 215
speakers
    basic peripherals, 25
    laptop ports, 507
speech recognition, 500
SpeedStep (throttling), Intel processors, 91
SpinRite utility, from Gibson Research, 254
splitters, 197
spot color, 538
Spybot Search & Destroy, from PepiMK, 622–623
spyware, 621–623
    need for, 409
    overview of, 621
    preventing, 621–622
    removing, 622–623
    threat analysis and, 602
SRAM (static RAM), 73
SS (single-sided) DVD, 284–285
SSE (Streaming SIMD Extensions), Pentium III, 82
SSL (Secure Sockets Layer), 626–627
ST connectors, fiber optic cable, 565
standalone role, network roles, 309
Standard Users, Parental Controls, 634–635
standards
    Ethernet, 556
    MPEG, 285
    printers, 543–544
    TIA/EIA UTP categories, 562–563
    Token Ring, 556
star bus topology, for UTP Ethernet, 560–561
star ring topology, for Token Ring, 567
star topology, 554
Start button, Windows OS, 339

Start menu, Windows OS, 339
startup disks. *See also* boot disks
startup disks, text mode errors, 326
static charge eliminator, laser printers, 539
static charging, in LCD displays, 472–473
static electricity, 22
static IP addresses, 584–585
static RAM (SRAM), 73
stealth viruses, 617
step-based approach, to problem solving, 655–657
sticks, of RAM. *See* RAM sticks
stop errors, Windows 2000/XP installation, 327
storage
    mass storage devices, 267
    RAM vs. permanent storage, 61
    stages of PC operation, 20
STP (shielded twisted pair) cable, 566, 567
stream loading, online games, 649
Streaming SIMD Extensions (SSE), Pentium III, 82
stripe set, 243
striped volumes
    combining dynamic disks into, 243
    overview of, 215
    with parity, 241
striping, RAID support on motherboards, 181
strobing, AGP and, 486
study
    developing study strategy, 9–11
    setting aside time for, 9
    techniques, 13
stylus
    for PDAs, 498
    for tablet PCs, 500
sub-pixels, in LCD displays, 471
subkeys, Registry, 365–366
sublimation, in dye-sublimation printing, 536
subnet masks, 580
subnotebooks, 498
Super I/O chip, 177
superscalar execution, Pentium Pro, 77
surge suppressors, 192–193
SuSE, Linux distributions (distros), 303

swap files, 367–370
    application execution error
        and, 370
    available RAM and, 368–369
    defined, 367
    moving location of, 369
    Performance Options in
        Windows 2000/XP, 415
swap partitions, 215
switches
    implementing UTP Ethernet
        and, 563–564
    laser printer components, 541
    overview of, 561
Symantec, PartitionMagic from, 256
symmetric multiprocessing
    (SMP), 371
synchronous DRAM (SDRAM),
    111–112. See also DDR-SDRAM
    (double data rate SDRAM)
sysprep (System Preparation Tool),
    325–326
system BIOS
    defined, 132
    hardware supported by, 132
    OSs working with, 294–295
system board, laser printers, 540
system bus speed, CPUs, 58
System Commander, by VCOM,
    211–213
System, Control Panel applets, 348
system crashes, threat analysis
    and, 602
system crystal
    CPU clock and, 58
    function of, 148–149
system files, boot process and, 377
system folder, 362
System Information, in System
    Tools, 355
System Management Model (SMM),
    90, 516–517
system memory access, 487
System Monitor
    overview of, 417–418
    Performance console and,
        360–361
system partition
    boot process and, 377
    files, 378
System Properties, Hardware
    tab, 349

system requirements, for software on
    CD-ROM accompanying this
    book, 679
system resources, 156–164
    COM and LPT ports, 161
    DMA (direct memory access),
        161–163
    I/O addresses and, 156–158
    IRQs, 158–161
    memory addresses, 163
    overview of, 156
System Restore
    creating restore points, 420–421
    restoring to previous time, 421
    in System Tools, 355–356
    turning off or managing disk
        space usage, 422
system ROM
    functions of, 134
    overview of, 131
system setup utility. See setup
    program, CMOS
System State data, backing up, 604
System Tools, 352–356
system tray
    location on taskbar, 339–340
    Safely Remove Hardware, 513
system unit. See also cases
    defined, 25
    identifying connectors on, 46
    opening, 37–38
    overview of, 36–38
system volume, boot process and, 377
System32 folder, Windows
    folders, 363
SystemRoot folder, Windows
    folders, 362–363

T

tablet PCs
    overview of, 500–503
    Ultra-Mobile PCs, 523–524
    Windows XP Tablet PC, 387
Take Ownership permission, NTFS
    permissions, 374
tape backups, 425
Task Manager
    CPU and RAM usage, 416
    process management, 417
taskbar, Windows OS, 339
TB (terabyte), 64
TCP/IP services, 580–581

TCP/IP (Transmission Control
    Protocol/Internet Protocol), 578–592
    APIPA (Automatic Private IP
        Addressing), 588
    configuring, 587–588
    default gateways, 582
    DHCP (dynamic host
        configuration protocol),
        584–585
    DNS servers, 582–584
    IPCONFIG, 585–586
    network addressing, 579–580
    as network protocol, 574
    NSLOOKUP, 586
    overview of, 578–579
    Ping, 585
    services, 580–581
    settings, 582
    tools, 585
    TRACERT, 586–587
    WINS servers, 584
tech toolkits, 655
tech utilities, Windows OS
    Administrative Tools, 359
    command line, 356–357
    Computer Management, 360
    Control Panel, 348–349
    Device Manager, 349–352
    Event Viewer, 360
    MMC (Microsoft Management
        Console), 357–359
    overview of, 347
    Performance console, 360–361
    right-click, 347–348
    services, 362
    System Tools, 352–356
technical support, on CD-ROM
    accompanying this book, 681
Technology Without an Interesting
    Name (TWAIN), scanner driver, 450
techs. See PC techs
Tektronix, 541
Telecommunication Industry
    Association/Electronics Industries
    Alliance (TIA/EIA), 562–563
telephone scams, social engineering,
    607–608
telephones, RJ-11 connectors, 562
Telnet, accessing remote systems, 581
temporary files, Disk Cleanup for
    managing, 248–249, 407–408
terabyte (TB), 64
termination, in Thicknet networks, 558

testing, in troubleshooting methodology, 656–657

text, hot keys for working with, 346

text mode errors, Windows OS installation, 326–327

TFT, 473

TFX12V power supply, 201

theft, physical, 608

thermal dye transfer printers. *See* dye-sublimation printers

thermal printers, 537

thermal units, in BTX motherboards, 175

thermal wax transfer printers, 537

Thick Ethernet (10Base5), 557–559

Thin Ethernet (10Base2), 559–560

threads, of programs, 72

threat analysis, 601–602

throttling, CPUs, 91

throw, projectors, 477

TIA/EIA (Telecommunication Industry Association/Electronics Industries Alliance), 562–563

TLDs (top level domains), 584

token passing, 565

Token Ring, 565–567
    cable and connectors, 566–567
    implementing, 565–566
    ring topology, 565
    standard, 556

toner cartridges, laser printers, 538

toner, laser printers, 539

ToniArts, EasyCleaner by, 408

tools
    anti-static, 22–24
    of PC techs, 21–22, 655

top level domains (TLDs), 584

topologies, network, 554–555

Total Seminars, 8

Total Tester, on CD-ROM accompanying this book, 679–680

touch screens, 458

touchpads, on laptops, 496–497, 523

TRACERT, 586–587

traces, motherboard, 168

trackballs, 34

TrackPoint devices, on laptops, 497

transaction logging, in NTFS, 372

transfer corona, laser printer components, 539

transfer modes, in IEEE 1284, 544

transformers, power supplies, 521

transistors, in CPUs, 75

Transmission Control Protocol/ Internet Protocol. *See* TCP/IP (Transmission Control Protocol/ Internet Protocol)

triad, RGB phosphors, 468–469

Trojans, 616

troubleshooting
    hard drives. *See* hard drives, troubleshooting
    keyboards, 445–447
    portable computers, 522–523
    scenarios, 650–651
    skill levels and, 14

troubleshooting methodology
    analysis, 656
    completing, 657
    overview of, 654
    testing, 656–657

TurboCache, from NVIDIA, 511

TurboTax, 20

turning gears, laser printers, 540

TWAIN (Technology Without an Interesting Name), scanner driver, 450

two partitions, 231–233

Types I, II, and III, PC Cards, 505–506

U

UAC (User Account Control), Vista, 633–635

UART (universal asynchronous receiver/transmitter), 435

UBCD (Ultimate Boot CD), 258

Ubuntu, Linux distributions (distros), 303

UDC (Universal Data Connector), 567

UDF (universal data format), 282

UL (Underwriters Laboratories), 192–193

Ultimate Boot CD (UBCD), 258

Ultra DMA mode, 163

Ultra-Mobile PCs, 503, 523–524

Ultralights, 498, 503

UMPC (Ultra-Mobile PC), 503, 523–524

unauthorized access, computer security and, 601

UNC (universal naming convention), 590–591

Underwriters Laboratories (UL), 192–193

Unicode, 354

uninstall program, 409–410

uninterruptible power supply. *See* UPS (uninterruptible power supply)

universal asynchronous receiver/ transmitter (UART), 435

Universal Data Connector (UDC), 567

universal data format (UDF), 282

universal naming convention (UNC), 590–591

Universal Product Code (UPC), 457

universal serial bus. *See* USB (universal serial bus)

UNIX
    history of, 303
    Mac OS based on, 302

unshielded twisted pair cable. *See* UTP (unshielded twisted pair) cable

unshielded twisted pair Ethernet. *See* UTP Ethernet (10/100/1000BaseT)

UPC (Universal Product Code), 457

updates
    device drivers, 351, 412–413
    OSs, 311

updates, Windows 2000/XP, 394–398
    Automatic Updates, 397–398
    Windows Update, 394–396

Upgrade Advisor, Windows XP, 313–314

upgrade installation
    vs. clean install, 307
    issues with Windows 2000/XP upgrade, 315–316
    performing install or upgrade of Windows OSs, 309–310

upgrade paths, Windows XP, 312

upgrades
    device drivers, 312
    portable computers, 504

UPS (uninterruptible power supply)
    overview of, 193–194
    shopping for, 195
    smart UPS, 194

USB Keyboard Support option, in CMOS, 445

USB thumb drives
    with fingerprint scanner, 457
    locating, 440–441
    overview of, 273–274

USB-to-serial dongles, 434

USB (universal serial bus), 436–442
    2.0 standard, 437–438
    card readers, 276–277
    configuring, 440–442

USB (universal serial bus) (continued)
    connectors, 27
    device power via, 28
    digital cameras plugging into
        USB ports, 453
    handheld devices and, 508
    host controller, 436–438
    hubs and cables, 438–440
    laptop ports, 507
    laptops and, 508
    motherboards and, 179–181
    networks, 568
    overview of, 436–438
    printers, 544–545
    speeds, 437
    upstream and downstream, 27
    webcams using USB ports, 455
User Account Control (UAC), Vista,
    633–635
user accounts. *See also* groups
    access control and, 611
    creating new user in Windows
        2000, 400–401
    default or built in, 398–399
    groups for controlling, 611–613
    Guest account, 398
    Local Users and Groups for
        managing, 399
    managing users, 401–405
    names in defining NTFS user
        accounts, 373
    NTFS, 372
    security and, 398
User Accounts applet, Windows XP,
    372, 401–405
user interface
    command-line and
        graphical, 297
    in OSs, 295–296
user interface, Windows OS, 336–347
    desktop, 336, 338
    hot keys, 346–347
    login screen, 336–337
    My Computer, 340–343
    My Documents, My [Whatever],
        343–345
    My Network Places, 345
    overview of, 336
    Recycle Bin, 345
    taskbar and Start menu, 339–340
    Windows Explorer, 343–344
Users and Passwords applet,
    Windows 2000, 372, 399–401

Users group, 373
UTP Ethernet (10/100/1000BaseT),
    560–564
    combo cards, 563
    full-duplex and half-duplex, 564
    hubs and switches, 563–564
    implementing, 562–563
    overview of, 560
    star bus topology, 560–561
    UTP (unshielded twisted pair)
        cable, 561–562
UTP (unshielded twisted pair) cable
    CAT levels, 562
    color chart for wiring, 563
    crossover cables, 564
    overview of, 561–562
    Token Ring and, 566–567
UVCView, 440–441

V

V (volts), 188
values, Registry subkeys, 365
vampire connectors, in Thicknet
    networks, 558
VCOM, Partition Commander
    Professional from, 256
vertical refresh rate (VRR), 466–467
VESA Local Bus (VL-Bus), 152
VESA (Video Electronic Standards
    Association), 31
VGA port, laptops, 507
VGA (video graphics array)
    beyond VGA, 485
    DVI to VGA adapter, 480
    overview of, 484–485
Via Technologies, 178–179
video
    common features of displays/
        monitors, 477–480
    CRTs. *See* CRTs (cathode ray
        tubes)
    displays, 465
    key terms, 491
    lab projects, 493
    LCDs. *See* LCDs (liquid crystal
        displays)
    My Videos folder, 345
    overview of, 464
    power conservation, 481
    projectors, 476–477
    quizzes, 491–493
    summary/review, 489–490

video cards, 481–488
    AGP, 486–488
    AGP bus and, 153
    beyond VGA, 485
    connectors, 31–32
    CPUs communication with, 647
    dual monitors supported, 480
    modes, 484
    motherboard connections,
        485–486
    overview of, 481–483
    PCIe, 488
    PCIe bus and, 154–155
    portable computing, 512
    for portables, 512
    shared memory and, 511
    summary/review, 490
    VGA standard, 484–485
    Vista and, 648
video displays. *See* displays
Video Electronic Standards
    Association (VESA), 31
video graphics array. *See* VGA (video
    graphics array)
video training, LearnKey online
    training, 680
virtual memory. *See* swap files
virus prevention, 617–618
virus shields, 616
viruses
    antivirus programs, 616–617
    overview of, 615
    polymorphics/polymorphs, 618
    signatures of, 617
    stealth viruses, 618
    threat analysis and, 602
    tips for preventing, 618–619
Vista. *See* Windows Vista
visual effects, Performance
    Options, 415
VL-Bus (VESA Local Bus), 152
voice recognition, 457
volt-ohm meter (VOM), 190
voltage
    changing voltage and multiplier
        CMOS settings, 137
    CPU, 75–76
    measured in volts, 188
    monitor repair and, 465
    testing AC voltage, 192
    testing with multimeter, 190
    US and international standards
        for AC, 189

voltage regulator modules (VRMs), 75–76
volts (V), 188
volume boot sector, 211
volumes. *See also* dynamic disks; partitions
    defined, 209
    mount points, 243–245
    simple volumes, 241
    spanned volumes, 241–243
    striped, 243
    types of, 214
VOM (volt-ohm meter), 190
VRMs (voltage regulator modules), 75–76
VRR (vertical refresh rate), 466–467

■ W

W (wattage)
    CPUs and, 84
    overview of, 188
    requirements of power supplies, 202
wait states, 73
WANs (wide area networks). *See also* networks
    overview of, 552
    TCP/IP and, 581
warranties, hard drives, 255
wattage (W)
    CPUs and, 84
    overview of, 188
    requirements of power supplies, 202
Web browsers
    pop-ups, spyware, and adware and, 619–620
    trusted authorities and, 627–628
Web cameras (webcams), 455–456
Webroot Window Washer, 606
Welcome screen, Windows 2000/XP, 317, 402
Wi-Fi (Wireless Fidelity). *See also* wireless networking
    network printers and, 545
    standards. *See* IEEE 802.11 standards
    wireless networking in laptops, 513
wide area networks. *See* WANs (wide area networks)
wide-screen monitors, 468

Windows 2000. *See also* Windows 2000/XP
    Add/Remove Hardware applet, 576
    color depth settings for displays, 483
    groups, 612–613
    history of Windows OSs, 299–300
    language and locale settings, 309
    log files, 328
    multiboot installations, 307
    Network Identification tab, 572–573
    Repair Options menu, 424
    software compatibility, 305–307
    Users and Passwords applet, 372, 400–401
    versions, 382
Windows 2000, installing or upgrading to
    clean install, 316–320
    hardware requirements, 312
    overview of, 311
    upgrade issues, 315–316
Windows 2000 Server, 308
Windows 2000/XP. *See also* Windows 2000; Windows XP
    Administrative Tools, 359
    APIPA (Automatic Private IP Addressing), 588
    APM/ACPI configuration, 518
    Backup or Restore Wizard, 603–604
    boot process, 377–378
    BOOT.INI, 379–381
    built-in drivers for USB devices, 440
    desktop, 338
    Disk Management, 215–216
    File and Printer Sharing, 575
    file sharing, 373–374
    GDI (graphical device interface) used for printing, 543
    IPCONFIG, 585–586
    login screen, 336–337
    Mouse applet, 447
    moving location of page file, 369
    My Computer, 341
    NTDETECT.COM, 381
    NTFS, 371–377

    NTLDR, 378
    OS organization, 370–371
    overview of, 370
    partitioning methods supported, 209–210
    peer-to-peer networking in, 570
    Registry Editor(s), 364
    security, 372–373
    sharing drives and folders, 588–590
    system folders, 363
    system partition files, 378
    TCP/IP settings, 582
    user accounts, 373–374
    XP versions, 383–385
Windows 2000/XP, maintaining, 394–409
    Automatic Updates, 397–398
    creating new users, 400–401
    Disk Cleanup for managing temporary files, 407–408
    Error-checking and disk defragmentation, 406–407
    key terms, 429
    lab projects, 432
    managing users, 401–405
    passwords, 405–406
    quizzes, 430–432
    Registry, 408
    security, 409
    summary/review, 427–428
    updates, patches, and service packs, 394–397
    user accounts and groups, 398–399
    Users and Passwords applet, 399–400
Windows 2000/XP, optimizing, 409–426
    ASR (Automated System Recovery), 424–426
    Backup utility (NT Backup), 422–423
    device drivers, updating, 412–413
    Device Manager, 414
    devices, 411–412
    devices, adding new, 414–415
    driver signing, 413–414
    ERD (Emergency Repair Disk), 423–424
    key terms, 429
    lab projects, 432

Windows 2000/XP, optimizing
  (continued)
    overview of, 409
    Performance console, 417
    Performance Logs and Alerts,
      418–419
    Performance Options, 415–416
    preparation for problems,
      419–420
    quizzes, 430–432
    resources, tracking, 416
    software installation, 409–410
    software removal, 410–411
    summary/review, 428–429
    System Monitor, 417–418
    System Restore, 420–422
    Task Manager, 416–417
    Windows components,
      adding/removing, 411
Windows 9x
    FAT32 released with Windows
      95, 223
    history of Windows OSs, 298–299
    for home user and small
      office, 381
    Network Neighborhood, 346
    upgrading, 315–316
Windows Classic style, 402
Windows Components Wizard, 411
Windows Defender, 622
Windows Embedded, 387
Windows Explorer, 343–344
Windows Firewall, 624
Windows installation CD
    adding/removing Windows
      components, 411
    partitioning and formatting
      with, 229
Windows Installer, 615
Windows Internet Name Server
  (WINS), 584
Windows Marketplace, 305–307
Windows Media Center
    installing Backup utility, 354
    in XP Media Center edition,
      383–384
Windows Mobile, 386
Windows NT
    for corporate environments, 381
    history of Windows OSs, 298
Windows OSs
    64-bit processing, 385
    Administrative Tools, 359
    APM/ACPI configuration, 518
    CD-media and, 282–283

Client for Microsoft
  Networks, 576
command line, 356–357
Computer Management, 360
Control Panel, 348–349
desktop, 336, 338
Device Manager, 349–352
Event Viewer, 360
folders, 362–363
history of, 297–302
hot keys, 346–347
key terms, 391
lab projects, 393
login screen, 336–337
MMC (Microsoft Management
  Console), 357–359
My Computer, 340–343
My Documents, My [Whatever],
  343–345
My Network Places, 345
network roles, 309
overview of, 335
Performance console, 360–361
quizzes, 391–393
Recycle Bin, 345
Registry, 363–369
right-click, 347–348
services, 362
sharing drives and folders,
  588–590
sharing printers, 591–592
summary/review, 388–390
System Tools, 352–356
taskbar and Start menu, 339–340
tech utilities, 347
user interface, 336
versions, 381–382
Windows Explorer, 343–344
Windows OSs, installing and
  upgrading
    automating installation, 320
    disk cloning for installation,
      325–326
    graphical mode errors, 327
    key terms, 331
    lab projects, 334
    lockup during install, 327–328
    performing install or upgrade,
      309–310
    post-installation tasks, 310–311
    quizzes, 331–333
    review and summary, 329–331
    scripting installations with
      Setup Manager, 320–325
    text mode errors, 326–327

Windows OSs, preparing for install or
  upgrade
    backing up/restoring data, 308
    clean install vs. upgrade, 307
    hardware requirements, 305
    image installation, 308
    language and locale
      settings, 309
    multiboot installations, 307
    networking role, 309
    overview of, 304–305
    partitions and file systems, 309
    planning post-installation
      tasks, 309
    selecting installation method,
      308–309
    software compatibility, 305–307
Windows Security Center (WSC), 634
Windows Server 2003, 301
Windows startup files, 377
Windows Update
    Automatic Updates, 397–398
    driver updates and, 412
    options, 398
    overview of, 394–396
    for security patches, 616
Windows Vista, 633–635
    command line, 357
    CompTIA A+ certification
      and, 12
    history of Windows OSs, 301
    other security features, 635
    Parental Controls, 634–635
    Registry Editor, 364
    semi-transparency of screen
      elements, 483–484
    UAC (User Account Control),
      633–635
    versions, 386
    video cards and, 648
    WSC (Windows Security
      Center), 634
Windows XP. See also Windows
  2000/XP
    64-bit processing, 385
    activation, 353
    Administrative Tools, 571–572
    applications, 294
    ASR (Automated System
      Recovery), 424–426
    color depth settings for
      displays, 483
    Fast User Switching, 405
    Files and Settings Transfer
      Wizard, 354

history of Windows OSs, 299–301
Home edition, 383–384
installing Backup utility, 354
language and locale settings, 309
Local Security Settings, 613
log files, 328
Media Center edition, 383–384
multiboot installations, 307
optical media and, 282
permissions in Home edition, 376
Professional edition, 383
resetting forgotten passwords, 406
scripted installation, 320–325
Security Center, 354–355
software compatibility, 305–307
System Properties, 350
System Restore, 355–356
user accounts, managing, 372, 401–405
versions, 382–383
Windows Firewall, 624
WSC (Windows Security Center), 634
Windows XP, installing or upgrading to
activation, 314–315
booting into XP setup, 314
clean install, 316–320
hardware requirements, 312–313
overview of, 312
registration, 314
software compatibility, 313–314
upgrade issues, 315–316
upgrade paths, 312
Windows XP Tablet PC, 387, 500
WINNT folder, 363
WINS (Windows Internet Name Server), 584
wired networks, installing and configuring, 575–592. See also networks
client configuration, 576–577
NetBEUI configuration, 577–578
NIC installation, 576
NWLink (IPX/SPX) configuration, 578
overview of, 575–576
sharing drives and folders, 588–590
sharing printers, 591–592
summary/review, 593–596
TCP/IP and. See TCP/IP (Transmission Control Protocol/Internet Protocol)
UNC (universal naming convention), 590–591
Wireless Fidelity. See Wi-Fi (Wireless Fidelity)
wireless keyboards, 445
wireless networking
laptops and, 513
troubleshooting laptops, 522
wireless networks
securing, 628–629
wireless networking in laptops, 513
wireless security, 629
words, bits of memory and, 60
workstations, 569. See also clients
worms, 616
Write, file and folder permissions, 375
WSC (Windows Security Center), 634

X

xD (Extreme Digital) Picture Card, 276
Xeon, Intel processors, 91–92
XT bus, 150

Z

Zelda game, 649
ZIF (zero insertion force) sockets, 67–68
zoom, optical and digital in digital cameras, 454

LICENSE AGREEMENT

THIS PRODUCT (THE "PRODUCT") CONTAINS PROPRIETARY SOFTWARE, DATA AND INFORMATION (INCLUDING DOCUMENTATION) OWNED BY THE McGRAW-HILL COMPANIES, INC. ("McGRAW-HILL") AND ITS LICENSORS. YOUR RIGHT TO USE THE PRODUCT IS GOVERNED BY THE TERMS AND CONDITIONS OF THIS AGREEMENT.

LICENSE: Throughout this License Agreement, "you" shall mean either the individual or the entity whose agent opens this package. You are granted a non-exclusive and non-transferable license to use the Product subject to the following terms:
(i) If you have licensed a single user version of the Product, the Product may only be used on a single computer (i.e., a single CPU). If you licensed and paid the fee applicable to a local area network or wide area network version of the Product, you are subject to the terms of the following subparagraph (ii).
(ii) If you have licensed a local area network version, you may use the Product on unlimited workstations located in one single building selected by you that is served by such local area network. If you have licensed a wide area network version, you may use the Product on unlimited workstations located in multiple buildings on the same site selected by you that is served by such wide area network; provided, however, that any building will not be considered located in the same site if it is more than five (5) miles away from any building included in such site. In addition, you may only use a local area or wide area network version of the Product on one single server. If you wish to use the Product on more than one server, you must obtain written authorization from McGraw-Hill and pay additional fees.
(iii) You may make one copy of the Product for back-up purposes only and you must maintain an accurate record as to the location of the back-up at all times.

COPYRIGHT; RESTRICTIONS ON USE AND TRANSFER: All rights (including copyright) in and to the Product are owned by McGraw-Hill and its licensors. You are the owner of the enclosed disc on which the Product is recorded. You may not use, copy, decompile, disassemble, reverse engineer, modify, reproduce, create derivative works, transmit, distribute, sublicense, store in a database or retrieval system of any kind, rent or transfer the Product, or any portion thereof, in any form or by any means (including electronically or otherwise) except as expressly provided for in this License Agreement. You must reproduce the copyright notices, trademark notices, legends and logos of McGraw-Hill and its licensors that appear on the Product on the back-up copy of the Product which you are permitted to make hereunder. All rights in the Product not expressly granted herein are reserved by McGraw-Hill and its licensors.

TERM: This License Agreement is effective until terminated. It will terminate if you fail to comply with any term or condition of this License Agreement. Upon termination, you are obligated to return to McGraw-Hill the Product together with all copies thereof and to purge all copies of the Product included in any and all servers and computer facilities.

DISCLAIMER OF WARRANTY: THE PRODUCT AND THE BACK-UP COPY ARE LICENSED "AS IS." McGRAW-HILL, ITS LICENSORS AND THE AUTHORS MAKE NO WARRANTIES, EXPRESS OR IMPLIED, AS TO THE RESULTS TO BE OBTAINED BY ANY PERSON OR ENTITY FROM USE OF THE PRODUCT, ANY INFORMATION OR DATA INCLUDED THEREIN AND/OR ANY TECHNICAL SUPPORT SERVICES PROVIDED HEREUNDER, IF ANY ("TECHNICAL SUPPORT SERVICES"). McGRAW-HILL, ITS LICENSORS AND THE AUTHORS MAKE NO EXPRESS OR IMPLIED WARRANTIES OF MERCHANTABILITY OR FITNESS FOR A PARTICULAR PURPOSE OR USE WITH RESPECT TO THE PRODUCT. McGRAW-HILL, ITS LICENSORS, AND THE AUTHORS MAKE NO GUARANTEE THAT YOU WILL PASS ANY CERTIFICATION EXAM WHATSOEVER BY USING THIS PRODUCT. NEITHER McGRAW-HILL, ANY OF ITS LICENSORS NOR THE AUTHORS WARRANT THAT THE FUNCTIONS CONTAINED IN THE PRODUCT WILL MEET YOUR REQUIREMENTS OR THAT THE OPERATION OF THE PRODUCT WILL BE UNINTERRUPTED OR ERROR FREE. YOU ASSUME THE ENTIRE RISK WITH RESPECT TO THE QUALITY AND PERFORMANCE OF THE PRODUCT.

LIMITED WARRANTY FOR DISC: To the original licensee only, McGraw-Hill warrants that the enclosed disc on which the Product is recorded is free from defects in materials and workmanship under normal use and service for a period of ninety (90) days from the date of purchase. In the event of a defect in the disc covered by the foregoing warranty, McGraw-Hill will replace the disc.

LIMITATION OF LIABILITY: NEITHER McGRAW-HILL, ITS LICENSORS NOR THE AUTHORS SHALL BE LIABLE FOR ANY INDIRECT, SPECIAL OR CONSEQUENTIAL DAMAGES, SUCH AS BUT NOT LIMITED TO, LOSS OF ANTICIPATED PROFITS OR BENEFITS, RESULTING FROM THE USE OR INABILITY TO USE THE PRODUCT EVEN IF ANY OF THEM HAS BEEN ADVISED OF THE POSSIBILITY OF SUCH DAMAGES. THIS LIMITATION OF LIABILITY SHALL APPLY TO ANY CLAIM OR CAUSE WHATSOEVER WHETHER SUCH CLAIM OR CAUSE ARISES IN CONTRACT, TORT, OR OTHERWISE. Some states do not allow the exclusion or limitation of indirect, special or consequential damages, so the above limitation may not apply to you.

U.S. GOVERNMENT RESTRICTED RIGHTS: Any software included in the Product is provided with restricted rights subject to subparagraphs (c), (1) and (2) of the Commercial Computer Software-Restricted Rights clause at 48 C.F.R. 52.227-19. The terms of this Agreement applicable to the use of the data in the Product are those under which the data are generally made available to the general public by McGraw-Hill. Except as provided herein, no reproduction, use, or disclosure rights are granted with respect to the data included in the Product and no right to modify or create derivative works from any such data is hereby granted.

GENERAL: This License Agreement constitutes the entire agreement between the parties relating to the Product. The terms of any Purchase Order shall have no effect on the terms of this License Agreement. Failure of McGraw-Hill to insist at any time on strict compliance with this License Agreement shall not constitute a waiver of any rights under this License Agreement. This License Agreement shall be construed and governed in accordance with the laws of the State of New York. If any provision of this License Agreement is held to be contrary to law, that provision will be enforced to the maximum extent permissible and the remaining provisions will remain in full force and effect.